D1225872

Praise for *Sunday in Hell*: *Pearl Harbor Minute by Minute*

The attack on Pearl Harbor was a profoundly bitter surprise for an unprepared America. It was an earth shaking event in a chain of devastating events perpetrated by the twentieth century's new totalitarians—the Axis powers of Nazi Germany, Fascist Italy and militarist Japan. This work revitalizes the cry, "Remember Pearl Harbor!" and records anew America's entry into World War II, the deadly, never-to-be-ignored lessons totalitarians leave in the archives of history's darkest hours.

> Gordon R. Sullivan
> General, US Army, Retired
> 32nd Chief of Staff

Bill McWilliams delivers a most readable history that immerses us in the depths of our Nation's darkest hour. Feel the shock and anger, the humiliation and devastation that roused the "Sleeping Giant" and inspired the greatest mobilization of spirit, and pride our nation has ever seen. This is the story of real people whose shattered lives became the stuff of the "Greatest Generation."

> General John P. Jumper
> US Air Force (Ret)
> Chief of Staff
> 2001-05

(continued)

A memorable history should read like an exciting true story, create clear visual images, and cause readers to feel they are among the people living the events. This work does. Bill McWilliams pulls us into the story, where we experience the sights, sounds, tastes, and smells of war, while feeling the powerful crosscurrents of emotion war provokes.

General Thomas R. Morgan
USMC (Retired)
Assistant Commandant
Marine Corps, 1986-88

Masterfully told; a powerful true story of the devastating events surrounding the Japanese attack on Pearl Harbor that propelled America into the most destructive war in human history. McWilliams' third major work after A Return to Glory *and* On Hallowed Ground *wrings inspiration and remembrance from sacrifice, valor and tragedy. Reading like an action-packed novel, this is truly history at its best.*

Colin Burgess
Award-winning Australian
military and spaceflight
historian and author

SUNDAY IN HELL

SUNDAY IN HELL

PEARL HARBOR MINUTE BY MINUTE

BILL MCWILLIAMS

OPEN ROAD

INTEGRATED MEDIA

NEW YORK

All rights reserved, including without limitation the right to reproduce this book or any portion thereof in any form or by any means, whether electronic or mechanical, now known or hereinafter invented, without the express written permission of the publisher.

Copyright © 2011 by Bill McWilliams

Cover design by Andy Ross

ISBN 978-1-4976-3882-2

This edition published in 2014 by Open Road Integrated Media, Inc.
345 Hudson Street
New York, NY 10014
www.openroadmedia.com

For Joey and Bob Border

Whose Lives of Love and Sacrifice Inspired This Book

CONTENTS

CHAPTER TWO

CHAPTER THREE

CHAPTER FOUR

CHAPTER FIVE

CHAPTER TEN

CHAPTER ELEVEN

CHAPTER TWELVE

SUNDAY
IN HELL

"When bad men combine, the good must associate; else they will fall one by one, an unpitied sacrifice in a contemptible struggle."

Edmund Burke
Thoughts on the Cause of
Present Discontents

FOREWORD

Sunday in Hell: Pearl Harbor Minute by Minute, is a fresh, new, meticulously-researched history that takes us through America's first fierce and most disastrous battle of World War II. Set in the historical context of the preceding ten years of the Great Depression, we see clearly our nation's steadfast hold on isolationism, and the rise of the 20th Century's new totalitarians, leading to the shattering Japanese attack on Pearl Harbor. Told by the people who lived its events, the attack abruptly thrusts us into the midst of war and all its powerful cross-currents of emotion. Then comes the bitter aftermath, and America's first dark days of struggle in the great, wide Pacific, where the fury began and as Admiral Nimitz related, "uncommon valor became a common virtue," inspiring a nation. In reading this history we learn anew why the words sacrifice, love, faith, patriotism, and "Remember Pearl Harbor," will forever reverberate through American history. In *Sunday in Hell*, we become acquainted with two brothers, both 1939 graduates of the United States Naval Academy (Annapolis) who room together aboard the Pacific Fleet's USS *Tennessee*. On board *Tennessee* in Puget Sound Navy Yard, the younger brother and a Marine reserve officer's daughter meet and begin a magnificent journey, while America lurches toward the cataclysm that forever changes the world. Throughout separate voyages to Hawaii on the *Tennessee* and the beautifully-appointed ocean liner, SS *Lurline*, we sail with them in the summer of 1941 into the relaxing, tropical warmth of the islands, as the winds of war blow ever-stronger. While *Tennessee* is engaged on rigorous Pacific Fleet training cruises, we learn of the growing tension between the Japanese Empire and the United States, sense the fury about to be unleashed and witness the last desperate efforts to avoid war. Every aspect of the attack on Pearl Harbor is viewed from a wide range of locations, vantage points and perspectives:

On the bridge of the destroyer USS *Ward*, when her crew fires the first shots of the Pacific war at a Japanese midget submarine.

Inside the cockpits of eighteen Douglas Dauntless (SBD) dive-bombers from Scouting and Bombing Squadrons Six, as they launch from the carrier *Enterprise.*

From the first moments of the crushing blows on military airfields throughout the island of Oahu to the savage attacks on the Pacific Fleet in Pearl Harbor.

With the attacking fighter pilots, torpedo and dive bomber crews in action over Pearl Harbor.

At the airfields while a small band of Army Air Force fighter pilots courageously scramble into the air against overwhelming odds.

In the rush to battle stations with ships' crews, beside men performing uncommon acts of courage, heroism and valor, as they fight to save their shipmates, themselves, and their ships.

And among the stunned, initially uncertain, and disbelieving civilian populace in Honolulu.

The attack's aftermath in December 1941, with its numerous reverberations on Oahu, the continental United States, across the wide Pacific and around the world follows. Three weeks replete with never told, seldom heard, or incomplete stories including the controversial declaration of martial law in Hawaii, and the immediate detaining of more than 400 suspected Japanese spies and sympathizers. Plus the aerial and sea hunt for the Japanese strike force while responding to the aggressive enemy submarine activity. *Sunday in Hell* will tell in vivid detail the inspiring responses of military and Hawaiian civilian populations filled with history that will shed new light on the events of 7 December 1941. This book will strengthen Americans pride in their nation as seen through the hearts and minds of those who lived it. For readers of all ages, from high school through retirement, the book brings a deep look into a generation whose sacrifice will echo down through the ages. It is the premier story of American citizens that quite literally saved civilization and our nation's hard won freedoms, when the new totalitarians of the twentieth century stalked the earth.

Thomas B. Fargo
Admiral,
USN (Ret)Former Commander,
U.S. Pacific Command (2002-2005)

AUTHOR'S EXPLANATION

Readers will see both traditional civilian and 24-hour military time keeping in this history. As an example, on board a company-owned ocean liner, a typical morning clock time will normally be expressed as 9:25 a.m. or 9:25 in the morning. On board a Navy combatant such as the battleship *Tennessee*, or in an Army unit war diary, the same time will be expressed as 0925 hours. At 9:25 p.m., in the evening, military time will be 2125 hours.

The Japanese flew three different types of carrier aircraft during the 7 December air raid. For ease of reading the aircraft will carry the nicknames given them later in the war. The Nakajima Type 97 BN2 carrier attack aircraft, which flew as a torpedo bomber and horizontal or level bomber in the attack, during 1942 was given the nickname "Kate" by the Allies. The Aichi Type 99 D3A1 carrier bomber, primarily employed as a dive bomber by the Japanese, in the same 1942 period earned the nickname, "Val." The Mitsubishi Type 0 A6M2, fast, highly maneuverable, heavily-armed fighter, was alternatively nicknamed the "Zeke," or "Zero" later in the war.

All Japanese names in the narrative, diplomats' names, ship and submarine commanders, airborne attack leaders, and crewmembers of ships and aircraft, are displayed in the Western convention. That is, the first and family names are reversed from what is normally expressed in the Japanese culture and language.

For readers unfamiliar with Navy, Army and Army Air Force terms and jargon, there are on the spot explanations throughout the narrative, with one exception. The terms "frame 88, frame 104, or frame 175," or other frame numbers will be in Chapters 5 and 6. Frame numbers assist in describing ship damage and where, more precisely, Japanese torpedoes struck ships the raiders successfully attacked.

To visualize the meaning of frames and frame numbers, imagine a ship in the process of construction, with no steel plates yet attached to its main members, or frames to form its complete hull. The ship's keel is the main bow to stern longitudinal structural member, at the ship's bottom, underlying the entire ship's construction. The keel is literally the ship's backbone.

Frames are the vertical cross-members attached to the keel and spaced at intervals, numbered progressively higher from bow to stern, and with the keel's length, give the ship its size and shape—as well as provide the framework for walls, or bulkheads, which are used to compartmentalize the vessel. Frame 1 is closest to the ship's bow and its highest numbered frame is closest to the ship's stern. The total number of frames increase with the lengthening of the ship.

PREVIEW

In 1930, Albert Einstein wrote in *What I Believe.* "A hundred times a day I remind myself that my inner and outer lives are based on the labors of other people, living and dead, and that I must exert myself in order to give in the same measure as I have received and am still receiving." For the people whose lives and deaths are recorded in the events described in this book, for this work and what was attempted in its writing, no words could better express my gratitude for all that was given by so many. Without the long ago labors of some, and without the assistance of so many others willing to give of their time and energies in the past seven years, this work would have been impossible.

One book above all others referenced in the bibliography helped in providing a springboard and roadmap to another lens through which Pearl Harbor might be viewed. For this work and its authors I write a deep and sincere thank you. Gordon W. Prange, whose thirty-seven years of research culminated in *At Dawn We Slept, The Untold Story of Pearl Harbor*, died in 1980, before his marvelous work was published. In consonance with his wishes, two of his former students, Dr. Donald M. Goldstein and Chief Warrant Officer Katherine V. Dillon, USAF (Ret.), collaborated, and continued the massive job of editing his multivolume manuscript totaling more than 3,500 pages into the classic it has become. Particularly valuable was the work's deep insight into Japanese plans and objectives, the thorough analysis of strategic and tactical errors and omissions, the thinking on both sides of the attack plan and execution—and the personalities of key leaders and participants on both sides. In no other source could be found the straightforward summary of the American government's and military's investigations and boards of inquiry into the Pearl Harbor disaster.

Through the lenses of the foregoing book, and seven others described in the acknowledgements, emerged yet another, complementary view of Pearl Harbor and its aftermath. From hundreds of sources come the words and voices of men, women, and children on Oahu that day, at sea and in the air, on the receiving end of the Japanese attack.

From Pearl Harbor's Pacific Fleet, Oahu's military and civilian airfields, Army posts and forts, and the numerous other targets of opportunity swept up in the horror-filled assault. From the attack's brutal realities and chaotic, shattering aftermath come stories seldom if ever told. From the island's populace, tourists in Honolulu and civilians in outlying towns and farming areas. From passenger liners at sea, a freighter under attack by a Japanese submarine before the air raid began. From Navy task forces at sea, and Pan American Airways' *Clippers* en route, the great passenger-carrying flying boats of that era—come the words and reactions of people abruptly engulfed in war's violent, deep, crosscurrents of emotion.

This is America's and The Territory of Hawaii's entrance into World War II, the humiliating, thunderous surprise and fierce first battle, the final lurch into the worldwide maelstrom. The surprise began amid ever-increasing tension, almost quietly, early on a Sunday morning.

On board the minesweeper USS *Condor*, a short distance outside Pearl Harbor at 0342 hours the morning of 7 December, Ensign Russell C. McCloy, *Condor*'s Officer of the Deck asked Quartermaster Second Class R.C. Uttrick, the helmsman, what he thought about "something in the darkness about fifty yards ahead, off the port bow." Uttrick peered through binoculars and said, "That's a periscope, sir, and there aren't supposed to be any subs in this area." This was the first contact, the day's prelude to the first shots and first blood of the Pacific war, signaled at 0650 hours by radio from the destroyer USS *Ward*, the sinking of a Japanese midget submarine just outside the entrance to Pearl Harbor.

At 0605 hours Japanese Admiral Chuichi Nagumo's Carrier Striking Force, from approximately 220 miles north of Oahu, had begun successfully launching their first attack aircraft, 183 planes. Thirteen minutes later, from approximately 200 miles west of Oahu, Admiral William F. "Bull" Halsey's Task Force 8, three cruisers and nine destroyers led by the carrier *Enterprise*, returning to Pearl Harbor—launched the first of 18 Douglas Dauntless Scout and Dive Bombers (SBDs) of Scouting Squadron Six (VS-6). Destination, Naval Air Station Pearl Harbor, on Ford Island.

At approximately 0830 ship's time, 0730 hours Hawaii time, en route to San Francisco on a northeasterly course, the SS *Lurline*'s Chief Officer, Edward Collins, stopped by the radio shack to have a chat with the officer of the watch, "Tiny" Nelson. Nelson was listening intently to communications traffic. Only a minute or so elapsed when Nelson began writing out a message on his typewriter. As he was listening and typing he called Collins' attention to read it. The message was an SOS, the international emergency signal from the 2,140-ton steam schooner SS *Cynthia Olson*, a flag-bearing American merchant vessel carrying a load of lumber, bound for Honolulu. She was approximately 300 miles off San Francisco, under attack by a surfaced submarine, later identified as Imperial Japanese Submarine, *I-26*. The last message from the freighter to the Matson Navigation Company's ocean liner stated she was under torpedo attack.

At Naval Air Station Kaneohe, on the windward side of Oahu, Aviation Machinist Mate Third Class Guy C. Avery was in his bunk on the sun porch of a bungalow when he heard the sound of a lone plane quite near the house. It passed and returned. "To hell with the Army," Avery thought. "Every day is the same to them." But the sound of the engine was different, and roused his curiosity. He reached the window in time to see "Zeroes [Japanese fighter aircraft] just beginning to fan out over the heart of the station and opening fire promiscuously." He shouted to his sleeping comrades, "The Japs are here! It's war!" To which one man replied, "Well, don't worry about it Avery. It'll last only two weeks." Avery checked his watch. It was 0748.

From Major Leonard D. Heaton, physician and surgeon at Schofield Barracks' Army Hospital. Writing in his diary the night of 7 December:

> The best and happiest days of our lives went up in the smoke of Pearl Harbor, Wheeler Field, and Hickam Field today. I wonder if, when and how they will ever return. I was standing with Capt's Bell and [Harlan] Taylor in front of my quarters about 8 o'clock this day. We were about to get in the car to pick up Col. Canning and thence to Queen's Hospital to attend a lecture by Dr. Jno. Moorhead of N.Y. who has been talking of traumatic surgery. We hesitated before entering the car because our

attention was called to the great number of planes in the air and some very loud distant noises. Soon one plane came quite close to us and in banking to come down our street I distinctly saw the rising sun insignia on his wings. Soon he was coming down the street with machine guns blazing away at us. We rushed into the house.

And later, after working tirelessly among four surgical teams throughout a long, bloody day into early evening, struggling to save lives, he added, ". . . Such wounds!!—eviscerations of brains, neck, thorax, abdomen—traumatic amputations, etc. No burns of any consequence . . . "

Surgical teams at Schofield Barracks treated 117 wounded that day. Thirty-eight of them died, most having arrived with fatal wounds.

Adjacent to Schofield Barracks, at Wheeler Field, in the first moments of the attack, Private Wilfred D. Burke, an aircraft armorer in the 72nd Pursuit Squadron, looked up to see an approaching Val dive bomber. "It was the first time I had ever seen a plunging dive bomber and it was an awesome sight. Nothing in warfare is more frightening. Hurtling down on us was the dive bomber being followed by another, while six or seven more were in echelon awaiting their turn. The leader pulled out right over us in a spectacular climbing bank. We could clearly see the rising sun of Japan on his wings and fuselage." In the succeeding minutes he saw firsthand the true horror and devastation caused by the attacking Japanese aircraft.

East from Ford Island, across Pearl Harbor's main channel, at the Navy Hospital, [nurse] Lieutenant Ruth Ericson saw sights and heard sounds she would never forget. ". . . The first patient came into our dressing room at 8:25 a.m. with a large opening in his abdomen and bleeding profusely. They started an intravenous and transfusion. I can still see the tremor of Dr. [Commander Clyde W.] Brunson's hand as he picked up the needle. Everyone was terrified. The patient died within the hour. Then the burned patients streamed in . . . " A total of 546 battle casualties and 313 dead were brought to the Navy Hospital before the day ended.

The navigator on the battleship USS West Virginia, Lieutenant Commander Thomas T. Beattie, wrote days later:

[The Captain and I] went out on the starboard side
of the bridge discussing what to do. During all this
time extremely heavy bombing and strafing attacks
occurred. The ship was constantly shaken with bomb
hits. The Captain [Mervyn S. Bennion] doubled up
with a groan and stated that he had been wounded.
I saw he had been hit in the stomach, probably by a
large piece of shrapnel, and was seriously wounded.
He sank to the deck, and I loosened his collar. I sent
a messenger for a pharmacist's mate to assist the
Captain. Just then, [at a time fixed as 0808], the
USS *Arizona*'s forward magazine blew up with a
tremendous explosion . . .

Aboard *Arizona* moments after the explosion Ensign James
Miller could see nothing but reddish flames outside. The sound
powered phones went dead, power to the [#3] turret failed, and
all lights went out . . . He stepped outside the turret to see what
the conditions were on the quarterdeck. He was stunned. "I
noticed several badly burned men lying on the deck and saw
Ensign Anderson, who had been Junior Officer of the Deck,
lying on the deck with a bad cut on his head." What he actually
saw was almost beyond comprehension, and was described by
another *Arizona* survivor.

. . . There were bodies . . . I'd seen them from above,
but it didn't register clearly until I got down on the
quarterdeck. These people were zombies . . . They
were burned completely white. Their skin was just
as white as if you'd taken a bucket of whitewash
and painted it white. Their hair was burned off; their
eyebrows were burned off; the pitiful remains of their
uniforms in their crotch was a charred remnant; and
the insoles of their shoes was about the only thing
that was left on these bodies. They were moving like
robots. Their arms were out, held away from their
bodies, and they were stumping along the decks . . .

By the time *Arizona* exploded, the battleship *Oklahoma*,
struck on her port side by four torpedoes was already listing

approximately 40 degrees, rolling slowly, relentlessly toward her death, trapping hundreds of men below decks, including Chaplain [Lieutenant], Father Aloysius H. Schmitt. The following week, he was to transfer to duty on shore. He helped save five men by lifting and pushing them through a porthole on the starboard side, while other men outside pulled them through—but lost his own life.

Standing outside the porthole helping pull men to safety was Marine Private Raymond J. Turpin of Waterloo, Alabama. He joined in the frantic rescue effort after it began, and carried a lifelong memory of Fr. Al. When the five men were safely out of the rapidly filling compartment, he reached for the Chaplain's hand in a second desperate rescue attempt. Fr. Al declined, saying, "Someone tried earlier to pull me out and I couldn't get through. I'm going to see if there are any others needing a way out." He never returned.

Deep in the bowels of *Oklahoma*, *Utah*, and all ships hit during the torpedo attack, the struggle to survive was immediate. Chief Water Tender, L.C. Bickley, whose station was in *Oklahoma's* engine room:

> . . . the word was passed to man all battle stations. I went to #2 Fireroom Pumproom and was starting pumps until water came in through the air ducts and flooded pumprooms. The hatch to #2 Pumproom was down [closed] and I couldn't get it up, so I dived and swam to #1 Pumproom and out. The lights were out and I couldn't see where the two men went that were with me. I got to H Division living compartment and water started coming in so I went out through a porthole in the wash room after the ship rolled over, and was picked up by a motor launch and put ashore in the Navy Yard. The only word I got over the phone was to get ready to get underway.
>
> Many men were lost in the lower [ammunition] handling rooms of turrets. Falling 14-inch shells killed and injured a great many. About 125 men remained in an air pocket in the shipfitters shop, but when the space was opened up, water rushed in as air rushed out. Only one man of this group saved

SUNDAY IN HELL   15

himself by swimming to the Chief Petty Officer
pantry on the third deck and out through an open
porthole . . .

On the west side of Ford Island, at 0812 hours, between the
time of the *Arizona* explosion and the capsizing of *Oklahoma*,
the heavily listing target ship *Utah*—formerly the pre-World
War I, thin-plated battleship of the same name—snapped her
mooring lines and capsized, the victim of two torpedoes in the
first moments of the attack. One man marked her death with
his valor, at the cost of his own life. Courage and valor were the
companions of many that day.

Lieutenant (jg) Hart D. "Dale" Hilton in [SBD] plane 6-S-7
with Radioman/gunner Second Class Jack Leaming in the rear
cockpit, led *Enterprise*'s plane 6-B-5 on the scouting mission in
sector 120 degrees, which took them well south of Pearl Harbor.
The first indication of trouble was the terse, excited message,
"DON'T SHOOT! THIS IS AN AMERICAN PLANE!" The first,
puzzled reaction by Dale Hilton and Jack Leaming was radio
silence had been broken. About a minute later came another
transmission . . . "Get out the rubber boat, we're goin' in!"

Aboard the cruiser *New Orleans*, below decks, in the mix of
crewmembers, low light, flashlights, periodic darkness, sweating,
undoubtedly much swearing and the occasional jolt of heavy
AA fire above, Lieutenant Edwin F. Woodhead, who was in
charge of the ammunition line during the attack, remembered,
"I heard a voice behind me saying 'Praise the Lord and pass the
ammunition.' I turned and saw Chaplain [Lieutenant Howell M.]
Forgy walking toward me along the line of men. He was patting
men on the back and making that remark to cheer them and keep
them going. I know it helped me a lot, too."

Less than two days outbound west northwest of Hawaii, Task
Force 12's aircraft carrier *Lexington*, the guide for ten other
ships in the task force, steamed toward the island of Midway.
Rear Admiral John H. Newton seemed somewhat less concerned
about the growing international tensions and Japanese threat in
the Pacific, though Task Force 12's mission was to deliver 18
aircraft from Marine Scout Bombing Squadron 231, to Midway.
His outlook changed abruptly, however, by the time Officer of
the Deck, Ensign Joseph Weber, entered a note in the *Lexington*'s
log: ". . . 0830 Received signal from CinCpac, 'Hostilities with

Japan commenced with air raid on Pearl.' Commenced zigzagging with standard zigzag plan . . . "

On board *Enterprise*, Officer of the Deck, Lieutenant John O.F. Dorsett noted in the carrier's log: ". . . 0900 On radio orders from SecNav, executed War Plan against Japan in view of unprovoked air raid on Pearl Harbor at 0800 this date. 0904 Commenced zigzagging . . . "

In San Diego, the aircraft carrier USS *Saratoga* arrived from overhaul at the Puget Sound Navy Yard in Seattle, Washington, and stopped all engines at 1120, 0920 hours Hawaii time. The Officer of the Deck, Ensign John P. Aymond, made three more entries in the log, before writing: "1144 War has been declared with Japan; air raid Pearl Harbor . . . "

From their apartment on Oahu, near Waikiki, Joey Border, 21-year old wife of Ensign Bob Border, assigned to the battleship *Tennessee*, started writing a letter home:

Dec. 7—Sunday

Dearest Family –

Here it is. We're at war with Japan and Hawaii is in the middle. I don't know if you'll ever receive this letter, but I hope that when you do, all this mess will be over. This morning the phone rang at 9 A.M. It was Bud Marron! a dr. on the Tennessee, who called to tell Bob that all naval officers were to report immediately. We couldn't quite believe it until we turned the radio on and there it was "Oahu is being attacked by enemy planes—please keep calm." Bob dashed out to Pearl Harbor. I hope he made it. Bombs have been falling at irregular intervals—one just hit about 5 blocks from here. I could hear the planes and the constant boom of the antiaircraft guns—the sky is dotted with puffs of smoke. Hickam Field is in flames and in that direction one can see the black smoke. Parachute troops have landed. Not many people have been killed—about 6 so far. A Japanese plane flew low over the streets of Wahiawa, machine-gunning everything and everybody. The Kaneohe Air Base is partially in flames and one of the main water lines has burst. A few are excited, but for the most part, everyone is calm. The radio stations have gone off the air, coming on for only official announcements. I am writing this from time to time throughout the day . . . It's sad, but I couldn't think of anything to say this morning when he left. All I shouted was— "Have fun. I love you." I know it won't be fun and he knows I love him . . . If any nasty Japs come around here, I have some very good butcher knives which I can use to good advantage . . .

Joey didn't complete her letter until the next day, and life became worse, much worse as this day wore on. She marked her envelope "Clipper," and Pan American Airways' *Philippine Clipper*, still bearing sixteen bullet holes from the 7 December Japanese attack on Wake Island, carried her letter as far as San Francisco, where it arrived on 10 December.

CHAPTER 1

The New Totalitarians

Dictators ride to and fro upon tigers
which they dare not dismount.
And the tigers are getting hungry.

Winston Churchill

On board the Matson Line's formerly luxurious SS *Lurline* the last days of December 1941, she earned the nickname of "Mighty Mouse" from the ship's crew and passengers. The *Lurline's* passengers included wounded, tourists, military dependents, non-essential government employees and their dependents, and civilian contractor employees' dependents being evacuated from the island of Oahu to the West Coast following the Japanese Empire's 7 December attack on Pearl Harbor. She was the spark for the women she called the "*Tennessee* twelve," wives whose husbands were crew members aboard the battleship USS *Tennessee*. Largely through the grapevine, and later from her personal observation of the event, the twelve learned the *Tennessee* had slipped out of Pearl Harbor with the battleships *Maryland* and *Pennsylvania* on Saturday afternoon, 20 December.

Unknown to her and the *Tennessee* twelve, the destroyers *Tucker, Flusser, Case*, and *Conyngham* preceded the three battleships out of the harbor, with orders to provide them a screen against attacks by Japanese submarines.

Departing under the greatest possible secrecy and designated Task Force 16 in sealed orders handed to Rear Admiral William S. Anderson, who was the Senior Officer Present Afloat and task force commander on board *Maryland*, the ships' sudden departure from Pearl Harbor created a stir. The *Tennessee* wives could only speculate as to their husbands' destination.

From 26 to 31 December *Lurline* sailed in Convoy Number 4032, one of the United States' earliest, World War II Pacific convoys, accompanied by two more Matson Line ships, the recently government acquired SS *Matsonia*, and the US Army Transport *Monterrey*, acquired by the Army in July 1941. Escorting the three Matson Line ships were the Pacific Fleet's Task Group 15.6, light cruiser USS *St. Louis* and two destroyers, *Preston* and *Smith*. Sailing through waters patrolled by Japanese submarines surrounding Oahu and near harbor entrances off the mainland's West Coast, *Lurline*, her sister ships and escorts, were moving at 17 knots, sometimes zigzagging, under equally tight secrecy and radio silence. No electronic signals of any kind to be sent ship to shore. Destination, San Francisco—a fact none of the passengers and nearly all the crew members knew. As was the case with Task Force 16, the movement of Convoy 4032 was highly classified.

Days and nights were tense, ships darkened. During daylight hours, when the weather and seas permitted, two Curtiss SOC Seagulls, catapulted off the *St Louis*, patrolled in planned patterns ahead of the convoy, searching primarily for submarines lying in wait, or the presence of Japanese ships or patrol planes launched from submarines or ships. Twenty-four hours a day, lookouts on board all the ships in the convoy constantly eyed the rough, wintry waters' surface with binoculars for tell tale signs of submarines, while destroyers aided their searches with hydrophones or SONAR, a relatively new electronic device in anti-submarine warfare. Life jackets in hand or worn by passengers and crew were mandatory on board the three Matson ships.

It's said that dynamite comes in small packages, and indeed, at five feet tall in a natural honey-blond, energetic, vivacious, smart, and determined woman, it does. Mary Joleen "Joey" Border lived the example. She was there, in Honolulu on 7 December, a barely twenty-one year old bride of less than five months that fateful morning. And now, here she was, back on the *Lurline* three months after she sailed on the same ship from San Francisco to Honolulu, to join her handsome, Navy officer husband, Ensign Robert Lee "Bob" Border—a 1939 United States Naval Academy graduate and crew member on the battleship *Tennessee*.

Joey and Bob had met in the junior officers' wardroom on *Tennessee* while the great ship named for the "Volunteer State" was in port at Puget Sound Navy Yard in December 1940.

Bob's older brother, Ensign Karl Frederick Border, who was his Academy classmate, was also his shipmate and roommate aboard *Tennessee* when Bob and Joey met. The world was aflame in Asia and Europe when they met, and their story was one among millions in a much larger story, a catastrophic event which swept up their lives and shook the world.[1]

The nine years preceding December 1940 were tumultuous. Growing in power, the 20th century's new totalitarians relentlessly pushed the world ever deeper into crisis. In the Far East, war began in September 1931 when Japan, ruled for five years by Emperor Hirohito, used the pretext of a minor incident on the South Manchuria Railroad to invade and annex Manchuria. Five months later Japan proclaimed the puppet state of Manchukuo. Having occupied Korea since President Theodore Roosevelt's arbitrated settlement of the Russo-Japanese War of 1905, they used the peninsula as their base to seize Manchuria.

Then, in 1933, the same year Franklin Delano Roosevelt first took the oath of office as the 32nd president of the United States, the Empire of the Rising Sun seized more of North China while the weak, divided nation, most of her provinces ruled by warlords, was mired in an expanding civil war between Chiang Kai-shek's Nationalists and Mao Tse-Tung's Communists. As the conflagration in Asia spread in the two years preceding 1933, the League of Nations debated, while in Japan, by terror and political pressure, the military took complete control of the government.

The Rise of Nazi Germany

In 1932, on the other side of the world, Germany's electorate accorded a new, dominant status to the rapidly growing National Socialist Party, Adolph Hitler's Nazis. Preying on the bitterness and disillusionment wrought by crushing reparations demanded by the Allies after Germany's World War I defeat, and economic collapse under the governing Weimar Republic, the Nazi Party appeared to offer Germans new hope. Though receiving only a third of the total, the Nazis, with fourteen million votes, had become the largest political party in the nation. Hitler previously vowed to rebuild the Nazi Party and achieve power by constitutional means. In January 1933, he achieved the last of his two goals when the former World War I general and aging president of the Weimar Republic, Paul von Hindenburg, appointed Hitler Germany's Chancellor. The next month, the Nazis used the Reichstag fire as an excuse to jail, beat and torture the Communists wholesale. They also gagged other political parties.

In the six years following his January 1933 accession he smashed democracy, dispossessed and ultimately liquidated Germany's cultivated Jewish population, and crushed party dissidents through terror or sometimes outright murder. He silenced the General Staff, seized the economy, and assumed direction of foreign policy. The rich Saarland, temporarily removed by the Allies from German administration after World War I, voted to rejoin the Reich.[2]

In September 1933, the Nazis held the first of their annual, giant Nuremberg rallies with their attending, huge, uniformed throngs—which assembled to carefully selected, inspiring martial music and the triumphant entry of the dictator, the likes of which the world had never seen. Filled with exciting pageantry and fervent, electrifying appeals to national pride, the rallies were the catalysts for renewing the glories of a Germany once again aggressively reasserting itself on the world stage.

In October 1933, claiming Germany was not given equality with other nations, Hitler took his country out of the League of Nations and the Geneva Disarmament Conference. By the end of the year, Hitler was Fuhrer, his ambition only temporarily satiated. In March of 1935 Hitler revealed a German Air Force already existed, and he provided for a peacetime army of thirty-six divisions.

In the United States—Isolationism

While events were spinning out of control in the Far East and Europe, the democracies struggled to extricate themselves from the strangle hold of economic collapse which followed the panic that engulfed America's Wall Street beginning 24 October 1929. The Wall Street disaster was felt throughout Europe, and on 11 May 1931, in the year Japan occupied Manchuria, Austria's powerful Credit-Ansalt Bank collapsed. On 21 September,

England abandoned the gold standard. World trade dwindled. Wages shrank fantastically, and Europe's growing number of unemployed workers joined the ruined middle class in following the Fascist, National Socialist and Communist movements, which thrived on despair.[3]

In the United States during the decade of the 1930s isolationism reached an all-time peak. It was the period for being cynical about war and patriotism. The commonly accepted belief was America had become involved in the First World War because we had been naive dupes of shrewd British and French propaganda. In the search for scapegoats for war guilt, the Senate's Nye committee investigated munitions makers, offering Americans these "merchants of death" as another conventional wisdom for the cause of war. The theme became a myth making the rounds in America's conversation, "Arms manufacturers deliberately fomented wars to increase the markets for their wares."

When the sound of aggression wafted across the oceans— from Manchuria, Ethiopia, and Spain—and began disturbing the populace, America insulated herself with neutrality laws, forbidding trade with either side in the conflict. It made no difference that our neutrality laws always seemed to harm the victim more than the aggressor. We thought we were safe. That was what mattered.[4]

By 4 March 1933, the day Franklin D. Roosevelt was sworn in following his November election defeat of Herbert Hoover, and little more than a month after Hitler became Germany's chancellor, twelve million Americans were unemployed. Roosevelt came in on promises of immediate relief, recovery and improvement. His makeshift New Deal grew in a curiously effective way, revitalizing the economy. He lowered tariffs, repealed prohibition, relieved pressure on the farmers, revalued gold, and initiated vast public works projects to take up the employment slack. Exuding self-confidence and galvanizing national faith, he brought a number of competent, imaginative men into office, and in his famous First Hundred Days concocted a new style and direction in Federal Government that would do more to change life in America than in any administration since Woodrow Wilson.[5]

On 25 January 1933, prior to the building of the Golden Gate Bridge and President Roosevelt's inauguration, a gleaming, white, luxury liner steamed through the Golden Gate on her first voyage into San Francisco Bay. Built by the Bethlehem Shipbuilding

Company at their Fore River Plant in Quincy, Massachusetts, and launched in 1932, the Matson Line's SS *Lurline* was the third of the company's three magnificent passenger liners. Her two Matson Line sister ships, SS *Monterey* and SS *Mariposa*, built in 1931, were already in service. Captain William Matson, founder and President of the Matson Navigation Company, named the first two *Lurlines* for his daughter, and though he died in 1917, her name was carried on this third magnificent liner. The splendid, fast ship was entering service between San Francisco, Australia and New Zealand.[6]

On 25 February the first United States aircraft carrier specifically designed for the purpose, the USS *Ranger* (CV-4), was christened at Newport News, Virginia, by Mrs. Herbert Hoover, whose husband was defeated in his bid for reelection to the presidency the previous fall. The U.S. had three other carriers, the *Langley* (CV-1), *Lexington* (CV-2), and *Saratoga* (CV-3), but they were ships that had been converted for use as carriers.[7]

The SS *Lurline* arrives in San Francisco on 25 January 1933, at the end of her maiden voyage. NPSSFHMML

Fascism's Rise to Power

In 1933 Italy, Fascism was thriving under Benito Mussolini, who formed his first Fascist Party cell in 1919. By 1922, the same year Berlin arranged the Treaty of Rapallo with Moscow, and the German Army's General Hans von Seeckt had already established secret training and arms manufacturing inside Russia in the Soviet towns of Lipetsk, Saratov, Kazan, and Tula; Mussolini's black-shirted bully boys had so cowed the Italian government he was able to make himself dictator. A new breed of tyrants had arrived on the world stage, complete with the presence of Josef Stalin in the Union of Soviet Socialist Republics.[8]

Totalitarianism was antithetical to everything democracy stood for, with its police state controlling the economic, political and cultural lives of its citizens. But until well into the 1930's, most Americans worried only about Communism. Many openly expressed admiration for Mussolini, who had "made the trains run on time," while Hitler was a man with a comical mustache who headed only a minority party and held no position of political power.[9]

In 1935 the United States was still struggling to overcome the disastrous effects of The Great Depression, but the population, hungry for good news, seemed hungry for even the illusion of good news if real progress couldn't be found. Economic gains registered in 1934 appeared to produce a heady effect on the nation.[10]

The appearance of economic progress sparked disagreements of all kinds. Labor and capital battled in a no-holds-barred brawl. President Roosevelt's New Deal suffered a stunning setback when the Supreme Court declared the National Industrial Recovery Act unconstitutional. Anti-administration forces then had effective ammunition to use against the New Deal, accusing it of being un-American, Bolshevistic, communistic, and socialistic. Major and minor rebellions among Democrats in Congress destroyed Party unity, making it difficult for the President to maintain control of his own supporters. In short, the nation was feuding.[11]

While the feuding continued, on 6 May 1935 the Works Progress Administration (WPA) was instituted under the authority of the Emergency Relief Appropriation Act, which passed on 8

April. On 11 May the Rural Electrification Administration was established by executive order to build power lines and finance electricity production in areas not served by private distributors. The Supreme Court struck down the National Industrial Recovery Act on 27 May, declaring it unconstitutional, invalidating the National Recovery Administration (NRA). The Court's decision implied any government attempts to legislate prices, wages, and working conditions were unconstitutional.[12]

At the 61st annual running of the Kentucky Derby on 4 May, Omaha, with jockey Willis Saunders aboard, won with a time of 2:05. Omaha and Willis Saunders continued their amazing performance by winning the 60th annual Preakness Stakes on 11 May, in a time of 1:58 2/5, and the 67th Belmont Stakes in 2:30 3/5 on 8 June. While Omaha and his jockey were making history on the racetracks, on 24 May, in major league baseball, the Cincinnati Reds and Philadelphia Phillies played the first night baseball game before 20,000 fans at Crosley Field in Cincinnati, Ohio. The Reds beat the Phillies 2-1. On 13 June, James J. Braddock won the heavyweight boxing championship on points in 15 rounds over Max Baer, an amazing comeback by a man considered "all washed up" by sports writers.[13]

So-called proletarian novels reflected conflicting social forces at work given impetus by The Great Depression. The upsurge in this form of novel found a receptive audience, and sparked the founding of a left-wing book club. The trend extended to the theater, the most conservative of the literary-based arts, and Clifford Odets electrified audiences with his glorification of the little man. Imaginative artists discovered American primitivism, which was stimulated by interest in African art. The Federal Music Project employed 18,000 musicians and sponsored thousands of free concerts. The film industry produced a plethora of epics such as "Mutiny on the Bounty," "A Tale of Two Cities," and one of the finest films of all time, "The Informer." Beginning 16 August the nation mourned the loss of the renowned humorist, writer, and film star, Will Rogers, who died with the internationally known, world-traveling aviator, Wiley Post, in an airplane crash near Point Barrow, Alaska.[14]

Founded in 1845, the United States Naval Academy at Annapolis, Maryland, accepted its ninetieth graduation class as Plebes—freshmen—in July 1935. Among the young men entering with the Plebe class were the two brothers, Karl Frederick Border, age 19, and Robert Lee Border, age 17. They were the sons of Captain Lee S. Border, USNA class of 1905. Entering her freshman year in high school, in Minneapolis, Minnesota was 14-year old Mary Joleen Springer, the daughter and only child of George and Charlotte Florence Springer. The paths of Bob and Karl Border, and Joey Springer would intersect five and a half years in the future, at the Puget Sound Navy Yard.[15]

In spite of increasing turmoil and international violence fomented by tyrants in Europe and the Far East, America held firm, rock like, continuing to insulate itself from the growing danger. With the great Atlantic and Pacific barriers to keep the wolves at bay, there was safety and comfort in tending to the nation's domestic needs.

President Roosevelt signed the Social Security Act on 14 August 1935. It established a Social Security Board to supervise payment of old-age benefits, such payments to be determined by the amount of money earned by recipients before their 65th birthdays. On 8 September a powerful demagogue in Louisiana and national politics, Senator Huey Long, was assassinated in the corridor of the state capitol in Baton Rouge, Louisiana, by Dr. Carl Austin Weiss, Jr.[16]

Japanese Aggression and Hawaii's Growing Importance in the Pacific

In the Territory of Hawaii the United States armed forces had long been present, having recognized the importance of Hawaii to military strategy even before annexation to the Union in 1898. American military and naval establishments in the islands grew gradually, with Army strength fluctuating between 13,000 and 15,000 in the decade leading to 1935. Japan's campaign of aggression in Manchuria beginning in 1931 gave impetus to improvements in existing posts and establishing new defenses.

In 1935 the Army reorganized its forces in Hawaii, and the War Department gave the islands priority among overseas garrisons in the posting of soldiers and distribution of munitions. The Army also established a Service Command, in part to deal with civilian problems in the event of war, and placed more emphasis on the role of civilian Hawaii in a Pacific conflict. Studies and military exercises envisioning war in the Pacific made clear wartime problems in Hawaii would markedly differ in three fundamental respects from the problems confronting the continental United States.

First, Hawaii was remote from sources of supply and would be affected by shortages of shipping space. A priority matter for the newly created Service Command was the food supply. Hawaii had historically depended heavily on the mainland for its food supply, a problem evident in World War I. The Service Command addressed the annual meeting of the Hawaiian Sugar Planters' Association (HSPA) on the security aspects of agricultural diversification, and the same year the HSPA appointed a diversified crops committee. The primary purpose of the committee was to explore the economic possibilities of crops other than sugar, but its studies and experiments took new directions as the international situation deteriorated. A shipping strike in 1936-37 would further emphasize Hawaii's vulnerability to limited ocean transportation.

Second, one-third of Hawaii's population was Japanese, approximately 155,000, and among them was an older alien group of 35,000. The remaining 120,000 were American citizens by birth, many holding dual citizenship due to legal complexities. Third, Hawaii was more than 2,000 miles nearer any Pacific front than the continental United States, clearly implying the islands were both an important point of defense, and a vital stepping stone to American operations in the far reaches of the Pacific.[17]

Additionally, major factors in the importance of the islands' geographic location would be the consequences of their loss. Their seizure by the Japanese would place an aggressive enemy astride America's primary sea and air routes to the Far East, effectively severing a major trade and supply line to outlying Pacific posts. Further, Hawaiian air and sea installations under Japanese control would provide them an advance base from which to strike the mainland.

In the period 1931-35, another factor was at work heightening the importance of Hawaii as an American bridge to Australia, New Zealand, and Asia. In November 1931, Juan Trippe, the visionary founder of Pan American Airways began to establish extensive international mail and passenger service to the Caribbean and then to South America using three S-40 flying boats, the first of two four-engine flying boats designed by the

Russian genius Igor Sikorsky. The S-40, with a range of 1,000 miles, could carry 50 passengers in relative comfort. Sikorsky's nearly three-times-longer-range S-42 entered Pan American passenger service to South America in August 1934. But Trippe's visionary drive didn't end with South America. He turned toward the Pacific to expand mail and passenger service.

Famed aviator Charles Lindbergh first convinced Trippe to seek the most efficient route, along the coast of Alaska to Japan, a distance of about 2,000 miles, but diplomatic troubles with the Soviet Union and Japan forced Trippe to consider alternative routes. Straight across the ocean from California to Hawaii, then to Midway Island and Wake Island, an uninhabited lagoon in the Western Pacific, was the most obvious route. From Wake Island, the route would be to Guam, and then finally to Manila in the Philippines. Though the U.S. Postal Service expressed only lukewarm interest in mail service along such routes, Trippe pressed ahead with his plans. In 1935, Pan American built airfields on Midway, Wake and Guam, and ran test flights across the Pacific using the S-42.

For the initial mail service flights, Pan American used the Martin M-130 flying boat, a thoroughly modern plane equipped

The Sikorsky S-42 flies over the towers of the not yet complete Golden Gate Bridge in San Francisco, departing for Hawaii on its 16 April 1935 survey flight. PAAR/UMLSCF

The Martin M-130 *China Clipper* over the port
of San Francisco. PAAR/UMLSCF

with state-of-the-art navigation systems and a range of 3,200 miles
(5,150 kilometers). Modeled like a hotel, with broad armchairs
and full meal service, it could carry as many as 52 passengers.
Trippe dubbed the first M-130 the *China Clipper*, though in truth,
Pan American landing rights were limited to the British colony of
Hong Kong, on the south coast of China.

While the Italian Army was seizing Ethiopia in far away
North Africa in October of that year, Pan American Airways was
planning to begin mail service across the Pacific with the *China
Clipper*, on 22 November 1935. With much fanfare the graceful
flying boat took off from San Francisco and flew to its new Pearl
City base in the Middle Loch of Pearl Harbor, on Oahu, then on
to Manila in the Philippines, with additional stops in Midway,
Wake, and Guam. After 59 hours and 48 minutes of flight across
the international dateline, and six days en route, the *China
Clipper* berthed in Manila on 29 November.[18]

While American's Pan American Airways was opening up
mail service to the Pacific and Far East, on 3 October 1935, a

modern day Roman Caesar and renegade socialist turned Fascist, Benito Mussolini, sent his Army into Ethiopia. In December 1934, anxious to prove his new Fascist Troops, he had provoked a skirmish at Walwal, near the Ethiopian border. Although Emperor Haile Selassie appealed for help to the League of Nations, The League had been virtually condemned to failure in 1919, when the United States Senate defeated President Woodrow Wilson's attempt to lead the nation into the world organization. Wilson had envisioned the League as an international forum to resolve issues and end war. Finally, the League could do nothing in 1935 because the remaining Great Powers refused to intervene. The war in Ethiopia lasted only six months but was marked by terrible atrocities.[19]

In 1936 events across the Atlantic and Pacific continued along the path of ever-deepening crisis. At the beginning of the election year, Democrats closed ranks and party leaders hailed the advent of good times. However, bad times continued for farmers when another scorching drought created a vast dust bowl and sent thousands westward in search of fertile land. On 2 March, Roosevelt signed the Soil Conservation and Domestic Allotment Act, which replaced the Agricultural Adjustment Act, previously invalidated 6 January by the Supreme Court. The new measure provided benefit payments to farmers who practiced soil conservation in a cooperative program to replace soil-depleting crops with soil-conserving crops.

Critics of the New Deal stressed the fact the national debt had been increased to twelve billion dollars since Roosevelt took office, while supporters countered with statistics of their own: an increase of thirty billion dollars in annual income. Labor warfare continued and unions discovered a new weapon in the sit-down strike.

While Hitler's Nazi regime continued to extend its reach and influence, the 1936 Olympic Games, held in Germany, would be the last the world would see for twelve years. At the 5-11 February Winter Olympics, the United States' team won two gold medals and placed fifth in the unofficial team scoring behind Norway, Germany, Sweden, and Finland. At the 5-16 August Summer Olympics, the U.S. won 20 gold medals and placed second in the unofficial team scoring, behind Germany. The star of the summer games was the U.S. Negro athlete, sprinter Jesse Owens, who won four gold medals—a stunning setback to Hitler and his Nazi

Party's "master race," and a step forward in black Americans' long struggle for racial equality in "the land of the free."

On 7 March, between the winter and summer games, Hitler sent his troops into the demilitarized Rhineland and began to fortify it. The Allies did nothing but mumble. Next he sent agents into Austria, and began to subvert that mountain nation of 6,500,000 people.

On 9 May the German Zeppelin Transportation Company's dirigible, Hindenburg, completed the first scheduled transatlantic dirigible flight, landing in Lakehurst, New Jersey. The craft, 830 ft long, 135 ft in diameter, and propelled by four 1050 hp Daimler Benz Diesel engines, had a range of 8,000 miles.[20]

The Spanish Civil War: Europe's Proving Ground for World War II

On 18 July the Spanish Civil War began, the wildest, bloodiest, and most heart-rending of the lesser conflicts leading toward a much larger conflict. Germany, Italy and Russia tested tactics, weapons and commanders after a handful of well-financed right-wing Spanish generals, headed by forty-four-year-old Francisco Franco, led a military revolt against the weak republic. Communist and liberal groups throughout the world joined to support the Republican militia, while Fascists and conservatives backed Franco. The Germans sent tanks, planes and 10,000 men to support Franco, the Italians 75,000. The Russians sent planes, tanks, and ammunition to the Republican forces, and some of their best officers, operating under aliases.[21]

As was written in C.L. Sulzberger's *The American Heritage Picture History of World War II*, "Spain aroused infinite passions and came to represent, in some weird prevision, the ideological fanaticism of World War II, so soon to explode. Before their own bodies and souls were torn on far greater battlefields, millions of people were caught in the emotional and symbolic vortex."

In October 1936, while the brutal, bitter Spanish conflict raged, Britain, France, and the United States maintained strict neutrality, Adolph Hitler and Benito Mussolini reached the agreement that created the Rome-Berlin Axis. Not surprisingly, Franco was victorious and then joined the Rome-Berlin Axis.[22]

In the same month, Pan American Airways inaugurated its first passenger flights across the Pacific, the largest ocean in the world, by carrying nine travelers round-trip from San Francisco to Manila, the route on which the first stop would always be the island of Oahu, Hawaii. Each passenger paid more than $1,400, an astronomical sum at that time. Soon after extending service to Manila and Hong Kong, Juan Trippe began pushing for routes to Australia and New Zealand. Though the British refused to grant landing rights to Australia, New Zealand was more cooperative. Pan American's *Clippers* would begin regular passenger services to New Zealand in March 1937, flying via Kingman Reef south of Hawaii, and American Samoa.[23]

In America's 1936 general elections, the New Deal received a huge vote of confidence. The Democrats increased their gains to three fourths of the seats in both Senate and House of Representatives, and President Roosevelt won reelection in a landslide.

Among books published in 1936 was the blockbuster novel, *Gone With the Wind*, by Margaret Mitchell, which sold 1,000,000 copies in six months, and in 1937 won the Pulitzer Prize; *Further Range* by Robert Frost, which included the poem "Two Tramps in the Mud Time;" and *The Big Money* by John Dos Passos, the third novel of his U.S.A. trilogy, which included *The 42d Parallel* (1930) and *1919* (1932). The foremost American dramatist, Eugene O'Neill, won the Nobel Prize for Literature.[24]

As 1937 began, the worst of the Depression seemed over. The New Deal entered a period of transition in which its measures lost much of their emotional impact. Voices were increasingly raised against the program despite administration attempts to press ahead. The inauguration of President Roosevelt on 20 January 1937 marked the first time the presidential inauguration was held on that date, and in less than a month, the President began efforts to change the composition of the Supreme Court.

On 5 February, after informing congressional leaders at a special Cabinet meeting in the morning, he sent a message to Congress at noon recommending revision of statutes governing the judiciary. Although the purpose was ostensibly to provide more efficient and younger judges in all federal courts, the President was charged with attempting to pack the Supreme Court, which in the past had invalidated hard sought parts of the New Deal legislative program. The following July the Supreme Court Bill was effectively killed when it was voted back into committee.

The American response to the conflicts exploding around
the world was increased isolation. On 1 May the United
States' Neutrality Act of 1937 went into effect, a law which
further tightened the 1935 Act and prohibited the sale of arms
to belligerents. The false sense of security the Act brought to
America would later prove more detrimental to the nation's
natural democratic allies than it would to totalitarians then
stalking the earth.

On 6 May, the same day the nation heard the first coast-to-
coast broadcast of a radio program, the dirigible Hindenburg
was destroyed by fire at its mooring mast in Lakehurst, New
Jersey. Herbert Morrison conducted the program, which aired the
Hindenburg disaster. The huge lighter-than-air-transport burst
into flames and fell to the ground in a few horrifying seconds,
marking the virtual end of transportation by dirigible. Six days
later Americans heard the first worldwide radio broadcast
received in the United States. Listeners heard the coronation of
King George VI of England. On 27 May the Golden Gate Bridge
in San Francisco, California was dedicated.

In sports, War Admiral, with jockey Charles Kurtsinger
aboard, won the 63rd annual Kentucky Derby on 8 May, with a
time of 2:03 1/5. A week later the two repeated victory in the 62nd
running of the Preakness Stakes in 1:58 2/5. Their third in their
triple crown triumphs came on 5 June in the 69th Belmont Stakes,
with a time of 2:28 3/5. On 22 June Joe Louis won the world
heavyweight boxing championship when he knocked out James
J. Braddock in the eighth round in Chicago. At the Wimbledon
tennis championship in England, J. Donald Budge won the men's
singles title. In the fifth annual baseball All-Star Game on 7 July,
the American League defeated the National League 8-3, the
League's fourth win. In Davis Cup tennis, Americans won the
championship on 27 July, defeating Great Britain four matches to
one. On 31 July-1 August the yacht Ranger successfully defended
the America's Cup, winning four straight races from the British
challenger Endeavor. In October the 34th annual World Series
was won by the American League's New York Yankees, four
games to one, over the New York Giants.

In August the first signs of a new recession became apparent
when a wave of selling hit the stock markets. After Labor Day,
the retreat sharpened, and many stocks fell rapidly. By 19
October, a demoralized market had reached the largest number

of transactions since 1933. In late summer, as the market slid, Congress passed and the President signed the National Housing Act, which created the U.S. Housing Authority for administering loans to small communities and states for rural and urban construction.

The American people were deeply affected by the Spanish Civil War. While the government took no official position on the conflict, a considerable portion of the public gave highly emotional support to the Loyalist, antifascist side. Hundreds of volunteers went to Spain, where they joined the Loyalist armies.[25]

Japan's "Special Undeclared War"

While the Spanish Civil War and Axis powers in Europe drew American attention to the east, to the west across the Pacific, Japan, in what was dubbed a "special undeclared war" brought much of Northern China and the Yangtze valley under control, pushing as far as the Wuhan cities. As Chinese resistance stiffened, Japanese blows became more widespread. Invading armies took the coastal cities and territories first, then moved up the rivers and spread inland. Begun in July 1937, the fighting in "The China Incident" lasted until November 1938.

Just after midnight in the early morning hours of 11 December 1937, one of the world's most luxurious cruise liners, the Dollar Line's SS *President Hoover*, ran aground on Hoishoto Island (now Green Island) off the east coast of the Japanese colony of Formosa. The *Hoover* was evacuating Americans from the Far East as a result of mounting tensions and the renewed Japanese offensive in China. She ran aground while en route south on the east side of Formosa, from Kobe, Japan to Manila in the Philippine Islands. With 503 passengers and an inexperienced crew of 330 on board, she was proceeding at night in unfamiliar waters, skirting her normal route and the port of Shanghai. To compound the ship's navigation hazards leading to the accident, the Japanese had turned out all their coastal navigation lights.

After firing flares, sending an SOS, approximately twelve hours of futile attempts to free the ship, and an apparent worsening situation, at low tide, 1 p.m., Captain Yardley ordered the passengers evacuated to the nearby shore. The early SOS alerted the US Navy in Manila and the destroyers *Barker* (DD-213) and *Alden* (DD-211) were ordered to speed to the *Hoover*'s assistance. At dawn on the 11th, the German freighter *Prussia*, arrived but there was nothing she could do. At 3 p.m., as the passenger evacuation was beginning, the Japanese heavy cruiser IJN *Ashigara* and an unidentified *Mutsuki* Class destroyer appeared on the scene to observe and protect the *Hoover*.

All the passengers were landed on the island within 36 hours, although the rescue was complex and harrowing in the heavy seas. At 12:45 p.m. on 12 December, the *Alden*'s crew sighted *Hoishoto* and signaled the Japanese cruiser asking permission to enter Japanese territorial waters. The USS *Barker* arrived shortly afterwards whereupon a Japanese naval officer boarded the *Alden* to formally grant permission on behalf of the Japanese government for the two ships to enter territorial waters and assist the *Hoover*. At 3 p.m. the same day, a Japanese ship, the *Toriyama*, arrived from Keelung carrying food and other necessities for the crew and passengers of the *Hoover*. On 13 December, the Dollar Lines' SS *President McKinley* arrived and the following day departed to Manila carrying 700 passengers and crew from the *Hoover*. By the time *McKinley* left on 14 December, a major international incident involving the United States and Japan was in progress.

On 12 December, as the Christmas holidays were drawing near, the Japanese Naval Air Force bombed and sank the American gunboat *Panay* (PR-5) in Chinese waters, sparking a crisis in U.S-Japanese relations. The Japanese invasion of China was proceeding up the Yangtze River. Most of the American Embassy in Nanking had been evacuated in November while the Chinese were abandoning the city, and the *Panay* had been ordered to remain nearby to provide protection and to evacuate the remaining US Embassy staff "at the last possible moment."

The last of the Embassy evacuees came on board 11 December and *Panay* moved upriver to avoid becoming involved in the fighting around the doomed capital. On 12 December, the Japanese Army ordered naval aircraft to attack "any and all ships" in the Yangtze above Nanking. Knowing of the presence of the *Panay*, the Japanese Navy requested and received verification of the order, prior to launching the attack. Shortly after 1:30 p.m., three Japanese Navy bombing planes flew overhead and released eighteen bombs, one of which disabled *Panay*'s forward 3-inch

American gunboat *Panay* (PR-5), sinking in the
Yangtze River, 12 December 1937. NHHC

gun, wrecked the pilothouse, sick bay and fire room, wounded
the captain (Lieutenant Commander J.J. Hughes) and several
others. Immediately after, twelve more planes dive-bombed and
nine fighters strafed, making several runs over a space of twenty
minutes. She fought back with her .30-cal. machine guns. By 2:06
all power and propulsion were lost, the main deck was awash and,
as Captain Hughes saw that his ship was going down, he ordered
her to be abandoned. Japanese planes strafed the boats on their
way to shore, and even combed the reeds along the riverbank for
survivors. Two of the three accompanying oil barges were also
bombed and destroyed.

The *Panay* survivors, kindly treated by the Chinese,
managed to get word through to Admiral Harry E. Yarnell, the
Commander-in-Chief, American Asiatic Fleet, and were taken on
board USS *Oahu* (PR-6) and the British vessel H.M.S. *Ladybird*
two days later. Two bluejackets and one civilian passenger died
of their wounds; eleven officers and men were seriously wounded.
The *Panay* was sunk, the three men killed, with a total of 43
sailors and 5 civilian passengers wounded. On 14 December the

American government demanded an apology and reparations. The Japanese complied immediately, but continued to wage war in China. The SS *President Hoover* and the US Navy gunboat *Panay* were both total losses.[26]

The news of the *Panay*'s sinking was a shock to Captain Lee S. Border, Bob and Karl Border's father, and brought back memories and an old sea tale to his Midshipmen sons at the Naval Academy. As a Navy commander serving in Chiang Kai-shek's China in 1925-28, their father had supervised the construction of the *Panay*, and the entire family, including nine-year old Bob and eleven-year old Karl had witnessed the exciting launch. Built by Kiangnan Dockyard and Engineering Works, Shanghai, China, and launched 10 November 1927, the gunboat was commissioned 10 September 1928. But there had been a hitch in her launch, an omen for superstitious sailors.

Launched sideways, sliding down rails, instead of the more traditional stern first, the special, more expensive grease for the rails, purchased in the United States and shipped to China, was pilfered by Chinese thieves and sold on the black market. Unknown to Captain Border, a cheaper substitute grease was used in *Panay*'s launch. When the signal came to release her restraints, she slid unceremoniously to a stop part way down the rails, in the words of superstitious sailors, "foretelling a dark end for the ship."[27]

By early March 1938, Adolph Hitler's agents in Austria had done their work well, and with the help of armed Austrian Nazis, in what was termed the Anschlus, he added Austria's land of 6,500,000 people to the German Reich. Again the Allies did nothing, and Hitler announced he wanted no more territory. On 11 March he explained to Benito Mussolini why he had absorbed Austria into the Reich, setting the stage for his move against Czechoslovakia, and the Munich Agreement that would follow 29 September.

While German tanks and planes were being tested in Spain, Hitler turned his attention to the great Slavic plains that the Teutons had long coveted as living space, Lebensraum. Within two weeks after the Anschlus, the funny little man with the mustache was planning to use the large German minority in the Czech Republic's Sudetenland to mount increasing pressure to collapse the Czech government and peacefully overwhelm a second, entire nation. By seizing Austria, he outflanked a ring of fortifications erected around conglomerate Czechoslovakia's western frontier. He had correctly reckoned the Allies would do nothing as long as their interests were not directly threatened.[28] In the United States economic adversity returned, leading to more government spending. The increase did ease the situation a little, but led to further disillusionment with the New Deal. On 16 February the second Agricultural Adjustment Act was signed by President Roosevelt. It maintained the soil conservation program; provided acreage allotments, parity payments, marketing quotas, and commodity loans to farmers, and authorized crop insurance corporations and the "ever-normal granary" proposals of Secretary of Agriculture Henry A. Wallace.

The continuing recession prompted passage of the Revenue Bill of 1938 by Congress, on grounds the tax concessions were needed to stimulate business. The bill reduced taxes on corporations and was supported by Republican and Democratic opponents of the New Deal.

In June President Roosevelt signed the Wage and Hours Act, raising the minimum wage for workers engaged in interstate commerce from 25 cents to 40 cents an hour. The act also limited work hours to 44 per week in the first year of the law, dropping to 40 hours the third year. In passing the law, Congress declared its power to ban interstate shipment of products made by unlawful exploitation of child labor.

The 10 April annexation of Austria by Germany, followed by Hitler's growing pressure on Czechoslovakia began affecting a shift in the American government's interest in foreign affairs. On 26 May the House Committee to Investigate Un-American Activities (HUAC) was formed. For the first time, isolationism vs. limited intervention became an active issue. Talk was widespread about the possibility of war, but few believed it likely. In September concerns were heightened when the European crisis was brought on by German demands in the Sudetenland, then part of Czechoslovakia.

Though President Roosevelt sent private memorandums to Britain, France, Germany and Czechoslovakia on 26 September, recommending arbitration, the Munich Pact was signed on 29 September by the Czech and the British prime ministers. In effect, the Pact surrendered the Sudetenland to Germany along with all Czechoslovakian fortresses on the frontier with Germany. British Prime Minister Neville Chamberlain, key figure in the negotiations

with Adolf Hitler, returned to England and announced he had
secured "peace in our time."

In 8 November's congressional elections the Democrats lost
seven Senate seats but kept a 69-23 majority, with four seats
going to minor parties. In the House Democrats lost 70 seats, for
a 261-164 majority, with four seats going to minor parties.

Technological advances continued at a steady pace in 1938.
James Slayter and John H. Thomas of Newark, Ohio, perfected
methods to manufacture fiberglass. The government issued patents
for nylon, the pioneer synthetic fabric and Du Pont manufactured
toothbrushes with nylon bristles, the first product to reach the
market. Scientists made further advances in atomic physics.

On 23 June, civilian air transportation in the U.S. came under
federal control with the passage of the Civil Aeronautics Act, which
established the Civil Aeronautics Authority as an independent
agency of the federal government. The agency regulated the
licensing of civilian pilots, use of airways, introduction of
new equipment, and rules of flight. Howard Hughes won the
International Harmon Trophy for his flight around the world in
the record time of three days, 19 hours, and 14 minutes.[29]

Pan American Airways Suspends
Pacific *China Clipper* Service

Using the Martin M-130 seaplanes, Pan American Airways had
become the dominant transoceanic airline. By the final months of
1937, the *Clipper* service had gained a reputation as a dependable
and elegant service that literally reduced the size of the world.
On regular flights across the Pacific, the bulk of the cargo was
mail, leaving room for usually eight to ten passengers who could
stretch out in three large compartments, and a larger, combination
lounge and dining salon. During the 18-to-20 hour flight from
San Francisco to Hawaii, passengers could enjoy cocktails in the
lounge and formal evening meals. Although uncomfortable in
comparison to current-day standards, passengers did not seem
bothered by the loud noise of the four engines that droned for the
total flight time of about 60 hours spread over five days en route
to Manila. So famous were the Pan American *Clipper* flying boats

that even Hollywood joined in the chorus of praise by producing a movie named "*China Clipper*," starring Humphrey Bogart.

Pan American's ambitious plans for expansion were tragically cut short, however, when two *Clippers*, the *Samoan Clipper* and the *Hawaiian Clipper*, crashed in 1937 and 1938 within six months of each other, killing all on board. With only two Martin flying boats remaining, the company was forced to cut its schedule by 60 percent. Public confidence in the *Clipper* service plummeted and passenger business dropped off sharply.

During the same period Pan American's monopolistic practices in the international market began drawing fire from many quarters, including pioneer aircraft builder Grover Loening, who resigned from Pan American's board, citing "the monopolistic aims of . . . one company in a tragic blunder of overexpansion, under-preparation and overworking . . . " The U.S. Department of Commerce subsequently withdrew its authorization for Pan American to use American Samoa as a landing point. The company's chief executive officer temporarily turned his attention to transatlantic routes.[30]

The US Navy Continues to Modernize

On 30 September 1937 the Navy commissioned the aircraft carrier *Yorktown* (CV-5) at the Naval Operating Base in Norfolk, Virginia. *Yorktown* was the second Navy combatant designed and built as an aircraft carrier. Under construction since 21 May 1934, sponsored by Mrs. Eleanor Roosevelt—the President's wife—*Yorktown* was launched on 4 April 1936. Nearly twice the length and displacement tonnage of the converted *Langley* (CV-1), the big, new carrier was fifty feet longer and displaced 5,300 tons more than *Ranger*. The second carrier in the *Yorktown* class, the *Enterprise* (CV-6), launched 3 October 1936 by Newport News Shipbuilding and Dry Dock Company, Newport News, was commissioned 12 May 1938.

In November 1938 the U.S. Army Signal Corps subjected their early radar to exhaustive tests by the Coast Artillery. Developed in 1936 and demonstrated before the Secretary of War in 1937, the new technology would prove to be invaluable to the nation's defense in the years to come.

During 14-18 November, delegates to the annual convention of the Committee for Industrial Organization met in Pittsburgh, Pennsylvania, formed the Congress of Industrial Organizations (CIO), and unanimously elected John L. Lewis president. On 13 December, the Works Progress Administration issued a report indicating federal relief dropped to 2,122,960, compared with 3,184,000 the previous year. The National Safety Council put the number of automobile-related deaths for the year at more than 32,000. About one third of the fatalities involved pedestrians. Collisions between motor vehicles accounted for almost 9,000 deaths.

In the meantime, movie attendance dropped 40% for the year. The top moneymaker of 1938 was "Snow White and the Seven Dwarfs," which made Walt Disney famous around the world, and became a film classic. On 30 October Orson Welles staged his radio play "War of the Worlds," based on the novel by H.G. Wells. The realistically performed news reports of an invasion from Mars caused widespread panic, demonstrating the power of the new medium to influence large numbers of people. Author Pearl S. Buck won the Nobel Prize for Literature with her novel, *The Good Earth*, another of her popular stories set in China.[31]

The Subtle Preparations for War in Hawaii

While attitudes in the continental United States toward accelerating international violence remained essentially unchanged in the mid-30s on into the year 1938, subtle changes began occurring in Hawaii. They began as undercurrents not directly related to war.

In 1935 a lava flow that threatened the city of Hilo on the "big island" of Hawaii, led to suggestions for formation of a major disaster council. In January 1938, an earthquake brought about a meeting of Honolulu city-county department heads and certain other persons to discuss "all phases of precaution against possible disaster." Only such disasters as "earthquake, epidemic, tidal wave or conflagration" were mentioned. While the word "war" wasn't publicly mentioned and discussions didn't result in action either, the seeds of organized preparation for a major emergency had been planted. Events involving Japan's deepening incursion into China would eventually be the catalysts for spurring Hawaii toward preparations for a possible attack on the islands.[32]

In November 1936, the first of three important events had been set in motion, which placed the Japanese firmly on the path to general war. The Japanese Army negotiated an Anti-Comentern Pact with Germany and Italy, intended to check the Soviets' ambitions in the Far East. Then came the Miyazaki Plan of 1936-37, which involved the expansion of heavy industry to enable Japan to wage a total war for three years. Next began the "special undeclared war" in China, when the Japanese clashed with Chinese forces outside Peking on 7 July 1937.

Japan's special undeclared war started with a series of successes in 1937, but began to bog down in late 1938. To initiate their 1937 campaign against coastal cities and territories, the Japanese had drawn down their garrisons in Manchuria. They were attempting to swallow a giant, and as Napoleon learned in Czarist Russia in the early 19th century, success at first mushroomed, then the enemy began to mount counterattacks using guerrilla warfare. By the end of September 1937, the Japanese had dispatched ten divisions to northern China, and five to Shanghai. The Chinese Nationalist Army evacuated Shanghai after 11 November 1937, and the Japanese moved against Nanking, which fell on 13 December amid scenes of mass murder, rape, torture and pillage.

Guerrilla attacks began in early 1938, and guerrilla war and banditry spread into Manchuria. During 1938, clashes with the Soviets erupted. The Japanese then faced the need for increasing security in Manchuria while continuing their aggressive offensive in China and avoiding further serious clashes with the Soviets.

Japan's drive deeper into China required expanded control of the Chinese population, and spawned a series of internal problems affecting trade, finance, and the need for a larger merchant fleet. The growing need for a merchant fleet for import and export was competing with a determined Naval rearmament program in overcrowded shipbuilding yards. Congestion in shipyards was causing massive construction delays in their Navy's most important fleet units, thus dragging out their preparations for three years of general war. A side effect in the eyes of the Western democracies was Japan's drive for expansion and dominance in the Far East appeared to be slowing. Japan could have her Miyazaki Plan to prepare for three years of war, but she couldn't have the plan and a war in China simultaneously. Then, beginning in August 1939, came a series of jolts that, for a time, disillusioned the Japanese and their now firmly-in-control, militarist regime.

On 23 August Germany signed a nonaggression pact with the Soviet Union, preparatory to the Wehrmacht's invasion of Poland nine days later. The signing effectively negated the Anti-Comentern Pact Japan had signed with Germany and Italy in 1936, and occurred as Soviet forces were quite literally taking apart Japanese forces in Mongolia, at the battle of Nomonhan. Defeat of the Japanese in Mongolia, disillusionment with Germany and a new-found respect for Britain and France, which had finally shown the will to resist Hitler, caused Japan to make for the sidelines after September 1939, the month general war exploded in Europe.[33]

Germany invaded Poland on 1 September. On 3 September Britain and France declared war on Germany. In response on 3 September, first Belgium, and then the United States—in a fireside chat by President Roosevelt—declared their neutrality, while on the same day thirty Americans died when a German submarine sank the British passenger ship *Athenia*. The following day, Secretary of State Cordell Hull advised U.S. citizens to travel to Europe only under "imperative necessity." On 17 September, as the German Army was driving east, deep into Poland, the Soviets struck west into Poland, completing the country's overwhelming, aggressive dismemberment by Nazi Germany and Soviet Russia.

At the beginning of 1939, America was remaining aloof from the struggles besetting the Europeans and Chinese. Historical novels had never been so plentiful. Among books published that year was *The Grapes of Wrath* by John Steinbeck, a powerful novel centered on an Oklahoma farm family who lose their farm to the bank and travel to California to seek work as migrant farm laborers. The book, described as a proletarian novel examined in moving detail the plight of the Okies, and by extension the plight of all people caught up in tragic circumstances not of their own making. The novel won a Pulitzer Prize in 1940 and was the basis for a motion picture classic.

Also published in 1939 was *Adventures of a Young Man* by John Dos Passos, the first novel of trilogy entitled District of Columbia; *The Wild Palms* by William Faulkner, a novel; *Captain Horatio Hornblower* by C.S. Forester; Collected Poems by Robert Frost; *Pale Horse, Pale Rider* by Katherine Anne Porter, a collection of stories; and *Abraham Lincoln: The War*

Years by Carl Sandburg, four volumes of history. On 1 May the Pulitzer Prize for fiction went to *The Yearling* by Marjorie Kinnan Rawlings; for biography, to *Benjamin Franklin* by Carl Van Doren; for history, *A History of American Magazines* by Frank Luther Mott; for poetry, *Selected Poems* by John Fletcher; and for drama, *Abe Lincoln in Illinois* by Robert E. Sherwood.

As the year progressed, film producers contended with the prospect of losing entirely the lucrative European market. Nevertheless, this was the year of "Gone With the Wind," one of the most expensive and most successful movies of all time.

On 10 May the Methodist Church issued a Declaration of Union which reunited some 8,000,000 American Methodists after 109 years of division. The conflict had begun in 1830 with the first of two major crises, which first separated the Methodist Protestant Church from the Methodist Episcopal Church over the question of Episcopal authority, and the second which further separated the Methodist Episcopal Church, South, from the Episcopal Church in 1844.[34]

Aboard the USS *Tennessee*—

On 1 June Midshipmen Karl Border and his younger brother, Bob Border, graduated with the US Naval Academy's class of 1939. Karl, who began keeping a diary when he entered the Academy the summer of 1935, recorded the event, intending to mark the beginning of a long, proud, happy life of service and camaraderie. On 24 June, the brand new ensigns reported aboard the battleship *Tennessee* (BB-43), in San Pedro, California, which had been her Pacific Fleet homeport since 1921. Their father, a senior Navy captain after 34 years of service, had, in the background, quietly intervened in behalf of his sons to obtain their assignments to the same ship after they graduated from Annapolis. Again, Karl captured the lifelong memory in his diary.[35]

Peacetime service in the battleship divisions, as on all Navy combatants, involved an annual cycle of training, maintenance, and readiness exercises. *Tennessee*'s yearly schedule included competitions in gunnery and engineering performance and an annual fleet problem, a large-scale war game in which most or all of the United States Fleet was organized into opposing forces

Captain (USN) Lee S. Border, USNA Class of 1905 (center),
and his two sons, Ensigns Robert L. Border (left) and Karl F.
Border, graduation day, 1 June 1939. Borders' Collection

**USS *Tennessee* (BB-43), Underway, 27 September 1939, with
roommates Ensigns Bob and Karl Border on Board. USN**

and presented with a variety of strategic and tactical situations to
resolve. Beginning with Fleet Problem I in 1923 and continuing
through Fleet Problem XXI in April 1940, *Tennessee* had a
prominent share of these battle exercises.

Yet her individual proficiency was not neglected. During the
competitive year 1922 and 1923, her crew made the highest
aggregate score in the list of record practices fired by her guns
of various caliber and won the "E" for excellence in gunnery.
In 1923 and 1924, her crew again won the gunnery "E" as well
as the prized Battle Efficiency Pennant for the highest combined
total score in gunnery and engineering competition. During
1925, she took part in joint Army-Navy maneuvers to test the
defenses of Hawaii before visiting Australia and New Zealand.
Subsequent fleet problems and tactical exercises took *Tennessee*
from Hawaii to the Caribbean and Atlantic, and from Alaskan
waters to Panama.[36]

Four days after Bob, Karl, and their classmates joined *Tennesse*'s
crew, and were readjusting to life on America's west coast—and in
the Navy's Battleship Force, Pacific Fleet—Pan American Airways

was reaching overseas again, this time from America's east coast. Transatlantic passenger air service began on 28 June when the *Dixie Clipper*, one of Pan American's huge, new B-314 flying boats, left Port Washington, Long Island, with 22 passengers aboard, and reached Lisbon, Portugal 23 hours and 52 minutes later.

While the German's 1 September invasion of Poland forcibly nudged the United States toward war allied with the Western Democracies, pragmatic reluctance fueled by the drag of lingering isolationism and a glaring lack of preparedness, continued to hold the nation in check. President Roosevelt's transfer of fifty destroyers to Great Britain, and his fireside chat declaring the nation's neutrality the same day 30 Americans died during the sinking of the British ship *Athenia*, clearly demonstrated the dilemma the nation faced.

Nevertheless, on 18 October, by presidential executive order, the United States closed all her ports to belligerent submarines. On 4 November the U.S. Congress passed the Neutrality Act of 1939, repealing the prohibition of arms exports in the 1937 law, and authorizing the "cash and carry" sale of arms to belligerent powers.

Ernest Orlando Lawrence of the University of California received the Nobel Prize in Physics for his development of the cyclotron and for subsequent discoveries in the field of radioactivity, specifically the study of artificially radioactive elements. With Lawrence's invention of the cyclotron, nuclear scientists had an invaluable instrument with which to produce subatomic particles required for study of nuclear reactions. The invention also proved to be a crucial milestone in the research and development of atomic weapons.[37]

Soviet Russia Turns Toward Estonia, Latvia, Lithuania, and Finland

The German-Soviet non-aggression pact of 23 August had assigned Stalin's Soviets Finland, Estonia, Latvia and (later) Lithuania as an "area of interest." Hitler cynically threw these small countries to Russia as a means of keeping his temporary ally occupied while he dealt with France and England.

Stalin rapidly absorbed Estonia, Latvia, and Lithuania by

forcing "mutual defense" pacts upon them, and then pouring in Russian troops to "defend" his new "allies." From Finland, Stalin demanded the Karelian Isthmus up to Viipuri, four small islands in the Gulf of Finland, the Finnish portion of the Rybachi Peninsula, and the use of Hango as a Russian naval and air base. He declared the concessions essential for Russian security, particularly in the Leningrad-Kronstadt area.

The Finns knew they had no hope of single handedly defeating the Russians, their historical enemy, but they did hope to hold out until other nations might be moved to come to their assistance or—failing that—to put the blood price too high for even the Muscovite stomachs. On 30 November, without a declaration of war, Stalin turned his air force loose on Finland's capital, Helsinki, and the second largest city, Viipuri. The Russians, though possessing overwhelming numbers and firepower, soon learned they were ill-prepared for the fierce, well-planned, coordinated defense by the Finns, and took bitter losses in a winter ground war that lasted into March 1940—when the Finns were forced to accept essentially the same terms demanded by Stalin prior to the Soviet attack.

Some 11,500 foreign volunteers—mostly Swedish, Norwegian, Danish, a few Americans, and a Hungarian battalion came to assist Finland, but needed extensive training and never saw action. Britain and France began preparing a 100,000 man expeditionary force but Sweden and Norway, holding fast to their neutrality, refused to let the Allies pass through their countries.[38]

The Germans Assault Denmark, Norway and Western Europe

Denmark and Norway were Hitler's next targets. The Germans' joint army-navy-air force planning began on 21 February while Russia was heavily engaged in Finland. Their task force weighed anchor on 7 April 1940 and two days later landed lightly equipped forces at Oslo, Kristiansand, Bergen, Trondheim and Narvik while Denmark was swiftly overrun to provide advance air force bases to support operations in Norway.

The Norwegians were ill-prepared and reacted slowly, but fought hard. By 3 May the Allies had been forced to evacuate

Norway. Sweden continued to maintain its strict neutrality in the face of the German and Russian onslaughts against their neighbors to the east and the west. The stage was set for the German assault on Holland, Belgium, Luxembourg, France and England.[39]

France and Britain were slow to mobilize and transition to war production following Germany's 1 September attack on Poland. Planning for defense of France and the lowland countries was hampered by the strict neutrality maintained by Holland and Belgium. By the time Hitler's Blitzkrieg struck the night of 9-10 May 1940, the British Expeditionary Force (BEF) in France numbered 394,165, but France and Britain had taken no significant offensive action following the German assault on Poland the previous September.

Five days after Germany struck, the Dutch surrendered. By 22 May the Germans drove to France's English Channel coast, isolated the BEF from the French armies, and invested the French coastal city of Calais—which surrendered on 27 May. On 28 May the BEF established a defensive perimeter around Dunkirk.

By 5 June the Germans, temporarily held back by a puzzling and controversial order from Hitler, entered Dunkirk, where the British Navy and hundreds of volunteer, civilian-manned boats— with covering air support of the Royal Air Force—had completed the evacuation of 338,226 British, French and Belgian soldiers from the beaches and harbor adjoining Dunkirk. Paris fell on 14 June, and three days later, France's former Chief of Staff and World War I hero, Henri Phillippe Petain, who had been recalled as ambassador to Spain and became Premiere, asked for an armistice.

The last week of the campaign had been an anti-climax. Hitler's Army marched triumphantly into Paris for the signing, where, on 22 June, the Fuhrer placed his signature on the humiliating treaty. Hostilities didn't cease until 25 June, when the Italians likewise signed.

Mussolini, eager to share in the spoils of victory, had declared war on 10 June, but it was the 20th before his generals were prepared to attack. Stalled at the border by the much weaker but more determined French, the Italians begged Hitler to advance troops from Grenoble toward the border. The Fuhrer's Army made only a half-hearted effort, and Italy went to the conference table without military conquests.

Thus ended the campaign in the West. Hitler's Blitzkrieg

shattered the Allied armies in Western Europe in six weeks and pursued them with a vengeance reminiscent of Napoleon.

Hitler now sought to coax and cajole Britain into suing for peace. Rebuffed, he ordered plans prepared for an invasion of England. The Germans named the plan "Operation Sea Lion," and changed it several times amid constant bickering between their Army and Navy. Never destined to be implemented, Operation Sea Lion was still-born because Herman Goring's vaunted Luftwaffe, the German Air Force, couldn't sweep the Royal Air Force from the skies and obtain air superiority over England.

Operating against newly developed radar and superior fighter planes, and employing their bomber and fighter forces less skillfully than they might have, the Germans suffered a decisive defeat in the critical Battle for Britain in the period 10 July-31 October. The courage and sacrifices of the valiant handful of British fighter pilots, augmented by relatively small numbers of Polish, Free French, Australian, Canadian, and American volunteer fighter pilots, spared England the ordeal of a German invasion.[40]

Hitler Looks to the East—But Other Axis Conquests Come First

Adolph Hitler and Nazi Germany now turned their attention eastward, where Hitler's partner in the dismemberment of Poland posed the only threat to German dominance of the Continent. Before attacking Soviet Russia, however, there were other conquests to be gained—in the Balkans and further south. As early as July 1940, Hitler—urged by Goring and Admiral Erich Raeder—began considering operations against the British in the Mediterranean. At the same time, he directed his planners to study an invasion of Russia. With the disastrous defeat of the Luftwaffe in the Battle of Britain, Hitler decided to transfer operations to the Mediterranean.

While Hitler's Wehrmacht (German Armed Forces) was engaged in France, the Russians seized Bessarabia from Rumania. Germany, after forcing the Rumanians to cede parts of Dobrudja to Bulgaria and Transylvania to Hungary, then combined with Italy to guarantee what was left of Rumania. These upheavals brought General Ion Antonescu to power, and on 7 October, at his request, German troops entered the country. Other moves by the Italians, against the British in North Africa, in Somaliland, the Sudan, Kenya, Libya—then Egypt, were precursors to the war's spreading into the Balkans.

Soon after the fall of France, Mussolini began a propaganda campaign aimed at establishing a pretext for an Italian invasion of Greece. Having seized Albania in 1939, Italy was ideally positioned for an invasion, but the Greeks refused to offer provocation. In spite of the propaganda campaign aimed at Greece, Mussolini seems to have preferred an attack on Yugoslavia as offering greater strategic advantages. Certain an assault on Yugoslavia would require German assistance, he sought Hitler's opinion in July 1940. Hitler emphatically refused whereupon Il Duce began concentrating on North Africa's Libya. But not for long.

By August 1940 his eyes were again on Greece. On 28 October his troops crossed the Greek border, and war came to the Balkans.[41]

Japan's Reawakening, America's and Hawaii's Growing Restlessness

Japan, uncertain and waiting upon events, had sidelined herself from the Rome-Berlin Axis and war on the other side of the world since September 1939, though her underlying problems remained unresolved. In the spring of 1940, however, one set of circumstances was no longer uncertain. Germany's shattering victory in northwest Europe—the overrunning of Denmark, Norway, Holland, Belgium, Luxembourg, France, and in the spring, poised to assault England—rekindled admiration and support for Germany within Japan, specifically within the Army. Japan's adherence to a treaty of alliance with Nazi Germany and Fascist Italy, the Tripartite Pact, followed on 27 September 1940.

The Pact committed Japan irreversibly to the new order reshaping the international community. Perhaps this was inevitable. The crushing defeat of France in May and June 1940 removed the European colonial empire's first line of defense in southeast Asia, French Indochina, and provided Japan maximum temptation at apparently little risk to herself. Within weeks of

France's defeat, Japan forced French authorities in Indochina and the British in Burma to close down supply routes to the Nationalist Chinese regime in Chungking. Japan had initiated a process that would end one year later with the crisis that was to lead to general war throughout the Pacific and southeast Asia.[42]

With the outbreak of war in Europe, in September 1939, the key political question facing the United States in 1940 became how to stay out of the conflict and still help the forces of democracy. Realizing America was facing a crisis, President Franklin D. Roosevelt decided to run for an unprecedented third term. At the Republican National Convention, the Grand Old Party nominated a political newcomer, Wendell L. Wilkie, whose plainspoken manner made him a powerful rival and contender. Roosevelt, nominated on the first ballot at the Democratic National Convention, would win in November largely because people felt it unwise to change an administration in dangerous times.

On 5 February, while Russia was continuing to press the assault on Finland, and Nazi Germany was pausing before launching attacks against Denmark and Norway, the Glenn Miller Orchestra recorded "Tuxedo Junction." His orchestra was well on its way to the pinnacle of success in the world of popular music, carried by a unique, romantic sound which became a staple for an entire generation of young Americans.[43]

As days and weeks rolled by and the shocking, precipitous collapse of the Allied defenses in Finland, Denmark, Norway, Holland, Belgium, Luxembourg, and France ended with the French asking for an armistice, America was turning ever-so-slowly to face the realization the continental United States could no longer remain isolated from the turmoil in Europe and Asia. In Hawaii the mood was somewhat more urgent. With additional support coming from the mainland and its armed forces, and at the urging of the growing military presence on the islands, the Territory was accelerating its preparations for possible attack.

In Washington on 28 June, Congress passed the Alien Registration Act, also known as the Smith Act. President Roosevelt signed the bill into law the next day. The legislation required registration and fingerprinting of aliens and made it unlawful to belong to any organization advocating overthrow of the U.S. government. Subsequent registration showed approximately 5,000,000 aliens living in the United States.

After Roosevelt was nominated for a third term and the Luftwaffe launched the German air campaign against England in August 1940, his administration accelerated specific measures to assist the Allies and build up America' s armed forces. On 3 September the U.S. gave 50 outdated, World War I, "four stacker" destroyers to Great Britain in exchange for 99-year leases on naval and air bases in Newfoundland and the West Indies. Still struggling with the siren call of isolationism, Congress on 16 September narrowly passed the Selective Service Act by the margin of one vote, the first peacetime draft law in American history. The law required registration of all men between the ages of 20 and 36, and provided for taking not more than 900,000 selectees each year, for one year of service. In 1941, Congress would extend the period of service to not more than 30 months, and lift the limit of 900,000 selectees annually.

Japan's revived aggressive moves against the French and British in Southeast Asia, followed by the 27 September signature on the Tripartite Pact with Germany and Italy, clearly indicated the crisis in the Far East was deepening. On 12 October President Roosevelt urged Americans to come home from the Orient, directing a seaborne evacuation. The directive greatly increased the sense of urgency which fueled the voluntary exits of American citizens from China, following Japan's invasion of 1931, its renewed assault in 1937, the subsequent evacuation of the American Embassy in Nanking and the sinking of the U.S. gunboat *Panay*.

On 5 November 1940, with his vice presidential running mate, Henry A. Wallace, Franklin D. Roosevelt defeated Wendell Wilkie for the presidency, propelling Roosevelt into an unprecedented third term. He won the electoral vote 449 to 82, and the popular vote, 27,244,160 to 22,305,198 for Wilkie. Socialist Norman Thomas received 100,264 votes; Prohibition candidate Roger W. Babson 57,812; Communist Earl Browder 48,579; and Socialist Labor candidate John W. Aiken, 14,861. In Congressional elections, the Democrats lost three Senate seats but kept a 66-28 majority, with two seats going to minor parties. The Democrats gained seven seats in the House of Representatives for a 268-162 lead, with five seats going to minor parties.

The 1940 census recorded the U.S. population as 131,669,275. Statisticians calculated the population's geographical center as two miles southeast by east of Carlisle, Indiana, in Sullivan

County. Average life expectancy was 64 years, a major increase from 49 years in 1900. Illiteracy reached a new low of 4.2% of the population, a decline of 0.1% from 1930, and a 15% drop from 1870. A survey determined 30,000,000 radios could be found in American homes.

Technological and medical advances continued, with the first publicly tested electron microscope at the Radio Corporation of America Laboratory in Camden, New Jersey, on 20 April. The Vought-Sikorsky Corporation completed the first successful helicopter flight in the U.S., by the experimental VS-300 on 15 May. Dr. Selman Waksman of Rutgers University, a pioneer in antibiotics, produced the first antibiotic developed in the U.S., actinomycin, found to be too poisonous for humans.

In 1940, author Richard Wright wrote a powerful novel, *Native Son*, considered by many to be Wright's masterpiece. The story was of Bigger Thomas, a young black drawn into crime and ultimately to execution as a murderer. Wright and Paul Green adapted the novel for Broadway the following year, a play which had a successful run. Wright's novel was among several important books published in 1940, among them, *The Hamlet* by William Faulkner, the first novel of a trilogy about the Snopes family; *For Whom the Bell Tolls* by Ernest Hemingway, set in Spain during that country's civil war; and *You Can't Go Home Again* by Thomas Wolfe, who had died in 1938. Critics found Wolfe's novel quieter and better organized than his earlier works.

Sports competition continued unabated in the United States while international competitions such as the 1940 winter and summer Olympics, Davis Cup and Wimbledon (tennis) were canceled. Indiana University won the National Collegiate Athletic Association basketball championship, defeating the University of Kansas 60-42 on 30 March. W. Lawson Little won the U.S. Open golf tournament on 9 June, and Byron Nelson won the PGA tournament on 2 September. Professional baseball's World Series went on as planned 2-8 October, with the National League's Cincinnati Reds defeating the American League's Detroit Tigers four games to three. On 8 December, in professional football's season-ending championship game, the National Football League's Chicago Bears defeated the Washington Redskins by the incredible score of 73-0.[44]

Collegiate football's year began on New Years Day 1940 with five bowl games played. At the Rose Bowl in Pasadena, California, the University of Southern California Trojans defeated the University of Tennessee Volunteers 14-0. In the Orange Bowl in Miami, Florida, it was the Ramblin' Wreck of Georgia Tech over the Missouri Tigers, 21-7. At the Sugar Bowl in Tulane Stadium in New Orleans, Louisiana, Texas A & M's Aggies played a close, exciting game against Tulane's Green Wave, winning 14-13. In the Cotton Bowl at Dallas, Texas, the Clemson University Tigers took the measure of Boston College in a close defensive game, 6-3. And in the Sun Bowl at Kidd Stadium at the Texas School of Mines, now University of Texas, El Paso, the Arizona State Sun Devils and Catholic University fought to a 0-0 tie. At the end of the fall 1940 football season, the University of Minnesota's Golden Gophers, with an 8-0-0 record, were selected as the mythical national champions, named as such by 10 of 14 organizations that ranked collegiate football teams of that era.[45]

In the War Department in Washington, DC, across the mainland, and in the Territory of Hawaii, secret planning and quiet, behind the scenes work to prepare for war was well under way. Military and civilian leaders conducted preparations carefully, thoughtfully, in a manner intended to avoid panicking citizens.

The Navy's Pacific Forces Move Forward and Hawaii Prepares for War

As the year 1940 began in Hawaii, the American Fleet's presence was a small unit at Pearl Harbor consisting of a carrier, heavy cruisers, and destroyers, called the Hawaii Detachment, the only force of consequence in the area. On 6 January Admiral James O. Richardson assumed command of the United States Fleet. In early spring Navy headquarters dispatched Admiral Richardson to Hawaii for the service's annual maneuvers, this year Fleet Problem XXI. On 10 April the fleet stood into Lahaina Roads, off the island of Maui.

When the maneuvers ended, the Fleet commander expected to take his armada, minus the Hawaiian Detachment, back to its homeport at San Pedro, California. The expected departure date of 9 May passed, and the Fleet remained in Hawaiian waters. Instead, on direction from President Roosevelt, the Navy Department kept Admiral Richardson and his fleet in Hawaiian waters, while finalizing a decision to move its base of operations from San Pedro to Hawaii.

The Chief of Naval Operations, Admiral Harold R. Stark, explained the delay to Richardson, attributing the decision to "the deterrent effect which it is thought your presence may have on the Japs going into the East Indies." From Richardson's perspective "the Fleet gradually drifted into staying in Hawaii," while the War Department concluded the "recent Japanese-Russian agreement to compose their differences . . . was arrived at and so timed as to permit Japan" to attack Oahu, "following the US Fleet's departure from Hawaii."

There followed a message from Washington to Major General Charles D. Herron, commanding general of the Army's Hawaiian Department, a message reading in part, "Immediate alert. Complete defensive organization to deal with possible transpacific raid . . . Maintain alert until further orders." Herron kept his forces on their toes throughout the summer, then the elevated readiness status gradually faded out.[46]

By 1940, food supply had actually become a serious problem in Hawaii. With the presence of the Pacific fleet and the arrival of defense workers, available shipping space was insufficient to maintain Island food stocks. Importers were given shipping space quotas. Appointment of a territorial committee to study the situation was urged and numerous attempts were made to obtain federal, local, or Army and Navy funds, but without success. At the request of the board of supervisors, Honolulu's mayor appointed a committee in July to analyze ways to meet the city's food requirements in the event of a tie-up of shipping because of labor disputes or other contingencies.

The committee found that Oahu produced only 15 percent of its normal food needs and stocked only a 45-day supply of imported food. It also recommended planning for wartime rationing and the appointment of a strong food commission. The committee completed its report near the end of August, and placed it on file.

In the fall of 1940, the Army took its food plan out of the secret category and presented it to plantation managers. The comprehensive program envisioned close control over production, storage, and distribution in the event of war. It approached the problem by considering the amount of food needed by Hawaii's civilian population and specified where in the islands it should be grown. It selected irrigated sugar lands because they provided more certain production than others. Both sugar and pineapple plantations set out experimental vegetable plots and intensively encouraged workers' individual gardens.

In September, the Pineapple Producers' Cooperative Association appointed an emergency food committee to work with the Army in maintaining a schedule of pineapple lands that could be used for food production. About this time the Hawaiian Academy of Science held a symposium, which brought out the inadequacies of Hawaii's food supplies and urged householders to stock their cupboards with food in order to clear needed space on retail shelves and in warehouses for storage of goods. The University of Hawaii agricultural experiment station, the University of Hawaii agricultural extension service, and the vocational agriculture division of the department of public instruction, which had been accumulating information on food crops and encouraging greater diversification of Island agriculture through the years, now intensified such work.

At the end of 1939 and during 1940, Honolulu physicians informally discussed the possibility of establishing a blood bank. In 1940 the Territorial Medical Association appointed a committee on preparedness and a representative to the National Committee on Medical Preparedness. The Honolulu Medical Society also appointed a preparedness committee, but its effort to arouse interest at that time met little success.

Further discussion of a major disaster council occurred in 1940. In July a new city-county committee openly discussed the possibility of "war in Hawaii." It considered a detailed plan of disaster relief and recommended a full-time secretary be employed. A new administration postponed action on the committee's report, which was submitted just before fall elections.

A new Provisional Police organization formed in July 1940 when the Army asked the mayor and the chief of police of Honolulu and the managers of Oahu plantations and utilities to plan for civilian participation in defending Hawaii against possible attack. Throughout the fall and winter, plantation employees, members of the American Legion, and utility workers trained in guard duty. By April 1941, 1,500 guards were ready for action, and in May more than a third participated in Army maneuvers. Most of the utilities had already taken some measures to protect their installations, and they now began erecting man-proof fences and floodlights around

Pan American Airways Boeing B-314 *California Clipper*,
over San Francisco with Oakland Bay Bridge and Treasure
Island in the distant background. PAAR/UMLSCF

their properties. As early as 1939 the board of water supply had
devoted bill stuffers to include such defense preparedness subjects
in monthly statements, as "what happens to water service under
bombardment." Beginning in 1940, many utilities employees were
finger printed, photographed, and blood-typed.

Island women had been knitting, sewing, and rolling surgical
dressings for England since the fall of 1939. After August 1940,
on recommendation of the Army, some of the dressings were kept
in Hawaii. The sewing corps rolled 145,000 surgical dressings
and knitted 6,000 garments and sent them to England by March
1941, when it was decided to hold all such goods in Hawaii.[47]

With the crashes of the two Pan American *Clippers* in a six-
month period in 1937-38, and the cessation of Southwest Pacific
flight operations, Hawaii had temporarily lost its air passenger
service. Pan American's chief executive officer, Juan Trippe, had
for a time turned his attention to transatlantic routes—but he did
not lose his determination to restore the *Pacific Clipper* service. In

a brilliant strategic move, he introduced the magnificent Boeing B-314 seaplane on the Pacific routes. The huge whale-shaped B-314 had already proved itself in the North Atlantic, and its range of 3,500 miles was perfect for the Pacific. In February 1939, the B-314 officially replaced the Martin M-130 flying boats on the Northern Pacific route. Later, in July 1940, Trippe finally reopened the South Pacific route that stretched from California, through Hawaii to New Zealand. The service would prove valuable to the Territory of Hawaii, in the years ahead.[48]

The Army Activates the Hawaiian Air Force

The U.S. Army Transport *Leonard Wood*, one of several ships leased to the Army to support the Pacific build-up and evacuation of American citizens, including State Department and military dependents, from the Far East, arrived in Hawaii on Saturday night, 2 November 1940. A tall gentleman walked down the gangway.

> . . . He had waving gray hair and thick brows shadowing pleasant eyes. His thin face with its oblong jaw, big nose, high forehead, and large ears looked more scholarly than military.

In his brilliant work, *At Dawn We Slept*, author Gordon W. Prange described *Leonard Wood*'s passenger, his background, and his mission in Hawaii.

> Major General Frederick L. Martin won his wings at the age of thirty-nine, when he was already a major. He completed courses at the Air Tactical School at Langley Field, Virginia, and the [Army] Command and General Staff School at Fort Leavenworth, Kansas. Then followed a series of command assignments. Further study brought him to the Army War College. After duty at Wright Field, Ohio, he took over command of the Third Bombardment Wing at Barksdale Field, Louisiana, in the spring of 1937 with the temporary rank of brigadier general.

On 1 October 1940, be became a temporary major general, and concurrently received his orders to command the Hawaiian Air Force, activated on 1 November . . . When he took over his new post, he ranked as the Air Corps's senior pilot and technical observer and had logged 2,000 hours of flight time.

Martin was not in the best physical condition and appeared older than his fifty-eight years. He had earlier developed a severe, chronic ulcer condition, which required surgery and undermined his health. As a result, he had not touched an alcoholic drink for years.

His assignment placed him in an ambiguous position. As commander of the Hawaiian Air Force he had direct access to Major General H.H. "Hap" Arnold, chief of the Air Corps, but he remained under the command of Short, a foot soldier to the soles of his boots. The situation could have been delicate, and indeed, Martin had received specific instructions from Arnold to end the undeclared civil war which had raged on Oahu between the Army, its Air Corps, and the Navy, and for which it appears some of the blame rested with the airmen.

Gordon Prange went on to write,

> To understand American commanders on Oahu in [the coming year of] 1941, one must see them in the context of the problems which bedeviled them. So Martin came to Hawaii bearing the olive branch. He took his role seriously and at times, in the interest of harmony, would abandon a point which his fellow airmen thought he should have followed up more vigorously. His eagerness to please, combined with a rather pedantic appearance and manner, caused some individuals to privately label him a "fuddy-duddy." But the estimate did the man less than justice, for he was a hardworking, dutiful, and loyal officer, although a worrier who fretted constantly lest he not accomplish enough.

With Martin's appointment, inter-service relations improved steadily throughout 1941.

Then Prange turned to Martin's Navy counterpart, an extroverted Irishman, Rear Admiral Patrick N.L. Bellinger, who had arrived in Hawaii on 30 October 1940.

He had a full thatch of dark hair parted on the left side, a rather long mouth and direct, bright eyes. He had a most distinguished flying career with any number of Navy firsts on his record. Now at Pearl Harbor, he held no fewer than five positions and theoretically answered to five different superiors, and . . . such assignments have never been rarities in the armed forces.

Bellinger was not a profound thinker, but he stood obstinately by his convictions and expressed them forcibly, constantly "beefing up" the letters his brilliant operations and plans officer, Commander Charles Coe, prepared for his signature. But he had no ounce of bluster in him, and his invincibly sunny disposition made him a general favorite. Like Martin, he was running a poor man's game and had no inhibitions about sounding off loud and clear even to the highest quarters about his troubles. On 16 January 1941, he wrote a strong letter to Stark:

1. I arrived here in October 30, 1940, with the point of view that the International situation was critical, especially in the Pacific, and I was impressed with the need for being ready today rather than tomorrow for any eventuality that might arise. After taking over command of Patrol Wing TWO and looking over the situation, I was surprised to learn that here in the Hawaiian Islands, an important naval advanced post, we were operating on a shoestring, and the more I asked the thinner the shoestring appeared to be.

. . . As there are no plans to modernize the present patrol planes comprising Patrol Wing TWO, this evidently means that there is no intention to replace

the present obsolescent type . . . This, together with
the many existing deficiencies, indicates to me that
the Navy Department as a whole does not view
the situation in the Pacific with alarm or else is not
taking steps in keeping with their view . . . [49]

After completing Fleet Problem XXI the spring of 1940, the
Tennessee proceeded to Puget Sound Navy Yard for overhaul,
then returned to her new home port, Pearl Harbor, arriving 12
August. Based at Pearl Harbor with *Tennessee* and the numerous
other ships of the Pacific Fleet was her sister ship, the *California*,
the second of two battleships in the *California* class; two older
battleships in the *Pennsylvania* class, *Pennsylvania* and *Arizona*;
and the *Colorado*, plus *Maryland*, *West Virginia* and *Nevada*,
which were the other three battleships in the *Colorado* class.[50]

After completing several scheduled training exercises,
Tennessee once again took courses and speeds out of Pearl Harbor
on 11 November, bound for Long Beach, California.[51]

Four days earlier, on 7 November 1940, the Tacoma,
Washington Narrows (suspension) Bridge began coming apart in
the morning hours, and eventually collapsed, with pieces tumbling
190 feet into Puget Sound. The bridge's collapse resulted from
a flawed engineering design, and followed a day of prolonged,
harmonic oscillations in high winds. Witnessed by automobile
and truck drivers and their passengers, other people who stood
on both sides of the Narrows, people in an airplane circling above,
and captured on film by newspaper reporters and moving picture
cameramen, the collapse of the modern engineering marvel made
headlines in newspapers, lead stories on radio, and on theater
screens across the nation, and came as a puzzling, disillusioning
surprise to the citizens of Tacoma, Seattle, Puget Sound Navy
Yard, Bremerton, and other nearby towns and cities. Thirteen
months after the incident, the west coast of the United States,
the entire nation, the Territory of Hawaii, and indeed the whole
world, would receive a far more profound shock, which would
forever change the course of world history.[52]

CHAPTER 2

A Diary of Happy Times

*Love is a canvas furnished by Nature and
embroidered by imagination.*

Voltaire

On 1 and 24 June 1939, Karl Frederick Border wrote that month's only two entries in the personal diaries he began keeping four years earlier when he and his younger brother, Robert Lee "Bob" Border, entered the United States Naval Academy at Annapolis, Maryland. As the sons of Navy Captain Lee S. "Hank" Border, USNA class of 1905, and his wife, the former Chettana Maud Nesbitt, all their lives they had been called "juniors" by Navy and Marine Corps families, as were the daughters of Navy officers. On 1 June, he wrote,

> Bob and I became Ensigns in the United States Navy this morning as Mother, Dad, and Grandma watched. Missy put on one shoulder mark and Alice the other . . . A fitting climax to a swell four years.

Missy was an affectionate name the family gave the boys' mother. Grandma was Grandma Nesbitt, Missy's mother, and a physician who had for years practiced medicine in Vallejo, California. The shoulder mark is the officers' black shoulder board bearing, in this instance, the ensign's insignia of rank worn by the most junior commissioned officers in the Navy. The ensigns' insignia is equivalent to the gold bar worn by second lieutenants in the Marine Corps and Army. Alice was one of many young women who at one time or another in the years ahead would admire Bob or Karl, the two handsome Midshipmen who, on graduation day, became Navy ensigns.

Karl's 24 June entry read, "Bob, Andy, Gene, Sully, and I reported aboard the Tennessee this afternoon for our first tours of duty as Naval officers. Swell ship."[1]

Ensigns Bob and Karl Border, after being commissioned at Annapolis, reported aboard the battleship *Tennessee* while she was moored in her Long Beach, California, home port. With them when they went aboard were Naval Academy classmates Andy Anderson, Gene Hayward, and Sully Graham, all fine young men. The Academy had long held deliberately high entry standards, as well as high academic, physical, moral, and conduct standards for its midshipmen—whom the Navy was educating and training to be its primary source of land-based, seagoing and aviation leaders in the Navy and Marine Corps.

The Navy, ever mindful of the role family played in the lives of its sailors, their lengthy seaborne separations from families, friends and sweethearts; and the rigors of life and training for war at sea, wanted to ensure its young commissioned officers became thoroughly familiar with their profession before they selected their brides. Their policy mandated newly commissioned officers not marry until they completed two years of service, a waiting period also intended to ensure two more years of maturity before making the important decision of choosing a partner for life.

Bob and Karl, 21 and 23 years of age, grew up loving Navy life. They deeply admired a father who, after graduating from the Academy in 1905, later obtained a masters degree in Naval architecture—ship design and building—from Massachusetts Institute of Technology, and was proud of both sons' achievements. Though ambitious, intensely competitive, and sometimes heatedly energized by sibling rivalry, the brothers were fiercely loyal to one another.

In their formative years, Navy and family life brought Bob and Karl international travel prior to and during the Great Depression—primarily to the Pacific coast, Far East and back. Growing up in a Navy family they gained a sense of adventure, solid discipline, powerful work ethics, and a deep appreciation and love of country. Their father, with his family, had been reassigned from Mare Island Navy Yard, at the north end of San Francisco Bay, California in 1922, to Puget Sound Navy Yard adjacent to Bremerton, Washington, across the Sound west of Seattle. From 1925-28 they were in China, where he was in charge of construction of seven river gunboats for America's Yangtze River patrols. The patrols protected shipping against river pirates.

In addition to deep, family attachments, both brothers were smart, good-humored and fun-loving, while Karl appeared to more easily charm the opposite sex, confidently believed he could, and routinely did. Karl wrote his more serious side into his diaries, while Bob, strong, equally confident, but the shy and quieter of the two, possessed the dryer sense of humor, and more closely held his serious side.[2]

Supervising a Civilian Conservation Corps encampment, part time, near Minneapolis, Minnesota, while Karl and Bob were being commissioned in the Navy, was Marine Corps Reserve Captain George I. Springer, who in his civilian pursuits was an office and school furniture salesman. George Springer and his wife, Charlotte Florence, an accomplished concert pianist who accompanied soloists playing with the Minneapolis Symphony Orchestra, and their 18-year old daughter, Mary Joleen, were native Minnesotans. They lived at 234 North Mississippi River Boulevard in Minneapolis. The city's orchestra performed concerts locally in the University of Minnesota's Symphony Hall, on campus in St. Paul. Nicknamed "Joey" by her parents, among Marine Corps and Navy families she would soon carry the label "brat," a term similar to Navy "juniors" but given to the sons and daughters of Marine and Army officers.[3]

Late summer of 1937, while Bob and Karl were at Annapolis, Joey Springer, still sixteen years of age, entered the University of Minnesota. In the spring of 1940, with war raging in Europe and the Far East, the Springer's lives, similar to the lives of an increasing number of Americans, began to change. In the fall, George Springer was recalled to active duty as a comptroller, an accountant and paymaster in the Marine detachment at the Puget Sound Navy Yard. On arrival, they moved into officers' quarters.

While among outsiders unfamiliar with the armed forces there was always talk and no small amount of exaggeration and gossip regarding bitter inter-service rivalries, inside the services the atmosphere was nearly always quite different. Routinely, inter-service respect, mutual admiration, camaraderie, cooperation, and even romance, flourished.

Ships, Beaus, and a Young Woman's Diary

December 1940 at the Puget Sound Navy Yard was a typically active month, but the pace had been picking up for more than two years. Though the war in Europe appeared far more threatening, in the minds of Americans on the west coast, it remained distant, far to the east, beyond the east coast, across the Atlantic. Yes, war was raging to the west, too, in China, and the Japanese were making threatening overtures in the southwest Pacific, but the great Pacific Ocean barrier made the fury loosed in the Far East seem more distant, less ominous. Besides, the War Department was already taking steps to strengthen the nation's Pacific defenses.

In a 14 December 1940, "Dear Frank" letter to President Roosevelt, a letter that didn't become public knowledge until years later, American Ambassador Joseph C. Grew, a friend of Japan, expressed his views about the growing differences between the two nations. The letter provides insight to the rationale behind decisions taken by President Roosevelt as relations worsened toward the end of the decade. "It seems to me increasingly clear that we are bound to have a showdown some day, and the principal question at issue is whether it is to our advantage to have the showdown sooner or have it later."[4]

To counter the growing unease caused by the aggressively expanding Japanese Empire, selected additional units of the Navy's Fleet, home-ported on the east coast until April 1939, barely two months before Bob and Karl Border graduated from Annapolis, were now bolstering the Pacific Fleet, cycling in and out of the Puget Sound Yard from San Diego, Los Angeles, San Francisco, and Hawaii. Among the ships entering and leaving the Sound periodically were the battleships *California*, *Tennessee*, *West Virginia*, *Maryland*, *Arizona*, *Nevada*, *Pennsylvania*, *Oklahoma*, *Colorado*, and the Pacific Fleet's three aircraft carriers, *Saratoga*, *Lexington*, and *Enterprise*.[5]

Ships bound for the Yard and its harbor near Bremerton, came through the entrance to the Strait of Juan de Fuca, between the state of Washington on the south shore, and Canada's British Columbia on the north shore, turning southeast as they proceeded through the Strait, then south toward the Yard for port calls, servicing, repair, modernization, or dry dock for overhaul. Families living in the Yard's quarters or small town of Bremerton could more conveniently reach Seattle by a short ferry ride rather than by highway and road which looped around the Tacoma Narrows miles to the south. Sailors on shore leave or travel orders from ships in the harbor, usually were taken to Seattle by ships' or Yard motor launches.

Other Navy combatants in the fleet, such as heavy and light cruisers, destroyers, destroyer escorts, minesweepers, and minelayers also entered and departed Puget Sound, as did freighters, tankers, supply ships, harbor service tugs, and fleet support vessels of various kinds.

The Sound and the Yard were veritable beehives, and heaven for 20-year old Joey Springer and her three closest girlfriends who viewed the crop of eligible bachelors aboard the great ships tied up, anchored, or in dry-dock, not just as eligible bachelors, but prime eligible bachelors. Among the objects of their attention, the junior officers on board the ships cycling in and out of a Yard, the feelings and intentions were reciprocated—at least in most instances. Long days and nights, weeks, and too often, months at sea—away from home—and in overseas ports of call, heighten the need for the feminine touch, care and love. For the most part, they were bright, courteous, disciplined, well-mannered, loyal, young men with sparks of goodness and ambition.[6]

Joey and her friends, often in the company of the ensigns of the fleet, frequented numerous ships' junior officer ward rooms for lunch or dinner; the Yard Officers' Club for lunches, dinners and dancing; parks, golf courses; and movies at the Yard theater, on board ship, or in Bremerton. Across the Sound, in Seattle, were waterfront saloons for drink and song, restaurants, and shopping areas that were magnets for the young women and their mothers.[7]

Added to the pleasant, busy lives of Joey and her friends, were the ski slopes and lodges of the beautiful giant, Mt. Ranier, a few miles southeast of Seattle. Hiking, picnics, dinners, dances, teas, card games, dice games such as backgammon, commonly called acey ducey, and parties, were all part of the social whirl and life of Marine Corps "brats" and Navy "juniors."[8]

The fleet's bachelor ensigns and lieutenants junior grade had a different label for these young women who daily came aboard ships and were at the center of a social life longed for as the men's

Mary Joleen "Joey" Springer, circa December 1940.
Borders' Collection

days at sea lengthened. "Yard engines" they were affectionately called, an apt term.

Since the early days of steam ships, "yard engines" were the small locomotives shuttling freight and coal-loaded cars from warehouses and transshipment points, through the yards servicing commercial and Navy harbor operations. Yard engines energetically hauled hundreds of tons of supplies, freight, and coal to piers, to be unloaded onto conveyor belts, carried on shoulders of stevedores, or hoisted by huge, crane-borne cargo nets to fill the holds and coal-fired boiler furnaces of steam ships. For more than a century yard engines pulled the cars filled with food, other supplies, and fire-released energy—coal—which sustained life on the high seas.[9]

As for the yard engines visiting the Pacific Fleet's combatants in the Puget Sound Navy Yard, they had a few nicknames they deemed appropriate for some of the more frequented ships. The good time, seemingly carefree ship, *California*, earned the nickname, "Alky Barge," and the *West Virginia*, with a too-long name, was the "Wee Vee," the same nickname given her by her crew.

When Joey Springer and her three closest friends were together they naturally compared notes on the behaviors and habits of the junior officers who escorted the yard engines, as well as the various groups of bachelors from each ship, who associated with one another while vying for the attention of young women who particularly caught their eye. Good fun and thoughtful prudence were Joey's and her friends' watchwords.[10]

The *Tennessee* Ensign

Joey noticed that among all the ships, she liked the officers on the battleship *California* for a singularly important reason. *California's* crew seemed more relaxed and fun-loving, less inclined to be serious about commitment and marriage. *California* was normally the flagship in the battleship divisions home-ported in Pearl Harbor, Territory of Hawaii, which meant whenever the battleships sailed together in task forces with escorts, screens of destroyers and cruisers, she flew the flag of the "S.O.P.A.", the Senior Officer Present Afloat, usually the task force commander, and normally a rear admiral. Perhaps that's the reason *California*'s crew was the more relaxed, confident, and fun loving.

But Joey and other discerning young women looking for commitment and eventually marriage were also interested in meeting young officers from other combatants, officers who, in the girls' judgments, were the more serious kind.[11]

The *Tennessee* was in port from 18 December 1940 until Christmas Day. As was often the case, during that week in port, Joey was invited aboard for dinner in the junior officers' wardroom. Dudley Adams, an ensign in the ship's company, invited, escorted, and introduced her to the officers joining them for dinner that evening. Among those he introduced was another young crew member and '39 graduate of Annapolis, Ensign Bob Border.[12]

Bob, an assistant division officer in a *Tennessee* anti-aircraft gun division of approximately eighty men, trained on, maintained and fired the ship's three-inch, AA guns. Still rooming with Bob on *Tennessee* was his brother, Karl. Consistent with the Navy's policy of keeping families together as much as possible, and with some help from their father before they graduated from Annapolis, the two brothers had been granted their request to serve on the same ship.[13]

When Joey met Bob on the *Tennessee* that evening, he was wearing a cast on his right forearm. The kick-back of an engine-starting hand crank on a Model A Ford in Long Beach, California, had cracked his right wrist. He believed he could persevere on duty with the fractured arm, but the ship's doctor saw matters differently, and put him ashore in the hospital when the ship tied up at the Yard. When next Bob and Joey encountered one another at a dance in the Yard Club she was with Dudley Adams again. Quietly, without her knowledge, Bob bribed Dudley for a date with her, a five dollar bribe he years later good-naturedly teased, "was a ten dollar bribe"—then again admitted it "was only five dollars, a lot of money in those days."[14]

Though he didn't mention the fact to Joey until some weeks after they were introduced, Bob was engaged—to a young woman named Gretna Price in Long Beach—to whom he had given his Naval Academy miniature class ring. Unknown to either Gretna or Joey, Bob's miniature was actually even more well-traveled, having been presented to Miss Lucy Pfahler at his Ring Dance in 1938, at the beginning of his first class (senior) year.

The reason for the withheld information was simple. The

dance of love. Bob Border had immediately been charmed by Joey, and he needed to bide his time with his closely held secrets for fear she would drop him if she knew he was engaged.

To Bob, Joey's personality sparkled. At a shapely, petite five feet tall, with natural, honey-blond hair, she was attractive, and alive with energy and spunk. Not just attractive, but lovely, vivacious, beautiful he believed—confident, self-reliant, observant, and smart, too. The bright wit, charm and humor came easily and shone like a beacon. There was nothing false or pretentious about Joey Springer. Though not at all brusque or abrasive, she came straight to the point in conversation. No holding back. Except for a few secrets of her own.[15]

Joey was engaged, too. Not one, but two had previously pursued her hand in marriage. While she was at the University of Minnesota, a dentist from Philadelphia proposed. She had met him while traveling with her parents. She didn't exactly say no, and neither did she say yes. Then there was the lawyer in Minnesota. Two birds in the bush might yield one in the hand. Anyway, a young woman had to be thoughtful to ensure a good catch. Men in the medical and legal professions were nearly always a good catch. Absent any knowledge of all this, Bob Border, the brother with the auburn red hair, a trim, lean, strong, five feet, seven inches tall, smart, and equally energetic was quickly convinced that here, in the person of vivacious Joey Springer, was a prize worth pursuing.[16]

Christmas season, 1940, was bright and cheerful in family quarters at the Puget Sound Navy Yard. In the Springer quarters, Christmas Eve was especially cheerful that year. Their "only," Joey, was home, home to stay instead of going back to the university for another semester. She was the center of love and attention in her family, the reason for Christmas cheer this yuletide season.

Winter's cold, moist air made brightly decorated trees and lights seem more festive. Open houses in many officers' quarters are a tradition at Christmas time, and Marine Captain and Mrs. George I. Springer's quarters were no exception.

Word of the open house spread quickly among the eligible junior officers on *Tennessee*. Bob and Dudley had spoken of her glowingly, and too much. Joey Springer is a beauty among the yard engines, has many beaus, and the Springers' home is a place to relax and enjoy life in port. Ensign Bob Border, captivated by her and still wearing the cast on his arm, wasted no time in accepting the invitation to join other young officers who were told of Christmas Eve open house at the Springers.[17]

Until Christmas Eve at the Springers, Bob hadn't heard Joey sing. At the age of sixteen, she sang in the chorus of the Minneapolis Symphony. She had grown up with classical music, having attended her first concert at the age of four. In conversation her voice was lovely, magnetic, and when she sang, the sound was marvelously clear, sweet, and flowed easily, with the confidence of a practiced lead singer—though she had never been a soloist. Her singing added to the charm and beauty Bob saw in her. Christmas Eve night, 1940, Bob and "Doc" Ward stayed late, vying for her attention.

Joey had other interests. Her dad had owned a light plane and taken her and her mother on flights. She wanted to take flying lessons for a private pilot's license. She liked to play golf, and during the open house made plans for a foursome on New Year's Day. Bob, overhearing the conversation, volunteered he played golf, too, and would like to join the round. "What about your cast?" Joey asked. He replied, "I'll caddie for you." She accepted. For Joey and Bob, good days and an exciting future were ahead.

Wednesday evening, 1 January 1941, she wrote her first entry in a small, pocket diary she purchased. She played golf with Bob in spite of a "terrific hangover." Small in stature, accustomed to ordering glasses of milk in restaurants and lounges, unaccustomed to alcohol's effects and not liking its taste, she had finally tried her dad's favorite evening cocktail, Scotch and soda. The Scotch hit her hard, with lingering effects and absolutely no sympathy from her father, but the golf game proceeded on schedule New Year's Day.

This first diary entry marked the beginning of an odyssey long remembered, a journey her diary will never let her forget. Her last entry, exactly one year in the future, will be the final entry in the only diary she kept her entire life.[18]

On New Year's day, more than 1,100 miles to the south of Puget Sound, *Tennessee* lay moored in Long Beach, one of three west coast ports the Pacific Fleet's battleship divisions frequented. Karl Border and two of his classmates had spent what Karl described as "one of his best Christmases ever," at Paradise Inn on Mt. Rainer, near Seattle. Joined by two young women they knew, they skied all day. They enjoyed the day so much the *Tennessee* boys had to hustle to get back to the ship on time for departure.

Their big home away from home was headed south, down the west coast toward more hospitable weather.

A week later *Tennessee* was in Long Beach. Karl took "Hunky," to a show and had an enjoyable day. Hunky was his "swell little gal" living near the port. He could count on a good day or evening out with Hunky every time *Tennessee* steamed into Long Beach for a brief stay.

Young women seemed particularly charmed by the trim, dark-brown-haired, athletic-looking Karl, who coached the *Tennessee*'s wrestling team. At five feet, nine inches tall, and a bit more muscular at 160 pounds, than his brother Bob who weighed in at 135, he was outgoing, gregarious, and loved to tease—a characteristic he sometimes carried to extremes. On one occasion during the brothers' high school days, his unmerciful teasing of Bob provoked an explosive response in which Bob bested his big brother. Karl found himself on his back, with an enraged Bob straddling his chest repeatedly banging his head on the concrete floor. Both came to their senses and recognized matters had got out of hand. From that time forward, the two accorded one another the greatest respect and loyalty, and Karl tempered his propensity to tease.

He also liked to gamble a few dollars now and then. The Stanford-Nebraska Rose Bowl game prompted a small, one-dollar wager with a fellow crewmember and friend, Ensign Les Hutchinson, with Karl's money on Stanford. Stanford's Indians won, a good beginning for Karl's year.[19]

Love, the Relentless Ensign, and the Cub Reporter

Thursday, Joey recorded her next social engagement in the Puget Sound Navy Yard, dinner on th *Nevada* with Delar V. Van Sand, a Yale graduate and ensign on the *Nevada*. Then off they went to the Yard Club for singing. On Friday, 3 January, golf again with the eager caddie, Bob Border, who refused to leave her to her own devices, or to forfeit escort duties to other suitors.

Saturday, she and her family went to dinner at the Metzgers. After dinner she went to a formal dinner dance at the Yard Club with Ensign Larry Baiada, a crew member on the *Arizona*, which was in port with the *Nevada*. While she enjoyed dances, including formal dances, formality didn't keep her from pushing the edge of stodgy convention.

Duke Ellington's and Bennie Goodman's jazz musicians were taking the music world by storm, providing another, more exciting escape from The Great Depression and the straight-laced, sterner stuff of the Navy's senior officers. The jitterbug had succeeded the Charleston as the fun dance of the exuberant younger generation of the thirties and early forties. In her mind—and in her diary—she had ". . . shocked all the old buzzards . . . " by jitterbugging with Larry Baiada at the formal dance.

Bob Border noticed the free spirit in her, and there was a goal at the end of his persistence. He had the Navy's two-years-active-duty-before-marriage rule in his sights, and the two years would end June 1, 1941—or was it May 31? Either way, he was determined to win her hand soon—maybe before the doctors sent him back to duty on *Tennessee*. Smitten. Love at first sight. He knew his departure couldn't be too many days in the future. His arm was rapidly healing. Thus, every moment of time with her was crucial. No holding back.

Sunday, another rainy day in Seattle, he received a phone call on board ship, inviting him to dinner at the Springer's. He didn't hesitate. He generally knew what to expect on Sunday afternoons in the Navy, two long-standing formal traditions also common in the Army and Marine Corps. Joey and her family soon learned the Sunday routine, still prevalent in the Navy when they arrived and settled in officers' quarters at Puget Sound. "Tea Fights."

Every Sunday afternoon Navy wives held formal teas at the Officers' Clubs, complete with receiving lines. The senior officers' wives took turns hosting the events. On Sundays as well, it was get out of the house and go to the tea, or elsewhere, or expect callers. Junior officers and their wives called at their captains' or admirals' quarters for a brief visit, each leaving one of their pre-printed calling cards on a silver platter located conveniently on a table or small chest near the entrance door.

If there were a trip to the Sunday "Tea Fight," and she wanted to attend, they would go. This day, no tea and they needn't stay around to greet callers if there were any, so he and the object of his growing affection were off to the Yard theater for the western movie, "Destry Rides Again." He escorted her home, they talked, said goodnight, and she wrote a letter. Then she ended her day explaining to her diary ". . . he's very nice but I love my Johnny." But Johnny, a letter writer himself, was a long way off, was writing less frequently, and definitely wasn't in the beehive of social activity Joey was thoroughly enjoying. Absence makes the heart grow fonder—of someone else.

Monday, after lunch at the Yard Club she and her mother took the ferry to Seattle for an afternoon of shopping, after which she met Delar V. Van Sand for dinner at the Press Club. From the Press Club, they went to see the movie, "Thief of Baghdad," followed by a stop-off at a waterfront dive for beer and songs.

Tuesday, Bob was back again, this time driving Joey and another of her girlfriends to lunch at Norma Hall's. This lunch was girls' time, with talk about their "loves," followed by letter writing. Bob returned to Hall's with Larry Baiada, picked up the two girls, and drove to the Yard Club for the evening.

While the social life was great fun, she needed a job to help pay her expenses and expand her interests. Bremerton was a small town, and with the Navy Yard next door, brats and juniors were aware finding a job might be difficult. She did have nearly three years as a student at the University of Minnesota, which should help. She liked to write, and was naturally curious about a broad range of subjects.[20]

Discussions with her dad yielded an idea. Cliff Pritchard, George Springer's friend, might be able to help her get a job at the Bremerton newspaper. Maybe an opening could be found. On 9 January, with Cliff Pritchard's intervention, fortune smiled on her. The editor needed a reporter for the city courthouse beat. She would follow cases in the local civil court, and write articles, a beat guaranteed to stimulate interest in the local community as well as gain her valuable writing experience.

Eight of the next ten days, Bob pursued Joey vigorously. Dinner, then to see the Harlem Globe Trotters' basketball team. The evening after her new boss took her to Port Orchard to help her learn the journalism and reporter's ropes, Bob came for dinner at the Springers. Then he took her to the Yard Club for dancing, and hamburgers afterward.

The next day, Saturday, out on the golf course with Bob again, always talking with one another. Later the same day she went shopping in Seattle with the *Nevada*'s Ensign Van Sand, afterward to a wonderful dinner at a French restaurant, Maison Blanc, then to a concert to see the Russians' Don Cossack Chorus. On the way home they went to the Rathskellers for drinks. She wrote later that evening the concert was "marvelous." Another week gone, but lots of dates, great fun, but just a bit too much wine that Saturday night. And there was something else. A slow, subtle change was coming over her. She was beginning to look far more thoughtfully at the young men pursuing her.[21]

The battleship *Arizona* (BB-39) at Puget Sound Navy Yard 18 January 1941. Behind *Arizona* can be seen the foretop (forward mast) and main top (main mast) of the *Nevada* (BB-36). The two ships were in Puget Sound for maintenance and upgrade. Joey had dinner on board *Nevada* in the junior officers' ward room with Delar V. Van Sand on Thursday evening, 2 January 1941. NPSAM

Before the next Saturday, she concluded Van Sand was a bore, and worse, she'd seen him disgustingly drunk. Sully Graham was fun but "too sexy." Bob Boyd, who had escorted her, broke the news he was engaged, and her Johnny was slowing down in letter writing. All the while, Bob Border stayed "steady on." He was with her almost every day—and she was beginning to see qualities in him she'd given short shrift to in her mind, and ignored in her diary.

After some Saturday work for the newspaper on the 18th, she and her mother gave a luncheon for five, before going shopping for shoes and a formal gown at the Washington Area Center, a large shopping district in downtown Seattle. Bob and his friend, Dan, spent the afternoon in bars, killing time, before going to meet

Joey, her mother, and Edith Pritchard for dinner at the Center—thence to the Ballet Russe and back to the Springer's quarters.

He had been thinking about Joey and the future the entire afternoon he and Dan had been hopping from one bar to the next. He had to be careful, keep his wits about him and avoid too much drink. He had known her barely a month, time was running short, he would have to leave for Hawaii and the *Tennessee* before too many more days, and he didn't want to lose this one.[22]

It had been a long day. She was tired, and about to say "goodnight," but it was time for a pleasant surprise. Bob, alone with her at last, softly, gently told her he wanted to give her his Academy miniature class ring. Indeed. He gave her a genuine surprise, nearly a profound shock.

Two engagements and now here is a bright, handsome, ambitious young, red-headed Navy officer becoming serious about her, most serious. An Academy graduate's miniature class ring, if accepted, is tantamount to an engagement though a marriage proposal doesn't necessarily come with a miniature. Nevertheless, the giving of a miniature is a wonderful Academy tradition coming from a Navy family proud of the Academy's and Navy's traditions. She liked him. He was fun. But love him? This will require some thought. She will have to avoid responding too quickly, either yes or no. He is here. He is fun. Don't chase him away. Give it some time. She held off giving an answer.

As for Bob, there was yet another factor to consider with the offer of his class miniature. He didn't have one. He didn't have the miniature he had previously purchased. He had given it—a second time—to Gretna, a second "engagement," in Long Beach. In the offer to Joey he was letting his second fiancée in Long Beach slip into second place, or perhaps no place.

Now what? Joey didn't say yes, and she didn't say no. Was this a "maybe"? He didn't know, but two facts were certain. First, a momentary stalemate was in progress. Second, he absolutely wouldn't quit. Time to redouble efforts to win her. It had been a whirlwind romance from Bob's perspective, but things would have to move faster.

Sunday morning, Joey arose late, and after breakfast the two took a long, leisurely walk, filled with warm, pleasant talk—getting to know one another better. They spent the afternoon playing cribbage, and she called it quits early that evening. Tomorrow morning was work, and Bob would be back again late Monday afternoon, to take her to dinner then a movie. After he took her home she wrote a letter, then to bed.

Earlier that Monday, 20 January, *Tennessee*, with Karl Border on board, got under way from Long Beach, bound for Pearl Harbor, with arrival planned the following Monday.[23]

In the meantime, no laying around the hospital wards for the sailor with the fractured arm. No time to waste. Too much fun to enjoy—with a beautiful, charming, young lady. Tuesday he came back to see Joey again. She had worked and written letters most of the afternoon before he arrived to take her to the Officers' Club. That night she crawled into bed at 1:00 a.m. after telling her diary she "got skonked," declaring in French, *mais oui*.[24]

Wednesday, here he came again. She worked that morning, played cribbage, went shopping, and bought a nice suede jacket. Then Bob took her to two movies, and they walked home in the dark afterward. It was a long, slow walk filled with more talk, and a stop to rest. Joey was tired, not feeling herself. It was cold and damp, but they were dressed warmly.

"Let's stop and sit here," he suggested. He didn't reveal the reason he suggested this location to sit, relax and talk. They stopped and sat down on the steps leading to the Yard's Quarters 2A, and talked at length. Joey sat next to him, close, warmth against the Northwest's cold, moist, winter air. The beautiful old quarters sat back from the residential street that ran southeast along a bluff overlooking the harbor. Below the bluff, lights in the Yard's harbor, on the ships, and channel marker buoys shined brightly. Bells on the bobbing and swaying channel markers occasionally echoed in the distance. Visible east across the Sound were the winking white and cream-colored lights of Seattle's residential areas, and a few, varied waterfront neon colors of the busy coastal city.[25]

For the first time, Bob began reminiscing about his days as a boy, long before he and Karl entered the Naval Academy. He spoke easily, with the quiet modesty he always reflected, and told her about his family's Navy life. She told him of her family, her life growing up in Minnesota before her dad was called to active duty at Puget Sound. Then conversation drifted to what each hoped and wanted for the future.

They would one day look back on that night in front of Quarters 2A as the magical evening when they began falling in love. However, he did not mention, and she would not learn

Puget Sound Navy Yard, late 1940. Second set of quarters left of flagpole is Quarters 2A, where the Borders had previously lived. Ships in the harbor include the aircraft carrier *Lexington* (CV-2) in the foreground, two battleships, and three cruisers. NAPAR

until months afterward that he and his family had twice lived in this set of quarters overlooking the harbor and the blue-green waters of the Sound. Joey was surprised again when he told her of Quarters 2A and their connection to his younger days. She had known little of his and his family's Navy life, and nothing of his past at the Puget Sound Navy Yard.

Life in the military is nomadic. The old quarters were perhaps the closest a Navy junior would ever come to the notion of "roots," a home at a single geographic location that represented permanency, happy times and long lasting, pleasant memories. When his father was stationed here on a second assignment, after they returned from Shanghai, China, his mother and father had given him the same bedroom. The first time he lived in that room, Bob was quite young, at the impressionable age of eight when the family left the Yard for China in 1925.[26]

Not so with Joey. Family life had been anything but nomadic for the Springers, but not easy. Life during the Great Depression was easy only for a few. No matter the economic strata a family might reside in, taking advantage of one's schooling and talents to provide income for the family and for education of children became an absolute necessity, for many an obsession. The Springers were blessed by comparison to the great majority of Americans, knew it, but were ever mindful of the cold, hard economic reality pressing on all sides of life. At least her dad had a job as a salesman, and was in the Marine Corps Reserve. Her mother gave piano lessons, played for soloists with the Minneapolis Symphony, and insisted she learn to play the piano and sing. The quality of Joey's singing led to her acceptance into the Symphony's chorus.

When she enrolled in the University of Minnesota in St. Paul, she lived in a dormitory three miles from home—and worked to help pay her expenses, tuition and books. She gave piano lessons and took other part-time jobs typing papers for other students, for pay, waiting tables and working a paper route to help pay the costs of her education. One small money-making endeavor she tried involved the early morning sale of fresh orange juice in the women's dormitory and sorority houses, the buildings where the daughters of wealthy parents lived on campus. She purchased a crate of oranges early each morning, cut each orange in half and squeezed fresh juice to deliver at fifty cents per glass, an extraordinarily high price, and a good return on any glass of juice during the Great Depression.[27]

An event in Joey's life she didn't mention to Bob that Wednesday night in front of Quarters 2A, told much about her will and determination to take risks in pursuing her goals—once she fastened on them. In the spring of 1940, before she left the University of Minnesota, the famed American Shakespearean actor, Maurice Evans, came to the university with a touring theater company, to perform a play. Several of her friends were among numerous adoring theater-goers who wanted autographs from the actor after the play, but he apparently intended to escape the crush of admirers to get to the train station. He ignored their pleas, and none obtained his coveted signature. After he left, Joey promptly wagered with her skeptical friends she could successfully retrieve his autograph. They accepted in spite of their doubts, after she persisted she would be successful. Off she went in pursuit of the fleeing celebrity, and caught up with him at the station.

She explained the circumstances, including the wager with her friends, and pleaded with him for his signature, whereupon Evans suggested she accompany him to the nearby eatery for a light lunch. He needed a bite before getting on the train. He purchased lunch for her and they enjoyed a pleasant talk while eating. When he excused himself saying he had to get on the train, he asked her to give him a paper napkin, which he autographed before saying how much he enjoyed the conversation, and "good luck." She proudly returned to the campus, showed the prized napkin and signature to her friends, collected proceeds from the wagers, and landed a reporter's brief explanatory article in the St. Paul newspaper, complete with a photograph of her displaying the prize.

But most of all, while Joey didn't tell Bob everything about herself that night, when she realized months later what Bob hadn't told her the same night, his modesty came to mind immediately. His dad had been the planning officer, responsible for building, repair, maintenance, and modernizing of many ships in the Navy's Fleet—and Bob never said a word. Status, as measured by the talents and achievements of those with whom he associated, even the achievements of the father he so deeply admired, awarded him no bragging rights. Bob didn't boast or brag. He simply worked, and worked hard—dutifully. Let the amount and quality of his work speak for who he was and the responsibilities he would be capable of carrying in the future.[28]

During their lengthy conversation that Wednesday night, they planned a ski trip to Mt. Ranier, to leave after she finished work on Saturday. They would obtain her parents' approval, stay overnight, separately of course, and return Sunday, the 26th. Thursday after work, she rounded up ski clothes for the trip, supplemented the collection with purchases, knitted for awhile, then helped her mother prepare dinner. Another of her admirers came for dinner, with a couple who were Springer family friends. Afterward Joey went with him to the club, returning home at midnight. The entire evening her mind was on the trip to Mt. Ranier on Saturday, Bob secondarily.

Friday, though she knew Bob was coming to dinner that evening, she was excited to learn the *California* was back in port. Another of her *California* beaus called on the phone. Ensign Robert D. "Kirk" Kirkpatrick, Jr., wanted to see her. When Bob came for dinner the two had little time alone. Family friends stopped by and later they joined in a game of Tripoli. She found the evening boring, undoubtedly in anticipation of the next day's trip to Mt. Ranier.

Saturday morning she worked at the paper. Then she and Bob

rode the ferry to Seattle, rented a car, and left for the Paradise Inn, the ski lodge on Mt. Ranier, where Bob had reservations for the night. It was Joey's first trip to the mountain. Snow was everywhere, and deep. To her the lodge and surrounding views were beautiful, beyond any she'd ever seen. Filled with people having a grand time, the entire area added excitement to the sense of complete relaxation and freedom both she and Bob felt. They played cribbage, socialized over cocktails and dinner, and retired to bed early—but not separately. Love and passion began sealing their lives and future that night.

The next day they were up at 8:00 a.m. and skied all morning. It was warm, superb weather on a perfect day after a wonderful evening. After lunch they started home about 3:00 and arrived near 7:00, tired—and happy. Such fun she proclaimed to her diary. When Bob left for the hospital, Joey collapsed into bed early. Tomorrow it would be back to work.[29]

Unknown to both, by the time she returned to work at the newspaper on Monday, the 27th, the Navy hospital at Puget Sound, and the 14th Naval District in Hawaii, where *Tennessee* was home ported, were already communicating regarding Bob's return to duty. The details to be worked out included when, how, and by what means he would return to his ship. Orders would soon be in his hands, directing him to proceed to the Naval Air Station at San Pedro, California, where he would receive further orders to proceed by air or sea transportation to Pearl Harbor.

From this time forward every day counted for Bob. Any uncertainty or lingering doubts Joey had about falling in love with him, he was determined to dispel. His departure was less than a week away. He had to spend every hour he could with her, every single day before he left for San Pedro, Hawaii and the *Tennessee*. At the same time, he was considerate and wise seeking Joey's hand. He pursued her parents as well, knowing that it was important to gain their trust and confidence. His behavior was genuine, as his attitude and feelings toward her mother and father were genuine. He was respectful and courteous to Captain Springer and Charlotte, and admired them both. He hoped they would be pleased to have him as their son-in-law, and was gaining their respect and confidence.[30]

On Monday, after Joey finished work for the day, he picked her up and they took the ferry to Seattle. After dinner at the Olympic Hotel, they went to see the movie, "The Philadelphia

Story," then returned to the Springer's quarters. For Joey it had been a lovely day. Tuesday, they drove around all afternoon and talked. That night she went to a movie, to see "Chad Hanna" with another suitor, "a nice fellow," and afterward, went with him to the Yard Club. Then home early.

Wednesday, Bob, Joey, Doc Weir and Zully Zullington played bridge all afternoon at Springer's, then went to dinner at the hospital where Bob was staying. After dinner, another movie, "Little Nellie Kelly." Thursday, the four of them played bridge at the hospital all afternoon, went to the Yard Club for dinner, then to see the film, "Cat and Canary." Friday, she and Bob played cribbage at her home in the afternoon, she prepared dinner for them, and they went to the movies again.[31]

In January 1941, the pace of defense preparations in the United States, its territories and overseas bases were continuing to quietly pick up momentum. On Monday, 7 January, the government established the Office of Production Management, and on 16 January, President Roosevelt asked Congress for an immediate appropriation of $350 million for 200 new merchant ships. In Washington, DC, on Wednesday, the 29th the American and British defense establishments began secret staff conversations to determine joint strategy in case the United States became involved in the war. The next day, Nazi Germany announced that ships of any nationality bringing aid to Great Britain would be torpedoed.[32]

None of these events were of great, overriding interest to Bob and Joey that month. Fun, getting to know one another, perhaps love, and more good times were better subjects to discuss—although neither were oblivious to world and national events which could adversely affect their lives.

Saturday, 1 February, after work, Joey went to the hospital to help Bob pack. That night they planned to eat dinner at the Yard Club, and dance afterward. She wanted the evening to be memorable, so had her hair done after helping him pack, then dressed in her new formal. The champagne and dancing were such fun, and Bob seemed "so darned nice." She was "so sorry" this was her last date with him.[33]

The same day he packed to return to Hawaii and the *Tennessee*, the Navy announced a major reorganization of the United States Fleet, a necessary step to accommodate and manage the Navy's expansion while preparing to face the growing threats to the nation. The reorganization revived the old names of Atlantic Fleet and Pacific Fleet, leaving the Asiatic Fleet unchanged. Admiral Husband E. Kimmel replaced Admiral James O. Richardson as Commander in Chief Pacific Fleet, with additional duty as Commander in Chief, United States Fleet. Patrol Force, United States Fleet, became Atlantic Fleet, and Admiral Earnest J. King Commander in Chief, Atlantic Fleet. Admiral T.C. Hart continued as Commander in Chief, Asiatic Fleet.[34]

Sunday morning Bob came to Springer's early for breakfast, bags packed and ready to leave. He and Joey went to church, had lunch, and caught the ferry to Seattle where he was to board a train for San Pedro. It had been ten glorious days for Bob, and he hoped she felt the same. He had seen her every single day, and almost every night, for hours on end. He was sure now more than ever he had found the girl he wanted to marry. Until now, she had said nothing to indicate she felt a serious attachment to him. He simply had to wait and see if she would respond by mail or telephone to his offer of his class miniature—maybe before he left San Pedro for Hawaii.

As the conductor announced "All aboard!" they embraced, kissed, and promised to write one another. He climbed aboard with his bags, took a seat at a window where they could see one another, and waved goodbye as the powerful engine gave its first gush of steam, roared and puffed to life, and slowly began moving south toward California. The image and reflection in the window, of this handsome, red-headed, young, smiling ensign, in his winter dress blue uniform was one moment in front of her and the next moment moving away, to disappear from view, perhaps never to be seen again. Joey immediately felt pangs of loneliness. But she soon buried them.

Ships and Airplanes

Monday, 3 February, as Bob's train rumbled steadily south, for Joey, it was back to work and the busy social whirl of the Yard engines. Work was on the Stetz case, a funeral home owner and mortician in Bremerton, who had been caught stealing jewelry and new clothes from cadavers—after the funeral ceremonies and the surviving family members had said goodbye to their departed loved ones. After she took a nap, came dinner aboard the "Alky Barge", the USS *California*, with Ensign "Wrinky." There she saw Ensign Herb Jones again, whom she had met in an earlier visit to the *California*'s junior officer ward room. In the afternoon she went roller skating with Bud and Dede.[35]

The next evening was to have been another date, but Joe K. called and broke it, saying he had contracted tonsillitis. For the first time in days, she had a quiet evening at home. Though "sooo tired" from all the happy days and evenings with Bob. But, Wednesday, 5 February was to be special, Charlotte Springer's birthday.

It was a lovely day. Bob, now in San Pedro, had ordered flowers delivered to Charlotte, and began writing a letter to Joey's dad asking for her hand in marriage. After work, Joey played golf, met Bud and Dede again, cooked dinner for her mother, and Herb Jones joined them for the birthday meal before they went to the movie, "Love Thy Neighbor." Before the year ended she would look back with sadness on the days she was in the company of Herb Jones, the young ensign from the "Alky Barge." For him, life would be brief.[36]

Although phone calls, letters and telegrams began to flow from Bob to Joey as soon as he left Seattle, she was still trying to keep him emotionally at arms length, be thoughtful about the future, and whether or not she would accept his offer to give her his class miniature. She busied herself with her newspaper editor's assignments, dates with other eligible young officers, lunches, dinners, shopping, golf, bridge and cribbage games, movies, letter writing, and knitting. Life as usual. Before Bob left she had begun interviewing in Seattle, searching for another job nearer shopping centers and a wider variety of entertainment available only in the city. The interviews and job search continued after he left.

In Minnesota, before the Marine Corps called George Springer to active duty, he had for a time held a private pilot's license, owned a light airplane, and on occasion taken Charlotte and Joey on trips. His always curious and active daughter fell in love with flying, and told Bob how much she enjoyed it. The interest was mutual, as Bob told her of his goal, to enter Naval aviation and take flight training at Pensacola Naval Air Station in the Florida panhandle, another place Joey had never seen.[37]

He wanted to be a Navy fighter pilot, flying off carriers. Her determination to again feel the satisfaction of flying came to life before he left for San Pedro. She scheduled a flight physical examination for Saturday, 8 February, and passed. The exam was the day after she played golf with Tom Ruddon, from the *California*, and joined Ensign Bill Seed for dinner aboard the aircraft carrier *Saratoga*, went to see the movie, "Philadelphia Story," and stopped off at the Yard Club afterward. But she would never take flight instruction or obtain her private pilot's license.

While Bob was nearing his California destination, other wheels were already turning. Shortly after he arrived, intending to end his engagement to Gretna Price, he learned Gretna was already living with a Navy Chief Petty Officer. He promptly wrote Joey a letter saying, "I'm available . . . " By Friday, 14 February, Valentine's Day, eight days before he reported aboard the destroyer *Morris* to return to Pearl Harbor and the *Tennessee*, matters were settled. Bob had chased Joey until she caught him.

She sent him a telegram with a proposal, "I love you. Will you marry me?" Low on funds, he borrowed money and immediately replied by wire, "I accept with pleasure. So happy now." She answered, "So glad. Love you." She played golf with L. Rankin all afternoon, was home for dinner, went to a movie with her dad, and told him of the telegram exchange with Bob. In her diary she wrote that night, ". . . am busy planning a wedding—with Bob."[38]

In San Pedro, Bob Border was ecstatic. Questions remained: when and where, and would they have time for a honeymoon? One fact was clear. The wedding wouldn't take place until the mandatory two years after commissioning, which meant on or after the second anniversary of his and Karl's graduation from Annapolis. When next would *Tennessee* be in port on the West Coast? He didn't know the ship's exercise and overhaul schedule. He would need to know as early as possible.

And there were other questions. Who would be best man? His brother Karl, of course. Who would give Joey away? He needn't have worried. There was a petite, energetic lady living with her parents at the Puget Sound Navy Yard, who would in the days ahead plan every detail of their wedding.

Bob had arrived at the San Pedro Naval Air Station on Thursday, 6 February. Saturday, 15 February, the Navy established Naval Air Station Kaneohe on Oahu's northeast shore. Six days later, after daylight on Friday, 21 February, the Hawaiian Air Force received its greatest single increase in assigned aircraft since its activation. Thirty-one P-36s, which had sailed from San Diego

on board the carrier *Enterprise*, took off from her broad flight
deck in flights of three while 10-15 miles off the coast of Oahu,
and flew directly to Wheeler Field. This launching of Army
fighters from the deck of an aircraft carrier was a historic "first"
in military aviation.

Led by flight commander Major George P. Tourtellot, the P-36s
were a spectacular sight as they roared in, three by three, making
near-perfect landings in precise formations. They taxied in front
of the hangars and drew up to form a line. Colonel Harvey S.
Burwell, Wheeler's commanding officer, strode to the side of the
flight leader's plane to offer his aloha and to extend his post's
hospitality. Major Tourtellot returned to the mainland aboard
the *Enterprise* the next day, but the 30 pilots who flew the other
planes were absorbed within the units of the expanding pursuit
wing. Among the arriving pilots were First Lieutenants Kermit A.
Tyler and Lewis M. Sanders, Second Lieutenants George S. Welch,
Othneil Norris, John M. Thacker, and George A. Whiteman—
who were all destined to have key roles in a drama to be played
out nine months later.

One day later, Ensign Robert L. Border, received the typed,
third endorsement to his basic travel orders, NA26/P16-4/00,
from the Commanding Officer, Naval Air Station San Pedro:
"1. Detached this date. Proceed without delay and report to
the Commanding Officer, *U.S.S. Morris* for transportation and
further transfer to the *U.S.S. Tennessee* for duty in accordance
with basic orders."[39]

At 2005 hours, Saturday, 22 February, he reported aboard
the *Morris* (DD-417), two days after twenty other men arrived
on the destroyer from the Naval Training Station San Diego for
travel to Pearl Harbor and further assignments to their ships.
Among the twenty were three sailors destined for the *Tennessee*,
two each for the cruisers *Savannah* and *Helena*, three for
the aircraft carrier *Yorktown*, and ten more for assignments
to destroyers. At 2345 hours the crew of the *Morris* began
preparing to get under way.

At 0002 hours on 23 February she weighed anchor, moved
slowly away from Berth 7, port of Los Angeles, toward the harbor
entrance. She led the Battle Force, Destroyer Division Seventeen,
accompanied by the destroyers *Buck* and *Roe*. Once clear of the
channel entrance into international waters, the three destroyers
formed an open order column, and steamed past Catalina and

Santa Barbara Islands. The *Morris*, carrying Destroyer Division Seventeen's Commander, then led the column's turn to port, set base course 258 degrees and standard speed 15 knots, bound for Pearl Harbor.[40]

It was winter, and the great Pacific's swells often run high, especially in winter's stormy weather—which all too frequently occurs. Destroyers, usually referred to as "Tin Cans" by America's sailors, and the "Tin Can Navy" by tough, hardened, destroyer crew members, are among the smaller combatants in any Navy. Under the best of weather conditions, when seas are relatively calm, destroyers' reputation for pitching and rolling is well known. Their reputation for a rough ride in rough seas is even better known. Frequently, new crew members and sailors tabbed for travel to their assigned ships via destroyers come aboard with some apprehension about possible seasickness—always an embarrassment to a conscientious seaman.

Seldom does a ship's course take her directly into or away from the movement of ocean swells. Courses directly against high wave motion result in heavy bow waves and exaggerated pitching, but little roll. Courses that take a ship at angles across rough or heavy wave motion induces both pitch and roll, but considerably lessens the severity of pitching. If seas are stormy and the ship's course takes it at angles across swell direction, pitching and rolling is irregular, sometimes appears wild, disconcerting, and can be disorienting, especially to the uninitiated.

But it was the destroyer's pitch, while plowing straight into heavy swells, which made crews and passengers seasick. Up, up, up, up the large, sometimes giant-like swell, followed by the long, sudden drop as the swell moved past the destroyer's center of gravity, she began rotating downward, the bow slamming down and cutting through the surface, on into the next swell— accompanied immediately by great walls of water crashing over the bow and forward main deck. When the going got rough, crews and passengers on destroyers had a rhyme they sometimes recited, to the tune of "Row, Row, Row Your Boat." "Roll, roll, roll, roll, roll you son-of-a-bitch; roll, roll, roll, roll, and you won't be able to pitch . . . " Bob Border remembers well his "cruise" to Hawaii aboard the *Morris*, though he was at sea only six days. "Everybody got seasick."[41]

For 0756 hours on Saturday, 1 March 1941, the *Morris's* deck log read "All engines stopped; approaching mooring. 0759

Moored bow and stern to buoy X23 Pearl Harbor, T.H . . .
1100 Ensign Robert L. Border, USN was detached to proceed to
USS TENNESSEE in accordance with basic orders . . . " Carrying
sea bags containing his uniforms, a few civilian clothes, toiletry
items, and personal belongings, Bob boarded a harbor launch
for transportation to the *Tennessee*. Glad to be returning to duty,
he had a happy smile for other reasons, and good news to give
Karl, which he had already conveyed to his mother and father by
phone and letter before he left Long Beach.

Karl Border was delighted to learn of his brother's return to
their ship, and greeted him warmly with a handshake, hug and
a brotherly slap on the back. After Bob broke the news of the
impending wedding to his surprised brother, and told Karl he
wanted him to be best man, he carried his bags to unpack in the
room they had shared before he went to the Puget Sound hospital
in December. They took the rest of the day to relax and catch up
on family news, shipmates and classmates, the coming wedding,
Tennessee and the Fleet exercises, spoke again of plans to go into
Naval Aviation training in Pensacola, and the world news. Karl
wrote in his diary that evening, "Bob came back about noon
today much to my surprise and pleasure. He looks fine and is
engaged to Joey Springer. What a man! We went over to Ford
Island, had a sunbath, swam, and generally took it easy. It's good
to have Minimus back."[42]

Early the same day, the Navy established the Support Force,
Atlantic Fleet, commanded by Rear Admiral Arthur L. Bristol,
Jr. Composed of destroyers and patrol planes, the Support Force
was to protect convoys in the North Atlantic, the lifelines to
the United Kingdom and free allies who had fled the Nazi's and
were still fighting the Axis powers in Europe. In the Balkans,
Bulgaria joined the Axis powers, after German troops occupied
the country.[43]

A Brother's Diary

No sooner did Bob rejoin his brother Karl and the crew of
Tennessee, than she put to sea on 3 March for nine days of training exercises with Battleship Divisions One and Three. The pace
of training exercises was relentless. Calls to General Quarters;

repelling submarine, destroyer, and air attacks, short range firing practice, night firing practice, damage control exercises, magazine inspections, fire drills, exercises of various material conditions, turns in column, turns to reform columns, launching and recovering planes, firing on towed targets, and crew physical conditioning.

While elements of the Pacific Fleet were at sea on 10 March, an increasingly aggressive Japan plunged deeper into Southeast Asia by successfully completing the role of mediator in the undeclared war between France and Indochinese nationalists and communists who were rebelling against French colonial control in Indochina. France, now under the heel of German occupation, with a collaborationist Vichy government administering the country, was no match for the German occupiers, the rebelling Indochinese, or the expansionist Japanese who had other designs. As a result of the mediated settlement, the Vichy government ceded territory to Thailand and gave Japan monopoly control of the Indochinese rice crop, as well as rights to the airport in Saigon.

When the Battle Force returned to Pearl 12 March, *Tennessee* was there only a few days. The day she returned, the Navy established the Corpus Christi Naval Air Station in Corpus Christi, Texas. While in Pearl once more, crew members', the ship's and Hawaiians' short wave and am radios were tuned into President Roosevelt's stirring 15 March "fireside chat" in which he delivered the administration's Lend-Lease message to the American people. He had signed the Lend-Lease Act into law on the 11th and changes to the "cash and carry" provisions of the 1939 Neutrality Act permitted transfer of munitions to the Allies. Karl and Bob, like hundreds of officers in the Armed Forces, considered his talk a virtual declaration of war against Germany, Italy and Japan, and Karl wrote in his diary that night, "Looks like we'll be in it soon."[44]

Tennessee put to sea again the night of the 17th, the ship darkened. Gas mask drills, fleet tactics with more turning and changing formations, variations of speed and courses, zigzagging, repelling night torpedo and destroyer attacks, catapulting and recovering aircraft, anti-aircraft drills and firing machine guns at balloons, once more became the routine. Participating in fleet tactics with the battleship divisions was the *Colorado*, sister ship and head of her class of combatants, which included *West*

Virginia and *Maryland*. The night of 19 March, while the Battle Force was exercising formation changes, two destroyers collided without serious damage, and returned to port.[45]

The Navy's Bureau of Personnel accepted Karl's and Bob's applications for aviation training at Pensacola. Forwarded to the Bureau by the 14th Naval District while *Tennessee* was in port, Karl's application spurred him to begin preparing for the anticipated change of career. He was delighted, went down to Radio One in the Communications Department and began "learning a bit of radio." Bob, who had initially been assigned to the communications department when they came aboard in June 1939, and was now in the 8th anti-aircraft gun Division, was the first of the two brothers to state his intent to leave the battleship division for Naval Aviation training. Because of his broken arm and a two and a half month's hospital stay at Puget Sound, he would have to wait longer to receive orders. The Battle Force briefly returned to Pearl Harbor 26 March, and put to sea again five days later.[46]

The next day, the 27th, the secret United States-British staff discussions in Washington ended. The discussions' result was the "ABC-1 Staff Agreement" which embodied the conflict's basic strategic direction in case the United States entered the war. On 28 March the British fleet defeated the Italian fleet in the Battle of Cape Matapan, with three Italian cruisers and two destroyers sunk, and several ships damaged. Sunday, 30 March, as tensions with the Axis powers in Europe mounted, the United States took possession of German, Italian, and Danish ships in United States ports.

Great Britain, the world's greatest parliamentary democracy, with lingering worldwide colonial interests, was standing almost alone in the face of the German and Italian onslaught in Europe, and the island nation's survival was of deep and growing concern for President Roosevelt and his administration. To strengthen defense of the North Atlantic sea lanes, which now constituted England's lifeline, on the 31st an American South Greenland Survey Expedition composed of State, Treasury, War and Navy Department representatives arrived in Godthaab, Greenland to locate and recommend sites for American military installations, and gather hydrographic information.[47]

While their ship was once more at sea on training exercises south of Oahu the first week in April, the brothers witnessed the recovery of an aircraft and its crew following an accident involving one of their ship's observation and scout and planes. The *Tennessee* and *Oklahoma* simulated firing on a beach protecting a simulated landing force on Kahoolawe Island, south of Maui on 4 April. The next day, while attempting to land in the relatively smooth water created on the ship's port side by *Tennessee*, in preparation for recovery aboard ship, plane #203, a new, low-wing monoplane—an OS2U Kingfisher—piloted by Lieutenant (jg) George Lawler, turned over. Fortunately, Lawler and his observer both safely escaped and the ship's company recovered the aircraft and its crew.[48]

There were three scout floatplanes on each battleship, and two on cruisers, including light cruisers. Landing and recovery of a floatplane on the high seas is sometimes a difficult and complicated procedure.[49]

Radar, a new technology, was secretly being introduced into the fleet for air and surface defense, and aircraft recovery, during periods of ships' maintenance and overhaul. On shore, also in secret, the Army was integrating ACR-270 radar systems in a four-truck package in Army anti-aircraft-artillery units' air defense systems. On Oahu the Army would have six such units in place in the months ahead.[50]

Aircraft carriers and seaplane tenders, such as the USS *Curtis*s, had first priority in modernizing the fleet with the Navy's CXAM radar for aircraft detection and gun-laying (locking on and automatically tracking targets while aiming guns), and battleships were next. Radar had a range of approximately 150 miles, straight line, and signals could radiate 360 degrees by sweeping the beam in a circle with antenna rotation, but couldn't reflect or "bounce off" surface targets or low flying aircraft beyond and completely below the horizon, which was approximately 14 miles from the ship's position on the ocean's surface.

Thus, while the Navy would later begin systematically modernizing the entire fleet with radar, the shipboard observation and scout planes remained the Naval gunfire combatants', as well as aircraft carriers' "eyes over the horizon," on the hunt for approaching enemy ships, submarines, and aircraft. From on board battleships and cruisers, the scout's normal mission profile was to be catapulted from the ship, and fly pre-planned search patterns directed by the Battle Force commander. When the mission was complete, the pilot would then land the aircraft on a relatively smooth ocean surface produced by the ship's turning maneuver, to be captured by a ship-towed sled, and hoisted aboard with a winch.

The launch and recovery of scout planes from cruisers and battleships usually required the ships to deviate from the convoy's course and speed, increasing speed of the ship to launch and decreasing speed below task force or convoy speed to recover the aircraft, while maneuvering at various courses and speeds to take advantage of wind and wave conditions. The catapult was deck mounted, and to launch the aircraft the catapult was trained (aimed) outboard, normally to port, 25 to 30 degrees, the ship accelerated and turned to permit the launch to be directly into the wind.

Catapult launches required particular attention to the ship's roll. It was vital to ensure the catapult fired while the ship was rolling opposite the direction of launch to avoid firing the

A Curtis SOC Seagull bi-plane is catapulted off a *St. Louis* class cruiser, 1942-3. Aircraft carriers and battleships received priority ahead of cruisers in modernizing scout aircraft squadrons, which were the airborne eyes of the fleet prior to the advent of radar. NHHC

plane directly into the water. As one sailor put it, "Those old compressed air cats were the equivalent of an oversized sling shot." The catapult was capable of accelerating the aircraft to approximately 60 plus miles per hour. There was little room for error in obtaining flying speed on launch.

The aircraft recovery, called "cast recovery," necessitated the full cooperation of all the deck divisions on the ships, were complex, and sometimes difficult and potentially dangerous, particularly when sea and wind conditions were marginal for flying operations. The recovery device was a towed sled equipped with two special vanes mounted on its underside to keep the sled riding away from the ship. The sled's distance from the ship was managed by a breast line controlled by the 3rd deck division, and it was their responsibility to keep the sled riding parallel with the catapult. Attached to the rear of the sled was a large manila net

Vought OS2U "Kingfisher" floatplane, of Observation Squadron One (VO-1). Being recovered by *Arizona* (BB-39), after a flight in the Hawaiian Operating area on the morning of 6 September 1941. The pilot, Ensign Lawrence A. Williams, is holding the belt of his rear-seat man, Radioman 3rd Class G.H. Lane, who is hooking up the aircraft to the ship's crane for recovery. This was the same type aircraft carried by all the battleships assigned to the Pacific Fleet. NA

similar to a cargo net. The sled was towed and controlled by a line from the 1st deck division, at the forecastle.

When the aircraft returned from its flight and was ready to land the sled would be streamed. The ship would then perform a wide continuous turn into the wind to create a smooth landing surface by forming a slick on the water. The pilot would make his landing approach on to the slick and rapidly taxi up on to the sled to engage the towing hook attached to the forward underside of his center float. Once engaged the pilot would reduce his throttle and be towed by the sled, while the ship straightened its course into the wind, and deck crews pulled the plane and sled toward the ship. The plane crewman would climb from the rear cockpit, straddle the pilot, and open the hatch in the wing center section to break out the hoisting sling. The crane operator would then lower the pelican hook to the plane crewman who's job it was to engage the hook with the hoisting sling. Once the plane was clear of the water, the pilot shut down the engine and the crane operator then raised the aircraft and swung it inboard placing it back on the catapult car where it was locked in place. The ship would then rejoin its formation.

At the same time the Navy was modernizing the fleet with radar, the newer OS2U Vought Kingfishers were coming into the fleet, replacing the SOC-1 Curtiss Seagulls, the old, slower, bi-wing, closed cockpit observation and scout floatplanes, which first began entering service on battleships and cruisers in 1935. Battleships received first priority in replacing the Seagulls, and cruisers were next in line.[51]

The war in Europe continued to spread. On 6 April Germany invaded Yugoslavia and Greece, and Italy declared war on Yugoslavia. The next day the Navy established an operating base in the Caribbean Sea, on the island of Bermuda. The increasing aggressiveness of German U-Boat (submarine) activity, attacking convoys in the Atlantic, necessitated building American bases further eastward toward Europe, to buttress and extend the depth of defense of the continental United States, while more effectively defending convoys.

On the 7th, the same day the Navy took formal possession of the new base at Bermuda, reinforcements were ordered dispatched from the Pacific Fleet to extend the Atlantic neutrality patrol further eastward from American shores. With one task force already being built around the carrier *Ranger* (CV-

4) at Bermuda, over the next six weeks the carrier *Yorktown*, battleships *New Mexico* (BB-40), *Idaho* (BB-42), and *Mississippi* (BB-41); light cruisers *Brooklyn* (CL-40), *Philadelphia* (CL-41), *Savannah* (CL-42), and *Nashville* (CL-43); five destroyers from Destroyer Squadron 8 and 6 destroyers from Destroyer Squadron 9, departed Pearl Harbor for duty in the Atlantic.[52]

In the Pacific, on the island of Oahu, the Navy and Army commanders, Admiral Kimmel and General Short, were urging the Hawaiians' civil government and populace to accelerate defense preparedness. Commanders of ships and military units worked with local community leaders and elected officials on a regular, cooperative basis, resolving a wide variety of questions, such as law enforcement, good order and discipline, morale and welfare of sailors, soldiers and airmen which invariably arise when adjacent communities lead different lives for different reasons, yet are interdependent. The spreading conflict in Asia was lending an increased sense of urgency to contingency planning for war.

Army Day, April 7, 1941, marked a milestone in the civilian preparedness program. At a luncheon sponsored by the Chamber of Commerce, General Short gave a talk that, in its somber tone and frank statement, threw a figurative bombshell.

He urged that the community hasten work that had already begun toward the production and storage of food, the organization of an emergency corps of doctors and nurses, and the organization of a police auxiliary to guard utilities and prevent sabotage. He urged the construction of bomb shelters for workers in the vicinity of essential industries, and characterized plans for the evacuation of women and children from probable areas of bombardment as "the most essential and difficult problem confronting the community."

His appeal to housewives to stock their cupboards with food aroused instant response. For six months home economists had been trying without success to finance publication of lists of foods to be stored by each household in order to provide an adequate diet for a given period. Now, the publications were not only financed but they attained wide circulation and response. Exhibits of the suggested foods were staged, talks were given, and articles were published . . .

A month later the Honolulu Chamber of Commerce estimated that there had been a 20 to 35 percent increase in the supply of food in private homes.[53]

The Hawaiian Sugar Plantation Association (HSPA) reported that the growth of defense industry jobs in Hawaii had brought jobs in the sugar industry to their lowest employment level since before 1900. Between January and April 1941 there was a decrease of 800 sugar workers, who had joined the exodus of islanders to "the gold mines" of Oahu. As defense construction increased, mainland workers, who began coming to Hawaii in small numbers during the period 1939 and 1940 seeking defense jobs, were being brought in large groups beginning the latter part of 1940.[54]

During periods in port, Bob and Karl, along with all the ships' crews in Pearl Harbor, paid scant attention to local news. Their interest was national and international news, which they knew had far greater effects on their lives and futures. Typically, in peacetime, life on military installations was almost a world unto itself. In both civilian and military communities, on and off the bases and posts, there was some social and official interaction, mainly the result of wives and families living on the economy because of insufficient government quarters on the installations.

Already sensitized to news of the growing international crises, many of the men and women in uniform in Hawaii, as in other overseas bases and posts, were far from home and separated from their wives and families. Even when off duty, they faced the prospect of recall for no-notice military exercises; national, regional, or local emergencies. As a result, they were vitally interested in mail from home, rest, relaxation, fun, sports and training competitions within and between ships' crews and military units and installations, and thoughts of the opposite sex. As the defense-related population in Hawaii grew, the ratio of men to women also grew.

While Bob ended his search for eligible young women, Karl didn't. His list of love interests seemed to lengthen the longer *Tennessee* was home-ported in Hawaii, or at frequently visited ports of call such as Puget Sound, San Francisco, and Long Beach. Jayne and Lois on Oahu, and Hunky in Long Beach occupied his thoughts, Hunky plus Missy and his dad—his letter writing. Movies, *Tennessee*'s wrestling team, which he coached and was a team member, tennis, golf, swimming, surfing, dinners, dances, writing short stories, occupied much of his time in port, as did pistol firing and wrestling competition between ships and among crew members, accompanied by modest, fun bets with competitors.

The brothers roomed together, lived life and served aboard ship together, joked, laughed, exchanged thoughts and ideas about duties, the wars in Europe and Asia, and their shipmates, but when in port normally went their separate ways among different sets of friends, shipmates and classmates for recreation and social life. Nevertheless, on special days, such as 13 April, Easter Sunday, they spent the day together, sunning, swimming, playing tennis, talking and thinking of home, family, and the girls in their lives—for Bob, especially Joey. The artist in Karl once more appeared, as he marked the day with his younger brother in his diary, "It has been half blue sky and half white clouds with hot sun to make swimming and tennis fun."

They mused about their dad and Missy moving into their new house at 126 Houston Street in Mobile, Alabama, and their dad's assignment as superintendent of ship building in the Navy yard in nearby Pasquagula, Mississippi. Both were now looking forward to their anticipated assignments to Pensacola Naval Air Station, in aviator's training—hopefully together. When Karl wrote their dad and Missy the next evening, he observed in his diary, "It will be swell when Bob and I get down there with them."[55]

While Bob and Karl enjoyed Easter Sunday 1941, Japan and the Soviet Union signed the Russo-Japanese Non-Aggression Pact. Four days later the German raider *Atlantis*, carrying an array of carefully hidden, powerful weapons including six 150-mm and one 75-mm guns, disguised as a freighter—and able to change her disguises to ships of different nations—sank the Egyptian steamship *Zamzam*, with approximately 150 Americans among the rescued passengers. *Fortune* magazine editor Charles J.V. Murphy and *Life* magazine photographer David E. Scherman were among the passengers sent back to Germany on a blockade-runner. The Germans allowed Scherman to take photographs but confiscated his film when the two men were taken to Europe. However, the photographer was able to smuggle four rolls of film back to the United States.

On 22 April, Congress authorized enlisted strength of the Navy to increase to 232,000. The following day a defeated Greece signed an armistice with Germany, the prelude to German airborne troops' invasion of Crete less than a month later. On 27 April, American, Dutch and British conferees in Singapore, meeting in secret, reached agreement on a combined operating plan in the event of war with Japan. The senior American representative was Captain W. R. Purnell, USN, Chief of Staff, Asiatic Fleet.[56]

Talk of war between Bob and Karl, and among *Tennessee*'s crew was part of daily conversation, while the brothers' heightened interest in Naval Aviation added another dimension to their private conversations, and Karl's entries in his diary. "Saw 'Flight Command' tonight on the quarterdeck with an appropriate accompaniment of our planes engaged in night flying. It [flying] will be sport." "The British are taking a licking in Greece despite a fine and brave stand. It looks pretty bad for them . . . The radio says tonight that the German troops marched into Athens this morning, a far cry from the days of Salamis or Marathon . . . We are in a little world all by ourselves out here and the war seems both remote and 'just around the corner.' Bob and I will be glad to get to Pensacola."

There were changes in fleet tactics, target towing, ranging and firing procedures intended to develop more rigorous and realistic training. The changes prompted crew reactions, changes back to the old system, some confusion and frustration. On 29 April Karl observed, "All hands are getting restless, wishing either for war or the old peacetime Navy."

In April, looking ahead to Pensacola, he asked to become more involved in shipboard aviation. On 3 May, two days before the ship returned to Pearl, he neared certification as a catapult officer when he sent two aircraft off the high catapult. Back at sea once more on 15 May, for eight days, Karl took his first catapult ride the last day of the deployment, when, sitting in the OS2U observer's seat, he was fired off the low catapult at 0500 hours, with Ensign Richard H. Hogan flying the aircraft. The experience again brought out the artist in him. "The sunrise was beautiful and combined with the mists on Oahu and the ships off Pearl to make a unique scene." Though Bob didn't seek certification as catapult officer, he too flew a mission off *Tennessee* as an observer in the rear seat of an OS2U Kingfisher.

Karl noted in his diary, President Roosevelt's 45-minute fireside chat on 27 May, while *Tennessee* was moored in Pearl Harbor. The violent, dictator-induced events around the world, particularly in Europe and on the Atlantic Ocean, had the eyes and ears of men and women in uniform. When radio announcers and newspapers alerted the nation to the President's speech, Americans everywhere crowded around radios, as they had done increasingly in the twenty months following the German invasion of Poland. The President spoke slowly, solemnly.

> ... The battle of the Atlantic now extends from the icy waters of the North Pole to the frozen continent of the Antarctic. Throughout this huge area, there have been sinkings of merchant ships in alarming and increasing numbers by Nazi raiders or submarines. There have been sinkings even of ships carrying neutral flags. There have been sinkings in the South Atlantic, off West Africa and the Cape Verde Islands; between the Azores and the islands off the American coast; and between Greenland and Iceland. Great numbers of these sinkings have been actually within the waters of the Western Hemisphere itself.
>
> The blunt truth of this seems to be—and I reveal this with the full knowledge of the British Government: the present rate of Nazi sinkings of merchant ships is more than three times as high as the capacity of British shipyards to replace them; it is more than twice the combined British and American output of merchant ships today.
>
> We can answer this peril by two simultaneous measures: first, by speeding up and increasing our own great shipbuilding program; and second, by helping to cut down the losses on the high seas.
>
> Attacks on shipping off the very shores of land which we are determined to protect present an actual military danger to the Americas. And that danger has recently been heavily underlined by the presence in Western Hemisphere waters of a Nazi battleship of great striking power.
>
> You remember that most of the supplies for Britain go by a northerly route, which comes close to Greenland and the nearby island of Iceland. Germany's heaviest attack is on that route. Nazi occupation of Iceland or bases in Greenland would bring the war close to our own continental shores; because those places are stepping-stones to Labrador

and Newfoundland, to Nova Scotia, (and) yes, to the northern United States itself, including the great industrial centers of the north, the east and the middle west.

Equally, the Azores and the Cape Verde Islands, if occupied or controlled by Germany, would directly endanger the freedom of the Atlantic and our own American physical safety. Under German domination those islands would become bases for submarines, warships, and airplanes raiding the waters that lie immediately off our own coasts and attacking the shipping in the South Atlantic. They would provide a springboard for actual attack against the integrity and the independence of Brazil and her neighboring Republics.

I have said on many occasions that the United States is mustering its men and its resources only for purposes of defense only to repel attack. I repeat that statement now. But we must be realistic when we use the word "attack;" we have to relate it to the lightning speed of modern warfare.

Some people seem to think that we are not attacked until bombers actually drop bombs on New York or San Francisco or New Orleans or Chicago. But they are simply shutting their eyes to the lesson that we must learn from the fate of every nation that the Nazis have conquered.

The attack on Czechoslovakia began with the conquest of Austria. The attack on Norway began with the occupation of Denmark. The attack on Greece began with occupation of Albania and Bulgaria. The attack on the Suez Canal began with the invasion of the Balkans and North Africa and the attack on the United States can begin with the domination of any base which menaces our security—north or south.

Nobody can foretell tonight just when the acts of the dictators will ripen into attack on this hemisphere and us. But we know enough by now to realize that it would be suicide to wait until they are in our front yard . . .

. . . Today the whole world is divided, divided between human slavery and human freedom—between pagan brutality and the Christian ideal.

We choose human freedom—which is the Christian ideal. No one of us can waver for a moment in his courage or his faith.

We will not accept a Hitler-dominated world. And we will not accept a world, like the post-war world of the 1920's, in which the seeds of Hitlerism can again be planted and allowed to grow.

We will accept only a world consecrated to freedom of speech and expression—freedom of every person to worship God in his own way—freedom from want—and freedom from terror.

Is such a world impossible of attainment?

Magna Carta, the Declaration of Independence, the Constitution of the United States, the Emancipation Proclamation and every other milestone in human progress—all were ideals which seemed impossible of attainment—and yet they were attained.

As a military force, we were weak when we established our independence, but we successfully stood off tyrants, powerful in their day, tyrants who are now lost in the dust of history.

Odds meant nothing to us then. Shall we now, with all our potential strength, hesitate to take every single measure necessary to maintain our American liberties?

Our people and our Government will not hesitate to meet that challenge.

As the President of a united and determined people, I say solemnly:

We reassert the ancient American doctrine of freedom of the seas.

We reassert the solidarity of the twenty-one American Republics and the Dominion of Canada in the preservation of the independence of the hemisphere.

We have pledged material support to the other democracies of the world—and we will fulfill that pledge.

We in the Americas will decide for ourselves

whether, and when, and where, our American interests are attacked or our security threatened.

We are placing our armed forces in strategic military position.

We will not hesitate to use our armed forces to repel attack.

We reassert our abiding faith in the vitality of our constitutional republic as a perpetual home of freedom, of tolerance, and of devotion to the word of God.

Therefore, with profound consciousness of my responsibilities to my countrymen and to my country's cause, I have tonight issued a proclamation that an unlimited national emergency exists and requires the strengthening of our defense to the extreme limit of our national power and authority.

The nation will expect all individuals and all groups to play their full parts, without stint, and without selfishness, and without doubt that our democracy will triumphantly survive.

I repeat the words of the Signers of the Declaration of Independence—that little band of patriots, fighting long ago against overwhelming odds, but certain, as we are now, of ultimate victory: "With a firm reliance on the protection of Divine Providence, we mutually pledge to each other our lives, our fortunes, and our sacred honor."[57]

The president's speech received banner headlines, and forcefully laid down American policy regarding the war in Europe. He declared an unlimited National Emergency, and his talk was anti-Hitler in every respect.

Two days later, the *Tennessee*'s gunnery officer told Karl he wanted him to take over the 5th Division, the starboard broadside gun crews. Karl was elated, and proudly announced to his diary what he undoubtedly said to the men who, at the call to battle stations, would man the guns, "We'll show them something or bust in the attempt."

Two weeks later the ship's crew learned they would be returning to the States temporarily, at a date not yet determined. On 17 June, Bob and Karl received word *Tennessee* was scheduled to be in Long Beach 10-24 July. The first thought that popped into Karl Border's head was Hunky, his Long Beach girl, while Bob's first thought was of Joey, and their wedding.

The next day, Noel Gayler from the *Enterprise* and the Naval Academy class of 1935 took Karl for a hop, circling completely around Oahu in an SNJ, a new low-wing monoplane, which was the Navy's version of the Army Air Force's T-6 basic trainer. Noel's father and mother had been long time family friends of the Borders. He demonstrated to Karl aerobatics and other basic flying maneuvers taught in aviation training, and gave him some "stick time" [control of the aircraft]—all of which Karl enjoyed immensely.

A letter from Missy was waiting when he returned to the ship. He would be going to the 7 September class at Pensacola, and Bob would enter in October. Great news, but "unofficial" news in a letter from Missy. No orders yet, but their dad was obviously looking out for their individual, family, and professional interests.

Wednesday evening, 25 June, Karl noted in his diary, "We shoved off this morning and started on maneuvers before sailing for Long Beach. Wonder how soon it will be before we come back to Diamond Head?" In the Battle Force leaving Pearl Harbor was the battleship *Colorado*, soon on her way to Puget Sound Navy Yard for major overhaul and modernization, which wouldn't be complete until spring 1942. Three days later, on 28 June, there was a tinge of brotherly love and nostalgia in his written remarks, "After two years Minimus and I are no longer roommates because the First Luff wants me up in the mast near the Fifth Division. Minimus has been a swell pal." Bob remained in the 8th Division, an anti-aircraft gun division, port side, his battle station aft, nearer the stern of *Tennessee*.[58]

In spite of their parting as roommates, everything was falling into place for Ensigns Bob and Karl Border. Bob and Joey could now fix their wedding date for July, while the *Tennessee* was in Long Beach. The Navy's required two year waiting period before marriage for its newly commissioned officers will have expired, and Karl could be Bob's Best Man at the wedding before leaving for Pensacola. If given fourteen days leave, which he was confident would be approved, there would be time for a honeymoon before Bob returned to the ship and sailed again for Pearl Harbor.

For Karl? His girl Hunky was in Long Beach. Fun. Aviation

training at Pensacola soon to follow, with the two brothers and Bob's new bride, the newest member of the Border family, near home during most of their time in flight training.

Wedding in a Long Beach Chapel

Life is filled with ironies. On Saturday, 1 March, the day Bob Border arrived in Pearl Harbor on board the destroyer *Morris*, Joey was at Mt. Rainier with one of the battleship *California's* fun-loving junior officers, Rink, and 16 other young men and women. They skied, partied, sang, danced, and she called the night ended and to bed at 11:15 p.m.

Rink had been pursuing her since *California* returned to Puget Sound in late January, but Bob had crowded him out, along with all potential suitors, until Bob left for the train ride south on 2 February. With Bob gone, Rink didn't waste any time attempting to fill the void. After all, engagements aren't final until wedding vows, when the chaplain says, "I now pronounce you man and wife." He joined a parade of admiring young officers smitten by Joey Springer's beauty and vivaciousness.

John Renfro, Tom Ruddon, Kirk Kirkpatrick and others sought her attention. She told none of them about her plans to marry Bob, accepted their invitations to their ships for lunch, dinner, or to golf rounds, skiing, and evenings out at the Yard club, movies, ferry rides to Seattle, dinner and shows in the city. She enjoyed the *California* boys' fun-filled company, and certainly didn't want to withdraw from social life, yet she kept them at arms length—gently, graciously. In fact, like all the Yard engines, she preferred visiting the junior officer ward rooms of all the larger ships, the aircraft carriers, battleships and cruisers. The calculus was simple. The larger the ships, the more eligible junior officers in the ward room for meals. But there was a destroyer in her future—without the worry of pitching, rolling, or seasickness.

Joey had earlier been aboard destroyers for dinner, but the USS *Monssen* (DD-436), with which she became acquainted, was new. She learned of the ship while it was under construction at Puget Sound Navy Yard, because the *Monssen's* first assigned skipper (ship's captain and commander) was a friend of the Springer family, as was his wife. Typically, the ship was quite small compared to the cruisers, battleships and aircraft carriers Joey regularly visited for meals and card games. The complement of officers and men numbered 276.

At 348 feet in length the new destroyer was 48 feet longer than a football field, 36 feet abeam (greatest width), thinly-armored, and light weight. She displaced only 1,630 tons. Her speed was typical of modern destroyers, 33 knots, nearly 38 miles per hour, almost twice the speed of the older, World War I-era battleships. Destroyers, like their larger, heavier kin, the light cruisers, were heavily-armed. They carried deck and turret guns, automatic rapid-firing, anti-aircraft weapons, depth charges, and torpedoes; were sleek, quick-accelerating, fast-attack escorts, submarine hunters and screens for convoys, battle or task forces. They were also close-in defense as well as plane guards for aircraft carriers when flight operations were ongoing, ready to aggressively attack submarines that might successfully slip inside the task force outer screen, or hurry to the rescue of downed aircrews in the vicinity of carriers. And in major surface engagements could be deadly, elusive adversaries to heavily armed enemies.[59]

By comparison *California* and her sister ship, *Tennessee*,

The destroyer *Monssen* (DD-436) Off the Puget Sound Navy Yard, Bremerton, Washington, 7 May 1941. NHHC

both commissioned in 1919, were heavily-armed and heavily-armored, including a thick, steel, "torpedo belt" at and below their waterlines; were broad abeam, and were slow, lumbering giants. Fully loaded and manned as the fleet flagship, *California* displaced 33,190 tons, was 624 feet in length, just over 97 feet abeam, with a complement of 1,407 officers and men. They bristled with destructive force, carrying the Navy's long range, surface and subsurface striking power.[60]

The captain and commander of the soon-to-be-commissioned *Monssen* was Lieutenant Commander Roland N. Smoot. His wife, Sally, had become Florence Springer's close friend, and Joey occasionally played golf with Sally, because Florence didn't play the game. Roland Smoot became George Springer's friend and occasional golf partner while Roland met and began training *Monssen*'s initial complement of officers and men for the 14 March christening. The Smoot's daughter and Navy junior, "Little Sally," was twelve years old, well mannered, and occasionally Joey looked after her.

After Joey attended the ship's commissioning ceremony on Friday, 14 March, she several times accompanied Ensign "Zully" Zellinger for dinner in the destroyer's wardroom, once in March, twice in April, once again in early May. *Monssen* was undergoing shakedown sorties out of Puget Sound, and would shortly begin sea trials. Her skipper would soon receive orders to take the ship to its assigned home port, probably San Diego, from where additional sea trials would continue and fleet operations begin. Given Germany's increasing, deadly U-boat attacks in the Atlantic, there was a strong possibility the *Monssen* might be sent to the Atlantic fleet.

On Monday, 7 April, Joey enjoyed dinner with Ensign Murphy aboard the *California* one more time. Two days later she and six of her friends, including Dede Dunbar and Norma Hall, went to the docks to see the battleship assemble her crew, cast off her lines, and leave Puget Sound. Joey cried, wrote in her diary that she cried, saying the ship's departure was "very sad," an unusual reaction for the tough, no nonsense, newspaper reporter who spent much of her work day chasing court cases through the Bremerton judiciary. She had spent many happy hours on *California*. The ship's bright, cheerful, fun-loving ensigns would be missed.

As always, she quickly pushed the brief period of sadness from her mind, devoting her thoughts and energies to the good times with her girlfriends and ships' junior officers at the Yard. Planning the wedding helped, too. She and Bob wrote one another often, and when she received letters from him, she quickly answered. He knew *Tennessee*'s next return to the West Coast was in the near future. He would let her know precisely when, as soon as the ship's schedule was known.[61]

In the first days of May, still uncertain of their wedding date, but able to plan and complete many of the other details for this once in a lifetime, joyful event, including the purchase of a dress, Joey came upon a ready-made opportunity to be near where Bob was convinced *Tennessee* would next visit a West Coast port— Long Beach. The ship wasn't scheduled for overhaul or dry dock in the Puget Sound Yard. The opportunity appeared when Lieutenant Commander Smoot received orders to bring *Monssen* and her crew south to the Long Beach and San Diego operating areas for sea trials.

Sally and Little Sal prepared to move to a rented apartment in Long Beach where the family could be near her husband, a way of life for Navy wives when husbands were at sea. Mother and Dad Smoot were in Long Beach, too, and a brother and sister-in-law were twenty miles away from where she and Little Sal would be staying. Sally knew of the wedding and after discussing the idea with Joey's parents, offered to bring her along to stay with them in Long Beach, perhaps until the wedding. Given the circumstances, including the likelihood of *Tennessee*'s short notice arrival in port, which would affect the Springers' ability to travel from Puget Sound to attend the wedding, Sally's offer seemed an excellent idea. First disclosed to Joey on 10 May, the idea was accepted and duly repeated to her diary on 12 May. ". . . I'm going with Sal!!"

The next week was a round of busy preparations and goodbyes, and on Saturday, 19 May, after waking at 4 a.m., the drive south began. Oregon and California were new to Joey. She had never been to either state and was looking forward to the trip. The Washington-Oregon scenery was wonderful, with forested hills and mountains, clear streams with lovely waterfalls flowing through the valleys. En route they passed a convoy of Army trucks moving north toward Fort Lewis, Washington. Across the great Columbia River they went, into Portland for lunch, then on to Klamath Falls—501 miles the tiring first day.

The next day, after rising at 6 a.m., Joey relieved Sally Smoot and took her turn driving to their overnight destination, Salinas, California. The further south they went the hotter it became, "hotter then hell," Joey thought. California reminded her of the Wisconsin Delta near her Minnesota home. The last day of the trip they ate lunch in a Malibu Beach restaurant, and pulled into Long Beach at 5:30 p.m. After another long day, she was relieved to unpack, have dinner with the Smoots, and fall into bed. Though tired, she was anxious to become acquainted with the city where she and Bob would marry, and lay awake for a time wondering what she would see the next day.

She had one day to shop, see the town, and relax before the 23d, when they would greet the *Monssen* as she arrived in Long Beach. That evening she had dinner in the ship's wardroom with Zully Zellinger.

The next three weeks were busy. Joey surveyed Long Beach, Los Angeles, La Jolla, San Diego, Tiajuana, Mexico; went shopping with Sally, sunbathing at the beach, to the movies, visited friends and relatives, saw comedian Jack Benny and his entertainment sidekick, Don Wilson, at the Marine Club, and continued to map out plans for the wedding.

Determined to recover Bob's first miniature class ring, she visited Gretna Price's mother to ask where Gretna might be. On 12 June, just days before she learned from Bob *Tennessee* would arrive in Long Beach on 10 July, the new, gold, class miniature ring he ordered for her, arrived.

They could now fix the wedding date, Tuesday, 15 July. All her activities and wedding plans, which included final measurements and fitting of the wedding dress, clothes for the honeymoon, church and scheduling of the hour, the minister, music, flowers, the wedding party, invitations and announcements, phone calls, reception afterwards, where they would spend their wedding night, the honeymoon location and reservations—all of it, with some advice and help from her mother and Sally Smoot, and letter exchanges with Bob, would have to be done by Joey. Bob and Karl would arrive on *Tennessee* with five days to spare. In spite of it all, to her it seemed the days dragged by. She wanted time to fly, but it dragged. And more surprises awaited her and Bob.

The first came on 23 June, when Lieutenant Commander Smoot jolted her with a letter implying Joey would have to leave their apartment. The letter gave no explanation, and Joey was offended, at least initially, when she grumbled to her diary, "Am taking a 'hint' given in Mr. Smoot's letter—guess I'll move." She didn't know, and he couldn't tell her or his family all the details, but he had received classified orders.

There were other reasons a move made sense, and Joey and Sally had discussed them. Buddy, their son, had come home from college for the summer, and he had a steady parade of friends coming through the apartment. Sally and her husband had frequent phone calls and telegrams from Navy friends and families coming through Long Beach, wanting to stop by and visit, or stay with them temporarily, on the way to a new assignment. But the more pressing reason was the near term departure of Sally's husband, Roland. Sally knew a few days later she and her family would be leaving for the East Coast on 28 August.[62]

On 25 June, Sally and Little Sal left for Coronado Island, across the bay west from San Diego. The *Monssen* was to leave San Diego on 27 June, assigned to the Atlantic Fleet. The day Sally and the children left for Coronado, Joey packed. News of the *Monssen*'s departure wasn't good for several reasons.

It meant Sally and her family would be leaving permanently, and Joey, not yet knowing when, had hoped Sally would be able to attend the wedding. The future Mrs. Robert Lee Border didn't have a car and would have to rely entirely on transportation by streetcars—which fortunately she'd been learning to do. She could get on with completing plans in spite of the inconvenience of no car.

She rose early next day, moved into another apartment down the street, bought a suit in Long Beach, went to the beach, and ended the day with the exciting news that *Tennessee* would be in port from 10 to 24 July. Bob would be granted fourteen days leave for their wedding and honeymoon.[63]

* * *

The second surprise was a jolt to Bob, and a circumstance over which he—and Karl, his intended Best Man at the wedding—had absolutely no control. When the force of seven battleships completed its exercises, and turned toward the West Coast on 3 July, it became apparent to Bob and Karl that the base course *Tennessee* was keeping probably wouldn't take the ship to Long Beach.

She had sheered out of the Battle Force, reduced speed to eight knots, and refueled the destroyer *Phelps*, on the starboard side from 0739 to 0900 hours, and from 1017-1100 took the destroyer *Aylwin* along the starboard side, to receive mail. At 1135 she commenced zigzagging, at 1255, ceased, then took up the base course of 160 degrees before turning port to 140. Two more turns at 1305 and 1414 hours, first, port to 107 degrees, then starboard to 125. Then, at 1505 hours *Tennessee* swung into formation with the aircraft carrier *Saratoga*, the fleet guide, turning to port again, and course 076 degrees. The remaining ships present in the task force she joined were the battleship *Colorado*; cruisers *Phoenix* and *Helena*; destroyers *Phelps*, *Farragut*, *Aylwin*, *Monaghan*, and *Dale*. At 1648 hours Molokini light, on a small island off Maui, came into view from *Tennessee*, 15 miles abeam her port side.

Then, at 0750 hours on 4 July 1941, Independence Day, ten minutes before Bob came on duty as Officer of the Deck, came the clincher. Ensign Charlie Morrison, the two brothers' friend from the Naval Academy's class of 1938, a year ahead of them, was the Officer of the Deck and signed the log entry. "Proceeded independently, destination San Francisco." *Tennessee* first sheered out of the task force and turned port to due north at a speed of 17 knots. Bob followed Charlie as OOD at 0800, followed by Karl at 1200 hours. Bob's deck log entry read: "0850 Changed course [starboard] to 053 degrees. 0930 Mustered crew at quarters. No absentees. Changed time zone from plus 10½ hours to plus 10 hours and set all clocks ahead ½ hour. 1030 Made daily inspection of magazines and smokeless powder samples, conditions normal."

Then, as Karl took the watch, he once more witnessed one of the Navy's great, at sea, traditions. When he signed the log four hours later, it read: "1200 [hours] Fired 21 gun National salute and broke Ensign [National flag] on main truck [foremast] in observance of Independence Day." To the seamen in the United States Navy, each of the ships on which they serve becomes both a temporary home on the high seas, and a sovereign moving island of America. An attack on their ship while at sea, is, to them, an attack on the United States and their home.

The evening of 6-7 July, Charlie Morrison came on duty again, as OOD, this time from 2000 to 2400 hours. Ensign Wood, who preceded him, briefed him that preparations were under way for a full speed run. Boiler #1 had been cut in at 1915 hours. The ship was on course 059 degrees when Charlie assumed Officer of the Deck responsibility.

At 2226 lookouts scanning the forward starboard quarter sighted a darkened ship bearing 040 degrees, distance two miles. The ship sighted turned on its running lights, and *Tennessee* challenged her. The reply was unintelligible. At 2230 the battleship turned starboard to 249 degrees and pursued. Ten minutes later she overhauled and identified the ship, the *Hoerg Merchant*, a Norwegian merchantman bound from San Francisco to Madras. Satisfied with the ship's identification, *Tennessee*'s commander ordered return to course 059. Gradually, throughout the period Charlie Morrison was on duty, the ship's speed increased from 15.5 to 18.9 knots, preparatory to the full power run.

When Bob Border took the watch at midnight, speed continued slowly increasing toward 20.1 knots, and at 0100, with all eight boilers on line, *Tennessee* commenced her full power run. Thirty minutes later vibrations were felt as rotor blades on the aft turbine began stripping. It was a major mechanical failure, necessitating reduced speed to 14.7 knots and eventually a trip to dry dock at Hunters Point in San Francisco Bay. Bob briefed Karl on the turbine failure when Karl relieved him to begin the 0400 watch.

The failure didn't alter the course or destination, however. At 1846 hours on Wednesday, 9 July, after passing through the cold, fog-shrouded entrance to San Francisco Bay, *Tennessee* anchored off Point Knox, near Sausalito, in 12 fathoms [72 feet] of water, with the ship on ten minutes notice to get underway. Over the loudspeaker system the crew heard the announcement liberty could be granted to those eligible. But, Karl noted, there were no boats available.

Bob Border took the 2000-2400 watch, with Karl next on the OOD duty roster. The next morning, at 0930, Bob left the ship on fourteen days leave, and ten minutes later was on the phone to Joey. He arrived in Los Angeles by train twelve hours later.

Having wired Joey on Sunday, the 13th, the next evening, at 1825 hours, Karl departed the ship on four days leave. The wedding in Long Beach remained on schedule for Tuesday evening, and he would be the Best Man—but not until he and the men in the 5th Division did some scraping on the ship's hull while she was in dry dock, he served two more tours of duty as officer of the deck, and he traveled overnight on the train from San Francisco to Los Angeles.[64]

Joey was ecstatic on receiving Bob's phone call, and he was deliriously happy to hear her voice, no matter that he was in

San Francisco and not Long Beach. They were thrilled and giddy with joy to see one another when he arrived that evening. They smiled broadly when they caught sight of one another at the train station, then laughed as they threw themselves into one another's arms and kissed sweetly, then more passionately. The ride back to Joey's apartment was filled with talk, and the talking extended until 2:00 in the morning.

Wedding plans, the first night in the bridal suite at the Villa Riviera, honeymoon at Lake Arrowhead, family, friends, classmates, the arrival of the miniature ring and how lovely it was, shipmates, the *Tennessee*'s schedule, the Navy and the possibility of war, Hawaii, aviation training in Pensacola, Bob's dad and Missy now a short distance from Pensacola, the possibility of Joey coming to Hawaii in the near future, her mother and father's being unable to attend the wedding because of the uncertainty of when and where it would be—everything under the sun two people deeply in love considered important to them, their future, and their lives together.[65]

All Joey's planning paid off which lifted both their spirits and made Bob more aware than ever he had picked, and been picked, by the perfect woman to be a proud Navy wife. Unsure of when or where *Tennessee* would come into port, Bob's bride-to-be had done all she could to permit last minute adjustments in wedding time and location, and had given the Episcopal priest, Dr. Drew Green, three alternative dates for scheduling—just in case—with the 15 July date as most likely according to the ship's sailing dates announced to the *Tennessee* crew.

Joey waked early the morning of the wedding, took her wedding dress and accessories, left them at Sally Smoot's, and met Karl for the first time in their lives, at the train station when he arrived. Their meeting wasn't strained at all. Both felt they knew one another, through Bob's mutually shared conversations and descriptions.

She took Karl to the hotel he planned to stay, and en route they talked animatedly about the wedding plans and rehearsal. The entire day, and the five preceding days, she and Bob were in a daze of infectious happiness. Everyone who encountered and talked with them, witnessed and felt their excitement, and this day especially, Karl was quickly swept up by the rising tide of joy.

Following the morning rehearsal, Joey picked up her new brown suit and hat, and the small wedding party went to the

Joey Springer in her wedding gown prior to the
ceremony, 15 July 1941. Borders' Collection

Army-Navy Club for a drink and their own, private wedding breakfast. Afterward she went back to Sally's and into a whirlwind of activity that Sally had to make a determined effort to slow down. Her son, Buddy, and two of his friends were at the Smoot's, and she knew Joey needed some rest. Later Sally prepared her a wedding dinner of vegetable salad and spaghetti. Joey had been dieting, shaving off inches in the right places, Sally believed, and needed some nourishment that would stick with her.

Joey took a leisurely bubble bath, they both dressed for the 8 p.m. ceremony, and arrived at St. Luke's just prior to the time Dr. Green requested. Sally, who helped Joey pick out "something old, something new (the wedding dress), something borrowed, and something blue," dressed in a style similar to Joey's. She wore a navy blue night dress and a blue, wrap-around turban with a yellow corsage of 14 Birds of Paradise, giving a "Navy blue and gold" appearance. She regarded Joey's white, mid-calf satin gown; white, wrap-around turban; and dainty, white, lace mitts as elegant and stylish, yet practical for future use. The large, single white orchid corsage Joey carried with her prayer book, added a lovely touch.

Bob and Karl were strikingly handsome in their Naval officers' dress whites, with the black shoulder marks bearing the ensign's insignia of rank. At Florence Springer's request and expense, Tom Seddon, came all the way from Minneapolis's Symphony Orchestra, where he was playing when Florence was accompanying the Symphony, played the organ at their wedding. By the time the ceremony began, the small chapel appeared nearly full because of friends, acquaintances, and a few of Sally's and Bob's relatives who were able to attend.

When Tom Seddon first started playing the traditional wedding march, "Here Comes the Bride," he miscued and stopped after a couple of notes, which, for a moment, flustered Sally. Fortunately, she later wrote Florence, she held in place with Joey at the entrance to the chapel. When he began playing a second time, the two hesitated momentarily, then Sally, with Karl to her right, urged they begin moving down the aisle. As they moved toward the altar at the slow, wedding march cadence, before them, Dr. Green stood on the altar step in his black robes and purple stole, Bible in hand. Bob waited in front and to the right side of the communion rail, standing, facing the center aisle, head turned toward and smiling warmly at Joey, with Sally and Karl coming down the aisle behind her. Within seconds, Joey and Sally both felt pride, and an unspoken attitude, "THIS is the way to do a wedding."

The ceremony was somewhat unusual that evening, because Sally had a double role in the wedding party, as both Joey's father and Matron of Honor. Sally and Karl came down the aisle behind Joey until she stopped in front of the altar step. When she stopped, Sally continued forward to Joey's left side to give her away. When the Reverend asked "Who is giving the bride's hand in marriage?" Sally replied clearly, "I am, in behalf of her father, George I. Springer." As Bob moved forward toward Joey's right side, Sally then, with little notice, took two short steps, slipping further left, taking Joey's prayer book and orchid, and doubled as the Matron of Honor. Such are the exigencies of the service, and life on the move in the Navy.

The wedding was a High Episcopal Mass, including a liturgy, alternate kneeling and standing at the communion rail, and the taking of communion. The reverend who officiated was diligent in counseling prospective brides and grooms in his parish, and prided himself in weddings that would last. During planning for this ceremony, he told Sally and Joey he was particular, investigated each situation carefully, wouldn't marry just anyone who requested his services, and had turned down many requests. He was more than proud that in the nearly forty years he had officiated at weddings, only two ended in divorce.

He was, as most experienced pastors are, thoughtful, thought-provoking, and eloquent in expressing God's word. In her letter to Florence three days later, Sally wrote, "Of all the weddings I have ever been to, I have never heard a ceremony read as beautifully as Dr. Drew read theirs. EVERYONE remarked upon it." In spite of his near perfection as a man of God, he wasn't without a sense of humor, which was evident twice during the ceremony.

When he came to the words, "Speak now or forever hold your peace," and the usual period of silence ensued, he said softly out of the corner of his mouth, just loud enough for the four in front of the altar to hear, "You are STUCK NOW." Until that moment, Sally, Joey, Bob and Karl, had all been feeling hearts pounding with excitement and some worry about making a mistake in their roles before God and everyone in the church. In all four, the Reverend's remark broke the tension and produced inward smiles. As to his thoughts about a lasting marriage, Joey's satin dress gave the good Reverend a sign all would be well with the newlywed Borders.

There was a soft carpet covering the kneeling step in front of the communion rail. The step's width was sufficiently narrow, and Joey's satin gown slippery enough to cause her knees to begin slipping off the step if she didn't kneel far enough forward. When she felt herself beginning to slip, rather than rising and attempting to scoot further forward, with her right arm she grasped Bob's left arm a bit more closely and tighter. Bob and Reverend Green both noticed her difficulty, and after a couple of instances, Bob, becoming concerned, reached around her waist and pulled her more tightly against his side when she knelt. The Reverend, pleased by what he observed, leaned over and whispered quietly to both, "This one is going to take . . . " And take it did, for two, long, wonderful lifetimes.[66]

The Navy Wife

Sally Smoot had promised Florence Springer she would write and tell her and George the whole story of their "only's" wedding. The letter, written three days after the happy event, was a masterpiece, the lifetime gift of an experienced, skilled, thoughtful and loving Navy wife, launching the young Navy bride on seas Joey and Bob had never sailed. She described in detail to Florence, all she had observed. The letter told of what was in the immediate future for Sally and her family, Bob and Joey, what she believed about Bob and their success in marriage, and what should be expected of a Navy wife. Laced with light humor, and bearing no resemblance to a lecture, it stated things simply, as they were, and were about to be.

July 18th

Dearest Florence –

Wednesday I took the "best man" to L.A.—and dropped my last house guest with her mother who also lives in L.A.—and returned home. I don't know when I have ever felt so LET DOWN as I did when I walked in the house. The house was ablaze with wedding flowers but I felt more like a FUNERAL personally. When Sally gets married it will be routine stuff and I will know all about what to expect etc.

Any detail that I forget to tell you about honey just sit down and write me a full questionnaire on account of I realize the many details that you are anxious to hear all about and I am liable to leave out something. Just anything you want more complete information on just shoot me the questions and I will answer them.

The paper had a little difficulty in getting the picture of Joey from Buffums—the wedding will be in the paper Sunday. I have ordered 20 papers. The Army-Navy Register is being notified about the wedding so it will come out in that. I will save one account for Joey to go in her scrap book—send one to the Borders—and the rest I will cut out and send you to do as you please with. The only thing I did forget that I regret terribly is that for a small amount I could have had a recording made of the ceremony and I know that you and George would have loved having that. I apologize. I feel very badly about not having thought of it in time.

As you know Bob arrived a week ago last night. The kids went around in a perfect daze of joy till the wedding. Their happiness was truly catching and I got a big kick out of it all too. Tuesday morning Karl arrived and we had our rehearsal. I'm just here to tell you they use too damned many people in a wedding ordinarily. Its very simple to be the father and matron of honor—you just give the bride away and zip over to the maid of honor place—and it's easy two shoes. Please don't think I'm speaking with levity about it because truly Florence the wedding was done perfectly and I will never get over regretting that you and George were not there. However under the circumstances I appreciate the whys and wherefores and only hope that I can make you see it thru my eyes so you feel as if you were actually there . . .

Sally then went into great detail telling of the events leading to the ceremony, the beauty of the wedding, and added,

> [When it was over] the bride and groom marched down the aisle with dignity with Karl and me hot on their trail. After the ceremony there were the usual congratulations and well wishes etc. and a happier couple you never saw in your put together life.—I delivered mother Smoot and the children to their respective homes and then Karl and Bess and Teddy and I went to the Pacific Coast Club. Shortly afterwards we were joined by the bride and groom. Again Joey looked adorable. She wore her new brown suit and accessories. The hat to that outfit is quite the most becoming that I have ever seen Joey wear. Karl broke out champagne and we toasted the newly weds. We hashed things over and talked awhile then at a quite modest interval the bride and groom excused themselves. By this time I was munching heartily on a chicken sandwich on account of I hadn't had time for dinner and if I was going to do any celebrating I felt the urge for a nice BLOTTER. Bess—Teddy—Karl and I "pub hopped" for a little while then I delivered Teddy to the dock and the best man to his hotel.
>
> I didn't get to see Joey and Bob Wednesday but talked to them over the phone. I had my taxi job to L.A. to do and by the time I returned they had left. When I returned is when I really felt let down. However I did laugh my head off. Here sat a note from Joey wherein she said that she was unable to find a pair of hose and her brown and white shoes but she would pick them up when she came back. Had they have been a snake they would have chewed her to bits because the shoes with the stocking stuffed in them sat in the closet just where shoes are kept. So I figured she was in a happy daze and though I hope she doesn't need them in Arrowhead her powers of looking were not clicking at that point . . .

Then Sally turned to her circumstance, the future, and how Navy wives live.

> For the first time in my life time has flown with Roland away. The combination of doing my own work and laundry—having mother and daddy Smoot in Long Beach who take a certain amount of time—plus my brother and sister in law twenty miles away—the time consuming interests of the children etc. I haven't had time to even look up some of the people who have visited and will visit have been people I'm devoted to and want to see as much as possible before I shove for the East because heavens only know how long it will be before I return to this coast.

> Despite the fact I don't feel it necessary to leave here before the 28th of Aug. I won't breathe easy till I get to Annapolis and get settled. Little Ruthie Kemper is driving East with us and is planning on being with me in Annapolis. When we get there and get settled we will both breathe a sigh of relief. Immediately we will pack bags and have them in readiness so SHOULD we receive a telephone call at anytime from Bath Maine to Key West we will be all set to get underway on the double in an endeavor to catch a glimpse of our respective husbands. An occasional glimpse is all we can hope for—but there is one thing sure and certain, we will never get said glimpse as long as we allow 3000 miles to remain between us and the East coast. Every time they hit the mainland after we get there we can make the best of a breakout here the break just fluffs and disintegrates into "what might have been." As for Roland he is well—and busy. The wives whose husbands are with the West Coast fleet lead a cream puff panty waist life in comparison with the East Coast. They see their husbands at least every six months—and they can count on mail. We don't know when or where we will see our husbands—have no idea where they are—go indefinite periods without mail and the set up is different in every way. We all have jobs to do and the jobs are full time affairs. If

we each and every one relieve our particular man
of any feeling of worry or responsibility relative to
the little woman and the kids at home—not leave a
stone unturned to do our share to continually boost
the morale of our particular man—in our humble
little way we contribute our share to a more efficient
officer OR enlisted man and ultimately to a more
efficient fleet. Thems my sentiments on the subject
and perhaps the eighteen years of being a Navy wife
has had something to do with the way my mind
works because I find that some of the younger ones
don't feel that way. Therefore I proceed to endeavor
to sell them that idea and I find after a few mental
pats on the back they catch on fast.

It is now Saturday morning and I have to run to
the market and make a noise like a housewife for
the time being.

I think Bob is a fine boy—both kids are lucky—
and I think that they will each serve as a balance for
the other one and that their marriage will work out
beautifully. I know you must feel rather lost at your
one and only having gone and gotten married—but
just the same girls do do that and when you come
right down to it you would have it that way . . .

We Smoots—tardily but sincerely—thank you
deeply for all you did for us before we left Bremerton.
It's too late for the official bread and butter letter
but the feeling of appreciation is there nevertheless.

Let me hear from you—and despite the fact it
takes me so long a time to get going on a letter I
usually make up for lost time once I get started.

My love to both of you—
Always—
Sally

Joey Border was now a Navy wife. Though she didn't read
Sally Smoot's 18 July letter to her mother until years later, she
immediately began learning the meaning of Navy wife when she
and Bob returned from their honeymoon a week after they left
the Villa Riviera for Lake Arrowhead. She had to find a new Long
Beach apartment to move into after Bob left for the *Tennessee*.

The great Pacific Ocean barrier was yet relatively calm when she delivered him to the Los Angeles train station early the morning of 24 July for his ride north to San Francisco. He arrived weary but happy and boarded the ship at 2215 hours.

Karl greeted him and noted he looked hail and hearty, very much like a married man, while in Long Beach, after Bob left, Joey packed, moved into the new apartment, unpacked, and went to dinner with Sally. After the months of anticipation, the thrills of a near perfect wedding and honeymoon, she couldn't so easily push away the loneliness that closed around her after Bob's departure. She did have something to look forward to, however. Bob, on board *Tennessee,* would be in Long Beach on Sunday, 3 August, for two more weeks. For Karl, the overnight cruise from San Francisco Bay to Long Beach, was his last night at sea aboard the battleship. On 19 July, after returning by train from Los Angeles, he received his orders to report to Pensacola. Bob, Joey and Karl will soon go their separate ways.[67]

Mary Joleen "Joey" Border, Navy wife, 22 July 1941. Borders' Collection

CHAPTER 3

Voyages

The sweetest of all sounds is that of the voice of the woman we love.

Jean de la Bruyere

Except for a period of less than three months in early 1940, Bob and Karl Border had served together on the battleship *Tennessee* for more than two years. The brothers had roomed together for all but five months. They were reluctantly now about to part company after growing up as Navy "juniors," graduating the same year from the Naval Academy, then serving as shipmates and roommates aboard the same great ship of the line. It was Wednesday, 13 August 1941.

That morning Joey left at 6:30 to drive Bob back to the ship. He had duty that day, while Joey attended a tea at Admiral Bagley's quarters and later prepared a spaghetti dinner for Karl and two couples who were mutual friends. Afterward, they all went to see the movie, "Reluctant Dragon."[1]

Joey and Bob knew well Karl's eagerness to enter Naval aviators' training at Pensacola.

His appetite for flying had been growing for some time and was whetted even more when Noel Gayler assigned as an aviator aboard the carrier *Enterprise* took him on the SNJ flight in the spring, circling lazily around Oahu. The flight was exciting, stimulating, further motivating him to fulfill his dream. Then came his OS2U flight while aboard *Tennessee*, with its catapult launch and recovery.

Not only was Karl going to be a Navy aviator, but he would have the good fortune of once again being near family while in training at Pensacola. His dad and Missy lived in Mobile,

Alabama, not far from Pensacola, and near the Pascuagula Naval Station, Mississippi, where his dad was Superintendent of Naval Ship Building.

But Joey also sensed Karl's reluctance to leave his brother and new sister-in-law, and she was pleased to let him stay at their apartment overnight his final two nights he could be with them. She was a Border now, and Bob and his brother were part of the Springer family as well. Family, that's what it was about. Love and family, in spite of the hardship of separations imposed by life in the Navy and Marine Corps.

Earlier that day, Karl, beginning to feel the pangs of saying "so long" to Bob and Joey, the blue water Navy, his friends, shipmates, senior officers he admired, and the *Tennessee*, noted in his diary,

> My last full day of duty, and quite a change from the day 26 months ago when John (Andy), Bob, Sully, Gene, and I reported aboard for duty. Bob and Joey are married and very happy. I've learned a bit about the Navy, and we are sort of at the parting of the ways. Sure is a pain to leave Capt. Reordan [*Tennessee*'s commander], Comdr Campbell [ship's executive officer], Blake, Dwight, Bob Shertz, Jim Conners, Bugs Moran, Jack Earle [classmates], Charlie Morrison and all the rest.[2]

Though Bob didn't keep written recollections of his days, he too was keenly aware of his older brother, "Maximus," departing on a different path, after nearly twenty-three years of growing up together.

On 14 August, Karl quoted excerpts from the orders he received in July.

> Upon receipt of these orders you will consider yourself detached from the USS Tennessee . . . report to US N.A.S. Pensacola, Florida for temporary duty under instruction in heavier-than-air craft as student naval aviator—detailed to duty involving flying . . . Detached this date. CE Reordan.[3]

Though he was remaining in the Navy, he was leaving one kind of life for another. He knew he would be aboard ships again, aircraft carriers primarily, an exciting prospect, but his mission would be quite different.[4]

He added,

> [I was] relieved . . . of the 5th division at 0910 and that was the end of a marvelous two years. Said goodbye to the boys in the division, and to the fellows, and headed for flying.

The same evening Karl stayed the night at Joey's and Bob's apartment, after driving Joey to Los Angeles for dinner and later seeing the Walt Disney movie, "Fantasia."[5]

The next day would be their last together for months. Bob returned to their apartment, Joey and he lent their car to a couple getting married, and Joey ironed clothes for her drive back to Puget Sound Navy Yard, Washington. They had one of Bob's friends over for lunch, then, after Karl made the rounds saying so long to friends, the three drove to Aunt Ramona and Uncle "Dutch" Heim's for dinner. Karl, who grew up knowing them as close, Navy friends of his dad's, found the Heims the same delightful friends of the family they had always been.[6]

When the three returned to the apartment, Joey packed, and all was in readiness for the parting. Joey was up at 6:30 a.m., Saturday the 16th, and packed their car, the first car they owned in their newlywed life. After Bob and Karl said "so long" to one another she drove Bob to Long Beach and they embraced, kissed, and waved goodbye as he left the dock on a motor launch to board *Tennessee*. As she watched Bob leave for the ship, she thought of their just repeated vow to always remain near as possible to one another. She again felt pangs of loneliness tugging at her, but this time quickly pushed the emotions aside.

She went back to the apartment and said goodbye to Karl as he went his separate way and later boarded a train for Mobile and Pensacola. Joey picked up Mrs. Smith and her "brat," as Joey called her—a child she considered not well-behaved, and her mother, whom Joey had agreed could ride with her back to Bremerton.[7]

Tennessee Sails Southwest

As Joey drove north toward Bremerton the first day of her trip home, those members of *Tennessee*'s crew on liberty began returning aboard to again bring her complement near full strength. At 1105, while preparations accelerated toward tomorrow's departure for Pearl Harbor, other crew members, using the stern-mounted crane and wench system hoisted the three OS2U aircraft aboard, plane numbers 201, 202, and 203, to be the ship's over-the-horizon scouts.

Three members of her crew left the ship, reassigned to duty aboard the battleship *Colorado*, and eighteen reported aboard *Tennessee* to replace men reassigned or had ended their enlistments in the Navy. And as always in Navy life, men bound for duties in Hawaii or on other ships in the Pacific Fleet came aboard to sail with her as passengers—working passengers—this day a total of 58. Forty-seven were destined for the submarine base at Pearl, ten for the destroyer auxiliary, *Dixie*, when next she arrived in Pearl Harbor, and one ensign with transportation orders to Pearl, where he would be further assigned to new duties.[8]

While Joey and Karl were en route on diverging paths away from Bob that day, and *Tennessee* prepared to get under way the next morning, President Roosevelt and Secretary of State Cordell Hull conferred with the Japanese Ambassador in Washington, DC, stating their prerequisites for resuming conversations with the Prime Minister, or arranging a Pacific conference. Less than three weeks earlier, the American government had frozen Japanese and Chinese assets in the United States, and one day later the Japanese government retaliated by freezing American assets in Japan.

Life and duty aboard ship, on an Army post, an Army Air Force operating base or Coast Guard station is far different than life in rural areas, small towns and cities across the United States. Sailors, soldiers, Marines, airmen, and Coast Guardsmen are more attuned to trouble spots in the world, which they know and understand may one day have a direct, personal impact on their lives as well as the lives of their families.

While Bob and Karl were on *Tennessee* together, news and

current events flowed to the ship's officers through classified, coded intelligence and command message traffic, as well as short wave and amplitude modulated (am) radio broadcasts which could be picked up when the ship was in line of sight range of an am broadcast station, or occasionally, when out of range, through "ionospheric bounce." (Under certain atmospheric conditions am radio broadcasts can be heard in faraway countries or continents, because the radio waves bounce or alternately ricochet off cloud layers and the ground or water.)

The importance of current events and international incidents was unmistakable to Navy "juniors" like Bob and Karl Border, Marine "brats" like Joey and the parents of both, especially when they were on duty. For young officers, sailors, and Marines off duty, and their wives, though ears were generally attuned to warning signs of danger, life was almost carefree, gay, filled with optimism, and talk of the future. They were still young, their worlds were what they could see, hear, touch, taste, and smell. The future often was now, little else, and life was geared to shutting out the bad news in the rest of the world. That was the world new bride Mary Joleen Border was in as she drove toward Bremerton, Washington, her father and mother, and her home in the Yard. As for Bob, he too missed his new bride, as *Tennessee* prepared to stand out of Los Angeles Harbor.

Joey made her way to Vallejo, California, approximately 30 miles northeast of San Francisco, dropped off Mrs. Smith and her daughter at a relative's home, and stayed the night with Grandma Nesbitt, Missy Border's mother, a physician who had been a general practitioner in Vallejo for years. The next morning, she picked up the Smiths and resumed the drive northward into Oregon. Joey's second day on the trip home, putting more and more distance between Bob and her, had already heightened her loneliness. Before the day ended matters would get much worse.[9]

In Long Beach, Captain Reordan prepared to muster *Tennessee*'s crew, while several more men, responding to orders, left the ship for new assignments, three to the battleship *Oklahoma*, one each to the carrier *Lexington* and the battleship *Nevada*. With *Tennessee*'s crew mustered at 0915, Captain Reordan ordered all hands assembled aft at 0940, preparatory for a burial at sea. She took departure from Los Angeles Harbor at 1014 hours, leaving nine men behind who failed to return and were reported absent without leave.

With colors lowered to half staff from 1014-1025, the ship's company committed to the deep the ashes of Mrs. Mary E. Farmer, cremated 14 May 1935, and the ashes of her late husband and former crew member, Chief Boatswain's [pronounced Bosun's] Mate Henry A. Farmer, cremated 23 June 1941. *Tennessee* had probably been Chief Farmer's home away from home for years, in Navy terms, a "plank owner," a sailor assigned to the ship as a member of her first crew when she was commissioned, and rose through enlisted ranks to become a Chief Bosun's Mate on *Tennessee* before he died. He loved the sea, and when his wife died six years earlier, he had decided they would be committed to the deep together, from his home at sea.

At 1025 *Tennessee* set course 248 degrees true, and at 1106 set standard speed at 15 knots, followed at 1145 with a change of course to 235 degrees. At 1200 hours Bob Border assumed the duties of Officer of the Deck for the succeeding four hours. Three minutes later, the great ship passed the West End of Catalina Island, abeam to port, and at 1317 passed Santa Barbara Island, abeam to starboard 7 miles. Bob's log entry reported sighting San Nicolas Island at 1445. Ten minutes after Bob's tour of duty ended at 1600, lookouts sighted the fleet auxiliary service ship *Medusa* (AR-1). *Tennessee* maneuvered to join Task Force 15, bound for Pearl Harbor. When the ships in the task force took stations in the formation, the fleet guide turned further to starboard, southwest toward Hawaii, course 250 degrees, speed 13 knots. The fleet guide was *Medusa*, leading the battleships *Tennessee* and *Maryland*, heavy cruisers *San Francisco* (CA-38) and *Portland* (CA-33), and the high speed minesweepers *Elliot* (DMS-4) and *Dorsey* (DMS-1).[10]

At 7:30 that evening, while Joey was driving in rain heading north from the small town of Chemsfelt, Oregon, her car was hit by another automobile, and rolled over twice before coming to rest upside down in a ditch beside the road. Though momentarily terrorized by the complete, shattering loss of control and the wild, tumbling scene viewed from inside the car, miraculously, the three occupants weren't injured.

Badly shaken, they hurriedly extricated themselves from the battered car. Joey and the passengers crawled through windows to escape. They were happy to be alive and unscathed, but it appeared the Ford might never be alive again. The car was badly damaged. After assuring themselves everyone was unhurt, Joey realized Chemsfelt was the nearest town, and she would have to hitch a ride back to find a place to stay. Dark was closing round them when they retrieved their suitcases and belongings from the car, and went their separate ways.

Mrs. Smith decided to hitch a ride in the opposite direction for her and her daughter, toward Eugene. Joey caught a ride the short distance back to Chemsfelt and after calling her father, telling him of the accident, that she and her passengers were unhurt, her predicament, and obtaining his advice, spent the night in a small motel's log cabin, a cottage-like arrangement Joey found suitable for this one night.[11]

On Monday, 18 August, she immediately contacted an insurance adjuster in Eugene, Oregon, to submit a claim. A kind truck driver, Mr. Burke, offered her a ride further north to Eugene, where, on the telephoned advice of her dad, she contacted a lawyer, Mr. Evans. Her goal was to wind up the necessary business in Eugene and make her way home to the Yard as soon as possible.

She had insufficient funds to pay the cost of a prolonged stay in Eugene. A rapid response by the automobile insurance company was essential, and an attorney could help her with the insurance company. He and the insurance adjustor also could make telephone arrangements to have the car towed to a nearby Ford garage, where the adjuster could, with the mechanics' assistance, evaluate the damage and obtain a cost estimate for possible repair. The idea of waiting for repair of the badly damaged car was out of the question. But it might be economically repaired and picked up later, if she found a way home.

After providing the attorney necessary information regarding the accident, Joey checked into a hotel and telegraphed Bob, aboard *Tennessee*, telling him of the accident, and she was uninjured. Still fretting about how to get home quickly, she reasoned the purchase of a used car from the insurance proceeds for their badly damaged car offered the necessarily rapid solution. She began a search for used cars, from which she planned to select one for purchase.

The day was exhausting, and Sunday had been frightening. When she returned to the hotel, Joey called her dad and broached the subject of a used car purchase. Visualizing his twenty year-old daughter dealing with a used car salesman, he promptly discouraged the idea. "Not only no, but hell no," he responded.

She ended her daily diary entry that night with the words, ". . . so lonesome and blue."[12]

On Tuesday she worked all morning with the attorney as he urged their insurance company toward a rapid settlement and payment of the claim. Still tired and emotionally drained, she napped all afternoon before again meeting with him briefly late in the day. She returned to her hotel room and wrote letters. Knowing Bob was on *Tennessee* and couldn't wire money through Western Union Telegraph, she wrote Karl, who arrived that same day at his parents' home in Mobile, near where his dad was beginning his duties in a new assignment.[13]

Later in the evening, Karl enthusiastically wrote in his diary, "Got home today, for the first time in two years! Mother and Dad are fine, and it's really swell to be with them." Accustomed to the neat, orderly, and polished four-year life of a Midshipman at the Naval Academy and more of the same in his two plus years aboard *Tennessee*, he couldn't help observing, "The house is fine but still a trifle disorganized." But another welcome home treat caught his interest and gratitude that first night with Missy and his dad. "Missy cooked tonight! What a dinner."[14]

It was Wednesday, 20 August, and *Tennessee*, with Task Force 15, churned steadily to the southwest toward Hawaii. Joey, now intent on assuring a rapid damage assessment and repair estimate, and having worked her reporter's beat in the Bremerton courthouse, wanted to ensure all was done quickly and "on the level" in both. She spent most of the day at the Ford garage, observing progress. Plainly, this entire knot of trouble was going to take longer to untie than hoped, and she was going to run short of cash.

She phoned Karl, and explained the circumstance. Karl was happy to hear Joey's voice, but stunned to learn of the accident. He hadn't yet received the letters she wrote, but would wire her some money as soon as possible tomorrow.

Before Joey's phone call came, he had driven to Pensacola and back with his dad, mother and their family Airedale dog, Bunky. They went to the launching of a new ship, the USS *Conqueror*. A family friend, Mrs. Ross, christened the ship, and in Karl's opinion she did an excellent job. Afterward, according to Karl, they ate a delightful lunch in Pensacola, and drove home.

After the call to Karl, Joey decided to relax with a drink and some socializing—in the company of a young gentleman named

Hal. An empty stomach, a too small frame, emotion-packed days and nights, and the drink hit her hard. When the socializing with another young man got too social, she ended it abruptly, walked to the hotel, got sick, threw up, and went to bed.[15]

The next morning the wire from Karl arrived transferring $15 to Joey, a blessing that would help tide her over until the insurance claim came through. She ate breakfast and Hal took her for a drive and a walking tour of his family's fish hatchery. He then drove her back to the hotel, and dropped her off. She ate lunch, napped, ate dinner, went to a movie, back to the hotel for bed, all the while wishing she were home. Time was dragging and she again was becoming impatient with progress toward home. The next day, Friday, would be different, she would see to that.[16]

Joey wasn't yet awake at 0400 hours, Hawaiian time Friday morning, as Combat Division Two neared the Islands on a course of 253 degrees true. Bob Border came on duty as Officer of the Deck for another four-hour stint, during which *Tennessee*, *Medusa*, *Maryland*, *Elliot* and *Dorsey* continued their fleet exercises and on board drills. A day earlier the two cruisers, *San Francisco* and *Portland*, left the formation on a southwesterly course. At 0600 Bob noted in the log that *Tennessee* came ninety degrees to port to a new heading of 163 degrees true, preparing for short range practice runs.

At 0815, shortly after Ensign Robert H. Wooding relieved Bob as Officer of the Deck, *Tennessee* began varying her courses and speeds, as Combat Division Two continued their short range practice runs. At 1030 she changed speed to 16 knots and at 1040 began a series of drills, the first, fire drill exercises for a simulated fire in the ward room. At 1042 the fire drills ended, and at 1051 a collision drill began, with a simulated collision on the port side, at frame number 57. At 1057 the collision exercise ended and three minutes later all emergency exercises ceased.

Undoubtedly, Joey tugged at Bob's thoughts throughout the day. He received her telegram telling him of the accident. Did she have their car repaired and was she on the way home? Though he couldn't know the answers to such questions, he knew she was a determined, strong-willed, young, Navy wife, one of the many reasons he loved her. She would find a way—and she did.

Joey haunted the insurance office all day, pushing for reimbursement sufficient to guarantee a train ride home. Ever outgoing, curious, and interested in others, during the day she met a sailor's wife and struck up a conversation. She phoned her dad to give a progress report, wrote some letters, sewed, and received the good news that tomorrow matters would be resolved—she would finally go home.[17]

After a difficult week, on Saturday morning her frustrating Eugene, Oregon transportation impasse came to an end. She received a check for $59, the sale price of Bob's and Joey's first automobile, wrecked, not repairable, and now headed for the junkyard. Two days earlier she wrote Karl in a letter, $575 would eventually be forthcoming from the insurance company to buy another car, but for now, she could buy a train ticket home.

"Am Going to Hawaii!!"

While on the train, thinking of home, the future, and Bob's increasing distance from her, her thoughts turned to a question which had begun nagging her before she, Bob and Karl parted company. "How can I get to Hawaii and join Bob?" With an ensign's monthly pay of $62 plus allowances, adding a few more dollars isn't a ticket to wealth and world travel. In her busy, optimistic mind and warm heart an idea and a plan began percolating. She had discovered another way. All things happen for the best, even life-threatening accidents.

During the hours of darkness early that Saturday morning, the Task Force guide, *Medusa*, and the destroyer *Dorsey* left Combat Division Two. Meanwhile *Tennessee*, leading the two-ship column, with *Maryland* 1,000 yards astern and the destroyer *Elliot* thirty degrees on the starboard bow at a distance of 1,000 yards, held course 253, periodically checking [turning to] 244 degrees. At 0310 hours she turned on her running lights for five minutes while passing through a rain squall.

At 0900 the crew mustered at quarters for role call and calisthenics—physical conditioning. There were no new absentees, but nine were still absent who had failed to report aboard when *Tennessee* left Long Beach on 17 August. There followed at 0930 a Summary Court Martial which lasted until 1055. A fireman first class had been absent without leave for eight hours and twenty-five minutes.

As was the daily routine, an inspection of magazines and

smokeless powder samples began at 1130. Conditions were normal. A weekly test of flooding and sprinkling systems came next, with satisfactory results. At 1300 condition Yoke was called for Group IV compartments, a material condition for damage-control during exercises and battle in which valves and doors pre-identified for condition Yoke are closed and "dogged down." At 1355, the ship was secured from condition Yoke.

At 1607 lookouts in the foretop sighted Destroyer Division Five, bearing 271 degrees, eight miles distant, steaming to join the formation as an inner submarine patrol, while the *Elliot* took station 8,000 yards ahead as a sound patrol. She was listening for submarines with her hydrophones. That night at 2307 hours, the glow of Molokai Light came into view, bearing 232 degrees, and a minute later Pauwela Light at 186.2 degrees true. The Task Force was nearing Oahu and Pearl Harbor.

To Joey's delight she finally reached Seattle by train late that Saturday afternoon. Her mother and dad met her at the station. As soon as they arrived at the family's quarters in the Yard, she began opening wedding gifts and letters. She took time out for dinner with her parents, talking with them and answering questions about her harrowing accident and related experiences on the trip home from Long Beach. Still excited and anxious to catch up on the news at home, in the Yard, and in the letters waiting for her, she stayed up until 2:00 in the morning. She punctuated her long day with the final words in her diary entry, "What a week!"[18]

Within two hours after Joey got out of bed Sunday morning, 24 August, *Tennessee*, with her husband aboard, arrived in Pearl Harbor and moored to quay F-7, on the ship's starboard side, with nine lines, two wire and seven manila ropes. For Combat Division Two, the week at sea en route from Long Beach to Pearl Harbor was a routine training exercise; nevertheless, as Karl Border's diary stated in the spring, Admiral Kimmel was keeping the fleet hard at work while war raged to the east and west across the oceans from the North American continent.

Monday began like old times in the Yard for Joey, running errands, a trip down town with a stop at the Bremerton newspaper where she had worked until she went to Long Beach to marry Bob. She called her friend, Peg, one of the "Yard engines" as the young ships' officers called them, wrote letters, asked another friend, Louise, to stay over for the night, then visited with her until late.

The next day it was up and into town, an all morning visit with Norma, after which she stayed for lunch. Joey next had her hair set, prepared dinner for her dad while her mother was away, wrote some letters, and visited with another of her friends, Dede Dunbar.[19]

Busy days and nights with friends in the Yard, trips to the PX—the Navy Exchange—and into Seattle for shopping. Lunches, five movies by 9 September—including "Shepherd of the Hills" and "Kiss the Boys Goodbye"—dinners at the Yard Club, family friends in for dinner with her parents, a party for 23 people she and her mother planned and prepared, games of Tripoli with friends and acey ducey with her dad, tea at Marine Colonel Carey's quarters. In spite of Joey's best efforts and all the energetically reengaged social life, loneliness was beginning to creep into her life.

Thursday, 11 September was an unusual day. Joey, responding to an invitation to tea, came aboard the battleship HMS *Warspite*, a famous British ship that brought the Puget Sound Navy Yard a visible reminder of the fury unleashed in Europe, Scandanavia, the Balkans, and on the surrounding seas.

Commissioned 8 March 1915, she was a *Queen Elizabeth*-class battleship that took part in the renowned World War I battle of Jutland on 31 May 1916, where she suffered 15 hits, heavy damage, 14 killed and many wounded, and survived three submarine attacks before she reached the port of Rosyth. The damage included a near disastrous temporary loss of steering which sent her steaming in two circles in the midst of the battle, and despite later repairs, left lingering effects on her steering mechanism all the ship's remaining service life.

Assigned in the Mediterranean theatre when Germany attacked Poland in 1939, she later returned to Britain's Home Fleet, where she participated in a variety of hunts for German capital ships that were acting as commerce raiders in the North Sea and Atlantic Ocean. In April 1940, *Warspite* served in the Norwegian Campaign, providing essential battleship support during the Second Battle of Narvik, when *Warspite* and numerous British destroyers attacked eight German destroyers trapped in Ofotfjord, near the port of Narvik.

Vice-Admiral William "Jock" Whitworth, leader of the

operation, transferred his flag to *Warspite* on the day the battle commenced. *Warspite*'s Fairey Swordfish, a bi-plane fragile in appearance, attacked and sunk the German U-boat *U-64*, to become the first aircraft to sink a U-boat in World War II. The objective of eliminating all eight German destroyers, who were running out of both fuel and ammunition, was achieved with minimum loss.

During the summer of 1940, *Warspite* transferred back to the Mediterranean theatre and fought in several engagements. The most important of these were the strategic victory at the Battle of Cape Matapan in March 1941, in which three Italian cruisers and two destroyers were sunk in a night action, and the Battle of Calabria in July 1940, in which she stayed afloat but was damaged several times. During the Battle of Calabria she was credited with achieving the longest range gunnery hit from a moving ship to a moving target in history. The hit was on the Italian battleship *Giulio Cesare* at a range of approximately 26,000 yards, nearly 14.8 miles.

Warspite also took part in the Battle of Crete, where she was badly damaged in the Kithera Channel by German bombers on 22 May. From there, the crippled ship sailed southeast to put into port in Alexandria, Egypt, along with the remainder of the British ground and naval forces, which were evacuated or withdrew following the successful but bloody German airborne invasion of Crete.

After undergoing temporary repairs, *Warspite* left Alexandria for the long journey to Puget Sound Navy Yard, where in August 1941, she began undergoing major repair and overhaul, including replacement of her main batteries of worn out 15 inch guns. Her crew was ready for rest, recuperation and liberty when they arrived in the United States, and their time at the Yard would prove enjoyable. Like the rest of the Americans at the Yard, in the small town of Bremerton, the city of Seattle and other nearby towns, the Springers were delighted to meet and welcome the British crewmen who were far from home, were already allies in spirit and action, and had seen firsthand the brutality of war at sea.

After Joey attended tea on the *Warspite* that Thursday, the same afternoon a few of the British officers enjoyed a fun-filled return visit to the Springer's quarters for the uniquely American treat of hamburgers, followed by a round of golf with the ship's Commander Aitkin.

All the renewed socializing with her Yard engine friends, and the young American and British officers in port with their ships, no longer seemed important, and felt repetitious. The British were too formal and stuffy, even snobbish, she concluded. She was restless, lonely, missed Bob terribly, and his feelings were equally strong.

In the middle of her growing restlessness came clouds and rain for three days beginning 31 August. The second day of rain brought her a miserable earache. To Joey, the entire Yard seemed dull by the end of the first week in September, except for Bob's letters. His letters filled her with longing to be near him. The first two arrived on 27 August, four days after she returned home. Since then she had written him several letters sprinkled with ideas of her using the $575 insurance reimbursement from their wrecked car for passage to Hawaii. He enthusiastically responded to her in a letter she received on 10 September. It seemed a grand, practical inspiration, and Bob could do his part at the other end. She took a day to broach the plan with her parents. Though reluctant to see her leave again, her dad and mother well understood and agreed.

She would book passage on an ocean liner out of a west coast port, probably San Francisco, travel by train to meet the scheduled sailing, and perhaps stop by to see Grandma Nesbitt in Vallejo, near San Francisco.

While she booked her departure and was en route, Bob could locate a furnished apartment to rent. He would have a place and his lovely new wife to come home to when *Tennessee* wasn't at sea, or he wasn't on duty when the ship was moored in Pearl Harbor. As for transportation, Honolulu had an excellent city bus system that could take them back and forth to Pearl Harbor and Joey anywhere she needed to go while Bob was at sea. If necessary Bob could borrow transportation from his Navy aviator classmates and friends while they were at sea with the carrier *Enterprise*. Bob and Joey didn't need a car to live on Oahu. The whole idea was warm, exciting, an invitation to be together again—as they had promised one another. Then came 12 September

A flurry of phone calls and telegrams: to book passage out of San Francisco on 18 September, on the Matson Line's SS *Lurline*, which twice monthly sailed the route San Francisco, Long Beach and Honolulu; to Bob, confirming the booking, departure and arrival dates; to the Borders in Mobile, telling them of their plans; to the Seattle railroad station for schedules, ticket cost and availability to Oakland, where she would go by ferry to San Francisco; to the local bus station for schedules and a ticket from San Francisco to Vallejo; and to Grandma Nesbitt in Vallejo to tell her of the voyage and Joey would like to spend the night of the 17th with her before she boarded *Lurline*.

Everything fell into place so quickly, she even had time to go into Seattle for a permanent. Full of love, pride and excitement, she wanted to look her best for Bob and the first ocean voyage in her life. To cap off a near-perfect day, Joey went with her parents to the quarters of family friends, the Shippey's, for dinner, and spent the evening in conversation, much of it about the days ahead and what the future held for Bob and her. Because of the war in Europe, the past two years had not been comforting, but today was special. She excitedly wrote in her diary, "Am going to Hawaii!!"[20]

On the day before Joey began preparing in earnest for the voyage to Hawaii, President Roosevelt announced an order to the Navy to attack any vessel threatening United States shipping or ships under United States escort. On 4 September the destroyer *Greer* (DD-145) had been attacked but not damaged while tracking a German submarine 175 miles southwest of Iceland, and on 7 September a German air attack sank the United States merchant ship *Steel Seafarer* in the Gulf of Suez.[21]

Despite increasing clashes with the German Navy and the Luftwaffe, to the American public, the wide Pacific seemed a formidable if not an impassable barrier against the expanding Japanese Empire pushing into Southeast Asia.

After completing trip preparations on 12 September, Joey was up early the next morning, went down town for more shopping, and then went out to dinner and dancing at the Yard Club with her family, until 2:00 a.m. On the 14th she packed most of the day, but found time to visit with one of Bob's classmates, Art Metcalf, before having tea at the Cohen's quarters, and to bed early.

The day of her departure she went down town with her mother to buy her train ticket, into Seattle for some last minute shopping, and then her mother saw her off on the train to Oakland. Joey noted in her diary that night, "hate to leave," but excitement and her effervescent personality took over. She met a baseball team and played bridge before retiring to the Pullman car for bed. The next morning it was up at 9:30 and breakfast in California before the train arrived in Oakland at 1:15 p.m.

From there she caught the ferry to San Francisco and the Matson Line passenger terminal, picked up her ticket for the *Lurline* and checked her baggage. Then she caught a taxi to Norma Warmie's where she had been invited to stay the night. She and Norma walked down town for dinner and shopping.[22]

Early Wednesday morning, a British trans-Atlantic convoy left America's east coast, bound for England, escorted for the first time by United States Navy combatants. Like all convoys plying the Atlantic to assist the desperately fighting English, this one's movement was cloaked in secrecy—although the convoy's sheer size and numbers made it easily observable by enemy spies and sympathizers living along the coast.[23]

A Cruise on the *Lurline*

On that same morning, Joey and Norma went back to San Francisco for more shopping. Joey bought some shoes, she and Norma looked at pictures, and met Bettie and Bill for lunch. Then tired and worn down by a cold, she went to bed for awhile. In the late afternoon Norma accompanied her to the bus station for the overnight trip to Vallejo to say goodbye to Grandma Nesbitt. The visit was short. After breakfast the next morning, she left for the return bus trip to San Francisco, to meet Norma again who saw her off at noon on the *Lurline*.

Joey had seen photographs of the *Lurline*, but the ship was even lovelier than expected. She was elated to learn she was boarding a beautifully appointed liner, a welcome, eye-pleasing respite in the hectic pace of travel. The 18,163-ton, 631-foot ship's elegant furnishings, mother-of-pearl inlays and beautiful wood-paneling lifted Joey's spirits and fanned her excitement. What a wonderful way to begin a voyage to happiness. Better yet, stateroom 333D was an inside room below the promenade deck, on a passageway, no portholes, approximately mid-ship, and therefore not as affected by the ship's pitch and roll in heavy seas.

After passing beneath the Golden Gate Bridge, and before *Lurline* set course for Hawaii, there was one more stateside stop in the ship's triangular route between Honolulu, San Francisco, and

Lurline's Grand Ball Room, with mother-of-pearl
inlays and beautiful wood-paneling. MNC

Los Angeles. Los Angeles Harbor, in Long Beach, was one of four west coast ports frequented by the Pacific Fleet, and Long Beach was the town where Joey and Bob married barely two months earlier—another pleasing reminder before sailing southwest to Honolulu.[24]

As Joey prepared to leave *Lurline* for the day, more than 2,228 miles to the southwest, in Pearl Harbor, *Tennessee*'s crew was preparing to get underway. Bob was now leading the 5th Division, the 5-inch broadside gun division Karl was commanding when he left for Pensacola on 17 August. As a Midshipman at the Naval Academy, Bob had had an unforgettable experience while on a summer training cruise, by obtaining an E—for Excellence— while acting as a gun division officer aboard a battleship during a firing exercise. The Academy superintendent publicized his achievement to the Brigade of Midshipmen, and his company's pennant carried the first E in living memory at Annapolis.

As part of the routine preparation for the ship's departure from Pearl Harbor, a day earlier a massive load of fresh vegetables and fruit was brought aboard, inspected and verified for quantity and quality, and placed in refrigeration along with 1,000 pounds of ice: the Wing Coffee Company, 1153 Smith Street, in Honolulu, delivered 4,000 pounds of oranges, 1,500 pounds of pears, and 10,000 pounds of potatoes; from Chun Hoon Ltd., Nuuana and School Streets in Honolulu came 750 pounds of tomatoes and 850 pounds of squash; the Tai Hing Co., 937-939 Kekoulike Street, Honolulu, brought aboard 1,500 pounds of apples, 800 pounds of carrots, 1,800 pounds of celery, 550 pounds of egg plant, and 1,000 pounds of sweet potatoes; and the Chung Chong Co., Ltd., 1276 College Walk, Honolulu, loaded 1,500 pounds of grapefruit, 425 pounds of lemons, 300 pounds of cucumbers, 1,700 pounds of lettuce, and 700 pounds of peppers.

On 19 September *Tennessee* was to proceed to its assigned operating area, to the southwest and south of Oahu, third in an open order column with three other battleships: *West Virginia* (BB-48), *Maryland* (BB-46) and *California* (BB-44). At 0732 hours she was underway, following *West Virginia* and *Maryland* out of Pearl, and at 0800 her crew mustered on station.

Five minutes later *Tennessee*'s "electrical gang," acting on orders from the bridge, energized the ship's degaussing coils, an essential defensive procedure normally taken before entering waters where electromagnetic mines are a threat. As soon as any metal-hulled ship begins moving through water it will begin building a mine-attracting electrostatic charge surrounding its hull. If ships are built with or without degaussing coils installed—which Naval vessels normally are—the longer such vessels proceed without energizing their degaussing coils, the greater strength the ship's magnetic field builds, increasing its vulnerability to an enemy's—or friendlies'—magnetic mines. Energized degaussing coils neutralize the electrostatic charge. Magnetic mines are designed with opposite polarity to their intended victims, and if a ship without operational degaussing coils passes too close, the mine can deliver a devastating and usually fatal explosive force below the water line, tearing a gaping hole in the hull of its victim.

After *Tennessee* cleared the entrance to Pearl Harbor, at 0835 she and the other ships in the column began zigzagging, a frequently-exercised defensive maneuver against possible enemy submarines lying in wait outside harbor entrances, along sea lanes, or in known fleet operating areas. Zigzags are preplanned. When the force commander signals their use, he designates which numbered plan will be followed. Each numbered plan, for example Plan #6, specifies different degrees of turn to be followed when the order to begin zigzagging is signaled to ships in the Battle Force.[25]

* * *

Joey took advantage of the *Lurline*'s day long stopover in Los Angeles Harbor to get her hair done, do some more shopping, and pick up the check from the insurance company, from which she could reimburse her dad for the loan to buy her ticket. Then it was back to the ship, drinks with Doc and Dot Ward, and dinner. At 10:30 p.m. the evening of 19 September, the Great White Ship, the pride of Matson's passenger liners, stood out from Long Beach, bound for Honolulu. Joey's and Bob's plan to be reunited was coming together. The world would soon be right again.

Saturday, 20 September proved a less enjoyable day, however. The sea was stormy and rough, and the obligatory lifeboat drill went as scheduled at 2:30 p.m. Joey, slightly seasick and still a bit tired from her excitement-filled journey, slept the rest of the day and recuperated sufficiently to keep company with Nat and Gina Bishop awhile before retiring for the night, and much needed sleep. The next day brought a fresh start. She felt rejuvenated.

Out of bed at 6:00 a.m. and a walk around the deck, drinking in the fresh Pacific air before breakfast, stimulated Joey and brightened her day. After breakfast she went to church, and following lunch played the traditional shipboard, deck game of Shuffleboard, other games, went to a concert, dinner, a movie, drank champagne, and danced—before retiring for the night. The day was grand.

After Sunday's busy social activities, Joey slept until 8:30 Monday morning, again walked the deck, took a light breakfast, then wrote letters. *Lurline* was now in a warmer climate, thus Joey decided to try out the ship's swimming pool. She sewed for awhile, took a bath, and joined Gina Bishop in a dinner for Gina's husband, Nat. Next came another concert. After dinner, she watched a movie, then went dancing again. This time she met and danced with a ship's crew member who, unknown to her, she would meet again three months in the future. His name was Mr. J.C. "Jack" Fischbeck, *Lurline*'s purser. After one more fine vacation day on the high seas, she was ready for another good night's sleep.

On Tuesday, she rose at 8:00. After playing shuffleboard in the afternoon with Brad again, she packed. This would be Joey's last

HAWAII

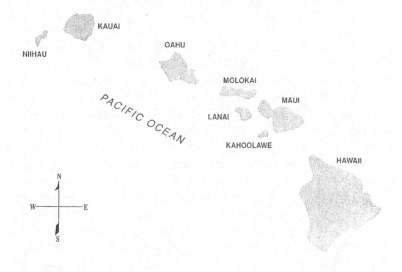

Hawaii

night at sea, since *Lurline* would arrive in Honolulu tomorrow. She was fortunate to be seated at the captain's table for dinner, a particularly gay evening in which she played Keeno, danced with Mr. Fischbeck again, and ended a long, happy day with bed at 1:00 a.m.

Wednesday, 24 September 1941, was the day she had eagerly awaited. Joey got out of bed early, at 5:30. She was excited. The islands were soon in view, first, the island of Molokai off the port beam, then as *Lurline* sailed past the island the call came over the ship's speaker system—Oahu's windward side (east coast) can be seen off the starboard bow. Passengers gathered at the ship's rails to gaze at Oahu's beauty, and enjoy the sights and sounds of the traditional Hawaiian welcome. By 8:15 *Lurline* had turned almost due west. First Koko Head then Diamond Head loomed clearly in the morning light, slowly moving past the starboard beam—not long before a tug pulled alongside and the harbor pilot came aboard to steer *Lurline* to her Honolulu berth.

Though Joey had never set foot in Hawaii, Bob had said beforehand he might be unable to meet her. The pace of fleet exercises had continued unabated throughout 1941 and didn't let up when the battle force returned to Pearl Harbor. Although for reasons of security the ship's crew wasn't routinely made aware of projected departures for exercises, the events of recent months told him he might be at sea when Joey's ship arrived in Honolulu. He was still aboard *Tennessee* on a training exercise, and Lieutenant (jg—junior grade) Walter J. Stencil, to whom Bob reported on the ship, had made arrangements for his wife, Anne, to meet Joey when the liner docked.

Joey walked down the gangway shortly after the *Lurline*'s 9:00 a.m. arrival. The traditional greeting of fragrant leis lowered gently over her head as soft music played by a Hawaiian band pulled her into the island's air of serenity. Anne went with her to pick up her baggage, then drove her to the apartment Bob rented for them at 250 Kaiulani, in southeast Honolulu—not far from Waikiki Beach, the Punch Bowl and Diamond Head. Joey's ride from the ship into their cozy furnished apartment was a marvelous beginning in a wonderful setting. She immediately found her surroundings much to her liking.

Bob and Joey had lived in Long Beach in their first rental for barely three weeks after they were married, before they and Karl went their separate ways. Having grown up the only sibling and a daughter, and now in a Marine officer's family, she was independent, self-sufficient, and easily adapted to the nomadic life of the military. She wasted no time in establishing their Honolulu apartment as their new home. She checked for items she needed to purchase to bring the warm feeling of home to the apartment.

Then Anne took her to shop for the items she listed, and from there to the grocery market to buy food—which also introduced Joey to the local stores and markets of interest. After unloading the car at Joey's, Anne drove her to her place for lunch, then returned her to unpack and straighten the apartment. From there she dropped Joey off at Mary Staley's for dinner. Lieutenant Poyntell C. Staley, Jr. a senior aviator who had come aboard *Tennessee* 16 November 1940, to fly one of the ship's scout planes, was Mary's husband. Joey, as a new Navy wife, was, for the first time being welcomed into the *Tennessee* family at the ship's home port, a welcome their brief stay in Long Beach hadn't permitted.

This transition was easy. This was the caring, military family life Joey had come to know and love. Adding to the warm glow already experienced on her arrival, she was now closer to heaven, on a near-mythical, romantic island with an unmatched, worldwide reputation for wonderful, year-around weather, gently swaying palms, beautiful evenings, dreamy sensual music, and tropical moonlight, all of which cast a spell on its thousands of annual visitors.[26]

While Joey was en route to Honolulu on *Lurline* from 19-24 September, the Battle Force composed of *Tennessee*, *California*, *West Virginia*, and *Maryland* worked tirelessly on various fleet training exercises and on-board emergency drills. The first night out, after using *Maryland* as a simulated target for Short Range Practice (SRP), *Tennessee* manned all fire control stations and searchlights for night battle practice. The next day she became the target for SRP, launched and recovered two of her planes, while continuing emergency drills.

On 21 September she took the lead in the column, with *California*, *West Virginia* and *Maryland* in that order, and at 0645 began the launch of all three planes for mail delivery and pick-up missions to Oahu and back. At 1655 *Tennessee* began maneuvering to recover the three planes and their crews, and at 1737 completed their recovery. Mail call soon followed, always an event of great interest and importance to men at sea.

During the day, *California* and *West Virginia* left the column for several hours, then rejoined, with *Tennessee* astern of *West Virginia*, and third in the column. The ship named for the Volunteer State ended her long 21 September training day by turning out of the column to become the target vessel for night battle practice.

The next day *Tennessee* catapulted her three planes again, the last, plane 202, launched to starboard at 0635, for anti-aircraft gunnery practice. At 0715, the ship's control (steering) was shifted from the bridge to the conning tower, where it would normally be shifted as soon as the ship's crew was called to "battle stations." Firing began with the starboard 3-inch batteries firing in string (one after the other), with gun #9 the first to fire, at 0739. At 0801 gun #3 from the starboard 5-inch broadside battery fired. Next, at 0828, *Tennessee* began another run, positioning to bring her 3-inch starboard guns to bear on the target, and at 0838 the battery fired. At 0846 another run with the 5-inch starboard battery firing at 0852.

At 0925 lookouts in the foretop informed the bridge they sighted a merchant vessel bearing two points on the starboard bow. *Tennessee* ceased firing to starboard, and shortly thereafter, at 0947, began another run to fire with her port batteries. After firing her 3-inch port battery at 0952, she ended her gunnery exercise with the 5-inch port battery firing at 1012 hours. At 1018 the conning tower returned steering to the bridge, and at 1100 the daily inspection of magazines and smokeless powder tests began, followed by the weekly tests of magazines, flooding and sprinkler systems.

Tennessee's commander, Captain Charles E. Reordan, held mast (disciplinary and court martial hearings) at 1100 while inspections and tests were in progress. At 1530 hours the ship maneuvered to begin recovering her three planes, and completed recovery of the last, 203, at 1557. Again, the long training day ended with the ship serving as target for night battle practice.

The next day, 23 September, Bob Border and *Tennessee*'s crew exercised their big guns firing at a surface target. Life is hard work and never dull aboard a Navy combatant. Repeated drills and exercises, nearly always timed, measured, and graded, keep crews battle-ready, and prepared for emergencies.

At midnight *Tennessee* steamed third in the column, astern of *West Virginia* and *California* on a south southwesterly course of 210 degrees true, at a formation speed of 10 knots. At 0034 hours, still following in column, she turned port 90 degrees, to course 120, and held that course for one hour before coming port another 90 degrees, to course 030. Exactly one hour later, at 0234, she changed course again, further port to true north, 000 degrees. The column was pointed toward Oahu and rendezvous with the target tow ship, the destroyer *Dorsey*.

At 0522 *Tennessee* lighted the oil-fed fires under boiler #3, and eight minutes later cut in boiler #3 to be ready to change speed. Twelve minutes later, at 0542, the foretop lookout called the sighting of *Dorsey*, bearing 042 degrees, towing the target for surface engagement. At 0600 hours, on signal from the Combat Force commander aboard *West Virginia*, *Tennessee* was ordered to proceed independently, turned starboard to a northeasterly course, 045 degrees, and accelerated to 15 knots, preparing to launch her scout planes.

She catapulted planes 202 and 203 at 0630 hours, with Lieutenant Staley, the pilot, and his observer, Radioman First Class Salter, manning 202; and Ensign Hogan, pilot, with Boatswain Mate Second Class Herbert, flying in 203. Five minutes later, the catapult successfully fired plane 201 airborne, piloted by Lieutenant Commander Claude W. Haman, with observer Radioman First Class Maloof aboard. At 0639 the ship began maneuvering on various courses and speeds to take position for short range firing of main and secondary batteries. At 0647 orders were passed from the bridge to cut in boiler #2, and at 0719 the bridge shifted control to the conning tower. All was ready to commence firing.

At 0735 hours *Tennessee* began her first run for short range battery practice, at the normal range of 1,200 to 1,500 yards from the target, with officers ordering string firing of the starboard 5-inch broadside battery. Gun #3 fired the first shot at 0741, and spotting and scoring began. Nine minutes later the big ship began another run, preparing, at officers' commands, to fire turret #3 (top turret, aft) in string. While turret #3 string firing was in progress the ship's crew mustered on station at 0800, followed one minute later with the thunderous roar and belch of smoke as turret #3 fired *Tennessee*'s first salvo of the exercise—all three 14-inch guns firing to starboard simultaneously. At 0805 the order came to cease fire and the ship maneuvered to begin the next run, at 0825, preparing to fire 5th Division's starboard forward group,

5-inch, broadside battery. The Division's four 5-inch guns and one 3-inch gun was under Bob Border's command.

They opened fire in string, the first shot at 0836, and kept a steady pace of fire—approximately four rounds per minute from each gun, until 0839, when, from the bridge, came the order "Cease fire!" One minute later another firing run began, with turret #3 again firing in string, followed eleven minutes later with #3's first salvo, then cease fire at 0855. Twenty-six minutes later, at 0921, the next run began, with 7th Division's two guns of the aft starboard 5-inch battery firing in string, with the first shot at 0927 hours, and the cease fire order coming two minutes later. Another run started at 0935, with turret #4 (lower turret aft) firing to starboard, followed by #4's first salvo at 0944, and a cease fire four minutes later.

Still maneuvering independently, *Tennessee* and the target, towed by *Dorsey*, began turning to port approximately 180 degrees, while the battleship's port side gun crews and turrets #1 and 2, prepared to open fire on command.

The next run started at 1051 for the port aft group of the two-gun, 5-inch battery of the 8th Division. The first shot was fired at 1056 and cease fire came two minutes later. Three minutes later, at 1102, *Tennessee* started another run with turret #2 firing in string followed by its first salvo at 1115 hours and cease fire at 1119. Eleven minutes later, following confirmation, the announcement came, "Target destroyed." Steering control was shifted from the conning tower to the bridge, and the remaining firing runs delayed.

Turret #1 and the port forward (6th Division's) 5-inch guns would not be able to fire short range practice until early Saturday morning, 27 September, shortly before *Tennessee* completed additional independent steaming and rejoined the remainder of the Battle Force to enter Pearl Harbor. The destroyer *Elliot* was the target tow ship.

At 1311 hours on Saturday, as *Tennessee* was easing toward berth F-6 in Pearl Harbor, and mooring an hour later, the ship's crew hoisted out motor launch #3 with the mail clerk and a working party aboard, proceeding at all deliberate speed to the Fleet Post Office. One of the first orders of business in home port—mail call.

This nine-day Battle Force exercise was memorable for Bob and Joey Border for more than one reason. Joey had been awaiting Bob's return to Oahu for three days after her arrival on *Lurline*. More important, the newlyweds were reunited in their new apartment and temporary home after being apart for forty long days and nights, all but two of those days coming after Joey's harrowing automobile accident south of Eugene, Oregon. To a delighted happy-to-be-in-port Bob Border had come his 5th Division's scoring E across the board in their gunnery exercises, a major reason *Tennessee* had the best overall score of all the ships in the Battle Force. News of the 5th Division's performance was good to bring to Joey, a point of professional pride for Bob, though he wouldn't learn of *Tennessee*'s standing first in the Battle Force for some time. It was a joyful reunion and a wonderful night Joey remembered in her diary. "God, it's wonderful to be with him!" she told her diary.[27]

Nevertheless, not evident to either Bob or Joey in the happiness of the moment, was an undercurrent of activity proceeding at a sometimes frustrating pace, preparations taken at the civil populace's deliberate, steady pace—and behind them, the military's relentless, more intense quest and urgings for contingency planning and preparations for a possible "orange attack," the military planners' terminology describing a possible Japanese attack on the islands.

The Gathering Storm

The day before Bob and Joey were reunited, the world's harsh realities of rising tensions and war in both Europe and Asia, pressed ever-closer to them and the people of Hawaii. The Navy ordered protection of all ships engaged in commerce in United States defensive waters—by patrolling, covering, escorting, and by reporting and destroying German and Italian naval forces encountered. Japanese naval forces weren't mentioned in the order because American Naval forces weren't nearly as active in the Far East as they were in aiding Great Britain in the Atlantic and Mediterranean. Further, since the sinking of the gunboat *Panay* in China's Yangtze River four years earlier, the Japanese had studiously avoided attacks on American shipping. And on Saturday, 27 September, the same day the Battle Force returned to Pearl Harbor, America launched its first Liberty Ship, the SS

Patrick Henry, the beginning of a massive building program
intended to supply the nation's emerging, desperately struggling
allies, while strengthening its own sparse Merchant Marine
Service.[28]

While the evacuation of American civilians and military
dependents from the Far East, Southeast Asia, and the Philippines
continued, as did defense preparations in Hawaii, to most
Americans, including those in Hawaii, the war in the Far East
remained distant, not an urgent matter. What's more Americans
believed their west coast well-protected against a possible Japanese
attack. They believed Hawaii to be an impregnable Pacific bastion,
with a ring of defended islands extending outward much further.
Midway Island was 1,380 miles to the northwest of Oahu, Wake
about another 1,260 miles west, southwest; Johnston Island a
white spear of land barely crested the waves 700 miles southwest,
with Palmyra 1,000 miles due south.

On Oahu, long before 1 October, defense preparations by local
Territorial Guard units had been in progress, training with regular
Army units in the Hawaiian Division, while units of the Pacific
Fleet repeatedly left port on exercises. The Army's Hawaiian Air
Force, activated 1 November 1940 and commanded by Major
General Frederick L. Martin, continued to lay the foundation for
the island's air defense system, with its primary mission being
defense of the fleet based at Pearl Harbor. That same November,
responding to the German air campaign against Great Britain
and the well-known and growing threat of Japanese sea power,
particularly carrier-based aviation and Japan's ability to conduct
amphibious landings, the Army deployed the federalized
California National Guard's 251st Coast Artillery Regiment to
Hawaii, to bolster the land and air defense of Oahu.[29]

The Army was proud of its preparations to defend Hawaii. The
Hawaiian Department was the Army's largest overseas department.
For more than three decades the Department had constructed
elaborate coastal defenses on Oahu. Beginning mid-1940, with
arrival of the Pacific Fleet, increasing war scares, the start of
selective service, numerous troop exercises, the mobilization of
the National Guard, the growth of Army strength, including the
Army Air Force, had been steady, toward an impressive strength of
43,000 soldiers by December 1941. The previous April, the Army
staff had already assured President Roosevelt: "The Island of Oahu,

due to its fortification, its location, and its physical characteristics, is believed to be the strongest fortress in the world."

On 1 October 1941, in the Army's Hawaiian Department, commanded by Lieutenant General Walter C. Short, the Army prepared to further strengthen its island base by activating the 24th and 25th Divisions from the old "foursquare" Hawaiian Division. The Department assigned the two divisions areas of responsibility for defense of the island, with the 24th defending the northern half and the 25th defending the southern half. However, behind the scenes, all was not well.

Despite the continuing push to strengthen the islands' defenses, there were a number of deficiencies, the most glaring of which was the same deficiency plaguing the continental United States' Western Defense Command—the lack of long range patrol planes. Hawaii needed 360 degrees of long range patrol coverage to ensure against a surprise carrier based air attack, which had been the most likely scenario emerging from military planners' studies and inserted into war game exercises. The necessary planes and crews weren't available to ensure a surprise carrier-based attack could be prevented.

Additionally, the Army and Navy in Hawaii had had a long history of divisive inter service rivalry, which General Marshall and Admiral Stark had previously recognized and vowed to improve. Marshall had given marching orders to improve the climate of cooperation to both Air Corps' Major General Martin, before he arrived in November 1940, and Lieutenant General Short, before he arrived to take command of the Department in February. For his part, Admiral Stark had been taking similar action with the Navy's Pacific Command. Though there had been definite improvements, not all the damage had been repaired, resulting in considerably less than the ideal in integrating the substantial defense capabilities the two services possessed on Oahu.[30]

On 7 October a letter came to Karl Border—Maximus—from Joey, the primary letter-writer in the newest of the Border families. In his diary he wrote, "Received a letter from Joey saying that the 5th division had gotten all E's. Swell work for Minimus and the boys! . . . "[31] Three months hence, early on a Sunday morning, the boys of *Tennessee*'s gun divisions 5, 6, 7, and 8, would fire at far more difficult targets under far different circumstances.

Two days later, at 2006 hours, *Tennessee*, with Bob Border

on board, was under way once more, bound for the Hawaiian operating area northeast of Oahu, and ten more days of Battle Force exercises with various units of the Pacific Fleet. Harbor pilot #4, with *Tennessee*'s commander, executive officer and navigator on the bridge, steered her clear of Pearl Harbor's entrance, then the pilot left the ship forty-two minutes after she pulled away from her berth. Though the nation was still at peace, as was typical for reasons of operational security and training, the ship was darkened and her running lights dimmed as soon as she left the harbor. Designated Task Force One, the fleet guide was the minelayer *Oglala* (CM-4) leading the formation at a speed of 12 knots on an initial easterly course of 090 degrees true. After clearing the southeast end of Oahu, Task Force One turned further port to 030 degrees at fifteen minutes after midnight.

Aboard *Tennessee*, at 0115 hours, lookouts in the foretop sighted a vessel bearing 040 degrees True (10 degrees off the starboard bow). At 0128 Molakai Light came in view, bearing 096 degrees (66 degrees off the starboard bow), at a distance of twenty-five miles. Two minutes later the order was given to turn on the ship's running lights to warn the vessel, identified as the SS *Makaweli*, a Matson Line freighter. In ten minutes *Tennessee* was well clear of *Makaweli* and the running lights were turned off.

As was also typical in fleet exercises, command guidance and operational security necessitated radio silence—except for emergencies. Messages were passed visually by signal flags, lights using Morse code, night and day, and as daytime back-up messengers. Classified intelligence information and Pacific Command guidance came shore to ship, to all independently operating ships and task forces, via encrypted messages. Again, unless there was an emergency, or specific command guidance requiring a reply, ships in this circumstance were operating in the "passive mode" as listeners and receivers only, and not radiating signals that could be picked up by an enemy, who could then triangulate and fix the transmitters' positions. Receivers of encrypted messages carried highly classified decoding "boxes" similar to the British enigma machines, with communications operators qualified to operate them.

In the ten days that Task Force One was at sea, *Tennessee* conducted numerous exercises in formations with *West Virginia*, *Pennsylvania*, *Maryland* and *Oklahoma* (BB-37); fueled the destroyer *Hull* (DD-350) on *Tennessee*'s starboard side; did more anti-aircraft firing; released a box-type kite for anti-aircraft firing by her .50-caliber machine guns and 5-inch/25 caliber anti-aircraft guns; conducted night and short range battle practices; periodically led the battleship column in exercises; and launched and recovered her scout planes in daylight exercises when weather and sea conditions permitted.

In all her days at sea, the crew's duty hours were long and demanding. When *Tennessee* moored at berth F-5 in Pearl Harbor at 1126 in the morning, Saturday, 18 October, liberty was on the mind of every sailor and many junior officers. There would be time for liberty, sixteen days, and, like other married junior officers whose wives had come to Hawaii, Bob was anxious to get home to Joey. As *Tennessee* slowed to enter the harbor and ease into her berth, he confirmed a ride home and packed a small bag to take with him. He left ship on a motor launch within minutes. When he arrived at their apartment at 1:00 p.m., he found Joey in bed, ill, and spent the afternoon looking to her needs and comfort.[32]

Though more than two weeks elapsed following *Tennessee*'s return to port on 18 October, that didn't mean sixteen days of liberty. The standard command policy was to keep at least 50 percent of the crew on board when ships were in port, which meant Bob would spend at least eight of those days on duty. If there were required training courses to attend ashore, such as qualifying in pistol firing, or he was assigned Officer of the Deck duties, they would eat into the time he and Joey could spend together. Life was never easy.

While Bob continued his duties during the ship's exercises at sea and in port, as well as his studies, training and tests as a junior officer intent on improving his professional skills and capabilities, Joey Border was becoming slowly accustomed to the life of a Navy officer's wife. Life in Honolulu and at Pearl Harbor was not unlike life at The Yard in Bremerton, except she was now fulfilling the role her mother fulfilled as the wife of a Marine officer.

She managed the household, keeping it orderly, neat, and clean; shopped at the market and department stores; and easily moved into the social circle of officers' wives who enjoyed one another's company, games of bridge and acey ducey, and cared for one another and their children while their husbands were on duty aboard their ships. Then there were the dinners and movies on board *Tennessee* with Bob; the officers' club at Pearl Harbor;

drinks and dancing at the well-appointed, inviting Honolulu vacation hotels like the Royal Hawaiian. There were noticeable differences however. He was the one man in her life now, no collection of beaus, and she told her diary frequently how she missed him when he was at sea or on duty when *Tennessee* was in port.

Having settled into the routine of a young Navy officer's wife, which included Bob's intervening absences while on duty aboard *Tennessee*, with Christmas less than two months in the future, and since she had worked as a reporter in Bremerton, she decided a job would break up both the household routine, the separations from Bob, and provide some extra cash for the holidays. While Bob was at sea in October, she began the job hunt and succeeded in finding full time employment as a receptionist and administrative assistant at the Canada Dry Bottling Company in Honolulu, for 80 cents an hour. Her first day of work was Monday, 27 October, the morning before Bob had four hours of duty as Officer of the Deck beginning at midnight.[33]

On 31 October, in Washington, DC, as relations between Japan and the United States continued to deteriorate, Secretary of the Navy Frank Knox signed a directive to the Chief of Naval Operations (CNO). Not made public, the directive's subject, "Evacuation Plan for Dependents of Navy Personnel from the Outlying Bases" would soon affect the entire populace in the Hawaiian Islands, and particularly on Oahu. Forwarded from the CNO, Admiral Stark, on 6 November, to the First, Fifth, Tenth, Thirteenth, Fourteenth and Fifteenth Naval Districts, and the Governor of Samoa, the directive was brief and clear.

1. Please direct the Commandants of the . . . Naval Districts, and the Governor of Samoa, to have plans prepared for the evacuation of dependents of, Navy service personnel, Navy civil service, and employees of Contractors engaged in Navy construction projects, from outlying bases under their respective jurisdictions.
2. When dependents of both Army and Navy personnel are present at the same base, coordination in planning will be obtained by means of a Local Joint Planning Committee, the recommendations of which will be forwarded through channels and

reviewed by the War Plans Division of the Chief of Naval Operations.

3. When appropriate, local plans should provide for: (a) utilization of returning troop and supply ships, acquisition of ships by charter or requisition; (b) the issuance of precautionary notices suggesting the return of dependents by available means prior to the date set for compulsory evacuation in order to avoid congestion and unavoidable inconveniences; (c) local evacuation in the event ships are not available; (d) limiting the amount of household goods that may accompany evacuees as necessary in case shipping space is limited, and storage of the remainder at Government expense until transportation is available; (e) dispatch notification to the Chief of Naval Operations at the time the evacuation is ordered, of the number of evacuees in order that funds may be made available for their transportation and reception; (f) alien dependents desiring to enter the United States should make application to the local American Consul for non-quota entry.

4. The Commandants of the above mentioned Naval Districts and the Governor of Samoa should be directed to comment upon the desirability of evacuating dependents from stations under their jurisdiction. They should also comment upon the effect of failure to evacuate dependents by M-Day from the point of view of the defense, food, and water supply, hospitalization, morale, and freedom of action.[34]

Before the directive from Secretary of the Navy Knox left the CNO's office bound for Hawaii, on Saturday, 1 November, Joey Border did her first Christmas shopping in Hawaii. Like the great majority of Navy wives, she was thinking further ahead than normal, to the holidays, about home and family.[35]

The Battle Force didn't put to sea again until 3 November, this time departing in Task Force One at 1204 hours. Between that Monday and her return to berth F-6 the following Monday,

Tennessee rendezvoused again with *Maryland*, *West Virginia* and *Pennsylvania* for fleet exercises.[36]

While *Tennessee* participated in training exercises in the Hawaiian operating area, in Washington, DC, at a 9:00 a.m. meeting on Friday, 7 November, Japanese Ambassador, Admiral Kishisaburo Nomura and his assistant met with Joseph W. Ballantine, American Secretary of State Cordell Hull's assistant, and relayed his government's expressed wish to resume conversations. He handed Ballantine a document which embodied Proposal A, a previously discussed set of conditions the Americans had found lacking as a basis for resolving the growing crisis.

That afternoon, at a cabinet meeting called by President Roosevelt, Hull spoke for some fifteen minutes on "the dangers of the international situation." He summarized the conversations with Japan, emphasizing that in his opinion, "relations were extremely critical and that we should be on the lookout for a military attack anywhere by Japan at any time."

Hull's words were tragically ironic. In Japan the Naval General Staff and Combined Fleet had just issued their operational orders. Three days later, the Combined Fleet began dispatching 30 submarines in five different groups on a steady march toward the east and southeast, while the 1st Carrier Striking Force began concentrating far to the north, in Etorofu Island's Hitokappu Bay—all subject to recall should there be an unexpected resolution of the crisis.

On 11 November, 10 November in Hawaii and the United States, two groups of Japanese submarines slipped out of harbors near the southern end of the main island of Honshu, nine from the Third Submarine Group, commanded by Rear Admiral Shigeyoshi Miwa, and five of Japan's newest submarines in a Special Attack Group. In the Third Group, the captain of submarine *I-8* was Commander (CDR) Tetsushiro Emi; *I-68's* captain was CDR. Otoji Nakamura; *I-69*, CDR. Katsuji Watanabe; *I-70*, CDR. Takao Sano; *I-71*, CDR. Rokuro Kawasaki; *I-72*, CDR. Ichiro Togami; *I-73*, CDR. Tan Isobe; *I-74*, CDR. Seiko Ikezawa; and *I-75*, CDR. Kiku Inoue.

The Third Group was ordered to sail from Saekai Bay to Kwajalein, where it would refuel before continuing its journey. Each submarine in the Group received a specific mission assignment, and left Saekai precisely at 1111, the eleventh minute after the eleventh hour of the eleventh day of the eleventh month.

The five in the Special Action Group were large, Type C.1 cruiser-submarines, all new, their construction completed within the preceding two years, each carrying a midget submarine mounted aft of the conning tower toward the stern of its carrier. The commander of the First Submarine Division, Captain Hanku Sasaki, had been unaware of the just completed modifications to his five submarines to carry the midgets until days before they sailed. He was astounded to learn their mission shortly after receiving the "strange orders" to pick up their submarines at Kure, and learning of the modifications they were undergoing with a 10 November target date to complete. In the Special Attack Group, the captain of submarine *I-16* was CDR. Kaoru Yamada; *I-18*, CDR. Kiyoshi Otani; *I-20*, CDR. Takishi Yamada; *I-22* CDR. Kiyoi Ageta; and *I-24*, CDR. Hiroshi Hanabusa. They were ordered to proceed direct to their mission area because their cruise speed was slower with the midget submarines mounted on their afterdecks, taking them longer to reach the operating area.

On 16 November, 15 November in Hawaii and the United States, the Second Submarine Group, commanded by Rear Admiral Shigeteru Yamazaki, and composed of submarines *I-1*, CDR. Eitaro Ankyu; *I-2*, CDR. Hiroshi Inada; *I-3*, CDR. Kinzo Tonozuka; *I-4*, Hajime Nakagawa; *I-5*, CDR. Etsuo Hichiji; *I-6*, CDR. Michimune Inaba; and *I-7*, CDR. Rinichi Koizumi sailed out of Honshu, their course east, northeast, until 28 November, Hawaiian time, when they were to turn southeast.[37]

* * *

Days at sea for the *Tennessee* were beginning to taper off as the month of December approached. The next departure was Tuesday, 18 November, when she got under way at 1558 hours and passed harbor entrance buoy #2 at 1650 for two days of exercises with *Pennsylvania* and *Nevada*.

Life in the armed services, especially during wartime, national emergencies, or periods of increased tensions in areas of the world considered vital to the nation's interest, frequently imposes inordinate, unexpected, short-notice demands on those who serve, and their families. In such circumstances families' ability to plan ahead is limited. Emergencies and short notice demands aside, life in the service normally requires planning ahead for holidays, birthdays and any other occasions important to families. Absences on temporary duty are usually scheduled weeks if not months in advance, and Bob Border knew the two-day exercise was coming. November 18 was Joey's twenty-first birthday.

Bob and Joey decided to celebrate this important first birthday since their wedding, one day early. When she returned from work, they played acey ducey, had dinner in the apartment, and Bob presented her a fountain pen, a purse and a manicure set, items she proudly recorded in her diary and etched in her memory.[38]

Tennessee once more returned to berth F-6 when she returned from the short exercise on Wednesday the 19th. One day later Japan's First Submarine Group departed Honshu, the formation commanded by Rear Admiral Tsutomu Sato and composed of *I-9*, CDR. Akiyoshi Fujii; *I-15*, CDR. Nobuo Ishikawa; *I-17*, CDR. Kozo Nishino; and *I-25*, CDR. Neiji Tagami. The Group's course was east, northeast until 28 November, when they too were to turn to the southeast.[39]

On Friday, 21 November, at 12:35 p.m. Pacific time, the 10,810-ton US Army Transport *Republic*, left San Francisco bound for Oahu, en route to the Philippines. On board were ground units of the 7th Bomb Group (Heavy), including the ground echelons of the 11th and 22nd Bombardment Squadrons (Heavy), which were bound for Java. The air echelons were to leave the Sacramento Air Depot in successive flights between 15 December and 1 January 1942. Just prior to the ship's departure from San Francisco, the *Republic* had come out of dry dock, where four 3-inch and one 5-inch gun had been mounted on her fantail. She was one of seven ships soon to form Convoy No. 4002, to leave Pearl Harbor for the Philippines, escorted by the heavy cruiser *Pensacola* (CA-24) and a patrol gunboat, a "sub chaser," the 1,922-ton *Niagra* (PG-52).

Saturday, the 22nd, at 5 p.m., the 6,481-ton US Army Transport *Willard A. Holbrook* departed San Francisco, to join Convoy 4002 in Oahu. Aboard the *Holbrook* were the 1st Battalion, 148th Idaho Field Artillery and the 2nd Battalion, 147th South Dakota Field Artillery. The convergence in Oahu of two Navy combatants and seven ships carrying men, equipment, crated airplanes, supplies and ammunition to the Philippines, was a convoy supported and approved by President Roosevelt, under the provisions of the Army's Pacific defensive war plan, Rainbow 5. The American-Japanese diplomatic crisis, already entering a crucial phase, was lending a new sense of urgency and caution as the United States continued building up its forces in the Philippines.[40]

The same Saturday, it was an early morning departure for *Tennessee*, at 0640 hours, for exercises with *West Virginia*, *California*, *Maryland*, and *Pennsylvania*, with return to F-6 at 1241 on Friday, 28 November, one day after Thanksgiving. This time, on return, *West Virginia* moored to *Tennessee*, outboard on *Tennessee*'s port side. For the next nine days both ships floated peacefully, side by side, with Ford Island to starboard of the Volunteer State's namesake.[41]

At 1030 hours Hawaii time on Tuesday, 25 November, while *Tennessee* was participating in the Battle Force exercise, Japan's Carrier Striking Force sortied from Hitokappu Bay, in the Kuril Islands. With the carriers *Akagi*, *Hiryu*, *Kaga*, *Shokaku*, *Soryu* and *Zuikaku*, were the battleships *Hiei* and *Kirishima*; heavy cruisers *Chikuma* and *Tone*; light cruiser *Abukuma*; destroyers *Akigumo*, *Hamakaze*, *Isokaze*, *Kagero*, *Shiranuhi*, *Tanikaze* and the *Urakaze*. Because of the lengthy journey, the Fleet took extraordinary measures to stuff additional fuel on board the carriers, to include stripping items considered unnecessary for the mission and the loading of barrels of oil wherever space could be found. Nevertheless, oilers would be needed to refuel the massive fleet steaming toward its rendezvous with destiny.

Accompanying the carrier force were the 1st and 2d Supply Groups and a patrol formation of three screening submarines commanded by Captain Kijiro Imaizumi; the *I-19*, CDR. Shogo Narahara; *I-21*, CDR. Kanji Matsumura; and *I-23*, CDR. Genichi Shibata. In the 1st Supply Group was the destroyer *Kasumi* and the oilers *Kenyo Maru*, *Kokuyu Maru*, *Kyokuto Maru*, and the *Shikoku Maru*. The destroyer *Arare* was with the 2d Supply Group, which included the oilers *Nippon Maru*, *Toei Maru*, and the *Toho Maru*.[42]

On 26 and 27 November, in Washington, there was a flurry of activity involving crucial meetings between Secretary of State Hull, Ambassador Nomura and Japan's Special Envoy, Ambassador Saburu Kurusu, as negotiations teetered on the edge of collapse.

On the morning of the 26th, Secretary of War Henry Stimson called President Roosevelt to confirm that the President had seen a G-2 (intelligence) report that a Japanese force of five divisions had embarked on 30 to 50 ships and the large fleet had been sighted southward-bound, near Formosa. Roosevelt had not

Japanese Ambassador Kichi Saburo Nomura and special envoy, Saburo Kurusu, leave the White House in late November 1941. NPSAM

seen the message and was furious when he heard its contents. He realized the Japanese, who ostensibly had been negotiating an entire truce and an entire withdrawal, had evidenced bad faith. They apparently had no intention of withdrawing. Late the same day, at 1645 hours, Nomura and Kurusu called on Hull. The meeting lasted two hours. At the very time they were talking the Japanese carrier strike force had been under way for twenty-four hours and had undergone its first en route refueling. The Japanese had activated their main war plan, and two invasion forces were on their way toward Malaysia and the Philippines.[43]

In San Francisco Harbor the morning of Thanksgiving Day, 27 November, the crew of the Matson Line's *Lurline* were in the final stages of preparing her for another long-planned voyage to Honolulu. The preceding day, at 10:00 a.m., several hundred students and faculty of Willamette University in Salem, Oregon, began a noisy, happy, excitement-filled rally at Salem's Southern Pacific train station. At 10:30, they were sending off twenty-seven members of the Willamette Bearcats' football team, plus Athletic Director and Head Football Coach R. S. "Spec" Keene, Manager

Dick Kernes, and Publicist Gil Lieser, to board *Lurline* for the voyage to Honolulu. Twenty-two of Salem's citizens accompanied the team, including Mrs. Keene, State Senator Douglas McKay and his daughter, Shirley, and nineteen others.

Coach Keene dreamed of this trip for years, and now it was a reality. The Bearcats, scheduled to play the University of Hawaii Rainbows on Saturday, 6 December, are to sail on *Lurline* with another football team, the San Jose State Spartans, from San Jose, California. The Bearcats and Spartans are scheduled to play one another in Hawaii on 16 December, with the Spartans playing the Rainbows between those two dates. The three round robin games were charity events planned and sponsored by the Shriners' Committee in Honolulu, in cooperation with the University of Hawaii.

Thanksgiving morning twenty-five members of the Spartan team were among the thirty-one people leaving San Jose by bus to the Matson Line terminal in San Francisco, accompanied by Coach Ben Winkelman, Manager Sebastian "Scrappy" Squatritto, yell leader Tommy Taylor, team photographer Bob McGevren, Mrs. Ed Wenberg, wife of team co-captain Ed Wenberg, and Lieutenant Dave Dorsey of San Jose, leaving the Navy's nearby Moffett Field for assigned duty in Hawaii.[44]

That same morning, at Pearl Harbor, Admiral Kimmel along with key members of his staff held an important conference in Pacific Fleet headquarters. Present was Rear Admiral Claude C. Bloch, Commandant of the Fourteenth Naval District and Task Force 4; Vice Admiral William F. "Bull" Halsey, Commander Aircraft, Battle Force (Task Force 2); Vice Admiral Wilson Brown, Commander Scouting Force (Task Force 3); and Rear Admiral Bellinger, Commander Task Force 9. Generals Short and Martin also attended, bringing Martin's chief of staff, Air Corps Lt. Col. James A. "Jimmy" Mollison. The conference principally discussed the question of whether or not to send Army Air Force P-40 fighter planes to Midway and Wake Islands and reinforce the garrisons with Army troops, or to keep the P-40s and troops to defend Oahu. The proposals had been under consideration in Washington and Hawaii for about a month.

The principle and awkwardness of "divided command" immediately surfaced in Kimmel's meeting, albeit good-naturedly, when Short hesitated to release the P-40s and troops from his control. "If I man these islands, I must command them," he declared. "Over my dead body," Kimmel retorted. "The Army should exercise no command over Navy bases."

"Mind you, I do not want these islands," replied Short amiably. "I think they are better manned by Marines. But if I must put troops and planes on them, then I must command them." As was pointed out in Gordon Prange's historical work, *At Dawn We Slept*, "A far more important underlying issue was any Army aircraft ferried to these outlying bases would have to be written off for use in the Hawaiian Islands. The distance was beyond the P-40's range of independent flight." General Martin therefore proposed sending some of his obsolescent fighters "because those were the ones we could afford best to lose." Short disagreed. " . . . if we are going against the Japanese, we want the best we have instead of the worst . . . "

"Jimmy" Mollison didn't like the scheme. "Our mission is to protect Oahu," he said, "and shipping out these Army planes will lessen our capability to do so." "Why are you so worried about this? Do you think we are in danger of attack?" asked Kimmel.

Mollison cautiously replied, "The Japanese have such a capability."

"Capability, yes," the Admiral conceded, "but possibility?" He next turned abruptly to his chief war plans officer, Captain Charles E. "Soc" Morris. "What do you think about the prospects of a Japanese air attack?"

"None, absolutely none," Morris replied firmly. There was more than Morris's response affecting Kimmel's thinking that Thanksgiving morning. The fact that the War and Navy Departments had authorized sending 50 percent of Hawaii's P-40s to Wake and Midway indicated to him authorities in Washington "did not consider hostile action on Pearl Harbor imminent or probable." In spite of the authorization and his interpretation of its meaning, he decided to keep the Army fighter planes on Oahu, and instead send a squadron of Marine F4Fs.

At 1430 hours, as General Short was returning from Kimmel's conference, Colonel Tige Phillips, Short's chief of staff, brought him a highly classified message which had just arrived in the Hawaiian Department. War Department Message No. 472, signed "Marshall," included another addressee, Lieutenant General James E. DeWitt, Commanding General, Western Defense Command, at The Presidio, in San Francisco, California. A similar message came through Navy command channels to the

Pacific Fleet Commander, Admiral Kimmel, from Admiral Stark, the Chief of Naval Operations in Washington, DC.

> Negotiations with Japan appear to be terminated to all practical purposes with only the barest possibilities that the Japanese Government might come back and offer to continue. Japanese future action unpredictable but hostile action possible at any moment. If hostilities cannot, repeat cannot be avoided the United States desires that Japan commit the first overt act. This policy should not, repeat not, be construed as restricting you to a course of action that might jeopardize your defense. Prior to hostile Japanese action you are directed to undertake such reconnaissance and other measures as you deem necessary but these measures should be carried out so as not, repeat not, to alarm civil population or disclose intent. Report measures taken. Should hostilities occur you will carry out the tasks assigned in Rainbow Five [the Army's basic war plan] so far as they pertain to Japan. Limit dissemination of this highly secret information to minimum essential officers.

When the conference adjourned, Admiral Halsey, except for a lunch break, stayed over until 1800 hours to visit with his Naval Academy classmate, Admiral Kimmel. During that visit, Admiral Stark's message to Kimmel arrived. Halsey and Kimmel discussed the potentially explosive crisis in the Pacific, and the imminent possibility of a Japanese attack. The next day the aircraft carrier *Enterprise* (CV-6), Halsey's flagship, was departing with a task force bound for Wake Island with the Admiral in command. The *Enterprise* was going to deliver the Marine F4F squadron to Wake Island.

Kimmel asked Halsey if he wanted to take the battleships with him. The presence of the battleships kept up the pretense of a routine mission. "Hell no!" Halsey retorted. "If I have to run I don't want anything to interfere with my running!" He felt America was going to be in a fight before he returned from Wake Island.[45]

It was late afternoon in San Francisco when Colonel Phillips handed General George C. Marshall's message to General Short. *Lurline* had departed San Francisco on her voyage to Honolulu. On board among nearly seven hundred passengers were the two college football teams and accompanying coaches, managers, and rooters. The Willamette University Bearcats from Salem, Oregon, and California's San Jose State University Spartans finally embarked for their long-anticipated round-robin games with the University of Hawaii Rainbows.

The *Enterprise* departed from Pearl Harbor on 28 November, in company of the heavy cruisers *Chester* (CA-27), *Northampton* (CA-26) and *Salt Lake City* (CA-25); the destroyers *Balch* (DD-363), *Gridley* (DD-380), *Craven* (DD-382), *McCall* (DD-400), *Maury* (DD-401), *Dunlap* (DD-384), *Fanning* (DD-385), *Benham* (DD-397), and the *Ellet* (DD-398). Her Carrier Air Group's normal complement of sixty-three planes included Bombing Squadron Six (VB-6) with 17 SBD-2 Douglas Dauntless dive bombers; Fighting Squadron Six (VF-6) with 16 F4F-3 Grumman Wildcat fighters; Scouting Squadron Six (VS-6) with 10 SBD-2s and 8 SBD-3s; and Torpedo Squadron Six (VT-6) with 18 Douglas TBD-1 Devastators and 2 SNJ-3s. On this mission, however, the Air Group was temporarily augmented with twelve Marine F4F Wildcats. Among crew members and aviators on the *Enterprise* there were no indications or premonitions of unusual events. They knew the mission was to qualify the Wildcat fighter pilots of Marine Fighting Squadron 211 (VMF-211), for carrier landings. However, the explanation of the mission included one crucial, attention-getting point not heard in living memory aboard the carrier. The fighters would be needed if the *Enterprise* lost her fighters or an emergency arose.

A former gunner and radioman, Jack Leaming, in *Enterprise*'s Scout Squadron Six (VS-6) described events in the succeeding twenty-four hours aboard the carrier.

> The Enterprise Squadrons took off from Ford Island the afternoon of November 28, and landed aboard Enterprise just off Diamond Head. The usual evening routine ensued . . . a movie, then lights out at ten.
>
> The next day began with relocating all our planes on the hangar deck. Upon completion, those in the flight crews went topside to watch the Marines qualify, from a safe vantage point of course, since

we expected the Marines to have some difficulty. They did not! They were Marines!

There were some tense moments, but the Landing Signal Officer, LSO, Bert Harden, would give them a wave off if they were not "in the slot" at correct speed and attitude. The procedure of landing aboard a carrier that is pitching and rolling, sometimes slowly, other times rapidly, requires practice, practice, practice, until one becomes as skilled as the world's most accomplished Olympic athlete. It requires quick thinking, split second timing, and coordination.

There were very few wave offs. On their third qualification landing, instead of taking off again, Captain Murray ordered that they be taxied to the bow of the ship, their engines cut, and all aircraft secured.

When the last Marine had landed, the Captain called the crew to quarters. Addressing us over the loudspeaker system, we were told he had been given a special envelope containing special orders upon departing Pearl Harbor from the Commander-in-Chief, Pacific Fleet [Admiral Kimmel]. This envelope was not to be opened until a specified time. That time had arrived. He read the orders to us.

"Henceforth," it began, "and to the completion of this mission, we will be operating as though under wartime conditions. Day or night, we must be ready for instant action. Hostile submarines might be seen or encountered. Everyone should be especially alert and vigilant at all times, especially while on watch." He ended by saying, "Steady nerves and stout hearts are needed now."[46]

At Pearl Harbor Saturday morning, 29 November, 0616 hours, the heavy cruiser *Pensacola* got underway in response to Task Force 15 Operation Order 15-41, with her skipper, Captain Norman Scott, the commander of Task Group 15.5. Dubbed "Operation Plum" when the effort was conceived, the convoy's destination was Manila, Philippines, to reinforce the Islands' defenses. Outside Pearl Harbor in advance of *Pensacola* was the other member of Captain Scott's task group, the patrol gunboat *Niagra*. The Pensacola turned right to 255 degrees after leaving the harbor entrance.

Also en route were the seven ships Task Group 15.5 would join to escort Convoy 4002: the 8,300-ton transport *Chaumont* (AP-5), carrying sailors, civilian workmen and cargo; the USAT *Republic*, carrying ground units of the 7th Bombardment Group (Heavy), destined for Java; the USAT *Meigs*, carrying a cargo of 52 crated, Douglas A-24 dive bombers and personnel of the 27th Bomb Group (Light); the freighter SS *Coast Farmer*, carrying trucks and ammunition; the SS *Admiral Halstead*, carrying 18 crated 24th Group P-40E pursuit aircraft; the USAT *Holbrook*, with three battalions of Idaho and South Dakota National Guard artillerymen and their 75-mm guns; and the Dutch ship MS *Bloemfountein*, carrying the Texas National Guard's 2nd Battlion, 131st Field Artillery and its guns. Cargo on the various ships included 340 vehicles, a half-million rounds of .50-caliber ammunition, 9,600 rounds of 37-mm antiaircraft shells, 5,000 bombs, and 9,000 drums of aviation gasoline.[47]

Early the same morning, while Bob Border was once more on duty aboard *Tennessee*, in Pearl Harbor, Joey Border, at home alone in their apartment, listened to the shortwave radio broadcast of the Army-Navy football game from Philadelphia, Pennsylvania. Though Bob had been an intramural soccer player at Navy, like all graduates of the Academy, he looked forward each year to the annual renewal of the classic football rivalry, which drew worldwide interest and attention throughout the Army, Navy, and indeed the entire United States. Now a Naval Academy graduate's wife, as well, she smiled and cheered quietly to herself, as the Midshipmen defeated Army's Cadets 14-6. Although she had expressed some mild frustration in her diary about the rain in Hawaii, she still regarded Oahu a beautiful island—and 1941 a truly wonderful year.[48]

Aboard *Lurline*, the passengers brimmed with pleasure at the thoughts of lovely tropical islands—home for some—while the men and women from Willamette and San Jose State Universities had similar happy thoughts, envisioning the beauty of the islands most had never seen, and football games filled with excitement.

Heavy cruiser *Pensacola* (CA-24) underway at sea, September 1935. Task Group 15.5 guide and command ship, was underway from Pearl Harbor, 29 November 1941. NHHC

The gunboat *Niagra* (PG-52) entering Pearl Harbor, 31 March 1942. She was the Task Group 15.5 sub-chaser escort for "Operation Plum." NA

CHAPTER 4

Prelude

If your sword is too short, take one step forward.

Admiral Marquis Heihachiro Togo

Christmas. Home. Family. Love. December is that time of year, no matter the circumstances and where an American might be. Monday, the first of the month, Joey was up and at work at the Canada Dry Bottling Company in Honolulu by 9:00 in the morning. There were more Christmas packages to wrap when Bob picked her up following his relief from duty. Thought and discussion with him after *Tennessee* returned from the last training cruise, had convinced her Saturday should be her last day at work. She had earned the extra cash she needed to supplement the purchase and shipment home of Christmas gifts and have an open house for the men in Bob's 5th Division. What's more they were anticipating his receiving orders at any moment for aviator training in Pensacola.

The same day, under the headline: TOKYO MINISTER SEES JAPAN MOVE INTO DUTCH EAST INDIES, the following excerpt from the United Press release appeared, datelined Tokyo, November 30:

> Lt. General Saburo Ando, a member of the Japanese War Council, predicted today that Japan will try to cut China's Burma Road and move into the Netherlands East Indies. As Holland itself had been completely occupied by the Germans, the Netherlands East Indies will be 'summarily treated' as soon as Japan decides to move into that area. Ando also singled out the U.S. as the only obstacle to the realization of Japan's East Asia 'Co-Prosperity Sphere.'

The Dutch East Indies still belonged to the Netherlands, a recognized ally of the United States. Japan was ignoring the risk of openly antagonizing America, and made what could be interpreted as a direct threat to attack the East Indies.

To Ando's prediction of Japan cutting the Burma Road—China's only remaining supply line from the outside world—the following opposing story appeared on the same day under the headline: U.S. PILOTS TO GUARD BURMA ROAD:

> In the near future, the vital Burma Road supplying China will be defended from Japanese air attack by an all-American air unit, composed of American planes, flown by American pilots under the Chinese flag. Japanese reaction to (this) is that it would be 'an example of the most provocative armed aggression,' and a 'direct hostile action.'

American pilots, volunteers flying "under the Chinese flag," would call themselves "The Flying Tigers." They would also be known as "The American Volunteer Group," and the AVG.

Another 1 December three-paragraph news release from the Japanese newspaper *Yomiuri* was startling. The first sentence claimed, "if the Hawaiian Islands did not exist, war between Japan and the United States would be impossible." The writer went on to say Japan's "use of armed force in the attainment of the 'East Asia co-prosperity sphere' was as justifiable as America's war for independence in 1776." Through war, he continued, "Japan is engaged in a similar struggle to emancipate the people of East Asia. U.S. takeover of Hawaii was really only an indicator of America's desire to now destroy Japan and control Asia."[1]

> Tuesday morning, front page headline stories from the *Los Angeles Times* indicated little let-up in the growing crisis. Under one headline, FDR CALLS NAVY AID IN ASIA CRISIS, was mentioned the president ". . . summoned Admiral Harold Stark, chief of U.S. Naval Operations . . . for a conference with Secretary of State Cordell Hull as the delicately balanced Oriental situation neared a critical stage . . . " Other headlines in Tuesday's *Times* read, AUSTRALIA FEARS CLASH

IN PACIFIC; AMERICAN FORCES ON ALERT IN
THE PHILIPPINES; CHINA EXPECTS JAPAN TO
INTENSIFY ACTION; SHANGHAI AMERICANS
AGAIN URGED TO LEAVE; BRITISH IN MALAYA
CALL   OUT   VOLUNTEERS;   and   JAPANESE
CIVILIANS PREPARE TO LEAVE HONG KONG.[2]

Tuesday for Joey was work and more Christmas shopping on
the way to *Tennessee* for dinner, after taking Mrs. Cubberley to
the Hickam Field officers' club for a drink. The coming holidays
brought back memories of last year's holidays, when she first met
Bob. She looked forward to the holidays on the beautiful island
of Oahu. Bob would have more time with her, and there were all
manner of things to do and places to go.[3]

The crisis, worsening over the next 24 hours, brought these
Wednesday headlines: U.S. DEMANDS JAPAN EXPLAIN
INDO-CHINA WAR MOVES, PEACE TALKS ENDANGERED;
TOKYO   WARNED   AMERICAN   NAVY   IN   PACIFIC
CAN SHOOT STRAIGHT; ALL U.S. MARINES OUT OF
SHANGHAI; and BRITISH CHINA COAST SHIPS ORDERED
INTO HONG KONG.[4]

On Wednesday, 3 December the *Lurline* arrived from the
second leg of her twice-monthly San Francisco-Los Angeles-
Honolulu triangular voyage, carrying the normal passenger
load, this time including the Willamette University and San Jose
State College football teams. The two teams, with their coaches,
cheerleaders, and small contingents of fans, along with the other
passengers, received the traditional, warm Hawaiian welcome
of band boys playing island music, leis, and hula girls before
loading luggage on buses for the Manoa Hotel near Waikiki—
where both teams made their headquarters. En route on late fall's
rough seas, both the Bearcats and Spartans suffered *mal de mer*,
and the coaches planned afternoon practices the day of arrival to
restart more intense conditioning and finalize game preparations.

Wednesday was a no-work day for Joey. While Bob was
on duty, she slept in until 10:00, went to the local market for
groceries, wrapped more Christmas packages, and cleaned their
apartment. In the afternoon she and Bob called on Lieutenant
Colonel William D. Bassett and Lieutenant Robert J. Foley
and their wives in the officers' quarters. Rear Admiral David
W. Bagley, the Combat Division Two commander, and his

staff, which included six officers, were temporarily assigned to *Tennessee* until 7 December. Colonel Bassett was the Combat Division's Marine Officer, and Lt. Foley, U.S. Navy, was one of the Admiral's two aides, as well as his Flag Secretary—the officer who directed the admiral's paperwork. (A Navy lieutenant senior grade is equivalent in grade to a Marine or Army captain.) Bob and Joey's calls on the two officers and their wives were in keeping with Navy and Marine Corps traditions, which included leaving preprinted cards, similar to business cards, containing their names and Bob's officer grade—ensign.[5]

In the states headlines were more of the same tense rhetoric, with the major headline predicting COLLAPSE OF PACIFIC PARLEYS EXPECTED. The sub-heading: "Hull Declares Japan's Policy of Expansion Has Prevented Peace Talks From Progressing." Headlines noted the soon-to-be enemies were continuing to evacuate what a few days later would become Pacific battlefields. American's were, . . . ADVISED TO LEAVE HONG KONG while 8,000 JAPANESE LEAVE PHILIPPINES FOR JAPAN. Another announced: TOKYO CALLS HOME ENVOYS TO MEXICO.[6]

The deterioration of United States-Japanese relations hadn't come overnight. The swift German conquest of Denmark, Norway, Holland, Belgium and France; the dramatic defeat and evacuation of the British Expeditionary Force from Dunkirk in 1940 followed by the bloody Luftwaffe air campaign against England; the German Navy's successful campaigns on and under the high seas; and the reinvigoration of the Berlin-Rome-Tokyo Axis had emboldened the Japanese militarists. The results were a renewed Japanese thrust deeper into China, and covetous, expansionist eyes cast on the Dutch, British and French colonies and protectorates in Southeast Asia. Slowly at first, then with an increased sense of urgency, the turn of events began pulling America—reluctantly—from its isolation. War was coming. Foot dragging and doubts began to fall away in 1940.

In October 1940 Congress approved calling the National Guard into federal service, and a bill followed permitting states to raise and maintain substitute forces called the State Guard. By October 1941, over 108,000 men had been recruited in thirty-six states.[7]

Since July 1941, the United States had been seriously preparing for possible war. The American government had established the Office of Civilian Defense in July, and printed War Department manuals on the procedures for protection against air attack. Approximately 80,000 American Legion and World War I veterans, from more than half the states—including all the states along both coasts—had begun organizing and training aircraft warning observers. In thirty-one states, Legionnaires established fifty-six schools to train aircraft spotters and wardens. Also under way by August were plans to train city police and firemen to handle various types of bombs.

While 1 December headlines traced deteriorating Japan-United States relations and evident failing negotiations toward an almost certain conclusion, other headlines that week told of accelerating American preparations for now-probable war. Headlines from a story in the *Los Angeles Times* said: HARBOR DEFENSE TESTED BY GUARD: Eighty Men Engage in Maneuvers Aimed Against Enemy Invasion. Authorities in New York warned of "the possibility of a sabotage attempt made along the busy Brooklyn waterfront . . . which embraces numerous defense plants, shipyards and three large bridges."[8]

Los Angeles Times headlines on 2 December warned: ARTILLERY UNITS MOVE TODAY FOR TEST OF AIR RAID DEFENSE: Gunners to 'Defend' L.A. from 'Attack' by Enemy Planes in State-wide Maneuvers. Fifty miles south of Los Angeles, the coastal city of San Clemente was informed it would receive its "Air Raid Instructions" that week. Former New York City Mayor Fiorello LaGuardia, the head of U.S. Civilian Defense was quoted: LAGUARDIA WARNS OF RAID DANGER.

On 4 December, under the headline, TROOPS FOR AIR RAID DEFENSE MANEUVERS TO ARRIVE TODAY, the writer disclosed details of the exercises: "4000 troops of the 37th Brigade from Camp Haan here for air raid exercises between December 11 and 16. Planes will fly as the theoretical enemy as well as interceptors. Will also test ground observers in spotting and reporting enemy planes to information center."[9]

When Bob and Joey returned to their apartment Wednesday, they ate dinner and played acey ducey. The day, like the rest of the week, was quiet and peaceful. That night they retired early, looking forward to a fun-filled evening on Thursday, 4 December, with dinner at the Western-themed Wagon Wheel Restaurant and bridge with John N. Renfro—Bob's Academy classmate and ship's secretary on *California*—and his wife.[10]

"Winds" Messages

While the recently reunited newlyweds Bob and Joey enjoyed the week with *Tennessee* in port, on Thursday, 4 December, the U.S. Navy's guarded, highly classified radio receiving station in Cheltonham, Maryland, intercepted a Japanese overseas "News" broadcast from Station JAP (Tokyo) on 11980 kilocycles. The broadcast began at 8:30 a.m., corresponding to 1:30 a.m. in Hawaii, and 10:30 p.m., 5 December, in Tokyo. The broadcast was probably in Wabun, the Japanese equivalent of Morse Code, and was originally written in syllabic katakana characters, a vastly simpler and phonetic form of written Japanese. It was recorded in Cheltonham on a special typewriter, developed by the Navy, which typed the Roman-letter equivalents of the Japanese characters. The Winds Message broadcasts, which Japanese embassies all over the world had been alerted to listen to in a 19 November coded message, was forwarded to the Navy Department by TWX (teletype exchange) from the teletype-transmitter in the "Intercept" receiving room at Cheltenham to "WA91," the page-printer located beside the GY Watch Officer's desk in the Navy Department Communication Intelligence Unit under the command of Navy Captain Lawrence F. Safford.[11]

The 4 December message was one of the last key intelligence intercepts the Navy was decoding and translating, in attempts to determine Japanese intentions and plans during their deteriorating diplomatic relations and negotiations with the United States. There was some delay and uncertainty in decoding and translating the message, which, as indicated in the Japanese government's 19 November message, would be contained in the Tokyo news broadcasts' weather reports. After considerable discussion of the 4 December intercept, senior Naval Intelligence officers concluded the message meant an imminent break in diplomatic relations with Great Britain, at least, and probably the United States—since the embassies had received instructions to destroy their codes. Code destruction and replacement was a routine procedure at regular, specified intervals throughout the year, but ominously, the most recent order to destroy codes didn't fit the normal pattern of Japanese behavior in managing their most secret codes.

But unknown to American intelligence another more ominous message had been sent to the combined fleet at 0730 hours on 2 December, Tokyo time, Monday, 1 December in Washington and Hawaii. Sent by Admiral Yamamoto's chief of Naval General Staff, Rear Admiral Matome Ugaki, it was to become one of the most famous messages in naval history. "Climb Mount Niitaka, 1208." It signaled that X-Day—the day to execute the Japanese war plan—was 0000 December 8, Japan time. Nagumo's task force received the information at 2000 hours, and at this hour was about 940 miles almost directly north of Midway, well beyond the arc of U.S. reconnaissance flights.[12]

Enterprise: Twelve F4F Wildcats to Wake Island

The morning of 4 December, at a position approximately 2,100 miles west of Pearl Harbor and 175 miles north of Wake Island, at 0450 hours, the carrier *Enterprise* sounded General Quarters and mustered all hands preparatory to beginning flight operations. At 0500 she ceased zigzagging, reduced speed to 18 knots, and at 0515 hours turned starboard to 354 degrees, into the wind, to begin launching aircraft. At 0529 hours the first of twenty-one *Enterprise* aircraft became airborne. First, were four Grumman F4F Wildcats—fighters—on combat air patrol. Next came three Douglas Dauntless SBD-3s as inner air submarine patrol. Third were fourteen more SBDs on a search mission.

Between 0630 and 0700, *Enterprise* radar detected a lone aircraft approaching from the south—a Navy Catalina PBY long range patrol aircraft with the mission of leading the twelve F4F-3s of Marine fighter squadron VMF-211 to Wake Island. The twelve pilots, already briefed, were prepared to launch, and at 0656 hours, 0956 Hawaii time, the first aircraft, with engine roaring at full power, and the flight control officer's hand signal, released brakes and lifted off to begin the final leg of the mission to reinforce Wake Island's garrison. At 0700, in the midst of the F4Fs' launch, lookouts spotted the PBY. Eleven minutes after the first Marine fighter lifted off, the last of the twelve was airborne, including their escorts, and Task Force 8 began an immediate

Carrier *Enterprise* (CV-6) en route to Pearl Harbor, 8 October 1939. Photographed from the cruiser *Minneapolis* (CA-36). NA

starboard turn from 354 degrees to Fleet course and axis 084 degrees to return to Pearl Harbor.

Six SBDs from Scouting Six, and the Air Group Commander, Lieutenant Commander Howard L. Young in a seventh SBD, accompanied the fighters toward Wake. Among the seven escorts was plane 6-S-7, with its crew: pilot, Lt. (jg) Hart D. Hilton and Radioman/gunner Second Class (RM2c) Jack Leaming. The escorts' instructions were to return to the ship upon sighting Wake Island on the horizon. Under no circumstances were any of the escorts to approach Wake any closer than instructed. The precaution was to avoid being recognized and placed in the vicinity by any hostile surface vessel or submarine.

In the minds of the Marine fighter pilots en route to Wake that morning, thoughts and questions about their future must have abounded. When they lifted off the Ewa Mooring Mast Field Friday, 28 November, to begin what they believed to be carrier qualifications aboard *Enterprise*, they were totally unprepared for the orders they would receive at the end of that day. They wore light summer flight suits, carried only a few toilet articles, and a towel. If they did not qualify for carrier landings the first day, they would be required to try again the next day. Consequently, they would need toilet articles for an overnight stay. The contents of the orders were so unexpected and remote the Marines were aghast.

Major Paul Putnam, the commander of VMF-211, had been called to the bridge. He was told that his men would be completely outfitted from *Enterprise*'s small store supplies. They could sign "chits" for articles they needed and purchased at the canteen.

Their gray fighters, that flashed in the sun, were to be painted Navy blue-gray above, so if seen from above, they would blend with the sea, and gray underneath, so if seen from below, they would blend with the sky. Complete overhaul of the engines, airframes, and guns was to begin immediately upon dismissal from quarters. Radio receiver and transmitter frequencies were checked for correctness.

Flight crews helped with the masking and painting of the F4Fs and checked the radio equipment. Mechanics pulled engine checks and overhauls. Using extra care to prevent possible jams, ordinance men belted ammunition for the four, fixed .50-caliber machine guns—two in each wing—for the Wildcats, and the .30-caliber free guns mounted in the rear cockpit of the SBDs which would escort the Wildcats toward Wake Island.

The voyage had been made in the utmost secrecy. Absolutely no one was permitted to discuss it or refer to it in any conversation— anywhere. Not even between shipmates, especially in a public place. The penalty for violation of this order, if there were a leakage of information, would be a General Court Martial.

Later, all the aircrews aboard ship were told not to maintain a log, carry any confidential material that could not be dispensed with hastily or totally destroyed in the event of an emergency, and not to precipitate any hostile action. They were to test fire their guns periodically on scouting flights to ensure proper and ready operation. They could drop smoke bombs and fire on them for accuracy if they chose. Above all, they were to maintain radio silence. No mistakes! Check the transmitter switches often!

Flight crews were given small sandbags, about four inches square, containing a message pocket, to be thrown onto the carrier deck in the event they made contact with any foreign ship or needed to communicate with their own forces while they were airborne. Some practiced dropping messages on the *Enterprise* deck while flying scouting missions.

Every precaution was to be taken. Do not fly close to foreign vessels lest they be detected. They were to fire on and destroy any unidentified ship or aircraft that approached the task force. It was known the Japanese fleet was at sea, and they might encounter them. All had realized history-making events were in progress, that internationally the situation was extremely tense and that the Japanese envoys were on their way to Washington for talks. Guns were to be manned and ready continuously. Each aircraft on a search mission would carry a 500-pound bomb.

Approximately one hour and fifteen minutes after takeoff, still early morning on 4 December, Wake became a barely visible speck on the horizon. A beautiful morning was beginning around the Island, as the escorts waggled their wings in a farewell gesture to VMF-211, and turned toward the *Enterprise*. During the return leg a storm was moving in, which could spell trouble for landings, but the carrier and her task force steered just clear of its edges, and the SBDs landed without incident. Task Force 8 was on the way back to Pearl Harbor.[13]

Aircraft Carriers *Lexington* and *Saratoga* at Sea

At 0400 hours Pacific Time, 0200 in Hawaii, on Friday morning, 5 December, Lieutenant Wellington T. Hines came on duty for a four-hour stint as Officer of the Deck, on the aircraft carrier *Saratoga* (CV-3). The ship was on course 180 degrees, standard speed 23 knots, at 199 rpm (shaft revolutions per minute), sailing south, singly, toward San Diego Harbor, continuing sea trials en route. After completing overhaul at the Puget Sound Navy Yard, her crew had begun loading ammunition and other supplies on 30 November, and, with its commander, Captain Archibald H. Douglas at the conn [ship's control], the ship got under way at 0902 on 2 December to begin sea trials preparatory to rejoining the Pacific Fleet in San Diego Harbor.

Now on course for San Diego the morning of the 5th with boilers 1 through 9 operating, at 0405 hours preparations for full power trials began, as boilers 10 through 16 were lit, one by one. At 0610, after generators and main engine set-up, the great ship began accelerating, her speed continuing to build

Carrier *Saratoga* (CV-3) launching planes, circa summer 1941,
as seen from the rear cockpit of a plane that has just taken off.
Aircraft on deck are Douglas TBD-1 *Devastator* torpedo
planes, probably from squadron VT-3. NA

until she reached 31.7 knots, 281 rpm, at 0713 hours—one hour
and three minutes after the run began. The crew kept her at
maximum power for twelve minutes, at a speed just under 36.5
miles per hour, nearly 150 percent of the maximum speed of the
battleships moored at Pearl Harbor.[14]

Early Friday morning, 5 December was more than busy at Pearl
Harbor, as well. On board the aircraft carrier *Lexington* (CV-2),
the electrical gang energized her degaussing coils at 0705, 0905
Pacific coast, and at 0728 the ship got under way, moving slowly
toward the harbor entrance. At 0750 the crew was ordered to
torpedo defense quarters, a standard operating procedure when
the ship left harbor. While on the watch that morning, Lieutenant
John R. Moore, the Officer of the Deck on *Lexington* noted the
following ships stood out of Pearl Harbor: the destroyers *Porter*
(DD-356), *Lamson* (DD-367), and *Drayton* (DD-366); the high-
speed minesweepers *Hopkins* (DMS-13) *Southard* (DMS-10); the
heavy cruisers *Chicago* (CA-29), *Astoria* (CA-34), *Minneapolis*
(CA-36), *Portland* (CA-33), and *Indianapolis* (CA-35). Three

Carrier *Lexington* (CV-2) Leaving San Diego, California, 14 October 1941. Planes parked on her flight deck include F2A-1 fighters (parked forward), SBD scout-bombers (amidships) and TBD-1 torpedo planes (aft). NA

of the five destroyers, *Porter*, *Drayton*, and *Lamson*, were later joined by two other destroyers, the *Flusser* (DD-368) and *Mahan* (DD-364), plus cruisers *Chicago*, *Astoria*, and *Portland*, with *Lexington*, the fleet guide, and together they became Task Force 12. Admiral Kimmel ordered the task force to move by a direct route to a point 400 miles 130 degrees (southeast) of Midway Island where *Lexington* would launch 18 gray, Vought SB2U-3 Vindicators of Marine Scout Bombing Squadron 231, which had been based at Ewa. The 18 VMSB-231 planes were to land at Midway to reinforce the island's garrison.[15]

The cruiser *Indianapolis* and five high-speed destroyer-minesweepers, the *Dorsey* (DMS-1), *Elliot* (DMS-4), *Hopkins*, and *Long* (DMS-12) were bound for an amphibious exercise at Johnston Island, southwest of Oahu, while the *Minneapolis* and four destroyer-minesweepers, *Boggs* (DMS-3), *Chandler* (DMS-9), *Hovey* (DMS-11), and *Lamberton* (DMS-2) were proceeding to gunnery exercises south of Oahu.[16]

At the conn when *Lexington* moved out of the harbor was

the commander, Captain Frederick C. Sherman, along with the Executive Officer, Commander Wallace M. Dillon, and the Navigator, Commander James R. Dudley. The carrier passed the channel entrance buoys at 0806 and brought the Vindicators from VMSB-231 aboard at 0940 hours. Commanded by Major Clarence J. "Buddy" Chappell, they landed aboard *Lexington* after a 1.7 hour flight from Ewa.

At sea, Task Force 12 then turned starboard to a course due west, 270 degrees, and at 1103 hours left the formation preparatory to landing the *Lexington* Air Group aboard the carrier. The ship maneuvered at various courses and speeds until 1202, when the last aircraft in the Group came aboard. During the recovery, at 1121, one fighter aircraft tailhook missed the arresting gear on landing, and the plane crashed into the barrier protecting aircraft parked on the forward flight deck. The pilot received slight facial lacerations. Following the Air Group landings, *Lexington* turned port, back to course 270 degrees and resumed her position in the Task Force formation.

Task Force 12 sailed with Rear Admiral John H. Newton, commander, Cruisers, Scouting Force, flying his flag from the cruiser *Chicago*. Unlike [Admiral Halsey on *Enterprise* when she sailed with Task Force 8 on 28 November], Newton had no indication that his mission might run into war. His orders being to reinforce Midway, then "return to operating area and resume normal operations," there appeared to him "no special significance attached to it other than reinforcement." He thought there might be some danger from submarines, so he kept to a speed of seventeen knots by day, zigzagged, and sent out scout flights to cover his advance. These were "normal operations in connection with training." Again, unlike Halsey, he "gave no special orders regarding arming of planes or making preparations for war other than had been routine."[17]

All three of the Pacific Fleet's three aircraft carriers were now at sea, *Enterprise* with Task Force 8, sailing on an easterly course toward Pearl Harbor, returning from her mission to strengthen the garrison at Wake Island; *Lexington* with Task Force 12, outbound from Pearl Harbor toward the west to reinforce the garrison at Midway with additional aircraft; and *Saratoga* steaming south along the mainland's West Coast to rejoin Pacific Fleet units in port at San Diego.

Far to the south of Oahu on 5 December, Task Group 15.5, the heavy cruiser *Pensacola* and gunboat *Niagra*, escorting the seven ships of Convoy 4002, "Operation Plum," crossed the equator, moving slowly at speeds approximating nine and one half knots, still on a southerly route bound for Manila, Philippines.

Approximately 960 miles north of Oahu on 5 December the Imperial Navy's Carrier Striking Force, with all its 32 ships darkened, refueled from the oilers *Toho Maru*, *Toei Maru*, and *Nippon Maru*, the carriers *Hiryu* and *Soryu* given priority. After the refueling was complete around 1130 hours, the three oilers of the Second Supply Group, in company of the destroyer, *Arare*, turned away to make for a designated rendezvous with the carrier force during return to the home islands. The next day, with the destroyer *Kasumi* escorting, oilers of the First Supply Group would refuel every unit in the carrier force before turning toward a designated rendezvous point for another refueling on 8 December. Once the Carrier Striking Force dropped off its remaining oilers, the formation would accelerate to 24 knots for its dash to a point approximately 200 miles north of Oahu.[18]

On Oahu: Boat Day, Charity Football, "Battle of the Bands" and Tranquility

"Boat Day" was in full swing at noon in Honolulu Harbor, on Friday, 5 December, when the *Lurline* prepared to sail to San Francisco on its twice monthly triangular voyage to San Francisco, Los Angeles and return. The gleaming white ship had arrived at her berth in Honolulu Harbor two days earlier carrying her normal passenger load, including the Willamette and San Jose State University football teams, with their coaches and small groups of fans and cheerleaders. The ship's crew and port authorities efficiently completed a rapid, two-day turnaround for *Lurline*'s return voyage to the States.

The 784 [outbound] passengers—a record number because the SS *Matsonia* had been converted to a troop ship, leaving almost no transportation to California—were in a festive mood. Socialite model Miss Marjorie Petty and University of Hawaii President Dr. D. L. Crawford were among the group, which consisted primarily of defense workers returning to their homes on the West Coast. Local singers, accompanied by the Royal Hawaiian Band, sang their favorite island tunes, hula girls danced, and fragrant flower leis were everywhere. Thousands of kamaaina residents joined the celebration surrounding the departure of Matson's "Great White Ship."[19]

Friday evening for Joey and Bob was dinner on *Tennessee* again, with another movie. Bob, scheduled for duty as Officer of the Deck early Saturday morning from 0400 to 0800 hours, enjoyed his time with Joey before driving her back to the apartment, kissing her goodnight, and returning to the ship.

As Officer of the Deck, Bob's one entry typed in the ship's deck log that was signed later by Captain Reordan, was at 0745 hours. "Commenced embarking Landing Force for Annual Military Inspection." After Bob completed and signed his entry, he stopped by his quarters, picked up personal belongings he needed, and left the ship for Pearl's main dock, across the harbor, via motor launch, for the drive back to their apartment, and a well-earned rest.[20]

On Saturday, 6 December, Joey's last day with the Canada Dry Bottling Company, she typed a two-page letter home, the first page on company letterhead stationery with the heading of INTER-OFFICE CORRESPONDENCE. Her enthusiastic letter told of Christmas plans including an open house for the men of Bob's 5th Division.

Dearest Family –

Just a note to go off on the clipper—or rather to be started and finished later because I just thought that the clipper doesn't leave till Dec. 12,—It's been raining ala Bremerton lately—with only one difference—I swear this is the craziest weather—The sun shines and the sky is a lovely blue with clouds floating around, and the rain comes down in buckets. Last night I went out to the ship for dinner and the movie. Bob drove me in. Twas a gorgeous night with the stars and clouds and a lunar rainbow and the rain came down and down. I received an announcement from the Skipton's of Gael's wedding. I have some Hawaiian print cocktail napkins which I'm going to send, but there was no card or address at all in the announcement. Do you have her address or her folks address? This is my last day at work—thank goodness. I haven't even started on my Xmas preparations. And there are going to be many. I don't know yet whether or not I'll be able to get a tree cuz there is a shortage of trees. They all have to be brought in from the Mainland. A 2-footer costs about $1.00 a foot. Whee. I'm having open house on Xmas day for all the men in Bob's division—there are about 70 to a division, but I think that only 25 will be able to come—some have to stand watch. I'm going to get a 28-lb turkey and have it roasted at one of the hotels—and have a large stocking— say would you please send out my big stocking? It will be just about right to hold all of the gifts for the men—just small things. I don't know where I'll put them, but if we have to park them on the stairs outside, we'll do it. Bob and I are compromising this year on Xmas. He has always opened his presents in the morning, but had never gone to church Xmas Eve—so he's going to church with me, and I'm going to wait till Xmas morning to open any of my things. Incidentally, dad, DO YOU HAVE THE NEGATIVES OR THE PRINTS OF THE THREE PICTURES I SENT YOU FROM LONG BEACH— two of which were taken on our honeymoon #1 and one of them taken in Long Beach. We have an album now, and I want those to go in it because they are the only ones we took in California. As long as we aren't coming back for Xmas, we'll probably be back sometime in January. Bob is going to put in for 30 days leave so that we'll have plenty of time to travel. Mom, I hope you haven't given away those sno-paks which I brought out from Minnesota because I'll probably need them in Minn. when we go back. I sent Auntie some Hawaiian jelly and jam besides the ivory pin. I think that Aunt Anna and Betty are the only ones I missed, and I'm sending them something via clipper. You never did tell me how those colored stills you took of me in wedding gown etal came out. Were they any good? I think that Bob would like to have one if they are good at all. And, dad, you never mentioned whether or not you received the check I sent for my bill at the Club and Bob's watch or whether or not it is on the way. What's the dope? If you didn't receive the check, we'll cancel it. I also ordered a Navy ring for Bob because he wants that more than anything—to the tune of $75—but I've earned enough to pay for it myself—I can't quite get used to the idea of buying Bob a present and then presenting him with the bill,——maybe that takes time. We had a letter from Missy last week—they can hardly wait for us to get to Pensacola as a matter of fact, Bob is getting pretty impatient himself. Must stop—have been rambling on for too long—though there isn't much doing in the office today . . . .

More later
Joey[21]

When kickoff for the football game between the University of Hawaii and Willamette University of Salem, Oregon began at 2:30 p.m. Saturday afternoon, the carrier *Lexington* and Task Force 12 were continuing on their heading west from Hawaii, bound for the designated launch area to reinforce Midway with additional aircraft. At the standard speed of 17 knots, occasionally reduced fleet speed of 10.5 knots and altered headings to conduct flight operations, the Task Force was approximately 480 miles west of Oahu.[22]

The carrier *Enterprise* with Task Force 8 had delivered the twelve Marine F4Fs to reinforce Wake Island, and was on a base course of 093 degrees, almost due east, approximately 540 miles west, southwest of Oahu, returning to Pearl Harbor. The destroyer *McCall*, was alongside starboard of *Enterprise*, refueling.[23]

Since its inception in 1920 the annual invasion of mainland football teams to play the University of Hawaii had become the largest, most important, and colorful sports spectacle in the Hawaiian Islands. A series of intercollegiate charity benefit games sponsored by the Aloha Chapter of the Shriners, the December sports contests between mainland schools and the Rainbows had grown in popularity and attendance in the 21 preceding years.

The history of the event included such notable colleges and universities as the University of Nevada, which sent their Wolfpack as the first visiting team, and took the measure of the Rainbows, 14-0; the University of Oregon, St. Mary's, Pamona, Oregon State, Colorado, San Mateo, Colorado State, Washington, Washington

State, Utah, South Dakota State, Utah State, Occidental College, University of Denver, Oklahoma, Idaho, Brigham Young, California, University of Southern California, Santa Clara, Drake University, College of the Pacific, San Diego State, the Green Bay Packers professional team, and more. The first game this year was being played on the same day of the month as the first game against Nevada in 1920.[24]

This year, the profits from the first game, between the Rainbows and the Bearcats, was for crippled children. The police fund would receive the profits from the second game, scheduled for Saturday, 13 December, between the Rainbows and the San Jose State Spartans. The Spartans and the Bearcats were to play one another the night of 16 December, before boarding *Lurline* for the return voyage to San Francisco, and trips home before Christmas.

From the visiting teams' arrival on Wednesday, through Saturday morning's 6 December issues, the sports pages of Honolulu's two major newspapers, the *Advertiser* and *Star-Bulletin* published a steady stream of articles about the Bearcat and Rainbow teams' and coaches' records, strengths and types of play expected of them; star players and their individual strengths, daily practice schedules, starting line-ups, and details and instructions for pre-game ceremonies.

The newspapers urged fans to be in their seats by 1:15 p.m., when a parade of 14 marching bands led by color guards with the flags of Hawaii and the United States, began assembling on the football field, the marching order based upon which bands had participated the most in the years since the event's inception. The Marine Band led the 14 onto the field, and the Shriners' crack drill team entertained the crowd at halftime, as did the massed bands playing together.

When the kickoff came at 2:30, the crowd had swollen to an estimated 24,000, the largest in the event's history, and just shy of the stadium capacity of 25,000. Giving away two inches in average height and six pounds per man in weight, the Rainbows, with a 7 and 1 record, were favored by 12 points over the Bearcats. The men from Willamette University sported an 8 and 1 record and clinched the Pacific Northwest Conference title, while leading the nation's small colleges in total offense of 430.5 yards per game, 300.8 passing and 129.7 passing. What's more, they outscored opponents 314 to 47 total points, and held six of their nine opponents scoreless.[25]

Before a stadium filled with excited football fans, the Rainbows and the Bearcats battled through a close first half, with Hawaii holding a slim 7-6 lead. As predicted, it was a wide open game. The Bearcats, using short and long passes, and multiple formations including a man in motion off the single wing with an unbalanced line, had so outplayed the Rainbows, however, that bettors had changed the odds to favor them for the second half finish.

In the second half, the Bearcats were unable to mount a consistent offense against a practiced, hard-nosed defense that included a game total of seven intercepted passes, by a pass defense noted for its weakness—and the Rainbows completely reversed their fortunes. The Hawaiian's stormed down the field in the first three and a half minutes of the third quarter to go ahead, 14-6, and locked the victory away with four minutes left, by punching over another touchdown.[25]

In the crowd watching the game were the San Jose State Spartans and their coaches, scouting their two opponents. The happy Rainbow fans now looked forward to the next game, on 13 December, while the Bearcats mentally began preparing to take the measure of the Spartans the night of 16 December.

Far to the southwest of Oahu, en route to Honolulu, was the American Presidents Line's SS *President Coolidge*, and a sister ship, the US Army Transport *General Hugh L. Scott*, formerly the SS *President Pierce*. Escorted by the Pacific Fleet's light cruiser, *Louisville* (CL-28), *Coolidge* and *Scott* were carrying passengers being evacuated from the Southeast Asian region due to rising tensions and the American government's urging employees and their dependents, as well as military dependents, to return to the United States.[26]

Saturday evenings on Oahu were normally filled with relaxed revelry, sprinkled with "happy hours" in the local hotel lounges and bars, dinners at restaurants and clubs, dances, floor shows, quiet gatherings with families and friends, and walks on the beaches. On the military installations, in the officers' clubs, enlisted recreation centers, and other locations on bases and posts, similar activities occur.

Tracing its origins to the early 1900s, the Navy's School of Music opened in Washington, D.C. in 1935 and operated in conjunction with the U.S. Navy Band. Students enrolled in the school in this era were interviewed in advance, selected for attendance, graduated in complete ensembles, and transferred aboard ship. For example, Band No. 13, until 1 December 1941, was on board the light cruiser *Raleigh* (CL-7) when it was temporarily shifted to the destroyer tender, *Dobbin* (AD-3). Band No. 22 was assigned to the battleship *Arizona*.

At Pearl Harbor, a crowd gathered at the new Bloch Recreation Center the night of the 6th for "The Battle of the Bands," the last elimination round of a Pacific Fleet music tournament begun the previous 13 September and held every two weeks, with the final competition planned for 20 December. The Bloch Recreation Center was a place designed to give the enlisted man every kind of relaxation the Navy felt proper—music, boxing, bowling, billiards, and 3.2 beer. Called by some "The Battle of Music," "The Battle of the Bands" featured Navy bands primarily from "capital ships" home ported in Pearl Harbor and those attached to shore installations in Hawaii. Four bands were to compete in each round of the tournament with one winner per round selected to perform in the final competition rounds. The *Arizona* band won the first round in September, and several of its members attended this night, to listen to their future "competition"—tonight's winner.

Each band performed a swing number, a ballad and one specialty tune, then played for the jitterbug contest. Competing this final night of the elimination round, were only three bands. As the men stomped and cheered, bands from the battleships *Pennsylvania* (BB-38) and *Tennessee*, and the fleet support ship, *Argonne* (AG-31), fought it out to go to the finals. The *Pennsylvania* band won, everybody sang "God Bless America," and the evening wound up with dancing. When the crowd filed out at midnight, many argued that the best band of the tournament thus far was the *Arizona*'s.[27]

The presence of two thirds of the Pacific Fleet in Pearl Harbor, with a considerable number of men from each ship's crew on liberty for the evening; the Army always present with it's units at reduced strength because of weekend passes and leaves, the Hawaiian Air Force standing down for the night before the somewhat lessened pace of weekend duties, adds to the already busy whirl of social activities and romance on the island. Despite the ominous, rapid, ratcheting up of tensions in the Pacific, and the quiet, hurried, usually one-on-one meetings involving senior officers and their key staff officers, this Saturday was little different than all Saturday's on Oahu. The threat of hostilities on Oahu seemed farfetched to all but a few.

Rear Admiral Claude C. Bloch, Commandant of the 14th Naval District spent his evening at home. He played golf in the afternoon, read for awhile, then, very tired, went to bed about 8:30 p.m. Rear Admiral Patrick N.L. Bellinger, the commander of Patrol Wings ONE and TWO and their attendant surface units, had an even less eventful evening. The flu had taken him down on Tuesday, and Sunday would be his first day up.

Some of the Army Air Force officers, including Major General Martin, attended a dinner party at the Hickam Field Officers' Club. Lieutenant Colonel James A. "Jimmy" Mollison, Martin's chief of staff, was at a similar function in the home of Lieutenant Colonel William C. Farnum. While there, at about 2230 hours, he received notice of a long-distance phone call from San Francisco saying that twelve B-17s would arrive at Hickam from the mainland at 0800 the next morning. Mollison called the duty officer to give him the estimated time of arrival. Because Mollison wanted to be sure he would be in the tower when they came in, he left the party immediately and went straight home.

Lieutenant General Short, the Hawaiian Department Commander, and Major General Durward S. Wilson, the 24th Infantry Division Commander were among those attending "Ann Etzler's Cabaret"—an annual charity dinner-dance which "one of the very talented young ladies had worked up" at Schofield Barracks Officers' Club. Before going to the club, a large group, including General and Mrs. Short, gathered at the home of Lieutenant Colonel and Mrs. Emil Leard for cocktails. The Shorts left the club with Lieutenant Colonel and Mrs. Kendall J. Fielder, Short's intelligence officer, between 10:30 and 11:00 p.m. and went straight home. They drove past Pearl Harbor, a magnificent sight with all its lights blazing. Short remarked to his G-2, "What a target that would make!" He had no idea his words would come true the next morning. He was looking forward to his usual Sunday morning golf game with Admiral Kimmel.[28]

Earlier in the day on 6 December, the newspaper headlines on the mainland declared: ARMY TO TRAIN 30,000 BOMBER CREWS A YEAR; HOUSE PASSES DEFENSE BILL to expand Army to two million; DEFERRED MEN MAY BE DRAFTED; and NAVY TO WAIVE MENS DEFECTS, indicating physical standards were being lowered for new recruits.[29]

When Joey arrived at their apartment following her last day at work, Bob was already home. They relaxed the remainder of the day, calling on the *Tennessee*'s junior medical officer and his wife, the Marron's, then ate dinner at the Kau Kau Corner before returning to their apartment to play acey ducey and retiring for the night. They slept soundly, happy to be together again, thinking of love, Christmas in Hawaii, and not too many days until the next exciting assignment—Naval Air Station Pensacola, Florida.[30]

The First Shots of the Pacific War

While Bob, Joey, and the people of Oahu slept peacefully the night of 6-7 December 1941, armed forces of the Japanese Empire moved undetected, ever closer to the Island of Oahu from the north, west, and south. To the north, Vice Admiral Chuichi Nagumo's Carrier Striking Force, composed of the First, Second, and Fifth Carrier Divisions, plus their combatant escorts, support ships, and submarine screens, bore down on the island through rough seas. The United States Pacific Fleet's long range patrol aircraft, concentrating their daily search patterns primarily in an arc from the south, clockwise through west to northwest of the island, hadn't crossed paths with or observed from a distance the large, powerful Japanese fleet narrowing the distance between itself and its intended targets.

To the south, as well as from the north and west, the oncoming foe was of a different form, moving quietly, submerged during daylight hours, and on the ocean's surface at night, submarines and midget submarines. The Japanese Naval General Staff had concluded the planned submarine attack was necessary to obtain subsequent cumulative effects. The first priority was given to the air attack by the Carrier Striking Force. "The principal aim of the Submarine Force was render the result of the air attack more effective."

Its primary operational duties were the secret preliminary reconnaissance of the Lahaina Anchorage and other strategic points in the Pacific; the tracking down and destruction of the enemy fleet, which might run out of Pearl Harbor escaping the air attack, and the interception of any counterattack against the Carrier Striking Force by the enemy fleet; participation of the Submarine Force in the attack by midget submarines against the enemy fleet in the harbor; and rescue of aircraft crews which might be forced down during the air attack.[31]

In the event the attack by the Carrier Striking Force on Pearl Harbor succeeded, the Submarine Force would maintain submarine patrol and reconnaissance of Pearl Harbor for a long period after the Carrier Striking Force withdrew to home base. Additionally, the Submarine Force would disrupt enemy surface traffic between the West Coast of North America and Hawaii and launch attacks on enemy air bases lying between Hawaii and the Samoan Islands. Screening ahead of the Carrier Striking Force were submarines, *I-19*, *I-21*, and *I-23*, which were under the direct control of the Strike Force Commander.

Exclusive of the three screening submarines, when the First, Second, Third and Special Attack Groups left Japanese ports in November, in command of the overall submarine operation was the commander of the 6th Fleet, Vice Admiral Shimizu Mitsoyoshi, who would be aboard his flagship *Katori*, stationed at the Kwajalein Atoll. Because the remainder of the large submarine

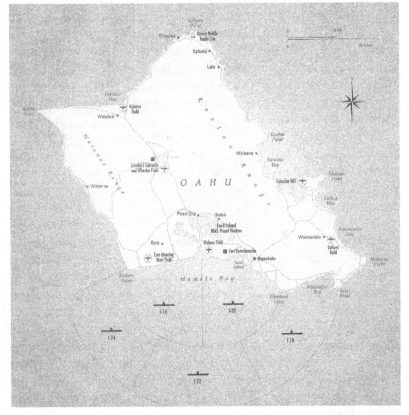

OAHU AND THE PARENT SUBMARINES

force would be in position at least 24 hours before X-day, he would maintain command until the air attack commenced, when all submarines would be under the Strike Force commander, Admiral Nagumo, for three days.

To complete their tasks and missions on and after 7 December, the First Submarine Group, consisting of *I-9, I-15, I-17* and *I-25*, was patrolling the sea northeast of Oahu, to track down and annihilate any escaping vessels, and be in readiness to intercept any counterattacks against the Carrier Striking Force. Assigned the same mission, the Second Submarine Group, composed of *I-1, I-2, I-3, I-4, I-5, I-6,* and *I-7*, was on patrol covering the area between and to the northeast of Oahu and Molokai, which was the primary passage and sea lane between the two islands, en route to and from Oahu and the West Coast of the mainland. Thus, on the morning of 7 December, these two missions initially interposed at some distance between them, two submarine groups along and directly astride the sea lanes from Oahu to America's west coast ports.

Patrolling south of Oahu, the Third Submarine Group, consisting of *I-8, I-68, I-69, I-70,*

I-71, I-72, I-73, I-74, and *I-75* had the same mission as the First and Second Groups, and in addition *I-72* and *I-73* were to perform a reconnaissance of the Lahaina Anchorage to determine whether or not major enemy ships were stationed there. By the morning of 7 December, the third Group was in position, the two submarines had completed their reconnaissance, reported no enemy units in the anchorage, and returned to stations south of Oahu. One other submarine in the group, *1-75*, was directed to remain on station near the northwestern most island of Niihau.[32]

In the meantime, the Special Attack Group's five carrier submarines, with their midget submarines, pressed toward assigned stations no greater then ten nautical miles from Pearl Harbor's entrance. Beginning midnight or shortly thereafter—the midgets' launch began. The five carrier submarines were large, Type C.1 cruiser submarines deployed on stations within defined sectors of a half-circle area adjoining the south shore of Oahu. The five sectors overlaid the restricted area just outside Pearl Harbor's entrance, an area in which no American submarine was to operate submerged.

In the inner two sectors at a range of 10 kilometers (6.2 miles) were *I-16*, to the southwest of Pearl Harbor's entrance, and *I-20*, at the same distance to the southeast. On the same bearing as *I-16* from the harbor entrance, at nearly 12.5 miles to the southwest, was *I-24*, with *I-18* on the same bearing as *I-20*, and the same 12.5 miles distance as *I-24*. The fifth cruiser submarine carrying a midget sub was *I-22*, which waited due south of Pearl's entrance, on the same roughly 12.5-mile radius as *I-18* and *I-24*.

The carrier submarines' maximum tonnage submerged was 3,561, considerably more than the American destroyers who later became their hunters. Each was 351 feet long, 30 feet abeam, had eight 21-inch torpedo tubes, and could carry twenty torpedoes. Additionally, each carried a 5.5-inch deck gun and two 25-mm anti-aircraft machine guns. Their two-shaft diesel engines gave them a maximum surface speed of 23.6 knots, and a maximum range of 14,000 nautical miles at 10 knots. They used two electric motors for submerged operation, yielding a maximum speed of 8 knots, and a range of 60 nautical miles at three knots. The submerged, most economical speed of 3 knots meant operating at that speed, the big submarines needed to surface in less than twenty hours to start their diesel engines and recharge the batteries for submerged operation.[33]

The first midget submarine launched was from *I-16*. Manned by Ensign Masaharu Yokoyama and Petty Officer 2nd Class Tei Ueda, the midget left at midnight. At 0116 hours, *I-22* released the midget commanded by Lieutenant Naoji Iwasa, leader of the midget submarines. At 0215, *I-18* launched the third midget, that of Ensign Shigemi Furuno and Petty Officer 1st Class Shigenori Yokoyama. At 0257, the fourth midget submarine was launched from *I-20*. This midget was commanded by Ensign Akira Hiroo and Petty Officer 2nd Class Yoshio Katayama. Last to launch was *HA-19* from *I-24* at 0333 hours. Commanded by Ens. Kazuo Sakamaki and Chief Warrant Officer Kiyoshi Inagaki, *HA-19* slipped off the deck of *I-24* some 10-1/2 miles off Pearl Harbor and headed for the lights of Honolulu.

The midget each cruiser submarine launched was a Type A "Midget," carried two crew members—normally an officer and one enlisted, two 18-inch bow torpedo tubes, and two torpedoes. They displaced 46 tons, were 78 feet in length, not quite one-third the length of their carrier submarine, and were a maximum circular diameter at the beam of 6 feet. Their 600 horsepower electric motor could push them to speeds of 23 knots surfaced and a substantial 19 knots submerged.[34]

Also approaching Pearl Harbor from the south, with its skipper,

Aerial photo of Pearl Harbor, view to the south, beyond
the harbor entrance, October 1941. NA

Commander Lawrence C. Grannis, was the USS *Antares* (AKS-3),
towing a 500 ton steel barge to Pearl from Palmyra Island. *Antares*,
an 11,450 ton ship with a maximum speed of 11.5 knots, was the
flagship of the 8th Training Squadron, and, as a utility auxiliary had
been used frequently in amphibious training with the Marines until
she was reclassified as a general stores ship in November 1940.[35]

Operating in the area outside Pearl Harbor the same morning,
under the command of Commander John B. Wooley, were ships
of the Inshore Patrol Command, the minesweepers *Condor*
(AMc-14) and *Crossbill* (AMc-9). The Patrol Command's duty
destroyer in the area was the USS *Ward* (DD-139), a World War
I vintage "four stacker." On 5 December, thirty-five year old
Lieutenant William W. Outerbridge proudly took command of
the *Ward*, and at 0628 on the 6th took his first sea command out
for a routine harbor entrance patrol. Less than twenty-four hours
later, the morning of 7 December, life for Outerbridge and the
Ward's crew changed abruptly.[36]

When the *Ward*'s new commander came aboard, he was well-
sensitized to the state of relations between Japan and the United

States. What's more the Patrol Command had received orders
that changed the rules of engagement under which the Command
would conduct their mission. Admiral Kimmel, reacting to the
top secret war warning message of 27 November, had issued new
orders to depth charge any submerged submarines found in the
restricted area outside the harbor entrance.[37]

Gordon W. Prange, in *At Dawn We Slept*, recorded the chain
of events that followed the deployment of the Japanese Empires'
midget submarines early the morning of 7 December.

> A waning moon peeked through the broken overcast
> to glimmer on the waters off Pearl Harbor. About "1-
> 3/4 miles south of entrance buoys," the minesweepers
> *Condor* and *Crossbill* plied their mechanical brooms.
> At 0342 something in the darkness "about fifty yards
> ahead off the port bow" attracted the attention
> of Ensign Russell G. McCloy, *Condor*'s Officer
> of the Deck. He called to Quartermaster Second
> Class R.C. Uttrick and asked him what he thought.
> Uttrick peered through binoculars and said, "That's
> a periscope, sir, and there aren't supposed to be any
> subs in this area."[38]

The *Condor*, with a mission to hunt for magnetic mines, hadn't the
means to take action, other than report the two men's observations
and conclusion to the *Ward*. While preparing his message to the
Ward Ensign McCloy chose two means of transmission to ensure
the destroyer received word of the intruder. At 0357 hours *Condor*
signaled by yardarm blinker and transmitted by radio: "Sighted
submerged submarine on westerly course, speed 9 knots." Aboard
Ward, on receiving the message, Outerbridge considered it likely
that *Condor* had in fact spotted a submarine, but he needed more
information. The following exchange ensued, monitored by the
Naval Radio Station at Bishop's Point:

> Ward: "What was the approximate distance and
>   course of the submarine sighted?"
> Condor: "The course was about 020 magnetic and
>   some 1,000 yards from the harbor entrance."
> Ward: "Do you have any additional information?"
> Condor: "Negative—no additional information."

Ward: "When was the last time you saw the sub?"
Condor: "Approximately 0350. It appeared to be
heading for the entrance."
Ward: "Roger that Condor. We will investigate."

At 0408 Outerbridge ordered "General Quarters" (Battle Stations), and *Ward* accelerated, while going on the hunt for the intruder. The search, conducted visually and by hydrophone, yielded no results and at 0435 Ward radioed, "No contact on unidentified sub. Securing from General Quarters." Since there had been a number of false alarms in the recent past, neither the *Ward* nor the Radio Station at Bishop's Point relayed the incident to their respective commands.

At 0458 the *Condor* and *Crossbill* were admitted to the base after the gate was opened. Unaccountably, the gate remained open until 0840 hours. Later that morning it would be learned that at least one midget submarine passed through the open gate.

The series of events beginning to the south of Pearl Harbor's entrance resumed when, beginning at 0615 Navy Patrol Squadron 14 (VS-14) launched the first of three PBY-5 aircraft from Kaneohe Naval Air Station to patrol assigned operating areas. Plane 14-P-1, Bureau No. 2419, flown by Ensign William P. Tanner, with co-pilot Ensign Robert B. Clark, Ensign David H. Butler (navigator), Aviation Machinist Mate First Class Oscar L. Windham (Plane Captain), Aviation Machinist Mate Third Class C.W. Mallard (2nd Mechanic), Radioman First Class Albert L. Moore (1st Radioman), and Radioman Third Class William McClintock (2nd Radioman) was airborne at 0630 and was flying toward its area patrol south of Pearl shortly after takeoff.

The *Antares* arrived off the entrance to the harbor at 0630, with Commander Grannis expecting the ship's rendezvous with a tug to which she would transfer the barge for tow into Pearl, then enter the harbor. It wasn't yet daylight. The tug wasn't in sight, and Grannis ordered a turn starboard, to the east. While the slow turn progressed, a suspicious object was sighted at some distance on the starboard quarter. As Grannis stated in his 10 December written report to Admiral Kimmel, "This object could have been a small submarine with upper conning tower awash and periscope partly awash and periscope partly raised but it could not be positively identified as such." Almost simultaneously, 14-P-1, with Ensign Tanner at the controls, was passing through en

USS *Antares* (AKS-3). NHHC

Minesweeper *Condor* (AMc-14). NA

route to their patrol area and was approximately one mile south of the harbor entrance, when the co-pilot, Ensign Clark, spotted the submarine. At first he had difficulty convincing Tanner he had seen a submarine. Finally, he did, and Tanner immediately turned toward it to mark its position with two float lights. In the meantime events were coming to a head. *Antares'* commander had made up his mind, and a radio message went to *Ward* at 0637 hours, monitored by the radio station at Bishop's Point.

> **Antares:** "Partially submerged submarine spotted 1500 yards off our starboard quarter . . . seems to be having depth control trouble . . . trying to go down."
> **Ward:** "Roger USS Antares . . . stand by." Then came—
> **Ward:** "Antares we have visual contact with the submarine."

Lieutenant (jg) Oscar W. Goepner, was *Ward's* Officer of the Deck. The destroyer's helmsman saw the strange object first. He and Goepner decided it was probably the conning tower of a submarine, though "they had never seen anything like it" in the Navy. "Captain, come on the bridge," Goepner called to Outerbridge. The destroyer's captain, who had retired to a makeshift bunk rigged in the charthouse after the prior stand down from General Quarters, was on the bridge in seconds to have a look—with a World War I style "tin helmet" on his head, pulling on a life jacket over a kimono and pajamas. Outerbridge concluded the object was trailing the *Antares*, apparently headed toward the entrance to Pearl Harbor, and couldn't be anything but a sub. But whose?

At 0640 Outerbridge ordered General Quarters. The destroyer once more came alive as the crew scrambled to battle stations, quickly brought up ammunition, and began loading the guns. *Ward* accelerated, increasing speed from 5 to 25 knots, and turned on a course placing *Ward* on a virtual collision course with the Japanese sub.

As she bore down on the target, about fifty yards to starboard, abeam the destroyer, the Number One 4-inch gun crew trained their weapon around, aimed and fired the first shot of the Pacific War, just missing over the top of the conning tower. Ensign Tanner, with his crew observing the action from the air, began positioning the PBY for a depth charge attack. As the destroyer sliced through the water at 25 knots passing close to the submarine, the Number Three gun atop the galley deckhouse fired, and the round struck the conning tower at the waterline, which was at the intersection of the hull and conning tower. When hit, the sub appeared to heel to starboard, and begin to slowly sink. Several of *Ward*'s crew saw the damage inflicted by the second round.

From their position, the PBY crew concluded that the second round had missed as well, but it hadn't. As *Ward* surged past the submarine, which appeared to go under her stern, the crew dropped four depth charges set for 100 feet, to the required accompaniment of four blasts on the ship's whistle. Unknown to *Ward*'s the PBY's crew, the sub was mortally wounded and sinking in 1,200 feet of water when Ensign Tanner released two more depth charges from the PBY, aiming for where he believed the enemy's bow might be.

The attack was at 0645 hours, and Outerbridge immediately reported his action to the Fourteenth Naval District watch officer. "We have dropped depth charges upon sub operating in defensive sea area." Deciding almost instantly he should have been more

Destroyers *Chew* (DD-106) and *Ward* (DD-139)
at Hilo Sugar Docks wearing her pre-World War II paint,
The Territory of Hawaii, 22 July 1941. NHHC

definite, he radioed a second message: "USS *Ward* to Com 14—
Have attacked, fired upon and dropped depth charges upon
unidentified submarine operating in defensive sea area. A direct
hit from our number three gun on his conning tower. Followed up
with four ashcans. Oil slick 300 yards astern visible on surface—
Lt. William W. Outerbridge, Commanding Officer USS Ward
DD-139." The radio at Bishop's Point logged the second call at
0653. The USS *Ward*, with the first shots of the Pacific War, drew
the war's first blood—and it was Japanese.

Ensign Tanner, orbiting above with his crew of six in the VP-14
PBY-5, noted the oil slick's discoloration of the water in the area
where the submarine was last seen, and at 0700 hours sent a coded
message to the Commander, Task Force Three, the senior task force
at Pearl Harbor. The commander of Patrol Wing ONE acknowledged, but not the Commander of Task Force 3. About fifteen
minutes later ComTaskForce 3 requested confirmation. Tanner
replied, claiming the kill, "Sunk one enemy submarine, one mile
south of Pearl Harbor." Though the *Ward* eventually received
credit for the sub's sinking, the action by Ensign Tanner was the
first attack against the Imperial Navy by a United States aircraft.[39]

In the next few minutes, the reports from VP-14 and the
Ward were passed from duty officers on Ford Island, in Patrol
Wing TWO, the Fourteenth Naval District and the Pacific Fleet
operations center, then to senior Fleet staff officers, triggering
discussions, questions, considerations that this may or may not be
the beginning of an attack, requests for confirmation, the hurried
drawing up of a search plan—to the northeast sector for patrol
aircraft, and finally, informing Admiral Kimmel. He had arisen
about 0700 hours, and on hearing the information, expressed
frustration that the information got to him so late, and immediately
decided he would come down to the center—and wouldn't meet
General Short for their usual Sunday morning golf game.

At no point in the telephone calls, increased activity in the
command centers, and relayed reports did the Navy inform
the Army, hence its airfields, air command centers, the Army's
information center, and anti-aircraft artillery or coast artillery
units, that a submarine had been attacked and apparently sunk
in the restricted area one mile outside Pearl Harbor. Nor was
the Fleet informed or given warning. As events unfolded, the
oversights probably would have made little difference. Time was
already running out.[40]

Launching to Strike: The First Wave

At 0500 hours, 7 December the Japanese heavy cruisers *Chikuma* and *Tone* each launched an Aichi Type 0 floatplane, with *Chikuma*'s tasked to conduct a reconnaissance of Pearl Harbor and *Tone*'s to scout the Lahaina anchorage, south of Maui, where the Pacific Fleet had occasionally been observed at anchor. Assuming it was empty, *Tone*'s scout was to search the area south of Oahu in the hope of locating any American carrier force that might be in the area. The seaplanes were not to overfly their initial objectives, but skirt them, and neither would they send their reports before the two strike formations had been dispatched.

On board the six carriers, aircraft engines were turned over after 0530, and as aircraft were manned at 0550 hours, approximately 220 miles north of Oahu, the carriers with their escorts were turning port, to east, into a 30-knot wind. Fifteen minutes elapsed while the carriers turned and accelerated to 24 knots to ensure sufficient wind speed over the flight decks to launch the heavily-torpedo and bomb-laden Nakajima Type 97 B5N2 carrier attack aircraft, later commonly called "Kates" by Americans. Seas remained heavy with carrier decks rising and falling some 40 feet, their bows crashing through waves and sending spray over the decks. Normally, in exercises, aircraft launch might have been cancelled, but war and operational necessity took precedence.

In fifteen minutes following the first launch at 0605 hours, the Carrier Striking Force launched 185 planes scheduled for the first wave: 43 fighters, the single seat, light, fast, agile, well-armed Mitsubishi Type 0 A6M2, later named "Zeke" or "Zero" by Americans, which carried two, rapid-firing 20-mm cannons and two 7.7-mm machine guns; 49 high level bombers, the Nakajima B5N2 "Kate," each with a crew of three—pilot, observer/navigator/bombardier, and radio operator/gunner— in addition to its bomb or torpedo load, and one flexible, rear firing 7.7-mm machine gun; 51 carrier bombers, the Aichi Type 99 D3A1, later known as "Vals," which carried a two-man crew of pilot and radioman/gunner, with a weapons load of bombs and three 7.7-mm machine guns, of which two were fuselage-

Japanese fighters, called Zekes or Zeroes by Americans, warm up their engines for launch. Lead plane is Lt. Saburo Shindo's Zeke on the *Akagi's* flight deck. NPSAM

Japanese Navy Type 97 (Kate) torpedo bomber on take-off roll from the aircraft carrier deck of either *Zuikaku* or *Shokaku* early morning 7 December 1941, with ship's crewmen cheering "Banzai!" NHHC

Japanese Navy Type 99 (Val) dive bombers prepare to take off from an aircraft carrier during the morning of 7 December 1941. Ship in the background is the carrier *Soryu*. NA

mounted, forward-firing and one the gunner in the rear cockpit flexibly fired; and 40 more "Kates" which could perform the dual mission of torpedo planes.

The astonishing efficiency of the launch was marred only by the crash of one fighter whose pilot was quickly rescued by a destroyer, and another fighter's abort due to engine trouble. Thus, by 0620, approximately seventeen minutes before the *Antares* radioed the *Ward* about the second sighting of the Japanese midget submarine attempting to slip into Pearl Harbor, the first wave of 183 airplanes, Zeke's, Vals, and Kates, were airborne and marshalling preparatory to the attack on Pearl Harbor and other key military installations on Oahu.[41]

The first aircraft launched were the Zekes. The first 15 were not part of the raiding force and were to maintain combat air patrol coverage for the Carrier Striking Force from 0600 to 0900, while the Zekes with the air strike provided observation and top cover for the Kates and Vals, which flew off after them. "The aircraft from the Japanese carriers circled outwards—those from carriers in the port column [of ships] circled counter-clockwise while those in the starboard column circled clockwise: aircraft from the *Akagi* and *Soryu* and the *Zuikaku* and *Shokaku* climbed to 1,100 feet while those from the *Kaga* and *Hiryu* climbed to 550 feet." The signal for the formation to set course for Pearl Harbor, given by the mission leader, Commander Mitsuo Fuchida, also signaled the beginning of the climb to cruising altitude. The Kate torpedo-bombers, formed on the left side of the stream and climbed to 9,200 feet. The Kate horizontal-bombers flew to their right at 9,800 feet, and the Val dive bombers, further right at 11,100 feet. The Zekes climbed to 14,100 feet and were free to range over all the bombers and torpedo planes, which were led by Fuchida's high level bombers.[42]

Enterprise: Scouts Launch

At 0618 hours, while Admiral Nagumo's six carriers were successfully launching the last few of 183 aircraft toward Oahu from a position 220 miles north, approximately 215 miles west of Oahu, the carrier *Enterprise*, steaming toward Pearl Harbor in company with her screens, submarine screens and plane guards in Task Force 8, launched the first of eighteen Douglas Dauntless Scout-Bombers (SBDs), bound for NAS Pearl Harbor, on Ford Island. Originally scheduled to arrive approximately noon on 6 December, Task Force 8 had been slowed by a strong Pacific storm. The storm compounded the delay, when one of the destroyers split a seam in the heavy seas, further delaying progress and necessitating the carrier's refueling of the destroyers after *Enterprise* and her escorts were clear of the storm. The task force's delay proved to be a tragedy-shrouded blessing.

The Air Group Commander, Lieutenant Commander Howard L. Young, with a flag officer, Lieutenant Commander Broomfield B. Nichol, in the rear cockpit, led off, followed by Young's wingman, Ensign Perry L. Teaff in aircraft 6-S-2, with Radioman/gunner Third Class Edgar Jinks in the rear cockpit, and continued on toward the Naval Air Station. In addition to Ensign Teaff's aircraft, from Scouting Squadron Six (VS-6), there were twelve other aircraft from VS-6 and four from Bombing Six (VB-6). The last plane was airborne at 0629. Their mission was to complete a ninety degree sector search, 045 degrees to 135 degrees true, to a distance of 150 miles ahead of *Enterprise*, and land at NAS Pearl Harbor.

At 0637 hours, as planned, fourteen aircraft rendezvoused with Lieutenant Commander Hallsted L. Hopping and his wingman, Ensign John H.L. Vogt, in aircraft 6-S-1 and 6-S-3 respectively, at Point Option, a planned, designated point in the airspace along the ship's projected track. At the rendezvous, they split into eight, two-plane sections, each section to search a ten degree sector, with the Air Group Commander and his wingman out ahead, the ninth section, in the center sector, 085 to 095 degrees, pointing directly at NAS Pearl Harbor on Ford Island.

Unknown to *Enterprise* and Lieutenant Commander Young, the allotted search sectors placed the northern five sections, including Young's, on courses that would intersect the tracks of the Japanese air armada bearing down on Oahu from the north. The Japanese aircraft were well outside the range of *Enterprise*'s radar and scout aircraft. In plane 6-S-7, the section lead responsible for

Douglas Dauntless SBD-3 scout bombers from the *Enterprise* (CV-6). Aircraft in the foreground is 6-S-14 from Scout Squadron Six (VS-6), and was flown by Ensign Edward T. Deacon, with Radioman/Gunner Third Class Audrey G. Coslett in the rear cockpit. Below the tail of 6-S-14 is 6-S-2, flown by Ensign Perry J. Teaff, with Radioman/Gunner Third Class Edgar P. Jinks in the rear cockpit. In this composite photo the *Enterprise* can be seen below the squadron. NHHC

searching the sector 115 to 125 degrees—which pointed to the south of Oahu and Pearl Harbor—were Lieutenant (jg) Hart D. "Dale" Hilton and Radioman/gunner Second Class (RM2c) Jack Leaming. Their wingmen in plane 6-B-5 were Ensign Edwin J. Kroeger, pilot, and RM2c Walter F. Chapman.

PLANE	PILOT	RADIOMAN	SECTOR
CEAG	LtCom Howard L. Young	LtCom Broomfield B. Nichol	085-095
6-S-2	Ens. Perry J. Teaff	Edgar P. Jinks, RM3c	
6-S-1	LtCom Hallsted J. Hopping	Harould "R" Thomas, RM1c	095-105
6-S-3	Ens. John H.L. Vogt	Sidney Pierce, RM3c	
6-S-4	Lt. Clarence E. Dickinson	William C. Miller, RM1c	105-115
6-S-9	Ens. John R. McCarthy	Mitchell Cohn, RM3c	
6-S-7	Lt(jg) Hart D. Hilton	Jack Leaming, RM2c	115-125
6-B-5	Ens. Edwin J. Kroeger	Walter F. Chapman, RM2c	
6-S-11	Ens. Carlton T. Fogg	Otis L. Dennis, RM3c	125-135
6-S-8	Ens. Cleo J. Dobson	Roy L. Hoss, RM3c	
6-S-10	Lt. Wilmer E. Gallaher	Thomas E. Merritt, RM1c	075-085
6-S-5	Ens. William P. West	Louis D. Hansen, RM3c	

(continued)

PLANE	PILOT	RADIOMAN	SECTOR
6-S-16	Lt(jg) Frank A. Patriarca	Joseph F. Deluca, RM1c	065-075
6-S-15	Ens. Walter M. Willis	Fred J. Ducolon, Cox	
6-S-14	Ens. Edward T. Deacon	Audrey G. Coslett, RM3c	055-065
6-B-9	Ens. William E. Roberts	Donald H. Jones, AMM3c	
6-B-3	Ens. Manuel Gonzalez	Leonard J. Kozelek, RM3c	045-055[43]
6-B-12	Ens. Frederick T. Weber	Lee E.J. Keaney, Sea1c	

Opana RADAR: Large Flight of Aircraft, Range 132 Miles

While the minesweeper *Condor* and the destroyer *Ward* were attempting to reacquire the Japanese submarine visually, or with hydrophone on the *Ward*, following *Condor*'s first reported sighting at 0350, five mobile SCR-270-B radars on Oahu were preparing to resume operations after being shut down for the night. Each radar (the acronym for radio detection and ranging) with its supporting equipment, mounted on four trucks, represented a new, still-developing and improving technology, which, in another form was on three ships in Pearl Harbor that morning, the battleships *West Virginia* and *Pennsylvania*, and the seaplane tender, *Curtiss*—in addition to the Pacific Fleet's three aircraft carriers now at sea, *Enterprise*, *Lexington* and *Saratoga*.

In July 1941 these [ground-based] radar sets began arriving on Oahu. Signal company personnel began assembling them at Schofield Barracks and then began learning how to operate them. Once assembled, [they were moved] to prepared sites throughout the island. The Signal Corps planned to activate six sets. On the

ISLAND OF OAHU, TERRITORY OF HAWAII,
7 DECEMBER 1941

morning of the [7th] five were operational, with the sixth still at Schofield. The five operational sets were at Kaaawa, Opana, Kawailoa, Fort Shafter, and Koko Head, and were connected by phone to the Information Center also located at Fort Shafter. The sets began operating at 0400 . . . except at Opana, which came on the air around 0415 due to a delay for generator maintenance first thing in the morning.

The Opana crew had been on duty since noon on Saturday. They divided their time between standing guard, maintenance, and operating the sets. The schedule called for each site to have a crew of three: one operator, one plotter, and one person to maintain the power generators. Because several units worked off commercial power and used generators as standby power, some crews cut back to two people per shift on the weekend. Opana had two crew members that Sunday morning.

. . . At 0613, radar at Koko Head and Fort Shafter began picking up sightings south of the island. Then at 0645, Kaaawa, Opana, and Kawailoa picked up a target approximately 135 miles north of Oahu. All three stations called the Information Center with the target, which were then plotted on the master plot board.[44]

The five plotters on duty within the Information Center the

hour before their shift was to end, saw nothing unusual in the reports. The Opana Mobile Radar Site, on a knoll in the foothills of the Koolau Range near Kahuku Point, the northern most point on Oahu, was manned by Privates Joseph L. Lockard from Harrisburg, Pennsylvania, and George E. Elliott, from Chicago, Illinois, who were billeted at Kawailoa, ten miles away. Lockard was the experienced operator, while Elliott was still learning the system.

Opana was generally regarded the best site. Thus, when the 0700 hours shutdown time arrived, and the oscilloscope recorded images suggesting that something was wrong with the set, Lockard and Elliott had to decide what to do. At 0702 the two men observed what Elliott insisted was a large flight of aircraft at an azimuth of five degrees, slightly east of due north, at a range of 132 miles from their site. Their observation was reported to the Information Center at Ft. Shafter, the conversation with Private Joseph McDonald taking eight minutes while the duty officer, Lieutenant Kermit Tyler, listened and learned more about the Center's day-to-day operation.

Private McDonald and Lieutenant Tyler were the only two men remaining on duty in the center. Tyler, who was a fighter pilot assigned to the 78th Pursuit Squadron at Wheeler Field, had arrived on Oahu in February flying one of the 31 P-36s off the *Enterprise* after the carrier had brought them from San Diego as part of the build-up of the 14th Pursuit Wing. When Tyler came on his second day of duty at the center at 0400 there were seven or eight enlisted men on duty, but by 0700 they had left the center, their work day ended. Tyler's first day had been on Wednesday, 3 December, from 1200 to 1600, when there was also a skeleton crew manning the Information Center.

Among the plotters who had left the center by 0700, were men who, during normal hours of operation, stood around a large table and marked on a map information called in by the five radar sites. During normal operating hours, the controller and pursuit officer on duty could sit on a large balcony and look down on these activities, and in theory, with ground to air communications, and communications with radar sites, outlying anti-aircraft batteries, pursuit operations, and Naval flight operations officers, manage an air defense battle. On 7 December, however, the integrated air defense system hadn't been fully developed within the Army's

Hawaiian Department, or integrated with the Pacific Fleet's considerable air defense and long range patrol capability.

Elliott's report logged at 0720 in the Information Center that morning so impressed McDonald that he suggested Tyler take the phone. This time Lockard, the experienced operator, spoke with Tyler, and called the blips the biggest sightings he had ever seen. Lockard later regretted he didn't express the "biggest sightings he had ever seen," as a number—"over fifty"—which would have convinced Tyler the sightings weren't B-17s.

According to Gordon Prange, in *At Dawn We Slept*, "It never crossed Tyler's mind that this incoming flight could be enemy aircraft. It could have been planes from a Navy carrier . . ." He remembered that on the way to the Information Center that morning he had listened to Hawaiian music on station KGMB. He recalled a bomber pilot friend had told him the station played this music all night whenever B-17s flew in from the mainland to Hawaii, acting as a beam for the planes' navigators. Lieutenant Tyler's second-hand information was correct insofar as there would be B-17s arriving on Oahu that morning, and the radio played Hawaiian music, which offered the crews' use of on-board radio direction finding sets on the final leg of their lengthy, over water flights from the mainland.

Tyler instructed the Opana operators to disregard the information and "not to worry about it." Elliot and Lockard continued to plot the incoming Japanese force until 0740, when the contact was lost in the background interference as the planes approached Oahu.[45]

Twelve B-17s to Hickam Field

At 2000 hours the night of 6 December, Lieutenant Colonel George W. Bicknell, the Hawaiian Air Force's senior intelligence staff officer, received a phone call from Lieutenant Colonel Clay Hoppaugh, the signal officer for the Hawaiian Air Force. "We have a flight of

B-17s coming in from the mainland. Will you put Station KGMB on the air all night so planes can home in on the signal?" Bicknell, already frustrated because of an inconclusive discussion with Generals Martin and Short, regarding the transcript of a puzzling, lengthy, suspicious, 3 December telephone conversation involving a Tokyo newspaper reporter and Mrs. Motokazu Mori, the wife of a Japanese dentist living on Oahu—snapped at Hoppaugh. "Why don't you have KGMB on the air every night and not just on the night we have airplanes flying? You folks have the money to do it."

"We'll talk that over some other time," Hoppaugh replied. Bicknell called KGMB and asked it to stay on all night. The people working at the station didn't know why, but the Air Corps paid when it asked for this service. Actually, it was common knowledge that whenever KGMB played music all night, aircraft flew in next morning.[46]

The first of the twelve-plane stream of B-17Cs and Es which would arrive singly over Oahu the morning of 7 December, at approximately ten minute intervals, had begun departing from Hamilton Field, CA, twenty-five miles north of the Golden Gate Bridge about the time Colonel Hoppaugh placed his 8:00 p.m. call to Bicknell. The flight into Hickam Field was to be the first leg of a long, over-water journey to Clark Field, near Manila, to reinforce General MacArthur's Far East Air Force in the Philippines. The estimated time of arrival was 0800 hours, 8:00 a.m.

As part of the American buildup in the Pacific, the Army Air Force scheduled 16 B-17s to deploy to the Philippines through Hawaii in late November 1941. The 38th Reconnaissance Squadron from Albuquerque, New Mexico, would supply eight aircraft and the 88th Reconnaissance Squadron from Fort Douglas, Utah, would furnish the remaining eight. The aircraft would take off from Hamilton Field, California, for the long flight to Hawaii. Modifications to the aircraft, installing long-range fuel tanks in the bomb bay, and high winds, combined to delay the flight until the evening of 6 December. General Marshall became alarmed over the delay, partly due to the increasing indicators that hostilities were imminent, and sent Major General Hap Arnold to California to impress upon the crews the urgency of their mission and the potential danger they faced.

Arnold personally addressed the crews from both squadrons. "War is imminent," he told them. "You may run into a war during your flight." "If we are going into war, why don't we have machine guns?" asked Major Truman H. Landon, flight leader in the 38th, and mission leader for the 16 aircraft movement to the Philippines. Arnold explained that the distance to Hawaii was so great, the B-17s needed to carry as much fuel as possible. The real danger would be during the second leg of the trip. Not only did the planes have no ammunition and their guns were still packed in Cosmoline, they carried only a skeleton crew of pilot, copilot, navigator, engineer, and radio operator, and filled the rest of the normal crew of nine with key squadron specialists such as crew chiefs, some maintenance technicians, the squadron flight surgeon, a combat photographer—along with several aviation cadets acting as navigators. It was a calculated risk that war would not start until after the aircraft arrived in Hawaii, where the protective grease would be removed from the guns and the aircraft armed for the final flight into the Philippines. Crew member totals on the 16 aircraft scheduled were 138, including 46 officers, 20 aviation cadets, and 72 enlisted men.

As the flight prepared to leave Hamilton Field, two aircraft from the 38th experienced engine trouble and didn't make the mission. One aircraft from the 88th had problems and aborted the takeoff. Once airborne, another aircraft from the 88th had problems and returned to Hamilton Field. In all, four B-17Cs and eight B-17Es, spaced about ten minutes apart, made the flight to Hawaii, with crews totaling 104, including 35 officers, 14 aviation cadets, and 55 enlisted men. Among the total was the 38th Squadron's new flight surgeon, Lieutenant William R. Schick, on Captain Raymond T. Swenson's airplane, and a combat photographer, Staff Sergeant Lee R. Embree, on board First Lieutenant Karl T. Barthelmess's aircraft.

The long flight over water was uneventful, and no one experienced any major difficulties. The Navy had positioned ships across the Pacific for the aircraft to use as directional indicators, and as they neared Hawaii, radio station KGMB was playing Hawaiian music for them to use in locating the island. Captain Richard H. Carmichael from the 88th contacted Hickam Field tower at 0745 but was still too far away, and the transmission was too garbled for anyone to understand.

A few minutes later the B-17s from the 38th sighted the Hawaiian Islands and spotted a flight of what they believed to be fighter aircraft coming to meet them. Thinking they were Americans, the pilots were glad to have escorts for the remaining miles into the field. Lieutenant Barthelmess and his crew were particularly pleased, and Sergeant Embree had his camera ready when two of the fighters with fixed landing gear swung toward

Two Japanese Navy Type 99, Aichi D3A (Val) dive bombers fly near a U.S. Army 38th Reconnaissance Squadron B-17E (Serial No. 41-2408) that arrived over Oahu from California in the midst of the Japanese air raid. The B-17 was piloted by First Lieutenant Karl T. Barthelmess. Photographed by Staff Sergeant Lee Embree. NA

a position aft of the big bomber. Everyone on board was startled by what proved to be a firing pass when the two opened fire with machine guns, then with their excess overtake speed pulled up above the B-17 off to the left side. Embree didn't know it when he snapped a photograph of the "escorts," but they weren't fighters. They were Val dive bombers heading toward the same destination—for far different purposes.

The first of twelve B-17 crews of the 38th and 88th had quickly learned the hard way their fighter escorts weren't American, the first of many costly surprises on and above the island of Oahu, and below the surface of the waters surrounding the island.[47]

CHAPTER 5

"AIR RAID, PEARL HARBOR. THIS IS NOT DRILL."

Any officer or non-commissioned officer who shall suffer
himself to be surprised . . . must not expect to be forgiven.

Major-General Sir James Wolfe

As aircraft in the first attack wave departed the Japanese Carrier Striking Force, the accompanying battleships and cruisers catapulted seaplanes into the air to patrol to the east, south and west of the carrier force. The entire surface force then turned south on their original course while the carriers were bringing up weapons-loaded aircraft from their hangar decks for the second attack wave.

At 0705 the carriers turned east into the wind a second time, and approximately ten minutes later began launching their aircraft in exactly the same order and using the same procedures as the first wave. One dive bomber from the carrier *Hiryu* didn't take off due to engine problems, and soon after take off, two more Vals and a fighter turned back with engine malfunctions. By 0725 the second wave was airborne with 167 aircraft, winging its way toward Oahu. In just 90 minutes the Japanese had launched 350 aircraft toward their targets.

Later, they launched 23 fighters to give combat air patrol coverage over the carrier force from 1000 until 1115 hours, and replaced them with 15 fighters from 1115 to approximately 1300, when the second wave was due to recover. For combat air patrol during the fleet's withdrawal from the launch area between 1300 and 1730, they launched 18 for the first period, then nine for the remaining daylight hours. They held no aircraft in reserve for a third attack.

During the first wave's approach to Oahu, a thickening 5,000-foot layer of clouds provided the aircraft protection from potential

Japanese Commander Mitsuo Fuchida,
Air Strike Mission Leader

observers. At 0733 the cruiser *Tone*'s seaplane reported the Lahaina anchorage was clear, and at 0735 the cruiser *Chikuma*'s seaplane informed the approaching aircraft and their carrier formation that nine battleships, one heavy and six light cruisers were in the harbor. Three minutes later the same seaplane scouting Pearl Harbor reported the weather conditions all but perfect for the attack. Aside from the almost flawless execution of the operation during this phase, the only matters worth noting were the sunrise, which apparently bore a striking resemblance to the Japanese naval ensign (flag) and drew an appropriately mystical response from the mission leader, Fuchida, and as author H.P. Willmott wrote "- an almost surreal addition—the fact that as the Japanese aircraft approached Oahu, some of the aircrews tuned in the local radio station. It was playing a Japanese song."

At 0740 hours, the first attack wave arrived off Kahuku Point. According to the Japanese plan of attack, if surprise was achieved, the Kate torpedo-bombers were to lead the assault. If no surprise, the dive bombers and Kate horizontal-bombers would lead in the hope they would attract the defenders' fire and make things easier for the slower, more vulnerable torpedo-bombers. Fuchida would make the decision as to whether or not surprise had been achieved, and would fire one red flare to indicate surprise, and two if no surprise, which would determine the type aircraft to lead in the attack.

Assured of surprise, at 0740 he fired one flare, then noted that Lieutenant Masaharu Suganami, one of the fighter group leaders, must have failed to observe the signal because his planes didn't take their proper formation. He paused for about ten seconds, and fired a second flare to alert Suganami, hoping the signal would be correctly interpreted. Lieutenant Commander Kakuichi Takahashi, leading the dive bombers, saw the second shot, and taking it for the double signal, accelerated immediately for his dive bombers' attack run on Ford Island and Hickam Field. Lieutenant Commander Shigeharu Murata, leading the Kate torpedo bombers, saw what happened. Although he knew Takahashi erred, he had no choice but to lead his torpedomen to their target as soon as possible. Takahashi was well on his way, however, and bullets and bombs, instead of torpedoes, would be the first weapons to strike the blows on Oahu.

While Fuchida ground his teeth in angry frustration over the human error interjected into the precise tactical plan he and others had so carefully worked out, he soon realized that the order in

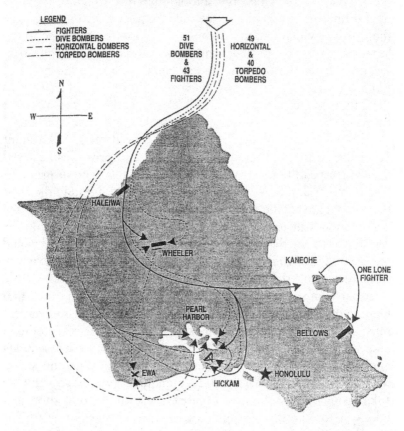

JAPANESE AIRCRAFT DEPLOYMENT FIRST ATTACK

LEGEND
— FIGHTERS
······ DIVE BOMBERS
– – HORIZONTAL BOMBERS
–·– TORPEDO BOMBERS

51 DIVE BOMBERS & 43 FIGHTERS

49 HORIZONTAL & 40 TORPEDO BOMBERS

WHEELER, EWA, FORD ISLAND, AND HICKAM HIT BY DIVE BOMBERS.
PEARL HARBOR HIT BY HORIZONTAL, TORPEDO, AND DIVE BOMBERS.
43 FIGHTERS ESCORTED BOMBERS DOWN THROUGH CENTRAL OAHU, THEN
BROKE OFF AND ATTACKED ALL INSTALLATIONS EXCEPT HALEIWA.
BELLOWS HIT BY ONE LONE FIGHTER.

Japanese Aircraft Deployment, First Attack.

which they attacked made little difference. Surprise was complete, and success assured. The only consideration remaining was degree.

Just northeast of Kahuku Point, the force formed into component formations, began changing altitudes, and turned toward the southwest to parallel the coast for a few miles. The 49 Kate horizontal bombers remained at their cruising altitude of 9,800 feet. The Vals climbed from their cruising altitude of 11,000 feet, to 13,000 feet. The Zekes, cruising and weaving back and forth above the Vals and Kates, at 14,000 feet, split into two groups, with 25 descending to 12,500 feet, and the remaining 18 continuing their descent to 6,500 feet. The 40 Kate torpedo bombers continued their descent from their cruising altitude of 9,200 feet to the lowest altitude possible, approximately 50 feet, as they closed on their targets. On reaching the Haleiwa area, the force split into two groups and took up separate headings toward their targets. The fighters were to race ahead of the Kates and Vals, and be in positions to sweep any enemy fighters from the air. The bombers assigned targets, necessary weapons loads against those targets, and direction of attack had been carefully coordinated, planned, mapped, studied and rehearsed.

Tactics for Surprise—and Deadly Weapons Loads

The Kates in both the first and second waves carried three different bomb loads. Forty in the first wave carried 800-kilogram (1,765 pounds), Type 91 torpedoes, one on each aircraft—specially modified with wood guidance fins for shallow water operation against the heavily armored Pacific Fleet combatants. Another 49 Nakajima Kates, the high-level bombers in the first wave, were loaded with 800-kilogram, specially modified, armor-piercing 16-inch naval shells, also for use against large ships. Thus, each high-level bomber in the first wave carrying the modified naval shell would have only one chance to hit its target.

The remaining 54 Kates, all in the second wave, carried a mixed load. Eighteen had two 250-kilogram (551 pound) bombs for land targets, and 36 carried one 250-kilogram bomb and six 60-kilogram (132 pounds) bombs, also for land targets. In addition all Kates carried a hand-operated, rear cockpit-mounted, 7.7-mm machine gun on a flexible mounting.

With a maximum speed of 235 miles per hour, Kates delivered their bomb loads primarily from the horizontal position, either at high altitude (around 10,000 feet) for those carrying the modified artillery shells, or at lower altitudes for those carrying smaller bombs, down to approximately 50 feet for those with torpedoes. Bombers with multiple bomb loads could drop them either singly, in pairs, or all at once depending on the targets attacked.

Fuchida had worked out a careful plan for the Kates in the first wave, to have the torpedo and high-level bomber forces each split to strike from two different directions simultaneously. Intending to increase the probability of a hit in delivering the single, 800-kilogram bomb from each Kate, he additionally instructed the high-level bombers to attack battleships tied up in pairs, rather than singly. He expected some of the ships to attempt escaping the harbor. To all the bomber crews he stressed the enormous additional benefit of sinking ships in the channel leading to the open sea, possibly blocking the entrance, and trapping the fleet inside the harbor.

The Val dive bombers in the first wave each carried a 250-kilogram land target bomb to strike airfields, and in the second wave, a 250-kilogram ordinary bomb for use against naval targets. Maximum speed was 240 miles an hour. In addition, each aircraft could carry two 60-kilogram bombs under the wings. Some eyewitnesses would later say they observed several dive bombers make multiple bomb runs, and these may have had the additional 60-kilogram bombs on board, although no Japanese records have been found supporting this claim. Dive angles during bombing attacks were an estimated 30-40 degrees with bomb release altitudes approximated 1,000 feet, and in some instances were as low as 300-400 feet. If additional dive bomb runs were made, they would probably be at shallower angles and lower release altitudes, appearing to ground or ship-based observers as "glide bombing." Each Val had two fuselage-mounted, forward-firing 7.7-mm machine guns, 500 rounds per gun, and a hand-operated, flexible-firing, rear cockpit-mounted 7.7-mm machine gun. After completing its bombing runs, the aircraft could make repeated strafing attacks.

The Mitsubishi Type 0 carrier fighters, were the Japanese Navy's best aircraft. On this morning, with a maximum speed of 310 miles per hour at 4,000 feet, they could outmaneuver anything stationed on Oahu. Armed with their two wing-mounted, rapid-fire 20-mm cannons, 60 rounds per cannon, and two 7.7-mm machine guns, 500 rounds per gun, mounted in the engine cowling, they also outgunned anything sent up against them. They each carried a centerline fuel drop tank to extend their range and time over the target area. Their primary mission was to protect the other aircraft against American fighters. After gaining air superiority, pilots would be free to attack targets of opportunity. They would meet little resistance and be largely free to wreak havoc on numerous targets.[1]

Fuchida, now solely in command of the Kate horizontal bombers, and the torpedo-bombers led by Lieutenant Commander Shigeharu Murata, continued toward Kaena Point. Before reaching the Point, Fuchida turned his formations further left, toward the south, staying west of the Waianae Mountains. These two groups continued in a wide turning arc, with the torpedo-bombers splitting again by turning more rapidly left, inside Fuchida's formation, before attacking Pearl Harbor. Fuchida's 49 horizontal bombers from the *Akagi*, *Kaga*, *Soryu*, and *Hiryu* swung south of the island, turning left toward their targets to make their bomb runs from southwest to northeast. Murata's 40 torpedo-bombers, turning inside Fuchida's force, split again with 16 from *Soryu* and *Hiryu* turning and descending east toward ships moored on the west side of Ford Island, and 24 from *Akagi* and *Kaga* swinging wide around and over Hickam, descending to attack Battleship Row, generally from southeast to northwest.

The group which first split from Fuchida's Kates and turned south to fly down the center of the island was composed of Lieutenant Commander Shigeru Itaya's Zeke's, escorting various units including the Val dive bomber force under Lieutenant Commander Kakuichi Takahashi. After separating from Fuchida, Takahashi's dive bomber force approached Wheeler Field from the north and slightly to the west, splitting into two more groups, 25 Vals from *Zuikaku* led by Lieutenant Akira Sakamoto targeted and further divided against Wheeler Field from the west and east, parallel with the runway and length of the parking ramp. Takahishi, seeing no evidence of air opposition, released the Zeke's from their top cover mission while his 26 Vals pressed on beyond Wheeler. Shigeru's 43 Zekes then accelerated, pushed ahead and split into three groups, 14 from *Soryu* and *Hiryu* to loop north and back toward the west and finally toward the south, to attack Wheeler. A second group of 11 from *Zuikaku* and *Shokaku* raced ahead and turned north toward Kaneohe— followed by 18 Zekes from *Kaga* and *Akagi*. Takashi's 26 Vals from *Shokaku*, after continuing past Wheeler, turned further left, toward the east, then back to the south toward Pearl Harbor as they separated into two groups of 9 and 17 to attack assigned targets at NAS Pearl Harbor and Hickam Field.

To the west of Pearl Harbor, at 0749 Fuchida gave his own formation of Kate level-bombers the attack order "*To, To, To*", the first syllable of *totsugekiseyo*, meaning "charge!" Four minutes later—and two minutes prior to the violent assault on the ships in Pearl Harbor—as Fuchida's horizontal bombers were turning onto the final approach for their bomb run, his radioman sent out the famous "*To-ra, To-ra, To-ra*" signal, the Japanese word for tiger. The carrier force and the battleship *Nagato*, Admiral Yamamoto's flagship in Japan's Inland Sea, picked up the signal at 0755, apparently due to favorable weather and ionosphere conditions.

Two minutes after Fuchida's command, "*To, To, To*," at 0751, the torpedo-bombers, led by Lieutenant Commander Shigeharu Murata of the *Akagi*, split into their four component groups. Sixteen Kates from the *Soryu* and *Hiryu* turned and began descending to attack ships moored west and north of Ford Island, while those from *Akagi* and *Kaga* flew to the southeast, turning left and descending in a wide arc around and across Hickam Field to come generally southeast to northwest across the harbor against the battleships.[2]

The Sinking of the SS *Cynthia Olson*

At approximately 0830 ship's time, 0730 hours Hawaii time, en route to San Francisco on northeasterly course, the SS *Lurline*'s Chief Officer, Edward Collins, stopped by the radio shack to have a chat with the officer of the watch, "Tiny" Nelson. Nelson was listening intently to communications traffic. Only a minute or so elapsed when Nelson began writing out a message on the typewriter. As he was listening and typing he called Collins' attention to read it.

The message was an SOS, the international emergency signal, from the 2,140-ton steam schooner SS *Cynthia Olson*, a ship

SS *Cynthia Olson*, first American flag-bearing merchantman sunk by the Japanese in World War II, a victim of submarine *I-26*. UDML

constructed by the Manitowoc Ship Building Company in Wisconsin, in 1919, and in 1941 operated in the lumber trade on the Pacific Coast. But on this day, en route from Tacoma, Washington since 1 December, she was under charter to the U.S. Army Transport Service, carrying lumber to Honolulu, Hawaii. This first message stated she was under attack by a surfaced submarine. The message was also picked up by a shore-based station on the Pacific Coast. The *Cynthia Olson*'s exchange with *Lurline* continued.

One of the cargo ship's final messages to *Lurline* stated they were under torpedo attack, and Collins asked Nelson to confirm the word TORPEDO. The brief reply stated it WAS a torpedo. "Tiny" had heard an earlier *Cynthia Olson* transmission giving her position in latitude and longitude, and he estimated her position as approximately 300 miles, bearing five degrees true, almost due north of *Lurline*.

The day before sending the SOS, the *Cynthia Olson*, captained by Merchant Marine Master Berthel Carlsen, was 300 miles off San Francisco, under way at 10 knots, when unknown to her crew, the Japanese submarine *I-26*, submerged at periscope depth and searching for potential targets, spotted and began tracking her. Commander Minoru Yokota, captain of the *I-26*, had been ordered to accompany *I-10* in reconnoitering the Aleutians, then after 5 December, to deploy to a point between San Francisco and Hawaii to report on American fleet units carrying reinforcements to Hawaii. Lastly, *I-26* was to destroy enemy merchant shipping after hostilities began.

The mission's duration sharply limited the big submarine's available space, including her hangar, because she was crammed with food and other supplies. Because of her overstuffed hangar, cargo and supply space, she carried only ten, old sixth year torpedoes of the seventeen she was capable of carrying.

The submarine continued following the *Cynthia Olson* southwest during daylight hours, while *I-26*'s navigator plotted the schooner's projected course. Yokota planned to surface at night, swing wide around her flank, pass her, and position his submarine along her projected course, to intercept and attack her at the moment hostilities were to begin on Oahu. The morning of 7 December, the submarine, having once more submerged to periscope depth prior to sunrise, intercepted the ship at exactly the projected point along her track. After Yokota established her nationality, *I-26* surfaced, and fired a warning shot. *Cynthia Olson*'s radio operator sent an immediate SOS, and the crew swung out her lifeboats. A shore station in California picked up the SOS at 0938 Pacific time, which was 0738 Hawaiian time.

Carlsen and his crew must have been profoundly shocked when *I-26* surfaced. The submarine was larger than their ship. Through binoculars the ship's officers were seeing a Junsen Type B.1 scout submarine 356 feet long and 17 feet abeam, 2,584 tons, and sufficient height—31 feet—to hangar a collapsible seaplane

Imperial Japanese Submarine *I-26*. IJN

that could be launched from a forward mounted, compressed air catapult, although on this mission the seaplane was left behind. The sleek, fast submarine was more than 100 feet longer than the *Cynthia Olson*. The *I-26* carried six forward torpedo tubes, an aft-mounted 140-mm (5.5-inch) deck gun, and two 25-mm antiaircraft machine guns.

The seaplane *I-26* normally took on her sorties, weighed 3,500 pounds, carried a crew of two, a payload of 340 pounds, and a rear-mounted 7.7-mm machine gun. The relatively light wood and metal-framed, cloth-covered wings and tail aircraft, had a top speed of 150 miles per hour, but normally flew at speeds near 85 miles an hour. When readied for launch, the wingspan was 36 feet. The engine was a Hitachi Tempu 9-cylinder, 340 hp, and the floatplane could remain aloft a maximum of 5 hours with an operating radius of 200 miles.

From a range of approximately 1,000 meters, *I-26* fired 18 rounds from her deck gun at the American ship, but the *Cynthia Olson* remained afloat. Twenty minutes after firing the first shot, *I-26* received Commander Fuchida's radioman's signal, "*To-ra, To-ra, To-ra*," submerged and fired a torpedo at the damaged target. The torpedo passed astern of the intended victim because the crippled ship was still making headway. The failure to hit *Cynthia Olson* with the single torpedo, caused Yokota to reassess his tactics. Only nine torpedoes left, and considerable time and distance remained on the assigned station off the United States' west coast. Yokota surfaced *I-26* again to open fire with her deck gun—this time with 29 more shells. The *Cynthia Olson* began settling. Yokota, concerned about a possible American air attack, decided the ship was sinking and *I-26* departed after being in the area a total of approximately two hours.

The *Cythia Olson*'s log of her final minutes preceded the last transmission to *Lurline* by the radio operator, and read:

0720 Watch relieved for breakfast.

Position by DR [dead reckoning] 1200 miles West of Cape Flattery, WA, Last position 145⁰ [degrees] 35' [minutes] W Longitude, 33⁰ 20' N Latitude, Cr [course] 278⁰, speed by log 10.4 Knots, Wind from SE, force 3, with low Easterly swell, clear, 15 miles visibility, stratocumulus clouds.

0725 Sighted submarine periscope, swung out boats, Onboard 33 Seamen, 2 U.S. Army Soldiers, total SOB [souls on board] 35.

0738 Under attack from surfaced submarine, sending SOS, answered by Matson's SS *Lurline*. All crew abandoning ship in lifeboats.

For the *Cynthia Olson*'s radio operator, time was running out after thirteen minutes. Undoubtedly, he was one of the last to leave the ship. The last message he sent to *Lurline*, confirming the torpedo attack, was sent before the surface attack that was fatal to his ship. The sequence of events also makes it clear the captain of the *Cynthia Olson*, Berthel Carlsen, did not command "All engines stop" when the first warning shot was fired. Nor did *I-26* hold its fire until the ship was abandoned. Emergency messages had continued while the submarine's rounds repeatedly slammed into the stricken ship—until she could no longer stay afloat. The *Cynthia Olson*'s Merchant Marine crew of 33 men, augmented by two regular Army privates, radio operator Samuel J. Zisking and medical technician Ernest J. Davenport, were never found. Records of Japanese submarine operations later disclosed *I-26* picked up no survivors. Records did disclose that Commander Shogo Narahara, the captain of Japanese submarine *I-19*, on Monday, 8 December, surfaced his boat when it passed through the area where the *Cynthia Olson* went down—and gave food to survivors in lifeboats. How many, if any, survived the sinking, and got into their boats but simply never made it to safety or were never found, and perished? No one will ever know. The vast Pacific keeps its answers in the deep—forever.

She went down approximately 1,000 miles northeast of Hawaii, while the first wave of the Japanese strike force was savaging American military installations and ships on the island of Oahu. She was the first American flagged merchantman sunk by the Japanese in World War II. Less than 45 minutes after "Tiny" Nelson received the *Cynthia Olson*'s SOS on *Lurline*, at 0915 Hawaii time The Great White Ship's skipper, Commodore Charles A. Berndtson, received word of another message, this one from Oahu. First transmitted from Ford Island at 0758 Hawaii time, 0858 on *Lurline*, the message was relayed around the world, and would become one of the most famous messages ever dispatched: "AIR RAID, PEARL HARBOR. THIS IS NOT DRILL."

In those minutes listening to and answering desperate calls for assistance from a ship too distant to save, and hearing the stunning broadcast from Oahu, *Lurline* sailed from peace into war. Nothing would be the same the remainder of this voyage to San Francisco—or ever—for her, her passengers and crew. What's more Commodore Berndtson and his officers now knew there was at least one enemy submarine, possibly more, lying in wait for their ship, between *Lurline* and San Francisco. She had no Navy escort, as her Matson Line sister ships had in traveling the routes from Hawaii to Manila and other Southeast Asian ports, and back to Hawaii. Much daylight remained and wartime precautions had to be taken without panicking the passengers.[3]

First Blows on Oahu—Shattered Military Air Fields and Aircraft

NAS Kaneohe Bay was home to three squadrons of Patrol Wing ONE, 36 PBY-5 "Catalinas," normally moored at waters edge, in hangars or on ramps, this morning with three on patrol. The squadrons were VP-11, 12, and 14. The morning was quiet and routine until a message arrived in the communications office. Lieutenant Murray Hanson vividly recalled what transpired.

> "Lieutenant, this is the comm. Office. You'd better come up here. One of your pilots just sent a message to the commander in chief that he bombed a submarine one mile south of Ford Island. CINCPAC sent him a Jig on it."
>
> I told him I'd be right up. I was leader of my division of VP-14, a Navy sea-plane patrol squadron, flying PBY-5 "big boats" assigned the dawn patrol that day. Stationed at the Naval Air Station, Kaneohe, Hawaii, I had just launched my planes to search at first light. I was killing time in our hangar, reading the morning paper, until the planes returned. I [was to] debrief the crews, service the aircraft and secure the hangar.

In naval communications parlance JIG means, "verify and repeat your message." The encoded contact report from my plane was so startling in its import that CINCPAC wanted him to recheck the encoding to make sure it had been done accurately, and then repeat the message to him. It was 7:30 Sunday morning. Kaneohe was 13 miles from Pearl Harbor and sheltered the bulk of the naval aviation—both land planes and sea-planes—in the islands at that time.

Waiting in his office for the message to repeat, the communications duty officer and I chatted and looked out the window toward Kaneohe Bay with the beautiful Koolau mountains in the background. It hadn't entered our minds that the message wasn't just a garble. Not until 10 seconds later. As we waited we saw and heard aircraft flying low over the station. The Army Air Corps had been flying maneuvers that week. He said to me, or I said to him (I'll never remember which), "This is the first time I've ever seen the army WORKING on Sunday." Then as one of the planes flew down past Lt. Northrup Castle's station boathouse and over our seaplane operating area, one of our aircraft anchored out there burst into flames. Almost simultaneously the intruding plane did a chandelle, and as it rolled away from us I clearly saw the MEATBALL—the rising sun insignia of the Japanese Naval Air Arm—on the wing of the deadly Zero!

It was now 7:52 am in Hawaii on December 7, 1941, and the dreaded but somehow expected moment had arrived—we were at war with Imperial Japan.

The Naval Air Station, Kaneohe, was new. Many of the military had not yet heard of it. Obviously the Japanese had. Some of the buildings were still incomplete and the station roads had not yet been paved. Only a few echelons of command had moved into the base . . .

In the Comm. Office, people responded with action. I ran downstairs to the station OOD's office shouting: "Japanese airplanes are attacking the station. Sound the alarm and call our commanding officer." (Cdr. Harold M. Martin, known as "Beauty.") It wasn't news to the OOD, but he found that we had no working alarm on station. Our makeshift general alarm was the workmen's steam whistle on the contractor's timekeeper shack. Since it was Sunday the shack was padlocked, and there was no steam for the whistle. No alarm!

When I called my squadron commander, LtCdr Thurston B. Clark, he was already awake and aware of the attack. He drove from his quarters to join me, his car strafed repeatedly all the way. He commandeered some guns from the OOD's armory and went outside. Never will I forget the spectacle of the squadron commander and me crouching behind the administration building, trying to shoot out of the sky with our heavy, awkward and inaccurate .45-caliber automatics, those 400-mile per hour ZEROS . . .

Aviation Machinist Mate Third Class Guy C. Avery was in his bunk on the sun porch of a bungalow when he heard the sound of a lone plane quite near the house. It passed and returned. "To hell with the Army," he thought. "Every day is the same to them." But the sound of the engine was different, and roused his curiosity. He reached the window in time to see "Zeroes just beginning to fan out over the heart of the station and opening fire promiscuously." He shouted to his sleeping comrades, "The Japs are here! It's war!" To which one man replied, "Well, don't worry about it, Avery. It'll last only two weeks."

Avery checked his watch. It was 0748. "We were struck first of all and about seven minutes before Pearl Harbor," he later wrote. "Our OD (officer of the day) called nearby Bellows Field to warn them and ask for help, but his call was regarded as a practical joke—but only for a few minutes, then it was too late." In fact, a Kaneohe contractor, Sam Aweau, had phoned Hickam and Bellows fields that the Japanese had attacked, but no one believed him.

Radioman Third Class James K. Poppleton from Pocatello, Idaho, was in his barracks ready room studying for his Radioman Second Class examination when he heard airplanes flying "very low." He glanced out the window toward the airfield, and similar

Sailors attempt to save a burning PBY at Naval Air Station, Kaneohe Bay, Oahu, during the Japanese air raid. This plane was set afire by strafing in the initial phase of the attack and was sunk in the second attack. Note dog observing the work. NPSAM

to Guy Avery wondered "Doesn't the Army know the war games are over for the weekend?" The next low flying airplane was so close, strafing the barracks area, Ken could see the pilot and the clearly visible rising sun on the fuselage. This was no air show. Kaneohe was under attack by Japanese aircraft.

The next minute after the second Zeke made his strafing pass by the barracks area Ken Poppleton was rushing toward the hangars to help protect the PBY's, their long range patrol aircraft. The distance from barracks to the ramp and hangars where the aircraft were parked was approximately one fourth of a mile. As he ran toward the flight line, he could see smoke rising from the ramp. He knew instantly planes were on fire. By the time he arrived at the hangar area, the first wave of eleven raiders had done their damage and left the area. When he arrived at the parking ramp, on the bay-side of the squadron hangar, he joined other sailors, first attempting to save as many aircraft as possible, with little success.

Kaneohe's popular commanding officer, Commander Harold M. "Beauty" Martin, had precious little with which to defend against the onslaught: 303 sailors, 31 officers, plus 95 Marines, including 2 officers. Ironically, Martin's mobile antiaircraft weapons had been rolled back to an Army installation on 5 December. Of Kaneohe's aircraft, four were moored in the bay about a thousand yards apart. The remainder were parked on the ramp except for four which were in Hangar No. 1.

VP-11 had twelve planes ready for flight on four hours notice, VP-12 had six on 30 minutes notice and five on four hours; and VP-14 the three on patrol, three ready in 30 minutes, four ready in four hours.[4]

In the first Japanese aircraft to attack there were five or six fighters, then after a brief lull, followed a few minutes later by five or six more, for a total of eleven. One group was led by Lieutenant Tadashi Kaneko, the other by Lieutenant Masao Sato. The first attacks were on the control tower on a nearby hill, and the four PBYs moored in the water. The next attacks were on aircraft parked on the ramp, the first being the wing commander's OS2U-1 Kingfisher. At the time a chief petty officer was turning over the propeller by hand. The Japanese apparently thought the aircraft was a fighter about to take off, and thoroughly riddled it.[5]

By the time Martin reached the administration building from his home, the first PBY moored on the water had begun to burn. Many of Martin's men were so new that he wondered how they would perform in combat. He needn't have worried. "It was remarkable," he said. "There was no panic. Everyone went right to work battling back and doing his job."[6]

Martin was right. During the initial Japanese assault on Kaneohe, Patrol Squadron 14's Chief Aviation Ordnanceman John W. Finn, from the same squadron as Lieutenant Tanner, who earlier in the morning flew PBY 14-P-1 that attacked the midget submarine outside the entrance to Pearl Harbor, began a series of actions spanning the first and second wave attacks, that would eventually lead to Finn's receiving the Medal of Honor, the nation's highest award for extraordinary heroism.

When the first wave of eleven Zekes left the area and men from his squadron rushed from their barracks to the ramp, Finn began to take charge. He and everyone else moving about the ramp among burning and wrecked aircraft knew instinctively more enemy planes would soon follow. If they couldn't launch their aircraft they had to do all they could to be ready to defend against the next assault. After first trying with little success to save the PBYs, they had begun pulling the .50-caliber machine guns from the port and starboard side-blisters of the wrecked and burning aircraft. On burning PBYs, it was a hot job that would soon get hotter.

The next problem to solve was to provide mountings for the machine guns. Inside the squadron's Hangar 2, the next large hangar to the east of Hangar 1, Finn ordered the metal smiths to fabricate tripods while he identified positions on the ramp, on the bay-side of the hangar, to place the tripods and mount the guns. He established locations inside the hangar for others, including Ken Poppleton, to begin belting .50-caliber ammunition and carry the none-too-light belts to the gun positions. During the lull between the first and second waves, the frantic ammunition-belting-and-carrying-to-the-guns activity proceeded, and triggered a lifelong humorous memory for Ken Poppleton.

Two of his squadron mates were the Mallard brothers. C.W. Mallard was the 2nd Mechanic and Aviation Machinist Mate Third Class on Ensign Tanner's PBY 14-P-1, that unknown to Ken Poppleton at the time, had about 1 ½ hours earlier dropped two depth charges in the attack on the Japanese midget submarine—among the "first shots of the Pacific War." Participating in the belting of approximately 50 rounds per belt and carrying of .50-caliber ammunition was C.W. Mallard's brother, a strapping six feet, four inch, Aviation Machinist Mate. "Duck" Mallard he was called by his buddies, a delightful nickname that both poked good fun at his last name and belied the physical strength of "Duck," who was also a crew member on another of the squadron's PBYs.

Ken Poppleton, a tall slender young sailor, weighed 165 pounds and when he attempted to carry the belted ammunition to the guns, he struggled to carry just one belt. Not so with "Duck" Mallard. Ken was astonished to see him effortlessly carrying two belts on each trip to the guns.

As for Chief Finn, he, like men in the other squadrons, would be ready with a gun and ammunition when the second wave, led by two flights of nine Kate horizontal bombers, followed by strafing fighters, roared over Kaneohe beginning about 0830 hours. He mounted a .50-caliber machine gun on an instruction stand between the squadron hangar and the bay in a completely exposed section of the parking ramp, which the enemy time and again subjected to bombing and later strafing in their follow-on attacks. With complete disregard for his own safety, he fought fiercely with telling effect. Though painfully wounded, he continued to man his gun until given a direct order to leave his post and seek medical attention. Following first aid treatment, though obviously suffering much pain and moving with great difficulty, he returned to the squadron area during the second wave, later actively supervising the rearming of the three returning VP-14 planes. Later in the war he would receive the Medal of Honor from Admiral of the Fleet, Chester W. Nimitz, in a ceremony on board the USS *Enterprise*.[7]

The Zeroes' first, low-altitude strafing passes at Kaneohe were deadly, and the effects of the remaining 32 in the first wave would prove devastating everywhere that morning. Each carried two rapid-fire 20-mm canons, one in the leading edge of each wing, and two 7.7-mm machine guns mounted on the nose of the fighter, in the engine cowling. To increase the amount of damage caused during their strafing runs, the Japanese loaded their ammunition in the following order: two armor piercing, one tracer; two armor piercing, one tracer; two armor piercing, one incendiary. With this loading the bullets would not only kill, but would shred thin metal, pierce light to moderately thick armor, gasoline and oil tanks, do fatal damage to vehicles, engines, aircraft and anti-aircraft guns—and start fires.

In the first eight minutes of the air assault on Oahu, the Zekes were commencing the near-total destruction of the Navy's long range patrol capability on the island. Follow-on attacks by Zekes and horizontal bombing Kates and additional fighters in the second wave would bring more death and destruction to Kaneohe Naval Air Station.

A Single Zeke at Bellows Field—A Warm-up for the Second Wave

Along the beach in Waimanalo to the southeast of Kaneohe, all was serene at Bellows Field until about dawn, when the acting first sergeant ran into the tent area to rouse the sleeping men, yelling that

Kaneohe had been 'blown all to hell.' Corporal McKinley thought he was crazy and just turned over in his bed. At 0810, someone called from Hickam Field and asked for a fire truck because they 'were in flames.' A return call disclosed . . . they had been attacked, so the Bellows fire chief left for Hickam with the fire truck.[8]

As follow-on to the swirling assault on Kaneohe, one lone Zeke piloted by Lieutenant Tadashi Kaneko, flew east over the water, and turned south, wide of the Hawaiian Air Force's Bellows Field, then turned in from the east, out of the sun, to make one strafing pass down a line of tents toward the west, perpendicular to the runway and roughly parallel with the beach. At Bellows the 86th Observation Squadron was equipped with two O-49 and seven O-47B observation aircraft. As he rolled wings level from his right turn to final approach for the attack, and glanced slightly to his left, he could see P-40 Warhawks from Wheeler Field's 44th Pursuit (Interceptor) Squadron, temporarily deployed for gunnery training. They were grouped together, lined up on the parking ramp, near the runway, in short rows.

On 7 November the P-40s of the 44th had begun deploying to Bellows for a month's aerial gunnery training. The training involved twelve of the squadron's aircraft and a complement of crew chiefs, assistants, armorers, radiomen, and other support troops. They flew a practice mission on Saturday, 6 December, but didn't immediately refuel their aircraft afterward. This was in line with the normal practice of the various squadrons conducting training at Bellows. When they finished on a Saturday afternoon, they usually waited until Sunday to refuel their airplanes. Also, during the week, before shutting down for the day, they normally cleaned the guns on the aircraft and armed them for the next morning—ready to go. However, on Saturday afternoons, they removed the guns from the aircraft to do a more thorough job of cleaning. Consequently, on this day, the P-40s at Bellows were parked wing-to-wing, low on fuel, and some had their guns removed. Only four of the 44th's officers were at the field that morning, and three were pilots. A B-18 bomber normally present at Bellows for target tow was on Molokai Island overnight, and would later fly back to Oahu in the midst of the second wave's assault.

It was approximately 0830 when the lone Zeke roared down

A lone Japanese fighter piloted by Lieutenant Tadashi Kaneko strafed this line of tents at Bellows Field during the first wave attack on Oahu. USAF

a line of tents, his 20-mm canon ammunition apparently gone, machine guns blazing. Private First Class James A. Brown from the medical detachment was slightly wounded in the leg. The Japanese now had the undivided attention of the men of the 86th Observation Squadron.

> The entire Casual Detachment got up, went over to the armament building, and drew Browning automatic rifles, Springfield [bolt action] rifles, and machine guns. Unable to find belts of ammunition for the machine guns, they tried aircraft machine gun belts but found they wouldn't work. The only other firepower available was a machine gun on an 0-47, [a single engine, two-seat aircraft] belonging to the 86th Observation Squadron and two 30-caliber antiaircraft machine guns which Hawaii National Guard personnel of the 298th Infantry positioned at the end of the runway. Everyone dispersed, jumping into ditches, behind buildings, or whatever shelter they could find.[9]

While the men of the 86th rushed to defend against the next onslaught, the three 44th fighter pilots were determined to get into the air as soon as possible. Squadron maintenance men scrambled to disperse, fuel and arm their aircraft.

Time was of the essence. In another half hour, the second wave's attack would bring much more than a single Zeke fighter strafing Bellows Field on one pass. Though none from the 86th died at Bellows Field that day, and only three were wounded on a field still under construction, two more of their number received wounds in the Japanese assault on Hickam Field—and two of the 44th's three pilots would die at Bellows, with the other wounded in desperate, vain, raging attempts to get airborne and strike back at the now-declared enemy.

The worst was in progress elsewhere, far worse. Between dawn, when the 86th's acting first sergeant told of Kaneohe's attack, 0810 hours, when the call for a fire truck came from Hickam, and 0830, when the Zeke roared through on a strafing pass, hell was visiting the island of Oahu. Wheeler Field, the home of the Hawaiian Air Force's air and fleet defense, the 14th Pursuit Wing, was the first Army Air Force field struck on Oahu. By 0900, when the second wave struck Bellows and completed their work on Kaneohe, the fierce Japanese attack on Pearl Harbor and other military installations on the island had become a never-to-be-forgotten, bloody, American national disaster.[10]

Plans to Counter Sabotage, Levels of Alert, and Training

The strafing pass at Bellows Field by the lone Zeke, and the initial reaction of the Field's defenders, was little different from the initial reactions of defenders at all Hawaiian Air Force installations on Oahu that morning, and was rooted in the preparations for war and training the command had received in the intervening months since July 1941. Zeke pilot Lieutenant Tadashi Kaneko was undoubtedly reconnoitering Bellows to learn if there were fighters deployed at the Field, intending to pass the information to the second wave. The Japanese were determined to first deal a hammer blow to the fighter and long range reconnaissance forces resident on Oahu, to protect the Japanese strike force—including the slower Vals and Kates—which would shatter the fleet and long range bomber and reconnaissance forces at Hickam and Kaneohe. The Army was far more concerned about sabotage than any other threat, such as air attack by two waves of Japanese carrier based aircraft.

With a philosophy that reflected his experience, Lieutenant General Walter C. Short, commanding general of the Hawaiian Department, demanded training in the basic infantry duties and skills for Hawaiian Air Force personnel not involved in flying. To accomplish this, the Department published a standing operating procedure in July that set up a six-to-eight week schedule in basic infantry training. When General George C. Marshall, Chief of Staff, questioned training Army Air Forces personnel as infantrymen, General Short countered that an enemy would not attack the Hawaiian Islands until after it had destroyed American air power and with the aircraft destroyed, large numbers of Hawaiian Air Force personnel would be available for infantry duty. Furthermore, General Short felt that the Hawaiian Air Force was overstaffed and more than half, or 3,885 out of 7,229 personnel, could be used as infantry after the invasion started.

(By 7 December, Hawaiian Air Force strength was 7,460.) He stated the training was to give these people something to do during exercises. General Short did not believe in using infantry to protect Hawaiian Air Force personnel who had nothing to do but sit around.

After setting up a program to insure all personnel would be trained to defend the island against a possible invasion, General Short began an intensive effort to protect the facilities against possible sabotage from the large Japanese population living on Oahu. To this end he created three alert levels aimed at providing the most appropriate defense response based on the forms of attack he believed the island would receive. Significantly, the first level, Alert Level One—and the one the Department was in on 7 December—was sabotage alert. During Alert One, ammunition not needed for immediate training would be boxed and stored in central locations difficult for an enemy to reach and destroy.

Thus, when the attack began, most antiaircraft ammunition was boxed and stored far away from the gun locations. At Wheeler Field, maintenance personnel not only removed the machine gun ammunition from the aircraft, they removed it from the belts so it could be boxed and stored in one location. Further, the aircraft were parked wing-tip to wing-tip, in neat rows on the ramp, instead of being dispersed into the approximately 125 earthen revetments constructed at Wheeler.

After being notified about an impending air attack against Hawaii, the Hawaiian Department would go to Alert Two. At this level, measures used in Alert One would remain in effect. In addition, personnel would activate the Air Warning Center, arm fighter aircraft and place them on alert; launch long-range reconnaissance, and arm and deploy antiaircraft units.

From this intermediate level, the entire Hawaiian Department would go to Alert Three when invasion seemed imminent. At Level Three, the command functions would move to underground facilities and available personnel would deploy to prepared beach defenses. General Short immediately decreed Alert Three after the 7 December attack began.[11]

The Alert Level One paralysis of no ammunition at the ready—plus no prior plan to disperse aircraft—rendered General Short's order meaningless in the face of the slashing, deadly air attack. Over the remaining military airfields, selected harbor installations and ships moored in Pearl Harbor, the first Zekes, Vals and Kates swarmed from multiple directions and altitudes. Startled, at-first-uncertain and disbelieving men on the ground and aboard ships, all disciplined and trained to respond in a crisis, and fight, were momentarily puzzled. Then they saw bombs or torpedoes released, the white-hot blinking of machine guns and 20-mm canons, the flash of orange insignia—"meatballs"—on the underside of wings or the sides of fuselages, heard a few shouted warnings, the roar of low flying airplanes, and the violent explosions of bombs or torpedoes in the stunning few moments before reality struck home. In the normal preparations for Sunday morning breakfast, church services, a weekend of liberty, lowered crew manning, absence of warning, and low defense alert condition, disaster quickly flourished.

While torpedoes, bombs, cannon fire and machine gun bullets tore into the attackers' primary target, the Pacific Fleet, setting off thunderous explosions, starting numerous fires, and a huge, all-consuming inferno on the battleship *Arizona,* the men on Army Air Force, Navy and Marine Corps airfields suffered their own brand of hell. Before one hour and forty-five minutes passed, total Army Air Force casualties on Oahu climbed to 163 killed, 336 wounded, and 43 missing. Of these, Hickam Field's losses were 121 killed, 274 wounded, and 37 missing. Out of 231 Hawaiian Air Force aircraft, 64 were destroyed, 93 damaged and only 74 were left in repairable condition. Hangars at both Hickam and Wheeler were severely damaged. An aircraft repair station in Hickam's Hawiian Air Depot was completely destroyed.[12]

Kate torpedo-bombers charged low across the water from the southeast and east, after passing at 50 feet altitude southeast of Hickam Field's hangar line, and past the south and north ends of Ford Island across the harbor from the west toward the main dock and ships in the north harbor, while other torpedo-bombers pressing in from the east and southeast unleashed devastating attacks on the battleships and other ships in the harbor. Val dive bombers and Kate horizontal bombers from the northeast and southwest almost simultaneously launched shattering dive-bomb and fighter attacks on aircraft and hangar facilities on Hickam Field, Ford Island, and nearby Marine Corps' Mooring Mast Field at Ewa—while to the northwest, Wheeler Field took staggering blows beginning moments following the assault on NAS Kaneohe Bay.

Disbelief, Bombs and Falling
Antiaircraft Rounds

To those living on the island's military installations, were residents in the surrounding hills, or tourists or vacationers who witnessed from a distance, or even close-up, first came curiosity borne of unfamiliar, confusing sights and sounds on a Sunday morning after a night of relaxing fun and, for the military and island residents, memories of months of drills. People living on Oahu had frequently seen extended military maneuvers punctuated with military police cars and jeep-led truck convoys of soldiers and towed artillery pieces moving on Oahu's roads, and columns of great ships of war sailing quietly, serenely in and out of Pearl Harbor. Military aircraft engaged in mock air defense exercises and gunnery training crisscrossing high above the island and over the water, and long range patrol aircraft leaving from their coastal moorings and airfields, looking for an enemy nearly all felt would strike thousands of miles to the southwest—preparations for war few believed in their hearts or minds would ever come to Hawaii.

From within Honolulu's residential, commercial, tourist centers and luxury hotels, where people were having early morning breakfasts and planning a day of sight seeing and pleasure, thoughts of war were even further away. To them, the discovery, recognition, and comprehension of a peaceful island's distant, deadly events came far more slowly. Their minds were riveted to a tranquil, south seas island paradise: motor launches, kayaks, fishing boats, yachts, sailboats, surfboards, swimming in the surf, island music, native music and hula dancers, fragrant leis, parties, exotic south sea and oriental restaurants, sumptuous island food; freighters, tankers, beautiful luxury liners plying in and out of the port of Honolulu, and the romantic lure of the growing air travel on the magnificent Pan American *Clippers* cycling in and out of Pearl City's calm, sheltered moorings inside Pearl Harbor.

To all who were outdoors, the distant, muffled, thunder, curious geysers of water in the harbor and in the ocean south of Waikiki and Honolulu Harbor, plumes of black smoke near and in Pearl Harbor, followed by momentary silence before the distant specks of climbing, diving and maneuvering airplanes—came slowly into focus. Momentary silence, disbelief, uncertainty, denial; questions to the island residents, and complete, totally incorrect conclusions were the reactions, as eyes slowly lifted skyward then shifted down ever so slightly, straining to see what was occurring ten to twelve miles in the distance, on the water and land below the swirling specks.

Seventeen-year old Frederick K. Kamaka of Hawaiian, Chinese and Norwegian extraction, was a junior at Kamahameha High School for boys, a private high school endowed by the kings and queens of Hawaii through means of the Bishop Estate, which at that time, owned 1/11th of the total land area of the islands. As an eleemosynary institution, it was restricted to Hawaiians only in attendance, with the minimum requirement being one-quarter Hawaiian at this time. Fred, whose father had sent him to the school to learn the latest in the woodworking field, for the family's growing ukulele manufacturing business, was "on duty" at the school that morning.

Kamahameha High School for boys was the closest thing to a true military institute and mechanical arts school that could be found in The Territory of Hawaii, and was similar to high school military institutes found on America's mainland. The boys lived in a dormitory, wore uniforms every day, had reveille every morning, retreat formation for flag lowering in the late afternoon, and heard Taps played every evening, signaling lights out. The routine included academics, drills and ceremonies—and drill competition—scheduled meals in the school dining hall, athletics, Sunday morning church services for religious training and morals education, and Sunday afternoon parades. Leading and managing the military education and training was an active duty Army officer, Lieutenant Ainsley Mahikoa, the resident professor of military science and tactics.

The morning of 7 December, Fred was at the usual Sunday morning breakfast, anticipating 10:00 a.m. church services, and the afternoon parade. The cadets sitting at his table were discussing the parade, knowing competition between companies would be keen this year. The parade and competition was especially important to Fred, as he was assigned to lead his squad for the company competition. Classmate Rowland Melim and Fred were dining room orderlies for the month, required to see that each assigned waiter cleared the tables after the breakfast meal and set up for lunch before being released to return to their dormitories to prepare for church and get their uniforms ready for the afternoon parade.

After securing the dining hall, the two left for their respective dormitories. Fred lived in the Kamehameha Dormitory, and as he crossed Bishop Hall Field, his thoughts dwelt directly on the fast approaching afternoon parade and his role as squad leader in the important competition. He felt strongly the rest of his company expected his squad to win. On reaching the Assembly Hall at the east end of Bishop Hall, he climbed atop the wall in front of the Hall, and as was his custom each morning, gazed at the view stretching before him.

His eyes swept from Diamond Head on the eastern end, past Waikiki Beach with numerous sailboats in the ocean, the dormant volcano crater, Punchbowl, the important places in downtown Honolulu, then past Aloha Tower where he could see two freighters waiting outside the entrance to Honolulu Harbor for a pilot to come take them into the harbor and dock. Finally his eyes came to rest on Hickam Field, about six miles distant, where he hoped to see some planes "taking off" but was disappointed. None were, though many were parked in rows on the concrete apron in front of the hangars.

Glancing westward past Pearl Harbor and the ships moored there, his gaze took him to Ewa Plantation's sugar cane fields and the Waianae Mountain Range that rose beyond Ewa. At that moment his eyes were attracted by a glint of reflected sunlight from an airborne mirror or metal sheet, from a northerly direction, above the mountain range. Looking closely, he noticed formations of planes arranged in the traditional "V" flight configuration, approaching the patch of clouds directly over Hickam Field and Pearl Harbor.

Suddenly, when the formation reached a point directly above the cloud mass, they began diving single file through the clouds toward Hickam Field and Pearl Harbor. The previous week, students and townspeople had seen some of the joint US service maneuvers being conducted, to include mock bombing of Honolulu Harbor on Friday, by planes from our aircraft carriers. After such exercises they usually landed at Ford Island, in the middle of Pearl Harbor. At first, Fred assumed the planes diving toward Hickam Field and Pearl Harbor were "our returning US planes." His attention and observant curiosity turned to surprise, then later to shock, when "puffs of dust" rose from the ground under the swooping planes over Hickam Field, and sounds of explosions rent the quiet Sunday morning.

As though Fred were watching and listening to distant lightning strikes and thunderstorms, he saw the puffs appear, followed nearly 30 seconds later by the sounds of muffled explosions, not thunder—the first at 7:55 a.m. While he was engrossed in the distant sights and sounds, Lieutenant Ainsley Mahikoa drove up in front of Bishop Hall, dressed in a civilian suit for church services. He came by to check his office's mail distribution box en route. When the lieutenant returned outside, a group of students was gathering, their attention drawn to events at Hickam Field and Pearl Harbor, and the lieutenant, curious as to what they were eyeing, joined them. Fred pointed out what appeared to be burning planes on the Hickam Field apron, visible bomb bursts on the ground, a sky filled with diving planes, and the faint sound of machine guns firing.

After watching the action for a moment, Lieutenant Mahikoa turned to Fred and said, "More maneuvers." He then went on to explain to all the students gathered, "The planes are probably from the carrier fleet which is absent from Pearl Harbor. Holes are dug into the ground and dynamite set off to simulate bomb bursts, and they are using smoke pots on the Hickam Field area instead of burning airplanes to make the action more realistic."

The crowd continued to gather, and students were now at their dorm windows, watching. About six minutes elapsed before all the guns at Pearl Harbor began to fire. Smoke puffs in the air began appearing, the first markers of flak bursts. As they watched from in front of Kamahameha High School, two planes were shot down in flames and others crashed into the water and on land. Fred excitedly pointed out to Mahikoa, "Look, we're shooting down our own planes."

Mahikoa's disbelief and maneuver explanations disappeared in a flash. He ran to the car, turned on the radio and turned the volume up. They all heard the announcement, which began playing over and over again: "This is the real thing—THIS IS WAR—Pearl Harbor is under attack—several planes have been shot down and they bear the insignia of the rising sun on their wings."

Over and over came the message, and the full significance began to strike deep in the minds of young men such as Fred

Kamaka and Lieutenant Mahikoa, who had minutes earlier been thinking of breakfast, clean-up after breakfast, the beauty of the island, maneuvers, mail boxes, church services, and an afternoon parade competition. Then something far more startling occurred.

As they listened intently to the radio broadcast, and stood transfixed, gazing at all that was happening, a totally unfamiliar sound intruded—similar to the loud whistle of an incoming artillery round heard in the sound system at a war movie. Mahikoa knew the sound instinctively, and shouted, "Hit the ground!"—throwing himself down in his nice, clean-pressed business suit. His cadets instantly followed his example, throwing themselves to the ground. None too soon.

Two expended, friendly antiaircraft rounds slammed into the retaining wall and exploded approximately 100 feet up the road, knocking a large hole in the wall and raining shrapnel over the area. No one was hurt, but other thoughts were now racing through young minds. Thoughts of a parade and a competition rapidly faded, swallowed in the realization that if the Japanese succeeded in capturing these islands, the boys of Kamahameha might never drill again. Within seconds several other rounds fell on the hillside above and below the school, but none came as close as the two that welcomed Kamahameha High School for boys to World War II that fateful morning. Others in Honolulu and surrounding communities wouldn't be so lucky, and the boys would grow up quickly.[13]

Inside residences or buildings, where windows afforded the smallest possibility of attention-getting views, and no accompanying, delayed sounds, recognition of the approaching, exploding inferno and life-changing disaster was far more slowly comprehended.

Hans Wiedenhoefer, a member of the San Jose State Spartans' football team, which left San Francisco on the *Lurline* Thanksgiving Day, was having breakfast in their hotel with the team. "Nobody knew what was going on. Some of us thought it was maneuvers. Others saw spouts of water in the harbor and a waiter told us he figured somebody was shooting whales. A couple of us took a walk down to the beach and when we saw one of those big bombs hit the water we knew it wasn't whale shooting and hustled back to the hotel. One of those bombs hit in the water about a hundred yards from the hotel and another one demolished a building a block away." He said the populace was calm, all went home quietly and there was no confusion. But to distant witnesses there was confusion, abundant confusion.[14]

Bill Ryne, halfback on the Spartan team, witnessed the same ". . . big spout of water in the harbor," and overheard the explanation about whales spouting. "Later we went to the beach but they wouldn't let us go into the water, and that afternoon we read in the paper of the attack. It was the first we knew of it." Tom Taylor, college yell leader who accompanied the Spartans said, "I thought the attack was a dress rehearsal for M-day." The team was preparing to take a bus trip around the island when the attack began, and when the buses didn't show up, Coach Winkelman investigated. He learned that all buses were being used by the military. This was the first he knew anything was amiss. "It was quite awhile before we realized what was happening," Star center, Wilbur Wool, said. "Then we only knew the islands had been attacked when someone told us. I don't know what the others thought then, but my first thought was about how I was going to get home."[15]

More than one person posed the same question. How was anyone going to get home? None knew of the orders issued to the 1st, 2d, and 3d Japanese submarine groups. None knew the location of the Japanese fleet devastating the American air and naval forces on Oahu. Where might the ships be to take them home? What Naval vessels would escort ships taking them through a Japanese fleet—wherever it might be—or Japanese submarines lying in wait for them?

Willamette University Bearcat's Coach R.S. "Spec" Keene was with his team eating breakfast in their hotel. "We saw water splashing in the harbor and asked a waiter what it was." "It's a whale spouting," he said. "We all trooped out to watch it, treating it as a joke. We didn't know until late in the afternoon what had happened." The team saw planes dropping bombs in the water but thought it was the US army and navy planes practicing "M-Day" maneuvers islanders had been talking about so much. Later, Coach Keene repeated, "No one became particularly excited. We didn't even know what was going on until almost five hours after the bombing started. Not even after we'd inspected a bomb crater two blocks from our hotel did we realize an attack had been made. We thought it was practice maneuvers by the army and navy air corps."[16]

Oregon State Senator McKay, who accompanied the Willamette

team to Oahu, later said, "We didn't know Hawaii had been attacked until we heard the president say so in his Washington, DC broadcast, although we had seen planes dropping bombs and had put aside as 'wild rumor' the story brought to the hotel by an eye witness of fire on Pearl Harbor and Japanese planes overhead." Indeed, a near-hysterical woman had driven from a vantage point nearer the spreading inferno, telling of airplanes, explosions, and fire on the waters in Pearl Harbor. Lorena Jack, "Miss Jack" to people at the university, remarked facetiously, "The Japs must be after us." She was later shocked to learn her facetious remark was a statement of fact. The rumor was no rumor, though later in the day, fear-breeding rumors ran rampant.[17]

With the exception of seven members of the San Jose football team who voluntarily stayed behind to help in the defense of the island, the two teams left the island twelve days later, never knowing that the Japanese were not deliberately dropping bombs in the water, or on Honolulu. Spent rounds from American 3-inch antiaircraft defense guns, fired mostly from ships in Pearl Harbor at Japanese aircraft attacking from the east, from the direction of Honolulu, were falling into commercial and residential areas, and exploding—adding to the carnage and heavy damage inflicted on Oahu. The ship, harbor and airfield defenders had no choice. It was war suddenly and violently entered, war brought to them. Fight back with everything at your disposal, kill or be killed.

To the northwest, south, southeast, and just southwest of Pearl Harbor, at Wheeler and Hickam Fields, Ewa—and at NAS Pearl Harbor, while the Japanese were battering ships in the harbor, they were simultaneously executing a classic air superiority attack on Oahu's Naval aviation and the Hawaiian Air Force. They systematically savaged aircraft caught on the ground, destroyed, badly damaged or set fire to hangars and maintenance buildings, supply depots, barracks, dining halls and tent areas, fuel and ammunition storage areas. The success of their onslaught, as at Kaneohe, and later at Bellows Field, would protect the first and second waves from effective fighter defense and leave Hawaii's air defense and long range patrol capabilities bloodied and in a shambles—but not completely destroyed. After the Japanese air assault ended, the Army's radar sites, fixed and mobile antiaircraft gun positions, and the Navy's antiaircraft guns aboard ships not sunk or badly damaged, remained operational. Casualties were relatively few in the Army's 24th and 25th Infantry Divisions and their supporting units. Not so on board ships and on Oahu's military air fields.

A Savaged Fighter Command

Wheeler Field, struck shortly before 0800, was home for the Hawaiian Air Force's entire pursuit (interceptor) force, which was the 14th Pursuit Wing, composed of the 15th and 18th Pursuit Groups. A successful attack on Wheeler would virtually assure air superiority. The Japanese took Wheeler Field completely by surprise, as they did every other installation on Oahu. No one on the ground sighted the oncoming Val dive bombers until they made their final turn for the attack.

Aircraft and maintenance facilities along the flight line were the primary targets. Supply depots, barracks and people anywhere in

Japanese Navy Type 99 carrier dive bomber (Val) in action during attack. A fearsome sight when viewed from the receiving end of its bomb delivery. NA

the vicinity of these targets, were secondary but also received devastating blows. The Japanese pilots were too well trained to waste their bombs and ammunition on insignificant targets. One bomb did land in the front yard of a house, but it was the result of a miss rather then a deliberate attack on the housing area.

Private Wilfred D. Burke, 72nd Pursuit Squadron said, "It was the first time I had ever seen a plunging dive bomber and it was an awesome sight. Nothing in warfare is more frightening. Hurtling down on us was the dive bomber being followed by another, while six or seven more were in echelon awaiting their turn. The leader pulled out right over us in a spectacular climbing bank. We could clearly see the rising sun of Japan on his wings and fuselage."

Burke, an aircraft armorer, had reluctantly got out of bed around 0700 that morning, in one of the tents on the hangar line. His boss, Sergeant Forest Wills, stirred resentment in Burke when he waked him on the only morning Burke could sleep late. He had promised Wills, a deeply religious man, he would go to church with him. "Deacon" Wills had become a good friend. As Burke put it, he "was sincerely concerned with my spiritual welfare, having observed that I was a worthless fellow given to drinking beer."

After eating breakfast in an unusually empty mess hall, Burke had some spare time before church and joined a group of men in the open quadrangle in the middle of the 72nd's tent area between Hangars 2 and 3, "shooting the bull." As they talked, a flight of planes passed to the west of Wheeler, heading toward Pearl Harbor. Someone said, "It's the Navy," but their idle observation soon turned to terror when Japanese airplanes almost directly overhead appeared to be diving toward them.[18]

Colonel Flood, the base commander, was in front of his quarters talking to some people when the attack began. He saw a bomb hit the Wheeler depot area and first thought someone out on maneuvers accidentally dropped it. Immediately afterward, a group of low flying airplanes sped by, only 50 to 75 feet off the ground. "You could almost hit them with a rock if you had it," thought Flood. When he saw the insignia of the Japanese rising sun, he knew what had happened and hurried down to the flight line. By then, hangars and aircraft were in flames, and a thick pall of black smoke hung over the area.[19]

Vals approaching first from the west, parallel to the parking apron, then from the east, then from both directions, releasing their bombs from 500 to 1,000 feet above the ground, delivered deadly explosive force. They released their bombs from one end of the hangar line to the other, scored direct hits on Hangars 1 and 3 and additional buildings in that area, setting fires. One bomb struck the 6th Pursuit Squadron barracks, entering a window on the second floor, where it exploded, caused considerable damage and numerous wounded.

The multi-direction attacks by the bombers and fighters added confusion and chaos to the abject fear and terror of defenseless men scrambling for cover and weapons to defend themselves against an enemy bent on destruction of the field's mission capability. Observations and recollections of events differed widely among those on the receiving end of the destructive weapons tearing Wheeler Field apart. According to some, the first place hit was the gas storage dump on the southwest corner of the base, where all of Wheeler's flammables such as gas, turpentine, and lacquer were kept. Most witnesses, however, reported that the first bomb struck Hangar 1, where the base engineering shops were located. The tremendous blast blew out skylights, and clouds of smoke billowed upward, making it appear the entire hangar was lifted

Planes and hangars burning at Wheeler Army Air Field, Oahu, soon after it was attacked in the morning of 7 December 1941, as seen from a Japanese Navy plane. NHHC

off its foundation. The explosion decimated the sheet metal, electrical, and paint shops in the front half of the hangar, but spared the machine and wood shops, and tool room, which were protected by a concrete-block, dividing wall.[20]

The bomb that hit Hangar 3 had struck the hangar sheltering the central ammunition storage area, where, because of the Hawaiian Department's Alert One status, the ammunition unloaded from aircraft, including rounds pulled from machine gun belts, had been stored. The hangar's exploding ammunition, going off like firecrackers in the flames, severely limited the ability to defend Wheeler Field against the continuing air attack.

Immediately behind the completed first wave of dive bombing attacks came the bombers, back again joining the fighters in follow-on, low level strafing attacks. The 72nd Pursuit Squadron tent area between Hangars 2 and 3 came under heavy attack.

Burke and his friends, as well as many other Wheeler men, fled from the strafing attacks in the tent and flight line areas, scattering in all directions. Burke headed for the married NCOs' (noncommissioned officers') quarters a block away, thinking the attackers were unlikely to waste their ammunition on family homes. As he ran across the street corner nearest his tent, a bomb struck the pavement behind him and killed several men. When he reached the first row of family housing, he placed his back against the wall of a house and looked back toward the hangars.

He was on higher ground and could clearly see the carnage and devastation. The dive bombers had regrouped, and with the fighters were methodically strafing planes of the 14th Pursuit Wing, which were lined up by squadron, wingtip to wingtip, in precise rows on the ramp. A thick pall of oily, black smoke from burning planes and hangars stretched over the flight line and hung almost as low as the tent tops that were left standing. The dense smoke screened the 46th Pursuit Squadron's P-36 fighter aircraft parked in the last row on the west end of the Wheeler flight line, preventing the Japanese from pinpointing them as targets.[21]

Private Henry C. Woodrum was in the food line at the mess hall when the attack began. After hearing the roar of an airplane passing low overhead, hearing a loud, window-rattling explosion that drew his gaze out the nearest window, he recognized the wing insignia of a climbing, turning Japanese aircraft, a Val dive bomber that had just released a bomb. A newcomer behind him, thinking it was a crash, commented, "Boy, that lieutenant sure hit hard!" "That's no crash," Woodrum shouted. "It's the Japs!" Others crowded around the window to have a look, then tried to rush outside at the same time, jamming the main entrance.

Woodrum took a shortcut by vaulting over a steam table and running through the rear of the kitchen, as a cook screamed obscenities at him. He dashed out the doorway into the loading dock, paused and looked upward. A low-wing monoplane seemed to be diving directly toward him. He froze as a bomb detached itself from the fuselage and arched downward, exploding nearby. The shock wave hurled him from the doorway, back into the building, across the hall, and through the open door of a walk-in storage area. Wet, smelly vegetables spilled on top of him from crates on the shelves. He made his way through the clutter back to the doorway, jumped off the dock, and ran toward the 14th Pursuit Wing Headquarters.

As he dashed up a steep slope leading to a construction site, where foundation trenches had been dug and lumber stacked ready for use, machine gun bullets raked the dirt in front of him. He scrambled behind a high stack of two-by-fours for protection. When the strafing stopped, he raised his head to look around and could smell the odor of burning oil. Across the way, almost every building along the flight line seemed on fire, and the Japanese pilots continued to strafe hangars, aircraft, and fleeing personnel.

The new P-40s were being blown to bits, their burning parts scattering along the ramp in all directions, setting other planes on fire. One P-40 fell in two pieces, its prop pointing almost straight up. A P-36 exploded, hurling flaming debris upon a nearby tent, setting it ablaze. A man ran from the tent, climbed into an old Plymouth, and drove only a short distance before being hit by a strafing aircraft. The car burst into flames, then exploded, but the driver jumped out in time, his clothes smoking, and ran into a building unharmed.

Private First Class Robert R. Shattauck wasn't as fortunate. A switchboard operator assigned to the 15th Pursuit Group's communications section, he and his buddies were eating breakfast when the attack began. They hurriedly left the mess hall and ran down to the tents where they lived. The first sergeant was there and told them to get out of the area since it was under heavy attack. Some stayed back to help fight fires, and the rest reported to the communications tent. Shattuck and Private Nelson were heading toward his duty station through the tent area when he was hit by shrapnel. One of his legs was torn off, and he died a short time later.

Back at the construction site, two men joined Henry Woodrum in taking cover behind the lumber pile. One was a young, crewcut lad, about 20 years old, who crawled to the end of the pile with his upper body extending beyond it. Although cautioned to get back before he got hit, he refused. "I can see 'em coming from out here." He began to laugh, treating the situation as a joke, but suddenly gasped and rolled halfway over, his body rigid, then quivering, before he flopped back on his belly and died. The rear gunners on the Japanese dive bombers had spotted Woodrum and others hiding among the piles of lumber. They began to take shots at them as the aircraft pulled out of strafing passes.

The men decided to take their chances and dash for the barracks, which was only one hundred feet away. One man reached the top of the embankment but was cut down by a line of machine gun bullets that stitched their way through the moist dirt, sending him tumbling into a motionless heap at the bottom of the slope. Woodrum and the others managed to make it to safety.[22]

When the brief lull came after the first wave of attacks, Wilfred Burke hurried back toward his tent. Reaching the street corner where the bomb that earlier had hit behind him had exploded, he was horrified to see six or seven bodies lying around. One had been completely denuded by the bomb blast, its head and one arm missing from the torso. When he reached his tent, he went inside to pick up his helmet and found two other men retrieving theirs. The helmets had only recently been issued and were the old World War I "tin hats." Before putting them on, all three men had to stop and take the time to lace in the helmet linings, indicating how unprepared they were for an attack.

A corporal ordered Burke to assist with casualties in the next tent, which was riddled with holes. The first man he saw was beyond help, crouched on the floor in a bizarre position of death, with part of his head missing. A seriously wounded soldier lay on his bunk with his abdomen ripped open by a bomb fragment, exposing his intestines. He was conscious and stared at them but didn't speak. They carried him on a stretcher to the dispensary. Several other wounded men had already been brought in and were on the floor awaiting medical attention. All were silent and uncomplaining. These were among the first of a seemingly endless stream of wounded, dead, and dying which would overwhelm available ambulance services on Oahu, and flood dispensaries, real and makeshift aid stations, infirmaries, and hospitals aboard ships in Pearl Harbor and on the island's military air fields—except at Haleiwa auxiliary field which lay in the bend of the northwest coast line, at the foot of the Koolau Mountain Range.[23]

Fighting Back in the Air . . .

The Japanese had planned to attack Haleiwa Field during the return to their carriers, but it was the one military airfield not touched by either wave of attackers. Lieutenants George S. Welch and Kenneth Taylor, two P-40 fighter pilots whose spirit would have been admired by Admiral Yamamoto, had just completed a night of poker games following a dance at the Wheeler officers' club, and picked up their chips about 0800. Their airplanes were at Haleiwa, three P-40s, in addition to four P-36s. When they heard explosions and the crackling of machine gun fire, they went outside to see what was going on, and recognized an air attack was in progress, Welch dashed to a phone, and called Haleiwa.

"Get two P-40s ready!" he yelled. "It's not a gag—the Japs are here." The drive from Wheeler Field to Haleiwa was a wild one. Zekes made three strafing passes at them—and missed. The two officers arrived at Haleiwa in nine minutes to find their fighters armed and waiting, propellers turning over. Without waiting for orders, they took off. With a few other pilots fortunate enough to get in the air from Wheeler Field, they pressed repeated attacks against the strike force—while often taking fire from American defenders on ships and the ground. Before the air battles were over, the small band of Hawaiian Air Force fighter pilots would exact a toll from the attackers, at no small cost to themselves.[24]

A Surgeon's Unforgettable Emergency Recall to Duty

Schofield Barracks, located next to Wheeler Field, also appeared to be under attack with all the aircraft flying in the area; however, other than isolated individual strafing attacks, on targets of opportunity, the Japanese did not specifically target Schofield and the 25th Infantry Division. Nevertheless, there were several strafing attacks at Schofield, on the Engineer, Artillery and Infantry quadrangles, the post hospital, and at least two attacks on officers' quarters. Unquestionably, the Japanese considered military housing areas valid, though lower priority targets. As a result of attacks at Schofield various other locations, two 25th Division soldiers were killed and seventeen were wounded.[25]

Major Leonard D. Heaton, physician and surgeon at Schofield's Army Hospital, and two other Army physicians, both captains assigned to the Schofield Hospital, were stunned to find themselves dangerously close to becoming casualties in two strafing attacks in the Schofield housing area. After dodging a Japanese fighter on the first firing pass down Major Heaton's street, by going inside the house, the three doctors and Sara Hill Heaton, his wife, again stepped outside—then had to scramble for cover inside the house a second time. Throughout the Sunday morning moments of shocked disbelief, their seven year-old daughter, Sara Dudley Heaton, was in their officers' quarters in bed, ill. Leonard Heaton wrote in his diary:

> Sunday—Dec. 7, 1941.
> The best and happiest days of our lives went up in the smoke of Pearl Harbor, Wheeler Field, and Hickam Field today. I wonder if, when and how they will ever return.
> I was standing with Capt's Bell and [Harlan] Taylor in front of my quarters about 8 o'clock this day. We were about to get in the car to pick up Col. Canning and thence to Queen's Hospital to attend a lecture by Dr. Jno. Moorhead of N.Y. who has been talking of traumatic surgery. We hesitated before entering the car because our attention was called to the great number of planes in the air and some very loud distant noises. Soon one plane came quite close to us and in banking to come down our street I distinctly saw the rising sun insignia on his wings. Soon he was coming down the street with machine guns blazing away at us. We rushed into the house.
> As long as I live I shall never forget my feelings and emotions when I saw and realized that these

were Jap planes and that we were in for the real thing. Something we never thought could ever happen to us here due to primarily our great naval force and implicit faith in such.

Back in the house Sara Hill inquired of the situation and I told her. Sara Dudley was sick with the nasal bronchitis and in bed. The four of us went back out on the sidewalk. Then we distinctly saw dive bombers and bombs over Wheeler Field and much black smoke in the direction of Pearl Harbor. There were many planes by now all over and around us. I remarked as must have many others before us in situations like this, "Where are our planes?" Whereupon another Jap plane came down our street spraying everything and everybody with machine guns. We rushed back into the house again and at this time I got an urgent call to come immediately to the hospital. I hurried off after comforting Sara Hill and Sara Dudley as best I could. The first wounded had arrived from Wheeler Field and we immediately set our operating teams in action . . .

The attacking Zekes that swept through the Schofield housing area left an indelible mark on the Heaton family's lives, and a souvenir to remind them of that day. An empty shell casing from an expended 7.7-mm machine gun was ejected from the aircraft and landed in their front yard, a family keepsake and reminder for the generations. Dr. Heaton wrote much more in his diary on 7 December, after working tirelessly among the four surgical teams throughout a long, bloody day on into early evening—struggling to save lives. Many could not be saved.[26]

After completing their bombing runs on Wheeler Field, the Japanese dive bomber pilots began making strafing passes on parked aircraft, which were lined up in rows perpendicular to the runway and ramp, ostensibly against the far greater threat of sabotage, which General Short and his senior Army commanders on Oahu had repeatedly emphasized in the preceding months—and was the procedure for aircraft parking in Alert One. Joining the dive bombers' follow-on strafing attacks, coming from the north and south, along the length of the rows of aircraft, came the Zeroes which had been released from their role of top cover for the bombers.

The wreckage of Captain Raymond T. Swenson's B-17C, Serial No. 40-2074, which burned in two after landing, following a Japanese fighter's airborne machine gun attack that hit its flare storage box. Flight surgeon, Lieutenant William R. Schick was aboard Swenson's aircraft, and with the crew members, escaped, was running to take cover, only to be fatally wounded by a ricocheting machine gun bullet from a strafing Japanese fighter. NA

The Japanese planes' ammunition loads of two armor piercing, one tracer; two armor piercing, one tracer; two armor-piercing, and one incendiary round, took a terrible toll, destroying and damaging numerous aircraft, starting fires accompanied with thick, black smoke—among aircraft caught on the ramp and in hangars. Many men who early recognized the enemy overhead and scrambled for cover or attempted to bring antiaircraft fire to bear wherever they could, fell victim to the onslaught—dead or wounded. The attacks included tent areas housing airmen between hangars and near maintenance facilities. At times there were over 30 fighters and dive bombers attacking Wheeler from every direction, a tactic used on every target complex on Oahu. The well-planned and executed tactic was designed not only to destroy fighter opposition on the ground and ships in the harbor, but to confuse and overwhelm gunners who might try to mount an effective antiaircraft defense. While aiming and firing in one direction at an airborne target, approaching fighter pilots pressing attacks at low altitude could see and cut down the defenders from another direction.

After making several strafing attacks on Wheeler, Lieutenant Akira Sakamoto led the dive bombers south to the Mooring Mast Field at Ewa, and inflicted more damage with their guns. The Zekes continued pressing their attacks on Wheeler a little longer, then left for other targets.

The dive bombers and fighters that struck Hickam Field were not the first indicators of an oncoming assault on the American bombers and reconnaissance aircraft at the large airfield complex. Moments before the inferno exploded on Hickam, some of Murata's Kate torpedo bombers from the *Soryu* and *Hiryu*, which, at altitudes of approximately fifty feet, attacked ships moored on the west side of Ford Island and the main docks on the east side of the harbor, made right turns over Hickam field, to exit the target area. They crossed Hickam after lead torpedo bombers from *Akagi* and *Kaga* flew at 50 to 75 feet, swinging wide to the southeast of the hangar line, but near Hickam, onto a southeast to northwest initial approach for torpedo runs against battleship row.

Coming on near parallel tracks toward battleship row, further to the north, were torpedo bombers from *Soryu* and *Hiryu*. Before anyone could react to the sounds of aircraft and explosions coming from Pearl Harbor or identify still low flying Kates, the fighters and dive bombers were upon Hickam. While the assault shattered and burned Hickam, all the other military airfields on Oahu, and their aircraft, the ships and men in Pearl Harbor were to confront their own special kind of hell.[27]

Similar to the initial attacks at Wheeler Field, the first targets [at Hickam] were those in and around the hangars but concentrated almost exclusively on the Hawaiian Air Depot. During the second wave the attacks widened to include hits on supply buildings, the consolidated barracks and dining hall, the base chapel, the enlisted men's beer garden, and the guardhouse all in just the first few minutes. This was in addition to machine gun attacks by both the dive bombers and the fighters on aircraft and personnel visible in the area. Within minutes the base was ablaze with many fires, and the Americans lost any chance of quickly launching aircraft to locate and attack the carriers.[28]

While the Val dive bomber's first bombs were ravaging Ford Island, Kate torpedo bombers, hugging the ground and water surface at 50 to 75 feet were rapidly approaching ships moored on both sides of Ford Island and in the harbor, and horizontal bombers were closing in at higher altitudes from the southwest and northeast—quickly followed by low level fighter attacks.

Among the first to feel the torpedo bombers' stings, were men and women going to 8:00 a.m. Mass at the Bloch Recreation Center at Fleet Landing, across the harbor to the east from where the battleships were moored. Pharmacist Mate Third Class Joseph Honish had weekend duty at the Naval Hospital. There was no chapel in the Navy Yard, so Joe and his buddy, dressed in "sailor whites," took the shuttle bus from the hospital to the Recreation Center, and were standing in line to enter the Center, when the first wave of torpedo bombers roared low overhead.

There was instantaneous reaction from the gathering crowd, heads and eyes up and rapidly turning around to see what this was all about. Another military exercise? The Army Air Force had just had an exercise yesterday. Then in a flash came different images and a different set of sounds Joe and his buddy would remember the rest of their lives. The startling red "meatballs" on the Japanese airplanes, followed immediately with the stunned reaction of the people walking up the steps. A sailor among them fell and a woman who was passing through the front gate walking toward the Center's front steps, went down, both at the instant sounds of the "pop, pop, pop" of machine gun fire reached the observers from above the fading roar of the low flying airplanes speeding away from them, across the water toward the battleships.

Rear facing machine gunners on the Kates, consistent with plans and briefings, were firing their swivel-mounted, 7.7-mm machine guns at targets of opportunity and, as a defensive measure, to keep potential gunners "heads down." The big, low, slow-flying Kates were taking both the offensive and defensive as their pilots flew them on their final dashes to torpedo release— then up, over huge ships and the naval air station on Ford Island Naval airfield, potentially bristling with antiaircraft guns. The gunners had scored hits within sight of Joe and his buddy. One machine gun bullet wounded the sailor climbing the steps, the other tore a large chunk of flesh from the inside of the woman's left thigh, taking her down.

People scattered or rushed inside the Center for cover, while some immediately gathered around the sailor, to assist him. Joe and his buddy rushed to assist the woman lying on the ground just inside the gate. It was a dangerous flesh wound, the bleeding had to be stanched, and she needed to be taken to the hospital immediately. She could soon be entering shock. They tore cloth from her petticoat, fashioned a tourniquet from it, commandeered a willing man and his automobile, lifted her into the car, and accompanied her in the race toward the Naval Hospital, through rapidly swelling traffic taking men to their duty stations.

En route they passed near the inside of the main gate to the Naval Base, and Japanese planes were still passing low overhead. As they raced by the main gate, they saw Marine guards with .45-caliber pistols drawn, firing at the airplanes roaring past them. They got their wounded patient safely to medical care, but had to leave her in hands that would help heal her wounds. The ride was wild, frightening, but the day was long from over for Joe Honish and his hospital "shipmate." For both, the horror of that day was just beginning. The parade of wounded, dead and dying was just beginning.[29]

In Pearl Harbor's Navy family housing area that morning, in a duplex at 501 5th Street West, across the street from three huge oil storage tanks and near the fleet's Bloch Recreation Center, were thirteen-year old Margaret "Peggy" Littmann, her fifteen-year old brother, Vincent, and her parents. Peggy's dad, Lieutenant Robert A. Littmann, was the communications officer on board the minelayer USS *Oglala*. The family, which included two older brothers not with the family—one still on the mainland, the other at sea when the attack occurred—had arrived on Oahu in September. Peggy's aunt, with a sixteen-year old son and just-born twins, all Peggy's first cousins, had taken her brother and parents in with their family pending availability of government quarters.

The Littmanns were also preparing to attend Catholic Mass. Peggy's dad was going to take them to the Honolulu Cathedral. Suddenly everyone heard a loud explosion. Peggy's 16-year old cousin ran outside to see what happened. He looked up, saw a low-flying airplane pass nearby, and immediately recognized the Japanese insignia on its wings. He dashed in the house and excitedly told everyone what he had seen. Peggy promptly went outside to see for herself, turned and saw another airplane fly past the house at low altitude. The next instant a shard of metal fell from the sky she had been gazing into, and landed about 3 to 4 feet from her—shrapnel or piece of something torn apart by an explosion. That was ample warning for Peggy. Fortunately no machine guns fired in her direction.

She retreated into the house. The sight that greeted her was even more sobering for a thirteen-year old girl. Her mother, Margaret, and aunt were on their knees in the bedroom, saying the Rosary. "Hail Mary, full of grace, blessed be thy name and blessed is the fruit of thy womb, Jesus. Holy Mary, Mother of God, pray for us sinners, now, and at the hour of our death . . . " Her father reacted quickly while the two women were praying, and began putting on his uniform, knowing he had to get to his duty station on board the *Oglala*. While the noise and intensity of the nearby battle raced toward a crescendo and prayerful fear was gripping the family, Peggy went to a window trying to see what was happening across the harbor.

Within moments, more planes were in the skies above Pearl Harbor, Ford Island, and to the south over Hickam. Explosions shook the area and gunfire could be heard. Her mother came to the window and stood behind her, watching the unfolding disaster where the battleships were moored. In a few short minutes they would forever etch in their memories the huge, fiery explosion that tore apart the *Arizona* at 8:08 a.m. and eventually took the lives of 1,077 of the battleship's officers and men. In her memory of so long ago she still sees the bodies blown from the decks of the *Arizona* and the repair ship *Vestal*, which was moored alongside, outboard of *Arizona*.

By the time Peggy's father reached his ship through the shocked, generally dazed first reactions and overwhelmed transportation of hundreds of others trying to get to the their ships and duty stations, the *Oglala* lay forlornly capsized, next to Dock 1010, near where she had been moored, outboard the light cruiser *Helena*. Lieutenant Littmann's normal duty station now lay under water, but his strong, internal call to duty urged him to somehow help—somewhere. He left the dock for the hospital, to offer his assistance.

By 2 p.m. the Marines set up a machine gun position in front of the house in which the Littmanns were staying, undoubtedly to defend against expected attacks on the nearby, giant fuel storage tanks—the entire family vacated their quarters and rode

Red Cross buses to the presumed safety of the Honolulu YMCA. Like everyone else on the island, they were experiencing the first, abrupt, wrenching change from peace on a beautiful tropical island, to the holocaust of war.[30]

South of Littman's temporary quarters, another bloody disaster was unfolding. To those at Hickam Field, the Japanese appeared to strike in three waves, though the carriers launched only two waves. Men working on the flight line and in the control tower that morning observed what they later described as "nine enemy single-engine, low-wing monoplanes carrying torpedoes" flying southeast of the hangar line, turning in a wide arc toward Pearl Harbor at an altitude of 50 feet. They were in two echelons, five in one, four in the second. Although these planes—Kates— were destined for Pearl Harbor, Val dive bombers came in shortly afterward and hit the technical buildings at the Hawaiian Air Depot, and the hangar line. After a lull, Japanese bombers returned around 0825 and struck again, with strafing attacks. Then once more about 0900, that time part of the carrier strike force's second wave of 167 planes.

With the first wave air attack by the Japanese, hell rushed in to Bomber Command's paradise. When they struck, Colonel Farthing, Hickam's base commander, was in the control tower awaiting the arrival of the B-17s from California. Lieutenant Colonel Cheney L. Bertholf, the adjutant general of the Hawaiian Air Force was with Farthing. In the tower the two officers had a panoramic view of the surrounding area, and watched what they believed to be Navy planes taking off from Ford Island and going around toward the Pearl Harbor Naval Base on the east side of the island. While watching the planes apparently taking off from Ford Island, they heard "a bunch of airplanes diving in, coming from about 10,000 feet." The two officers recognized they weren't Army planes and concluded they were Marines.

The planes dived on Pearl Harbor. Farthing saw a black object leave the first plane and hit with an explosion. As the plane recovered from the dive it rolled into a turn, heading directly toward Hickam. While it was in the turn, the base commander and the adjutant could see the orange "meatball" insignia of Japan, "The Land of the Rising Sun." Bertholf immediately rushed down from the tower to sound the alarm. Farthing came right behind him and saw the airplane, a Val, approaching at about 25 feet, firing its guns. Rounds struck the No. 3 (right inboard) engine of a B-17 parked on the ramp, setting it on fire, and setting some B-18s ablaze on the same strafing pass. The aircraft were parked so close together that when one was hit, probably by an incendiary round or tracer, they all seemed to catch fire—when the reality was the streams of machine gun rounds from guns on both wings of the dive bomber were tearing through the entire line of aircraft.

The Val flew past, ceased fire, reversed hard, made another pass across the field, and seemed to be firing at Colonel Farthing, the only person in the area at that time. He hit the dirt and stayed there the remainder of the first wave attack.

The first wave of enemy planes to attack Hickam approached over Fort Kamehameha and scored direct hits on the Hawaiian Air Depot's large hangar, destroying much of its contents. The depot restaurant was a total loss, but supply buildings were untouched except for scattered machine gun bullets, shrapnel, and flying debris.

The B-17s' Welcome to Oahu . . .

Captain Gordon A. Blake, Hickam's base operations officer, had been in his office in the operations building since 0700 preparing for the B-17 arrival. His good friend, Major Roger Ramey was there, too, partly in his capacity as A-3, operations officer in the Hawaiian Air Force, but mostly because his classmate and close friend, Major Truman H. Landon, was leading the incoming flight of 38th Reconnaissance Squadron B-17s. Blake and Ramey were sitting there "chewing the fat" and listening to reports coming in to the tower when they suddenly heard a loud explosion. Dashing outside, they saw a dive bomber with the Japanese insignia on the underside of its wings pulling up almost directly overhead after bombing the Hawaiian Air Depot.

Blake's first thought was to get the B-17s down safely, so he ran to the tower to guide them in. The twelve Flying Fortresses and their crews, four B-17Cs, older models, and eight newer, differently-configured B-17Es never before seen in Hawaii, began arriving singly at intervals of up to ten minutes. Throughout the attack they came, unwittingly scheduled into a dangerous, chaotic nightmare. Low on fuel and totally defenseless, except for whatever evasive, maneuvering skills the pilots might possess, the aircraft commanders of the big, four-engine Fortresses, were taking their cues from Hickam tower and aircraft in the stream ahead of them. When asked for landing instructions the tower controller calmly gave wind direction, velocity, and the runway on which to land, as though it were any other day, occasionally reporting that the field was under attack by "unidentified planes." The calm voice gave some steadiness and assurance to men who soon recognized they were in serious trouble.

Lead B-17 crews in the 38th Reconnaissance Squadron's six airplanes, in some ways, may have been more fortunate, but undoubtedly they didn't think so. They were contending with Japanese fighters making firing passes before the defenseless bombers could touch down on the runway at Hickam. The Japanese attacked at least five aircraft in the two arriving squadrons, and destroyed two of them—both in the 38th. Miraculously, five of the 38th's six landed at their planned destination, with the last to arrive recovering at Bellows, all while the furious Japanese attack was in progress.

Nearing the end of 13-hour flight, Major Landon and his crew were the first to fly into the inferno about to erupt at Hickam—and was already in progress on and around Ford Island. From Pearl Harbor, Chief Machinist's Mate (AA) Harry Rafsky, enlisted aide to Rear Admiral William L. Calhoun, commander, Base Force, saw the big bombers approaching and thought they belonged to the enemy. He said to himself, *Jesus Christ, the Japanese are really coming in now!*

Landon was pleased to see a group of planes flying toward his airplane from the south, at a higher altitude. *Here comes the Air Force out to greet us*, he thought. At that instant he saw the planes rolling into a diving turn toward their B-17E, setting up for an attack, the red "meatball" clearly evident on their wings. A voice over Landon's intercom barked, "Damn it, those are Japs!" They rapidly closed on their target, swinging toward the tail of the bomber, machine guns blazing.

Landon evaded the attackers on their first attempt at a shoot-down, but his troubles weren't yet over. As he turned to land, Gordon Blake warned from the control tower, "You have three Japs on your tail." Landon looked back and confirmed Blake's observation. The Zekes were doggedly hanging onto his plane, and to make matters worse, the gunners on the ground, unfamiliar with

---

the B-17E, added to the hail of fire coming their way. Nevertheless, Major Landon landed the lead aircraft safely, with no one killed or wounded. In spite of such "fortune," war's brutal randomness had its effects on the second 38th aircraft to land at Hickam, and the last, Captain Robert H. Richard's B-17C, aircraft serial number 40-2049, which finally attempted recovery at Bellows.

Captain Raymond T. Swenson, aircraft commander and pilot of B-17C, aircraft serial number 40-2074, was the second to attempt landing at Hickam Field. He circled, trying to get landing instructions. On board were one aviation cadet, four enlisted men, and three other officers including Lieutenant William R. Schick, who was the squadron flight surgeon assigned to the 38th a few days prior to the B-17s' departure from Hamilton Field.

Second Lieutenant Lee E. Metcalf, 23rd Bomb Squadron, was new to the Hickam B-17 squadron, having received his pilot's wings one month earlier. He was on foot heading for the flight line, crossing the railroad tracks on "Hangar Boulevard," looking down in stunned disbelief at pieces of bodies near where a bomb had hit. He looked up to see a B-17 making a landing approach with a Japanese fighter in hot pursuit, attacking the bomber. Metcalf was unaware he was watching Swenson attempting to land while evading the attacker. To Metcalf it appeared the B-17 overshot the runway due to excessive speed, and had to "go around" and try again. On board the aircraft, however a far more serious problem would soon erupt.

A bullet fired by an attacking Japanese fighter pierced the radio compartment, igniting a bundle of magnesium flares and wounding Schick in the leg. Fortunately, no one was killed by the enemy fighter's guns. However, seconds later, the big plane was afire inside and would soon become a blazing torch from mid-fuselage to the tail section. To escape the flames, the crew moved to the front of the plane.

Now fearing a mid-air explosion, Swenson radioed the tower he was coming in for an emergency landing. He knew there would be no more "go arounds." Again, briefly, fortune was still on their side. The attack on Hickam was in its early stages, and the runway was clear of bomb craters and debris. Descending through a storm of Japanese tracer rounds and now increasing American antiaircraft fire, Swenson and his co-pilot, Lieutenant Ernest Reid, kept the crippled, burning Fortress under control, all the way to a near-perfect touchdown. But during the touchdown and landing rollout, the plane's fuselage, weakened by the fire's intense heat, cracked and broke apart aft of the cockpit and forward of the aft wing root. The front section of the Fortress skidded to a stop, nose pointed more sharply skyward, with the disconnected tail section coming to rest some distance away.

The crew jumped from the wrecked aircraft, finding themselves in the middle of the airfield, hundreds of yards from shelter, with a fierce battle raging. They split up. One group made for the hangar line where airplanes and buildings were exploding and burning. The other group, which included Lieutenant Schick, sprinted for the grass on the Honolulu side of the field, where Lieutenant Bruce Allen and his eight men, the first B-17 crew to land after Landon's, and shortly before Swenson's aircraft, were hugging the ground as Japanese bullets thudded around them.

As Schick's group dashed across the runway, the pilot of a Japanese fighter strafing the airfield caught sight of them, aimed, and opened fire, missing them all—except for a ricochet which struck Schick in the face.

Later, at the Hickam Hospital, Captain Frank H. Lane, the acting hospital commander, came across Schick in the middle of the confusion wrought by the attack and flood of dead and wounded coming into the hospital. Lane remembered,

> He was a young medical officer who had arrived on the B-17 bombers from the States during the raid. When I first noticed him he was sitting on the stairs leading to the second story of the hospital. I suppose the reason my attention was called to him was that he was dressed in a winter uniform which we never wore in the islands, and had the insignia of a medical officer on his lapels. He had a wound in his face and when I went to take care of him he pointed to the casualties on litters on the floor and said, "take care of them." I told him I'd get him on the next ambulance going to Tripler General Hospital [at Fort Shafter], which I did. The next day I heard that he died after arriving at Tripler.

Four other men on Swenson's crew were wounded that day: Aviation Cadet G.C. Beale, Private Bert Lee, Jr., Master Sergeant LeRoy B. Pouncey, and 2nd Lieutenant Homer Taylor.

First Lieutenant Robert H. Richards, flew the last 38th aircraft in line attempting to land his B-17C at Hickam, but repeated Japanese fighter attacks harassed him so badly he aborted the landing and headed east out to sea. The Zekes riddled the airplane and damaged ailerons. He tried to lose his attackers along the southern coast of the island, turned, and roared over Waimanalo Bay toward Bellows' short fighter strip. By the time Richards slowed the giant for a landing into the wind, the Japanese attackers' first major assault after the lone Zeke raked the tent line about 0830, would soon be ripping into Bellows.

No one at Bellows knew of the B-17s' arrival at Hickam that morning, and certainly no one at Bellows expected to see a large four-engine bomber suddenly appear on final approach for landing, pointed toward the ocean. Richards was descending on short final when crew chief Earl Sutton taxied his P-40 across the runway heading for a dispersal area, crossing in front of the rapidly closing bomber. Richards had no choice. He added power, pulled back on the yoke, and executed a "go around," undoubtedly desperately low on fuel, with engines badly overworked and overheated following a flight of more than 13 hours. No time to make a full 360-degree circuit and land into the wind.

Sergeant Covelesky recalled:

> No one was aware of the flight of bombers arriving from the states, and to see that approaching monster trailing smoke from its right engines . . . was mind-boggling. Our asphalt landing strip at Bellows was hardly long enough to accommodate our P-40s, much less a B-17; and when he made an approach from the ocean downwind, we knew we were in for a breathtaking crash landing. Even though his wheels were down, he flared out and touched down halfway on the strip, knowing he wouldn't be able to stop, retracted the wheels and slid off the runway over a ditch and into a cane field bordering the strip.

Fire trucks and an ambulance converged on the aircraft. The B-17 crew immediately went to work salvaging the bombsight, that it wouldn't fall into enemy hands should the Japanese invade the island. Private Lester A. Ellis of the 86th Observation Squadron was ordered to position himself on the runway, armed

The US Flag flies over Hickam Field during the attack on Pearl Harbor and other major targets on Oahu. Note the burning consolidated barracks buildings in the background. NPSAM

with a Springfield rifle, and shout warnings whenever enemy aircraft started strafing runs. They wouldn't have long to wait. The second wave was already on the way to visit Bellows with far more deadly attacks than one Zeke strafing a tent line.

The 88th Reconnaissance Squadron's six B-17E aircraft and their crews were more fortunate. They lost no airplanes, and had no casualties. Warned of the attacks at Hickam, by radio transmissions between the tower and the 38th Squadron's six airplanes, only three landed at the destination field. The remaining three went elsewhere. Two, commanded by Captain Richard H. Carmichael, the squadron's lead aircraft commander, and Lieutenant Harold N. Chaffin, passed up Hickam and flew to Haleiwa Auxiliary Field, which the Japanese planned to attack on their way back to their carriers—but had chosen otherwise. First Lieutenant Frank P. Bostrom piloted the third aircraft, and after attempting several landings at Hickam, only to be attacked each time by Japanese fighters, headed for Barbers Point and eventually flew to the northern part of the island—where the defenseless bomber was again attacked by the Japanese. Desperate to find anyplace reasonably level and long enough, Bostrom landed his bomber safely on Kahuku Golf Course, with rapidly repairable damage, and no injury to crew members.

After the eight B-17s landed at Hickam, Blake left the control tower to see Major Landon, whom he had known as a cadet, so he could pass instructions to get their planes ready in case higher authority assigned them a mission. He rode out to Landon's revetment on the back of a fancy motorcycle driven by a large Hawaiian man wearing a big, wide, studded leather belt. The cyclist and other members of the Honolulu Motor Club had appeared on the scene to offer their help.[31]

The First Attack on Bomber Command

Private Edward E. Hall of Greenwood, South Carolina enlisted in the Army two months after Germany invaded Poland. A truck driver in the 13th Quartermaster Truck Company, Aviation, at Hickam, he normally hauled food, clothing, equipment and other supplies issued from the Hawaiian Air Force depot warehouses to other base and outlying units. On Thursday he returned from approximately two weeks of maneuvers. He stood Saturday morning inspection, and volunteered to come in around 0700 hours Sunday for some extra "Kitchen Police" (KP) duty—to earn needed supplementary cash. His unit's mess hall was at a temporary location, because the permanent building was being refurbished, necessitating use of a compressor with a field stove for cooking breakfast. His friend, Alex, was working with him.

"Hey! Hall! Alex yelled. You going skating tonight?" Going skating was the only thing on Ed Hall's mind. Before he could answer, a loud noise interrupted the conversation. Believing it to be the compressor, he dismissed it. There was no mistaking the explosion heard next. It sounded as if the hangars were being bombed directly across the street. He ran to the back door to look outside, just in time to see Hangar 7 blown up, with debris flying in every direction. Out of the corner of his eye he saw men running out of the nearer Hangars, 2 and 4, scattering, while pieces of asphalt flew everywhere.

Instant shock and fear. His first reaction was to take cover underneath a large sink inside the building. Then more explosions followed by a momentary pause. He walked outside and looked up, startled to see an airplane flying "the wrong way," directly toward him, across the runway and parking apron, coming northwest, machine guns firing. He stood momentarily transfixed while the deadly bullet trail came toward him. Abruptly, the firing stopped as the pilot pulled the airplane's nose up sharply to avoid power lines. Ed turned and dashed into the building, fleeing with a lifelong memory. A thin power line had saved his life. Alex, Ed and everyone inside rushed through the front door to take cover underneath roof overhangs in the next line of one story supply buildings, away from the flight line, and adjacent to the two story wood barracks of Splinter City—the name given to the approximately 28 two-story, barracks buildings by the men who lived in them.

They dodged bullets as they ran around building corners and hid beneath overhangs, hoping they were hidden next to buildings not worthy targets for bombers, and could remain unseen by low flying enemy pilots hunting machine gun targets. Another brief pause. Ed stepped away from the wall to look again. Someone grabbed his clothes and pulled him back. "Get outta there! You'll get killed!" No sooner was he pulled back under cover than another Japanese plane strafed the building they were hiding against, and bullets tore a chunk from the corner of the overhang. Enough. Enough for one day. Enough for a lifetime.

For Ed Hall, and all the men in the 13th Quartermaster Truck Company, Aviation, who survived the attack on Hickam Field, these first frantic, fear-filled minutes were just the beginning of three days of non-stop duty, work too often filled with tragic and macabre sights—and the smell of death.[32]

Days before the attack, Brigadier General Jacob H. Rudolph of the 18th Bombardment Wing had scheduled a flight of B-18s for "some of the youngsters who had not completed B-18 training." He had more airplanes than pilots assigned, so this Sunday morning flight provided the opportunity to give them an extra hour of training. Twenty-four men were in the hangar, moving the bombers out in preparation for an 0800 takeoff, when the Japanese attacked, scored a direct hit, and killed twenty-two of them outright, while seriously injuring the other two. Outside,

Master Sergeant Dave Jacobson was changing a B-18 tire on the ramp. He disappeared without a trace when a bomb hit.

After the first wave, all Hawaiian Air Depot officers came in and assisted with fire fighting, salvaging material, and other requirements. Approximately 100 civilian employees also reported for duty, including Mr. Phillip W. Eldred, purchasing clerk for supply, who was strafed and killed on his way to the depot. Another employee, Mr. John B. Gordon Bankston, suffered temporary paralysis in his left arm, when hit by a piece of flying shrapnel.

Private First Class Robert P. Chase, an aircraft mechanic assigned to the 23rd Bomb Squadron, awoke from a deep sleep to the thunderous roar of exploding bombs and watched in utter disbelief as enemy aircraft repeatedly strafed the barracks. Private Ira W. Southern got up to the sound of what he thought was heavy artillery gunfire. This was not unusual, since target sleeves were regularly towed close to Hickam; but the noise seemed louder, sharper and more erratic than usual. After grumbling that target practice should be held sometime other than Sunday morning, he strolled over to the windows to look outside.

He could see a plane, flying at an altitude of about 500 feet, coming toward the barracks but thought nothing of it until he saw a large object drop from the plane. The next thing he knew, there was a terrible explosion, and the engine repair depot across the street seemed to disintegrate. At the same time, he noted with horror that the plane pulling out of the dive was clearly marked with the Japanese rising sun insignia. A sudden explosion drowned out the roar of the plane overhead. A low-flying plane had dropped a bomb through the window, tearing a huge hole in the floor and filling the barracks with flying shrapnel.

Chaos reigned as shocked, panic-stricken men milled around in all directions. More and more earthquake-like shocks rattled the building as the enemy planes expended their bombs. The racket of explosions, shouting, and yelled orders to vacate the barracks was deafening. Southern went to his locker to get his gas mask but was so nervous, he couldn't work the combination to the lock. He finally got the locker open, slung his canister gas mask across his shoulder, and headed down the stairwell toward the supply room to get a gun and some ammunition. As he reached the ground floor landing, he saw that several dying and wounded men had been dragged inside the building for protection. The supply room was locked, so the men broke open the door, only to find that the rifles were all neatly locked in the racks.

They somehow broke the locks, grabbed Springfield (bolt action) rifles and Colt .45 semi-automatic pistols, found the ammunition stored in boxes on the shelves, and dragged several boxes to the floor. Bombs that hit nearby were sending fragments of shrapnel flying through windows of the supply room, so they lay on the floor while filling their bandoliers, then dashed outside the barracks and began firing fruitlessly at the bombing, strafing enemy planes.

Others who fought back included Sergeant Stanley McLeod, who stood on the parade ground, east of the consolidated barracks, firing a Thompson submachine gun, alongside Corporal William T. Anderson. Both men lost their lives. A soldier kneeling near some bushes, took potshots at the attacking planes with a bolt-action Springfield rifle. Staff Sergeant Doyle King fired his submachine gun from under a panel truck. Master Sergeant Olef Jensen of the 72nd Bomb Squadron directed the emplacement of machine guns, and one of his crews under Staff Sergeant R.R. Mitchell claimed credit for shooting down an enemy plane.

Technical Sergeant Wilbur Hunt set up twelve .50-caliber machine guns in bomb craters near the barracks, then unexpectedly got the gunners he needed. A bomb had blown off a corner of the guardhouse on the west side of the consolidated barracks, next to the fire station, releasing all the prisoners, who dashed over to Hunt and said they were ready to go to work. He immediately put them on the guns. On the ball diamond, north of the fire station and guardhouse two men set up a machine gun on a tripod between home plate and some trees along the edge of the field. Suddenly a wave of high-level bombers—Kates—released their deadly loads of high explosives and they fell right on the ball field, scoring a direct hit on the gun, killing both men instantly.

By the time the next wave of attackers came, ground defenses were going full blast. In addition to the parade ground and the barracks area, guns were set up on the hangar line and even around the flagpole at post headquarters. Green troops under fire acted like veterans and displayed amazing courage. A corporal sped across the parade ground to help man a machine gun that was entirely in the open without any protection whatsoever. Halfway there, he was strafed by a low-flying Japanese plane.

Mortally wounded, he kept on trying to reach that machine gun but fell dead on the way.

Time and time again, as the machine gunners fell, others rushed to take their places. One man managed to lug—no one knows how—a machine gun to the top of one of the hangars that hadn't been bombed and was perched up there, popping away at the strafing planes. On the apron in front of the hangars, a "mild-mannered private first class who was an orderly room clerk" climbed into a B-18 and mounted a .30-caliber machine gun in the nose. The gun was unstable, because the mount was made for an aerial gun; but he braced it against his shoulder and kept up a steady stream of fire. An enemy plane flew low, strafed the B-18, setting it afire with incendiary rounds. There was no way for him to escape, and spectators nearby said he did not even seem to try, but kept on firing. Long after the flames had enveloped the nose of the plane, they heard his screams and saw the tracer bullets from his machine gun mounting skyward.

The valiant men who fought to defend the base were exceptional individuals, well deserving of the honors they later received, posthumously in many cases. The average and very normal reaction to the attack, however, was fear, confusion, and panic. There were a few extreme cases, such as the "Little Lord Fauntleroy of a second lieutenant" found hiding in the bomb dump, crying with fear and nerves; an unnamed officer of fairly high position who "went all to pieces after the attack and had to be sent back to the states on a stretcher;" and a private first class who also had to be evacuated to the mainland, "crying and combative," for years of psychiatric care. These individuals just did not have the temperament to withstand the horrors of battle and were probably more deserving of pity than scorn.

The 17th Air Base Group's William Melnyk and two of his friends fortunately ate an early breakfast, escaping the carnage that would soon visit the Hale Makai, and were sitting around one of the beds in the big, consolidated barracks relaxing and chatting. The noise of a low flying aircraft caught their attention, and one remarked, "It looks like the Navy is practicing dive bombing us again." Then came a loud explosion less than a minute later. They, like Ed Hall at the temporary mess hall in Splinter City, rushed outside to see what was going on. While standing on the stairway landing at the end of Wing G, looking toward Wing F, they witnessed the same shattering scene Ed Hall saw, a bomb hit Hangar 7 and explode. The concussion blew all three of them off the landing onto the ground. As they got to their feet, they heard the squadron first sergeant yelling for everyone to get out. They ran toward the parade ground, which soon began filling with men coming out of the barracks, some clad only in their underwear. Then a Japanese bomber, a Val, flying so low that the pilot and rear gunner were clearly visible, began strafing the area with its two 7.7-mm cowling-mounted machine guns. Men were soon falling or running in all directions.

In the 18th Bomb Wing's second floor bay, Russell Tener pulled on a pair of trousers and rushed down the stairs with many others, heading toward the grassy parade ground. They were fleeing buildings for open areas, believing they would be less exposed because the dive bombers were targeting buildings, including the huge consolidated barracks. Clearly audible to Tener were the whistling sounds of falling bombs, mixed with the frightening sounds of exploding bombs and machine gun fire. He recalled thinking he joined the Army and chose an assignment to Hawaii as a vacation at government expense, and now he would be lucky to get through this day alive.

In the meantime, Melnyk, who had rushed to the parade ground and was greeted by the onslaught of strafing Japanese planes, dashed for the shelter of the new barracks in Splinter City—a concentrated block of 50 wood frame buildings, approximately 28 of them two story barracks—just north of Hangars 2 and 4, and east of the parade ground. He stayed there a short time watching some men shooting at the Japanese planes with .45-caliber pistols, then left the area, returning across the parade ground to the big barracks to report to the supply room where he worked. The sights that greeted him en route were more devastation, and more destruction coming—burning aircraft along the hangar line, and high above an approaching flight of level bombers. They were Kates. He dashed for the protection of the barracks and later learned that some of the Kates' bombs landed in Splinter City, close to where he was standing, killing several men.

When Melnyk reported to the supply room, he was immediately assigned the duty of passing out rifles and ammunition to men in his squadron. Another wave of bombers flew over and a bomb exploded between Wings E and F, shaking the building. A moment later someone came running in, shouting, "I need help; the lieutenant has been hit!" Melnyk went with him. First Lieutenant Malcolm J. Brummwell, the squadron adjutant, who had taken command of the headquarters squadron, 17th Air Base Group, when First Lieutenant Howard F. Cooper, the commander, who earlier, still in his residence, was seriously wounded by shrapnel. Brummwell was bleeding across the chest, moaning with pain. Concerned about broken water mains and loss of water pressure on the base, Brummwell and two airmen had just obtained aluminum kitchen containers to get water before the supply failed, when he was struck down.

They carried him to the supply room and laid him on a counter while someone called the hospital for an ambulance. It arrived shortly and they were instructed to bring him out. When they slid him off the counter he fell toward Melnyk, who grasped him, with his bleeding chest against his own. They carried him to the ambulance, laid him on a stretcher, and slid him inside. The ambulance driver and assistant then turned toward Melnyk, believing he was also wounded, because of all the blood on his shirt.

"Take it easy now and get into the ambulance." A protesting Melnyk replied there was nothing wrong with him. The driver soothingly said, "I know, I know," and kept forcing him inside. Melnyk finally climbed into the vehicle, then crawled over the driver's seat, went out the front door, and started to walk away. The ambulance driver believed he was in shock and began chasing him, yelling at him to come back—but finally gave up, returned to the ambulance, and drove the wounded officer to the hospital. Lieutenant Brummwell later died of his injuries.

Two bombardier aviation cadets from Texas were newly assigned at Hickam Field. They wore blue uniforms with wing insignia on their caps, and were soon to be commissioned as second lieutenants. When the attack began, they had no assigned place to report but felt they should "do something," so they headed toward the consolidated barracks to see if they could help. While crossing the baseball field, they looked up to see bombs falling directly at them. They hit the ground, and the bombs exploded close by. Falling debris struck and wounded one cadet, who wore his arm in a sling for awhile and later received a Purple Heart. The other cadet was unhurt but lost his cadet cap for which they looked high and low after the attack. He had promised his Texas girl friend she could have the insignia on it when he was commissioned.

Private First Class Gabriel W. Christie, 19th Transport Squadron, like Ed Hall in the 13th Truck Company, lived in the two-story wooden barracks of Splinter City. Gabriel had become accustomed to the sound of blasting dynamite from construction projects in the Navy area, and thought nothing much about the first explosion he heard—the sound of the first hit on the Hawaiian Air Force Depot. Going out the back of the barracks, he saw some men standing around outside watching planes circling over Pearl Harbor, and joined them—then saw one of the planes drop a bomb. He wondered how the Navy could practice so close to their home quarters without endangering their men. On seeing the Japanese insignia of the red-orange sun on the wings of another plane that dived lazily down, dropped a bomb, then pulled away in a right turn, he thought it didn't seem right for the Navy to be using a foreign power's emblem in their war games. Not until a third plane dived, dropped a bomb, then flew over Hickam strafing people caught in the open, did it finally dawn on him that they were actually under attack.

Chaos followed, and men had difficulty reconciling conflicting stories. Most 19th Squadron personnel remembered running to the supply room for guns and ammunition. Private First Class George J. Gabik recalled that when they arrived the supply sergeant refused to give them anything, so they "just eased him aside with a little force," broke down the door to the weapons room, and grabbed .45-caliber ammunition, which is all they had. Christie, who probably arrived later, recalled seeing one of the lieutenants in the supply room when they got there, issuing .45-caliber pistols and the few Thompson submachine guns that were available.

The lieutenant, identified as the squadron adjutant and a Reserve Officer Training Corps graduate from the University of Hawaii, later became a subject of sharply differing recollections, some men indicating his actions, words, and orders cost lives. Whatever the facts might have been, according to Christie, the officer asked them to assemble in the middle of the parade ground in order to distribute .45-caliber ammunition, which had been loaded in a small panel truck. The lieutenant also asked for a volunteer to drive the truck back to the parade ground, and Christie offered to do so. After he delivered the ammunition, the officer asked him to stay with the truck in case he needed it, and to drive it off the parade ground and park it along the curb.

Airmen who began congregating on the parade ground scattered when the Japanese planes commenced their bombing and strafing runs. Many ran back toward Splinter City, just east of the parade ground. A PX warehouse was one of the buildings in that area, and facing it was a little fruit and vegetable stand operated during the workweek by a Japanese couple. Christie, momentarily paralyzed with fear as he stared at the approaching enemy planes, turned and ran for his life. He passed the parked truck he had been instructed to stay with, and leaped under a metal sink located at one end of the fruit and vegetable stand. The bomb bursts came closer and closer, and the concussion from one blast caused the corner of the building to collapse over the sink. Looking across the way, he saw the truck burning fiercely. Nearby 55-gallon drums had been perforated by shrapnel from exploding bombs, and their position had protected him from injury.

He then saw Private First Class James I. Lewis, a member of his squadron, lying on his back under the PX warehouse. To Christie, Lewis looked so calm that Christie envied his courage, wishing he could be like him. He later learned Lewis was dead, killed by the shrapnel that struck him in the back.

From his position between the street and the 19th Squadron barracks, First Sergeant McCuiston, heard one explosion after another. The last was a deafening blast that seemed to lift him off the ground. After getting to his feet, he turned to run, hoping to find a better shelter before the next bomb fell. A few feet away, two dead airmen lay face down. The legs of one were severed at the buttocks, and his blood soaked the ground. The other had a massive head wound from an object which had passed through him from the left temple to just above the right ear, and his brains were lying on the ground. The horror of the moment distracted him. He failed to notice his own left shirt sleeve and the front of his shirt were bloodstained from wounds, which fortunately he learned were minor.

Other 19th Squadron members wounded near the parade ground were Pfc. Gabik, who was struck by a piece of shrapnel on his left leg, and Staff Sergeant Sidney C. Howe of the radio section, whose left arm was nearly blown off. An ambulance picked up both men during a lull in the attack and transported them to the base hospital. They received a shot of morphine before being taken to Tripler Hospital at Fort Shafter. Another man in the 19th, Sergeant Jack O. Ehrke, helped carry wounded men from the parade ground despite being wounded himself by several pieces of shrapnel in his back. He later received the Distinguished Service Cross for his action.

The flow of dead, dying and wounded coming into the Hickam Hospital was under way within minutes after the attack began, soon overwhelming the small 25-bed facility.

On the flight line, 19th Transport Squadron men acted to save their two C-33 aircraft. One was riddled so badly by enemy machine gun fire, the men later named it "Patches." Second Lieutenant L. A. Stoddard received the Silver Star for taxiing "Patches" to the safety of a revetment while it was being strafed. The other C-33, just out of maintenance, had no fuel in its tanks. Private First Class Samuel D. Rodibaugh and some other squadron men pushed it across the runway to the grass area. No sooner did they move the airplane when three Japanese planes roared across the field on a strafing pass. They hadn't time to get to satisfactory cover, so they hit the ground and lay motionless.

In the meantime, Technical Sergeant Arthur C. Townsend took matters into his own hands, obtained a small truck, and asked Second Lieutenant John E. Roesch to help him get some ammunition and a machine gun, after which they headed out to the bunkers. After dropping off some ammunition, they proceeded across the runway, which was being heavily bombed and strafed, reached the far side, set up their machine gun, and began firing at the Japanese.

To cool the weapon, Townsend shot a hole in his World War I helmet, making a funnel out of it, so that nearby water on the ground could be scooped up and poured into the small hole in the water jacket of the machine gun, permitting them to fire away until all the ammunition was exhausted. Sergeant Townsend and Lieutenant Roesch later received the Silver Star for heroism in action.[33]

Zekes and Vals Rake Ewa

At the Marines' Mooring Mast Field, Ewa (pronounced Eva), on the southwest coastal plain of Oahu, near Barbers Point, the first wave hit as the Japanese began their deadly assault on Ford Island and the ships in Pearl Harbor. At 0740, when Fuchida's air armada closed to within a few miles of Kahuku Point, the forty-three Zekes split away from the rest of the formation, swinging out north and west of Wheeler Field, the headquarters of the Hawaiian Air Force's 18th Pursuit Wing. Passing further south, at about 0745 the *Soryu* and *Hiryu* divisions executed a hard, diving turn to port and headed north toward Wheeler. Eleven Zekes from *Shokaku* and *Zuikaku* simultaneously left the formation and flew east, crossing over Oahu north of Pearl Harbor to attack NAS Kaneohe Bay. Eighteen Zekes from *Akagi* and *Kaga* headed toward what the Japanese called *Babasu Pointo Hikojo* (Barbers Point Airdrome)—Ewa Mooring Mast Field.

In the officers' mess at Ewa, the officer-of-the-day, Captain Leonard W. Ashwell noticed two formations of aircraft at 0755. The first looked like eighteen "torpedo planes" flying at 1,000 feet toward Pearl Harbor from Barbers Point, but the second, to the northwest, comprised "about 21" planes just coming over the hills, from the direction of Nanakuli, also at an altitude of about 1,000 feet. Ashwell, intrigued by the sight, stepped outside for a better look. The second formation, of single-seat fighters, the two combat units from *Akagi* and *Kaga*, flew just north of Ewa and wheeled right. Then, flying in a "string" formation, they commenced firing. Recognizing the planes as Japanese, Ashwell burst back into the mess, shouting, "Air Raid . . . Air Raid! Pass the word! He then sprinted for the guard house to have "call to arms" sounded.[34]

The eighteen Zekes, two divisions of nine each, their belly tanks plainly visible, had descended from over the Waianae Mountains, rolled out of their turns into the string formation and came straight at Ewa from the north, northwest at an altitude of 1,000 feet, descending toward altitudes as low as 25 feet.

Corporal Earl Hinz, who joined the Marine Reserves in Minneapolis in 1937, while attending the nearby University of Minnesota, had been called to active duty with his entire Marine reserve squadron on 16 December 1940. Ordered to San Diego to join with two other squadrons to form Marine Air Group Two as part of an Expeditionary Force, they arrived in Hawaii on the carrier *Enterprise*, and later were designated Marine Air Group (MAG) 21. He helped build the operating base out of dusty sugar cane fields near Ewa. By mid-July 1941, when ground and flight operations were in progress, the men at Ewa were quite certain war with the Japanese was imminent, but none knew where it would begin. They were still building and expanding the base when the attack came, and by the date of the attack, there were only two or three revetments built, and no airplanes occupied them.

At 0755 the morning of the attack, Ewa's bugler sounded: "Assembly for Colors." It was customary to stand at attention when Colors sounded, but this time that posture lasted only moments before Earl Hinz and everyone else realized they were under attack by airplanes bearing the "red meatball" insignia of the Japanese Empire. No one at Ewa had to be told "man your battle stations." Everyone dispersed at double speed, Earl to his station on the base's only fire truck.

They were in the cantonment area when "Assembly for Colors" and the attack came, and were about a half mile by road from base operations and the flight operations control tower—which was atop an approximate 100-foot steel tower originally erected as a mooring mast to service the giant airships (dirigibles) the Navy constructed in the 1930s. During flight operations, the fire truck was normally parked near the operations building, close to the control tower.

As he was closest to the truck, Earl started its engine, while the crew chief jumped on. He headed down the road toward base operations and the runway where the Marine Air Group's forty-eight planes were parked following Saturday's inspection. The men realized halfway to the runway that the first wave of fighters had set fire to many of the parked airplanes—too many for one ancient fire truck to handle. Suddenly, the truck's steering became sluggish, as though the rear tires were flat. A Zeke had made a firing pass on the truck and shot up its rear tires. He braked to a stop, they jumped out of the vehicle and took cover underneath it, waiting until the first eighteen Zekes ceased their attacks.[35]

Lieutenant Commander Shigeru Itaya, from the carrier *Akagi*, led the 2nd Combat Unit's nine, and Lieutenant Yoshio Shiga from *Kaga*, led the 1st Combat Unit's nine from the carrier *Kaga*. They were targeted against Ewa and Hickam, and roared across Ewa, low, in the string formation, right down the short, wide, northwest-southeast runway, where all MAG 21's combat aircraft were parked in neat, straight rows, wingtip to wingtip. With machine guns and canons chattering, they scored numerous hits and set fires among the parked aircraft, then pulled up, over the trees, Itaya's pilots going straight through toward Hickam Field after one pass. Unlike Itaya and his pilots, Shiga's unit reversed course to make blistering strafing passes on the parked aircraft from the opposite direction. They made at least eight strafing passes, concentrating their attacks on the aircraft.

At one point during the follow-on strafing passes Yoshio Shiga found himself facing a lone Marine, firing back at the Zeke and its 7.7-mm machine guns with a pistol. According to author Gordon Prange, who interviewed the former pilot after the war, Shiga mentally ". . . paid him a good respect."[36]

After the first eighteen fighters had done their work, Earl crawled from beneath the fire truck, looked at the flat tires, left the vehicle and hurried on foot toward base operations.

Ten or fifteen minutes after the initial attacks by Itaya's and Shiga's Zekes, two more fighter units followed, eight from the 3rd Combat Unit led by Lieutenant Masaharu Suganami from *Soryu*, and six from the 4th Combat Unit led by Lieutenant Kiyokuma Okajima from *Hiryu*. These fourteen had come south to Ewa from Wheeler, after their devastating attacks on the 18th Pursuit Wing. Val dive bombers leaving Wheeler with empty bomb racks also visited the Marine Air Station to complete their work with more strafing passes using their two cowling-mounted machine

Burning aircraft on the ramp, Mooring Mast Field at Ewa.

guns. The Zekes and Vals coming from Wheeler concentrated on buildings and people, not even sparing hospital tents.[37]

Between the first and second attacks, which began at approximately 0835, when the Zekes and Vals came south from Wheeler, the Marines hurriedly began preparing for what they knew would be a follow-on air attack and possibly an invasion. Before the hard hit base could get reorganized to mount a successful antiaircraft defense from the ground, the Japanese returned. In the midst of the preparations for the third attack which ended about 0915, Earl was surprised to see the fire truck at its normal alert position near the tower, its tires obviously repaired or replaced.[38]

At Ewa, one parked aircraft after another was destroyed or set on fire in the initial onslaught, exacting a toll of nine of eleven F4F fighters and eighteen of thirty-two SBD-1 scout bombers. Men rushed out of their tents and ran through the fire for their planes, intent on pulling them away from the fires. The area flamed with blazing puddles of gas spilled from tanks.[39]

Ewa's primary fire truck driver, Corporal Duane W. Shaw, who apparently had the tires repaired or replaced after Earl Hinz left for the base operations area, knew the planes already burning at the end of the runway couldn't be saved. He hoped to save valuable equipment such as guns and spare parts. He raced the bright red truck out onto the exposed runway and was caught in the third attack. The 1930 vintage vehicle refused to go over 42 miles per hour, and was immediately attacked by fighters roaring low over the runway from the north. A strafing Zeke shot off the rear tires again, ending his valiant try in a screech of shredded rubber. When an officer complimented him afterward for having driven into a hail of bullets, Shaw said, "Hell, Lieutenant, I saw a fire, and I'm supposed to put 'em out."

When their old fire truck succumbed to the relentless strafing attacks, its crew abandoned it, and went their separate ways on foot to get guns, ammunition and further orders.[40]

By the time the final attack by Val dive bombers occurred beginning about 0930, Ewa's Marines were well along in preparing to defend against further attacks. The base commander, Lieutenant Colonel Claude A. Larkin had issued a written order signed by the executive officer, Lieutenant Colonel William J. Wallace, outlining unit responsibilities for air and ground defense of Ewa:

UNITED STATES MARINE CORPS
HEADQUARTERS, MARINE AIRCRAFT
GROUP TWENTY ONE,
2ND MARINE AIRCRAFT WING, FLEET
MARINE FORCE, EWA, OAHU, T.H.

December 7, 1941

1. (a) This group has been attacked by air and it is reported that the enemy is still in the vicinity so that a ground attack is probable.
(b) The U.S. Army is covering and protecting all territory outside of the perimeter of EWA FIELD.
2. This group will immediately take designated positions to protect this field by manning machine gun emplacements and establishing patrol around the field.
3. (a) VMJ-252 man machine guns at the tower. When alert is sounded the remainder of the squadron will assemble in area No. 1.
(b) VMF-211 man machine guns as shown on chart. When alert is sounded the remainder of the squadron will assemble in area No. 2.
(c) VMSB-231 man machine guns as shown on chart. When alert is sounded the remainder of the squadron will assemble in area No. 3.
(d) VMSB-232 man machine guns as shown on chart. When alert is sounded the remainder of the squadron will assemble in area No. 4.
(e) HQ&SS-21 man machine guns as shown on chart. A patrol of twelve men, or as many as necessary, will keep continuous watch around the perimeter of the field during daylight. When the alert is sounded the remainder of the squadron will assemble in areas No. 5 and No. 6.
(x) When alert is sounded all men will assemble with arms, ammunition and accouterments.
2. Assembly areas will be prepared for defense and personnel will be prepared to attack on orders.

3. One spare crew for all machine guns will be in reserve in the vicinity of machine gun positions.
4. All personnel will draw gas masks.
5. All personnel will keep dispersed in and out of assembly areas.
6. Ammunition will be drawn from central ordnance, the guard house or squadron ordnance departments.

Commander, Marine Aircraft Group 21
Headquarters Office
Message Center, Headquarters Office

BY ORDER OF LIEUTENANT COLONEL LARKIN
Official:

S.E. RIDDERHOFW.	J. WALLACE.
Major, U.S.M.C.	LtCol., U.S.M.C.
Operations & Training Officer.	Executive Officer[41]

The attacks on Ewa weren't yet over. The second wave would soon follow, but the base defenders would be better prepared for the final round, and the attack's aftermath.

CHAPTER 6

Inferno, Carnage, and Valor:
Attack on the Pacific Fleet

ETERNAL FATHER, STRONG TO SAVE
WHOSE ARM HATH BOUND THE RESTLESS WAVE
WHO BIDS THE MIGHTY OCEAN DEEP
ITS OWN APPOINTED LIMITS KEEP
OH HEAR US WHEN WE CRY TO THEE
FOR THOSE IN PERIL ON THE SEA

From the Navy Hymn

At a point roughly opposite Haleiwa Field, Commander Mitsuo Fuchida signaled the general attack at 0750. One minute later Lieutenant Commander Shigeharu Murata called on his torpedomen to execute their attack. Northwest of Ewa the torpedo bombers split into two groups of eight planes each under Nagai and Matsumura and continued their accelerated descent toward the west side of Pearl Harbor. Another flight under Murata and Lieutenant Ichiro Kitajima, composed of two groups of twelve planes each, flew southeast, then turned north and northwestward in a wide arc over Hickam Field and headed directly for the battleships on the east side of Ford Island. By the time the second two flights of twelve swung wide and roared over Hickam Field, they had descended to their target attack altitude of approximately 50 feet.

Each torpedo group attacked in formations of twos and threes. Each pilot had been instructed to close in on his target, even at the risk of his life. He would make additional runs if his observer-bombardier thought he might miss. After several passes, if the observer couldn't get a good sighting, the pilot would use his good judgment and choose another target. Forty Kate torpedo bombers were now rapidly approaching their low altitude dash to weapons release, two groups of eight fanned into flights of two or three, from the northwest—with their major targets moored on the west side of Ford Island; two groups of twelve subdivided and fanned into flights of twos and threes, from the east and southeast, their targets, the battleships.

These latter two groups were the planes men at Hickam Field saw fly low and fast across the southeast side of the field just prior to the dive bomb and strafing attacks on the bomber command base—and two of the twenty-four Kate torpedo bombers were seen by 13-year old Peggy Littmann and her 16-year old cousin standing for a few moments outside his parents' Navy officers' quarters.

Commander Fuchida, now opposite Barber's Point with his high-level bombers, flashed *Tsu, tsu, tsu* on the Kate's radio-telegraph, a signal similar to his earlier *To, to, to*, but this time only to his group. The deadly noose was closing around Ford Island, Pearl Harbor, and the United States' Pacific Fleet.[1]

Awaiting confirmation of the submarine sinking report from a PBY aircraft in VP-14, Patrol Wing TWO's Lieutenant Commander Logan Ramsey stood near a window of the Ford Island command center, watching the color guard prepare to hoist the flag. Lieutenant Frank Erickson, U.S. Coast Guard, the Ford Island duty officer, was also watching Marine Corps Privates First Class Frank Dudovick, James D. Young, and Private Paul O. Zeller, march up and take post for Colors. Satisfied that all looked in order outside, Erickson stepped back into the office to check if the assistant officer-of-the-day was ready to play the recording for sounding Colors on the loudspeaker.

At about 0755 the scream of a plane diving over the station caught Lieutenant Commander Ramsey's attention. He turned to Lieutenant Richard Ballinger, the command center duty officer, and said, "Dick, get that fellow's number, for I want to report him for about sixteen violations of the course and safety regulations." Each man looked out separate windows to follow its track. "Dick, did you get his number?" Ramsey asked. "No, but I think it was a squadron commander's plane because I saw a band of red on it," replied Ballinger.

"Check with the squadrons and find out which squadron commanders' planes are in the air," Ramsey ordered. That exact instant Ballinger reported, "I saw something black fall out of that plane when it completed its dive."

Exactly at 0757 an explosion reverberated from the hangar area, and Ramsey's expression immediately changed. At the same instant, Lieutenant Erickson heard two explosions in rapid succession, sending him running to the window. He reached it just in time to see a Kate torpedo bomber fly past 1010 Dock, coming toward Ford Island, and release a torpedo, which moments later struck the battleship *California.*

Hearing Ballinger's report of "...something black...out of that plane, brought an immediate reaction from Ramsey. Instinctively, he exclaimed, "Never mind the squadron commander, Dick. That was a Jap plane and a delayed action bomb." Ramsey raced across the corridor to the radio room and ordered all radiomen on duty to send in plain English: "AIR RAID, PEARL HARBOR. THIS IS NOT DRILL."

At exactly 0758 one of the most famous radio messages ever dispatched clicked over the airwaves and reverberated around the world. Admiral Kimmel's headquarters followed with a similar message, but it was Lieutenant Commander Logan Ramsey who first sent the words that waked the United States of America from its long sleep.

As the dive bombers pressed their attacks, Ramsey dispatched a second message ordering all patrol planes to assigned sectors. The objective was to locate the Japanese Fleet. He was unaware how futile the effort would be. He called his boss, the Patrol Wing TWO commander, Rear Admiral Bellinger, who was at his quarters on his first day out of bed since his bout with the flu. "The Japanese are attacking!" The skeptical response came, "You wouldn't kid about a thing like that," and Ramsey had some difficulty convincing Bellinger he wasn't kidding.

The Japanese already had complete control of the air over Ford Island and were everywhere else savaging the Navy's and Army Air Force's capability to search for the carrier strike force. He frantically tried calling Patrol Wing ONE at Kaneohe, to get their PBYs in the air, but their situation was already worse than Ford Island's. They were scrambling to save what they could. The sky over Ford Island and Pearl Harbor swarmed with Japanese planes. Within a few minutes Takahashi's dive bombers destroyed about half of Ford Island's complement of carrier-based planes, and made a shambles of the hangars. By the time Ramsey finished his call to Kaneohe the waters lapping at Ford Island, were alive with desperate rescue activity.

Ford Island's commanding officer, Captain Shoemaker, arrived at the seaplane parking apron, jumped out of his car and gazed at an appalling spectacle of flaming aircraft and the hangar burning fiercely. Scarcely one plane remained undamaged on the apron. He caught sight of a petty officer and some sailors ducking behind what protection they could find. He put them to work pulling untouched aircraft away from the fires. That was about all they could do, for when the Ford Island fire fighters arrived, there was no water pressure. *Arizona* had sunk on the water mains.

Shoemaker's particular nightmare was the chance of a catastrophic explosion of the tanker *Neosho*, moored starboard side to Berth F-4, Ford Island. She was berthed near the fuel supply and had just finished discharging aviation gasoline to the dock only five minutes before the Japanese struck. The tanks held gasoline, not oil. If they were hit, and the tanks or ship blew up, the nearby battleships *Maryland*, *Tennessee* and *West Virginia* would have been turned into infernos. An alert ensign had turned on the water sprinklers above the giant tanks, and *Neosho's* skipper, Captain John S. Phillips, had everything under control. By 0810 her antiaircraft batteries were firing, but Shoemaker had to sweat thirty-two more minutes before he could see his nightmare relieved. By 0842 *Neosho* was finally on course to Berth M-3 at Merry's Point.[2]

Rear Admiral William Rhea Furlong heard the sounds of Takahashi's dive bombers over Ford Island—although the sounds of airplanes flying over the island weren't unusual. In command of Battle Forces Pacific, a fleet of service vessels, Furlong was also the Senior Officer Present Afloat (SOPA) in the mine forces that morning. Strolling along the quarterdeck of the ship where he lived, his flagship, the minelayer *Oglala*, he was awaiting the call to breakfast. He paid little attention to the roar of engines until he saw a bomb drop. He was gazing northwest from *Oglala* when the bomb drop captured his attention. *What a stupid, careless pilot*, he said to himself, *not to have secured his releasing gear*. The bomb exploded in a shower of water and earth at the water's edge at the southwest end of Ford Island.

As the pilot pulled his airplane out of the dive and rolled into a hard turn, Furlong saw the red ball of the Rising Sun, and reacted instantly. "Japanese! Man your stations!" he shouted. At his

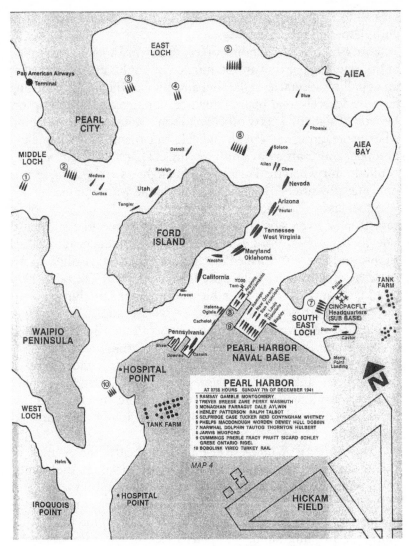

Diagram of ships in the harbor when the attack began.

command *Oglala* flashed the alarm: "All ships in harbor sortie." Furlong's gaze, initially drawn northwest by the dive bombers over Ford Island, probably never saw Murata's and Kitajima's Kate torpedo bombers charging low across the harbor, from the area of Merry's Point. They were screened from Furlong's view by the Kates' low altitude and distance from *Oglala*, and the torpedo bombers' axis of attack from the vicinity of Merry's Point. Nor did he apparently see or hear the explosions of the first strikes on *Oklahoma* and *West Virginia*, which came almost simultaneously. The torpedoes' first explosions in the hulls of both ships shot geysers of water 600-700 feet in the air.

But worse, in the next minute or two, *Oglala*'s crew topside, gazing northwest toward the explosions and fires burning on Ford Island would have their eyes fixed in disbelief by the approach of another Kate, low over the water speeding directly at them from around the south end of Ford Island, to deliver a torpedo aimed at the old, thin-plated minelayer. Dropped close in, at a range of approximately 500 yards, that one torpedo would have painful, near-disastrous effects on both *Oglala* and the light cruiser, *Helena*.[3]

In these, the earliest moments of the assault on Ford Island and Pearl Harbor, the battleships *Oklahoma* and *West Virginia*, moored on the east side of the island bore the brunt of the torpedo attacks, which came in the shattering first five to six minutes of the raid. The multiple attacks on *Oklahoma* and *West Virginia* saved the *Maryland* and *Tennessee* from similar fates. *Oklahoma*, moored at Berth F-5, outboard to port of the *Maryland*, which was berthed next to Ford Island, and *West Virginia*, similarly moored to port, outboard of *Tennessee*, offered the most tempting targets to the torpedomen. *Oklahoma* and *West Virginia* took all the torpedoes tracking toward the two pairs of ships.

Arizona, berthed approximately 75 feet astern *Tennessee*, near Ford Island, was shielded to a lesser degree by the repair ship *Vestal*, which was moored outboard to port, bow to stern, from the *Arizona*. *Nevada*, moored singly in open water, 75 feet astern of *Arizona*, and *California*, adjacent to Ford Island, nearer the south end of the island, and further toward the harbor entrance from *Maryland* and *Oklahoma*, drew fewer of the Kates' waterborne missiles. Nevertheless, one or two torpedoes, with the bomb hits the two battleships suffered, were enough to eventually put both *Nevada* and *California* on the bottom of the harbor.

The Japanese had devoutly wished to find the Pacific Fleet's three aircraft carriers in the harbor. Their normal berths were on the west side of the island, but this morning the berths held lower priority targets. The Japanese strike force's scout plane had earlier transmitted confirmation of the carriers' absence while Fuchida's first wave was en route. In four berths were the old battleship *Utah*, then a remotely controlled target ship—which took two torpedo hits just prior to *Oklahoma* and *West*

Photograph taken from a Japanese plane during the torpedo attack
on ships moored on both sides of Ford Island. View looks about east,
with the supply depot, submarine base and fuel tank farm in the right
center distance, in the first moments of the attack. Note the absence
of flak bursts, an indicator of complete tactical surprise, though ships'
crews were manning battle stations and were en route to guns. A
torpedo has just hit USS *West Virginia* on the far side of Ford Island
(center). Other battleships moored nearby are (from left): *Nevada*,
Arizona, *Tennessee* (inboard of *West Virginia*), *Oklahoma* (torpedoed
and listing) alongside *Maryland*, and *California*. On the near side of
Ford Island, to the left, are light cruisers *Detroit* and *Raleigh*, target
and training ship *Utah* and seaplane tender *Tangier*. *Raleigh* and
Utah have been torpedoed, and *Utah* is listing sharply to port. In the
lower left is the seaplane tender *Curtiss*. Japanese planes are visible
in the right center (over Ford Island) and over the Navy Yard at
right. Japanese writing in the lower right states that the photograph
was reproduced by authorization of the Navy Ministry. NPSAM

Virginia—the seaplane tender *Tangier*, and the light cruisers USS *Raleigh*, also struck by a torpedo, and *Detroit*, which escaped the fate of *Raleigh*. Two of the Kates by-passed ships on the west side and instead swung around the south end of the island and released their weapons, aiming for the *Oglala* and cruiser *Helena*, which was moored at 1010 dock, inboard of *Oglala*, where the *Pennsylvania* was normally moored.

In those first deadly five to six minutes, Japanese aircraft carrying forty torpedoes, sixteen by Kates initially flying west to east, twenty-four by Murata's and Kitajima's crews coming from the south, southeast and northeast were converging on their targets. The Japanese officially claimed 23 hits out of 40 delivered. The first hits came to *Oklahoma* and *West Virginia* almost simultaneously. *Arizona*'s fatal blow came at the hands of a Kate high level bomber minutes later.

The Capsizing of USS *Oklahoma* (BB-37)

As on nearly all the ships along the line of battleships, on *Oklahoma*, the first indication of an air attack was the explosion of bombs dropped on Ford Island by three Val dive bombers. The three Vals were seen by crew members on the *Utah*, which was moored on the west side of the island, closer to the Vals' approach from the southwest. The first bomb completely missed the island's southwest shoreline, falling in the harbor short of its Ford Island target and shooting a harmless geyser of mud and water 200 to 300 feet in the air. Admiral Furlong on *Oglala* saw the bombs falling from the same flight of Vals. The next bomb struck the southwest hangar on the island.

With shocked attention initially riveted to the west and southwest, to events on Ford Island, few men among *Oklahoma*'s crew saw the first death-dealing Kates coming low across the harbor from the southeast and east, releasing their modified, Type 9, shallow-water torpedoes, and beginning their pull-up to avoid collision with the ship's superstructure. *Oklahoma*'s Ensign Herbert F. Rommel was an exception.

His attention was also first drawn to the bombs exploding on Ford Island, but he caught sight of another more ominous event—a Kate torpedo bomber flying west to east from over the south end of Ford Island launching a torpedo that passed beneath the minelayer *Oglala* and struck the light cruiser *Helena* (CL-50). "The ship was hit about midships and the explosion seemed upward with many splinters. I ran aft and passed the word, 'A cruiser has just been sunk. These are real bombs and real torpedoes. Man the anti-aircraft battery!'" It was already too late.

By the time alerts were shouted, torpedoes were in the water. No time to react and more Kates followed behind, coming at the largest, most exposed targets among the battleships: *Oklahoma*, *West Virginia*, *Arizona*, *Nevada*, and *California*.[4]

Worse, as indicated in Bob Border's officer of the deck entry in

Torpedo planes attack "Battleship Row" at about 0800 on 7 December, seen from a Japanese aircraft. Ships are, from lower left to right: *Nevada* (BB-36) with flag raised at stern; *Arizona* (BB-39) with *Vestal* (AR-4) outboard; *Tennessee* (BB-43) with *West Virginia* (BB-48) outboard; *Maryland* (BB-46) with *Oklahoma* (BB-37) outboard; *Neosho* (AO-23) and *California* (BB-44). *West Virginia*, *Oklahoma* and *California* have been torpedoed, as marked by ripples and spreading oil, and the first two are listing to port. Torpedo drop splashes and running tracks are visible at left and center. White smoke in the distance is from Hickam Field. Grey smoke in the center middle distance is from the torpedoed USS *Helena* (CL-50), at the Navy Yard's 1010 dock. Japanese writing in lower right states that the image was reproduced by authorization of the Navy Ministry. NPSAM

the 6 December, *Tennessee* deck log, the battleships in Division 1, were undergoing inspection by the First Battleship Division Commander, Admiral Isaac C. Kidd, who was on board *Arizona* that weekend. As a result, *Oklahoma* was freshly painted, and bulkhead doors, hatches, and passageways were open, which under routine, in-port conditions, would have been closed. Some of the guns' firelocks had been removed [the mechanism in the breech of the gun that contains the firing pin]. Further, while "ready ammunition" storage boxes near the guns were supposed to be full, with enough to keep gun crews firing until magazine-supplied shells were available, in several cases, gun crews didn't have readily available or couldn't find the keys to unlock the boxes. A few boxes had been emptied for the inspection. Already at the lowest levels of alert and ship condition statuses, the opened compartments and locked ready ammunition boxes gave additional margins of luck to the attackers and portended some costly delays in response by defenders.

By 0803, barely eight minutes after the first calls to general quarters, most of the slow, lumbering Kate torpedo bombers, throttles undoubtedly full open, had come and gone, wreaking havoc on the battleships and a few other ships in the harbor, with their claimed 23 torpedo hits in the 40 they carried. Added to the devastating effects of those first eight minutes, and in the succeeding nine minutes were Kate high level bombers, Val dive bombers, and strafing attacks by the Zekes as well as the Vals—after the Vals had completed their dive bomb passes.

Lieutenant Jinichi Goto, squadron commander of *Akagi*'s torpedo pilots closed on his target, the *Oklahoma*.

Gordon Prange, who years later interviewed Goto wrote,

> Suddenly the big ship loomed directly before him. "I was about 20 meters above the water . . . when I released my torpedo. As my plane climbed up after the torpedo was off, I saw that I was even lower than the crow's nest of the great battleship. My observer reported a huge waterspout springing up from the ship's location. Ararimashita! [It struck!] he cried. The other two planes in my group . . . also attacked Oklahoma."

Prange described in some detail the last minutes of the stricken *Oklahoma*.

Electrician's Mate First Class Irvin H. Thesman was ironing a pair of dungarees in the power shop when the public address system blared out: "Man your battle stations! This is no shit!" Although startled by such uninhibited language over the ship's PA, Thesman thought it just another drill. So he grabbed a bag of tools and a flashlight and dogtrotted to his station in the steering gear compartment.

Two hits in rapid succession had already torn into *Oklahoma*'s vitals. Boatswain Adolph M. Bothne found both the aircraft ammunition ready boxes and the fire and rescue boxes locked. He picked up a hammer and a cold chisel from a gear locker. At that moment "a third torpedo hit in the middle of the ship, and the ship started to list noticeably . . . " Bothne "had to walk uphill to go to the starboard side, and after they had the ready boxes open there and the ammunition out they had no air to load the guns, and one of the men said there were no fire locks on the guns."

Hastening toward his battle station in Turret No. 4 [lower turret, aft] amidships, Gunner's Mate Second Class Edgar B. Beck decided there was no point in continuing on his way because "it was clear that we were going over." So he decided to concentrate on helping his buddies through the shell hoist, their only means of escape. He knew that when the ship capsized, the 14-inch shells, which weighed 1,400 pounds, would break loose and crush to death anyone in their path.

Oklahoma's executive officer, Commander Jesse L. Kenworthy, was the senior officer aboard. He and the ship's first lieutenant, Lieutenant Commander [William H.] Hobby,[Jr.], concluded "that the ship was fast becoming untenable and that an effort should be made to save as many men as possible." So Kenworthy ordered Abandon Ship and directed the men "to leave over the starboard side and to work and climb over the ship's side out onto the bottom as it rolled over."[5]

The *Oklahoma*'s surviving officers and men gave additional insight to the rapid, disastrous capsizing of their ship. With the first warning of the attack the call was sounded to man the antiaircraft batteries and the crew went to general quarters. Men not assigned to battle stations and not otherwise engaged to support battle stations constituted a reserve force, and in the call to general quarters under air attack were to proceed to the third deck, two decks below the main deck, for safety reasons.

While air or sea battle on the open seas made such a procedure appear logical, this day, with *Oklahoma* moored in Pearl Harbor, exposed to torpedo attack from the port side only, the procedure would add to the bitter losses incurred in the ship's capsizing. She began to list to port immediately after the first hit. It heeled to an angle of 45 degrees after the third hit. Great quantities of oil and water which covered the major portion of the weather decks— all the topside decks exposed to the elements—were forced up by the explosions, while oil poured into the harbor through the gaping holes opened in *Oklahoma*'s portside hull. The huge outpouring of thousands of gallons of oil from the nearly-full, bomb and torpedo-ruptured tanks of *West Virginia* and *Arizona* soon added to the thick scum of oil flowing out with the tide, along side the battleships.

Although the antiaircraft batteries were being manned within moments after the call, and the ready ammunition boxes were being opened, because of the rapid heeling of the ship and the oil and water on the decks, it was impossible to effectively service the guns. None of the 3-inch and 5-inch guns were able to open fire. One .30-caliber machine gun on the port side superstructure deck opened fire but the gun was almost immediately knocked out by the first torpedo hit forward. Two or three additional torpedo hits were felt.

For men rushing topside after the first three torpedo hits and "Abandon ship" call, the rapidly increasing list coupled with the water and oil mixture, created slippery, almost impossible conditions for those trying to scramble "uphill" to the starboard side. They couldn't remain on their feet. Electrical power was lost after the second torpedo hit, and the capsizing ship went almost totally dark inside, below the main deck—except for a few areas where battle lights briefly remained on or crew members were able to grab flashlights.

Below the third deck the situation quickly became desperate, especially for crew members deep in the ships lower decks, passageways, shops, engine and fire rooms, gun turrets and ammunition handling rooms; and for those who, as a result of routine training drills, took cover below the third deck on the port side.

As flooding accelerated on the port side, men found normal escape routes rapidly submerged, forcing them to move laterally through a limited number of passageways, toward the starboard side—trying to find escape routes. To compound their struggles to find a way out, when the call to general quarters came, many bulkhead doors and hatches had immediately been closed and "dogged down" in attempts to seal off watertight compartments and inhibit flooding.

Assistant Pay Clerk Daniel L. Westfall wrote, telling of the oncoming death of a once-proud ship of war, and the fearful circumstances her crew faced:

> At the time of the attack I was in my room shaving. The word was passed, "Away Fire and Rescue Party," just as I was leaving my room the second word was passed for all hands to man their General Quarters Stations closely followed by a shock of a hit. I glanced at my clock as I was leaving my room and noticed the time was a few minutes before 8:00 A.M.
>
> I started for my station in Radio Central; as I was passing along the third deck up a port ammunition passageway, I felt two more hits. The lights went out in the passageway except for one battle light [dim, red lights activated when the ship is ordered darkened], and two panel lights in the boat crane machinery space.
>
> By the time I reached the compartment abreast the armory the ship had picked up a 10-15 degree list to port; there were a couple of battle lights on in this compartment. Water and oil were bubbling up along the junction of the bulkhead and deck of

the electrical workshop, port side. Repair personnel were busy closing watertight doors.

When I reached Radio Central, personnel there had just started evacuating on the orders of the Communications Watch Officer. Radio equipment was apparently out of commission as I noticed many pieces of equipment knocked over or dangling by wires. Back up on third deck all lights were out and only a few flashlights were available. About this time word came along from man to man to "Abandon ship." I helped a partially incapacitated man [up] to the second deck and then joined in a line passing injured men along to the ladder by the dental office. I lost all knowledge of time while here, but after some minutes, Ensign [Thomas A.] McClelland, who was beside me in the line, said he was feeling faint and then collapsed. I noticed other men dropping around me. I stooped over to pick up McClelland but when I stooped over I got dizzy and fell. I seemed to be paralyzed from the waist down, had great difficulty breathing, but had enough strength in my arms to drag myself to the ladder and up a couple of steps [toward the main deck] before collapsing completely. [Fuel oil fumes are mentioned on other ships as being causes for such collapses.]

After passing out I had only flashes of consciousness until mid-afternoon. When I recovered I was at the Naval Air Dispensary on Ford Island. Shortly thereafter I joined a bunch of men going over to the BOQ [Bachelor Officers Quarters] at the air station and started a check on survivors from the supply department.

Westfall probably never learned the names of the men who saved his life.

Marine Second Lieutenant William G. Muller, Jr. wrote:

I had just returned aboard ship on the 0745 motor boat; the boat came alongside the gangway at approximately 0750. On reaching the Junior Officers' mess the word came over the loud speaker system, "Air attack, all unengaged personnel seek cover, these are real Japanese bombers." I could hardly believe that this was a real attack but the excitement and reality of the voice convinced me to move. I left the mess and started aft, first stopping off at my room to get my pistol. My room is on the starboard side, just aft of the Junior Officers' mess. I left my room and went over to the port side to enter the third deck via a hatch just adjacent to the Warrant Officers mess. A line had been formed by this time and men were pouring down into the third deck. I finally found an opening in the line and started down the ladder. I had just reached the third deck and was almost opposite the ladder when the first torpedo hit. The explosion came from the vicinity of the Wardroom and was not a violent one. The line was still moving down on the third deck and I was opposite the Communication Office [Radio Central] when the second torpedo hit. This explosion caused violent repercussions and the whole ship seemed to tremble. I figured the hit was almost adjacent to where I was standing.

By this time I decided to leave as water was beginning to flood into the third deck and the ship started listing to port. I assume there were a couple hundred personnel in that third deck and only a few of us were able to reach a hatchway in time. Two more torpedo hits were sustained by the time I was able to work my way back to the hatch I had entered and to get up to the second deck. The ship was about 35 to port by this time and the decks were too slippery and steep to walk on. I worked my way to starboard by use of dogs and fittings on the bulkhead. During this time I heard the last two explosions which were somewhere amidships or aft. There were six torpedo hits that I heard in all.

With difficulty I made the starboard side and climbed into my room which I knew had an open port. The porthole was almost overhead and I climbed through it, slid down the side which inclined about 50 and jumped into the water.

SUNDAY IN HELL 297

Ensign Joseph M. Doherty was in the Junior Officers' Mess when Lt. Muller arrived:

> . . . I left the Junior Officers' Mess for the third deck. On the way down the ladder, the first bomb or torpedo hit. Before I ever got to the Communications Office, oil was pouring into the compartment A-122-P from a hole near frame 60. We had no time to set Zed ["Zed" or "Condition Zed" refers to closure of all watertight hatches and doors] and I guess there were four or five hits in about five minutes. The ship listed to port and oil was knee deep on the third deck after the first five to seven minutes.
>
> Bunks and bedding interfered considerably with people trying to get around. They were all over the deck at all angles and in everyone's way. The ladder to the second deck was bent and twisted and the lights went out after approximately the fourth hit. I got out a port on the second deck . . .

Deep in the bowels of *Oklahoma*, *Utah*, and all ships hit during the torpedo attack, the struggle to survive was immediate. Chief Water Tender, L.C. Bickley, whose station was in *Oklahoma*'s engine room, wrote:

> . . . the word was passed to man all battle stations. I went to #2 Fireroom Pumproom and was starting pumps until water came in through the air ducts and flooded pumprooms. The hatch to #2 Pumproom was down [closed] and I couldn't get it up, so I dived and swam to #1 Pumproom and out. The lights were out and I couldn't see where the two men went that were with me. I got to H Division living compartment and water started coming in so I went out through a port hole in the wash room after the ship rolled over, and was picked up by a motor launch and put ashore in the Navy Yard. The only word I got over the phone was to get ready to get underway.
>
> Many men were lost in the lower [ammunition]

handling rooms of turrets. Falling 14-inch shells killed and injured a great many. About 125 men remained in an air pocket in the shipfitters shop, but when the space was opened up, water rushed in as air rushed out. Only one man of this group saved himself by swimming to the Chief Petty Officer pantry on the third deck and out through an open porthole . . .

Excerpts from Chief Machinist Second Class Irvin M. Hull's statement, told the story of one of the shipfitters mentioned by Chief Water Tender Bickley:

The lights were out. I went to the shipfitter shop and tried to get up the hatch leading to the Chief Petty Officers' quarters, but water washed me back. The ship had listed 90 to port so I tried to swim out through the same hatch but was washed back again and landed in the C100s along the Conveyor. I dogged down the door to the shipfitter shop. The ship listed another 90 thus being all the way over. We had about 125 men in the C100s. After four hours, the men tore the door off the shipfitters shop. Water and oil came into the C100s and rose to waist level. I swam to the CPO pantry and out a port hole. None came with me. I left the ship about 1300, five hours after the ship sank.

Shipfitter First Class William T. Link, Jr., was one who did escape, and wrote:

Time was short and in such time word was passed, "Japanese Airplane Attack All unengaged personnel seek cover on the third deck—Set condition Zed— Man your Battle Stations."

By sending men to seek cover on the third deck, jammed ladders prevented quick access to repair stations and also crowded repair stations.

Repair I was never fully manned and three men were dropping [closing] large hatches. Oil made it necessary to turn nuts with wrenches.

Chain stanchions secured with nuts could not

be removed in the short time we had and hatches were not closed at all. Countless parts [of the ship] were not closed because of the necessity of using a wrench to turn the slick oily nuts.

I never did hear "Abandon Ship" and Repair I did not all escape.

I escaped through a port in A Division living space, had no trouble, and ran around or up to the bottom of the ship. I obtained a life jacket out of the water along side of the ship and put it on. I helped another sailor back on the ship and was pulled on the ship again myself by Seaman Second Class Birnel. Then I swam to the rescue boat. I did not dive off the ship, only shoved off into the water. I was never excited but was covered with oil.

Seaman First Class Daniel Weissman was in the lower [ammunition] handling room of #4 turret, the turret nearest the stern.

After the first hit, I went to the shell deck. The lights went out and the ship started to turn over. I went [back] to the lower handling room and followed a man with a flashlight. I entered the trunk just outside the handling room on the starboard side. The lower handling room flooded completely. Water entered the trunk. I dove and swam to the bottom of the trunk and left the ship through the hatch at the main deck and swam to the surface.

Oklahoma had continued to heel rapidly. At Bosun Bothne's direction approximately 150 men made their way to the starboard blister ledge, and remained. The ship seemed to hesitate, until the fourth torpedo hit. When struck, it bounced up, and when settled down, turned over through an angle of about 135 degrees. The rollover past ninety degrees occurred at 0815, after the first torpedo struck at approximately 0756. As she rolled, men climbed over the starboard side and bottom, and many went into the water to swim to the *Maryland*. In those desperate nineteen minutes, from among her complement of 1,353 officers and men,

461 were trapped in their capsized ship, with most compartments rapidly filling with water.[6]

In the aft steering compartment, Electrician's Mate Irvin Thessman and seven other men dodged tumbling lockers and spare parts as the ship rolled and they climbed up the starboard side. He was twenty-five, the oldest among them, and felt responsible for his shipmates. The call to general quarters automatically meant material condition Zed was declared, which mandated a maximum effort at damage control, the closing and "dogging down" of all doors, hatches, ports and valves marked with a "Z" to make compartments as watertight as possible. The sealing of their compartment, didn't shut off the flow of water.

It began to trickle through the ventilation system supply line into aft steering, and Thessman and his shipmates, in attempting to tighten the Zed fitting on the supply line, broke it. They hurriedly stuffed rags in the line and lashed a checker board in place over them. They established and maintained communication with men in Radio IV and the Lucky Bag,* by tapping morse code on the bulkheads. The wait for rescue began.

Chaplain, lieutenant junior grade, Father Aloysius H. Schmitt this day was to serve his last Mass on board *Oklahoma*. The following week, he would have been transferred over to duty on shore. He had gone three decks down to prepare for the service and to hear confessions. Suddenly, in a matter of moments it seemed, he felt four tremendous explosions. Four torpedoes had struck the port side of the *Oklahoma*. The lights went out when the second one hit. Father Al, with those in the compartment with him, made their way out and tried to get up to the starboard side where they hoped they could find an open porthole. They did.

Al Schmitt assisted men out the porthole. He earlier tried to get through, pushed upward by men inside and pulled by men outside, and couldn't. When they recovered his body weeks later, they learned he had attached some of his ecclesiastical gear to his belt, and that was prohibiting him from getting through the porthole. Realizing there were other men who had come into the

---

* Lucky Bag. 1. A traditional name for a space or container for stowage of articles found adrift. Unclaimed articles aboard ship are periodically sold at auction from the lucky bag, with the money made going to the ship's recreation fund. A sailor losing something might be lucky enough to find it in the lucky bag and reclaim it. 2. Title of the yearbook for the midshipmen at the Naval Academy.

compartment and they were prevented from escape, he had men outside push him back in, and those inside pull him back, where he continued to help others to safety.

Four weeks after the attack, in a Protestant service in San Francisco, a Jewish sailor told how he lived because a Catholic Chaplain had pushed him out a porthole.

For more than one reason, another crewmember who was the last to see Father Al alive carried vivid, indelible memories throughout his life. Marine Private Raymond J. Turpin, born in Waterloo, Alabama, the ninth of ten children in the Turpin family, served on one of the starboard side secondary batteries, a 5-inch broadside gun not normally used in defense against an air attack when the battleships were at sea. On this day, in port, his gun's limited usefulness in an air attack was exacerbated by a rapidly capsizing ship and the battery's location on the side nearest the *Maryland*, opposite the side being attacked by the torpedo bombers.

In the frantic, violent few minutes leading to the death of *Oklahoma*, Ray Turpin three times narrowly escaped death, helped save five other men, escaped to the *Maryland*; while covered with oil, fed ammunition to a new, four-barrel antiaircraft machine gun crewed by some of his shipmates who had also escaped and joined that great ship's gun crews; watched with excited pride as his shipmate-gunner poured fire into an already smoking Japanese attacker; and spent much of the rest of the battle in a shower—then in hospital pajamas.

While such memories are often sources of lifelong thankfulness, wry good humor and sometimes great pride, in battle they are tempered by other, terribly painful and frustrating memories difficult to bear. For Ray, the most painful of all was to watch helplessly through the porthole at a compartment rapidly filling with water as *Oklahoma* continued slowly rolling to her death, and Father Al, the last man in the compartment, declining to take his hand in a second desperate rescue attempt—saying "Someone tried earlier to pull me out and I couldn't get through. I'm going to see if there are others needing a way out." Ray remembers Father Al's face, how close he was and yet so far—barely three or four feet, and an eternity.

Having cleaned up on a Sunday morning, dressed in his marine khakis, gone to breakfast and returned to the marines' compartment on the third deck, on the starboard side, near

Oklahoma's stern, Private Ray Turpin—like everyone else on board—was momentarily stunned when he heard "Air attack! Man all antiaircraft batteries! This is no shit!" The shocking language he had never heard over the ship's speaker system, never expected to hear, and the serious urgency of the voice, energized him and everyone in his compartment though he couldn't believe the turn of events on a Sunday morning. Since this wasn't a call to general quarters, and instead they were under air attack, all of the secondary battery crews made for the second deck, where they had to run forward toward midships, then go down through a hatch onto a ladder to the third deck, and take cover during the raid.

While they were en route the first torpedo struck *Oklahoma*. Immediately thereafter came the call, "General Quarters! Man your battle stations!" The reaction was swift and automatic, and for the first time, probably saved Ray's life. He and the other gunners reversed course, and headed back up to the second deck, ran aft toward the stern, up the ladder they normally climbed to reach the weather deck [main deck], out the hatch, then raced forward toward midships, and their battle station—the secondary battery.

As Ray and five other men were running forward toward their gun they could hear an aircraft roaring low overhead behind them, near or just beyond the ship's stern. The sound caused him to glance over his right shoulder as he ran. He saw the attacking airplane—a Kate torpedo bomber—pulling up to avoid collision with *Oklahoma*'s, *Maryland*'s, or perhaps *West Virginia*'s superstructures.

The man running behind Ray hollered at him, "Were you hit?"

Unaware of what transpired behind him, he replied, "No, why'd you ask?"

The voice behind him shouted, "He strafed us!"

As the Japanese aircraft flashed up and over the *Maryland*, the Kate's rear-facing gunner, consistent with mission plans, opened fire with his 7.7-mm machine gun, and raked the deck on which Ray Turpin and his shipmates were running.

A startling revelation. This was real, all too real. Neither Ray nor the other five men slowed down. His life may have been saved a second time when the Kate's gunner missed him.

The *Oklahoma* was fatally wounded by the second torpedo, which knocked out electrical power, communications, and

303 Sunday in Hell

brought complete darkness to the men fighting for their lives below the weather deck. Worse, because the ship's speaker system and sound-powered telephones were knocked out when electrical power failed, the command to "Abandon ship!" had to be passed by word of mouth. More than a few men in passageways below the weather deck never heard the command, and consistent with all the drills they had participated in, continued downward toward the third deck, until it became obvious they had better extricate themselves to survive.

Topside, where it was becoming increasingly obvious the ship was going to capsize, crewmembers made decisions to leave without ever hearing the "Abandon ship" order. When the ship's list was approaching forty-five degrees and continuing, Ray Turpin had already made up his mind she was going to roll over. He also decided he had no desire to jump or dive into the water as hundreds of other shipmates were doing—in spite of the continuing air attack. The huge volume of oil spilling from *Oklahoma*'s ruptured fuel tanks was not only a deepening scum on the surface on the port side, which he couldn't see, it had permeated the water and was appearing on the starboard side. Men who dove or jumped into the water between the *Oklahoma* and the *Maryland*, were surfacing and swimming, covered with oil. Adding to the grim scene in the water between the two ships was more oil from the torpedoed *West Virginia*'s ruptured tanks, drawn toward and around *Oklahoma*'s hull by the wind and outgoing tide.

Just before the list reached forty-five degrees, Ray simply walked down the starboard side of the ship from the railing near and below his assigned secondary battery, and sat down at the intersection of the ship's starboard side and blister. (A blister is a built-in or modified-in bulge, which creates a void external to the hull of a man-of-war to protect its hull against mines, bombs, and torpedoes.) He sat facing toward the stern of *Oklahoma*. He could see the bows, main batteries and superstructures of *West Virginia* and *Tennessee*. Looking between the two ships, he could see *Arizona*, directly astern of *Tennessee* approximately seventy-five feet. He sat momentarily frozen, considering what to do while the air raid's fury swirled above and around him.

The thunder of *Maryland*'s guns drew his attention. He turned, and looked upward over his left shoulder to see high above, six Kate horizontal bombers in formation, tracking up the battle line from the southwest. *Maryland*'s and *Tennessee*'s gunners who saw the formation early enough to elevate and apply sufficient lead to their guns were firing at the approaching wave of raiders. He saw their bombs release almost simultaneously, one from each, and plunge toward the ships astern of *Oklahoma*. Transfixed, he watched the bombs fall, and one disappeared into *Arizona* in the vicinity of her number 1 and 2 turrets. One explosion followed a moment later by a gigantic explosion tolled the death knell of *Arizona*. He felt the instantaneous rush of hot wind past him and stared in shocked disbelief at the huge puff of black and gray smoke mixed with a giant mushrooming fireball, as debris, bodies, and body parts lifted high in the air and rained on the quarterdecks of the torpedoed and burning *West Virginia*, the largely obscured repair ship *Vestal*—moored stern-on adjacent to *Arizona*—and the thus far relatively unscathed *Tennessee*.

In his field of view looking past the stern of *Oklahoma* toward the shattered *Arizona*, men were walking up *Oklahoma*'s side and hull as she rolled further, then sliding down or jumping into the oily water. A strange, surreal scene. Others pulled from the water after escaping from the upper decks were beginning to climb up the rotating hull as she continued to roll and settle. Suddenly, among those he could see while gazing toward the stern of the ship, he heard men hollering, some calling for help. He became aware men were calling for help from inside a third deck porthole, and others standing around the porthole were responding reaching inside to grab hands and arms, attempting to pull men through the porthole.

The ship was continuing to roll slowly but relentlessly toward ninety degrees. He instinctively got on his feet and moved further aft to assist them. Rescue activity was already frantic when he arrived, and, one by one Ray, and men he didn't know, pulled five to safety through the fifteen-inch porthole. Unknown to him, before he arrived to help, one of those the rescuers attempted to save was Father Al.

None of the five were easy, though the young men attempting to escape certain death were generally small and slender. The men inside the compartment had nothing to stand on or brace themselves against. Helping, giving a boost from inside the compartment, was Father Al. All the men striving to be rescued could do was be lifted up by men inside with them, who perhaps were already treading water if they had nothing to stand on. The men being rescued grasped the outer edge of the porthole with their hands, held on, and pulled up part way toward the porthole. They couldn't possibly "chin themselves" through the narrow opening. One or more men standing or kneeling outside on each side of the porthole would grasp wrists, then forearms, then upper arms, pulling them up high enough through the porthole to get arms underneath their armpits, then around their chests, working them ever higher until they could pull their waists, hips and legs completely through and get their footing on the side of the ship. Then the rescuers reached for the next man.

One taller, heavier, young sailor was in a desperate circumstance. Ray and another man began pulling him up, but he was overweight and his broader width and size were wedging him in the porthole—although his potential rescuers had straddled the porthole and were pulling him agonizingly higher, step by step, raising him far enough to get their arms around his chest while other eager hands pulled up on his arms. The rescuers were pulling, tugging and rocking back and forth from side to side, with all they had. While they pulled and moved him from side to side, Father Al pushed from below.

They could hear the sailor's body bearing the extended pressure, his joints and bones hyper-extending, popping and cracking, and with one man on each side at his back, were rocking him from side to side trying to pull him through. His body was emerging from the compartment black and blue with scrapes and bruises. He was in great pain, but cried, "Don't stop! Keep pulling!" With great relief they finally pulled him free, and he, like the others was quick to leave the porthole and abandon the ship, which was now on its side, about to roll further—while Ray Turpin reached to no avail for the hand of the last man he could see inside the compartment, Father Al.

When the good Father left to look for others he could help, Ray hesitated, waiting for what seemed a long time. He was hoping to see him reappear. He didn't, and he would never see him again. Ray Turpin had done all he could. He had to leave to save himself. Reluctantly turning away, he saw a heavy, approximate three-inch in diameter mooring line that tied *Maryland* and *Oklahoma* together.

From beyond his location on *Oklahoma*'s now-horizontal starboard side, the line ran up at an incline from a tie further toward the stern of the capsizing *Oklahoma*, angling upward toward *Maryland*'s weather deck, almost directly below the bridge of *Maryland*. The line, which normally ran almost level spanning the standard eight-foot space between the two ships, was now under great and increasing tension as the *Oklahoma* settled lower on its port side, its upper deck and superstructure compartments continuing to flood at a rapid pace. The rolling *Oklahoma* was literally pulling *Maryland* away from the quays to which she was moored on her starboard, Ford Island-side, and downward ever so slightly into a shallow list to port.

Ray was determined. He was not going to jump into the oily water. The line would be his salvation, and while the battle raged, he started across, up at an angle, hand over hand, hanging below the huge line, hands nearer the *Maryland*, with feet wrapped over the line, holding fiercely and climbing with his hands and arm strength. His head was hanging down so he could look back and slightly to his left, toward his goal. He was almost there, nearing the ship, when he heard "Cut the line!" shouted from an officer on *Maryland*'s bridge. To his utter astonishment and frustration, when he glanced back to see where the line disappeared over the edge of *Maryland*'s weather deck, there stood a chief petty officer poised with a fire axe in his hands.

"But Sir!" the chief shouted back at the officer, "There are guys on the line!"

Without hesitation came the more loudly shouted reply, "Cut the God damn line!"

Also without hesitation, and with Ray Turpin looking on helplessly at a bad dream, the chief turned and with three or four heavy swings of the axe, the huge line abruptly parted under great tension. It propelled Ray Turpin back a short distance toward the *Oklahoma* as he fell approximately fifteen feet into the oily water with heavy, coiling, entangling rope falling on top and submerging him. He didn't know what happened to the men coming behind him on the mooring line, but he was stunned by his fall and at the same time suddenly fighting to free himself from the tangle of rope pulling him further beneath the surface of the oil-blackened water.

Somehow, holding his breath, he struggled free, swam furiously upward, and lunged for the surface, where he emerged, nearly exhausted, covered with a coat of oil and gasping for air. Turning around while treading water, he looked further forward toward the bow of *Maryland* and caught sight of a one-inch rope line dangling down her side. He tried to swim toward it, but he was so exhausted he was in danger of going under. A tall, lanky sailor who was a powerful swimmer saw him struggling and came to his aid. He helped him to the line, and Ray, now re-energized, attempted to climb it hand over hand. He couldn't.

When he gripped the line, no matter how hard, and started to pull upward, his hands slipped down. He looked more closely at the line. The lower end had oil on it, probably from men who had already pulled themselves to safety. The tall, strong-swimming sailor once again came to his aid, and literally boosted him high enough that he could grasp the line above its oiled surface. The instinct for survival and adrenalin took over, and Ray Turpin, now oblivious to his exhaustion, rapidly climbed hand over hand, straight up the ten to fifteen feet, and with no one on the *Maryland*'s weather deck to grasp a hand or pull on the rope, he somehow climbed aboard and got to his feet—still covered with oil.

He glanced around, and everyone on the ship's deck was busy, heavily engaged in the fight against the raiders. He wanted to get into the fight, saw a gun crew operating a recently installed 1.1-inch, four-barrel, antiaircraft machine gun—part of the "upgunning" and strengthening of the Fleet. He walked toward it, and to his surprise, three of the men on the weapon were marines from his *Oklahoma* gun crew. One was the trainer, who was a small, energetic, aggressive fighter firing the gun. Another was the pointer. He knew two of them by their last names, Fuller and Alexander. The third man was dropping loaded ammunition clips into the guns, which maintained a high rate and volume of fire when the trigger was pulled.

"Can I help?" Ray asked above the noise.

"Yeah, grab some clips, load 'em, and drop 'em in the guns when the others empty!"

Ray felt reinvigorated. He was finally fighting back at the raiders who had so devastated his ship, obviously killed many of his shipmates, and tried to kill him and his buddies. Still oily and wet, he watched in admiration as the feisty little *Oklahoma* gunner, operating a *Maryland* gun, successfully poured fire into a low flying Japanese aircraft that was already trailing smoke, and was turning north toward the area of Pearl City—probably to crash and burn. He couldn't see the final result, for more than one reason.

Ray felt a tap on his shoulder, and turned to see a *Maryland* doctor, the ship's senior medical officer—a physician and Navy lieutenant commander—standing behind him. "What happened to you?" he asked.

"Sir, I just came off the *Oklahoma*."

"*Oklahoma*? What happened to the *Oklahoma*?" he asked.

Ray pointed toward where the great ship had been visible only minutes earlier, "It's sunk."

The doctor, who obviously had just come on deck for the first time since the attack began, looked in the direction of the main channel—where *Oklahoma* had been moored—and for a moment stared in disbelief. "My God!" he exclaimed. Then, beckoning Ray, he said, "Come with me. I want to examine you."

The doctor, Lieutenant Commander John F. Luten, had undoubtedly been setting up *Maryland*'s primary aid station below decks after general quarters sounded, probably treating the first wounded on the *Maryland*, and perhaps some of the oil-soaked men scrambling off the *Oklahoma*. From his training and experience at sea, he certainly knew an oil-soaked body was not only not good for the lungs and heart, but was also a potential matchstick under the right conditions. What probably he didn't know yet was Japanese machine gunners had tracers loaded at intervals in their machine gun belts. Ray protested, to no avail, while the doctor led him to the ship's primary aid station below deck.

After telling a busy corpsman [medic] to clean the oil off the young marine, he needed to examine him, the doctor left the aid station. The corpsman seemed to remain preoccupied, paying little attention to the task the doctor had given him. The battle was still raging topside, so Ray took advantage of the opportunity to continue the fight, left the aid station, and returned to the gun where the crew was firing at every raider they believed to be in range. His second attempt to join the fight was no more successful than the first.

Shortly, Dr. Luten reappeared at the same 1.1-inch battery, this time in no mood to be evaded. "What are you doing here? I told you to get cleaned up. I want to examine you. Come with me," and he took him below again, to the aid station.

This time, the ship's senior medical officer gave the corpsman a more forceful, direct order. "I told you to clean this man up. I'm going to examine him." Duly chastised by the sharpness of the doctor's tone, he told Ray to take off his clothes, get in the shower, and wash off the oil. When he handed the corpsman his wet, oil-soaked khaki's, the corpsman lifted them above the large medical trash basket, about to let go—whereupon Ray protested, "What am I going to wear?"

"When you get out of the shower I'll give you a pair of pajamas."

And so it was that a young marine who had acquitted himself with such courage, bravery, and typical Semper Fi pride, in a morning filled with frantic dashes to battle stations, violent explosions and almost unending sounds of battle, fear, blood, terror at the thought of drowning, desperate rescues, suffocating oil in the water, and near-death experiences, spent the rest of the 7 December air raid fighting in hospital pajamas, apparently quite healthy.

When at 1100 hours that morning the last, single, low-flying enemy aircraft suddenly roared across the ruins of the Pacific battle line before returning to its carrier, Ray Turpin's initiation into World War II was complete. Before the day ended, he was on Ford Island, dressed in Navy "utilities," the traditional sailor's

The overturned *Oklahoma* (right) and *Maryland* (BB-46)(left) In the background white smoke rises from *West Virginia* as her fires are brought under control after the attack. *Arizona* burns fiercely in the background. Note that rescue operations are underway on the upturned hull of *Oklahoma* and the main deck of *Maryland*. NPSAM

dark blue bell-bottom trousers and lighter blue shirt, and slept in an aviation hangar that night. When he left two days later, he was still in Navy utilities, and firmly convinced he wanted to leave battleships for good—for marine aviation. He did, and never looked back—except for the memories of a good priest of incomparable courage and valor, other brave young Americans who risked their own lives to save others, chance events that intervened to save his life, desperate young sailors he helped save; and a strong, brave young sailor he never knew, who twice came to his rescue.

Attempts to rescue the men trapped in *Oklahoma* began immediately after she capsized, and continued while the attack was in progress. Two of *Oklahoma*'s crew, Ensign Francis C. Flaherty, U.S. Naval Reserve, of Charlotte, Michigan, and Seaman First Class James R. Ward of Springfield, Ohio displayed uncommon courage and valor in those desperate minutes. They were in two different gun turrets, when the two men heard the Abandon Ship order verbally passed to them and realized the ship was going to capsize. Both remained in the turrets to which they were assigned, each holding a flashlight so the remainder of the turret crew could see to escape. In saving their lives each man sacrificed his own.

Both posthumously received the nation's highest award for valor, the Medal of Honor.

Undoubtedly, there were others on board *Oklahoma* who showed no less courage and valor, but they shall forever remain nameless, for none who observed their actions lived to tell of their deeds.[7]

The *West Virginia* (BB-48): Down

On *West Virginia*, in the moments *Oklahoma*'s crew first sounded general quarters, Ensign Roland S. Brooks, officer-of-the-deck, saw what he thought was an internal explosion on *California* and on *West Virginia*'s loudspeaker ordered "Away Fire and Rescue Party!" He followed with a second announcement, "Japanese are attacking, all hands general quarters!" and rang the general alarm.

The flame and smoke he first saw actually came from the

burning hangar on Ford Island. Brooks' order started men hurrying topside, and undoubtedly saved hundreds of lives. Circumstances on the ship Navy men affectionately called the *Wee Vee* were about to deteriorate rapidly, as *Oklahoma* was plunging headlong into crisis before the crew could unlimber her guns. While the attention of *West Virginia* men topside was drawn toward the explosions on Ford Island, coming low across the harbor from the east and southeast were Murata's and Kitajima's torpedomen.

Soon after Murata's and Kitajima's flights swept through dropping their weapons, Matsumura, who had led sixteen Kates toward the west side of Ford Island and found no suitable targets, circled round the island and struck *West Virginia* with his torpedo after one previous pass at the battleships failed to yield good aim.[8]

The ship's executive officer, Commander Roscoe H. Hillenkoetter, was in his cabin, dressing, when Brooks passed the first order on the loudspeaker. Approximately thirty seconds later the executive officer heard "General Quarters" sound, and at the same time, 0755, the Marine orderly rushed into Hillenkoetter's cabin and announced, "The Japanese are attacking us." As the Marine was telling him of the attack, Hillenkoetter felt two heavy shocks on the hull of *West Virginia*. It seemed as if these shocks were somewhere forward on the port side. He rushed from his cabin. By the time he reached the quarterdeck [the open main deck at the stern of the ship] the ship was beginning to list rapidly to port. He proceeded along the starboard side until just forward of #3 turret [top turret, aft], when there was a third heavy shock felt to port.

The planes on top of #3 turret caught fire. Fire covered the turret's top, and began spreading toward the quarterdeck. The quarterdeck sentry informed Hillenkoetter that the captain had already gone to the bridge, so the executive officer remained aft to assist in extinguishing the fire around #3 turret, and on the quarterdeck. A fourth heavy explosion threw the executive officer flat on the deck. Throughout this time the ship continued to list, and Hillenkoetter estimated the list to be 20-25 degrees. He called to the sound power telephone watch to tell Central [damage control] to counter-flood, but he was uncertain whether or not the word got through.

Then Hillenkoetter saw a flash of flame about fifteen feet high somewhere forward on *Arizona*, and had just got to his feet when there was another "terrific flash of flame from the *Arizona*, the second flash higher than the foretop," the high mast nearest *Arizona*'s bow and aft of the #1 and #2 turrets, and the bridge superstructure. Burning debris of sizes from a fraction of an inch up to five inches rained on the quarterdeck of *West Virginia*.

Although the devastating hit to *Arizona* was not the first hit she had taken, unknown to *West Virginia*'s Executive officer, at that instant he had just witnessed the death blow to *Arizona*—a 1,765-pound bomb delivered by a Kate horizontal bomber, from an altitude of approximately 10,000 feet. The converted 16-inch artillery shell had penetrated the main deck, immediately adjacent to and between the heavily armored #1 and #2 turrets, deep into the forward black powder magazine, exploded, and set off a huge secondary explosion in the main magazine.[9]

Lieutenant Commander John S. Harper, *West Virginia*'s First Lieutenant and Damage Control Officer, had just turned out of his bunk when he heard the loudspeaker call to general quarters. At the same time he heard guns being fired. Almost immediately he felt the ship shake from a heavy explosion that seemed below and forward. He ran forward to his battle station, Central Station, a central, armored compartment, located forward and below the bridge and conning tower, from where he was responsible for receiving battle damage reports, establishing priorities, and issuing orders to repair parties. During Harper's run to his battle station via the starboard side of the second deck and down through an armored hatch into compartment A-420, he felt further heavy shocks to the ship as more torpedoes struck *West Virginia*—but couldn't recall how many. He noted that men were proceeding to their stations with a minimum of confusion.

On reaching the third deck in compartment A-420, he saw water entering the port side through the junction of the port bulkhead and the deck. At this time the ship was already in a considerable list. He continued down in Central Station, and as he arrived he heard Ensign Kelley, the assistant navigator, passing the word to set condition Zed, an initiative by the young, inexperienced officer Harper mentally noted was highly commendable. After arriving at his battle station, and throughout his few minutes in Central Station, Harper was unable to establish communications with the captain, either in the conning tower or on the bridge, and communications with damage control parties were intermittent.

The inclinometer showed a list of approximately fifteen

degrees when Repair II and Repair IV reported via sound powered telephone that the third deck was being flooded from the port side. Over the loudspeaker and sound powered phone simultaneously, Harper immediately ordered "counter-flood all voids on the starboard side." About the time he passed the order, all power went off the ship, causing him to conclude the loudspeaker system wasn't operating. The water flooding port side had caused the auxiliary power generator to fail, which temporarily, then later permanently, shut down the ship's electrical power. As on *Oklahoma*, darkness began engulfing *West Virginia* crewmen manning battle stations below the main deck—while the ship was increasing its list and settling.

Momentarily Harper received word via a messenger from Repair II and IV they were commencing to counter-flood. The order to counter-flood had come from the assistant gunnery officer—this day also the senior gunnery officer aboard—and former assistant damage control officer, Lieutenant Claude V. Ricketts, whose battle station was on the bridge with the captain. By this time, the inclinometer was off scale, and Harper estimated the maximum list at 28 degrees to port. Within a few moments, before counter flooding began to take effect, he would face one of those desperate, agonizing decisions no officer ever wishes to confront.

Water began pouring down the trunk, a ventilation and repair access leading to Central Station. The watertight door to the trunk was closed and dogged—tightened or clamped to maintain watertight integrity—however, the door was closed with one dog in a position that couldn't be tightened, and water began to enter Central. As Harper and his men were attempting to stanch the flow of water into Central Station, men from the forward distribution room and Plot, the ship's operational control center, were entering Central Station through the open starboard communicating door. They were covered with oil and water. But Harper couldn't recall any water entering the door into Central. As the ship's list increased, next came men banging and hammering on the port door from the trunk leading into Central Station. They wanted into Central Station.

Harper shouted the question, "How much water is in the trunk?" They replied, "It's getting high!" Then came the agonizing decision and reply. Counter-flooding seemed to be taking effect. The men in Central Station still had communications via messenger through the starboard door. Harper refused to allow his men to open the port door into the trunk, and directed the men outside to try to get through Plot and around the starboard side to enter through the starboard door that wasn't yet leaking water. At the same time, he directed Repair II to attempt to open the armored hatch above the trunk to let the men escape. Repair II reported back. There was about three feet of water above the hatch, and they were unable to open it. Harper's pained reaction carried in his memory to *West Virginia*'s action report, and undoubtedly the rest of his life: "I believe these men were lost, as I am quite certain no further personnel entered central through the starboard door." But there was no time to stop and reflect.

By this time, water was pouring into Central. Communication had been reestablished with Rapair II and Repair IV. Harper ordered all except the telephone talker to evacuate via the armored tube leading to the conning tower. All left, Ensign Archie P. Kelley being the last of the group. Harper and telephone talker, Yeoman Second Class Rogers, remained. Again, Harper mentally took note, and wrote of Rogers' coolness and attention to duty in communicating "without the slightest trace of excitement, and in every way in the manner in which he had been taught."

Main Control came on line, reported a number of men trapped in one of the engineering compartments, and requested a repair party attempt to burn a hole in the deck to allow the men to escape. Harper passed the information to Repair IV, certain he'd given correct information to Repair IV. He received acknowledgement, but at this moment, communication with all but Repair I failed. The port side of Central Station was now six feet under water, and the entire compartment was flooding rapidly. Harper informed repair I Central Station was being abandoned, and Yeoman Rogers went up the ladder followed immediately by Harper, who made his way to the Flag Bridge.

On reaching the bridge he was told the Captain was seriously injured, and went to the cot where he lay. He reported to Captain Bennion that the ship's list had been stopped, that starboard voids had been counter-flooded and the ship would remain upright. He then left the bridge and went down to the forecastle.

For Lieutenant Commander John Harper that day, there would be more painful decisions, and at the end, when he had done all he could for *West Virginia* and her crew, he was unable to control the onset of trembling, and felt the cold, clammy symptoms of shock.

Counter-flooding and determined fire fighting saved *West*

Virginia, while her guns continued firing as long as possible. As Lieutenant Commanders Hillenkoetter and Harper later wrote, Lieutenants Ricketts' and White's initiative and actions throughout that bitter day, were particularly noteworthy—although the two senior officers made it clear their comments in no way were intended to diminish what so many others accomplished under the worst possible circumstances.

Ricketts was sitting at breakfast in the wardroom when assembly was sounded and the fire and rescue party called away. Almost immediately, as he was leaving the wardroom, he heard general quarters sounded. As he went up the ladder [stairs] to the starboard side of the quarterdeck, he heard word being passed verbally, "The Japs are attacking." As he reached the quarterdeck, he felt the ship being hit. "She was shaken some, but I was not knocked from my feet." His next thought was instead of actual torpedo hits the vibration might be caused by bombs falling close aboard.

He went up the starboard side of the boat deck to the antiaircraft battery, which was being manned. Ensign Hunter was already at the 5-inch battery, his assigned battle station, and as Ricketts passed on his way to the Fire Control Tower—his battle station on the bridge—he told Hunter to open fire as soon as possible. The Fire Control Tower was locked, so Ricketts and other men assigned to the tower broke it open. Control of the AA batteries for ship defense from the tower wasn't possible. Communications were already intermittent, and soon failed. Enemy aircraft were launching attacks from multiple directions, dive angles, and altitudes, making it impossible to effectively shift, coordinate and concentrate fire. Batteries would have to fire under their own local control, at fleeting targets of opportunity.

Captain Bennion arrived on the bridge from the conning tower, his normal battle station, when the ship had already been hit by more than one torpedo, and the list was rapidly increasing. Ricketts knew there were probably few C&R officers ([damage] control & repair) on board, and said, "Captain, shall I go below and counter-flood?" He replied, "Yes, do that." Ricketts went down through an area he called "Times Square," and asked Seaman First Class Billingsley to help. The two men hurried down to the main deck, then aft along the starboard side, and down to the second deck through the escape scuttle in the hatch in front of the Executive Officer's office. The hatches in the vicinity were closed with escape scuttles open. He saw wounded being brought up the hatches forward. The ship was now listing so heavily that on linoleum decks it was impossible to walk without holding on to something.

The two men reached the third deck by a ladder at frame 87 starboard and went forward to the first group of counter-flood valves. Billingsley went aft and got a crank for operating the valves. When he came back he brought two more men with him, Rucker and Bobick, shipfitters from Repair III. Billingsley and Ricketts began counter-flooding while the other men assisted at other valves. When Ricketts was assured counter-flooding was well under way, he told Rucker to counter-flood everything on the starboard side until the ship was on an even keel. It wasn't long before the excessive list to port began to decrease. Rucker later told Ricketts he had not previously received orders to counter-flood, but he and Bobick had already decided they should, and had opened valves into two voids in Repair III. Ricketts, like Lieutenant Commander Harper, took mental note of the initiative and good judgment by the two seamen, and later wrote of what they did to help save their ship.[10]

At this juncture Ricketts was unaware another young officer, Lieutenant (jg) Harry B. Stark, saw the immediate need for counter flooding, and took the initiative along with other men, to keep *West Virginia* from capsizing.

Certain counter-flooding was successfully underway, Ricketts hurried back to the boat deck AA battery and learned all the ready ammunition had been expended. He went to Times Square and began forming an ammunition train, a line of men intended to pass ammunition from the magazine, well below the main deck, to the guns, opening necessary hatches along the way. However, when the hatch to the third deck compartment A-420 was opened, he found it flooded. He again closed the hatch, and abandoned further attempts to obtain ammunition. The settling *West Virginia*'s AA batteries fell silent one by one, their ready ammunition boxes empty, and as they did, the ship's crew turned their attention to retrieving the wounded and moving them to safety and medical care.

Ensign Thomas J. F. Ford, who had been assisting Ricketts with the ammunition train, led men from the train, and others, to evacuate wounded from the second deck. While the evacuation was beginning, Ricketts received word the Captain was seriously wounded and needed attention. He dispatched Ensign Jacoby and

Seaman Second Class S.F. McKnight forward for a pharmacist mate to come to the Flag Bridge, and assist the Captain. Ricketts then went to the bridge, and found Ensigns Powell P. Vail, Jr., and Victor Delano with Captain Bennion, who was lying in the starboard doorway leading to the Admiral's walk. He had a serious abdominal wound, with his intestines exposed, a large piece of metal from a bomb explosion on the *Tennessee*, having passed through his abdomen.

Chief Pharmacist Mate Leslie N. Leak arrived with a first aid kit and dressed the wound as best he could. They put their Captain on a cot and moved him under shelter aft of the conning tower, where he remained during the second air attack. Ricketts and other officers and enlisted men worked feverishly that morning to shelter the dying Captain, make him comfortable, and try to comply with his wishes, while gently as possible, often at the last moment, moving him away from the encroaching fire and suffocating smoke, attempting to transfer him to the *Tennessee*. In the days after the attack, Lieutenant Ricketts wrote poignantly of him.

> The Captain deserves the highest praise for his noble conduct to the last. Although in great pain he kept inquiring about the condition of the ship, whether or not we had any pumps running, etc. He was particularly concerned about fires on board and the oil on the surface of the water. I assured him that everyone was doing everything possible to fight the fire and control the damage. He did not want to be moved and after the fire started kept insisting that we leave him and go below. For a short time after he was wounded it would have been possible to lower him down, but his wound was so serious I knew he would be better off with as little handling as possible. Leak concurred with me in this opinion. However, when the fire broke out around the after part of the bridge structure I moved him regardless, because of the suffocating smoke and the approaching fire.[11]

Lieutenant (jg) Frederick H. White was in the wardroom when the fire and rescue was called away by bugle. He ran for the quarterdeck, and the first thing he saw on reaching topside was a Japanese plane passing over the *Oklahoma*, from which a column of water and smoke was rising. As he ran forward he stopped at the Deck Office and sounded the general alarm just as the first torpedo struck the *West Virginia*. En route to his battle station in secondary forward, he noticed no one in charge of the AA battery on the boat deck where the crews were manning the guns, so he remained there and took charge of the battery, breaking out the ready service ammunition, forming an ammunition train, and getting the starboard guns firing under local control.

By the time the starboard batteries were firing the ship had received three or four torpedo hits, throwing oil and water over the decks, and rapidly increasing the list toward 25 degrees—which made gun crews' footing precarious. As the list progressed port guns couldn't be elevated sufficient to be effective, and their crews were brought to starboard. Flooding below decks soon caused the loss of air pressure used to clear barrels and reload before firing. The loss required starboard guns to be depressed by hand-crank, barrels rammed clean, reloaded by hand, and re-elevated by hand-crank before firing the next round. The result was a substantially slowed rate of fire.[12]

As aircraft in the flights of two or three Kate torpedo bombers pulled up and passed low over the battleships, after releasing their torpedoes, their aft-facing gunners raked the decks of the ships with machine gun fire. Immediately behind the torpedo attacks from the port side, came the Kate high-level bombers, coming in five and seven-plane V-formations, at 10,000 to 12,000 feet, from the northeast and southwest, tracking slightly offset along the longitudinal centerlines of the moored battleships. Within two to five minutes following the first attacks, defenders on numerous ships in the harbor were opening fire.

Throughout the desperate struggles on the battleships following the torpedo and level bomb attacks, Val dive bombers unleashed their fury on them, many returning to follow up with strafing passes. Like the Kates, when the Vals delivered their bombs and pulled out, aft-facing gunners raked the ships' decks as well. In the mix of swirling attackers were Zekes in high speed strafing passes with 20-mm cannons and 7.7-mm machine guns blazing.

In spite of the fury of the Japanese onslaught against the battleships, to the American gun crews' everlasting credit, until their guns couldn't be fired because ammunition was no longer available, or insurmountable circumstances overwhelmed servicing the guns, discipline was excellent.

When ammunition in ready service boxes was expended, White went below on the starboard side to see if more ammunition could be brought up from the magazine. In compartment A-511 he found water up to the airports on the port side, the hatch between A-511 and A-420 open, but A-420 filled to within inches of the hatch. He saw a great many injured men lying on deck or in the water in A-511, and having concluded no additional ammunition could be supplied to the batteries, turned his attention to rescuing the wounded. He ordered his detail to evacuate the wounded to Times Square. He then returned to Times Square where Ensign Ford was in charge of secondary battery, which was no longer engaged, and ordered secondary battery personnel to evacuate all injured from the second and main decks to Times Square. From there he returned to the AA battery on the boat deck, reported to Lieutenant Commander Johnson, the communications officer, told him that ammunition couldn't be brought up, and informed him of the situation below deck.

At this point White encountered Lieutenant Commander Harper who instructed him to go to the bridge and bring down the Captain, who was wounded. He assisted Lieutenant Ricketts, Ensign Delano and several other men in moving Captain Bennion to safety to the rear of the conning tower, which was heavily armored. While others improvised a stretcher, White and a seaman manned #1 and #2 machine guns forward of the conning tower. By the time the second wave of attackers arrived, White and *West Virginia*'s surviving, able-bodied crew were engaged with another deadly enemy—fire.[13]

While *West Virginia*'s executive officer and first lieutenant were hearing the call to general quarters and rushing toward their battle stations, the ship's navigator, Lieutenant Commander Thomas T. Beattie, sprang into action.

> About five minutes to eight I was in the wardroom just finishing breakfast, when word came over the loudspeaker from the officer of the deck, "away fire and rescue party." This was followed immediately by a second announcement over the loud speaker, "Japanese are attacking, all hands general quarters," and the alarm was rung.
>
> I heard several dull explosions coming from other battleships. Immediately I left the wardroom

and ran up the starboard passageway to the bridge. The Captain was just ahead of me proceeding in the same direction.

At this time the ship listed at least five or six degrees and was steadily listing more to port. The captain and I went to the conning tower, our battle station, and at this time dive bombing attacks started to take place and numerous explosions were felt throughout the ship. Upon testing our communications with Central Station and to the guns we found they were disrupted. I suggested to the Captain as long as no communications were in the battle conning tower that we leave there and attempt to establish messenger communication and try to save the ship. We went out on the starboard side of the bridge discussing what to do. During all this time extremely heavy bombing and strafing attacks occurred. The ship was constantly shaken with bomb hits.

The Captain doubled up with a groan and stated that he had been wounded. I saw that he had been hit in the stomach, probably by a large piece of shrapnel, and was seriously wounded. He then sank to the deck, and I loosened his collar. I sent a messenger for a pharmacist's mate to assist the Captain.

Just then, [at a time fixed as 0808], the USS *Arizona*'s forward magazines blew up with a tremendous explosion, large sheets of flame shot skyward, and I began to wonder about our own magazines and whether or not they were being flooded. I posted a man with the Captain and went down to the forecastle where a number of the crew and officers had gathered. I got hold of a chief turret captain to immediately check on the magazines and flood them if they were not flooded at this time. Large sheets of flame and several fires started aft. Burning fuel oil from the USS *Arizona* floated down on the stern of the ship. Just then the gunnery officer, Lieutenant Commander [Elmer E.] Berthold came aboard and I asked him to try to flood the forward magazines. I dispatched another gunner's mate to flood the forward magazines. Shortly thereafter

I was informed that the after magazines were completely flooded but that they were unable to flood the forward magazines, as the water was now almost to the main deck.

I then sent word to Lieutenant Ricketts and Lieutenant (jg) White, who were now on the Flag Bridge with the Captain and told them I was very anxious to get the Captain on the forecastle and send him to the hospital, and to get some lines and a stretcher and lower him down from the bridge.[14]

Lieutenant Commander Doir C. Johnson, the Communications Officer, had seen Beattie on the forecastle and reported to him. [forecastle pronounced folk-sul: partial deck toward the bow, one level above the main deck]. Beattie directed him to go to the bridge and bring Captain Bennion down. Lieutenant Commander Harper, having evacuated Central Station, gone to the bridge and reported the ship's condition to Captain Bennion, arrived on the forecastle at this time. Wounded men were being brought to the forecastle and loaded into boats. Johnson, who saw a large, black seaman carrying wounded sailors to the forecastle, directed the sailor to come with him, and went to the bridge where he found the captain lying on a cot in full uniform, wounded. The pharmacist mate had dressed his wound as best he could. Johnson, believing he'd found the right man to carry the captain to safety, had brought the big, well-built, mess attendant, Doris Miller, intending to have him pick up the captain and carry him below.

Miller, who had been the ship's heavyweight boxing champion, had arisen at 0600 and was collecting laundry when general quarters sounded. He headed for his battle station, the antiaircraft battery magazine amidships, only to discover that torpedo damage had wrecked it, so he went on deck. Because of his physical prowess he was assigned to carry wounded fellow-sailors to places of greater safety, and to the forecastle for evacuation by boat to the hospital ship, USS *Solace*, or the Navy Hospital. When Lieutenant Commander Doir C. Johnson and Miller arrived on the bridge to move Captain Bennion, the mortally wounded commander of *West Virginia* insisted on staying where he was—on the bridge.[15]

Beattie continued, "They sent word back that the Captain

This image is of Captain Mervin S. Bennion. He was the
Captain of the *West Virginia*. He was born on May 5, 1887
in Vernon, Utah, and attended the US Naval Academy. He
posthumously received the Medal of Honor. NPSAM

was very much against being moved and that he preferred to stay where he was."

Nevertheless, the dying captain's final order was the only one his men ever disobeyed. He remained conscious, asking alert questions to the last. Gordon Prange, in *At Dawn We Slept*, recounted, "After [the Captain] died, Johnson saw Miller, who was not supposed to handle anything deadlier than a swab [a mop], manning a machine gun, 'blazing away as though he had fired one all his life.' As he did so, his usually impassive face bore the deadly smile of a berserk Viking."[16]

As Captain Bennion lapsed into unconsciousness and his life ebbed away, Beattie left the bridge and descended to the forecastle:

> I then saw the First Lieutenant, [Lieutenant Commander John S. Harper], on the forecastle and told him I thought he was now Commanding Officer. [Neither man knew the ship's executive officer was on board in the after part of the ship. Beattie asked Harper] if he had been able to close any watertight doors and do any counter flooding. He told me that the ship was counter flooded, and Central Station had to be evacuated due to flooding. No other damage control measures were possible.
>
> He then asked me to look after all evacuation of the wounded. I had the men on the forecastle search those parts of the ship which were still accessible for the wounded men. Large numbers were brought on deck and loaded in boats that were along side and were sent to Ford Island, the [hospital ship] *Solace* and the Naval Hospital. During all this time the ship was being subjected to heavy divebombing and strafing attacks. I then told the men on the forecastle whenever they saw an attack coming to get under cover. The ship had listed over about fifteen degrees and was resting on the bottom. Water level had risen to above the level of the main deck and it was impossible to get on this deck or below.
>
> At about this time a large oil fire swept from the *Arizona* down the port side of the *West Virginia*. We had no water on board as the fire mains and machinery were out of commission and we were

unable to do any fire fighting at all. I got into a motor launch to go to the stern of the ship to investigate the fire. The smoke was so heavy I could not see aft of the bridge. As I got into the boat a sheet of flame swept on top of us and we barely managed to get free of the fire. I then had the boat take me aft. The burning oil on the water then swept by the ship and I managed to return to the quarterdeck. I realized then that the ship was lost . . . [17]

Lieutenant (jg) Stark, was in his room, GG, the third stateroom counting aft on the starboard side of the half deck, in the third watertight compartment from aft. He was getting up from his bunk when he heard "Away Fire and Rescue Party," followed by General Quarters. He heard and felt three violent explosions in quick succession immediately following the loud speaker calls, and the ship started listing to port. Grabbing an armload of clothes he ran forward and found only one man on the half deck manning the repair phone to Central Station. The two men started closing watertight doors working from aft toward the bow, although he recalled he didn't check the aft door leading to the airplane crane room, which normally should be shut.

As he dogged down [closed water-tight] the door forward of his room he heard something "let go" in the compartment, some leak starting violently. By that time there were a few more men in the compartment above. He dropped [opened] the large watertight hatch over the space above and crawled out through the escape scuttle to reach the third deck. When he emerged on the third deck, he was greeted with an abrupt skid down the listing deck to port, into about four feet of water covered with a scum of oil.

He decided to work his way along the starboard side of the third deck to see if counter-flooding was in progress. He was certain there was no danger of sinking in the shallow water, but there was great danger of capsizing to port—the list was increasing. He dropped down into the trunk to the steering motor room, intent on ensuring counter-flooding was in progress. Fire and grains of burning powder showered around him. With the help of a Marine sentry, the two extinguished the small fire, but they couldn't completely shut the hatch leading down into the steering motor room. The door seemed jammed though almost shut. He sent the marine up to shut the hatch over him

Doris Miller, Mess Attendant 2nd Class, USS *West Virginia*,
just after being presented the Navy Cross. NPSAM

as he undogged [opened] the starboard door to enter the mess attendants' compartment. Someone helped him close the door, as he recognized for the first time that it was completely dark except for the glimmer of a flashlight forward.

He groped his way along the deck to the next compartment through the open door, and found the damage control locker. Seaman Third Class S.F. Puccio had broken into the locker and was hunting for counter-flood cranks. Stark and Puccio each found one, and flashlights. Stark told Puccio to flood forward while he went aft. He ran back into the aft compartment and started cranking, which would force valves open to permit flooding. For some time they worked to flood three voids, watertight compartments separated from other compartments and designed into the ship to increase its buoyancy.

Unnoticed at first was their inability to build sufficient pressure to open the valves, before men began falling to the deck and passing out, overcome by fuel fumes. The valve settings were open, but the men were too weakened to crank the valves open. Stark abandoned attempts to counter-flood, grabbed someone and told everyone else to haul somebody out the starboard hatch on the quarterdeck, just aft of the deck's break. Everything went temporarily black until he woke up under the overhang of #2 turret, his normal battle station. His head ached fiercely, he couldn't breathe, and all his extremities tingled as if they had been asleep and were just awakened.

He learned from Chief Turret Captain Crawford, that no one was in gun control, and started for that station with the starboard guns seemingly "firing in his face." It was the first time Stark realized the antiaircraft guns were firing. He ran to Lieutenant Ricketts on the boat deck by a number three antiaircraft gun and asked him if he needed men. "Yes, on the antiaircraft ammunition supply." He noticed several antiaircraft officers on the battery and it was functioning "wonderfully." He got back under the overhang of the turret, but the hatches were closed. He attempted to open the right tail hatch, passed out from exertion and was unable to tell Crawford to get men on the antiaircraft ammunition train.

He lay there trying to breathe, confused, once more unsure about the passage of time—until Crawford returned, told him the ammunition train was flooded, that all boat deck ammunition was exhausted, and the Captain had ordered "Abandon Ship." He made sure #2 turret was evacuated, then remembered "hitting the water" from the forecastle. He tried to swim but was too weak. Gunners Mate Second Class E.F. Clover and Seaman First Class H.C. Hitcher, in his division, held him up and dumped him in a life raft. The next thing he remembered he was in the Ford Island dispensary.[18]

Lieutenant Stark's recollections spanned the pause between the first and second waves of the Japanese attack. By the end of the first wave, West Virginia's life as a fighting ship was drawing to a temporary close, but there was more to come. And though her captain was dead, along with many others, his selfless leadership, courage and valor enshrined him in the memories of his crew, and he would in the future receive the posthumous award of the Medal of Honor. The brave, young, black mess attendant, Doris Miller, who had worked tirelessly to save many others in those first desperate minutes, came to carry his mortally wounded Captain from the bridge, and though turned away, went on to fight fiercely that morning—and received the Navy Cross.

West Virginia, saved from a permanent grave by her crew's immediate counter-flood initiatives, wouldn't go down without a fight. The struggle below the main deck continued at a furious pace, while gunners were manning antiaircraft batteries that, except for machine guns, would soon be depleted of ammunition and rendered unserviceable. As the ship's list to port increased, batteries on the port side had to be abandoned—while dive bombers and fighters attacked from different directions at varying dive angles.

What's more, thousands of gallons of oil pouring from the stricken Arizona, the settling West Virginia, capsized Oklahoma, and paralyzed California, were already dealing deadly fumes and oil covered bodies to sailors fighting to save their ships and lives. Soon the oil-fed conflagration consuming Arizona, drawn relentlessly along the line of battleships by the outgoing tide, aided by the northeast wind, would pose deadlier threats to West Virginia, Tennessee, and Maryland, while California's crew, moored further southwest toward the harbor entrance, with the ship's hull torn by torpedoes and bombs, would fight her fires while fighting for survival.

Throughout the period after West Virginia's guns fell silent and evacuation of the wounded began, at the direction of Tennessee's acting commander, men on Tennessee became progressively more involved in fighting West Virginia's spreading fire to keep it confined forward while helping the wounded across from West

A fireboat pours water onto the burning battleship *West Virginia* BB-48 following the attack by Japanese naval aircraft. The USS *Tennessee in* background. NPSAM

Virginia's starboard side. They came by the hundreds, 344 before the morning ended, many coming across on a 5-inch gun tube. Finally came the difficult decision to abandon ship.[19]

As the huge, thick, gray and black, plumes of smoke began obscuring battleships on the east side of Ford Island, the Japanese inflicted more death and destruction amid the terrible scene below them. Val dive bombers that had released their bombs, continued to join the Zekes in strafing attacks up, down, and across the lines of ships.

Arizona (BB-39) and *Vestal* (AR-4): Sudden Death and Uncommon Valor

Moored at Berth F-7 when the attack began was the 600-foot long, 31,400-ton *Arizona*, with the smaller, 466-foot, 12,585-ton repair ship *Vestal* tied close, bow to stern, portside, outboard of the battleship. Similar to the other battleships that morning, *Arizona*'s fuel tanks were approximately 95 percent full, slightly less than 660,000 gallons of oil. One boiler was operating to drive a generator for auxiliary power. And like all the other battleships moored in the harbor, her powder and ammunition magazines were full.

Vestal was providing scheduled tender upkeep for the period 6-12 December. Rear Admiral Isaac C. Kidd, Commander, Battleship Division I, and Captain Franklin Van Valkenburgh, *Arizona*'s commander, were on board the battleship when the officer of the deck, Ensign Henry D. Davison, sounded the three-blast, howler alarm signaling an air raid. *Vestal*'s captain, Commander Cassin Young was also present aboard his repair ship when officer of the deck Davison, sounded *Arizona*'s general quarters at 0755.[20]

Typically, when a combatant is in port on a normal routine, the Officer of the Deck's duty station is on the quarterdeck, aft, rather than forward, on the bridge. On *Arizona*, after sending a messenger down to take the 0800 reports to Captain Van Valkenburgh, Ensign Davison was preparing to hoist the colors at the stern when he heard airplanes which sounded like dive bombers overhead. He looked through his binoculars to the southwest and saw the red dots on the wings, but for a moment still couldn't believe what his eyes told him—until he saw some bombs falling. He saw the first bomb hit near the air station on Ford Island, sounded the air raid alarm, and notified Captain Van Valkenburgh.[21]

The Captain came on deck and hurried toward the bridge. Lieutenant Commander Samuel G. Fuqua, the ship's First Lieutenant [third in succession to take command in an emergency] and Damage Control Officer, was in the senior officers' wardroom eating breakfast when the air raid alarm sounded. He immediately got up from the table, went to the phone and instructed Davison to sound general quarters. He then ran up to the starboard side of the quarterdeck to see if Davison had received word. He cut back through the wardroom and went out the port hatch just in time to see a low-flying Japanese plane go by, firing machine guns. Fuqua returned to the starboard side of the quarterdeck, and ran forward toward his battle station, Central Control, in the conning tower. As he was running, he glanced up and saw a bomb dropping which appeared to be falling near him.[22]

The next thing he remembered was lying on his back, waking up about six feet from a hole in the deck, after apparently being knocked unconscious by a bomb which struck the face plate of #4 turret on the starboard side, glanced off, and went through the deck just forward of the captain's hatch, penetrating the decks and exploding on the third deck. When he came to and got up off the deck the ship was a mass of flames amidships on the boat deck, and the deck was awash to about frame 90. He saw men running out of the fire toward the quarterdeck, some with severe burns, others jumping over the side to escape the searing flames. The antiaircraft battery and machine guns were apparently still firing.[23] The bomb was among the first of eight which struck *Arizona* during the raid, and when Samuel Fuqua regained consciousness, he learned a far worse disaster had visited the ship.

He proceeded to the quarterdeck, and with the assistance of the #3 and #4 turret crews, who were forced out on deck by fumes, smoke and flooding below, attempted fighting the fire spreading aft from the boat deck onto the quarterdeck. Pressure in the water mains was gone, and the men gathered all the CO_2 fire bottles from the port side—about fourteen of them—and held back the fire.[24] They were beginning a long struggle filled with nightmarish sights, sounds, and odors—while trying to save the lives of shipmates, many enduring their final moments, sometimes hours, of incomprehensible pain and suffering.

The great majority of the *Arizona* crew who lived to tell theirs and their ship's stories, were those with battle stations aft. Ensign Douglas Hein was one of few men who went forward and last saw and lived to tell of seeing Captain Van Valkenburgh and Admiral Kidd alive. He left the junior officers wardroom and went to the boat deck when general quarters sounded. As he made his way toward the signal bridge, he noted that some of the forward antiaircraft gun crews were firing. He saw Admiral Kidd on the signal bridge, then went up to the navigation bridge. When he arrived, the only other two men present were the Captain and the Quartermaster (the ship's helmsman). He overheard the Quartermaster ask the Captain if he wanted to go to the conning tower, but Captain Van Valkenburgh was making phone calls and didn't want to leave the bridge.

The Quartermaster reported a bomb had just struck #2 turret, when suddenly the whole bridge shook like it was in an earthquake. Flame came through the bridge windows, which had been broken by gunfire. The foretop, tilting forward and collapsing the bridge and its superstructure following the violent explosion, continued to shake the bridge while the three men tried to get out the port door at the after end of the bridge—but couldn't. They staggered toward the starboard side and fell on the deck just forward of the wheel.

Hein, finally able to raise his head, turned and saw the port door open. He got up and ran to it, ran down the port ladders, passing through flames and smoke. He descended halfway down the signal bridge ladder, found it bent back under the top half, and jumped to the boat deck. He then climbed down a hand railing to the galley deck. The intensity of flames and smoke on the boat and galley decks were decreasing. He walked aft and down the ladder to the port quarterdeck, crossed to the starboard side and down the officers' ladder to the barge.[25]

Ensign Jim D. Miller, whose battle station was #3 turret, got up about 0745, and was dressing when Ensign Davison sounded the air raid alarm. Miller heard only one blast on the alarm instead of three, which was odd, as though someone had accidentally touched the switch. He felt an explosion near the ship, which seemed like a "no-load" shot off No. 2 Catapult. When two more explosions quickly followed, he decided it wasn't a catapult shot. Then he heard word passed to set Condition Zed below the third deck.

Jim Miller slipped on a uniform and hurried down to the third deck to check his assigned watertight doors and hatches, still not convinced an air raid was in progress. As soon as he returned to the second deck from the lower wardroom, he met a gunner's mate who told the ensign he was trying to find the magazine keys. Miller went to the Captain's Cabin to call him and get the keys if possible, but the Captain had already left for the bridge. Miller then looked in the Gunnery Officer's stateroom to see if he could get the keys from him, but he wasn't there either. By that time, the gunners mate had left him, heading down to the third deck.

Miller heard general quarters sounded. He went to his battle station in #3 turret, through the lower ammunition handling room, to the booth, took the turret officer's station and manned the sound powered phones to Plot. Communications to Plot were good, but he heard no other turrets on the line. Shortly after he reached the booth and was on the phone, the turret was shaken by a low intensity explosion. Within moments another far more powerful explosion shook #3 turret, reverberated throughout *Arizona*, and showered death and destruction on her decks and the decks of *Vestal*, *West Virginia*, and *Tennessee*.[26]

Battle stations in *Arizona*'s aft, particularly the two heavily-armored turrets had this morning saved many lives and for the moment sheltered their occupants from the horror that swept across *Arizona*'s decks, ripped through the ship's vitals, broke her back, tore her apart forward of the superstructure, and opened the forward compartments to near-instant, massive flooding. Over 1,000 men perished within moments when the 1,765-pound bomb officially credited to a Kate high-level bomber pilot, Tadashi Kusumi, from the carrier *Hiryu*. Within twenty-four hours, the huge explosion, captured on film, became an image indelibly seared into the nation's memory, and with other devastating photographs taken in Pearl Harbor and on Oahu that day, forged a rage unifying the American people like no other event in the nation's history.

Smoke poured in through the overhang hatch, and Jim Miller could see nothing but reddish flames outside. The sound-powered phones went dead, power to the turret failed, and all lights went out. After a verbal check in the dark, he concluded the turret was not yet half manned.

When the bomb hit and glanced off the side of #4 turret, penetrated down to the third deck and exploded, the crew in Miller's lower handling room—including Ensigns Guy S. Flannigan and Jennings P. Field, jr.,—was shaken up, and water began coming in the lower handling room. Gases from the explosion were filling the turret from the overhang hatch and openings in the lower room. He stepped outside the turret to see what the conditions were on the quarterdeck. He was stunned. Six days later, he wrote dispassionately, "I noticed several badly burned men lying on the deck and saw Ensign [Lawrence D.] Anderson, who had been Junior Officer of the Deck, lying on the deck with a bad cut on his head."

What he actually had seen was almost beyond comprehension, and was described by another *Arizona* survivor, after the explosion adjacent to and far below #2 turret had sucked the life from so many.

> I remembered not to touch the hot ladder rails as I raced . . . onto the quarterdeck . . . There were bodies . . . I'd seen them from above, but it didn't register clearly until I got down on the quarterdeck. These people were zombies . . . They were burned completely white. Their skin was just as white as if

you'd taken a bucket of whitewash and painted it white. Their hair was burned off; their eyebrows were burned off; the pitiful remains of their uniforms in their crotch was a charred remnant; and the insoles of their shoes was about the only thing that was left on these bodies. They were moving like robots. Their arms were out, held away from their bodies, and they were stumping along the decks . . . [27]

The violent horror on *Arizona*, vividly described by this one survivor, told of walking dead, yet didn't adequately describe the excruciating agony of the ship and the great majority of her crew. After the explosion lifted and broke *Arizona*'s back, and opened her forward passageways and compartments to massive flooding,

Forward magazines explode on *Arizona* (BB-39), after she was struck by a Japanese armor-piercing bomb. At far right is the mainmast of *Oklahoma*, heeled over to port approximately 40 degrees, toward capsizing. Slightly to the left of *Oklahoma* are the forward turrets of *Tennessee* (BB-43), with the rest of that ship covered by the blast from *Arizona*'s explosion. At far left is the bow of *Vestal* (AR-4), moored eight feet outboard of *Arizona*. NA

men not knocked unconscious, instantly killed or burned to death by the huge explosion and fireballs that roared into the shattered bow below #1 turret and aft beneath #2, were scrambling toward upper and main decks any way they could.

Men whose bodies were being consumed by fire were fleeing aft to get out of it, or jumping over the side to quench the flames. Those who leaped into the hopefully cooling water quickly found oil floating to the surface all around them. But the huge majority still struggling to survive below the main and second decks couldn't escape the flooding, were trapped in compartments and passageways, and drowned as the ship settled rapidly down by the bow, mercifully upright for those able to survive. At least a few were able to escape upward through open hatches, then swim out from under the oil and fire floating on the surface of the water. The *Arizona* sank in nine minutes.

Adding to a scene akin to Dante's Inferno, was the sight of flames rapidly spreading on the oil-covered surface of the waters surrounding the forward two-thirds of the ship, and spreading toward the stern, against the wind. Her tanks had been violently ruptured and a monstrous fireball applied to the fuel oil. Sailors blown overboard who survived the explosion's power and had no choice but to struggle directly to the surface, were confronted by a 6-inch thick scum of oil with rapidly spreading fire—and emerged on the surface covered with oil, their flesh potential match sticks waiting to be ignited if the flames made lingering contact.

The sight of desperately burned and wounded men which greeted Ensign Miller, a turret not completely manned and filling with suffocating gas, with all power off, convinced him he and his men could do nothing toward repelling the attack. He sent word into the #3 turret for all hands to come outside and fight fires, and all came out. But the battle was just beginning.

Scarcely twenty minutes had passed since the Japanese raiders first struck the Pacific Fleet in Pearl Harbor. Though the oil-fed fire surrounding *Arizona* was pulled relentlessly toward the harbor entrance by the outgoing tide and pushed by a nearly 9 mph east wind, and would soon spread toward an already fire-tortured *West Virginia* and her somewhat shielded sister-ship, *Tennessee*, there was some saving grace for *Arizona's* surviving crew members. The same tide and wind, plus determined firefighting with all the fire bottles the surviving crew could find, helped retard the fire's progress toward the ship's stern, and kept the quarterdeck relatively clear—where survivors could congregate for rescue and transportation of the burned and wounded.[28]

Ensign Flannigan, whose battle station was in the lower room of #3 turret, Miller's turret, was in his bunkroom when the air raid alarm sounded. Everyone in the bunkroom thought it was a joke to have an air raid drill on Sunday. He wasn't yet dressed. Then he heard an explosion. He climbed into khakis and a pair of shoes. Then general quarters sounded, and he made for his battle station in the lower room of #3 turret.

Condition Zed was being set below decks as he hurried to his station. Just as he and his men got down the ladder leading to the passageway between the lower rooms of #3 and #4 turrets, the bomb exploded on the third deck between the two turrets. When the explosion occurred he felt a whish with a gust of hot air—and sparks flew. The lights went out. A nauseating gas and smoke immediately followed. When they reached the lower room door of #3 turret, the door had already been closed and dogged from the inside. They were unable to get out of the passageway. He beat on the door for what seemed like minutes, until someone finally opened it.

They got all the men they could find in the passageway, into the lower room, and then dogged down the port door through which they entered. They were unable to close and dog down the starboard door to the passageway between the two turrets because the explosion had sprung it.

The air in the turret remained fairly clear for a time, but finally gas or smoke started coming into the room. The men got concerned and restive but obeyed when Flannigan and Ensign Field ordered them to keep quiet. They found a flashlight and saw the turret was misty with smoke. A hissing sound began immediately afterward, and a hurried search began, to find the source—air leaking from holes in the transverse bulkhead of the lower room. That meant air was being forced through the bulkhead holes by rising water.

Ensign Field tried to get Central Station [damage control] on the ship's service phone, but the phones were out. Flannigan tried the sound powered phone, and it was also out. Smoke continued to worsen, and they collectively decided they would have to abandon the turret's lower room. He and Fields sent men up the ladder to open the hatches to the electric deck, [ammunition] shell room and [gun] pits. At first they had difficulty opening the first hatch, and were coughing heavily when it was finally opened. The two ensigns sent their men up to the pits on the double, leaving two with Flannigan and Field. The officers sent the two men ahead of them, and Field went up the ladder behind them, followed by Flannigan. By the time the last two finally left, water was about eight inches deep in the lower room, and rising.

They closed and dogged hatches behind them as they progressed upward to the gun pits, where Flannigan took charge while he sent Ensign Field out on deck to assist Lieutenant Commander Fuqua. Then Flannigan saw smoke entering the pits through the pointers and trainers telescope slots. He urged the men to take off their shirts and stuff the openings with their clothes. Shortly, Field passed instructions from Ensign Miller to come out on deck and assist in fighting fires. When he and his men stepped outside, they saw for the first time what had happened to the *Arizona* in a few short minutes. The ship seemed to be afire from the boat deck forward—while the ship's First Lieutenant, Lieutenant Commander Fuqua, was moving about on the quarterdeck,

Arizona burns fiercely after her forward magazines have exploded, and *Vestal* has already moved away under her own power. Note collapsed foremast. NPSAM

calmly determining priorities, assigning firefighting and rescue tasks, looking to the wounded, and giving directions. Responding to Fuqua's direction, Flannigan and his men unlashed the life raft on the starboard side of #3 turret and threw it in the water.

By this time, the boat deck was awash up to the edge of the quarterdeck, as the ship continued to settle. He sent the men aboard the raft and shoved it off, then was called aft to help wounded into the barge for Ford Island.[29]

Ensign Anthony R. Schubert was shaving in the wardroom head when he heard the air raid siren briefly sound over the loudspeaker system, followed by the word, "Air Raid." At the same time he could hear scattered gunfire. He went to his starboard-side room and looked out the port, where he saw several low-wing monoplanes at low altitude flying away from the line of battleships moored forward of *Arizona*, apparently having finished a bomb or torpedo attack. He then heard the general quarters alarm and the word passed for general quarters. He put on a pair of dungarees and slippers to go to his battle station, forward, in Secondary Conn.

During this brief period there were several explosions which filled the air with fumes vented out the port. The worst explosion, which, at 0808 marked the death of *Arizona*, filled the inboard end of the room with flame and left a residue of orange smoke that continued to vent out the port. By this time the ship was down by the bow and sinking so rapidly that the lines from the ship to the after quay were snapping. He took a breath of air from out the port and went into the passageway, aft, and up through a stores hatch which had been blown open. He went aft to the quarterdeck and found Lieutenant Commander Fuqua directing operations. He assisted in opening hatches and retrieving the wounded, chiefly burn cases, and putting them in launches bound for the hospital ship *Solace*.[30]

While surviving *Arizona* crew members were laboring tirelessly and courageously to save their shipmates and ship, the Japanese attacks on the battleships continued. The first wave of the Japanese assault was nearing an end, and the great ship was already dead. But more would come before the morning ended.

When the survivors of *Arizona* began gathering their thoughts and writing recollections a few days after the attack, above all others the name of one man was fixed in their memories and flowed from their hands, though he would never be one to cite his own behavior as anything but his duty. Lieutenant Commander Samuel G. Fuqua's calm, cool, deliberate, steadying presence and influence was a magnificent force for good in the midst of horror. Guiding and directing young officers and sailors throughout nearly an hour and a half of air attack, he worked side by side with them, fighting fires, rescuing men who emerged from the flames and smoke, on fire; preventing others suffering great pain from jumping over the side to certain death; loading boats, launches and barges with wounded and burned to take to dispensaries and hospitals.

Fuqua recalled afterward that he and the men assisting him had moved approximately 70 injured and wounded men to safety and subsequent evacuation. He also remembered assuming during the rescue and evacuation that Captain Van Valkenburgh and Admiral Kidd had proceeded forward to battle stations at the call to general quarters. To ensure the two senior officers hadn't returned to their cabins while the injured and wounded were being evacuated, he asked Ensigns George B. Lennig and Jim Miller to go to their cabins and check. The two cabins were waist deep in water when Miller and Lennig arrived to find neither man present.[31]

E.C. Nightingale, a Marine Corporal, saw Fuqua on deck and wrote that he seemed "exceptionally calm." He added, "Charred bodies were everywhere."

First Class Petty Officer D.A. Graham wrote:

> Mr. Fuqua was the senior officer on deck and set an example for the men by being unperturbed, cool, calm, and collected, exemplifying the courage and traditions of an officer under fire. It seemed like the men painfully burned, shocked and dazed, became inspired and took things in stride, seeing Mr. Fuqua, so unconcerned about the bombing and strafing, standing on the quarterdeck. There was no "going to pieces" or "growing panicky" noticeable, and he directed the moving of the wounded and burned men who were on the quarterdeck to the motor launches and boats.

Captain Van Valkenburgh, Admiral Kidd and Lieutenant Commander Fuqua were three men on the *Arizona* who later received Medals of Honor, the Captain's and Admiral's awarded posthumously. The citation accompanying the First Lieutenant's award, spoke eloquently of an officer, who in a crisis became an extraordinary, steadying, rocklike leader, and a bright shining light for *Arizona*'s surviving crew members:

> For distinguished conduct in action, outstanding heroism, and utter disregard of his own safety, above and beyond the call of duty during the attack on the Fleet in Pearl Harbor, by Japanese forces on 7 December 1941. Upon the commencement of the attack, Lieutenant Commander Fuqua rushed to the quarterdeck of the U.S.S. *Arizona* to which he was attached where he was stunned and knocked down by the explosion of a large bomb which hit the quarterdeck, penetrated several decks, and started a severe fire. Upon regaining consciousness, he began to direct the fighting of the fire and the rescue of wounded and injured personnel. Almost immediately there was a tremendous explosion forward, which made the ship appear to rise out of the water, shudder and settle down by the bow rapidly. The whole forward part of the ship was enveloped in flames which were spreading rapidly, and wounded and burned men were pouring out of the ship to the quarterdeck. Despite these conditions, his harrowing experience, and severe enemy bombing and strafing, at the time, Lieutenant Commander Fuqua continued to direct the fighting of fires in order to check them while the wounded and burned could be taken from the ship, and supervised the rescue of these men in such an amazingly calm and cool manner and with such excellent judgment, that it inspired everyone who saw him and undoubtedly resulted in the saving of many lives. After realizing that the ship could not be saved and that he was the senior surviving officer aboard, he directed that it be abandoned, but continued to remain on the quarterdeck and directed abandoning ship and rescue of personnel until satisfied that all personnel that could be had been saved, after which he left the ship with the [last] boatload. The conduct of Lieutenant Commander

Fuqua was not only in keeping with the highest
traditions of the Naval Service but characterizes him
as an outstanding leader of men.[32]

Aboard *Vestal*, the ship which shielded *Arizona* from multiple
torpedo attacks like those suffered by *Oklahoma* and *West
Virginia*, there was more agony—and men of courage and heroism.
Author Gordon Prange carefully researched and wrote of *Vestal*'s
initial response to the dive bombers' attack on Ford Island.

As luck would have it, Vestal's officer of the deck
was Chief Warrant Officer Fred Hall, who the
previous night had predicted a Japanese attack on
Pearl Harbor. Hall immediately recognized the red
disk under the bombers' wings and ordered, "Sound
General Quarters!" But the ship's Quartermaster,
jaw at half-mast, stared at Hall as if he had lost his
mind. "Goddamn it," howled the officer, "I said
'Sound General Quarters!' Those are Jap planes up
there." And he himself pulled the signal at 0755.

At the sound of general quarters gun crews rushed to man the
3-inch antiaircraft, four 5-inch broadside, and two .30-caliber
machine guns. In his 11 December action report, Commander
Young recalled that *Vestal*'s 3-inch AA and machine guns opened
fire approximately 0805, the 3-inch firing three rounds before the
breech jammed. The gunners cleared the jam and fired one more
round before *Arizona* violently exploded.

When the death blow fell on *Arizona* thirteen minutes into the
attack, *Vestal*'s skipper, Commander Cassin Young, miraculously
survived, though he and approximately 100 of *Vestal*'s crew were
literally blown off their ship's decks, over the starboard side, into
the harbor. While the great majority of the repair ship's sailors
swept overboard survived the powerful shock wave radiating
outward across *Vestal*, *West Virginia*, and *Tennessee*, there were
casualties and more stories of lives saved, and men fighting back
in the face of the deadly assault.

In the early moments of the attack, men on *West Virginia*'s
deck looked up to see a flight of Kate high-level bombers flying
over them from the southwest tracking on a path offset slightly,
paralleling the centerline of the pairs of battleships. The high-

level bombers had come almost immediately behind the Kate torpedomen's low altitude attacks from the southeast and south, releasing their bombs at an altitude of approximately 10,000 feet. The lead bomber did excellent work in accounting for wind offset and range at bomb release.

Two bombs struck *Vestal* about 0805, approximately the same time the 3-inch AA and two machine guns opened fire. The first bomb was on the starboard side, away from *Arizona*, at frame 44. It penetrated three decks, passed through the upper crew space and stores compartments, exploded in a lower stores hold, cut fire main and crew electrical cables, buckled a watertight hatch, wrecked the lower hold and started a fire. Heat from the fire necessitated flooding the forward magazine, which contained 100 rounds of target and approximately 580 rounds of service 5-inch ammunition. The bomb didn't puncture the ship's hull.

The second bomb hit on *Vestal*'s opposite side, to port, at frame 110, further aft, close to *Arizona*, and did near-fatal damage to her hull. It passed through the carpenter shop, shipfitter shop, shipfitters' locker room, fuel oil tanks, and left an irregular hole in the hull approximately five feet in diameter, just inboard of the bilge keel. Flooding with fuel and water began immediately and eventually progressed up to the level of the carpenter shop. Commander Young's recollections of the first moments of the attack implied that at least two other bombs from the same bombing run struck *Arizona*—one the fatal blow resulting in the disastrous secondary explosion that swept *Vestal*'s 3-inch AA gun crew overboard, killing one of its members.

The huge explosion and its accompanying fireball savaged *Vestal*'s port side aft, bent stanchions, port lenses, broke windows, rained debris, bodies, and body parts on the decks and ignited oil-fed fires on the water's surface between the two ships. The fireball also instantaneously ignited fires aft and amidships on three of *Vestal*'s life rafts, six mooring lines, a gangway; and burned paint work. On the afterdeck lay the bodies of two men. Cassin Young concluded in his 11 December statement, "These men may have been either *Arizona* personnel blown over by magazine blast or members of *Vestal* after gun crews: they were burned beyond recognition."

The explosion and fireball which first swept men off *Vestal*'s topside decks, then showered debris, destruction and death on her, had a shattering effect on some of her crew. Immediately after two bombs had torn into her came the explosion, fires within and topside on *Vestal*, and in the water between the two ships—and indications their ship was taking water and beginning to list. To compound the fear of an imminent, perhaps far worse disaster, she was still tied close to *Arizona*, a much larger, more powerful ship, which was rapidly settling, her forward half a roaring inferno. Amid the shock, disbelief, and confusion were a few moments of a commander nowhere in sight, which caused some of her crew to decide to abandon ship.[33]

Some of the crew members headed for the gangway on the starboard side, intending to leave the ship down the side shielded from the fire. They met their captain coming back on board.

The encounter was unforgettable, a story that would be proudly told by one of *Vestal*'s wounded crew members to passengers on the SS *President Coolidge,* and to a newspaper reporter in San Francisco on Christmas Day. The account was also described to men who later recommended Commander Young receive the Medal of Honor for his courage and leadership that terrible morning.

Commander Young swam to the gangway and emerged from the water just as some of his crew had started to clamber down. Covered with oil from the slick, he blocked their path and shouted, "Where in the hell do you think you're going?" When they said that they were abandoning ship, Young ordered them back to their stations, bellowing, "You don't abandon ship on me!"[34]

There was more fighting by *Vestal*'s crew as the Japanese raid continued, and more ship and life saving decisions made by their feisty commander. When he wrote of *Vestal*'s actions on 11 December, it was his sad duty to tell of six identified dead; three unidentified dead, including two possibly from *Arizona*; seven missing; and nineteen hospitalized. He said, "About twenty percent of those hospitalized are seriously injured, suffering primarily from burns and fractures."[35]

The Death of USS *Utah* (AG-16) and Saving of Light Cruiser *Raleigh* (CL-7)

At 0812, at berth F-11, bow pointed northeast on the west side of Ford Island, the mooring lines restraining the *Utah* snapped and she rolled to port on her beams, ending her long career as first a battleship, and finally, a radio-controlled target ship. When she was lost, 58 members of her crew who were on board that morning were lost with her, all but a few entombed in a ship never refloated.

Moored where aircraft carriers normally berthed in Pearl Harbor, she took two torpedoes port side, when 16 Kates from the carriers *Soryu* and *Hiryu* fanned in two groups of eight low across the harbor from the west and northwest. Like the torpedo bombers coming toward the battleships from the opposite direction, the Kates came in flights of twos and threes against selected targets—but not without some frustrating mistakes by eager young Japanese pilots.

Lieutenants Heita Matsumura and Tsuyoshi Nagai, both squadron leaders, led the two groups of Kates, with Matsumura having specifically instructed the crews to avoid *Utah*—which would be a waste of precious torpedoes. But the two leaders brought the 16 in so low it was probably difficult for inexperienced crews flying formation off their lead aircraft to divide their attention and identify desired targets visually early enough to make necessary course adjustments—if they had tentatively selected their targets. Nagai and Matsumura early recognized the *Utah* and passed her by. Other torpedomen passed up targets on the west side of Ford Island, and circled round to launch their weapons at the battleships. Matsumura was angered at his young pilots' waste of torpedoes.[36]

Nagai changed course and flew over the southern end of Ford Island, aiming for 1010 dock on the east side of the harbor, expecting to see a more lucrative target, the battleship *Pennsylvania* (BB-38). She too was absent from her normal berth, and Nagai would have to settle for smaller targets—the minelayer *Oglala* and light cruiser, *Helena*.

About 0755, two Kates flown by Nagai, and an eager, young, inexperienced Lieutenant Tamotsu Nakajima were flying at altitudes as low as 50 feet toward *Utah*, from the west. Nakajima thought he saw a torpedo hit *Utah* and followed suit. On board the ship, members of her crew were directing their attention to three airplanes in formation, coming from the south toward Ford Island, diving low over the south end of the island and dropping bombs. They were undoubtedly the same Val dive bombers and bombs seen by Admiral Furlong from the quarterdeck of *Oglala*, officers on the decks of *Oklahoma*, *West Virginia* and *Arizona*, and in Naval Air Wing TWO on Ford Island when the attack on the Fleet began.

Aboard the light cruiser *Raleigh* (CL-7), moored at berth F-12 directly ahead of *Utah*, bow also pointed northeast, men were about to hoist the colors at the stern, when the Officer of the Deck, who evidently saw the approaching aircraft, concluded this was "part of a routine air raid drill," and called the antiaircraft gunners to their stations. But just then, about the same time two torpedoes slammed into *Utah* in quick succession, near Frame 84, a torpedo struck the *Raleigh* midships at Frame 58, flooding the forward engine room and Nos. 1 and 2 firerooms. Another passed forward of her bow, about ten yards astern of the light cruiser, *Detroit* (CL-8), moored further ahead of *Raleigh*, at F-13. The torpedo sank in shoal water near Ford Island.

On *Raleigh*, Seaman First Class Frank M. Berry ran for the ship's alarm, but it didn't go off because electrical power promptly failed after the torpedo exploded. While *Raleigh*'s crew rushed to battle stations, manned their guns to battle the attackers, and began the fight to avoid capsizing, *Utah* began listing hard to port, her crew struggling desperately to save themselves and one another. With two gaping holes torn in her aging hull, she was taking water at a far more rapid rate than *Raleigh*. Within moments after the second torpedo hit, she was listing approximately 15 degrees. About four minutes later the list was approximately 40 degrees and increasing.

Commissioned as Battleship No. 31 on 31 August 1911, after her keel was laid down in 1909, she served on numerous wartime and diplomatic missions, until under the terms of the Washington Naval Treaty she was selected in 1931 for conversion to a target ship. On 1 April 1932 *Utah* was recommissioned in Norfolk, Virginia, as a radio controlled target ship, and during the following eleven and a half years served in many training and test roles, including a machine gun school, bombing target, target tow, combatant target ship, and embarked and transported marines as a troop ship. She came to Hawaiian waters in April 1941, and after a modernizing overhaul at Puget Sound beginning in May, to make her a more effective target ship, sailed for Hawaiian waters again on 14 September. She completed an advanced antiaircraft gunnery cruise in Hawaiian waters shortly before returning to Pearl Harbor the first week in December.

When the Japanese struck the morning of 7 December, the captain and executive officer were both on shore leave, and the senior surviving officer on board was the Engineering Officer,

Lieutenant Commander Solomon S. Isquith. When the attack came, and continued for nearly two hours, Isquith and every man on board were eventually, painfully reminded circumstances made it impossible for the ship's guns to fire a single round against her attackers—and they had no weapons with which to defend themselves. In the most recent training cruise, she had been engaged in operations as a bombing target and all her 5-inch and 1.1-inch guns were covered with steel houses. All .50 and .30-caliber machine guns were dismounted and stowed below decks in storerooms, all ammunition was in magazines and secured, and two layers of 6-inch by 12-inch timbers covered the decks for protection against practice bombs.

A defenseless ship and crew were only the beginnings of mounting frustration, anger, and tragic loss—among men who acted with great courage and heroism, with more than one risking or giving up his own life to save others. On *Utah* in Pearl Harbor that morning, were magnificent, inspirational men, exhibiting extraordinary acts of self-sacrifice that would be repeated time and again in a mounting catastrophe.

When Lieutenant Commander Isquith saw the abrupt list begin after the first torpedo hit *Utah*, he concluded the ship was going to capsize. What's more, he must have known the crew couldn't defend the ship, and even if guns were serviceable in minutes, there wouldn't be time to open fire.

He immediately passed "All hands on deck and all engine room and fireroom, radio and dynamo watch lay up on deck and release all prisoners." (On board ships, sailors punished as a result of a "captain's mast," a disciplinary proceeding under the Articles of War, are locked in "the brig"—or jail, which was usually well below the main deck.) Isquith, seeing the rapid increase of the list after the second torpedo hit, ordered all hands to the starboard side, the high side, to escape the danger of loose, tumbling timbers fatally pinning or injuring men attempting to scramble topside to save themselves.

He then passed the word for crew members to equip themselves with life jackets, direction that proved impossible for many. Life jackets were in canvas bags stored with miscellaneous gear in rooms above the main deck, which required men to go up ladders—where they would encounter storerooms with shifting, spilling and mixing contents—then, if they could find a life jacket, have time to escape. Worse, in the midst of scrambling for life jackets those first few moments, a bomb apparently released by a Val dive bomber, struck the port "aircastle"—superstructure—of *Utah*.

Fast on the heels of prior orders to the crew, and the frantic first few moments after the torpedo hits, came a report from the engine room. Steam had dropped, they couldn't cut in the drain pumps, the port engine room was flooded, and the starboard engine room was taking water rapidly, the water at that time being above the high pressure turbine and reduction gear—though the lights were still on in the engine room.

The starboard engine room watch cleared the starboard engine room. The No. 2 fireroom, with No. 4 boiler steaming, reported steam dropping rapidly and additional burners cut in to hold steam. The second torpedo hit put out all fires. The fireroom watch then abandoned the fireroom, closed the quick closing fuel oil valve, leaving the auxiliary feed pumps operating but slowing down due to lack of steam.

Isquith wrote in the USS *Utah*'s action report, dated 15 December,

> By about 0805, the ship listed to about 40 degrees to port. Lights were on. No report had been received from the dynamo [generator] room; word was again passed, 'All hands on deck and abandon ship, over the starboard side.' The crew commenced getting over the side, the ship continuing to list but somewhat slower. The planes were now returning from a northerly direction flying low and strafing the crew as they abandoned ship.
>
> Observing the strafing and the moving of the timbers and loose gear in the aircastles, I directed the crew divide into three groups, one group going up the ladder leading from the starboard aircastle to the captain's cabin stateroom, and one going up the ladder leading from the starboard wardroom country near the wardroom pantry to the forecastle. A large number of these men escaped through the ports in the captain's cabin.
>
> Lieutenant (jg) Philip F. Hauck, Machinist Stanley A. Szymanski, and myself were the last to leave the ship going through ports in the captain's cabin. At this time, about 0810, the ship was listing about 80 degrees to port and the planes were still strafing the

ship, mooring lines were parting, and two motor launches and the motor whale boat were picking up men in the water. Many were observed swimming to the north and south of Pier FOX-11, and as planes were still strafing the men were ordered to the sides of the keys for some protection.

At about 0812, the last mooring lines had parted and the ship capsized, the keel plainly showing. All men picked up by the ship's boats were taken ashore to Ford Island and ordered to return and pick up any men still swimming about.

On reaching shore on Ford Island, all hands were ordered into trenches that had been dug there for some Public Works Project, in order to protect themselves from strafing planes. Noting that many men were wounded, Commander Gray H. Larson, (MC), U.S. Navy, with KERNS, Jean W., HA1c., U.S. Naval Reserve, who had brought a first aid kit ashore with him, set up a first aid station in the quarters of Lieutenant Church (CEC), Building No. 118 Ford Island. Commander Larson, GRAY, CPHM., and two other pharmacist's mates proceeded with the first aid treatment of all men who had been injured and necessary cases were sent to the Naval Air Station Dispensary in Naval Air Station trucks supplied for this purpose.

While in the trenches, a short time later, knocking was heard on the ship's hull. At this time planes were still strafing and dropping bombs. I called for a volunteer crew to return to Utah to investigate the knocking heard. Machinist Szymanski and a volunteer crew consisting of Chief Assistant Medic MacSelwiney and two seaman, names unknown, returned to the ship and located the tapping coming from the void space V-98, under the dynamo room. They answered the knocking with knocks on the outside which in turn were answered by knocking within the ship.

Etched indelibly in the memory of Lieutenant Commander Isquith that terrible morning, were several brave men, who on 15 December he singled out for exceptional conduct under fire.

In numerous ships that same morning, there would be many unforgettable men like those commended by the *Utah*'s engineering officer: (jg) P.F. Hauck, U.S. Navy, for assisting in getting men safely out of the ship without thought of his own safety; Machinist S.A. Szymanski, U.S. Navy, for rescuing Fireman Second Class John B. Vaessen by cutting a hole in the bottom of the ship while planes were still strafing; Fireman Second Class John B. Vaessen, US Naval Reserve, for remaining at his post in the forward distribution room without thought of his own safety, to keep lights on the ship as long as possible while realizing full well the ship was going to capsize; Chief Assistant Medic (Pharmacist Assistant) Terrance MacSelwiney, U.S. Naval Reserve, for operating a motor whale boat making trips to and from the ship during cutting operations without regard to his own safety from strafing planes, and for inspecting the engine room, clearing out the watch and securing

USS *Utah* (AG-16) torpedoed by Japanese aircraft, listing heavily to port, about to part her mooring lines and capsize off the west side of Ford Island, during the attack on Pearl Harbor, 7 December 1941. Photographed from seaplane tender *Tangier* (AV-8), which was moored astern of *Utah*. Note colors half-raised over fantail, boats nearby, and sheds covering *Utah*'s after guns. NA

the engineering plant prior to abandoning ship while aware the ship was going to capsize; and Chief Watertender Peter Tomich for ensuring that all fireroom personnel had left the ship and the boilers were secured prior to his attempting to abandon the ship.

The modest engineering officer played down another memory and important detail he left out of his 15 December report. While acting as the ship's commander looking after the safety and survival of Utah's crew, then leaving the ship at the last possible moment, he nearly waited too late, thus risking his own life. He climbed on a table anchored to the deck in the captain's cabin, preparing to exit through the same port through which he'd observed many men escape. About to lose his footing and balance, only an extra reach and grasp through the port by the men who had just preceded him saved him from possibly losing his own life. But it was Chief Watertender Peter Tomich whom Isquith and others remembered most of all.[37]

A 48-year old immigrant born in Ljubuski, Austria-Hungary on 3 June 1893, in what later became Yugoslavia, then Bosnia and Herzegovina, he first served in the U.S. Army in World War I, then enlisted in the U.S. Navy in 1919, and initially served on the destroyer Litchfield (DD-336). By 1941 he became the Chief Watertender on Utah, and came with her to Pearl Harbor in September. As the Utah began to capsize, he remained below, securing the boilers and making certain other men escaped, and in so doing lost his life. For his acts of "distinguished conduct and extraordinary courage" he posthumously received the Medal of Honor.[38]

While Utah's crew struggled to escape a defenseless, rapidly capsizing ship, the Raleigh's crew fought a similar but ultimately successful battle to avoid the same fate—and were by no means defenseless against the Japanese onslaught. One of the first men into action on the guns was twenty-two year-old Ensign John R. Beardall, Jr., son of President Roosevelt's naval aide.

The torpedo's explosion against Raleigh's hull awakened him. He hurried to the quarterdeck in his red pajamas, and one of the first things he saw was "those big red balls . . . and it didn't take long to figure out what was going on." Within five minutes, his port antiaircraft battery, and the starboard antiaircraft battery controlled by Ensign James W. Werth, had their ready ammunition boxes open and their 3-inch, 1.1-inch guns, plus .50-caliber machineguns manned and firing.[39]

When Raleigh's Officer of the Deck first noticed aircraft

diving toward Ford Island, and called antiaircraft gun crews to their stations, believing it was a "routine drill," Captain Robert B. Simons, *Raleigh*'s commander, was in his cabin drinking a cup of coffee, and the Executive Officer, Commander William H. Wallace, was on shore leave. When the torpedo hit, Simons "heard and felt" a dull explosion in the ship. He looked out the airport in his room, saw "the water boiling amidships," promptly hurried toward the bridge, and met Lieutenant Robert H. Taylor en route—who told him "the Japanese are attacking the fleet." Simons mentally noted, and later wrote, "The guns were magnificently handled; all hands from chief petty officers to mess boys volunteering to fill out the regular gun crews and keep ammunition supplied."

When he arrived on the bridge the ship's crew had already been called to general quarters and she had begun to heel over to port. He was told "an airplane torpedo had struck #2 fireroom, flooding it, and that #1 fireroom was the steaming fireroom, but all fires went out due to water and oil." He immediately directed the damage control party, under Ensign Herbert S. Cohn, USNR, and Carpenter's Mate R.C. Tellin, USN, to counterflood to bring the ship to even keel. In spite of the crew's taking prompt action to right her, to Simons it appeared *Raleigh* would capsize in the 45 feet of water in which she was moored. He and his crew, like a crew on an under-powered airplane unable to safely hold altitude, took extraordinary measures. In his 13 December action report he described what happened next:

> Orders were given for all men not at the guns to jettison all topside weights and to put both airplanes in the water first. Both planes were successfully hoisted out by hand power alone, and were directed to taxi over to Ford Island and report for duty, along with the aviation detail on board. The senior doctor was directed to report to the hospital ship USS *Solace*, to aid in caring for the injured and wounded from other ships (we had no dead and only a few wounded on this ship) . . . A signal was sent to send pontoons and a lighter from alongside the *Baltimore* to this ship, and they were delivered expeditiously and secured to our port quarter with steel hawsers under the ship and acted as an outrigger. Extra

The cruiser *Raleigh* (CL-7) is kept afloat by a barge lashed alongside, after she was damaged by a Japanese torpedo and a bomb, 7 December 1941. The barge has salvage pontoons *YSP-14* and *YSP-13* on board. The capsized hull of *Utah* (AG-16) is visible astern of *Raleigh*. NA

manila wire lines were run to the quays to help keep the ship from capsizing.

Our torpedoes, minus their warheads, were pushed overboard by hand and beached at Ford Island. Both torpedo tubes, both catapults, the steel cargo boom, were all disconnected and jettisoned by hand power. Also, all stanchions, boat skids and life rafts and booms were jettisoned. Both anchors were let go.

. . . When it appeared the ship might not capsize or sink, Ensign [James] J. Coyle, USN, of the *Raleigh*, was told to see if he could find an oil bottom that was free of water and to raise steam in either #3 or #4 fireroom, as water was getting in to the after engine room and #3 and #4 firerooms, and if they were flooded there would be little hope of keeping the ship afloat. This was done and the pumps were started.

Meanwhile the gun crew on topside kept up a heavy and accurate fire . . .

Raleigh's skipper reported that the ship's gunners registered hits on five Japanese aircraft they saw destroyed during the raid.[40]

But defending and saving their ship wasn't all they did. When *Utah*'s surviving crew began efforts to locate men trapped in their ship's capsized hull, *Raleigh*'s sailors came to their assistance. They furnished an oxy-acetylene torch and crew to cut the hole in *Utah*'s hull, which permitted rescue of Fireman Second Class John B. Vaessen. Captain Simons, *Raleigh*'s commander, later wrote in admiration of Vaessens first reaction when he was pulled from *Utah*'s hull. ". . . as soon as he took a deep breath, [he] insisted on going back to see if he could rescue any of his shipmates."[41]

Dock 1010: The Struggle to Save *Oglala* (CM4) and *Helena* (CL-50)

At 0755, when Rear Admiral William Furlong realized Japanese aircraft were dropping bombs on Ford Island, and shouted to *Oglala*'s on-deck crew, "Japanese! Man your stations!" he was rushing to command *Oglala* flash the alarm: "All ships in harbor sortie."

In his haste to sound the alarm to the ship's crew and all ships in the harbor, he probably didn't see Lieutenant Tsuyoshi Nagai's Kate torpedo bomber coming low across the water from the west, abeam *Oglala* and aiming directly for her. The old minelayer, built in 1907, and acquired by the Navy in November 1917, was moored port side, eight feet outboard from the light cruiser *Helena*, Berth B-2, 1010 Dock, with both ships bows toward the southwest, 210 degrees, toward the harbor entrance. The ship's captain, Commander Edmond P. Speight, wasn't aboard *Oglala* when the attack came, and the executive officer, Commander Roland E. Krause was in command.

Nagai had led seven other Kates and their three-man crews toward targets on the west side of Ford Island, but bypassed them, intending to release his torpedo against the battleship *Pennsylvania*, normally moored at 1010 Dock. She wasn't there. When Nagai did recognize her, from intelligence and target study, she was in Dry Dock No. 1, directly ahead of *Oglala* and *Helena*, with the destroyers *Cassin* and *Downes* in the dry dock ahead of *Pennsylvnia*. The new dry dock west of *Pennsylvania* wasn't occupied, and the floating dry dock just west of the new dry dock, held the destroyer *Shaw*. For Nagai, a torpedo attack on *Pennsylvania* was now impossible, thus he bore in on *Oglala*, with the silhouette of the much larger, adjacent *Helena* visible but partly shielded by the minelayer two-thirds her length and less than forty percent her tonnage. While *Oglala*'s crew was running to battle stations, they sighted Nagai's approaching Kate.

On *Helena* at 0755, Signalman's Mate First Class C.A. Flood was on watch, on the signal bridge. Flood, recently on assignment to the Navy's Asiatic Station, saw the same planes as did Admiral Furlong on *Oglala*, at an altitude of approximately 4,000 feet over Ford Island. Flood had no need to see the "red ball" insignia of the Rising Sun. He instantaneously recognized the Val dive bombers' silhouettes, and notified *Helena*'s Officer of the Deck, Ensign William W. Jones. Without hesitation, Jones activated the alarm, sounding general quarters, while passing the word over the loud speaker, "Japanese planes bombing Ford Island. Man all battle stations and break out service ammunition." Some on *Helena* also spotted the approaching Kate.

Approximately 500 yards from *Oglala*, Nagai released his torpedo. To crew members on both ships, the torpedo appeared aimed at them. No time to react. Guns not yet manned, or ready ammunition boxes opened. The torpedo wake, appearing on the harbor's surface well behind the weapon's actual position in the water, was tracking straight and true. Prepare for impact. Then came surprise. No hit on *Oglala*. Instead, the torpedo passed beneath *Oglala*'s fifteen-foot, seven-inch draft and at 0757 a violent explosion amidship on *Helena* tore a large hole in her starboard side and bottom, at approximately frame 75, about eighteen feet below the water line, while lifting the fireroom plates and rupturing the port side hull of *Oglala*.

As the Kate climbed up and over the two ships the radioman-gunner in the rear cockpit raked the two ships with his rear-facing machine gun. According to the *Helena*'s crew, there was a simultaneous strafing pass by other attackers. The torpedo's explosion and strafing attacks instantly killed an unknown number of *Helena*'s crew, who were running through passageways and on deck, to battle stations. While the men on *Oglala* were far more fortunate in terms of casualties—none killed and two wounded that morning, one of them on the battleship *Pennsylvania*—both crews immediately began struggles to keep their ships afloat, and within three to five minutes batteries on both ships mounted a furious antiaircraft defense.

On board *Oglala*, the explosion's shock threw crew members out of their bunks, knocked out the generator circuit breaker, cutting electrical power to the ship; jolted the engine room flushing pump off its foundation; and started rapid flooding in the fireroom and engine room forward on the port side.

When the explosion overpressure ruptured *Oglala*'s hull, starting immediate flooding, the minelayer's fireroom watch, led by Fireman Second Class J.K. Johnson, shut down the boiler fires to avoid boiler explosion, closed watertight doors, and abandoned the fireroom. She was without electrical and engine power, her crew unable to activate pumps, couldn't get her underway to get clear of *Helena*—and flooding couldn't be countered though later inspection revealed the ship was at the time, temporarily dry forward of the engine room.

Approximately three minutes later, a Val dive bomber pilot miraculously missed both ships with a bomb that fell in the eight-foot space between them, just forward of *Oglala*'s fireroom. While it wasn't a direct hit, and no flash or flame started fires on her with either explosion, the bomb's explosion added to the damage already inflicted on both ships, increased the rates of flooding, and metal splinters [shrapnel] wounded several men on *Helena*.

Though *Oglala* was in material condition Baker when the attack came, with ports and hatches open for crew comfort, on orders, the crew immediately rushed to set material condition Afirm and readiness condition Zed, closing ports, hatches and watertight doors. Nevertheless, flooding continued, albeit slowly, in the old, not well-compartmented ship—through air circulating systems, unsealed bulkheads, and some ports later found to have been missed in the crew's haste.

Gunners rushed to battle stations on both ships, and *Oglala* called for assistance from *Helena* to man her forward gun. Three men crossed on the gangway to assist, and two more later crossed to assist in handling her aft mooring lines. On one occasion early in the action, the Mount Captain on a 5-inch *Helena* battery, requested *Oglala*'s officers and men to clear their bridge, because he desired to fire through it—and it was done.

The Mount Captain's dilemma and request mirrored similar problems existing wherever ships were moored close together in the line of battleships, at 1010 Dock, or in destroyer and mine warfare ships' "nests" that morning. In the first minutes of the stunning surprise attack, the raiders used low level tactics and varying axes of attack to press close to their targets before weapons release. This often required already rushed defenders to depress their guns so low they risked firing into the superstructure of the adjacent ship. In so doing, the Japanese were, in the beginning, effectively silencing a significant number of the larger combatants' antiaircraft guns. As the hellish morning wore on, that circumstance would change.

At 0830, with the raiders' first-wave assault still in progress, the minelayer's engine room reported extensive flooding. Commander Krause, on receiving the report, noted the ship was settling by the stern, and listing to port five degrees, with the list increasing. Her fate was sealed, but he needed to get the ship clear of *Helena* before giving the order to abandon her, else she would capsize into the cruiser, causing more damage, silencing its starboard guns for certain, and pinning her in place—if not doing fatal damage to a major combatant already crippled by the torpedo.

Admiral Furlong, on board as the Commander Minecraft, Battle Force, asked *Helena* for submersible pumps, but learned *Oglala* had lost electrical power due to engine room flooding and couldn't use her pumps. He hailed two harbor tugs which were working with a dredge in the channel. Beginning about 0850, during the lull between the first and second wave, the tugs started pulling *Oglala* aft, clear of *Helena*. By 0900, about the time the second strike wave descended on Pearl Harbor, she was secure to 1010 Dock, astern of *Helena*.

By 0930, with her list increasing through twenty toward forty degrees, her wire lines parting, the crew, unable stay on their feet, were sliding off the deck, and the gunners could no longer service the 3-inch gun. The machine guns were taken ashore, and Commander Krause and Admiral Furlong ordered "Abandon Ship." Admiral Furlong, Krause, and the gun crews were the only men remaining. When the ship was about to roll over, Furlong ordered the gun crews to leave the ship, and the two officers left with them. The three men from *Helena*, who had been sent to service her forward gun dived off *Oglala* and swam back to their ship to resume their duties—as did the two who went aboard to assist with her aft mooring lines. At or slightly before 1000 hours, *Oglala* rolled over on her port side in thirty-six feet of water, shearing off the bridge structure and main mast when they struck the dock.

Four men from *Oglala* weren't through fighting when they were ordered to abandon the capsizing *Oglala*. Chief Engineer's Mate A. Zito took two men, manned a drifting motor launch, and proceeded across the harbor to the damaged battleships where he assisted in rescuing crew members and fighting fires, remaining at his volunteer duty station until the following morning. Communications Mate Third Class Lowell Pennell went to the dry-docked *Pennsylvania*, where he was wounded while assisting a 3-inch antiaircraft battery mount defensive fire.[42]

In the meantime, on *Helena*, a different, yet equally desperate struggle was in progress—and crew members on both ships helped one another fight the common enemy. But the fate of *Helena* and many of her crew, as compared to *Oglala*, made abundantly clear that the Japanese were intent on destruction of the Pacific Fleet's major combatants present in Pearl Harbor.

As on all the ships struck in the first minutes of the attack, nearly all *Helena*'s damage and casualties occurred before the guns on the ten thousand ton ship were able to open fire at approximately 0801. Though crewmembers were rushing to general quarters, closing and dogging down watertight doors, hatches, ports, and running to their guns, the initial response wouldn't be nearly enough. The torpedo's explosion killed and wounded most of the one hundred casualties later reported while they were running to battle stations. Twenty-six were killed outright and five more of the fifty later sent to the Naval Hospital, died. Six wounded were from bomb splinters and machine gun strafing, two of which were fatal.

Deep below the main deck the 1,765-pound torpedo's explosion knocked the turbo generator out of commission, cutting the ship's electrical power—including power to her antiaircraft defenses. After the explosion tore through her hull and severed the wiring to the main and 5-inch batteries, water poured through the gaping hole, rapidly flooding one engine room and one boiler room. The ship went dark below the main deck for approximately one to two minutes, then came to life again. During that period crew members continued toward their battle stations in the dark.

Damage control and engineers swiftly restored electrical power by starting the forward and aft diesel generators. At the same time others in the engineer and damage control party isolated the flooding by closing all hatches and watertight doors to flooded areas, then shored bulkheads adjacent to the flooded compartments. Continuing their repair work, they ran power lines and pressure hoses over the top of flooded compartments to connect aft and forward electrical boards and the fire mains, secured boilers and firerooms affected by flooding, lighted aft boilers, and started auxiliary generators.

The explosion also knocked out fire main pressure, started small fires on the third deck, tore numerous shrapnel holes through the structure above the water line on the starboard side, punctured thirteen fuel tanks, a reserve fuel tank, two water tanks, and a diesel tank. Leaking fuel increased fire hazards up to the third deck level. Repair parties quickly suppressed the small fires, then took measures to reduce fuel tank leaks, fire and fume hazards, to include the issue of gas masks and protective clothing to the crew as soon as possible.

Considerable difficulty was experienced in attempts to maintain gunfire control circuits. On four occasions electrical fires resulted in the Plotting Room and on another occasion in the forward [electrical] distribution room, but the fires were quickly put out—keeping power always available at the gun mounts.

Men not manning guns or in damage control and repair parties assisted in moving wounded to the sick bay, as medics promptly converted the sick bay into an aid station to treat the wounded until they could be evacuated to the hospital. Settling of the ship eventually caused flooding of the sick bay to six inches deep, by water backing up through drains in three different areas of the sick bay—forcing transfer of the forward aid station to the ward room.

There were many good reasons Captain Robert H. English, Helena's commander, wrote glowingly of his crew's performance in his 14 December report to the Commander-in-Chief, U.S. Pacific Fleet: "Every man and officer on this ship conducted himself in a meritorious and exemplary manner. All were cool, determined, resourceful, vigorous and individually and collectively conducted themselves with no hint of confusion or hysteria and with no thought of danger to themselves."

There were many to be cited for all they had done to save and fight their ship, while saving one another, especially in those first few minutes that became painful yet inspirational, lifelong memories for each and every one on *Helena*. In his report he quoted words written by the 5th Division Gunnery Officer, Ensign David L.G. King:

> Because every man of the 5th Division did his duty I feel it impossible to mention or commend any single person without a resulting injustice to the others. But in fairness it seems nothing but proper to commend Seaman First Class R.D. Greenwald, who died at his station as [gun] trainer during the action. Other commendations must include the entire roll call of the crew for the 5th Division.

Captain English continued:

> The Forward Boiler personnel on watch proved to be a typical example of American courage and discipline. An explosion blew out a fuel tank behind the steaming boiler; the personnel knew not what it was but proceeded to put to rights a distorted situation in the dark, with guns firing, water pouring through a bulkhead, and super-heater temperature alarms and horns blowing due to short circuits. With all this they continued their work of securing the fireroom with water up to their chests before abandoning. After abandoning the room they dogged down the hatches and reported to the Repair III party for further duties.
> They were Ensign [Norman E.] Westphal and Chief Watertender [Jasper M.] Westbrook.

Quickly down nearly five feet by the bow, badly damaged, stabilized, but not sunk, *Helena* continued to fight, and when the second wave of 167 Kates, Vals and Zekes swept in at 0900, her crew's withering gunfire added to the volume of steel exploding in the skies over Pearl Harbor and the surrounding areas—keeping raiders at a more respectful distance. During the long brutal two hours that morning, Captain English reported *Helena*'s gunners contributed to the destruction of seven enemy aircraft.[43]

View from Pier 1010, looking toward the Pearl Harbor Navy Yard's dry docks, with the destroyer *Shaw* (DD-373)—in floating dry dock *YFD-2*—and battleship *Nevada* (BB-36) burning at right, 7 December 1941. In the foreground is the capsized minelayer *Oglala* (CM-4), with cruiser *Helena* (CL-50) further down the pier, at left. Beyond *Helena* is Drydock Number One, with the battleship *Pennsylvania* (BB-38) and the burning destroyers *Cassin* (DD-372) and *Downes* (DD-375). NA

CHAPTER 7

"Praise the Lord and Pass the Ammunition . . ."

We will either find a way or make one.

Hannibal

In the first moments of the attack, with battleships *Maryland*, *Tennessee*, and *Arizona* inboard of *Oklahoma*, *West Virginia*, and the repair ship *Vestal*, the three inboard battleships appeared to have escaped with little damage. Then, immediately following the Val dive bombers' and Kate torpedo bombers' initial onslaught, came mission leader, Commander Mitsuo Fuchida, with his Kate high-level, horizontal bombers—on their initial bomb run from the southwest, up the line of battleships, toward the northeast.[1]

The Kates came in formations of five, six, or nine, the latter in three flights of three airplanes each in a V of Vs, which to the ground observer appeared as an arrowhead without a shaft. The lead aircraft was at the point of the arrowhead. The Japanese, in planning and training for the attack, were convinced the formation yielded the highest percentage of hits, consistently up to 33 ½ percent. The eager and energetic Kate bombing team who convinced Japanese war planners this was the bombing formation to use at Pearl Harbor were Chief Petty Officers Akira Watanabe and Yanosuke Aso.[2]

After giving his attack signal to the high level bombers, Fuchida, as planned, dropped back from the lead position to better observe the action, yielding to the number two plane in the formation— with two of its crew members Watanabe and Aso, who developed the tactics for bombing success. On the formation's first pass over the line of battleships, what Fuchida believed to be air turbulence prevented satisfactory aiming for bomb release. Nevertheless, number three's 1,765-pound bomb fell from it shackles, and Fuchida watched as it exploded harmlessly in the water. He wrongly assumed number three had blundered and shook his fist in rage. The disappointed bombardier indicated by gestures that enemy fire had jarred his bomb loose. The formation turned to circle back for another approach in the stream of Kates flowing high above Pearl Harbor, up the line of battleships.

Fuchida immediately felt remorseful for jumping to conclusions, but there was no time for wasted emotions. His own plane suddenly rocked, severely jolted by a flak burst somewhere close. "Is everything all right?" he cried out to his pilot. "A few holes in the fuselage," came the reassuring response. American sailors and junior officers had raced to their shipboard guns and broken out their service ammunition with astonishing speed.[3]

Because the raiders attacked with no warning, from multiple directions, altitudes, and dive angles in a sharply compressed time period, defenders' responses were necessarily controlled locally, at the gun batteries, rather than centrally on each ship. The return fire seemed ragged at first, with the wrong type of ammunition and fusing, flak bursts and direct fire rounds generally well short of gunners' targets—with a few notable exceptions. Nevertheless, Japanese air leaders were surprised at the rapidity of the American response, while American officers were unstinting in praise of their gun crews' initiative, discipline, devotion to duty, and speed in mounting a fierce defense. As the assault continued, effectiveness of defenders' fire increased, though some crewmembers on ships in overhaul or repair had had little or no antiaircraft firing practice for months.

Commander Midori Matsumura ran into the same unexpectedly rapid response from American gunners. He had led the Kate torpedomen against the ships on the west side of Ford Island, then bypassed them, and circled to go after targets among the battleships. He made his second pass on the battleships, and again wasn't satisfied. He circled at low altitude again, this time fastening on *West Virginia*, and still delivered one of the first blows to her. By that time, guns were blazing, and Matsumura and his crew were fortunate to have avoided the hail of steel fired into the air above and across Pearl Harbor. Gordon Prange, in *At Dawn We Slept*, wrote of Matsumura's vivid recollections.

"A huge waterspout splashed over the stack of the ship and then tumbled down like an exhausted geyser . . . immediately followed by another one. What a magnificent sight!" So impressed was Matsumura that he told his observer to photograph the scene. But the man misinterpreted the order and blazed away with his machine gun, wrecking the antenna of his own plane.

"By this time enemy antiaircraft fire had begun to come up very fiercely. Black bursts were spoiling the once beautiful sky," Matsumura recalled. "Even white bursts were seen mixed up among them." The white smoke came from harmless training shells as the Americans hurled everything imaginable at the Japanese, while seamen smashed the locks of the ships' magazines. Now those magazines began to yield their deadly harvest, and Matsumura soared away, picked up a fighter escort, and headed for the rendezvous point.[4]

On board the destroyer *Blue* (DD-387), which during the attack got under way with only four officers on board—all ensigns—one of her officers, Ensign Nathan F. Asher, was on the bridge and never understood how his men "got their ammunition from the magazines to the guns in the fast and swift manner that they did." A few awakened with Sunday morning hangovers but later said "they had never sobered up so fast in their lives."[5]

On the dry-docked *Pennsylvania*, which had three propeller shafts removed, the crew had been excused from antiaircraft drills. Machine guns in the foremast were manned, and gun crews were available to man all antiaircraft batteries, thus guns commenced firing between 0802 and 0805. As time passed, a considerable number of seamen from other ships, such as *Oglala*, the destroyer *Chew* (DD-106), the destroyer tender *Dobbin* (AD-3); the light minelayers *Tracy* (DM-19), *Sicard* (DM-22), and *Pruitt* (DM-22), voluntarily came aboard *Pennsylvania* to assist in manning guns, forming ammunition trains and fighting fires. Sadly, among the many sailors who came aboard *Pennsylvania* from six different ships to help defend and save her, the fleet, and one another, eleven died as a result of the Japanese air attack, as did 18 men from the battleship's crew.[6]

Similar to *Blue*, destroyers such as *Tucker* (DD-374), *Reid* (DD-369), *Monaghan* (DD-354), *Aylwin* (DD-355), *Dale* (DD-353) and *Farragut* (DD-348); *Worden* (DD-352), *Hull* (DD-350), *Dewey* (DD-349), *Phelps* (DD-360) and *MacDonough* (DD-351); *Patterson* (DD-392), *Ralph Talbot* (DD-390) and *Henley* (DD-391); destroyer minelayers such as *Gamble* (DM-15), *Montgomery* (DM-17), *Breese* (DM-18); destroyer minesweepers *Trever* (DMS-16), *Zane* (DMS-14), *Perry* (DMS-17) and *Wasmuth* (DMS-15), moored in "nests" in the East and Middle lochs of the harbor; or in dry docks, such as destroyers *Cassin* (DD-372), *Downes* (DD-375), and *Shaw* (DD-373), near *Pennsylvania*, across the main channel to the east of Ford Island; the cruisers *Detroit* (CL-8), near *Raleigh*, seaplane tenders *Tangier* (AV-8) and *Curtis* (AV-4) west of Ford Island in the Middle Loch; *Phoenix* (CL-46), northeast of Ford Island, near Aiea Bay; and the light cruiser *Honolulu* (CL-48); three submarines, the *Dolphin* (SS-169), *Narwhal* (SS-167), and *Tuatog* (SS-199); and three patrol boats on the east side of the harbor moored at docks in the Southeast Loch, all added to the increasingly fierce volume of gunfire anytime an airborne target appeared within range.[7]

From Tragedy—Inspiration

The heavy cruiser *New Orleans* (CA-32), moored inside Berth 16 on the south side of the Southeast Loch, bow in, undergoing engine repairs, was taking power and light from the dock when the first Val released its bomb that fell harmlessly off the south end of Ford Island. The *New Orleans*' Chaplain, (Lieutenant jg) Howell M. Forgy, a six foot, two inch, athletic-looking native of Philadelphia, Pennsylvania, was still in his bunk gazing out the port-hole at the morning sky, thinking about the sermon he would deliver to the officers and men two hours later. He felt the cruiser jarred slightly.

He had chosen "We Reach Forward," based on Paul's words: "Forgetting those things which are behind, and reaching forth unto those things which are before." He planned to tell them, through the words of Paul, that their fate lay in the days ahead and not in those that had passed. Again, the heavy cruiser moved slightly.

He concluded a tug was probably shifting the ship to another berth. Then another little noise challenged the tranquility of the Hawaiian morning, a muffled tat-tat-tat, he described as similar to a "... boy ... running a stick along one of those white picket fences back home." Then the silence suddenly exploded with the deafening clang-clang-clang of the general alarm. His first reaction typified thousands of reactions in Pearl Harbor that morning. "I wondered why the officer of the deck could never get it through his head the fact that the general alarm was not to be tested on Sundays."

He then recalled, "The clang-clang-clang continued stubbornly, and the shrill scream of the bo'sun's pipe beeped through the speaker. 'All hands to battle stations! All hands to battle stations! This is no drill! This is no drill!'" Still not convinced, he next concluded, "This must be some admiral's clever idea of how to make an off-hour general quarters drill for the fleet realistic." He dressed and sauntered toward his battle station in sick bay—going down ladders bucking a line of marines pulling on their jackets, panting and swearing unprintable things about general quarters—hurrying up through the hatch to their battle stations at the machine guns and AA batteries topside. Everyone was grumbling about general quarters, especially at this hour, when their Sunday-morning-after-Saturday-night liberty was interrupted so abruptly.

When he arrived in sickbay, Lieutenant Commander Edward Evans, a World War I and China veteran, and the senior medical officer, came behind him, cinching up his tie. When the "doc" stepped through the door, his face expressed worry. Chaplain Forgy asked, "What's it all about, Doc?" "I don't know," the doctor said. "I just saw a plane falling out of the sky. It was burning." The Chaplain told him he thought that was carrying a drill pretty far. Dr. Evans turned his head slightly to the side, glancing past him, then, "I don't know, Padre. This might be the real thing."[8]

Topside the reaction of the *New Orleans*' crew was already beginning to typify the frustration, anger and fierce response to the Japanese naval aviators' onslaught. From their furious response and the cruiser's battle came words that in the months ahead, inspired one of the songs that lifted the spirits of a nation still reeling from the 7 December disaster.

In his 13 December report of actions taken, *New Orleans'* commander, Captain James G. Atkins, with evident pride, recounted events on a heavily armed ship carrying nine 8-inch, eight 5-inch, and eight .50-caliber machine guns—that wasn't ready and in no condition to fight. The crew had not engaged in target practice since June, and fully 40 percent had little or no gunnery experience—many having never fired machine guns or big guns. What's more, the antiaircraft battery directors were off the ship that morning, requiring the 5-inch guns to operate under local control. Nevertheless, Atkins recalled, ". . . throughout the raid [they] fought the ship with the coolness and steadiness of a Veteran crew."

After crewmembers sighted Val dive bombers attacking Ford Island, *New Orleans* was promptly called to general quarters at 0757. At a time Captain Atkins recorded as 0805, looking aft, they sighted Japanese torpedo bombers—probably a second, follow-on flight that had swung round from the west side of Ford Island after learning the carriers weren't there. The Kates were spotted on the port quarter, over the Southeast Loch, flying low past the ship's stern, on headings taking them toward the battleships. They were passing southeast to northwest near the docks and berths of what became known as "the bowling alley"— which opened toward the battleships across the main channel next to Ford Island, and was a good track to follow from the air. It was also the perfect terrain and water feature for pilots' use as an initial point for their low level approach to torpedo release.

New Orleans men standing on the ship's quarterdeck looking aft, opened fire with rifles and pistols when the first flight they saw passed near, right to left past the stern, while below decks men were scrambling to bring up electrical power and steam to first begin, then continue operating the 5-inch AA gun batteries. Because the ship was undergoing engine repair, all fires and boilers were shut down, and power and light was being fed from the dock. Yard power to the dock either failed or was cut off, which caused the ship to go dark, and shift to battery power. The changeover to battery power momentarily shut off the lights. Then soon after the lights came on, they began dimming. It became a race against time to raise steam before battery power was exhausted, and all the while men were working in engineering spaces, magazines and ammunition passageways, using flashlights.

In the meantime others broke out ready ammunition to feed the guns, and began setting up ammunition trains—men passing ammunition by hand, from magazines below, through handling rooms, up hand-operated hoists, to the guns above. While engineers and fireroom crews took emergency action to fire up boilers for steam to run the generators and air compressors, and operate gun batteries, the lack of power, lighting and air pressure temporarily held the rate of gunfire in check. Gunners had to elevate and traverse the tubes with hand-cranks, clear the tubes with rammers instead of compressed air, load and fire the guns by hand. But open fire they did, albeit at slower rates, using all the .50-caliber machine guns and 5-inch AA guns they could muster.

The *New Orleans'* crew's determination to open fire with all their AA batteries, in addition to machine guns, and give the enemy all they could became a magnet drawing men from nearby ships and smaller harbor craft that had no gun batteries available. Seeing her guns in action, they rallied to her from her sister ship, the heavy cruiser *San Francisco* (CA-38), across the dock from *New Orleans*, to the east in Berth 16; the light destroyer-minelayers *Preble* (DM-20) and *Tracy* (DM-19), moored directly ahead of her in Berth 15; and *Pruitt* (DM-22) and *Sicard* (DM-21), moored directly ahead of *San Francisco*. Other men who were returning to ships perhaps deemed beyond help, or were awaiting assignments to another ship and simply wanted to help—and had climbed aboard a *West Virginia* motor launch—and many more from small craft in the yard, came aboard *New Orleans* to assist.

San Francisco, *Preble*, *Tracy*, *Pruitt* and *Sicard* were all in various states of overhaul, with machinery partly disassembled and skeleton crews present for duty, keeping all from firing their larger AA batteries. On *Tracy*, a small band of destroyer men assembled three Lewis

.30-caliber machine guns and two .50-caliber machine guns and defended their ship as best they could, while others headed for the *New Orleans*, and later, after the air raid, a party of ten went to assist in fighting fires aboard the stricken battleship *California* (BB-44). A large number of *Preble's* crew hurried to assist men on the *Pennsylvania* in handling ammunition, fighting fires and assisting the wounded. Men from *Sicard* went to assist the destroyer *Cummings* (DD-365), and others to *Pennsylvania*.[9]

San Francisco was awaiting dry dock to clean her heavily fouled bottom, and her engineering plant was largely broken down for overhaul. Ammunition for her 5-inch and 8-inch guns were in storage, and her 3-inch guns removed, to be replaced with four 1.1-inch quadruple mounts. Her .50-caliber machine guns were being overhauled. Only small arms and two .30-caliber machine guns were available. Men on her crew were anxious to help in some way, and chose to help the men on her sister ship.[10]

These were the ships and men of which Captain Atkins wrote, "In addition to the splendid fighting spirit shown by the officers and men of the USS *New Orleans* . . . Their willing, cool, and courageous help greatly increased the volume of fire from this vessel. The example of these men rallying to help where they best could was in keeping with the best traditions of the service."[11]

Later brought to Atkins' attention, was another seemingly unimportant event that received no mention in his report. It was indeed an event that would echo down through the years.

Chaplain Forgy, after hearing "Doc" Evans say this might be the real thing, said, "I think I'll run topside and take a look, if you don't mind." At first transfixed by the destruction he was witnessing, he watched the battle unfold. It appeared every gun on *New Orleans* was now firing. The noise was deafening. Across the harbor, he saw diving Japanese aircraft in seemingly slow glides to bomb release, then abrupt pullouts and climbing turns toward the sea, explosions, fire, thick palls of smoke, enemy aircraft falling in flames, tracers, and flak bursts. He saw an enemy aircraft hit, fall and crash in the vicinity of the naval hospital, and heard the ship's gunners shout "like freshmen at the first touchdown of the day."

With Lieutenant Frances Lee Hamlin, the main battery officer (his 8-inch guns unsuited for AA fire), he went to the wardroom, and, at Hamlin's urging, began closing and dogging port holes. As they closed them, the room and all areas below deck became darker until they had to feel their way down passageways toward sickbay, where emergency lights were on. He lost Hamlin in the dark but found his way into sickbay, where he reported to Dr. Evans and told him, "You're right, Doc. This is the real thing." The doc was pacing back and forth in the room, his face white and grave. The noise from above told him more than the chaplain could. He had been through it all before, and he knew the heartbreaking stream of broken human beings that would keep coming into that little sick bay until this war was history.

Then outside Chaplain Forgy heard the booming voice of a big gunner's mate named George. "Get those God Damn lines down the hatch to the magazine," he shouted. Suddenly the impact of their helpless situation hit the chaplain. *New Orleans* had been under a temporary overhaul, and the ammunition hoists were without power. The gunners topside were ducking machine gun bullets and shrapnel, training their guns manually, by sheer guts and sweat, and they had no ammunition other than the few shells in their ready boxes.

The sharp voice of Lieutenant Edwin F. Woodhead could be heard, gathering every man in sight—shipfitters, big turret men, the repair parties—every one who had no specific job at the moment. "Get over by that ammunition hoist," he ordered. "Grab those five inch shells and get them to the guns!" The big 5-inch shells, weighing close to a hundred pounds, were being pulled up the powerless hoist by ropes attached to their long, metal cases.

Chaplain Forgy saw a "... tiny Filipino messboy, who weighed little more than a shell, hoist it to his shoulder, stagger a few steps, and grunt as he started the long, tortuous trip up two flights of ladders to the quarterdeck ... " where the shell was needed. The chaplain recalled, "A dozen eager men lined up at the hoist. The parade of ammunition was endless, but the cry for more kept coming.

He saw a Jewish boy from Brooklyn reach for a shell before he had caught his breath from the previous trip. Sweat from his face no longer came in drops, but came in a steady stream down the ridge of his nose, splashed to his chin, and fell away. His legs tried to buckle under him, but he wouldn't let them. He knew they were putting everything they had into the job, and it was beginning to tell on them. He wished he could boost one of the shells to his shoulder. The cool metal of the shell casing against his neck and shoulder would feel good. He would be busy and feel better inside. "But a chaplain cannot fire a gun or take material part in a battle." There was little time for reflection, but he did the next best thing.

Below decks, in this mix of crewmembers, low light, flashlights, periodic darkness, sweating, undoubtedly much swearing and the occasional jolt of heavy AA fire above, came a man walking up the line of sailors who were passing ammunition. He was Lieutenant (jg), Chaplain Howell Forgy. Lieutenant Woodhead, who was in charge of the ammunition line during the attack remembered: "I heard a voice behind me saying, 'Praise the Lord and pass the ammunition.' I turned and saw Chaplain Forgy walking toward me along the line of men. He was patting the men on the back and making that remark to cheer them and keep them going. I know it helped me a lot, too," he said.

The lyrics and chords of the song, "Praise the Lord and Pass the Ammunition," written by Frank Leosser in 1942, became one of the World War II anthems that inspired a generation of Americans in the most destructive war in human history.[12]

To the east of *New Orleans*, in Berth 17, the light cruisers *St. Louis* (CL-49), closest to *San Francisco* but across the dock, and *Honolulu* (CL-48) outboard to port—to the east of *St. Louis*, made their presence felt. At 0756, two of *St. Louis*'s officers observed what they described as ". . . a large number of dark colored planes heading towards Ford Island from the direction of Aiea. They dropped bombs and made strafing attacks. At the same time a dark olive drab colored plane bearing the aviation insignia of Japan passed close astern and dropped a torpedo." It was the same torpedo bomber sighted by the crew of *New Orleans*, and fired at with their rifles and pistols because her AA guns weren't yet in service.

The *St. Louis* went to general quarters at once and manned its entire battery. Her commander, Captain George A. Rood, reached the bridge at approximately 0800, and by that time the ship's .50-caliber machine gun and it's 1.1-inch, four-gun battery were already manned, in action, and delivering a full volume of fire. He ordered that steam be raised immediately on six boilers, for a speed of 28 knots, and preparations be made to get under way at the earliest possible moment. Yard work on the 5-inch mounts was in progress, and the crew set about removing all interferences, to have the battery in operation as soon as possible. She would get underway at 0931, and before the morning passed, fired 207 rounds of 5-inch, 3,950 rounds of 1.1-inch, and 12,750 rounds of .50 caliber ammunition. Much more would be added to her story later that morning, and in the remaining weeks of December.[13]

Across the "bowling alley," to the northeast, at the submarine base, officers and men on watch aboard the submarines *Dolphin* (SS-169), *Narwhal* (SS-167), and *Tuatog* (SS-199), the submarine tender *Pelias* (AS-14), two seaplane tenders, the *Thornton* (AVD-11) and *Hulbert* (AVD-6), and six patrol boats, PT-20, 21, 22, 23, 24, and 25, shouted warnings such as "Man the guns!" and rang alarms bringing crews to battle stations against air attack. Gun batteries on these nine vessels fired thousands of rounds of ammunition, first at torpedo bombers in the early minutes of the raid, then later in the first and second wave attacks, at dive bombers, level bombers and fighters going after other ships in the harbor. By the time the fourth torpedo bomber passed near the submarine base, gunners were beginning to get the range, azimuth and lead necessary to score hits. Because the Japanese were concentrating their assault on the larger combatants in the harbor, none of these defenders received damage or casualties throughout the morning.

Men on the *Dolphin* saw and heard the 0755 dive bomb attack on Ford Island, sounded general quarters, and five minutes later opened fire with machine guns, automatic rifles and shoulder-fired rifles at Kate torpedo bombers passing over the water astern

The submarine *Narwhal* (SS-167) defending against Japanese raiders. In the background is the cruiser *St. Louis* (CL-49) getting underway. Note the probable Japanese fighter aircraft in the distance, appearing to be directly above the *Narwhal* image. NHHC

of all three submarines, some of the attackers as close as a 100 or 150 yards. *Dolphin's* crew was witnessing and reacting to the same low-flying torpedo bombers seen by men on the *St Louis, Honolulu, San Francisco* and all the ships moored on the south side of the East Loch. His submarine moored portside, bow in, to Pier #4, Berth S-8 at the time of the attack, *Dolphin's* skipper, Lieutenant Commander Gordon B. Rainer, writing in his 12 December report, recounted the reports to him from the Duty Officer. ". . . the planes were flying very low . . . and were readily identified by large red balls on each wing."

The *Narwhal* in Berth S-9, similarly reacted, with its two .50-caliber and two .30-caliber machine guns, and ready ammunition easily accessible on the bridge and in the conning tower. Her skipper, Lieutenant Commander Charles W. Wilkins, wrote in his 12 December report, "The Dock Duty Chief at the gangway saw the first bomb drop and explode on Ford Island. He immediately sounded the Air Raid Alarm." The duty section, under the command of the Duty Officer, mounted and manned the antiaircraft guns and opened fire in four minutes. He continued:

> By this time torpedo planes were coming in at low altitudes and fire was directed at the nearest of these targets. Thereafter, firing was continued at every opportunity when enemy planes came within effective range. One enemy torpedo plane, at which numerous ships, including *Narwhal*, were firing exploded and crashed in the channel about 100 yards astern of *Narwhal* prior to launching its torpedoes. Personnel are reasonably sure that *Narwhal* scored hits on one other plane which came under our fire and banked and turned at close range. This plane emitted white smoke and appeared to be wobbly as it disappeared low in a direction over the Navy Yard Officers' Club.

From the submarine *Tautog* moored at Pier #2 came confirmation of perhaps the first ship to open fire against the raiders inside Pearl Harbor—and possibly the first valid claim of a shoot-down of one of five Kate torpedo bombers lost in the first wave of attackers. In his 12 December report, Lieutenant

Commander Joseph H. Willingham, Jr., described *Tuatog*'s circumstance and what his crew observed.

> On 7 December, 1941 *Tautog* was moored at pier two U.S. Submarine Base manned by one section of Submarine Division Sixty-One relief crew. *Tautog* had returned from a 45-day patrol on 5 December and only one fourth of the regular crew was on board. At 0750 several men on deck observed three planes flying in the general direction of the U.S. Navy Yard from over AIEA fleet landing. When the first plane dropped a bomb and turned revealing the insignia, it was realized that an attack was being made. General Quarters was sounded immediately and about 0755 the first .50-cal. machine gun was brought into action. Torpedo planes, some of which passed very close astern of *Tautog* had commenced an attack on Battleships moored at Ford Island. At about 0758 the fourth plane in line burst into flames with a loud explosion when about 150 feet astern of *Tautog*. Tracers from the after .50-cal. machine gun and the starboard .30-cal. machine gun were going into the fuselage of this plane at this time. U.S.S. *Hulbert* was also firing at this plane. It is certain that it was hit repeatedly by *Tautog*, no other ships in the vicinity had opened fire. Somewhat later in this attack a second plane was brought down in the same general area but at longer range. *Tautog* was firing at this plane but it is believed that it was hit by *Hulbert*. Other attacks were too distant for effective machine gun fire from *Tautog* . . .
>
> Battle stations were manned, the ship was rigged for diving, completely sealed except for ammunition access and made ready for getting under way. One plane was shot down.
>
> No losses or damage.
>
> It is considered that the situation was recognized promptly and the available armament brought into action expeditiously. Lieutenant W.B. SIEGLAFF, U.S.N. in charge of the relief crew section, assisted by Ensign R.F. STROUP U.S.N.R. and Ensign R.L.

FARRAR, U.S.N.R., attached to *Tautog* handled the situation competently until return of the other ship's officers about 0830. Machine guns which brought down the plane were manned by:
MIGNONE, P.N. TM2c U.S.N.
DIXON, I.H. GM1c U.S.N.
FLOYD, W.E. EM1c, U.S.N.
Hulbert, moored at pier 1, U.S. Submarine Base, was the first vessel in the harbor observed to open fire. By 1000 all except 10 of the crew of *Tautog* was aboard. By 1700 the ship was fueled, and provisioned for extended operations with all of the crew aboard.[14]

Reports from the seaplane tenders *Hulbert* and *Thornton*, and the submarine tender *Pelias*, similarly described the first moments of the torpedo attack on the battleships. Eighty-five percent of *Thornton*'s crew was on board, including four ensigns, one of whom was the gunnery officer. Moored portside to dock at Berth S-1 when the dive bomber attack on Ford Island began, the ship's general alarm sounded immediately, sending the crew to air defense stations, including Machine Gun Battery Control, and Control for Repair. Four .50-caliber machine guns, three .30-caliber Lewis guns, three Browning Automatic Rifles, and twelve .30-caliber Springfield rifles, constituted her air defense capability.

At 0758, the same time reported by *Hulbert*'s commander, *Thornton*'s skipper, Lieutenant Commander Wendell F. Kline, reported opening fire, with both ships firing .50-caliber machine guns at a torpedo bomber that burst into flames and fell in the water, with its torpedo falling clear of the aircraft, without being launched.[15]

With his ship moored at Berth S-3, *Hulbert*'s captain, Lieutenant Commander James M. Lane reported sharing in the downing of the torpedo bomber, and stated he believed his vessel was the first to open fire on the attackers proceeding west toward the battleships, and that no other ships were firing at the plane when it was brought down. As did the commanders of many other ships in the area, the two submarine tenders' conflicting reports during the swirling, hectic and confusing first wave attack presented numerous overlapping claims for credit in shoot-downs of Japanese airplanes.[16]

Later during the raid, the three tenders and the submarines

would defend the tanker *Neosho* from Japanese aircraft strafing her while she was en route from the dock near the fuel tanks on Ford Island, to a safer berth at Merry's Point.

The crews of six patrol boats in Motor Torpedo Squadron One, moored in Berth S-13, rushed to battle stations while machinist mates started air compressors to operate the two, twin .50-caliber machine gun turrets on each boat. The crews of *PT-20, 21, 22, 23, 24,* and *25* were eating breakfast on board the barge YR-20 when the Squadron Duty Officer, Ensign Nile E. Ball, who was standing on the barge when he noticed numerous airplanes with the insignia of the rising sun diving on the battleships. A chief petty officer near him remarked, "They look like Japs." An instant later the first bomb exploded and he realized they were Japanese. He ran to the barge and gave the order "Man the guns!" He later told the Torpedo Boat Squadron commander the men responded immediately, and in addition to starting the air compressors, manning the guns and opening fire, others started belting additional ammunition.

Similar to the reports of other commanders and duty officers on ships moored at the submarine base, Commander William C. Specht, the Torpedo Squadron commander, claimed credit for his men crewing the squadron's PT boats in the shoot down of two torpedo planes, one carrying its torpedo, the other apparently having earlier released its weapon.[17]

The two submarines and two seaplane tenders each claimed to have hit and downed a torpedo bomber, claims that couldn't be verified. The overlapping claims from the ships moored at the submarine base and throughout the harbor were entirely understandable. The defenders' surprise, shock, and reactive excitement in the swirling air attack by numerous aircraft from multiple directions, altitudes, and angles of approach, and the locations and distances of the hundreds of participants and observers viewing the same events were major factors in their claims. Moreover, defenders were fighting fiercely, in a rage, and were eager to claim any victory over the machines and enemy they saw killing and wounding their shipmates, blowing up and sinking their American ship borne homelands and savaging their territorial island paradise. It was virtually impossible to confirm what ships, and which guns should receive credit for specific shoot downs. Conversely, there was no question whatsoever as to the huge volume of fire thrown at the attackers in the approximately one hour and fifty minutes of the attack on the Pacific Fleet in Pearl Harbor.

One fact is inescapable however. The Japanese lost five torpedo bombers, all from the carrier *Kaga*, all from among the twenty-four that came across the southeastern part of Hickam Field, over the East Loch to attack the battleships. By funneling the Kates from *Kaga* and *Akagi* through "the bowling alley" they found themselves running an extended gauntlet of fire from both sides of the alley, whereas the sixteen from *Soryu* and *Hiryu* swept across the West Loch toward *Utah*, *Raleigh*, *Detroit*, and *Tangier*, where defenders' attention was at first, mostly riveted to Ford Island, and defenses weren't nearly as heavy, concentrated and potentially deadly.

Nevertheless, the Japanese losses from the first wave, with all their attacks on airfields and the Pacific Fleet were relatively small compared to the enormous damage they inflicted in the first fifteen minutes: one Val and three Zekes, plus the five Kates, nine of the total that would fall from the skies over Oahu that morning. By the time the second wave of 167 aircraft launched their assault, gunners on the ships, ground and in the air were more practiced and exacting in the price they made the enemy pay. Inexperienced antiaircraft gunners were learning how to lead the enemy when firing. Gunners on the ships and ground, and a small number of airborne fighter pilots, downed twenty more. Significantly, but not known at the time, 111 or more attacking aircraft from the two waves sustained various degrees of damage and a total of twenty were eventually pushed over the sides of their carriers, into the deep Pacific.[18]

The 15 February 1942 report from the Commander-in-Chief Pacific, to the Secretary of the Navy, summarized the speed, volume and fury of the Pacific Fleet's antiaircraft response to the Japanese raiders: "Although a battery condition of readiness for ships had not been designated from the Naval Defense Plan, the first batteries opened fire less than two minutes after the attack was initiated. All batteries, except those on ships undergoing overhaul, had taken up fire within approximately seven minutes after the attack was initiated."

Reports assembled as of that date, indicated the Fleet expended 284,469 rounds of ammunition of all types, with the bulk of rounds fired, 272,556 from .45, .30 and .50-caliber guns. The remaining 11,913 came from 1.1-inch, 3-inch, and 5-inch guns.[19]

As the bitter day wore on, Pearl Harbor's and Oahu's defenders would begin to learn, sadly, their fierce defense wouldn't stop the carnage and devastating losses on the ground and in the harbor, and would cause "friendly fire" deaths on military installations, in Honolulu and its surrounding communities, and in the air over Oahu—the painful prices of a successful surprise air attack, and war.

Into the Maelstrom: *Enterprise*'s Scouting Squadron Six (VS-6)

At 0720 in the morning, following his 0618 launch from the flight deck of *Enterprise* approximately 215 miles west of Oahu, Lieutenant Commander Howard L. Young, *Enterprise*'s Air Group Commander, was airborne in his Douglas Dauntless SBD-3, with his rear-seat passenger, Lieutenant Commander Bromfield B. Nichol, USN, Tactical Officer attached to the staff of the Commander Aircraft, Battle Force. Admiral Kimmel's staff had informed Nichol that the Commander-in-Chief wanted to see him as soon as he landed at Ford Island. Flying the Group commander's airplane and 6-S-2, to search sector 095-105 degrees, the next sector south of Young, were the VS-6 squadron commander, Lieutenant Commander Hallsted L. Hopping in 6-S-1, with his Radioman/gunner First Class Harould Thomas; and on Hopping's wing in plane 6-S-3 was Ensign John H.L. Vogt, with Radioman/gunner Third Class Sidney Pierce. The remaining fourteen SBD-3s, in seven flights of two, like the two senior officers' flights—all equipped with two, cowling-mounted .50-caliber machine guns, and one flexible, aft-firing .30-caliber machine gun mounted in the rear cockpits—were already spread into their respective scouting sectors.

Young was continuing toward NAS Pearl Harbor, ahead of the thirteen other planes from

VS-6 and four from VB-6, and was one of the squadron's nine, two-plane sections, intending to complete the scouting mission in support of Task Force 8 and *Enterprise*, and recover the squadron in advance of Task Force arrival at Pearl Harbor. His wingman in plane 6-S-2 was Ensign Perry L. Teaff, with Radioman/ gunner's Mate Third Class Edgar P. Jinks in the rear seat. Teaff was comfortably spread in a tactical formation to permit both crews to scan the ocean surface and surrounding skies. The two sections on either side of Young's were just over the horizon, not visible to the four men.

When Young sighted the tanker to starboard at 0720, he was proceeding on an easterly course. Upon investigation it proved to be the SS *Pat Doheny*, out of Los Angeles, owned by the Richfield Oil Company. Proceeding on their assigned track of 090 degrees, he sighted and passed the submarine *Thresher*, accompanied by the destroyer *Lichtfield*, at 0740—the same time Fuchida fired the first red flare, northeast of Point Kuhuku, signaling the Japanese first wave to assemble into their attack formations.

At 0810 Young's flight passed Kaena Point abeam to port, his position, 20 miles west of Oahu. By 0810, the Japanese Kate torpedo bombers had completed most of the destruction and death caused in their deadly torpedo attacks; Wheeler and Hickam Fields, NAS Kaneohe Bay and the Mooring Mast Field at Ewa were ablaze, with many airplanes destroyed or beyond repair, and hundreds dead and wounded. *Oklahoma* was listing heavily to port, soon to capsize. *West Virginia* was settling, its crews battling to avoid capsizing while fighting fires, Japanese bombers and fighters. *Arizona* had been shattered in one terrible instant, killing more than 900 men in minutes, and was a raging inferno. *Vestal* was fighting the air defense battle while fighting fires, struggling to avoid sinking or being consumed by the fire fed by *Arizona*'s ruptured tanks. *California* and *Nevada* had been struck with torpedoes, and were battling fires and enemy airplanes.

Maryland and *Tennessee*, though relatively unscathed, were deeply absorbed in fighting the air defense battle as best they could, rescuing hundreds of men forced to abandon *Oklahoma*, *West Virginia* and *Arizona* while warding off the oil-fed inferno creeping toward them from *Arizona* and *West Virginia*. And on the other side of Ford Island, *Utah* was two minutes away from capsizing, the cruiser *Raleigh* was fighting the air defense battle while trying to avoid capsizing as well. In between, Ford Island was a shambles and in flames with nearly all its airplanes and hangars destroyed or damaged, while on the east side of the harbor, the cruiser *Helena* and minelayer *Oglala* were blazing away with their AA guns, while *Helena* was trying to stay afloat and *Oglala* was starting to list toward capsizing into *Helena*.

At 0820 Young passed to seaward (south) from Barber's Point, and at that time saw approximately a squadron of planes circling Ewa in column. Believing them to be Army pursuit planes, he gave them wide berth, decreasing his altitude to 800 feet and continued toward NAS Pearl Harbor.

At a point mid-way between Ewa and Ford Island he noticed considerable antiaircraft fire ahead. At almost the same instant he was attacked from the rear, without warning, by Japanese planes. Recognizing the insignia of one plane that had completed a dive on him—he immediately dove toward the ground zigzagging. Nichol didn't have sufficient time to man the free gun in the rear cockpit. The SBD's fixed guns were loaded and charged but Young had no opportunity to use them. He didn't recognize with certainty the planes that attacked him, and at first described them as "low-wing monoplane fighters with retractable landing gear." They were Japanese fighters, Zekes.

Perry Teaff's plane was attacked at the same time but neither he nor his gunner, Jinks, were hit, though their plane absorbed several hits. In spite of the now wild ride, Teaff stayed with his flight lead, circling with Young's plane, low over a cane field to the North of Pearl City. To Young it became immediately evident the flight was also under AA fire regardless of which direction he led them. He didn't have sufficient fuel to return to the ship had he been able to get away from the island.

Hoping the two SBDs would be recognized as friendly, he decided to make a low approach to the Ford Island field and land—it seemed he had no alternative. Nevertheless, until he landed, their plane was subjected to heavy AA fire from ships and shore batteries in spite of recognition maneuvers and lowered wheels and flaps for landing. Young estimated his landing time was about 0835, approximately ten minutes after the first wave of attackers began withdrawing from their assault to rejoin at their Barber's Point rendezvous, and return north to their carriers. Teaff, subjected to the same harrowing AA fire decided to turn away just prior to landing. He finally landed later under the same conditions. Throughout the wild melee, the Air Group Commander was unable to establish communications with the Ford Island control tower.[20]

There was good reason for the tower's failure to respond. After he landed, he could see what wasn't entirely visible or understandable until he got on the ground. At Ford Island, the hangars, and planes on the ramp and in the hangars, were wrecked. There were numerous fires. The nearby battleships were in the grip of an inferno, with huge black clouds of smoke rising from *Arizona*, burning oil on the water, and the settling, burning *West Virginia* and *California*. The sky was being obscured by giant clouds of black and gray smoke.

A massive rescue operation was already under way. Crew members on several major combatants were desperately fighting to save their ships. Gunners on board ships and on Ford Island were still fighting furiously to down or drive off any aircraft they believed might be attackers. It was "shoot first and ask questions later." To make matters worse, few men firing at any aircraft considered within range had received sufficient training in aircraft recognition, and couldn't distinguish friend from foe when they weren't under attack.

Inspection of Young's plane revealed several bullet holes through the wings but no serious damage.

Thus began VS-6's return to Oahu early the morning of 7 December 1941. Not yet known to the Air Group Commander, matters had already deteriorated and were rapidly worsening. Former Radioman/gunner Second Class Jack Leaming, who became a prisoner of war on 4 March 1942, was personally involved in the return of his squadron to Pearl Harbor, meticulously researched, and wrote of the men in VS-6, and the four airplanes in VB-6 who were with them that morning.

Lieutenant Commander Hopping's wingman, Ensign John H.L. Vogt, with Radioman/gunner Third Class Sidney Pierce in plane 6-S-3, were apparently killed. At the time, there was little information available to explain what occurred. Hopping, who was flying a track further south than Young, but behind him, also investigated the tanker *Doheny*, seen by the Air Group Commander at 0720. Hopping, spotting the ship 20 miles "broad on his port bow," signaled Vogt in 6-S-3 to remain outside gun range while he investigated. He made contact with the ship at 0730, and also identified her as the *Pat Doheny*. When Hopping completed his investigation, Vogt's 6-S-3 couldn't be found. Hopping completed the sector search alone, and set course for Barbers Point.

When a short distance from Barbers Point, Hopping observed heavy smoke ahead, over Pearl Harbor and Ewa. Just as he caught sight of the smoke, he heard a frantic radio call several aircraft in his squadron also heard—Ensign Gonzalez's pleading voice saying, "Do not attack me. This six baker three, an American plane!" The same voice continued on telling his gunner to break out the boat as he was landing in the water. When abreast of Ewa Hopping sighted Japanese airplanes attacking the airfield.

He immediately broadcasted a report that Pearl Harbor was being attacked by Japanese aircraft, a report apparently heard by few in the squadron. He rolled into a high speed dive to low altitude and headed for Ford Island, and landed at 0845 amidst a hail of friendly fire.

Vogt, apparently still airborne at that time, remained separated from his flight lead, and eventually encountered Japanese Val dive bombers from *Kaga* or *Hiryu* near Ewa. As events would prove, Marine Lieutenant Colonel Claude A. "Sheriff" Larkin, Ewa's commander saw Ensign John H.L.Vogt's SBD and a Val collide in mid-air. Vogt and Radioman/gunner Third Class Sidney Pierce bailed out, but at too low an altitude. Both died in the trees when their parachutes failed to fully deploy. Neither of the Japanese crewmen escaped from their Val when it crashed.

In spite of his missing wingman, the squadron commander wasted no time when he landed at Ford Island. He began preparing to take his men and their planes back into the war now raging around them. But, it would take time to learn how many would be available for the next mission they would fly that day—find and attack the Japanese fleet.

Flying the northernmost track, 050 degrees, were two of the four SBDs from VB-6, *Enterprise*'s bombing squadron. It was common practice to assign them to participate in the scouting mission. In the lead plane from Bombing Six, 6-B-3, was Ensign Manuel Gonzalez, pilot, with Radioman/gunner Third Class Leonard J. Kozelek, in the rear cockpit. Ensign Frederick T. Weber, pilot in plane 6-B-12 with Seaman First Class Lee E.J. Keaney, the radioman/gunner in the rear cockpit, flew Gonzalez's wing.

Gonzalez and Weber sighted nothing on their first leg. About twenty miles past the island of Kauai, they completed their search mission and turned to a heading toward Oahu. Shortly after turning, Weber instructed Keaney to tune in radio station KGU in Honolulu to get some homing practice. Approximately twenty-five miles from Oahu, Weber sighted a large group of planes "milling around" between three thousand and four thousand feet. At first, he thought they were Army planes and continued to watch them for a few minutes. He was flying about five hundred yards on the right wing and five hundred feet above Gonzalez. When next he looked toward his flight lead, he couldn't locate Gonzalez. He rolled into a turn and circled, attempting to visually sight him again, then made four or five "S" turns over the position he had last seen him.

He glanced ahead and saw a plane at the same altitude and course the two had been flying. He tried overtaking the plane, assuming it was Gonzalez. Approximately two thousand yards astern of the aircraft, it began a 180-degree turn toward him. Weber concluded Gonzalez was helping him overtake and rejoin. He rolled into an easy turn to port to cut off his presumed leader and slide toward regaining his position in the tactical formation. When the plane was ahead on Weber's right, it abruptly increased its bank toward 90 degrees, pulling into a tight, high-G turn toward him. Then he saw the large red circle on the topside of the left wing. Reaction was instantaneous, and training took over.

Weber pushed his throttle full open while abruptly reversing his turn to starboard, rolling into a diving turn, passing well underneath the enemy. He was changing his direction opposite the enemy's and accelerating into an inverted high-speed dive to separate from the raider—by pulling his airplane's nose down while inverted, then rolling his wings level to begin pulling out of the dive before colliding with the water. He leveled off twenty-five feet above the water, having put insurmountable distance between his plane and the enemy's, and evaded an attack. Gonzalez and Weber had intruded upon the rendezvous point of the Val dive bombers that had completed their first wave attack and were returning to their carriers.

Weber's pilot report recalled the foregoing events occurred between 0810 and 0830. He estimated there were forty to fifty Japanese planes in the group. He never heard Gonzalez's transmission, "Don't shoot!" because he had instructed Keaney to change the radio frequency to station KGU, Honolulu, to take a bearing and practice homing on the station. The circumstance wasn't unusual, since the squadron was routinely ordered to maintain radio silence, and was well-disciplined to do so. Later, on reaching Barber's Point, Ensign Weber joined on plane 6-S-10.

Lieutenant Wilmer E. Gallaher, and his Radioman/gunner First Class Thomas E. Merritt, were flying their mission in the assigned sector for track 080 degrees, the sector just north of the

Air Group Commander's search area. On Gallaher's wing in plane 6-S-5 was Ensign William P. West, with Radioman/gunner Louis D. Hansen in the rear cockpit. They had completed their 150-mile leg that ended between Kauai and Oahu and turned south for Oahu. Shortly after turning, Gallaher, flying at five hundred feet and obtaining a bearing on station KGU, saw several planes rendezvousing ahead at approximately 1,500 feet. He thought they were U.S. Army planes.

After obtaining the bearing, he returned to the squadron's voice frequency and heard White-16, the squadron commander, Lieutenant Commander Hopping, broadcast Pearl Harbor was being attacked. Immediately thereafter he heard Manuel Gonzalez transmit, "Don't shoot, I'm a friendly Navy plane!"— or words to that effect. Gallaher continued to Oahu and arrived about 0835.

Ten minutes earlier, Lieutenant Clarence E. Dickinson, a 1934 Naval Academy graduate and pilot in 6-S-4 with Radioman/gunner First Class William C. Miller in the rear cockpit, and Ensign John R. McCarthy in 6-S-9 with Radioman/gunner Third Class Mitchell Cohn, had completed their search of sector 110 degrees, the sector south of the squadron commander, Hopping. Dickinson and McCarthy were approaching Barbers Point from the south at 1,500 feet, after Dickinson had turned north and instructed Miller to take a bearing off a Honolulu radio station to be certain they were on the correct heading.

As they approached Barbers Point, about ten miles west of Pearl Harbor, Dickinson saw numerous shell splashes in the water near the entrance to the harbor. Looking for the source, he saw a cruiser and three destroyers about three miles off the harbor entrance, but they weren't firing guns. Looking upward he saw numerous AA bursts above Pearl Harbor. Ewa's Mooring Mast Field was afire and sending dense smoke as high as 5,000 feet over Barber's Point. Smoke was also rising from the *Arizona* and covering the channel area. Completing his scan of the channel area, he saw no other planes.

He instructed McCarthy to come alongside and started climbing. They leveled off at 4,000 feet over Barber's Point and hadn't seen any enemy planes, "but was very shortly attacked by two Japanese fighters as we headed towards Pearl Harbor." McCarthy, seeing the approaching Zekes, slid behind, underneath and across to Dickinson's left, so his gunner could get a better shot at the fighters. Unfortunately, the fighters opened fire at a time that took McCarthy's aircraft right into the bullet stream—just as Dickinson rolled into a left turn to give Miller a better shot. When Dickinson rolled into his left turn and checked his wingman, he saw McCarthy's plane below, smoking. It had caught fire from the right side of the engine and the right main fuel tank. He lost speed and dropped about fifty yards astern and to Dickinson's left. Dickinson could see McCarthy attempting to regain control of his plane as 6-S-9 slowly circled to the left, losing altitude.

Dickinson lost sight of McCarthy and Cohn but in a few seconds sighted their plane below, just as it struck the ground. He saw a parachute had opened at about 200 feet with the occupant apparently safe. McCarthy's leg was broken in his escape. Plane 6-S-9 crashed and burned near Ewa. Cohn went in with the aircraft. (Later, Cohn's remains were buried at The Punchbowl, mistakenly identified as unknown.)

Dickinson and Miller, now without a wingman to help ward off their attackers, found themselves under fire from four or five enemy planes, the nearest less than one hundred feet away. Miller reported he had been hit, followed by another report, as Dickinson recalled, ". . . I think it was just as the wing caught fire."

"Are you all right, Miller?"

"Mr. Dickinson, I've expended all six cans of ammunition." Then he screamed. To Dickinson it seemed ". . . as if he opened his lungs and just let go. I have never heard any comparable human sound. It was a yell of agony. I believe Miller died right then. When I called again there was no reply." Dickinson looked aft and saw a Japanese plane on fire slowly losing altitude but didn't actually see him hit the ground. He was able to get in two short bursts from his fixed guns when one enemy plane overshot them and pulled ahead.

Dickinson's left fuel tank was on fire and he learned his controls had been shot away when he attempted to roll into a right turn. He told Miller to jump but he didn't reply. The plane entered a spin to the right at approximately 1,000 feet. As it started to spin, Dickinson made the necessary preparations and bailed out. His parachute operated normally and he had the good fortune to have it open—and open low enough the Japanese hadn't the time to attempt to attack him in his parachute, or the Marine gunners on the ground near Ewa mistake him for an enemy and open fire. He also was fortunate to come to earth virtually unhurt on the freshly graded dirt of a new road, a narrow aisle through the brush to the west of Ewa Field.

After attempting to hitch a ride in a red automobile van driven by a Japanese man, who refused him a ride and fled the area, he walked and ran a quarter mile to the main road bordered by cane fields, and flagged down an automobile containing a couple headed to Fort Weaver for a picnic. They picked him up and after he explained the circumstances and pointed to the "Japanese planes" flying above, took him to Pearl Harbor.

Later, as he related his experience and Miller's death, tears rolled down his cheeks. He was undoubtedly recalling the tragic irony of their conversation on the flight deck of *Enterprise* just before they launched that morning.

Dickinson was already seated in the front cockpit, and as was the normal routine, the last thing Miller did while standing on the wing before climbing into the rear cockpit each flight was help Dickinson adjust and check his pilot's radio cord. "Mr. Dickinson, my four years' tour of sea duty ends in a few days and there's a funny thing about it."

"What's that, Miller?"

"Out of twenty-one of us that went through radio school together, I'm the only one who hasn't crashed in the water. Hope you don't get me wet today, Sir."

"Miller, next Saturday we all go home—for five months. So probably this is going to be our last flight together. Just stick with me this morning and first thing you know we'll be on Ford Island runway. We'll taxi up to the hangar, step down, and your sea duty will be over and done with. That's all we've got to get by—this morning's flight."

Dickinson and Miller had been flying together since April 1941, and both were from North Carolina. Dickinson described Miller as ". . . a boy about twenty-one or twenty-two; tall, with dark hair and fair complexion." He was from Thomasville. In discussions they often sought to identify mutual acquaintances back home, although they never came closer than to find acquaintances bearing the same family names. They had a mutually respectful officer-enlisted man relationship seldom encountered, and their constant trying to find mutual acquaintances was an indication of their regard for one another.

As the preceding events involving Scouting Squadron Six

were unfolding, the Japanese second wave was conducting its air attack. Dickinson and the couple who gave him a ride endured, and survived a strafing attack. He got out of their car at the entrance to Hickam Field and succeeded in returning to Ford Island. Miller was unable to leave the plane and died in the crash. The crash site was found several days later and his body was recovered.

Ensign Edward T. Deacon in 6-S-14 with Radioman/gunner Third Class Audrey G. (Jerry) Coslett in the rear cockpit, and Ensign William E. Roberts in 6-B-9 with Aviation Machinist Mate Third Class Donald H. Jones searched in sector 050 degrees. Their first contact with Japanese aircraft was approximately twenty miles west of Kaena Point. About thirty fighters were seen in a long column formation on a northwesterly course about one hundred feet off the ocean surface.

Deacon thought they were P-40s but couldn't distinguish any markings on the wings although they passed within four hundred yards of them. They were either returning to their carriers at low altitude on a heading intended to mislead potential followers, preparing to double back for another string of strafing passes across western Oahu's airfields, or positioning themselves to take up escort roles for bombers returning from their targets. Regardless, the enemy planes made no attempt to attack.

Deacon and Roberts proceeded on course 105 degrees to Barber's Point at five hundred feet altitude, and arrived at 0833. After circling once, Deacon heard Gonzalez's transmission, "Don't shoot!" Then, he and Roberts charged their guns and climbed to 1,000 feet heading for Luke Field because Ford Island was obscured by smoke from Ewa. As they passed Ewa, they noticed about twenty dive bombers heading directly for them at the same altitude. The dive bombers had just pulled out of dives against targets on Ford Island and were headed toward their assembly area over Barbers Point.

Deacon led the two SBDs in a dive for a low level run toward Hickam Field, passing over Fort Weaver at about 200 feet. Defenders on the ground opened up with .50-caliber and 20-mm machine guns, hitting both planes. Deacon's engine started to sputter and lose power. From 200 feet, insufficient altitude to bail out, they were going down. With little altitude or time to make a decision, he landed the airplane, full stalled, in about two feet of water just short of Hickam Field. Undoubtedly they were thrilled to be alive, but any such feelings quickly passed. No sooner had he landed than Deacon and Coslett were again under fire, this time rifle and machine gun fire from the beach, about 200 yards distant.

A number of shots came into the cockpits. One struck Coslett in the right wrist and another hit him in the right side of the neck. The bullets that hit the front cockpit nicked Deacon's left leg in the thigh and cut the parachute straps at the cushion. To stanch the bleeding from Coslett's wrist, Deacon pulled the rear seat radio cord loose, and used it as a tourniquet on his right forearm. Then he broke out the life raft and paddled about 100 yards to the crash boat that was in the channel. The crash boat took them to the Hickam Field dock where an ambulance carried them to the Field Hospital. There Coslett received emergency treatment, followed by transfer to Tripler Army Hospital at Fort Shafter.

Ensign Roberts, with Radioman/gunner Jones, had stayed on Deacon's and Coslett's wing until Deacon was forced down by friendly fire. He remembered well those final, approximate thirty minutes of their scouting mission, with some variance in perception and detail.

He stated that upon completion of the first leg, about ten miles north of Kauai, they turned for Barbers Point. At 0820 he sighted the same formation as Ensign Deacon, headed toward Kauai. He passed near a small, detached group of airplanes, observed they were painted a green color similar to that used on U.S. Army aircraft, and concluded they were Army. The relevance of the red circles didn't occur to him until later. One plane came quite near and waved his wings in passing.

At 0830, Roberts and Deacon were over Barbers Point. Roberts observed the smoke rising from Ewa and Pearl Harbor and perceived them to be cane field fires. He followed Deacon toward Hickam and suffered the same friendly fire. As he watched Deacon nose up and then lose altitude, he saw white smoke or gasoline streaming from his leader's left wing. He lost sight of Deacon as he went down, and immediately turned his attention to Hickam Field, a very short distance dead ahead. To his good fortune, he landed safely.

Lieutenant (jg) Frank A. Patriarca in 6-S-16 with Radioman/gunner First Class Joseph F. DeLuca in the rear cockpit, and Ensign Walter M. Willis in 6-S-15 with Coxswain Fred J. Ducolon, in the rear cockpit as gunner were in the sector with the center track of 070 degrees. Both arrived at Barbers Point about 0825.

They proceeded down the coastline to a point just east of Ewa and turned in to make a normal approach to Luke Field at 1,000 feet altitude. During this time, Patriarca saw Ewa burning and numerous planes overhead. Deluca called his attention to the AA fire over Pearl Harbor and to the geysers of water along the coastline.

As Deluca was passing his observations to his aircraft commander, Patriarca caught sight of tracer bullets flying past their plane. A plane over Ewa was reflected in the sun as it went up on its wing, revealing the red meatball markings. He realized the Japanese were attacking Oahu, and at that moment, the flight he was leading. He turned and dove for the coastline at full throttle while broadcasting the attack.

Patriarca shed his attackers and decided to return to the *Enterprise* using the ship's 0600 Point Option position. When he made the decision, he turned to see Willis and Ducolon, in

6-S-15, were no longer with him. He searched for the *Enterprise* but couldn't find her, and decided to return to Pearl Harbor. Throughout his search and the beginning of the return to Pearl Harbor, he heard no further messages. His fuel supply was running low and he landed at Burns Field on the island of Kauai. Patriarca and Deluca returned to Oahu on 12 December. No trace of Willis or Duculon has ever been found.

Lieutenant (jg) Hart D. "Dale" Hilton in plane 6-S-7 with Radioman/gunner Second Class Jack Leaming in the rear cockpit, led Ensign Edwin J. Kroeger from Bombing Six in 6-B-5, with Radioman/gunner Second Class Walter F. Chapman in the rear cockpit, on the scouting mission in sector 120 degrees, just south of Lieutenant Dickinson and Ensign McCarthy.

Ensign Carlton T. Fogg, pilot in 6-S-11 with Radioman/gunner Third Class Otis L. Dennis, and Ensign Cleo J. Dobson with Radioman/gunner Third Class Roy L. Hoss in the rear cockpit were in sector 130 degrees, just south of Hilton and Kroeger. They were the southern-most flight in the scouting mission.

The first indication of trouble was the terse, excited message, "DON'T SHOOT! THIS IS AN AMERICAN PLANE!" The first, puzzled reaction by Dale Hilton and Jack Leaming was radio silence had been broken. Who? Why?

About a minute later came another transmission. "Get out the rubber boat, we're goin' in!" Jack Leaming recorded his reaction to the second message. "What the hell is wrong with that crazy

SOB? He's breaking radio silence! He had forgotten to keep his transmitter switch off! What was happening somewhere close? What was wrong?" The first transmission seemed more a yell of desperation, a frantic plea rather than a plea for mercy. The second carried the sound of resignation, and preparing for an inevitable result. Kroeger and Chapman in Hilton's flight, Fogg and Dennis, Dobson and Hoss heard the same transmissions but the words were garbled and unintelligible, stirring curiosity. What's going on?

The two planes south of Hilton and Kroeger came into their sector and Kroeger came alongside in 6-B-5, wanting to know the content of the message. Naval aviators, strongly disciplined to maintain radio silence were accustomed to 'talking back and forth' by pulling into close formation and using hand signals, including Morse Code. A pat on their heads with an open hand is a dash and the closed fist is a dot.

Flying in close formation, wingtips just a few feet apart, they asked, "What was that transmission, who was it?" None knew the answer. Leaming responded that he and Dale had received the message garbled as well. Hilton told Leaming to tell them to return to their stations, and they slid back and out, to their tactical formation. As they were maneuvering back into position Jack Leaming picked up a strange odor. It smelled like gunpowder, but where was it coming from? They were at 2,000 feet and there wasn't anything in sight but the ocean and scattered clouds. Hilton maintained heading for Barbers Point and the odor intensified. As the four airplanes came nearer, all eight men could see smoke billowing up from Oahu.

Two immense, thick columns of smoke were rising, forming a cloud in the air over Pearl Harbor. Jack Leaming could see fires. The scene appeared chaotic. The first thought through most minds was, "What the hell is the Army doing having maneuvers on a Sunday morning?" At first confused and perplexed, there was only one conclusion. We had been attacked! A war had begun! But, by whom? The answer would come shortly.

They were near the end of their mission and approaching Barbers Point, as were five other airplanes. Three came in a V formation: Gallaher and Merritt in 6-S-10, West and Hansen in 6-S-5; and Weber with Keaney, Gonzalez's wingman, in 6-B-12. Moments later Fogg, with Dennis in 6-S-11; and Dobson with Hoss in 6-S-8 joined up. Lieutenant Gallaher took the lead, and the seven circled at an altitude of 400 feet. Overhead at approximately 4,000 feet a number of enemy fighters were seen but they didn't attack.

Gallaher decided to withdraw off shore to the south approximately ten miles. There they again orbited, while observing the battle to the north. The SBD, though state of the art technologically, was a scout and dive bomber. Though its rear cockpit radioman/gunner could swivel his seat 360 degrees inside a steel circle on which his single gun or twin .30-caliber guns were mounted, and it carried two guns in the nose cowl which could be fired by the pilot, it was much slower at a maximum speed of approximately 245 miles per hour, less maneuverable, and far more lightly gun-armed than the Zero or Zeke. Choosing to charge into a fight with them was extremely unwise.

Gallaher saw the enemy beginning to depart the target area at approximately 0830, but antiaircraft fire over Pearl Harbor remained heavy until a brief pause in the raid occurred between approximately 0845 and 0900. Though their orders were to recover at NAS Pearl Harbor, on Ford Island, Gallaher decided to land at Ewa instead. The other six followed him, arriving about the time the second wave of enemy aircraft renewed the attacks at Pearl Harbor and Oahu's military air fields. The seven *Enterprise* SBDs' time on the ground at Ewa was brief.

No sooner did Gallaher roll to a stop, when a marine jumped up on the wing and advised him not to stay on the ground, as they had been heavily machine gunned and had lost nearly all their planes. So, the seven all took off, and headed for Ford Island. As they approached the channel, they encountered heavy fire. A destroyer dashing out of the harbor, doing what seemed to Jack Leaming to be thirty knots, an unprecedented spectacle in a five mile speed zone, opened fire with 1.1-inch, .50-caliber, and .30-caliber guns. He saw one tracer flash past above them. Reality set in, with a huge boost of adrenalin. First came anger.

There were no hits but he let fly with all the profanities he knew, and reached for the Aldis lamp to flash the answer to the challenge for that hour. The Aldis lamp is routinely used to flash signals in Morse Code when approaching a ship at sea, or another aircraft, to determine if it is friend or foe. Aircraft would never approach any ship or other aircraft within gun range prior to being challenged by that ship, or challenging the ship. Never until the challenge and proper response does either know if the other is friend or foe.

The Aldis lamp delivered a bright, intense light visible for miles, even in bright sunlight. It had a pistol grip with a trigger that was used to send the Morse Code in flashes of light. A short interval for a dot, and a lengthy flash for a dash. Each hour the letter for the challenge and the response changed.

Jack Leaming pointed the Aldis lamp at the bridge of the destroyer and flashed the letter P as rapidly as possible, denoting the answer to the challenge at that hour. He didn't challenge or wait for the destroyer to challenge! There was no time for that. He was scared, scared as hell, didn't want to die, just wanted the destroyer to quit shooting and let Dale Hilton land the airplane.

They were already very low when Dale kicked right rudder, rolled into a bank to the right, and dove for the ground in a right turn. When he pulled the nose and wings level, Jack could have sworn they were no further than fifty feet above a cane field. The cane field became a green blur as they accelerated out of the area.

The challenge and reply for the day and hour was M and P, in Morse Code. Jack was flashing "P" as fast as his finger could press the trigger. The men on the destroyer apparently didn't see the signal. But fortunately, when Dale Hilton rolled the SBD into the diving right turn, the gunners saw the stars on the wings, and ceased firing. Jack Leaming recalled, "But, by then we were out of range. Gone! And I will never forget the challenge and reply as long as I live!"

When Lieutenant (jg) Hilton turned away from the destroyer's storm of AA fire from the channel leading to Pearl Harbor, his decision was made. They would take their chances at Ewa, they did, and landed there safely. From the seven Gallaher had led from Ewa toward Ford Island, four had made the same decision, and returned to Ewa. Fogg and Dennis, in 6-S-11; Kroeger and Chapman in 6-B-5; and 6-B-12 with Weber and Keaney.[21]

True, the Lord's ammunition was being passed, but the gunners on the ships and the ground were mad as hell, too. Five planes from VS-6, and one from VB-6 had been lost—six of eighteen—at least one of them shot down by friendly fire, with a total of eight men dead, and two wounded. Sadly, several more good men would pay the price for the gunners' fury before 7 December ended.

California (BB-44): Flagship Wounded

When the first dive bomb attack struck Ford Island at 0755, there was immediate reaction on the battleship *California*, flagship of Admiral William S. Pye's Battle Force. *California* was closer to the first bomb's impact than all the battleships, and there was no doubt in anyone's mind what was occurring. Officer of the Deck, Ensign Archibald T. Nicholson, Jr., activated the ship's general alarm, which signaled general quarters and battle stations, and over the speaker system gave the order, "Set condition Zed." "Set [Material] condition Yoke," soon followed.

Lieutenant Commander Marion N. Little, the ship's First Lieutenant (third in line of command) was the senior officer present on board, when the raid began. He immediately hurried to the bridge, took command, and ordered ". . . Man the battery and prepare to get under way." By 0800 the main and auxiliary steam lines were warmed.

Lieutenant Commander Frederick J. Eckhoff, Navigator, relieved the Officer of the Deck and assisted the commanding officer. Lieutenant Commander Henry E. Bernstein, Communications Officer, had the head of department duty aboard ship, rushed immediately to insure keys for the magazines were broken out and ammunition supply was started. The senior Gunnery Officer was Lieutenant George Fritschmann, who manned Control [of the guns] and took charge of all batteries. All other officers and men aboard promptly went to their battle stations and established communications between Conn [ship's command and control], Fire Control, Central Station, Main Control, and their subsidiary stations. The remainder of the crew rushed to battle stations or to safety below decks, opened ready ammunition boxes, and far below decks began opening magazines to feed a steady flow of ammunition to the guns before ready ammunition boxes near the guns were emptied.

When general quarters sounded, and "Set condition Zed" came over the speaker system, the crew began closing open manholes, hatches, bulkhead doors, and all other openings marked with a "Z", while topside, almost simultaneously, a formation of enemy planes raked the ship with a strafing pass. Before the strafing pass ended, the torpedo attack began as torpedoes struck *Oklahoma* and *West Virginia*.

Like *Arizona* and other battleships, *California*'s states of material and battle readiness were less than desirable for the circumstance, additional factors of good timing and luck favoring her attackers. The shocking speed of events made it virtually impossible for the crew to close and dog down openings to watertight compartments in sufficient time, which was to eventually prove disastrous for the ship, though she didn't suffer the number of torpedo hits taken by *West Virginia* and *Oklahoma*.

As did other crews on the battleships, her officers and men on deck that morning momentarily had their attention first drawn to the southwest, west and northwest toward Ford Island, by the Val dive bomber passes, with the thunderous explosions that followed bomb impacts. Then came the near-instantaneous, follow-on strafing attack on their ship. While *California*'s men briefly fixed their gaze on Ford Island and then took cover to avoid machine gun bullets, to the southeast through east, twenty-four Kate torpedo bombers were fanning out, their pilots taking tactical spacing between aircraft, scanning with their eyes, talking to one another, sorting, selecting and—two of them—rapidly closing, fifty feet above the ground and water, toward *California*.

California was moored singly, southwest along the extended line of battleships, past the tanker *Neosho*, further toward the harbor entrance. The ship lay in forty feet of water, with her bow pointed toward the harbor entrance, starboard side to Berth F-3, with boiler #1 in use for auxiliary purposes. Below the forty feet of water was another ninety feet of mud, covering its coral base. She was fueled to 95 percent capacity, approximately 660,000 gallons of oil, and was in the lowest material condition for damage control, X-Ray, with five of ten voids—areas normally closed watertight—open, preparatory for maintenance work.

When the fuel tanks were filled to 95 percent, leaks had been discovered, and repair parties had sealed the five on the starboard side—but the five on the port side were still open, not yet repaired. Additionally, the ship was in readiness for an inspection, with a high percentage of her manholes open. Though the command "Set [Material] condition Yoke," had early been communicated to the crew when general quarters sounded, what occurred within the ensuing ten minutes overwhelmed their ability to save *California* from eventually settling to the bottom of Pearl Harbor.

At machine guns #1 and #2, both manned and designated the "ready guns," were 400 rounds of ammunition when general quarters sounded. Ammunition ready boxes for the 5-inch antiaircraft guns held 50 rounds. All 5-inch, 3-inch antiaircraft guns and .50-caliber machine guns were ready to load and use, but the battery wasn't manned. More significantly, like the *Nevada*, she was moored singly, "in the open," not hampered by being moored next to a sister ship. Her gun crews had more freedom of movement in tracking and firing at the raiders swirling in the air above the harbor.

The first enemy planes to come in range of their guns were Kate torpedo bombers coming from the east. Machine guns #1 and #2 opened fire on them at 0803. Recognizing the high volume of antiaircraft fire that would be quickly needed, and a soon-to-be acute shortage of ammunition, from central control came orders to expedite ammunition to the guns. Two minutes later, two torpedoes exploded virtually simultaneously against *California*'s port side, aft of midship, approximately frame 110, tearing a gaping hole about forty feet long, extending from the first seam below the armor belt to the bilge keel.

Almost simultaneously, another torpedo exploded toward the port bow, about frame 47, tearing a large, irregular hole covering an area of about twenty-seven by thirty-two feet, with the top of the hole six feet below the armor belt. Massive flooding of compartments near the holes started immediately, and she began to list to port. Without hesitation, Lieutenant Commander Little ordered counter flooding to limit the list to four degrees, while crew members rushed frantically to close and dog down hatches, bulkhead doors, and open manholes to limit flooding to as few compartments as possible. Shortly thereafter, about 0810, #2 and #4 5-inch AA guns opened fire, just as the ship's electrical power and lights started failing.

Forward in the vicinity of Forward Ordnance Repair, nearby the ruptured fuel tanks on the port side, the third deck commenced flooding with fuel. The strength of the fumes were such as to overcome the ammunition party attempting to expedite the delivery of ammunition. The rupture of fuel oil tanks forward introduced water into the fuel system and before it could be cleared, light and power on the ship was lost at a critical time. The flooding of compartments near the torpedo hits prevented access needed to adequately control damage, the ship lost power and compressed air to her guns, pumps couldn't be started until later, and *California* was soon temporarily paralyzed, her crew unable to continue preparations to "get under way" or keep up their normal rate of AA fire.

At call to general quarters, Gunner's Mate Jackson C. Pharris, of Columbus, Georgia, hurried to his battle station on the third deck, where he was in charge of the forward ordnance repair party. At 0805, the first torpedoes to slam into *California* exploded almost directly under his station, stunning and severely injuring him. The explosion hurled him against the overhead and back to the deck, causing a concussion. The explosion was followed at 0810 by the loss of power and light to the ship. Quickly recovering, he acted on his own initiative, undoubtedly aided with flashlights or lights from power temporarily supplied by auxiliary generators, to set up a hand-supply ammunition train for the antiaircraft guns. The train supplied ammunition obtained from Magazine A-231 ½-M and passed through handling room A-233-M and up Hoists #11, #21, #13, and #23 by hand operation. Men in this vicinity were overcome with fuel fumes and had to be removed. Pharris, with replacements from the broadside gun crews, succeeded in removing the overcome men and getting sixty-two antiaircraft rounds from the magazines to the larger guns.

Ensign Edward R. Blair, Jr., with a ten-man working party, obtained 1,600 rounds of belted .50-caliber machine gun ammunition from the magazine in the torpedo hold forward, before that compartment flooded. No further ammunition could be obtained from the ship's magazines during the raid, and the *California*'s crew immediately began seeking ammunition from other ships to help defend her.[22]

With oil and water rushing in where the port bulkhead had been torn from the deck, with many of the remaining crew members overcome by oil fumes, the ship without power and the speaker system to pass orders, and listing heavily to port as a result of a second torpedo hit, Pharris ordered the shipfitters to counter flood. Twice rendered unconscious by fumes and handicapped by his painful injuries, he persisted in his desperate efforts to speed up the supply of ammunition and at the same time repeatedly risked his life to enter flooding compartments and drag to safety unconscious shipmates who were gradually being submerged in oil. He saved many of his shipmates from death and was largely responsible for keeping the *California* in action during the attack. From the perspectives of other men in *California*'s crew, his heroic conduct, inspiring leadership, valiant efforts, and his extreme loyalty to his ship and her crew, reflected and enhanced the finest traditions of the Navy. As a result, he later received the Medal of Honor.[23]

In those first few minutes of the rush to battle stations, manning the guns, the torpedo attack and resulting massive flooding, twenty-six year old Machinist's Mate First Class Robert R. Scott from Massillon, Ohio, got to his assigned station in the compartment where the ship's air compressor operated, and serviced the guns. When it was evident the compartment was rapidly flooding, the remainder of the men inside evacuated, and urged him to leave. He refused, saying words to the effect, "This is my station and I will stay and give them air as long as the guns are going." The flooding continued and he continued operating the compressor until it failed—too late for him to save his own life—after he provided life protecting service for his shipmates and his ship through a higher rate of antiaircraft gunfire. He posthumously received the Medal of Honor, ". . . for conspicuous devotion to duty, extraordinary courage and complete disregard of his own life, above and beyond the call of duty . . . "[24]

At 0815, just ten minutes after the crew started fighting the flood of water into *California*'s compartments, to keep her alive with power and lights—and some hope of getting under way—men topside on her after and quarterdecks, glancing toward the northeast at the destruction wrought among the battleships, engaged an image they probably would never forget—the final rollover of the capsizing *Oklahoma*. The image that would be forever burned into their memories was approximately 150-200 men walking, running up her starboard side, slipping, and some falling back into the water, as they scrambled for safety and survival on her upturning keel. As she rolled on her side other men who had, at the last moment, escaped from compartments beneath the water's surface, through portholes, hatches, passageways, bulkhead doors, and from the starboard weather decks, bobbed to the surface, swimming, treading water and oil, trying to find anything permanent to grasp and pull themselves to safety.[25]

As if the capsizing of *Oklahoma* wasn't enough, just beginning to creep slowly toward the men in the water was a river of oil-fed fire pulled relentlessly toward the harbor entrance by the outgoing tide and aided by a ten miles per hour wind from the east—all from the roaring inferno on and around *Arizona*, which had been ignited by the violent 0808 explosion. And it was the same ungodly scene witnessed from different angles by hundreds of men topside on ships much closer to *Oklahoma*—*Maryland*, *Tennessee*, and the embattled *West Virginia*. The fire, which slithered closer to an already burning *West Virginia* and began consuming men blown into the oil covered water, would eventually threaten *Tennessee*, *Maryland*, and finally *California*.

At 0820 a bomb's near miss shook *California* so severely that some men believed the ship had been hit by another torpedo. The overpressure and bomb splinters from the close-in explosion unquestionably caused more damage and accelerated flooding. The main radio compartment promptly flooded, had to be abandoned, and nearby compartment A-518 started to fill with oil from the ruptured fuel tanks.

Three times in the hour beginning 0815, the ship came under attack by Val dive bombers coming successively from the west toward the starboard bow, from the southwest—dead ahead—and from the south toward the port bow. The near miss explosions along the starboard side caused minor sized holes amidships between the armor belt and gallery deck. At 0825 her 5-inch AA battery took a flight of Kate horizontal bombers under fire, as four bombs dropped by Kates fell harmlessly between *California*'s bow and the northern quay of Berth F-2. Five minutes later she wouldn't be so fortunate.

At 0830, barely five minutes before the *Enterprise*'s Lieutenant Commander Young survived withering "friendly fire" and landed the first of VS-6's SBDs on Ford Island, a Japanese Val dive bomber scored a devastating direct hit abreast of *California*'s casemate #1, starboard side, at frame 59. The bomb penetrated the main deck and exploded on the second deck starboard, causing numerous casualties among men in the ammunition train established several minutes earlier. The explosion also caused a raging fire amidships on the second deck extending from frame 51 to 77, and the main deck from frame 51 to 87. The fire remained largely uncontrolled for more than an hour due to the loss of pressure on the fire main, and the lack of sufficient extinguishers to cope with it until tugs came alongside to supply fire protection. The bomb hit also compounded the general flooding on the second deck and into the machine shop by destroying the watertight integrity of the first and second decks between frames 26 and approximately 100,

USS *California* (BB-44) The scene is from the southeastern side of Ford Island, looking northeasterly, with *California* (BB-44) in right center, listing to port after being hit by Japanese aerial torpedoes and bombs, and a river of oil-fed fire about to engulf her in flames. NHHC

and between the second deck and the machinery spaces on the third deck reached by the large centerline hatch about frame 65.

At approximately 0810, just prior to loss of the ship's power and light, Control ordered all 5-inch broadside battery crews to assist 5-inch AA crews with their ammunition supply. Among the groups who moved to assist the AA gunners by forming a hand-supported ammunition train, were Ensigns H.C. Jones, William F. Cage, and Ira W. Jeffrey, a party from Repair V, and Marine Private Arthur E. Senior.

Senior clamored down to the division where he saw twenty-three year old Ensign Herbert C. Jones, of Los Angeles, California, who celebrated his birthday on 1 December, standing at the foot of the ladder, where he had organized and was directing the ammunition train to the AA gunners after the mechanical hoists were put out of action by the power loss. For almost twenty minutes Senior and the others toiled under Jones' direction until the bomb exploded on the second deck at 0830 fatally wounding

Jones, while setting *California*'s second and first decks afire and plunging the compartment into darkness. Acrid smoke filled the compartment, and Senior reached for his gas mask, which he had lain on a shell box behind him, and put it on. Hearing someone say: "Mr. Jones has been hit," Senior flashed his flashlight over the ensign's face and saw that "it was all bloody. His white coat had blood all over it." Senior and another man then carried Jones as far as the M Division compartment, but the ensign wouldn't let them carry him any further. "Leave me alone," he gasped insistently, "I'm done for. Get out of here before the magazines go off!" Soon thereafter, however, before Senior could get clear, he felt the shock of an explosion from down below and collapsed, unconscious. Private Senior survived the ordeal. Jones lost his life, and "For conspicuous devotion to duty, extraordinary courage, and complete disregard for his own life, above and beyond the call of duty . . . " he posthumously received the Medal of Honor.[26]

The men supplying ammunition to *California*'s AA gunners still refused to give up their efforts to keep the guns firing in spite of the bomb's devastating explosion and the spreading fire—which was to take more lives. Some men continued desperate efforts to get ammunition through passageways being steadily consumed and eventually blocked by fire. Radio Electrician (Warrant Officer) James T. Reeves of Thomaston, Connecticut, who was two days short of his forty-sixth birthday, on his own initiative, had moved to assist in supplying ammunition by hand when the hoists were put out of action at approximately 0810. When the bomb exploded, setting the fire, he held his station in the ammunition train, continuing to pass ammunition until he was overcome by smoke and fire, which resulted in his death. "For distinguished conduct in line of his profession, extraordinary courage and disregard of his own safety . . . " he posthumously received the Medal of Honor.[27]

At 0845 Vice Admiral William S. Pye, Commander, Task Force One; and the ship's Executive Officer, Commander Earl E. Stone came aboard *California*, and Stone temporarily took command. Task Force One, should it be sent on a mission, included Battle Force Divisions Two and Four with six battleships; Carrier Division One, with one aircraft carrier—which was at sea; Cruiser Division Nine, with five light cruisers; Destroyer Flotilla One, with sixteen destroyers plus a destroyer flotilla flagship and two other flagships, one for each of two squadrons; and Mine Division One, which included the *Oglala* as flagship, plus four destroyer-minelayers.[28]

Approximately 0825, the first wave of attacks had begun to taper off, and the number of enemy aircraft over Pearl Harbor began dwindling toward a fifteen-minute lull which began approximately 0845, with some attacks still in progress. With her magazines flooding, the continuing high rate of AA fire, and additional attacks probable, Pay Clerk H.A. Applegate and Electricians Mate Third Class B.F. Pavlin went by motor launch, under fire, to other ships to obtain more ammunition.

Throughout the fierce fight topside, and in spite of the large, out-of-control fire; flooding and the rush to arrest flooding, men weren't giving up on the order to get under way. By the time Admiral Pye and Commander Stone came back on board, men working determinedly on *California*'s machinery restored electrical power, light, and pressure on the fire main by lighting off four boilers with cold oil and natural draft. In the process they were isolating the after power plant, and within twenty-five minutes would be ready in all respects to get under way.

Hopes were high. Getting under way seemed a real possibility, but it was not to be, as other unforeseen factors would intervene. *California* was slowly sinking in spite of the determined efforts of her crew, while further astern, to the northeast on line of battleships, other men were fighting hard to save their ships and get under way while battling the Japanese raiders.[29]

Battleships *Maryland* and *Tennessee*: Gunners and Rescuers

Of all the battleships in Pearl Harbor, both the *Maryland* (BB-46) and the *Tennessee* (BB-43) received the least damage in the attack. Moored inboard of *Oklahoma* and *West Virginia* respectively, both escaped the hammer blows the Kate torpedo bombers dealt to the five other battleships. *Maryland* and *Tennessee* each received two bomb hits, and suffered fewer killed and wounded than any of their six sister ships, including *Pennsylvania*, which was in dry dock across the harbor. Their escape from the fates which befell the other capital ships was fortuitous in more ways than one, for they became the guardians and rescuers for hundreds who were driven from, or ordered to abandon, the desperate circumstances which converged on *Arizona, West Virginia, Oklahoma* and later, on *California* and *Nevada*.[30]

As with *Oglala* next to the cruiser *Helena* at 1010 Dock, *Vestal* was moored eight feet outboard from *Arizona*, as were *Oklahoma* and *West Virginia* moored outboard of *Maryland* and *Tennessee* respectively, barely eight feet between the two pairs of parallel battleships. All the battleships' bows pointed southwest toward the harbor entrance, and *Vestal's* bow pointed opposite, to the northeast. *Arizona* lay directly astern of *Tennessee*, approximately seventy-five feet, with *Vestal* alongside *Arizona* directly astern of *West Virginia*. The 31,600-ton *Maryland* was moored starboard side to Berth F-5, using #3 boiler and after machinery space for auxiliary power. The quays, like the ships moored to *Arizona*, *Maryland* and *Tennessee*, were also close to the inboard battleships, approximately eight feet toward Ford Island.[31]

Maryland was the flagship for Commander Battleships, Rear Admiral William S. Anderson, and his staff of twenty-one officers. Most were on board when the raid began.

One of the first men on the *Maryland* to catch sight of the Val dive bombers' attack on Ford Island was twenty-two year old Seaman First Class Leslie V. Short from Garden City, Kansas, who listed his home address as Noel, Missouri. Like all men assigned to gun crews on any ship under attack when the raid on Pearl Harbor was in progress, he was at great risk, subject to wounds or death each time a horizontal bomber, dive bomber, torpedo bomber or fighter targeted his ship, and attacked toward her bow. The swarming enemy aircraft were striking from nearly 360 degrees of the compass, low level, high level and at varying dive angles and speeds. The result was heavy casualties among gun crews and ammunition trains on ships hardest hit. Fortunately, Short survived the attack unscathed. The forward machine gunners on the *Tennessee* weren't so fortunate.

Although Leslie Short hadn't been called to his duty station, after breakfast he went to his Group "A" Machine Gun Station, forward, on the bridge superstructure, below the bridge, and just above the top of #2 turret—to write letters home and address some Christmas cards. Suddenly, he ". . . noticed planes diving on the Naval Air Base nearby [Ford Island]." At first he thought they were Americans ". . . in a mock diving practice attack." Then he saw smoke and flames rise from a building, looked closer, and saw they weren't American planes.

Leslie Short sprang into action. He broke out an ammunition belt from the nearby ready ammunition box, loaded the belt into his machine gun, charged the gun, glanced to his left, toward the east, and saw two Kate torpedo bombers which had just released two torpedoes apparently aimed at *Oklahoma*. He opened fire on the nearest plane, firing past *Oklahoma*'s forward superstructure, and above her forecastle, saw flames and smoke burst from the Kate, then saw it veer off to its left falling toward the Navy hospital across the harbor. He next turned his gun on the trailing Kate, saying later, "I think I also hit the second plane which I aimed at immediately after shooting at the first one but by then was so busy that I cannot say for sure." He had opened fire on the Kates before the ship's general quarters alarm sounded at 0752.[32]

When general quarters sounded, word went out immediately to set conditions Yoke and Zed and make all preparations to get underway. Preparations to get under way included instructions for the Conning Tower to take control of steering and engines as soon as possible.[33]

In those first fifteen to twenty-five minutes, until *Oklahoma* capsized at 0815, her superstructure effectively masked *Maryland*'s portside antiaircraft batteries located adjacent to *Oklahoma*'s upper deck superstructure—except for enemy aircraft approaching from high overhead, directly from the southwest and northeast, up and down the line of battleships. The portside batteries were unable to acquire and fire on targets approaching the battleships low on *Oklahoma*'s and *Maryland*'s port beam.

Ensign William O. Beach, the communications staff duty officer on the Commander Battleships Staff, had just finished breakfast and was sitting in the ward room when he heard Leslie Short's first brief burst of machine gun fire, followed immediately by the sound of general quarters. He walked to one of the open ward room ports and looked out to see "a plane swoop up over the *Oklahoma* and *Maryland*, the plane having evidently just dropped a torpedo." He walked aft to the Flag Office where he encountered Ensign William F. Bradway, Jr., another staff communications duty officer, getting what information he could from Radio Central and telephoning it to Flag Plot. Beach left the Flag Office and went up the ladder to the port side of the quarterdeck, saw the *Oklahoma* already listing, and fifty or more

Japanese aircraft in bombing attacks on ships in the harbor, Ford Island and Hickam Field.

A group of men standing near #3 turret on *Oklahoma*'s starboard side, asked Beach for orders. He told them to dog down the open hatch leading to *Oklahoma*'s Officer Country, forward on the starboard side, then get below the protective deck. Beach then went forward and up to the Flag Bridge where he decided there was nothing he could do in Flag Radio, so stayed out on the bridge to take Lieutenant Commander Horne's place as best he could, until Horne, the staff communications officer, returned to the ship. *Oklahoma* was moments away from capsizing.[34]

Commander William F. Fitzgerald, Jr., Operations Officer, Staff of Commander Battleships, was undressing, ready to take a bath, when he became aware of nearby intermittent explosions. He quickly pulled on his trousers, grabbed a hat and blouse [uniform coat], and started topside. He was hardly out of his room when general quarters sounded. He immediately proceeded to the Flag Bridge, telling all men he encountered en route to "man their battle stations and be calm."

When Fitzgerald arrived topside, about 0800, he noticed smoke, flame and many explosions throughout the harbor. He could hear machine gun fire from the *Maryland*, and *Oklahoma* was still upright, but listing perceptibly to port. His first glance didn't tell him she was going to roll over. Heavy explosions continued. Upon arriving on the Flag Bridge, he immediately checked with Captain Donald C. Godwin, *Maryland*'s commander, to see if he was making all preparations to get underway. Godwin replied he was.

Shortly after Fitzgerald arrived on the Flag Bridge, Captain Worral R. Carter, Chief of Staff, said, "We can't do much good up here. Let's go down to the guns and give them a hand." Both proceeded to the 5-inch AA batteries and split up, each one doing what he could to assist in organizing the gun crews, ammunition parties, and assigning stations to men not otherwise engaged. During all this time the flame, smoke and noise were unending. There was some 5-inch gunfire on the *Maryland* when he arrived at the guns, but it was impossible to tell just who was firing. He then concentrated on getting guns in action that hadn't yet opened fire. Time was approximately 0810.

He noticed Lieutenant (j.g.) Robert S. Mandelkorn, the staff assistant material [supply] officer and gave him a series of directives such as ". . . organize a party to obtain steel helmets for all men topside, get [compressed] air to the batteries and spare tools for the guns . . . " By 0815, just as the *Oklahoma* rolled on her port side, there was sufficient air pressure to use the power rammers on *Maryland*'s starboard battery, but not until an appreciable interval afterwards did the port battery obtain sufficient air. In the meantime the port battery fired by hand power. Numerous men from *Oklahoma* swam to the *Maryland* and upon coming aboard, Fitzgerald immediately assigned them to gun stations or the ammunition party.[35]

Captain Godwin, *Maryland*'s commander, wrote of his crew's and Leslie Short's actions in an 11 December report to the Commander-in-Chief, Pacific Fleet, "Though the conduct of all hands aboard this vessel during the air raid on the morning of Sunday, December 7, 1941 could be classified as meritorious, outstanding was the action of Leslie Vernon Short . . . Short, a machine gun striker 22 years old, truly demonstrated the spirit of men behind the Navy guns . . . "

Captain Godwin's comments were valid in every respect. Both *Maryland* and *Tennessee* opened fire within five minutes after the attack began. Because the two ships suffered no serious degradation of their abilities to generate steam and electrical power, their AA batteries continued heavy defensive fire through the second wave attacks whenever raiders appeared in range through the heavy clouds of smoke intermittently obscuring visibility.[36]

With forward machine guns already in action, the remaining gun crews scrambled to their batteries, and others went to their stations in Central Control. Ship Fitter First Class Andrew J. Geiser was among the first arriving at his battle station in Central Station, and quickly recognized the gravity of the situation. On his own initiative he took action to avoid a possible disaster by immediately ordering the aviation gasoline stowage compartment flooded. It was well he did. Later, a bomb struck *Maryland*'s forecastle directly above the gasoline stowage, and his initiative prevented a probable catastrophic explosion and fire.[37]

By 0803, a torpedo had struck *Nevada*, one had passed beneath *Vestal* and torn into the bottom of *Arizona*, and three or more each had already slashed into *West Virginia* and *Oklahoma*. Across the harbor to the east, another torpedo had zipped beneath *Oglala* into the cruiser *Helena*. On the west side of Ford Island, *Utah* was nine minutes from capsizing, and the *Raleigh*'s crew—

their ship struck by one torpedo at virtually the same instant *Utah* was struck by two—was beginning the struggle to avoid capsizing.

At 0805, as two torpedoes were slamming into *California*, and the forward and aft .50-caliber machine guns were already in action on *Maryland*, her 1.1-inch AA and 5-inch batteries opened up on the enemy—but, in the case of the 1.1s, not without the initiative of Ensign William J. Manning. There were no ready ammunition boxes installed to support the recently installed, four-gun, 1.1-inch antiaircraft batteries, which could put out a high volume of devastating AA fire. Manning raced to the 1.1-inch ammunition magazines below decks, broke the magazine lock, set up and started an ammunition train of men not assigned AA gun stations, and began passing ammunition to the guns by hand.[38]

Captain Godwin, *Maryland*'s commander, praised the two senior staff officers on duty aboard *Maryland*, Captain W.R. Carter and Commander W.F. Fitzgerald, Jr., who hurried to assist the crew in rapidly opening fire on the enemy, helping to activate the 5-inch AA battery. He also wrote words of praise in behalf of Coxswain Charles G. Anderson and Gunners' Mate Third Class Raymond A. Heitzman, of whom Commander Fitzgerald had said, "The actions of these two men were outstanding in every respect." Captain Godwin stated they "were cool, intelligent and efficient" under fire, promptly organizing and operating their 5-inch gun. In his report, he claimed *Maryland* gunners downed seven enemy planes, four being quite definitely confirmed.[39]

At 0808, while *Utah* was four minutes from capsizing on the west side of Ford Island, *Arizona*'s forward magazine violently exploded, showering *Vestal*'s, *West Virginia*'s and *Tennessee*'s after decks with burning powder, oil, and debris, and igniting an inferno on *Arizona* which rapidly spread in the water around the stricken battleship. The fires started on *Arizona* and *West Virginia* sent heavy palls of smoke skyward that helped intermittently obscure all four ships from the eyes of enemy raiders, while degrading the ability of gunners to see and defend against attackers swirling overhead.

At 0815, while the topside battle was being waged, *Maryland*'s Conning Tower took steering and engine control while preparations continued to get under way. At the same time, with the *Oklahoma* capsizing to port, the situation on *West Virginia*, off *Maryland*'s port stern approximately eighty-five feet, was deteriorating rapidly, with her captain dying, the ship settling, fires raging out of control, and counter flooding initiated to keep from capsizing.

Though *Maryland*'s crew had received the same 0810 signal to get under way, as had *Nevada*, *California*, and other ships in the harbor—and by 0838 was standing by all lines to cast off—getting underway had become a virtual impossibility. *Maryland* was rendering badly needed assistance to desperate men from the capsized *Oklahoma*, and Admiral Kimmel would issue a countermanding instruction to battleships before *Maryland* could sortie. In *Nevada*'s sortie, and the enemy's swarming attacks on her, the Commander-in-Chief of the Pacific Fleet realized she, or any other battleship, could be sunk in the channel and possibly block the entire harbor.

Later, in a 15 December confidential mailgram to Admiral Kimmel, Captain Godwin described what *Maryland*'s crew had observed throughout the morning of 7 December:

. . . FIRST ATTACK WAS DIVE BOMBING OF HANGARS ON FORD ISLAND AT ZERO SEVEN FIFTY X SIX PLANES FROM SE PASSED DIRECTLY OVER SHIP AT AN ALTITUDE OF ABOUT TWO THOUSAND FEET X RISING SUN INSIGNIA CLEARLY VISIBLE X DIVING ANGLE TWENTY TO THIRTY DEGREES PULLING OUT AT ABOUT FIVE HUNDRED FEET X SECOND WAS TORPEDO ATTACK ON BATTLESHIPS FROM PORT BEAM AT ZERO SEVEN FIFTY-FIVE X NO ACCURATE OBSERVATIONS ON NUMBER OR METHOD DUE TO POSITION OF SHIP INBOARD OF OKLAHOMA X APPEARS THAT OKLAHOMA WAS HIT FIRST AND CALIFORNIA LAST X DIVE BOMBING AND STRAFING ATTACKS BY FORTY TO FIFTY PLANES ON ALL SHIPS UNTIL ABOUT ZERO EIGHT THIRTY X DIVE ANGLE APPROXIMATELY FORTY DEGREES X ATTACKS WERE MADE BY INDIVIDUAL PLANES FROM VARIOUS DIRECTIONS X AFTER LULL OF TEN TO FIFTEEN MINUTES CONTINUED TO UNTIL ABOUT ZERO NINE THIRTY X BOMBS FROM DIVE BOMBERS

SMALL OR INTERMEDIATE CALIBER X AT
ABOUT ZERO NINE HUNDRED HORIZONTAL
BOMBING ATTACK CAME CONSISTING
OF TWO GROUPS OF SIX PLANES EACH AT
ALTITUDE OF ABOUT ELEVEN THOUSAND
FEET X ONE GROUP CAME FROM ABOUT
TWO HUNDRED DEGREES TRUE OTHER
FROM ABOUT ONE FIFTY TRUE X BOMBS
DROPPED WERE HEAVY CALIBER X HOLES
INDICATE STRAFERS USED FIFTY CALIBER
AND THIRTY CALIBER X NO EVIDENCE OF
HITS BY LARGE GALIBER BUT OBSERVERS
CLAIM FIRE FROM SOME PLANES INDICATE
LARGER CALIBERS USED X OCCASIONAL
DEFLECTION OF TRACER FROM PLANE
SHOT AT INDICATES POSSIBLE ARMORING
OF VULNERABLE PARTS.[40]

A massive rescue operation was already in progress among the battleships and elsewhere—and the protective cover of *Maryland*'s undamaged AA batteries would prove vital, as Japanese planes continued attempts to strafe the hull of the capsized *Oklahoma*, motor launches engaged in rescue, and other ships along the east side of Ford Island. She had plenty of ammunition to offer, yet more trouble was ahead for the *Maryland*, including requesting more ammunition, while *Tennessee*, from the outset, had entered a more difficult circumstance.

When the attack came, the *Tennessee* was moored starboard side to interrupted quay F-6, with two wire hausers and seven manila lines, with *West Virginia* tied to *Tennessee*'s portside with one wire hauser and seven manila lines. Boiler #1 was steaming for auxiliary purposes. While *Tennessee* was fortunate in that she was shielded from torpedo attacks by *West Virginia*'s portside mooring, other factors quickly conspired to nearly victimize her along with her five less fortunate sister ships. One particularly searing point had become evident on all the battleships, and indeed on all the ships in the harbor.

All the at-sea drills, various training exercises against simulated aircraft and submarine attacks, task force formation maneuvering, and gunfire training under centralized control, was of little help in this enemy onslaught. The defenders were caught moored, frozen in place, unable to move, with insufficient steam up to quickly get underway. Stationary targets rather than at sea, where they could otherwise maneuver to spoil tracking solutions, evade bomb and torpedo hits, would be able to zigzag, weave, make hard turns, and change speeds.

To make matters worse, ships like the *Pennsylvania, San Francisco, Honolulu,* and numerous destroyers were undergoing overhaul, had no boilers lit; were dependent upon electrical power, water and telephone from the docks—which were quickly lost; and as a result their antiaircraft defenses were in various states of degradation, a condition aggravated by the engineering activities in progress during overhaul. For ships not undergoing overhaul, normally only one boiler was kept in operation for auxiliary purposes, and a single hit in the wrong area could quickly cause the temporary or permanent loss of electrical power, and the immediate degradation of antiaircraft defenses because of the shift to manual operation of guns and turrets.

The primary offsetting factor was ships' antiaircraft gunners' tracking and firing solutions were less complex because they were on an essentially stable gun platform taking the enemy under fire, rather than at sea on a pitching, rolling, and maneuvering platform—which probably would have lowered the cost to the enemy.

The *Tennessee*'s Officer of the Deck, Ensign Donald N. Kable, was nearing the end of his 0400 to 0800 tour of duty when the Val dive bombers first struck Ford Island. As a result of repetitive enemy strafing attacks, before the morning ended, Kable was carried below for medical treatment, the only officer aboard *Tennessee* seriously wounded.

Tennessee's commander, Captain Charles E. Reordan, wasn't aboard when the attack began. Neither were the Executive Officer nor First Lieutenant, Commanders Colin Campbell and Joyce A. Ralph. Lieutenant Commander John W. Adams, Jr., the gunnery officer, assumed temporary command of the ship. Ralph, third in line to assume command in an emergency, when at his battle station was Damage Control Officer, but this day, in his absence, Lieutenant Robert R. Moore took responsibility as the acting DCO.

Lieutenant Commander Adams wasn't on the bridge when the first indications of the attack came over the loud-speaker system, "All hands to general quarters." While proceeding topside a messenger informed him Japanese planes were bombing the fleet. As he ran to the bridge, he shouted to the officer-of-the-deck to get the ship in condition Zed as quickly as possible. When he arrived in Conn I [primary control], on the bridge, he found the interior communication circuit talkers were at, or manning their stations. He directed main control to get underway as soon as possible, and also directed central station to pass the word over the loud-speakers to get the ship in condition Zed as fast as possible. The direction went out over all fire control battle circuits. By this time he was able to establish communication with air defense, and received a report that that the antiaircraft batteries were fully manned and engaging the enemy planes.

From that time until the executive officer and captain returned to the ship he received various reports over the interior communication system, and various directives from higher authority, which he coordinated to all departments as the reports and circumstances indicated at the time.

After ensuring general quarters was sounded and instructions issued to set Condition Zed, Ensign Kable rushed to his battle station, where he was the Control Officer on the .50-caliber machine guns. Within five minutes *Tennessee*'s antiaircraft batteries opened fire, but ran into the same difficulties first encountered on *Maryland*.

The *West Virginia*'s parallel mooring and superstructure rendered some of *Tennessee*'s portside AA batteries useless against raiders approaching low on *West Virginia*'s port beam. Fires broke out on *West Virginia* within moments after she absorbed her first torpedo hits. After *Arizona*'s explosion at 0808, heavy smoke from the fires on *Arizona* and *West Virginia* combined to complicate *Tennessee* gun crews' abilities to visually acquire and track enemy raiders coming from any direction, while also complicating Japanese attempts to visually acquire and attack targets obscured by the smoke.

When general quarters sounded, 17-year old Seaman Second Class J.R. Johnson from Salt Lake City, Utah, was below decks completing mess duty as a cook, cleaning up the general mess [enlisted crew's mess hall] by 0800 hours—after providing breakfast for approximately twenty men. Assigned to *Tennessee*'s E Division "electrical gang," anytime *Tennessee* departed or entered port, J.R. Johnson left his normal duty station, manned the ship's degaussing gear and activated it as a routine anti-magnetic mine procedure. This day, because *Tennessee* was in port, at the sound of general quarters, he immediately proceeded to his normal duty station, which was also his battle station—the electrical drive station in #3 engine room. No sooner did he arrive than word was passed to "make all preparations to get underway."

For the next one and one half hours, while gun batteries up above kept up their fire, he and many others toiled to get both plants and six boilers ready to move their ship away from berth F-6, and out of the harbor. As was the case with *Maryland*, other factors intervened to pin *Tennessee* in her berth for several days.

Early during the bombing and strafing attacks on the battleships, two bombs struck *Tennessee*, the first forward, splitting the hoop on the #2 turret's center 14-inch gun, rendering the gun inoperative and in need of replacement. Though the damage wasn't heavy, the explosion's splinters tore into the nearby forward machine gun nest, just above the turret, and directly below the bridge, killing three men outright and wounding several others. A fourth later died as a result of his wounds, before he could be evacuated.

The second hit, a 1,765-pound bomb dropped by a Kate horizontal bomber struck aft, wrecking the catapult on top of #3 turret and penetrating five inches of armor. The second bomb could have been disastrous—but luck was with *Tennessee* and her crew. As the bomb descended it sheared off the starboard after yardarm of the mainmast, then entered the turret and exploded with a low order detonation, breaking up and sending pieces into the turret booth and left gun chamber. Flames from the explosion shot into the booth and into all three gun chambers. The turret crew had just manned their stations and were in the process of closing all flame-proof doors and hatches when the bomb struck. Almost immediately *Tennessee*'s crew entered a different kind of struggle.

Arizona's shattering explosion rained burning powder, oil and debris on *Tennessee*'s and *West Virginia*'s quarterdecks, ignited raging oil-fed fires on the water's surface, and rapidly exacerbated *Tennessee*'s predicament. Due to the pull of the outgoing tide and the east wind's push, the surface fire swept toward *Tennessee*, spread around her stern, and started a fire on her port quarter. Intense heat from fires on *West Virginia* and *Arizona*, and the fire on *Tennessee*'s quarterdeck, began buckling *Tennessee*'s outer port quarter and stern shell plates and increasing fire hazards below deck—until fire broke out in the officers' wardroom and quarters. The situation continued to deteriorate.

At first unknown to *Tennessee*'s crew, the combination of multiple torpedo hits, exploding on *West Virginia*'s port side, forcing her toward *Tennessee*, *West Virginia*'s substantial list to port before counter flooding began to right her, raised *West Virginia*'s starboard side until her torpedo belt could be seen through *Tennessee*'s portside general mess portholes. As *West Virginia* settled, her starboard side pressed up against the camels on *Tennessee*'s port side and pinned her against the quay's on her starboard side. (A camel is a large bumper hanging over the side, between two ships moored close together, or next to docks, to keep the two ships apart or avoid direct contact with docks.) *Arizona*'s fire spreading on the water toward the stern of *Tennessee*, and in between the burning *West Virginia* and *Tennessee*, was steadily increasing the danger to *Tennessee*. Fire fighting parties deployed hoses and went to work below decks struggling to put out the extremely hot fires.

Lieutenant Commander Adams directed that some fire hoses be turned toward *West Virginia*, to aid in pushing the fire forward and rescue men from the stricken ship. During the bombing, *Tennessee*'s #3 motor boat was sunk, and #2 motor launch burned and sank when caught in the oil fire from *Arizona*. Like *Maryland*, however, *Tennessee*'s troubles were just beginning, and the enemy's second wave was yet to come.[41]

While the battle raged in the Southeast Loch, and men were struggling in the Middle Loch to save *Raleigh* and men trapped in the capsized *Utah*, another kind of battle was erupting on the west side of Ford Island.

Battle in the Middle Loch: The Sinking of a Midget Submarine

At 0726, while the USS *Ward*'s report of depth charging a submarine outside the harbor entrance was still winding its way through the Pacific Fleet's staff, the 1,850-ton destroyer *Helm* (DD-388) departed Berth X-7 bound for a buoy in the West Loch, preparatory to deperming. All hands were at special sea detail stations, and both her boats were manned and in the water, with instructions to follow the ship to the West Loch, which was past the Middle Loch on further toward the harbor entrance.

Deperming was called degaussing on the battleships, which, to defend against magnetic mines, had degaussing system's designed into the ships' architecture to reduce the magnetic charges on steel hulls traveling through water. Battleships' crews activated degaussing systems each time they entered and departed a harbor, and as needed in other areas where the mine threat was elevated.

The smaller, lighter combatants, such as destroyers, "depermed" using an external system, in which electrical coils were, on a scheduled basis, wrapped at intervals around the beam of the ship, and activated to reduce the built-up electrical charge. It was standard procedure to remove magnetic compasses and electric chronometers when ships were scheduled into deperm, and this day *Helm*'s crew left those units aboard the destroyer *Blue*, moored next to *Helm* near Aiea Bay.

By 0755 the *Helm* had passed the Middle Loch, proceeded down the main channel south of Ford Island, turned to starboard, into the West Loch channel, and headed toward the deperming bouys.[42]

Moored at berth X-14 in the northern most area of the harbor, approximately 900 yards east of the Pearl City peninsula in a nest of four ships in Destroyer Division Two, was the destroyer *Monaghan* (DD-354), her bow on a heading of 025 degrees. The 1,500-ton *Monaghan*, designated the Division's "Ready Duty Destroyer," was fully manned, on one-hour notice to get underway. Moored close to her starboard side, left to right, were three more destroyers in the *Farragut* class, the *Aylwin* (DD-355), *Farragut* (DD-348), and *Dale* (DD-353).

At 0751 the watch [duty] signalman on *Monaghan*'s bridge received a visual message from the Commandant, 14th Naval District, "PROCEED IMMEDIATELY AND CONTACT WARD IN DEFENSIVE SEA AREA." He transcribed the message, and handed it to the communications messenger, who delivered it to the radioman on watch in Main Radio, on the bridge. At approximately 0755, the radio messenger delivered a rough copy to the communications officer, Ensign John W. Gilpin, who was in the wardroom finishing breakfast. Receipted and logged in Main Radio at 0752, the message was the command's response to the *Ward*'s report of its attack on a submarine in the defensive sea area just outside the entrance to Pearl Harbor.

On receiving the dispatch, Gilpin noted the time group for message dispatch was 0248 local, and hurried to the bridge to find out why it had not been sent down sooner. The signalman assured him it had just been received, the time of dispatch an apparent error. Gilpin looked again at the message, agreed with the signalman's conclusion, turned to go below and encountered the executive officer, Lieutenant Harry J. Verhoye. The executive officer immediately ordered, "Make all preparations to get underway," and passed the message to *Monaghan*'s captain, Commander William P. "Bill" Burford, who was in his cabin. Ensign Gilpin went below to obtain the confidential chart and books preparatory to getting underway, and stopped by the "radio shack" to ensure they used the right harbor radio frequencies during departure. Just after he arrived one of the radio strikers burst in and incredulously asked if "it was a drill or air raid." Gilpin stepped outside and went to the outboard door, which faced west—just as the general alarm sounded. He saw two torpedo planes coming in from the northwest, toward Ford Island, but continued below to get the charts and books.

At 0755, as Ensign Gilpin was receiving the message in the wardroom, an excited crew member reported to Burford that Japanese planes were in Pearl Harbor. Burford stepped out onto the portside deck, looked to the north, northwest and saw a large cloud of dense black smoke rising from the vicinity of Schofield Barracks, turned to look south across the harbor, and saw a Kate torpedo bomber attack the *Utah*. At 0800 the general alarm sounded and word came on the speaker system to go to general quarters, while the engineer officer in the engine room responded to orders to get up steam on all boilers for emergency sortie.

One minute earlier the *Helm* logged, "First enemy plane sighted in shallow dive over Ford Island, headed northwest. Observed first bomb hit on hangar at southwest end of Ford Island. Called crew to general quarters. Executive Officer went below to assist in opening magazines and getting ammunition to guns." Almost simultaneously *Helm*'s crew sighted torpedo planes approaching from the direction of Barbers Point.

They came in low, passed over the West Loch channel, and several of their radiomen-gunners, facing aft in the Kates, strafed *Helm* as they passed—a greeting other Kate gunners administered to a liberty boat returning from Pearl City to the light minelayer *Montgomery*, in the Middle Loch. All the Japanese gunners' rounds missed the *Helm* by a few feet. As with other ships in the Middle and West Lochs, *Helm*'s gunners hadn't time to react.

Her forward machine guns, the only guns that could bear on the approaching Kates, were coated with grease and had to be cleaned before they could fire.

Helm's skipper, Commander Chester E. Carroll, Jr., immediately ordered "Back engines," and began maneuvering the ship out of the loch to head for the channel entrance. At 0805 her after machine guns opened fire at planes over the main channel, followed shortly by the forward machine guns firing at passing torpedo planes, and at 0807, the 5-inch battery—all with no hits. At 0810 she was in the main channel steaming toward the harbor entrance, when the port machine gun, manned by Gunner's Mate Second Class W.C. Huff, hit a plane approaching from the south. The plane veered sharply, caught fire, and crashed behind trees near Hickam Field. Commander Carroll ordered all boilers lighted off, and at 0813 *Helm* steamed past the gate vessel, accelerating toward 25 knots.

At 0817 *Helm*'s crew sighted the conning tower of a submarine to the right of channel, northward of Buoy #1, and Carroll ordered open fire, "pointer fire," but the submarine submerged before guns could swing and aim at the target.[43]

On board the destroyer *Monaghan* at 0800, Commander Burford inquired of the status of officers in the other ships in the nest of four destroyers and issued orders to commence firing from all ships as soon as they were capable—as well as orders to send boats ashore for their officers. *Monaghan*'s First Lieutenant and Torpedo Officer, Ensign Paul W. Gill, immediately sent a man below to bring up the firing locks for the guns, then sent repair party men forward and aft on the 341-foot ship to break the locks on all magazines, while he started organizing ammunition transfer.

He then placed Ensign Raleigh C. Christian in charge of "extra men"—those not assigned a battle station, while others were detailed to take charge and perform necessary tasks to get the destroyer underway as soon as possible. Gill was sent by Ensign George V. Rogers to belt .50-caliber ammunition, while Chief Boatswain Mate Jones took repair men and part of Gun #3 crew to take in the motor whaleboat and gangway. Two repair-party men were sent forward and aft in charge of petty officers to stand by and take in forward and after lines with the help of Guns #1 and #5. Boatswain Mate Second Class Meadows and the Gun Captain of Gun #3 were placed in charge of the ammunition train for that gun. Guns #1, #2, and #4 had ammunition on the way up. Guns #1 and #2 had no power on the hoist, and an electrician's mate was sent forward to solve the problem. Coxswain I.C. Switzer was placed in charge of bringing up Gun #5 ammunition, while Ensign Christian brought up .50-caliber ammunition and belted it.

At 0808, by radio and visual signal, the commander, Destroyer Flotilla 1, ordered Destroyer Division Two, which included all the destroyers in *Monaghan's* nest, to establish the Offshore Patrol. Responding to the radically changed circumstances, the command's order revised the direction previously given *Monaghan's* commander—to assist the *Ward*.[43]

At 0814 ships in the nest began firing on the enemy horizontal bombers with both machine guns and 5-inch batteries. There was not yet electrical power to *Monaghan's* guns or ammunition hoists. Crews operated guns by manual control and brought ammunition up by hand and manual hoisting, until steam was up. In response to a flag hoist on the cruiser *Detroit*, she was underway at 0827, backing from her mooring. After backing clear of the nest, she moved ahead in a starboard turn toward the south, accelerating to ten knots and maneuvering to sortie from Pearl Harbor via the North Channel.[44]

As Val dive bombers launched their first attacks on Ford Island at 0755, at virtually the same minute sixteen Kate torpedo bombers from *Soryu* and *Hiryu* were fanning out, approaching their target areas, low from the west and northwest, across the harbor between Pearl City and Ford Island. Five from *Soryu* pressed toward *Utah*, *Raleigh*, *Detroit* and the seaplane tender *Tangier* (AV-8), all moored on the west side of Ford Island. They were the torpedo bombers seen by Commander Burford, *Monaghan's* skipper, and Ensign Gilpin, the communications officer on *Monaghan*.

Further south, a smaller number of Kate torpedo bombers from *Hiryu* swept low over the water just west of Pearl City, then across the water on the west side of the Middle Loch, down the channel and around the south end of Ford Island toward 1010 Dock. En route they flew low near the seaplane tender *Curtiss* (AV-4) moored at Berth X-22, the repair ship *Medusa* (AR-1), moored at Berth X-23 approximately 400 yards northwest of *Curtiss*, and a nest of four high-speed minesweepers moored further northwest of *Medusa* less than 100 yards. The bows of all six ships pointed northeast, roughly the same direction as the destroyers in the nest with *Monaghan*. From starboard to port at Buoys D-7 and D-7-S, the four minesweepers were: the *Perry* (DMS-17) nearest *Medusa*, *Zane* (DMS-14), *Wasmuth* (DMS-15), and *Trever* (DMS-16). As the Kates crossed the water just to the west of Pearl City one or more radio operator-gunners facing aft in the Kates had strafed a liberty boat returning from Pearl City to the light minelayer *Montgomery* (DM-17).

Moored to Buoy D-3 in a nest of four more ships approximately 500 yard further west of *Trever*, also bows to the northeast toward Pearl City, were from right to left, the light minelayers *Ramsay* (DM-16), *Breese* (DM-18), the *Montgomery*, and *Gamble* (DM-15).[45]

The Kate torpedo bombers flew past the ten ships on the west side of the Middle Loch channel while the ships' crews' attention was first drawn to the dive bomb attacks on Ford Island—to the east—and passed too quickly for any of the ships' antiaircraft batteries to react. Unlike Captain Clifton A.F. Sprague on *Tangier*, and consistent with direction from the fleet's Commander-in-Chief, the other nine commanders had dutifully ordered ammunition be removed from ready boxes and stored in magazines. The silence of the ships' guns on the west side of the Middle Loch would end in approximately four minutes, while adjacent to Ford Island, gun crews on the seaplane tender *Tangier* saw the Kates coming, and were the first to fire on them.[46]

At 0755, the 11,760-ton *Tangier* (AV-8) was berthed at F-10 on the west side of the island, with her bow pointing 230 degrees true—roughly the same direction as the battleships on the other side of the island. Directly astern of the 492-foot ship, at Berth F-11, was *Utah*, oriented stern to stern with *Tangier*. *Tangier* had arrived at Pearl Harbor with her complement of 1,075 officers and men on 3 November, assigned to Patrol Wing TWO, with the mission of servicing the Wing's flying boats. Her crew routinely serviced approximately twenty of the long range patrol aircraft, providing gas, oil, machine gun ammunition and 500-pound bombs. Using cranes the *Tangier* could hoist the big, two-engine, Catalina PBY Flying Boats on deck for maintenance or overhaul, then return them to operation.

At 0758 *Tangier*'s klaxan sounded general quarters, and shortly before 0800 all guns that could be brought to bear on airborne targets, opened fire. Among the targets were three Kate torpedo bombers closing in on *Utah*, *Raleigh*, and *Detroit*, logged at

0803, a startlingly rapid response that was no accident. Captain Sprague, *Tangier's* commander, was a hard-boiled, proud naval aviator, and in his 2 January 1942 report to the Commander-in-Chief, Pacific Fleet, wrote, ". . . the first of the Japanese planes passed along port [east] side of ship headed to Ewa, at about 400 feet, its orange insignia clear, leaving no uncertainty that this was a real attack . . . It was [my] impression that this ship was the first to open fire, or surely among the first."

When the order came early in the week of 1 December, for the Battle Fleet to be ready for Admirals' Inspection beginning 8 December, with ammunition taken from the ready boxes locked in the ships' magazines, Sprague told his gunners' mates to keep the ammunition in the ready boxes. He had "come out here to fight a war!" If one of the brass hats came to visit his ship the admiral would have to signal the ship first for side boys at the gangway, then he—Sprague—and the crew would hide all the ammunition before the admiral came on board.[47]

The executive officer, Commander George H. DeBaun, counted five Kate torpedo bombers releasing torpedoes near the white spar bouy in the north side of the channel in the attacks on *Utah*, *Raleigh*, and *Detroit*, and received a *Tangier* crewman's report that one of the torpedoes passed just clear of their stern, between *Utah* and *Tangier*. Torpedoes were released at a range of approximately 400 yards. After the torpedo attack the crew took advantage of a slight lull to check all watertight doors, hatches, ports, and fire hoses. Chiefs and officers checked damage control parties, ammunition supply and belting parties and redistributed personnel to eliminate bottlenecks. The only change made was to assign 5-inch [non-AA] gun crews and ammunition supply parties to augment 3-inch AA and .50-caliber machine gun ammunition and belting parties.

At 0820, *Tangier* signalmen saw the visual dispatch from Commander-in-Chief, Pacific Fleet, "Make preparations to get underway," and by 0830 she was ready, while across the channel to the west a chain of events was set in motion that led to the sinking of a Japanese midget submarine in Pearl Harbor's Middle Loch.[48]

The battle began at 0830, when crew members on Mine Division Four's 1,215-ton high-speed minesweeper *Zane* sighted a "strange submarine 200 yards astern of *Medusa*." *Zane's* crew, already at general quarters and having opened fire on the raiders with their AA guns at 0802, immediately loaded Gun #4 and signaled the Commander-in-Chief, Pacific Fleet, who, at 0832, signaled to all ships in Pearl, "Japanese submarine in harbor." *Zane* couldn't fire, however, because the rounds would have struck *Perry*, moored next to her, to starboard.[49]

A few moments earlier, men on the after deck house of the *Perry*, sighted the intruder "heading toward the Middle Loch and swinging toward the moorings of *Medusa* [and] *Curtiss* . . . " They promptly manned their after-deck-mounted #4 battery, an unusual-size, 4-inch gun, and fired two shots. The first was well over. The gun crew reset range to 300 yards, and fired the second round. No one saw the fall of shot or projectile splash, but the crew concluded the second round passed through the submarine conning tower or hull and contributed to the midget submarine's sinking. As was noted in the ship's action report of 22 December, 50 yards to the east of *Perry*, "The *Medusa* was also firing on the same enemy."[50]

The *Medusa*, 484 feet long, and displacing 10,620 tons, and the seaplane tender *Curtiss*, 527 feet long and displacing 8,671 tons, were more tempting targets for Japanese raiders attacking in the Middle Loch, consequently both were subject to repeated air attacks as the morning progressed. Lieutenant Commander John F. P. Miller, *Medusa*'s Repair Officer, was the senior officer aboard and acting commander. In his 16 December Action Report, he wrote:

> About 0755 I heard a loud explosion, and looking out the port of my room, saw what appeared to be the hanger on the South end of Ford Island in flames and a large column of black smoke reaching into the air.
>
> The General Alarm was sounded immediately and all hands went to General Quarters. On my way to the bridge I gave the magazine keys to the Gunner's Mate on duty with orders to open the forward magazine, then the after magazine.
>
> On reaching the bridge orders were given to the engine room to get ready to get underway immediately. I then proceeded to the Signal Bridge where Mr. [Ensign Charles T.] Foley was in charge of Fire Control. He was mounting two .30-caliber machine guns, one on each end of the Signal Bridge.

At approximately 0805 the first shot was fired by the *Medusa* from #5 3-inch A.A. gun. From this period on I have no estimate of time but both A.A. guns and both machine guns kept up continuous fire during attacks . . . During the [first] attack it was reported that a submarine periscope was sighted about 1000 yards on our starboard quarter or about 500 yards astern of the *Curtiss*. I gave orders to open fire on the periscope—shortly afterward the *Curtiss* opened fire . . . "

Miller next observed an explosion "at a small dock astern of *Curtiss*," and concluded the submarine fired a torpedo at the dock. Instead, he had seen the impact of a shot fired at the submarine by the destroyer *Monaghan*, now accelerating down-channel toward the submarine. Miller continued, "The submarine then broached to the surface with conning tower in plain sight. Many shots could be plainly seen hitting the conning tower from both *Medusa* and *Curtiss*. While being shelled the submarine appeared to be backing toward the *Curtiss* . . . "[51]

Medusa's Forward Battery Officer, Ensign Robert M. Rocktaschel, had a clear view of the submarine's maneuvering as it moved out of the North Channel further west into the Middle Loch.

The submarine was sighted as it rounded the stern of the *Curtiss* and started up this loch. At first only its periscope was visible and it was immediately fired upon. Gun #1 [a forward-mounted gun] was loaded and ready for firing with the exception of primers which were stored in the pyrotechnic locker and by the time these were procured it was too late to use this gun. However, machine guns and gun six opened fire on the submarine with three inch anti-aircraft projectiles as solid shot was not available. The submarine went behind our stern and then either by turning around or by backing down started out of the loch back to the main channel. When it came into the training [gun traversing] field of Gun #5, part of the conning tower was visible above the water. As it neared the stern of the *Curtiss* a destroyer [*Monaghan*] came down the main channel and made to ram it. The submarine's conning tower was on the starboard side of the destroyer . . .

The *Curtiss* went to general quarters at 0750, and reported having been immediately strafed by Japanese fighters. At 0803 her gunners commenced firing .50-caliber machine guns, followed two minutes later with 5-inch batteries firing under local control. All guns were ordered to "fire individually on any target making an offensive approach." As indicated in his 16 December action report, Captain Henry S. Kendall, who was not on board his ship during the attack, at 0808 *Curtiss*'s acting commander ordered the engine room, "Underway emergency." At 0825 Japanese bombers attacked *Curtiss*, and two minutes later the engine room cut in boilers number 1, 2, and 4. Though enemy raiders scored no hits in this first attack, *Curtiss*'s crew had tested her main engines at 0835, and the Engineering Department told the officer in command they were ready to get underway—the new seaplane tender, commissioned in November 1940—didn't get underway that day. The second wave of attackers took a heavy toll on her and her crew.

At 0836 crew members sighted the submarine's periscope on their starboard quarter, distance 700 yards, and 5-inch guns were ordered to "Fire on the submarine." Gun #3 fired one over and two just short and directly at the periscope. Gun #2 opened fire. At 0840 the submarine surfaced showing its conning tower and a section of its bow, then fired a torpedo up North Channel toward the onrushing *Monaghan*. *Curtiss*'s Gun #3 twice hit the conning tower with their 5-inch rounds. Then at 0842, the order came "Cease firing on submarine." *Monaghan* was closing fast on the intruder.

At 0833, before she could depart her berth, *Tangier*'s crew had reported to Captain Sprague a Japanese submarine was in the harbor channel. Just before *Curtiss* ceased firing on the submarine, the *Tangier*'s crew first sighted it 800 yards off their starboard bow. Across the channel to the west, action was escalating rapidly to a climax. Nevertheless, *Tangier*'s eager 3-inch, #1 antiaircraft gun crew got off six rounds by 0844, when Captain Sprague ordered cease fire "due to fouling of the target by *Monaghan*."[52]

On board *Monaghan*, maneuvering to turn down the North

Channel on various headings, Commander Burford's signalman called his attention to a flag hoist on *Curtiss* indicating the presence of a submarine. "Well, *Curtiss* must be crazy," Burford responded. "That may be, Captain," the crewman conceded, but what is that down there?" Burford followed his gesture off the starboard bow and saw "an over and under shotgun barrel looking up at him." Others on the bridge sighted the submarine's periscope and conning tower approximately 300 yards off the starboard quarter of *Curtiss*.[53]

At 0837, when abreast of Buoy 7, the submarine was bearing 230 degrees true at a range of about 1200 yards from the destroyer. *Monaghan*'s Gun #2 fired one shot which either missed or ricocheted, and struck the derrick barge moored off Beckoning Point, approximately 700 yards astern of *Curtiss*. The hit started a small fire on the derrick. Burford promptly ordered, "All engines ahead flank speed and full right rudder." Word was passed that "it was intended to ram the submarine—then distant about one thousand yards." At the helm, Chief Quartermaster Dewey E. Williamson was directed to head for the submarine when he gave assurance that he saw it.

The turn toward the submarine at first overshot the heading to successfully ram, but the helmsman corrected back to hold a collision course, which held *Monaghan* on a track slightly convergent with *Curtiss*, to pass approximately 100 yards to *Curtiss*'s starboard.

From *Monaghan*'s bridge, *Tangier*'s 3-inch AA gun and *Curtiss*'s 5-inch and machine guns could be seen firing vigorously at the submarine. Just after 0840, with its conning tower and bow clearly visible, the submarine turned sharply toward the destroyer and at range of about 75 yards fired a torpedo at *Monaghan*. With the submarine's bow inclined upward, the torpedo broached twice, once about two feet into the air, fell back into the water, stabilized, began tracking along a line that would split the distance between the two ships, ran parallel past the starboard side, approximately 20-30 yards from *Monaghan*— and struck the north bank, throwing a geyser of water 200 feet in the air.

At 0843 collision was imminent, the south shore and the derrick barge were looming closer, and word was passed over the speaker system, "Standby for shock forward." The crossing angle for ramming was approximately 40 degrees.

The executive officer, Lieutenant Verhoye, who had been listening to the communications from the bridge, on his own initiative had already ordered and supervised preparations to drop depth charges. At the call to general quarters, he had rushed to his normal battle station, Battle Two [aft steering], then later moved to Gun #5, aft, when the submarine's sighting was reported. When he heard "We are going to ram," Verhoye ordered "Standby depth charges, set on 30 feet."

Chief Torpedoman's Mate G.S. Hardon, on watch at the port depth charge racks, and Torpedoman's Mate Second Class A.F. Parker on the starboard racks were ready.

Hardon had been topside and saw bombs dropping on Ford Island when the attack began. He recognized immediately it wasn't a drill, and didn't hesitate. He hollered "General quarters!" and sent nearby men aft for machine gun ammunition. As soon as ammunition arrived, he put Torpedoman's Mate Second Class Dorsett and several firemen to work belting ammunition, then sent Parker aft with instructions to stand by depth charge racks and "get some ready for dropping." He then turned his attention to charging torpedoes with Torpedoman's Mate First Class Varnado—until he heard the call, "Submarine . . . " He promptly left Varnado to continue charging torpedoes, and went aft to the depth charge racks.

When he arrived, he found Parker had already set the depth charges to 30 feet. He had set one at 30 feet, but uncertain of the channel's depth asked Lieutenant Verhoye before setting the remainder at the right depth for release. Hardon had only to verify the correct settings, then stood by after Parker cut the safety lines, letting the charges into their traps.

From the bridge the submarine was seen to disappear beneath the bow, while from the stern it appeared to Hardon the submarine would cross under the stern. Ensign P.W. Gill, the First Lieutenant and torpedo officer, fully expected substantial damage forward, with a good possibility of losing the forecastle if *Monaghan* hit the submarine a solid blow. He hastily organized a repair party to isolate the damage. As *Monaghan* passed over the submarine, there was a brief insignificant list to port and Gill felt only a slight jar as she struck a glancing blow causing the intruder to slide aft along the starboard side. Gill sent a repair party below to check for damage, then hurried toward the forecastle anticipating a need to drop anchor in an attempt to snub the ship and keep it off the oncoming mud bank.

Without orders, as the submarine passed beneath the stern, Chief Hardon released one depth charge, and the executive officer told him to drop another. He was about to drop the third, when he felt the ship brush the mud beneath her.

Immediately after ramming the enemy, Burford commanded, "All engines back emergency full speed. Full left rudder." The depth charges violently exploded approximately 0844, about 50-100 yards astern of *Monagahan*. On the forward decks of the *Curtiss* and from the *Monaghan*, men standing aft on the *Curtiss* could be heard cheering wildly after the ramming and depth charge explosions.

To *Monaghan*'s port side, in the North Channel, her sister ship, the destroyer *Dale* (DD-353), which had followed close behind her in leaving the destroyers' nest, and observed *Monaghan*'s starboard turn and acceleration to attack the submarine, stopped just prior to the successful ramming and depth charging—then resumed accelerating toward 25 knots to exit the harbor.

From the *Medusa*, Lieutenant Commander Miller observed, "The first depth charge appeared to drop right on top of the submarine as the volume of water shooting into the air was heavily colored with a black substance. The second charge did not have the black coloring." The *Curtiss*'s commander saw air bubbles and an oil slick come to the surface where the depth charges exploded. From the *Trever*, the first depth charge appeared to "roll the submarine over." Lieutenant (jg) Hart Kait, *Monaghan*'s gunnery officer, reported, "The first explosion brought the submarine's bow and superstructure into full view."

Burford's "All engines back emergency full speed," and "Full left rudder," though carried out promptly, was insufficient to check the ship's headway. Burford waved off Ensign Gill and the #1 gun crew's intended use of the anchor as she eased slowly to port, into shallow water over the mud bank, and her starboard bow struck a slight blow to the derrick barge moored at Beckoning Point. Burford ordered "All engines stop," and the ship came to full stop with the derrick just forward of the bridge. Chief Hardon, aware *Monaghan* was going to run aground, had again taken the initiative and wisely decided not to drop a third depth charge.

An oxy-acetylene tank on the derrick was burning. A man

stationed on the forecastle sprayed the blaze with fire suppressant from an emergency fire bottle, to keep the additional tanks from exploding. The stream of suppressant had no appreciable affect on the fire.

Burford ordered, "All engines back." On attempting to back clear of the derrick, the barge's bow began to swing out as if to follow the ship. Burford realized *Monaghan* had snagged her bow on one of the barge's mooring lines. While backing, endeavoring to free the ship from the mooring line, a second submarine alert occurred from within the tense, excited crew. Gun #2 trained on a target off the port bow and fired one round at what turned out to be a black cage buoy.

Burford reversed the engines once more and eased forward, holding left rudder. He then ordered back again, this time more on the port engine, the bow continuing slowly to port. Then forward again, engines full ahead, still full left rudder, and this time she pulled away, cleared the barge by several yards, and broke free of the mooring line. Still in shallow water with her bow continuing to port, she struck the mud bank, but didn't slow. Within seconds the *Monaghan* was clear of the mud bank, and at 0847 swung into the deeper water of the North Channel. She fell in about 1,500 yards astern her sister ship, the *Dale*, at 0908 passed the entrance buoys, and proceeded out of Pearl Harbor to her assigned station—Offshore Patrol. Behind her, the second wave of air attacks had begun, and word was passed for the crew topside to take cover and lay down. No Japanese planes attacked her. The aft repair party found one small hole in the hull, at starboard plate D-205-L, and immediately shored the hole to stop leakage.

"It was a hectic few minutes," Burford later recalled. "There was that sub coming directly at me, and I at him, and all that speed, and the firing by others, and a number of ships out ahead of me in restricted maneuvering space, and all that Japanese air attack behind us and our antiaircraft fire, their planes—God, a lot was going on in just a few minutes of time."

Throughout the ship, and behind her etched in history, the *Monaghan* left indelible memories of a second, small victory on a terrible day. On the bottom of the west side of the Middle Loch, lay a Japanese midget submarine, its two-man crew dead. The *Medusa*'s acting skipper, Lieutenant Commander Miller wrote of Commander Burford, "The Commanding Officer of the *Monaghan*

The destroyer *Monaghan* (DD-354) deliberately rammed, depth charged and sank a Japanese midget submarine in the Middle Loch, the morning of 7 December 1941. Off Mare Island Navy Yard, 17 February 1942. NA

The seaplane tender *Curtiss* (AV-4) and repair ship *Medusa* (AR-1) photographed from the deck of the *Tangier* (AV-8). *Medusa* is on the right. *Curtiss*, has just been struck by a crashing Japanese aircraft, hit by AA fire while flying low, just east of *Tangier*, over the western edge of Ford Island. The pilot started an immediate right turn toward the *Curtiss*, apparently intent on a final, suicidal attack on the ship. The timbers in the water are from the capsized target ship *Utah* (AG-16), which had capsized at her berth, astern of *Tangier*. NHHC

should be commended for the promptness with which he made the attack, and the excellent seamanship displayed in very restricted waters." *Tangier*'s Captain Sprague wrote, ". . . this was a fine piece of work and the Commanding Officer of the *Monaghan*, in my opinion, should be commended for an excellent and rapid action."[54]

For his actions that terrible morning Commander Burford received the Navy Cross, and the *Monaghan* crew carried glowing memories filled with great pride.

Nevada the Brave: Her Colors Emerge Into the Sunlight

Moored at the northeastern most berth on east side of Ford Island, the 27,500-ton battleship *Nevada* (BB-36) was the eldest, by a few months, of all the battleships in Pearl Harbor. Though the eldest, along with other sister ships she had been back-fitted with anti-torpedo protection that made her fairly well resistant to warhead explosion. She lay starboard side to the interrupted quay wall, berth F-8, with six manila lines and two wires holding her in place. Boiler #2 provided steam to generate auxiliary power.[55]

Ensign Charles W. Jenkins, the Officer of the Deck on the *Nevada* was ending his 0400 to 0800 watch, looking forward to some well-earned rest, when unforeseen circumstances changed his plans. His first entry in the deck log for the four hour period, read: "0700 Received following stores for general mess: From Oahu Ice & Cold Storage Co.—2000 lbs. ice. Inspected as to quantity by Pay Clerk J.W. Cooper, USN, and as quality by Pharmacist Mate First Class A.F. Bond . . . " With the undetected Japanese air armada still twenty minutes from their initial strike on Ford Island, the second and final entry for the period was at 0735, and listed the names of six seamen who left the ship for temporary duty in Honolulu, with the Shore Patrol—the Navy's law enforcement arm.

The entries had been typed and signed though he had one more duty to perform before he was to be relieved by the oncoming duty officer—morning colors on *Nevada*. This final task, raising the American flag on the fantail-mounted staff before going off duty, began a far more frantic four-hour additional tour of duty, from which there would be no relief, no rest, and would be filled with indescribable, fear-filled moments of death, destruction, and unforgettable, inspiring memories. It's unlikely he had time to stop and make accurate notes as time passed, because *Nevada*, like all but two ships in the line of battleships, was quickly in an all-out struggle for survival. When he had time to draft his report covering the period 0800–1200, the first sentences in the neatly-typed, signed *Nevada* deck log for 7 December, summarized events in the crew's fight to save their ship and one another, while battling repeated attacks by Japanese aircraft:

> 0800 Made morning colors, with guard of the day and bugle. 0801 Japanese aircraft commenced surprise attack on U.S. Pacific Fleet present in Pearl Harbor, and on U.S. Army Air Base [Hickam Field]. Aircraft approached at low altitude, strafing ship. Went to General Quarters; set material condition ZED; Lieut-Comdr. Francis J. Thomas, USNR, acting commanding officer; Ensign [JOSEPH] K. TAUSSIG, Jr., USN, acting as air defense officer. Officer-of-the-Deck remained aft and took charge of Repair ONE . . .

At the sound of general quarters, the crew began scrambling toward their battle stations. Two machine guns forward and two aft were already on continuous watch, and the 5-inch antiaircraft battery was partially manned for the routine daily 0800 battery and fire control check when the first strafing attack swept the line of battleships—before *Nevada*'s surprised gunners could react. No sooner did the flight of strafing aircraft roar over the top of her superstructure, than Kate torpedo bombers were seen approaching on the port beam from the direction of Aiea Landing. At 0802, as the first Kates came in range both forward and aft machine guns opened up, concentrating their fire to great effect.

The gunners saw one plane fall to machine gun fire and crash about 100 yards off the ship's port quarter, without dropping its torpedo. A second Kate released its torpedo at a range of 200 to 400 yards and safely over-flew the ship as the pilot, with throttle wide open, pulled the nose up to avoid collision with the superstructure. Typically, the radioman-gunner in the rear cockpit of the Kate, fired machine gun bursts at *Nevada*'s decks as the pilot pulled up and over the superstructure.

A third, seen to disintegrate in a violent explosion before torpedo release, was believed to have taken a direct hit, perhaps on the torpedo it carried. Gunners on *Nevada*'s 5-inch broadside battery, which opened fire at 0803, believed they had brought the torpedo bomber down. Another witness believed the explosive direct hit on the Kate, also brought down its wingman—the Kate that crashed 100 yards off the port quarter—before its torpedo could be released. Once *Nevada*'s batteries opened fire, they fired almost continuously until approximately 0820, when a brief lull occurred.

At 0803, before the officers responding to general quarters arrived on the bridge, Chief Quartermaster Robert Sedberry, on his own initiative, ordered the engine room to "Make all preparations to get under way," immediately followed by the torpedo's explosion into *Nevada*'s port bow at frame 42, tearing a huge hole in her outer plates, from frame 38 to frame 45 in length, and about thirty feet in depth. The violent explosion also tore a hole in lower blisters A-32-V and A-34-V, ruptured upper blisters A-66-V and A-68-V, and caused another small split opening at about frame 36, extending three feet in width and ten feet down from the second deck, and in spite of the anti-torpedo protection, triggered flooding in the immediate vicinity of the hit. During the same, frantic two minutes Ensign Jenkins observed what he believed to be flames on board the minelayer *Oglala*, across the harbor at 1010 dock. The flames were instead on the light cruiser *Helena*, which had been struck approximately five minutes earlier by the torpedo that passed beneath the minelayer, moored outboard of the cruiser.

By 0805 *Nevada* was listing slightly to port following the torpedo hit, and men rushed to set condition Zed to contain the flooding. Up above, on the gun decks, spotters sighted Fuchida's horizontal bombers approaching from the southwest, up the line of battleships, on both bows, at altitudes of approximately 10,000 feet, and anti-aircraft batteries (5-inch and .50-caliber) took them under fire. One minute later, at 0808, several bombs fell close aboard to port of *Nevada*, near-misses fortunately—and at almost the same instant *Arizona* exploded violently, apparently hit during the same bombing run by the Kates. At 0808 Damage

Control passed word to counterflood starboard voids C-5, 7, 11, and 19-V to halt *Nevada*'s progressive list.

By 0809 the men at *Nevada*'s Conn observed that the violent explosion which tore apart *Arizona* had ignited a huge inferno that was rapidly spreading oil-fed flames on the surface of water around the stricken ship. The fire had spread to *Vestal*, moored close to *Arizona*, after the explosion had already ignited fires on her. The explosion and spreading fire gave urgency to the commanding officer's decision to get *Nevada* under way as soon as possible—to avoid further danger due to *Arizona*'s proximity. The scene they were observing worsened when they noted explosions (torpedo hits) coming from *Oklahoma*, moored next in line toward the harbor entrance, directly ahead of *West Virginia*'s bow. Within moments they could see a heavily listing *Oklahoma*, rapidly increasing her list. About 0810 *Nevada* received a signal from the harbor signal tower for all ships to get under way and stand out of the harbor.

Getting under way required sending a line handling detail, to "single up all lines," that is, release all except necessary single mooring lines to quays to continue holding the ship in place until steam was of sufficient pressure to turn her two propeller shafts. At the height of the first Japanese onslaught, forty-seven year old, Chief Boatswain (warrant officer) Edwin J. Hill of Philadelphia, Pennsylvania, led the line handling detail of ten men, went down the gangway into the harbor and swam, under fire, from the ship to the quays, to single up all lines, while on board, below decks, fires were being lighted under boilers #1, 3, 4, and 5. As Chief Boatswain Hill and his detail went about their duties, at 0815, men topside forward on *Nevada* saw the same searing image seen from *California* at the other end of the line of battleships, the wrenching sight of the capsizing *Oklahoma*.

By 0820 Chief Hill's detail singled up all lines, started swimming back to the ship, and the air attack slackened somewhat as preparations continued to get underway. At 0830 men on *Nevada* observed the *Vestal*'s forward lines being cut, on orders of *Arizona*'s Lieutenant Commander Fuqua. Though undergoing heartbreaking toil on *Arizona*'s quarterdeck, Fuqua and *Arizona*'s survivors had the presence of mind to look to the care of other men and their ship. It was *Arizona*'s Aviation Machinist Mate First Class Donald A. Graham who, in the face of intense fire on her deck, repeated bomb passes and strafing

USS *Vestal* (AR-4) beached on Aiea shoal, Pearl Harbor, after the Japanese raid. She is listing from damage caused by two bombs that hit her during the attack. NA

attacks, carried out Fuqua's orders and persisted in cutting the forward lines mooring *Vestal* to his fatally damaged ship. The *Vestal*'s aft lines had already parted, and, listing to starboard with all lines cut from *Arizona*, she was getting underway, standing toward Aiea Landing.[56]

Then, air attacks surged again, and a bomb struck *Nevada*'s bridge, penetrating to the forecastle, resulting in severe shock accompanied by flareback and increased flooding below the main deck. Fire broke out on the bridge structure and below. In spite of the fire, at 0832 the engine room cut in boiler #5 on the main steam line, and three minutes later, though they had to secure boiler #2 due to smoke and gas, reported ready to get underway. Then circumstances once again abruptly changed, and boilers #3, 4, and 5 had to be secured due to smoke in the firerooms. Determined to get underway the engine room watch immediately relit the fires under boiler #5, Chief Hill's detail cast off *Nevada*'s lines, and the boiler took up the load needed to begin slowly backing her away from the berth, into the channel. The time was 0840.

After backing the ship into the channel, with Lieutenant Commander Thomas at the Conn, Lieutenant Lawrence E. Ruff, the acting navigator in the conning tower, and Chief Quartermaster Sedberry at the wheel, orders were given to the engine room, all ahead, and *Nevada* began moving at various courses and speeds to conform to the channel, to stand out of the harbor. As she moved down-channel, the starboard AA ammunition conveyor failed and an ammunition train formed to pass ammunition from the main deck to the battery by hand.[57]

Below decks Machinist Mate Donald K. Ross from Beverly, Kansas, who intended to celebrate his thirty-first birthday on 8 December was fighting another kind of battle, trying to ensure electrical power was available to the ship and its gun batteries. The fire caused by the bomb which penetrated the bridge area, was making the forward dynamo room increasingly untenable due to smoke, steam, and heat. He forced his men to leave that station and performed all the duties himself—until blinded and unconscious. Upon being rescued and resuscitated while the ship was proceeding down-channel, he returned and secured the forward dynamo room and proceeded to the after dynamo room where he again was rendered unconscious by exhaustion. Again recovering consciousness he returned to his station where he remained until directed to abandon it. "For distinguished conduct in the line of his profession, extraordinary courage and disregard of his own life . . . " he later received the Medal of Honor.[58]

Clear of the inferno raging along the line of battleships, *Nevada* eased past a shattered, fire-ravaged *Arizona*, a burning *West Virginia*, and *Tennessee* fighting fire licking at her stern, the capsized *Oklahoma* with her upturned hull, a relatively unscathed *Maryland*, through the intermittent clouds of smoke shadowing the harbor and spreading across Ford Island.

In *At Dawn We Slept*, Gordon Prange gave readers a powerful description of what the men on *Nevada* saw and felt as she passed the line of once proud battleships. The description also told of the fighting spirit of *Arizona* men who had just suffered the fearsome experience of a ship torn apart and sunk, and an unknown number of shipmates' lives instantaneously snuffed out.

> . . . When Nevada limped past the blazing *Arizona*, someone saw three survivors swimming nearby and tossed them a line. They climbed up and helped man

Nevada's starboard 5-inch gun. Heat from the burning battleship was so intense that the gunners had to cover their shells with their bodies lest they explode.

The capsized *Oklahoma* was "another terrifying and shocking sight." To some witnesses the fate of *Oklahoma* was the crowning horror of the day, worse even than the volcanic eruption aboard *Arizona*. The explosion of a battleship, although an awesome thing, was comprehensible. It even had a certain tragic grandeur. But for a battlewagon to overturn was unthinkable; it affronted human dignity. Something of this horrified incredulity held [the navigator, Lieutenant] Ruff in its grip as *Nevada* moved abreast of the overturned vessel.[59]

View of "Battleship Row" as probably seen by the crew of the *Nevada* (BB-36) when she steamed down the main channel during the Japanese raid. *West Virginia* (BB-48) is at the right sunk alongside *Tennessee* (BB-43), with oil fires shrouding them both. The capsized *Oklahoma* is at the left, alongside *Maryland* (BB-46). Crewmen on the latter's stern are using firehouses to try to push burning oil away from their ship. NPSAM

Though *Nevada*'s crew experienced a momentary lull in attacks, they were far from being out of danger. Above the harbor, Lieutenant Commander Takashige Egusa's Val dive bomber pilots, just arriving in the second wave, caught sight of her moving to escape, and recognized a golden double opportunity—to sink a battleship, and at the same time block the channel and bottle up Pearl Harbor. High above the scene, mission Commander Mitsuo Fuchida, who remained orbiting the scene in his Kate horizontal bomber, asked his pilot to roll into a steep bank for a better look. "Ah, good!" he thought. "Now just sink that ship right there!" At 0850 ". . . the Japanese bombers swarmed down on us like bees," Ruff later remarked. *Nevada*'s gunners, who had kept up almost continuous AA fire since approximately 0830, now concentrated their batteries against an enemy determined to sink her in the channel.[60]

In spite of the deadly sights and sounds shattering the air above Pearl Harbor that Sunday morning, made worse by the violent explosions, spreading inferno, death, and heavy palls of smoke along battleship row, on Ford Island, across the harbor, and on Hickam Field, inspiration sailed with *Nevada* as she moved down-channel toward the harbor entrance. Though the men at her guns, on and below her decks hadn't a moment to notice the nation's colors routinely raised at her stern, those who caught sight of her from a distance would carry a memory never to be forgotten. One lone, great ship, the first and only battleship able to get underway, was parading her colors through hell, emerging periodically in the sunlight, her crew determined to save her and fight another day. And though her struggle wasn't yet over—they did save and resurrect her, and she did fight—many other days.

USS *Nevada* (BB-36) headed down channel past the Navy Yard's 1010 Dock, under Japanese air attack during her sortie from Battleship Row. Photographed from Ford Island. Small ship in the lower right is the seaplane tender *Avocet* (AVP-4). Note fuel tank "farm" in the left center distance, beyond the Submarine Base. NHHC

CHAPTER 8

The Second Wave

*First gain the victory, and then
make the best use of it you can.*

Admiral Viscount Nelson

The first wave began withdrawing at 0830, having lost nine aircraft. Five Kate torpedo bombers were the price extracted for savaging the Pacific Fleet's battle line. Air superiority over the island of Oahu was won at the cost of one Val and three Zekes. In addition, seventeen Vals, eleven Zekes and a minimum of eighteen Kates were damaged to some degree. While an overall total of 55 aircraft lost or damaged from a total of 183 seems relatively large, the raiders did enormous damage and won an overwhelming victory in their first strike. The second wave of 167 aircraft was approximately half way to their target area when Commander Mitsuo Fuchida's radioman-gunner tapped out the now-famous signal "To-ra! To-ra! To-ra!" on the Kate's radio-telegraph.[1]

Like the first wave, the second flew at staggered altitudes for greater maneuverability and better interception of enemy aircraft. The Japanese planned for strategic and tactical surprise. They anticipated the greatest damage to the capital ships would probably occur in the first few minutes of the strike due to hoped-for surprise and the planned 40 torpedoes and 50, single 1,765-pound bombs dropped by 50 of the 90 Kates allocated to the first wave.

They also anticipated the use of Kates in the low-altitude torpedo bomber role in the second wave would expose the slow, lumbering aircraft to heavy losses with little additional benefit. No torpedoes. Second, they planned to send the high-level, horizontal-bombing Kates entirely against the airfields, concentrating follow-on strikes to assure destruction of long range patrol and bomber aircraft and their support facilities at Kaneohe, Ford Island, and Hickam. A total knockout of the Navy and Air Force's long range patrol and bomber capabilities would greatly lower the odds of finding and seriously damaging their strike fleet.

To better accomplish their objectives the Kates in the second wave carried mixed loads of two 550-pound bombs, or one 550-pound plus six 132-pound bombs, instead of one 800 kilogram bomb, giving better area coverage on the airfield targets. They could salvo all their bombs in one pass or make multiple passes on targets, releasing one or more bombs at a time, depending on defenses they encountered.

Not only did the second wave include no torpedoes or heavy bombs on the Kates because of the different targets to be attacked, the Japanese sent only 54 Kates, whereas the first wave attack plan included 90. The fifty-four high-level Kates, divided into two groups of twenty-seven, passed in and out of clouds at 10,500 feet, on the starboard wing of the armada. The mission of Lieutenant Commander Shigekazu Shimazaki's Sixth Group, from the carrier *Zuikaku*, was to complete the destruction at Hickam Field. Lieutenant Tatsuo Ichihara led the Seventh Group from *Shokaku*. Ford Island was the target of 18 of his planes, while the objective of the other 9 was NAS Kaneohe Bay.

Below Shimazaki's Kates, at approximately 3,000 feet, and slightly to starboard—to the west—flew Egusa's 78 Val dive bombers. Again, though the Vals could carry considerably less ordnance than the same number of Kates, and the Japanese knew American gunners' blood would be boiling, they made a tactical decision to shift mission responsibility toward the faster, more maneuverable dive bombers in the second strike, after sending only 54 primarily against airfields in the first wave. Organized into four groups, their mission was to concentrate on as many ships as possible and wreck them beyond repair. Egusa led seventeen planes from *Soryu*. Lieutenant Michio Kobayashi was to lead another eighteen from *Soryu*, but engine trouble kept him aboard the carrier. Lieutenant Takehiko Chihaya commanded the Eleventh Group of eighteen dive bombers from *Akagi*, while Lieutenant Sakuro Makino led twenty-six from *Kaga*.

Lieutenant Saburo Shindo led 35 Zekes, weaving back and forth, providing top cover above the bombers. Shindo led the First Air Control Group from *Akagi*, Lieutenant Yasushi Nikaido

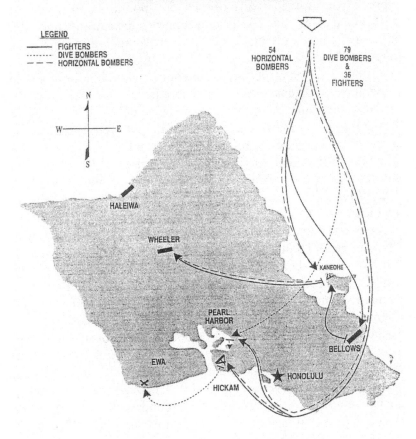

JAPANESE AIRCRAFT DEPLOYMENT
SECOND ATTACK

LEGEND
— FIGHTERS
⋯⋯ DIVE BOMBERS
– – HORIZONTAL BOMBERS

54
HORIZONTAL
BOMBERS

79
DIVE BOMBERS
&
35
FIGHTERS

N
W—E
S

HALEIWA

WHEELER

KANEOHE

PEARL
HARBOR

BELLOWS

EWA

HONOLULU

HICKAM

WHEELER, KANEOHE, BELLOWS, HICKAM, AND
PEARL HARBOR HIT BY FIGHTERS.
HORIZONTAL BOMBERS HIT KANEOHE, HICKAM,
AND PEARL HARBOR AND STRAFED WHEELER.
DIVE BOMBERS HIT PEARL HARBOR AND
STRAFED HICKAM AND EWA.

Japanese Aircraft Deployment, Second Attack.

the second from *Kaga*. Lieutenant Fusata Iida headed the Third Air Control Group from *Soryu*; and Lieutenant Sumio Nono led the Fourth Group from *Hiryu*. Besides cutting the enemy from the skies over Oahu, Nono's and Iida's fighters were to strafe Kaneohe, Bellows Field, and NAS Pearl Harbor, on Ford Island.

One fact was abundantly clear in Shindo's mind. His task would be more difficult than Itaya's in the first wave. The enemy wouldn't be surprised. The time lag of approximately thirty minutes between the end of the first attack and the beginning of the second would be enough to enable U.S. Forces to man their defenses in greater strength. Further, American gunners would be mad as hell, more practiced, their anticipation of enemy tactics improved, and their accuracy increased. Shindo's fears were well-founded. As the second wave approached Oahu, Japanese group leaders could plainly see tell-tale brownish puffs of smoke—flak bursts over the island.[2]

Because the Japanese carrier strike force had sailed further east from the first launch, before launching the second wave, the second wave approached the island and their targets generally from over the eastern half of the island, with twenty-seven of the high level Kates swinging in a wide arc over Koko Head, and approaching their Hickam Field targets from the southeast, from above Fort Kamehameha.[3]

When Shimazaki ordered his second wave to deploy into attack formations at 0850, defenders' guns were already warmed up. When he gave the order to "Attack!" almost five minutes later, the defense was something to reckon with.[4]

A Recall to Duty

At 0854 the lead elements of the second wave Vals began their follow-up attacks at Pearl Harbor, while Kate high level bombers and Zeke's struck Kaneohe and Hickam by 0900—and Zekes only struck Bellows. At 0855 Bob and Joey Border's phone rang in their upstairs apartment. Bob picked up the receiver. Lieutenant (jg) John R. "Bud" Marron, a doctor (Medical Corps) and the assistant medical officer on the *Tennessee*, was on the line. Bud told Bob all naval officers were to report to duty. The Japanese were attacking the Fleet.

Bob, in stunned disbelief, hung up and repeated to Joey, "The Japanese are attacking the Fleet." He raced to get dressed. Joey asked him what was happening. "The Japs are bombing the Pacific Fleet! I have to report for duty!" "What did you say?" came Joey's startled response. "The Japs are attacking Pearl Harbor, and l have to report to duty. Turn on the radio." He pulled on his underwear, socks, and trousers, buttoned and tucked his shirt in his trousers, grabbed his belt, tie, billfold, and cap. While he was dressing, still in disbelief, they heard an announcer saying "Oahu is being attacked by enemy planes. Please keep calm." He rushed downstairs taking two or three steps at a time. Joey couldn't think of anything to say but, "Have fun" and

"I love you," words that later in the day struck her as completely inadequate.

Joey stood silent as he stormed out the front door and hurried to the old jalopy Noel Gayler had loaned them. She thought for a moment then turned to listen to the radio. The attack had been under way for more than an hour, and Honolulu radio had already begun emergency broadcasts, periodically reminding the population that Japanese aircraft were attacking Pearl Harbor, Hickam Field and other military installations on the island.

Noel Gayler, a pilot on the *Enterprise* who had previously taken both Bob and Karl on airplane rides, routinely left his old car with Bob and Joey when the *Enterprise* was at sea. It was often their primary means of transportation. This day Bob drove on a wild ride to the dock, into the teeth of a traffic jam. Army, Navy, Marine and Army Air Force men were scrambling to their duty stations, as hundreds of recalled Navy men tried to get through the main gate into the Yard and to their ships. He was forced to take a roundabout route across the harbor to the *Tennessee*. Fires started by *Arizona* were drifting down-harbor, uncontrolled fires were burning forward and amidships on *West Virginia*—with heavy, dark plumes of smoke occasionally obscuring *Tennessee* from view.

He made it to the docks without being strafed by Japanese fighters, but the traffic coming into the Naval Base was heavy— six lanes wide at the main gate. After all the emphasis on the likelihood of sabotage, Bob thought it odd that the Shore Patrol waived in speeding automobiles without checking identification. He drove to a vacant lot near the dock where *Tennessee*'s motor launches normally loaded and unloaded men going to and from the ship. None were in sight. He waited, then heard coxswains on other boats calling, "All boats! All boats!" He took one of these, and went to Ford Island to make his way aboard ship.

All he could see were motor launches from other ships moving about the harbor, huge columns of smoke almost obscuring the wreck of *Arizona*, the sinking *West Virginia*, the forlorn *Oklahoma* capsized, with *Tennessee* occasionally appearing when the smoke momentarily allowed a glimpse. *California* was down by the stern with the river of fire from *Arizona* heading toward the stricken ship, and it appeared *Nevada* was aground on the near side of the harbor, close to the drydocks. At least *Tennessee* and *Maryland* weren't sinking, but he was to learn *Tennessee*'s motor launches and whale boats had all been damaged or consumed by fire, and fires were burning below the quarterdeck.

By the time Bob arrived at his 5th Division duty station, the

The Japanese second wave flew into a veritable hornets' nest of fleet air defense fire. View of Pearl Harbor looking southwest from the hills to the north. Taken during the Japanese raid, with anti-aircraft shell bursts overhead. Large column of smoke in lower center is from the *Arizona* (BB-39). Smaller smoke columns further to the left are from the destroyers *Shaw* (DD-373), *Cassin* (DD-372) and *Downes* (DD-375), in dry docks at the Pearl Harbor Navy Yard. NA

second wave of attackers had finished their work—but long days and sleepless nights were just beginning for survivors of the attack. When he came aboard, his 5th Division had been directed to assist in fighting the fires on *Tennessee*'s after deck. *Arizona*'s fires doggedly persisted, illuminating *Tennessee* as a relatively unscathed, inviting target while the entire island of Oahu was blacked out each night.[5]

Pennsylvania, Cassin, Downes, and Shaw: Attack on the Dry Docks

During the first wave attacks the battleship *Pennsylvania* (BB-38) and destroyers *Downes* (DD-375), *Cassin* (DD-372), and *Shaw* (DD-373), though hemmed in in drydocks on the east side of the harbor, remained relatively free of heavy attack and initially sustained much less damage than ships moored adjacent to Ford Island, or the *Helena* and *Oglala* at 1010 dock astern of *Pennsylvania*. As the attack progressed, the raiders increasingly turned their fury on *Nevada* steaming slowly down-channel, the settling *California* in Berth F-3 across the channel, and these four ships in dry dock.

When the raid began, the *Pennsylvania*, 31,400 tons and 608 feet long, was in Dry Dock No. 1 with three propeller shafts removed. The much smaller destroyers *Cassin* and *Downes*, each 1,500 tons and 341 feet in length were directly ahead, side by side, toward the south in the same dock, with *Downes* to starboard. *Shaw*, a same-size *Mahan* Class ship, was in the old *New Orleans* floating dry dock (YFD2), just beyond the new, empty dry dock to the west of No. 1, and next to the main channel. Though the much larger, heavily armored battleship was a prime target for the Japanese, the three, thin-plated destroyers, were far more vulnerable to catastrophic damage from bombs of any size—and eventually paid a heavy price.

The battleship's crew had been excused from antiaircraft drills, and because of being in drydock wasn't scheduled for Sunday drills. However, gunners manned the machine guns in the foremast, and a Conditional Watch of antiaircraft crews was available, but not on the guns. The ship was receiving steam, power and water from the Yard. *Pennsylvania*'s commander, Captain Charles M. Cooke, Jr., was aboard, as was the First Lieutenant.

Captain Cooke, writing on 16 December using his recollections and the reports submitted by officers and men in his crew, described the attacks as seen from *Pennsylvania.*

> First call to colors had been sounded, when about 0757, explosions were heard on the end of Ford Island abreast drydock #1. When [the] second explosion took place, it was realized that an air raid was in progress. Men started proceeding to their stations and "Air Defense" was sounded. Shortly after, general quarters sounded. Condition "YOKE" was set as soon as stations were manned. In many cases men knocked off locks of ammunition ready boxes and ready stowages, not waiting for keys. 0802—Attack by torpedo planes came in from West and South, attacking OGLALA and HELENA and battleships across the channel. Number of planes not recorded, estimate 12 or 15.
>
> 0802 to 0805 (Exact time not known). PENNSYLVANIA commenced firing at enemy planes,—reported as first ship opening fire by personnel on board. All anti-aircraft batteries were rapidly brought into action. After release of torpedoes three planes came in low from the port beam, strafing PENNSYLVANIA,—strafing attack not effective. During torpedo attack, one enemy plane was observed to burst into flames about 2,000 yards on the starboard bow.
>
> Dive bombing attacks, torpedo attack on Pearl Harbor and dive bombing attacks on Hickam Field continued.
>
> Sometime between 8 and 8:30 a.m. the NEVADA was observed to be getting underway and had reached a point about on the PENNSYLVANIA'S starboard quarter, distant about 600 yards when a dive bombing attack was observed to be approaching the PENNSYLVANIA on the port bow, 10 to 15 planes coming in succession, low altitude. This was between 0830 and 0900. This attack apparently was directed at PENNSYLVANIA and the two destroyers in the dock. These attacking planes were taken under

heavy fire. Just before reaching PENNSYLVANIA, about two-thirds appeared to swerve to the left, a number of them dropping bombs at the NEVADA, with some misses ahead and some misses astern, and at least one hit apparently in the vicinity of the bridge. The NEVADA was observed to stop.

At the same time, other planes of this attack passed to port and over the PENNSYLVANIA and dropped bombs which fell in the water beyond the caisson [the temporary structure at the aft end of the drydock, beyond Pennsylvania's stern]. Except probably for machine gun bullets it is believed that the PENNSYLVANIA was not hit during this attack.

One of the dive bombers dropped a bomb on the SHAW in the floating drydock, setting it on fire . . .

The first two of three bombs to hit the *Shaw* were devastating. The attacking Vals, from the "10 to 15" approaching from port to starboard in the formation described by *Pennsylvania*'s Captain Cooke, released them at approximately 1,000 feet, in a steep dive. They struck the machine gun platform just aft of 5-inch gun #2; penetrated the gun shelter platform, forecastle and main decks; and exploded in the crew's mess room on the first platform deck. Though a considerable number of crewmembers were on liberty because the ship was in drydock, casualties were heavy among a full complement of approximately 155 men.

The third bomb, which struck the *Shaw* about the same time, came from a Val approaching in a shallower, approximate 30-degree dive, more from the port quarter [east]. It struck the port side of the destroyer's superstructure deck, passed through the corner formed by the aft side of the radio room and the port side of the stores office, entered the supply office, went out through the starboard aft corner of the office, and overboard through the starboard rail just above the main deck—without exploding within the ship.

Fire broke out at once as a result of the first two hits. Oil from ruptured fuel tanks spread in the areas near where the fires broke out, and poured into the dock below. The fire soon spread, fueled by the ship's burning paint and oil from the blown tanks. Twenty minutes later the forward magazines blew up—a spectacular, violent explosion seen for miles, which appeared to rival the terrible shattering of *Arizona*. The explosion literally lifted the forward portion of the ship off its blocks, severed the ship's bow at about frame 65, with the exception of some bottom structure, and rained debris on the surrounding docks.

The dry dock was deliberately flooded to help quench the fire and prevent more damage. As it sank, the bow of *Shaw* toppled over to starboard and went down with the dock. The Yard tug *Sotoyomo* was also in the dock and sank with it. As the dock sank, oil from ruptured tanks burned on the water surrounding the ship. A strong wind from the stern aided crewmen who saved the after portion of the ship.

The *Shaw*'s crew never had a chance to effectively enter the fight against the raiders. They spent all their efforts attempting to save one another and their ship, and paid a terrible price.

Sailors stand amid wrecked planes at the Ford Island seaplane base, watching as the destroyer *Shaw* (DD-373) explodes in the center background, 7 December 1941. The seaman in the foreground is Bob Barrigan, from Oklahoma City, Oklahoma, a crewmember on the seaplane tender *Tangier*. *Nevada* (BB-36) is also visible in the middle background, with her bow angled toward the left and her colors visible to the right. Planes present include PBY, OS2U and SOC types. Wrecked wing in the foreground is from a PBY. NPSAM

Twenty-four men were killed outright or died of wounds, and many more were wounded, some seriously, as a result of the bombing, ensuing fire, and explosion. The *Downes* and *Cassin* were suffering similar fates, but not quite so severe.[6]

Similar to *Shaw*, *Downes* and her crew remained untouched the first hour of the attack on Pearl Harbor. Like the *Pennsylvania*, the *Downes* was receiving steam, electricity, fresh and salt water "over the dock" from Navy Yard sources. Work was in progress on the stern tubing, strut bearings, shell plating forward, replacement of tripod mast with stick mast, and various minor jobs. Large sections of shell plating had been removed on both sides forward, preparatory to substituting heavier plate.

When the raid began, 142 enlisted men and five officers were on board, with four officers and four enlisted on authorized liberty. The commanding officer, Lieutenant Commander William R. Thayer; Executive Officer, Lieutenant William O. Snead; Engineer Officer, Lieutenant William A. Hunt; and Gunnery Officer, Ensign John B. Balch were on liberty. Lieutenant (jg) Jefferson D. Parker was duty officer, senior officer on board, and thus the acting commander.

Typical of ships in dry dock, the *Downes*'s ammunition and gun readiness were considerably less than desired. Her 5-inch guns' breech plugs and tripping latches had been removed for alteration, and 310 rounds of 5-inch ammunition removed to the Naval Ammunition Depot to permit yard work in connection with depth charge stowage. The remainder of the 5-inch ammunition was distributed throughout all magazines. Fifty caliber machine guns had been dismounted and stowed in a locker, and all belted .50-caliber ammunition removed to the Ammunition Depot to permit yard work. The remainder of .50-caliber ammunition was in forward magazines, unclipped. She had twelve torpedoes with war heads fitted in tube mounts, with air flasks bled down. Eight depth charges were in racks, six fire suppressant tanks charged and mounted, and several voice powered [battle] telephones in repair. After receiving reports from all officers and men on board during the attack, the ship's captain, Lieutenant Commander Thayer summarized events leading to the *Downes* virtual destruction that morning.

Several men on deck, including the Chief Petty Officer with the day's duty, sighted the Val dive bombers coming out of the clouds to attack Ford Island. The Chief immediately ordered the sounding of general quarters and notified Lieutenant (jg) Parker. The crew rushed to their stations, set condition Afirm, closing all doors, hatches, and manholes to maintain watertight integrity—except where prevented by the temporary ventilation ducts forward. They checked closure of sea valves, and began intense efforts to prepare the ship for fighting.

The machine guns were quickly readied for firing, and work began on assembling the breech plugs of the 5-inch battery. Ammunition details broke out ammunition for both the machine guns and the 5-inch guns. Because there was no belted ammunition, they obtained two magazines from the *Cassin* to open fire as soon as possible. Yard power was lost at 0810, necessitating ammunition trains be formed to pass ammunition by hand. The lines worked in total darkness until flashlights could be obtained, and as a result no tracer ammunition could be found. Men not occupied, which included men of the engineers' force and most of the 5-inch gun crews, belted machine gun ammunition. The 5-inch crews continued to supply and belt ammunition until their guns were ready to fire.

The speed with which the crew armed the *Downes*'s antiaircraft guns to fight, gratified their skipper. Eager machine gunners opened fire within fifteen minutes after the raid began—aiming at the high-level bombers that were well out of effective range. The result was a "cease fire." In the meantime, the 0810 power failure sent several men from the engineers' force, under Chief Machinist's Mate Charles B. Johnston and Chief Electrician's Mate James M. Raidy, scrambling to start the emergency diesel generator. Working by the light of the battle lanterns, at 0823 the engineers were able to take power and light from the emergency generator. Switches activated power to the ammunition hoists, and afterward the hoist for Gun #2 brought up ammunition.

With the loss of yard power, no power was available for the operation of the 5-inch battery and battery director; however, as soon as Gun #3 was ready (about 0845), the crew loaded it by hand and fired a test shot to see how the ship would stand the shock of firing while dry-docked. The test was successful, and Ensign Richard W. Robinson, who had been in charge of the forward machine guns, took charge of Gun #3 and stood by to open fire in local control. Ensign Richard L. Stewart had been sent to control the aft machine guns. Ensign Richard Sebbo took control of the forward machine guns. Ensign Comly was in charge of the ammunition details, and Lieutenant (jg) Parker directed operations from the bridge. *Downes* and *Cassin* were both ready and eager to battle the raiders after the first wave passed without damage, but in minutes the two destroyers suffered shattering blows that took both out of the fight.

At 0850, a six minute lull had begun. The raiders' second wave, with Lieutenant Commander Takashige Egusa's Val dive bombers in the lead, was about to descend on the ships in the drydock, and on the *Nevada* coming down-channel toward the harbor entrance. Lieutenant Parker was asked if the *Downes* was ready for the dock to be flooded. After a quick check, he replied in the affirmative. At 0857, as *Shaw* was being struck, hell came to visit both destroyers, and it was miraculous that the two ships together didn't suffer the wounded and loss of life that wracked the *Shaw*.

Three Val dive bombers approaching from the southeast attacked *Pennsylvania*, *Downes* and *Cassin* in a steep dive— three of the 10 to 15 the *Pennsylvania*'s Captain Cooke described. The remainder rolled into dives and veered to their left, striking *Shaw* and aiming to attack and sink the *Nevada* in the channel. *Downes*'s forward and aft machine guns immediately opened fire on the three Vals pressing toward Dry Dock No. 1. All the dive bombers were taken under intense fire by the ships they were targeting, as well as gunners on any ship in range of the attackers.

At the same time, *Downes*'s 5-inch, Gun #3 was attempting to take the first of five flights of attacking high level horizontal bombers under fire. They were tracking toward the battleships and were seen to release bombs just after passing the dry dock. Parker asked the *Cassin*'s commander, the senior destroyer officer present, for permission to test fire the gun. The gun got off one round just before a bomb hit the dry dock between *Downes* and *Cassin*, abreast *Downes*'s Gun #5, killing two men outright. The explosion ruptured the diesel fuel oil tank, set it afire, and stopped the generator. The ship was without power or lights. Fire instantaneously enveloped the aft part of the destroyer, and flames spread rapidly, covering the after deck house and gun shelters. Heat was intense.

The repair party and gun crews quickly manned fire hoses, and turned water on the flames. The flow was insufficient, a problem soon corrected, but the men found the water ineffective— spreading the fire rather than suppressing it. Within minutes the fire was out of control. In the engine room, Chief Machinists Mate Johnston, with other men, successfully fought several small fires until they were overwhelmed and Johnston ordered them to abandon the engine room at 0912.

Topside, Lieutenant Parker ordered the crew to abandon the aft part of the *Downes*. He was unaware flames were already driving men off the ship. He ordered the aft magazines flooded, but didn't have time to confirm the order was carried out. A few seconds later, at about 0920, he concluded the situation was hopeless and ordered "abandon ship." Shortly after Parker gave the order to abandon ship, another bomb hit between the *Cassin* and *Downes* abreast the bridge structure setting the quarterdeck and forward part of the *Downes* afire.

In the meantime Johnston, having abandoned the engine room, had raced to the main deck and he and Chief Electricians Mate Raidy fought the fire until nearly everyone else was off the ship. Raidy stayed fighting the fire too long and too close, and suddenly found his clothing in flames. Johnston rolled him on the deck to put out the fire, the two men left the ship, and Raidy, undeterred, later manned a hose on the dock and continued fighting the fires until he was taken to the hospital with serious burns.

Above and below decks, in the face of bombs, strafing, and the huge, racing fire, heroics abounded. Pharmacist Mate Third Class Adam A. Balzak continued dressing a man's wounds at the aft battle dressing station with flames all around outside. He barely escaped in time. Chief Pharmacist Mate Shirley W. Richardson tried to lead several men off the ship, but they were lost. Machinist Mate Second Class William Ernst tore a burning shirt from a shipmate, probably saving his life, then Boatswain Mate Lewis Hite helped save the same shipmate by leading him part way off the ship—then returned to connect fire hoses, and later chased other men off the ship in time to save them.

Chief Gunner's Mate Henry E. Cradoct was largely responsible for the speed with which the machine guns were mounted, ammunition belted and supplied to the machine guns, ammunition delivered to the 5-inch battery, and 5-inch guns #2 and #3 made ready to fire. Charles M. Hooke, Elmer S. Stadelman, James J. Foundation, and Eric L. Thompson, all Seamen First Class, manned the forward and aft machine guns and displayed remarkable courage and coolness in the face of grave danger. Remaining topside, in action at their stations—as long as possible—in spite of the fire, bombing and strafing, all firing their guns whenever targets were available.

Fireman Second Class Edward T. Kwolik remained on the ship in the face of grave danger, even after being ordered off. He stayed to keep a fire hose on the after engine room hatch, to permit men in the engine room to escape. Seaman Second Class Paul O. Postlethwaite was injured while checking the setting of condition Afirm prior to reporting the ship ready for the dock to be flooded. He continued his duties, fighting fire in the ship, then, forced to leave the ship over the fantail, fighting fires from the dock until hit by fragments and severely wounded.

Lieutenant Parker attempted to personally check that all men were off the ship, but the flames, fed by diesel and fuel oil, the ship's painted surfaces, and fanned by the wind, swept diagonally across the ship, setting it on fire from bow to stern. Most of the men escaped over the brow [temporary bridge or ramp between the ship and dock], located on the second deck just forward of the chart house. Some had been trapped and driven off the ship over the fantail. As the last survivors were leaving the ship, another bomb struck the bridge, completely destroying the director platform, bridge, and chart house.

Having released all their bombs the Vals returned with strafing attacks, and when they ended, some of the *Downes* men, like Raidy, went to the windward side of the dock and manned hoses. Others assisted in moving the wounded to the hospital or first aid stations, while several others, including two gunners' mates, went to the marine barracks to assist in giving out arms and ammunition. The two shortly returned to take up stations where they might fire on attacking planes.

Soon after the ship was abandoned, a violent explosion occurred amidships at torpedo tube #3, tearing a large hole in the side and main deck in the vicinity of the tube mount, demolishing the number two stack, and sending fragments onto the *Pennsylvania*'s bow. As the fire progressed, powder from the forward magazines blew out through the sides of the ship, and 5-inch ammunition in the gun shelters exploded periodically, sending out frequent showers of metal fragments in all directions. Parker and several men tending hoses received wounds from the fragments. The explosions became so dangerous that, for a few minutes, it was necessary to abandon the hoses, which were futile against the fire at that time. Later the hoses were concentrated on the sterns of *Cassin* and *Downes*, to save the depth charges.

The *Downes* lost twelve men killed or died of wounds. Many others were wounded, most due to burns. In his 17 December Action Report, *Downes*'s skipper, Lieutenant Commander Thayer was effusive in his individual praise of twenty-one men, including Chiefs Johnston and Raidy, and Lieutenant Parker. In his descriptions of what they had done individually and collectively, he used such characteristics as performance of duty, knowledge of skills and training, leadership, coolness, good judgment, resourcefulness, courage in the face of grave danger, energy, loyalty, complete disregard for their own safety, and determined actions under fire. In large measure he summarized much of what could be said of crew members on every ship attacked in the harbor that morning.

Once he surveyed the damage inflicted on the *Downes*, he knew he would never again command her and her crew. He would go elsewhere and serve. He ended his report with these words:

> The ship was lost, but . . . [I have] . . . naught but praise for the officers and men of the crew who fought her under such unfortunate circumstances. They did their utmost to inflict damage on the enemy, working against almost insurmountable odds. They did all in their power to save the ship from fire. They showed they were real shipmates with a concern for each other's safety. They were loyal and determined. Their primary concern during the engagement was to get the guns in action, and their biggest regret was that they couldn't meet the enemy in a fair fight at sea. I am proud to have commanded the U.S.S. Downes.[7]

Cassin fared little better than *Downes*, except for the number of casualties. At approximately 0750, as *Cassin*'s skipper, Lieutenant Commander Daniel F.J. Shea, stepped from his cabin to go below to breakfast, Chief Gunner's Mate Ernest L. James, dashed into the passageway and said, "Captain they are here, bombing Hickam Field." Shea stepped aft and out the starboard passageway door, and about 100 feet away from the starboard side of drydock #1 he saw an airplane with large red discs on the bottom of its wings—at an altitude of approximately 100 feet.

He immediately ordered Chief James to sound general quarters and started for the bridge. There was no power on the general alarm so James had the word passed verbally. Fifty caliber machine guns prepared to open fire, but similar to the other destroyers' guns, *Cassin's*

5-inch AA guns were undergoing modification. Men had to be dispatched to the Navy Yard to see if parts could be obtained for the 5-inch battery.

At 0800 Shea saw a Kate torpedo bomber coming down in a glide to about 75 feet on a course paralleling the dry dock a short distance from its port side. On reaching the channel the Kate turned slightly left, heading straight for the *California*, across the main channel—where the pilot released the torpedo at a range of approximately 200 yards from the battleship. The Kate kept going and disappeared from sight.

A few moments later the *Helena* opened fire, followed by the *Pennsylvania*. *Cassin* and *Downes* opened up with .50-caliber machine guns. Both the executive officer and gunnery officer were ashore, as was the sound powered telephone talker who, when normally at his station, relayed commands and information. Shea called by voice down to Gun #2 to expedite retrieving breech plugs at the Navy Yard if possible, and ordered men to seek protection of gun shelters, as he had no guns to fire. Some stayed out from cover to see what was going on. Others assisted repair parties who led out hoses and stood by for handling damage.

Approximately 0810 he saw a Japanese plane, low and descending with a tail of flame 50 feet long, parallel to the *Pennsylvania* and *Downes*, and disappear over the trees to crash near the hospital. A few minutes later five high altitude bombers passed overhead at approximately 12,000 feet, from forward aft and let go large bombs after they passed No.1 Dry Dock.

Shortly, Shea saw Captain Charles D. Swain and Lieutenant Commander Bernard E. Manseau coming down to the drydock, and went to meet them. They requested he close up both destroyers preparatory to flooding the dry dock, though about 30 ports below main deck forward were off because, like *Downes* and *Shaw*, *Cassin* was about to have heavier plating installed.

He directed all hands, except the machine gunners, close up the ship as quickly and completely as possible—portholes, bulkhead doors, hatches, manholes, from the lower decks up, similar to setting condition Zed. The crew responded rapidly, though having to cut numerous power cables leading from one compartment to another, before dogging down doors. Closing up the ship also necessitated disconnecting leads from large portable blowers forward, which had been set up for fresh air circulation during work on the plates.

Shea returned to the bridge when he was certain the closing was satisfactorily underway, just in time to see a second flight of high level bombers pass overhead, apparently tracking toward the battleships. Then about 0830 *Pennsylvania* signaled via semaphore [hand held signal flags], "Senior destroyer officer report aboard." During the sending of the message, intense gunfire from *Pennsylvania*, *Cassin* and the enemy, interrupted the signalmen, causing them to seek cover and try twice to send and acknowledge receipt of the message.

Now assured the ship's closure was well underway, he left the *Cassin*'s bridge for *Pennsylvania*, having secured the phones and called a signalman to notify Ensign Frank M. Culpepper, next in line of command, that he would be right back. When he was almost to the bow of *Pennsylvania*, the *Downes* was hit on the after deckhouse by a small bomb. Smoke and dust were rising as he ran along the dock. The 3-inch AA on *Pennsylvania* was firing fast and efficiently. He climbed aboard the battleship amid terrific blasts of fast-shooting guns, climbed to the conning tower then to the next level above, to Captain Cooke.

Cooke asked him if *Cassin* was preparing for flooding of the dock, stating that even without *Pennsylvania*'s propellers he wanted to get it flooded. Shea answered "Yes" and left, believing Captain Swain and Lieutenant Commander Manseau had not seen Cooke at the same time they saw him about flooding.

Between Shea's arrival on *Pennsylvania*'s brow and his departure for *Cassin*, the *Downes* was hit hard, at 0857, and huge flames erupted all over her, and on the starboard side of *Cassin*. As he ran forward toward his ship, he saw a gaping hole in the dock where a bomb had hit at 0906, abreast of *Cassin*'s stern, and the hole was emitting clouds of smoke. He skirted the hole on the run. The flames convinced him the fire couldn't be successfully fought, and as soon as he passed the hole and the stern of the ship he started waving men off *Cassin*. He had felt a sharp increase in the heat emanating from both the hole and the ship as he passed her stern, and feared a magazine explosion.

Word had already been passed to "Abandon ship," and crew

members were passing the command throughout the ship as they converged toward the brow from forward and aft. Unknown to Shea at the time, his earlier orders to "close up the ship" preparatory to flooding the dry dock, had been life-saving to his entire crew. As he had previously ordered, they had worked from the bottom up, and were nearly all topside when they received and began passing the order to abandon ship.

He soon learned there was no water to fight the fire. The #3 .50-caliber gun was on fire because it lacked cooling water, and there was none in the men's wash room due to interrupted service from the Yard. When he passed the stern of *Cassin*, moving forward, he continued waving men off the ship repeatedly shouting for them to "Step out! Step out!" He arrived at the brow as the last group of men came off the ship. Ensign Culpepper, Shea's designated acting commander, was the last man.

Shea saw what he believed to be a hole in the brow, and later learned a small bomb had passed through the brow and ship without exploding—just ahead of Ensign Macon E. Callicott as he was leaving the ship. Another small bomb was believed to have hit in the galley [kitchen] passage as well—with no casualties. Nevertheless, the near-miraculous survival of *Cassin*'s crew wasn't assured yet.

After the entire crew was off the ship, within a few minutes the first hose arrived from the Yard, then others. Shea directed the first six or eight hoses be kept on the port side of *Cassin*. Wind was carrying flames and heat away from them, over the *Downes*. Because there were no hoses on the side nearest *Downes*, fires raging on *Cassin* were impossible to fight from the starboard side of the drydock. He concentrated fire hoses on *Cassin*'s depth charges and torpedo tubes to keep them from exploding. Several times everyone had to retreat before the intense heat and fragments from small explosions tearing at *Cassin*, but they pressed forward again each time, trying to keep the flames from causing far more violent explosions.

Shortly after the last surviving crewmember left *Downes* at approximately 0920, and flooding of the dock was just beginning, the violent explosion occurred in *Downes'* torpedo tube #3. Flames shot about 60 feet in the air, hurling fragments in all directions and practically tearing hoses away from fire fighting parties—which consisted of men from *Downes*, *Cassin* and Yard employees. All hands retreated from the dock and sprawled on the road. Lieutenant Parker, a few feet to Shea's right, was hit, as was Fireman First Class C.L. Talbert, to his left. He first thought Parker's neck badly cut because it was bleeding heavily, and directed him and Talbert to the hospital in a nearby small truck. Within a short time Parker was back, minus his coat and his head bandaged, rejoining the fire fighting forces.

Cassin, also undergoing replacement of a large number of her forward plates, finally slipped from her keel blocks and rolled to starboard, into *Downes*. The two ships' fires were brought under control approximately 1045, after the raiders withdrew to their carriers. However *Cassin* was far more fortunate than her sister ship in terms of crew losses. Because she took no hits from exploding bombs, and her skipper and crew could react more deliberately in retreating before the fire, she lost not one man and only a few were wounded.

Commander Leland P. Lovette, commander of Destroyer Division Five, and the *Cassin*'s executive officer, arrived after both ships were abandoned and the fires were still raging. With one quick look, Lovette told Shea to take charge of *Cassin* and *Downes* as he would go at once to the *Reid* or *Conyngham* to sortie. He returned in about ten minutes to say he was going out on *Cummings* and would take about 25 men from *Cassin*, to include the best gunnery and torpedo personnel. About 60 went to *Cummings*, but 40 returned.

Lieutenant Commander Shea wrote of his crew, on a ship he would never again command:

> The conduct of the men was superb, particularly the quiet overall supervision by the Chief Boatswain Mate, [JOHN] T. STRATTON, who seemed everywhere at the same time directing closure and abandoning. At no time was there any fear or panic, but merely rage not only at an enemy attack but at inability, after months of training, to be able to return fire. The entire crew behaved in accordance with the best traditions of the Service.[8]

The battleship *Pennsylvania* didn't suffer the near fatal damage which shattered the two destroyers, and their sister ship, the USS *Shaw*, but sadly, losses among her crew and men from several other ships who rallied to help defend against the Japanese onslaught,

were heavier. Beginning at 0830, the engine room watch lighted
fires under #4 boiler, but raising steam on board was hampered
because of smoke coming from a cold boiler. The smoke interfered
with antiaircraft fire, so its effects had to be minimized.

At 0906, bombs delivered by aircraft in the second wave,
from the second flight of Val dive bombers, struck *Pennsylvania*,
the dry dock on the starboard side of the battleship, and
Downes simultaneously. The hit on the dry dock was near the
bow, abreast Frame 20. Another hit on the drydock was port
side, probably at the same time, caused the gaping hole that
Lieutenant Commander Shea ran past returning to *Cassin*.
The only direct hit on *Pennsylvania*, a 550-pound bomb, was
devastating. Boatswain Mate Andrew Hoover experienced the
deadly randomness of war when the bomb plunged through the
battleship's decks and exploded.

When the air raid began, Andy was at the Navy's Receiving
Station at Pearl Harbor, awaiting reassignment after serving on the
heavy cruiser *Astoria* (CA-34). Like many at the receiving station
awaiting travel home, to technical schools, or reassignment to
other ships, the attack angered him. He saw the violent explosion
which sank the *Arizona*, the raging fires on the sinking *West
Virginia*, and the upturned hull of the capsized *Oklahoma*. He
joined with five other seamen from other ships, destroyers he
remembered, wanting to assist somewhere, because ". . . we all
felt we should be doing something more than being spectators."
They concluded they couldn't get back to their ships. He couldn't
return to the *Astoria*. She had left Pearl on 6 December with Task
Force 12, led by the *Lexington*, carrying aircraft to reinforce
Midway Island. Other men at the Receiving Station were going
by vehicle to other ships moored in the East Loch. The men knew
their crews would be shorthanded, and would need help to get
their guns firing. As a result, during the lull between the first and
second wave of attacks, Andy and the five other men hitched a
ride on a flatbed truck that took them to dry dock #1, where they
boarded *Pennsylvania* to offer assistance.

En route, there was little conversation, and not much time
to get better acquainted. He wouldn't remember the names of
the destroyers he believed the five had come from. If the men
introduced themselves to one another, they wouldn't remember
their names either. They were attentive to the skies above,
watching for more enemy planes, and to the fierce fires raging on

Ford Island and the battleships. They witnessed from a distance the violent explosion of the *Shaw*, could see *Nevada* getting underway toward the harbor entrance, and as the truck passed 1010 dock, nearing the *Pennsylvania*, they saw the listing mine layer *Oglala*, and the torpedoed cruiser *Helena*.

When they climbed the brow of *Pennsylvania*, there wasn't the usual Officer of the Deck to report to—no formalities—and men were too busy to ask who they were. Instead, the six simply walked across the deck, port to starboard, where an antiaircraft gun crew near the door to the marines' quarters told them to go below, through the watertight door behind them, the urgency heard in the words, "The planes are coming again." As they crossed the deck, Andy saw the *Nevada* still moving toward the harbor entrance, now almost abeam the *Pennsylvania*.

When he went through the door and down the ladder, he passed through the compartment below 5-inch Gun #7, and was sent on to the next deck to join an ammunition train. He had just reached the bottom of the ladder on the third deck, and turned around to help pass along antiaircraft ammunition on a conveyor composed of rollers, when the 550-pound bomb penetrated the boat deck above. It ripped through the deck inside the protective shield, just aft of 5-inch Gun #7. After passing through the boat deck, it detonated in the compartment below, the Marines' quarters, blowing a 20-foot by 20-foot hole upward through the boat deck, and another similar-size hole downward through the casemate deck. [A casemate is the protective, steel shelter for a gun crew.] The explosion blew out the bulkhead just aft of Gun #9, put the gun out of action, wrecked a considerable part of the galley equipment, and caused fuel oil from the service tank to run into the decks below.

The bomb hit on the dock cut yard power, and subsequently power on the ship for lights and gun operation, which was taken up by the ship's storage batteries. At the same time, fire main pressure received from the yard was cut off. The ship's lights went out until the shift to battery operation, and it was almost pitch black below. Fire erupted in the casemate and on the main and second decks, and was difficult to put out. Fire fighters were forced to use a large number of extinguishers because the fire mains lacked pressure, and painted cork lining bulkheads were hard to extinguish.

Explosion blast and fragments dished in the main deck and

The wrecked destroyers *Downes* (DD-375) and *Cassin* (DD-372) in Dry Dock One at the Pearl Harbor Navy Yard, soon after the end of the Japanese air attack. *Cassin* has capsized against *Downes*. *Pennsylvania* (BB-38) is astern, occupying the rest of the drydock. The torpedo-damaged cruiser *Helena* (CL-50) is in the right distance, beyond the crane. Visible in the center distance is the capsized *Oklahoma* (BB-37), with *Maryland* (BB-46) alongside. Smoke is from the sunken and burning *Arizona* (BB-39), out of view behind *Pennsylvania*. *California* (BB-44) is partially visible at the extreme left. NA

penetrated the second deck. Three-inch ammunition was being passed through the compartment on the main deck just forward of the clipping room, serving the 3-inch Gun #3 on the quarterdeck. At the time of the explosion, boxes containing 24 rounds of 3-inch ammunition were in this compartment, and the blast perforated eight cartridge cases of 3-inch projectiles, causing the propellant powder to burn—but none exploded.

The bomb's explosion also dished the casing of the ammunition hoist to the 5-inch battery putting the hoist out of action, and raised the platform for operation of 5-inch Gun #7, which was adjacent to the large section of the deck blown up. After the explosion the gun couldn't be trained [swung in azimuth] to the limits of its train forward. Fragments on the boat deck struck a 40-foot motor sailing launch in the skids, perforating the sides in a number of places. The motor launch probably saved some men manning port guns.

Casualties. Therein lay the irony of the single bomb hit on the *Pennsylvania*. When the bomb exploded at 0906, she suffered much greater loss of life than did the *Tennessee* and *Maryland* combined, each hit by two bombs while their crews fought to avoid their ships' destruction along with *Oklahoma*, *Arizona*, and the *West Virginia*. On 16 December Captain Cooke reported the explosion at casement #9 caused the deaths of "about 26 men and two officers," including six Marines. "Twenty-nine more were wounded," he wrote, all but a few with "multiple wounds or severe burns." One officer, *Pennsylvania's* First Lieutenant, Lieutenant Commander James E. Craig, was killed when probably passing through the compartment to carry out specially assigned duties aft. Lieutenant (jg) Richard R. Rall, the junior medical officer, was at the battle dressing station in the Warrant Officer's Mess Room, when killed.

Among the dead were the men at the gun near the bulkhead door Andy and his five brief acquaintances went through to go below for reasons of safety. Because the bulkhead door was left open, the blast and enough of the death-dealing fragments were funneled through the open door to kill the entire gun crew.

But a greater irony was the fate of eight men from five different ships who, joined the fight assisting the dry docked *Pennsylvania*, and gave their lives trying to help other men defend their ship and shipmates. From the destroyer *Chew* (DD-106), Seaman Second Class Mathew J. Agola and Fireman Third Class Clarence A.

Wise. From the destroyer tender *Dobbin* (AD-3), Gunners' Mate First Class Andrew M. Marze. From the light minelayer *Pruitt* (DM-22), Radiomen's Mate Third Class George R. Keith, and from light minelayer *Sicard* (DM-21), Seaman Second Class Warren P. Hickok. From their sister ship, the light minelayer, *Tracy* (DM-19), there were three from among approximately fifteen dispatched to assist the battleship's crew: Seaman First Class John A. Bird, Radiomen's Mate Third Class John W. Pence, and Seaman First Class Laddie J. Zacek.

Among the eight were the five men who rode with Boatswain Mate Andrew Hoover from the Receiving Station to the *Pennsylvania* because ". . . we all felt we should be doing something more than being spectators." *Pruitt, Sicard* and *Tracy* were moored near the cruisers *St Louis* and *New Orleans*, undergoing overhaul—with most of their antiaircraft guns and much of their ammunition not available for use. The five from the Receiving Station, along with the other three from *Tracy*, paid with their lives. Irrespective of the circumstance, Andy Hoover was the lone survivor, and carries the lifelong memory of that day and five young men whose lives were cut short by one of war's terrible ironies.[9]

After the bomb hit, a Chief Gunners' Mate came through the passageway where men had been killed asking for volunteers to clip .50-caliber ammunition. Andy volunteered, went into a small room, and began clipping approximately 10,000 rounds of .50-caliber ammunition before a chief gunners' mate stopped him. He lost track of time, and when he was later asked to "help clean up" up on deck, the second wave had departed.[10]

At 0920, while Andy was still below decks, the dry dock began flooding as the crews of *Downes* and *Cassin* were abandoning their ships. The *Downes* and *Cassin* were afire stem to stern, their surviving, able crew members were on the dock fighting the fires. In spite of their best efforts, oil on the water surface of the flooding drydock transmitted fire to the paint on the starboard bow of *Pennsylvania*. The hot fires caused aluminum paint in two of *Pennsylvania*'s forward compartments to melt and flow to the bottom of the compartments, threatening to expand internal fire damage. Fire parties brought the battleship's forward fires under control, while the raging fires on the two destroyers started the series of smaller, ammunition explosions, leading to the powerful torpedo warhead explosion on *Downes* at 0941. Debris rained on *Pennsylvania*'s forecastle, including a torpedo tube weighing between 500 and 1,000 pounds.

After crews abandoned the shattered, burning destroyers *Shaw*, *Downes* and *Cassin*, the *Pennsylvania*, submarine *Cachalot* (SS-170), astern of *Pennsylvania* and ahead of *Helena* at Berth 1 on the east side of the main channel; the seaplane tender *Avocet* (AVP-4)—moored at Berth F-1, directly across the main channel to the west, from *Helena* and the capsizing *Oglala*—and the *Maryland*, could best lend gunfire support to the struggling *California* and *Nevada*, who both came under withering dive bomb and horizontal bomb attacks from the second wave. All continued to send high volumes of antiaircraft fire at the enemy raiders, whenever the Vals, Kates and Zekes came in range.[11]

Pearl Harbor Shipyard Floating Dry Dock #2: *Shaw* burns after being bombed. *Nevada*, repeatedly struck by dive bombers, and ordered not to proceed from the harbor, has been deliberately run around. Her stern is swinging toward the center of the main channel, pulled by the tide. The seaplane tender *Avocet* is in the foreground. NPSAM

California and Nevada Down

In *Nevada*'s deck log, Officer of the Deck, Ensign Charles W. Jenkins, summarized the ship's savaging by Val dive bombers as she continued toward the harbor entrance in the face of the oncoming second wave. At 0850 Lieutenant Commander Egusa's Vals concentrated their initial assault on *Nevada*, resulting in five bomb hits on her forecastle, three forward, one on the boat deck and one on the superstructure. The bombs penetrated the forecastle, "exploding below decks, one or two near crews galley. Fires broke out forward and amidships." From other vantage points in the harbor the entire area forward of the bridge appeared to be in flames. Flooding increased, with water rising above the floor plates in firerooms #1 and 2, and into fire boxes, requiring isolation of the two firerooms.

One dive bomber even ignored the tanker *Neosho* (AO-23) which, at 0840, having off-loaded some of her aviation gasoline, began backing from her mooring near the storage tanks on Ford Island, moving across the main channel toward Berth F-3 at Merry Point—just as *Nevada* began backing from her mooring to move down channel. Witnesses to *Neosho*'s odyssey were greatly relieved she never received a hit, and gave all the gunfire support to her they could, including ships and submarines moored in the East Loch's submarine base. Other gunners in range of attackers going after both *Neosho* and *Nevada* added to their defense.[12]

At 0905, both *California* and *Nevada* received a signal not to proceed out of the harbor. *Nevada*'s acting skipper, Lieutenant Commander Francis J. Thomas, immediately ordered "All engines stop" and passed the word to Chief Boatswain Edwin J. Hill to make preparations to anchor.

Chief Boatswain Hill and his line handling detail responded, moving toward the ship's bow. Among the 10 to 15 dive bombers *Pennsylvania*'s Captain Cooke described attacking the drydocked battleship and destroyers *Downes* and *Cassin*, were those that turned slightly to their left, and bore down on *Nevada* as Chief Boatswain Hill and his men went forward on the forecastle. The results of the multiple attacks were devastating.

At 0907, the same minute *Pennsylvania* was struck by a single bomb that killed twenty-eight men and wounded an equal number, *Nevada*'s deck log recorded, "Received bomb hit on forecastle, killing Chief Boatswain Hill (blown overboard) and an unknown number of men. Numerous near misses of bombs at this phase of the action . . . " The deck log continued, factually describing the crew's untiring efforts to keep fighting and keep her afloat as the Japanese pressed their attacks:

0908 Backed [engines] emergency full speed. 0910 Grounded bow of ship intentionally between floating drydock [near the destroyer *Shaw*] and channel buoy #24, starboard side to beach, ship grounded on even keel. Stopped. Exact position not definite, due to intense smoke. Personnel casualties being transferred to Repair One. 0915 Captain [Francis W. Scanland] returned aboard. 0920 Shifted ship control to Battle TWO [aft steering]. Two harbor tugs moored alongside forward to assist in fighting heavy fires forward. 0925 All personnel not on A.A. guns or broadside, engaged in fighting fires forward and amidships. Casualties being transferred to [hospital ship] SOLACE and Naval Hospital, Pearl Harbor. NEVADA A.A. battery firing intermittently on enemy planes. Approximately 0925 flooded all magazines. 1000 Secured forward high pressure air compressors due to smoke and flooding. 1015 No progress being made in overcoming fires forward. Rigged additional hoses from aft and tugs. Due to trim forward, NEVADA stern began swinging toward middle of channel. 1020 Harbor tugs secured hoses, cast off forward, and pushed stern toward beach to prevent blocking the channel. Unsuccessful attempts made to anchor; both windlasses and wildcats jammed with wreckage from bomb hits. 1030 Secured forward dynamos and low pressure air compressors due to smoke. 1035 (about) Ship floated off beach and drifted toward western side of channel. Air attacks ceased. Backed both engines two-thirds to move the ship to western side of entrance channel and avoid possibility of blocking channel. 1045 Grounded on western side of Pearl Harbor entrance channel, starboard quarter aground, bow south. Buoy #19, 30 yards off starboard bow. Soundings: Bow 9 fathoms, stern 2 ½ fathoms. Harbor tugs used to push bow toward beach to clear channel. Final position with bow about 15 yards from buoy #19. Ship began to list to starboard. 1130 Restarted low pressure air compressors as smoke had cleared. Continued fire fighting on forecastle and amidships assisted by two harbor tugs forward. Ship listed 4 degrees to starboard . . .

The log went on to describe the damage inflicted on *Nevada* during the entire action. In addition to the torpedo hit on the port bow in the first minutes of the attack, at least six bombs struck the forecastle forward of #1 turret, at least two bomb hits

Nevada (BB-36) beached and burning off Waipo Point after being hit forward by Japanese bombs and torpedoes. Her pilothouse area is discolored by fires in that vicinity. The harbor tug *Hoga* (YT-146) is alongside *Nevada*'s port bow, helping to fight fires on the battleship's forecastle. Note channel marker buoy against *Nevada*'s starboard side. NA

forward of the stack, in the bridge structure, and at least two aft of the stack in the boat deck. Bombs wrecked casemates 4 and 9, put broadside gun #9 out of commission, wrecked the forecastle to forward of #1 turret, including all anchor handling gear, the wardroom and officers' country forward on the main deck.

The extent of damage below these spaces wasn't known until later, but was evidently considerable. All spaces below and forward of the wardroom were flooded. Fire completely gutted the navigating and signal bridge structure. The canteen was destroyed, with minor damage in the vicinity of the incinerator room and laundry. A bomb wrecked the ship's galley as well as the boat deck above where the bomb penetrated. An undetermined number of blisters were ruptured, with a torpedo hole about frame 40. Extensive damage to electrical wiring occurred due to explosions and fire.

When *Nevada* backed across the channel and finally ran aground, stern first, on the west side of the channel, flooding continued and there was no way to stop it. She was sinking by the bow, but her main deck remained above water, and her AA guns remained operational. Her final list was eight degrees to starboard. About 1530, fires were under control and at 1550 the crew removed the dead, 29 of them, including 2 officers. Captain Scanland reported 100 men wounded and 17 missing at the end of the day. Among the wounded were five officers and 10 marines.

The final count of those who were killed in action or died of wounds would climb much higher—a total of 58, including eight marines.

Captain Scanland climbed aboard *Nevada* late in the action, when his ship was aground on the east side of the channel. When the battle ended the pride he felt for the entire crew was evident in his 15 December report to the Commander-in-Chief, Pacific Fleet.

> The Commanding Officer finds it extremely difficult to single out individual members of the crew as deserving of special praise. Every officer and man aboard, without exception, performed his duties in a most commendable manner and without regard to personal safety. The courage and spirit of the antiaircraft gun crews, where the bomb hits caused most of the casualties, was of the highest order. Every man on the ship carried on in accordance with the best traditions of the service.

It is considered that Lieutenant Commander Francis J. Thomas, U.S. Naval Reserve, the Commanding Officer during the greater part of the attack, is deserving of special commendation. This officer got the ship underway within forty minutes and headed down channel. Although the Nevada had been torpedoed and had received one or two bomb hits, Lieutenant Commander Thomas correctly decided that it was urgently necessary to get underway to avoid destruction of the ship due to proximity of the Arizona which was surrounded with burning oil and afire from stem to stern. Throughout the action Lieutenant Commander Thomas cooly and calmly fought the ship despite many bomb hits and casualties. After the attack and for two days afterward, Lieutenant Commander Thomas performed damage control duties in a most creditable manner although near the point of exhaustion by his two days of strenuous work.

Chief Boatswain Edwin J. Hill, U.S. Navy, killed in action, is deserving of the highest commendation possible to be given for his skill, leadership and courage. At the height of the attack he led his line handling details to the quays, cast off lines under fire, and then swam back to the ship. Later, while on the forecastle attempting to let go the anchors, he was blown overboard and killed by the explosion of several bombs. His performance of duty and devotion to duty was outstanding.

Ensign Joseph K. Taussig, jr., U.S. Navy, is deserving of the highest commendation for his extraordinary display of courage, leadership, and devotion to duty. Being the senior officer present in the A.A. battery, he immediately took charge of that battery and directed its fire even after damage had severed all cables between his director and the battery, and he had been very seriously wounded by a bomb explosion. Despite efforts of the personnel of the A.A. director to take Ensign Taussig to a battle dressing station and insisted on continuing his control of the A.A. battery and the continuation of fire on enemy aircraft. He was finally removed from the director by the director crew and hospital corpsmen who had been sent for. It was necessary to lower Ensign Taussig by lines in a stretcher to the boat deck, as other means of descent had been cut off by a serious fire in the bridge structure. It is considered that Ensign Taussig's actions were beyond the call of duty and that his performance of duty is deserving of recognition.

Ensign Thomas H. Taylor, U.S. Navy, took station as battery officer on the port A.A. battery. At this station he afforded an outstanding example of leadership, devotion to duty, and valor. Under fire from strafing attacks, bomb explosions in the immediate vicinity, and serious fires that exploded one ready ammunition box in the starboard 5-inch A.A. battery, wounded by fragments, burned, shell-shocked, and completely deafened due to broken eardrums, he continued to direct the fire of his battery in an effective manner. His presence of mind in playing a hose on the ready ammunition boxes that were becoming red heat from the proximity of fires, avoided heavy damage to the battery. His activities are deserving of the greatest praise.

Among others that should be mentioned are –

Lieutenant Lawrence E. Ruff, U.S. Navy, for his invaluable assistance as acting Navigator to Lieutenant Commander Thomas, and assistance in an excellent performance of ship handling.

Chief Quartermaster Robert Sedberry, U.S. Navy, for his calm and effective handling of the wheel and his foresight in ordering the engine room to prepare to get underway before the arrival of officers on the bridge.

Solar, Adolfo, Boatswain's Mate First Class, U.S. Navy, for his initiative in effective handling of the A.A. Battery, early opening of fire by that battery until battery officers arrived, and his skill in keeping his own gun firing almost continuously at enemy planes. His leadership, initiative, and valor were beyond the call of duty, and his death by fragments was keenly felt.

Neundorf, W.F., jr., Seaman First Class, killed in action, as gun captain of No. 6 A.A. gun, gave an example of leadership, skill, and bravery that is remarked upon by all who observed it.

. . . The performance of duty of the Medical Department under difficult conditions is most gratifying, and the members of that Department exhibited the same courage and devotion to duty under fire as any other member of the crew. The dead and wounded were quickly and effectively handled.

As removal of the dead began at 1530 hours, the colors were lowered to half-staff, then were returned to full staff when the last of the dead were taken from the ship.

With twenty-nine years of service in the Navy Chief Petty Officer (Chief Boatswain) Edwin J. Hill had celebrated his 47th birthday on 4 October 1941. Among those killed during the last savage, dive bomb attack that morning, his name, acts of courage and heroism are etched forever in the annals of American history—and live in the memories of the officers and men who were aboard the USS *Nevada* on 7 December. The citation accompanying the posthumous Medal of Honor received by his surviving family, reads as follows:

For distinguished conduct in the line of his profession, extraordinary courage, and disregard of his own safety during the attack on the Fleet in Pearl Harbor, by Japanese Forces on 7 December 1941. During the height of the strafing and bombing, Chief Boatswain Hill led his men of the line-handling details of the U.S.S. *Nevada* to the quays, cast off the lines and swam back to his ship. Later, while on the forecastle attempting to let go the anchors, he was blown overboard and killed by the explosion of several bombs.

Nevada's troubles weren't over yet. As the day drew to a close and she continued to slowly settle, at 1830 fire broke out on the forecastle again. All hands turned to fighting fires. At 2100 fires flared once more on the forecastle, and were finally brought under control at 2300. Meanwhile, like *Nevada*, as the battle raged during the enemies' second wave of attacks, fire and water were becoming *California*'s other nemesis—and she too finally went down.[13]

At 0900, shortly before Captain Joel W. Bunkley, the commanding officer, returned aboard *California*, and as dive bombers were resuming intense attacks, she was heavily shaken by what seemed a violent explosion of unknown origin—probably a near miss on the starboard side by a bomb from the flights of dive bombers—seen by crews on *Pennsylvnia* moments earlier. A large issue of smoke came from *California*'s starboard side gallery deck. In spite of the explosion's severity gunners on *California* and the small seaplane tender *Avocet* (AVP-4), moored at Berth F-1 on the west side of the main channel further toward the harbor entrance, continued firing at the second wave of Kates and Val dive bombers now bearing down on *Nevada*, *Pennsylvania*, the destroyers *Downes* and *Cassin*, and the five battleships remaining on the east side of Ford Island.

In the two hours following the onslaught of the raiders' first wave, the wind-driven-and-tide-pulled river of oil-fed fire spreading from the shattered forward section of *Arizona* nearly overwhelmed *Arizona*'s few survivors holding back the conflagration on her quarterdeck—and forced *Nevada*'s and the crippled *Vestal*'s crews to get their ships underway to avoid further damage. As the fire drifted toward the harbor entrance it threatened to destroy *West Virginia*, *Tennessee*, and *Maryland*, moved past the capsized *Oklahoma* and through the berth vacated at 0842 by the tanker *Neosho*. As time approached 1000 hours the fire pressed relentlessly toward the sinking *California*.

Captain Bunkley, who had come aboard to assume command, watched the oncoming fire, increasingly concerned for the safety of a crew already hard hit with casualties. When it appeared the fire would completely envelope *California*, he decided they should temporarily abandon her, and with the approval of Admiral Pye, at 1002 ordered "Abandon ship." Flames having cleared the ship, at 1015 he cancelled the order, crew members manned battle stations topside, a large number of men returned from the beach to resume work, and others remained to obtain additional fire fighting equipment on Ford Island. The crew fought the fire with all available fire equipment on board, and that obtained from Ford Island. Shortly thereafter, the yard tug *Nakomis* came alongside starboard, forward to assist in fighting fires, while Admiral Pye, the Commander Battle Force, left *California* with his staff, shifting his flag to the submarine base.

Extensive salvage operations of movable gear began. The ship was listing about eight degrees to port. The engineering plant suffered no mechanical or electrical casualty that would have prevented its operation during the engagement. However, the fire in A-611 produced sufficient heat and smoke in the forward engine room to make it operational only with great difficulty.

At 1400 hours the submarine rescue vessel *Widgeon* came alongside and sent divers down to examine damage to *California*'s hull in the vicinity of frame 47. The fleet paymaster removed funds and records from the ship, and shortly before 1730 the crew began removing official records and papers from the ship to Ford Island for safekeeping. The auxiliary minesweeper *Bobolink* (AM-20)

Crew abandoning the damaged *California* (BB-44) shortly after the end of the Japanese raid, as burning oil drifts down on the ship, at about 1000 hours on the morning of 7 December 1941. The capsized hull of *Oklahoma* (BB-37) is visible at the right. NHHC

joined in assisting *California*, pulling alongside *Widgeon* at 1730 to use her pumps to pump dry selected, flooded compartments.[14]

In his action report dated 13 December Captain Bunkley summarized *California*'s casualties: 5 officers killed, 6 wounded; 48 men killed, 58 wounded; and 45 missing. He named 17 men, 4 of them officers as ". . . outstanding in their work during the battle," in supplying ammunition and removing wounded. Three of their number had been killed, including two ensigns. He cited 52 more "For outstanding work in removing wounded trapped in either closed compartments or in compartments afire." Two others received praise for obtaining ammunition from other ships while under fire, the senior medical officer for treatment of wounded ". . . although burned about the face and arms from fires nearby his station," one gun captain for coolness and example under fire which "instilled confidence in the men about him," and another for his outstanding work as acting damage control officer.[15]

The final count of men killed, died of wounds, and missing later declared dead from the deadly attacks on the *California* reached 102, including four marines and five officers.[16]

The flagship *California*—the battleship and junior officer crew members Joey Border had so admired and had said a tearful goodbye to in January—was down for now, but she would be back to fight again.

Following Through on Their Pearl Harbor Mission—and Into a Hornets' Nest

While Val dive bombers leading the second wave concentrated their attacks on *Nevada*, *Pennsylvania* and the destroyers in the dry docks, other flights zeroed in on targets to the north and west of Ford Island. The seaplane tenders *Tangier* and *Curtiss*, the repair ship *Medusa*, the light cruisers *Raleigh* and *Detroit*, and the destroyer tender *Dobbins* felt their sting, but not without a growing price.

At 0850, crewmen on *Tangier* sighted the lead formations of the second wave coming in from the southeast, and shortly afterward their ship became the target of repeated dive bomb attacks. Moored aft of the capsized *Utah*, with her bow pointed toward the harbor entrance, she, along with *Curtiss* and *Medusa*, both across the channel to the west, were larger than nearly all nearby ships except the cruisers *Raleigh* and *Detroit*—and were inviting targets. But the attackers met sharp resistance.

Vals approaching their targets on an axis from the southeast to northwest, and attacking ships moored east or west of Ford Island, or strafed targets after bomb release, found themselves running into a veritable hornets nest of gunners. The second wave was quick to learn American gunners on the island and on the decks of ships everywhere were getting the range, azimuth and lead necessary to increase the toll taken from the raiders.

Shortly after 0850 gunners on the *Tangier* claimed to have shot off the tail of one aircraft just after it had passed abeam to starboard, and reported the "plane crashed in [the] Middle Loch in back of *Curtiss* and *Medusa*. The plane was hit by .50-caliber machine gun bullets and the tail was shot off by the 3-inch forward [AA] battery." The *Tangier*'s 2 January 1942 action report also stated its gunners "Riddled another Japanese airplane, which went out of control and crashed on the shore line, near Beckoning Point."[17]

Aboard *Raleigh*, lying further to the northeast dead ahead of the capsized *Utah*, her crew was still struggling to avoid *Utah*'s fate after the first wave's successful torpedo attack on the two ships. Nevertheless, when the second wave's glide bombing and strafing attacks began in the Middle Loch shortly after 0900, *Raleigh*'s and *Detroit*'s gunners again met the attackers "with a warm reception"—while *Raleigh*'s crew feverishly worked to keep her afloat and avoid capsizing.

In spite of the Vals' combined dive bomb and strafing attacks, the fierceness of the cruisers' antiaircraft defense helped assure all but one of their bombs were near misses, and there were no fatalities on either ship. One bomb glanced off *Raleigh*'s #7 3-inch ready ammunition box, went through the carpenter shop, then through an oil tank, piercing the skin on the port quarter below the water line, and finally detonated on the bottom of the harbor about fifty feet from the ship. When the raiders returned to their carriers, in addition to all *Raleigh*'s crew accomplished in saving their ship, they reported hits on five Japanese airplanes which they believed fell to their guns and the guns of other defenders. The *Raleigh*'s gunners expended 266 rounds of 3-inch ammunition, 3270 rounds of 1.1-inch [four-barrel gun], and 9990 rounds of .50-caliber ammunition.[18]

Detroit's crew, their ship fortunately unscathed throughout the raid, manned and fired all their .50-caliber and 3-inch antiaircraft guns, expending 422 rounds of 3-inch, and approximately 10,000 rounds of .50-caliber ammunition.[19]

Further west, across the channel in the Middle Loch, the seaplane tender *Curtiss* was about to be visited by hell—twice.

According to *Curtiss*'s commander, at 0905 one of three planes pulling out of a dive over Ford Island was hit by *Curtiss* gunners, set afire, and crashed into her starboard side against #1 crane—forcing the crew to temporarily abandon #3 gun. The plane disintegrated, the gas tank exploded, and the plane burned on the boat deck. After the midget submarine attack, and an enemy airplane slamming into her, *Curtiss*'s troubles still weren't over. The Val's attack and ensuing crash had been seen from an entirely different perspective by men on the *Tangier*.

Tangier's Captain Clifton A.F. Sprague stated in his 16 December action report that at 0910 his crew observed another group of approximately 27 aircraft approaching from the raiders' second strike force, and they "... riddled another Japanese plane, flying up our port side [generally parallel to *Tangier*], engine caught fire, then part of fuselage forward of pilot burst into flame, pilot got his plane around 90 degrees to right and from the Commanding Officer's observation, deliberately crashed into *Curtiss*. Plane crashed into *Curtiss* near after stack, into boat crane and A.A. gun station and started a good size fire."[20]

The three reports, and yet another from *Medusa*, highlighted the difficulty of deciding which gunners should receive credit for Japanese planes shot down during the attacks on Pearl Harbor and the six airfields targeted on Oahu. The skies above the harbor, more than above any other military installation on Oahu, were filled with death-dealing gunfire from every direction within moments after the first attack began, and the volume of fire slackened only during brief periods when no airplanes were visible to gunners. From the instant the attack began, on through the night of 7 December, any aircraft, friend or foe, received the same reception, as the men from *Enterprise*'s VF-6 Squadron so painfully learned that night. In most instances, in the air above Pearl Harbor, it's likely that Japanese aircraft shot down received multiple hits from antiaircraft guns from two or more ships. And it was this same relentless volume of fire that fell from the air and took its toll on civilians and a few military, in the surrounding areas.

Lieutenant Commander John F.P. Miller the repair officer and acting commander on the *Medusa*, and Ensign Robert M. Rocktaschel, the forward battery officer, wrote of the air attack in the Middle Loch:

> . . . The majority of planes attacking the *Medusa-Curtiss* sector were flying at an altitude of not over 400 feet; a few were not over 100 feet . . . [On the second attack] . . . the plane, having been set afire, deliberately crashed into the USS *Curtiss* . . .
>
> Two other planes nosed down to dive bomb the *Medusa* and the destroyers [light minelayers and high-speed minesweepers] on our port hand. Both of these were brought down. One cut in two just before starting to level out and crashed on the east bank on this loch. Neither of these planes released their bombs.[21]

At 0912 a group of Val dive bombers under heavy fire attacked the *Curtiss* and *Medusa*. During the attack, one bomb hit the *Curtiss's* stern mooring buoy, one fell short, and one hit the ship on the starboard side of the boat deck. Two fell approximately twenty-five feet off *Medusa's* starboard bow, and two more fell off her port quarter. Fortunately, the *Medusa* remained unscathed.

During this round of attacks, *Medusa's* crew observed a Val dive bomber fly low across the bow of their ship about 200 feet. Her gunners opened fire with .30-caliber machine guns and a barrage of fire came from ships in Mine Division Three, moored to the west of *Medusa*. The heavy fire struck home. Crews watched as the aircraft took hits and descended into the water about 1,500 yards on *Medusa's* port beam, near the Pearl City dock. Civilians "reported two Japanese swimming around a plane capsized in the water." The minelayer *Montgomery* dispatched a motor whaleboat to the scene to investigate and when they arrived, only one, the pilot, was still afloat. He was several times motioned into the boat, but refused to obey, instead finally reaching inside his jacket. On seeing the enemy pilot's threatening gesture, Seaman First Class D.F. Calkins shot him, and he immediately sank.

The bomb that struck *Curtiss* was more deadly than the suicidal, "I'll-take-some-enemy-with-me" attack by the doomed

Val pilot and his gunner which had apparently been hit by *Tangier*'s defensive fire. The bomb passed through the carpenter shop, radio repair shop, entered the hangar and detonated on the main deck level. The explosion destroyed bulkheads, decks, equipment and fixtures within a radius of 30 feet from the point of detonation, and started numerous fires which destroyed equipment in the hangar, upper handling room of #4 gun, battery, ship movie booth, and radio transmitter room. The explosion and fires caused numerous casualties. *Curtiss*'s crew, like the men on the capital ships, suddenly found themselves fighting to save their ship and one another while battling the enemy.

Radioman's Mate First Class R.E. Jones and Radioman's Mate Second Class J.G. Raines were in the radio transmitter room with two of their shipmates, Dean B. Orwick and Benjamin Schelect, both Radiomen Second Class. The bomb's explosion knocked over several transmitters. One fell across Dean Orwick's legs and Ben Schlect was caught under another. The transmitter room immediately filled with flame and smoke from the film and smoke from the fire in the movie projection room directly below. Jones and Raines rescued Orwick, then made several desperate, unsuccessful attempts to remove Ben Schlect. Dean Orwick later died of his wounds.

Ensign Ralph G. Kelly was in the immediate vicinity of the bomb explosion, and though wounded, displayed great courage and devotion to duty as he continued directing the midship repair party while working tirelessly to bring the fires under control and remove wounded and dead from the wreckage.

Ensign Gordon K. Nicodemus, Jr., the after battery officer at Gun #3 when the engagement with the midget submarine occurred, was directing his gun crew when the Japanese pilot turned his doomed, burning Val dive bomber, clearly aiming for *Curtiss* and impact near their battery. They were forced to abandon the gun. He then displayed unusual courage, leadership, and devotion to duty in directing fire fighting and reorganizing his crew to continue fighting the gun. Ship Fitter First Class H.C. Dorsett was tireless and fearless. His thorough knowledge of the ship and equipment, his industry and devotion to duty, contributed to successful rescue of many wounded, and controlling damage to the ship.

Curtiss's captain, Commander Henry S. Kendall, in his 16 December 1941 action report, cited the "distinguished conduct" of several other men among his crew who demonstrated great courage and devotion to duty during the attacks on the seaplane tender. At 0927 the aft engine room was out of commission and evacuated due to heavy smoke, broken steam lines, and water from overhead. During the engagement, when it was clear the safety of their ship was in question, Chief Water Tender J.H. Mosher, Chief Machinist Mate F. Beach, and Machinist Mate First Class S.F. Safranski returned to the evacuated engine room, disregarding the steam, acrid smoke filled compartments, and their personal safety, to start pumps to clear the engine room of water. With complete disregard for their personal safety, J.A. D'Amelio and Robert R. Bieszcz, both Seamen First Class, continued fighting fires on the boat deck while repeatedly exposed to strafing attacks by enemy planes. Others were recognized for their actions in saving wounded shipmates.

Curtiss, with five officers and 55 men on shore leave from a complement of approximately 1,195 was hard hit. In addition to 20 fatalities, including two unidentified, a total of 33 went to the hospital and the hospital ship, *Solace*, 25 more wounded stayed aboard, and one was reported missing. Later, one more was added to the list of killed in action.[22]

From 0913 to 0920, during the same period Vals attacked the *Curtiss*, more dive bombers swarmed *Tangier*, but fortunately all five bombs, delivered by five different planes, missed their target. No plane dropped more than one bomb and no two planes dropped at the same time. The first fell off *Tangier*'s port bow— on Ford Island—because the pilot didn't press his attack. The other four planes released their bombs from about 300 feet in shallow dives and all were close misses, two forward, one about fifteen the other about twenty feet off the starboard side; two aft, about twenty and forty feet off.

Captain Sprague stood, with no thought to take cover, and was able to watch the two bombs forward, from instant of release to water impact. They appeared to be 250-300 pound bombs. He felt sure they were going to be hits and was surprised by the resulting small amount of damage. A dull thud was felt throughout the ship and Captain Sprague ascribed it to the bombs burying themselves in the mud, which muffled the force of the explosions. Fragments struck the ship in 42 places, with no serious damage. There were no penetrations below the water line, and only three men on deck received wounds—all superficial. No more planes came near *Tangier* after 0920.[23]

At 0910, while other Vals were attacking in the Middle Loch, more unleashed bomb and strafing attacks in the northern sector of the harbor. Their targets included five nests of destroyers in which twenty destroyers were moored, two destroyer tenders within two of those nests; the light cruiser *Phoenix* (CL-46) moored singly at Berth C-6 about 200 yards off the north shore near Aiea Bay; and the hospital ship *Solace* (AH-5), moored first at Berth X-4 until it shifted to Berth X-13 at 0900, away from the destroyer tender *Whitney* (AD-4) and her five destroyers. Five destroyers lay at Berth X-2 alongside the destroyer tender, *Dobbin* (AD-3), approximately 700 yards slightly off the starboard bow of the cruiser *Detroit*. Five more lay alongside the tender *Whitney* (AD-4) at Berth X-8 approximately 1,400 yards on the bow of *Detroit*.

In a nest at Berth X-11, approximately 700 yards east of *Monaghan* were three destroyers: *Henley* (DD-391), *Patterson* (DD-392), and *Ralph Talbot* (DD-390). After the destroyer *Helm* left its mooring for the West Loch, at 0726, the destroyer *Blue*

Seaplane tender *Tangier* (AV-8), Japanese bomb explodes
some twenty feet off the starboard side of the ship,
forward of the bridge, causing minor damage during the
Pearl Harbor air raid, 7 December 1941. NHHC

(DD-387), was moored singly at Berth X-7 approximately 100 yards east of *Whitney*, and two of Destroyer Division 80's four ships, the *Allen* (DD-66) and the *Chew* (DD-106), were at Berth X-5 with the old decommissioned ship, ex-*Baltimore*—used for storage—about two hundred yards east of *Solace*. The other two ships in Destroyer Division 80 were the *Ward*, still on patrol outside the harbor entrance, and the *Schley* (DD-103), which was in overhaul at the Navy Yard's Berth #20.[24]

In attacking moored destroyers the Japanese were indeed stirring hornets' nests. While the "Tin Can Navy's" ships appeared more vulnerable to torpedo and bombing attacks due to thinner armor plating when compared with the cruisers and battleships, they were like angry porcupines in an air attack—especially when moored close together in port. It was a reinforcing lesson the Japanese attacking ships in the Middle Loch were learning at the same time, when withering volumes of fire came from two cruisers, *Raleigh* and *Detroit*; two seaplane tenders, *Tangier* and *Curtiss*, the repair ship *Medusa*; four destroyer-minesweepers and one destroyer-minelayer.

The number of antiaircraft guns available per square foot of deck area was multiplied considerably when two or more destroyers were moored together. They could put out an enormous volume of supporting fire for one another, though raiders' low level and low angle approaches from either starboard or port hampered the ability of gunners to open fire for fear of hitting ships moored alongside. What's more, when underway, destroyers operating singly or in formation added speed, maneuverability, and relatively small size as targets to their prickly air defense capabilities.

At 0755, when the attack on Ford Island instantly galvanized the Pacific Fleet's command structure to action, a signal was sent from Destroyer Flotilla 1 to Destroyers, Battle Force, "ANTI-AIRCRAFT BATTERY TAKE AMMUNITION CONDITION OF READINESS ONE." With recall of personnel in progress, at 0808 Rear Admiral Robert A. "Fuzzy" Theobald, the commander of Destroyer Flotilla 1, ordered Destroyer Division Two to establish an offshore patrol.[25]

Monaghan, earlier ordered to sortie in response to the destroyer *Ward's* report of having depth charged a submarine outside the harbor, was the first destroyer in Division Two to depart the nest at Berth X-15. *Dale*, *Farragut* and *Aylwin*, soon followed

SUNDAY IN HELL 477

Monaghan—the ship that veered out of the north channel and sunk the midget submarine in the Middle Loch—while *Dale*, close behind and momentarily stopped while *Monaghan* depth charged the submarine, proceeded past her in the North Channel.

Moored at Berth X-2 in a nest with five destroyers was the destroyer tender *Dobbin*, with all their bows on headings approximating 053 degrees. At 12,450 tons fully loaded, and 484 feet in length, *Dobbin* stood out as a tempting target beside the five smaller ships close to her port side. In sequence proceeding west the five ships of Destroyer Flotilla One were: *Hull* (DD-350), *Dewey* (DD-349), *Worden* (DD-352), *MacDonough* (DD-351), and *Phelps* (DD-360). All but *Phelps* were 341 feet in length, and *Phelps* was 380 feet. All the destroyers were undergoing routine servicing or overhaul by *Dobbin*'s crew.

In the first wave assault on Pearl Harbor, the Japanese had concentrated on the capital ships, but the second wave's mission "to concentrate on as many ships as possible and wreck them beyond repair" expanded their reach to the remaining relatively untouched ships.

Bandsman Ira "Ike" Schab, who was in *Dobbin*'s Band No. 13, and the night before had attended the Battle of the Bands, had just dressed after taking a shower, and had closed his locker about 7:45. He was thinking of an expected visit from his brother, who was assigned to a Naval Radio Station a few miles distant, at Wahiawa. The *Dobbin*'s band, as was normal practice, was to play for church services that morning. Ike was jolted from his morning's thoughts by the clang, clang, clang of the ship's general alarm, which could be heard in spite of the absence of a speaker system. Next came the Chief Bo'sun's Mate "piping down" from the weather deck, and shouting loudly after each piping, "Away the fire and rescue party!" Ike's battle station was in the machine shop, but normally hadn't an assigned duty there, so decided to go topside and see what was going on.

When he arrived, he looked toward the port quarter, down the west side of Ford Island, where a week earlier the band had been on board the *Raleigh*. He saw smoke rising from *Utah*, which was already listing from its two torpedo hits. Ike knew almost instantly the Fleet was under attack, and hurried below to the machine shop—his battle station—and "broke into" an ammunition train to help out. He handed out machine guns and mounts to the crew's gunners, and was later sent to the magazine to pass ammunition for the ship's two 3-inch and one 5-inch guns. At six feet, one inch in height, and weight of 165 pounds he had to carry boxes of ammunition which weighed just under 200 pounds. He had no trouble at all. He was more than excited, and his adrenalin was pumping. The ship confronted little trouble during the first wave of attacks, but matters quickly worsened when the second wave broadened their attacks. Nevertheless, the *Dobbin* and her destroyers acquitted themselves well.

At 0910, during the same period Vals were pressing dive bomb attacks against *Nevada*, *Pennsylvania*, *California*, *Curtiss*, *Tangier*, *Medusa*, *Raleigh*, and *Detroit*, three Vals came in low on the starboard quarter of *Dobbin*.

Heavy antiaircraft fire from *Dobbin* and the nest of destroyers caused the pilots to alter their approach, and each of their three bombs were near misses, one on the starboard quarter, one astern of the tender, and one on the port quarter. Unlike the near misses in the attacks on *Tangier*, *Medusa*, and *Raleigh*, fragments from these near misses tore into the crew of *Dobbin*'s 3-inch Gun #4 located on the aft end of her boat deck and caused minor damage elsewhere, including destruction of #1 Motor Whale Boat hull, damage to three radio transmitters, and a number of small holes through decks, bulkheads, and booms.

Killed in action at Gun #4 was Coxswain Howard F. Carter of Lakeside, California. Mortally wounded were Torpedoman's Mate Third Class J.W. Baker of Oklahoma City, Oklahoma, who died later that afternoon; and Fireman First Class Roy A. Gross of Oak Park, Illinois, who died near midnight on the 7th. Wounded were Coxswain Edwin J. Brumley and Seaman Second Class Clarence M. Ouellette. Ironically, *Dobbin*'s fourth loss that day, Gunners' Mate First Class Andrew M. Marze, whose wife, Doris Grace, was at Pearl Harbor, was killed in action by the single bomb hit on *Pennsylvania* at 0906, minutes before the near misses on the destroyer tender caused three more fatalities at his ship's Gun #4.

When the raid began at 0755, *Dobbin*'s commander had immediately sent their motor whaleboats to the landings, and they were in continuous service wherever needed, an action duplicated by numerous ships in the harbor. They became part of a voluntary, ad hoc transportation and rescue operation that began during the raid and continued in spite of bomb attacks, periodic strafing attacks, explosions, white-hot fires on stricken ships, falling fragments and spent ammunition from bombs and antiaircraft rounds raining on the harbor area. Tug boats, fireboats, dredges, supply and garbage haulers, motor whale boats, motor launches, captain's gigs, and numerous other harbor craft were all over the harbor as the raid progressed.[26]

In the nest of destroyers adjacent to *Dobbin*, the destroyer *Hull* (DD-350) was typical of reactions to the raiders' attacks. When two Kate torpedo bombers in the first wave came low across the harbor fifty yards astern at 0758, one minute after general quarters sounded, the gangway watch opened fire with .45-caliber pistols. At 0805 #4 machine gun opened fire, and two minutes later #1 Gun, a 5-inch antiaircraft weapon, opened fire, followed two minutes later by #5, #2, #3 and #4. No. 2 machine gunner, while firing at a plane on the bow saw it ignite and crash into a cane field in flames. He stated as far as he knew he was the only gunner firing on the plane when it caught fire. Another Japanese raider, a Val and its 50-100 lb. bombs, crossed the bow of the nest and was seen to smoke and crash in Aiea, with an attendant explosion. At 0830, Hull reported two Vees of three each high level Kates, appeared intermittently directly overhead, through clouds, at about 10,000 feet. The ships opened fire with all guns, the formation broke up and dropped their bombs in cane fields.

The tugs and larger yard auxiliaries fought raging fires on the *Arizona*, *West Virginia*, *California* and *Nevada*; moved ships such as the *Oglala* before she capsized, helped move the *Nevada* before she could sink in the main channel, assisted the *Raleigh* to keep her from capsizing, and performed other salvaging tasks—often at great risk. The smaller boats transported men returning or recalled to their ships, moved men from ship to ship and ship to shore; transported survivors, wounded and dead, taking them to the docks or the hospital ship *Solace*; moved reallocated ammunition ship to ship or from the Ammunition Depot in the West Loch to ships; transported portable pumps to ships like the *California*, *Nevada,* and *Raleigh*; took welding equipment from ship to ship and divers from the submarine base to the capsized *Oklahoma* and *Utah* to attempt locating and rescuing men trapped in their upturned hulls; transported men to fight fires on ships such as *California* and *Nevada*.[27]

While the second wave of Vals continued to take its toll at Pearl Harbor, at a considerably elevated cost, the Kates and

Zekes administered the final devastating blows to five of Oahu's military airfields.

The Second Time Around: Air Fields

The Hawaiian Air Force's fighter command at Wheeler Field, bomber command at Hickam, and the 21st Marine Aircraft Group at Ewa had been shattered by the first wave's Vals and Zekes, though a few courageous fighter pilots, including three at Bellows Field, remained intent on striking back as best they could. While the Japanese raiders in the second wave bravely pressed their attacks into a storm of antiaircraft fire from the Pacific Fleet in Pearl Harbor, the relatively defenseless Kaneohe, Bellows and Hickam fields were being visited by hell a second time. Strike leader Mitsuo Fuchida, who had been orbiting over Oahu assessing the damage, thought he might take over the second wave and direct its attack. On observing Shimazaku's and Egusa's having the situation so well in hand at Pearl Harbor, he let Shimazaku go ahead while he continued to observe results.[28]

To the north Shindo's Zekes bore in first. Swinging slightly to the west, they divided into two groups. Half reversed course to pass over Kaneohe from the northwest. The other half went straight for Hickam and Ford Island. Over Kaneohe the first eighteen-plane group again split in two. Nine Zekes strafed the float plane installation, then turned west and machine-gunned Wheeler Field. The other nine flew on southeast, past Kanehoe to Bellows.[29]

Lieutenant Colonel Leonard D. Weddington, Bellows Field's commander, was at his home about a mile from the post when his driver rushed to inform him of the raid. The colonel immediately left for Bellows and was there when here came the Japanese with more than one Zeke. Nine fighters in three groups of threes in V formations, led by Lieutenant Sumio Nono, approached from the north about 0900 and attacked for approximately fifteen minutes. The raid consisted of gunfire only and started with a diving attack by all nine planes, after which the three-plane formations peeled off and began strafing from various directions.

Nono and his eight other Zeke pilots had discovered unexpectedly big game at this small, outlying auxiliary field.

They strafed parked aircraft, hit a gasoline truck, attacked P-40s caught trying to get airborne, shot two down, and seeing the B-17 that turned away from Hickam during the first wave's assault and crash landed during the lull between the lone Zeke's strafing pass and Nono's second wave, repeatedly strafed it.

Private Forrest E. Decker of the 428th Signal Maintenance Company, Aviation, at Bellows visiting friends, saw the gas truck's tanker burst into flames immediately. He recalled, "One man, whether brave or just stupid, ran to the vehicle, pulled the release lever, got into the cab and drove the tractor away from the tanker." They waited for it to explode, but it never did. It had so many holes in it that it just burned itself out.

Using bolt-action Springfield rifles and clip-loaded Browning automatic rifles, Bellows' ground defense forces fired back at the Japanese but inflicted no damage. Private First Class Raymond F. McBriarty and Private William L. Burt of the 86th Observation Squadron grabbed a gun and ammunition from the armament shack, mounted the gun in the rear cockpit of their squadron commander's parked 0-47 aircraft, and loaded the gun with ammunition. They were putting ammunition into the plane's fixed guns when the attack started. They "hit the dust" when the [nine Zekes] struck, then crawled in the cockpit and expended 450 rounds on the attacking flights of three during their low-level strafing passes. They later received the Silver Star for gallantry in action.[30]

Men of the 44th Pursuit Squadron rushed to disperse, fuel, and arm their twelve P-40 Warhawks lined up on the edge of the runway. Only four of the squadron's officers were at Bellows that morning, and three were pilots. They wanted to get in the air immediately, though their aircraft were not completely armed. Lieutenant Phillips, the armament officer, insisted that all six .50-caliber guns be fully loaded before any aircraft took off. When Nono's nine Zekes appeared and began raking Bellows with strafing attacks, the three determined pilots saw no choice but to ignore his wishes.

Second Lieutenant Hans C. Christiansen started to get into the cockpit of his plane. An enemy machine gun bullet struck him in the back. He fell at the feet of his astonished mechanic, Corporal Elmer L. Rund, who was standing by the [trailing edge] of the right wing. Blood gushed from a large hole in the life jacket of the fatally wounded pilot. Rund and his crew chief, Joe Ray, ducked under the aircraft for protection from the strafing attack by the Japanese planes, which seemed to come from all directions.

In the meantime, 2d Lieutenant George A. Whiteman ran up to a P-40 that was still being loaded with ammunition. He told the men to get off the wing because he would fly the plane as it was. He started the engine and taxied out onto the runway, leaving so quickly that the armorers hadn't time to reinstall the gun cowlings on the wings. Whiteman began his takeoff run. Two Zekes immediately spotted him, and rolled in to attack. He managed to get his slowly accelerating Warhawk off the ground approximately 50 feet before enemy planes closed sufficiently from high on his tail to open fire. He tried to turn inside the two fighters to spoil their tracking solution and cause them to overshoot his flight path, but the P-40 hadn't enough speed and altitude to successfully make a hard turn and evade. His attackers' bullets struck the engine, wings, and cockpit. The Warhawk burst into flames. He attempted a last ditch belly landing on the beach, but his left wing hit the sand, the airplane cart-wheeled, broke up, and a tremendous ball of fire erupted.

Staff Sergeant Cosmos Manning carried a large fire extinguisher down to the wreckage, and others followed in a hopeless rescue effort. Black smoke rose in a thick column from the crash site, marking the funeral pyre of Lieutenant Whiteman. Staff Sergeant Edward J. Covelesky, a P-40 crew chief, had thrown himself down on top of a sand dune to hide in the vegetation when the strafing attack began. He picked himself up and ran down to the beach area, where he saw the only trace of the P-40 was a few scattered pieces of metal surrounding an ugly black patch of smoldering sand. Fourteen years later, Sedalia Air Force Base in Missouri was renamed Whiteman AFB in honor of Lieutenant Whiteman.

The third pilot at Bellows, 1st Lieutenant Samuel W. Bishop, taxied into position, turned his Warhawk toward the ocean, and began his takeoff roll directly behind Whiteman. He saw Whiteman's plane go down burning after a burst of gunfire tore into the engine and cockpit. A deep rage engulfed him as he got airborne. He held the P-40's gun trigger down as Japanese planes swarmed around him. As he retracted his landing gear and hugged the water, trying to gain speed, the Zekes clung tenaciously to him and shot him down in the ocean about a half mile offshore. Despite a bullet wound in his leg, Bishop managed to get out of his plane and, with his Mae West keeping him afloat, swam to shore.[31]

When the crew flew their crippled B-17C aircraft out of the fury engulfing Hickam and made an emergency landing at Bellows Field, their long ordeal wasn't yet over. Bellows had had one lone fighter attack during the Japanese first strike, but fully expected more. By the time the bomber slid off the runway on its belly, word had spread at Bellows of attacks at Pearl Harbor, Wheeler, Kaneohe, and Hickam. The B-17 crew had been caught in the middle of the attacks on Hickam and had seen from a distance some of the devastation wracking Pearl harbor. Everyone anticipated a possible landing of Japanese troops. The weary, beleaguered bomber crew immediately began work to salvage the still-secret, new bomb sight and remove the stowed, still-greased guns they were going to mount for the last leg to the Philippines. The guns were later set up for ground defense.

Private Lester A. Ellis of the 86th Observation Squadron was positioned on the runway as a lookout near the crash-landed B-17 when the Japanese second wave appeared at Bellows.

The crippled, crash-landed B-17C, which diverted from Hickam to avoid repeated attacks by the Japanese raiders. The pilot made an emergency, downwind landing at Bellows Field and retracted the landing gear during roll-out. The crew counted 73 bullet holes in the bomber after the airborne attacks while attempting to land at Hickam, followed by attacks at Bellows Field by nine Japanese fighters. NPSAM

When sent to his post, he was ordered to give a shouted warning to the plane's crew, and Bellows men assisting them, should the enemy return and begin strafing runs. Lieutenant Nono's nine Japanese fighters' repeated attacks gave him more than enough times to shout, and each time everyone near the downed bomber ran for cover. After the Japanese planes left, the bomber crew counted 73 bullet holes in the B-17. Though considered repairable, the airplane was instead used for spare parts, and never repaired. The crew suffered two seriously wounded, Staff Sergeant Lawrence B. Velarde and Sergeant Vernon D. Tomlinson.[32]

Nono's Zekes did enough damage at Bellows. In addition to the wounding of the medical detachment's Private First Class James C. Brown in another lone Zeke's early morning "out of the sun" strafing pass down the line of tents, the deaths of Lieutenants Christiansen and Whiteman and the wounding of Lieutenant Bishop—all three from Wheeler's 44th Pursuit Squadron—two more men from the 86th Observation Squadron received wounds at Bellows. Two others received wounds at Hickam in separate attacks. When Nono's nine Zekes departed Bellows, he wasn't through. Not yet.[33]

In Nono's group of Zekes Sublieutenant Iyozo Fujita was on his first combat mission. The night before, when he was aboard *Soryu*, the pleasant-faced young fighter pilot was keenly aware this would be his first mission, and expected it to be his last. He drank several bottles of beer to bring on sleep, then took a bath. Before the early morning launch, he donned clean clothing to go into battle spotless, like the samurai of old. Then he pocketed a picture of his deceased parents. He told himself he was completely in the hands of fate—but now, having successfully come off a damaging attack on Bellows, he had passed his first test, was still alive, and was following Nono on his way to Kaneohe.

They streaked back to the Naval Air Station, where nine of Shimazaki's Kate horizontal bombers already had the field under attack, coming in at much lower altitudes than the 10,000 feet or more flown by the first wave of bombers over Pearl Harbor. The Zekes in the first wave had been able to confirm there were no heavy antiaircraft guns defending Kaneohe. The second wave of Kates approaching at the lower altitude carried a mixed load including two 550-lb bombs, wouldn't be threatened by big guns—and their bombing could be more accurate.[34]

The first wave's eleven Zekes had done heavy damage at Kaneohe and shocked the Air Station into full alert. The Japanese fighters' 7.7-mm machine guns and 20-mm cannons, armor-piercing ammunition loads interspersed with tracers and incendiary rounds, killed and wounded men scampering to mount a defense; damaged and started fires on aircraft and vehicles, and in hangars. The 20-mm rounds exploded on impact, sounding like bombs, and did much heavier damage. Officers and men rushed to their duty stations and Lieutenant Commander Buckley and a considerable number of men were in Hangar 1, which housed Patrol Squadrons 11 and 12. Buckley was supervising the supply of weapons and replenishment ammunition.

Twenty-five minutes after the first wave departed, Iida's nine Zekes from the second wave swirled overhead above the bombers, staying out of the way and providing cover, while bombs dropped by Ichihara's second-wave Kates fell with telling effect. Each released a pair of bombs in each pass from altitudes between 1,000 and 1,500 feet. Two bombs hit and exploded in Hangar 1, destroying the four PBYs inside; two close alongside near the southeast corner, and one dud fell inside. The five bombs caused the most casualties suffered in all the attacks. Another bomb destroyed the Air Station's only fire truck.

Immediately behind the nine bombers came nine more led by Lieutenant Tsutomu Hagiwara. At this point men on the ground who observed the bombers' attacks became uncertain whether or not the second nine Kates dropped any bombs at Kaneohe. "So much smoke was in the area and people [were] stunned by the first wave [of bombers] . . . " Observers on the ground concluded, if the second group didn't release their bombs, the lead observer-bombardier had probably been killed because his aircraft had taken considerable punishment from a high volume of machine gun fire aimed at the lead aircraft. They had seen the tracers hitting the aircraft. If the second group of Kates didn't drop, the first group made another bomb run, aiming for the other hangar—and were far less successful. By then resistance was fierce. Some bombs fell between the hangar and the water, causing holes in the parking ramp. The rest fell in the water, not a tribute to the raider's bombing accuracy. Explosions in front of the open hangar doors heavily damaged airplanes inside and set them on fire.

Twenty year-old Aviation Machinist Mate Clifton E. Dohrmann

woke up to war at Kaneohe when the first wave came that morning. Clif was in his bunk in Patrol Squadron 11 barracks in the foothills, about a mile from the flight line, when he awakened to what sounded like bombs going off. He and other men went outside to see what was going on, looked toward Kaneohe Bay and saw Filipino contractor personnel running away from the airfield toward the foothills. Then he saw aircraft he knew to be Japanese Zeroes attacking the Air Station. More men came outside, the word spread rapidly, and then Clif and others went back inside to pull on their uniforms and hurry on foot to their duty stations.

As he neared Hangar 1 and its engineering shop in the northwest corner, his duty station, he found himself running for cover inside the huge building. The first wave had come and gone. Bombers were coming, the beginning of the second wave. The hangar housed aircraft from patrol squadrons VP-11 and VP-12. Men were scurrying to find weapons to fire, or for cover anywhere they could find it, as were drivers of any vehicles and the small flight line tractors pulling flatbeds picking up wounded and dead. Bombs from the Kates were exploding uncomfortably close, near the hangar. Running beside him was another man. Clif didn't know who he was and neither of them had time to stop and get acquainted. They never did become acquainted.

As they neared the huge hangar door, the first of the two bombs to hit Hangar 1, penetrated the roof, exploded on the concrete floor, and sent a piece of shrapnel tearing through the door, instantaneously leveling the man next to Clif. It tore off his leg. Fear, shock, training and the survival instinct took over. There was nothing Clif could do. The wounded man would be picked up. He had to get to his duty station in engineering.

Guns. Men arriving in engineering needed guns. The squadron's airplanes had been badly damaged by the first wave of Zekes. All four PBYs moored in the water were on fire. Crews couldn't possibly get any Catalinas safely in the air when fighters were waiting for the Kates to finish their work. Clif and others rushed to Ordnance, Patrol Wing ONE's armory, to get rifles, pistols, machine guns, and ammunition, anything they could to fight back. It was locked, but someone quickly arrived with keys.

Clif's engineering boss, Chief Aviation Machinist George Roy Jackson, grabbed a
.50-caliber machine gun and ammunition and headed for the

ramp. Clif and another man took a .50-caliber machine gun, a
tripod and ammunition and went out the single door adjacent
to Ordnance, facing Kaneohe Bay, near the northeast corner of
Hangar 1. The Japanese fighters in the first wave had strafed east
and west, up and down the line of PBYs parked wing to wing
between the ocean and the hangars. Men were fighting fires on
several of the airplanes, still targets for the second wave now
savaging the Air Station. The two defenders would need some
protection.

Clif remembered engineering was modifying VP-11's aircraft,
installing armored seats for the pilots and other crew members.
The two men rushed enough armored seats onto the ramp to
form them into a semi-circle facing the ocean, with Hangar 1's
high concrete block and stucco wall at their backs for protection.
Clif quickly set up as the gunner on the right, facing the Bay,
inside the protective semi-circle. His volunteer assistant gunner, a
crew member on one of VP-11's Catalinas was to his left, almost
aligned with and in front of the hangar's side entry door, near
Ordnance. He was to be the ammunition bearer and feed the
ammunition belts into the gun.

At this point, in which brief minutes seemed an eternity,
bombers were still on the attack. Chief Jackson was on the ramp
firing his hand-held .50-caliber machine gun at Kates as they
roared overhead. On the bay-side of Hangar 1, Clif fired short
bursts at raiders he believed he might have a chance to hit. They
saw no hits.

Then another explosion just as Clif was squeezing off a burst.
Another bomb inside the hangar. Again, shrapnel tore through
the door, this time from behind his squadron mate. The man
pitched forward, face down, pulling the ammunition belt with
him, which jammed the machine gun. Clif turned to see a hole in
the man's back, a hole he felt he could stick his entire hand into.
Clif's participation in antiaircraft defense was over. His squadron
mate needed immediate medical attention.

He ran out on the ramp in front of the huge hangar door
looking for one of the flight line tractors picking up wounded.
Now came the fighters, from behind him, then seemingly from
every direction. He found someone to help him, and lifted the
wounded man onto the flatbed. He feared the man was mortally
wounded, but at least he was on his way to medical care. Clif
hadn't time to dwell on the subject. Fires caused by the Kates'

Wrecked automobiles, some still burning, beside a damaged
hangar at Naval Air Station, Kaneohe Bay, Oahu, during
or soon after the Japanese air attack. NHHC

bombs and the Zeke's cannon and machine gun fire set Hangar 1
ablaze, and the huge structure burned until only its steel skeleton
was left.

It was shortly after 1000 hours and it was all over at Kaneohe—
or was it? Obvious question. "Where had the Japanese come
from?" "Might they land troops?" Logic said troops might not
be far behind the air attack. Before night came, Clif and other
men from Kaneohe were in the hills above the Air Station, armed
with rifles and machine guns, in hurriedly-dug defensive positions,
while closer to the beaches, civilians—mostly volunteers, others
motivated by the declaration of martial law—were digging trenches
and filling sand bags, fully expecting a Japanese invasion.[35]

In VP-14's hangar, after the 18 Kate level bombers of the
second wave passed, Radioman Third Class Ken Poppleton and
others were more fortunate, and they knew it. They believed the
small amount of fire power they marshaled had kept their hangar
from being struck by the bombers. Hangar No. 1 to the west

of theirs took multiple bomb hits, and was the hangar where Kaneohe's defenders sustained most of their casualties.

Ken and his squadron mates spent the next hour assessing what else they might need in case another attack occurred. He checked the teletype for any communications telling them what to expect next. He found a message from Ensign Tanner's PBY, 14-P-1, reporting their attack on the midget submarine. He took the message from the machine and delivered it to their squadron commander. His radio instructor caught sight of him and ordered him to the "Radio Shack" (message center) at the headquarters of Kaneohe Naval Air Station. "We need all the help we can get."

He spent the next ten hours on the circuit between Radio Honolulu and Radio Washington. The circuit was an intercept circuit to keep NAS Kaneohe Bay and Patrol Wing ONE informed of official communications, and was an alternate communications node in case Pearl Harbor lost it's capability to transmit and receive.

No sooner did he start monitoring traffic than it became clear people at Radio Washington, receiving messages, were hard to convince an attack was in progress. Not until Pearl Harbor had a temporary power loss during the second wave's attack, and Kaneohe took control of communications, did Radio Washington accept that an attack was in progress.

Ken Poppleton slept and ate at the "Radio Shack" for the next two days, and only then returned to his squadron. He wouldn't fly as a crew member on a PBY again until after the middle of December.

Before he left the hangar for his new temporary duty station that morning, the second wave of Zekes came roaring in for further attacks, having come from their assault on Bellows Field. Though one launched a strafing attack on the VP-14 hangar, it caused no serious damage and cost the Japanese pilot his life.

Aviation Machinist Guy Avery recalled the Zeroes "cruised around over us, firing sporadically at any likely target." They strafed homes, cars, pedestrians. "Particularly did they harass the firemen who were fighting the blazes among the squadron planes standing on the ramp." Lieutenant Iida went after the station armory, making his pass just as an aviation ordnanceman named Sands stepped out of the side door and fired off a burst with a Browning Automatic Rifle, emptying the clip. A crusty aviation ordnanceman 2nd class of the old school, he called to men inside the armory, "Hand me another BAR! Hurry up! I swear I hit that yellow bastard!"

As Iida moved in for the kill, the defiant sailor "emptied another clip" and escaped Iida's bullets, which "pockmarked the wall of the building." Iida broke off the attack, turning to overtake and rejoin the fighters who had reformed and were headed toward a mountain gap and additional attacks on Wheeler Field. It was nearly over at Kaneohe, but not quite.

En route to rejoin the remainder of his fighters, Iida saw a spray of gasoline begin to flow from his plane. He undoubtedly believed he might not make it to Wheeler to continue the mission, and was certain he wouldn't make it back to *Soryu*. In *At Dawn We Slept* Gordon Prange told the story of Lieutenant Iida:

> No doubt this was the moment when Iida, faithful to his preachings, pointed first to himself, then to the ground, thus indicating he was going to plunge into the enemy.
>
> A sailor saw him returning and, evidently considering Iida Sands' particular pigeon, shouted, "Hey, Sands! That sonofabitch is coming back!" Sands grabbed a rifle; Iida roared straight at him. Ignoring the bullets splattering around him, Sands "emptied the rifle at the roaring Zero . . . Iida ceased his fire a moment before passing over Sands' head . . .
>
> The Zero crashed into a road winding up a round, flat-topped hill and struck the pavement about five feet below one of the married officers' quarters, "skidded across and piled up against the embankment at the opposite side." The impact ripped out the engine, turned the plane upside down, and shattered Iida's body to pieces. Avery was convinced that mercifully the pilot died before the crash because he took Sand's fire head-on and seemed to lose control of the airplane at the last instant.
>
> Horror-stricken, Fujita watched Iida's plunge to death. He mistakenly credited his friend with "crashing straight downward in the midst of a flaming hangar on Kaneohe Air Base."
>
> One other Japanese aircraft fell at Kaneohe, but the defenders could not identify the pilot, for the

plane crashed into Kailua Bay. Iida and his unknown
comrade probably would have counted their lives well
lost. Kaneohe was about as wrecked as wrecked can
be . . . Of Kaneohe's thirty-six PBYs, three on patrol
escaped, six were damaged, the rest destroyed . . . [36]

One of the three PBYs on patrol, 14-P-2 (Bureau No. 2418),
was repeatedly attacked by nine Japanese aircraft about 1000
hours while the Japanese raiders were withdrawing to their
carriers. The attack put numerous bullet holes in the aircraft, but
it remained airborne, in commission, and, for the Navy, became a
major indicator of the direction the search for the carrier striking
force should take later that morning.[37]

Eighteen sailors and two civilians were killed, and eleven,
including two officers, were seriously wounded in the attacks at
Kaneohe. Among the dead were four officers and thirteen sailors
from Patrol Squadrons 11, 12, and 14, and a sailor from the
Air Station headquarters. The destructive assault on Patrol Wing
One sharply increased the probability the Japanese carrier task
force would not be found.[38]

Fujita re-formed the remainder of Iida's group and led them
toward Wheeler Field, fiercely intent on avenging his friend's
death. To his surprise, vengeance was interrupted by machine
gun fire from American fighters.

Land, Reload, and Into the Air Again:
P-40s and P-36s on the Attack

By the time Lieutenants Welch and Taylor drove at break-neck
speed from the Wheeler officers' club to the auxiliary field at
Haleiwa—while dodging three strafing attacks—their two P-40s
were waiting, guns loaded, and engines running. They scrambled
into the air at approximately 0830. As they lifted off the runway,
the raiders' first wave was just beginning to leave the hostile
airspace over Pearl Harbor and Hickam Field to rendezvous over
Barbers Point and return to their carriers. Others that had early
run dry of bombs and ammunition, and rejoined in formations,
were already en route to their carriers. The first wave of Zekes
targeted against Kaneohe, and the Vals and Zekes targeted against

Wheeler had done their work well, and gone to secondary targets to use their remaining machine gun ammunition.[39]

Ground control directed Welch and Taylor to head for the southern tip of the island where Japanese in the first wave were continuing their strafing attacks on Marine Air Group 21 at Ewa. In the initial attack, the raiders sent thirty-two fighters in successive attacks on the base, with two groups of nine each targeted against Hickam with attacks on Ewa en route. The thirty-two had already departed Ewa, when Welch and Taylor arrived in the area, but two groups of eight and six targeted against Wheeler Field as well, with follow-on strafing attacks at Ewa, were still in the vicinity of Ewa when the two P-40's arrived. Additionally, some of the attacks on Ewa were Vals which had dive bombed Wheeler Field, had 7.7-mm machine gun ammunition remaining, and were specifically targeted against Ewa for follow-on attacks.[40]

As Welch and Taylor pressed south toward Barbers Point they spotted a group of enemy planes in a long line, and both pilots jumped into the line at or near the end, and probably closing forward in the line, began shooting down aircraft. He recalled, "I made a nice turn out into them and got in a string of six or eight planes. I don't know how many there were . . . and I was on one's tail as we went over Waialua, firing at the one next to me, and I pulled out. I don't know what happened to the other plane. Lieutenant Welch, I think, shot the other man down." Welch added, "We took off directly into them and shot some down. I shot one down right on Lieutenant Taylor's tail." Each got two confirmed kills during this first engagement. Taylor fired on a third raider but didn't see the crash. Both were running out of ammunition so returned to Wheeler Field to reload.[41]

Welch and Taylor were returning to Wheeler totally unaware of the wild cheering that greeted their aggressive attacks on the Japanese aircraft in the air within sight of Ewa. Between the first and second wave of attacks, the Marines hastily assembled an antiaircraft defense, ready to return fire on Japanese planes firing out the last of their machine gun ammunition against the field. The defense included mounted machine guns and World War I, 1903 Springfield bolt action rifles.

A group of marines improvised a gun mount from a scout plane, shot down one Zeke, and hit a number of others. Although one enemy loss was credited to ground fire, it was in the air where hope sprang anew. They watched as ". . . several US Army Air Corps planes from an outlying base engaged the enemy, downing two 'meatballs' right over our heads and three a distance away. The resulting cheers from Marine ground defenders blanked out other battle noise for the moment."

Against that total, when the second wave of raiders finished their work, the attackers had destroyed or temporarily knocked out nine of Ewa's eleven F4F fighters, eighteen of thirty-two scout bombers, and six of eight utility aircraft. Casualties were four killed in action, and thirteen wounded.[42]

The first wave's attack on Wheeler destroyed most of the 42 total destroyed P-40s (37 P-40Bs and 5 P-40Cs), and damaged many more of the 99 total on the island. Sixty-four were in commission prior to the attack, and only 25 remained in commission after the raid ended. The older, slower, less capable P-36A Hawks being phased out of the Army Air Force's inventory were toward the west end of the ramp, almost obscured by heavy smoke and relatively untouched by the raiders. Of 39 P-36As at Wheeler, 20 were in commission prior to the attack, the raiders destroyed four and damaged several others, leaving 16 in commission.

When the attack began and men fled the flightline area, Colonel Flood, the base commander, had ordered mission support units to return. They were needed to salvage as many airplanes as possible from the parking ramp and hangars, and all other mission essential items such as ammunition, aircraft in hangars for maintenance, engines that had been removed, spare parts, and machinery and tools from shops. Aircraft ground crews and men from support units returning to the flightline began moving aircraft away from the fires, and dispersing the few remaining P-40s to revetments, then came back to salvage as much ammunition as they could, while others were preparing mostly P-36s for flight.

Hangar 3 had taken a direct hit from a dive bomber. In the hangar were tons of ammunition taken from all aircraft on the flightline and centrally stored to reduce the possibility of sabotage. The hangar was on fire. The fires triggered small, secondary explosions which continued for several hours, making ammunition retrieval for loading difficult and dangerous at best.

By this time there were many more pilots available than aircraft ready to fly. It became a contest as to who would get which P-36. A simple system evolved in which the pilots ran for the planes when a call came through to scramble them. The first one arriving got the cockpit. One pilot accused another of not running very fast, and a fistfight ensued. The armorer, Private Wilford Burke saw the humor of the situation and took comfort in knowing that he wasn't the only one with "cold feet."

First Lieutenant Lewis M. Sanders picked three experienced pilots and told them to grab the first available aircraft and follow him for a four-ship attack. Lieutenants John M. Thacker and Philip M. Rasmussen stayed by their aircraft until they were ready to go, then jumped in and began to taxi. Lieutenant Othneil Norris helped get an airplane ready, but left to go get a new parachute. Second Lieutenant Gordon H. Sterling, Jr. spotted the unattended aircraft, jumped in and taxied out to join Sanders and the other two pilots. The practice of grabbing any aircraft ready to fly happened several more times before the day ended.

Airborne about 8:50, minutes before the second wave of Vals descended on the the *Pennsylvania*, other ships in the Navy Yard, and the *Nevada* moving down-channel, Sanders led the flight east toward Bellows Field. Spotting the Japanese second wave of Zekes coming from over Kaneohe on their way toward Wheeler, the four P-36s immediately engaged. Unknown to Sanders and Sublieutenant Fujita, with surprise bursts of machine gun fire, Sanders and his three flight members interrupted Fujita's intended vengeance for the loss of his friend and flight leader, Lieutenant Iida, who had just lost his life at Kaneohe.

Sanders got on the tail of a Zeke and shot it down. Coming off the attack, he saw Sterling in hot pursuit of another fighter that was diving toward the water. Behind Sterling another Zeke had entered the fight and was shooting at Sterling. Sanders came up behind this aircraft and opened fire. Rasmussen observed the four aircraft. The plane Sterling was attacking crashed. Sterling, close behind, also plunged into the sea, shot down by the Japanese on his tail. Sanders meanwhile set fire to the fighter that shot down Sterling, but Rasmussen didn't know whether it, too, went into the water.

Just before witnessing Sterling's death, Rasmussen had charged his guns, only to have them start firing on their own. While trying to stop the guns from firing, a Japanese aircraft passed directly in front of him and exploded. Things began to happen fast after that, and he soon had two Zekes on his tail. He took evasive action and lost them in cloud cover. Meanwhile, Thacker dove into the battle, only to discover his guns had jammed and wouldn't fire. He kept making passes at the Japanese until hit several times, then broke off the engagement and returned to base. Sanders found himself alone with a Zeke and was quickly losing the flying contest. Deciding that discretion was the better part of valor, he broke off the one-sided contest and headed back to Wheeler Field.

In Fujita's account of the engagement, he "poured bullets into an enemy fighter below him, and the American plane disappeared in a trail of black smoke. Another American—"a P-40 or P-36"— came at him, all guns blazing. Fujita took his adversary's fire straight on, and though winged by antiaircraft fire and now with a shot up engine, he fired at another plane. All around him his "comrades engaged in a slashing dogfight with other American fighters." "The Zekes handled beautifully and consistently outmaneuvered U.S. interceptors,"—but the Japanese had as much as they bargained for. Fujita decided enough was enough, rocked his wings to signal rejoin, and they sped off to rendezvous for the return to *Soryu*. So far the Americans had managed to get six fighters airborne and had shot down seven Japanese with loss of one P-36.

From that point on, the story became confusing. Pilots were taking off individually from two different fields and then joining up after getting airborne. Takeoff times were difficult, if not impossible to verify. About the same time Sanders' flight was mixing it up with Fujita's Zekes near Kaneohe, Welch and Taylor were ready to head out on their second mission that morning.

Wheeler was in turmoil when they landed. Welch recalled, "We had to argue with some of the ground crew. They wanted us to disperse the airplanes and we wanted to fight." As the armorers were loading ammunition, the Japanese came back. The ground crews had to run for cover. Welch got off first, and just as Taylor was ready to go the second wave hit Wheeler Field. Taylor waited until what he thought was the last in the line of Zekes and took off after them, guns blazing. Just after he got airborne, another Japanese got on his tail and opened fire. For a few seconds it looked grim, but Welch had stayed in the immediate area, saw the attack on Taylor and came to the rescue. He got behind the Zeke that was shooting at Taylor and scored his third kill for the day.

The shootdown shook Taylor free and allowed him to gain some altitude. Though wounded in the attack he was still able to fly, so he continued attacking Japanese aircraft wherever he could find them, damaging at least one more. Meanwhile, Welch headed back to Ewa and got a confirmed kill on another Japanese, bringing his total for the day to four.

While Lieutenants Christiansen, Whiteman, and Bishop were futilely attempting to get airborne at Bellows, resulting in the deaths of Christiansen and Whiteman and the shootdown and wounding of Bishop, Haleiwa auxiliary on the west side of the island launched aircraft as fast as pilots showed up. Lieutenants John Dains and John Webster both got off at different times in P-40s, while Lieutenants Harry Brown and Robert Rogers each took off in P-36s. From Wheeler Field, Lieutenants Malcolm Moore and Othneil Norris entered the fight by flying P-36s. Brown and Rogers headed for Kahuku Point. There they engaged the enemy without any confirmed kills, though Rogers damaged one enemy aircraft.

From there they joined with Moore and Webster and headed west. Webster damaged one aircraft over Kaena Point, but couldn't confirm a kill. Japanese fighters cornered Rogers, but Brown plowed into the fight, shooting down one attacker. The action started winding down as the Japanese began withdrawing. Moore opened up on one retreating aircraft but didn't down it. Brown closed on the smoking aircraft and fired. Like Moore, however, he was unable to score a hit to down him, and the enemy got away.

One mystery still remains concerning the action that occurred in the air that Sunday morning. Radar operators at the station at Kaawa watched a P-40 shoot down a Japanese Zeke during the height of the battle. The operators were positive the American aircraft was a P-40, and they identified it both from its distinctive silhouette and the sound of its engine. None of the pilots that survived that morning's action remembered flying in the Kaawa area.

The only pilot whose action was unaccounted for was Lieutenant John Dains, who flew two missions that morning in a P-40. Both times he was separated from the other American fighters and fought by himself. After landing the second time, he switched to a P-36 and joined up with George Welch for a third mission. Neither pilot spotted anything because by that time the Japanese had cleared the area so they decided to return to

Wheeler Field. On the return flight, antiaircraft guns at Schofield Barracks opened up on the two aircraft and killed Dains.

There were three plausible explanations. First, the radar operators could have been mistaken in what they saw. Second, some other P-40 pilot downed the Japanese plane and was unaware where the action occurred. Third, John Dains did get the enemy plane as ground personnel observed and just never got the chance to tell his story.

The Japanese would concede twenty-nine aircraft from all causes that morning. The Hawaiian Air Force claimed ten of those losses with four more probable and two Japanese aircraft damaged. If Dain's kill is added to the list, the score comes out eleven destroyed in air-to-air combat with a loss of four American planes, which were flown by Whiteman, Sterling, Bishop, and Dains.

Gordon Sterling was the only Army Air Force pilot lost in

Photograph taken 17 December 1941. Nine Japanese planes were shot down by these five young Army Air Force officers during the Japanese attack. Left to right they are-2nd Lt. Harry W. Brown, who bagged one Japanese plane; 2nd Lt. Philip M. Rasmmussen, one plane; 2nd Lt. Kenneth M. Taylor, two planes; 2nd Lt. George S. Welch, four planes; 1st Lt. Lewis M. Sanders, one plane. Lts. Welsh and Taylor received Distinguished Service Crosses. UHHL

air-to-air combat with the enemy, and it appears he downed the fighter he was chasing before he crashed in the water. The Japanese downed two during the pilots' desperate attempts to get airborne at Bellows Field: George Whiteman, who was killed, and Samuel Bishop taking off behind Whiteman. Friendly fire downed John Dains. He didn't survive.

Could American fighter forces, both Air Force and Navy have inflicted much heavier losses that morning had they received strategic or tactical warning? The results after experiencing total surprise, certainly suggest they could. However, to place the air battle into perspective it's important to remember the Japanese had committed over half their force just to deal with the American fighters. They preplanned an on-the-spot decision to discard their fighter-top-cover defense system if they encountered no reaction en route to the target area. This meant the few interceptor aircraft that did get airborne that morning hit an almost unprotected attacking force.

Welch and Taylor's encounters over Ewa during their first flight provided an example of this. Had the American forces met the Japanese from the beginning, the Japanese force over Ewa would certainly have had fighters flying top cover for them, thus diverting them away from the targets they attacked and decreasing the damage to aircraft and airfields on the ground. As Sanders discovered over Kaneohe, the P-36 was no match for the Zeke, and without special training, neither was the P-40. But these are matters of speculation.

More important under the circumstances that morning was how the men of the Hawaiian Air Force responded. From the most junior man on the ground to the best fighter pilot in the command, everyone did the best they could with what they had. They were caught by surprise, but they most certainly never gave up. And most assuredly, the United States Navy certainly never gave up. From their ships and airplanes they gave the raiders far more than anticipated.[43]

The Japanese second wave plan included no fighters or bombers specifically targeted against Wheeler Field, probably a reasonable decision in terms of additional damage that might be gained. As events proved, the base was already in a shambles. Iida's two groups of Zekes totaling 17 aircraft from *Soryu* and *Hiryu*, given free reign for targets of opportunity after hitting their primary targets at Bellows and Kaneohe, were headed toward rendezvous in the vicinity of Ewa for return to their carriers. After the loss of Iida at Kaneohe, Sublieutenant Fujita had led one group toward the rendezvous, and ran head-on into Sanders' flight of P-36s, where the Japanese lost one or two more, possibly diverting his group from further attacks on the fighter base—while other Zekes pressed toward the rendezvous before returning to their carriers.

Men on the Wheeler flightline who raced for cover, and Taylor's scrambling takeoff in which he nearly was shot down, were seeing the last gasp of the Japanese attack on Wheeler Field. Sanders and others in the small band of fighter pilots that managed to get airborne, pointed toward Kaneohe, can be credited with avoiding further death and destruction at Wheeler Field as a result of the encounter with Fujita's Zekes.

While sadly, VS-6 from the *Enterprise* lost eight crew members and five dive bombers in the Japanese hornets' nest the SBDs had the terrible misfortune to fly into that morning, to his everlasting credit, one of VS-6's gunners, Radioman First Class Miller, who lost his life, unquestionably downed one of the first wave's Zekes. One other SBD, 6-S-14, went down, hit by "friendly fire," but both crew members, Ensign Deacon and Radioman Third Class Coslett, survived.

Had the Pacific Fleet, Navy and its aviators, the Fourteenth Naval District, and the Army's Hawaiian Department had strategic or sufficient tactical warning, results would probably have been quite different. Scouting Squadron Six, other aircraft from Task Force 8, Navy and Marine aircraft on Oahu, along with bombers and fighters from the Hawaiian Air Force would have been able to greet the Japanese carrier strike force far north of Oahu—perhaps before they ever launched their aircraft. Pearl Harbor might have been emptied of Naval combatants and all antiaircraft defenses on Oahu, plus the Air Force's interceptor squadrons primed and ready for the kill.

But reality was quite different on Oahu, in the air and surrounding seas that day. Through a chain of tragically incredible oversights and events, laced with bad luck, neither adequate strategic nor tactical warning occurred, and disaster followed. Near Pearl Harbor, the Japanese second wave was bringing hell back to Hickam Field and Ford Island a second time.

In the second wave, the Japanese carriers *Shokaku* and *Zuikaku* sent thirty-six Kate horizontal bombers over the Hickam-Ford Island-Pearl Harbor area, at approximately 10,000 feet, nine of the thirty-six specifically targeted against Hickam. In addition, Zekes from *Akagi's* 2d Attack Unit, led by Lieutenant Saburo Shindo, planned to deal more death and destruction to an already battered Hickam Field.[44]

The rush to pick up wounded and dead all over Oahu and take them to the nearest aid stations, clinics and hospitals started almost immediately when the raid began. At all airfields, while ambulances and medical facilities were almost immediately overwhelmed, military men and women, and hundreds of other on-the-spot volunteers assisted any way they could. As was the case at Kaneohe, where flight line tractors pulling small flatbed trailers hauled wounded to the nearest medical facilities and temporary aid stations, on Hickam Field vehicles of every conceivable type—bread wagons, milk wagons, hand carts, trucks, private cars—were commandeered to augment the ambulance fleet and transport wounded to the base hospital. All available men in the immediate area were pressed into service to help load the injured. At the Hickam parade ground, they stacked the most badly wounded on top of each other in the back of an ambulance and rushed them to the hospital.

Private First Class Raymond L. Perry of the Army's 29th Car Company was on temporary duty at Fort Armstrong in downtown Honolulu when the first attack occurred and everyone was scrambling around trying to get away from the antiaircraft shells raining on the city. They were experiencing what young Frederick Kamaka, his schoolmates, and junior ROTC instructor at Ft. Kamehameha School experienced. The larger antiaircraft guns on ships at first were using contact fuses instead of time fuses on the rounds fired toward the east from Pearl Harbor, at raiders, and expended rounds were exploding on impact with the ground. Perry, "tired of being shot at," learned vehicles were needed at Hickam to transport wounded to Tripler Army Hospital at Ft. Shafter, and quickly volunteered to go.

Two military policemen on motorcycles escorted their convoy of five trucks to Hickam Field. They proceeded along Hangar Avenue, past the consolidated barracks, and pulled into the area between Hangars 9 and 13. With the help of Army Air Forces personnel, they began loading wounded men into their trucks. Then at 0845, someone shouted, "Here they come again!" and everyone took cover in the closest hangar doorwell.[45]

Kate level bomber and Val dive bomber formations were

closing toward Hickam, Pearl Harbor, and Ford Island from the southwest into the wind. Twenty-seven of the fifty-four total Kates carried two 550-pound bombs, and the twenty-seven others carried mixed loads of one 550-pound, and six 132-pound bombs. The first nine over Hickam were again devastating.[46]

After the explosions and firing subsided, Perry and the other volunteers went out and found all their trucks completely demolished. Of the seventeen men they had picked up, only three were still alive. Earlier, someone had taken a bed sheet, painted a large, red cross on it, and attached it to the top of the center truck. All it proved to be was an aim point for the attackers.[47]

Hangar 15, which housed base engineering, suffered considerable damage, with many personnel wounded and killed, but Hangar 17 had only minor damage. Bombs wrecked Hangar 11, killing nearly all the 11th Bomb Group's armament and aircraft maintenance technicians. The attack shattered Hangar 7 and slightly damaged Hangar 9, but left Hangars 3 and 5 intact. The Japanese also destroyed all the tugs and gas trucks in the gas storage area but failed to damage the underground fuel tanks. A target folder later discovered with a downed Japanese plane showed the tanks in the area where the ball diamond was located.

That area was in fact the original site planned for the tanks; however, over a year before the attack, a change in plans resulted in placing them elsewhere and building a baseball field in that location. Consequently, the ball field was bombed instead of the underground fuel storage tanks. The same target folder identified the base operations building as the officers' club, so the nerve center was spared, as were Hangars 2 and 4, which had been completed just a few months before the attack.

Hickam's big, new consolidated barracks was a major target, and was reported as the most heavily bombed on Oahu. It shook repeatedly with the force of explosions for what seemed like an eternity. The first bomb took a heavy toll, instantly killing thirty-five men who had been eating the late breakfast in the large mess hall, the Hale Makai, but remained after the attack began, believing they would best be sheltered from the assault. Trays, dishes, food, and body parts splattered everywhere. Injured survivors crawled through the rubble to safety. More bombs hit and exploded, and the concussion killed all the Chinese cooks who sought protection in the freezer room.

Infantry-trained noncommissioned officers ordered airmen

to disperse from the big building to lessen the possibility of multiple deaths from a single explosion, but tragically, many who left were killed by strafing or bomb fragments. Except for wings or sections that took direct hits, the consolidated, concrete-reinforced barracks actually offered the best protection, and was the most resistant to fire.

Russell Tener, who had fled the consolidated barracks for the perceived safety of the parade ground, and was making his way across the grassy area when pandemonium erupted. Pilots of low-flying Japanese aircraft sighted the mob of men, turned toward them, machine guns blazing while Val dive bombers were releasing their bombs. He ran toward the base chapel, and found the wood-frame building no longer standing—leveled by a direct hit, leaving only the concrete entry steps. Joe Nelles, the Catholic Chaplain's assistant and Russell Tener's friend, went to the chapel early every Sunday morning to prepare the altar for Mass. Joe was Russell's immediate thought when he saw the Chapel had

Strafed Fire House on Hickam Air Field with two fire trucks outside and debris from the attack This vivid photo shows the damage to Hickam Field's fire station. Note pockmarks of machine gun fire on the side of the building. NPSAM

been destroyed. Russell's fears were later confirmed—Joe had been killed in the Chapel.

On the other hand, unbelievable though it may be, a few took advantage of the chaos caused by the attack. A small group of men who took shelter under a nearby building were shocked to see an airman looting the post exchange (PX) after it was shattered by bombs. He emerged from the PX with a case of beer and cartons of cigarettes, started across the parade ground toward the consolidated barracks, but was cut down by a strafing Japanese plane. As he fell, beer cans and packs of cigarettes flew in all directions. At the consolidated barracks, amid all the death and destruction, looters helped themselves to items belonging to others. When Ira Southern returned to his third-floor bay after the attack, he found several of his personal items missing, including his new Zenith portable radio.

In the midst of the horror and incidents of looting inevitably came humor. The first sergeant in Ed Hall's truck company exploded in a rage, when, after he had endured the first two attack waves, he witnessed the destruction of the nearby Snake Ranch beer garden when it took a direct bomb hit and was demolished. This was too much. Shaking his fist at the sky, he screamed, "You dirty sons-a-bitches! You've bombed the most important building on the post!"

Base fire department crews responding to the scene wrought by the Japanese first wave faced a formidable task, with fires blazing in the hangars, aircraft, barracks, and numerous other facilities. Broken water mains from bomb blasts, which also hit the fire station itself, crippled their efforts. Rushing to answer calls for assistance, Private First Class Howard E. King, a hoseman, had just manned one of the fire engines when his crew chief, Sergeant Joseph J. Chagnon, suddenly yelled , "Look out!" Before King could move, there was a blinding flash, and something hit him like a ton of bricks. He found himself lying in a prone position, his leg shattered, peering through the smoke and could barely make out the twisted engine. Chagnon was dying.

Fire Chief William L. Benedict also suffered injuries when blown sixty feet by a bomb, then strafed by a Japanese pilot. Searchers at first couldn't find him. Then a young soldier told the chaplain that the fire chief had died in his arms, so Mr. Benedict's name appeared on the list of dead. He was finally found, bleeding in twenty-three places from shrapnel about two hours after the attack began. He later read his own death notice when a doctor at Tripler showed him a newspaper clipping prematurely announcing his death.

Under a memorandum of agreement, twenty-two fireman from Honolulu Fire Department companies responded when the alarm rang, calling for help at Hickam Field. When they reached Hickam's main gate on Kamehameha Highway, the first wave of the attack was over. The fire fighters saw dead, dying, and wounded bodies lying everywhere. The multistory concrete barracks off the main street was burning fiercely. An underground gas main at the base's entrance had been hit, was spewing flame dozens of feet into the air, and aircraft hangars and a quarter-mile long row of planes parked outside were also ablaze. On reporting to the Hickam fire station, they discovered that the station had been bombed and was in a shambles. One fire engine, driven about twenty feet out onto the ramp, apparently when the driver was trying to respond, was badly chewed up by a strafing enemy airplane. The driver was dead, slumped over the steering wheel. The other engine—King's and Chagnon's—never got out of the station. Thus the firemen from Kalihi Engines 4 and 6 (Palama and Kalihi stations) suddenly found themselves to be the only force available. Shortly afterward, however, Engine 1 from Honolulu's Central station on South Beretania Street arrived to assist.

A bomb dropped by the first wave of attackers struck Hickam's primary water main, leaving an enormous crater rapidly filling with water and no functional fire hydrants. Lieutenant Frederick Kealoha, in charge of the Honolulu Fire Department companies on the scene, had just decided to try drafting water from the bomb crater when the second wave of level bombers, followed almost immediately by Lieutenant Shindo's fighters, appeared overhead. He screamed at the fire fighters to take cover, and they scattered in all directions. For the next fifteen minutes, "Hell rained down from the skies in the form of whistling bombs and screaming machine gun bullets, seemingly strafing everyone and everything in sight."

The quarter hour seemed to last forever, as the firemen tried to make themselves invisible to the Japanese. When the second wave attack was finally over, the fire fighters hesitantly emerged from their hiding places and began to assess the latest round of death and destruction. Captain Thomas S. Macy, Captain John

Carreira, and Hoseman Tuck Lee Pang were dead. Lieutenant Kealoba and Hoseman Moses Kalilikane were critically wounded. Also wounded were Hosemen John A. Gilman, Soloman H. Naauao, and George Correa. The remaining firemen did little fire fighting for awhile, concentrating instead on providing aid to the injured men.[48]

The desperate efforts to remove wounded from ships and shattered airfields under fire, and take them to hospitals and other medical facilities was beginning to accelerate when the last of the straggling Japanese raiders were leaving the air over Oahu approximately 1000 hours, heading for their carriers. Numerous American ships, destroyers, minesweepers, minelayers, and patrol boats—the smaller ships—had left Pearl Harbor or were preparing to steam for the harbor entrance by the time the Japanese departed.

Underway . . . the Last Two Torpedoes, and More Enemy Planes

At 0817, when watch officers on the bridge of the destroyer *Helm* sighted the conning tower of a submarine toward the right (west) side of the channel, northward from buoy #1, they were still inside the harbor entrance. It was the first sign of more trouble with midget submarines attempting to enter Pearl Harbor, and probably the same submarine sunk twenty-four minutes later by *Monaghan*.

At 0819, as the *Helm* was accelerating out of the harbor, another submarine conning tower surfaced off Tripod Reef bearing 290 degrees, distance 1,200 yards from buoy #1, and one minute later the destroyer opened fire.

The gunners scored no hits but saw several close splashes. To *Helm*'s crew, the submarine appeared to be touching bottom on a ledge of the reef, in the line of breakers. While still firing at the submarine, it apparently slipped off the ledge and submerged. Things were happening fast, and they weren't all good.

While taking the sub under fire, and radioing a plain language report of the submarine to CinCPac on 2562 Kilocycles, the main contact relay on the power panel for the ship's steering motor short-circuited. Orders were given to shift to hand steering, and the crew began maneuvering the ship by the engines. The short caused the main circuit breakers to open, taking all light and power off the ship for about one, most crucial minute.

At 0821 men on the after guns and amidships observed a torpedo pass close under the stern on a northwesterly course. Because power was momentarily off the ship, the sound-powered phones dead, and no one verbally or by messenger passed the word, their observation didn't reach the *Helms*'s bridge until well after the torpedo's near miss. Not until 0824 was the shift to hand steering complete.

By 0830, as the first wave's aircraft were beginning to depart for their carriers, the *Helms*'s two confrontations with enemy submarines were in the past. She was steaming on various courses and speeds off the harbor entrance, steering by hand, firing intermittently at enemy planes, searching for enemy submarines, and observing numerous large splashes close at hand—undoubtedly large caliber, expended antiaircraft rounds, salvoes of bombs falling, or aircraft crashes as a result of the fierce battle raging above harbor and Hickam Field.

For 0900 hours the *Helms*'s 11 December 1941, Action Report for the Japanese attack read, "Destroyers commenced sortie." And indeed they did, as did other ships ordered to stand out of Pearl Harbor during the attack—to patrol assigned areas, and attack the enemy if found.[49]

The destroyer *Monaghan* was underway at 0835, and changed course en route to sink the midget submarine in the Middle Loch. Coming fast behind her, pausing at 0844 while *Monaghan* rammed and depth charged the submarine, was the destroyer, *Dale*, which then resumed speed and raced out of Pearl approximately 1,500 yards ahead of *Monaghan*. The *Blue* (DD-387) got underway at 0847, cleared the harbor entrance at 0910, and forty minutes later initiated the first of three depth charge attacks on underwater sound contacts, four and six miles respectively, south-southeast of Diamond Head. Her crew reported sinking or damaging a submarine, which couldn't be confirmed.

The *Farragut* (DD-348), in the north harbor destroyer nest with *Monaghan*, was underway at 0852, en route to the harbor entrance, just as the raiders' second wave was descending on the battleship *Nevada* and numerous other ships. Lieutenant Edwin K. Jones, the regularly assigned engineer on board the ship, was the senior officer on board, and acting commander. The other four officers on board were ensigns. Lieutenant Commander George P. Hunter, the ship's commander, was ashore on liberty, and was verbally ordered by Rear Admiral Robert A. Theobald, Destroyer Flotilla One's Commander, to take command of the destroyer *Hull* (DD-350). *Farragut* and nearly all others were "running the gauntlet " of swarming enemy aircraft. At 0921, she was subjected to a strafing attack that did slight damage topside. Shortly afterward, while proceeding through the channel abreast of Hickam Field one of her crew, according to witnesses, brought down a Val dive bomber with a .50-caliber machine gun. *Farragut* cleared the harbor entrance at 0927.

The minelayer *Ramsay* (DM-16) left her berth in the nest of minelayers in the West Loch at 0855. While churning toward the harbor entrance, she took a Japanese plane under fire, and claimed its destruction. The destroyer *Aylwin* (DD-355), with Ensign Stanley B. Caplan the senior officer aboard, and Ensign Hugo C. Anderson cooperating, was underway from the northern area of the harbor at 0858.

The USS *Phelps* (DD-360), in the destroyer nest alongside the destroyer tender *Dobbin* in berth X-2, East Loch, was underway at 0926, not long before the Japanese attackers began withdrawing, and cleared the harbor at 0950. At 1010, with Japanese raiders still withdrawing, the light cruiser *Phoenix* (CL-46) got underway from Berth C-6, but due to a series of conflicting signals, first returned, started again, turned around once more, then finally got underway at 1030 to clear the harbor. Following *Phelps* from the destroyer nest at 1040 was the *Worden* (DD-352), after taking a jarring near miss from a bomb which exploded about fifty yards astern, and her crew having claimed credit for downing a Val dive bomber. The *Phelps* would soon join the light cruiser *St. Louis* as a submarine screen.[50]

At 0756, moored port side to the light cruiser *Honolulu* in Berth B-17, Navy Yard, with six manila lines and one wire line to *Honolulu*, was the light cruiser, *St Louis*—boiler No. 8 steaming for auxiliary purposes. The bows of both cruisers, inside the slip, were pointed southwest, toward the harbor entrance, both were receiving service from the dock—*St Louis*, fresh and flushing water, and telephone from the Commander-in-Chief, Pacific Fleet. On *St Louis*, the Junior Officer of the Watch, Gunner Wilfred G. Wallace, observed a large number of dark colored planes heading in the direction of Ford Island from Aiea, which was off the stern, almost due north. As they passed over Ford Island they appeared to "drop missiles which caused flame and smoke but no sound." Immediately afterward "a dark green plane with a red circle on its tail," recognized as a Japanese plane, passed astern from port to starboard. A Kate torpedo bomber. At 0757 *St. Louis* went to general quarters to repel the air attack. At 10,000 tons and with a normal complement of approximately 888 men, she was the first of the larger ships in Pearl Harbor to escape her berth and put to sea.

At 0806, after observing the initial attacks on Ford Island, *St. Louis*'s commander, Captain George A. Rood, responding to a CinCPac signal, ordered "Commence all preparations to get underway, full power, emergency" and the engine room lighted fires under boiler numbers 1, 2, 5, 6, and 7. While the engineering department was lighting boilers to develop steam to drive her large turbines, at 0810 her gunners topside opened fire with 1.1-inch and .50-caliber machine guns.[51]

St Louis was to have been in port for about a week for boiler repair. "Yet the men did jig time in getting those boilers ready so we could get up steam," said Rood. Repairmen cut a hole about four feet in diameter in the side of the ship to pass gear in and out. Before she could get under way, they had to close the hole and weld it securely. Their efficiency paid off, permitting them to get under way more rapidly.[52]

At 0820 her crew sighted a single Japanese torpedo bomber approaching at low altitude, "from two points on the port bow," [approximately 24 degrees to the left of the bow] on course directly toward the slip. Apparently, the Kate pilot had made prior attempts to target one or more of the battleships, and consistent with Commander Mitsuo Fuchida's guidance regarding satisfactory aiming for torpedo release, was coming in several minutes behind other torpedo-carrying Kates. The tardy approach to his target would prove the attacker's undoing.

Twenty-five minutes into the raid, every gunner in the harbor who remotely believed he had a shot, would aim to bring the Kate down. *St Louis*'s gunners opened fire with her 1.1-inch antiaircraft guns and were certain they hit the plane, setting it afire. It rolled into a turn to the left, trailing fire and smoke, and went "behind a building on the starboard bow." The downing of the Kate, launched by the Japanese carrier *Akagi*, was claimed by several ships and their gunners—all seeing the same event from different perspectives.

At 0846, the coxswain's crew singled up all lines, and at 0855, boilers were cut in. At 0909, from among the second wave of seventy-eight, swarming Val dive bombers attacking numerous ships throughout the harbor, particularly *Nevada*, *California*, the dry docked *Pennsylvania*, *Cassin*, *Downes*, and *Shaw*, and other ships in the Naval Yard, came a single Val carrying its one 550-pound bomb, pressing an attack from the port beam.

The bomb penetrated the dock and exploded abeam frame 40, fifteen to twenty feet from the ship, well below the water's surface, between the dock and the *Honolulu*. It was a damaging near miss causing *St. Louis*'s bow to lift on a swell of water, while causing considerable damage to *Honolulu*'s hull. Rood felt the *St. Louis* bounce, and the blast knocked down Commander Carl K. Fink, Rood's executive officer. Though not a direct hit, the explosion caused flooding in *Honolulu*'s nearby staterooms and magazines, damaged power and fire control systems, and cut

At the right in the image, at approximately 0940 hours while the attack is still in progress, is the cruiser *St. Louis* (CL-49), moving down-channel toward the harbor entrance. Following her in the background is an unidentified destroyer. In the left foreground is the bow of the slowly settling, listing battleship *California*, and in the background is the burning, sinking *West Virginia* and shattered, fiercely burning *Arizona*. NA

power for elevating, train, hoists, blowers, lighting circuits, and power cables to Turrets I and II. Most of the flooding resulted from rupture of a magazine flood sea chest. [normally used to flood magazines in an emergency] *St Louis*'s 1.1-inch gunners believed they had hit the Val as it pulled away.[53]

Though neither ship suffered any killed or seriously wounded in the air attacks, *St. Louis* was headed for a rendezvous with the last Japanese midget submarine to fire torpedoes in the attack on Pearl Harbor.

At 0931, with Captain Rood at the conn; the Executive Officer, Commander Carl K. Fink; and the Navigator, Lieutenant Commander Graham C. Gill on the bridge, *St Louis* began backing out of her slip in the direction of the capsized *Oklahoma*, underway from *Honolulu*'s starboard side. Maneuvering down-channel on various courses, standard speed 15 knots, Rood edged his cruiser toward the open sea. He didn't pause to maneuver around a dredge with its steel cable extending to Dry Dock #1. Instead he ordered emergency full speed and "hit the cable a smashing blow and snapped it like a violin string."[54]

Power to train her 5-inch guns came on at 0947, and at 1004 she cleared the channel buoys and entered international waters, accelerating toward 25 knots—just as men at battle stations on the bridge sighted two torpedoes approaching on the starboard beam. Rood ordered an immediate change in course to begin zigzagging, while the conning tower of a submarine was sighted on the starboard bow, distance about 1,000 yards.

The two torpedoes exploded, one shortly behind the other, approximately two hundred yards from their intended victim, having struck a reef near buoy #1. *St Louis* commenced firing with her 5-inch battery. The first two salvos were believed to have hit the conning tower. At 1007 she ceased firing when the submarine either sank or submerged. The cruiser set course to the south according to a modified zigzag plan, at 25 knots, 262 r.p.m., while signaling word of the attack to Commander-in-Chief Pacific Fleet's operations center, and other American ships in the area.[55]

The sortie of *St Louis* was the last major ship action at Pearl Harbor. Egusa's Vals, bomb racks empty, flew off to strafe Ewa, Hickam and Ford Island, while above, except for random strikes by aircraft using up the last of their ammunition loads, the attack was over. The second wave cost the Japanese six Zekes and fourteen Vals. Many others were hit but escaped.

Commander Mitsuo Fuchida, in his Kate, orbited over the fearful scene, assessing the damage and rounding up stragglers. His badly shot up plane had circled for about two hours. As a good leader should, he waited until the last of the rearguard fighters flew out of sight returning to their carriers, before he headed for *Akagi*. He couldn't obtain an accurate damage report because he couldn't see through all the smoke obscuring his vision. Despite the smoke, he reported to the rejoicing Admiral Nagumo success beyond his wildest dreams.[56]

At 1010, Captain Rood ordered the destroyers *Blue*, *Phelps*, and *Lamson* to act as an anti-submarine screen for *St. Louis*, and six minutes later sighted four enemy aircraft high overhead on a parallel course. He ordered open fire, saw no hits, and ordered "Cease fire" at 1018. At 1115 the crew sighted five more enemy planes on the port beam position angle of about 70 degrees, and antiaircraft guns again opened fire, then ceased firing two minutes later. At 1134 *St Louis* ceased zigzagging and turned right to course 270 degrees. At 1145 three more enemy aircraft came into view, bearing 010 degrees, almost due north, and *St. Louis* commenced firing. Cease fire came one minute later as *St. Louis* and her submarine screen began zigzagging according to standard Plan 6. At 1210, she turned right to base course 357 degrees, almost due north.

At 1213 she commenced firing at four enemy aircraft on the starboard beam, position angle 60 degrees, then ceased firing at 1215. Twice more, at 1218 and 1233 St Louis fired at enemy aircraft on the starboard side, and each time ceased firing in one or two minutes. At 1235 she exchanged calls with a ship "hull down," bearing 300 degrees. It was the cruiser *Minneapolis*, with two destroyers. At 1238 the crew sighted three more ships, bearing 345 degrees, distance twelve miles. In the early afternoon the four ships joined with the cruisers *Detroit* and *Pheonix*, continuing first on a northern course, then to the west. They had been instructed to rendezvous with the carrier *Enterprise* and Task Force 8, and did so late in the afternoon.

At 1530 hours, Captain Rood ordered the crew mustered. Events had unfolded at a furious pace, with little time to take stock of crew status and many other factors important in the readiness for battle at sea. Roll call revealed the hasty departure from Pearl

Harbor under fire had resulted in eleven officers and fifty-seven men left behind for a variety of reasons, not quite ten percent of the ship's complement. During the day, St Louis's gunners expended 207 rounds of 5-inch antiaircraft ammunition, 13,950 rounds of 1.1-inch, and 12,750 rounds of .50 caliber ammunition.

There had been no casualties on the St. Louis, a blessing the entire crew would soon know—if they didn't already. They had fought furiously, as did all the other crews on all the other ships, had come dangerously close to a direct hit from a Val dive bomber, had seen the swirling action over the entire harbor, seen the horror confronted by the battleships and their crews, and witnessed the devastation occurring on Ford Island, Hickam Field, and the nearby dry docks. In a final bit of blessed irony, a coral reef may have saved the ship and its crew from two torpedoes, and a totally unexpected, last minute disaster. From all St. Louis's crew observed that morning and her one final 7 December irony came her nickname, Lucky Loo—for the duration of the war.[57]

Over a hundred miles behind them, the agonizing reality of what occurred on Oahu between 0755 and 1010 hours the morning of 7 December 1941, had in one, cryptic sentence been flashed across the islands and around the world. And on Oahu the true horror of a visit from hell was just beginning to sink deeply and forever in the memories of all present on the island that day.

CHAPTER 9

Aftermath: 7 December

Men with sharpness of mind are to be found only
among those with a penchant for thought.

Shiba Yoshimasa

W hen the Japanese attack on Pearl Harbor began, *Enterprise* and Task Force 8 were approximately 200 miles west of Oahu, at 0730 had changed course to the east, 090 degrees, and were reducing speed from 20 to 14 knots preparatory to launching aircraft. At 0800 the first airplane was airborne, and the cycle of launching and recovering aircraft continued while she changed course first to due north, then starboard back to 075 to recover the last plane at 0851.[1]

At the time of the attack, the Japanese strike fleet was approximately 200 miles north, northeast of Oahu, and about 320 miles northeast of Task Force 8. Having just launched the second wave, Nagumo's force would remain in that general area until approximately 1300 hours when it would turn to a northwesterly course of 330 degrees and accelerate to 26 knots, to put distance between the fleet and Oahu. It was the highest speed the fleet attained the entire voyage.[2]

Undoubtedly, *Enterprise* had received the 0757 broadcast from Ford Island, "Air raid Pearl Harbor. This not drill," quickly retransmitted by Admiral Kimmel's staff. At 0900, while the Japanese raiders' second wave was swarming over Pearl Harbor, Hickam, Ewa, Kaneohe, and Bellows, Admiral Kimmel at Pearl Harbor and Admiral Halsey aboard *Enterprise* received radioed orders from the Secretary of the Navy, "Execute War Plan against Japan in view of unprovoked air raid at Pearl Harbor at 0800 this date." Everything had changed in that first hour. Everything.

As the day continued the world of America's restrained years of isolation was turning upside down. Aboard *Enterprise*, and throughout Task Force 8's senior officers, far different concerns and questions entered the worlds of Pacific Fleet combatants at sea—and now at war.

At 1618 hours, after a day of intense activity the *Enterprise* Officer of the Deck, Ensign Jack A. Holmes, logged the sighting of Task Force 3, three heavy cruisers, one light cruiser—the *St Louis*—and twelve destroyers "broad on the port beam." At 1640 he logged, "Observed anti-aircraft fire on port beam," while at that same minute, Lieutenant Elanzo B. Grantham, OOD on *St. Louis*, logged, "Commenced firing at enemy aircraft on port quarter." At 1646, Grantham wrote, "Sighted aircraft carrier bearing 220 degrees, identified as *Enterprise*." The two task forces were converging while flight operations were still in progress.

At 1642 *Enterprise*'s crew launched the first airplane, and seven minutes later, the last aircraft in the afternoon operation cycle left the flight deck. At 1702, just as the first airplane from an earlier launch was landing, and the carrier was on course 061 degrees, into the wind, Ensign Holmes wrote, "Submarine reported bearing 305 degrees, distance approximately 6,000 yards. Changed course right to 120 degrees." Orders immediately followed, signaled to the task force and passed to the *Enterprise* crew. The signal to the task force, probably sent with hoisted signal flags, was all ahead flank speed, turn port to 090 degrees. The turn was executed at 1704. Sunset would be at 1712, twilight at 1737, when the last discernible horizon would be visible. The *Enterprise* went to general quarters, slowed, changed headings and speed again, and resumed landing aircraft at 1726.[3]

The three cruisers *St. Louis*, *Phoenix* and *Detroit*, plus *Northampton* which was from Task Force 8, and their destroyer submarine screens, were all on the high seas by mid-afternoon, free of the disaster that befell Pearl Harbor and all the military airfields on Oahu. On the four cruisers and their destroyer escorts that afternoon, the carrier *Enterprise* and other ships in the expanding Task Force 8, its commander, Admiral William H. "Bull" Halsey; the carrier's commander, Captain George D. Murray; and other senior commanders and their staffs were wondering, "Where is the Japanese carrier strike force?"

What course and speed are they traveling? Are they near? Are they south or southwest of Oahu? Northwest? Due west? North or northeast of Oahu? Long range patrol capabilities on Oahu are in a shambles, sharply reduced to small numbers. Do our on-board scouts have the range to find the Japanese carrier force? Which areas do we search? Do the Japanese know where we are? Have their submarines or scout planes found us, when we were unaware of their presence, and reported our position? Do we have the strength to engage if we find them or they find us? We have one carrier. Given the reported large number of aircraft participating in the attack, they must have considerably more than one carrier, which implies a powerful strike force.

Similar questions abounded at Pacific Fleet headquarters in Pearl Harbor, and at the Army's operations and information centers at Ft. Shafter, and in the Hawaiian Air Force's fighter and bomber operations staffs—before the last Japanese airplanes turned toward their departure headings. Not too surprisingly, senior members of the rapidly mobilizing territorial and Honolulu city governments and home guard were asking similar questions of themselves and the American military commands.

Does the enemy strike force include troops and troop transports? Will they attempt to land troops on Oahu or other Hawaiian Islands? How many ships and planes do they have, and what type? What else are they planning? Will they send more raiders, destroy the fuel tanks and submarine base, and attack power plants and other similar targets? Destruction of the oil storage tanks would be devastating, and destruction of submarines caught in the harbor would further hamper any counterattack against the Japanese fleet. Whatever the answers, one thing was certain. The enemy came completely undetected, struck with devastating strategic and tactical surprise, left without being followed or found, and left Pearl Harbor and military airfields on Oahu in shambles.

By the time the raiders flew away to their carriers, the Honolulu radio stations were going silent, ordered to shut down because they could again be used as homing beacons for Japanese aircraft should there be another strike. The *Honolulu Advertiser* wasn't able to print due to press shutdown, and the *Star-Bulletin* took up the slack publishing three extras that day.[4]

No one knew the real toll of death and destruction that first morning, and many among the military and civilian populations wouldn't know for years—but it was staggering. Eight battleships, three light cruisers, three destroyers, and four auxiliary craft either sunk, capsized, heavily damaged, or damaged generally—eighteen vessels. Naval aviation suffered heavy losses: thirteen fighters, twenty-one scout bombers, forty-six patrol bombers, three utility craft, two transports, and one each observation/scouts and training craft. To this must be added the *Enterprise* VS-6 Squadron airplanes shot down that morning.[5]

The Hawaiian Air Force took a terrible beating as well, with losses totaling four B-17s, twelve B-18s, two A-20s, thirty-two P-40s, twenty P-36s, four P-26s, two OA-9s, one O-49, plus one B-24 on station being specially equipped for a Philippines-based reconnaissance mission. Additionally, eighty-eight pursuit planes, six reconnaissance aircraft, and thirty-four bombers had been damaged. At first it appeared all those damaged were wrecked, but 80 percent were later salvaged. The Japanese also received an unexpected bonus with the destruction of two B-17s arriving from Hamilton Field, bound for Hickam. Nevertheless, they didn't know the real extent of the damage. Unfortunately for the Japanese Navy and their militarist government, neither did they realize the significance of the targets they failed to strike.[6]

Where Is The Japanese Fleet?

Admiral Nagumo stood on *Akagi*'s bridge peering into the sky. About 1010 hours "black points appeared far to the south one after another." The first wave was returning, some in formation, some singly. The flight decks of all six carriers came to life, each preparing to land its planes.

Throughout the morning the weather had steadily worsened. High seas and shifting wind directions made landings difficult. Carrier crews pushed a few badly damaged planes into the sea to clear the flight deck for fuel-starved planes and their crews circling impatiently overhead. Before the day was over the Japanese would be able to tally their losses, information to help Admiral Nagumo decide whether another strike was possible—either today or tomorrow. In the meantime, the second wave began landing at 1115, with the last airplane to recover at 1214. As returning aircraft were found to be operational for another mission that day, they were being refueled and rearmed for fleet defense, in case the enemy launched a counterstrike.[7]

Of the 350 aircraft launched from the six carriers that morning, twenty-nine were shot down and 111 received varying degrees of damage, some during landings, with approximately 20 beyond repair and pushed over their carriers sides. Fifty-five aircraft had been held back for combat patrol (covering the fleet), or reserve, thirty Zekes launched at 0600, and recovered by 0900. Twenty-three Zekes launched at 1000, for recovery prior to 1300 hours. Based on information available, apparently 210 aircraft would be available for a second attack, with 55 again kept for combat patrol.[8]

Lieutenant Tomatsu Ema, who had led the dive bomb attacks on Wheeler Field, landed his Val aboard *Zuikaku*, where his colleagues and admirers "went wild with joy when the first reports came in." Ema felt relieved and glad that he survived the attack. But he didn't think all was over. He believed the enemy might launch a counterattack. He and the rest of the carrier's airmen thought the war would go well for Japan. At least now they had a chance.[9]

Commander Mitsuo Fuchida's Kate was guiding two escorting Zekes back to the carrier, fighters that would have been lost had they not tagged along. On the return flight, Fuchida's mind centered on thoughts of a second attack that same afternoon, as soon as the remaining aircraft could be refueled and rearmed. As his pilot counted off the miles returning to *Akagi*, Fuchida mentally tabulated priority targets for destruction: the fuel-tank farms, the vast repair and maintenance facilities, and possibly a ship or two bypassed that morning.[10]

Meanwhile, *Akagi*'s Air Officer, Commander Shogo Masuda, was on the flight deck near the bridge, with Lieutenant Commander Shigeharu Murata, who led the first wave's Kate level-bombers. All the flying officers were reporting to them, and Masuda was tabulating the results of the attack on a large blackboard.

Commander Minoru Genda, from the beginning, the creative genius most responsible for shaping Admiral Yamamoto's plan, hurried down from the bridge once or twice, relaying the word to Nagumo and Rear Admiral Ryunosuke Kusaka, Nagumo's Chief of Staff. Both admirals impatiently awaited a final tabulation. During one of Genda's visits to the blackboard, assembled pilots urged a second attack. Genda listened but offered no opinion.[11]

Excitement rose to a fever pitch around *Akagi's* blackboard. An accurate assessment was the immediate concern of all the pilots and observers, but they also discussed American resistance to the first wave. All agreed that reaction, "considering all the facts on that morning, was surprisingly quick." They also agreed that the great success could not have been possible without surprise.[12]

About noon Fuchida's pilot landed on *Akagi's* rolling, pitching deck. An elated, smiling Genda wrung Fuchida's hand, then rushed back to the bridge. At that moment a sailor ran up with a message that Nagumo wanted to see Fuchida immediately, but Fuchida decided to wait until he correlated his observations with those of his flight leaders. He carefully scanned the blackboard and listened to the reports of about fifteen flying officers as he sipped a cup of tea. After listening to their observations, he was satisfied theirs tallied closely with his. He could give his superiors a fairly accurate assessment. At that moment another messenger informed Fuchida that he was to report to Nagumo, and hurry.[13]

When he arrived on the bridge he found Kusaka, Genda, and several other key staff officers gathered with Nagumo. Fuchida planned to give a formal briefing listing events chronologically, but Nagumo interrupted impatiently: "The results—what are they?"

"Four battleships sunk," Fuchida replied. "I know this from my own personal observation. Four battleships damaged," he added. He then listed by berth and type the other ships his airmen had struck. Again Nagumo interrupted, "Do you think that the U.S. Fleet could not come out from Pearl Harbor within six months?"

The question made Fuchida uneasy, but he owed the admiral the truth. "The main force of the U.S. Pacific Fleet will not be able to come out within six months," he answered. Nagumo beamed and nodded.

Kusaka resumed the questioning. "What do you think the next targets should be?" The question implied an aggressive intent, and Fuchida answered quickly. "The next targets should be the dockyards, the fuel tanks, and an occasional ship." There was no need to attack the battleships again.

Kusaka then took up the possibility of an American counterattack. Fuchida and Genda assured him the Japanese controlled the air over both Oahu and the sea. Commander Tomatsu Oishi, Nagumo's senior staff officer, next spoke up. "Is the enemy in a position to counterattack the task force?" Again, the direct question put Fuchida on the spot, but he knew he must be as forthright as possible. "I believe we have destroyed many enemy planes, but I do not know whether we have destroyed them all. The enemy could still attack the Fleet." Oishi didn't answer.

Nagumo: "Where do you think the missing U.S. carriers are?" Fuchida explained he couldn't be certain, but they were probably training somewhere at sea, and added that by this time the carriers had received word of the attack and would be looking for the task force. The suggestion wasn't a pleasant one for Nagumo, and Oishi fretted too over a possible counterattack. He turned to Genda for his opinion. Genda replied easily, "Let the enemy come! If he does, we will shoot his planes down."

With a few words of praise, Nagumo dismissed Fuchida. Genda continued. He wasn't satisfied the job was finished in spite of Fuchida's impressive damage report. He knew his airmen had given Japan an opportunity that would never come again, and he wanted to finish the job. But he didn't advocate another major strike that afternoon. The planes had already been refitted to attack ships at sea in case the Americans launched a counterattack. To hit Pearl Harbor again would require changing armament again. The change would hold up takeoff until dark. Sea and weather conditions had degenerated sufficiently to create even more difficult circumstances for launch and recovery, would cause confusion, and possibly result in numerous casualties.

Additionally, *Lexington* and *Enterprise* were still at large. Genda believed in his mind that, "Nagumo would have been a standing joke for generations if he had attacked Pearl Harbor again," without first ascertaining their location. He urged Nagumo, "Stay in the area for several days and run down the enemy carriers."

But Admiral Nagumo saw otherwise regarding the attack and withdrawal plan. He had risked Japan's First Air Fleet, and his ships had come through without a scratch. He didn't want to tempt fate again. The First Air Fleet continued northwest, toward refueling and home waters while *Enterprise* headed toward directed search areas to the southwest of Oahu.[14]

Among the Japanese senior Naval officers, from Admiral Yamamoto and his staff, on down, immediately after word of the success and decision to return home was made, in the months ahead there would be numerous lengthy discussions about the wisdom of Nagumo's decision not to strike Oahu a second time. The purpose of Yamamoto's attack plan was to secure the

Japanese Empire's left flank for six months against an incursion by the American Pacific fleet, while they drove south and southeast to achieve their greater objective and continued to maintain and build their fleet. They were convinced they would be able to hold off or defeat a weakened Pacific fleet long enough to cause the Americans to sue for peace rather than continue a prolonged fight.

Nevertheless, after first accepting Nagumo's decision as the on scene commander, Yamamoto observed to Vice Admiral Jisaburo Ozawa on the island of Truk in late 1942, "Events have shown that it was a great mistake not to have launched a second attack against Pearl Harbor." By failing to exploit the shock, bewilderment, and confusion on Oahu, by failing to take full advantage of its savage attack against Kimmel's ships, by failing to pulverize the Pearl Harbor base, by failing to destroy Oahu's vast fuel stores, and by failing to seek out and sink America's carriers, Japan committed its first and probably greatest strategic error of the entire Pacific conflict. American Admiral Nimitz would later point out that had the Japanese destroyed the fuel tank farm, which was all above ground, the Pacific Fleet would have been forced back to the United States' west coast. There was no other source of fuel in the Hawaiian Islands.[15]

* * *

The carrier *Lexington*, guiding Task Force 12 and still plowing toward reinforcement of Midway when the attack at Pearl Harbor occurred, had received an 0830 signal from CinCPac. Logged by the OOD, Ensign Joseph Weber, the signal read, "Hostilities with Japan commenced with air raid on Pearl Harbor." *Lexington*, immediately went to general quarters and launched aircraft to begin searching for the Japanese strike fleet. Shortly thereafter the task force was ordered to turn around and proceed toward the southwest to hunt with Task Force 8, in a different area. Admiral Kimmel must have been concerned about his two carriers being widely separated, and was clearly reacting to the presumed strength of the Japanese strike fleet, by moving the task forces into positions where they could support one another.[16]

In another twenty-four hours most of the men of *Enterprise*'s Task Force 8, who delivered the twelve Marine fighter planes to Wake Island, would hear, then see firsthand, some of the marks of death and destruction, learn more of staggering losses, see the residual scars and horrors of huge explosions and fires, a devastated

Hickam Field and Naval Air Station on Ford Island, capsized and sunk ships with trapped men in the hulls of *Oklahoma* and *Utah*, possibly *Arizona* and *West Virginia*; witness the desperate attempts to rescue them; and the fire still burning on *Arizona* and illuminating *Tennessee* and *Maryland* at night.

The damaged *Pennsylvania*, shattered destroyers *Downes*, *Cassin* and *Shaw*, all battered in the dry docks; the *Maryland* and hemmed-in *Tennessee*; the capsized minelayer, *Oglala*, and the grounded, listing *Vestal*. The continuing relentless efforts to save *California* and *Nevada*, still slowly sinking or in danger of capsizing, see men still picking up shattered bodies and body parts on ships and from the harbor's oily waters.

Late the afternoon of 7 December, neither Admirals Kimmel at Pearl Harbor, Nagumo on *Akagi* leading the Japanese strike fleet, Halsey in *Enterprise*'s Task Force 8, nor Rear Admiral John H. Newton in *Lexington*'s Task Force 12, knew their adversaries' locations. For the Americans on Oahu the situation wasn't as simple as it was for Nagumo, and time available to find the enemy's strike fleet began rapidly running out when the Japanese force turned to course 330 degrees at 1300. By 1700 hours Nagumo's strike force would be approximately 350 miles north of Oahu.

Throughout the hours after the attack, it was far from clear to the Americans the Japanese effort was spent. Of necessity the defenders had to divide their battered military forces to conduct a rescue and recovery operation, a search and strike operation, and yet ensure their remaining forces were able to defend against another attack, which might include the landing of troops. With fires burning the remainder of the day, some for several days, wounded were being tended, intense efforts were underway to rescue men trapped in the capsized *Oklahoma* and *Utah*, learn if survivors were inside ships sunk upright in shallow water, find the hundreds of missing, and the dead which had to be retrieved and buried.

The majority of American military anticipated either follow-up strikes or a full-scale landing. Throughout the rest of the day there were numerous false alarms, compounded by civilian-owned radio stations gone silent which would have helped quell the rumors sweeping both the civilian and military populations. There were numerous false alarms about landings, paratrooper landings, renewed air attacks, a Japanese fleet coming around the east side of the island, and enemy aircraft carriers seen southeast of Diamond Head and south of Barbers Point. There was at least one case of warships engaging non-existent aircraft, and inevitably, there were reports of non-existent or wrongly identified ships.

Consistent with the incredulity and shock that rippled throughout the Oahu civilian and military populations when the attack began, one account stood out. Honolulu's mayor, who stated he could see fires on the ground, shells bursting in the skies, and detonations, and that he watched the attack for half an hour and "then got a little suspicious." More pertinently, although at first there was disbelief and numbness induced by shock, the Americans fought back furiously.

In spite of the disbelief and turmoil, the overall story was one of officers and men who were absent from ships and bases on weekend passes or liberty, making their way to command posts and action or battle stations, to find them already functioning.[17]

Though the response gathered intensity and fierceness as time slipped by, it was fragmented, uncoordinated, and not nearly as effective as it might have been had strategic and tactical warning been received, defense readiness and alert status elevated in advance of the attack, and information pooled and assessed during and immediately after the attack. Finally, American command and control arrangements did reassert themselves as the day wore on.

As war always does, especially when total, disastrous surprise is achieved, its powerfully-generated emotions bring out the worst as well as the best in men and women. Long-buried racial prejudice's and hatreds came pouring out, given bitter impetus when men saw shipmates, close friends, squadron members, or roommates cut down in a bloody heap, blown apart, burned to death, or drowned in fire-swept, oily water right before their eyes. Angry, mistrustful attitudes toward the Japanese as a people—including Japanese-American (*nisei*) citizens—buried and long simmering in the local and military populations in Hawaii came boiling to the surface during and after the attack.[18]

A Zeke made a series of ineffectual strafing passes against the heavy cruiser *Northampton*, off the island of Kauai, while on Niihau one Zeke pilot put down expecting to be rescued by Japanese submarine [I-75], stationed near the island for that purpose. Instead he found himself a prisoner of the Hawaiian population. He enlisted the help of a Japanese alien and a *nisei*, and the pilot sought to recover the papers that had been taken from him. The result was an episode in which homes were burned and Hawaiians seized as hostages or shot before the Japanese airman was finally killed and the *nisei* killed himself.[19]

There was in fact a burning passion to ferret out the enemy's carriers and exact grim retribution for the blood spilled this Sunday morning. At first Admiral Kimmel's instinct told him that the enemy's ships lay northward, and at 1018, a few minutes after the *St. Louis* passed the entrance of Pearl Harbor outbound, he advised his forces at sea: "Search from Pearl very limited account maximum twelve VP [patrol squadron] searching from Pearl. Some indication enemy force northwest Oahu. Addressees operate as directed by Comtaskforce Eight [Halsey] to intercept enemy. Composition enemy force unknown."[20]

Ironically, a few minutes earlier, about 1000 hours, Patrol Squadron Fourteen's PBY

14-P-2, one of Kaneohe's three patrol planes that launched beginning at 0615 that morning, was attacked by nine Japanese aircraft. When Ensign Otto F. Meyer, Jr. and his crew of six departed Kaneohe, they had been assigned a search sector west, northwest of Oahu. When attacked, they were approximately 30 miles northwest of Kaena Point, Oahu's western most point, and had heard the prior dispatches indicating hostilities had commenced. On hearing the dispatches, Meyer ordered the gun stations manned and made ready for immediate use—except for the "tunnel gun" (tail gun), which was made ready but not manned.

When the nine aircraft were first sighted, Meyer was flying the PBY-5 at 1,000 feet, and they were about six miles distant on the PBY's bow, crossing from starboard to port, and were about 500 to 1,000 feet higher than the big patrol plane. He initially described them as "low wing monoplanes with retractable landing gear," which meant there were no Val dive bombers among the nine. Then, as they crossed his bow, he recognized they were in a shallow turn to their port, gradually toward the PBY, and they appeared to be SBDs. But their turn to port continued, placing them on a course parallel to but opposite the PBY's direction of flight. Meyer increased power to 2300 RPM and 33 inches of manifold pressure, while increasing speed and descending in altitude to 20 to 30 feet above the water. Distance between the PBY and the nine aircraft decreased rapidly, and as they were about to disappear from Meyer's field of view high on the port side, he asked the waist gunners to report the planes' actions. No sooner did he make the intercom call when he heard, "They're coming in!"

Meyer ordered the gunners to ". . . lock and load and follow the planes with their guns, but don't fire until directed." A few seconds later, he saw tracers striking the water about 100 feet forward of the PBY's bow and passing about 30 feet from the hull on the port side. One of the gunners reported the planes were firing at them, and Meyer directed return fire.

The first few planes attacking came from astern and above in a very shallow dive, most pulling away to the side from which they were attacking, while they avoided passing forward of the PBY's tail. Nevertheless, the "Rising Sun" insignia was plainly visible as they rolled away and pulled up from their intended victim. The attacks continued: coming in from the beam at about twenty degrees angle of elevation and some at about seventy degrees; directly overhead in a vertical dive; from the (stern) quarter; and from almost directly astern, but not in such a position that the PBY's tail offered the enemy cover.

Nearly all the attackers except one were Zekes, Meyer noting he and his crew could see streams of smoke coming from the upper cowling, as they were firing from fixed, nose-mounted guns firing through the propellers. There was one exception, and after the mission, Ensign Meyer reported, "At least one of the attacking planes was a two seater for it pulled up on a parallel course, range about 100 yards and from about sixty degrees off our port bow, fired back at us from a single flexible gun and then retired." His PBY had been attacked by a Kate horizontal bomber, which was evidently leading, and being escorted by the fighters, back to their carriers.

Meyer's report also indicated the fighters didn't press their diving attacks, and probably pulled up earlier on each firing pass because the PBY's belly was so close to the water.

When the Kate retired from its attack, Ensign Meyer promptly executed a sharp 180 degree turn to starboard to head toward Oahu. From at least one of the enemy planes, the crew observed a streamer of smoke, but there was no way of knowing if 14-P-2's gunners had inflicted damage. The attacking group appeared to rejoin and were lost in the haze astern before their retiring course could be determined.

During the five to six minute engagement one of the radiomen transmitted word of the attack by voice radio, while gunners struggled to defend the aircraft. Later the first and second radiomen transmitted word of the attack by key on both circuits they were guarding.

At the outset of the attack the starboard gunner found that his machine gun would fire only one round at a time. He had to recharge the gun for each round. During the attack, he succeeded in replacing his .50-caliber gun with the .30-caliber gun from the tunnel hatch, and fired about fifty or sixty rounds from his gun. The rotating hatch locking lever on the bow turret broke off during the action, and the bow gunner had nothing to assist him in holding the gun against the slip stream. His efficiency was thus greatly impaired.

The PBY took at least eleven hits, four in the tail section, one of which would likely have been fatal to a tail gunner. None of the other seven hits did prohibitive damage. Having shed the pursuing enemy and returned to within four or five miles of Oahu, Ensign Meyer and his crew reversed course and continued their assigned search mission to a distance of approximately 380 miles, finding nothing but clouds and whitecaps. In the meantime, at Pearl Harbor and Kaneohe, the scramble was on to find additional aircraft from among the remaining undamaged Navy and Army Air Force planes on Oahu to dispatch in the search for the Japanese carrier force.

At Kaneohe, radiomen in the communications section lost contact with 14-P-2 and nothing further was heard from Ensign Meyer's crew until mid-afternoon. When contact couldn't be re-established following word of the attack, VP-14's boss, Lieutenant Commander Thurston B. Clark apparently assumed the airplane was down, and sent the remaining two VP-14 PBYs airborne to both cover the unfilled "hole" and search for the "missing" PBY. Unfortunately, Admiral Bellinger wasn't informed of that decision, and continued working to send more airplanes to the same search area. Because of difficulties and delays in communicating with Kaneohe at the outset of the attack, Bellinger's ability to coordinate patrol wing search activities was hampered.

The painful reality was the American command on Oahu didn't know the direction from which the Japanese carrier force and airplanes had come. Commander Joseph J. Rochefort, chief of the Pearl Harbor intelligence unit learned the Japanese commander "bore either 357 or 178 [degrees]." Because of "a limitation of aircraft operations he could be expected to be found within 200 miles." Direction-finder readings, always ambiguously opposite in their presentations, suggested the enemy was either due north or south, and the commands, long inclined to look to the south, southwest and west as likely avenues of approach by an enemy expanding into Southeast Asia, eventually concentrated their search to the south.[21]

Captain Charles E. "Soc" McMorris, boss of Kimmel's War Plans Division was "inclined strongly to believe that the attack had come both from the northward and southward . . . " Because the American carriers at sea were "already in the southward area," War Plans "felt that the chance of intercepting the northern route was probably quite remote, while the chance of of intercepting the southern route looked, at least, to hold some promise . . . " Kimmel made the wrong choice, and at 1046 notified Halsey's Task Force 8, "D/F [direction finder] bearings indicate enemy carrier bearing 178 from Barbers Point."[22]

When Commander Charles Coe reached his office on Ford Island he was told "to get on the operational telephone, call Army Air, and find out where the hell the Japanese planes were coming from and try to get any other information." Coe did his best, but everything was chaos, confusion and demoralization at the time. "Lines were not manned," he said, "and I could not get through to anybody." The entire situation suggested that even had they found Nagumo's carriers, they couldn't do much about them. Commander Coe said, "We were simply not in a position to retaliate."

Other indicators pointed northward. When Major Landon was leading the B-17s into Hickam from the north, northeast that morning, he noticed that some of the Japanese airplanes were flying in the same direction. After he reported to Hawaiian Air Force headquarters, he tried to interest someone in his information, but it seemed to him nearly everyone was more interested in fitting helmet liners into helmets in anticipation of another attack than in locating the Japanese force and hitting it before it could launch further strikes.

The Opana Station Radar plotted a clear northbound track for the withdrawing Japanese aircraft, which the control center at Ft. Shafter recorded at 1027 and 1029, but according to Major General Martin, "there was no indication of that course being an important one at that time." In fact, no one brought it to his attention until they analyzed the history of the control chart sometime later.

In the meantime, during the morning, senior Navy operations officers apparently concluded the strike force lay to the north, because in early afternoon, the remaining airplanes in *Enterprise*'s beleaguered VS-6 launched a planned, briefed search north from Ford Island and Oahu, a search that proved to be too little too late, and probably would have been suicidal had they encountered the Japanese strike force.

Their fruitless good fortune was augmented with searches by other Navy aircraft, some launched by Pacific Fleet ships that departed the harbor during the attack, others with Task Force 8, plus unarmed utility aircraft dispatched or commandeered by determined and brave Navy pilots. Back at Ford Island, VP-21's Ensign Theodore W. Marshall, at the BOQ when the attack started, commandeered a squadron truck. After driving between the quarters, the enlisted barracks and NAS Pearl Harbor, ferrying officers and men to their battle stations—practically oblivious to the bomb fragments and strafing that nearly riddled the vehicle—Marshall proceeded to the flight line. Although unfamiliar with landplanes he climbed into a Grumman F4F Wildcat. Finding that it had been damaged by strafing, Marshall, undaunted, spotted a Douglas TBD-1 (Bureau No. 0289, an ex-*Enterprise* machine that had been assigned to the Battle Force pool on November 18), climbed in, and started the engine. Despite being as unfamiliar with the Devastator as he was with the Wildcat, Marshall took off and attempted to track the Japanese planes as they retired from Pearl. For 150 miles he tried to keep up with the enemy, until his flagging fuel state compelled his return to Ford Island, where he landed the lumbering plane successfully. For his heroism that day, he received the Silver Star.

On the *St. Louis* Ensigns Raphael Semmes, Jr., and Maurice Thornton took off in their obsolete Curtiss SOC biplanes during the raid and unsuccessfully attacked a formation of Val dive bombers. Neither man had taken along a radio-gunner, and Thornton ran out of gas during the return flight, necessitating his rescue by a destroyer on 9 December.

The courage of Marshal, Semmes and Thornton matched that of the pilots of the utility squadrons who took off in VJ-1s and Sikorsky JRS-1s. Ensign John P. Edwards took up the first followed by Lieutenant (jg) James W. Robb, Jr., Lieutenant Gordon E. Bolser, and Ensign Nils R. Larson. Lieutenant (jg) Wesley H. Ruth with Aviation Chief Machinist Mate (Naval Aviation Pilot) Emery C. Geise as his co-pilot in JRS-1 (Bureau No. 1063), encountered a Zeke from *Shokaku* 200 miles off Oahu in what was probably the last engagement between the U.S. Navy and Japanese planes on December 7. For courageously piloting utility amphibians armed only with Springfield rifles, Edwards, Robb, Bolser, Larson and Ruth were all awarded the Navy Cross.

While the brave men accompanying them in their scratch crews received appropriate recommendations, too, only one—Sergeant Thomas E. Haley (USMC)—would receive the Navy Cross. Haley had quit the *Oklahoma* after she had been ordered abandoned, helped rescue his shipmates from the oily water, and then manned an antiaircraft gun on board the *Maryland*. Once on Ford Island, he unhesitatingly volunteered to go up in one of the Sikorskys, armed with only a rifle and still wearing only the skivvies in which he had swam away from the capsized battleship.

In addition, pilots of other SOCs proved that courage and initiative were not just the preserve of the fighter pilot. Lieutenant Malcolm C. Reeves and Ensign Frank H. Covington, from the heavy cruiser *Northampton* in Task Force 8, searching for the Japanese west of Oahu, experienced more success in the unaccustomed role of dogfighters as they battled a Zeke and sent it away trailing smoke. Nevertheless, in spite of the dogged searches individually launched or dispatched, the early search efforts looked primarily south to find the enemy fleet.

By 1127 four of Hickam's A-20 bombers from the 58th Bombardment Squadron (Light) had taxied out and were ready for takeoff. Led by Major William J. Holzapfel, Jr, they were carrying loads of 300 pound bombs in their bomb bays, after a wild scramble on the ground by men who braved the Japanese raiders' onslaught to get some slightly damaged airplanes ready to fly, then first load 500-pound bombs, then download them and reload with 300-pound bombs for the mission. The Navy had no instructions for them, so General Martin gave them the mission of finding the carrier that was south of Barbers Point. The takeoff and flight of these "first-off-the-ground," Douglas, twin-engine bombers was the most inspiring sight of the morning for the downtrodden Hickam troops.[23]

The large vessel in the location specified for the A-20s to

attack was the heavy cruiser *Minneapolis*, on her way home from the Fleet operating area. Her commander instructed the radio room to advise Kimmel, "No carriers in sight." Somehow it came out "Two carriers in sight." Fortunately, the A-20 pilots heading toward *Minneapolis* recognized her.[24]

Another United States cruiser, the *Portland*, had a narrow escape that afternoon. The commander of "a squadron of seaplanes returned from Midway" reported a Japanese carrier and destroyer "well south of Pearl Harbor." Virtually every member of Kimmel's staff quizzed the pilot, who insisted he knew it was a Japanese carrier, because "he saw the Rising Sun painted on her deck . . . and she had the plan of a heavy cruiser painted on her deck as camouflage." The location plotted proved to be almost exactly that of Vice Admiral Wilson Brown's task force, returning from Johnston Island with five old destroyers converted to minesweepers. CinCPac immediately directed Brown "to get that carrier."

Brown replied that he believed his cruiser *Portland* had been bombed. Unable to credit the reply, headquarters radioed *Portland*: "Were you bombed this afternoon?" Came the reply, "Yes, a plane dropped two bombs narrowly missing me astern."

Captain "Blondie" Saunders, who had been named provisional commander of all B-17s, led a three-plane formation from Hickam. They also started off in search of the Japanese carrier force. One aircraft had to abort, however, when his tail wheel started to vibrate and the copilot mistakenly grabbed the lever locking the elevators instead of the tail wheel. This resulted in raising the tail of the B-17 high enough prior to takeoff to ruin all four propellers. The two remaining B-17Ds, piloted by Saunders and Captain Brooke E. Allen, took off at 1140, circled around Diamond Head, and before the day ended were in the air for about seven hours.[25]

Pilot, aircraft commander, and acting squadron commander, Captain Allen, flew his

B-17 off the Hickam runway in Saunders' flight of two, and after arriving in the vicinity of Diamond Head followed official intelligence and headed south, despite his private conviction that his prey was northward. That morning, when he heard the first explosions on Hickam Field, he rushed out of his house in his bathrobe, "exposing his nudity," just in time to see a Zeke completing a strafing pass down his street. Frantically waving his arms and shaking his fists, he shouted, "I knew the little bastards would do it on a Sunday morning! I knew it!" Heading south he in time sighted "this beautiful carrier," which, according to Allen, fired on him. So he went into a bomb run. But suddenly, in Allen's words, "God had a hand on me because I knew this wasn't a Jap carrier." He had spotted *Enterprise*. Allen pulled out of range, put his compass on "N," and decided to try the northern direction, but had no luck.

He turned back toward the south and again saw *Enterprise*, now much nearer to Oahu. Two Navy Wildcats intercepted his B-17 and looked it over suspiciously as he started back to Hickam. How close he came to the carrier force he never knew but "returned with minimum fuel and a heart full of disgust that I had been unable to locate them." The timing suggests his initial swing south toward *Enterprise* had been just long enough for Nagumo's carriers to speed north beyond his reach.[26]

Saunders remembered, "the military forces on Hawaii had seen B-17s around the island for six months but they really let go at us, like we were public enemy number one. I thought we were going to be shot down by our own forces."

A second flight of three A-20s launched at 1300, led by First Lieutenant Perry S. Cole, with Technical Sergeant O'Shea as bombardier and Rod House as gunner. They too were unsuccessful in the search for the carriers. Crew members did get a dramatic view of the damage inflicted by the raiders, plus 20 to 30 holes in their aircraft from alert but angry, frustrated, uncontrolled gunners inadequately trained in aircraft recognition.[27]

Sometime after the first American carrier hunters launched, the Hawaiian Air Force received a map recovered from the body of a Japanese pilot shot down near Fort Kamehameha. The map had approximately ten courses laid out on it to a point northwest of Oahu, which indicated they had either left the carriers there or expected to return to carriers in that direction. General Martin dispatched planes northward in the afternoon, as did the Navy's VS-6, and they found nothing. The remainder of the day was spent preparing to fend off another attack, particularly a follow-through amphibious landing.[28]

Captain Waldron, provisional commander of all B-18s, participated in the search with two aircraft, taking off at 1330 in a northwest direction. His B-18 carried six 100-pound bombs and two .30-caliber machine guns. Men from the 31st Bomb Squadron made up the crew. The B-18 was obsolescent, its bombing capability primitive, and defensive guns completely inadequate. Waldron later considered it fortunate that they didn't find the Japanese carrier force. "I wouldn't be here if I did," he said.

He and his crew also faced heavy antiaircraft artillery fire when he brought their bomber back to Hickam. Although they were operating on radio silence, the routine procedure, he finally got on the radio and said, "This is Gatty, your friend! *Please let me land*! That went on for some 45 minutes to an hour before he finally got clearance to land.

While Gatty Waldron was out on the search with his B-18, Lieutenant Colonel James A. "Jimmy" Mollison, Major General Martin's Chief of Staff, was working frantically to establish the Hawaiian Department's emergency headquarters in Aliamanu Crater. He was hurrying to meet a 1430 deadline for occupancy. He also felt responsible for Martin, who possessed both personal courage and good sense. But Martin's ulcer drained him of resistance, and the attack shattered his morale. At about 1500 Martin began to show signs of being overwhelmed, and turning to his chief of staff, stammered, "What am I going to do? I believe I am losing the power of decision." Mollison, realizing his good chief had reached the end of his rope, immediately arranged for Martin's admission to the Hickam Field hospital, with orders no one was to disturb him. He had a private phone installed at Martin's bedside so he could communicate with the general when conditions demanded.

At Wheeler, as soon as available fighter aircraft could be patched together and serviced, they were sent up to patrol the skies. They, too, encountered heavy antiaircraft artillery fire, especially over Pearl Harbor, then faced a barrage of rifle and machine gun fire when approaching Wheeler to land. One mission flown by an assortment of ten 15th Pursuit Group planes joined to escort Saunders' and Allen's B-17s on the search north-northwest of Oahu, in a 200-mile sweep for one and one half hours, landing at dusk. Another was a twilight scramble by Lieutenant Aloha and other 18th Pursuit Group pilots who took off from Wheeler to investigate a bogey (an unknown), with instructions to climb as high as they could and fly toward Diamond Head. The flight commander, First Lieutenant Charles H. MacDonald, asked what they were supposed to be going after. When the control tower operator told him it was a bright light over Diamond Head, he asked, "Doesn't anybody know that Venus is bright out there this time of year?" With that parting question they aborted the mission and returned to Wheeler.

One other Hickam aircraft landed at Mooring Mast Field Ewa after dark, a B-23 Dragon, a type of aircraft scarce in the Army Air Force. The B-23 was a twin-engine bomber, complete with bomb bay doors, intended to replace the Army Air Force's outmoded B-10 bomber, and looked somewhat like the Douglas DC-3 transport—but proved to be obsolescent before it could be brought into service. Only a small number were manufactured and entered service at a few bases. Nevertheless, the lone Dragon out of Hickam, with its small bomb load and few defensive machine guns, plus an aggressive crew, joined the search late that day, and returned toward Hickam that night, dangerously low on fuel—so low in fact, the aircraft commander decided to recover at Ewa.

At Ewa, the Marines had taken a beating along with everyone else, and hadn't any operative runway lights, or radio transmitters in their control tower. While they set up defenses against

Mooring Mast Field at Ewa, with the aircraft control tower in its Airship Mooring Mast, the mast outmoded due to cancellation of the Navy's airship program. Photographed 13 February 1941. USMCASC

possible follow-on attacks, they also set out flare pots along their remaining primary runway, on one side only, nearest the control tower. Using the Aldis lamp's red and green signal system, and their radio on "receive only" channels, they could receive emergency landing requests from inbound friendly aircraft.

In came the B-23 Dragon in the early dark of night, aircraft running lights on and blinking, it's crew requesting an emergency landing due to low fuel. The tower operators gave the pilot the green light on final approach, and watched progress down final approach, until they recognized much to their dismay, that the pilot assumed the flare pots were on the right side of the runway—his right—when they were instead on the left side of the runway. The Dragon was bearing down toward a touchdown off the runway, heading directly toward the control tower and vehicles parked in front of it. A last minute, frantic red light was flashed at the B-23 with a whole lot of momentary angst over whether or not the already-worried crew saw the red light waving the Dragon off.

Fortunately, the Dragon's crew saw the red light, and realized their wrong assumption. But matters were desperate. The crew applied full power for the go-around and pulled up into a hard climbing turn to the right, a short downwind opposite the

An Army Air Force bomber – one of the obsolescent, never-massed-produced B-23 Dragons—low on fuel, landed at Ewa at night after searching for the Japanese strike fleet. USAFM

direction of landing, then turned another 180 degrees to a short final approach. The aircraft touched down safely and during the landing rollout, its running lights suddenly went out, both engines sputtered, then quit. Dark and silence.

Marines who had jumped into vehicles to go out to meet the airplane on the runway were startled to see its lights fade and engines stop, but sped up to the aircraft, not certain what to expect. The pilot's side window opened, as did an access door to the airplane, and the Marines were invited to come aboard. They did, and were promptly greeted with multiple "thanks" and an offering of "spirits," whereupon the two services' members imbibed freely.

It had been a hell of a day. Like the crew of the inadequately armed B-18 that was out hunting the Japanese fleet, the B-23 Dragon was pitifully unprepared, unescorted and wouldn't have survived an encounter with much more capable Japanese aircraft, or the blistering antiaircraft defense Nagumo's fleet would have mounted had the Dragon found them. Then on top of the worrisome afternoon search had come the revelation the airplane was flying at night after a frightening day, desperately low on fuel, and could be shot down by "friendly guns," or land "in the drink." Prior to the mission, the crew likely concluded, "If we have to go, we might as well go happy, and laugh all the way."[29]

In addition to the unrecorded B-23, Army Air Force A-20, B-17, B-18, B-23, P-40, P-36, and O-47 aircraft flew 48 fruitless sorties in a frustrating search for the enemy carriers. As the cold and weary aircrews from Hickam climbed stiffly out of their airplanes that evening, they were anxious to find something to eat. Many had not eaten since the previous night. The enlisted men learned that the base hospital had the only hot food around, so they headed that way. The hospital was dimly lit with blankets draped over the windows for blackout purposes. After eating some stew, the men walked back to their units.

Beginning the next day, prior long-range patrol patterns, in search of the withdrawing Japanese strike force, and for follow-on defensive patrols, would begin to change for the Navy and Army Air Force in Hawaii, and evolve into a coordinated plan for both—under the control of the Navy's Patrol Wing TWO. By 21 December enough B-17s would be flown out of California to Oahu to bring the heavy bomber force to a full-group strength of forty-three planes. To make the improved, far more extensive patrol operation possible the Navy began transferring three squadrons of reconnaissance aircraft from the Atlantic to Hawaii as soon as it could, and the Army Air Force would routinely hold 18 of its heavy bombers as a striking force ready for action on 30-minute notice.[30]

Scouting Squadron Six Joins the Search

While the Army Air Force was dispatching aircraft to search for the enemy on 7 December, the men of *Enterprise*'s VS-6, under the guidance of the Commander, Task Force 8 and the control of Patrol Wing TWO, were preparing to use as many of their remaining aircraft as could be mustered following their harrowing landings at Ford Island, Ewa and Hickam. The Air Group Commander, Lieutenant Commander Young, had been the first to land at Ford Island approximately 0835, through a hail of friendly antiaircraft fire, much aimed at his plane and originating from as close as fifty yards. He and Lieutenant Commander Nichol, who was on Admiral Kimmel's staff, immediately reported to Kimmel, where Young informed him of the position of the *Enterprise* and their squadron's mission.

Landing after Young at Ford Island, at approximately 0845, was the squadron commander, Lieutenant Commander Hopping. He set about obtaining fuel for his airplane and making arrangements to refuel and rearm the squadron's airplanes, including one 500-pound bomb each. After reporting to Patrol Wing TWO and learning Young was at CinCPac, Hopping received orders from Wing operations to search an area south of Barbers Point where a carrier had been reported.

In the meantime, Young received orders to report to Patrol Wing TWO to help with the search for the enemy carriers, and began taking stock of the number of aircraft he would have available to participate in the search. He counted thirteen total from VS-6 and VB-6. He was ordered to send nine planes to search sector 330 degrees to 030 degrees to a distance of 175 miles, a 60-degree sector straddling due north. The remaining aircraft were to investigate reports of hostile ships and sampans south of Barbers Point. If found the SBDs were to attack with bombs and gunfire. Young also sought and received permission to remain in the Ford Island control tower to maintain radio contact with *Enterprise* and aircraft conducting the search—a well-intentioned plan that would eventually prove futile because of low-power limitations of control tower radio transmitters.

At 1030 Hopping took off from Ford Island and flew toward Barbers Point. From there he flew tracks west twenty miles, south twenty miles, west sixty miles, south twenty miles, east sixty miles and back to Ford Island. He made no contacts except with our own ships and sampans. During the return, he received orders from the *Enterprise* to "refuel, rearm and rejoin," meaning rejoin the search for the enemy. Hopping acknowledged the orders and passed them to plane 6-S-7, crewed by Lieutenant (jg) Dale Hilton, pilot, and Radioman/Gunner Second Class Jack Leaming, who, with two other VS-6 SBDs, had landed at Ewa between 1000 and 1015 following repeated attempts to land at Ford Island during the air raid. Jack Leaming continued, describing events as they unfolded for VS-6, which was once again to be in the air, this time to join in the search for the Japanese strike force.

At 1145 Hopping landed at Ford Island and reported to the commander of Patrol Wing TWO that there were no Japanese surface craft within the rectangle covering the area 100 miles west and 60 miles south of Barbers Point. He also told him of the orders he received from *Enterprise*, whereupon, as Patrol Wing TWO had directed the Air Group Commander, Hopping was to take nine of his aircraft to search the 60-degree sector to the north.

By the time Hopping landed, the first flight of four Army Air Force A-20s had been airborne nearly twenty minutes, directed by General Martin to search the same general area Hopping had just searched—both tasked to search in response to the same report. Neither Hopping nor Major Holzapfel, leading the A-20s, was aware of the overlapping directives they received, nor were they monitoring or communicating on the same radio frequencies.

While Hopping gathered his squadron's remaining planes and their crews for the search mission, Lieutenant Clarence E. Dickinson arrived on Ford Island following a harrowing automobile ride to Hickam, then to the docks across the main channel from Ford Island. The civilian couple who picked him up not far from Ewa after he bailed out of his burning SBD, had driven him back to the entrance to Hickam Field, and dropped him off. En route to Hickam, Japanese fighters were strafing the road they were traveling, and made a pass on their car—but missed. The three saw the car 50 feet ahead of them hit by the same airplane on the same strafing pass, apparently killing the two people inside. Later they saw other vehicles that had been attacked along the same road. Throughout the trip back to Ford Island, Dickinson worried about the fate of his Radioman/gunner, William C. Miller, though the circumstances of those last desperate seconds before bailout caused him to fear the worst.

When Dickinson rejoined his squadron on Ford Island and learned of their search mission, he had only one thought—to fly the mission. He didn't tell his commanders of his harrowing ordeal that morning. He didn't want to give them a reason to leave him behind. He just needed another airplane, and would later quietly solve the problem of a radioman/gunner to fill in for the missing Bill Miller, who hopefully was found alive and well. With some help, Dickinson solved both problems, and joined with eight other SBDs to complete the mission. His selfless act later became known to Commander Young, the *Enterprise* Air Group Commander, and on 15 December he wrote in his "Report of Action with Japanese Air Force at Oahu, T.H.,"

> Lieut. C.E. Dickensen, USN, Scouting Squadron Six, after having been attacked by superior numbers of Japanese planes and under constant AA fire from the ground was forced to bail out, his plane having caught fire. In the midst of the third attack on Pearl Harbor, he made his way to Ford Island Field and immediately upon arrival there manned another plane and participated in the 175 mile search flight. At this time his ordeal of having been shot down was not known to his superiors and no mention of the same was made by him to anyone at the time, thus displaying a superb courage, stamina, devotion to duty, unexcelled logic and coolness in action. It is requested that this officer be given an official commendation for his performance of duty.[31]

When Lieutenant Dale Hilton landed and went to get further orders at Ewa, he told Jack Leaming to cover the star on the wing with brush and camouflage the plane as best he could. As

Jack was completing the task, a fuel truck arrived and he had to remove some of the fresh paint to fill the tanks. Minutes later, Marines arrived and armed their plane with a 500-pound bomb. They still had a full load of machine gun ammunition. The Ewa commanding officer sent word to CinCPac and Patrol Wing TWO of their availability for a mission.

Hilton and Leaming in 6-S-7, with 6-B-5 and 6-B-12, received orders to join some B-17s from Hickam Field at 1115. A fourth VS-6 aircraft, 6-S-11, with Ensign Fogg and Radioman/Gunner Third Class Dennis remained at Ewa by orders of Wheeler Control until 1000 the next day, when the Patrol Wing TWO operations officer directed Fogg to return to Ford Island. That left three SBDs ordered to join with the B-17s. The three took off from Ewa in time to rendezvous with the B-17s at 1115, and circled west of Ford Island at 2,000 feet, again dodging "friendly" ground fire. The B-17s were nowhere in sight, and the SBD crews concluded that they had left earlier—when, in fact, Saunders' and Allen's two B-17Ds didn't get airborne until 1140.

As Hilton and his flight of three SBDs were coming to the conclusion the B-17s had already departed, Lieutenant Commander Hopping, their squadron commander, reported he was over Barbers Point. Hilton called him and gave him their position. Hopping ordered all planes to return to Ford Island to refuel and rearm. They landed at about 1130, and began preparing for the search to the north of Oahu. Years later, after spending more than three years in Japanese prisoner of war camps, Jack Leaming would write of that mission:

> The feelings arising from this assignment ran the gamut of human experience. Anger, fear, bravado, futility, hopelessness, and the confrontation with death were nearly overwhelming. [Nine] of us against an unknown number of surface ships and aircraft.
>
> Every second in the air was fraught with anxiety, apprehension, anger, and searching the skies for the enemy. The situation grabbed our whole being, your thoughts and feelings. The past alternates with the present. The determination to destroy and obliterate the men and force that wreaked this havoc upon our

fleet and shipmates superceded even personal safety. Now, those years of practice would be tested.

It was a great relief to be back with men from the squadron, but it was not a pleasant experience upon learning what had happened to some of our shipmates. The most astounding tale was that of Lieutenant Dickinson.

While Dale [Hilton] attended the briefing at the Command Center, I stayed with the plane. It was parked near a revetment close to the *Arizona*. As I busied myself looking the plane over and waiting, I watched a parade of injured and dead pass by me. When I looked out over the harbor, it was covered with oil more than six inches thick.

Ford Island was not the place we left. The *Nevada* was beached near the channel entrance. Men were diving in a sea of oil alongside her, coming up hands first to spread the oil, and then their heads would appear as they looked for shipmates who were injured.

The *Utah* had capsized at her moorings just behind where [the *Enterprise*] usually tied up. A destroyer had blown up in dry-dock across the channel. Several battleships were resting on the bottom, their main decks awash. Men were still fighting raging fires. Hangars were reduced to skeletons, as were planes inside them, PBYs, three or four squadrons of them, destroyed. Mess attendants were wearing captains' four striper coats. If you saluted an officer he called you a crazy S.O.B. Hours before, he would have put you on report if you did not.

There were screams of men still hurt, unattended, still dying . . . men running around crying like babies, in a state of shock, cussing. The air blue with their oaths, screaming, "Let me at those yellow bastards!" or "They killed my best buddy!"

Every second that stretched into minutes reflected and affirmed that the unquenchable struggle for life is timeless and the hope and faith that bind men together in their most hopeless hour is of the Divine.

War pumps you up. A uniform suddenly becomes

radiant and destruction is the goal. It is easy to do and gets easier the more you do it. The squadron, your buddies, the ship become more important than yourself. You become more vindictive and brutal. Becoming a POW accentuates these feelings.

The transition from peace to war was sudden, unbelievable. It was a beautiful, sunny Sunday morning, certainly not an appropriate setting for killing. All of a sudden you seem to realize that life itself is a defeat, a constant, incessant, losing game. But, somehow, you summon the courage to continue, to accept what is, run with it, and hope the future will be brighter.

Ewa Field and Ford Island looked as though some crazy producer had set it up for a film production . . . this was not for real . . . but IT WAS! This, the great U.S. Fleet, had been reduced to nothing in minutes. What was all this bombast about how invincible we were. And you wondered what in the hell you would do if they came back.

In the meantime, Lt. Dickinson was scouting around for an airplane to participate in the search. LtCmdr. Young had been injured and could not fly, so Dickinson was assigned the CAEG's plane. Then, he had another problem, who was going to man the rear cockpit and free gun!

Well, he lucked out again. An aviation machinist's mate third class, Jim Young from VP-22 [Patrol Squadron 22] was ready, eager, and willing to avenge the injuries of shipmates and the destruction of his PBY squadron. I can still see him in his dungarees and undershirt talking his qualifications and almost demanding to go. He was told to get permission from his commanding officer and he did, in record time. LtCmdr. Young had received orders to send nine SBDs to conduct a search for the Japanese fleet. When Jim Young returned with his C.O.'s okay, we were ready to go.

At 1230, Dale and I, with eight others searched a sector of 330 degrees true to 030 degrees true from Kaena Point looking for the Japanese Fleet.

We were in three groups of threes. Our sector was from 330 to 350 degrees. Lt. Dickinson and Ensign Weber from VB-6 were with us. Our orders were to attack any enemy we encountered. If ever there was a suicide mission, this was one . . .

Upon our return from the scouting hop at 1530, we immediately took off again for the Big E. As we were walking out to man our planes, I encountered Lt. Gallaher. He asked me if I was going to "ship over" [go home since his enlistment was about to end] and I said "Hell, no!" I extended my enlistment for two years the last days of December. I thought the war would be over in no time and that was long enough.

When we landed aboard, we were mobbed with questions about Pearl Harbor. As we answered questions, the answers were met with disbelief. The presence of Jim Young [from VP-22], who everyone knew was not a member of the squadron, and his description of the morning events convinced everyone that our answers were true. Halsey determined that Pearl Harbor needed all the aerial defense that could be given if there should be another attack. He ordered us to return to Ford Island.

After we returned to Ford Island, the *Enterprise* had sent out an attack force of TBDs [Douglas Devastator torpedo bombers from Squadron VT-6], SBDs with smoke tanks [carrying 100 pounds of hydrofluoric acid] to screen their attack, with a cover of six fighters, F4Fs, based on a report from a shore based direction finder that there were enemy ships off Oahu. [The slow moving Devastators, carrying torpedoes, could cruise no faster than 90 knots, not far above stall speed for the SBDs and F4Fs. Thus the SBDs flew above the TBDs, weaving back and forth in S turns at a higher speed, and the F4Fs flew above covering both groups, also making S turns. Because of the S turns, neither the SBDs nor the F4Fs were able to navigate during the mission and had to rely entirely upon the TBDs for safe return to the ship.] The report [of enemy ships] proved to

be false. After an extensive search, it was discovered
to be our cruisers and destroyers that had left Pearl
Harbor for the safety of the open ocean.

Night had fallen by the time their mission was
completed and they returned to the ship. [The
Enterprise had to show a searchlight for the
returning aircraft to find her.] They all landed
aboard safely [except for 6-T-13, a torpedo bomber,
which crashed into No. 1 barrier with no damage]
but the fighters were low on fuel and were ordered
to land at Ford Island . . . [32]

The *Enterprise* had launched the force of torpedo and dive
bombers, escorted by six fighters, beginning at 1642 hours, just
two minutes after the carrier's OOD, Ensign Jack A. Holmes, had
logged observing the *St. Louis*'s antiaircraft fire as the cruiser and
other ships approached to join with Task Force 8. The last aircraft
was airborne seventeen minutes later, and the launch was in
response to the same, earlier direction finding readings on which
prior searches had been based. At 2010 *Enterprise* turned on her
breakdown lights to land the returning aircraft. Seven minutes
later the first airplane landed, and at 2038 Devastator 6-T-13 hit
the barrier, delaying the final aircraft to land until 2113.

While the landings were in progress, the destroyer *Hull* (DD-
350), which had left Pearl Harbor, joined the Task Force at 2045.
At 2115, with speed at 15 knots, *Enterprise* began zigzagging
according to plan No. 6, and turned off her running lights ten
minutes later. It had been a long day of hectic flight operations,
with painful losses, but they would soon learn of more losses.

As the *Hull* was joining the Task Force, the landings of the
six fighters from *Enterprise*'s VF-6 were in progress on Oahu,
landings that would ironically have tragic consequences.[33]

The 7 December search for the Japanese carrier strike force,
from bases on Oahu was essentially over and unsuccessful,
while the search for Nagumo's fleet and "the enemy below,"
submarines, continued from the Pacific Fleet's two available
carriers and their task forces. No one will ever know if or how
close the Americans came to finding the strike force that day. By
nightfall the enemy fleet was far to the northwest, bound for their
refueling rendezvous, and wouldn't reappear again until two

weeks later, when they diverted part of their task force to aid in overwhelming Wake Island's defenders.

From the start, had all the American's search efforts been concentrated to the north, both from Oahu and from the large, rapidly-assembled carrier task forces, they might have caught their quarry before they could escape—perhaps in the midst of refueling and rearming, when the enemy couldn't launch an adequate airborne defense. On the other hand, had the Americans found the fleet, using the small forces they launched at various intervals from bases on Oahu, their ability to inflict serious damage would have been doubtful at best.

The two B-17s with fighter escorts, and perhaps a flight of three among the nine SBDs in VS-6 probably came close to sighting Nagumo's fleet miles ahead of them to the northwest, but by the time they approached the limit of their search ranges, his fleet was over the horizon, beyond their visual reach. Had they found the fleet with sufficient fuel remaining to attack, probably neither of the two forces was sufficient to successfully penetrate the fighter defense the Japanese could mount. Finally, were they fortunate enough to surprise the strike force, they likely would have suffered grievous losses from the fleet's bristling antiaircraft guns before being able to conduct successful bomb attacks.

Punishment for the Japanese carriers and their Naval aircraft involved in the attack on Oahu and Pearl Harbor would have to wait for months, but not quite the six months Admirals Yamamoto and Nagumo had sought in protecting the flank of the Japanese Empire's drive deep into Southeast Asia.

Added to the tragic turn of events in the attack and attempted counterstrike, the failure to find the large Japanese force, the lingering uncertainty as to exactly where they might be and what more they might have planned, coupled with the raiders' total surprise and glowing success on Oahu, had far more serious consequences than were generally known at the time. The resulting uncertainties and their reverberations were particularly evident in Hawaii, and spread like wildfire through the military chains of command and across the continental United States.

While the Navy and Air Force commenced the frantic but ultimately frustrating search for the Japanese carriers, a desperate rescue and recovery operation was in progress on Oahu, along with movement of the wounded and dead to proper medical care and disposition.

Saving Lives and Counting Losses

When the tally of killed and wounded was finally complete, in reality not until many days afterward: 2,335 military and 68 civilians had been killed or died of wounds, a total of 2,403. In addition, 1,143 military and 35 civilians were wounded, or 1,178 total. The totals included "friendly fire" dead and wounded.

The devastating total of 3,581 killed and wounded, plus an unknown number who received minor wounds and medical treatment and weren't recorded, or didn't bother to seek medical attention, tell nothing of the human suffering and family losses. Exploding bombs and torpedoes, and powerful, fire-setting machine gun and cannon rounds, plus exploding ammunition magazines, fires feeding on huge oil tank ruptures and attendant massive fuel spills from ships, parked aircraft loaded with fuel and fuel storage areas, resulted in shattered and dismembered bodies, making many of the dead impossible to find or identify, and maiming many of the wounded for life.

Compounding the problem of identifying the dead was the fact that prior to World War II men and women in the military weren't issued "dog tags," later required and so well known in the American military. Consequently and tragically, the cumulative effect was approximately 670 unknowns were eventually buried in 252 different locations in the Punchbowl Cemetery on Oahu, and all but one remains unknown to this day.

A thoughtful examination of the attack's aftermath clearly indicates the Japanese fighters and dive bombers specifically targeted fire stations, and the red-painted fire fighting equipment and their crews, with the military purpose of permitting their incendiary and tracer rounds to cause as much damage by fire as possible. Deep penetrating, high-explosive bombs and torpedoes tore through heavy armor plating on ships to both set massive fires and cause flooding. Armor piercing, tracer and incendiary rounds penetrated thinner armor plating on ships, and tore through key targets of all types on airfields, with devastating fire-starting effects. The tactics and selected weapons loads paid off for the attackers.

The threat of fire on board ships is always a matter of great concern, a reason for frequent inspections and improvement of equipment, fire fighting and damage control drills. Ships are in fact enormous, high-powered, high-energy-driven floating cities loaded with hundreds of thousands of gallons of flammable fuel, and Naval combatants are literally floating arsenals and ammunition depots with redundant safety systems, horizontal partitions (decks), vertical partitions (bulkheads) on both sides of compartments, and procedures designed around them to avoid catastrophe.

There were numerous fires on airfields, but few were as deadly and massively fatal as on the ships. Fires on ships, and on the surface of oily waters injected a different kind of horror into that day, and into the tortured memories carried in the years ahead. The images of the walking dead seen on the *Arizona* and men struck down or trapped by exploding bombs and horribly burned or nearly consumed by fire on the battleships *West Virginia*, *Nevada*, *California*, *Nevada*, and *Pennsylvania*; the destroyers *Shaw* and *Downes*; the repair ship *Vestal*, moored to *Arizona* when the attack began; and the seaplane tender *Curtiss*. Some were burned to death before the eyes of their comrades and others who could only stand by helplessly, unable to reach them, bodies burned beyond recognition, and others burned beyond any hope of surviving, unrecognizable and lingering in slow deaths.

Added were the wrenching visions of drowning shipmates who had been hopelessly trapped by their capsizing and sinking ships, or drowning beneath the six inch oily scum fed by massive, ruptured fuel tanks that spread over the waters' surface surrounding the battleships.

The tidal wave of casualties coming from ships, airfields, the city of Honolulu, and outlying areas at first seemed beyond comprehension and initially overwhelmed temporary available transportation, aid stations, designated medical treatment centers aboard damaged and sinking ships, receiving clinics, hospitals, the hospital ship *Solace*, ambulance and volunteer transportation, doctors, nurses, emergency rooms, operating rooms, pharmacies, morgues, cemeteries, and casualty identification and notification systems. While total bed capacity at the existing military and civilian hospitals was far more than sufficient to eventually absorb the influx of wounded and dying, it came at the expense of convalescing patients who had to move to make room.

Scheduled training and no-notice exercises prepared military and civilian doctors, nurses, medics, ambulance, firemen and supporting medical staffs to respond calmly and professionally to the stream of casualties, but it was, in some instances, impossible to keep up with the numbers pouring into the primary and back-up treatment centers. The number of severely wounded inevitably increased beyond the capability to give them immediate, possibly life-saving treatment.

As the streams of dead and wounded poured off the ships, airfields, and other locations, the task of identifying the dead, dying, and the units or ships they came from was all too often impossible. The urgency of getting the badly wounded to treatment overcame on-site note taking or record keeping. Many men carried no identification, frequently because it was left behind when they rushed to battle stations or fled impossible circumstances. Some volunteered to assist on other ships such as *Pennsylvania*, then turned up missing, and it took days to find out what happened to them. Many of the wounded couldn't be found by their unit supervisors and commanders for days, and in some instances, men were declared dead who were only slightly wounded, and instead were "missing" somewhere in a hospital.

Many men were dismembered in violent explosions, their bodies separated from any form of identification they might have carried. Others were burned beyond recognition, along with any hope of identification. The recovery and rescue work, official records, and accounts of efforts by doctors, nurses, medics and volunteers tell the story. Both the Army's Hawaiian Department, Office of the Department Surgeon, and the Navy's Medical Department at Pearl Harbor were well prepared and responded magnificently to the crisis they confronted.

Immediately, at the Hawaiian Department's Station Hospital at Schofield Barracks—which serviced Wheeler Field—the Station Hospital at Hickam Field, and Tripler General Hospital in Fort Shafter, as casualties began coming in, sixteen civilian surgical teams, previously assigned and organized, were dispatched to various hospitals to assist in the care of battle casualties. Additional people promptly went to open up Kamehameha School and Farrington High School as auxiliary hospitals. The same day, the Hawaiian Department issued orders to open St. Louis College as a hospital. Plans for the conversion of these schools into hospitals had previously been made, and if the battle had continued their use as auxiliary hospitals was available. Four Provisional General Hospitals and six Hawaii District Hospitals, added to three large military hospitals offered the possibility of 3,472 normal beds available, with emergency and expansion beds totaling 5,340 and 7,009 respectively—more than enough to accommodate the influx of wounded that day.[34]

At the Station Hospital at Schofield Barracks, the second largest of the Army hospitals on Oahu, Major (Doctor) Leonard J. Heaton, Medical Corps and Chief of Surgical Services, arrived at the hospital minutes after he was recalled to duty. Just prior to the telephone call, he and his family and two other physicians had dodged machine gun bullets in the Heaton's front yard, fired from a Japanese fighter that made two passes down the street in front of their family quarters. For months he and the men and women in the hospital planned and prepared for such an emergency. The Hospital staff rapidly cleared convalescent patients from beds to make room for the arriving wounded. In his diary he described what he and his operating teams faced beginning just thirty minutes after the first bomb fell on Wheeler Field:

> The first wounded arrived from Wheeler Field and we immediately set our operating teams in action. We worked all that day up until early evening. I had already set up 4 of these teams on paper and they started to function as all were present. We were not caught short on personnel or equipment. Such wounds!!—eviscerations of brains, neck, thorax, abdomen—traumatic amputations, etc. No burns of any consequence. No cardiac or neurological operated cases . . . [35]

Surgical teams at Schofield Barracks worked tirelessly, treating 117 wounded that day. The speed with which the wounded were handled and the calm thoroughness of their treatment had much to do with the saving of life and limb. Thirty-eight of them died, most having arrived with fatal wounds. No cases of gas gangrene developed or caused deaths, a form of deadly infection in wars past, and a tribute to a new, simple life-saving procedure begun by Dr. Heaton and later recognized and used throughout the Army.[36]

Hickam Station Hospital, which had opened only a few weeks before, was built of reinforced concrete three stories high, with wide, tropical screened porches on three sides. In the back, connected to it with a ramp, was a building that housed medical department personnel, a kitchen and a mess hall. Seriously ill patients were normally sent to Tripler General Hospital. Hickam's hospital staff consisted of seven medical officers, five dentists, seven nurses and forty enlisted men. The hospital had a capacity of thirty-two beds, which could expand to sixty, and couldn't possibly handle the stream of casualties that flooded it that morning. Consistent with emergency planning and direction given to all Army hospitals on Oahu, dentists at Hickam were immediately drafted as auxiliary medical doctors.

Captain Frank H. Lane, the acting commander, was an Army Air Force flight surgeon living with his wife, Carmen, and their two sons in family housing located only a short distance from the Pearl Harbor boundary. Awake shortly before 0800 that Sunday morning, he was preparing to take his family to church and had just finished dressing when he heard a loud explosion. His first thought was one of the oil storage tanks on the hill had exploded. He looked out the bedroom window, and saw a cloud of black smoke in that direction, which seemed to confirm his conclusion. He ran downstairs and out the back door, just in time to see a small plane marked with the rising sun insignia of Japan flying slowly by, slightly above the tops of the two-story houses. He could plainly see the pilot and thought at that time that a Japanese carrier must be in Hawaii on a diplomatic mission.

As the plane flew toward Ford Island in Pearl Harbor, more explosions occurred. Then another plane flying in front burst into flames and fell in the water. Only then did Captain Lane realize an attack was underway. He called to his wife to stay inside, ran to his car parked behind their quarters, and drove to the hospital about four blocks away. By then, the high-pitched whine of diving planes, the chatter of machine gun fire, and the roar of exploding bombs filled the air.

As Captain Lane parked his car on the street in front of the hospital, the medical officer of the day, Captain Andre d'Alphonso, arrived in an ambulance with a wounded soldier. The captain was at the flight line to meet the incoming B-17s, to spray them for bugs, and certainly didn't expect to treat victims of an enemy attack. About the same time, a severely wounded soldier came in, carried on a door, conscious, but with a good part of his abdomen and hip cut out by a piece of shrapnel. Captain Lane felt he was beyond hope, but to reassure him, sent him on to the operating room, telling him he would be fixed up.

By this time all available personnel were reporting to the hospital. The entire hospital staff came in, including those who had been on night duty and were just relieved at 0700 that morning. Filipino orderlies Maguleno H. Jucor, Torihio Kendica, Cosme R. Echanis ran through a hail of machine gun fire and bombs to get to their duty stations. Hospital patients left their beds and either went home or joined in helping with the flood of casualties. All phones in the facility were busy with calls for help. The trucks and drivers augmenting the fleet of seven ambulances began a regular pickup of injured at the consolidated barracks, mess hall, and the flight line, where most of the casualties were occurring, then made regular runs to Tripler.

Among those assisting in picking up the wounded along the flight line was Private Ed Hall, from the 13th Quartermaster Truck Company (Aviation), who, during the first minutes of the attack had escaped with his life while on volunteer kitchen police duty, a short distance from the hangars. He began shuttling a company truck up and down the flight line area during the lull between the first and second waves, picking up wounded and dead and taking them to the Hickam hospital. He continued as the second wave of raiders came in from the direction of Fort Kamehameha, but on one occasion, had to stop, jump out of his truck and crawl underneath it to take cover. As the day wore on, and most all the known casualties had been taken to the hospital, he and the men assisting him, turned their energies more and more to evacuating dependents and their personal belongings off base, removing debris, and transporting needed supplies. He was beginning three days of virtually non-stop, exhausting duty.

When the first of the injured began coming in to the hospital, they found the hospital staff prepared and waiting. Surgeons performed numerous emergency operations to remove bomb fragments. One of the dentists, Lieutenant Robert Lee Kushner, turned surgeon that day, working alongside Lieutenants White and Garret and all the other medics who put in long, continuous hours of duty. They didn't know how long the raid would last, so didn't fill the beds at Hickam, instead evacuating the wounded to the much larger, better-equipped, 850-bed Tripler Hosptial as fast as they could. They sent the wounded on after administering first aid, which, except for emergency surgery, was limited to applying tourniquets, splints, bandages, and giving morphine. The pharmacy prepared morphine in syringes holding ten doses each and didn't have time to change needles between patients. Every few minutes, a medic would go out and check the corpses being stacked in the back of the hospital to make sure that none of the living was among them.

Sometime during the attack, a delayed-action 550-pound bomb landed on the front lawn of the Hickam Hospital, about fifty to seventy feet from the building. Shortly, the air was filled with the acrid smell of the explosives from the bomb, and a number of people yelled "Gas! Gas!" adding to the tumult and confusion. Hickam's nurses, including Monica E. Conter and M. Kathleen Coberly, provided a calm, steadying influence in seeing to the needs of their patients—and won the praise and admiration of all who witnessed their hard work.

This was the first time that Army nurses had been on the front line of battle. Always in the past they were in evacuation hospitals at least ten miles behind the lines. Annie Gayton Fox, who was the nurse in charge that day, later received the Purple Heart, not for wounds, but for bravery. She was believed to be the first woman to receive the medal since it was revived as an award of honor by President Roosevelt.

Hundreds of casualties arrived at the Hickam Hospital that day, but two made a special impression on Captain Lane. The first was a soldier that walked in the front door under his own power. One arm was completely gone but he waved his remaining arm in greeting, still managing to wear a smile on his face. The other was the young flight surgeon, First Lieutenant William R. Schick, who was on Captain Raymond T. Swenson's B-17 and received a face-wound from a ricocheting Japanese machine gun bullet, refused treatment in deference to others he believed more seriously wounded—an act that apparently cost him his life later that day, at Tripler Hospital.[37]

Navy and Marine Medical Services Were Ready

In Pearl Harbor and on Ford Island circumstances for the wounded and the people transporting and caring for them were more complex and difficult, primarily because of the frequency of burn patients. The wounded, dying and dead on ships presented a special problem—how to move them from often-isolated, badly damaged, flooding or burning compartments to designated medical treatment areas on the ships while they were still under attack—or rescue crew members from sinking, burning, or badly-damaged ships, and move them across water to medical facilities where more comprehensive care was available. To their everlasting credit, as had the Army, the Navy had prepared well for the medical emergency that came 7 December.

Between 1939 and 1941 Pearl Harbor had been fortunate in receiving unusual attention from the Surgeon General and the officers who assisted him in the Bureau of Medicine and Surgery in making plans for the Medical Department. When the facilities of the Pearl Harbor hospital became overcrowded in 1940, an intense effort had been made to add to bed capacity, equipment, supplies, and trained people in the Hawaiian area. Although the Naval Hospital at Pearl Harbor had a normal bed capacity of approximately 250 and was one of the best equipped of the eighteen hospitals then in commission, a new hospital that would be removed further from military installations and be less subject to destruction in case of air attack had been planned and was actually under construction at the time of the Japanese attack.

Because of the great concentration of naval personnel and the activities of the Fleet in the Hawaiian area, the Surgeon General requested and secured permission to send out to Pearl Harbor the Navy's second Mobile Base Hospital, a type of transportable facility which was the most significant organization developed by the Navy Medical Department during the pre-war emergency. To add further to the hospital facilities in the Hawaiian area, the hospital ship *Solace* (AH-5) arrived in Pearl Harbor shortly after the Mobile Hospital and was in port when the Japanese struck. For the horror inflicted on the battleships moored on the east side of Ford Island, the *Solace* and all the Navy's medical facilities would be a God-send.

The less damaged *Maryland* and *Tennessee* became avenues of escape to Ford Island for survivors of the shattered, blazing *Arizona*; the fire-ravaged, sinking *West Virginia*, and capsized *Oklahoma*, while others of their crews, with no other way out, leaped into the oil covered waters that quickly surrounded the battleships, attempted to swim to safety or were picked up by the numerous boats fishing survivors from the waters.

The boats evacuated many of the wounded and burned men

from the ships, and those rescued from the water, to the *Solace*; to the dock where the repair ship *Argonne* (AG-31), flagship of the Base Force, was moored; or to landing C near the U.S. Naval Hospital.

After the first wave air attack the main battle dressing station of the *Argonne* was moved to the secondary battle dressing station, where the injured men from the ship were treated. Later, the medical department of the *Argonne*, aided by medical personnel from other ships, received a large number of wounded and burned men at the dock where the ship was moored. In the open, under fire, about 150 cots were set up on the dock to take care of the injured men evacuated from ships or rescued from the water. Subsequently, under the direction of the Base Force surgeon, personnel moved the cots and medical material to the Officers' Club in the Navy Yard, which was less exposed to enemy fire. By 1030, a "field hospital", supplied and equipped by *Argonne*, was set up. The dock continued in use as a clearing station for the wounded. The most severely wounded went to the Naval Hospital. Less severe cases went to the Mobile Base Hospital, or to the field hospital at the Officers' Club.

When the watch officers on *Solace* realized an air raid was in progress, they sounded general quarters and took action to close all watertight doors and ports, including cargo ports—except the two at the gangways, to call away rescue parties. The crew prepared all hospital facilities and supplies for maximum service, put together 50 beds in the emergency ward, began moving patients from lower to upper bunks, and discharging to duty 141 patients. They witnessed the huge explosion and fire on *Arizona* and immediately dispatched two motor launches with rescue parties. Other boats were lowered and sent on similar duty.

Approximately 0820 hours boatloads of casualties began to arrive, and medical personnel, with available men from the deck divisions, immediately moved to take care of them. After wounded began coming aboard at a rapid rate, 23 were taken care of in the 50-bed emergency ward compartment. At 0900 the ship got underway, after slipping its forward and after moorings, and shifted from berth X-4, near the destroyer tender *Dobbin* and her nest of destroyers, to berth X-13, in the clear.

Though the Japanese didn't attack the prominently-marked, white hospital ship the entire raid, the rescue parties in motor launches #1 and #2, including their stretcher parties, performed heroically in the face of grave danger in picking up numerous casualties and returning them to the care of Solace's doctors, nurses and corpsmen. The Japanese were less generous toward some of the smaller boats plying the harbor, made random strafing passes on some of them, and at least one was sunk by a bomb.

In their first trip the rescue parties boarded the burning Arizona while its crew was abandoning ship, and worked with Lieutenant Commander Fuqua, and side by side with other surviving crew members in rescuing burned and injured casualties found on its deck, some very close to the flames. They picked up three more wounded, clinging to a camel, and rescued a man swimming in oily water that was aflame.

After unloading at the Solace, #2 motor launch made two trips to the burning, sinking West Virginia and brought back casualties to the Solace. Then came another trip to West Virginia, where the battleship's First Lieutenant and Damage Control Officer, Lieutenant Commander John S. Harper, had taken charge and was directing the carrying of wounded men abandoning ship. Afterward the launch took up patrolling and rescue duty until approximately 1100 hours.

On its second trip, #1 motor launch rescued several more men from the stern of Arizona, and more casualties from West Virginia. On its fourth trip, the West Virginia's executive officer, Commander Roscoe H. Hillenkoetter came aboard the launch following the "Abandon ship" order, and at his request picked up some men in the water and transferred them to a gig. Shortly thereafter, when many men had jumped into the water after an explosion on board West Virginia, the motor launch picked up over three dozen more.

As the rescue of wounded and others abandoning Arizona and West Virginia progressed, the sea of fire spreading on the oily surface and being pushed and pulled toward the harbor entrance by the wind and tide made rescue work even more perilous. Flames covered the water's surface moving around and near West Virginia, and were getting close to #1 motor launch, scorching its sides when Fireman Second Class F.C. Ley, the boat engineer, jumped into the water to rescue a struggling ensign. The Coxswain had to get into the water to quench his own smoldering jumper. With this boatload delivered to the Solace and a quick change of clothes for its crew, the boat took Bowman M.G. Carpenter,

The hospital ship *Solace* (AH-5) in Hawaiian waters. Her crew was heavily involved in rescue as well as hospitalization of wounded during and after the attack. NA

and a salvage party to the capsized *Oklahoma* where it remained until midnight.

Each of the *Solace's* motor launches carried a crew of four, plus stretcher parties of nine and eleven men respectively on #1 and #2 boats, and all were commended by name in the *Solace* commander's 12 December action report. Assisting the *Solace*-assigned medical officers part of that first day were six medical officers from other ships, one civilian doctor from the U.S. Public Health Service, and five volunteer nurses. In addition to the ship's chaplain, a Protestant and two Catholic chaplains from *Nevada* and *Tangier* came aboard to help and remained most of the first two days.

The *Solace* admitted a total of 132 patients on board on 7 December. About 80 received first aid treatment only. Twenty-eight patients, 26 of whom weren't identified, died. At the end of the day, the number of occupied beds was 177, with 253 unoccupied.[38]

There were 28 chaplains on Oahu that morning. Nine were

Army, 19 were Navy, and on board the 94 ships in the harbor that weekend were many more. By one means or another, all found themselves ministering to the needs of people affected by the attack. When it began, Chaplain Bill Maguire, Fleet Chaplain (for the forces afloat), was standing on the dock at the officer's landing, awaiting the motor launch to take him to the fleet flagship, the battleship *California*, for an 8:30 Mass. The chaotic events he witnessed while on the landing, including the savaging within minutes of the battleships moored next to Ford Island, delayed his departure and cancelled the Mass he was to give. Finally, Bill Maguire was able to get aboard a motor launch to the *California*, but the launch had to detour to a destroyer temporarily because some enemy planes attacked anything moving on the water.

When he arrived at the *California*, it was apparent the *Arizona* was gone, the *Oklahoma* was gone, the *West Virginia* was on fire and sinking, and the *California* would be next to sink. There were numerous wounded on *California*, and they had to be removed. The ship's chaplain, Ray Hohenstein, was among the wounded, and was to be the only other wounded chaplain that morning other than the two fatalities, Chaplain Kirkpatrick on *Arizona* and Chaplain Schmitt on *Oklahoma*. Ray Hohenstein was in the port side of the *California* when struck by shrapnel. He was moved to the starboard side just before a bomb struck the port side. For a time a rumor swept the ship, "Our chaplain has been killed." Contrary to the rumor, he was evacuated to Aiea Hospital, and in the meantime, Bill Maguire was given a motor launch and a crew and began to ferry casualties from the *California* to the Naval Hospital.

He made three runs before the "river of fire" drifting toward the *California* from the *Arizona* and *West Virginia* presented a barrier which caused the temporary "Abandon ship" ordered by the *California*'s commander, Captain Bunkley. Chaplain Maguire swam toward the shore and waded through the muck onto Ford Island. He corralled 15 trucks, got mattresses and blankets out of a nearby Bachelor Officers' Quarters, and laid them in the back of the trucks. Sailors abandoning the *California* were bringing the wounded onto shore—men who had been blown off the ship by exploding bombs, others who had tried to swim through the fire—and placing them on the trucks. He next commandeered a ferry normally used to transport persons from the harbor docks to Ford Island, moved the trucks from the island to the dock, and dispatched them to three different hospitals.

Except for the *Arizona* and *Oklahoma*, typical of the medical services rendered on the more severely damaged or sunk ships was the *Nevada*. Aboard her 116 men were wounded seriously enough to require hospitalization. Thirty-three were known dead, and eighteen were missing. After the first lull in the attack, about 65 casualties received emergency treatment at the forward, amidship and after dressing stations until these stations had to be evacuated to the sick bay. In the ship's sickbay between twenty and thirty cases received treatment.

Throughout the ship, patrol party corpsmen were busy administering first-aid. Two of these were recommended by the senior medical officer for their bravery and performance beyond the call of duty. Men on the crew who had previously received first-aid instruction, gave valuable assistance to the medical department in rendering emergency treatment to the wounded and burned men. The dead were collected astern. Attempts were made to identify each body before it was tagged and transferred to Pearl Harbor Hospital. Immediately after the attack there was neither time nor facilities for keeping paper records on either the living or dead transferred to the hospital.

After the battle was over, the sickbay of the *Nevada* had to be moved to the mess room of the chief petty officers. When this area flooded the next day, the medical department was again shifted. A first-aid station was established under the overhang of #4 turret on the main deck aft. On the beach, about fifty yards off the starboard quarter, two tents were set up, supplied and equipped. Health records from the Nevada were sent to the Receiving Barracks "for separation and forwarding."

Ashore, immediately after the attack, first-aid stations were set up quickly in the Receiving Barracks, Recreation Center, Yard dispensary, Officers' Club, Submarine Base dispensary, Naval Air Station dispensary, and Marine Barracks. The Section Base dispensary at Bishop's Point helped the Army to care for men from Hickam Field.

Ford Island Naval Air Station estimated that about 200 injured and burned men from the station and ships were given first aid at the dispensary before they were sent back to duty or to a hospital. About 130 patients were transferred to the Pearl Harbor Naval Hospital and the Aeia Plantation Hospital. Patients were evacuated starting about 1045, with an effort to move critical cases first, and by 1430 all the most seriously wounded were transferred. Seven men who died before they could be evacuated and a dead Japanese aviator were sent to the morgue at the Naval Hospital.

The number of casualties at Kaneohe Naval Air Station was seventeen dead and sixty-seven wounded. As quickly as wounded men could be brought to the station dispensary, they received emergency treatment. The dispensary was "inadequate to care for the 75 or 80 wounded requiring hospitalization," and a large number had to be sent elsewhere. Since evacuation to the Pearl Harbor Naval Hospital was initially out of the question because of insufficient vehicles available and already overloaded treatment facilities, about forty men were sent to the Kaneohe Territorial Hospital for the Insane. Subsequently, they were transferred either to the Pearl Harbor Hospital or back to the station.

At the Ewa's Mooring Mast Field, the hospital tents that housed the sickbay and dispensary were "set on fire by incendiary ammunition," and "a large quantity of equipment and medical supplies" were "damaged by enemy gunfire." Under the direction of the medical officer of Marine Aircraft Group 21, the fire was extinguished and a burning canvas which covered the medical stores was removed. Despite the fire, casualties were taken from the field between attacks and given prompt treatment by the medical officer and his assistants, who continued to work with their damaged equipment while exposed to enemy machine gun fire. The most seriously wounded men were evacuated to the Ewa Plantation Hospital. Compared with other stations subjected to attack, the number of casualties suffered at Ewa was small. Thirteen men received wounds, three were killed during the attack, and a fatally wounded man died five days later.

The Naval Hospital at Pearl Harbor was only slightly damaged during the attack. Although located near major military installations, the hospital was not hit by any bombs. A crashing Japanese airplane moderately damaged the roof of the laboratory building, destroyed about one-half of the animal house, and set a vacant quarters building on fire, virtually destroying it. But the fire was brought under control by fire fighters and didn't spread to other buildings. The only casualty suffered by the hospital was Pharmacist's Mate First Class Arthur W. Russett who was killed by machine gun fire in the Navy Yard while returning to the hospital from liberty.[39]

In an oral history, Navy nurse, Lieutenant Ruth Ericson, described what happened that morning:

> Two or three of us were sitting in the dining room Sunday morning having a late breakfast and talking over coffee. Suddenly we heard planes roaring overhead and we said, "The 'fly boys' are really busy at Ford Island this morning." The island was directly across the channel from the hospital. We didn't think too much about it since the reserves were often there for weekend training. We no sooner got those words out when we started to hear noises that were foreign to us. I leaped out of my chair and dashed to the nearest window in the corridor. Right then there was a plane flying directly over the top of our quarters, a one-story structure. The rising sun under the wing of the plane denoted the enemy. Had I known the pilot, one could almost see his features around his goggles. He was obviously saving his ammunition for the ships. Just down the row, all the ships were sitting there—the [battleships] *California* (BB-44), the *Arizona* (BB-39), the *Oklahoma* (BB-37), and others. My heart was racing, the telephone was ringing, the chief nurse, Gertrude Arnest, was saying, "Girls, get into your uniforms at once. This is the real thing!" I was in my room by that time changing into uniform. It was getting dusky, almost like evening. Smoke was rising from burning ships. I dashed across the street, through a shrapnel shower, got into the lanai and just stood still for a second as were a couple of doctors. I felt like I were frozen to the ground, but it was only a split second. I ran to the orthopedic dressing room but it was locked. A corpsmen ran to the OD's [Officer-of-the-Day's] desk for the keys. It seemed like an eternity before he returned and the room was opened. We drew water into every container we could find and set up the instrument boiler. Fortunately, we still had electricity and water. Dr. [CDR Clyde W.] Brunson,

the chief of medicine was making sick call when the bombing started. When he was finished, he was to play golf . . . a phrase never to be uttered again. The first patient came into our dressing room at 8:25 a.m. with a large opening in his abdomen and bleeding profusely. They started an intravenous and transfusion. I can still see the tremor of Dr. Brunson's hand as he picked up the needle. Everyone was terrified. The patient died within the hour. Then the burned patients streamed in. The USS *Nevada* (BB-36) had managed some steam and attempted to get out of the channel. They were unable to make it and went aground on Hospital Point right near the hospital. There was heavy oil on the water and the men dived off the ship and swam through these waters to Hospital Point, not too great a distance, but when one is burned . . . How they ever managed, I'll never know. The tropical dress at the time was white t-shirts and shorts. The burns began where the pants ended. Bared arms and faces were plentiful. Personnel retrieved a supply of flit guns from stock. We filled these with tannic acid to spray burned bodies. Then we gave these gravely injured patients sedatives for their intense pain. Orthopedic patients were eased out of their beds with no time for linen changes as an unending stream of burn patients continued until mid afternoon. A doctor, who several days before had renal surgery and was still convalescing, got out of his bed and began to assist the other doctors. **Do you recall the Japanese plane that was shot down and crashed into the tennis court?** Yes, the laboratory was next to the tennis court. The plane sheared off a corner of the laboratory and a number of the laboratory animals, rats and guinea pigs, were destroyed. Dr. Shaver [LT JG John S.], the chief pathologist, was very upset. About 12 noon the galley personnel came around with sandwiches and cold drinks; we ate on the run. About 2 o'clock the chief nurse was making rounds to check on all the units and arrange relief schedules. I was relieved around 4 p.m. and went over to the nurses' quarters where everything was intact. I freshened up, had something to eat, and went back on duty at 8 p.m. I was scheduled to report to a surgical unit. By now it was dark and we worked with flashlights. The maintenance people and anyone else who could manage a hammer and nails were putting up black drapes or black paper to seal the crevices against any light that might stream to the outside. About 10 or 11 o'clock, there were planes overhead. I really hadn't felt frightened until this particular time. My knees were knocking together and the patients were calling, "Nurse, nurse!" The other nurse and I went to them, held their hands a few moments, and then went on to others. The priest was a very busy man. The noise ended very quickly and the word got around that these were our own planes.

The first wave of about twenty Japanese planes, Kate torpedo bombers, came over the hospital about 0745. They passed immediately over and to the channel side of the hospital buildings. Traveling at high speed at or below 150 feet, none of the planes fired upon the hospital or made any attempt to bomb it. Their speed was so high that the men who saw them, and who were at first uncertain of their identity, hadn't time to warn the intended victims of the attack.

Members of the hospital staff were recalled to duty immediately, to "report to the hospital." As it was Sunday morning, many of the medical officers were at home. The commanding officer, executive officer, and the other men who lived on the reservation were the first to arrive. Medical officers who were not on the reservation were longer in reporting, but by 0915 the entire staff of the hospital was on duty. Medical officers and corpsmen from ships which had suffered damage during the attack reported intermittently throughout the morning. The two surgeons from the Mobile Hospital were assigned to one of the surgical teams of the hospital. Lieutenant Ericson's oral history mentioned the doctor of the Medical Corps who was convalescing after a major operation and voluntarily returned to duty. He worked until he became exhausted at the end of the third day. A large number of civilian women who had nursing or first-aid training volunteered to assist the twenty-nine Navy nurses. A total of 114 registered nurses were supplied through the local Red Cross and as many as 26 of these were on duty at one time. About eight or ten nurses who were wives of enlisted men were of valuable assistance.

Soon after the first attack, special measures were taken to protect the hospital, and arrangements for receiving a large number of casualties were made. At about 0800, stations for air attack were manned. Ambulances and fire-fighting equipment were dispersed so as to avoid total destruction in case of a hit. All battle dressing stations in the wards and the operating suite were set up by 0815. Medical officers, as they arrived, were sent to various dressing stations. Four operating teams were assigned to the main operating suite. A station for minor injuries was established in a vacant building formerly used as nurses' quarters. Patients in the brig and the locked ward were released.

To make more room for casualties, ambulatory patients were transferred to two old frame buildings and five hospital tents in the rear of the hospital. Convalescent patients who "requested that they be returned to duty" were permitted to return as best they could to their commands. The three hospital ambulances, ambulances from other stations, military and civilian trucks, personal cars, and delivery wagons were used to transport casualties to the hospital. Motor transportation was managed by the Navy Yard garage, where a pool of all vehicles was formed. The device of the pool enabled cars to be sent out in an orderly way to places that needed and could effectively utilize ambulance service.

Civilian as well as military personnel assisted in the transportation of casualties. Under fire and "with no thought of possible injury to themselves or their automobiles," civilians "spontaneously cooperated in promptly bringing casualties to the hospital." The first casualties arrived at the hospital within ten minutes after the first attack, and by 0900 they were coming into the hospital in a steady stream. Under the supervision of the commanding and executive officers, casualties were distributed to the main operating suite or to any one of the twelve wards where empty beds were available. A receiving ward would have caused a "hopeless bottleneck," and was not used.

Although an effort was made to send acute surgical cases to the surgical wards and fracture cases to the orthopedic wards every ward received a variety of cases. The great majority of patients with burns were sent to the medical wards. A regrouping of cases according to type of injury was not attempted during the day of the attack.

Accurate records for the patients admitted to the hospital could not be kept. The rate was much too rapid at first for the men to be properly tagged and for information such as the name, next of kin, and religion to be recorded. Not until the afternoon was it possible to begin recording admission data. Even then the necessary information could not always be obtained. None of the patients wore metal identification tags; and the service, health, and pay records of men were frequently missing. Furthermore, many patients who were unconscious when admitted to the hospital died before they could be identified.

A total of 546 battle casualties and 313 dead were brought to the hospital on 7 December. Approximately 452 casualties were admitted to the hospital in less than three hours. Of the total admissions, 93 came from battle stations aboard ships, temporary first-aid stations ashore, and several plantation hospitals in the vicinity of Pearl Harbor. A record was not kept of more than 200 men who received first-aid for slight injuries and were returned to duty immediately without being admitted to the hospital. The census of patients in the naval hospital at midnight, 7 December, was 960.

Identification of the dead and preparation of bodies for burial began at about 1100 of the day of attack. This most unpleasant work was done by a detail under the supervision of a hospital pathologist of the Medical Corps, who was assisted by an officer of the Dental Corps, and an officer of the Hospital Corps. Identification was slow, difficult, and sometimes impossible. None of the men wore metal identification tags, and the clothing of some of the men was marked with several different names. Some of the bodies were so badly charred or mutilated that they could not be identified from physical features; fingerprints could not be taken from some of the men because their fingers were missing or badly mangled; and only portions of some bodies were brought in.

A systematic procedure for keeping record on the dead was followed. On the Navy form for reporting deaths all available data, including fingerprints and names if possible, were recorded. Each body, whether identified or not, was tagged with a serial number. This serial number was also placed on the Navy form for reporting deaths, the grave marker, the casket, and on the canvas wrapping, if used.

All bodies, except those of identified officers, were placed in plain wooden caskets. Bodies of officers were placed in standard Navy caskets in order that they might later be disinterred and shipped home if desired. Burials began on 8 December in Oahu Cemetery, Honolulu. Two officers of the Chaplain Corps and two civilian priests from Honolulu rendered proper religious rites at the hospital and at the funeral ceremonies held each afternoon in the Oahu and Halawa Cemeteries. The brief military ceremony held at the burial grounds included a salute fired by a Marine guard and the blowing of taps by a Marine bugler.

Supplies at the Naval Hospital were, in general, sufficient to take care of the unprecedented demands created by the Pearl Harbor disaster. Shortages of dried plasma and tannic acid developed because of the great number of burn cases. Additional wet plasma was obtained from the blood bank established at the Queen's Hospital, Honolulu; and other supplies were requested by dispatch and flown from the West Coast by plane.[40]

Rescues In the Harbor

When the attack began the USS *Tern* (AM-13), a harbor auxiliary was alongside the north end of 1010 dock undergoing upkeep by the repair ship *Argonne*, with the work due to be complete 9 December. All the *Tern*'s machinery was dead and she was receiving steam, water and electricity from the dock, but her crew immediately began preparations to get underway while opening fire with .30-caliber Lewis machine guns at 0805. Under repeated strafing attacks, with her bow pointed east, and unable to open fire with her 3-inch guns because *Argonne* blanked them out, at 0943 she was underway as the raid was tapering off—picking up survivors in the harbor. She received 47 survivors, and at 1050 commenced fighting the fire raging on *Arizona*. Shortly she received orders from the *Maryland*'s commander to shift her firefighting effort to *West Virginia*. Then *Tern*'s commanding officer was placed in charge of fighting the fires on *West Virginia*, where she remained until 1430 hours on 8 December, when the fire was finally put out.[41]

Motor launches #1 and #2 from the training ship *Rigel* (AR-11), moored at berth 13 adjacent to the destroyer *Cummings*, and the light minelayers *Preble* and *Tracy*, also undertook rescue assistance when the attack began. *Rigel* had no power available, due to a conversion in progress, replacing power units, boilers, generators, and other machinery. She was receiving the essential services of steam, electricity, fresh and salt water, and compressed air from the Navy Yard, with approximately half the officers, including the captain and executive officer, plus one third of the crew on shore with authorized leave or liberty. She had no armament installed hence could take no offensive or defensive action, but an ensign and four men quickly volunteered to participate in rescue operations during the devastating attack on the battleships. They manned motor launch #1 and succeeded in saving between 50 and 100 men from the *West Virginia*. Motor whale boat #2 wasn't so fortunate.

No sooner did the boat and its five-man crew, including its ensign boat officer get underway from its berth under the starboard bow of *Rigel*, when a light bomb (132 pounds) dropped by one of the raiders struck the port quarter of the boat, and cut all planking from capping to keel in two. The bomb exploded underwater after passing through the boat, throwing all five men into the water. Two received serious injuries and were hospitalized—and *Rigel's* troubles were not yet over.

Shortly after the bomb sank motor launch #2, another exploded on contact with the water surface, near the stern of the ship, midway between piers 13 and 14. Fragments tore approximately 150 holes varying in size from 2 ½ to ¼ inch in diameter, in the port quarter of the ship, between frames 120 and the stern. The explosion wounded and hospitalized five crew members.[42]

The struggles on board *West Virginia*, *Tennessee*, *California*, *Nevada* and *Maryland*—fed and complicated by the terrible destruction and unrelenting, huge fire on *Arizona*—stretched from hours into days after the fighting ended approximately 1000 hours. At 0930, as wounded were beginning to be evacuated from *West Virginia*, *Tennessee's* Engineering Department reported ready to get under way, but *Maryland* hadn't moved, and *Tennessee* couldn't back out of her berth either. At 0940, Commander Colin Campbell, the executive officer, returned aboard *Tennessee* from his quarters, assumed command from Lieutenant Commander

Adams, and immediately contacted the officers on the bridge of the *West Virginia*, to ask if her magazines had been flooded—to which the reply came that they had flooded the aft magazines but couldn't be certain the forward magazines were flooded because their second deck was under water. Campbell told them their "magazines must be flooded at all costs, as this ship was relatively undamaged and must be saved." At 0948 the Engineering Department was ordered to "Standby." Three minutes later a burning ammunition lighter (small ammunition carrying boat) with its top blown out was seen floating on the starboard beam of *Tennessee*, between the ship and Ford Island. Damage Control ordered a hose played on it, and by 0955 the fire appeared under control, with no ammunition visible through the hole in the lighter's top.[43]

Aboard *Tennessee*, at 1002 Damage Control ordered flooding of aft magazines 306, 310, and 312 to reduce the possibility of meeting the same fate as *Arizona*.[44]

Throughout the latter part of the air raid, Chief Boatswain Mate Lewis W. Adkins, in charge of the after repair party, had remained exposed to the repeated air attacks while leading the fire fighting work on and below the quarterdeck. Just prior to 1000, as the flooding of the aft magazines was about to begin, Seaman Second Class J.R. Johnson, from the electrical gang, along with other crewmembers, was directed aft to assist Chief Adkins in fighting the fires. The sights and sounds that met Johnson when he went topside were surreal.[45]

At 1005, on *West Virginia*, barely eight feet away on the port side of *Tennessee*, the crew was preparing to abandon ship. The oil-fed fire from the *Arizona* that had been blazing at the stern of *Tennessee* had just gone out, mostly due to its steady, relentless progression past the sinking *West Virginia* and the capsized *Oklahoma* toward the *California* and the harbor entrance. Flooding of the magazines would soon progress to the point that *Tennessee*'s pumps had to be activated, pouring large streams of water out openings in the stern, just below the quarterdeck.

The *Arizona* was aflame all over. A fire on the bow of *Maryland* had just been put out after erupting four minutes earlier. Large fires were blazing on *West Virginia* and her officers and men were making their way around the out-of-control fires to both port and starboard, carrying their wounded and dead—including their captain—to escape and be rescued. In the water around *Arizona*

Dense smoke rises from the forward and midships portion
of the *Arizona*. Just ahead of her (L-R) the sinking *West
Virginia* outboard with the slightly damaged *Tennessee*
inboard, pumping streams of water from flooded aft magazines
through openings just below her quarterdeck. NPSAM

were rescue boats from *Solace*, while other boats were picking up
Arizona and *West Virginia* crewmembers who were in or near the
oily, flaming waters. *Oklahoma* survivors were standing or sitting
on the overturned hull, and rescue parties were taking them off,
while others were already listening for the sounds of hammering
on the hull from possible survivors trapped inside her.[46]

Particularly seared in J.R. Johnson's memory was the moment
when he and the men with him caught sight of a sailor from either
Arizona or *West Virginia* who had come to the surface nearby,
after first flailing and pushing the oil and fire aside with his hands
before surfacing for air. He was blackened, either by oil, flame
or both. The best they could do to help him was turn the stream
of water on and around him until he looked around, could take
another deep breath, dive and swim out from under the hell he
found himself in. Johnson would never know if he lived or died.

At 1020, while he played the hose on the quarterdeck fire, other
men from Bob Border's 5th Division gun crews were directed to
assist in fighting the fire. At 1027, fire fighting parties looking

forward from the port side of the quarterdeck, could see men coming across a 5-inch gun from *West Virginia* to *Tennessee*. About 1030 the fires were under control on *Tennessee*, and a decision was made by Captain Reordan, who had come aboard a half hour earlier, to move the ship forward as much as possible to increase her distance from *Arizona*'s fire.[47]

Both of *Tennessee*'s engines' revolutions per minute were increased sufficient for five knots speed, and the ship didn't move. That's when Captain Reordan and the crew realized they were apparently wedged in position by the settling *West Virginia*. Shortly, he decided to keep the engines running at five to ten knots to roil the waters astern and keep the fire pushed away from the *Tennessee*. The huge propellers continued to turn most of the rest of the day, an added measure to save her.

At 1032 men on *Tennessee*'s bridge saw clearly that *Arizona*'s crew was abandoning ship. None knew at that moment the extent of the catastrophe that had consumed the great ship, nor did they know just how extensive had been the losses on *Oklahoma* and *West Virginia*. At 1033, just thirty-one minutes after *Tennessee*'s aft magazines were ordered flooded, she was down six degrees by the stern, which indicated a huge volume of water had been poured into the ship's magazines to keep her from suffering the fate of *Arizona*.[48]

About this time the 110-foot garbage scow, *YG-17*, a harbor auxiliary commanded by Chief Boatswain's Mate L.M. Jansen, approached the *West Virginia* from the main channel. Acting without orders and on his own initiative Jansen nudged *YG-17*'s bow up against *West Virginia*, near her bow, fire hoses ready, and began pouring water on the burning ship. Jansen held firm fighting the fires in the face of periodic explosions of fire-ravaged ready ammunition boxes. For twenty-four hours, Jansen kept his crew's streams of water cascading onto the raging fires, this first morning alternately moving his vessel along the edge of the fire floating on the surface, then in close again, all the while relentlessly attacking the *West Virginia*'s white hot fires. Shortly after 1100 hours the *Tern* joined the fight to suppress *West Virginia*'s fires, which remained a threat to *Tennessee* as long as they burned. Jansen's "gallant conduct" was observed by several senior officers aboard the ship he and his crew fought so hard to save, and they, including the Commander Battleships,

Admiral Williams S. Anderson, officially took note of his work in the Action Reports and statements they signed on 11 December.[49]

As the morning progressed 344 of *West Virginia*'s crew climbed or were assisted across, forward, to the *Tennessee* from their settling ship, and sixty-nine of their number returned to assist in rescue and fire fighting efforts. Ninety-nine men from the devastated *Arizona* came aboard and were soon moved from *Tennessee* to Ford Island, the Naval Hospital or other medical facilities for treatment or reassignment. Two *Oklahoma* survivors and one from *Vestal* reported aboard *Tennessee*. Forty-nine from the capsized minesweeper *Oglala* came aboard *Tennessee* to assist and perhaps get into the fight. A few others, who couldn't get back to their ships, came to assist: one each from the destroyers *Gridley* and *Balch*, one who couldn't get back aboard the light cruiser *St Louis*, and yet another volunteer from the Receiving Station.

Added to the four deaths on *Tennessee* that morning were twenty-three wounded, including one officer and two Marines. Though not large numbers when compared with losses on other ships, the loss of any man was too much, and the men who lost their lives would be forever etched in their shipmates' memories.[50]

While *Tennessee*'s crew was fighting fires to ensure her survival, the *Maryland*'s crew, though also concerned about the fire on and around *Arizona*, *West Virginia*, and threatening *Tennessee*, increasingly devoted their attention to the plight of *Oklahoma*'s crew. Many of her surviving crew swam from the capsizing and later upturned hull to be helped aboard *Maryland*. Commander Edgar P. Kranzfelder, one of Admiral Anderson's staff officers assigned to the *Maryland*, helped begin the desperate efforts to save men trapped in the overturned ship.

He was with another Battleships' staff officer, Commander Lorenzo S. Sabin, Jr., in the Moana Hotel in Honolulu when, at approximately 0820, they received a call from the telephone operator telling them an emergency existed at Pearl Harbor, that they should return to their ships as soon as possible. They proceeded to the harbor as expeditiously as they could and arrived aboard *Maryland* about 0925, while the second wave's attack was still in progress. Kranzfelder went immediately to the bridge, and shortly after arriving, a man from *Oklahoma* contacted him saying assistance was required on *Oklahoma*, and there was an urgent need for cutting equipment.

At this time Lieutenant (jg) Robert S. Mandelkorn proceeded aboard *Oklahoma* to assist in the rescue work, and Kranzfelder told Admiral Anderson he believed he could be of assistance in connection with the rescue work. Anderson responded telling him to do all he could to release any entrapped men. Before leaving the *Maryland*, he obtained a copy of the *Oklahoma* booklet of plans for use in connection with the cutting of holes in the ship's hull.

With Mandelkorn's assistance Kranzfelder organized the rescue group, which rigged lines from the bilge keel at intervals along the bottom, established telephone communication with the *Maryland*, and quickly rigged an air supply line from *Maryland* to *Oklahoma*. They removed strainers from main injections and overboard discharge in an attempt to gain access to the engine room. Through a small overboard discharge connection in the hull, they established contact with two men trapped in the evaporator pump room, then passed food and water to them. Using information obtained from them about their location in the ship, and the aid of the plans booklet, it was possible to determine the best locations to cut holes in the ship's bottom.

Except for the reserve fuel feed bottoms, practically the entire bottom of *Oklahoma* consisted of oil tanks, requiring considerable care in choosing where to cut holes with an oxyacetylene torch to avoid the fire hazard gushing oil would precipitate. Fortunately, the information given the rescue party by the trapped men was correct, and entrance holes were cut in a cofferdam—a void space designed into ships to isolate one space from another and prevent oil or other liquids from getting into a compartment near a tank.

In the meantime, Lieutenant Commander William L. Benson, the engineer officer on *Oklahoma* had arrived to take charge of the rescue operation. Since Kranzfelder considered his and Mandelkorn's services would be required in connection with the remaining battleships in distress, the two returned to the *Maryland*, where Kranzfelder reported to Admiral Anderson that Benson was now in charge of the rescue work. Benson would keep Kranzfelder advised of progress and any additional equipment assistance needed.[51]

Equipment wasn't all that was needed. A need for divers was evident, more divers than were now available at Pearl Harbor.

Pearl's Divers

At the Pearl Harbor submarine base, the full complement of Navy divers gathered during the attack, and a new Salvage Unit was being established at the Naval Shipyard with Warrant Officer Albert Calhoun the designated Officer in Charge. Before the Japanese raiders departed Oahu en route to their carriers, a call had been placed to San Diego asking for qualified divers. The newly formed salvage unit which hadn't anywhere near the necessary number of divers to complete the enormous amount of salvage work it confronted in the harbor, had asked for assistance.

In San Diego, Metalsmith First Class Edward C. Rayner, and his "Navy best buddy," Robert 'Moon' Mullen had both attended a one-month diving school during the summer and were assigned back to their parent unit, the Destroyer Repair Unit, to which they had been assigned since May 1941. Some of Rayner's and Mullen's buddies won their division softball tournament the morning of 7 December and joined the losing team for soft drinks at the base gedunk stand (or soda fountain) after the game. The radio in the corner was blaring out swing tunes when suddenly an announcer interrupted the program with a special bulletin: "Pearl Harbor was bombed by the Japanese at 8 a.m. today, Hawaiian time."

Everyone at the soda fountain was incredulous over the news. They shook their heads and muttered doubts that this could happen to their Navy. Rayner's disbelief turned to white-hot anger as the reality of the attack registered in his mind. America is at war! A feeling of excitement welled up in him. By God we'll kick their butts, he thought. He couldn't wait to get at the enemy. He had no idea of the horror he was so eager to encounter.

The repair department sent word to all the divers to report to the office at 1200 hours, 1000 Hawaiian time. He hurried over to the barracks to clean up then report for duty. After showering, he shaved, changed into his working uniform, and reported to his division officer, Lieutenant George Dawnes, in the repair office. After all the divers assembled, Dawnes told them something big was in the wind for them, that he would have more information on the matter after the all-officers meeting scheduled for 1300. At 1400, noon Hawaiian time, Dawnes again herded the divers into his office and closed the door. He began,

> Men, you have two hours to get packed and be in front of your barracks. A bus will pick you up at 1630 and transport you to Naval Air Station, Coronado. You will be making a long flight tonight. I am not at liberty to tell you where you are going or how long you will be gone, or even if you will return to San Diego. You are directed not to make any phone calls to your families or to girlfriends before you leave. You can send them a postcard when you arrive at your final destination. As the senior petty officer, Raymer will be carrying your service records, sealed orders, and pay records with him. Good luck to you. Get moving; you don't have much time!

They filed out of his office, and hurried to the barracks. As Raymer and Moon packed their sea bags and ditty bags, they speculated on the secret mission, and agreed, from all evidence, they were bound for Pearl Harbor. In hindsight, Rayner recalled, "We were naively unaware of the number of ships sunk or damaged. The president had described only minimal damage in his brief statement regarding the attack, except for the sunken battleship *Arizona*."

The Navy bus picked them up promptly, made the short trip across San Diego Bay by ferry, and dropped them off at the seaplane ramp in the air station at 1700. They trooped aboard the waiting PB2Y aircraft, a big four-engine seaplane, with their personal belongings. Already on board were four Army colonels, three Navy captains, and several civilians. Raymer and the eight other divers were the only enlisted men aboard.

The plane taxied out into the bay and took off immediately as the nine sailors settled down on the floor, using their sea bags as headrests. The pilot informed the passengers that cruising speed would be 150 knots, and they should arrive at their destination in approximately fourteen hours. The noise and vibration from the plane's engines were deafening. It was impossible to speak above them or be heard. The divers had to be content to sleep, read, or be silent with their thoughts.[52]

Pan American *Clippers*: Three Changed Flight Plans, One *Clipper* Destroyed

Pan American Airways' huge four-engine, *Anzac Clipper*, a Boeing B-314A flying boat,

NC 18611, with a crew of ten and seventeen passengers, including three women, was 450 miles—two hours—from landing at Pan American's Pearl City terminal on Oahu. The passengers were asleep, the crew at stations. All was well—until the Radio Officer, W.H. Bell, informed Captain H. Lanier Turner and the First Officer, Ed Sommers, of the air raid at Pearl Harbor. The *Anzac Clipper*, also carrying relief pilot Guy F. McCafferty as a crew member, was one of three Pan American Clippers airborne over the Pacific Ocean when the Japanese attacked Pearl Harbor and other targets on Oahu. The fourth, Pan Am's *Hong Kong Clipper*, a Sykorsky S-42, was at Hong Kong's Kai-tak airport being readied for an early morning departure to Manila on its regular schedule between the two cities.

The *Anzac Clipper* had departed Pan American's Treasure Island Terminal in San Francisco Bay at 5:00 p.m. the evening of 5 December on the first leg of a planned 14-day round trip to Singapore. An hour and forty-five minutes into the flight, the *Clipper* developed engine trouble, requiring an engine shut down and a return to base. The flight was rescheduled for the same departure time the next day, 6 December, and was again delayed.

According to one story, the delay was due to one of the passengers, who went to his daughter's dance recital and was held up in traffic. Therefore, the plane was held at Treasure Island for his arrival. Another report said there was a minor maintenance problem that took an hour to clear. Regardless of the reason, as a result of the delay, the *Anzac Clipper* departed for Honolulu an hour and a half behind schedule. The fifteen-hour flight was uneventful until Bell heard the startling message about the bombing. He shortly confirmed to Turner the raiders were Japanese.[53]

Far to the south, southwest of Oahu, toward New Zealand, on another Boeing B-314, the *Pacific Clipper*, First Radio Operator John D. Poindexter, taking down Morse code dispatches, also heard the first reports of the air raid at Pearl Harbor, and quickly informed Captain Robert Ford. The *Pacific Clipper* had departed Treasure Island on 2 December and landed the next morning at the Pearl City terminal to refuel before continuing toward its New Zealand destination, with stops at Canton Island; Suva; Noumea, New Caledonia; and Auckland. The morning of 7 December, the flight from Noumea to Auckland was routine until two hours outbound from Noumea, when Poindexter received the first report.

Then came a simple two-word message heard by the radio operators on both the *Anzac* and *Pacific Clippers*. "Plan A," a prearranged signal that all Pan Am aircraft in flight were to maintain radio silence, land at their next scheduled destination, and await instructions.

Aboard the *Pacific Clipper* en route to Auckland, first engineering officer Homans K. "Swede" Rothe's reaction was stunned disbelief. He later recalled, "It seemed incredible that the news could be true. It might have been a mistake or maybe only a test." It was neither, and Captain Ford reached into his flight bag for the sealed emergency orders that all Pan Am captains had begun carrying when the political situation started to deteriorate in the Far East. Captain Ford immediately briefed his crew that the airline would now be operating on a wartime basis and they would continue to Auckland, New Zealand.[54]

On the *Anzac Clipper*, Captain Turner and his crew knew that landing at the Pearl City terminal was out of the question. Undoubtedly another thought crossed his mind as well. Had they departed San Francisco on time, rather than an hour and a half late, they might have been a large, obvious, inviting target in the vicinity of Oahu, in the midst of the Japanese attack.

Turner immediately pulled out his sealed envelope. The instructions were clear: Get the aircraft to a safe harbor as quickly as possible, offload the passengers and camouflage the aircraft. He decided to land in Hilo Bay, off the Naniloa Hotel at Hilo, on the Big Island of Hawaii. Hilo Bay offered a protected harbor, the farthest from Pearl Harbor, and was approximately 200 miles southeast of Oahu. He ordered the passengers into the lounge and briefed them regarding the attack and change in destination. There was no panic or hysteria.[55]

The passengers included Prime Minister Saw of Burma, and his secretary, Tin Tut; G. MacDonald of London, England; F.W. Brown III, Washington, DC; Robert S. Prescott, Washington,

DC; J.C. Montgomery, Cleveland, Ohio; Joyce Granner and Bernice LaMarr, 1302 North King St., Honolulu; Edward R. Loeg, Fredericks Hall, Virginia; A.C. Weier, Hongkong; R. Bagaj, Benares City, India; Clifton Norris, Hasbrouck Heights, New Jersey; Sidney P. Johnson, San Francisco; Dr. V.G. Clark, 513 Hawaii Trust Bldg., Honolulu; Lt. Harry Paller, Washington, DC; and Randolph Crossley of Honolulu.

After arriving in Hilo, Turner was ordered by Pan Am to complete the required maintenance as quickly as possible, offload the mail and return with any passengers who wanted to return to the security of San Francisco. When he announced he was going to refuel and return to San Francisco as soon as possible, not a single passenger wanted to make the flight. All decided to take their chances and make their way to Honolulu, thence to their destinations any way they could. After the passengers made their decisions he told them they could remain in Hilo hotels. All but one chose to stay at The Naniloa. Randolph Crossley stayed in the Volcano House.

The crew attempted to camouflage the aircraft but rain washed the water-soluble paint away. The aircraft was refueled, and Turner put three additional 55-gallon drums of aviation gasoline aboard, in case they had to divert on the way back to San Francisco. Turner accepted mail from the Hilo Post Office to carry to the mainland, and he and his crew took off the afternoon of 8 December and flew the *Anzac Clipper* 2,400 miles back to Pan Am's Treasure Island base in San Francisco.

On the return trip they ducked into clouds whenever the opportunity presented itself, although they saw no enemy aircraft or ships. En route they learned via radio of the impending blackout in San Francisco, but were well prepared to land anywhere from Seattle to Mexico.[56]

The *Philippine Clipper*, a Martin M-130 under the command of Captain John H. Hamilton, a lieutenant in the Naval Reserve, was en route, twenty minutes outbound from Wake Island to Guam when the radio operator received the news about the attack on Pearl Harbor. Commander W. Scott Cunningham, the Navy officer in charge of Wake, sent Hamilton a message suggesting he return to the island. Hamilton ordered the crew to dump about 3,000 pounds of gasoline, to get down to the maximum landing weight, and returned—as Pan American's packet of emergency instructions directed. Among the passengers was a military mission, a Flying Tigers pilot—and a cargo of airplane tires, all destined for China.

On landing, about forty minutes after takeoff, Hamilton went to Cunningham's office while the aircraft was being refueled. Cunningham cleared him to take off again, subject to his orders and suggested the crew take a patrol flight with F4F Wildcats escorting, before leaving for Midway, which Hamilton agreed to do—with a 1300 hours takeoff. Commander Cunningham, an experienced aviator, laid out a plan that included escorting the *Clipper* with two F4Fs from VMF-211, and sufficient fuel for the *Clipper* to conduct the search, and the flight to Midway, with a reserve. The Japanese had other plans.

At 0710 that morning, 8 December, thirty-four Japanese Mitsubishi G3M Type 96 "Nell" land attack planes of the Chitose Air Group lifted off from the airstrip at Roi, in the Marshall Islands. Shortly before noon they came in on Wake at 13,000 feet. Clouds cloaked their approach and the pounding of the surf drowned out the noise of their engines as they dropped down to 1,500 feet and roared in from the sea. Lookouts sounded the alarms as they spotted the twin-engine, twin-tailed bombers a few hundred yards off the atoll's south shore, emerging from a dense bank of clouds. They attacked Wake Island just prior to noon, and within ten minutes the area was a shambles. (The raid at Wake was 7 December and just prior to 2:00 p.m. Hawaiian time. Wake Island is across the international dateline.)

Hamilton, who a few minutes before the raid began had left Commander Cunningham's office just arrived at the hotel by car, and due to construction had to walk—looked up to see the oncoming Nells. He ducked into one of the drain pipes, and later recalled they came in nine-plane, close formation. The first nine started by machine gunning the construction camp. The second nine began the bombing, dropping what appeared to him to be small bombs of about 150 pounds. He said, "The bombs fired the hotel, destroyed the Pan American buildings and dock, but didn't hit the *Clipper*. However there were 16 bullet holes in the plane. By good fortune no bullets struck a vital spot."

The garrison at Wake Island took a terrible blow in the air attack, which was to become a daily ritual. Warned at 6:50 a.m. the morning of the Japanese attack on Pearl Harbor, the 1st Marine Defense Battalion, which numbered 449 men including the twelve VMF-211 pilots delivered by the *Enterprise*, had arrived on the Island 19 August. The garrison was still building its base and defenses, and had not yet received its radar, which was still in Hawaii. Lacking radar, and with no revetments to protect the aircraft from bombs, the garrison immediately went on wartime footing, and it was decided to keep four of the twelve Wildcats airborne on patrol as a hedge against surprise attack. One two-plane section, Captain Henry T. Elrod and Second Lieutenant Carl R. Davidson flew north, Second Lieutenant John F. Kinney and Technical Sergeant William J. Hamilton flew to the south, southwest at 13,000 feet. Both sections were to remain in the immediate vicinity of the island.

Visibility was poor, and the four Wildcats failed to spot the Japanese aircraft. Seven of the eight Wildcats on the ground were destroyed. Worst of all, VMF-211 lost twenty-three men dead and eleven wounded, including two pilots killed, from among fifty-five total aviation personnel on the ground. No Japanese aircraft were lost. At one stroke, VMF-211 lost 75 percent of its aircraft and over 60 percent of its personnel. Pan American's base suffered a knockout blow.[57]

In the book, *Pan American's Pacific Pioneers, The Rest of the Story*, author Jon E. Krupnick, recorded the "Report of Attack on Wake," written by John B. Cooke, the manager of Pan Am's Wake Island base.

> After the bombing attack was over, I was bleeding some about the face and body, but a quick check assured me I had no injury of consequence.
>
> I then left what was left of the building to see how others fared, proceeding directly to the hotel about a half block distant. This framed building of 40 rooms and spacious lobby and dining room was badly battered and one wing was already ablaze. Several minutes search revealed no one there and in leaving I noted what appeared to be all of the white Pan Am personnel on the dock or approaching it and the Clipper's engines were being started.
>
> At first it seemed to me to be a bit cowardly to think of leaving, but there would have been no purpose in remaining. Every Pan Am building had been hit and several were burning. Power was gone

and radio was gone, all was gone. The station had been rendered useless.

A check revealed 16 bullet holes in the Clipper, but miraculously, somehow, the gas tanks and engines were not damaged. To leave meant saving the airplane and ourselves so we left.

Thirty-seven of us [including crew members], plus fuel, made a terrific load for the Martin. The first try for take-off failed, as did the second. For a third, the safety factor was nil as already the engines had been full throttled longer than cylinders ordinarily stand. But Captain Hamilton promptly taxied back for another try. This time he kept full speed the entire length of the runway. When the point had been reached where it was either take off or crash, the plane lifted and retained sufficient altitude to cross the island. We then skimmed the water for several hours. Necessarily, and to better avoid detection. At nightfall we took a respectable altitude that remained well aloft until we neared Midway, which we reached at midnight . . . [58]

Ten Pan Am Chamorro employees from Guam were killed in the attack on Wake Island. As soon as the bombers left Wake and the damage assessment was complete, Captain Hamilton cancelled the proposed reconnaissance flight, and ordered the M-130 stripped of all extraneous equipment and cargo. With the passengers aboard, he lifted off for the 1,185-mile flight to Pan Am's blacked out base at Midway, and was about forty miles from their base when he reported seeing two warships heading away from Midway. When he landed just prior to midnight, he learned the island was shelled that afternoon.

They left Midway a little over an hour later, this time with the destination Pearl City on Oahu. For a time, they took a course toward the alternate landing area at Hilo, fearing they wouldn't be cleared to land at the Pearl City terminal. They were then informed the way was clear at Pearl Harbor.

The escape from Wake Island by the *Philippine Clipper* was one piece of good fortune in the midst of an attack that foreshadowed a far greater disaster for Wake Island's defenders fifteen days hence. Departing from Pearl City, Hawaii, the afternoon of 9

The *Philippine Clipper*, after landing at Pan Am's Treasure Island terminal in San Francisco harbor, 10 December 1941. The aircraft landed in San Francisco still carrying the 16 bullet holes from the Japanese attack at Wake Island. UML

December Captain Hamilton flew the *Philippine Clipper* under radio silence to Pan Am's base at Treasure Island, and arrived 10 December. All except the crew and one company executive, Frank McKenzie, airport maintenance engineer, were left at Honolulu, where they were evacuated to the mainland by ship.[59]

The *Philippine Clipper*'s return trip had been harrowing, but the experience of Captain Hamilton, his crew and passengers wasn't quite as unnerving as were the travails of the *Hong Kong Clipper*'s Captain Fred S. Ralph, his crew, and passengers. On hearing of the Japanese attack on Pearl Harbor, the Pan Am man in charge of the company's interest in the China National Aviation Corporation, William Langhorne Bond, ordered the *Hong Kong Clipper* to fly to an inland lake near Kunming, but before the plane could be readied for departure, the Japanese struck Hong Kong. Just six hours after Commander Mitsuo Fuchida's air armada began savaging Pearl Harbor and other military targets on Oahu, the *Hong Kong Clipper* lay tied at her dock at Kai-tak Airport on Kowloon Peninsula, when Japanese bombers passed over the city, unloading their bombs on the airport's runway and firing incendiary bullets, setting the Sikorsky S-42 on fire. The airplane burned to the water's edge, the Pan Am *Clippers'* only casualty of the war due to enemy action.

The *Pacific Clipper* landed safely at Auckland, New Zealand that day, then continued and completed an unplanned, but necessary 31,500-mile around-the-world odyssey, landing at the LaGuardia Marine Air Terminal on 6 January 1942.[60]

The SS *Lurline*, Homeward Bound in Wartime Conditions

When the *Anzac Clipper*'s Captain Turner learned of the Japanese attack that morning, forty minutes before their estimated time of arrival at Pan American's Pearl City terminal, the SS *Lurline* was still on course toward San Francisco. Everything had quietly begun to change for *Lurline*'s officers and crew some minutes earlier. Her skipper, Commodore Charles A. Berndtson, and First Officer John Van Orden had been told of the exchange of messages with the SS *Cynthia Olson* by *Lurline*'s Chief Officer, Edward Collins.

After Collins notified the Commodore and First Officer, and Van Orden had plotted the *Cynthia Olson*'s position: about 300 miles bearing 005 degrees true from *Lurline*, Collins returned to the radio shack. At that time he found Mr. Nelson copying another message, this one from the U.S. Navy. The message exchanges with the *Cynthia Olson*, which began at 8:30 a.m., 7:30 on Oahu, raised several important but unanswerable questions, until 10:15, when Collins returned to bring Berndtson the Navy message telling of the Japanese attack on Pearl Harbor.

Collins recalled, though the messages from the *Cynthia Olson* were most unusual, ". . . we were shocked to receive the Navy message that we were at war. When Commodore Berndtson read the war message, his face mirrored the shock and deep responsibility he immediately recognized to be his." On receiving word of the Japanese attack, Berndtson and his officers realized immediately a Japanese submarine must have attacked the *Cynthia Olson*, and there could be no doubt there was at least one enemy submarine between *Lurline* and San Francisco.

After a quick consultation in the chart room, Berndtson decided that two obvious orders must be executed without delay:

change course to get off the Great Circle Route (the most direct route between two points on the earth's surface) and increase to full speed. These two decisions were *Lurline*'s best available defense against submarine attack. She carried no deck guns, no radar, no submarine detection gear, and no airplanes to catapult and scout ahead for submarines or enemy surface craft that might be lying in wait. The only sensors available to her were the eyes of watchful crewmembers and passengers.

Naval and military officers aboard were gathered together, they were informed of the situation and a staff formed to enforce military security.

The commodore told Collins to inform the Chief Engineer, Ray Sample, what had occurred and to increase to full speed. Collins went aft to Sample's quarters and found him at his desk working over his morning reports. When Collins told him the Japanese had attacked Pearl Harbor, ". . . we were at war," and the commodore wanted all boilers on line for full speed, Ray Sample didn't question or comment—he simply got up from his desk and left his quarters. The only thing heard from him was the closing of the elevator door as he took the quickest and shortest way to the engine room to prepare for flank speed, *Lurline*'s full 22 knots.

Berndtson and Collins decided other shipboard measures were necessary during the remaining daylight hours. What needed to be done had to be done quickly and efficiently. The passengers could be briefed on the turn of events later. The two officers got the deck gang together, instructed them to break out all the paint in the paint locker, and immediately begin painting the windows on the decks, to black them out so that no lights from the inside would be detected by enemy craft. Fortunately, there were considerable quantities of blue and other dark-colored paints to darken the vessel.

Commodore Berndtson ordered the chief steward to close bars and remove the liquor to the store rooms. According to Collins, "The passengers were amazed to see what was going on. Perhaps some of them surmised that we were at war . . . " Unquestionably, the passengers were more than a bit curious, and among them there must have been an undercurrent of rumors and growing apprehension. But Collins observed no hysteria, undue excitement or outward alarm. They clearly knew that something unusual had occurred when crew members proceeded to paint the inside of windows in the public rooms and the portholes in their own rooms, and when crew members removed electric lamps to dim the interior of the ship.

At 5:00 p.m., Commodore Berndtson assembled the passengers in the First Class Lounge and told them what had happened. He told them what he knew of the attack at Pearl Harbor, and frankly stated he didn't know which port the vessel would be instructed to dock—either San Francisco or Los Angeles. Passengers were told to surrender all radios and other electrical apparatus because they could be used by Japanese submarines to locate our position. They were then advised that the situation was serious, but there was no reason for undue alarm.

They were asked to expedite their meals in order to reduce the time they would be grouped in one area—and at all times to carry their life preservers. This last instruction before opening up to questions, must have been particularly sobering. There had been the obligatory life boat drills on leaving Honolulu, the precautionary norm under any circumstance when beginning a voyage. But this was markedly different. "At all times carry life preservers." Not a pleasant order to ponder.

When the commodore asked if there were any questions, a somewhat strained silence ensued. Finally, an elderly woman said she was booked for Los Angeles and if the ship was going to stop in San Francisco, how would she get there? The captain responded saying he was unable to advise her on how to get to Los Angeles, as he was hoping only that he could get her to San Francisco. His answer seemed to break the tension among the passengers, and they all had a hearty laugh.

As darkness settled in, a watch of six able seamen was set on the leeward side of the bridge deck, to be available for night time emergencies requiring experienced sailors. In the steward's mess room about twenty men from the steward's department were on station throughout the night, available for emergencies in the vessel's interior. Fortunately, none occurred, and there was no need to use any of these men during the three nights voyage.

Though the crew welcomed the night and the darkness, neither gave the measure of security hoped for, because it was a period of the full moon. The sky and the atmosphere were unusually clear. The moon reflecting on the water was a ribbon of silver from horizon to horizon, with the now-all-too-beautiful white hull of the *Lurline* illuminated by the moonlight. They felt as though the periscope of every Japanese submarine was watching them.

The tense race for safety was undoubtedly remembered for a lifetime by those aboard—the great white ship shining in the bright moonlight, racing for home at her full 22 knots while her passengers in life jackets scanned the horizon, hoping for a protective blanket of fog or a heavy rainstorm.[61]

At 2:00 a.m. the morning of 10 December, the *Lurline* slipped under the Golden Gate Bridge, just as air raid sirens plunged the city into darkness for the second time that night. She docked at 3:27 a.m. and by daylight the passengers were cleared completely through the necessary inspections.

At noon, 11 December, company officials handed her over to the U.S. Maritime Commission under a demise charter arrangement wherein Matson's ship, crew, and supplies were placed at the disposal of the Government, with Matson operating the ship under order either of the U.S. Navy or U.S. Army Transport Service as the sub-charter changed from voyage to voyage.

In a few short days, the SS *Lurline*'s bright, white coat would receive multiple coats of admiralty gray, specifically intended to better hide her from the enemy. The outward change would be matched by dramatic changes inside. All trappings of luxury disappeared, along with openness and the sweeping grandeur of a once-proud cruise liner built for happiness and relaxation on the high seas. War was closing round her evermore tightly, while to the southwest of Oahu, three other ships which had received word of the attack on Pearl Harbor, were on course for Honolulu: the American Presidents Line's SS *President Coolidge*, the U.S. Army Transport *General Hugh L. Scott*—formerly the *President Pierce*—and the United States Navy's light cruiser, *Louisville* (CL-28).[62]

The Cruiser, the President and the Former President

The 9,050-ton *Louisville*, under command of Captain Elliott B. Nixon, left Manila Harbor on 25 November and steamed south to Tarakan, Netherland East Indies (Borneo), where she stayed 27-28 November, refueled, then, on the 28th sailed east, northeast, under orders to rendezvous with and escort the *Coolidge* and *Scott* to Honolulu.

On Saturday, 29 November, at 0904 hours, while on an east,

Light cruiser *Louisville* (CL-28) off the Mare Island
Navy Yard, California, 26 May 1942. NA

southeasterly course of 110 degrees, the watch on *Louisville*'s
bridge sighted the superstructure of the *Scott*, distant about 21
miles, and four minutes later sighted the *Coolidge*, commanded
by Captain Henry Nelson, 18 miles distant. Both ships were
off *Louisville*'s starboard quarter and the cruiser was on a
converging course. At 1130 she joined with the two larger ships
to escort them to Honolulu, with *Coolidge* in the lead as guide,
and continued east, southeast toward Goode Island, Australia
and Pago Pago, the capital of American Samoa. At the time the
three ships rendezvoused, the carrier *Enterprise* with Task Force
8, was two days west out of Pearl Harbor, en route to deliver
the squadron of F4F Wildcat fighters to the garrison at Wake
Island.[63]

On board the ten-year-old, 21,936-ton liner *Coolidge*, only
fifty-four feet longer than the 600-foot, sleek, faster, cruiser
Louisville, were missionaries, Manila businessmen; several
score young Chinese, believed en route to join others of their
countrymen at Army Air Force training centers; Russian and
British diplomatic figures who had left China ahead of the

renewed Japanese drive deep into that country; U.S. military and diplomatic dependents who left China, Japan, the Philippines and other southeast Asian countries, voluntarily leaving on urging of the State Department; an American businessman, John J. Waldron, a World War I veteran who had been in China eighteen years, developed a thriving carpet business, and by chance had left the Chinese capital for Shanghai to arrange for shipment of a $25,000 cargo of raw materials to America; and many others. A luxury cruise ship capable of providing service to a maximum of 988 passengers, *Coolidge's* normal complement of 290 officers and men was expecting a reasonably routine voyage to Honolulu and on to San Francisco in spite of the tension in the Far East.[64]

On board the smaller, slower *Scott*, the crew's outlook on the voyage was little different. The *General Hugh L. Scott*, built in 1921, was received by the Army on 31 July 1941, modified to carry troops, had made a prior trip to the Orient to reinforce the American forces in the Philippines and bring Americans home. The *Scott* arrived in San Francisco from Manila on 31 October. At 535-feet length and displacing 12,579 tons, she could carry up to 2,470 passengers, and had been sent back to Shanghai on one more trip to evacuate Americans leaving East and Southeast Asia.

On 7 December the three ships were on course 051 degrees, at standard speed 16.5 knots, near maximum speed for *Scott*, when at 0815, on the bridge of *Louisville*, Officer of the Deck Ensign Henry F. Lloyd logged, "Word received of Japanese attack on U.S. territory and declaration of war on U.S. and Great Britain." Speaking to a newspaper reporter in San Francisco eighteen days later, Milton McManus, an officer on board the *Coolidge*, told of the passengers' and crew's reactions to the news.

> They first heard the United States had declared war on Japan. "The boys in the crew thought that was elegant. We'd been waiting for it, ready for it, and now we were in it. Most of the boys were tickled pink." There was little worry at first. A good part of the crew consisted of Japanese-Hawaiians, but right off the bat they held a meeting, counted noses, and announced they were 100 percent behind the captain. "Just tell us what we got to do," they said. "It'll be done."

The Presidents Line's *SS President Coolidge* photographed before she was purchased from the Dollar Line. NPSSFHMM

US Army Transport *General Hugh L. Scott*, formerly *SS President Pierce*. NPSSFHMM

And it was done. In a record-breaking effort, they camouflaged the entire ship in two days—two days while they were lunging through heavy seas in their race back home. They blacked out portholes, splashed paint over the decks and sides, and cut their radio-sending equipment out of commission. On board, life went on. Just before the ship crossed the international date line, a Chinese mother gave birth to a little girl. The ship's officers were nominated as godfathers-in-general and the ship's cook put on a celebration.[65]

The SS *President Coolidge* and U.S. Army Transport *General Hugh L. Scott* arrived in the port of Honolulu mid-afternoon, Tuesday, 16 December. After seeing her charges safely to the entrance of the port, the *Louisville* continued on to Pearl Harbor, and at 1701 hours moored adjacent to the cruiser *Salt Lake City*, at berth C-3. The sights that greeted the *Louisville*'s crew as they entered Pearl Harbor were almost beyond comprehension. The stark evidence of the Japanese attack's destructive power, and the massive salvage work in progress, seemed to mock their long, tame, escort mission from Manila. With powerful, after-the-fact visual images, war had come to the crew of the *Louisville*.[66]

From the decks of *Coolidge* and *Scott*, at first nothing seemed drastically different in the port of Honolulu—except there was heavy military presence and considerably more than the usual bustle on the docks. In the next three days, that too would change as they learned more of the devastation that had visited Oahu, and the newest passengers to join their company came aboard for the return to San Francisco. While there had been some justifiable excitement and anxiety building in the days since 7 December, those feelings would pale in comparison to the tension felt beginning Friday, 19 December.

By the time the two ships arrived in Honolulu, news had spread. No one knew where the Japanese fleet had gone but the search was continuing. There had been successful attacks and ships sunk by Japanese submarines in the waters around the Hawaiian Islands. The enemy below was having some success, and when *Coolidge* and *Scott* next sailed from Honolulu, they would be entering far more dangerous waters.

CHAPTER 10

"... A Date Which Will Live in Infamy ... "

*Let us set up a standard around which
the brave and loyal can rally.*

Winston Churchill

Islanders distant from the scenes of terror and destruction were slow to realize an attack was in progress. Explosions were muffled, the drone of airplanes not unusual, and the dark smoke over Pearl Harbor, Ford Island, and Hickam, Ewa, and Wheeler Fields mingled with early morning low clouds.

In Honolulu, at 17 seconds past 8:04 a.m., radio station KGMB interrupted a concert program to recall all Army, Navy, and Marine Corps personnel to duty. The station repeated the order at 8:15 and 8:30, and police and firemen were called at 8:32. The first reference to an actual attack came at 8:40. "A sporadic air attack has been made on Oahu ... Enemy planes have been shot down ... The rising sun has been sighted on the wingtips!"

The word "sporadic" apparently misled many listeners, who confused it with the common Army term "simulated." Oahu's maneuver-conscious residents were accustomed to the term "simulated" and many assumed this was just another Army and Navy exercise. But some telephoned stations to ask for details, and the volume of calls began harassing already-busy announcers who were trying to convince listeners of the perils in the morning's events. One announcer shouted into his microphone, "This is no maneuver. This is the real McCoy!"

As time passed announcements became more urgent. By noon, the order recalling all service personnel had been broadcast by each radio station a dozen times; however, many residents didn't have their radios on, were indoors, or were quietly having breakfast and had no idea of the events in progress. Tourists, such as the Willamette and San Jose State Universities' football teams, were also having breakfast or enjoying the scenery before taking scheduled sightseeing bus trips—and weren't listening to radios. The announcements summoned doctors, nurses, and volunteer aides, civilian workers of the Army and Navy, and employees of various firms. Motorcycles and trucks were called to first aid stations. Radio stations barked orders and warnings every few minutes:

> The United States Army Intelligence has ordered all civilians stay off the streets. Do not use your telephone. The island is under attack. Do not use your telephone. Stay off the streets. Keep calm. Keep your radio turned on for further news.
>
> Get your car off the street. Drive it on the lawn if necessary, just so you get it off the street.
>
> Fill water buckets and tubs with water, to be ready for a possible fire. Attach garden hoses. Prepare to take care of any emergency.
>
> Keep tuned to your radio for details of a blackout which will be announced later.
>
> Here is a warning to all people throughout the Territory of Hawaii and especially on the island of Oahu. In the event of an air raid, stay under cover. Many of the wounded have been hurt by falling shrapnel from antiaircraft guns. If an air raid should begin, do not go out of doors. Stay under cover. You may be seriously injured or instantly killed by shrapnel falling from antiaircraft shells.

At 10:00 a.m. mobilization of the Territorial Guard was ordered. Formation of the Guard had been discussed ever since the National Guard was called to active duty in 1940. There was some doubt whether the governor had the power to form one until he was given authority by the legislature in late October 1941. The University of Hawaii Reserve Officer Training Corps (ROTC) was called to duty, and its members became the nucleus of the Hawaii Territorial Guard. Other youths, including many from high school ROTC units, were rapidly enlisted, and by nightfall the guard numbered thirty-five officers and 370 men. Among the high school

ROTC youths was seventeen year-old, junior student Frederick K. Kamaka, and others from the Kemahameha Schools.

At about 11:00 a.m. a radio announcement summoned all the American Legionnaires. Within an hour, 300 to 400 veterans of the Spanish-American War and World War I assembled at their clubhouse. One Legionnaire reported his early morning activities as follows, bringing a bright spot of humor to an otherwise dark, confusing time:

> Got out my Winchester rifle and 30 rounds of ammunition. Found to my dismay that I had forgotten how to load it. Started downtown, as I anticipated landing parties, parachutists and street rioting. Realized that I might be mistaken for a rioter or a guerilla myself, so went back home and got my old uniform out of the moth balls, on the theory that it would be helpful in reassuring some group of civilians, in case I should have to deal with any who were more excited and scared than I was myself. Couldn't find various items, and couldn't remember how to put on insignia. Got mad and bawled out the members of the household. Was told to go on out and fight the Germans instead of the women folks at home. The dog spied my Sam Browne belt on the lanai, and dragged it over to the guava bushes in the next lot to chew it at leisure. Recovered it and spanked the dog. Started downtown again and stopped in the Legion to find out what was best to do. There were already about 75 of the comrades there and more arriving every few minutes.

Two truckloads of men were sent to police headquarters for assignment to various duties, and another group helped at fires near the Legion clubhouse. By 4:00 p.m. organization had been completed, with each man assigned to an eight-hour watch. Most of the veterans were assigned guard duty. One detachment answered S.O.S. calls, and cared for dud bombs. Others helped the Engineers, and some went to the waterfront.

Governor Joseph B. Poindexter, broadcasting over station KGU, proclaimed a state of emergency, and at 11:41 a.m., the Army ordered the Honolulu commercial broadcasting stations off

Governor Joseph B. Poindexter, The Territory of Hawaii. HA

the air to prevent their beams being used to guide enemy planes. The silence was ominous, even more nerve-shattering than the announcements, and led nearly everyone on Oahu to twist radio dials in search of more information. On police radio frequencies they heard patrolmen being ordered to investigate a steady stream of alarming reports. For days thereafter, many radio sets on Oahu remained on. A week later commercial stations resumed their regular schedules, but in the meantime residents kept their radio sets on all the time, tuned to police broadcast frequencies— except when advised to turn to commercial stations for special announcements.

Nine times KGU and KGMB returned to the air that day, for periods varying from forty-five seconds to five minutes.[1]

While it can be said that the raiders concentrated on targeting and attacking the American military and their installations with their bombs and generally stayed clear of attacks on the civilian populace, as is always the case in war, even that otherwise admirable military quality of disciplined restraint went by the boards in some instances. Japanese naval fighter aircraft, loosed from their intended force protection role after Fuchida saw the strike force had achieved complete surprise, had their share of less disciplined, over-aggressive pilots who randomly attacked civilian vehicles and aircraft in outlying areas near military installations. There were a number of attacks on civilian vehicles traveling roads and streets, similar to those seen by Lieutenant Dickinson when he hitched a ride to Hickam Field with a man and his wife, after Dickinson's *Enterprise* SBD was shot down.

An argument can be made that there was possibly incorrect target identification, or simply a Japanese intelligence-identified connection between military capability and the civilian airport near Hickam. Whatever the case might have been, Zekes made at least one strafing pass on the runway, parking ramp and buildings at John Rodgers Airport. Killed in the attack was long-time instructor pilot and later-named Hawaiian aviation pioneer, Robert L. Tyce, who was in front of a plainly marked, civilian DC-3 passenger aircraft, manually turning over the propeller when he was struck down.

Three soldiers from F Battery, 251st Coast Artillery (AntiAircraft) had the misfortune of continuing their flying lessons out of John Rodgers Airport that morning, in two clearly marked civilian airplanes. They were flying over the waters off Ewa Beach when

Japanese fighters in the first wave swirling around the Ewa Mooring Mast Field, attacked them. Both aircraft were shot down, and crashed in the ocean. The bodies of Sergeant Henry C. Blackwell, Sergeant Warren D. Rasmussen, and Corporal Clyde C. Brown were never found.[2]

Another pilot, Machinist Mate Second Class M.F. Poston, a student pilot who was a crew member aboard the *Argonne* in Pearl Harbor, was flying a light aircraft at 6,000 feet from Halewia to John Rodgers Airport. The aircraft, belonging to KT Service, was attacked over the Pali, and Poston's engine and propeller were shot away. He managed to bail out and survive. He landed beyond the Pali, was picked up by deputized civilian police, who returned him to the Honolulu Shore Patrol, where he was questioned and returned to his ship.[3]

While the raid was in progress women and children in the military and civilian housing areas on the Navy Yard, and at bases and airfields, had begun wondering where to go and what to do, though many had been told to "stay inside—this is the safest place"—when their husbands rushed to their duty stations.

In Honolulu, similar questions, and the added destruction and death wrought by at least forty expended antiaircraft rounds, plus at least one bomb that fell in the city or into surrounding areas. As had happened to Frederick Kamaka, the boys in his dormitory, and their Junior ROTC instructor, Lieutenant Ainsley Mahikoa, at the Kamehameha School shortly after 8:00 a.m., "bombs" were falling elsewhere in the city. Shortly before 9:30 a.m., a projectile exploded near the driveway of the Governor Poindexter's residence, Washington Place at Beretania and Richards Street, sending shrapnel through the shrubbery and across the street to kill a pedestrian. Later, after the governor had gone to his office at Iolani Palace in downtown Honolulu, not far from his residence, a shell burst in the corner of the grounds there.

The *Honolulu Star-Bulletin* in the first of four Extra editions, reported an unidentified Chinese man killed by the "bomb" across the street from Washington Place, in front of the Schuman Carriage Company, where windows were broken.[4] Timing of the incident suggests that Governor Poindexter was in fact on the phone with President Roosevelt when the bomb, or antiaircraft round, exploded near Washington Place. Gordon Prange wrote in *At Dawn We Slept,*

During the afternoon Roosevelt telephoned Governor Poindexter on Oahu. While they were talking, suddenly the governor "almost shrieked into the phone." Roosevelt relayed the message to the men clustered around him. "My God, there's another wave of Jap planes over Hawaii right this minute."[5]

For a considerable time, people living in Honolulu and surrounding areas were certain the Japanese had deliberately bombed the civilian population. A total of at least fifty-seven civilians are known to have been killed on Oahu, nearly fifty required hospitalization, and about 230 were less seriously injured. An undetermined number later died of injuries, and a few casualties weren't listed in available records. Investigations revealed the great majority of victims in Honolulu were the result of "friendly fire."

The Waipahu and Ewa sugar plantations, next to Pearl Harbor, and the town of Wahiawa, adjoining Schofield Barracks, saw a lot more action from enemy aircraft than did Honolulu. At Waipahu, machine gun bullets, shrapnel, and shells started two cane fires, riddled the sugar mill, hit the plantation hospital in four places, went through the roof of the company store, exploding in an

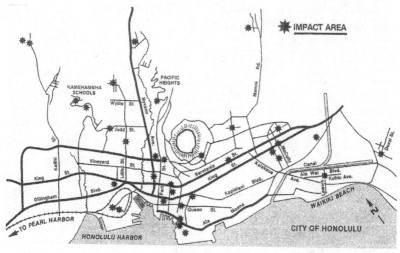

Damage in the Honolulu area, most from falling friendly fire antiaircraft rounds.

electric supply warehouse, and narrowly missed many houses. In nearly all of the fields of tall cane, many of which concealed terrified women and children, shells buried themselves—dozens of them in some concentrated areas—blasting holes in the ground the size of barrels and flattening cane for several square yards. At Waipahu two were killed and thirty-seven wounded.

At Ewa, after strafing the nearby Marine airfield, enemy planes machine gunned the plantation's main street, the mill and power plant, and some thirty houses, and started two cane fires.

At Wahiawa, low-flying planes strafed stores and cars, wounding several people. Patients overflowed from Dr. Merton H. Mack's small private hospital into Red Cross headquarters in the rear of the Wahiawa fire station. An enemy plane crash in a pineapple field near the town did little damage, but another started a fire which destroyed five small houses before the blaze could be brought under control by a handful of firemen and a Boy Scout bucket brigade. Bodies of the four crewmen from the two downed aircraft were buried in the Wahiawa cemetery. At Wahiawa, three were killed and nine wounded.

At Aiea, between Honolulu and Pearl Harbor, the plantation's fire department fought a house fire and two cane fires, one of which was caused by the crash of an enemy plane. Waialua was quiet but the plantation hospital received two patients, both of whom had been struck by bullets fired by strafing enemy aircraft.[6]

In Honolulu thirty-two men, women and children were killed and many more wounded, nearly all the result of expended antiaircraft rounds falling into the city and residential areas. The randomness of the sad incidents is seen in the ages of those lost. Among the casualties were seven children, eight years old and younger, who were killed or died of injuries, including the youngest, three-month-old Janet Yumiko Ohta and seven-month-old Eunice Wilson. Seven more ranged in age from twelve to nineteen years, and the remaining eighteen ranged in age from twenty to the oldest, Ai Harada, who was fifty-four years.

In Ewa, six-year-old Yaeko Lillian Oda, and thirty-four year-old Francisco Tacderan lost their lives. Robert Tyce, the flight instructor, was thirty-eight when he was killed by the Japanese fighter's machine guns at John Rodgers Airport. At Kaneohe Bay, Kamiko Kookano, thirty-five, and Isaac William Lee, twenty-one, were struck down. In Pearl City, Rowena Kmohaulani Foster was only three when she died. In Whiawa, Richard Masaru Soma was twenty-two, and Chip Soon Kim was sixty-six. In Waipahu, Tomoso Kimura was nineteen.

Seven more civilians lost their lives on the installations they had gone to support, or where they normally worked as Federal employees. The Honolulu Fire Department lost three at Hickam Field: John Carriera, fifty-one, Samuel Macy, fifty-nine, and Harry Tuck Lee Pang, thirty. August Akina, thirty-seven, and Philip Ward Eldred, thirty-six, died at Hickam. Tai Chung Loo, nineteen, was killed at Pearl Harbor, and Daniel La Verne, twenty-five was killed at Red Hill.[7]

Civilian Medical Services
Answered the Call

Months before 7 December, the Hawaii Territorial Medical Association and the four county medical societies had set up Preparedness Committees to plan and prepare the Territory of Hawaii and civilian physicians in case the United States entered the war. The Preparedness Committees were part of the M-day (mobilization day) plan activated the morning of the attack, when calls had gone out to doctors, nurses, and ambulance services.

Within minutes after the first bomb dropped on Pearl Harbor, hasty telephone calls to Honolulu officials set the well-planned civilian defense machinery in motion. The police switchboard officer was so skeptical of the first reports that he called the Pearl City station by radio to verify. Assured it was no hoax, he issued an alarm calling all police officers, police reserves, men with special badges, and even those on pension and retirement. They were desperately needed. Throughout the day unprecedented volume swamped ten men in a dispatch room usually staffed by three.

The first volunteer agencies to get into action were the medical and ambulance services of the Major Disaster Council. This council was an official organization of the City and County of Honolulu, formed in June 1941, as an outgrowth of several years of increasing concern over the possibility of wartime bombardment. The service established its office by 8:30 a.m., ordered litter frames installed in trucks volunteered as emergency ambulances. By 9:05 a.m., doctors and nurses were on their way to Tripler General Hospital at Fort Shafter in response to an Army request. By 9:15, eight first aid stations had reported in readiness, and five minutes later forty-five truck-ambulances were speeding to Hickam. At county, corporate and private hospitals, clinics and aid stations the response was gratifying, as doctors, nurses, volunteers and Red Cross workers tended to both military and civilian casualties who came in or were transported in for treatment.[8]

The plantation hospitals at Aiea, Ewa, and Waipahu received a total of more than 130 Navy casualties. The City-County Emergency Hospital received 104 patients between 8:36 a.m. and 8:17 p.m., The Queen's Hospital emergency unit, fifty-three. Many attack victims were brought in dead or dying. About forty of the more critically injured were hospitalized at Queen's, which, filled to capacity, hastily sent 100 of its 339 patients home to make room for the wounded. Leahi Home likewise discharged 105 of its 480 patients to provide beds for any further emergency.[9]

Most Army doctors rushed to the scenes of the bombings to provide field care for the wounded soldiers before sending them to Tripler. There, civilian doctors and nurses, Army nurses, and volunteer helpers performed most of the operating-room and ward duties. Appalling shortages and tremendous confusion arose as the seriously wounded arrived at Tripler in a steady stream until early afternoon. The entrance stairs to the hospital became spattered with blood.[10]

Not until late afternoon were sufficient supplies obtained from the Major Disaster Council, the Red Cross, civilian doctors' offices, and from the Army itself, whose ample stocks were kept under lock and key, and were delayed by red tape. Until then, doctors doing major surgery borrowed scissors back and forth from one table to another. They ran out of operating gowns and worked in pajamas and underwear. They tied rags about their faces as masks, and for two or three hours had to operate without gloves.[11]

The Major Disaster Council had distributed two shipments of medical supplies to first aid stations before the war. A third allotment, which was still unpacked at the time of the attack, was distributed to hospitals and first aid stations by a hundred volunteers. Surgical instruments were sent to Tripler, where shortages became evident among the operating teams mobilized to meet the emergency. The Red Cross rushed 17,000 surgical dressings to Navy hospitals and a similar number to Tripler. The City-County Emergency Hospital loaned sulfa drugs to the armed forces. Unfortunately, the council's supply of narcotics, stored in a safety deposit vault in compliance with federal laws, could not be obtained until 8 December.[12]

Most civilian physicians called were asked to come to Tripler, to which other Army hospitals, mostly Hickam's new, smaller hospital, were sending patients because of limited local surgical capabilities, numbers of physicians, nurses, and available beds. Some were called into Queens Hospital, and other medical facilities designated in the prewar planning. Tripler's doctors, nurses, corpsmen and orderlies, similar to other military hospital staffs were stunned and nearly overwhelmed by the initial flood of severely wounded which began to arrive that morning.

The response of Honolulu surgeons to a call from Tripler was immediate and en masse. By coincidence, many of them were assembled at the Mabel L. Smyth auditorium to hear Dr. John J. Moorhead, a visiting authority on traumatic [wound] surgery—the same lecturer Dr. Leonard D. Heaton, the surgeon from the Schofield Barracks was to have heard before a Japanese fighter made two passes down the street in front of his married officer quarters, just before 8:00 a.m. Dr. Moorhead began his lecture about 9:20, because some of the physicians had come in late, some, such as Dr. Arthur G. Hodgins, filled with excitement. No sooner did he begin his lecture with the scriptural quotation, "Be ye also ready, for in the hour that ye know not, the Son of Man cometh," when the door was thrown open and Dr. Jesse Smith announced from the rear of the hall that surgeons were wanted at Tripler immediately. Dr. Moorhead and his entire audience answered the call. Eventually, many of them were asked to provide their remembrances of December Seventh.

Similar but not entirely typical of the fourteen civilian physicians' recollections of that morning was Dr. Arthur G. Hodgins, a 1897 graduate of the University of Toronto and licensed in Hawaii in 1899 in the practice of obstetrics and gynecology. He was planning to attend the lecture by Dr. Moorhead. Dr. Hodgins drove from his home in Pearl City to Honolulu, nine miles distant. En route he could plainly see the attack in progress. When he arrived for the lecture shortly before 9:00, there was much curiosity, uncertainty and outright dismissal of reported observations among physicians waiting to hear Dr. Moorhead. With the notable exception of his apparently unwarranted criticism of Colonel Edgar King, the commander of Tripler Army Hospital, Dr. Hodgins' recollections, taken in interviews and published in a six-part series, "Remembrances of December Seventh" in the *Hawaii Medical Journal*, 1947-48, are not unlike those of sixteen other physicians, most of whom went to Tripler to offer their services.

On the morning of December 7, 1941, he and his wife and his servants were at their place on "The [Pearl City] Peninsula" located next to the Pan American [*Clipper* Terminal] on the middle loch of Pearl Harbor. They had finished breakfast and he was waiting to bring his servants into town for the weekend when he heard the first bomb drop on Pearl Harbor. He rushed out and saw the dropping of the bomb and the anti-aircraft fire and the smoke beginning to rise from the other side of Ford Island about one mile away. About 8:15 to 8:30 they were ordered to get out, and he left with his servants for Honolulu. Near Aiea he picked up a sailor who told him that the city was under attack and that three of our ships were down and burning. Hodgins came to his office and unsuccessfully tried to call his wife, and then proceeded to the Mabel Smyth Memorial Building for the lecture of Dr. Moorhead. He arrived there shortly before 9:00 o'clock, and found several others of the medical profession there, including two Army medical officers from Schofield. He described what he had heard and seen, and the Army officers said they had just come by that way and there was nothing to it, and they went on into the meeting. Two other Army officers from Schofield came in and were immediately contacted by telephone and ordered to return to their quarters. Dr. Hodgins went into the hall and informed the first two medical officers from Schofield of the orders, but they paid no attention to him and sat still.

About five minutes after Dr. Moorhead began his lecture, Dr. Jesse Smith came in and announced that twelve operating surgeons were wanted at once at Tripler General Hospital. Dr. Sam Brown of Hilo, having no transportation, asked Dr. Hodgins to take him to Tripler. They had considerable trouble getting through, because everyone was taking to the road to see what was going on at Pearl Harbor. [Dr. Hodgins was seeing mostly military men voluntarily, or on telephone or radio recall, returning to their duty stations.] The first five surgeons to arrive at Tripler were Drs. Strode, R. 0. Brown, Sam Brown, Moorhead and Hodgins. They reached Tripler about 9:30 and were met by Major Spitler, who said, "They caught us with our pants down." Subsequently Drs. Halford, Batten, Osorio, Black and others arrived. Dr. Hodgins and Dr. R. 0. Brown were directed to the Maternity floor by some Major. Dr. Halford and some of the others did most of the major surgery. When they went to get ready for surgery and had their clothes off, there were no operating suits, and he worked most of the day in his B.V.D.s. Later in the day someone found some pajamas for them to wear. They wore the same gown nearly all day and simply washed off their gloves between cases except when they got an occasional change of gloves. There was very little equipment. They had about three sterile towels for each patient, and their instruments were extremely limited. They each had two or three hemostats, and there was perhaps one operating saw in the house. There was plenty of sulfa drugs on hand but they had a great deal of trouble getting anesthetists, there being only two or three at the hospital, and consequently they did most of their surgery under local anesthesia. They were short of suture material and dressings. The Maternity department was very ill equipped to do the major surgery, so that they did not handle anything except shrapnel wounds and amputations.

They did not see Col. King the entire day.

He stated that the Army medical officers were acting as traffic officers, directing the ambulance drivers where to take patients, but that they made no apparent attempt to act as a triage to separate the urgent surgery from that less urgent. He said that no army surgeon did any surgery the first day.

Their first case was an amputation of a leg and the repair of a urethra torn by shrapnel. Dr. Brown, a urologist, desired to use a sound to make this repair, but they were unable to find one. Dr. Halford finally found a silver catheter but they were unable to use it, and Dr. Brown decided to drain the bladder suprapubically. The patient was a fat man and they had only a single retractor to hold the wound open, and Hodgins had to use his finger to supply the deficiency. A catheter was fastened in place and that night the patient was brought back to be catheterized, but Dr. Hodgins didn't know why.

On one occasion, apparently when the instruments had been reduced or changed, a man with a crushed arm was brought in which required amputation, and they had to refuse to do the amputation because of lack of instruments. "They were totally unprepared for any emergency such as that; Queen's would have been better prepared."

He stated that every operation was done by the civilian surgeons, and they cleared up most of the heavy work the first day, although there was some delay in getting to some of the patients of perhaps three to four hours. The blood and plasma was supplied by the local blood bank, and Dr. Fennel remained at the hospital giving the blood and plasma as rapidly as he could.

When Black got there he had to go back and get his own instruments.

The next day he returned to the hospital and offered his services and left his name and address for call, but was not called again.

They continued to work until about 4:00 p.m. He returned to the peninsula to find that his wife had packed up but the guard had refused her permission to leave. He talked the guard into letting them go to their sons in Dowsett Highlands, where they arrived at dark.

He advised that I see Mr. Al Castle, head of the Red Cross, about the work that they had done for about a year before the "blitz," and that Col.

King had done everything he could to discourage their work as being entirely unnecessary. He stated further that he thought Col. King had done more against the civilian hospitals in the city than any other individual; e.g. Queen's Hospital was overcrowded and he would not allow them to put up a temporary structure to house about fifty patients because the hospital was in a danger zone. He demanded that "Queen's Hospital keep thirty beds vacant at all times for an emergency." Again Leahi Home for Tuberculosis was overcrowded and had a waiting list, but was well equipped and staffed, but Col. King insisted on building another hospital at Wahiawa and manned by men who had not taken care of tuberculosis, instead of adding to Leahi. Asked if he thought there had been a marked increase in tuberculosis, he said No. He felt that the chlorination of the water was entirely unnecessary, as the water supply came from artesian wells and had never given any trouble.

When asked who were the men who deserve the credit for the medical civilian preparation, he said the Committee of Judd, Strode and others.

Dr. William Winter, who read Dr. Hodgins' recollections in the series titled "Reminiscences of December Seventh," wrote a letter to the editor of the *Hawaiian Medical Journal* and took strong exception to Hodgins' characterization of Colonel King's and the Army's work at Tripler and in the civilian community.

To the Editor:

In connection with the article, "Reminiscences of December Seventh:" I wish to make a rather a strong statement.

According to the text of this article the late Dr. Hodgins saw fit to make the following remark under oath, "Col. King had done everything he could do to discourage their work [i.e., that of the Red Cross—Ed.] as being entirely unnecessary." This appears on page 50 of the JOURNAL, Volume 7, Number 1, and has reference, I believe, to the work done by the

Medical Preparedness Committee in conjunction with the American Red Cross.

I wish to state clearly and without fear of contradiction that the above quotation is as far removed from the truth as it is possible for a thing to be.

I can remember distinctly the tall gaunt figure of Col. King on the platform of the Mabel Smyth auditorium one Sunday morning in April, 1941. He was chewing what was alleged to be tobacco and he said this: "Gentlemen, it is highly probable that there will be a war in the Pacific in the not too distant future. I can conceive of a carrier-based raid directed against the island of Oahu which might easily result in 2,400 major casualties. Are you prepared to care for these casualties? I don't believe that you are."

He then urged us to throw our whole-hearted support into the work of setting up medical aid stations. Dr. Robert B. Faus had already done considerable work in this direction, and Col. King urged that this work be continued. The question of equipment for these stations was a very difficult one. No funds were available from any source for such a purpose. Col. King knew this and told us, that although the United States Army could not supply us with funds, it could supply us with equipment, and that he would see to it that the Army did it, and it did. Thus much of the equipment in our medical aid stations came from Col. King.

Moreover, Col. King arranged for men from the various army services to address us on different subjects at our Sunday morning meetings. Each man who came to us was an expert in his own field. Men spoke on Chemical Warfare, War Gases, the Construction and Operation of Decontamination Units, Gas Masks, etc. This too came as a result of Col. King's interest.

Our Sunday morning meetings began in the latter part if March, 1941, and continued until the time of the attack. Col. King attended many of these meetings and was always most anxious to help us and was most generous with his counsel and advice.

Lastly, my own association with the preparedness program was sufficiently intimate for me to say beyond all peradventure of doubt that what Dr. Hodgins had to say concerning Col. King's attitude toward medical preparedness is not true.

WILLIAM WINTER, M.D.
34, Young Hotel Bldg.
October 24, 1947

Dr. Homer Izumi's and Dr. Harold Johnson's experiences were markedly different than Dr. Hodgins.'

[Dr. Izumi] had come to Honolulu a few days before to complete preparations for moving to Honolulu and was staying with his friend Dr. Harold Johnson.

December 7, 1941, dawned bright and clear, and, highly optimistic about his plans, he packed to return home by the 8 o'clock plane. Dr. and Mrs. Johnson and their son Larry drove him to John Rodgers Airport, arriving there about 7:30. About 10-15 minutes after arriving they noticed clouds of smoke and heard gun fire over the Pearl Harbor area. A few planes were flying in the same vicinity and one was seen to burst into flames and plunge toward Pearl Harbor.

Directly overhead they also noted a flight of planes wheeling and circling in loop formation tit-tat-tatting at each other. In the course of all of its loops this formation swooped down to within about 150 feet of them and they noticed that one of the planes had red dot markers on its wings. Dr. Izumi remarked, "Gee, Harold, that looks like a Japanese emblem!" "Yeh, don't they get realistic nowadays," replied Johnson as he hoisted his boy Larry to his shoulders and said, "Look, Larry, look!"

Immediately after this event the Maui plane was announced and Dr. Izumi boarded it. Waving goodbye to his friends through the plane window, just as they were preparing to take off, he noticed someone running across the landing field, coming from the nearby Andrew Flying Service hangar and shouting something which immediately caused the farewell crowd gathered near the plane to run for their cars. Then the door of the plane was opened and all passengers were asked to get out. Dr. Johnson, who, like the rest of the farewell crowd had started to leave the airport, had returned by the time Dr. Izumi had disembarked. The cause for the sudden excitement was the fatal shooting of a man near Andrew's hangar, apparently from the firing of the planes which had just a few minutes before so closely zoomed overhead. [Unknown to Dr. Izumi, the man killed was the civilian flight instructor, Robert Tyce.]

Because Dr. Izumi thought the shooting was due either to an accident or to some fanatical attempt, he lightly passed off Dr. Johnson's attempt to persuade him to leave the airport, feeling that things would soon be taken care of and he would be able to fly on to Maui. As Dr. Johnson reluctantly drove off, Izumi realized that he and a few airport attendants were the only ones around. A tall, lanky Scandinavian stood with him as they looked and talked about the possible seriousness of conditions over Pearl Harbor way.

By now this area was a billowing mass of black smoke and flames and occasionally a flaming plane was seen plunging downward into the area. Heavy gunfire and explosions were heard all over, and the seriousness of the entire affair dawned on Izumi and his Scandinavian acquaintance with a sudden outburst of gunfire from the keawe-tree-covered areas surrounding John Rodgers airport. The whining sound of falling bombs which landed on the ocean side of the take-off field further convinced them of the urgency to get going. This thought was suddenly interrupted by the appearance of several huge droning planes flying very low, coming at them from the direction of the sea. Sensing real danger, they made a dash for safety—away from the administration building into the open—and frantically realized the only protection was that of a small tree planted in the center of the parking circle.

Unconsciously, throughout this entire excitement, Dr. Izumi had gingerly carried a box of fancy pastries intended for Maui consumption. Peculiarly, as he and his friend dashed for the tree, his first thought was to protect the delicate pastries—his second thought, one of misgiving, that he hadn't kissed his son Allan goodbye when he left Maui for Honolulu. As he dove for the protection of the tree—still carefully hugging his box of pastries—he found his lanky Scandinavian companion had beat him to it and was frantically trying to encircle his over six-foot frame around the tree trunk which Izumi flashingly realized was only about six inches in diameter. The next moment found Izumi and his pastries very much in competition with his lanky companion for the protection of the small tree. As the huge planes roared just overhead, they both buried their faces in the ground, peering up as they passed to see, first that their protecting tree was practically leafless, and second that the planes bore American insignia. The immediate relief was followed by pride and a feeling of security at the sight of the huge U. S. bombers. Later they found out that these bombers had flown in from the mainland and were unarmed, but the sight of them at that moment gave them courage to gather their wits and bags, secure a car, and leave the field.

After getting back to Dr. Johnson's home, Izumi and the Johnsons observed from the front porch the maneuvering of our ships trying to head out of the harbor for the open sea while many planes hovering over them tried to drop bombs on their decks.

Following this short period of watching, Dr. Johnson, who was in charge of the west Honolulu O.C.D. (Office of Civilian Defense) units, left to open up and activate his unit, while Izumi helped rig up a bomb shelter in the yard. The following day and for the next 5 or 6 days Izumi worked in the Farrington O.C.D. unit and helped in the care of some patients who had been evacuated from Tripler to Farrington. About a week or ten days after the attack Izumi was given permission to fly back to Maui. Upon arrival at John Rodgers airport, one of the attendants, recognizing him as one of the December 7th refugees, told him that after he left the airport his plane had been machine-gunned by enemy planes.

Dr. Stewart F. Steele, M.D., interviewed both Izumi and Johnson and recorded their experiences.

> Dr. Harold Johnson, a dermatologist was living in upper Kalihi Valley on December 7. His classmate, Dr. Homer Izumi, had been in Honolulu to hear the lectures of Dr. John J. Moorhead and he was planning on taking the 8 o'clock morning plane to his home on Maui, carrying with him a number of pies and cakes for his wife. They arrived at the airport at about 7:30 A.M. when they became suddenly aware of a large flight of twenty or thirty planes coming in from the direction of the Molokai

channel. About five minutes later they heard heavy explosions and saw flashes from the direction of Pearl Harbor, and huge columns of smoke began to rise from that area. They saw one of the planes suddenly catch fire in mid-air and plunge earthward. He remarked to his wife, "Just think, there goes a young lieutenant burning to death and think of the poor family that's left."

The airport officials had meanwhile gone on top of the building to see what was going on. A small private plane had taxied to the end of the runway for taking off when a Japanese plane suddenly swooped in and machine-gunned it, killing the pilot. The plane then turned and swept across the airport immediately above the airport station at such a low attitude that Dr. Johnson thought he could have thrown a baseball into the cabin. The "rising sun" on the wings was easily observed. There was difference of opinion as to whether it was a practice attack or whether it was it was the real thing. Suddenly one of the airport officials came in telling everyone to lie on the floor. Dr. Johnson had his wife and small child with him and told Dr. Izumi he felt he should take them home and he didn't believe the plane would leave for Maui. Dr. Izumi, however, felt sure the plane would take off and refused to leave the airport.

He therefore left Dr. Izumi at the airport and drove home, going along Dillingham Boulevard. He stated that the boulevard was absolutely clear. On arriving home they filled the bathtub with water, as well as some buckets, and then turned off all the public utilities in case of damage. About one-half hour later Dr. Izumi came back in a taxicab. He said that after they left the shrapnel began to fall allover, and he with his boxes of pies in both hands went out and tried to hide behind a small tree.

Dr. Johnson and Dr. Izumi thereupon proceeded to Dr. Johnson's regular station, which was supervisor of the first aid stations in the west portion of Honolulu. It was necessary for him to go from one first aid station to another, but his quarters were in Palama where Joe Lam was the medical director. He saw the people who were brought in from a car in which a child had been killed and the others injured by exploding shrapnel. He covered the headlights of his car with blue cellophane and spent the night of December 7 making the rounds of his stations. Once during the day he drove home to see that the family were in good shape, and returned home for breakfast on the morning of December 8.

On 20 December, Dr. S.R. Brown rendered a matter-of-fact report to the Hawaii County Medical Society, in the form of a lecture, recounting the events of that morning. It was detailed in telling of the terrible wounds among the mostly twenties young men who were brought to Tripler for treatment. His lecture was also published in its entirety in the series contained in the 1947-48 *Hawaiian Medical Journals*. He began:

> I feel rather diffident in having occasioned this meeting; however, I have had certain opportunities, and it has appealed to me that, if I could pass along any benefits or knowledge that I had acquired, it was my duty to do so, particularly as Society affairs in part accounted for my being in Honolulu. We may think they won't hit here again. That attitude might be unfortunate, so I thought it better be now and not next month.

> If I am unable to tell you anything today that will be of benefit it will not be from lack of opportunity, but rather inability to observe and deduce from my observations.

> I will take up my connection with events while in Honolulu in a rather chronological manner. On the Sunday morning of the 7th of December there was a meeting at 9:00 o'clock at the Mabel Smyth Memorial Building to hear a lecture by Dr. Moorhead, that had been postponed from the previous day. Just before the lecture, while gathered outside the lecture room, Dr. Hodgins arrived from Pearl Harbor, very excited, telling of

hearing bombing and seeing a cruiser lying on her side and burning at Pearl Harbor. His information was received in rather a disbelieving way, so much so that he proceeded himself to believe that what he was seeing was anti-aircraft practice, and we went in and sat down at the lecture. However, there seemed to be an uncertainty in the air from that time. Dr. Moorhead began his lecture by mentioning that he had served in France in the last war and that if the opportunity came he wanted to do his bit again in any capacity which he could. After a few minutes one or two individuals were called from the lecture, and then an announcement was made through the loud speaker that surgical teams and medical help were wanted at Tripler. We then, of course, realized that something was happening. I got in the car with Dr. Hodgins and we started toward Tripler, which is on the old road out of Honolulu toward Pearl Harbor. Traffic going out was already dense, consisting of the greater part of men from the various posts who were trying to return to duty.

After some delay owing to traffic, we reached the hospital and went up to the operating floor. Certain surgical teams, which had previously been arranged for under the civilian defense committee of the Medical Society, were arriving and ready to work. Dr. Moorhead and myself, having no previous connections, teamed up together and were assigned to a table. Already the wounded were covering the floors of the halls and available space leading to the theatre.

My observations from now on will be largely the product of my association with Dr. Moorhead over the next two days, and it is on this authority of that association that I am talking today. When I mentioned to him that I expected to quote my experiences and hoped that I would not misinterpret his opinions, he was good enough to say that he was quite willing to take a chance on that.

> I cannot possibly recall to you all the cases. I will
> just mention a few cases, which will bring out all the
> points that I want to make as I go along from here.

He went on to tell of the first patient that came to them, who had a traumatic amputation of the hip. One leg had been shot off right through the hip joint, leaving a stump of the femur about three or four inches long. In each case he told of the treatment given, the apparent short-term results, and that records were kept of each and all subsequent cases. The next case was a compound fracture of the tibia and fibula with a large part of the calf shot away. The decision was to amputate below the knee.

Dr. Moorhead, who had served on the battlefields in France during World War I, and had teamed with Dr. Brown when they arrived at Tripler, was circulating among the tables in the three, second floor operating rooms, giving counsel and advice to surgeons who were working over young men with wounds most of the doctors had never seen before. His advice helped in making difficult decisions on whether or not to amputate, as well as how to treat the wounds before and after surgery. Dr. Brown noted ". . . there were a large number of amputations performed those days."

The next case he described was a compound fracture of the femur, above the knee, in which the projectile had traversed the thigh transversely and wasn't lodged in the tissues. The decision was to save the leg. Next described was a gunshot wound to the abdomen, in which a .30-caliber-size bullet had entered the back, downward, missing the spine, and was lodged on the right side under the liver.

He recalled that on Monday morning, after a few hours off, Dr. Moorehead said, "Now let's review a bit. What did we do yesterday [on the abdomen wound] that, if we had to do over again, we would do differently?" In addition to treatment for shock, other subjects related to the complex wound were discussed. Then Dr. Brown turned to discussion of a "sucking" chest wound, its treatment, and what was learned; a debilitating shrapnel wound in the groin area, and removal of "foreign bodies"—mostly small pieces of shrapnel—from tissues. He closed by saying:

> We have been discussing war surgery, and in these
> days civilians are almost equally involved. Your

case today may be pushed along for the casualty of tomorrow, so you have no assurance of opportunity to follow up with advice or correct any omissions of today; therefore, complete and correct first treatment means saving of life and limb, and will greatly shorten the average hospitalization and disability.

To again briefly list the means: (1) Treatment of general condition-shock, hemorrhage, et cetera. (2) Investigation of wounds in all their possible extensions. (3) Complete debriding. (4) The efficient use of sulfa drugs, locally and by mouth. (5) No suturing for closure. (6) Vaseline gauze to keep wounds open, not for packs. (7) Records to go definitely attached to the patient.

I can't close without mentioning the men who were "taking it." Most of them were lads in their twenties. Their attitude may be summed up in the words self-control and cooperation. They showed it in the quiet way they took an anesthetic, yes, and in the quiet way they came out of anesthetic. It greatly lightened the work, and without doubt improved their chances. They were admirable.[13]

Martial Law Declared

The M-Day Act, a far-reaching measure which had been passed by a special session of the territorial legislature barely two months before the attack, went into effect at 11:15 a.m. when Governor Poindexter proclaimed a defense period over radio station KGU. He was erroneously told he would have to cut short his radio broadcast, that Japanese planes were coming in on the beam. Immediately, he issued a defense act rule creating an Office of Civilian Defense to exercise all the power conferred by the M-Day Act. (The Hawaii Office of Civilian Defense was different from the federal office of the same name and also from the defense councils of the various states.) Committees of the Major Disaster Council, already hard at work, were absorbed by the new OCD organization, and the MDC coordinator became the OCD director for Oahu.

General Short visited the governor at 12:10 to ask for martial law. He told of the damage at Pearl Harbor and the military airfields, and his fears that the Japanese would attempt a landing the next morning, aided by local saboteurs. He assured the governor that martial law was "absolutely necessary" to implement the orders which the military could enforce. While the governor had wide powers under the M-Day Act, he could enforce them only through civilian agencies, and their facilities would have been inadequate in the face of invasion or uprisings. Governor Poindexter was reluctant to relinquish control to the Army, but felt that conditions were so alarming that he must defer to the judgment of a military man. He promised General Short an answer in an hour and placed a telephone call to President Roosevelt in Washington.

The call came through at 12:40. Following instructions from the Navy censor already on the job, the operator asked the governor, "What are you going to talk to him about?" She refused to complete the connection until a superior finally told her it was all right to let the governor talk to the president.

Secretary of the Territory Charles M. Hite, who listened in to all the governor's calls that day, noted in his diary:

> Operator most difficult to handle, persisted in cutting short the talk, kept interrupting. Gov. managed to inform President Japs had attacked and about fifty civilians killed. Badly needed food and planes. Roosevelt marvelous—said he would send ships with food and planes already ordered. Gov. said Short asked for martial law and he thought he should invoke it. President replied he approved. Gov. said main danger from local Japs.

When General Short returned, the diary continues:

> He requested and urged Martial Law, saying for all he knew landing parties en route . . . Said attack probably prelude to all out attack—said otherwise all government and business functions to continue as usual. Gov. said he would accede and asked Short how long in his opinion such status would continue. Short said he unable to say, but if it

developed this was a raid only and not the prelude to a landing, Martial Law could be lifted within a reasonably short time. Trouble was he didn't have complete reports, he himself in the dark and could not afford to take chances. Short obviously under great strain—Gov. calm and collected. Gov. signed Declaration. When Short left Gov. said never hated doing anything so much in all his life.

The governor assumed that the "reasonably short time" might be thirty days. It is probable that General Short did not at the time expect martial law would continue for three years. The governor and the general both issued proclamations that had been in an Army file as early as March, 1941. The governor's proclamation, in accordance with powers given him under the Organic Act, placed the territory under martial law and suspended the privilege of the writ of habeas corpus. It went further, requesting the commanding general to "exercise the powers normally exercised by judicial officers"—a step the legality of which was to be debated for several years. The general's proclamation told the populace:

> The imminence of attack by the enemy and the possibility of invasion make necessary a stricter control of your actions than would be necessary or proper at other times. I shall therefore shortly publish ordinances governing the conduct of the people of the territory with respect to the showing of lights, circulation, meetings, censorship, possession of arms, ammunition, and explosives, the sale of intoxicating liquors, and other subjects.

At 4:25 p.m. came the announcement on the radio. The Islands had been placed under martial law and the office of the Military Governor of Hawaii had been assumed by Major General Walter C. Short, Commanding General of the Hawaiian Department. The stations repeated General Short's statement twice in English and, for the benefit of aliens, once in Japanese. Later, blackout orders came over the air: "Please turn out your lights . . . Hawaii is observing a complete blackout.[14]

At 5:16 p.m, the following Signal Corps message went from

Ft. Shafter to the White House, and was received at 11:06 p.m. Washington time:

> THE PRESIDENT THE WHITE HOUSE
> WASHINGTON D C
>   I HAVE TODAY DECLARED MARTIAL LAW THROUGOUT THE TERRITORY OF HAWAII AND HAVE SUSPENDED THE PRIVILEGE OF THE WRIT OF HABEAS CORPUS PERIOD YOUR ATTENTION IS CALLED TO SECTION SIXTY SEVEN OF THE HAWAIIAN ORGANIC ACT FOR YOUR DECISIONS ON MY ACTION.
>   POINDEXTER[15]

The president, who, under the circumstance, gave his verbal approval on the phone, later that day asked the U.S. Attorney General, Francis Biddle, for his legal opinion regarding Governor Poindexter's action. On 9 December the attorney general responded after reviewing and quoting the pertinent paragraphs in the statutes, stating in the final paragraph of the letter, "I believe that the action taken is appropriate . . . "[16]

The declaration of martial law, still a controversial subject to this day, was believed by many to have been made without the president's knowing the full implications of the decision and his approval. Specifically, author Gwenfread Allen, in the book *Hawaii's War Years, 1941-45*, stated on page 36:

> The governor, in accordance with law, notified the president by radio that he had declared martial law and suspended the right of habeas corpus. President Roosevelt radioed his approval on December 9. (But the governor said nothing in his message about the Army assuming judicial functions, and copies of the controversial proclamations evidently were not sent to Washington until 1943. *It is doubtful whether the president saw them, even then.*) [Emphasis added.]

While President Roosevelt might not have seen the copies of the proclamations, he was clearly made aware that martial law included the military governor's assumption of the Territory's judicial function. Attorney General Biddle's 9 December opinion, addressed to the president and sent to the White House along with the proposed message reply to Governor Poindexter, stated in the next to last paragraph:

> I am advised that a Military Governor and an Associate Military Governor have been appointed; that all civil courts have been suspended until further notice; that a Commission to advise the Military Governor, consisting of Governor Poindexter, the Territorial Attorney General, the Mayor of Honolulu, and a prominent businessman, has been designated; and that the United States Attorney and a member of the Provost Marshall's staff have been designated military prosecutors.

The president initialed "O.K. FDR" below the attorney general's signature block, and on 9 December the message formally approving the governor's action was dispatched at 4:02 p.m. by U.S. Government cable:

> HONORABLE JOSEPH B. POINDEXTER, GOVERNOR, TERRITORY OF HAWAII, HONOLULU, HAWAII.
> YOUR TELEGRAM OF DECEMBER SEVENTH RECEIVED AND YOUR ACTION IN SUSPENDING THE WRIT OF HABEAS CORPUS AND PLACING THE TERRITORY OF HAWAII UNDER MARTIAL LAW IN ACCORDANCE WITH U.S.C., TITLE 48, SECTION 532 HAS MY APPROVAL.
> FRANKLIN D. ROOSEVELT

Again, before the message was dispatched, the president wrote his initials, "FDR", enclosed in quotation marks, next to his name.

On the same day, Attorney General Biddle sent a memorandum to President Roosevelt, with an accompanying draft censorship bill, proposed to be sent to Congress. The draft bill was in response to direction from the president to Mr. Biddle a month earlier to form a committee "to consider War Censorship and make an appropriate recommendation to you."[17]

As a result of the attack on Pearl Harbor censorship in Hawaii was already in effect, as Governor Poindexter and the

Territory Secretary learned when the governor placed his call to President Roosevelt. Censorship was just one of many martial law ordinances proscribed on Oahu and throughout Hawaii on 7 December. One of General Short's priorities for action was saboteurs, and their potential for aiding possible landings of Japanese troops.

Potential Saboteurs Taken Into Custody

At noon the Japanese Consulate in Honolulu was placed under guard. Breakfast was served at the Consulate at 8:30 a.m., and the Consul-General was still unaware of the attack. In *At Dawn We Slept*, Gordon Prange recorded what happened at the Consulate that morning:

> One of the *Star-Bulletin's* reporters of Japanese ancestry "begged . . . to be allowed to go out on the street and cover the news." Riley H. Allen, the editor, feared the young man "might be shot or locked up." Then Allen "finally decided that we would send him out to the Japanese consul and bring back what news he might find there." This reporter was probably Lawrence Nakatska, who dropped by the consulate that morning in search of a story.
>
> Like so many others on Oahu, the consulate's members had anticipated a leisurely Sunday. [Consul General Nagao] Kita and [and his deputy Otojiro] Okuda had an engagement to play golf with a friend. At about 9:00 [native Hawaiian guide and chauffer Richard Masayuki] Kotoshirodo, hearing the distant thundering, walked the short distance from his abode to the consulate "to find out what all the commotion was about." He discovered Kita, Okuda, and others of the staff already assembled, looking worried. [Takeo] Yoshikawa, [a trained intelligence officer who was Japan's top spy in Hawaii], appeared shortly, in shirt sleeves, hair mussed and clothes wrinkled. He remarked that it was a "noisy morning." He wanted to go up to the

heights to see what was happening, but Kita forbade him to leave.

Kita refused to admit to [the reporter] Nakatsuka that a Japanese attack was in progress, let alone make a statement about it. The reporter hurried back to his office for a copy of the day's extra and brought it to Kita as evidence. The blazing headline WAR! OAHU BOMBED BY JAPANESE PLANES was Yoshikawa's signal for action. He and [Sainon] Tsukikawa [the secretary of the code room], dashed for the code room, where they began to burn material furiously.

After leaving [General] Short's headquarters, [Lieutenant Colonel George W. Bicknell, [the Hawaiian Department's chief intelligence investigative officer], arrived at his office downtown, where he found his people issuing ammunition and small arms. [Robert L.] Shivers, [the head of the FBI office in Hawaii], was there, astonished and "scared all the way through," like almost everyone else. He and Bicknell wanted to pick up Japanese suspects immediately but were unable to do so because the provost marshall could not provide the necessary trucks and MP guards. This delayed the plan for several hours. "Bob Shivers and I were running around like two wild Indian dogs," Bicknell recalled.

At about 1000 or 1100 Shivers asked Police Chief Gabrielson to put a guard around the consulate "for the protection of the consul general and the members of his staff and the consular property." Gabrielson turned the assignement over to Captain of Dectectives Benjamin Van Kuren and Lieutenant Yoshio Hasegawa. When they and a few colleagues arrived at the consulate, they found uniformed police officers with sawed-off shotguns already on guard. Kita stood in the driveway at the rear of the building, holding the *Star-Bulletin* extra.

Van Kuren and his men trooped in through the back entrance. In the code room the police "found a wash tub on the floor" in which the Japanese were burning documents. The police also salvaged a brown "bellows type envelope" full of undestroyed papers. They brought their find to the FBI, which in turn gave it to Naval Intelligence . . . to work on.[18]

The police seized five burlap sacks of torn papers, plus the envelope of untorn papers.

The consul, finally convinced of the attack, gave his last newspaper interview in Hawaii just before the guards were posted. He warned Japanese residents to be calm and law abiding.[19]

Immediately after martial law was declared, Army Intelligence, assisted by the Federal Bureau of Investigation, and police began arresting residents considered dangerous. Because one third of the total population in the Islands was of Japanese ancestry, internal security in case of war with Japan had long been a matter of official concern. Cards had been prepared with the names and addresses of Japanese suspects, and were divided among thirteen squads of officers. Within three hours after the declaration of martial law, nearly all the Japanese suspects considered most dangerous were in custody at the Immigration station.[20]

There would be more taken into custody the next day, as security agencies, augmented with additional volunteers, expanded the net to include Caucasian suspects—practically every German and Italian alien in Hawaii, with the exception of the aged and infirm. Members of the San Jose State football team volunteered to assist police, and several participated in arresting Japanese aliens. A San Francisco member of the San Jose squad, a former Lowell High School player, Hans Wiedenhoefer, told of working with the police.

> Next day we joined the police force, were given steel helmets, arm bands and riot guns, and assigned to various police posts for eight hour shifts along with regular members of the force. I was working with a Hawaiian policeman when we got a call to raid a place which had a powerful short wave radio set in it. It was pitch dark, there wasn't a light and you couldn't see the front of your nose.
>
> We closed in and found the radio equipment all right but four fellows we were supposed to nab weren't there. Apparently, two of them had been

tipped off because we found a note from them warning the other two to beat it.

The Hawaiian policeman told me I had better stay there and keep watch and then he left me. For a few minutes my knees knocked pretty hard, and when I heard somebody fooling around a window in the next room I just rushed in there, aimed and took a shot.

He said he couldn't tell whether he hit the target but he said it felt pretty good to see several policeman come rushing up after he fired. Later, Wiedenhoefer and Gray McConnell, in company with a regular policeman, made four arrests.[21]

By the end of the day on 8 December, 482 persons were in custody on Oahu—370 Japanese, ninety-eight Germans, and fourteen Italians.[22]

Evacuations to Safer Areas—The Prelude to Seaborne Evacuations

Before the attack was over, many women and children rushed in automobiles from military installations to the comparative safety of Honolulu. Throughout the day and night, trucks and busses of the evacuation committee of the Major Disaster Council moved others from Army posts and from nearby civilian areas. At 1730 hours the 25th Infantry Division Artillery commander ordered area commanders to prepare all families for evacuation from Schofield Barracks to Honolulu, that trucks were on the way.[23] About 4,000 evacuees were housed at Hemenway Hall at the University of Hawaii and at ten public schools designated by the evacuation committee, while some evacuees moved in with friends. At Waipahu, 500 hundred crowded plantation club houses, the Hongwanji School, and public schools, while 100 were taken in to private homes. A total of 2,100 volunteers, including many public health nurses, social workers, teachers, Red Cross aides, and recreation workers, assisted in the evacuation.[24]

The field commanders at Hickam and Wheeler, Colonels Farthing and Flood, had all women and children evacuated.

Some had already departed on their own in private automobiles seeking the comparative safety of Honolulu or other outlying areas. At Hickam a loud speaker blared, "Get all women and children off the base." Ira Southern and others helped search the houses and found women and children under beds, outside, or already preparing to leave. They boarded Honolulu Rapid Transit Company busses and trucks provided by the evacuation committee of the Major Disaster Council. Some evacuees moved in with friends. The remainder stayed at the University of Hawaii's Hemenway Hall, at public schools designated by the evacuation committee, in private homes of families who had volunteered to house them, and at other places such as plantation clubhouses and Hongwanji School in Waipahu.[25]

John M. Sardis, a civil engineer who worked for the Army Corps of Engineers, and his wife Sherry, lived in a housing area near Hickam Field. The terrible destruction at Hickam and in Pearl Harbor brought them fear, rumor and great uncertainty. The military informed them they had to evacuate to a safer area the afternoon following the attack. They took a few personal belongings and went to Kamehameha School in a convoy of private automobiles, escorted by the military. On arriving at the school they settled into a boys' dormitory room and John was sent back to work to begin inspecting damage on Hickam. Rumors were immediately pervasive, the first one being "Japanese paratroopers had landed."

On Monday following the attack, they were permitted to write messages to families on the mainland to inform them "we were OK."

One oddity which struck John when he began assessing damage at Hickam, was the Japanese had repeatedly dive bombed the baseball field adjoining the Fire Station—a matter of considerable curiosity. John was certain the Japanese believed that an underground fuel storage area lay beneath the baseball field. He knew plans had originally been to locate the tanks there, but were finally installed elsewhere on the airfield. He was equally certain Japanese agents had been active on Hickam, and events later proved him correct. A map of Hickam was found on the body of a Japanese pilot, and it indicated the fuel storage area was underground, beneath the baseball field.

Sherry and John stayed at the school approximately two weeks. Husbands went to work each day. The wives asked to do volunteer work with the Red Cross. They were told the Red Cross had run out of bandages, and the wives received instructions on what size to cut up sheets to use as bandages for the wounded. They didn't use the phones, and generally stayed in doors at night—blacked out. John's movement by car at night was limited, and he drove the first night with a piece of blue cellophane covering the top half of each headlight. Afterward, consistent with martial law orders, he painted both headlights blue, except for a small horizontal slit across the middle of each one.

All entertainment stopped, schools were ordered closed until further notice, school seniors and juniors patrolled the school grounds without arms, patrols were everywhere, and military convoys were on the streets every day, moving troops back and forth. During that two weeks Sherry was asked if she wanted to be evacuated to the mainland, and she politely refused telling them "No, she wanted to stay on the island and support her husband and the war effort as long as he worked there."

At the end of the two weeks, they were permitted to return to their house. The military had appropriated their quarters but took them back to move their personal belongings to another set of quarters. In spite of it all, she remembered the experience as one of close cooperation, working together, and the strong feeling of doing something important for her country.[26]

Approximately 2:00 p.m. the Red Cross came to the officer's quarters of Lieutenant Robert Littmann, the communications officer on the *Oglala*, which had capsized that morning. Lieutenant Littmann, having seen he could do nothing when he arrived at the dock where *Oglala* lay, went toward the Naval hospital where he had seen a Japanese airplane crash. While he was gone, the Red Cross came to evacuate his wife, son, daughter Peggy, and Peggy's aunt and her family, by school bus, from their officers' quarters to the Honolulu YMCA.

When they arrived, the YMCA was bedlam. Swarming with wives and small children, many deeply worried about their husbands' and fathers' safety, they wondered what would happen to them after being uprooted from their homes and taken to an unfamiliar location. After about two hours, Peggy's father came to the YMCA to take the family home. Women anxiously gathered around him, asking about their husbands. There was little he could tell them. When his family returned to their quarters, they covered the windows with tar paper to black them out, and he painted the car headlights with blue lacquer. It would be February before Peggy, her mother and brother would return to the mainland.[27]

At Schofield Barracks, the Army surgeon, Dr. Leonard Heaton, entered additional recollections in his diary for the long, tortuous day of 7 December:

> . . . I got Sara Dudley [his seven year-old daughter] to the hospital in the morning—the only place for her because all the women and children were being corralled in the 19th Infantry barracks and she was sick. I checked on them and they were comfortably situated in Ward 16. We heard various rumors from time to time thru the day, i.e., two Jap carriers sunk, 15 Jap troop transports off Barbers Point, etc. A confusion of ideas and statements. I was awfully tired having operated straight thru all day . . .

And in his 8 December entry, he referred to the evacuation of families from Schofield Barracks, logged in the 25th Division Journal, ". . . All the women were taken to Honolulu during the night . . ."[28]

Troops on the Move

Hawaii's presumed impregnability had vanished in two hellish hours. The inability to locate and counterattack the Japanese strike fleet heightened fears of another air raid and a follow-on landing of troops. Having severely crippled American air and naval forces in Hawaii, not only had the Japanese Navy stripped away the islands' aura of impregnability, they created a new strategic equation that reverberated to the highest levels of the American military establishment and government. Both the Hawaiian Islands and the mainland's west coast could possibly be in the Japanese crosshairs.

The Japanese onslaught of 7 December almost severed the American lifeline to the Philippines, which, along with Wake, Guam and Midway Islands came under attack the same day. The lines of communication to Australia were also in jeopardy. To complicate the problem handed the Americans, the Japanese

Navy ringed Oahu with submarines, moved submarines across the sea lanes from Hawaii close in to the west coast, placing nine on patrol near key harbor entrances. A by-product of the attack was near-frenzied war hysteria that was absent sufficient facts and filled with rumors, which swept the mainland, and particularly gripped the west coast. The reaction was amplified by the military's release of unconfirmed reports and rumors, and the news media's unwitting, yet sometimes questioning complicity in the same practice.

As a follow-up to the defenders' stinging losses, had the Japanese launched a successful third strike, they could have done enormous strategic damage, far more than they achieved with the first and second wave. If they mustered enough force to strike the fuel storage tanks, docks, harbor repair facilities, and power generation plants, the United States' lines of communication and supply to Australia and all other forward bases would have been more severely limited if not severed completely. If the enemy struck hard and did little else but destroy the storage tanks, an immediate fuel crisis would have occurred, at least temporarily forcing the entire Pacific Fleet back to the mainland's west coast. There were no other significant sources of fuel oil in the islands.

September 1941, the War Department prescribed an impressive allotment of antiaircraft artillery weapons: 84 mobile and 26 fixed 3-inch guns for high altitude firing, and provision for replacing some of them as soon as possible with more modern weapons; 144 of the newer 37-mm automatic weapons; and 516 caliber .50 antiaircraft machine guns for action against low-flying aircraft. By then also the department had four antiaircraft regiments, and it was scheduled to receive a fifth before the end of the year. Actually three of the four regiments present were at little more than half strength, and the equipment on hand was considerably less than that allotted, amounting to 60 mobile and 26 fixed 3-inch guns, only 109 antiaircraft machine guns, and only 20 of the 37-mm automatic weapons.

With the strength available, Army antiaircraft units on Oahu had the ability when deployed to give some protection against high-flying horizontal bombing planes along the south coast (from Diamond Head to west of Pearl Harbor) and around Schofield Barracks and Wheeler Field. The 37-mm guns had been in Hawaii for almost ten months before ammunition for them arrived on 5 December 1941, and there had been very little for the antiaircraft machine guns, so that firing practice for even the small number of guns available for defense against dive or torpedo bombers or other low-flying planes had been more or less out of the question.

About half the mobile 3-inch guns were assigned action stations on private property, and in practice sessions during the months before the Japanese attack the gun crews kept to nearby roads and carefully refrained from trespassing. Except during practice sessions the guns and the regiments that manned them were concentrated in three areas some distance from their battle stations, and at all times after May 1941 ammunition for the guns remained in the Ordnance depot. Only the fixed 3-inch guns, with ammunition boxed but close at hand, were ready for near immediate action. The rest depended on getting several hours' advance warning of an impending attack.[29]

Shortly after the attack began, and throughout the remainder of the day on Oahu, late but hurried, long-planned defense measures were being taken by both the Army and Navy. Though the 24th and 25th Infantry Divisions reacted immediately, as did antiaircraft artillery units, by the time the air raid ended, their planned defense positions still weren't yet manned and ready. The sharp losses sustained in long-range patrol and fighter aircraft, while not totally debilitating, increased the risks of another successful Japanese air attack—if they had made such a decision. Rapid troop moves on the ground, and around the clock alert were essential, and began immediately, increasing the demand on already strained transportation and communication nets.

The entire island went to high, tense, "hammers' cocked" alert. Though too late to do any good during the raid, ground radar sites went to round the clock operation. Antiaircraft batteries in the 251st Coast Artillery, fresh off maneuvers the week prior to the raid, were all inside the artillery's camps and compounds to protect against sabotage when the attack came. The order to go to "Alert Level 3"—prepared to meet an all out air attack and invasion—wasn't issued, until 0823. Two minutes later electric power was lost, and all communications ceased for five critical minutes before communications were established with Fort De Russy, and a communications truck left camp for Hickam Field. While not deployed when the attack began, all were deployed and in place by 1900 hours. The deployed AA batteries, added to the remaining fighter defense capability at Wheeler, now dispersed into revetments and at auxiliary fields, with a number on rapid reaction alert, was sufficient to make the Japanese pay to fight their way into the air over the harbor again.

Under the Oahu defense plan the 24th Infantry Division had responsibility for the northern half of Oahu and the 25th Infantry Division had responsibility for the southern half of Oahu including Pearl Harbor and Honolulu. The 27th Infantry Regiment was responsible for the southeast portion of Oahu, including Honolulu. The 35th Infantry Regiment had the defense of Pearl Harbor, the southwest and western portion of Oahu and the 298th Infantry Regiment had the eastern shore of Oahu. The Hawaiian Department went to Alert Level 3 as the attack occurred and as early as 0930 units of both divisions began quickly moving to their assigned defense sectors. At 1245 the 35th Infantry reported its 1st Battalion in beach positions, 2d Battalion at Schofield Barracks, the 3d Battalion in position at Ft. Shafter, less Company I, which was in nearby beach positions.[30]

With the possibility of another Japanese air raid or invasion, the first order of business was to quickly bring air defenses up to full readiness while constructing permanent beach fortifications including pillboxes and revetments as well as stringing thousands of yards of barbed wire on the beaches. On the air fields, while antiaircraft batteries set up to defend against a possible follow-on raid, Army Air Force and Navy men scrambled to get as many aircraft as possible in commission, dispersed into revetments where they existed, on alert and ready to fly, while cannibalizing parts from destroyed or heavily damaged aircraft to complete additional repairs and bring more aircraft into service. On 8 December, with Ewa's runways relatively undamaged, an Army Air Force fighter squadron with 12 aircraft and 183 men transferred to Ewa until the runways at Wheeler could be repaired.

Because a goodly portion of the defensive positions were on private land the Army had been unable to construct more permanent defensive fortifications at these locations. [Due to the imposition of Martial Law,] no such restrictions existed after the attack and an intense effort was undertaken to improve fortifications covering likely amphibious landing sites. Besides manning the beach defenses the units of the 25th Division also guarded key non-military installations on the southern half of Oahu as well as aided in the enforcement of the Martial Law that had been put into effect after war was declared.

Of additional concern was providing protection for the some twenty thousand women and children who were military dependants of service personnel stationed on Oahu. Fearing additional air attacks on Schofield and Wheeler and shortly after the Schofield units had deployed to their defensive positions, buses and trucks evacuated Schofield families to schools, hotels and homes in Honolulu and some to homes in the hills of Wahiawa.[31]

Preparations to meet the expected Japanese invasion included the formation of four infantry companies comprised of Wheeler Field personnel, headed by four Army Air Forces officers who had been in the infantry before. They were deployed around the field and instructed "to watch for anybody that might come in." Also, a battalion of infantrymen from Schofield Barracks arrived to guard the airfield, at which time Colonel Flood turned his ground personnel over to the Army major in command of the battalion.

At Hickam, Hawaiian Air Force personnel defended the airfield and bomb dump against expected Japanese invasion. Outside the military posts, army troops took up defensive positions around the main islands to thwart anticipated attempts to land from the sea. Possible aircraft landing areas were blocked with old trucks, scrap boilers, large tree branches, and other obstacles. If materials were unavailable, furrows were plowed. Trenches soon crisscrossed beautiful parks, pineapple fields ready for harvest, and even school playgrounds far too small for any plane to use. All civilian airports were taken over by the armed forces, and all private planes were grounded.[32]

* * *

At 9:00 p.m. on Saturday, 6 December, in the continental United States, at Fort Lewis, Washington, a train waited at the siding to board the 161st Infantry Regiment. The soldiers of the 161st were bound for their port of embarkation, San Francisco. The regiment had been detached from the 41st Division in early November, and its members informed they were going to the Philippines. Brought up to full strength in the months preceding the departure date by filling mostly with volunteers, and a few non-volunteers from the Division's 162nd, 163rd, and 186th Regiments, the men in the 161st really wanted to go—but some were sent elsewhere. Thirty-six Chinese and Japanese soldiers were transferred, some with tears in their eyes.

Five young enlisted men who later banded together to write

a history of the 161ˢᵗ, recalled the sense of fun and adventure which motivated them toward a Philippine assignment, and what occurred in the ensuing thirty-six hours following their arrival to board the train. They recorded one historical fact about their regiment just prior to telling of the train trip to San Francisco.

ON THE 9ᵀᴴ DAY OF MAY, 1898, THE 161 HAD VOLUNTEERED AS A UNIT AND SAILED FOR THE PHILIPPINES IN THE SPANISH-AMERICAN WAR. SIX DAYS AFTER LANDING THE 161 WAS IN ACTION ON THE FRONT LINES, SUFFERED 12% CASUALTIES AND WAS CITED FOR VALOROUS CONDUCT IN THE BATTLE OF SANTA ANNA. IN 1899 THE REGIMENT SAILED FOR HOME, SPENDING A WEEK IN JAPAN ENROUTE. NOW WE WERE ON OUR WAY BACK.

"We weren't war-mad—bullets and bayonets scarcely entered our minds. We wanted adventure, and we figured the war was going East and we were going West—so what the hell? We were going to the Philippines to sit under a palm tree and live the life of Riley."

Telling of the 6-7 December train ride, Private Paul R. Shepard; Privates First Class Elson L. Matson, Jerome N. Eller, Bernard G. Rico; and Staff Sergeant Keith G. Crown wrote:

... It was cold and we were bundled up in overcoats, warmed with all the liquor we had been able to get hold of. With our packs on our backs and our barrack bags secure in the baggage car (a bag of clothes, one of alcoholic accessories) one by one we filled the cars.

The black night settled in around us; the lights from the train gleamed out, and the few people at the siding waved farewell. The couplings groaned and pulled as our train started to roll ...

TROOP TRAINS ARE A LIFE BY THEMSELVES, KITCHEN IN BAGGAGE CAR, MAGAZINES AND LITTERED PAPERS ALL OVER, A THICK

BLUE CLOUD OF CIGARETTE SMOKE. HERE AND THERE, A POKER GAME, PUNCTUATED BY A BURST OF PROFANITY OR A SURPRISED CHUCKLE TO ACCOMPANY AN UNEXPECTED FULL-HOUSE. THE NIGHT OF THE 6TH PASSED ON WITH A WORLD OUTSIDE AND A WORLD OF OUR OWN MOVING ALONG ON STEEL TRACKS.

TOWNS FLASHED BY IN THE DARK OF MIDNIGHT AS THE SOUTHERN PACIFIC CLICKED ALONG—PORTLAND, SPRINGFIELD, THE WILLAMETTE RIVER. THE MORNING OF DECEMBER 7TH DAWNED.......

Some of us were sitting in the smoking car playing poker. Nothing had changed; we were pretty chatty.

"I figure we're doing a smart thing—the war's going one way and we're going another."

"Just think of the big money exchange we're going to get out of our money over there in the Orient."

"Yeah, boy, those trips to China."

Most of all we mentally reveled in the easy life we were going to lead.

Shortly after noon the train stopped for a few minutes at a small station a few miles north of Klamath Falls, Oregon. The station master rushed out, "Say, have you guys heard? The Japs have bombed Pearl Harbor!"

Disbelief spread through the outfit. "Just what in hell was that guy talking about?" Our train started to move again. At Klamath Falls we were greeted by newsboys selling "Extras" with headlines screaming the news that the Japs had bombed Pearl Harbor. The railroad dispatcher had sent a message through for all trains to move cautiously—"Pearl Harbor has been bombed!" A couple of portable radios picked up faint flashes of news.

There began a lot of excited moving about the cars: "What was it?" "Did you get that? They bombed Pearl Harbor!" "Just another Orson Welles broadcast!"

And the poker games continued.

At Dundsmuir, California everything was confirmed.

> Double guards were put on the doors. Porters, conductors, soldiers tried to argue it wasn't so—inside us the belief deepened it was so.
>
> Machine gunners and pistol men demanded bayonets. In a matter of minutes peace was lost, the lethargic peace-time soldier awoke with a jolt. Live ammunition was issued throughout the train. From front to rear of the long train speculation buzzed as to our future. There was much singing until late at night—"Over There" and "There's a Long Long Trail A-winding . . . "[33]

When the 161st arrived in Oakland by train the morning of 8 December, the 34th Infantry Regiment had been encamped at the Army's Presidio in San Francisco, but was undergoing some major changes as a result of orders received the previous evening. On 7 December its equipment had already been loaded on the Matson Line's SS *Monterey* and *Matsonia*. The 34th, selected the outstanding regiment in the Carolina Maneuvers of 1941, was preparing to board the two ships on Monday, the day the 161st arrived. They, like the 161st, were on secret orders embarking for the Philippines. At 1800 hours on 7 December, the 34th received orders revoking their embarkation, and on Monday unloaded its equipment from the two ships and transported it to the Presidio by truck. Their destination was about to be changed.[34]

A Letter Home

At Pensacola Naval Air Station, Ensign Karl Border, now well along in flight training, wrote in his diary the evening of 7 December,

> Japan bombed Pearl Harbor today while their envoys were still talking peace, the traitorous skunks. Wonder how Bob and Joey are making out, and what the old Tennessee is doing tonight? The Japs have declared war and we will tomorrow, so now we're in it. Hope Minimus is o.k.

On Oahu, when Joey and Bob were jolted awake by the phone call from Lieutenant (jg) J.R. "Bud" Marron, one of the doctors on board the *Tennessee*, they were at first in disbelief. Their first thought was to turn on the radio. Announcers were repeating word of the attack as Bob hurriedly dressed and stormed out the downstairs door to return to duty. Joey was left to learn for herself what was occurring all around their apartment's neighborhood, and on the island. She heard radio announcers periodically repeating the refrain that Pearl Harbor and Hickam had been attacked by airplanes bearing the insignia of "the rising sun," all Army, Navy and Air Force personnel should report to their duty stations; along with announcements calling for policemen, firemen, medical and volunteer services to come to their place of work.

One profound shock followed another so rapidly the impact was difficult to absorb and almost impossible to understand. Yesterday had been so peaceful, so wonderful. Christmas had been just around the corner, with more shopping, plans for a party for the boys of the *Tennessee*'s 5th Division. So much to look forward to—Christmas in Hawaii. Now it was all changing. But not until night, and the next day, and the next night, and the next day, and on and on, would it begin to fully sink in. Warm, tropical Hawaii, with its dreamy music and gaiety; cocktail hours, sumptuous dinners and dancing in lovely hotels in Waikiki; the beach and clear Pacific waters, dinners and movies on the *Tennessee*; movies on the *West Virginia*, tea parties, golf, tennis, calls on senior officers and their wives, the gracious formality and peacetime traditions of the close-knit Navy family—all of it—gone.

Her first impulse after Bob left was the product of her experience as a newspaper reporter. She had written home yesterday, but she began writing another letter home, describing what she was seeing, which by this time was the second wave's attack. After the first page of descriptions, she began including more of what she was hearing over the radio—then told her dad and mother she was writing the letter "from time to time throughout the day." As the day wore on, she went to the apartment of Lieutenant Robert J. Foley, the aide to Admiral Bagley, to ask his wife what she had heard. There seemed little Joey could do but worry about Bob and his safety, and busy herself in their apartment. She didn't complete her letter until Monday, when she also knew martial law, including censorship, had been imposed throughout the Territory of Hawaii. She had to be thoughtful about the messages she conveyed to her parents.

Dec. 7—Sunday

Dearest Family –

Here it is. We're at war with Japan and Hawaii is in the middle. I don't know if you'll ever receive this letter, but I hope that when you do, all this mess will be over. This morning the phone rang at 9 A.M.. It was Bud Marron! a dr. on the Tennessee, who called to tell Bob that all naval officers were to report immediately. We couldn't quite believe it until we turned the radio on and there it was "Oahu is being attacked by enemy planes—please keep calm." Bob dashed out to Pearl Harbor. I hope he made it. Bombs have been falling at irregular intervals— one just hit about 5 blocks from here. I could hear the planes and the constant boom of the antiaircraft guns—the sky is dotted with puffs of smoke. Hickam Field is in flames and in that direction one can see the black smoke. Parachute troops have landed. Not many people have been killed—about 6 so far. A Japanese plane flew low over the streets of Wahiawa, machine-gunning everything and everybody. The Kaneohe Air Base is partially in flames and one of the main water lines has burst. A few are excited, but for the most part, everyone is calm. The radio stations have gone off the air, coming on for only official announcements. I am writing this from time to time throughout the day. The latest news is Kanehoe Air Base has been completely wiped out. 21 Jap ships have been sighted off Barbers Point— about 30 miles from the island. We are prepared for a bombardment at any time—the antiaircraft guns are still at it. It's still hard to realize that this is it. Of course I'm anxious about Bob, but I thank God that he is on a battleship and not in the air. It's sad, but I couldn't think of anything to say this morning when he left. All I shouted was—"Have fun. I love you." I know it won't be fun and he knows I love him. Then I cleaned the house, baked a cake, and read a magazine. Now I'm going to do dishes. If any nasty Japs come around here, I have some very good butcher knives which I can use to good advantage. Yesterday I took a pill for constipation and the funny part of it all is that if a bomb does hit the place, I'll probably be sitting in the biffy—which seems to be my main occupation—

Joey discontinued the letter home until Monday, and Saturday night wrote in her diary,

Woke up at 9—Bob had to go back ship—U.S. at war with Japan—Oahu attacked and bombed—parachute troops landed—Hickam in flames—also Kaneohe—Radios off—black-out night—to Foley's—home—spent night at Barb. M[orrison]'s—bed at 9—no lights.[35]

Fear, Anger and Tragedy: Hell Revisited on Good Men

In the meantime reality of war and all it meant was getting through to the general population, and the information was coming nearly all by word of mouth. Men and women who had seen fires and damage at Pearl Harbor or the airfields, been called to duty with the Territorial Guard and other agencies, or volunteered their assistance to medical facilities and transportation serving wounded and dying, were telling what they participated in or witnessed.

In spite of the tough wording of the martial law declaration, the civilian populace didn't hesitate to voluntarily assist Army units in digging trenches, bunkers, and filling sandbags in defensive positions the 24th and 25th Division's battalions were assigned to defend. Such activity freed up men carrying weapons to better prepare to do their duties should the Japanese attempt to land troops. Not until nightfall however would the full impact of the day's terrible events hit home all across Oahu.

When night came, it multiplied the nagging fears of another

attack. The tension was palpable. But there was something else. Boiling anger, deep resentment, and a mounting fury laced with a determination to strike back. It was a fury that stretched all across The Territory of Hawaii, and when General Short issued a comprehensive set of orders accompanying the Martial Law announcement, the orders added more tension to the mix. The orders were printed in the *Honolulu Star-Bulletin*'s 3rd Extra that afternoon:

If you are ordered by military personnel to obey a certain command, that order must be obeyed instantly and without question.

Avoid the slightest appearance of hostility in words or act.

Certain enemy agents have been apprehended and detained.

Civilians who go about their regular duties have nothing to fear.

All citizens are warned to watch their actions carefully, for any infraction of military rules and regulations will bring swift and harsh reprisals.

Prisoners when captured, will be turned over to the nearest military patrol, military guardhouse, police patrol or police station.

Information regarding suspicious persons will be telephoned to the provost marshal at Honolulu 2948.

A complete blackout of the entire territory will go into effect at nightfall tonight.

Anyone violating the blackout by showing a light will summarily be dealt with.

All civilian traffic except in case of dire emergency, will cease at dark.

In this emergency, I assure you that the armed forces are adequately dealing with the situation and that each and everyone of you can best serve his country by giving his whole hearted cooperation to the military and civilian governments.

Further instructions regarding civilians will be issued as need arises.

Keep your heads and do your duty as Americans.[36]

With radio stations silent, rumors started and remained rampant. People had been urged to stay off the phones to keep from jamming the lines. Literally thousands of men unaccustomed to routinely carrying or manning loaded weapons were now deployed throughout the island on full alert in fixed sentry or gun positions, or on patrol.

Air raid wardens patrolled nearly every city block in Honolulu, the ranks of the prewar group having been swollen by hundreds who had responded to radio appeals that morning. The youths of the Hawaii Territorial Guard stood lonely alert at twenty-five strategic locations.

The governor, the secretary of the territory, and the governor's private secretary grabbed a short rest at Washington Place. In his diary, Secretary Hite noted: "Dinner in dark pantry. Outside flares from Pearl Harbor plainly visible from lanai. During the night machine guns on Punchbowl kept firing at planes."

At a plantation hospital crowded with civilian and service casualties, a nurse wrote of the night of 7 December:

> It was a strange experience indeed working through long black hours with feeble assistance of a blue-covered flashlight which cast a weird shadow on the faces of the patients already unrecognizable by the charred flesh and violet purple coloring of Gentian violet. We spent the night stumbling up and down corridors, sneaking in doors to prevent the escape of dim light from the heat cradles, feeling for feeble pulsations in temples or wherever flesh was intact. The only natural part of the strange night was the intermittent crying of babies in the nursery at times when they felt they were entitled to food regardless of bombings.[37]

Seventeen-year old Frederick Kamaka told of his being called to guard duty that evening:

> About 2:00 in the afternoon, Lieutenant Mahikoa ordered all members of the school's rifle team to report to him, and I reported as directed. We were told that because of the possible invasion of the islands by the Japanese we would be assigned duties

to guard the girl's school area, the school's water tanks above the campus and the trail between the tanks and the school campus. He also advised us that all the ROTC 03 Rifles in our Armory had been taken for use by the Honolulu Territorial Guard to man the beaches around Oahu and to protect against possible landings by Japanese invasion troops. Without our ROTC weapons to use on our guard missions, we would have to use the .22-caliber rifles of the school rifle team, and 12 and 16 gauge shotguns, plus personal weapons that the Kamehameha teachers and staff possessed.

We were put on shifts of two hours with two students assigned on each shift to guard important water tanks, an assignment I received. I was assigned to guard the area above the water tanks and my companion guard was given the area below the tanks. Guarding during the first afternoon shift was fine, but when night came, we could imagine that there could be an enemy behind every swaying bush and tree. Then when the announcement was made of possible enemy paratroopers being dropped in the hills to disrupt or take over facilities like our water tanks, it increased tensions. Soon my fellow guard member and I found ourselves with our backs against each other as we tried to complete our tour of duty. About midnight, the rains came to add to our discomfort, soaking us to the skin as we were not issued raincoats. We didn't dare close our eyes for a minute while on our two-hour guard shift.[38]

Lieutenant Colonel Herbert H. Blackwell, an antiaircraft brigade executive officer who, after going without sleep for more than thirty-six hours following the attack, then slept for a few hours Monday night, recalled the nights, the tension, and anger in a letter home he began writing his family two days after the attack:

The first nights after the attack guards were posted everywhere, and it was extremely dangerous to go out at night, for fear of being shot . . . Monday night

I went to my quarters for a few hours of rest, and it sounded like a battlefield. Rifle and occasionally machine gun fire was heard on all sides, occurring about every one or two minutes. With much of the population here Japanese the threat of sabotage is great. However, these soldiers on guard were shooting on bushes when the wind would sway them, at any suspicious sounds, which may have been made by animals, etc. Whenever they heard or saw anything that did not respond to their challenge they shot at it . . . Fortunately, so far as I know only one of our own soldiers has been shot, which I think is very remarkable. I shall be very glad when we have a little moonlight again . . . No one gets very excited anymore. You would be surprised to see how our soldiers react to all this. Although they have been on duty almost continuously, with very little sleep or rest, enduring hardships, they are the happiest lot you ever saw. They all are just itching for the Japs to return, now that they are ready for them. You can't get one to go to sleep as long as there is any suspicion of attack. They are afraid they will miss a chance to get revenge. I will tell this little incident before I close.

The other day I saw three soldiers bringing in a suspected Jap spy which they caught under suspicious circumstances. The Jap was sullen and slow in following directions. One soldier was behind him with his bayonet pressing against his behind, and every now and then he would give him a slight push to speed him by. In either side was a soldier with a bayonet pressed against his ribs. When ever they wished him to change direction the bayonet was pressed into his off side, and he would immediately respond. He could not understand English so the soldiers resorted to this method of directing him. From the expressions on the faces of these soldiers I could see that they would have liked to have used the bayonets more violently. They were exercising extreme self-control. You need have no fear of the fighting spirit of our soldiers . . . [39]

Since the consolidated barracks at Hickam had been destroyed, many enlisted men slept that first night under trees, in the open under blankets, in pup tents, in any unlocked family quarters, or whatever shelter they could find. Members of the 17th Air Base Headquarters Group relocated for the night to an essentially undamaged wooden school building near the water tower. As friends were reunited, they rejoiced, then grieved for those who were killed or seriously wounded. After dark nervous men challenged anyone in sight and shouted at every shadow. Trigger-happy soldiers, sailors and Air Force men fired tracer bullets into the sky at the slightest provocation. Throughout the night, everyone was jumpy, convinced that the Japanese would be back to capture the island.[40]

It had been raining steadily at Wheeler since noon, and the troops were muddy and miserable that night. Charles Hendrix was shaking from head to foot, the first time he had ever been cold in Hawaii. Then someone yelled "Gas!" and pandemonium erupted until each man found his gas mask and put it on, adding to his discomfort and misery. In the eerie darkness, trucks crept about slowly, their lights dimmed by sheets of carbon paper taped over the headlights. Shots rang out as sentries fired at shadows and sometimes at each other, often not even waiting for a response to their challenge. The sign and countersign the first night of war were "George Washington" and "Valley Forge"— for sentries calm enough to listen.[41]

The long night wore on. Suddenly, someone thought he saw a Japanese and then was sure he saw a Japanese, and fired. The result was a long, continuous wave of rifle fire as everyone in the Wheeler-Schofield perimeter fired simultaneously. Thousands of rounds of ammunition arched harmlessly into empty fields, serving only to ease some of the tension. Then, on the narrow-gauge railroad tracks running through the field, a locomotive pulling a few cars chugged its way into a siding. As it stopped armed guards jumped down and said they saw no Japanese on the way from Honolulu, then marched up the street to the 14th Pursuit Wing headquarters. The Hawaiian train crew stayed in the cab, afraid to leave for fear of being mistaken for Japanese, so Private Woodrum and another person took them some coffee.

A few minutes later, a loud hissing sound pierced the night and someone shouted at the top of his lungs, "Gas! Gas!" Everyone donned gas masks, looking strange with their bulging eyepieces and dangling throat tubes. A sergeant came back after investigating and ripped off his mask, shouting, "Take'em off. It's just that damned engine letting off steam." Everyone cursed the train crew.

A little later, a command car came through the gate and parked at the edge of the field. Several men climbed out and began walking toward Woodrum and others in the group, with a man in the center who obviously was the leader. Seeing the glitter of rank on the officer's shoulder, they started to come to attention, but the man held out his hand and said, "At ease, men, at ease." Some one came out of the cook tent with a blue flashlight, and they saw stars on his shoulders. It was Brigadier General Howard C. Davidson, the 14th Pursuit Wing commander, who in the midst of the raid that morning was down on the flight line working feverishly beside his men, disengaging undamaged airplanes to move them away from the river of fire engulfing the Wheeler flight line and hangars.

He told them "We're going to be all right even though we took a beating." He didn't think the Japanese would return, but said, "we would be more ready for them if they did." With him were three pilots who got off the ground and shot down some Japanese planes—Lieutenants Taylor, Welch and Rasmussen. They answered all the questions asked, while the general stood back and listened, interjecting a remark occasionally, watching as the men began to relax a little. This seemed to be the main reason for the visit. Finally, General Davidson said there were other people to see before the pilots could sleep, and they all walked back to the command car and drove away.[42]

At Bellows, members of the 298th Infantry worked all night putting gun emplacements and stringing barbed wire on the beach, expecting a Japanese landing at daylight. Others without critical jobs were mustered into guard duty, both on the beaches and within the field. Three days later, much to the relief of the Army Air Force men, infantrymen took over sentry duties. All had been alarmed at the number of shots fired for no reason other than nerves and inexperience.

On the first night, for example, a call was put out that "the Japs were landing on the beach" and everyone was ordered to fix bayonets and head out there. As the first of their group topped the sand dunes, beach guards opened fire, fortunately for them, over their heads, then informed them that the reported landing was false. Tension and panic caused several near tragedies even in the tent area, so it was not safe to walk around. Consequently, most of the men stayed all night in foxholes dug in the sand.[43]

The first night after the attack, several factors combined to pile another tragedy on top of a day overflowing with tragedy. The still-burning *Arizona* bathed Pearl Harbor in an eerie, flickering light, causing the crews of *Maryland*, *Tennessee* and all the other relatively undamaged ships still in the harbor to be more than a bit concerned. On the upturned hull of the *Oklahoma*, rescue operations were in progress, with men trying to cut their way through to desperate, terrorized sailors trapped inside her.

While unscathed ships were darkened and the rest of the island was blacked out, the one burning ship provided a beacon for enemy planes that might be launched against Pearl Harbor in a night raid. All the ready ammunition boxes on the ships were full, and gun crews waited restlessly, many anxious for the enemy to dare show himself again. They were ready, on the ships particularly, on Ford Island; in the now-deployed 251st Coast Artillery antiaircraft batteries, including a battery deployed on Ford Island; 24th and 25th Division Army units deployed to nearby beach areas, and everywhere on Oahu.

Adding to the tension was the still-prevalent fear of sabotage; the all-too-frequent sounds of random, night-time gunfire in outlying areas, caused by hair trigger reactions; rumors of approaching airplanes and ships, reports of enemy paratroopers which began during the morning, the reasonable assumption of a possible invasion; and thousands of inexperienced, heavily armed men deployed throughout the island, on high alert, angry, frustrated, and ready for a fight. Then came the totally unexpected approach of six F4F Wildcat fighters from the *Enterprise*'s Fighting Squadron Six (VF-6), setting off a firestorm of antiaircraft fire. The result was a wrenching friendly fire incident that to this day many believe was antiaircraft fire against more Japanese raiders.

The tragic train of events was set in motion during the recovery of the nineteen TBD-1 torpedo bombers, six SBD scout aircraft and the six F4F fighters aboard *Enterprise* when they returned from a search for the Japanese strike force. The standard launch and recovery sequence for carrier operations was to launch the fighters first, and land them last if possible, to ensure the slower, more vulnerable aircraft had fighter cover throughout the mission. The first launch for the mission was at 1642 hours, still daylight, when the lead fighter left the carrier's deck, and the first recovery of the torpedo bombers began at 2017, night time, three hours and thirty-five minutes later. At 2038, torpedo bomber 6-T-13 crashed into No. 1 barrier on the *Enterprise*. There were no injuries or damage, but there was a delay in clearing the aircraft and barrier. The delay, and night carrier landings, which are always more difficult, stretched out the recovery unacceptably for the waiting fighters. Because of low fuel state they were diverted to Ford Island. It wasn't until 2113 hours that the mission's last aircraft, and the last aircraft for the night of 7 December, came aboard *Enterprise*—about the same time the furious barrage over Pearl Harbor and Ford Island was taking its toll on VF-6.[44]

On Ford Island, Lieutenant Commander E.B. Wilkins, the operations officer, earlier received word friendly airplanes were approaching to land. He sent out reliable men in cars, motorcycles and other means of transportation, to warn all riflemen and machine gunners to hold their fire. After several false alarms as to the immediacy of the approach, he received word leading him to believe the planes would be landing in a short time. He again ordered word passed to the defense forces, having particular regard to men stationed adjacent to the southwest portion of the field, from which direction the planes would normally approach. Wilkins then drove to the west side of the field, known as the Luke Field side, and took a position well out on the warming platform at hangar #133 to direct planes to their parking area and give what service might be needed.

After a few minutes he saw planes approaching from the general direction of Hickam Field. At first he saw only four planes in sections of two each. An instant later he saw that one section had three planes and heard one of the men nearby say "There's six of them." He reported he never saw the sixth plane, but all running lights were burning and the planes appeared to be flying up the Pearl Harbor Channel. He recalled they must have been in the close proximity of Hospital Point when he heard the first shots fired. He went on to write on 10 December, "In less than five seconds the entire Pearl Harbor area was firing. The planes flew up dry dock channel at an estimated 300 feet altitude until they disappeared from my view at a point a little northeast of the administration building. "

Lieutenant Frank A. Erickson, US Coast Guard, was in the landplane control tower when the six Enterprise planes were fired upon, as was Lieutenant Commander Young, commander of the *Enterprise* Air Group, who assumed control to bring the planes in. Two flood light trucks with lights on were stationed at the southwest end of the runway and green lights were placed at the northwest end to mark the corner of the runway. Erickson reported the following traffic passed between the tower and the planes:

> TOWER: Turn on your running lights, make the approach from Barbers Point. Come in as low as possible.
> PLANE: (Believed to be Blue 18, the lead aircraft): Am making one pass at the field.
> TOWER: Do not make a pass at field. Turn on running lights and come in as low as possible.
> BLUE 18: (To planes in formation): Close in, I am going to make one pass at the field. (The planes were then approximately over the dry dock channel).
> TOWER: Do not make pass at field, come straight in. (At this time firing started apparently from surface vessels).
> ONE OF THE PLANES: What the hell is wrong down there?
> TOWER: Turn off your lights and beat it. (One plane got on the field during the firing). Later instructions were again given to approach low from Barbers Point with running lights on and come straight in. Only one other plane from this group managed to get in.

No one knows which gun or ship fired the first rounds, but when the firing began, it was deadly. For the time, 2101 hours, the *Maryland*'s Navigator, Lieutenant Commander Hugh W. Hadley, logged "Aircraft with running lights approached ship in bombing position and not in landing position for Ford Island. All ships opened fire . . . " At 2108, he recorded, "Commander Patrol Wing TWO ordered 'Cease fire.'" Two minutes later, CincPac and Patrol Wing TWO ordered "Disregard cease fire." The countermanded order introduced confusion into an already volatile circumstance. Astern of *Maryland*, *Tennessee*'s navigator, Lieutenant Commander Jasper T. Acuff recorded, "At 2104 commenced firing on planes crossing over ship. 2109 ceased firing . . . "[45]

When the six *Enterprise* aircraft approached Ford Island, the 251st Coast Artillery's Battery G was in position at the submarine base, with Battery H on Ford Island. At 2003 hours seventy-five Marines armed with ten .30-caliber and eight .50-caliber machine guns reinforced Battery H. At 2054 came the moonrise, beginning to add more light—and shadows—to the night. According to the 251st War Diary, at 2115 both batteries, and undoubtedly the reinforcing Marines, opened fire.[46]

At 2049 the 25th Infantry Division, now deployed in its planned defensive sectors sent a FLASH message to all division units. "Unidentified plane flying low toward Pearl Harbor. Received from Wailupe." Someone had reported sighting the inbound F4Fs. At 2103, with VF-6 aircraft passing near Hickam, another FLASH: "Enemy attacking Hickam Field." At 2106: "Enemy planes attacking Pearl Harbor." Then at 2112, another message to the Division: "No instructions regarding friendly planes rocking wings as means of identification. 5th Column tactics [sabotage tactics] suspected." At 2116 another FLASH message: "Enemy planes flying toward Schofield toward Newark. (and how!)" Then, finally, at 2128, FLASH: "To all stations; those are our planes trying to land—pass along to all sectors—this report from Navy."[47]

The message was too late. Jack Leaming, the Radioman-Gunner from *Enterprise*'s

VS-6 and had been on the nine-plane search for the Japanese strike force that afternoon, was on Ford Island for the night, in the unit's hangar, and had just been assigned a cot next to an ensign when the night exploded into furious gunfire. He grabbed his flight gear and ran for 6-S-7, his airplane. He recalled, "Outside every available machine gun and AA battery around was firing at some incoming planes. I arrived outside in time to see a plane crash and explode north of Ford Island. Then, another trying to land was fired [caught on fire] over the dry dock area and the pilot bailed out." The explosion north of Ford Island was Ensign Herbert H. Menges' F4F slamming into a house in Pearl City, then into a nearby gully. The plane he saw "fired over the drydock area" was Ensign Eric Allen's.

Reported in numerous ship's deck logs, seen and heard from almost every area south of Oahu's mountain ranges, and from

Honolulu to the southern and southwestern shores of the island, perhaps if nothing else, the fierce reaction demonstrated that the enemy—if they chose to strike again—would probably have paid dearly—even though they wouldn't be attacking with aircraft running lights blinking.

Four of the six airplanes from Fighting Squadron Six, were shot down within five to eight minutes, resulting in the deaths of three pilots, and the injury of a fourth. A fifth pilot attempted to land at Ewa, but his engine quit, probably due to fuel starvation or engine damage, and he parachuted to safety. With running lights on, the flight had apparently taken spacing in two sections, with the lead aircraft pulling ahead to make the low pass during the descending approach to Ford Island—to give each section adequate spacing and lateral separation on landing roll out on the wide runway. Unfortunately, taking spacing for landing, with two sections of aircraft on a slow, final approach, had just the opposite effect in terms of safety. The still-angry, hair-trigger, hornets' nest of gunners observing their approach, guns armed and ready, could concentrate fire on each section, and on each airplane one at a time when the formation scattered. But that wasn't all. The storm of antiaircraft fire had other sad consequences.

Ironically, on board the USS *Argonne*, moored bow-toward-the-northeast across the main channel from Ford Island, there were two other casualties. At 2116, Seaman Second Class Pallas F. Brown who that morning narrowly escaped with his life from the capsizing *Utah*, was killed by a .50-caliber machine gun bullet fired from somewhere to the west. The stray round passed through the port side of *Argonne* at frame 70, struck another *Utah* survivor, Seaman First Class W.A. Price, in the left arm before mortally wounding Pallas Brown.[48]

The flight's former second in command that night, wrote of his experiences years later when he was Captain Jim Daniels, United States Navy, retired, in Kailua, Hawaii:

> I was to be second-in-command of a flight of six F4F-4 fighters from the USS Enterprise that were to escort 19 torpedo planes and six scout planes on our way to find the Japanese Fleet, which a report said had been located.
>
> Unfortunately, the report was erroneous, as we

later found out. However, we were launched and
went out some 200 miles.

It was dark when we returned to the ship and
my flight leader talked to the Enterprise, and asked
permission to land. The ship said ". . . go into Pearl
Harbor," and gave us coded direction.

We turned on the heading toward Pearl.
Everything was blacked out except burning ships,
which we thought were burning cane fields. It was
8:30 Sunday night.

As we passed Diamond Head we turned toward
Ford Island in a loose formation and were given
permission to land. Most of our gauges had been
indicating we were running out of fuel for the last
20 minutes.

When we broke formation in preparation for
landing, everything in Pearl Harbor opened up on us
with their antiaircraft batteries. The sky was ablaze
with gun tracers . . . I called the Ford Island tower
and told them I was coming in. I put my wheels
down and headed right back over the harbor about
50 feet over the water.

I roared right past the foretop of the Nevada.
They turned all their guns on me but nothing
connected.

Moments later I touched the runway. I overshot,
[and landed long]. There were two crash trucks in
front of me at the end of the runway. I slammed
on the brakes and spun around in a full circle on
the green of the golf course just beyond the field.I
taxied back up the field. A Marine gunner sprayed
the plane with bullets. He just missed my head.

Of the six planes and pilots I was the only one to
land intact: three others were killed.

After this frightening experience, I went to the
BOQ to find a bed. I could see and hear the Arizona
still burning. I wanted to call my wife who was
staying east of Pearl City but assumed with all the
damage around that there would be no telephone
service. I picked up the phone anyway, and to my

surprise got a dial tone. To my complete surprise I dialed my number and got through to my wife.

I was the luckiest man in the Navy on Dec. 7, 1941.[49]

Wheeler Field personnel, armed and waiting for the feared invasion, witnessed the spectacular display of firepower from Pearl Harbor and Hickam triggered by the approach of F4Fs from *Enterprise*. Thousands of tracer bullets and rounds of antiaircraft fire crisscrossed the sky, which to witnesses, appeared to light up like an orange sheet of flame.

The F4Fs came toward Ford Island on a long final approach, heading approximately 020 degrees. Men manning gun positions along the beach to the south and southwest of Hickam Field, and on Hickam, undoubtedly heard and sighted the inbound aircraft and may have opened fire first. Lieutenant (jg) Francis F. Hebel, the squadron commander, was leading the flight, flying Bureau Number 3906, attempting to land at Ford Island, when his plane was hit by friendly ground fire.

Lieutenant Hebel turned left approximately forty-five degrees, toward Wheeler Field, adjacent to Schofield Barracks, apparently hoping to land there. He flew along the Schofield perimeter, and two .50-caliber machine guns positioned north of the highway began chattering away. He appeared to be attempting a forced landing in a pineapple field, when his plane began to slowly roll over before it nosed down, skidded, cart-wheeled and broke in two.

Shortly afterward a second aircraft flying roughly the same route crashed further up the gully from the first. Ensign Herb Menges' aircraft, Bureau Number 3935, had been hit by friendly ground fire while attempting to land at Ford Island. Like his flight leader, he turned left apparently hoping to land at Wheeler Field. He was killed in Pearl City when his plane crashed into a house and came to rest in the gully almost on its back, its canopy smashed, the pilot hanging suspended through the opening.

Wheeler field men saw the airplanes crash, uncertain if they had brought them down, and were the first to arrive at both crash sites. The first aircraft they reached was in the gully. They stopped abruptly upon seeing the insignia on the fuselage, which identified the plane as U.S. Navy. Several men eased the pilot from the aircraft and laid him down.

Others raced on toward the airplane in the pineapple field,

which they quickly realized was U.S. Navy also. They carried both pilots to the highway, and waited for the ambulance called to take them to the Schofield Hospital. Both pilots were believed to be dead on arrival at the hospital, but one wasn't. Lieutenant Hebel was apparently one of the last two patients operated on by Dr. Leonard Heaton in the surgeon's Schofield Barracks Hospital operating room late that night. Dr. Heaton remarked in his diary for 7 December, "Got very little sleep that night. We had two bad cases in—one a . . . flyer shot down over Schofield by our own guns—he died shortly after leaving the table . . . "[50]

One of the two .50-caliber gunners was certain he had shot down at least one of the planes. He had been depressed all day after seeing some close friends killed in the barracks during the attack that morning. All day long he wanted to kill Japanese so badly that when the chance came he took advantage of it. When he learned that the plane he believed he had shot down was American, he fell apart.[51]

Ensign David Flynn, was flying Bureau Number 3909 attempting to land at Ford Island when his plane was hit by friendly ground fire. He turned left toward the southwest and the Mooring Mast Field at Ewa, intending to land there. His engine quit four miles from the field, and he successfully parachuted to safety. He was found ten days later in Tripler Army Hospital, with a broken leg.

Ensign Gayle Hermann, flying Bureau Number 3982, dead-sticked his airplane [landed his plane with a dead engine] onto the Ford Island golf course, just beyond the far end of the runway, after the aircraft took a 5-inch shell through the engine. Fortunately, the shell didn't explode on contact, but passed through the engine—or he would probably have been killed. The airplane was badly damaged but he "walked away from it" uninjured.

Ensign Eric Allen was flying Bureau Number 3938, attempting to land at Ford Island, when his plane was hit and soon caught fire. He turned right, apparently crossing over the damaged and sunk battleships on the east side of the island, and was above the main channel when the aircraft exploded and he bailed out. He was hit by a .50-caliber machine gun bullet. The harbor auxiliary, *Vireo* (AM-52), was alongside the *California* doing salvage work when Ensign Allen fell astern the *Vireo*, whose crew picked him up and identified him as an *Enterprise* aviator. The ship immediately sent a message to assure harbor control that the planes in the air were *Enterprise* planes. Ensign Allen was transferred to the *California*, and then to the Naval Hospital, where he died.[52]

Later that evening, Jack Leaming came across a small group of women, and two or three of them were crying. He learned they were the widows of the three pilots who had been killed.[53]

Two More Small Victories: Another Midget Submarine and The First Prisoner of War

On board the *Maryland* and other ships in the harbor, at 0035 hours the morning of 8 December information was received that friendly patrol planes would take off in the Pearl Harbor Channel between 0100 and 0200 and that Army and Navy aircraft would take off one hour before dawn. "Army designated 0600 as friendly dawn." In spite of the messages traffic, heightened tension and hair triggers kept guns banging away at reported "enemy aircraft" repeatedly until finally, at 0558, the commander of Patrol Squadron 14 messaged, "All U.S. Planes in air."[54]

At 6:00 a.m., 8 December—4:00 a.m. in Hawaii—the Southern Pacific train carrying the Philippines-bound 161st Regiment from Ft. Lewis, Washington, pulled into San Francisco. The four soldiers who in September 1944 began writing the regimental history, recalled,

> . . . Up and down the line of cars, heads stuck out of windows, necks craned to see the sights, to wave back at beautiful girls in housecoats and pajamas. With our necks still craned, we rolled under the Oakland Bay Bridge with its big pylons and towering steel gray supports. It wasn't long before our gripes made us wish we'd never heard of San Francisco.
> . . . Heavy weapons companies and Service Company had already arrived in San Francisco and were quartered on Angel Island. We waited on board the train as the nation listened to President Roosevelt's speech . . . [55]

He began his address at 12:30 p.m. Eastern time, 9:30 a.m. in

San Francisco, 7:30 in Hawaii. All over the United States, Hawaii, and many other parts of the world people gathered around radios and listened.

He began speaking at 12:30 p.m. Washington time, and his speech lasted eight minutes. It took Congress thirty-three minutes to act on his request for a declaration of war on Japan. The Senate voted 88 to 0, the House 388 to 1. Representative Jeannette Rankin from Montana, was the lone dissenting vote, and earned the distinction of being the only member of Congress to vote against entry into both world wars.[56] The president's speech was measured, yet powerful:

> Mr. Vice President, and Mr. Speaker, and Members of the Senate and House of
> Representatives: Yesterday, December 7, 1941— a date which will live in infamy—the United States of America was suddenly and deliberately attacked by naval and air forces of the Empire of Japan.
> The United States was at peace with that Nation and, at the solicitation of Japan, was still in conversation with its Government and its Emperor looking toward the maintenance of peace in the Pacific. Indeed, one hour after Japanese air squadrons had commenced bombing in the American Island of Oahu, the Japanese Ambassador to the United States and his colleague delivered to our Secretary of State a formal reply to a recent American message. And while this reply stated that it seemed useless to continue the existing diplomatic negotiations, it contained no threat or hint of war or of armed attack.
> It will be recorded that the distance of Hawaii from Japan makes it obvious that the attack was deliberately planned many days or even weeks ago. During the intervening time the Japanese Government has deliberately sought to deceive the United States by false statements and expressions of hope for continued peace.
> The attack yesterday on the Hawaiian Islands has caused severe damage to American naval and military forces. I regret to tell you that very many American lives have been lost. In addition American

ships have been reported torpedoed on the high seas between San Francisco and Honolulu.

Yesterday the Japanese Government also launched an attack against Malaya. Last night Japanese forces attacked Hong Kong. Last night Japanese forces attacked Guam. Last night Japanese forces attacked the Philippine Islands. Last night the Japanese attacked Wake Island. And this morning the Japanese attacked Midway Island. Japan has, therefore, undertaken a surprise offensive extending throughout the Pacific area. The facts of yesterday and today speak for themselves. The people of the United States have already formed their opinions and well understand the implications to the very life and safety of our Nation.

As Commander in Chief of the Army and Navy I have directed that all measures be taken for our defense.

But always will our whole Nation remember the character of the onslaught against us. No matter how long it may take us to overcome this premeditated invasion, the American people in their righteous might will win through to absolute victory. I believe that I interpret the will of the Congress and of the people when I assert that we will not only defend ourselves to the uttermost but will make it very certain that this form of treachery shall never again endanger us.

Hostilities exist. There is no blinking at the fact that our people, our territory, and our interests are in grave danger. With confidence in our armed forces— with the unbounding determination of our people— we will gain the inevitable triumph—so help us God.

I ask that the Congress declare that since the unprovoked and dastardly attack by Japan on Sunday, December 7, 1941, a state of war has existed between the United States and the Japanese Empire.[57]

President Franklin Delano Roosevelt signs the Declaration
of War against the Empire of Japan. NPSAM

On Oahu 8 December, dawn passed without the reappearance of the enemy, but early morning airborne patrols were launched, searching for the Japanese strike force. At Bellows Field, several of the 86th Observation Squadron personnel, including First Lieutenant Jean K. Lambert, spent the night in the operations shack listening to the radio. The Hawaiian Department Headquarters alerted them to begin reconnaissance flights after dawn. Between 0600 and 0700 preparations were underway for the first missions when a call came from the control tower alerting them to "something strange in the water, out by the reef, of the beach end of the runway."

Major Charles B. Stewart, the squadron commander, sent Lambert and First Lieutenant James T. Lewis up to see what it was. As soon as their 0-47 aircraft was airborne, Lewis began circling the reef area while Lambert crawled down into the "greenhouse," the plane's observation belly, to get an unobstructed view. It wasn't light enough to use the aerial camera, so he just scanned the ocean with his naked eyes and quickly saw a Japanese midget submarine.

A Japanese midget submarine lies beached near Bellows Field the morning of 8 December, on the windward side of Oahu. The midget's mother boat was submarine *I-22*. NPSAM

The surf was high, and the big waves rolled the sub to an upright position, allowing Lambert to see the conning tower. The sub was obviously hung up on the reef, and there was no sign of life. Lambert immediately called Major Stewart on the radio to describe the scene below and told Stewart he would make one or two sketches of the sub, since the light was insufficient to take pictures. Stewart approved and gave instructions to them to get back after they had seen enough. They circled at low altitude for another ten to fifteen minutes, returned to Bellows and briefed the major, who then called Department Headquarters to report the situation.

In the meantime, Lieutenant Paul S. Plybon, Executive Officer of G Company, from the 25th Infantry Division's 298th Regiment—which had bivouacked for weeks in the ironwood grove at the end of the Bellows runway, took Corporal David Akui with him on beach patrol just before dawn. When it was light enough, he scanned the bay through his high-powered binoculars and saw what he believed to be a lobster stake near the entrance to the reef. As they watched, a wave broke on the "stake," revealing the top of the submarine's conning tower.

About that time, there was a flash of white when a big comber broke in front of them, and they saw it was a man struggling in the surf. They waded out and brought him in when the next wave washed him closer to shore—and learned they had captured the commander of the sub, Ensign Kazuo Sakamaki. He had been fighting against the giant waves for some time and finally lost consciousness.

They took him to the operations shack and provided him a blanket, as he was cold and exhausted. Major Stewart again called Hawaiian Department Headquarters, this time to report the sub's officer was in custody. In a very short time, Second Lieutenant Lee E. Metcalf of the 23rd Bomb Squadron at Hickam Field arrived at Bellows, accompanying a military intelligence staff member, to pick up the prisoner.

In the course of his interrogation, Sakamaki stated he was twenty-four years old, an officer of the Japanese Navy, and a graduate of the Imperial Naval Academy. He was the commanding officer and navigator of the midget sub. His shipmate, Kiyoshi Inagaki, was the engineer, and had drowned in the rough surf. (His body washed up on the beach three days later.)

Sakamaki was greatly distressed over the "disgrace" of being captured and begged to be killed. He stated that he wished to commit suicide and had not done so at the time of landing on shore because the possibility had remained of making good his escape and rejoining the Japanese Navy. Now that he was disgraced he did not want his name or ship information to be sent back to Japan. Ensign Kazuo Sakamaki was the first prisoner of war captured by the United States in World War II and became known as POW No. 1.

Sakamaki's midget sub, which had an inoperative gyrocompass, had been depth-charged by two destroyers, twice struck a reef at the Pearl Harbor entrance, and finally drifted east until it lodged on the coral reef off Bellows Field. About mid-morning on 8 December, some Navy officers arrived at Bellows to look at the submarine, then recommended to their senior officers that the sub be freed from the reef by dive bombing around it. A little later, a Navy plane flew over and dropped a few bombs in the vicinity of the submarine, with no visible effect. It was almost noon.

The 86th Observation Squdron had a huge raft, constructed of heavy lumber with empty 50-gallon drums as flotation gear, which was usually anchored out by the reef for swimming and other activities. That day, however, it was up on shore for maintenance. Practically everyone in the squadron donned swimming trunks and helped launch the raft, after first affixing a steel cable to the submarine's bow area, then attached the other end of the cable to a huge bulldozer used for construction work at Bellows.

The bulldozer then reeled in the cable on the drum attached to it and dragged the midget off the reef and up onto the beach. Shortly afterward, a Navy technical intelligence unit from Pearl Harbor arrived with an 18-wheel flatbed trailer and hauled away the sub. So it was that little Bellows Field in Waimanalo had the honor of capturing not only the first prisoner of war for America but also the first "prize" of war. This, after a long day of tragedy, confusion, loss of life, and despair, provided a glimmer of optimism and hope. It was another step on the long road back.[58]

While the early morning sighting of the midget submarine was generating excitement at Bellows Field, on board the *Maryland*, where the crew could see the fires still burning on the shattered *Arizona*, at 0930 hours, a message to the Pacific Fleet in Pearl Harbor, from Admiral Kimmel, was posted throughout the ship.

"Your conduct and action have been splendid. We took a blow yesterday. It will not be a short war. We will give many heavy blows to the Japanese. Carry on."[59]

Divers Arrive to Aid in Rescue and Salvage Work

During the same period, the big, four-engine PB2Y seaplane carrying nine Navy divers, four Army colonels, three Navy captains and several civilians from San Diego was nearing Oahu after a long, overnight flight.

Metalsmith First Class Eward C. Raymer, the senior petty officer among the divers, carried with him the records of Robert "Moon" Mullen, his closest Navy "buddy," plus those of Tony Salvatore, Andy Davis, Bill Rush, Ben Apple, Jimmy Willson, Martin Palmer, and Cameron Walker.

The aircraft commander came on the speaker, reporting that the landing site had been changed from Ford Island in Pearl Harbor to NAS Kaneohe Bay, on the windward side of the island. He told the passengers there were a lot of nervous gunners in and around Pearl Harbor and four or five carrier aircraft from the *Enterprise* had been shot down the previous evening. He also noted that during night patrols armed sentries were shooting first and asking questions later. The pilot advised them that dawn would be breaking soon and he would make a flyby of Pearl Harbor, keeping out of gun range on the way around the island to Kaneohe Bay.

Edward Raymer recalled his reaction as he peered out the window during the flyby.

> We were awakened by the pilot's voice. He reported that he had just made contact with two U.S. Navy fighter aircraft that would be escorting the plane into Oahu. Our estimated time of arrival was thirty minutes away . . . The sun was just coming up out of the ocean when Oahu came into view. I was numbed by shock and disbelief at the panorama of wholesale destruction below. The airfields of Wheeler, Hickam, and Ford Island had been burned out. Damaged

planes were tossed about like abandoned toys
on their runways. Pearl Harbor was a disaster.
Although the ships could not be identified, it looked
as if there were at least twenty, either damaged or
sunk, and most of these appeared to be the pride
of the Navy, the battleships . . . I stared in horror at
America's terrible loss. There is no longer any doubt
in my mind about our final destination or what our
job would be.

After their plane landed, a Navy bus transported them across
the island to the Receiving Station at Pearl Harbor. They were
issued lockers and bunks in the last barrack in the row of
buildings, and were the only occupants. The Officer of the Deck
directed them to report to the newly formed Salvage Unit at the
Pearl Harbor Naval Ship Yard. Warrant Officer Albert Calhoun,
the designated officer in charge, looked tired and harassed. He
told his new charges he hadn't closed his eyes for twenty-four
hours.

Raymer handed their records to his new supervisor, and
inquired of their diving assignments. The bosun ordered them
to take a truck and pick up four sets of diving gear from the
submarine base. When they returned he sent them to 1010 dock,
where they selected a suitable sampan from the dozen that were
tied up. Alien Japanese fishermen had owned them but they had
been confiscated earlier by the U.S. government. Aliens weren't
permitted to own boats in Hawaii.

They selected a seventy-foot craft, installed a diving air
compressor, and outfitted it with two complete sets of deep-sea
diving gear. After spending three hours equipping the boat, they
reported back to Calhoun. They took seats in a room adjoining
his office, and Raymer gazed out the large windows lining the
room, aghast at the morbid scene of destruction in the harbor.

Before I start on the list of damaged and sunken
ships, I need to find out a little more about each of
you. Right now all I have is a list of names and a pile
of service records. My boss, Lieutenant Howard E.
Haynes, whom you will meet later, will want to
know about your Navy background, what your
specialties are, qualifications, et cetera. So just hit

the high points and keep it brief. Raymer, let's start with you and work clockwise around the room.

"Raymer, metalsmith first class. Much of my experience has been welding, and I am a qualified pressure hull welder. I served aboard the *Vestal*. I have practiced underwater arc welding and cutting with a gas torch." Following his remarks, the rest of the divers indicated their repair specialties and work experiences.

Calhoun then said, "Welcome aboard the Salvage Unit. You will be attached to this command on temporary additional duty, which may not be so temporary judging from the amount of diving work you see before you." The bosun read them a directive from the commander in chief, Pacific, that ordered all repair facilities to get the least damaged ships back in fighting condition first. He also told them that their primary work would involve raising the sunken battleships, since few of the ships afloat suffered underwater damage.

To the best of Raymer's knowledge no one had ever raised a battle-damaged battleship before. No salvage histories or guidelines were available to educate the divers. The divers' perceptions of what was involved in raising such a ship were very restricted. From a practical and logical viewpoint, Raymer opined the exterior holes in the hull must be made watertight first. Then the interior of the ship would be emptied of water by pumping or being blown dry with compressed air. But Raymer had no idea how all this would be accomplished or how long it would take.

Calhoun then launched into an account of the attack the day before and reviewed the damage suffered by the sunken battleships. The last ship on the list was the *Oklahoma*. He said she was struck amidships on her port side by seven torpedoes. A gash two hundred feet long had been opened in her hull and she took a thirty-degree list to port, bursting her mooring lines to the *Maryland*, inboard of her, and rolled upside down. Four hundred men were trapped inside and maximum efforts were under way to rescue them.

The bosun gave them their assignments for the afternoon. They were to proceed to the *Oklahoma* and report to Commander Kenworthy. If he had no diving work for them, they would proceed to the *Nevada* and report to Lieutenant Commander Thomas. They climbed into the sampan and headed out through the dead sea of bunker oil strewn with flotsam and wreckage. Bill Rush inched the sampan through the debris until they reached the *Oklahoma*. As they pulled alongside, Raymer wondered out loud if it was possible that anyone was still alive in the hulk.

There was tremendous activity around the *Oklahoma*. Floodlights had been set up and the bottom hull was crawling with sailors and shipyard workmen. Pneumatic hammers reverberated against the steel bottom plates, beating out a cadence that could be heard around the harbor. It sent a message of hope to the men trapped below, assuring them that help was on the way. Raymer's buddy, "Moon" Mullen, asked one of the workers why they were chiseling out holes in the bottom when a cutting torch would be so much faster. The worker replied that they had tried that yesterday and the toxic fumes from the burning paint killed two trapped men. Now the only safe way to rescue the men was to chisel holes in the bottom hull. The nine divers also learned eight men were rescued just thirty minutes before the divers arrived and had been sent to the hospital for observation after their terrifying experience. Commander Kenworthy didn't need the divers on *Oklahoma*, so they proceeded to the *Nevada*.

All told, thirty-one sailors were released from their underwater tomb before rescue efforts were abandoned. Machinist Mate Second Class W.F. Staff, was one of the last men rescued at 2:00 a.m., Tuesday, 9 December 1941. His statement testifies to the mounting terror the survivors experienced.

> Sunday morning at 0750 on 7 December 1941, I was in the Carpenter Shop when the general alarm was sounded. I immediately went along the starboard side of the third deck to my battle station. I felt several explosions on the way to Repair II. When I got to Repair II I took my phones and went to get a flashlight but they were locked up so I went on down to A-28, the forward air compressor room, and started to set Zed. There was an electrician's mate and fireman also, Centers, J.P., Machinist Mate Second Class and myself in the compartment. When

the lights went out the fireman and electrician's mate started to go out the Zed hatch which had been set by Repair II; they were yelling and screaming. Water and fuel oil were coming down the hatch. I tried to stop them from opening the hatch, but couldn't.

The next thing we knew we were all under water and oil. Centers and myself were the only ones that came up. It took us some time in the dark to find out that we were back in A-28 and the ship had capsized.

We then tried to get into the linen storeroom. It was on the starboard side and was out of the water. The storeroom was locked and it took several hours to beat the lock off with a wrench that we found on the air compressor. We could not get into the storeroom as gear must have been wedged against the door.

We tried to get into a small storeroom which was in the overhead, but it was also locked and we could not get into a position to beat it off.

About Monday noon we heard tapping and we answered them. After so long they were right overhead and we could hear them talking. When they started to cut into us it let out air and we were under air pressure, the water came up as our air escaped. The water came up and ran out of the hole they were cutting, and they left. But we still had about six inches of air space. We tried the linen room again and it gave a little. Apparently the water had cleared the gear away from the door, we went in and started tapping again.

The rescuers soon got out to us again, and we left the ship at 0200 Tuesday morning. I wish to thank these men for their hard work in rescuing us: Chief Bosun Mate Keenum, Shipfitter First Class Thomas, Carpenter's Mate Second Class Harris.

When the nine divers arrived on *Nevada*, the senior officer aboard, Lieutenant Commander Thomas, directed them to sound the sunken hull at thirty-foot intervals. To accomplish this, they lowered a diver from the sampan to a depth of twenty feet. Swinging a five-pound hammer, he rapped the hull three times, then stopped and listened for an answering signal. They took turns for five hours. No answering signal was ever heard. Tired and filthy after their disappointing mission, they piled into the sampan and headed for 1010 dock. Tuesday, they met their new diving officer, Lieutenant Haynes, and in a session with all nine, he gave them new assignments—and later had a private session with Raymer.

Haynes told the divers about some of the hazards they could expect to encounter on the ships, but he was careful to point out that no one could identify all the dangers because few, if any, divers experienced diving inside a battle-damaged ship strewn with wreckage. He emphasized that floating oil, sediment, and debris in the water would make underwater lights useless. Diving inside the ships would be done in complete and utter darkness, requiring them to develop a keen sense of feel, great manual dexterity with tools, and a high degree of hand-to-brain coordination. Since the Navy had no safety precautions for such a situation, they would be required to devise their own.

Lieutenant Haynes then took Raymer aside to speak to him privately. He explained to Raymer the diving crew would rarely have a diving officer attached, and even then, he would not be experienced in salvage work. He then paused, lit his pipe, puffed a few times until the tobacco glowed, and told Raymer that over his objections, the senior salvage officer had assigned the exterior hull work to the Pacific Bridge and Shipyard's civilian divers. Interior work on the ships was to be the responsibility of the Navy divers because they were familiar with the insides of battleships.

Afterward, Haynes gave the nine divers their assignments: dynamite the concrete quays that pinned the *Tennessee* against the *West Virginia*, and sound the hulls of the sunken ships to insure that no one was trapped inside them. Rescue of any possible survivors took precedence over every other operation. He also pointed out they would not be diving deeper than forty-five feet within the ships, and could stay down all day and not be concerned about bends or other diving illnesses. Raymer noted that he neglected to discuss the possibility of performing their necessary bodily functions after hours underwater, but they soon learned how to cope with that.[60]

On Monday, 8 December, while the divers were arriving on Oahu and beginning their difficult, dangerous work, the people on the island were relieved at having passed a long, anxious night. Nevertheless, it was also the beginning of more sad days, for the first of hundreds of funerals began on Monday. Joey Border returned to the Border's apartment, and later continued her letter home. She was now aware of martial law, food rationing, and censorship, and had to choose her words carefully to avoid the censors' returning the letter.

> Home again. The 2nd day of war has started. I tried to send a cable to you this morning, but the telegraph office accepts no messages—either coming in or going out. We were bombed slightly last night— the entire area effected a complete blackout. I went over to Barbara Morrison's for the night. It certainly was odd sitting around in the dark from 6-9—the only news we got was from mainland stations. Everything is calm today with the exception of planes which constantly fly overhead and occasional antiaircraft fire. The Japs have been taken care of in this vicinity, but there was plenty of damage done in Pearl Harbor and the surrounding area—I don't know how many canoes were hit—2 were sunk— and about four disabled—ours comes in the 2nd category—The dead and wounded have mounted to 360 so far—this is really interesting something to tell my grandchildren. Food is being rationed out to prevent serious shortages. Bob is safe wherever he is—the Exec got word in somehow that everything aboard was O.K.—so I know that he's all right. Quite a few of the families have had to evacuate to the schools because their homes were gutted or destroyed by bombs –
>   I haven't done much but write you, clean and play A-D [acey-ducey] with Barby
>   —I guess I'll have to think up a few appropriate games to play in the dark—The water is contaminated, evidently the work of saboteurs, so we have to boil all water before using. Mom, you went thru the last war, but I'll bet you never had to wonder whether or not the planes which flew overhead were yours. It's quite an experience—there's no sense in getting

frightened—so I just sit back and enjoy it, putting it down in my diary for future remembering—Hell nor high water could get me out of Hawaii now. I'm staying right here so that I'm at least near Bob. I wish I could be on the ship with him. Well, must do my marketing for the day. Write soon, darlings, and don't worry about me. If any bombs fall around here, I'll just duck under the bed—! Merry Christmas—! Maybe I'll still see you in Feb.! Love Joey—

She wrote on the envelope, <u>VIA</u> <u>CLIPPER</u>, mailed it Monday afternoon, and the letter was postmarked in Bremerton, Washington, 13 December. It had been carried from Pearl City to San Francisco, arriving 10 December via Pan American's *Philippine Clipper*, which returned through Oahu still carrying its sixteen bullet holes following the Clipper's narrow escape from Wake Island on 7 December.[61]

On 8 December, a day of deepening sadness, the funerals began. Joey would attend five of them in the days ahead, including the 11 December funeral for the *California's* Ensign Herbert C. Jones, who had come to her parents' quarters in Puget Sound Navy Yard the past January. Joey was unaware that he would be nominated to receive the Medal of Honor for his valor that terrible day.[62]

Army dead were buried in the cemetery at Schofield Barracks. The Navy buried 328 in its plot at Oahu Cemetery in Nuuanu Valley, 18 at Kaneohe Bay and 204 in a new naval cemetery which it established at the time by purchasing twenty-five acres at Red Hill, near Aiea.Mixed with all the loss, sadness, frustration and anger about the visible dead and wounded, were the missing. When the final count of dead and wounded was reached, 1,606 of the presumed dead were missing who were finally declared dead. The missing were lost in the following categories: Army 3, Army Air Force 15, Marine Corps 66, Navy 1,522. The greatest losses of missing occurred in the Navy, on the *Arizona*, followed by the *Oklahoma*, and *Utah* where, on the three ships, it was impossible to recover hundreds of bodies. The final death toll on *Arizona* was 1,177, including 73 Marines and 1,104 Navy; on *Oklahoma* 14 Marines and 415 Navy; *Utah* 58 Navy, for a total of 1,577.[63]

A Bright Light at the End
of Another Dark Day

The morning of 8 December the heavy cruisers *Northampton* (CA-26) and *Chester* (CA-27), both of which had accompanied *Enterprise* to Wake Island, stood in to Pearl Harbor at 1111 and 1132 respectively, while the ships' stunned crews crowded topside decks and gazed at the destruction the Pacific Fleet had absorbed twenty-seven hours earlier. Later, approximately 60 miles to the southwest of Pearl Harbor, at 1452 hours, *Enterprise* was also preparing to enter Pearl Harbor. With Task Force 8, she had delivered the twelve F4Fs to Wake Island, and safely returned to help seek Pearl Harbor's attackers. The intent was to put in to port as close to dark as feasible, refuel, refill her aviation fuel storage tanks, load provisions and supplies, and leave prior to sunrise, the most likely time of attack by the enemy.

Few, except some of her aviators who had landed at Ford Island or Ewa, had seen the destruction wrought by the Japanese attack. Timing for arrival and departure would allow the crew to see some of it—enough to make a lasting impression. But there was something else—the spirits of the men who had endured the destructive power of the Japanese attack nineteen hours earlier. They needed to see what the Japanese had failed to find, a shining example of the now-fully-emerged backbone of the Pacific Fleet— the fast carrier.

While recovering her last airplanes between 1425 and 1452, the commander, Captain G.D. Murray ordered "Set Material condition Affirm." At 1447 her electrical gang cut in the degaussing coils, while the carrier turned from 076 degrees, starboard to course 090 degrees, all engines full, 20 knots, 189 r.p.m. At 1453 she sounded general quarters, at 1500 changed speed to 18 knots and commenced zigzagging according to plan No. 2, then ceased zigzagging at 1557 and returned to base course 090 degrees. One minute later she turned port to 055 degrees, then at 1620 turned further port to north.

Unknown to *Enterprise* and her crew, lying ten miles south of Diamond Head observing traffic in and out of Pearl Harbor was the Japanese submarine *I-70*, whose captain, Commander Takao Sano reported to the Submarine Force commander, Vice Admiral Shimizu Mitsoyoshi aboard the command ship *Katori*, stationed on the Kwajalein Atoll, that they had sighted an American carrier entering Pearl Harbor. Submarine *I-8*, whose captain was Commander Tetsushiro Emi, picked up Sano's signal and relayed it to other submarines in the Oahu operating area. Commander Sano's signal told Admiral Mitsoyoshi that at least the *Enterprise* was in the area, and might offer herself a prize target when she left Pearl Harbor again. After maneuvering at various courses

The heavy cruiser *Northampton* (CA-26) steams into Pearl Harbor on the morning of 8 December 1941, her men observing the devastation wreaked by Japanese planes the previous day. From her bridge, Rear Admiral Raymond A. Spruance silently looked on. His reading and studying about war had not prepared him for the awful sight that lay before him. That evening, he emotionally and tearfully related his feelings to his wife and daughter. Apparently, though, he never spoke of it again. *Northampton* was at sea with Vice Admiral Halsey's Task Force 8 on the day of the attack, returning from the delivery of 12 Marine F4F fighters from VMF-211 to Wake Island. Photographed from Ford Island, looking east toward the Navy Yard, with dredging pipe in the foreground. NA

and speeds standing into Pearl Harbor, at 1647 *Enterprise* passed between entrance buoys Nos. 1 and 2.[64]

She entered the channel with all available men at parade along the edge of the flight deck, amidst cheers and hurrahs from those aboard the ships in the channel.[65] She was an inspiring sight that filled flagging spirits with great pride and hope for the future. All of Task Force 8 was alive and well, ready to fight, while at sea, so were *Lexington* and all her escorts—and, coming from San Diego with her deck and hangars full of aircraft, also escorted, *Saratoga* was underway, headed west, southwest toward Oahu.

At 1743, *Enterprise* moored starboard side to the quay walls at berth F-9, on the west side of Ford Island, with the seaplane tender *Tangier* dead ahead in berth F-10, and the capsized *Utah* beyond *Tangier* at berth F-11. The oiler *Neosho*, came alongside to port one minute before midnight, and began refueling *Enterprise* at 0015 hours, 9 December. At 0055, she began receiving aviation gasoline. While refueling was in progress lighters came alongside with provisions and supplies. At the same time trucks arrived dockside with more provisions, and the entire crew, including enlisted aviation personnel, participated in an "all hands evolution." Aviation personnel were told if an alert occurred they were to return to their planes. On the east side of Ford Island, while the refueling and provisioning of *Enterprise* was in progress on the west side, the last of the rescues of *Oklahoma*'s trapped crew members occurred.

The entire operation to get *Enterprise* ready for sea again, went like clockwork, and at

0300 the crew started preparations to get underway. At 0315 refueling ceased, and *Neosho* was underway from alongside at 0353. *Enterprise* had taken on 463,000 gallons of fuel oil, and 61,000 gallons of gasoline, and at 0420 the carrier was underway from berth F-9. At 0556 she passed entrance buoy No. 1 to port and turned port on a southeasterly heading of 154 degrees, soon to assemble with her screens. She had come triumphantly into Pearl Harbor for a few brief hours, a witness to the harbor's wreckage, and left like a ghost slipping into the early morning darkness. Behind her she had left a bright light of hope for the future.[66]

The enemy had other ideas and designs.

CHAPTER 11

Reverberations

*We have already arrived at the place of our destiny,
and now courage must finish the labor of constancy.*

General Jose de San Martin

The *Lurline* arrived in San Francisco 10 December. While she was en route from Honolulu, came 7 December with its two wrenching messages, the first *Lurline* received from the sinking *Cynthia Olson* and the second forwarded from the battered NAS Pearl Harbor on Ford Island. War. Life aboard *Lurline* and all American ships had immediately changed.

Already in San Francisco harbor were two more of the Matson Line's ladies, the *Matsonia* and the US Army Transport *Monterey*, two ships the Philippines-bound 34th Infantry Regiment had already begun to board prior to 7 December—before the regiment's embarkation orders were revoked at 6:00 p.m. that day, and the regiment began to offload pending a change in orders. The elegant *Lurline*, a ship of gracious living and cruising on the high seas between San Francisco, Los Angeles and Honolulu, in the next six days began a rapid conversion to a troop ship, most of it completed the first four days, a metamorphosis already begun on *Matsonia*, and on the *Monterey* when she was chartered by the government on 3 December.

The three cruise ships not only outwardly changed colors to make them more difficult for the enemy to observe day or night, workmen swarmed almost every passenger deck and hurried to convert her, inside, for wartime missions.

The sumptuous furnishings of staterooms and public rooms were all removed . . . exquisite mother-of-pearl

Matson Navigation Company's SS *Matsonia* before
conversion to a troop transport. MNC

Soldiers' bunks, four high and consisting of canvas lashed to
pipes and supported by chains, comprised the sleeping quarters
for troops on the *Matsonia* after she was converted. MNC

inlays and beautiful wood-paneling were boarded up ...
murals and other decorative effects were necessarily left
exposed to the ravages of crowded wartime use. Then
tiers of bunks were installed, and the efficient, plain
equipment of fighting craft, and the ship's gleaming
hull was covered with coats of admiralty gray.[1]

The hurried conversion stripped from them all the trappings
of floating hotels that catered to passenger relaxation and
enjoyment. War was bringing an abrupt, new reality which
demanded an austerity few cruise ship passengers and crews had
ever experienced—except for those who had sailed on troopships
to Europe and back during the World War I era.

The US Army Transport *Monterey* was chartered by the government
on 3 December 1941 with plans underway to convert to a troop
transport and carry troops to Manila, Philippine Islands. When
news of the Pearl Harbor attack came she was in San Francisco
harbor, where she was relieved of her cargo and reloaded with plane
parts and other vital war material. All three Matson liners were
diverted to Oahu, departing in Convoy 2005 on 16 December with
troops and war materials to reinforce the 24th and 25th Infantry
Divisions against a possible Japanese invasion of the island. MNC

Over time at the beginning of this war, passenger-carrying capabilities of the great ocean liners quadrupled, or even quintupled. Workmen revamped first class suites and cabin class staterooms to sleep far greater numbers, cabin class eight to nine people instead of two, suites more than double the stateroom numbers. They mounted multiple-stacked, stretched canvas bunks with no mattresses in areas and compartments where none previously existed. Twenty-six large life rafts tied just below the promenade decks of each ship, thirteen on starboard and port sides augmented the sixteen big lifeboats mounted on the on the upper deck. *Lurline's* peacetime design for 701 passengers eventually stretched into a maximum wartime capacity for 3,851, the older, smaller *Matsonia* from 577 to 3,028, and *Monterey* from 728 to 4,150.

Porthole glass and view windows were painted over, and everything possible done to prevent light from escaping the ship when dark, including weather-induced dark. Caution, regulatory, and command signs went up in the passageways, on bulkhead

Lurline, fully converted to a troop transport, leaving Brisbane, Australia on 11 September 1945, with 3,560 persons on board, including Australian war brides. MNC

doors, near ladders, and on compartment walls (bulkheads) facing decks—nearly all intended to make the ship and its wartime voyages as safe as possible while making life in crowded conditions organized, disciplined and livable.

Elegant dining rooms became large, antiseptic mess halls with self-service cafeteria trays, hand-carried utensils, and lines outside the dining room doors replacing linen-covered, individually-served dining tables with formerly fine china, silverware, waiters, headwaiters and maitre des. Kitchens and kitchen staffs expanded and meals were served rapidly, in shifts, with punctuality demanded by circumstance. Bars, libraries, dance floors and entertainment stages, writing rooms and lounges were turned to more practical uses, including more bunks. Overstuffed chairs, sofas, rattan (bamboo) furniture of any kind, hardwood tables, and wooden dining room chairs were removed, replaced by austere, metal, wear-resistant folding chairs and tables.

The proud cruise ships were transformed to exude a different form of pride, to carry thousands of young men, and a few women—mostly nurses, their personal possessions and uniform items in duffel bags, and the military equipment and supplies required to travel with a combat ready regiment. Antiaircraft guns mounted fore and aft, each of sufficient caliber, muzzle velocity, and flexible mounting to successfully defend against attack by a surfaced submarine, plus machine guns, gave the big liners some fangs they had never before cultivated or grown. To the crews of the liners, the abrupt changes must have been disconcerting and causes for some anxiety at best. To more than 100 crewmembers on *Lurline* alone, in their first wartime return to Hawaii, the changes, plus the enemy they faced, became worrisome and increasingly demoralizing.

When the *Lurline* arrived in San Francisco, the 161st Infantry Regiment had already arrived by train from Fort Lewis, in Washington state, and was encamped at the Presidio. As previously indicated, the 34th Infantry Regiment had already offloaded from *Matsonia* and *Monterey* on 8 December, and returned by truck to the Presidio. The 34th, its secret orders for the Philippines revoked, and still waiting for revised orders, had in the meantime been given other defense missions along the west coast.[2]

On 9 December, the 34th's Company E traveled south by truck convoy, ordered to guard duty at Monterey, California. The 3rd Battalion remained at the Presidio in San Francisco, under the operational control of the Presidio's commander. On 10 December, Company C proceeded to guard duty at Benicia Arsenal in the San Francisco Bay area, where in the first twenty-four hours after the attack on Pearl Harbor, 125 separate truck convoys were loaded and dispatched, leaving the Arsenal's stock of ammunition, small arms and high explosives completely exhausted. On the same day, one platoon from Company G left for an assigned mission in Paso Robles, California.[3]

Each night beginning 7 December, federal authorities, including military, mobilized civilian defense wardens, and civilian authorities imposed a blackout on the west coast, a measure imposed in the Hawaiian Islands the same night. In those first days, as in Hawaii, on the mainland outlandish rumors aided by erroneous reports from the armed forces, fueled sometimes humorous, sometimes hysterical, and sometimes tragic reactions to events requiring rapid but careful evaluation and thoughtful responses.

Donald J. Young's book, *December 1941, America's First 25 Days at War*, vividly describes the shock first visited upon the mainland United States, particularly the west coast, by the Japanese attack on Pearl Harbor:

> Few American's old enough to remember December 7, 1941, have forgotten exactly where they were and what they were doing when they received word of the Japanese attack on Pearl Harbor.
>
> It is doubtful that the announcement, made throughout the United States over radio, through loud-speakers at pro football games, in theaters, and even in churches, was delivered under anymore dramatic circumstances than at a small, insignificant American Legion baseball field in picturesque Ojai, California. It was there that a game was to be played between the Ventura American Legion Post and the U.S. Army team from Fort MacArthur in Los Angeles.
>
> In the middle of the pre-game flag-raising ceremony, with the players and crowd standing solemnly at attention and the Fort MacArthur band poised to strike up the National Anthem at the moment Old Glory reached the top of the flagpole, a man in civilian clothes was seen running across the field towards

the officer standing in front of the Army contingent, Lieutenant Colonel Fred Wright. When he reached the startled soldier he handed him a telegram.

"What's this?" asked the somewhat irritated athletic officer. "Couldn't you have waited until the ceremony was over?"

Wright tore open the envelope and read its contents. "My God," he gasped, "I can't believe it."

Turning to face the band, his arm upraised to stop them from striking up the National Anthem, Wright solemnly announced, "Men, let me have your attention. We have been ordered back to our post. Japan has attacked the Hawaiian Islands. Into your trucks on the double."

You can bet it was "into your trucks on the double" at military posts throughout the United States that day, particularly on the Pacific Coast. All leaves were canceled. Servicemen away from their bases were ordered to report to the nearest military post. Headlines in special addition papers up and down the coast, in anticipation of an attack, typically as in the *Los Angeles Examiner* announced PACIFIC COAST ON WAR BASIS FROM ALASKA TO MEXICO.

Brigadier General William O. Ryan, commanding officer of the Fourth Interceptor Command—which was responsible for air defense from Oregon to San Diego—ordered all civilian observers to report to their observation posts immediately and "see that it is fully manned at all times."

All private planes on the coast were grounded and the licenses of civilian pilots suspended until further notice. In addition, the Navy announced that all planes flying over naval bases, except air stations, would be "regarded as hostile and fired upon without warning."

The Coast Guard, which upon the attack immediately became part of the U.S. Navy, ordered all ships into the nearest port "pending clarification of the situation."

Major General Joseph Stilwell, later of the Burma Campaign fame, was commanding officer of the Fourth Army's III Corps, whose responsibility it was to provide beach defense for the Pacific Coast, from Monterey to San Diego.

Stilwell and his wife were entertaining his III Corps staff officers at their home in Carmel when they first heard of the attack on

Pearl Harbor. Later that night the General scribbled the first entry into what would become his wartime diaries. His comments on what happened that day and the subsequent 15 days, as much as anything recorded, give insight into the confusion, anticipation and fear that existed within the military during the first few days of the war. It can be seen in the December 7 entry, where he wrote: "Japs attack Hawaii. 3pm: Goode phoned. Jap fleet 20 miles south, 10 miles out of Monterey. 3:30: phoned White at (Fort) Ord; to send reconnaissance troops down Highway 1 (to look for possible Japanese invasion force).

Another general of more prominence at the moment than Stilwell—General Harold H. (Hap) Arnold, chief of the U.S. Army Air Forces—was notified of the attack under quite different circumstances.

Several miles outside the city of Bakersfield, in California's San Joaquin Valley, General Arnold and Mr. Donald Douglas, president of Douglas Aircraft Company of Santa Monica, had been hunting quail all morning, when a small plane with the words KERN CO. SHERIFF painted on the fuselage began circling them.

"Hope you've got your hunting license with you, General," said Douglas jokingly.

Moments later the plane flew directly over and the pilot dropped something out of the window. The hunt was over. It was a note announcing the attack on Pearl Harbor.

As further reports of Japanese attacks throughout the Pacific reached the ears of Americans anxiously listening to their radios that day, the country began to react.

An example of the military activities that took place up and down the coast in reaction to the news of the attack can perhaps be best understood by closely examining what happened at Fort MacArthur and in the Los Angeles area.

At Fort MacArthur, protector of the important Los Angeles Harbor, plans already worked out in eventuality of such an emergency, known as "M-Day" (Mobilization Day), went into effect immediately after news of the attack on Pearl Harbor was received at 11:35 a.m. This included manning all coast artillery and antiaircraft guns, blockading the harbor entrances, establishing road blocks and check points at key roads, intersections, bridges, tunnels, and gates leading to vital aircraft plants, naval shipyards and military bases. Los Angeles Sheriff Eugene Biscailuz quickly mobilized the city's already organized major disaster task force of 10,000 civilian volunteers for use when necessary.

The baseball game at Ojai wasn't the only "ball game" in California where people found out about the Japanese attack on Pearl Harbor. That morning a game was being played in Griffith Park in Los Angeles between the Paramount Studio nine and a local Japanese team. During the third inning, the small crowd was suddenly doubled when a group of stern-looking men in suits came and stood behind the Japanese bench. It wasn't until the end of the game, however, when the entire Japanese team was taken down town for "questioning," that Paramount was told the strange spectators were "G-men," and that Japan had attacked Hawaii. (Of all the arrests of Japanese to follow, probably those made during the first week following the attack on Pearl Harbor were the most legitimate, as they were based on information collected by the FBI and the ONI—Office of Naval Intelligence—before the war started.)

Since the largest contingent of Japanese in the United States resided in southern California—including a community of 5,000 at Terminal Island's Fish Harbor, in the middle of Los Angeles Harbor—many, if not most, of the M-Day precautions were those against sabotage. As an example, the Southern California Edison Company turbine electric plant at Long Beach, the biggest in the world, was immediately encircled by troops. In Hollywood, a team of FBI agents was sent to guard the National Broadcasting Company station and transmitter against possible sabotage or espionage. Guards at Douglas, Lockheed, Vega and North Armerican aircraft factories were doubled and tripled. In fact, 150 Los Angeles police officers had to be sent to San Pedro later in the day to augment the heavy call for guards. All ships at dock in Los Angeles Harbor were ordered to move away from shore and into the outer anchorage, as a precaution against sabotage of both vessels and docks. Fire stations throughout the harbor area stood with doors open, ready to roll upon the first sabotage alarm.

Every radio station and newspaper in the Los Angeles area was pressed into service to call soldiers and sailors back to their units. As noted in the *Los Angles Examiner*, "Thousands of sailors and officers were in homes ashore on leave, when radios gave the startling news of the Hawaiian bombardment and then the order to report to their stations. They slid into uniforms and kissed wives, sweethearts and mothers in hasty farewells, not knowing when they would return." The Army also made calls, including one for all men recently discharged from the service having reached the age of 28. Like it or not, they were "back in."

At Fort MacArthur, the "alert" signal sent gun crews swarming to the roofs of numerous harbor structures, buildings and even 200-foot smokestacks to man antiaircraft and machine gun nests.

Tremendous activity was noted inside the fort itself; within an hour trucks were rushing through the area with supplies and ammunition for gun crews manning heavy coastal defense positions.

Colonel William W. Hicks, harbor defense commander at Fort MacArthur, ordered, "strong scouting forces . . . out of the fort at noon on assignments to patrol the entire coast to an undisclosed distance north of the fortified area."

Two thousand soldiers from Camp Haan in Riverside, at Fort MacArthur for advanced antiaircraft training and war games scheduled to start on December 11, were dispersed as needed throughout the city. Six hundred alone went to the Douglas Aircraft plant in Santa Monica as guards.

Telephone company crews laid direct lines into the fort for exclusive use by the Army, and to separate all top priority military messages from civilian calls. A three-way telephone circuit was set up between Fort MacArthur and Fort Winfield Scott in San Francisco and Fort Rosecrans in San Diego to facilitate liaison between the three posts.

Navy patrol boats that had been operating within the harbor area put out to sea under secret orders. Six of those that left were on their way to perform probably the least enviable duty of all those ordered out on 7 December. They were ships of the U.S. Navy's advanced warning system—the Offshore Patrol—that, from their assigned patrol area 150 miles off the coast, would hopefully be able to radio the location of an approaching Japanese attack force before they were blown out of the water.

This "expendable" force was made up of 100-foot long commandeered pleasure yachts, manned by naval personnel, and equipped with radios and a few machine guns. For the simple reason that sailboats didn't need to be refueled, they were selected for the job. Several of these sleek ships, in uncharacteristic battleship gray, would patrol the 400 mile section of the Pacific Coast between Guadelupe Island of Mexico and Point Conception, California, and more would operate from Conception to San Francisco, all the way to British Columbia.

A message announcing the closing of the harbor between 6 p.m. and 6 a.m. until further notice was made by the Navy. In addition, Navy and Coast Guard ships were stationed at the harbor entrance to turn back pleasure and commercial ships as they attempted to leave. It was reported that 50 of those sent back were fishing boats from the Fish Harbor Japanese fishing fleet.

People crossing from Terminal Island to San Pedro on the municipal ferry found "grim Army guards gripping bayoneted rifles awaiting them at the landing," where they were sent "through a line of guards and FBI agents, who diverted those of Japanese or Oriental appearance into a wired enclosure."

From there they were hustled away under guard, some back to confines of the island, others to the Federal Prison on Terminal Island for questioning. In fact, the island's Fish Harbor Japanese community itself became a virtual concentration camp for the 5,000 residents, as truckloads of Army troops carrying fixed bayonets cordoned off the area within the first hour after news of the attack.

As one could imagine, it wasn't only at Fish Harbor where things were getting rough for the Japanese. In Norfolk, Virginia, site of an important naval base, Colonel Charles B. Borland ordered every Japanese in the city arrested. Civil Aeronautics Authority Chairman Robert Hinkley announced that no Japanese nationals would be allowed on commercial airline flights within the continental United States. In fact, any Japanese attempting to book passage from the United States to neutral Mexico would automatically be arrested by the FBI.

Both the FBI and ONI had been zeroing in on Japanese spy activities on the Pacific Coast since the mid-1930s. Lists of known Japanese spies and spy suspects had long since been compiled by both organizations when Pearl Harbor was attacked, prompting an immediate round-up that very day. Probably because of the large concentration of Japanese on Terminal Island, the largest number of arrests—40—were made in Los Angeles, with an unconfirmed report that 260 more were listed for "internment" as a result of extensive FBI investigations over the past year. By the end of the day, 28 had been arrested in San Diego, 25 in San Francisco, 20 in Seattle, a dozen in Portland and two in Tacoma. Before the day was over, 736 Japanese aliens in the United States and Hawaii would find themselves behind bars or barbed wire. This was out of 80,000 Japanese nationals listed as residing within the continental United States, and the 41,000 in Hawaii.

In anticipation of needing prisons to intern the large number of Japanese nationals that could be arrested, California's State Finance Director, George Killion, offered the use of all 12 of the state's federal government relief camps.

In Sacramento, California, an incident occurred that day which was probably the last of its kind for a long while in the United States—a Japanese attacked an American. Mr. Raymond Schneringer, a 46-year-old World War I veteran, had been discussing the attack on Pearl Harbor with a friend on a street corner in downtown Sacramento when a young Japanese, overhearing the conversation, hit him in the jaw. "Just after I said 'then we'll let the Japs have it,' the fellow sprang at me, hit me in the jaw and ran away before I could get up." Given what happened in the Pacific earlier that day, this was recorded as the first "war casualty" to occur in the United States.

The only other "defiant" act committed by a Japanese that day happened when the Japanese consul in San Francisco, Yoshio Muto, allegedly tried to burn his house down. Some say that he was trying to burn his secret files so fast that the fire got out of hand . . . [4]

The first day of war on the west coast was wild, and it would be days before matters would begin settling toward a routine of realistic vigilance and disciplined responses. The next day, along with President Roosevelt's speech asking Congress for a declaration of war, the panicked round-up of Japanese all over the United States, but particularly on the west coast, continued.

Along with its continuing round-up of Japanese nationals and sealing its country's borders to prevent the departure of anyone of Japanese extraction, the government seized and closed all Japanese banks, businesses, newspapers and radio stations and transmitters in the United States. All Japanese fishing boats were also seized.

In California, Gov. Culbert Olson, panicked by the knowledge that 75 percent of the Japanese in America resided in his state, readied a previously prepared proclamation notifying all members of the Japanese race to remain off the streets until their loyalty to the United States had been established.

"Segregation of Japanese residents in sympathy with the Imperial government of Japan should be made," he said. "They should be put up in bodies of concentration. We must do that as a duty to ourselves and to the Japanese that are loyal to the U.S."

Unbeknownst to Governor Olson, who was dissuaded from

issuing his proclamation only because it would have a serious effect on the vegetable and seafood supplies in the state, two months later, not only Japanese loyal to the Imperial government, but all Japanese, would find themselves in his "bodies of concentration."

While awaiting that fateful decision, Japanese in the United States were quickly learning that any combination of having Japanese features and a camera was considered a "fatal" combination.[5]

As in Hawaii, across the mainland, and particularly the west coast, the round-up of German and Italian aliens got underway Sunday afternoon. In Los Angeles, the FBI arrested sixty by the end of Monday, including Hermann Schwin, a German-American bund leader on the west coast, and Hans Diebel, a German youth group leader.

The Chinese community in Seattle, observing reactions toward the Japanese throughout the United States, and particularly on the west coast, wisely ordered identification cards for all local Chinese to as they said, "distinguish us from Japanese to avoid any unpleasantness."[6]

There were numerous incidents of overreaction. In New York, Mrs. Hedda Basham, furious after reading of the attack on Pearl Harbor Monday morning, went to her antique and curio shop, took everything off her shelves bearing a "Made in Japan" label, and smashed it with a hammer.[7]

If there was one place in America where overreaction could be counted on, it would be on college campuses. One of the first to take action was the University of Idaho, in the small, isolated northern Idaho town of Moscow.

It started Sunday afternoon. University President Harrison C. Dale, after hearing of the attack on Pearl Harbor, announced that the school was going on a "war footing." All the Army ROTC students at the Lindley Hall dormitory were called out to guard the university's supply of military equipment, about 200 obsolete Springfield rifles. If the Japanese would have invaded the University of Idaho that night, their failure to take the campus would have been attributed to only one thing—disbelief. For what they would have seen was a bunch of military cadets marching around the campus carrying "broomstick" rifles. It would appear that President Dale just couldn't trust college boys with real guns.

The only other reaction noted occurred at fraternity house at the University of California at Berkeley . . . The barely noteworthy reaction involved a sign hanging from an upstairs window of the Sigma Nu fraternity house, which said: "IF YOU THINK WE'RE WORRIED, YOU SHOULD SEE OUR TOKYO CHAPTER."[8]

What happened at Pearl Harbor left no one in America unaffected. The Society of Composers, Authors and Publishers in New York City, notified everyone of its members on Monday morning to go to work and produce fighting songs. "We want Americans to remember Pearl Harbor," one of the officers said. A song of that very same title, "Remember Pearl Harbor" was written shortly thereafter.[9]

Don Reid wrote the lyrics and teamed with Sammy Kaye to write the music, they recorded it with the Republic Music Corporation, and applied for international copyrighting of the song before the end of December 1941. It was an instant success, and coupled with "Praise the Lord and Pass the Ammunition," composed in 1942, became the primary fighting songs to inspire and unite the nation.

One segment of the American populace that didn't need patriotic songs to get it going, was its able-bodied men. A story in the San Francisco Chronicle, is one that probably could have been printed in city newspapers all over the country that night.

To men of the United States, the declaration of war against Japan today meant one thing: Stand aside, let me in!

Young men, with and without jobs and families, kids with or without parental consent, old youths with honorable discharges and ancients bursting with zeal demanded spots in the fast-growing ranks.[10]

While the American civilian population wondered, discussed and anticipated its fate in the brand new, day-old war, so did its military, particularly on the vulnerable Pacific Coast. In San Francisco, the main enlistment stations went on 24-hour, 7-day-week schedules.

In the northernmost reaches of Alaska, Brigadier General Simon B. Buckner, commander of the Alaskan Defense Command, swallowed real hard at what he saw that morning. "At dawn," he said, "I watched our entire Alaska Air Force take to the air so as to not be caught on the ground. (It) consisted of six obsolescent medium bombers and 12 pursuit planes."

General Stilwell, after a quick stop at his office at the Presidio at Monterey on the 8th, went on to San Francisco to see his boss, Lieutenant General John DeWitt, commanding general of the entire Pacific coast. While there he received a phone call from Washington about his ammunition supply. "Almost a hatful," noted Stilwell in his diary later, followed by the somber words, "Much depressed."

By the time he returned to the Presidio at 6 p.m., there were signs that gave everyone on the coast reason to be "depressed," even frightened.

It actually began very early that morning, [8 December], with a 3 a.m. message from the 9th Coast Artillery Headquarters at Fort Winfield Scott in San Francisco to Forts MacArthur and Rosecrans in San Diego, that "the main Japanese fleet was at latitude 38 degrees, 48 minutes north longitude, 132 degrees, 5 minutes west, on a bearing of 281 degrees." Approximately 165 miles west of San Francisco.

At noon the Navy reported a destroyer and aircraft between San Clemente and Santa Catalina Islands, and an unidentified battleship 15 miles southeast of Sunset Beach. In response to those sightings, a 3:45 p.m. message from Headquarters of the Commandant, 11th Naval District in San Diego to its base in Long Beach, read:

> Take every precaution against surprise raiding attack by surface vessels and aircraft from direction 5 to 15 miles southwest of Sunset Beach to San Clemente Island. Information (also) forwarded to Harbor Defense Command (Ft. MacArthur) and Interceptor Command, Los Angeles, with instructions from Assistant Commandant 11th Naval District (Long Beach) to ask General Ryan (CO 4th Interceptor) to send out planes to investigate.

At 5:45 p.m., two hours later, while contemplating how to react to the 3:45 message, Fort MacArthur received the following communiqué from the 11th Naval District in Long Beach.

> Message received from San Diego stating we may expect an attack at dawn.

As much as possible, Fort MacArthur was ready. Gun crews on the four giant 14-inch coastal guns and the 12-inch mortars were standing by. Two mammoth 14-inch railway guns stood manned and ready. Observers and lookouts were in position from Point Vicente on the tip of Palos Verdes Peninsula to Costa Mesa, some 25 miles to the south. Antiaircraft guns were manned and searchlight crews were standing by to illuminate either the sky if an attack came from the air, or the beach should an invasion be attempted. In front of the giant concrete parapets protecting the 14-inch guns on Fort MacArthur, no less than 24 machine gun nests had been dug and manned. To those who knew, their purpose was all too ominous. Should the Fort's heavy guns be captured intact, some of them could be turned on Los Angeles itself. It's bad enough to know the enemy has landed, but quite another to learn you are being shelled by your own guns.

As the evening wore on, the messages got progressively worse, with tension and dark expectations. At 6:17 p.m. the Harbor Defense Command switchboard at Fort MacArthur lit up again. Another message, this time from 4th Interceptor Command. And this even blacker than the first two. It warned:

> Attack by enemy aviation, sub and surface craft imminent tonight. All precautions will be taken against surprise.

Not that an attack by all three—planes, submarines and ships—wasn't enough, at 7 p.m. the real bombshell was dropped. This message, relayed from the Assistant Commandant, 11th Naval District in Long Beach, reported:

> San Francisco and Seattle are being attacked.

Although reactions are not recorded, there can be little doubt that this announcement hit with the impact of Pearl Harbor. Questions like: "Did 'being attacked' mean invasion, too?" and "Would the Japanese attack the entire West Coast or just Seattle and San Francisco?" were certainly on everyone's lips.

For the next three hours all remained quiet, except for the telephone. Every time it rang, everyone jumped, then held their breath and crossed their fingers. Finally, at a little before 10 p.m., a message came in at Long Beach from Adm. Harold Stark, chief of Naval Operations, in Washington. It stated that secret intelligence information gathered there indicated:

. . . an attack on the West Coast by the same (currently attacking San Francisco and Seattle), or another raiding force (likely) as soon as Jap ships can get into position . . . Attack expected to be by dive bombers and torpedo planes probably accompanied by submarine attacks from inside the harbors. Attack will be pushed home with great vigor. You will take steps so far as lies within your power in cooperation with Army to prevent repetition of success at Hawaii and destroy enemy carriers. Most dangerous period believed first daylight hours. Consult Army as to measures they will undertake. All ships at Navy Yards or otherwise will so far as possible make Readiness Condition One and during the night Readiness Condition Two for antiaircraft batteries. Keep all possible compartments closed. Mount and man all available machine guns of whatever caliber. Arrange for effective air raid alarms and air raid drills. Concentrate available aircraft and vessels for scouting approaches to Puget Sound, San Francisco and Los Angeles-San Diego to report to Army Air Force for defense duty. Army will station pursuit (planes) at naval air stations. Keep CNO advised.

Along with the San Francisco and Seattle attack message, it is doubtful the Navy or any other branch of the military had ever received communication with such frightening implications to the security of the United States. (Unknown to the American command, of course, the closest Japanese warship or plane at that moment was some 4,000 miles away in the Pacific, with no thought at all of striking the American mainland.)

While the reaction on the West Coast rose in intensity the 7th and 8th, on and after 7 December General Marshall and his staff worked feverishly to strengthen the West Coast defenses. A pursuit group from Michigan began arriving in the Los Angles area on 8 December, but it was the reinforcement of antiaircraft defenses that received the most attention during the week after the attack. By 17 December nine additional antiaircraft regiments were rushed from various parts of the United States to the West Coast, and, with some assistance from Marine Corps units, vital installations in the Seattle, Portland, San Francisco, Los Angeles and San Diego areas received at least some antiaircraft artillery protection. The Army also moved two additional divisions and many lesser types of ground combat and service units to the West Coast before the end of December and made the 3rd Division, already there, available for defense use.

With the entire coast alerted on the 8th but not yet under attack, as erroneously reported, the Pacific Northwest, San Francisco, Los Angeles and San Diego braced themselves for the worst.

Up in British Columbia, the mayor of Victoria had already warned everyone "the situation is serious. The Japanese are off the Aleutian Islands, and we may expect an attack at anytime."

Seattle, which in March boasted that it was the first American city to successfully stage a practice blackout, again was the first to turn out their lights—some of them, that is. When all the lights in downtown Seattle didn't go off, people took things into their own hands. An angry crowd, which had grown to about 3,000 in number before it was over, roamed downtown streets throwing bottles, bricks, and, in some cases, trash cans through store windows whose lights were still on.

For an hour and a half, shouts of "turn out the lights," and "this is war," arose from the mob, which moved from one illuminated store to another. Some were heard chanting, "We want blackout, we want blackout!" One man was so angered by a flashing neon sign that he smashed it with his bare fists. Police finally broke up the demonstration after threatening to use fire hoses, but not until thousands of dollars of damage had been done and all the lights were extinguished.

It's no wonder after what happened that nothing was mentioned in the papers about the effectiveness of the special group of city air raid wardens, fitted with roller skates with little red lights on the undersides so people could see them during blackouts.

Like Seattle, the Portland area, too, was blacked out. A few miles outside the city a squad of soldiers was guarding a key highway bridge over the Columbia River. After the blackout order was given, the sergeant in charge had to send one of his men to tell the residents of a nearby house to darken their lights.

"Turn on your lights and be quick about it!" shouted the soldier, pounding heavily on the front door.

The startled homeowner opened the door, took one look at the soldier and bolted through the house and out the back door, shrieking to his neighbors, "run for your lives, the Japs are here!" Seems the soldier who banged on the front door was Private A. Takahashi, a Japanese-American.

Six hundred and fifty miles south, in San Francisco, blackout hysteria among the civilian populace was not the biggest concern. One woman, for example, complained to police about ". . . a crazy man prowling around my place shouting 'lights out.'" Another declared, "People can't sleep with all that noise. Can't they keep those sirens quiet?" Another questioned, "When sirens sound, does it mean they've shot down a plane?" One wanted to know, "What's all the noise, did Japan quit already?" A woman asked why they were using searchlights. "There's no fog."

One person at least, a Mrs. Ann Stewart, took the meaning of the sirens and searchlights seriously—a little too seriously in fact. A resident of a downtown hotel, Mrs. Stewart had opened a window to see if she could see enemy planes, but in the excitement, leaned out too far and slipped, falling seven floors to her death on the street below.

If not hysteria, what Seattle and San Francisco did have in common, however, was confusion. But not if you read the headlines in the papers, which proclaimed things like: JAPAN PLANES NEAR S.F.—4 RAID ALARMS; ENEMY PLANES SIGHTED OVER CALIFORNIA COAST; FOE PLANES FLY IN NIGHT OVER SAN FRANCISCO; and REAL THING IN WEST, ARMY SAYS. Although the headlines sounded very certain, the military surely wasn't.

Things started with a 6:40 p.m. [night time] air raid alarm in the San Francisco area from a report that "strong forces" of hostile aircraft were approaching the coast. As a precaution, to keep enemy planes from homing in on radio beams, in case of an air raid, all radio stations in the Bay area went off the air.

The third alarm, sending radio stations off the air about 1:30 a.m. [9 December], alerted police 20 minutes later that "unidentified planes had been detected approaching the coast." At 2:06 a.m., the "yellow alert" message was sent from 4th Interceptor Command headquarters at the Presidio.

At 2:13 a.m., another blackout was ordered. Eight minutes later the Army reported that "the planes are heading toward shore and so far as we know they are still coming.

At 2:50 a.m., the "blue" stand-by signal came down, and five minutes later, the "red" enemy overhead signal. This was it.

"Almost immediately," recorded the San Francisco Chronicle, "the roar of planes were heard. Reports of dogfights proved without foundation, however, and at 3:37 a.m. the 'all clear' was sounded."

No less than two squadrons of enemy planes, numbering 15 to a squadron, reportedly crossed the coastline west of San Jose, where they separated. One squadron scouted south, and the other reportedly headed north up the San Francisco Bay, over the naval ship yards at Mare Island, and then turned back to sea in the vicinity of the Golden Gate Bridge.

General Ryan, commanding officer of the 4th Interceptor Command, was even more specific.

> The southern formation turned north 20 to 30 miles off the Monterey Peninsula shoreline headed for the Golden Gate. The northern formation started circling in the Pt. Reyes area about 20 miles off shore. Some of the planes of the southern formation came in close enough to the shore to be heard passing Fort Barry. They joined the northern formation about 20 miles off Pt. Reyes. The combined formation then turned south toward the Golden Gate, about 20 miles off shore.

The Army reported that "in all probability an enemy carrier was lurking off the coast, perhaps 500 to 600 miles out." "No doubt they came from a carrier," said Lt. Gen. John DeWitt, "but it would have moved after they launched and would rendezvous at another spot." Planes and ships scouted the area for the enemy carrier, but it could not be found. Some American planes reportedly followed one of the Japanese squadrons out to sea, but no shooting was reported.

Of course, there were no Japanese planes over San Francisco that night, however, General Ryan's response to whether there really were enemy bombers was, "Well, they weren't Army planes, they weren't Navy planes, and you can be sure they weren't civilian planes. There was an actual attack." To make it cautiously unanimous, Capt. Walter K. Kilpatrick, chief of staff of the 12th Naval District, said it "certainly wasn't a drill."

To the question of why no bombs were dropped, General DeWitt said that "they could have been on reconnaissance duty and gathered information for later use." General Ryan's answer was that "they were 'homing in' on the radio broadcasts, and then these were turned off, they didn't know what to do, and so they went away."

San Francisco Mayor Rossi, meanwhile, publicly—but prematurely—congratulated the "loyal citizens who heeded tonight's air raid alarm." Prematurely because, according to one San Francisco paper the next day, residents had to "buy all the morning papers off the news stands to find out what they were supposed to do in a blackout."

By the time the day was over, however, General DeWitt made sure they knew. Headlines in the *San Francisco Chronicle* announcing: DEWITT BLASTS S.F.'S FIRST BLACKOUT AS 'FLOP,' laid the groundwork for what followed. "You people do not seem to realize we are at war," he began. "So get this: last night there were enemy planes over this community! They were enemy planes! I mean Japanese planes! And they were tracked out to sea. You think it was a hoax? It is damned nonsense for people to assume the Army and Navy would practice such a hoax over San Francisco. We will never darken this community nor sound an alert unless enemy planes are threatening. When you hear the signal, TURN OUT YOUR LIGHTS. You can thank God bombs were not dropped. Remember, San Francisco is so full of military objectives that the whole city is a target. Don't be jittery. Learn to take it. You've got to take it. And if you can't take it, get the hell out of San Francisco now before it comes. The Pacific Coast is in the war," he said, and suggested, "it might have been a good thing if Jap planes had dropped some bombs . . . to jolt the city into a realization of that fact."

In one final blast about leaving lights on, the General said if he couldn't ". . . knock it into (their) heads with words, (he'd) turn (them) over to the police for them to knock it in with clubs."

Although not attacked publicly, General DeWitt had also placed a call to Alcatraz's warden, James Johnston, and asked him why he hadn't turned the lights out in the prison last night. Since the prison was a "federal institution," said Johnston, "he couldn't turn them off without government permission."

"Who in hell do you think the Japs are at war with," yelled DeWitt, "the city of San Francisco? I represent the U.S. government, and I say turn out your God Damn lights next time!"

"As long as we know when and from whom to take our signals," said the cowed Johnston, "Alcatraz lights will be turned off from now on."[11]

Underneath the Golden Gate bridge and into this environment on 10 December sailed the SS *Lurline*, with her greatly relieved crew and grateful passengers. There was good reason for their collective sigh of relief. There had been no doubt since receiving the messages of Sunday morning three days earlier, that they would be sailing through dangerous waters the remainder of the voyage to San Francisco. The message exchanges with the *Cynthia Olson* early the morning of the 7th had made it abundantly clear one or possibly more submarines lay between *Lurline* and San Francisco. The balance of the day, and the remainder of the trip home, *Lurline*, her crew and passengers worked to get home safely, aware the ship was a potential target for submarine attack.

While reasoned examination and calculations of the facts, and the considerable mountain of information and intelligence now existing or pouring into the Chief of Naval Operations staff in Washington, and Naval District command centers on the west coast and Hawaii indicated the likelihood of a carrier-based air attack, ship to shore bombardment, or invasion was unlikely on the west coast, stations on the west coast did hear *Cynthia Olson*'s emergency transmissions before she went down. In his Monday, 8 December speech requesting Congress for a declaration of war President Roosevelt had specifically mentioned ". . . American ships have been reported torpedoed on the high seas between San Francisco and Honolulu." It was a speech heard and rebroadcast all around the world.

The Enemy Below

The Navy had no way of knowing precisely the number of Japanese submarines participating in the attack on Pearl Harbor. As described in chapter 3, there were in fact 30 submarines in five groups, including the Special Action Group of five of Imperial Japan's newest undersea boats, Type C.1 cruiser-submarines carrying one midget submarine each. Large, potent combatants, the mother boats were 351 feet long, 30 feet abeam, 18 feet hull depth and at the cruising speed of 10 knots had a maximum range of 14,000 miles. Running on the surface using two-shaft diesels, their maximum speed was 23.6 knots, and submerged running on two electric motors, their maximum speed was 8 knots, with a range of 60 nautical miles at the submerged cruise speed of 3 knots. Thus, one of their most important limiting characteristics was a maximum of 20 hours submerged at cruise speed before they had to surface to operate their diesels and recharge their batteries.

Nevertheless, displacing 2,184 tons standard, 2,554 tons full, and 3,561 tons submerged, their armament was substantial: eight 21-inch torpedo tubes, twenty torpedoes; one 5.5-inch and two 25-mm antiaircraft guns. Having launched their midget subs beginning 2300 hours 6 December, inside a radius of 20 nautical miles from Pearl Harbor's entrance, they intended to rendezvous and recover their newest secret weapons the night of the 7th.[12]

By nightfall on the 7th, the U.S. Navy was certain at least one, and perhaps two midget submarines slipped inside the harbor before the one was believed sunk in the Middle Loch by the destroyer *Monaghan*. It was believed at the time that at least one, possibly two more had been sunk outside the harbor entrance, and perhaps another near Diamond Head. Another was found beached in the surf off Bellows Field the morning of the 8th, its commander captured, while the commander of mother boat *I-22*, Commander Kiyoi Ageta, and the commander of the midget submarines embarked, Captain Hanku Sasaki, waited in vain for their offspring to return. The five large submarines, including the *I-16*, *18*, *20*, and *24*, had been ordered to remain south of Pearl Harbor on a surveillance mission, observing American vessels leaving and entering Pearl, while waiting to return to rendezvous with their five pups. When the midgets didn't return on schedule the evening of the 7th, the five searched all night, then returned a second, and finally a third night, before returning home empty-handed.

Undoubtedly, the Office of Naval Intelligence was able to learn much regarding midget submarine operations from Prisoner No. 1, the Japanese lieutenant and midget sub commander captured in the surf off Bellows Field—at least up to the point where the midget subs were to rendezvous with their mother boats. But he likely didn't know the content of orders given the large cruisers' commanders regarding operations after retrieving the midgets. Whatever the information he divulged under interrogation, it was unlikely the newest "secret weapon" the Japanese had sprung at Pearl Harbor, their only five submarines now capable of carrying five midgets, would be placed at further risk by diverting the larger boats to attacks on shipping.

After completing the air attack on Hawaii, and the carrier strike force withdrawal northward began, Admiral Nagumo released the three submarines which had been accompanying his force as the Patrol Unit, and directed them to return to the command of the Submarine Force. The Patrol Unit, composed of *I-19*, *I-21*, and *I-23*, was then assigned to the direct command of the 1st Submarine Group, composed of *I-9*, *I-15*, *I-17*, and *I-25*. Also on the 8th, Admiral Yamamoto, the Commander-in-Chief of the Japanese Combined Fleet, proceeding according to their war plan, ordered Admiral Nagumo to relinquish command of all the submarine forces which supported the carrier strike force, placing them under the direct command of the Combined Fleet's Submarine Force.

The expanded 1st Submarine Group of seven submarines now lay north of Oahu, while the carrier *Enterprise* was preparing to enter Pearl Harbor the evening of the 8th, to refuel, take on aviation gasoline, food, water and other provisions. As *Enterprise* maneuvered to enter Pearl Harbor, unknown to her crew, the 3rd Submarine Group's *I-70*, lying four miles south of Diamond Head reported to Admiral Mitsoyoshi, the Submarine Force commander at Kwajalein Island in the Marshalls, they had observed an enemy carrier entering Pearl. The signal received from *I-70* on the 8th, had broken a puzzling silence from the boat, after it failed to respond to a message from Mitsoyoshi the night of the 7th. The message the evening of the 8th, would be the last signal ever received from *I-70*.[13]

In the meantime, U.S. Naval Intelligence and fleet commanders were confronted with the need to make a prudent set of assumptions regarding their operations. Sizable Japanese submarine forces were on station in waters around the Hawaiian Islands, along the sea lanes between Hawaii and the Philippines via Midway and Wake Islands, Hawaii and Australia, Hawaii and U.S. mainland west coast ports, and were probably on or en route to stations off key West Coast port entrances.

In the twenty-four to forty-eight hours after the attack, patrols and task forces operating in waters surrounding Hawaii, reported a substantial number of known or suspected contacts with the undersea enemy, more than confirming the presence of possibly numerous enemy submarines. In the period 7-15 December, the *Enterprise* and its Task Force 8, operating to the south and southwest 7-8 December, and north through the northeast of Oahu 9-15 December, recorded by far the largest number of enemy submarine contacts when compared to the Pacific Fleet's *Lexington* and *Saratoga* carrier task forces operating during that same period.

In fact, it was no wonder that in those first days and weeks of guarding the islands and sea lanes, the green and eager sailors and young officers of *Enterprise* and its destroyer screens reported a dozen submarines a day where there were none or very few. To the inexperienced eye peering anxiously through binoculars, it was easy in the daytime to mistake the far off ripple of white caps or dolphin fins for a periscope moving parallel with the tops of swells. At night a playful porpoise just below the surface, coming straight at the bow of ship, with luminous phosphorescent bubbles sliding from his nose and stretching out behind him, can make the mouth of the saltiest destroyer skipper go dry for a moment, fearing he was confronting a death-dealing torpedo. And to the men manning the new submarine electronic listening devices, later known as SONAR, the return from a whale gave nearly as good an echo as a submarine, and showed about the same speed and depth.

The number of reported submarine contacts those first days and weeks, coupled with repeated calls to battle stations and depth charges fired, became a matter of concern to Admiral Halsey, the Task Force 8 commander. Finally, he sent a message comforting his commanders with the thought ". . . if all the reported torpedo wakes were real, the enemy submarines were now out of torpedoes and must return to base and reload." He added, ". . . too many depth charges are being expended against neutral fish."[14]

The carrier *Saratoga's* getting underway from San Diego on 8 December immediately augmented the Fleet—increasing the number of American carrier task forces in the Pacific from two to three, but she reported no submarine contacts until she began operating out of Pearl Harbor.

The *Saratoga*, fresh out of overhaul, had just arrived in San Diego on 7 December, when the attack on Pearl Harbor occurred. She rapidly refueled, filled up with aviation gas, brought her crew and air group up to strength in men and planes; loaded ammunition, food, water and other provisions, and was underway, bound for Pearl Harbor, 0958 hours 8 December, escorted by three destroyers from Destroyer Squadron 50, the *Dent*, *Talbot*, and *Waters*. While the carrier *Lexington*, with Task Force 12, turned around and headed back toward Oahu, searching for the Japanese strike force, the Japanese were also making adjustments to war plans based on the changing situation.

On 9 December, *I-69*, which had been ordered to lay off Pearl Harbor to rescue midget submarine crews the night of the 8th, unsuccessfully attacked a cargo ship, then was depth charged— also unsuccessfully. Off Barbers Point, the submarine became entangled in a submarine net, and Lieutenant Commander Watanabe's crew struggled for hours before finally breaking free. Submerged for 39 hours, all hope of *I-69*'s rescue ended. The incident confirmed to the Submarine Force Commander that the Americans had taken extraordinary precautions in southern Oahu, including the laying of submarine nets between Diamond Head and Barber's Point, and Mitsoyoshi ordered the 3rd Submarine Group, already stationed south of Oahu, to move further south.

On the same day, *I-6*, on station in the Kaiwi Channel, between Oahu and Molokai, reported two heavy cruisers and a *Lexington* class aircraft carrier heading northeast. The *I-6* had in fact seen the *Enterprise* and Task Force 8, in company with the heavy cruiser *Salt Lake City* (CA-25), and destroyers *Fanning*, *Balch*, *Benham*, *McCall*, and *Gridley*. The Submarine Force commander, Vice Admiral Mitsoyoshi, ordered the 1st Submarine Group, still north of Oahu, and the *I-10* and *I-26*, the latter having sunk the *Cynthia Olson* the morning of the 7th—to track down the aircraft carrier which ". . . evidently was moving toward the United States."[15]

On 10 December, Admiral Mitsoyoshi made another slight change in the Japanese operational plan. The Special Attack Unit came under his command, instead of the 1st Submarine Group as planned, and was ordered to abandon the search for the five midget submarines and return to Kwajalein. The 2nd and 3rd Submarine Groups were to continue observation of Hawaii. The 3rd Submarine Group, consisting of *I-8, 68, 69, 70, 71, 72, 73, 74,* and *75*, was to return to Kwajalein on or about 17 December, and the 2nd Submarine Group was to continue to observe the whole island of Oahu alone after that date.

The 1st Submarine Group, plus the *I-10* and *I-26* were to continue to track the enemy fleet toward the United States mainland and

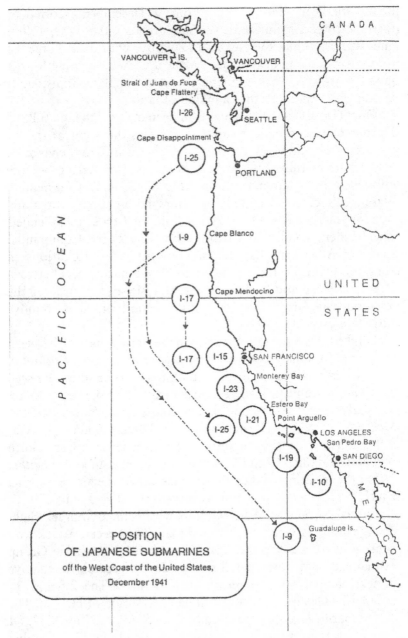

Positions of Japanese Submarines off the West Coast
of the United States, December 1941.

sink the carrier. Upon receipt of orders, the 1st Submarine Group of seven submarines, plus the *I-10* and *I-26* attached, surfaced and racing at flank speed, took up the chase of *Enterprise* and Task Force 8. During the period 7-10 December only a few Japanese submarines, including *I-6*, reported discovering the "enemy aircraft carrier, cruiser and destroyer and none of these achieved any direct attack results." The chase was to no avail.

Resigned to that fact, Admiral Mitsoyoshi designated the nine submarines as Submarine Force Detachment, and ordered them to commence operations against shipping off the west coast of the United States. The submarines' stations would be: *I-26* off Cape Flattery; *I-25* off Cape Disappointment; *I-9* off Cape Blanco; *I-17* off Cape Mendocino; *I-15* off San Francisco; *I-23* off Monterey Bay; *I-21* off Estero Bay; *I-19* off Los Angeles; and *I-10* off San Diego. The position and track of Task Force 8, and its subsequent, frequent surface and underwater contacts with the Japanese submarines beginning the morning of the 9th, suggest more than "a few" submarines encountered Task Force 8 in the five days after *Enterprise* stood out of Pearl Harbor. While both forces were underway on the 10th, the Empire of Japan lost its first major submarine sunk by American fire in World War II.[16]

The Sinking of *I-70*

At 0553 that morning *Enterprise* and its task force, after having passed between Oahu and Molokai on the 9th, was continuing its search toward the north and northeast along the sea lane toward the mainland's west coast, and launched her first group of planes to fly the morning search patterns. They were looking for Japanese surface ships, aircraft or submarines. It was to be a day of frequent contacts with enemy submarines, intense flight operations, sightings of submarine periscopes as well as submarines running on the surface, enemy torpedo wakes sighted tracking toward *Enterprise*, aggressive depth charge attacks by *Enterprise*'s submarine screening destroyers, a zigzagging task force, sharp changes in speed from flank speed to engines stop, and abrupt changes in direction at flank speed with the great ship heeled over twenty to thirty degrees opposite the direction of turn. The day began with a bang.

The last aircraft among the first group to launch lifted off at 0602. They were from Bombing Squadron Six, and within seventeen minutes of the first launch, one aircraft from

VB-6 sighted an enemy submarine running on the surface. At 0618 *Enterprise* began launching a second group, and completed the launch three minutes later. While the second launch was in progress at 0619, SBD 6-B-17, from VB-6 reported a submarine at latitude 22 degrees 30 minutes north, longitude 156 degrees 30 minutes west, course 080 degrees true—a course nearly due east. At 0630 hours, the plane's crew reported they bombed the submarine.

The pilot, Lieutenant (jg) Edward L. Anderson, with Radioman/gunner Third Class S.J. Mason in the rear cockpit, was searching an area forty miles south of *Enterprise* at 300 feet altitude. In his action report of 15 December, he wrote,

> . . . sighted a wake made by [an] enemy submarine. The vessel was close and [the] conning tower [was] sighted above water. The submarine was making a crash dive. I pulled up to 800 feet over the enemy and released a 1000 pound bomb which was seen to explode approximately 50 feet aft and somewhat to port of the submerging submarine's conning tower. Oil appeared on water. No further evidence of submarine.[17]

The last aircraft airborne in the morning launch was at 0621. At 0627 hours, Ensign Clifford R. Walters, flying SBD 6-B-2 from Bombing Six, reported sighting a Japanese submarine bearing 020 degrees from point option, the point from which the squadron dispersed to begin flying search patterns. He had reached the end of the search mission's first navigation leg, and after rendering a report and being informed that ten surface vessels he had spotted were Task Force 1, detached from Task Force 8 to meet *Saratoga* and escort her to Pearl Harbor, he turned toward the *Enterprise*. In his 13 December action report he recounted what occurred:

> . . . While en route back to the ship, I saw a submarine on the surface. Tracking the submarine in the sun, I was able to see it was large, no flag, and traveling at about 16 knots. I decided to bomb it in

a glide bomb but the higher winds pushed me into a dive bomb attack and with little flaps. I dropped the bomb at 1800 feet and was unable to pull out until about 600 feet because I was traveling at a speed of about 240 knots. The submarine submerged just before I was in firing range with the .50-caliber fixed guns. He submerged slowly and blew many bubbles on descent. The 1000 pound bomb landed about 40 feet on the starboard quarter. I believe shrapnel hit the submarine as the bomb had an instantaneous fuze. My Radioman, IVANTIC, J.J., RM3c, strafed the submarine with his .30-caliber free machine gun as we pulled out of the dive. I remained over the spot for a few minutes and the submarine did not surface again, so I returned to the ship. I saw no oil on the surface.[18]

Ensign Walters' action report suggests he probably had attacked and damaged the *I-70*. His Imperial Majesty's submarines *I-25* and *I-70*, were two of the Japanese combatant's attacked by *Enterprise* aircraft that morning. *I-25* reported being attacked with a depth charge by a TBD-1 "Devastator" of VT-6, but dove to 130 feet, and the depth charge exploded above her, causing no damage. After waiting thirty minutes, *I-25* returned to periscope depth and was attacked a second time, and again dove to 130 feet, causing the depth charge to explode above her, with no damage.[19]

The *I-70* was less fortunate. She had been damaged by a bomb released by an SBD in the early morning attack, damage that forced Commander Sano's decision to surface, and continue running on the surface. Considerably smaller and carrying less firepower than the Type C.1 cruiser subs that carried the midgets launched into Pearl Harbor, the Type 6A submarine built in 1934 was 336 feet long, 27 feet abeam, with a hull depth of 15 feet; displaced 1,400 tons normal, 1,785 full, and 2,440 tons maximum submerged; carried a 4-inch instead of a 5.5-inch gun; six instead of eight torpedo tubes; and 14 instead of 20 torpedoes.[20]

The end came in the early afternoon 121 miles northeast of Cape Halava, Molokai, Hawaiian Islands, at latitude 23 degrees, forty-five minutes north, longitude 155 degrees, thirty-five minutes west. Lieutenant Clarence E. Dickinson, the pilot who

Japanese submarine *I-70*, after sustaining
damage in a pre-war collision. IJN

had, himself, been shot down by swarming Japanese fighters over
Oahu the morning of 7 December—costing the life of his radioman/
gunner—had his opportunity for payback, and succeeded. He
struck with one dive bomb pass, and the submarine sank, leaving
four sailors in the water who later perished.[21]

Lieutenant Dickinson, writing in his 1942 book, *The Flying
Guns*, had no way of knowing the identity of the submarine he
and his Radioman/gunner sunk that day, but vividly recalled the
sequence of events leading to *I-70*'s destruction.

> . . . the morning scouting flight picked up three
> or four submarines on the surface. Three or four
> seen in the area covered by the scouting flight
> logically meant that there were an awful lot of Jap
> submarines around. So, about 11:30 in the morning
> of December 10, Admiral Halsey decided to send
> three planes to each place where a submarine had
> been sighted. I was detailed to make this flight.
>
> At that time no one had been assigned to me in
> place of Miller, [my radioman-gunner killed over
> Oahu the morning of 7 December.] So I took a lad

named [Thomas E.] Merritt, about twenty-one; very nice looking. This young man turned out to be an extremely reliable radioman and gunner, one of the best in the squadron. But this was going to be his first chance for revenge.

The submarine I was to hunt for was supposed to be about 125 miles north of Pearl Harbor. However, when I had flown about 75 miles south I wasn't expecting to find the submarine waiting for me; that was only my starting point, really. It had been seen at six o'clock approximately where I was by a half hour past noon. Where could it have gone in the Pacific Ocean in six and a half hours? I decided the best thing to do was to fly a rectangular course around the position where the sub had been last sighted and give emphasis to the north and east. I went twenty miles south, then traveled thirty miles on a leg to the east, then began the leg forty miles north. I had left the carrier at noon. It was now about half past one. Nothing but sky and water anywhere in sight.

The wind was blowing pretty much of a gale. There were white-capped waves, but visibility was excellent. I could see twenty-five miles in any direction, possibly thirty miles. Just as I reached the north corner of my rectangle, lo and behold! Way over to the northeast about fifteen or eighteen miles away there was a great big submarine running on the surface. It was pushing to the northeast just as fast as it could go. It was obviously a submarine but it looked to me to be the biggest I had ever seen. I talked to the carrier immediately.

"This is Sail Four . . . Have sighted submarine. Am attacking."

The carrier acknowledged my message. I was already heading toward the sub. I was about 800 feet off the water then and to make a good dive bombing attack I would have to climb up to 5,000 or 6,000 feet at least. So I started climbing. I suppose I was climbing while I was talking with the ship. Now, to go straight ahead fifteen to eighteen miles in a scout bomber is one thing, but it is something else to go a mile up while you are going eighteen miles ahead; moreover I was flying right into a heavy wind. It would probably take six or eight minutes for me to get into position to do my job. I had certain chores to do in connection with my craft of bombing. I had to "arm" the bomb mechanically before I dropped it. I had to do certain things to it that would make it explode on contact. Threaded through the fuse of that 500-pound bomb I was carrying were what we call "arming wires." These arming wires have to be pulled out of the fuse before the bomb is dropped, else it will fall as a dud. When the wires are pulled out, two parts of the fuse move into position, the "vanes" on the fuse rotate properly and on contact the bomb explodes. Consequently the height of futility in bombing is to neglect to arm your bomb. The arming of the bomb is the pilot's job, but to make sure that none of us forgets in the excitement of the attack, it has been made a part of the gunner's duty to check with the pilot just as your partner checks you against a possible renege in a bridge game when you fail to follow suit by asking politely, "No spades?"

I had plenty on my mind climbing to a good diving position. I didn't see how I could stand the disappointment were the Jap to submerge. Next thing I knew he was shooting at me; just as soon as I was within gun's distance of him the sub had opened up with two deck guns, four or five inchers. The Japs manning those guns were not especially good shots but, after all, this was the second time within three days that I had been shot at and I was a little tired of being on the receiving end. I was getting sensitive, I suppose. However, I had fine faith in that bomb. It is quite an effective weapon if you drop it close enough. Right beside the submarine, in the water, is best.

Those anti-aircraft bursts were giving me just a touch of headache. There wasn't a great deal of danger from them but they were annoying. I was climbing as hard as I could and then young Merritt called over our radio. "Is the bomb armed, Mr. Dickinson?"

I was busy in my cockpit just that second and did not respond. "Mr. Dickinson, is the bomb armed?" I feel sure I must have said yes a couple of times but this kid back of me wasn't going to have a failure on his hands. I was climbing and estimating the situation every instant. The Japs were shooting. Merritt was prompting. "Be sure the bomb is armed!" "Look here," I said, "the bomb is armed. For God's sake! Relax! Maybe we can get this submarine. Take my word for it, the bomb is armed."

Those aboard ship hadn't realized how far I had to go when I reported I was attacking. However, when I was about half way to where I was determined to get, there was a voice in my ears, asking for a report. Was I making progress? With the Jap shooting at me, with my deep concern for fear the submarine would disappear before I could lay my egg and further rasped by Merritt's well-meant solicitude, I was in no mood to be heckled by the ship. So I told them I would report the progress of my attack as soon as I had time to drop the bomb.

I suppose the Jap's two deck guns had fired at least twenty-five anti-aircraft shells at me. I had had him in sight for almost eight minutes. Yet he had made no attempt to submerge. All he was doing was turning to the right a few degrees. Obviously there was something wrong with him. He had been bombed once before that day. The plane from our carrier that had found him at six o'clock in the morning had dropped a bomb fairly close to him. So I believe he could not submerge. I can't imagine a submarine skipper in his right mind staying on the surface to fight a plane rather than dive. Even when I was three or four minutes away, in good working order he might have submerged easily. He did not, so I believe that he had previously been damaged.

Those two deck guns, one forward, one aft, were big enough to sink anything but a battleship. But they were firing a couple of machine guns, too. These were mounted on the platform of the oval, tank-like conning tower. For the second time in three days I could see the head-on, deadly jewel wink of machine guns but the flashes from the muzzles of those two anti-aircraft guns were yellow as lemon cream. Nevertheless the black explosions that occasionally washed a slight tremor into the plane quite definitely were not lemon pies.

I was measuring the sub's course, measuring my height and getting nicely set when my gunner spoke again. "Is the bomb armed, Mr. Dickinson?" This time I said, rather gently, I think, "Yes." Then I dived. I had a pretty good dive. All the way down I could see the heathen still shooting. Their faces looked brown, not yellow. I wasn't close enough to see expressions because I was probably as much as thirty stories higher than the Empire State building when I acted. At the left-hand side of the cockpit there is a handle, the bomb release. You simply pull this back so that it travels an inch or possibly an inch and a quarter, until it will go no further. There is no click or jar but you know you have dropped your bomb.

By the time I was able to pull out of the dive, and turn to get my plane's tail out of the way of my eyes it was probably fifteen seconds before the bomb struck; it struck right beside the submarine, amidships.

I saw first of all only one gun was firing. I suspect the bomb explosion had killed the Japs at the other gun. In a further space of seconds I had the plane turned and was flying back towards the sub. It had stopped, had no perceptible headway and had started to settle, as nearly as I could tell, on an even keel. The fact she had no forward motion satisfied me right then this was not a dive. She was settling! A little more by the stern than forward. In about three-quarters of a minute after my bomb struck the sub had gone under the water.

The chances are, I think, that the bomb explosion caused the submarine to open up underneath. That would kill her speed. Filling amidships would cause her to settle more or less on an even keel. Right after she disappeared, from her amidships, as near as I could tell, there was an eruption of oil and foamy water, like the bursting of a big bubble. Seconds later, fifteen or twenty, I suppose, there was a second disturbance; another bubble-like eruption of foam and oil churned to the white-capped surface of the sea. This time I saw some debris. I reported to the carrier what I had done and what I had seen. But I was careful to say that "possibly" the submarine had been sunk. You simply can't be sure on such evidence.

During the flight back to the carrier the young man in the rear seat and I discussed the probabilities. "Looks like we got him, Mr. Dickinson." "Yes, I think we did."

"That's certainly pretty nice, huh?"

If you had seen Pearl Harbor you would think so, too. I said to Merritt: "Glad you didn't let me forget to arm that bomb."

This was no time to lose the ship but as I approached the position where I estimated she would be all I could see was a big rainstorm covering the area. I circled the storm without seeing a trace of the carrier. I felt certain she was in the storm but I had a feeling it would be easy to get lost in such weather. At such a time! I had things to talk about. I finally plunged into the rainstorm and there was the carrier.[22]

The day proved hectic for Task Force 8 and the quarries she sought. In addition to the two bombing attacks on surfaced submarines and the sinking of *I-70*, there were seven other confirmed contacts with enemy submarines, which included non-stop air operations, periscope and conning tower sightings, two torpedo wakes clearly observed aiming for *Enterprise*, two depth charge attacks by screening destroyers, and gunfire at one submarine observed on the surface by the cruiser *Salt Lake City*. Throughout the day the two forces were constantly searching and maneuvering for shots at one another, or to spoil shots, weaving, zigzagging, changing speeds and directions.[23]

The day after the loss of *I-70* and Task Force 8's heavy engagement with the Japanese submarines in the vicinity of Oahu, Vice Admiral Mitsoyoshi was aware only that he had heard nothing from the submarine's commander, and the boat's status was still uncertain. Nevertheless, looking ahead to operations off the West Coast of the United States, and answering to directives from Imperial General Headquarters, he issued a detailed order to the Submarine Force Detachment now moving toward the coast. On Christmas Eve night, *I-15*, *I-9*, *I-10*, *I-17*, *I-19*, *I-21*, *I-23*, *I-25* and *I-26* were to each surface and fire 30 shells on selected targets. Rear Admiral Sato, aboard *I-9*, was charged to execute the order.[24]

Several facts were evident in Task Force 8's high number of active encounters with Japanese submarines 7 through 13 December. The enemy submarines were in the waters around Oahu in force, astride the sea lanes between Hawaii and the mainland, and an unknown number were now moving toward the west coast. They would probably arrive on stations off the west coast about 17 December. Between the 10th and the 17th, the enemy would begin taking a toll on shipping.

While *Enterprise* and the ships and planes of Task Force 8 were aggressively pursuing enemy submarines north and northeast of Oahu on 10 December, the carrier *Saratoga*, which departed San Diego 0958 hours the morning of 8 December, bound for Pearl Harbor, was refueling the three destroyers in her submarine screen, one at a time. From Destroyer Division 50, they were the *Talbot* (DD-114), *Waters* (DD-115), and *Dent* (DD-116), all World War I "four stackers." *Saratoga*, which began flight operations on the 9th, on the 11th dispatched *Talbot* to pick up the two-man crew from an SBD, plane number 3-B-2, from Bombing Squadron Three (VB-3). The aircraft went down 50 miles distant, and another plane in the flight reported the two men were in their rubber boat.[25]

On 12 December at 1335 hours, *Talbot*, *Waters* and *Dent*, were relieved of screening duties and turned back to San Diego when the ships of Task Force 1, which had been sent by CinCPac to escort and screen *Saratoga* on into Pearl Harbor, took stations in the formation. The ships in the now-strengthened task force were the heavy cruiser *Minneapolis* (CA-36), and the newer, more modern destroyers *Tucker* (DD-374), *Selfridge* (DD-357), *Case* (DD-370), and *Conyngham* (DD-371).[26]

Saratoga entered Pearl Harbor and moored at pier F-9 at 1037 the morning of 15 December without having logged a single submarine contact the entire sortie from San Diego to rejoin the Pacific Fleet in Hawaii. Less then twenty-four hours later, at 1226 on 16 December she was underway again, turning west southwest, soon to join Task Force 14 and deliver additional aircraft to Wake Island. At 1350 hours, while outbound initially to the southeast, *Saratoga* logged the sighting of Task Force 8 and the *Enterprise*, which was proceeding to Pearl Harbor for refueling and provisioning for further operations.[27]

While *Saratoga* and her newly formed task force were en route to Pearl Harbor from San Diego, Task Force 12, with the *Lexington*, was returning from the cancelled delivery to Midway of 18 Marine Vought SB2U-3 Vindicators from VMSB-231 squadron at Ewa. On orders from CinCPac, Task Force 12 turned around the morning of 7 December to search for the Japanese carrier strike force while maneuvering toward Pearl Harbor. At 1152 hours, as *Lexington* and her screens were steaming northwest toward the harbor's entrance, the heavy cruiser *Indianapolis* (CA-35) reported a torpedo wake on the cruiser's port side and the task force began maneuvering to avoid additional torpedo launches at *Lexington*.[28]

At 1621 hours, another submarine contact was reported on *Lexington*'s starboard bow, and she changed course left to avoid a torpedo wake that had been sighted. Escorting destroyers attacked the intruder with depth charges. Unknown to *Lexington* and Task Force 12, the depth charge attacks had taken their toll on the Japanese submarine *I-68*, whose captain was Commander Otoji Nakamura.[29]

Ordered to patrol on a station 20 to 50 miles southwest of Pearl Harbor, Nakamura vainly attempted more than once that day to penetrate the submarine screen and torpedo *Lexington*. For his trouble *I-68* was repeatedly hammered by 21 near miss, depth charge attacks. The attacks were uncomfortably close to being fatal for *I-68* and its crew. The last attack wrecked many of the submarine's battery cells, and caused flooding in her aft torpedo tubes. Nakamura decided to terminate *I-68*'s first patrol against the United States Navy, in support of the Combined Fleet's Pearl Harbor operation, and brought his crippled submarine limping slowly back to Kwajalein, where it arrived on 28 December—a long, and undoubtedly tense 15-day journey for the crew.[30]

Following another rapid turnaround, *Lexington* was again underway from Pearl at 1357 hours on 14 December, and at 1732, saw *Saratoga* and her task force disappear over the horizon as she returned to refuel, take on aviation fuel and provisions, for the next sortie. Steaming on a southwesterly course as part of Task Force 11, by shortly after midnight the morning of 17 December, *Lexington* and the commanders of all the task force's ships knew they were embarked on a raid on the Japanese-held Marshall Islands, in support of *Saratoga's* planned delivery of additional aircraft to Wake Island.[31]

Saratoga left Pearl on 16 December, steaming toward the west, southwest with four destroyers providing plane guard duties and submarine screen: the destroyers *Blue* (DD-387), *Henley* (DD-391), *Helm* (DD-388), and *Bagley* (DD-386). At 1215 on 17 December, she commenced joining Task Force 14, a powerful force consisting of the heavy cruisers *San Francisco* (CA-38), *Astoria* (CA-34), and *Minneapolis*; destroyers *Mugford* (DD-389), *Selfridge*, *Patterson* (DD-392), and *Ralph Talbot* (DD-390); the tanker *Neches* (AO-5) and seaplane tender *Tangier*. Finally, *Lexington* and Task Force 11, supporting *Saratoga* and Task Force 14 were about to take the fight to the enemy.

The Gatherings

On Wednesday, 10 December, while *Enterprise* and Task Force 8 aggressively disrupted Japanese submarine operations to the north and northeast of Oahu, initiatives undertaken to move the Pan American Airways' *Anzac Clipper's* passengers from Hilo on the Big Island, to Oahu, were about to bear fruit.

The attack on Pearl Harbor, and its aftermath, including the declaration of martial law, brought Hawaiian Airlines and all civil aviation traffic to a temporary dead stop. Availability of direct communications with sources of supply, mainland and elsewhere, was suddenly non-existent. Until Wednesday following the Japanese "visit," the only usable aircraft available to Hawaiian Air was the line's one S38, an old amphibian. It had taken three days to get a DC-3 back in service. Another of the line's DC-3s was shot up so badly it would be weeks before all the parts needed could be obtained. What's more, the declaration of martial law had placed the line's operation at the disposal and under the control of the Army Air Force command at nearby Hickam Field.

Matters were made far more complicated by the fact the

islands, and especially Oahu, remained at high alert, uncertain of the Japanese strike fleet's whereabouts, and for the most part convinced the enemy would surely follow up their success with an attempted, more devastating knock-out blow.

While the airline's owner, Stan Kennedy lobbied to convince officials that the islands required some inter-island transportation, and his people should provide the service, both civilian and military authorities were trying to work out the details of how martial law should be invoked to maintain an effective society. During the same period, the *Anzac Clipper*'s passengers isolated at Hilo, 200 miles to the southwest, made known their plight.

The afternoon of the 7th, in an exclusive interview with the *Hilo Tribune-Herald* newspaper reporter, Ricardo Labez, the Burmese Prime Minister expressed his intent to telephone Secretary of State Cordell Hull in Washington, DC, regarding further transit to his country. Unquestionably, his call, among several others made, alerted senior government officials to the circumstances of the stranded passengers, and they in turn asked the Army and Navy to assist them. People at Hickam, who, due to the declaration of martial law, had hurriedly been assigned to control all future Hawaiian Airlines' flights, were also eager to see one of their planes get airborne.

The morning of the 10th, Hawaiian Air's senior captain, Sam Elliott, received a call from Hickam Field concerning the need for a flight southeast to Hilo via Maui. "Can you do it . . . say, by Thursday?" the Hickam officer asked Elliot. "It will mean a flight without any incoming weather reports along the way; no tower communications; no way you may use the radio to alert Maui and Hilo stations. Worst of all, we have no knowledge concerning the possible presence of enemy forces."

"Sounds a little spooky, but I'm sure we can handle it. Give us a day and a half to get ready," volunteered Elliott.

The stated priority for scheduling the Hawaiian flight hinged upon military need—their representatives to communicate directly with County officials and scattered military detachments on Maui and the Big Island. Besides the military officials headed outbound from Honolulu were several sugar company executives from Maui and Hawaii island plantations, and Dr. Homer Izumi from Maui, temporarily trapped by the Japanese attack.

Within an hour, Elliott caught up with Jimmy Hogg, the line's junior captain, who was helping clean up and get the airline flying again, after the attack. Hogg listened to Elliott's description of the project requested by the Army Air Force.

"After Sam's explanation concerning all the hazards a pilot could run into, he asked me if I wanted the flight," Jimmy said. "I asked him: Goddamn, Sam, you're really scratching the bottom of the barrel, aren't you?"

Sam didn't reply to the question.

"Why don't you take it, Sam?" asked Jim, grinning when he asked the question.

"Galdarn it, DO YOU WANT IT OR DON'T YA?" That's the final statement Jimmy said he got from Captain Sam.

"Yeah . . . O.K., I'll go," smiled Jimmy.

At wakeup on Oahu 11 December, DC-3 Number 10 was ready to go. Low clouds and rain blanketed the channel between Oahu and the island of Molokai. No one in Honolulu had any idea what the weather would be like further east, only that it would likely get worse on Maui and the Big Island as the day progressed. Hogg's landing on Maui would—and was a complete surprise to Valley islanders. The unsure populace and its militia might take the approaching airliner sneaking below the clouds as a possible Japanese bomber.

As Sunday night and the tragic "friendly fire" incident amply demonstrated, war and guns, and the dangers inherent in nervous, inexperienced people carrying them, pose grave dangers. The kind of dangers few understood. Nobody knew what kind of war to expect or from whence it would come. Thousands of men throughout the islands felt an obligation to their families, men who would shoot first and ask questions later. Following the air attack on Oahu, any airplane was under suspicion and fair game until identified otherwise.

Jimmy Hogg said it was that latter thought that set hard on his mind. He knew all about the problems of Hawaii's weather. When it rained with visibility down to a mile or less, you got down on the water and picked a course for your next landfall, keeping one wary eye peeled for muddy surf, the other watching the clock. B.J. Hogg was no beginner at that. It was foul weather navigation as he had learned it during hundreds of flight hours in the old amphibians.

Hogg's first sight of Molokai came right on schedule. Laau Point five degrees off the nose, a mile of mud-streaked surf in between. He followed the shoreline five miles then turned further

SUNDAY IN HELL 705

southeast for Lanai's Keana Point, the western most part of the pineapple island.

Reaching Lanai amidst a brief moment of sunlight, Jim made the left turn that would carry the DC-3 along the island's northern beach until he reached Lanai's northeastern point. A heavy rain shower blocked any view of Maui, his first stop, but Jimmy maintained visual contact with the water. To that point Jimmy considered the flight as being "duck soup." No different from the old days. Even had leaks in the cockpit. He thought, "They'll look at me and believe I was so scared I wet my goddamn pants." He guessed there was a chance he might before the flight was over.

In three minutes Jimmy calculated he would be nearing the Maui shoreline. The moment he made contact it required a sharp right turn to fly past the historic Pioneer Inn and the huge banyan tree that marks old Lahaina town. Jimmy, now flying the shore on a southeasterly heading was still in rain showers and just below a ragged cloud layer.

Within minutes his concentration on the course changes his route required became more critical. He was still in heavy to moderate rain. Definitely not an aid to visibility. Particularly when the last twelve miles of his route was known as whale country—where the deep waters of Maui's south shore meet the rising slopes of the island's western mountains.

As he turned and banked to maintain flight over the shorebreak, he was gradually turning eastward. Having momentarily forgotten the Army colonel's warning that he may receive fire from folks on the ground who wouldn't know a DC-3 from a Japanese bomber, he refreshed his thinking and quickly turned slightly seaward. He hoped he'd be out of range of anyone but a sharp-shooting deer hunter, yet still within sight of Maui's shore. He realized that once he struck the shoreline at Lahaina, phone calls could easily pass along his presence.

Within minutes he rounded the point just south of Stan Kennedy's original Maui airport—Maalaea. That meager strip of tidal land carved out of an adjacent stand of kiawe trees that had taken Kennedy just three days to complete. Now Jim's more advanced DC-3 would use Puunene airport, less than three miles from Maalaea, a bigger and better airfield, built by the federal government two years previously and suitable for either the Sikorsky amphibs or the new Douglas DC-3s.

The skies throughout most of the island's central valley were relatively clear, visibility better than eight miles, most of the approaching rain squalls had yet to arrive.

"What the hell?" was Jimmy's first reaction as he started to approach the field. Trucks and vehicles, and all kinds of obstructions were blocking the runways.

Without radio contact with the airport, Jim had no idea how he was going to convince people on the ground he was on their side and deserving of a chance to land. He circled for half an hour before the blockade was removed. Upon landing, he was greeted by Army or national guardsmen carrying weapons at the ready and pointed in his general direction.

Jim parked the DC-3 and shut down the engines. His Maui passengers had deplaned but were apparently being restrained from leaving the scene. When Jim stepped out he was confronted by an Army sergeant whose first words were: "Permission to inspect your aircraft, sir?"

Jim gave him an O'K, "but what the hell is it for?"

"My orders, sir," replied the no-nonsense sergeant. The sergeant continued, explaining that Hogg was lucky he didn't get hit when he came along the shore from Lahaina. "Coming up the coast from Lahaina, flying right down on the water nobody could tell who the hell you were and everybody was trying to shoot you down." He told Jim he suspected some of the local people didn't know one airplane from another, and maybe Hogg ought to know most Mauians had prepared for the worst, "if you know what I mean."

"Maybe it was a good thing it was raining because I don't think they hit us," Hogg responded. The two walked around the airplane and learned it had escaped without a scratch.

Jim had no trouble understanding how close they came to serious trouble, and made clear to the sergeant this same DC-3 might be landing on Maui about three hours from now en route to Honolulu. He made a polite request asking the sergeant to try and keep his boys in line. "This plane's already been shot up by the Japanese," added Hogg.

The incident at Maui turned out to be the worst scare Jimmy had. The flight to Hilo proceeded much like the first half of the trip, right down above the waves. The runways at Hilo airport had also been blockaded, but all obstructions were quickly removed once Hogg circled the field. Once the plane landed, a friend of Hogg's named Bones Richardson and other National Guard members came forward.

"Jim," said Richardson, "Damn good thing I recognized the tail end of that airplane as you went by because we were ready to blast you out of the sky." These were tense times indeed.

Captain B.J. Hogg picked up all of Pan Am's passengers, each of them happy to finally see progress after their unexpected and rather extended visit to Hilo. But Jimmy wasn't quite ready to believe all his possible troubles were over. He still had to get back into what could be called the military complex of Honolulu, an area still barely recovering from the nasty surprise foisted upon the island by the Japanese attack.

Communications between the islands had yet to be authorized, but at least Jim knew what the weather would be—and he knew that Maui's airport could be expecting some of the bad stuff he flew in earlier. If he had to fly low again he had to be more concerned over all of those touchy people with guns.

Hogg reminded himself "If guns were an issue on Maui, what the hell am I up against when I return to the island of Oahu?" What if the Honolulu weather was the same as when he left? He'd be a target for all those nervous, real-life, gun-toting people who had firsthand evidence of what war is all about. Five days earlier they had seen what air power could do. Making a low shoreline approach back to Honolulu could be inviting more bullet holes than the few he was likely to get from the Maui people.

As it turned out, he needn't have worried. Jimmy and his passengers made it with only a minimum of difficulty. By the time he brought the Pan Am passengers in to John Rodgers Airport late that day, the light cruisers *St. Louis* and *Phoenix* (CL-46), in Task Group 15.2, were outbound from Pearl Harbor, the *St. Louis* underway from berth C-5 at 1600 hours, the *Phoenix* three minutes later from C-6, destination San Francisco. Once there, their tasks were return to Honolulu and Pearl Harbor, each to escort a convoy from San Francisco to Honolulu, complete with destroyer anti-submarine screens, less than one day apart.[32]

At 1639 hours, with her commander, Captain George A. Rood at the conn, *St. Louis* was proceeding at the harbor speed limit, *Phoenix*, with her commander, Captain Herman E. Fischer at the conn, astern preparing to fall into column when at sea, and still not clear of the entrance, when a patrol plane dropped a smoke bomb off the starboard bow of *St. Louis*, and reported submarines near the smoke bomb. A destroyer attacked the submarine with depth charges and the plane attacked with bombs, while both ships promptly accelerated to flank speed, 31 knots, and commenced zigzagging. At 1644 *St. Louis* cleared the channel, and six minutes later eased her speed down to 29 knots, followed by another reduction to 25 knots at 1700 hours as destroyers *Southard* (DD-207) and *Wasmuth* (DD-338) reported for duty as screening vessels. After leaving the harbor, instead of turning east to pass between Oahu and Molokai, the two, in column with *St. Louis* as guide and *Phoenix* on station astern 1,000 yards, turned starboard to 270 degrees, then later further right to 348 degrees, to pass between Kauai and Oahu, and finally to course 030 degrees true.[33]

Before the two cruisers departed Pearl Harbor and ran headlong into submarines waiting at its entrance, CinCPac's intelligence officers had undoubtedly picked up emergency signals from the freighter SS *Lahaina*, about 700 miles northeast of Oahu, and passed the contents and their intelligence assessment via ultra messages to the two combatants' captains. Naval intelligence and operational commanders were also aware of the sinking of the *Cynthia Olson*. From the preceding four days following the air raid had come numerous reports of enemy submarine sound contacts, sightings, and torpedo attacks in waters around Oahu and along the first 100 to 200 miles of the route to the mainland—plus one midget beached near Bellows Field, and reported claims of sinkings of at least four other submarines, including two other midgets. The *Cynthia Olson* and freighter *Lahaina* were ample warnings of what lay between Oahu and the west coast. Task forces and convoys to and from the mainland wouldn't be pleasure cruises, and matters got worse as the days of December progressed.

On 3 December, the 5,642-ton Matson Line freighter, *Lahaina*, had left Ahukini, Kauai, for San Francisco, carrying 745 tons of molasses and 300 tons of scrap iron. When Captain Hans O. Matthiesen received word of the 7 December Japanese attack on Pearl Harbor, his first reaction was to instruct his 34-man crew to turn the vessel around and head back to Kauai, following orders from the U.S. Navy to return to the nearest U.S. port. Three days later, Matthiesen received an urgent radio message directing the ship to reverse course and proceed to the continental U.S., which was apparently considered safer than Hawaii, with its submarine- infested waters.

While responding to the situation and direction he received, it occurred to Matthiesen that Japanese bombers headed for Pearl Harbor probably passed directly over the ship but could not see it in the stormy weather. To remain hidden from view, he ordered the ship's crew to mix all paint in the lockers together to produce a dull gray color. He then instructed crewmembers to repaint the ship from the stack down and to place a sack of raw potatoes in each of the life boats.[34]

In the afternoon of 11 December, 1941, while the *Lahaina* was about 700 miles northeast of Oahu, the Japanese submarine *I-9*, one of four Imperial Navy submarines scouting the ocean far to the northeast of Oahu and heading toward the west coast, surfaced on her starboard side and fired a warning shot across the vessel's bow. Embarked on *I-9* was the commander of the 1st Submarine Group, Rear Admiral Tsutomu Sato. Captain Matthiesen and his crew were confronting one of Imperial Japan's startlingly large, newer submarines, 367 feet in length, 31 feet abeam with a hull depth of 18 feet. Completed 13 February 1941, *I-9* displaced 2,434 tons standard, 2,919 full, and 4,149 tons maximum submerged, with six torpedo tubes, 18 torpedoes, one 5-inch deck gun, two 25-mm antiaircraft guns, and could carry a light seaplane in a hangar beneath the conning tower. Like other submarines of the same type engaged in the Pearl Harbor operation, the *I-9* left her seaplane at home, because the long-range journey required additional cargo space in the empty hangar for food and other supplies. The captain of *I-9*, Commander Akiyoshi Fujii, conserving the boat's torpedoes, had given the order to surface and open fire with its deck gun, which hit the ship about eight times.[35]

Captain Matthiesen wrote of *I-9*'s attack shortly after the incident.

> "He came up on our starboard quarter right out of the sun, where you try not to look because it hurts your eyes," said Matthiesen. "He fired a shot. I saw it hit, then another . . . " Third Mate Douglas McMurty, who at noon had surrendered his watch to the second mate, was asleep when the attack began. "I raced for my emergency station, the number one lifeboat on the starboard side, and hoisted myself up." A shell then exploded below the wooden boat, tossing McMurty aside. The next rounds destroyed

the deckhouse and bridge. "They knew exactly what they were shooting at," said McMurty, who quickly ran to the other lifeboat.

According to Matthiesen, it was a strange feeling to be shot at but be unable to shoot back. "He didn't give us any time to get into the lifeboats. The first shell went right through the starboard lifeboat." After giving the order to abandon ship via the port lifeboat, Matthiesen returned to his quarters to retrieve a bag with marine instruments. He dropped the bag and his cigarettes to a crew member in the lifeboat, and was going over the rail to let himself down when another shell hit the quarters he just left, setting the forward house afire. "We were no sooner under the port quarter, sitting there, when a shell came right through the ship, landed about 50 yards away in the sea, and then exploded."

The men in the 24-foot lifeboat rowed frantically, attempting to stay near the shelter of the burning freighter, where they couldn't be seen. Their task was made even more difficult because the 17-person lifeboat was carrying 34 men. Then the submarine's nose appeared around the edge of the ship. "I could see them on deck, watching like hawks," wrote Matthiesen, who ordered his men to

The Matson Line's freighter, *Lahaina*, sunk by Japanese submarine *I-9*, on 11 December 1941, about 700 miles northeast of Oahu. MNC

be quiet. "The first guy who makes any kind of a movement gets brained," was his order. Then the submarine backed within 40 or 50 yards of the ship, and the deck gun fired into the *Lahaina*'s engine room, which immediately began to fill with water. As the submarine turned away, the men could hear some of the Japanese submarine's crew cheering and yelling, "Banzai!"

The cheering and yelling of "Banzai!" a term that had its origin in a different language and sound in ancient China, where it was customary to pay respects to the emperor, is a derivative of the term picked up in ancient Japan, where it was modified as it echoed down through the ages to modern times. Literally, it translated "Ten thousand years," and was used to bless the emperors in East Asia in ancient times. Heard by Captain Matthiesen and his crew, it had already been heard thousands of times in armies, navies and among peoples subjected to the Japanese militarists onslaught in China, the south and southwest Pacific regions in the decade leading to the attack on Pearl Harbor. With shouts of "Banzai!" still ringing in his memory, Mattiesen continued with his account.

All night the ship drifted and burned, with the entire sky red from the flames leaping as high as 100 feet. At dawn, however, the crew saw that the ladder was still intact and the engineer's house appeared unburned. Matthiesen and a group of his men then boarded the ship to look for provisions. With the ship listing and burning, the men hustled 15 blankets, a case of eggs, 25 pounds of carrots, several dozen lemons and apples, five loaves of bread, a case of biscuits, butter and 10 gallons of water. "We had a hell of a time with that case of eggs, but we did it," wrote Matthiesen. Hurriedly, the men left the ship as the midship-house exploded in flame and debris. At about 10 a.m., the vessel turned on her side and slid into the sea, as the crew solemnly gave her their final farewell.

Matthiesen decided to head for Maui, which he estimated was about 700 miles south. In the 10-day struggle for survival that ensued, four men died, the last just before the survivors sighted land. The captain wrote in his log, "We brought his body in to Maui and buried it there."[36]

The day *Lahaina* went down before the guns of *I-9*, and the *St. Louis* and *Phoenix* left for San Francisco, there were numerous submarine warnings passed from CinCPac to ships afloat. Task Force 8, operating to the north and northeast of Oahu 9 through

11 December, repeatedly encountered, pursued, and attacked Japanese submarines aggressively pressing their own efforts to penetrate *Enterprise*'s anti-submarine screen and launch torpedo attacks on the carrier. That pattern continued daily until *Enterprise* entered Pearl Harbor late afternoon, 16 December, the Tuesday the cruiser *Louisville* escorted the *President Coolidge* and the US Army Transport *General Hugh L. Scott*, with their war-wary passengers into Honolulu from the Philippines after their lengthy voyage to a temporary respite. The *Coolidge* and *Hugh L. Scott* were now three days from the next leg of their journey to San Francisco.

In the nine days following their Pearl Harbor operation, the Japanese Combined Fleet was beginning to learn that American anti-submarine warfare was considerably more effective than anticipated. The results came from experience gained in the Navy's cooperative operations and technology-sharing with the British Royal Navy, plus the anti U-Boat and convoy work with the British in the Atlantic.

The 10-11 December warnings proved valid for the *St. Louis* and *Phoenix* racing toward San Francisco twenty-four hours later on course 057 degrees, when at 1619 hours on the 12th, lookouts on *St. Louis* sighted a submarine periscope wake bearing almost due east at range 4,000 yards. Submarines *I-1*, *I-2*, and *I-3* were still on station in the Kauai Channel. The two cruisers went ahead flank speed, 31 knots while changing course almost 70 degrees left, to 350 degrees true, putting rapidly increasing distance between them and their potential attacker, and frustrated any hopes of a torpedo attack. They knew the enemy's slow submerged speeds would leave them far behind the cruisers, and even at night, on the surface, the enemy subs' maximum speeds couldn't close the gap.[37]

What's more, no submarine commander in his right mind, enemy or friendly, with one or two 5-inch guns and two antiaircraft guns was going to surface and duel with even one cruiser, day or night, never mind two cruisers.

* * *

On the 12th, far to the south, southwest of Oahu, Task Group 15.5, the *Pensacola* Convoy, was still plowing steadily southward. The task group commander had received a message shortly after the attack on Pearl Harbor diverting the convoy into Suva in the Fiji Islands, pending a decision on the nine ships' final destination.

While the convoy was en route, intense deliberations by the War Department's Joint Army and Navy Board, and President Roosevelt, yielded a decision not to attempt sailing into the teeth of the Japanese advance into the Philippines. Having slowly and steadily made its way at speeds from nine to nine and one half knots to conserve fuel, Captain Norman Scott's cruiser, with sub-chaser *Niagra*, received the message confirming the decision. They were to escort the convoy to Brisbane, Australia on the northeast coast of "The Land Down Under."

On the 13th, they turned southwest and put in to Suva, and at 1420 hours on the 14th [13th in Oahu] held a conference aboard *Pensacola* to review the orders they received, coordinate plans for arrival and follow-on activities in Brisbane. Attending were Brigadier General Julian Barnes, U.S. Army, Convoy Commander Troops; Colonel Johnston, U.S. Army, Chief of Staff; Commander Davenport Browne, USN, Convoy Commander; Commander G.C. Clark, USN, Convoy Vice-Commander; Lieutenant Alexander J. Gray, Jr., USN, Naval Observer in Suva; the American Consul and the Commanding Officer, Royal New Zealand Air Force Detachment at Suva. At 1640 hours *Pensacola* was underway again, bound for Brisbane, and at 1703, the convoy, with *Niagra* to follow, was underway, standing out of Suva.

* * *

At 1650 on the 12th, *St. Louis* and *Phoenix*, now well clear of the Kauai, Channel slowed to 20 knots and turned starboard to course 130. No sooner had they slowed to a speed of 20 knots, when at 1652 *Phoenix* signaled *St. Louis*, "submarine to port," and they again turned just over 70 degrees port, to 057, while accelerating to 25 knots. Twenty-three minutes later, back starboard to course 042 degrees. San Francisco was yet four days distant.

Most assuredly, with the declaration of war, runs to San Francisco and back would not be pleasure cruises—although *St. Louis* and *Phoenix* were fortunate on this run. The sleek, fast cruisers had forged ahead of the slower moving Japanese submarines, which had to run submerged during daylight hours, and wouldn't be on station off the west coast until 17 December. Nevertheless, caution was never thrown to the wind, for on the 13th, when they were a day short of the midpoint in their dash to San Francisco, each cruiser launched all four of their scout planes during the day, on a coordinated schedule to give their task group airborne anti-submarine search coverage ahead, virtually every minute of the entire daylight period. Before and after launch and recovery of aircraft, the two commenced zigzagging to spoil tracking and ranging by any submarine that might have slipped in close, ahead of them, undetected.

The rest of the trip neither *St. Louis* nor *Phoenix* logged the presence or suspected presence of Japanese submarines. The 14th, 15th, and 16th, they launched no scout planes. At 1725 hours on the 15th, just as the command "darken ship" went to the two crews, lookouts on *St. Louis* sighted two destroyers, the *King* (DD-242) and *Humphreys* (DD-236), both World War I-era "four stackers," which shortly joined the formation—*Humphreys* on the starboard bow, *King* on the port bow—as submarine screens the final fifteen hours of the run to San Francisco.

* * *

Far southwest of Task Group 15.2, on Oahu, Saturday, 13 December was a day of deepening sadness for Joey Border and many others. Bob, who, on arrival aboard *Tennessee* as the second wave of attackers was withdrawing, had been completely absorbed by the crisis and his resulting duties, yet knew full well Joey would be worried and wondering about his safety. He couldn't call her from the ship as he could before war came to the islands, and so when he had a few spare minutes wrote her a letter instead, which she was greatly relieved to receive on Wednesday the 10th. She hadn't seen or heard from Bob since a few, shock-filled minutes after he stormed down the stairs and out the front door for the ship while the air raid was still in progress. Happiness and marital bliss disappeared with him.

A pall hung like a dark cloud over the beautiful islands. Except for the martial law proclamation and official announcements, most of which were requests or orders, the radio fell silent the afternoon of the 7th, took days to return to reasonably normal broadcasting, and with the lengthening silence immediately came a rash of foreboding rumors. Words were of enemy paratrooper landings, more air raids, the Japanese fleet's presence just off shore, enemy amphibious landings on beaches, sabotage, "bombs" falling in Honolulu, all coupled with the reality of terrible damage to the fleet and airfields, a devastating loss of life all across the island—and especially in the harbor and on the air bases.

Newspapers were the only halfway reliable sources of information, and in many instances they were reporting rumors as fact. News and accurate factual information were scarce. Joey could go to several reliable sources of information, however. Her closest friend, Barbara Morrison, was the wife of Lieutenant (jg) Charles H. Morrison Jr., who was Bob's *Tennessee* shipmate and supervisor from the Naval Academy's class of 1938. Barbara was the daughter-in-law of Navy Captain Charles H. and "Mother Morrison," as Joey called her. "Mother Morrison" was quite religious and hovered over her son and daughter-in-law, always concerned for their care, safety and well-being.

The Morrison's had just arrived on Oahu for Captain Morrison's new assignment and were awaiting government quarters at Pearl Harbor when the attack came. Fortunately, Charlie and Barbara had rented a house within easy walking distance of Joey's and Bob's apartment, and the day of the attack Joey went to Barbara's to spend the first night, avoid being alone, and, considering her lessons as a cub reporter in Bremerton, Washington, to learn more about what was going on at Pearl Harbor. Most of all she worried about Bob. Did he safely reach the *Tennessee*? Was he alright?

More fortunately, "Mother Morrison" knew Joey was alone in the Borders' apartment, and insisted that Barbara look after Joey, plus ensure she was both welcome and could always come to Barbara and "Mother Morrison's" for assistance. This was the Navy family's way. Perhaps even more important, Captain Morrison was an officer who firmly believed in keeping his family informed regarding life, health and well-being in the Navy, short of divulging activities clearly requiring military secrecy's silence.

Mixed with all the shocking and painful news of Oahu's 7 December was the declaration of martial law, military vehicles and vehicle convoys constantly on the move, trench digging and sandbagging, the calls for police, Red Cross, hospital, and other volunteers; blood donations; guards seemingly everywhere wearing helmets, battle dress and carrying rifles with fixed bayonets; air raid sirens and drills, nightly blackouts, food hoarding first—then food, pharmacy and gasoline rationing, curfews, movement of military dependents off the bases to safer, temporary shelters; schools closed and children out of sight; and Joey's complete dependence on scarce public transportation or any officers' wives and friends who might have automobiles they could drive.

For Joey and any other bus or automobile passenger familiar with the great battleships of the Pacific Fleet, a ride toward or past the Navy Yard brought terrible sights and constantly sad reminders. Shattered, burned airplane hulks and buildings at Hickam Field and incomprehensible, nightmarish views across the harbor toward Ford Island. Most of the grand, beautiful ships Joey had come to know and go aboard for pleasant afternoons and evenings in Pearl Harbor and in times past in Puget Sound and Long Beach were lifeless derelicts. *Tennessee*, Bob's ship, thank God, from a distance looked to be untouched, as did *Maryland*, which on the 10th had been moved from her berth in front of Tennessee to another pier across the harbor to the east. But there were the sickening, grotesque sights of the shattered and burned *Arizona* astern of *Tennessee*, and the upturned bottom of *Oklahoma* next to *Maryland* until *Maryland* moved across the channel. On the channel side next to the relatively unscarred *Tennessee*, sat the battered and badly burned *West Virginia*, her main deck awash, and further distant, *California*, then beyond, across the channel from Hospital Point, *Nevada*, all forlornly sitting on the bottom of Pearl Harbor. Beginning the morning of the 12th, the damaged *Pennsylvania* could be seen back at her normal mooring, to Dock 1010, having been returned from the dry dock. Then had come the funerals beginning the 8th.[38]

All week had come the sad funerals followed by funeral processions weaving through the streets and along the highways toward freshly dug graves in cemeteries. There were hundreds of freshly dug graves, and throughout the week men labored feverishly to stay ahead of the pace of burials. Many of the dead couldn't be identified, their gravesites temporarily affixed with numbers indicating they were "unknown." Kaneohe buried 18 unknowns. Joey attended five funerals at Navy cemeteries, and Saturday the 13th was the absolute low point in what she told her diary was the "Most awful week I've ever spent."

Ensign Herbert Jones' funeral was first thing Saturday morning, the 13th. She remembered well the young ensign from the *California*. He, along with others had come to the Springer's quarters in Puget Sound Navy Yard on 5 February for an evening of relaxation and fun. Joey went by bus to the Navy chapel at Pearl Harbor, and went with the funeral procession to the new Red Hill Cemetery where he was laid to rest with full military honors, a Marine Corps honor guard, and a bugler playing the mournful sound of "Taps." She would long remember standing on the elevated sloping terrain in the newly opened Red Hill Cemetery near Aiea, her gaze sweeping the terrible sight of Pearl Harbor, past the as yet, unmanicured surface scarred by numerous freshly dug and covered graves.

The words spoken of him at the service vanished into achingly sad memory. She was unaware he would be long remembered by his shipmates, young sailors and Marines touched by his bravery, valor, unhesitating concern for others when he first fought to save them, then was mortally wounded—and again only thought of others while he was dying.

When the funeral was over she went to Barbara Morrison's and told her of this fifth and hopefully final funeral, then caught the bus to Queens' Hospital to give blood, a gesture she hoped would contribute something, but only exacted more futility from an already dark day that was ending a dark week. When she arrived to give blood, she was eye witness to a scene that had been in progress ten hours a day, every day since the attack.[39]

> . . . Although only 253 persons had responded to the blood bank in all the months before the attack, now 400 and 500 a day clamored to give blood. The bank had been geared to taking two or three persons an hour; now it processed 50 donors an hour . . . Short cuts consistent with safety were made. Equipment was improvised or borrowed from chemical laboratories of the University of Hawaii and industrial firms. The Hawaiian Sugar Planters' Association and the Pineapple Producers' Cooperative Association sterilized equipment and processed blood into plasma.

Another eye witness to the sudden increase in volunteer blood donors, wrote:

> Men and women waited in line for hours. Soldiers stood their guns with fixed bayonets in our surgery hallway and rolled up their sleeves and helped; sailors gave their few precious hours of liberty to wait their turn. Mothers asked strangers to hold small children and took their turns on the surgery

tables. Civilian defense workers from Pearl Harbor
and workers from Red Hill, red-eyed from long
hours of welding, stopped by to donate before
snatching a few hours rest. The whole crew and
passengers from a Dutch ship came in a body to
help their American allies, then hastened back to
journey across a perilous sea.

A crew of husky iron workers in their oily work
clothes came en masse; whole crews from dry docks
and inter-island ships. Dock workers and society
folks waited in line to do their part. Sugar and
pineapple plantation employees came direct from
their work in the fields.[40]

But Joey's time in line waiting to give blood was for naught.
When the volunteer technician attempted to find a vein in the
small arm where veins could barely be discerned, she could only
repeatedly insert the needle trying to hit the small, elusive target.
Frustrated, they both gave up and Joey left with multiple needle
pricks that left her more disconsolate at being unable to do her part.
She took the bus back to her apartment, where a call came from
Charlie Morrison on board *Tennessee*—obviously prompted by
Barbara's and "Mother Morrison's" concern for her. She learned
she couldn't yet come to Pearl Harbor, but tommorow would
be different. Bob would be able leave the ship for the first time,
Sunday, at Pearl Harbor. With that piece of good news, and a
letter from a friend in the states, she went back to Louise Foley's
to spend the night.

Sunday the 14th she again made the bus trip to Pearl Harbor,
this time with eager anticipation in spite of the depressing
wreckage visible along the way. The sight of Bob approaching
the dock on a motor launch lifted her spirits. She was thrilled to
see him, know that he was safe, and even more thrilled to learn
he could come home to the apartment for a few hours. They rode
the bus together. She was full of questions, and en route he told
her of what he had seen and had to do, the losses, and all he had
learned and been involved in, including the hard damage repair
and salvage work in progress on the battered ships. But for now,
that was all behind them. That night, when she went to Louise
Foleys, she told her diary she and Bob had a *glorious afternoon*
before he left for the ship at 4 p.m.

It was 9 p.m. in Pensacola, Florida, where Karl Border would return on Monday. He was nearing completion of his aviation training, and would soon be receiving his Navy wings of gold. He was spending Sunday night at home "with Missy and dad," and they had received good news that day, which he noted in his diary—a telegram from Joey's father. ". . . Received a telegram from Captain Springer saying Bob and Joey are safe! Thank God!" The Springers had received Joey's 7 December letter, which she completed and mailed via *Clipper* on 8 December.

On Monday, the 15th, life was slowly returning toward normal for Joey, but relaxing wasn't easy and a "return to normal" wouldn't really come to Oahu until war's end. For now, the islands remained on high alert, with the night blackout still in effect. That evening, for the first night since the 7th, she could once again at least listen to the radio. But other factors were operating in the background to bring more of war's wrenching change to life in the Navy—and in a tropical paradise.[41]

Orders to Evacuate

In the Navy's Pacific Fleet headquarters and the Army's Hawaiian Department, joint planning to evacuate military dependents and non-essential government employees and their dependents, began after the 31 October memorandum from Secretary of the Navy Knox arrived in Hawaii six days later, 31 days in advance of the Japanese attack. The result? When 7 December came, there was no evacuation plan. But planning, preparing, and doing, heretofore virtually non-existent, abruptly accelerated. The attack lit a blowtorch underneath Navy and Army staff officers, and retired Navy Captain Max M. Frucht, the territorial representative to the U.S. Maritime Commission, who suddenly had the additional duty of manager of the evacuation thrust upon him.

The memorandum had instructed, "have plans prepared for the evacuation of dependents of, Navy service personnel, Navy civil service, and employees of Contractors engaged in Navy construction projects, from outlying bases under their respective jurisdictions," then went on to say, "When dependents of both Army and Navy personnel are present at the same base, coordination in planning will be obtained by means of a Local

Joint Planning Committee, the recommendations of which will be forwarded through channels and reviewed by the War Plans Division of the Chief of Naval Operations."

To complete the evacuation, the memorandum outlined the alternative means.

> When appropriate, local plans should provide for: (a) utilization of returning troop and supply ships, acquisition of ships by charter or requisition; (b) the issuance of precautionary notices suggesting the return of dependents by available means prior to the date set for compulsory evacuation in order to avoid congestion and unavoidable inconveniences; (c) local evacuation in the event ships are not available; (d) limiting the amount of household goods that may accompany evacuees as necessary in case shipping space is limited, and storage of the remainder at Government expense until transportation is available; (e) dispatch notification to the Chief of Naval Operations at the time the evacuation is ordered, of the number of evacuees in order that funds may be made available for their transportation and reception; (f) alien dependents desiring to enter the United States should make application to the local American Consul for non-quota entry.

Secretary Knox also ordered,

> The Commandants of the above mentioned Naval Districts and the Governor of Samoa should be directed to comment upon the desirability of evacuating dependents from stations under their jurisdiction. They should also comment upon the effect of failure to evacuate dependents by M-Day from the point of view of the defense, food, and water supply, hospitalization, morale, and freedom of action.

M-Day, abruptly, harshly delivered on 7 December, had come and gone with a thunderous, earthshaking roar, and the need to evacuate Oahu had become far more immediate, complex and difficult to manage. The insipient, pre-attack belief in the military commands on Oahu that the primary, if not the exclusive, threat to Hawaii was sabotage following the outbreak of war, had brushed away any sense of urgency to publish precautionary notices encouraging voluntary evacuation by dependents.

Now, after the devastating attack, the question had become—especially for tourists—"How are we going to get home?" Despite the almost instantaneously-prevalent, powerfully-motivated feeling throughout the island of working together against a common enemy, fear and tension were now present in the questions hovering over tourists and others feeling trapped on the islands. The abrupt, massive, relocation of dependents and others to safety from on and near military installations, during and after the attack, had been an additional rude shock, and a foretaste of things to come.

Adding to everyone's discomfort was the unadvertised but "word-of-mouth," spreading reality that expended projectiles fired during the fierce antiaircraft defense had killed and wounded many in Honolulu and surrounding areas. While the next time, the enemy could deliberately attack Honolulu and all the other towns, as well as likely military targets, and everyone might, just might, have warning to take cover, the depressing thought of being killed by your own defenders' guns didn't help civilian or military morale.

The problem and related questions now were "How many are we going to have to evacuate to the mainland, who are they, what are the priorities to be given in evacuating them, how soon and on what ships are we going to place them?" Short notice, rushed, effective communication with many people, in the face of an immediate need for the utmost secrecy regarding ship movements, plus congestion and inconvenience were to become a way of life. Placing announcements and press releases in newspapers and on the radio regarding ship departures and arrivals, could result in ship sinkings and heavy loss of life. The phrase "loose lips sink ships," which later became more than a slogan, was deadly serious.

What's more, the brutal attack suddenly added to the list of evacuees. The more seriously wounded in the attack, along with accompanying doctors and nurses; widows and children of men killed and those still carried missing in action, entered into the equation, all with higher priority than non-essential government employees, military dependents and employees of contractors.

Tourists had come by sea on the vessels plying in and out of Honolulu from the mainland and points further west, including the two mainland football teams from San Jose State and Willamette University. En route from Manila by way of American Samoa, and due to arrive on the 16th, were the *President Coolidge* and *Hugh L. Scott*, escorted by the *Louisville*, the two American President Liners already laden with passengers who had left further distant shores, many voluntarily returning to the United States.

Compounding the circumstances, was the immediate, serious threat of Japanese submarines. The threat, expected if war broke out, first becoming evident an hour before the air attacks on Oahu, was punctuated with the sinking of the *Cynthia Olson* 1,000 miles to the northeast, then the sinking of the Japanese submarine *I-70* north of Oahu and the Matson Line's *Lahaina*, the latter two on the 11th. The initial blows on the 7th were followed by a rash of increasing submarine attacks on Navy task forces and on unescorted vessels in the shipping lanes between Hawaii and the West Coast—as well as in the waters adjoining Oahu and surrounding the islands.

A leisurely, planned, voluntary evacuation by single, unescorted, unarmed vessels was now out of the question. The Pacific Fleet suddenly had thrust upon it, what undoubtedly had been part of contingency planning—all shipping to and from the mainland, and further toward American bases in the Pacific, had to be escorted by Naval combatants with well-prepared and well-led anti-submarine capabilities. Fortunately, the Navy was already improving those capabilities as a result of the Atlantic Fleet's support and assistance of the British, plus the Atlantic neutrality patrols undertaken earlier in the year.

Added to the immediate problem were the virtual destruction of all the Navy's long-range patrol aircraft on Oahu, and the termination of Pan American Airways' burgeoning civil air travel route from the mainland through Oahu to faraway points in the Far East and the Southwest Pacific. A small number of Pan American *Clipper* passengers from the two planes which had been forced to divert and turnaround from their planned routes, now were on Oahu, a number of them seeking a way back to the mainland.

The afternoon of 12 December retired Captain Frucht, whose office was on the 7th floor of the Aloha Tower in Honolulu, asked Mr. Randolph Sevier, the manager of the Steamship Department of Castle & Cooke, Limited, which ticketed commercial ship passengers, to make office space available for Frucht and his staff. Frucht asked for locations that would facilitate their management of the evacuation. Late that same afternoon, Sevier replied by letter, offering a 14x20-foot office space on the first floor, near Castle & Cooke's passenger department.

For the moment, the form of transportation to be furnished for evacuees was unknown, and Sevier advised Frucht to avail himself of the services of their Passenger Department. Though Sevier seemed to acquiesce to Frucht's request, to satisfy his company's management procedures, he also wanted the retired captain's request and any other such requests to come from Rear Admiral Bloch, the Commandant of the 14th Naval District, and suggested the wording to be used. The move continued to be held up by bureaucratic nonsense despite Admiral Bloch's written request to Sevier on 14 December, worded precisely as Sevier asked.

Planning moved ahead, undoubtedly at a frantic pace in spite of the delayed move. But the delay exercised by Castle & Cooke, and acquiesced in by Frucht in the face of a full blown crisis, was the first indicator of trouble ahead. Twelve days later Admiral Bloch's patience would run dry. [42]

On the 12th, Frucht had been given the estimated numbers of dependents to be evacuated to the mainland, from both the Army and Navy. On 15 December, Frucht received revised numbers totaling an estimated 10,000 Navy-related dependents and General Short sent Lieutenant Colonel Casey Hayes to Frucht's office with revised numbers totaling 4,996 Army-related, which were passed to Admiral Bloch in a memo. The questions remained, who would be the first to depart on orders, and what would be the assigned priorities? [43]

While the evacuation planning was in progress Japanese submarines were continuing to make themselves felt. The night of the 14th, twenty-nine miles north, northeast of Oahu, off Cape Makapuu, the Norwegian freighter, *Hoegh Merchant*, which had left San Francisco for Manila, and on 8 December, had been rerouted to Honolulu, stopped to await daylight before proceeding to the port. She carried 7,500 tons of general cargo including 100 tons of explosives. Japanese submarine *I-4*, captained by Commander Hajime Nakagawa, found her in the dark, torpedoed, and sank the stationary ship. Fortunately there was no loss of life, and all 40 of her crewmembers were picked up by the minesweeper *Trever* (DMS-16), which brought them into Honolulu the same day. [44]

On 15 December, with *Coolidge* and *Hugh L. Scott* one day from arrival in Honolulu, Admiral Bloch, already showing frustration, wrote to Admiral Kimmel, the Commander-in-Chief:

> I propose to immediately start to evacuate the dependents of Navy and Marine Corps personnel in Hawaii.
>
> In order that I may have people available to go on the first transportation available, I request that you take necessary steps to have about 500 dependents of Navy and Marine Corps personnel attached to the Fleet register with the Transportation Office in the Navy Yard, giving their names, addresses, and other data that may be required in connection with this movement.
>
> I suggest that the first ones taken be on a voluntary basis and that all notices put out be so communicated as not to cause panic among dependents.
>
> At a later date, I hope to get an office established up town so that this registration can take place up there. At the present time this seems to be impracticable.[45]

On the 16th, the day of *Coolidge*'s and *Hugh L. Scott*'s arrival in Honolulu, and the same date the three Matson Liners' departed San Francisco, Bloch's Chief of Staff wrote a brief memorandum to go district-wide in the 14th Naval District: "Dependents of Navy Personnel desiring evacuation to mainland should register as soon as practicable with District Overseas Transportation Office, Pearl Harbor or with the Office of Captain M.M. Frucht, USN (retired), in the Castle and Cooke Building, Honolulu, T.H."[46]

By 16 December, an evacuation order had been announced and received in all the civilian, Navy and Army organizations affected by the order. On the same day, Frucht readied a press release for the 17th containing the order's key provisions.

> Evacuation from Oahu to the Mainland will begin at once for all wounded who are able to travel, tourists, and dependents of Navy personnel, civil employees and defense employees, with priority

in that order, it was announced yesterday by Capt. M.M. Frucht, U.S. Navy evacuation officer.

The number of persons to be evacuated was not disclosed. "Navy lists of wounded and personnel dependents have been completed," Capt. Frucht said. "Tourists and family dependents of civil defense employees must register. There is a deferred list to include dependents employed by the government or on government projects, and dependents of employees who have permanent homes here."

Registration is to begin immediately, and evacuations will begin right away, Capt. Frucht said. Capt. Frucht's telephone number is 66752.

The official notice issued from Capt. Frucht's office follows in full:

"The Navy Department has directed the evacuation from the island of Oahu to the mainland in the following priorities:

1. Wounded.
2. Tourists.
3. Dependents of Navy Personnel.
4. Civil employees' dependents
5. Defense employees' dependents

Of the above categories the following will be placed on the deferred lists:

1. Dependents employed by government or on government projects.
2. Dependents of employees who have permanent homes here.

Persons coming in the second priority will register at the Honolulu Gas Company with Commander H.W. Boynton. Registration for the third, fourth and fifth priorities will be taken in the building of Castle and Cooke, Limited; in the Navy Housing Projects by Lt. Commander S.B. Wood, and in the Overseas Transportation Office, Pearl Harbor, by Commander Barrett. The registration will consist of obtaining the names of dependents, the local residence, household effects, if any, and whether they desire to leave as soon as convenient or wish to be placed on deferred lists for evacuation."[47]

Similar sets of instructions went from the Army's Hawaiian Department, telling department members and their dependents what must be done to obtain passage on ships evacuating Army wounded, dependents, and civilian employees' dependents. The beginning of the evacuation, though far too late in planning, was gathering momentum, but there was much more to do—and much confusion. Because planning for the evacuation began barely 31 days prior to the attack on Pearl Harbor, and had progressed slowly, Frucht and his staff, now trying to get organized, were being progressively overwhelmed by tasks needing prompt attention.

There were numerous additional considerations and details which had to be worked out in the last minute crush and scramble to begin evacuating the more than twenty thousand which would eventually leave through the port of Honolulu—beginning with the departure of the first convoy on 19 December.

There were many questions to be answered, such as how many people could be accommodated on each ship? The limitations for all the passenger-carrying vessels would be lifeboat and life raft capacity and the ship's ability to accommodate that number with sleeping areas, food, water and life jackets. The *Coolidge* and *Scott* were already carrying passengers when they arrived on 16 December, though some number would disembark because Hawaii was their destination. Ships arriving from San Francisco in the coming days and had been quickly converted to troop ships capable of carrying increased passenger loads, would be disembarking all their passengers—the reinforcing troops, equipment and supplies, and could accommodate far more than *Coolidge* and *Scott*.

How would the evacuation be funded? Who fit the definition of tourist and how was their passage to be paid? How much would be charged per person for the one-way trip? Who might have to pay their own way? What household effects could be shipped? Could pets go with their owners? Could automobiles be shipped? Individual appeals were already pouring in, some asking to be exceptions to the evacuation order, others not on the priority list who were appealing because they wanted to escape the threat of renewed attacks. Some saw the tourist priority as a way out, and were quite willing to fraudulently pose and apply as "tourists."

Three new questions arose from the appeals and requests

for exceptions to the evacuation orders. How should appeals and exception requests be submitted? To whom should they be sent, who should decide and respond? As planning continued the people and military commands on Oahu received another shock—though not entirely unexpected.

Cutting the Lines

Not only was the nation and the world stunned by the calamity that befell the Pacific Fleet, the Army and Army Air Force on Oahu, there were less apparent, even more devastating, long range effects that followed. The relief of the Army, Army Air Force and Navy commanders on Oahu, the several follow-on, high-profile investigations into what occurred, the resulting media coverage, and the need to protect operational security, masked the far more ominous effects that impacted the course of the early war in the Pacific. Behind the necessary mask of secrecy and operational security, far more serious trouble was in the offing.

The blistering surprise attack, followed by the inability and now-badly-crippled, Oahu-based forces to search for and find the Japanese strike force, shook the senior military leaders' and the Roosevelt administration's confidence in the Pacific's military commanders as well as the nation's intelligence services. To compound the seriousness of the situation, Oahu, the United States' first and most valuable stepping stone to Midway, Wake, Guam, the Philippines, and the far reaches of the Pacific, immediately appeared in grave jeopardy.

Where had the Japanese strike force come from and how did they come close enough to Oahu to deliver the body blows without being detected—then slip away? The answer soon came, but too late. Might they be able to repeat the strike? Oahu's defenders had been weakened by the heavy blow, especially in long range patrol and pursuit aircraft. Then there was the seemingly, now-unanswerable question, might the Japanese have the force and logistical capability to instead, invade, seize, and hold Oahu, and all its military installations? Was there something missed in knowing the actual strength of the Japanese Navy, including their aviation and Naval infantry? If they possessed the capabilities, the

United States forces could indeed be driven back to the mainland, and the war made even longer and more difficult.

Even more painful to consider, should the Japanese follow up their attack with another air attack that destroyed or heavily damaged the oil and aviation gasoline storage tanks on Oahu, the Pacific Fleet, Army and Army Air Forces could be forced back to mainland ports, bases and airfields—unless sufficient escorts and tankers could be mustered to ensure fleet, air operations and power generation were secured and sustained until the damage could be repaired.

In fact, almost immediately it became clear that the most direct line of communications and logistical support to MacArthur's forces in the Philippines had been effectively severed by the Pearl Harbor disaster. And unless prompt, strong action was taken, the line of communications and logistical support to Australia and New Zealand—with Australia the southern route from Hawaii to the Philippines—was also in danger.

As the Japanese rapidly plunged deeper into the south Pacific, the situation worsened when the Asiatic Fleet commander, Admiral Thomas C. Hart, stated a few days later he couldn't guarantee the safety of troop and supply ships, including tankers, his fleet was ordered to escort to the Philippines. He was confronting harsh reality. His fleet consisted of 3 cruisers, 13 World War I-era destroyers, 6 gunboats, 6 motor torpedo boats, 32 patrol bombers, and 29 submarines. A regiment of marines, withdrawn from Shanghai, also joined the defending forces late in November 1941.

The Japanese struck far south into Thailand and Malaya the day they struck Pearl Harbor, took Guam on 10 December, and landed two regiments on northern Luzon in the Philippines the same day. They held the World War I mandate of the Marshall Islands, which included Kwajalein, due south of Wake Island, and began almost daily bombing raids on Wake, indicating they were preparing to take the island. After Wake Island the next step east toward Hawaii was Midway.

The first hidden indicators of far more serious trouble were the rapid, but highly classified decisions immediately following the 7 December attack to reroute the 34th and 161st Regiments from their Philippine destinations, to Oahu. The *Pensacola* Convoy, Convoy No. 4002, which left Pearl Harbor on 29 November, was sailing via the southern route to Manila, to give wide berth to

Japanese holdings in the Marshall Islands, south of Wake Island. With the highly successful air attacks on Pearl Harbor, followed by the air raid on Wake Island, and nine hours after Pearl Harbor, on bases in the Philippines, the convoy was immediately diverted southward from its course. Later the convoy commander was instructed to proceed to Suva in the Fiji Islands, where it was to remain until a final decision regarding its destination. On 12 December, after much discussion in Washington, the convoy was ordered to Brisbane, Australia, a second proximate, but for good reason, highly classified harbinger of far more serious trouble for General MacArthur's forces in the Philippines.

In the history, *U.S. Army in World War II*, author Louis Morton described the ongoing discussions involving the *Pensacola* Convoy and the Philippines.

> . . . The convoy was immediately ordered to put in at Suva in the Fiji Islands until a decision could be made on its ultimate destination.
>
> The decision was made on 9 December at a meeting of the Joint Board. The chief planners of the Army and Navy, Brigadier General Leonard T. Gerow and Rear Adm. Richmond K. Turner, wanted the convoy brought back immediately to Hawaii to reinforce that badly battered garrison. General Gerow's position was more extreme than that of his naval counterpart. He suggested that if the convoy was not sent to Hawaii it should be brought back to the United States. Following discussion, the Joint Board approved the plan to recall the *Pensacola* convoy to Hawaii.
>
> While the safety of the Hawaiian Islands was undoubtedly of prime importance, the decision to bring back the *Pensacola* convoy was, in effect, an abandonment of the Philippine Islands. General Marshall was willing to concede the importance of Hawaii, but felt keenly the obligation to send help to General MacArthur. He had already assured the USAFFE commander on the afternoon of 7 December that he had "the complete confidence of the War Department," and that he could expect "every possible assistance within our power." On the

morning of the 10th, "concerned with just what to say to General MacArthur," he discussed the Joint Board decision with Mr. Stimson. He confessed that "he did not like to tell him [MacArthur] in the midst of a very trying situation that his convoy had had to be turned back, and he would like to send some news which would buck General MacArthur up."

At a White House meeting later that day, the question of the *Pensacola* convoy was again discussed, and the President indicated his desire that the vessels should continue to the Far East. He referred the matter back to the Joint Board, and at its meeting that afternoon the Board decided to send the convoy on to Brisbane, Australia. The Army members reversed their stand of the previous day and expressed the opinion that Hawaii could be supplied from the United States. They now wished, they said, to make every effort to send aircraft, ammunition, and other critical material to the Philippines.

On 12 December the commander of the *Pensacola* convoy was ordered to proceed to Brisbane, his later movements to be determined "following arrival and depending upon the situation." At the same time, the U.S. military attaché in Melbourne, Col. Van S. Merle-Smith, was notified of the impending arrival of the vessels and given instruction to be passed on to the senior Army commander in the convoy, Brigadier General Julian F. Barnes.

In these instructions, General Barnes was ordered to place himself under MacArthur's command and told that his principal task was to get the aircraft, men, and supplies in the convoy to the Philippines as quickly as possible. Upon arrival in Australia, he was to assemble the A-24s immediately and send them north to the Philippines. [A-24s were the Army Air Force version of the Navy's SBD dive-bombers.] Before unloading the other troops and supplies, he was to find out from the Navy if the vessels could be escorted northward. If they could not, they were to be unloaded in Brisbane and used "as the situation dictates," with the first priority given to the defense of the Philippines.

On 13 December, General MacArthur received the welcome news that reinforcements were on the way. Immediately he conferred with Admiral Thomas C. Hart, commander of the Asiatic Fleet, which was charged with defense of the Philippines and Guam, on the possibility of escorting the ships from Brisbane to Manila. He emphasized to Hart the necessity for bringing in supplies and reinforcements and explained how limited were the resources at his disposal. "I suggested," he reported to the Chief of Staff, "that he [Hart] should endeavor with his own surface forces and with assistance of Australian and Dutch naval and air forces to bring in the present convoy and keep my line open."

But Admiral Hart's answer was extremely discouraging. He pointed out that the British and Dutch were fully engaged trying to hold Singapore and the Malay Barrier and that he could not take the responsibility of protecting the convoy with the weak forces at his disposal. The Japanese, he believed, would have established a complete blockade of the Philippine Islands before the convoy could arrive. "In effect," MacArthur reported, "he [Hart] seemed to be of the opinion that the islands were ultimately doomed." MacArthur's own view was that there was no serious obstacle to the safe convoy of vessels from Brisbane to Manila "provided reasonable naval and air protection are furnished."

While the matter of the *Pensacola* convoy was being settled in Washington, MacArthur made specific requests for reinforcements based upon his ideas for offensive action. On the recommendation of General Brereton he asked for 300 pursuit planes, together with air warning equipment. If the aircraft in the *Pensacola* convoy could be ferried to Luzon and be ready for operations by 1 January, he felt he could meet the immediate situation with 250 dive-bombers. At this time, 14 December, he first advanced the idea that the planes be brought within operating distance of the Philippines by means of aircraft carrier. He asked also for additional .50-caliber ammunition and suggested that it be brought in by the dive-bombers or by Pan American Airways planes shuttling between Australia and the Philippines. Altogether, he declared, he had or would soon have fourteen airfields capable of accommodating the aircraft he was requesting.

The receipt of the specific requests in Washington resulted in immediate action. General Gerow, in a personal note to General Marshall, pointed out that the *Pensacola* convoy was due in Brisbane very shortly and an immediate decision on the Navy's willingness to convoy the vessels northward was necessary. "If the ships can go directly to Manila, the supplies, except aircraft, should not be unloaded in Australia," Gerow noted. "Admiral Stark is the only one that can make the decision."

Marshall had already discussed this problem with Stimson, who felt that to abandon the Philippines would "paralyze the activities" of the Allied forces in the Far East. The question was discussed at the White House, and the President instructed the Navy to do all in its power to assist the Army in reinforcing General MacArthur. General Marshall thereupon assured MacArthur that there would be "no wavering in the determination to support you." Although naval losses had complicated the problem of reinforcement, he declared that fighters and bombers would be rushed to the Philippines as quickly as possible.

Quick action followed the President's instruction to send help to the Philippines. Orders were issued to load the transport *Polk* in San Francisco harbor and the *Coolidge,* due in port soon, with pursuit planes and ammunition and dispatch them immediately to Australia. Two additional shipments were scheduled to reach Brisbane early in January. The arrival of these vessels would place in Australia 230 aircraft. At the same time, two Pan American *Clippers* were loaded with .50-caliber ammunition and dispatched to Australia via the South Atlantic-Africa route. Fifteen heavy bombers were also immediately diverted to MacArthur, and a flight schedule was established which would give him three planes a day until the new year. The sum of $10,000,000 was made available to the future commander of the base in Australia to enable him to carry out his mission of supporting the defense of the Philippines. On 17 December, Brigadier General Dwight D. Eisenhower drafted a plan to build up an Australian base, and by 18 December Marshall was able to inform MacArthur that the War Department "is proceeding with utmost expedition to provide necessary supplies at base with early emphasis on most critical items."

On 22 December the *Pensacola* convoy with its valuable cargo of aircraft, artillery battalions, guns, bombs and ammunition arrived in Brisbane. It was still a long way from Manila, but the first leg of the journey had been completed. A way now had to be found to send the planes and supplies from Australia to the Philippines.

The program to reinforce the Philippines was in full swing. The necessity for reaching a decision on the destination of the *Pensacola* convoy had raised the question of reinforcement immediately on the outbreak of war and brought the issues into sharp focus. But the settlement of this question had raised broader strategic problems. These were not so easily solved.[48]

New Army and Navy Commanders in Hawaii

On 16 December, the date Captain Frucht announced the evacuation order, the *Louisville* led the *Coolidge* and *Scott* safely into Honolulu, and *St. Louis* and the Matson Liners departed San Francisco for Oahu, the Army and Navy relieved Generals Short, Martin, and Admiral Kimmel. Gordon Prange, in *At Dawn We Slept* described what occurred.

On the morning of the 15ᵗʰ, Secretary of the Navy
Frank Knox met at the White House with President
Roosevelt, Secretary of State Cordell Hull, Secretary
of War Stimpson and several others, where the
President gave Knox penciled notes covering all
the information about the attack which he thought
"could then, with the security of the nation at stake,
be released to the public."

Later that day, Knox released his report to the
press and public. He listed the losses, including
Arizona, Utah, Cassin, Downes, Shaw, and *Oglala*
and the damaging of several other ships, including
Oklahoma. This was not entirely candid but, in view
of later salvage operations, not too far off the mark.
He also listed casualty totals, which exceeded the
number of dead but underestimated the wounded.

Replying to questions, Knox expressed the belief
that "between 150 and 300 planes took part in the
attack, too many to have come from a single aircraft
carrier, that "apparently none was land-based,"
and that so far as known, "none was flown by
Germans." He further declared that "a rumor that
the Navy had been forewarned" was untrue. Above
all, he stressed the record of personal heroism. "In
the Navy's gravest hour of peril, the officers and
men of the fleet exhibited magnificent courage
and resourcefulness . . . " But the secretary had to
acknowledge the dominant, brutal truth:

> The United States services were not on the
> alert against surprise air attack on Hawaii.
> This fact calls for a formal investigation which
> will be initiated immediately by the President.
> Further action is, of course, dependent on
> the facts and recommendations made by the
> investigating board. We are entitled to know
> it if (A) there was any error of judgment
> which contributed to the surprise, (B) if there
> was any dereliction of duty prior to the attack.

Knox's report to Roosevelt and the American people followed an extraordinary, highly classified trip to Oahu by Secretary of the Navy Knox.

The night of 7 December Knox had, on his own, decided he must go to Oahu, conduct a personal—but obviously official— visit to Oahu, to determine the extent of the damage and if possible to find out why the Japanese had caught U.S. forces unprepared. After securing the President's permission, he and a small party including his aide, Captain Frank E. Beatty, departed Anacostia Naval Air Station, California, at the south end of San Francisco Bay, on Tuesday morning, 9 December and arrived safely at Kaneohe Naval Air Station on the 11ᵗʰ. Lieutenant Commander "Beauty" Martin, Kaneohe's commander, met the Navy Secretary at the seaplane ramp. Martin found the secretary friendly but intensely serious, eager to get to the bottom of the ugly business. He showed Knox and his party the devastated air station, the wrecked PBYs, the burned hangars, and the officers and men "trying to salvage something out of the wreckage."

Secretary Knox met Admiral Kimmel in Honolulu, at the Royal Hawaiian Hotel, and they proceeded to the Admiral's quarters. He invited Knox to stay with him, but the secretary politely declined, in view of the "investigative nature of his visit." He had given orders "that he would not be the guest of any senior officer on Oahu."

The group from Washington observed an atmosphere of apprehension on Oahu. Captain Beatty, Knox's aide, described the Hawaiian command as "definitely security minded" with conversations "carried on in whispers" and "much glancing around lest their words be overheard." Post attack shock was still evident among many, and everyone recognized the danger inherent in the island's exposed position. General Short deployed everything in the Hawaiian Department to stop a possible invasion. One top officer thought the attack had been a hit-and-run strike. A senior officer among the Hawaiian Department engineers "became almost paranoid about the Japs' return." He "was really quite obnoxious with his prophecies of doom . . . "

The Islands were far from alone with their anxieties. In Washington, Rear Admiral Richmond K. Turner, Assistant to the Chief of Staff, United States Fleet, on 9 December in an operations message, informed Kimmel:

> . . . Because of the great success of the Japanese raid
> on the seventh it is expected to be promptly followed
> up by additional attacks in order (to) render Hawaii
> untenable as naval and air base in which eventuality
> it is believed Japanese have forces suitable for initial
> occupation of islands other than Oahu including
> Midway Maui and Hawaii . . .

> Until defenses are increased it is doubtful if Pearl
> should be used as a base for any except patrol craft
> naval aircraft submarines or for short periods when
> it is reasonably certain Japanese attacks will not be
> made . . .

Pearl Harbor presented a grisly picture to Secretary Knox
and his group of visitors, "the shambles of the Battle Line of the
world's mightiest fleet." Foremost in their minds, however, "was
the human loss and suffering." During the visit, they watched
men remove bodies from the oil-covered waters while others
worked briskly "clearing up wreckage and preparing for another
attack."

Later General Short met with Knox at Kimmel's quarters and
talked with him for approximately an hour and a half to two
hours. He briefed the secretary concerning the status on Oahu
before the attack, the air strike, and harped heavily upon the fifth-
column activities. Knox needed no convincing regarding Hawaii's
Japanese. At the end of his trip he reported to Roosevelt: "The
activities of the Japanese fifth columnists immediately following
the attack, took the form of spreading on the air by radio dozens
of confusing and contradictory rumors concerning direction in
which the attacking planes departed, as well as the presence in
every direction of enemy ships." In reality, the Army and Navy
on Oahu required no Japanese assistance in generating confusing
messages on 7 December.

In contrast with misapprehensions about the local Japanese,
the commands already had a good idea of the composition
of the attacking force. Papers discovered on a Japanese plane
which crashed indicated a strike force of six carriers, three heavy
cruisers, and numerous auxiliary craft including destroyers and
other vessels.

There were questions and frank exchanges of answers regarding warning messages thought to have been transmitted to and received by the commands the night before the attack. Obviously these men were discussing no previously unknown dispatch which satanic forces withheld from its addressees. They were talking about the famous warning which General Marshall sent in association with Admiral Stark not on the night of 6 December, but arrived shortly after noon on 7 December for one very good reason. The message from Tokyo upon which it was based was not received, decoded and translated by the U.S. Army until the morning of 7 December.

Admiral Kimmel was equally honest with Knox in other ways, and so was General Short. Both admitted that they had not expected an air attack and the Japanese caught them unprepared and unawares. Kimmel had regarded a submarine attack as "the principal danger from a Japanese stroke without warning . . . "

Knox's findings regarding the state of readiness to defend against a carrier strike seriously disturbed him. In an 18 December letter he wrote, "It is simply incredible that both the Army and Navy could have been caught so far off first base . . . They evidently had convinced themselves that an air attack by carrier born [sic] planes was beyond the realm of possibility, because they made no preparation whatever for such an attack." Believing in an American repulse of a nonexistent third wave attack at "about eleven o'clock" on 7 December, Knox was sure that had the defenders been ready, they would have beaten off the initial assault. [It's important to note, the "nonexistent third wave attack" was the tragic friendly fire incident involving the six F4F Wildcat fighters from *Enterprise*'s VF-6 the evening of 7 December.]

Kimmel was still Commander-in-Chief, still concerned with the war situation, and could see some positives in the circumstance. The oil tanks had escaped destruction, as had his machine shops, what he referred to as his "Navy behind the Navy." And above all else, his invaluable carriers escaped damage. On 10 December he sent a reply to Admiral Stark's office, responding to Rear Admiral Turner's OPNAV message of the previous day, emphasizing he and his command were ready for action:

> Since the appearance of the enemy in this area all tactical efforts with all available forces have been vigorously prosecuted toward locating and destroying enemy forces, primarily carriers. Our heavy losses have not seriously depleted our fast

striking forces nor [sic] reduced morale and determination. Pearl must be used for essential supply and overhaul facilities and must be provided with additional aircraft both army and navy also relief pilots and maintenance personnel. Pearl channels clear. Industrial establishment intact and doing excellent work . . .

A gargantuan cleanup and repair task remained. Further devastation greeted Knox and his party on Ford Island, but the most painful sight of all were the hundreds of wounded at the Naval Hospital, some "so terribly burned and charred as to be beyond recognition." That evening, Thursday, 11 December, Governor Poindexter joined the group at dinner in the blacked-out hotel, and they sat up most of the night discussing what they had seen and "planning for the morrow."

The next morning Knox visited the Hawaiian Department's command post for an extensive briefing. On this occasion he didn't "indicate in any way that he was not satisfied" with what Short had done. He spent about two hours in the command post, and after picking up casualty lists, photographs of the damage, and various Japanese souvenirs, Knox and his party left for Kaneohe that afternoon and shortly took off for the mainland. As soon as his plane touched down at Washington, he hurried to the White House. The original copy of his report carries the notation in Roosevelt's handwriting, "1941—given me by F.K. 10 P.M. Dec. 14 when he landed here from Hawaii. FDR."

No Army report similar to Secretary of the Navy Knox's ever surfaced. Secretary of War Henry L. Stimson and General Marshall had dispatched an Army investigative team to Oahu, Colonel Charles Bundy and Major General Herbert A. Drague, a senior Army Air Force officer, aviation pioneer, and former commander of the First Air Force, intending him to replace Short. Tragically, blind chance took charge. Weather was atrocious and on 12 December their bomber went down over the High Sierras. The wreck wasn't found for months. Given this circumstance, Stimson accepted Secretary Knox's findings. To preclude one service from bearing the brunt of any allegations, and aware the Army was charged with defending Oahu and the Pacific Fleet, he knew the Army had to take its medicine along with the Navy.

General Marshall acted swiftly when Colonel Bundy and

Army Air Force Lieutenant General Delos C. Emmons was already on Oahu 17 December 1941, leading an investigation team dispatched to the island by General Marshall when he was directed to relieve and replace General Short, effective that day. USAF

General Drague's aircraft went missing. He wanted an airman to replace Short, and named Army Air Force Lieutenant General Delos C. Emmons, who was in San Francisco at the time, and recommended Colonel J. Lawton Collins as Emmons's chief of staff.

Stimson announced Martin's and Short's relief on the 17th, one day after Kimmel, Short and Martin were informed of their relief. He in effect was taking his position "side by side with Knox as to the absence of preparedness on December 7th." He explained that this action "avoids a situation where officials charged with the responsibility for the future security of the vital naval base would otherwise in this critical hour also be involved in the searching investigation ordered yesterday by the President."

Emmons, already on Oahu, relieved Short on 17 December. The change of command was quiet, unpublicized, without ceremony and without hard feelings between the two officers.[49]

Admiral Chester W. Nimitz, Kimmel's replacement, would arrive on Oahu mid-morning, Christmas Day, after a 17.2 hour flight from San Diego.

CHAPTER 12

Surprise Departure, and
" . . . Am Going Home"

*Something must be left to chance; nothing
is sure in a sea fight above all.*

Admiral Viscount Nelson

At 0833 the morning of the 16th, *Phoenix*, still in column aft of
St. Louis, passed beneath the Golden Gate Bridge, and at 0840,
began proceeding independently for Mare Island Navy yard.
Moments earlier *St. Louis* passed the submarine net, and at 0842
Phoenix passed the net, not long before turning port, up San
Francisco Bay to the north, and then through the Carguinez Strait,
to moor in Mare Island Navy Yard. As *Phoenix* maneuvered
toward Mare Island, *St. Louis* logged, "Alcatraz abeam to port" at
0844 and "anchored in Naval Anchorage, San Francisco Bay . . ."
at 0904.[1]

St. *Louis*'s stay in San Francisco was brief and hectic. She
received 9,374 gallons of diesel fuel, and 60, one-pound cans of
chili. The commander received 99 apprentice seamen and 101
more experienced sailors reporting on board and logged them
in by name, bound for the receiving station at Pearl Harbor,
replacements for Pacific Fleet ships and shore installations
battered in the 7 December attack.

There was a new urgency, a completely transformed sense of
mission among the *St. Louis* crew. They had been targets of the
enemy and personal witnesses to the shattering attack on Pearl
Harbor. Bombs, bullets and torpedoes had been unleashed at
them, experiences to remember the rest of their lives. Shortly,
St. Louis and her crew departed, leading the Pacific Fleet's first
wartime troop convoy on a dash to Oahu, bringing thousands

of troops, their equipment and ammunition. A good mission bringing a powerful sense of purpose and a feeling of deep satisfaction.[2]

At 1615 hours Pacific coast time, twenty-five minutes before *St. Louis* got underway to leave San Francisco, the cruiser *Louisville*, now approaching Oahu, logged sighting of Diamond Head 16 miles distant, slightly east of north. Three hours earlier the destroyer *Reid* had taken up position as submarine screen for the *Coolidge* and *Scott*—to escort the two ships on into Honolulu. At least six Japanese submarines were still on stations arrayed northeast to northwest of Oahu, and the passengers and crews on the two ships had already been introduced to wartime precautions on board the passenger liner and Army transport when word came of the attack on Pearl Harbor. They were about to be shocked by the sharply different welcome they would observe, when compared to previous arrivals at one of the world's most beautiful, tranquil vacation lands.[3]

In San Francisco at 1640, with sunset minutes away, *St. Louis* was under way again, with Captain Rood in command of Task Group 15.6, escorting Convoy No. 2005, the *Lurline*, *Matsonia* and *Monterey*, with anti-submarine screen the destroyers *Lawrence* (DD-250), *Preston* (DD-379) and *Smith* (DD-378). *St. Louis* was in the lead, with *Lurline*, the convoy guide, *Matsonia* and *Monterey* in column at 1,000 yards interval astern of *Lurline*, and *Lurline* 1,000 yards astern of the cruiser. The *Lawrence* was temporarily in the column, 1,000 yards ahead of *St Louis*, *Smith* 1,000 yards on the starboard bow, and *Preston* the same distance on the port bow.

Aboard *Lurline* were the 2nd and 3rd Battalions of the 161st Infantry Regiment, plus regimental headquarters and support units, a total of 3,292 troops plus a very heavy load of bombs, ammunition and other military supplies. On *Matsonia* were 29 officers and 850 enlisted men of the 1st Battalion, 34th Infantry Regiment, plus regimental headquarters and the 145th Field Artillery Battalion, and support troops, for a total of 3,277 men—plus bombs, munitions and airplane parts. Aboard *Monterey* were 93 officers and 2,281 enlisted men of the 2nd and 3rd Battalions, 34th Infantry Regiment, and other men bringing the total to 3,349. She also carried airplane parts and other war materials.

All the Army units on board the three Matson Liners had been en route to the Philippines from their Army posts when

Cruiser *St. Louis* (CL-49), the command ship for Task Group 15.6, escorting Convoy 2005, which left San Francisco on 16 December 1941—the first wartime convoy to leave the West Coast for the Pacific Theater. Off Mare Island Navy Yard, 6 March 1942. NAPR

Destroyer *Preston* (DD-379), submarine screen for Task Group 15.6 and Convoy 2005. Cropped photo at the Mare Island Navy Yard, 15 August 1942. NA

Destroyer *Smith* (DD-378), submarine screen for Task Group 15.6 and Convoy 2005. Off Mare Island Navy Yard, 28 July 1942. NAPR

they left for San Francisco, but immediately after the attack on Pearl Harbor and before departure in Convoy 2005, their orders had been changed, diverting them from their original destination to instead augment the 24th and 25th Infantry Divisions of the Hawaiian Department. Remaining units of the 1st and Provisional Battalions, 161st Regiment, with their equipment, would follow the next morning in Task Group 15.7, with *Phoenix* leading and in command of the task group.

At 1652, *St Louis*'s Officer of the Deck, Ensign Lawrence G. Lewis, logged passing under the San Francisco-Oakland Bay Bridge, 1657 passing Treasure Island—the home terminal of the Pan American *Clippers*—one mile abeam to starboard, 1705 hours passing Alcatraz one mile abeam to starboard, and at 1720 passing under the Golden Gate Bridge. For people on shore and crossing the bridges, observing the majestic sight of a departing wartime convoy of three great, admiralty-gray, former cruise liners, a cruiser and three destroyers leading them through San Francisco harbor, out through the Golden Gate and away from the west coast, the sight must have stirred strong emotions.

There can be no doubt that Ensign Lewis and many other men on the ships in Task Group 15.6 and Convoy 2005, bound for Hawaii and looking up at the magnificent engineering miracles they passed beneath, at the flickering early evening lights of San Francisco, and the shores of San Francisco Bay, wondered to themselves if they would ever see those sights again—or their homeland. Soldiers on the three liners saw the same sights, and must have been moved by the same thoughts. But very few young men mention their innermost thoughts or dwell on such things for long, if ever, not even in war—a blessing given what lies ahead.[4]

That morning, *Phoenix* had moored starboard side to Mare Island's berth 21 at 1040 hours. At 1100 hours, Captain Andrew D. Denney, the Captain of the Yard, came aboard to pay an official visit to Captain Fischer and departed twenty-five minutes later. At 1138, the oil barge *Contra Costa* came alongside and began refueling the *Phoenix*.

At 1636, four minutes before *St. Louis* got underway to return to Hawaii, *Phoenix* began taking on ammunition, including 62 catapult charges, 4500 rounds of .50-caliber armor piercing and tracer bullets, and 4500 rounds of .30-caliber tracer bullets. By 1718 she had taken on 7,301 gallons fuel oil, and at 1757 was underway to the San Francisco Naval Anchorage, where she anchored at berth C-3 and remained until early the next morning.

At 0636 hours on the 17th, nine minutes after the destroyers *Cushing* (DD-376) and *Perkins* (DD-377) were underway, *Phoenix* was underway leading Convoy 2004 from San Francisco to Honolulu. The two destroyers were joined by a third, the *Humphreys* (DD-236). The four combatants were escorting three more ships, a convoy that on the 18th would double in size.

Departing from San Francisco in Convoy 2004 was the *Aldebaran* (AF-10), the Navy's new, 13,910-ton supplies and stores ship commissioned in January; the USAT *Tasker H. Bliss*, a 12,568-ton transport, formerly the American Presidents Line's SS *President Cleveland*, leased by the Army 31 July and now capable of carrying 2,435 troops; and the troop transport SS *President Garfield*, also formerly a ship of the American President's Line. On board the *Tasker Bliss* was the 1st and Provisional Battalions of the 161st Infantry Regiment. The *Aldebaran,* which had begun loading ammunition within hours after the 7 December attack, was carrying a full load of ammunition in her holds, and transporting 104 seamen to new assignments in the Pacific Fleet.[5]

The departure of the *Bliss*, carrying the men of the 161st is poignantly recorded in the Regiment's history:

The stern of the *Bliss* churned away from the pier, just as our last kitchen stove swung aboard. The pier grew smaller and smaller and the Bay began to get choppy. The Bridge, the one we long afterward dreamed about, passed over-head.

America was dropping away from us at nine knots. We leaned far out on the rail of the ship and watched her—a great, long line of rich purple stretching from one horizon to the other as far as the eye could see. The early morning sunlight struck brilliantly against ranch houses and villages along her West coast, etching them in white against purple. And lighthouses stood forth from her shores, and evaded the grasping white fingers of the ocean.

For once we didn't feel like starting a crap game, or reading, or playing cards, or even talking, because we were leaving her behind. Why, lots of us had just crossed her, speeding on endless gleaming rails from the biggest city on earth and from colonial villages in the East. We had passed over the Mississippi that almost cuts America in two. Through rolling green meadows we had come, past red barns, and white farmhouses. Then through the mysterious desert, silent and shimmering with heat, and great white bones of tremendous animals a million years old baked deep in her clay. Near the coast America reached for God, her mountains disappearing into clouds. We had built a beautiful bridge there, and had passed under it an hour ago.

OUT TO SEA ON THE MATSON LINERS, AHEAD OF OUR SHIP, THE BLISS, THE 161 HAD MADE ITS RENDEZVOUS—WITH THE FIRST WAR CONVOY TO LEAVE THE STATES . . . [6]

At 0830, approximately 200 nautical miles ahead of *Phoenix* and her convoy, and holding a standard speed of 15 knots, *St. Louis* signaled the ships she was escorting to begin zigzagging according to Plan No. 21. The convoy's base course was 229 degrees when the "execute [begin zigzagging]" was signaled. On board each of the Matson Liners was a Navy communications detachment, including enlisted signalmen and one ensign each who could encode and decode messages sent and received by radio, understood and could send visual signals, as well as control and provide information on the correct degrees of turn using the various zigzag plans.

At 1430 on Wednesday, the 17th, in Convoy 2005, the *Matsonia* mustered all their troops at the ship's lifeboat stations and the crew instructed them in the use and adjustments of their lifebelts, and gave them general instructions for all cases of emergency—an abandon ship drill that would be repeated the 18th and 19th. All day, until 1710 hours, the five-ship formation continued zigzagging, holding 15 to 17 knots and a base course of 230 degrees. A few minutes before zigzagging ceased, from the bridge of the *St. Louis* came the order for "darkened ship" and at 1715 the officer of the deck sounded general quarters, as the dusk anti-submarine routine settled in.

Light cruiser *Phoenix* (CL-46), the command ship and lead escort for Convoy 2004. In this photo she steams down the main channel off Ford Island's burning battleships, past the sunken and burning *West Virginia* (BB-48), at left, and *Arizona* (BB-39), at right, approximately 1110 hours the morning of 7 December 1941. NHHC

Captain Rood's defensive zigzag against possible submarine attack was warranted, for the Japanese submarines ordered forward to stations off the entrances to West coast harbors were completing their long journeys. If their navigators tracked and calculated their positions correctly, they were swinging onto their stations, where they could silently wait and launch attacks on shipping.

At 1300 the same afternoon, *Phoenix* and Convoy 2004, which had been holding course 235 degrees and a speed of 15 knots, turned port to 205 degrees, then further port to 180 degrees at 1700 hours, went to general quarters, and began zigzagging. They were diverging to the left from the track taken by *St. Louis* and Convoy 2005. After darkening the ship three minutes later, at 1800 hours the *Phoenix* convoy ceased zigzagging, then an hour later turned right to 198 degrees.[7]

Around midnight, well behind the two convoys pressing toward Oahu, the skipper of Japanese submarine *I-15*, Commander Nobuo Ishikawa, ordered the crew to surface her, to recharge the batteries. They were near the Farallon Islands and the patrol station they were to keep, and once surfaced, he gave the crew a chance to come see the lights of San Francisco.[8]

[th], the destroyer *Lawrence* left *St. Louis*'s formation to return to San Francisco, while from the Los Angeles port of San Pedro, and from San Diego, at 0230 the same morning, Destroyer Division Seventy, escorting three more ships, was under way to join *Phoenix* and Convoy 2004.

Aboard *Phoenix* at 0705, the first two of four scout aircraft were catapulted to begin search patterns along the projected convoy course, looking for tell tale signs of submarines or enemy surface vessels. Two hundred miles ahead, *St. Louis* launched one aircraft at 0730 and another at 0738, both on similar scout missions. At 0840, while *St. Louis*'s scouts were still airborne, one of Convoy 2005's screening destroyers, *Smith*, reported sighting a submarine on the cruiser's port quarter, and immediately proceeded toward that location. In one minute *St. Louis* signaled the convoy to zigzag according to Plan No. 21, while *Smith* continued toward the target area to begin dropping ten depth charges. The results of her attack were unknown, but the sighting, if valid, confirmed a crucial fact undoubtedly reported in coded message traffic early that morning. Japanese submarines had arrived off the United States' West coast and were initiating attacks on American shipping.

At 0830 and 0850 respectively, the morning of the 18th, the ships from San Pedro and San Diego were sighted by *Phoenix*. By 1045 hours, the *Phoenix* was on station 2,000 yards ahead of the 13,529-ton transport, *Harris (AP-8)*, out of San Diego, and two oilers, out of San Pedro, which accompanied *Harris*—leading the formation of three columns of two ships each, on a course of 257 degrees, toward Oahu. The distance between columns was 1,000 yards. The left column was the 24,830-ton fleet oiler *Platte* (AO-24) with *Garfield* 2,000 yards astern; the center column *Harris* with *Aldebaran* 2,000 yards astern, and right column, the 24,830-ton sister-ship of *Platte*, oiler *Sabine* (AO-25), with *Bliss* 2,000 yards astern.

Each tanker carried nearly its maximum capacity of diesel oil, fuel oil, and gasoline, a total of 146,000 barrels—or approximately 8,030,000 gallons—to be discharged into storage tanks in Honolulu, at Hickam Field, and in Pearl Harbor. The *Harris* was carrying supplies, military equipment and provisions in its cargo holds, a company of 177 marines from the headquarters, 2nd Marine Division, with their unit equipment; a detachment of 33 medical corpsmen and two doctors, 74 Navy, Marine Corps and Army officers, and six civilians including two doctors.

At 1308 hours, *Phoenix* and Convoy 2004 also were alerted to a submarine's presence—a submarine that came perilously close to launching a successful attack. The convoy and escorts came to general quarters, and began zigzagging while one of the two destroyers, *Cushing* or *Perkins*, maneuvered toward the submarine to drop depth charges. The intruder penetrated the formation close enough to the rear of the center column of *Harris* and *Aldebaran*, in column behind *Harris*, to fire torpedoes, which passed underneath the stern of the *Aldebaran*—fortunately a near-miss. A single torpedo penetrating and exploding in the hull of the *Aldebaran*, which was carrying a full load of munitions, could have had disastrous consequences.[9] The encounter undoubtedly was sobering to Captain Fischer, the task group commander.

The morning of 18 December, the first two convoys of the Pacific war to leave the West coast, precursors of a tidal wave of men and materials of war which would eventually flood Oahu and the Hawaiian Islands, were steadily making their way toward building a huge staging base for war against the Empire of the Rising Sun. And while they were en route to Oahu, similarly headed southwest toward Brisbane, Australia from Suva in the

Fijis, was Convoy 4002, the cruiser *Pensacola*, the gunboat-acting-as-subchaser *Niagra* and seven other ships carrying four artillery battalions, airplanes, ammunition, and other supplies for war—the precursor of another tidal wave which would build up a second, huge allied base in the "Land Down Under."

The Enemy Below—Revisited

But the war was just beginning. Far to the north, behind Convoys 2004 and 2005, the Japanese launched the first submarine attacks off the United States' West coast. The enemy submariners committed to the Pearl Harbor operation, still relatively inexperienced in attacking shipping of any nation, gained immediate attention on 7 December with the sinking of at least one and possibly two midget submarines just outside Pearl Harbor, one and possibly two penetrating inside the harbor, and the sinking of the *Cynthia Olson* by *I-26*, 1,000 miles to the northeast in the sea lane between Oahu and Puget Sound. The morning of the 8th another midget had beached and been captured near Bellows Field. Japanese submarines followed up with repeated, but unsuccessful attacks on Navy combatants leaving Pearl Harbor, then threw themselves pell mell into repeated, but again unsuccessful attacks on *Enterprise*'s Task Force 8, northeast of Oahu. The result of their attempts to attack *Enterprise* was the 10 December loss of *I-70*.

Then *I-9* sank the Matson Line freighter *Lahaina*, 700 miles northeast of Oahu on 11 December. On 13 December *Lexington*'s Task Force 12 had encountered and repeatedly depth charged *I-68*, unknowingly causing severe damage and the submarine's limping withdrawal to Kwajalein. Early the morning of 14 December, *I-4* sank the Norwegian motor ship *Heough*, in the approximate 40-mile-wide Kaiwi Channel between Oahu and Molokai.

Though not yet known to the Navy, after dark on 17 December, 200 miles south of Oahu, *I-75* torpedoed and sank in approximately six minutes, another Matson freighter, the 3,252-ton SS *Manini*. The sinking was so rapid, her crew had no time to send an emergency signal. On 18 December, *I-72* torpedoed and sank the 5,113-ton American merchantman SS *Prusa*, 150 miles south of Oahu. The torpedo wrecked the *Prusa*'s engines and she went down in approximately five minutes, another sinking which happened so rapidly there was no time to send an emergency signal. In both instances the crews drifted in life boats for days before they were picked up—and provided the first pieces of information regarding the Japanese submarine attacks south of Oahu. The attacks off the mainland's West coast began with less success.[10]

The morning of the 18th, far north, astern of *St. Louis*'s Convoy 2005, at 0130 hours, just fifteen minutes before the destroyer *Lawrence* left the formation to return to San Francisco, the Union Oil Company tanker *L.P. St. Clair* was moving south from Seattle, just opposite the mouth of the Columbia River. A gun flash a few hundred yards to starboard, toward the open Pacific, attracted the skipper's attention. As soon as a second flash occurred, Captain John Ellison concluded they were being fired upon by an enemy submarine, and ordered "hard a port," for the entrance to the Columbia River.

The first of a series of undersea boat attacks off the Pacific coast was underway. Though the best Commander Neiji Tagami's Japanese submarine *I-25* could do in the darkness was fire ten wildly aimed shots at the fleeing tanker, in the next seven days American merchantmen encountered close to a dozen more attacks. Few ended so futilely as *I-25*'s first encounter.

About an hour before dawn on the same morning, off Cape Mendocino, north of San Francisco, as *I-17* moved quietly along the surface, one of its lookouts spotted a ship approaching. Commander Kozo Nishino, ordered an attack on the American freighter, *Samoa*, on her way to San Diego with a load of lumber. Allotted only one torpedo per merchant ship, Nishino decided to begin the attack using the boat's 5.5-inch deck gun and use the torpedo only if necessary.

Moments before the *Samoa* crossed the bow of *I-17*, the merchantman's First Mate John Lehtonen, on watch at the time, spotted a dim light from the approaching enemy sub and yelled down to Captain Nels Sinnes, "A submarine is attacking us!" Nels, who had been asleep, sat bolt upright in his bunk, quickly pulled on his trousers and shirt, grabbed a life jacket and yelled into the crew's quarters for everyone to report to their lifeboat stations. Crewmen were tearing the canvas covers from the lifeboats as the Japanese opened fire. Sinnes later recalled, "Five shots were fired at us. One, apparently aimed at our radio antenna, burst in the air above the stern. Fragments fell to the deck."

The Japanese commander, unsatisfied with the results of the gun attack from his pitching deck, ordered a torpedo fired at 70 yards. Seconds later, the freighter's captain recalled,

> We saw the telltale wake of a torpedo coming directly at us amidships. It was too late to do more than just wait for our destiny. [Then] the miracle happened. The torpedo went directly beneath us, didn't even touch the hull and continued beyond. A short distance away it exploded. There was a huge shower accompanied by smoke and flames. Fragments from the torpedo fell on our deck.

In retrospect a combination of three things saved the *Samoa* and her crew. Two were the darkness and the torpedo's explosion away from the ship. Nishino, unable to see whether the torpedo had hit the ship, moved in closer to check it out. In the dim light, with the Japanese sub less then fifteen feet away, the third bit of good fortune came into play. Sinnes explained,

> Shortly after the attack the sub hove to about 40 feet away. Visibility was extremely poor and I couldn't make out the flag or anybody on board. There was a shout: 'Hi ya!' from the submarine. I replied, 'What do you want of us?' There was no answer. Then it disappeared, evidently thinking that we were sinking on account of our heavy list to port.
> The list was due to the fact that the engineers had been shifting water in the ballast tanks. We lost our No. 1 lifeboat a couple days before in a storm, part of which was still hanging from its davit. He evidently thought . . . [we were] sinking on account of this and left us alone.

Sinnes was right. Commander Nishino did radio the flag submarine, *I-15*, off San Francisco, that he had sunk an American merchantman. *Samoa* floated quietly until daybreak at 7 a.m., then headed at full speed for San Diego, arriving two days later.

An additional Japanese submarine made its presence known on 18 December. The incident was also recorded by Donald J. Young in his book, *December 1941, America's First 25 Days at War*.

An hour earlier, about a day's sailing to the south, a small, 70-foot-long commercial fishing boat out of San Pedro, the *Jacky-Joe*, was about to get underway for Santa Cruz Island, some 75 miles up the coast off Ventura. Owner, builder and skipper, Andy Mardesich, along with his younger brother, Mike, and engineer, Tom Johnson, had anchored at the Catalina Island Isthmus that night, before heading for Santa Cruz to do some fishing.

As Mike steered the little ship along the shaded shoreline of the island, a boat was seen about 10 miles out heading into the Catalina Channel. Deciding to "get in on his luck," Mike instinctively headed for what Andy by now had identified in his binoculars as "a strange, black-colored fishing boat." Five minutes later, the *Jacky-Joe* broke out of the shade into the early morning sunlight, at which the "fishing boat" they were watching abruptly disappeared. "My God, it's a sub," shouted Andy, "Let's get the hell out of here!"

The nearest help appeared 30 miles away in a cluster of fishing boats across the channel off the Palos Verdes Peninsula. Mike turned hard to starboard and gunned the little fishing boat toward safety. About halfway across, however, one of the engines blew. Since use of the radio was restricted to "only if you are sinking" conditions, Andy decided to head back for San Pedro. Limping in at six at night, too late to get inside the harbor before the antisubmarine nets were drawn, Mardesich was taken by boat by the U.S. Coast Guard into the U.S. Navy section base to make his report. In all probability he had seen the arrival of the sub *I-19*, the Japanese boat ordered to attack merchant shipping off Los Angeles Harbor.[11]

"The President's Lady" Sails from Honolulu: Task Force 15.2

For Joey Border, the 15th, 16th, 17th and 18th, continued to drift slowly back toward normal, if anything could ever be normal again. Beginning Monday the 15th, Joey could now at least sleep in her apartment each night, listen to the radio each evening, relax a bit, read and write letters. On the 16th she went shopping down town, came home and wrapped Christmas presents, went to the food market, and straightened the apartment. Bob had told her there were indications *Tennessee* might be leaving soon, so on the 17th she cleaned the apartment, and had her hair done. They had decided to celebrate Christmas on the 18th.[12]

More and more each day, the effects of martial law could be felt. Because of the tight cloak of secrecy and censorship that had wrung down on any information about ship and airplane movements, either commercial or military, or troop movements and training on the islands, it was difficult to know what was going on. She didn't know, and few did, that the *Coolidge* and the *Scott* were to arrive on the 16th. Nor did she know that the Navy was preparing to move not only *Tennessee*, but *Maryland* and *Pennsylvania* out of Pearl Harbor.

Bob indeed sensed the ship would be departing in the near future—but when or to where he hadn't the slightest notion. Perhaps they would be heading west into war. All the signs were there. Long hours of duty and work, hurried damage repair, the push to get *Tennessee* moved away from *West Virginia*, *Arizona*, and *Oklahoma*. Scheduling of departures and disclosures of destinations were now closely held secrets—if known at all by ship's commanders.

Beginning on the 8th, the three battleships had been given priority for repair above and below the waterline to return to service pending repair of heavier battle damage, and activities had been moving at a feverish pace. The *Maryland* and *Pennsylvania* could readily be moved, but the *Tennessee* had to be freed up because she was still pinned in place against the quays by the sunken *West Virginia*. On the 8th the oiler *Ramapo* (AO-12) moved from Berth B-12, Pier 14, making way for the move of the first battleship. On the 9th divers were divided into teams to more efficiently expend their time and energies on higher priority tasks. One group began systematically sounding the sunken *Utah*, *Oklahoma*, and *West Virginia* for men who might still be alive, trapped in the double hulls, and possibly be rescued. The sounding work, performed at depths of no more than twenty-five feet was nevertheless difficult and extremely tiring.

In parallel, divers examined the hulls of *Maryland* and *Tennessee* and began repairs of small holes caused by bomb near misses. At 1030 the morning of 10 December, *Maryland* eased carefully out from between Berth F-5 and the overturned *Oklahoma*, and proceeded under her own power to Berth 12, Pier 14 in the Navy Yard, vacated by *Ramapo* on the 8th. At 0845 the morning of the 12th the *Pennsylvania* was backed out of dry dock, moored portside to Dock 1010, and immediately began receiving food and water on board. On the 13th she began refueling. To make space available to *Tennessee*, the cruiser *San Francisco* vacated Berth 17, *St. Louis* and *Honolulu* having been moved from adjacent berths—the *Honolulu* into dry dock. To free up *Tennessee*, divers drilled holes in the concrete quays holding her against the *West Virgina*, and dynamited them.

Additionally, pumping of both water and some oil from the partially flooded *Tennessee* was necessary to ensure her hull was clear of the harbor's bottom. At 0827 the morning of the 13th divers commenced hull inspections to determine if the ship was clear of the bottom all around, and reported at 1130 she was clear to move out. All the while repairs continued, including replacement of buckled shell plating that contained 1,500 feet of cracks and 2,000 loose rivets caused by the intense heat from *Arizona*'s, *West Virginia*'s, and *Tennessee* fires.

At 0802 the morning of the 16th, the day *Coolidge* and *Hugh L. Scott* arrived in Honolulu, *Tennessee* began shifting berths. U.S. Navy Tug No. 153 moored to her at 0810, cast off at 1115, and after the battleship cast off lines from F-6 at 1200, she was carefully inched forward out from between *West Virginia* and Berth F-6, through *Maryland*'s Berth 5, between the Berth 5 quays and the capsized *Oklahoma*, and finally moored at Berth 17, across the harbor to the east, at 1525 hours.[13]

Wednesday evening, 17 December, the chief nurse at the Naval Hospital called one of her nurses, Navy Lieutenant (jg) Ruth Erickson, into her office and told her to go to her quarters, pack a bag, and be ready to leave at noon Thursday. Ruth asked where she was going, and in reply the chief nurse said she had no idea. The commanding officer had ordered her to select three nurses and they were to be in uniform. Navy nurses as yet had no outdoor uniforms, thus would wear the regular white ward uniforms.[14]

On Thursday, the 18th, men previously temporarily assigned to *Tennessee* in the days after the attack, began returning to their ships, normal duty stations, or the receiving station at Pearl Harbor. Because Bob sensed the ship's departure could come any day, he sought every opportunity to see Joey or talk with her on the phone. Bob came home to the apartment again at 11:30, they celebrated Christmas as they had planned, before he left for the ship at 4 p.m. She listened to the radio that evening then went to bed, aware that tomorrow might bring Bob's departure to heaven knows where. The whole world had changed. Neither he nor Joey knew if his pending assignment to Pensacola for aviator training would become the hoped-for reality. *Tennessee* still had an almost full load of fuel, her magazines and ammunition ready boxes had been replenished. Perhaps she was receiving temporary repairs to join a task force that would seek out the enemy.[15]

The same morning, the 18th, at the Naval Hospital, in their ward uniforms—capes, blue felt hats, and blue sweaters—nurses Ruth Erickson, Lauretta Eno, and Catherine Richardson waited for a driver to pick them up at their quarters. When he arrived and inquired of their destination, they still had no idea. They went by the Officer of the Day's desk and picked up their priority orders, which directed them to one of the piers in Honolulu. They were to go aboard the 21,936-ton *President Coolidge* along with a number of corpsmen from the hospital and prepare to receive patients. Eight volunteer Red Cross nurses from the Queens Hospital in Honolulu were attached to the 12,579-ton *Hugh L. Scott*, at the next pier. The Navy nurses calculated *Coolidge's* medical supplies for a ten-day period.[16]

When the two ships arrived in Honolulu from their perilous voyage from Manila, they were already carrying hundreds of evacuees, including women, children, missionaries, government officials, businessmen, Army and Navy officers and many Chinese aviation cadets. Among the evacuees from the Far East were Royal Leonard of the China Aviation Corporation, formerly personal pilot to Chiang Kai-shek; V.M. Zubilin, going to Washington to be third secretary of the Soviet Embassy; Mrs. V.M. Zubilin; J. Thyne Henderson, formerly first secretary of the British Embassy in Tokyo, en route to Chile. An added surprise children, wounded and other passengers would eventually learn, were two Panda bears sent from Madame Chiang Kai-shek, a gift to the United States China Relief organization.[17]

On arrival, the world cruise ship, and her smaller, accompanying American President's Line vessel were placed immediately at the disposal of the military to transport Navy and Army wounded back to the mainland. Two Navy doctors on board as passengers were placed on temporary duty orders to tend to the wounded, and were glad they could be of assistance. Into the two ships' already overcrowded deck spaces were jammed additional scores of the hundreds waiting to leave the islands, including tourists, most of the former passengers from the two Pan American *Clippers* turned back by the attack; all but seven of the football players from San Jose State, the entire Willamette University football team, and the coaches and fans that accompanied both teams; many expectant mothers, widows and children of men killed in the attack, and servicemen's dependents.

In the period after their arrival on the 16th both ships were converted into semi-hospital ships. Bunks were added to sickbays. Crews gave up sections of their quarters for the wounded. Additional space for attack survivors was prepared in one of the steerage compartments. Cots lined the sides of passageways and filled the *Coolidge*'s spacious lounge, from which furnishings had been removed. The ship's nursery was likewise converted into sleeping quarters. Cots filled staterooms, so closely placed there was no space left for passage.

The Naval Hospital brought the requested supplies the 18th. Then came the nurses' arduous task of preparing beds for the patients, checking supplies, organizing nursing watches, planning meals for helpless men, positioning adequate medical supplies near the most critical cases, and the thousand other details associated with such a tremendous first venture. On the *Coolidge*, Catherine Richardson took the 8 a.m. to 4 p.m., Ruth Erickson's duty ran from 4 p.m. to midnight, and Lauretta Eno was on from midnight to 8 a.m.

On the 18th, information regarding the evacuation of tourists went to hotels and other locations where they were staying. There were approximately 1,000 tourists on the island, and lead time was needed to notify as many as possible to come to the correct pier the morning of the 19th.[18]

During that tense and fearful period it was not known from hour to hour whether another attack might hit Hawaii. Yet out of the awful confusion, through the efforts of these hastily recruited Red Cross nurses under command of Navy nurse Catherine Richardson, came final readiness for arrival of the stretcher cases.

Beginning early the morning of the 19th, passengers watched from the ship and pier in stunned, solemn silence as the wounded were brought aboard. The approximate 800 passengers on the *Coolidge*, who had come from Manila, and had heard of the bombing of the Philippine capitol as well as Pearl Harbor, and had gone through the en route transition from peace to war, until this moment hadn't seen the direct effects of war. They now confronted a far more sobering sight. The services' commands decided that patients who would need more than three months treatment should be transferred. Ruth Erickson noted, "Some were very bad and probably should not have been moved." There were men hideously burned by explosions and fire. There were fracture cases wearing body as well as limb casts. There were sightless men, their eyes covered with bandages.

They came to the piers in the Navy's blue and Army's tan ambulances. The 30 critically burned patients brought to *Coolidge*, and those with multiple fractures, were sent to the sickbay. The remaining 95 carried by the *Coolidge* were distributed in the lower deck quarters already prepared. Wounded officers were placed in staterooms. Meanwhile, no doubt, similar preparations and patient loading were in progress on the *Scott*, which took aboard 55 stretcher cases in addition to approximately 150 Army dependents and other civilians ordered to leave Hawaii.

Although every assistance was given by ship's personnel, the responsibility for trying to keep the fearfully injured survivors alive until they reached adequate medical facilities was entrusted to seven Navy doctors, the *Coolidge* surgeon, and eleven Red Cross and three Navy nurses.[19]

Early Friday morning, the 19th, the pace of activity on *Tennessee* picked up considerably. On the docks in Honolulu, final preparations were underway for the departure of the *Coolidge* and *Scott*, to be in the first convoy from Oahu to the mainland, carrying evacuees to safety. Many of the remaining passengers added to those who had arrived on the ships, received one to two hours' notice to board, though notification had begun on Thursday.

Coach "Spec" Keene from Willamette University had been trying to find a way back to the states for his football team and their fans ever since the attack, and that morning had two hours to round up his team and get them to the right pier in the port of Honolulu. The Willamette team had volunteered to guard key facilities for the U.S. Army engineers, while the San Jose State team was supporting the Honolulu police in law enforcement and security duties, as well as assisting in searches for Japanese aliens. Some thought they might be stranded in Hawaii for six months, or for the duration of the war. The women who came to cheer for Willamette and enjoy Hawaii, after two days had volunteered to assist at the Army's Tripler General Hospital, working as nurses' aids. They washed dishes left in the kitchen since the attack, carried trays, bathed the wounded and assisted nurses with dressings for the wounded. All had to be on board the morning of the 19th.[20]

Military dependents generally had further to travel from the military installations to the port of Honolulu, and most who boarded that morning probably had registered for departure, as Admiral Bloch and the Army's Hawaiian Department had requested. The military men and government employees assigned to units on the island, and who had dependents living there, frequently participated in telephone recalls during training exercises. Thus the call-ups and messages that went out to dependents to report to the piers the morning of the 19th resulted in more rapid notification. Mrs. Catherine Conroy, with her six year old daughter Rosalie, whose husband was Master Sergeant John J. Conroy of the Army Air Force, hadn't seen her husband for a week, because dependents had been locally evacuated to safety from Schofield Barracks after the attack. She and Rosalie were finally permitted to return to their quarters to pack, preparatory to evacuating to the States—and received five hours notice.

Notices came to evacuees by phone and messengers, to hotel rooms, restaurants, movie theaters, beauty shops, homes, apartment buildings, military unit's headquarters, and dependents' quarters. Seven football players from San Jose State declined to leave, and, wanting to do their part in the war effort, volunteered instead to stay on with the police force. The chief of police liked their work and offered them $165 a month salary.[21]

While the morning's activities were in progress on *Tennessee*, Bob Border undoubtedly saw or later learned two destroyers and a cruiser had left Pearl Harbor. The first was at 0933, the destroyer *Reid* (DD-369), whose captain was Lieutenant Commander Harold F. Pullen. The second, *Cummings* (DD-365), whose skipper was Lieutenant Commander George D. Cooper, got underway at 0939, and the 7,050-ton light cruiser, *Detroit* (CL-8), at 0955.

Entering the harbor at 1152 that morning, trailing an escort, was the 14,225-ton attack cargo ship *Procyon* (AK-19), which arrived after a seven-day dash from San Francisco under classified emergency orders. The *Procyon* was carrying a precious cargo of blood plasma and medical supplies, moored at 1248, and began cargo unloading after 1500 hours.

At the outbound *Detroit*'s conn when she left Pearl Harbor at 0955, was her commander, Captain L.J. Wiltse, and on the bridge was her navigator, Lieutenant Commander R.E. Elliott. On leaving Pearl Harbor's Berth F-13, Captain Wiltse opened his sealed instructions. San Francisco was Task Force 15.2's West Coast destination.[22]

Approximately 1100 hours, with the older, slower *Scott*, the guide leading *Coolidge*, the two ships were underway from Honolulu to rendezvous with *Detroit*, *Cummings* and *Reid* just outside the harbor. Because of reported submarine activity in recent days, Task Force 15.2's route to San Francisco would be decidedly different. Maneuvering at various courses and speeds the Navy's three combatants were in formation with the two passenger carriers at 1158 hours, speed 15.5 knots, on a westerly course of 267 degrees.

On board *Coolidge* and *Scott*, as soon as the ships left the harbor and while maneuvering to join formation, passengers were served lunch, and not long afterward, assembled on the promenade decks to receive the mandatory briefings at their assigned lifeboat stations—and the even more sobering instructions regarding the carrying, donning, and wear of life jackets.

Typically, instructions were, "Carry or wear of life jackets is mandatory at all times when moving about the ships. We are at war, and this is not simply a drill. The winter seas will be rough at times. There have been reports of submarine attacks and submarines may be lying in wait. Should submarine alerts occur you will be ordered to don your life jackets. Be ready to don your life jacket at any time and move quickly to your lifeboat station if told. Follow the crew's instructions without question."

Following boat assembly and life jacket instructions, with ships now in the open sea, about 1,500 passengers were receiving their second, and more intense welcome into wartime sailing under threat of submarine attacks. While there was elation at the thoughts of finally going home, many, already somewhat affected by what they had just heard, were becoming reacquainted with the unpleasant, discouraging mealtime after-effects of rolling and pitching decks. As if that weren't enough, as the day wore into night, they would feel the effects of repeated zigzagging, blacked out ships with less than desired ventilation, and the beginning of mixed, unpleasant odors from seasickness, medications given the wounded, and burnt flesh oozing body fluids in spite of bandages

Cruiser *Detroit* (CL-8), command ship of Task Force 15.2 convoyed the *Coolidge* and *Scott* from Honolulu to San Francisco, departing 19 December 1941. Off the Mare Island Navy Yard, 18 February 1942. NAPR

Destroyer *Cummings* (DD-365), submarine screen for Task Force 15.2. Off Mare Island Navy Yard, 4 March 1942. NAPR

and ointments intended to assuage the terrible burns some men had received.

Detroit, with *Scott* and *Coolidge* in column, spaced 800 yards astern of the cruiser, with *Reid* and *Cummings* on opposite flanks, held their westerly course until 1314 hours then the formation came further starboard to 310 degrees and began zigzagging using plan No. 33. They were entering the Kauai Channel and were beginning their passage between Oahu, to the east, and Kauai to the west. If Japanese submarines on stations in the vicinity of Oahu, sighted the Task Force, they apparently couldn't position themselves for attacks, and didn't report its sighting. While there was no submarine alert given the passengers that first afternoon, many knew why the ship periodically zigzagged and explained the procedure to others. To the uninitiated, zigzagging equated to a submarine alert.

At 1533 zigzagging ceased and four minutes later the five ships swung further right to course 015 degrees true, or 15 degrees east of north. To reduce the likelihood of submarine attacks, the task force was now positioned on a track approximately 65 miles west of the normally busy sea-lane leading from Oahu, through the channel between Molokai and Oahu, to San Francisco. At 1603 zigzagging resumed, and ceased nearly two hours later, when darkness had closed round Task Force 15.2. At 1700, while zigzagging was in progress the *Reid* logged a friendly plane over the convoy, undoubtedly assisting the search for any signs of submarines while providing protective cover for the convoy. This was the first night out, and the task force hadn't yet experienced a submarine alert.[23]

The Willamette University and San Jose State football teams were berthed in steerage, and had hammocks for sleeping. The women who accompanied the teams were in third class cabins with Chinese, Turks and others fleeing the war. The long, tense journey, and last leg home for thousands had begun, while ahead, off to starboard, over the horizon, the cruiser *St. Louis,* destroyers *Smith* and *Preston* were escorting Convoy 2005, the Matson Line's *Lurline, Matsonia* and *Monterey* carrying 9,918 men in the opposite direction, base course 243 degrees, bound for Oahu.

All day the 19th, Convoy 2005 had pressed toward Hawaii, mostly at a speed of 19 knots, on course, four times zigzagging, and beginning at 0623, *St. Louis* kept at least one of her four scout planes airborne, until 1501 hours. To spoil a possible submarine attack, she again initiated zigzagging at 1558, shortly before sunset. Throughout the day, no submarine alerts or attacks occurred.[24]

Behind *St. Louis* and Convoy 2005 was the cruiser *Phoenix*, with destroyers *Perkins* and *Cushing*, and the six ships of Convoy 2004, which, for good reason, each day was falling further behind *St. Louis*'s convoy. *Phoenix*, on leaving San Francisco, deviated toward the south at first, out of the normal sea lane, until she rendezvoused with *Platte*, *Sabine* and *Harris* the morning of the 18th, then, turned right to a base course of 257 degrees, the course toward Oahu. *Phoenix* and Convoy 2004 had to keep a slower speed of 15 knots because of the maximum speeds of the ships she and the two destroyers were escorting. The larger convoy's slower ships necessitated more zigzagging and more frequent launch of scout aircraft to ensure they remained free of submarine attacks following the early afternoon torpedo attack on *Aldebaran*, the 18th.

The cold, hard facts were, the surface speed of a Japanese submarine that might be tailing the convoy and traveling on the surface at night would permit it to possibly overtake, pass, and position itself to attack. The tankers *Platte* and *Sabine*, and the *Aldebaran*, once already attacked and missed, carrying munitions, would have been especially tempting targets to Japanese submarines were they able to penetrate the convoy's submarine screen. Fortunately, Convoy 2004 encountered no submarine alerts or attacks on the 19th. On Oahu, as the day came to a close, Joey and Bob Borders' lives were about to take another surprising turn.

Joey had learned of the evacuation order, but had no idea when she would be affected by it. Word had spread of the *Coolidge*'s and *Scott*'s departure that morning. She went down town, stopped by Mary Marron's, then saw Dot Thorpe, before again going to Pearl Harbor by bus that afternoon to meet Bob for a half hour visit at the boat landing, and then registered as required by the evacuation order.

He told her of the continued activity on *Tennessee* and the possibility they would be leaving any day. He reiterated he had no way of knowing when the ship might leave or where it would go. They spoke of the future, quietly, and of love, the need to stay close, talk often as possible by phone, and write letters when no other means of communication were available. Their love and steadfast determination to remain close as humanly possible were what mattered, what sustained them. When they parted and she returned to the apartment, she called him once more to tell him how much she loved and missed him each day. From the apartment she went to Fran Atkins' for the night. By the time she went to bed, she had made up her mind. When Bob left she was going home as soon as possible, and she told her diary, ". . . Am going home."

Task Force 16: Dash to Resurrection

At 1100 hours the morning of the 20th, *Tennessee*'s crew began hoisting the first of three scout planes on board, two with their pilots and observers, another indicator of preparations to get underway. If Bob were on deck to notice, his curiosity would have been further aroused by the fact *Pennsylvania* and *Maryland* were also hoisting airplanes aboard, as they normally would if they were going to sortie.

Ford Island, where battleships in port normally sent their scout planes for maintenance and to continue search or training missions while the ships were in port, had, like all airfields on Oahu, taken a terrible beating. During the attack the Pacific Fleet's long range patrol wings had been shattered, and the Fleet needed every available scout aircraft—no matter its range—to help protect it. *Maryland* had lost one of its scout airplanes, which went missing on the 8th while conducting a search mission. But clearly, the battleships, already damaged, needed scout aircraft on board to search ahead of them, wherever they might be headed. The acting commander of the Pacific Fleet was taking a calculated risk with Task Force 16.[25]

At 11:30 a.m. Hawaii time, the same morning, 1:30 p.m., Pacific coast time, another submarine attack was beginning, twenty miles off California's Cape Mendocino, 225 miles north of San Francisco. This time Commander Nishino's *I-17* wouldn't miss, though he believed his crew had sunk the American freighter *Samoa* two days earlier. And this time, not only did the submarine's torpedo strike home and permanently disable the empty Sacony-Vacuum Oil Company tanker, *Emidio*, five of the ship's crewmen died as a result of the attack.

The skipper of the *Emidio* received a report called down to him from the bridge. A sub had been sighted about a quarter of a mile off the stern and closing. Captain Clark Farrow, attempting first to outrun the raider, ordered "full speed and dumped ballast, but . . . had no chance to escape. We were rapidly overtaken," said Farrow. "The sub was making 20 knots. I (then) tried to get behind her but (it) reversed course and kept after us."

Farrow realized the situation was hopeless and ordered his radio operator, W.S. "Sparks" Foote, to send an S.O.S., which he did, accompanied by the words, "Under attack by enemy sub." No sooner was the message tapped out on the wireless, than *I-17* fired the first shot with it's deck gun, which carried away the radio antenna. Two more shots struck the *Emidio*, one of them destroying one of the lifeboats still hanging in its davits on deck.

"The captain (then) ordered us to take to the lifeboats," one of the crewmen said later. "Three of the crew—R.W. Pennington, Fred Potts and Stuart McGillivray—were attempting to launch one of the boats when a shell struck it, spilling them into the water. Other boats were put over the side to search for the three missing men, but we couldn't find them."

With the exception of four men still on board, and the three lost over the side, what was left of the 36-man crew rowed away from the endangered ship. About ten minutes later, after a parting shot at the life boats, the *I-17* abruptly submerged. A couple of minutes later two airplanes explained the reason for its sudden disappearance. "It may have been 10 or 15 minutes after the S.O.S. when the two Army bombers came roaring overhead from the coast," said Farrow later. "To us in the lifeboats it was a welcome sight. One of the airplanes, circling where the sub had gone down, dropped a depth charge. We couldn't tell if it hit it or not."

It didn't. But Captain Nishino and *I-17* hadn't finished the job. He decided to risk a second attack by the American planes for one torpedo shot at the abandoned tanker. "We were still looking at where the sub went down," continued Farrow, "when we saw its periscope slowly push up above the surface. While still partially submerged it fired a torpedo from 200 yards. We could see the trail as it sped straight for the ship. It struck with a loud explosion."

On board *Emidio*, radioman Foote, who had quickly jury-rigged another antenna, was just preparing to send a second S.O.S. when the torpedo hit. Foote, undaunted by the blast, dutifully tapped out his S.O.S., adding the words, "Torpedoes in stern," then calmly made his way to the main deck and jumped overboard.

In the engine room, three men had either not heard or ignored the abandon ship order, and were still attending to their duties when the torpedo struck. Oiler B.F. Moler, astoundingly saw it penetrate the engine room bulkhead, passing so close to him he could have reached out and touched it. Fireman Kenneth Kimes and Third Engineer R.A. Winters likely had no chance to see it. "It exploded on the other side of the engine room and killed Kimes and Winters outright," Moler told an examining medical officer the next day at the Eureka naval base section. Despite three broken ribs and a punctured lung, "I somehow swam and climbed up to the upper deck and jumped overboard." Life boats picked up both Moler and Foote.

The submarine's captain was right by thinking he was risking a second attack by American bombers if he showed himself too soon. "Back came the planes as the sub sank out of sight again," continued Farrow. "One of them dropped another depth charge. There was a big blast and plenty of smoke. That may have hit here, we figured, for we didn't see her again."

The depth charge missed again, and at 3:05 a.m. the morning of the 21st, the Coast Guard cutter *Shawnee* encountered *I-17* while searching for the *Emidio*'s crew. Through a series of events that could only be described as "fortunate" the *Shawnee* avoided a battle with the submarine she and her captain, Chief Boatswain Garner Churchill, and the volunteer crew of four would have lost.

At 6:45 a.m. on the 21st, the *Shawnee*'s crew sighted the foundering tanker. They saw no life boats, and there was no sign of life. At 8:10 a.m., a Navy patrol plane arrived and signaled Churchill back to the coast. He arrived back at the Humbolt Bay Lifeboat Station at 12:45 that afternoon, some 13 precarious hours after he had left, only to learn *Emidio*'s crew had been picked up by the Blunt's Reef Lightship. Despite the torpedo hit, the *Emidio* didn't sink. Several days later, it ran aground on a pile of rocks off Crescent City, California, approximately 85 miles north of where it had been torpedoed.[26]

There was yet another submarine attack off the West Coast the afternoon of the 20th. About the time the *Emidio* crewmen put their oars in the water to begin their agonizing 14-hour "pull" to safety through a rainstorm and rough seas, the Japanese submarine *I-23*, on station some 330 miles south, off Santa Cruz, began stalking the 6,771-ton American tanker, *Agwiworld*. At 2:15 in the afternoon, the Richfield Oil Company's tanker was headed north, some 20 miles off Monterey Bay and 75 miles south of San Francisco, when an explosion off the stern of the ship brought its captain, Frederick Goncalves, running to the bridge.

About 500 yards to the west, directly in line with the sun, Goncalves saw what appeared to be a submarine. "I ordered the helm hard to port and headed straight for (it)," the captain said, "but when the second shot came, I put the helm hard over the starboard and presented my stern to the sub." Although the enemy boat, whose captain was Commander Genichi Shibata, was much faster than the *Agwiworld*, Shibata had a dilemma. In an attempt to overtake the fleeing American tanker, the submarine would be running in a heavy ground swell, and with decks awash Shibata could lose his entire gun crew. The swell would limit the gun crew's accuracy as well.

Perhaps one other factor gave Shibata pause, and prevented him from closing further while attacking *Agwiworld*—the probability the Japanese had overheard the tanker's distress call to the U.S. Navy. Whatever the reasons, *I-23* remained at 500 yards, firing at least six more shots at the now zigzagging American. "The sub didn't chase us into port exactly," Captain Goncalves said. "We zigzagged around, maneuvering always to present the smallest target possible. The sub circled and dodged, trying to get broadside of us, but never succeeded. As we neared land and the sub fired the last of its eight shots—four of which splashed water onto the deck—it quickly submerged."

Meanwhile, on shore several Monterey peninsula residents unknowingly witnessed the attack. A story in the *Monterey Herald* that evening said: "Scores of golfers playing seaside courses reported today they had observed the tanker with huge clouds of smoke pouring from her funnel, fleeing toward Santa Cruz and zigzagging wildly, but most of them thought little more about it."

Although not reported anywhere else, according to the logs of the *I-23*, Commander Shibata wasn't through that day, not yet. Not long after his unsuccessful pursuit of *Agwiworld*, the sub encountered "an old gunboat" a few miles out of Monterey, and another "chase" ensued. Although Shibata's "old gunboat" turned out to be a harmless fishing boat, the Japanese still gave chase, firing intermittently from their 5.5-inch deck gun until registering a hit on the ship's rudder. Leaving their victim going harmlessly around in circles, much to the glee of the enemy gun crew, *I-23* put to sea.

Flagship of the Japanese submarine force attacking the West

Coast shipping was *I-15*, on station forty miles west of San
Francisco, off the Farallon Islands. Though Commander Nobuo
Ishikawa's logs indicate *1-15* made no sightings or attacks during
its eight days on station, it possibly was involved in a slight collision
on the 20th with an Oakland garbage scow, named *Tahoe*.

The 37-year-old converted lumber ship had dumped its weekly
load of Oakland city garbage off the Farallons and was heading
back for port. Telling the story of the encounter, the scow's
captain, William Vartnaw, said some of his crew sighted what
appeared to be a periscope and part of a sub's superstructure
break water directly ahead less than 60 yards.

There wasn't enough time to change course or stop, so the
Tahoe ran into the sub, scraping its way across the hull to the
other side. The crew raced to the stern to get another look at
what they hit. Nothing could be seen. His ship leaking badly with
an 80-foot-long gash torn in her hull, Captain Vartnaw was able
to bring her safely to the Oakland Scavenger Service dry dock
that night.

According to the 1992 writer of the story, ". . . the Navy refused
to officially accept the [*Tahoe* crew's] story. Besides, how would it
look to the rest of the country—and the Navy—if the first blow to
a Japanese sub had come from an old garbage scow?" Apparently
ignorant of the enormous complexities, difficulties and outright
terror associated with submarine and anti-submarine warfare,
and of course, along with everyone else, equally ignorant of the
losses and damage inflicted on the Japanese submarines operating
in Hawaiian waters during the fourteen days beginning with the
Japanese attack, he went on to add sarcastically,

> Unmindful of the Navy's stance on the matter, a
> newspaperman from the San Francisco Chronicle
> wrote the following poem in tribute to the old
> scow's moment in the sun:
> The Tahoe's back on the job today,
> She's ruined a sub, her crewmen say;
> The Tahoe rides the waves today,
> A queen for sure in her own sweet way.

On the 21st, as Task Forces 15.2 and 16 plowed steadily
northeast toward home, both commanders undoubtedly received
coded warnings of submarine attacks, and locations of the

attacks, as rapidly as information became available. The public was made aware with headlines in the San Francisco Chronicle and other coast newspapers: REPORT: SUBS STRIKE TWICE OFF COAST, and TANKER'S LIFEBOATS SHELLED BY JAPS, 'RUTHLESS,' SAYS CAPTAIN. Another claimed: PLANES ATTACK COAST RAIDER and TWENTY-TWO MISSING IN SEA RAID OFF COAST.[27]

Before the attacks off the California coast began the afternoon of the 20th, Joey, who wouldn't learn of them until a day later, was in Honolulu shopping. When she returned to the apartment, she called Bob, and during the conversation told him she would go to the Morrisons' quarters at Pearl Harbor to visit Barbara. The Morrisons had moved in during the week and Barbara was there helping her mother and father get their new home set up. After lunch she caught a bus to the Navy base.

Early to mid-afternoon, Joey and Barbara sat down near the living room window, which gave a clear view of Pearl Harbor—set up and began playing a game of acey-ducey. Soon engrossed in the game and conversation, they didn't notice four destroyers proceeding at intervals down the main channel toward the harbor entrance. The first to get underway from Berth X-8, at 1430 hours, was the *Tucker* (DD-374), with her captain, Lieutenant Commander William R. Terrell at the conn. The *Flusser* (DD-368) followed, captained by Lieutenant Commander William G. Beecher, Jr, departing Berth X-11 five minutes later. Next came the *Case* (DD-370) from Berth X-8 at 1444, with her captain, Lieutenant Commander Robert W. Bedilion on the bridge. The last destroyer in the column moved away from Berth X-8 at 1453, the *Conyngham* (DD-371), with Lieutenant Commander Henry C. Daniel at the conn.

The frequent departures and arrivals of destroyers in Pearl Harbor were routine, and seldom gained notice. The number of their destroyer patrols had increased greatly since the 7 December attack, joining in a growing, steady stream of motor torpedo boats, submarines, mine sweepers, cruisers, the fleet's three carriers, and support ships in and out of the harbor.[28]

Joey's and Barbara's conversation continued, dwelling on what their husbands seemed to be saying the past two or three days, when and where they might be going, and their plans to go home. Was it reasonable to expect the *Tennessee* and the remaining two battleships would be committed to war so soon after being struck by Japanese bombs? They could see the three great ships moored in the harbor. *Tennessee* and *Maryland* were in berths, bows-in, starboard sides to piers in the Southeast Loch, on the east side of the main channel—the same side of the channel as *Pennsylvania*, which was moored portside at her pre-attack berth at 1010 Dock, in the location temporarily occupied by the cruiser *Helena* when she was torpedoed. *Oglala* still lay forlornly capsized astern the battleship.

There had been much shifting of ships to different berths to accelerate repair, salvage, and previously-scheduled overhaul work. The torpedo-damaged cruiser *Helena*, had been moved into the drydock after *Pennsylvania* vacated it on the 12th. The oiler *Ramapo* vacated Berth 12 Pier 14, which *Maryland* moved into on the 10th. The cruisers *Honolulu* and *San Francisco* had been moved into dry dock, opening up Pier 17 for the *Tennessee's* move on the 16th.[29]

The ladies could no longer board any of the ships to see for themselves the state of varnished wood quarterdecks, canvas shaded forecastles and quarterdecks, heavily painted hulls, brightly polished metal fittings, cleanly swept and mopped passageways, capped gun muzzles, and canvas covered guns. Gone were lunches and dinners in the wardrooms and movies on the decks under starry tropical skies. Gone were Sunday afternoon receiving lines and teas, calls and calling cards at senior officers' quarters, the polite formalities sometimes scoffed at by both. Long-standing customs and traditions of the Navy, swept away, many of them forever.

Gone was golf at country clubs, tennis, picnics in the parks, dinners and dances at the Yard Club and Royal Hawaiian Hotel. Boating, surfing—gaiety. Gone, all gone. Time was terribly important now, life deadly serious, a matter of survival and catching fleeting moments of happiness. Guns were no longer silent. The staggering flow of funerals had begun. But now, on this Saturday afternoon, at one of the first light moments for Joey in nearly two shattering weeks, in the midst of a game of acey-ducey, surprise snapped them both from unpleasant thoughts and melancholy revelry.[30]

At 1542 hours, the battleship *Maryland*, with two tugs on her port side, began to move. She was underway, backing out of Berth 12 at Pier 14. From where Joey and Barbara were sitting, she was across the Southeast Loch, toward Hickam Field, moving slowly,

Destroyer *Tucker* (DD-374), submarine screen for Task Force 16. Off Mare Island Navy Yard, 14 March 1942. NAPR

Destroyer *Flusser* (DD-368), submarine screen for Task Force 16. Off Mare Island Navy Yard, 12 January 1942. NAPR

Destroyer *Case* (DD-370), submarine screen in Task Force 16. Off Mare Island Navy Yard, 20 February 1942. NAPR

stern first, generally toward them. Then she began to turn while backing, pushed and nudged by the tugs, slowly into the Loch, presenting her starboard side and hiding the tugs from anyone who might see her from the north. A pause, and then she began moving forward, toward the main channel, and turning to port.

Glancing up from their game periodically, Joey suddenly caught sight of *Maryland*, and called her to Barbara's attention. A few short minutes later, she glanced again, certain, since the war had begun, the battleships would no longer sail singly. The *Tennessee* was moving. She reasoned correctly. At 1555, *Tennessee*, also with two tugs, Numbers 119 and 129, fore and aft on her port side, began backing and turning out of her berth at Pier 17. Joey and Barbara sat, quiet, both enthralled and at once let down again, while the slow motion drama unfolded before them. At 1600 the tugs guiding both *Tennessee* and *Maryland* cast off as *Tennessee* inched forward, ever-so-slowly, pointed toward the main channel, and as she approached a position abeam Pier 14, she too began turning to port, to fall in column astern of *Maryland*.

The two battleships had both eased past *Pennsylvania*, when at 1624, with Navy tugs 142 and 146 on her starboard side pulling, turning and guiding, she too began slowly moving away from 1010 Dock and forward into the main channel, toward the open sea. A majestic, breathtaking sight, and the end of an era. Presently, with the exception of the *Colorado* in Puget Sound Navy Yard for overhaul and modernization, they were only three survivors among nine of America's Pacific battle line—and they were leaving Pearl Harbor. All three battleships would be changed, and never look the same.[31]

From an earlier, fading era they had come, like the more recent era of the great Pan American flying boats, the *Clippers*, now savaged by the leading edge of warfare in the modern era, of fast carrier task forces and the long range striking power of naval and land-based aviation, and the rapid construction of airfields on islands. Yet, these three battleships, plus *West Virginia*, *California* and *Nevada* were only bent, not broken. Resurrection was coming, but for now, neither Bob nor Joey knew where *Tennessee*, *Maryland*, and *Pennsylvania* were headed, or what the future held for the three great ships and the lives of two young people in love, and in war.

One by one they exited Pearl Harbor, and one by one began zigzagging, turning in column to westerly headings with *Maryland* as Task Force 16 guide. Patrolling, periodically zigzagging, watching, listening, and waiting for them outside the entrance to Pearl Harbor were the four destroyers, *Tucker*, *Flusser*, *Case* and *Conyngham*.

The first to take station on the battleships was the last destroyer out of the harbor, *Conyngham*, on the inner submarine screen for *Maryland*. At 1644 *Maryland* began zigzagging using Plan No. 6, after turning on a base course of 255 degrees, and three minutes later *Case* was in position, screening on her starboard beam. At 1717 *Maryland* went to flank speed, while *Flusser* was closing at 25 knots to screen *Tennessee*, and was in position at 1721. At 1724 *Maryland* turned to 280 degrees, a course west northwest. One minute later she changed course to the right due to a submarine being reported by a patrolling destroyer not in the formation. Her crew heard depth charges being dropped as she commenced zigzagging again on the 255 base course. While *Maryland* was zigzagging, *Tucker*, the first destroyer in Task Force 16 to leave the harbor was the last of the destroyers to take up her screening position on the guide of the battleship column. Having left the possible enemy submarine far behind, *Maryland*, *Tennessee* and *Pennsylvania* and their four screens ceased zigzagging at 1826.[32]

Tennessee's crew didn't yet know their mission or destination, Captain Reordan probably withholding information until well clear of potential submarine attacks in the area near Oahu. Were they headed west for a raid on Japanese-held islands? If so, where and when? Were they going to rendezvous with a carrier task force? The westerly heading caused numerous questions, which for a few hours wouldn't be answered—not until after Lieutenant Walt Stencil was on the bridge as Officer of the Deck. Undoubtedly there were mixed emotions to go with the questions. Many were ready to fight, eager to strike back at the enemy. The battle line had taken a terrible, humiliating, bloody beating, and suffered the heaviest losses of all the ships in the Pacific Fleet. Every battleship in the task force had been struck by bombs and bullets, all but these three by torpedoes, and all had taken casualties. The *Tennessee* had suffered less than others in the line, four killed and twenty-one wounded. Nevertheless, to strike back hard was the natural response.

Over two hours after the westerly heading was established, *Maryland*, with the Senior Officer Present Afloat, Rear Admiral William S. Anderson, signaled a starboard turn to 350 degrees. They were turning north to pass between Oahu and Kauai. Again, if Japanese submarines were on station in the Kauai Channel, and sighted the task force, they neither attempted to attack, nor reported a sighting. Then, at 2321 hours the formation turned further starboard, to slightly east of north, 010 degrees true. It appeared they might be going home, but uncertainty lingered.[33]

* * *

About an hour before dawn on the 21st, an army sentry at the tiny Hawaiian village of Spreckelsville, Maui, spotted a flare, bringing a detachment of troops of the 299th Infantry to investigate. At daylight, they could see a boat loaded with men approaching shore. The officer in charge ordered his men to "prepare to repel enemy landing party." A few minutes later he rescinded the order, however, when they identified the occupants of the boat as civilians. They were what was left of the crew from the Matson Line freighter, *Lahaina*, sunk on 11 December by the Japanese submarine *I-9*.

For exactly nine days, 15 hours and 30 minutes, according to

Captain Matthiesen, the survivors rowed and sailed their over-crowded 20-foot lifeboat, until they reached Spreckelsville that morning. They had kept a daily log of their journey, telling of their perilous days at sea. It is a wonder they survived the ordeal.[34]

At 0545 hours on board *Tennessee*, still on base course 010 degrees true the morning of the 21st, general quarters sounded, and at 0611, as a precautionary measure Task Force 16 began zigzagging. At 0729 *Maryland* sighted a Catalina PBY, a long range patrol aircraft out of Oahu, off the port beam. More than hour after the PBY disappeared from view, and still plowing generally north at 0840 the *Tucker* reported sighting a submarine, bearing 330 degrees from *Tennessee*. The formation of three battleships and four destroyers began making various courses and changed to flank speed, 18 knots, then at 0858, began zigzagging again, followed by a reduction in speed to standard, 15 knots.

Once more during the day the formation zigzagged, but there were no more submarine alerts that day, no launching of scout planes, and at 1803, after holding a heading of due north, the formation turned right to 069 degrees. At 2000 hours the *Conyngham* left the formation to return to Pearl Harbor, singly. When she peeled out of the formation, the submarine screen adjusted positions, with the *Case* dead ahead of *Maryland*, *Tucker* on her port beam, and *Flusser* on her starboard beam. There could be no doubt. Task Force 16, less *Conyngham*, was going home. Puget Sound or San Francisco. Battle damage repair for the three dreadnaughts, probably modernization. Back to the mainland, at least temporarily.

Bob Border could relax, smile, take the assignment to Pensacola, and become a naval aviator. The hard, dark, painful days and terrible nights in Pearl Harbor were already beginning to fade, but would never go away. He would miss the *Tennessee*. Many of the ship's crew would scatter to new assignments, many whose paths he would not cross again—but some he would see again. She was a good ship, filled with many wonderful memories of good men, his brother, Karl, and other good sailors, all with great pride in a great ship of the line. *Tennessee* would come out of overhaul and modernization a better, more powerful ship. She would be back. And Bob would be able to repay the Japanese by flying fighters. It would take time, but he would get there.

What's more, Joey had told him on Saturday in their last phone conversation that when he left Pearl Harbor, she was going home as soon as she could be evacuated. Their promises to one another were paying off. He was certain he would see her again before too many days and weeks elapsed. They would be together again, and be able to visit with Joey's dad and mother, Captain and Charlotte Springer, his dad and Missy in Mobile, not far from Pensacola. Seven or eight more days—or less, to the West coast.

The morning of the 21st, at 0700 hours, Task Group 15.2, composed of the cruiser *Detroit*, the destroyers *Reid* and *Cummings*, escorting *Coolidge* and *Scott*, was holding steady about 500 miles ahead and slightly east of Task Force 16, when the *Reid* left the formation to return to Pearl Harbor. When the destroyer left the formation, *Scott* held her position as convoy guide, with *Coolidge* astern, in column, destroyer *Cummings* on *Scott's* port bow, and the *Detroit* on *Scott's* starboard bow.[35]

On board *Coolidge* and *Scott*, life was less than pleasant for the wounded and their attending nurses and doctors. Water had to be conserved. No bathing for able-bodied passengers. There was a movie in a blacked out compartment the previous night, and the passengers, though crowded and still wrestling the heavy sea's discomforts were making the best of a difficult, tense situation. But the doctors and nurses couldn't avail themselves of the entertainment. On *Scott* Red Cross nurse Margaret Logan, described conditions they faced.

> None of this small medical force had ever worked under such conditions and most of them felt utterly helpless, exhausted and desperate. Few, possibly, ever expected to reach their destination.
>
> As the ship pitched and rolled, neither medications nor food could be given properly to a majority of the patients. Feeding alone took precious hours that seemed to never end as nurses patiently forced drop by drop or spoonful by spoonful of liquids through the blistered and bleeding features of men completely swathed in bandages.
>
> Of all passengers aboard, the missionaries probably were of the greatest assistance. They rotated 24 hours daily in helping feed this tragic cargo. They sat for hours trying to calm the ones suffering from shock. They answered every call and hardly could have done more.

With an absolute blackout ordered throughout the ship at each sunset, the already overburdened ventilating system seemed to stop. Sweeping in nauseating waves down passageways and into every corner, the sickening impact of mixed odors from putrifying flesh that oozed through bandages, medicines and antiseptics, food, unwashed bodies and oil fumes often became too much for even the bravest of nurses.

Stumbling to the upper decks through cluttered passageways and up endless darkened ladders they would snatch a few moments of solitude and breath deeply of the salt air before hurrying back down to their work in the stifling confines of those too sick to know or care what happened.[36]

There were others who volunteered to help the nurses and missionaries with the wounded, the football players from Willamette and San Jose State, and the ladies who accompanied the teams. Previously confined to steerage, word of their assistance reached the *Coolidge*'s captain, and he granted them "the run of the ship." Some levity arrived in a difficult circumstance when passengers learned of Madame Chiang Kai-shek's two panda bears on board. During the day, when seas weren't too rough, to the delight of parents and their children who sailed on *Coolidge*, the pandas performed on deck in the fresh salt air.[37]

All day the 20th, *St. Louis* and Convoy 2005, had pressed on courses toward Oahu, speeds varying between 19 and 20 knots, after zigzagging for approximately forty minutes beginning 0623 that morning. With *Lurline* still the guide, *St. Louis* 1,000 yards ahead, and *Matsonia* and *Monterey* in column aft of *Lurline*, the destroyers *Smith* and *Preston* maintained submarine screen positions on *St. Louis*'s starboard and port bows respectively. Then came the morning of the 21st. When dawn neared, the two destroyers dropped back to positions on the flanks of *St. Louis*.

The convoy was approaching the Kaiwi Channel, between Oahu and Molokai, an area where Japanese submarines were known to have been patrolling. Prior submarine contacts and attacks in and northeast of the channel, mandated extra precaution to ensure no attacks on the three troop-laden ships. At 0525, *St. Louis* rang general quarters for standby, set material conditions, and at 0550 began maneuvering on various courses and speeds to catapult scout aircraft. At 0600 and 0605 the first two aircraft were in the air to conduct searches.

Back on station after the launch, and with the ship lighted at 0624, *St. Louis* signaled zigzag, Plan No. 21, and began the formation's first turn one minute later, convoy speed 20 knots, base course 255 degrees. At 0640, *St. Louis*'s watch sighted the destroyers *Waters* (DD-115) and *Dent* (DD-116), which had escorted the carrier *Saratoga* from San Diego to Pearl Harbor, beginning the day after the Japanese attack. The two were approximately 30 degrees off the port bow five miles distant, coming into the convoy. Shortly they took up additional stations in the submarine screen, *Waters* 1,000 yards on the port beam of *Matsonia*, and *Dent*, 1,000 yards on the starboard beam of *Monterey*.

At 0700 four patrol bombers from Oahu flew into positions overhead as escort planes, and at one minute intervals beginning at 0805, *St. Louis* launched her two remaining scout planes, 9-CS-19 and 9-CS-17. After the launch, they flew ahead of the convoy to search, relieved planes 9-CS-18 and 9-CS-20, and they proceeded into Pearl Harbor for landing. With the gathering of escorts around Convoy 2005, there is little doubt the crews and passengers on *Lurline*, *Matsonia* and *Monterey* were pleased by what they were witnessing. At 1210 the destroyer *Talbot* (DD-114), which had also escorted *Saratoga* from San Diego, joined the escort, and twenty-six minutes later the watch on *St. Louis* sighted Molokai, slightly more than ten degrees off the port bow.

The convoy wouldn't be considered out of potentially troubled waters until safe in the ships' respective harbors. At 1310 hours Oahu was sighted approximately 30 degrees off the starboard bow, and a minute later the *Lamson* (DD-367), a destroyer routinely engaged in patrolling in the vicinity of Oahu, took up escort and a sub screen station. *St. Louis* signaled zigzag again, at 1410, turning to course 180 degrees before cessation at 1430, and a turn starboard to 300 degrees, before heading west to place Diamond Head five miles distant on the starboard beam.

Throughout the approach to Oahu, past Diamond Head, and into the port of Honolulu, the decks of the Matson liners were increasingly crowded with soldiers seeing the Hawaiian Islands for the first time, and particularly the island they would be defending in the months ahead. After a long, sometimes rough, tense trip in close quarters, excitement and expectations were high, and conversations animated.

On the docks, expectations and excitement were equally high. The welcoming party of Oahu's leaders and dignitaries were seeing the arrival of the first reinforcements to the island after a devastating attack, followed by two weeks of tense, high alert; massive clean-up and salvage, population moves to safety, schools shutdown, tending to wounded, hundreds of funerals, troops with fixed bayonets and more in machine gun positions seemingly everywhere or in truck convoys constantly on the move; rumors, word of frequent submarine sightings and attacks, the daily drone of airplanes overhead from dawn to dark, and ships pouring in and out of Pearl and Honolulu Harbors. Welcoming parties, it appeared, would never be the same. The music, smiles, leis, and warm greetings were there, but the sights and sounds somehow felt different, a bit less cheerful, muted by war. Nevertheless, for the soldiers leaving the ships, the welcome was exciting.

St. Louis, *Preston* and *Smith*, left Convoy 2005's three Matson troop carriers, as they turned toward Honolulu's harbor. The cruiser entered Pearl Harbor, waiting with engines stopped briefly at 1605, until the submarine net was opened, and at 1615 crossed over the net. At 1650 she moored at Berth C-S-5, while in the port of Honolulu, *Lurline*, having eased close to Pier 24 at 1551, was moved gently toward the Pier by a harbor tug, and moored at 1642. *Matsonia* edged close to Pier 28 at 1536, and moored at 1648. *Monterey* arrived adjacent to Pier 20 at 1542, and moored at 1704. As soon as gangways were in place, the thousands of soldiers on board began disembarking by units, and awaited transportation by trains, each unit assigned locations for the night.[38]

Men of the 161st Regiment who were on board *Lurline*, and later contributed to the unit's history, described their arrival in this first convoy:

. . . ON SUNDAY, 21ST OF DECEMBER, 1941, THE HAWAIIAN ISLANDS CAME INTO VIEW. MEN ON THE DECKS WATCHED THE DIM ISLANDS ON THE HORIZON. OAHU LOOMED ON THE STARBOARD, RISING OUT OF THE

MISTY BLUE-GREEN WATERS AS A CRUMPLED
CROWN OF A HAT ABOVE ITS BRIM.

At 3:30 the convoy passed around Diamond Head.
There was the famous Waikiki Beach glaring in the
sunlight. Palm trees lined the beach—the first palm
trees seen by many of us. The ships cut down their
speed and fairly drifted. We crammed the decks to see
the sights—the beautiful Royal Hawaiian and Moana
Hotels on the beach amidst glamorous splendor; the
buildings of Honolulu, the various colored houses
clustered on green slopes of tall hills, fertile valleys
in between.

The three grayed Matson liners set into the
harbor of Honolulu about 4:30. Aloha tower; the
piers; machine gun emplacements on the buildings
of the water front. The men remained on deck as
bands played and a welcoming party appeared on
the docks.

Night came on black as pitch. We lounged in
the water-front yards with our equipment until the
freight trains arrived to take us on a long, miserable,
crowded ride to an unknown destination.[39]

The 34th Infantry Regiment headquarters and the 1st Battalion
went to Fort Shafter for the night, the 2nd Battalion nine miles
to Hickam Field, and the 3rd Battalion the long trip to Bellows
Field, pending further assignments in support of the 24th
Infantry Division, in the northern half of Oahu. The next day,
as preparations continued for sending the second evacuation
convoy to San Francisco, the 34th Regiment was ordered to
Schofield Barracks, to be in place not later than 1800 hours,
with the 3rd Battalion remaining at Bellows one more night. The
headquarters company, anti-tank company, service company and
2nd Battalion moved into the 19th Infantry Quadrangle, and the
1st Battalion into the 21st Infantry Quadrangle. On the 23rd, the
3rd Battalion relocated from Bellows Field, rejoined the Regiment
at Schofield Barracks at 1700 hours, and quartered in the 31st
Infantry Quadrangle.[40]

The evening the first convoy arrived in Honolulu, the 161st
Infantry Regiment, assigned in support of the 25th Infantry
Division's defense of the island's southern half, sent its 2nd

Battalion to Fort Shafter, and the 3rd Battalion traveled to Hickam Field. On the 23rd, one day before the *Phoenix* and Convoy 2004 arrived bringing the rest of the 161st, Captain Gaylord E. Treat and forty-eight Company H men departed on a task force for Christmas Island.[41]

The day the *Lurline* moored at Pier 24, the same day *Tennessee*'s Bob Border first learned the West Coast was Task Force 16's destination, Joey began preparing in earnest to return to the mainland. Up at 7:30 a.m., she read for awhile, started to pack, then rode a bus to Pearl Harbor to visit "Bobbie" (Barbara) Morrison. Barbara came back to her apartment with her for the night, they "popped a cork," drank, and listened to the radio. They talked of their husbands, wondering where they were and how they were doing. They reminisced, talked of the terrible two weeks beginning two Sundays ago, wondered where the future would take them, and if the four of them would be together again. These were perilous times, and almost daily, something new and different happened to change yesterday's plans. Bed came early, at 9:00 p.m.

Monday, 22 December, Joey believed she and Barbara were leaving the next day. They were up at 7:00, Joey prepared breakfast, completed her packing, and the two played acey-ducey. They went to a movie with Dot Thorpe, then shopping before she returned to the apartment for her last night in Honolulu. A letter from her dad was waiting, a warm response to her 6 December letter and the harried, two-day letter home she wrote beginning the day of the attack.

December 17, 1941

Joey dear: -

You will never know what your letter meant to me and to mother. We were worried no end and to find out that you were O.K. as well as Bob just put the sun back in the sky. Someday (and I hope it is soon) we can get together and go over the whole situation. Just to answer a few questions—yes I sent your watch—yes I received your check and cashed it (thank you) no I didn't send any Xmas presents to you and Bob. We are holding them here until we know they will reach you.

Mother and myself are both well and happy now

that we know you and Bob are O.K. I sent wires to mother Border and Grandma Nesbitt as soon as I heard from you. I sent the cable before I received your cable. Your presents to us also arrived O.K. The birthday presents were swell honey—just like you to pick things that appeal to me. Mother was mighty fine to me also on my birthday—gave me a flask of face lotion (imagine—but then the flask can be used after the lotion is gone) And pinky came thru with an Acey-Ducey set that will really knock your eyes out. In a leather case with classy do-dads and dice to match. Boy was I glad.

Naturally there isn't much news here to tell you. The whole situation is so unbelievable that we have hardly gotten our feet on the ground yet. Jim Holman wired me on Tuesday about you. Also Cronins. Many letters have been received—Gina—Aunt Mate—Aunt Vern and others all asking had we heard from you. Jerry Lynch called—the whole staff very interested. The Col. has been a constant inquirer as well as the Shippys and others. After all trouble is a great leveler.

This letter is a bit incoherent but I am writing as thought comes to me. Your attitude makes me proud of you—more than I can put into words. What ever the past has been—the little things we called trouble—all dim now as we take up to our task in the present and carry the ultimate end of victory for our Country. Your ancestors have been in every major trouble this country has ever had and now you are part of the great group giving and enduring hardships for the only thing that counts—a free country and republic where a man may call his soul his own. And to know that Bob is my son now and a part of the fine group that are giving that others may enjoy—makes me proud. May God protect you both from harm and guide you through troublesome times.

I have no idea when this letter will reach you. Regardless of failure of mail service—remember that mother and I are constantly thinking of you and hoping that the day will come soon when we can get together as in the past. God bless you both honey— keep a stiff upper lip honey and do your stuff.

Always thinking of you

your Dad

From Capt. Geo. I. Springer[42]

The morning of the 22nd, as Joey contemplated her leaving for home, Admiral Shimizu postponed the Christmas Eve shelling of targets on the West Coast, and the cruiser *Detroit*, with destroyer *Cummings* in Task Group 15.2, continued their escort and screening duties, maintaining the starboard bow and port bow positions on *Scott*, with *Coolidge* in column astern of *Scott*. Course 058 degrees, speed 16 knots, bound for San Francisco. They were half way in their voyage to San Francisco, and commanders had been warned of the increasing submarine attacks off the West Coast. Given the acceptable weather and the fact they were approaching an area of increasing threat, caution was an absolute necessity in defending the ships and people in the convoy.

Shimizu's order to delay the scheduled Christmas Eve attack to 27 December occurred on the 22nd, the same day Headquarters, Combined Fleet learned of the arrival of the battleships *New Mexico* (BB-40), *Mississippi* (BB-41) and *Idaho* (BB-42) off the West Coast. Reacting to information later proved to be false, Mitsoyoshi, undoubtedly with his headquarters' agreement, ordered *I-9*, *I-17*, and *I-25* to intercept the task group which was expected to arrive in Los Angeles on 25 December. The order had the effect of concentrating most of the nine submarines south of San Francisco, with *I-9* and Rear Admiral Sato having to move all the way from Cape Blanco, well south down the coast, when the bulk of the convoy traffic was transiting in and out of San Francisco.

Detroit sounded general quarters at 0540, flight quarters at 0613, and catapulted plane #1 at 0630, plane #2 at 0639, recovering them at 1006 and 1018 respectively. During the period the scout planes were conducting their normal, "inverted triangle" search ahead of the convoy, another submarine attack occurred off the West Coast.

This time, the attack was just off treacherous Point Arguello, California, which on the morning of 8 September 1932, had become the graveyard for seven lead ships of a U.S. Navy destroyer squadron. Submerged less than two miles off the point, approximately 55 miles northwest of Santa Barbara and well south of San Francisco, Japanese submarine *I-21*, its skipper Commander Kanji Matsumura, had been lying in wait of a target for two days. Their wait was about to end, for coming up the coast to cross west of their position, was Standard Oil Company tanker *H.M. Story*.

Walking the beach of Point Arguello that morning was a woman whose name was withheld by the Navy. She, along with Jack Sudden, a young high school student from nearby Lompoc, witnessed the attack.

Sudden, rabbit hunting along the Southern Pacific railroad tracks at the time, said that at around 8:30 a.m., 7:30 on board the *Detroit* convoy approximately 900 miles distant, he "heard a dull explosion and saw smoke rising from the sea. At first I couldn't tell what it was," he said, "but a few minutes later heavy smoke began to settle over (the) water like a smoke screen. To the northwest of the screen and about three miles from shore I could see the tanker speeding up the coast . . . I later saw a long dark object leave the smoke screen heading in the general direction of the ship. Watching the object—that must have been a torpedo—it closed the gap between itself and the ship and at times came to the surface and kicked up a white spray. The last I could see of the torpedo, it passed in front of the ship."

The explosion first attracting Sudden's attention had come from *I-21*'s deck gun, but the heavy smoke screen put out by the fleeing tanker made it impossible for Matsumura's gun crew to see the target, forcing him to submerge and use a torpedo. The woman witness, with the aid of binoculars, could see the submarine plainly. "It was between the tanker and the shore when I saw it," she said, "less than two miles away. I saw what I thought were three torpedoes fired from the submarine at the ship, but they all went behind it. The tanker then went full speed ahead, with heavy black smoke pouring from her funnel."

Not long afterward planes arrived and dropped several bombs. "They were so heavy that when they exploded they shook the ground where I was standing," she continued. "The explosions raised great columns of water."

SUNDAY IN HELL 785

Residents of the small coastal village of Surf, about eight miles north of Point Arguello, were attracted by the bombing, and saw the tanker as it rounded the point. As it drew even with the little town, a large seaplane landed alongside as the *Story* hove to. Several persons from the plane were seen boarding the ship. Frustrated by his failure, Matsumura headed north, where, unknown to him, he would find hunting much better.

While submarine attacks off the West Coast were continuing on the 22nd, the *Pensacola* Convoy, which had been diverted from its original destination of Manila in the Philippines, was closing on Australia's safe, northeastern harbor in Brisbane. The convoy had completed a lengthy, slow, 23-day passage south, while beginning 9 December, the American Joint [Army-Navy] Board in Washington, with President Roosevelt's approval, deliberated its final destination, and communicated the changed destination to the convoy on 12 December.

As Task Group 15.2 held a course of 058 degrees and a speed of 16.5 knots most of the 22nd, and pressed closer to the areas off San Francisco where submarines might be encountered, *Detroit* and *Cummings* continued to receive no underwater contacts, nor did the convoy zigzag that day. Nevertheless, at 1352, *Detroit* again sounded flight quarters and catapulted planes #1 and #2, to conduct searches along the convoy's projected course, recovering them at 1611 and 1620. Most of the night passed uneventfully.[43]

In the early hours of Tuesday morning, the 23rd, the daily routine for Task Group 15.2 held out prospects for a relatively uneventful run into San Francisco Bay. That prospect was shattered by a later warning of another submarine attack, 65 miles further north of Point Arguello. At 3 a.m., the Japanese submarine *I-21* had found another target, and Commander Kanji Matsumura, unable to identify his target in the dark, ordered the sub's deck gun crew to fire on the Richfield Oil Company's empty tanker, *Larry Doheney*.

Six miles away in the small beach community of Cayucos, at the northern edge of Estero Bay, the shot awakened Mrs. Roy Genardini, wife of the town's constable. Twenty seconds later a second shot was heard. On board the 7,038-ton *Doheney*, no one was asleep after the first shot. The skipper of the tanker, Captain O.S. Brieland, asleep when the first round was fired, was already on the bridge directing the ship's maneuvers when the second round came. Both missed, while Brieland frantically zigzagged his 20-year old into the night.

After a few minutes, Commander Matsumura was about to call off the chase, after finding the darkness and *Doheney*'s fishtailing maneuvers too much, when a lookout sighted the tanker inside 200 yards with its port side exposed. Matsumura quickly ordered a torpedo fired.

Still in her bed in Cayucos, Mrs. Genardini was just about convinced the shooting was over, when she was suddenly jarred by an explosion that, in her own words, "nearly threw me onto the floor." In the city of San Luis Obispo, thirteen miles inland, lights could be seen coming on in homes all over town, as people reacted to a sudden rattling of doors and windows. They were to learn the concussion came from a Japanese Long-lance torpedo that exploded after missing the *Larry Doheney*.

With the miss, a frustrated Matsumura broke off the chase and submerged. However, his frustration at being outrun by two American tankers in two days, would be more than vindicated in less than two hours. About the time *I-21* disappeared below the surface, another American tanker, the Union Oil Company's *Montebello*, was pulling away from the company wharf some 20 miles south, off Avila, on its way north with a cargo of gasoline. An hour and a half later it would find itself in a life or death race with a frustrated Japanese submarine commander with vengeance on his mind.

At 5:30 a.m., William Srez, on watch on the *Montebello*, alerted her captain, Olaf Eckstrom that they were being stalked by what looked to be a submarine. Eckstrom had been the ship's first mate, until five hours earlier. At midnight, her previous commander abruptly resigned, giving the command to Eckstrom.

"I saw a dark outline on the water, close astern of us," said the new captain later. "Srez was right. It was the silhouette of a Jap submarine, a big fellow, possibly 300 feet long. I ordered the quartermaster at the wheel, John McIsaac, to zigzag. For 10 minutes we tried desperately to cheat the sub, but it was no use. She was too close . . . (and) let a torpedo go when we were broadside to her."

"The torpedo smashed us square amidships," said Srez, "and there was a big blast and the ship shuddered and trembled and we knew she was done for."

Fortunately for *Montebello*, the torpedo hit the only

compartment not loaded with gasoline. "The men wouldn't have had a chance if any other hold was hit," said Eckstrom. But it did knock out the radio, "and I could not wireless for aid."

"The skipper was cool as a snowdrift," interjected Srez. "He yelled an order to stand by the lifeboats and then an order to abandon ship, and there was something in the way he gave those orders that made us proud to be serving under him."

As the crew responded by lowering lifeboats, the submarine opened fire with its deck gun at nearly point-blank range. "The sub then began to shell us," continued the captain. "There was from eight to 10 flashes. One . . . hit the foremast, snapping it. Another whistled by my head so close . . . I could have reached out and touched it. But there was no panic, no hysteria. We got all four lifeboats into the water. Splinters from one of the shells struck some of the boats, but by some kind of a miracle, none of us was wounded."

Meanwhile, the gunfire and explosion of the torpedo attracted attention from the nearby shore. Clint Spooner, a rancher on the tip of Point Estero, six miles away, phoned the sheriff's office that he had seen "three flashes of light and three minor explosions in the dark, and an enormous flash and a loud explosion." Elsewhere up and down the isolated coastline, people were heading for the water's edge for a view of the "goings on."

Another person wishing to get a view of the "goings on" was Captain Eckstrom himself, who, unsure if the *Montebello* was going to sink, ordered his lifeboats "to lie a short distance from the ship. But 45 minutes later, just as the dawn was breaking, she went down."

Two residents of the tiny coastal town of Cambria Pines witnessed the sinking from shore. "She upended like a giant telephone pole and slowly settled into the sea," said Mr. M.L. Waltz, the editor of the Cambria weekly paper. "But there was no fire or explosions about the ship that we could see."

Mrs. Harold Waite, from her home on a hill above Cambria Pines, saw the stern of the tanker "lift suddenly from the water and then disappear." After that, a heavy fog and later a rainstorm prevented anything else from being seen from shore. What they missed was seeing 36 men in four lifeboats rowing frantically for shore. The marauding *I-21*, with its still-frustrated captain, continued firing his deck and machine gun at the helpless American merchantmen until poor visibility forced him to retire.

Although no one was hit or wounded, the boat holding the captain and five other crewmen was hit.

"Shell splinters hit our boat," said Bill Srez, "and she began to leak like a sieve. We began rowing shoreward, with some of us leaning on the oars for all we were worth and the others bailing." Slowed noticeably from its leaking hull, the captain's lifeboat was soon well behind the other three, who, two hours later, were picked up by Standard Oil tugboat *Alma* and launch *Estero*, dispatched from nearby Estero Bay.

Fighting fatigue, rough water and a leaking boat, it wasn't until noon, some six hours since the sinking, that Captain Eckstrom, his first and second mates, the ship's fireman, and seamen Srez and John T. Smith, hit the shore at Cambria. "We were caught in the surf," said Srez, "and the lifeboat capsized and we got all wet. Some of the boys were scratched up by the rocks. The captain nearly drowned." The ordeal of the 8,000-ton *Montebello* was over, but not forgotten.

Angry crew members cursed the Japanese, Srez vowing "As soon as I dry out, I'm going to look for another ship. Those Japs haven't scared me yet and they never will." Eckstrom said, "I'm proud of the men under my command. God bless 'em, they behaved like American seamen. I only hope the Navy gets that Jap sub before she gets another American ship."[44]

While the attacks were in progress further south, Task Group 15.2 was continuing on a course of 070 degrees, still holding 16.5 knots. On board *Detroit*, general quarters sounded at 0600, flight quarters at 0655, and at 0714 and 0721 scout planes were in the air again. At 0840 hours, the relative calm aboard *Scott* and *Coolidge* abruptly changed, when the destroyer *Cummings* signaled the convoy, "submarine contact, bearing 155 degrees true"—approximately on the starboard beam of the convoy, and in the direction from which an enemy submarine might approach.

Cummings left the formation to investigate. *Detroit* immediately signaled evasive course and speed changes, and aboard the two liners, the submarine alert brought orders for mandatory wear of life jackets, and more than passing excitement to harried passengers. Though the destroyer shortly reported the contact as apparently false, the passengers' worries weren't relieved. They were entering the final 48 hours of a perilous journey—a journey few on *Scott* and *Coolidge* would ever forget—and the attacks were continuing, capturing headlines up and down the West

Coast, headlines above stories that would soon be read in Hawaii newspapers, and repeated on radios.[45]

Later the 23rd, Japanese submarine *I-9* was coming to the end of a three day harassment of a small 944-ton Texas Company tanker, *Idaho*, heading south toward Long Beach. The *I-9* had arrived at its assigned position off Cape Blanco, Oregon, on 17 December, after sinking the Matson Line freighter the *Lahaina*, on 11 December, 700 miles northeast of Hawaii. On the 20th, after hunting proved non-existent near the Cape, *I-9* signaled the flag submarine, *I-15*, off San Francisco, and was ordered toward the Panama Canal.

Not long after getting under way down the American coastline, the *Idaho* was spotted moving in the same direction. For the next three nights and two days, *I-9* hounded the small ship, forcing it to zigzag in constant fear of being torpedoed. The second night, Commander Akiyoshi Fujii sent a message in international code demanding the tanker identify itself. The captain responded by ordering full speed ahead. The *Idaho*'s ordeal ended December 23, when it reached the port of Long Beach.[46]

In Honolulu on the 23rd, preparations for the departure of the second evacuation convoy were proceeding at a lurching, almost chaotic pace, although Joey Border was certain she would be leaving for home that day. Packed and ready to go, she went down town, only to learn departure would be the next day. The entire day was hectic for her. The back and forth was wearing, both physically and emotionally. Excited, anxious to get started, carrying and loading luggage in transportation, rushing to ensure being on time, attempting to check-in and process—then disappointment. Back to the apartment, where the only saving grace was a letter that arrived from Sally Smoot, who had given her away at Bob's and Joey's wedding in Long Beach in mid-July. Behind the scenes at the Port of Honolulu, not visible to Joey and all other evacuees preparing to leave, there was much confusion as to who would do what, and who would give direction in managing the evacuation.[47]

The intent in loading for the second convoy to San Francisco was to carry the maximum number of evacuees allowable. The first convoy could carry a relatively smaller number because *Coolidge* and *Scott* brought a normal passenger load into Honolulu, and the ability to accept wounded and additional passengers on the two vessels was limited.

The second convoy, disembarking a full load of troops, unit equipment and supplies from the three Matson vessels, could carry a much larger number of evacuees. By the 22nd, the Fourteenth Naval District had counted 15,313 people, exclusive of wounded, needing evacuation, the Army's Hawaiian Department submitted a total of 4,996, not counting wounded, and the District Chief of Staff informed the evacuation manager by letter on that date.[48]

But there were problems the evacuation manager, Captain Frucht, didn't anticipate, which needed to be quickly resolved. Further, he and his small staff and the Castle and Cooke office were giving conflicting guidance in preparing for departure.

The *Lurline* was short of crew members. The Fourteenth Naval District's Port Director, who controlled the movement of all ships in and out of Honolulu's port after martial law was declared, asked the District's Personnel Officer in a 23 December letter to provide 100 Navy enlisted men to be put on board *Lurline* to assist with the passengers and ". . . to help work the ship." He explained, "The *Lurline* is 70 short of her crew and the morale of the civilian crew is reported not too high." He went on to say, "This movement should be accomplished today. The *Lurline* will shift to Pier 11 early Wednesday morning, December 24th. All passengers must be aboard by 1300, that date." The Navy augmented *Lurline*'s crew, but on the 23rd, Castle and Cooke, Limited, established a different date for loading passengers on *Matsonia*.

After the *Matsonia* arrived on the 21st, Castle and Cooke, which was managing ticket sales for the evacuation, learned that the ship, managed and equipped by the Army, had been stripped of beds, and had only cots and standee bunks available for passengers. Captain Frucht didn't learn of the problem until the 22nd, when he was informed by the ticketing agency the ship had no beds, mattresses, blankets, or any bedclothes. There were approximately 750 to 1,000 tourists signing up to leave Oahu, including those who had already left on the first convoy. Castle and Cooke wanted to know, could tourists, who were the next priority behind the wounded, be brought aboard *Matsonia*? Further, what was the maximum passenger load allowed on the ship, and which service, Army or Navy, would be paying shipping and ticket costs? Could automobiles, pets and other personal belongings be evacuated on this vessel? What would be the allowable charges for tourists—adults and children—boarding Matsonia?[49]

In a memo to Admiral Bloch on the 23rd, Captain Frucht told

the District Commandant, that the Army had authorized 900 mattresses to be obtained from Fort Armstrong, and they would be delivered to the *Matsonia*'s captain, who would sign for receipt of the mattresses. He then asked Admiral Bloch to inform him as soon as is practicable, the number of Navy evacuees to be on *Lurline*, that he could release additional, unused spaces to Castle and Cooke—and in the same memo telling the Commandant *Matsonia*'s cargo is being discharged, and the estimated time to complete the work is tentatively Christmas Day, Thursday, the 25th.

The same morning, Fucht called Mr. A.J. Pessel, the General Passenger Agent at Castle and Cooke, and told him the "the *Matsonia* will be handled by the Navy; that Castle and Cooke are to accommodate tourists on the *Matsonia*; that [you] are to start selling tickets for the *Matsonia*; and that [you] are to inform passengers to go aboard the vessel at Pier 28 not before Thursday, December 25th, at 1 P.M. and not later than Thursday, December 25th, at 4 P.M. Later in the day, Pessel wrote a letter to Fucht, confirming the contents of the conversation.[50]

While the passenger loading difficulties were being ironed out in Honolulu on the 23rd, and word of submarine attacks off the West Coast were flooding the newspapers and radio news broadcasts, Wake Island fell, bringing more bad news of defeat. Having bombed Wake Island almost daily since 7 December, and seen their first invasion fleet driven off with heavy losses on 13 December, the Japanese returned on the 22nd with powerful forces, including carriers, to ensure they took the island.

Admiral Pye, acting CinCPac, alerted to increased Japanese air activity in the Marshall Islands, including the presence of one and possibly two enemy carrier task forces, had called off the surprise raid on Jaluit in the Marshalls, and changed the mission of Task Force 11 (*Lexington*). They were to turn north to support a possible engagement with the Japanese forces or evacuation of Wake by Task Force 14 (*Saratoga*). *Saratoga* was still 430 miles distant when the powerful Japanese force landed and began overwhelming the island's defenders. At 0652 the morning of the 23rd, Commander Winfield S. Cunningham, the Navy's commander of the island's defense force, sent his final message to Admiral Pye, reflecting the situation as he knew it: "Enemy on island. Several ships plus transport moving in. Two DD [destroyers] aground." Later in the day, Pye, engaged by message with the Chief of Naval Operations, receiving additional information of possible enemy battleships with their carriers, and fearing he was risking one, possibly two of the Pacific Fleet's three carriers, after the heavy losses sustained at Pearl Harbor, called off any attempt to evacuate the defenders, and directed the two carrier task forces to retire to the east.

Author Robert J. Grossman recorded the reactions of men in Task Force 14 when word reached them they were to reverse course:

> [Vice Admiral] Frank Jack Fletcher's Task Force 14, meanwhile, was right on schedule, and was in fact further west than Pye knew. His ships fully fueled and ready for battle, Fletcher planned to detach the *Tangier* and two destroyers for the final run-in to Wake, while the pilots on board the *Saratoga* prepared themselves for the fight ahead. Fletcher, not one to shirk a fight, received the news of the recall angrily. He ripped his hat from his head and disgustedly hurled it to the deck. Rear Admiral Aubrey W. Fitch, Fletcher's air commander, similarly felt the fist-tightening frustration of the recall. He retired from the *Saratoga*'s flag bridge as the talk there reached "mutinous" proportions.

As word of the recall circulated throughout Task Force 14, reactions were pretty much the same. Pye's recall order left no latitude for discussion or disobedience; those who argued later that Fletcher should have used the Nelsonian "blind eye" obviously failed to recognize that, in the sea off Copenhagen, the British admiral could see his opponents. Fletcher and Fitch, then 430 miles east of Wake, could not see theirs. They had no idea what enemy forces they might encounter. The Japanese had beaten them to Wake.

Of the 449 Marines (1st Defense Battalion and VMF-211 detachments) who manned Wake's defenses, 49 were killed and 32 were wounded. Of the 68 Navy officers and men, three were killed, five were wounded and the rest taken prisoner. The small, five-man Army communications detachment suffered no fatalities and were all taken prisoner. Of the 1,146 civilians involved in construction programs on Wake Island, 70 were killed and 12 were wounded. Five of Wake's defenders were executed on board

Nitta Maru. With the exception of nearly 100 contractors who remained on Wake Island, all the rest joined Wake's Marines, sailors and soldiers in prisoner of war camps.[51]

In Hawaii the same day, Admiral Bloch, responding to increasing submarine attacks, especially on unescorted United States as well as foreign flag vessels—and the need to establish tighter control and increased security of commercial operations—sent a letter to steamship owners, operators, and agencies of the Territory of Hawaii regarding movements of commercial vessels. Distributed to Castle and Cooke, American Factors, Ltd.; F.L. Waldron & Co., Norton Lilly Co., Inter-Island Steamship Navigation Co., Theodore H. Davies Co., C.C. Brewer & Co., Alexander & Baldwin, Lowers & Cooke, Haw'n Pineapple Co., Lt.; and Contractors Pacific Naval Air Bases, the letter provided clear, unambiguous guidance:

1. No movements of United States or foreign flag commercial vessels, regardless of type and tonnage, will be undertaken beyond harbor limits in the Fourteenth Naval District, except as authorized by the Port Director, Naval Transportation Service, Fourteenth Naval District.

2. Steamship owners, operators and agents are hereby enjoined to see that no information on such movements is transmitted by telephone, telegraph, cable, or radio, except as may be authorized, and in manner prescribed, by the Port Director.

3. Instructions covering the above will be issued by addressees to their sub-agencies on outlying Islands of the Hawaiian Group.[52]

On the American West Coast on the 23rd, the *Los Angeles Times* announced under the headline: COAST DECLARED A THEATER OF WAR, that the rash of enemy submarine attacks had prompted Lieutenant General John DeWitt, commanding officer of the Western Defense Area (California, Oregon, Washington, Nevada, Utah, Idaho, Montana, Arizona and Alaska) to define his command as a "theater of war."

That morning, on board the ships in Task Group 15.2, reports had come over the radios about the submarine attacks off the West Coast, bringing the trip home from Oahu to a tense climax. Although the ships' crews and passengers had taken daily precautions of darkened portholes and blackouts beginning at 5 p.m., more elaborate precautions were ordered. Passengers were told to sleep with their clothes on, to carry their life belts with them at all times, even during meals. Some elected to wear them all the time. The report of submarines and the resulting orders spread panic among cases of hysteria and borderline shock patients. A fearful madness seized some who were helplessly immobile in body casts. Many passengers remained awake all night, unable to sleep.[53]

On the 23rd, Task Force 16, composed of *Maryland, Tennessee, Pennsylvania* in column, with destroyers *Tucker, Flusser* and *Case* screening began the day holding course 053 degrees true, and speed 15 knots. After Tennessee sounded general quarters at 0613, two minutes later the formation, responding to *Maryland*'s flag signal, commenced zigzagging and continued until 0843, before resuming course 053 degrees to catapult *Tennessee*'s scout plane No. 201. The formation resumed zigzagging at 0848 and continued zigzagging until nearly 1300 hours. Admiral Anderson, the Senior Officer Present Afloat, on board *Maryland*, was taking no chances with his three battle-damaged ships. Though *Pennsylvania*'s radar was operational, he wanted to keep scouts out front of his Task Force during daylight hours of suitable weather.[54]

The Missing

The same day, in the town of Coatsville, Pennsylvania, a letter was received by Mr. Roy White, from his son, Navy seaman Lloyd White. The letter, dated 13 December, said he was safe and well, but had been through "a trying ordeal." Ten days earlier, on the 13th, the same date of his son's letter, a telegram was delivered to the family of Lloyd White, notifying them that he had been "lost in action." His father, Roy, after reading the telegram, threw it down, saying, "it isn't true. They had me reported dead for 11 months in France during the first World War and I wasn't. Neither is Lloyd." And he wasn't.

Lloyd White was one among many first reported dead in the attack on Pearl Harbor, and later found alive. Like so many others on 7 December, he was prematurely declared dead, when an inadequate search for his whereabouts, an insufficient waiting period after the search, and a wrong assumption led to the wrong conclusion and a grievous error in notifying his parents of his death. This painful incident and other similar cases in the days following the attack on Pearl Harbor, led to important changes in who, how, when and under what circumstances casualties would be reported to families.[55]

Submarine sightings and attacks continued off the West Coast on Christmas Eve, although most people went about decorating their trees, listening to Christmas carols, doing last minute chores, and, other than hearing an occasional news broadcast or glancing at a headline in the paper, could momentarily forget the state of affairs around the world.

Two miles off Long Beach, California, at 6:25 a.m., the lumber schooner *Barbara Olson* was steaming towards San Diego when a violent explosion occurred about 100 feet off its seaward side. No one on board the ship knew what caused the explosion, but about four miles away, outside the Long Beach harbor entrance, the loud report attracted the attention of lookouts on the Navy sub chaser *Amethyst* (PYc-3). On Japanese submarine *I-19*, lurking one mile closer to Long Beach, on the landward side of its target, Commander Shogo Narahara knew what caused the explosion. He had just ordered the crew to fire its first torpedo of World War II, and it passed underneath the *Barbara Olson* and exploded on her seaward side.

The *I-19* had been one of the three submarines patrolling out front of Admiral Nagumo's carrier strike force, and now, with this first missed shot, Commander Narahara had the undivided attention of the *Amethyst*'s captain, who sounded general quarters one minute later. The event, noted in the sub-chaser's log, read: "At 0625 sighted an explosion that threw smoke and spray approximately 300 feet into the air. At 0626 sounded general quarters. At 0730 secured from general quarters and set condition Baker." *Amethyst* headed toward the area of the attack, but was unable to detect the intruder. The *I-19* and *Amethyst* would meet again, about four hours later, while 975 miles north off the mouth of the Columbia River—about the same time *I-19* missed the *Barbara Olson*—three Army Air Force B-25 bombers took off from McChord Field, near Tacoma, Washington, for submarine patrol off the coast.

The three pilots, Lieutenants Brick Holstrom, Ted Lawson and Bill Whitty passed over their initial point, the mouth of the Columbia River, at the assigned 1,000 feet altitude, and fanned out in three different directions. About 12 miles out, Lieutenant Holstrom, forced to drop down to 500 feet because of poor visibility, spotted what looked to be a submarine. After radioing he had sighted a sub, he initiated an attack. Unfortunately, his bombardier, Lieutenant George Hammond, had forgotten to re-adjust his bombsight for the lower altitude, and the first 300-pound bomb overshot. By the time Holstrom set up for his second pass, the submarine was diving, so Hammond let go his entire load.

"I saw one bomb hit in front of the conning tower," said top turret gunner Clarence Gillingham. "Another went just to the side of the sub. It had been underwater but the hit brought it back up near the surface, then (it) went back down again. I could see air bubbles and oil. We radioed we had hit the sub and were returning to base."

Lieutenant Ted Lawson, alerted by Holstrom's message, arrived in time to see him drop his bombs. "We saw him circling and dropping his bombs," said the young lieutenant, "and by the time we got (there), oil was coming up in greasy bubbles, as if something was throwing up under water. The sinking was confirmed." The next day, newspapers blared the sinking, but the "confirmed sinking" never occurred. Records later revealed the Japanese lost no submarines off the West Coast. The only submarine in the area was the *I-25*, which was untouched by the attackers and later in the war made her presence felt again.

At 0605 Hawaii time on the 24th, 0805 on the West Coast, Task Group 15.7, composed of *Phoenix*, *Perkins* and *Cushing*, plus the *President Garfield*, the *Tasker Bliss*, *Aldebaran*, *Harris*, and oilers *Sabine* and *Platte*, in Convoy 2004, commenced zigzagging on a base course of 215 degrees true. At 0644 lookouts on *Phoenix* sighted the destroyers *Lamberton* (DD-119) and *Long* (DD-209), coming to join the formation and add to their submarine screen.

Instead of passing through the Kaiwi Channel between Oahu and Molokai, the normal, most direct route from San Francisco, the convoy had for most of the 23rd, kept a more westerly course, and was approaching Oahu from the northeast, crossing north of the island, planning to transit the Kauai Channel. They knew submarines were patrolling in both channels, but fleet operations and commanders undoubtedly believed there was advantage in taking the longer, less "normal" route into port.

This slower moving convoy, after having had good weather and relying on scout airplanes from *Phoenix* all day the 18th through the 22nd to reduce the chances of a submarine attack, on the 23rd and 24th had to move through rough weather, with rain showers, squalls and a high sea state—unsuitable for launching scout planes. The two additional destroyers arrival, with their anti-submarine capabilities, and zigzagging, were the best tactical defenses available to hedge against a sub attack in the latter stages of the convoy's passage to Oahu. At 1100 hours on the 24th, lookouts sighted the Barbers Point Light 16 miles distant, almost due east of *Phoenix's* position.

At 1315, ships in the convoy began proceeding independently into Pearl and Honolulu Harbors. Beginning at 1415 hours, *Aldebaran, Harris, Phoenix, Cushing* and *Perkins* moored safely in Pearl Harbor, while destroyers escorted the *President Garfield* and the *Tasker Bliss* into the Port of Honolulu to debark the remainder of the 161st Regiment, with its unit equipment and supplies. The oiler *Platte* moored starboard side to Pier 31, Standard Oil Dock, Honolulu Harbor, at 1415, preparatory to discharging her fuel oil cargo. At 1438 the oiler *Sabine*, following the other ships into Pearl Harbor's entrance, moored to buoys off Hickam Wharf, and just prior to 1700 hours began discharging gasoline to the dock.[56]

Meanwhile, in the waters off Long Beach, California, *I-19*, which had gone undetected after its unsuccessful attack on the *Barbara Olson*, moved to new hunting grounds a few miles north off Point Fermin. The submarine's skipper, Commander Narahara, was angry, but not for the same reason Commander Matsumura of *I-21* had been angry—the missed shot. It was something else. What irritated him was the lackadaisical attitude Americans had shown for the war since *I-19* arrived off Los Angeles Harbor on the 18th.

On two different occasions, he sent messages to the flag sub *I-15*, off San Francisco, in which he used the word contemptuousness to show his irritation. The first one told of how lights displayed by automobiles, homes and businesses on the night they arrived were so bright that a newspaper could be read from the deck of *I-19*. The second one, sent on Sunday night the 21st, told of the crowd of sunbathers with brightly colored umbrellas who had arrogantly lined the beaches that day.

It was 10:00 a.m. on the 24th. Entering the Catalina Channel some five miles north of the waiting enemy submarine was the 5,700-ton McCormick Steamship Company freighter *Absoroka*, on a heading for San Diego with a load of lumber. In a few minutes she provided *I-19* the opportunity for its first kill of the war. After *Absoroka* entered Catalina Channel, a telephone call came into the San Pedro Coast Guard station from a local resident, William Anderson, who reported he had just seen a submarine from his home on the bluffs near Point Fermin. He told them he had seen what appeared to be a small fishing vessel offshore near his home; however, it "seemed to be riding too smoothly for the heavy sea that morning." The Coast Guard's response was unresponsive. "Maintain watch and call back with a progress report." Fifteen minutes later, any derisive musings that might have come from the men on duty at the station, quickly vanished.

By 10:30, the unsuspecting *Absoroka* was off Point Fermin. The Point's famous 77-year-old lighthouse was clearly visible less than a mile away. Army Sergeant James Hedwood and his machine gun crew, manning a position on the point just below the lighthouse, were watching the ship as it passed. "We were looking at the lumber schooner when suddenly we saw a fountain of water spout 100 feet into the air at the stern." The force of the explosion spun the boat around some 220 degrees, "with its stern to the sea and its bow facing toward land."

Seaman Joseph Scott, on board *Absoroka*, was the first to see the sub that got it. "It was mid-morning and all hands were up and around, when I looked off to port and saw a whale. At least I was about to say 'look over yonder, a whale,' when I changed my mind and yelled, 'there's a God Damn Jap submarine!' You know how a guy will lose control and cuss at a time like that, caught by surprise and all."

"Well, she was coming head on. Then her periscope went up and she shot a torpedo. I've seen torpedoes coming at me before. 'They've wasted that one,' says I.' Sure enough it went wide, but right on its heels came another. 'Oh, oh, that's bad,' says I, because I could see this one was going to get us." Scott's comment about having seen torpedoes "coming at me before," was no exaggeration. At sea since his early 20s, the 48-year-old veteran had no less than four merchant ships torpedoed out from under him on four consecutive voyages in World War I.

"Well sir, in those torpedoings, as I recall 'em, there was always a bang or blast and a bump. But this one was a sort of slow jar, with nothing but a rumble because she was hit below the water line."

Harry Greenwald, Marshall Mansfield, Herbert Stevens and Joseph Ryan, were working on the starboard side, routinely checking the lashings on the particularly heavy deck load of lumber she was carrying moments before it struck. One of them glanced up in time to see the wake. "Torpedo!" he yelled, pointing toward the stern of the ship. Everyone looked up. "I knew (it) was going to miss us and broke into a grin," said Greenwald. "But my grin froze because the second 'fish' followed the first one quicker than it takes to tell it."

The second torpedo struck with tremendous impact about 50 feet aft of the beam, knocking three of the four men into the sea. The fourth, Joseph Ryan, was able to ride out the blast, which according to one observer, threw tons of lumber into the air "as if a man were throwing match sticks around." Amazingly, in a matter of seconds, Harry Greenwald, one of the three men blown overboard, was back on deck. As he struggled to the surface after his sudden dunking, much to his surprise, the rail over which he had just been hurled was close enough for him to grab. "The deck (rolled) over so far from the explosion," said Greenwald, "that her deck went under water. I grabbed the rail as the ship shuddered and righted herself (and) was carried up as she swung back." Mansfield, one of the other men tossed overboard, pulled himself back on board by rope.

The third man, Herbert Stevens, who had injured his leg in the blast and subsequent fling into the sea, began yelling for help. Heeding his call up on deck, Joe Ryan dashed to the rail, picked up a coil of heavy mooring line and tossed it toward Steven's bobbing head.

Ryan had begun pulling him toward the ship when it happened. Unknown to the merchant veteran of 46 years, the explosion had snapped the lashings anchoring the deck load of lumber behind him. As he was leaning over the rail drawing his injured comrade towards the side of the ship, a 10-foot wall of lumber teetered and then fell, striking him heavily on the back of the head and neck, killing him instantly, his lifeless body tumbling overboard with hundreds of board feet of lumber.

Oiler James O'Brien, a little further forward when the torpedo hit, said the blast, "knocked me off my feet and made me goofy for a minute. Because the sub had the glare behind her, we couldn't have had a chance to escape. She had a perfect target."

Radio operator Walt Williams, in the communications shack on the aft end of the boat deck when it happened, was literally blown out of his chair onto the floor by the blast. Seconds later, said Williams, "Captain Louie Pringle notified me to send out the SOS signal, and the message that we'd been torpedoed. Two messages I didn't have to be told to send."

Down in the pantry, the ship's cook, Thomas Watkins, was basting a roast for the noonday meal when the torpedo struck. "The galley seemed to turn upside down and the last I saw of the roast, it was hash," said Watkins. Although it wasn't Sunday and they weren't due into port until late that night, Watkins had been wearing his best Sunday suit under his cook's whites all morning because, as he said, "I had a hunch we might get the same thing that happened to the *Montebello*."

The fact that the *Absoroka* suddenly seemed destined to sink out from under him appeared secondary. "I found myself out on deck worrying about my good clothes," he said, "and remember saying to myself, 'Thomas, be careful and don't get your Sunday suit wet.'" He didn't but had he been in lifeboat No. 2, he would have. It capsized with two men in it, but they were picked up by boat No. 1.

Down in the boiler room, meanwhile, one of the crewmen was hurriedly wrapping the severely burned hands of Frank Johnson before starting to the main deck. Johnson was just opening the door of one of the boilers when the blast occurred. "The burners flared back and the fire poured out all over," he said. "I couldn't tell what caused it."

Out on deck, crewmen had already lowered the lifeboats. No need to wait for the order to abandon ship, the old *Absoroka* had already settled up to the main deck.

Not long after Walt Williams' distress call, planes showed up and dropped bombs near where the sub was last seen. On the heels of the bombing, the *Amethyst* arrived on scene again, and began dropping depth charges. Neither bombs nor the pattern of 32 depth charges showed results.

As the day wore on, seven of the 33-man crew rescued from the *Absoroka*, including Captain Pringle, had come back on board. Seeing that the old ship was not in any immediate danger of sinking because of the buoyancy of its cargo of lumber, Lieutenant Commander Hans B. Olson tied up his U.S. Navy tug and gingerly towed the ship in and beached her on a strip of sand below Fort MacArthur.[57]

In Honolulu Christmas Eve morning, Joey Border was again certain this was the day she would leave Oahu for home. She went to the dock and was told to go home and wait. She waited, but no word came, and she once more remained frustrated—unaware the *Matsonia* was still offloading cargo while Crown and Cooke sought answers regarding the maximum passenger load *Matsonia* could carry.

The answer finally came that day when Captain Frucht sent a letter to Castle and Cooke, saying the lifeboat capacity of *Matsonia* was 976, that in addition the life rafts were capable of holding in excess of 400—therefore the number of passengers should be limited to 976 persons. In the meantime Joey went to Barbara Morrison's for dinner and the night, and played acey-ducey with Barbara one more time. She voiced her frustration to her diary, "heleva Xmas Eve."[58]

On Christmas Eve, off the West Coast, the cruiser *Detroit*, leading Task Group 15.2 pressed ever closer to its destination, San Francisco, while nine Japanese submarines, excluding *I-9*, which had been ordered toward the Panama Canal, remained on station, most well south of the entrance to San Francisco Bay. His Imperial Majesty's submarine crews had been looking forward to the night of the 24th, because they had been given an order by Admiral Shimizu, commander of the 6th Fleet, to bring a special Christmas gift to Americans residing near key targets up and down the coast.

But on the 22nd, Admiral Mitsoyoshi, responding to orders from Admiral Yamamoto, Commander in Chief of the Combined Fleet, postponed the attack until the 27th, the 26th in the United States. As Task Group 15.2 pushed toward the Golden Gate, *I-15* remained somewhere in the vicinity of the Farallon Islands, which were about 30 miles off the entrance to San Francisco Bay. Submarine *I-17*, which had started south toward Los Angeles on the 22nd, when American battleships were reported to be arriving Christmas Day, remained on station further west of *I-15*, but apparently neither observed, or chose not to approach or report the presence of the convoy.[59]

That bleak Christmas Eve, the convoy had held an easterly course, keeping a sharp lookout, with all passengers ready at a moment's notice to react should an attack occur. *Detroit* launched no planes, and the convoy zigzagged only once, late in the afternoon.

During the days and nights preceding Christmas Eve, an appeal to passengers on the *Coolidge* brought more clothes, books, magazines and cigarettes than the wounded could use. There had been movies every other night, and dancing on alternate nights. Some passengers had taken swims in the ship's pool, despite the increasingly cold winter air. Games were played almost constantly, and volunteers read to wounded unable to see. Barbers in the group volunteered their services free, giving shaves and haircuts. Every means available had been used to keep morale up, while during the days, when passengers were on deck, they watched the sea for tell-tale periscopes. The danger lay like a pall over the ship, and at no time was vigilance relaxed.

On this day especially, the passengers, determined to keep spirits up and tension and fear at bay, held a Christmas party before the ship was darkened for the night. They sang Christmas carols and were able to give a few gifts, most gifts prepared weeks ago. There was neither candy nor nuts for the children, and only a few toys that had been put aboard at the last moment by busy Red Cross workers. There were far more children than gifts. One passenger described the Christmas party as "sad." The attack sent widows with children home on the two ships.

Not all was sad however, as young men seriously wounded but not broken in spirit, livened up the trip—and the party—with wise cracks and humorous banter. Almost all had shown improvement on the trip. Their cheerfulness deeply impressed the passengers. One young sailor whose right leg had been amputated above the ankle saw a friend whose left leg had been similarly amputated. He sent him a note that said: "How about a dance?"

The football players from San Jose State and Willamette University, who had volunteered to assist in caring for the wounded and cheering the downcast throughout the crossing, continued to lift spirits during the party. One had earlier made light of his being billeted in steerage, saying if a torpedo had hit the ship, it would come into his living room. The last blackout of the convoy came at 5:00 p.m., after the Christmas party.[60]

That night the nurses lost one of the wounded, an older man, Boatswain's Mate Second Class Alvin Albert Dvorak of Minneapolis, MN. He had been badly burned, and was losing intravenous fluids faster than could be replaced. *Coolidge*'s destination now was San Francisco with 124 patients and one deceased.[61]

At midnight, with *Cummings* still on the port bow of *Scott*, *Detroit* on the starboard bow at the same 1,500-yards distance, and *Coolidge* astern of *Scott*, they continued to hold to the easterly course. At 0120 hours the convoy entered heavy intermittent squalls and rain showers, with lowered visibility shrinking to 1,000 yards, then 800 yards, until the *Coolidge* disappeared in the haze astern of *Cummings*. Aboard *Detroit*, after the long, tense night, general quarters sounded at 0600. General quarters on *Detroit* began the wake-up from restless, almost impossible sleep on *Coolidge* and *Scott*, and a flurry of activity. Passengers, told they were nearing the coast, knew the Golden Gate would soon come into view.[62]

At first light Army bombers from the Western Defense Command, joined in escorting the convoy, similar to what had been done when the *St. Louis* and Convoy 2005 came into Honolulu on the 21st.[63]

Early morning of Christmas Day brought relief to Red Cross nurse, Margaret Logan, who described what occurred that morning as *Scott*'s passengers began realizing they were near the end of a long, dangerous journey.

> As a Christmas gesture, perhaps an expression of thanksgiving, there was a scramble to buy gifts for the wounded. All on board contributed something, from the lowliest cabin boy to the slightly rumpled official. The store on the *Coolidge* was bought out by breakfast time. Each patient and nurse received at least one gift—clothing, cigarettes, toilet articles, or some useful present.[64]

At 0635 the electrical gang on the *Detroit* activated the degaussing coils. Twenty minutes later the watch sighted the Farallon lights six miles distant, slightly aft of the port beam, and after signaling the turn to the convoy, came port to 020 degrees. *Detroit*'s crew turned on her lights at 0721, followed immediately by the other ships in the convoy, and at 0755 the watch logged sighting the San Francisco lightship slightly east of north. Then came varying courses and speeds to enter the inland waterways. Task Group 15.2, soon to pass beneath the Golden Gate Bridge, was about to arrive home.[65]

They Came From the Early Morning Mist . . .

Long before the ships docked at the Embarcadero, classified, coded messages had been received in the Twelfth Naval District, sent from the Fourteenth Naval District, undoubtedly copied to the Chief of Naval Operations in Washington, DC, telling the District Commandant to plan for and expect the arrival of wounded and other evacuees from the attack on Pearl Harbor. Task Group 15.2's estimated date and time of arrival was probably communicated via message as well, with information regarding the wounded and other categories of passengers on board the *Coolidge* and *Scott*. By the time the two passenger-carriers docked, preparations were made for handling them—and as much as possible, for keeping tight secrecy on the convoys transiting San Francisco.

Soldiers with rifles, sailors with pistols, and policemen closed off the area and kept the public, including reporters, behind wood barricades set up two to three blocks from the Embarcadero. In advance of their arrival, ambulance after ambulance rolled onto the piers. Army trucks arrived, laden with stretchers.

Already painted admiralty gray, they came like ghosts gliding out of the gray morning mists, from their passage beneath the Golden Gate Bridge. *Cummings* had pulled ahead of the convoy to enter the channel into San Francisco Bay, followed by *Detroit*—and the larger *Coolidge* astern of *Scott*. Passengers topside who first glimpsed the Golden Gate and the San Francisco skyline, for the first time in weeks felt safe. Everyone on board the ships was happy to be home at last. The two escorts left *Scott* and *Coolidge* as the big ships slowed and turned toward their moorings at the Embarcadero. *Detroit* anchored at Berth No. 1, San Francisco Bay, at 1015, after *Cummings* came into Berth Number 4 at the San Francisco anchorage at 0950.

Passengers on *Coolidge* and *Scott* were asked to wait until the wounded going down the gangway were taken off the ships before they debarked. The city's Health Director, J.C. Geiger, had dispatched four emergency hospital ambulances to rush any critical cases that might need immediate blood transfusions to the San Francisco Hospital blood bank. Red Cross nurses and workers, more angels of mercy, arrived to help, and to take charge of the large number of civilian evacuees the ships brought in. They were a welcome, cheerful sight bringing fresh donuts and coffee. Taxicabs were allowed through the barricades, but were kept at a distance while the wounded were taken off the ships. Reporters, in writing their stories, were forbidden to name the ships in print or photographs, what time they arrived, or when they might depart.

In the cold, drafty air, the grim task of unloading the casualties began, a slow, steady procession of men swathed in bandages, flat on their backs on stretchers, carried down the gangplanks, gently lifted into waiting, white Navy and tan Army ambulances. Within minutes after the ships docked, some of the wounded were on the way to local hospitals. No sooner did one ambulance load and pull away, than another pulled forward to receive its patients.

Though local civilians and newsmen had to stay behind the barricades, and couldn't get near the wounded, one reporter asked a policeman to describe what he had seen. "I saw them. I saw what bomb blasts and shrapnel did. I saw what were once fine, husky lads. And it hit me, like a Joe Louis punch in the pit of the stomach." There were young women waiting there, and one of them asked a sailor on guard at the barricade, "Do you know whether Johnny Thompson is aboard? He was an aircraft gunner . . . or something." "I don't know nobody," the sailor said, and moved on.[66]

Some of the Navy ambulances went on ahead to Mare Island. Simultaneously, the long task got underway of transferring other Navy patients not needing emergency care, to two lighters—ferries on which cots had been set up. They were being taken to the Mare Island Naval hospital, accompanied by the nurses who came with them on the *Coolidge*. Transfer to the first ferry was complete close to noon, and the trip up San Francisco Bay to the Napa River, to Mare Island, began, with the second following about 2:00 p.m.[67]

In the meantime, passengers went down the gangways to a city more than well-prepared to meet and assist them. First came children, some with their mothers, some alone. They were the families of Navy and Army men, some of whom had been killed in the attack. Set up on the docks were canteens to give hot coffee to the women and hot chocolate to the children, while they waited in the cold morning air to process through customs. Mrs. Philip A. Coxon and her Red Cross workers greeted them and began providing warm clothing for children clad in clothes too thin for mainland climates.

After the women and children cleared through customs the Red Cross nurses and workers escorted them to waiting automobiles that whisked them to various quarters where they found Christmas cheer, candy and toys for the children. If additional clothing was needed they got exactly what they needed from Red Cross supplies. If boys needed sweaters, they received sweaters. If girls needed dresses, they received dresses. Two layettes were provided for two babies born on board the ships.

Through the combined efforts of the Red Cross and the National League for Women's Service, the latter an organization created in World War I, stations had been set up and an organization had been completed for getting evacuees to relatives or friends. The Women's City Club and Hospitality House in Civic Center were ready to aid navy wives and children. The Western Women's Club and the Women's Athletic Club were prepared to perform similar services for army evacuees. From Mrs. Alvin Wade, assistant hostess at Fort Mason, came an urgent appeal for volunteer nursemaids and women to care for evacuated children.

Civilian passengers needing assistance went to the California School of Fine Arts, where they were fed, clothed and cared for. Any civilians ill or injured were taken to hospitals by city ambulances. Soon evacuees were dispersing to the city's hotels, to the homes of friends and to the many stations established for them. There was intermittent drizzle. Taxicabs had received numerous calls, were unable to keep up with the demand, thus causing some waiting and extended transportation delays for some of the evacuees leaving individually for other destinations.

Nevertheless, by 4:30 p.m. the docks were clear, and many of the passengers were on their way to their stateside destinations. The parents, friends and fans of the San Jose State and Willamette University football teams received joyous Christmas presents in phone calls of the teams' safe arrival in San Francisco.[68]

The San Jose team scattered for homes and late Christmas

celebrations, with only one being from San Francisco. Left behind on Oahu, voluntarily, were seven of their team members, who hired onto the Honolulu Police force: Bill Donnelly, Ken Stranger, Don Allen, Jack Lercari, Fred Lindsay, Chet Carsten, and Paul Toguetti. The Willamette University team, coaches, and fans boarded a Southern Pacific train bound for Salem, Oregon. When they arrived home the next day, over 1,000 Salem and university people gave them a roaring, emotional welcome.[69]

The first ferry carrying wounded arrived at Mare Island at 4:30 p.m. and nurses on board helped take the patients to their wards. Had not the San Francisco Red Cross hurriedly collected a large box of sandwiches from every available store open on Christmas Day, none of the patients and nurses on the ferries would have eaten from breakfast until the second arrival at Mare Island that night. At Mare Island, the last of the Navy patients were placed in ambulances shortly before midnight and taken to the hospital.

The nurses stayed in nurses' quarters that night. While at Mare Island, a doctor asked Lieutenant Ericson, "For God's sake, Ruth, what's happened out there? We don't know a thing." He had been on the battleship *Arizona*, and was detached only a few months prior to the attack. The first convoy of wounded had ended but the trip back for the nurses was scheduled to start the next morning, December 26.

Back down the Napa River they went, passed through the barricaded San Francisco waterfront, now reinforced with barbed wire, and reported aboard the transport, USS *Henderson* (AP-1), for return to Oahu for another cargo of wounded.[70]

The Battle of Los Angeles

The Christmas Eve torpedo attacks on the freighters *Barbara Olson* and *Absoroka*, near Los Angeles, coupled with resulting newspaper headlines and radio reports, raised fears among the West Coast civilian populace and increased Army and Navy harbor defense vigilance and alert levels markedly. Though Japanese submarines operating off the coast were already feeling the pinch of decreasing fuel reserves, had informed Admiral Shimizu, and received orders canceling the postponed night deck gun attack on shore installations, the lingering pall of fear they created in a one week spate of attacks brought one last battle to the minds of military men unfamiliar with submarines and submarine warfare.

The action began approximately the same time as the last ferry carrying wounded left San Francisco's Embarcadero for the Mare Island Naval hospital. The alert level and sequence of events are found in excerpts from the Harbor Defense Command Post log of the 3rd Coast Artillery, commanded by Army Colonel William W. Hicks. The "submarine" which provoked the action can be found in the Christmas Day log of the *Amethyst*, which had been heavily involved in the previous day's actions.

At 0055 in the morning, Colonel Hicks, reacting to the preceding day's attacks near Los Angeles Harbor, ordered, "One gun at each 155 [battery] and the AA positions will be on Class 'A' alert and will be prepared to fire on any submarine immediately upon identification." Trouble began nearly 13 hours later, at 1347, when the command post received a report from an artillery observer co-located with a searchlight on the Redondo Pier. "Light #2 thinks they see sub off of barge." The "barge" was the old, decommissioned, four-masted, barkentine schooner, *Kohala*, which for years had been used by the city of Redondo Beach as a commercial fishing barge.

Three minutes later, the command post received a report from another observer at Palos Verdes, "Light #3 identified sub 150 yards off of barge—it is bobbing up and down." Light #2 then reported "Barge is 1 ½ miles west of Redondo Pier," and two minutes later, at 1355 ". . . sub still bobbing up and down 1 ½ miles West of Redondo."

At the same time, to one of the batteries on Palos Verdes, came an order from the command post, ". . . turn the 155 [mm gun] around so you can reach sub off Redondo, check with Rocky Point and see if they can see it, and swing gun to bear on it." Six minutes later the observer on the Redondo Pier reported the "214th is shooting at sub with small arms. Coast Guard Cutter [*Amethyst*] is crossing in front of Point Fermin at top speed." Four minutes afterward, at 1405, the command post, having alerted both Navy and Army units involved in harbor and coast defense, received the report, "Army has dispatched 3 bombers to 1 ½ miles off Redondo Beach to bomb submarine."

In succeeding minutes the observer on Redondo Pier repeatedly insisted the bobbing object was a submarine, "still see sub but it is sinking a little bit," "sub still bobbing up and down," "Sub is drifting off a little bit," "Sub 200 yards from barge due south," "Bomber approaching sub," "bomber didn't see sub and continued on," Sub in same position, bomber returning to target," Two Navy bombers overhead," "Bomber up high circling," "Army plane dropped bomb but missed," "Army let go another stick of bombs," and "Army bombers dropped 2 bombs."

The repeated bomb misses and repeated insistence the target was a submarine remaining in the area, resulted in an order from Colonel Hicks, ". . . one gun from 75-mm battery at Inspiration Point to emplace on pier at Redondo Beach and open fire on reported submarine." The command was increasingly convinced the submarine was the same boat that attacked the two freighters on Christmas Eve, had probably been damaged in the subsequent bomb and depth charge attacks, and was attempting to hide behind the barge while making repairs.

A heavy bomber came overhead, followed some time later by two Navy planes that dropped bombs at 1500 hours and reported sending "their best observation plane now." The sub, reported as having disappeared four minutes earlier, was reported again as "emerged and is drifting toward Rocky Point 2,000 yards out of field of fire."

Finally, at 1541 the 75-mm gun from F Battery was in position on Redondo Pier, set up, sighted the target, and the battery commander, Major Miller, was ordered to open fire. Between 1548 and 1555 ten rounds were fired before the gun jammed. The Navy sent another plane to mark the target, and the jam was cleared, but visibility was decreasing, and eventually deteriorated sufficiently that searchlights were unable to illuminate the target area.

Off Long Beach at 1540 hours, the *Amethyst*, twice a late participant in anti-submarine actions, received a report of the ongoing action, prompting her skipper, Lieutenant (jg) Donald A. Nienstedt, to head for Redondo Beach to "destroy an enemy submarine." The *Amethyst*'s log tells the rest of the story.

> At 1656 target designated by aircraft, appeared to be periscope, opened fire (with 3-inch deck gun), closing in. At 1702 ceased firing, no casualties. (Puzzled at the apparent lack of response from the enemy sub, despite the shelling, bombing and now depth charging), at 1706 lowered boat to investigate

target which proved to be roof off a small fishing
vessel with galley chimney attached. At 1808 picked
up boat and took target in tow. At 1815 tow carried
away in heavy weather.[71]

The battle of Los Angeles was over, but for others a different
sort of battle ended on Christmas Day, for different reasons. In
Davenport, Iowa, on 16 December, Mr. and Mrs. Frank Baxter
received a telegram from the War Department announcing that
their 21-year-old son, Eldon, had been killed at Pearl Harbor.
Earlier this Christmas day the doorbell rang again. This time the
postman handed them a special delivery letter from Honolulu.
He had brought the greatest Christmas present ever delivered to
them: a letter from their son, saying he was alive and well.

In Alameda, California, Mrs. Annie Werson, a widow, was just
sitting down to Christmas dinner with her four sons and three
daughters, when the doorbell rang. When she opened the door,
there stood a messenger from Western Union, the second time in
ten days he had been there. The first time he brought a telegram
saying her 27-year-old son, Bert, had been killed at Pearl Harbor.
What message could he be bringing this time? When Mrs. Werson
opened the envelope, she read nine of the sweetest words she
would ever see: "Gather around the Christmas tree and think of
me. It was signed 'Bert.'"

Unbelievably, this or a similar scene happened that day to
the families of Frank Rom of Queens, New York; Joe Maloney
of Malden, Massachusetts; Curtis Fransworth of Leominster,
Massachusetts; Dale Burley Jr. of Munising, Michigan; and David
Mills of Morristown, Pennsylvania. Seven of America's young
men returned to the world of the living from the muck of Pearl
Harbor. On what better occasion could such news be received
than on Christmas Day?

In an effort to prevent a repeat of these painful incidents, on
December 21, Army and Navy officials ceased reporting missing
men as dead. Mr. and Mrs. John Rauschkalb, of New York,
triggered this more common sense approach, after they returned
from a memorial service for their 22-year-old son John Jr.—who
was reported killed at Pearl Harbor—and found a letter from
him saying he was alive and well. Despite their happiness on
learning their son was alive, the days of unnecessary grief and
sadness prompted Mr. Rauschkalb to send a telegram to the War

Department complaining bitterly of the current policy. From that day forward, if a man were missing, the War Department telegram reported him that way, and he was kept in the missing status until facts derived from careful investigation clearly indicated he should be presumed dead.[72]

On Christmas Eve, the new Commander-in-Chief, Pacific Fleet, a passenger on a huge Navy flying boat, left San Diego, bound for Oahu. In the months and years ahead, much good would come from his command and leadership in the Pacific.

CHAPTER 13

Three Matson Ladies Plus
Escorts: Convoy 4032

Joys divided are increased.

Josiah Gilbert Holland

Mid-morning Christmas Day, a huge, four-engine, Navy PB2Y-2 Coronado seaplane, a big brother to San Francisco's Pan Am *Clippers* and the Catalina PBYs stationed at Kanehoe and Ford Island, winged its way southwest to northeast, on a track parallel and comfortably east of Pearl Harbor's main channel. Piloted on the long, over water flight from southern California by Lieutenant Bowen F. McLeod and Ensigns Frank L. DeLorenzo, Ross C. Barney, and Thomas Robinson with engineering crew member Warrant Machinist Mate Clarence L. Pearson, Bureau Number 1635 left San Diego 17 hours earlier bringing the new Commander-in-Chief, Pacific Fleet, Admiral Chester W. Nimitz, to take the reins of command from the acting Pacific Fleet commander, Admiral Pye. The pilots invited Admiral Nimitz to the flight deck and asked him if he would like to observe the damage and destruction inflicted by the Japanese. He eagerly accepted, and was seated in the left hand pilot's seat, where the plane captain normally sat. They made wide, left turn circles over Pearl Harbor as well as Hickam Field, giving him a clear unobstructed view of the scene.

Many of the ships in the harbor the day of the attack were either with task groups or on patrol. Except for the five battleships resting on the harbor bottom, most of the rest had shifted berths or were in dry dock. In plain view, one after the other, as the aircraft flew east of the harbor on the first pass were the *Nevada*, *California*, the capsized *Oklahoma*, the badly burned and settled

Admiral Chester W. Nimitz arrived in Pearl Harbor on
Christmas Day 1941, and took command of the Pacific
Fleet in a 31 December ceremony. NPSAM

West Virginia and the shattered *Arizona*. On the far side of Ford
Island, the upturned bottom of the *Utah* was clearly visible. On
the near side of the main channel, still in their dry docks, could
be seen the shattered destroyers *Cassin*, *Downes*, and *Shaw*.
Though there were no more fires burning in the harbor, the tide-
made trail of oil leaking from the sunken ships of the battle line,
and six-inch clouds of oil floating elsewhere in the harbor added
stark reminders of the horror of 7 December.

As they circled wide of Ford Island and Hickam Field, the admiral
and the six-man crew, who were also viewing the destruction for
the first time, saw skeletons of what were once hangars, and flight
lines filled with the junk of what had been military airplanes.
Admiral Nimitz just kept shaking his head and clucking his tongue.
Ensign DeLorenzo wondered if he felt as the crew did. "Those
dirty bastards! Somehow, someway, we are going to make them
pay!" What was in the admiral's mind, and what would be his
demeanor as he viewed the destruction still evident and considered
the great responsibility he was undertaking?

The answer came when they landed. Admiral Nimitz took the time to shake the hand of every member of the crew, thank them for the comfortable flight, and apologize to each one for taking them away from their families on Christmas Day. DeLorenzo's thoughts were lifetime memories. What a giant of a man. What a great leader to take over the Pacific Fleet![1]

After Admiral Nimitz's airplane landed in Pearl Harbor Christmas morning, and while passengers were leaving the Embarcadero in San Francisco, Joey Border, after one more game of acey-ducey on Oahu, with Barbara Morrison, the two left to board the *Lurline*. Finally, she was leaving—but she didn't know precisely when, nor did she know the destination. There were no tickets which gave the time, date of departure, or destination. All she knew was the date and time period in which to board. The clamp-down on secrecy was working.

They were among the first to begin boarding at 1:00 p.m., Honolulu time, but had to wait until 6:00 to be assigned staterooms. Their baggage had been delivered to the dock in the morning, before they boarded. Joey's baggage consisted of a light travel case and a steamer trunk which held the young married couple's most cherished possessions, including such items as the ceramic angels she planned to have for their first Christmas together.

She was told her baggage would be delivered to her stateroom after the passengers boarded between 1 and 4 p.m. The result was a long wait in the area where the belongings were being held. She took advantage of the wait by introducing herself and striking up conversations with other women—and taking brief naps on the baggage. The last twenty-four days had drained her. Sleep beckoned and she welcomed it, especially since the waiting continued.

When her baggage was finally picked up for the walk through the passageways and up the ladders or stairways to her stateroom, for the first time she was able to look closely at the inside appearance of *Lurline*. It definitely didn't appear the ship Joey remembered when she sailed on her grand voyage from San Francisco in September. She was seeing the transformation of the ship that occurred in San Francisco between 10 and 16 December. Partly, but not entirely, she was now seeing a troop ship. Painted gray on the outside, on the inside the ship seemed equally gray and austere. Gone were virtually all the trappings of a luxury cruise liner, and as the evacuees continued to come aboard, it became apparent the ship would be far more crowded.

Strikingly, except for the relatively small number of tourists returning to the mainland, all the passengers were women and children. On further reflection, the thought wasn't pleasant. All the women and children were going home—somewhere—while their husbands, fathers, sons, brothers, fiancées, and lovers were staying behind to fight a war, and an enemy that had come and gone without a trace after delivering staggering death and destruction on a sleepy Sunday morning.

Some of the women were new widows, their husbands killed during the attack, or died of wounds, their children without fathers. Without question, many more of the women and children leaving on *Lurline* would lose husbands and fathers in the months ahead. Then there were the islanders who had married men in the Navy or Army. They were going home, too, to homes and families they had never seen or met, a country they had never seen or lived in, and in most instances, hard winter climates never experienced—nearly all without benefit of warm clothes. And to make matters worse, the news had been full of headlines about submarine attacks in the seas around the islands and off the West Coast near port entrances.

When Joey, with her travel case and the baggage handler, arrived at her assigned stateroom, he put the steamer trunk in the cabin and left. She promptly decided she didn't like the room. The passenger list was obviously incomplete. There were more evacuees than the list of names given the ship's crew. As had been the case with the *Coolidge* and *Scott*, and now for security reasons deliberately so, hundreds of passengers had only two hours notice of their departure. She quickly scouted nearby cabins, found one she liked better, and dragged her steamer trunk and travel case to it. What a change!

She didn't know *Lurline*'s destination, or when the ship would leave. They could be sailing to any port from San Diego to Seattle. Staterooms for six, not two or three. Find a bunk, put a suitcase, child or both on it, and claim it. No twin or double beds, no springs or mattresses, no sheets, one pillow, find a bunk among the two stacks of three, fold-out, taut canvas cots bolted to the cabin walls—each holding one blanket. Joey's petite size mandated a lower bunk, which she gladly claimed. She then read the rules posted in every cabin.

No smoking except in designated areas. Wear lifebelts or carry them with you at all times. No fresh water baths or showers, except for babies—and the wounded when they were brought aboard. Bathe in saltwater only. One glass of drinking water per day, which Joey wryly observed to herself, she might use to drink, bathe, or brush her teeth. Then came the first meal aboard *Lurline*, the troop ship.

There was a small Christmas tree on a table in the center of the "dining salon," which was no longer a dining salon. The small tree was the only concession to Christmas. No reserved dining tables with pre-arranged or assigned dinner partners. No menus. No freshly washed, clean, white tablecloths, folded white napkins, polished silverware, saucers and coffee cups, wine glasses, champagne glasses, or water goblets. No waiters to serve individual tables or place settings. Wait in line outside the dining room until tables are vacated. Cafeteria style. Get in line, take a tray, a paper napkin maybe wrapped around some silverware, and eat what's put in front of you. Find a friendly or recognizable face, and hopefully a place to sit near them.

Before Joey went to sleep that night, she summed up her experiences to her diary: ". . . awful mess—met some gals—bed at 10—heleva Xmas—it isn't the same ship—Fooey . . . "[2]

Indeed, Admiral Bloch, the commandant of the Fourteenth Naval District, apparently considered management of the evacuation an "awful mess" as well. On the 26th he had had enough, and sent a letter classified as "RESTRICTED," to the newly arrived Commander-in-Chief of the Pacific Fleet, Admiral Nimitz.

Subject: Evacuation of dependents
1. Evacuation of dependent personnel is not proceeding satisfactorily. The main cause of this is the inability of the Officer-in-Charge to handle the situation. Manifestly efficient evacuation is a necessity for the maintenance of morale. The Commandant has no officer under his command suitable to put in charge.
2. It is therefore requested that the Commander-in-Chief, Pacific Fleet furnish a suitable officer to take charge of the evacuation of personnel. Services will probably be required not over three months.

C.C. Bloch[3]

Retired Captain Max Frucht, who was managing the evacuation not only faced an increasingly difficult situation and the frustration of Admiral Bloch, he and Crown and Cooke were beginning to receive written appeals from people claiming to be tourists who weren't really tourists, wives appealing the order to evacuate, and others pleading to be evacuated who were frustrated because they had been told to wait.

Up at 7:00 the morning of the 26th, Joey Border awoke to continued, rushed preparations for departure. She saw the wounded brought dockside in ambulances, up the gangways, most moved to what had once been *Lurline*'s ballroom. Crewmembers, and medics on board temporarily Christmas Day, had assisted two nurses and a doctor in setting up cots, and organizing medical equipment and temporary medical supply cabinets. When the more severely wounded needing round the clock care were carried aboard, they were placed in the ballroom-turned-temporary hospital, and those who were ambulatory and could reasonably care for themselves were placed in nearby staterooms.

Up on deck that morning, she noted something else as the moment for getting underway approached. No Royal Hawaiian Band standing on the dock playing the traditional Hawaiian music. No Hawaiian singers. No dancers. No confetti. No leis. No send-off. No long, low blasts on the ship's horn. No crowds of well-wishers, except for a few husbands, fathers, and friends—all kept at a distance.[4] The secrecy clamp was tight, and holding firm. Guards wearing helmets and combat dress, carrying rifles, sandbagged machine gun positions visible and manned. The island was still beautiful, but the warm, sensual, welcome of the September tropics and the tourists' send-offs were absent, gone to war.

As for the crews of *Lurline*, *Matsonia* and *Monterey*, they undoubtedly had received advance word from their ships' captains, and were more than impressed by the passenger load they were taking on board. Convoy 2005 from San Francisco to Honolulu 16-21 December, had carried troops and their unit equipment and supplies to reinforce the islands' defenses. There was an air of anticipation and excitement among the young soldiers. They had been trained to fight, were disciplined yet fun-loving, had marvelously positive attitudes, found ways to entertain themselves, and, as the first reinforcements to arrive in Hawaii, eagerly received the trappings of a Royal Hawaiian welcome. Though it would take time for the reality to sink in, this large group of passengers was totally different, a passenger load they had never experienced.

Except for tourists, Kamaainas—old time Island residents—and the wounded leaving on this second convoy, virtually all others were women and children, nearly all the wives and children of Navy, Army, and Army Air Force men, plus wives and children of government employees and contractor employees. Among them were a number of widows and children of men killed in the attack or died of wounds.

Typical of passengers boarding was Mrs. June Cowee of Kansas City. She was a half mile from Pearl Harbor and was awakened by a terrific explosion that morning. She and her family saw several planes go down in flames, didn't know what to do, so they jumped in their car to get away—only to see Japanese planes strafing vehicles and people on the road, including a milk truck in front of them, the driver struck down when he got out of the truck and ran to hide in a cane field. Another was Mrs. Andrew Jackson Roberts, whose husband was a Navy quartermaster. She had two sons, 4-year-old Michael, and 2-year-old Tony. Michael was old enough to be frightened by the air raid, was tight-lipped and reluctant to talk, and Tony was too young to understand. Mrs. Roberts had been on Oahu only six weeks when ordered to evacuate and had seen her husband only two nights after being apart for one year.

Ten-year-old Dwight Agnew Jr., son of a naval officer, boarded wearing his lifebelt, a special lifebelt that had been worn by a merchant captain whom Dwight's dad had rescued, along with the captain's crew. The captain had been wearing it when his ship went down, and he gave it to Dwight, who had been wearing it ever since. With his mother, Mrs. Thelma Agnew, he was going back to the mainland, intent on wearing the lifebelt all the way home.

Mrs. Gertrude Schuessler of Chicago was going home to her mother's, bringing three children, Noel, 10, Merrily, 6, and Gerta, not quite 2. Her husband was a medic, who was on his way to his ship, and got to the boat landing at Pearl Harbor about five minutes before the attack began. He spent the rest of the day tending wounded. When the bombing started, Mrs. Schuessler and her children rushed to a neighbor's home which looked more like a stronghold than theirs. She tried to prepare her children for an austere Christmas, telling them that because of "conditions, Santa couldn't get to Hawaii on his surfboard . . . "

Joyce Parry of Salt Lake had only a couple of hours to pack. When she did, all her bags were shunted off somewhere. For the entire trip her wardrobe was green slacks, two donated sweaters, a pair of pajamas and a coolie jacket. Because of short notices to leave, some women came aboard with their complete personal belongings and clothes in paper sacks.

Among the wounded was 20 year-old J.R. Trammell, a farm boy from Oklahoma, who was in his ship's galley when a torpedo struck, and he took shrapnel in both legs. Five men in the galley with him were hit. Two of Trammell's shipmates were among the wounded loaded on *Lurline*, L.E. Pullman of Southgate, California and W.A. Schiller of St. Louis, Missouri. They were in a gun crew on deck when a bomb exploded, and shrapnel wounded all but two of the 12-man crew.[5]

Mrs. Therese Hall, 22, came aboard the *Monterey* with 3-month old twins, Priscilla Brenda and James Lennard. Her husband, M.L. Hall stayed behind in his Army Air Force unit, and Mrs. Hall was already weary from struggling to carry the two young twins when she came on board. Mrs. Arthur A. Fahrner, wife of a quartermaster sergeant at Hickam Field, brought their five children. They had just sat down for breakfast when the Japanese attacked, and were evacuated immediately to the University of Hawaii. She had seen Japanese planes falling in flames, deliberately diving into the hangars on Hickam. When she returned home three days later, temporarily, to get some things, she found their breakfast table just as they left it. Mrs. Nuela Norman arrived on her ship with her left arm in a sling, injured during the attack, and a child wounded in the attack and wearing a cast on his leg, was carried on board by his mother.[6]

Mrs. Dorothy Lloyd was an office worker in Honolulu. She was going home to her family in Long Beach, intent on warning people stateside about what they were up against, that they couldn't afford complacency. She was also proud of what the taxi drivers of Oahu, the "cabbies," had done in response to the attack. In her memory were the polyglot lot of Chinese, Malay, Korean, and even Japanese cabbies, typical of Hawaii, who loaded their taxies with sailors and officers and drove right into the inferno that was Pearl Harbor to get men to their guns. They didn't stop to ask for fares, either.

Mrs. W.L. Hayes, niece of Colonel Frank Kuhn, stationed at Honolulu, and wife of an Army Air Force lieutenant was pregnant and came aboard the *Monterey* knowing her time for delivery was near. She let people know her husband shot down two Japs.

Two other passengers on the *Lurline* were brown-eyed, 2 year-old Dickey Thompson, and his mother, Mrs. Ruby Thompson, a pretty, fresh-faced 20 year-old with pain in her eyes. Dickey's real name was Richard, and he probably didn't grow up remembering his father, Petty Officer First Class Robert Thompson of Atlanta, Georgia, who was killed at Pearl Harbor, his grave the blue Pacific waters. His body wasn't recovered. Ruby was angry. She knew how her husband died. His shipmates told her. She firmly believed her husband died because someone on Oahu talked too much.[7]

While there some feelings of relief among many at the prospect of leaving the war torn island, especially among the women and children, there was little joy. Joy evaporated Sunday morning, 7 December. The women were leaving their husbands, fiancées, brothers, sons, and lovers behind, the children, their fathers—all to futures of uncertainty, danger and fear. The war's violent, frightening beginning had been a profound shock in a tropical paradise, followed by the wartime pall of martial law and rationing, blackouts, round-the-clock alerts, repeated sirens and air raid warnings, the daily sounds of airplanes roaring overhead, the fears of additional air attacks, or landings of enemy troops, the silence of the radios for days, the consistent flow of bad news and defeat blaring in newspaper headlines, the flood of rumors, their men wrenched from them with no warning or knowledge of where they were going or when they would be back. It had been compounded by abrupt local, temporary evacuations from homes and quarters to "safer areas," and now, after all that had transpired, "you are being ordered to leave," short notice evacuations, leaving the islands for good, leaving loved ones behind, often with hardly time to say personal goodbyes.

To make matters worse, it was Christmastime, a time when families normally came together in celebration. But on the ships these two days they were greeted with more austerity, no entertainment such as dance bands, singing groups, and vaudeville troupes—although the Red Cross and other local volunteers did everything they could to help out in a difficult if not chaotic situation.

In Pearl Harbor that morning, four ships of the Pacific Fleet were preparing to get underway while crews on the *Lurline*, *Matsonia* and *Monterey* were loading passengers and cargo, and making last minute preparations to depart from the port of Honolulu. At Pearl Harbor, the first was the high speed destroyer-minelayer *Breese* (DM-18), which left Berth D-5 in Pearl Harbor's Middle Loch at 0711, carrying mail—orders—for the high speed destroyer-minesweeper, *Southard* (DMS-10). *Southard* left Pearl Harbor at 1535 on Christmas Day, assigned to a patrol area outside the harbor.

When *Breese* left early the morning of the 26th, she was followed by the destroyers *Preston*, at 0830, and *Smith*, at 0837, both moored in Berth Xray 12, alongside the destroyer-tender *Whitney*. *Preston* and *Smith* had been tasked to proceed with the light cruiser *St. Louis*, underway later from Berth C-5 at 0929 hours. The Navy combatants comprised Task Group 15.6, to escort Convoy 4032. At 0915, shortly before *St. Louis* got underway, the *Breese* pulled alongside the *Southard* outside the harbor, and passed the mail to her ordering *Southard* to temporary duty as an additional convoy screen.

The escort duty was expressed in the Commander, Task Force 15 Operations Order 19-41, dated 25 December 1941. Captain George A. Rood, the *St. Louis*'s commander, who had led the three Matson vessels and the destroyers *Preston* and *Smith* from San Francisco in Convoy 2005, was on the cruiser's bridge when the ship went to general quarters at 0955 prior to leaving the harbor entrance.

The *Monterey*, under the command of Elis R. Johanson, was under way from Honolulu's Pier No. 20 at 1009 hours after four days of offloading cargo and taking on cargo including provisions and passengers' belongings, such as some automobiles approved for shipment home. Aboard her was a total of 804 Army and Army Air Force wives, children and casualties of the raid. Of this group 240 were under twelve years of age. At 1047, the *Breese* took the position of screening vessel on *Monterey*, and, hugging the shoreline, at 1110 they passed Diamond Head Light, abeam to port one mile.

Having completed cargo loading at 3:30 a.m. the morning of the 26th, then embarking the last of her 836 passengers—nearly all women and children—*Matsonia*, commanded by Frank A. Johnson, was underway from Pier No. 28 at 10:19. The

Lurline left Pier 11 at 10:27, aided by tugs *Mathilda* and *Foss* and logged having "SAILED" at 11:30, the time she was in the convoy formation. The *Monterey*, eased away from Pier 20 by tugs *Mikimiki* and *Matilda*, left her moorings at 10:41. As Joey Border would soon learn, because the evacuation and loading had been so hectic, Commodore Berndtson and the crew hadn't an accurate count of the passengers on board *Lurline*.

At 1125 the *St. Louis* was on station in the convoy, 1,000 yards ahead of *Lurline*, the convoy guide, with *Matsonia* and *Monterey* in column astern of *Lurline*, and *Smith*, *Preston*, *Breese* and *Southard* acting as anti-submarine screen on both flanks of the column. The course was 090 degrees true, speed 17 knots, when, five minutes later, the formation began zigzagging, and continued zigzagging on base course 090 degrees until 1201, when, after signaling the formation, at 1238 the *St. Louis* entered the convoy into a port turn, to 027 degrees—then commenced zigzagging at 1244. Task Group 15.6 and Convoy 4032 were proceeding east, around Diamond Head, then turning to the northeast to pass between Oahu and Molikai, two days after the nine-ship Convoy 2004, Task Force 15.7, had returned to Honolulu, passing north of Oahu, and south through the Kauai Channel, then east into Pearl Harbor and Honolulu.

At 1314 hours the *Preston* reported a submarine contact, and *St. Louis* immediately began maneuvering the formation to evade, while the destroyer proceeded to investigate, and four minutes later reported the contact false. At 1332, *St. Louis* again signaled zigzag according to Plan No. 21. Once more, if submarines *I-4*, *I-5*, and *I-6*, were on stations in or northeast of the Kaiwi Channel, they either didn't sight the convoy, or if they did, didn't attempt to attack it or report its presence. Captain Rood was taking no chances, and continued the formation zigzag. Nevertheless, the report of a submarine, followed immediately by evasive action increased tensions and raised fears among passengers. To compound the immediate submarine alert, the weather was rough, with swells running higher than normal. Joey and many other passengers felt seasick—and the voyage was just beginning.[8]

On board the *Matsonia*, logged between 3:00 and 3:15 p.m., while the formation maneuvering was in progress northeast of Oahu, Captain Johnson ordered the passengers and crew mustered at their respective lifeboat stations, drilled in the proper use and adjustments of their life belts, and given instructions for all cases of emergency, including submarine attack.[9]

While *Lurline* pitched, rolled, and plowed steadily northeast through rough waters, Joey settled in, continued to get acquainted with other women in her stateroom, and wrote in her diary that evening—"got glamorized." She also told her diary before climbing into her not-so-soft bed at 11:00 p.m., "thousands of women and children."

That observation, now recorded in writing and repeated again in the mind of a young, energetic former newspaper reporter, called up ideas and initiatives for the rest of the trip home. After all, if Joey had learned anything, it was that Navy wives, because of the nomadic lives they necessarily lead, have to be self-reliant, positive, sometimes even aggressive, no-nonsense, and at the same time, be cooperative and loving. If you don't know what's going on, find out. Be inquisitive. Ask questions—lots of questions. Let others know what you learned. Work together. Take care of one another. Help one another. Be thoughtful and compassionate. Stay busy, occupied, constructive, to keep your mind off yourself and the disappointments that can make life miserable—if you let them. Make the most of what you have. Don't dwell on the dangers and fears. Know what you have to do when there's an emergency, and that's it. Don't bitch and complain. Think ahead, plan ahead, get organized, and stay ahead.

The greatest submarine threats were at dusk and dawn, in the day's fading light and the morning's first light. Enemy submarines normally ran on the surface at night, using their diesel engines to charge their batteries while making much faster speeds than when submerged. Because of the lowered visibility at night, no patrol planes present, and ships normally running darkened, the submarines were also less likely to be seen. If there was an encounter, it usually was accidental and close-in, as were the cases in some of the early morning attacks between the 18th and 25th of December.

Convoys normally made less average speed in the daytime because they often zigzagged for prolonged periods, while at night, they steadied on course and moved as rapidly as feasible. Invariably, with the dawn came caution, increased alert and more eyes scanning the sea through binoculars, telescopes—and periscopes.

The morning of the 27th was no different on board the *St. Louis*.

Weather was satisfactory to launch scout planes. General quarters sounded at 0600 hours, and at 0630, the crew catapulted the first of two airplanes in quick succession, while signalmen prepared the convoy to begin zigzagging at 0644. Not yet 24 hours into Convoy 4032's journey to the West Coast, two events related to Japanese submarine operations around Hawaii and the West Coast were in progress, one of which, unknown to the convoy commanders, would have a direct bearing on the relative safety of the six ships.[10]

Well behind the convoy at 0515 hours, 25 miles south of the island of Kauai, the destroyer *Allen* (DD-66), which was on patrol in Hawaiian waters, picked up all twelve survivors in Lifeboat No. 1, from the Matson Lines' freighter, *Manini*, which had been sunk in a torpedo attack at dusk on 17 December, approximately 200 miles south of Honolulu. The *Manini*'s Second Mate, George W. Jahn was the senior officer on the lifeboat, and all who scrambled onto it survived the ordeal after the ship went down in minutes.

The near miraculous recovery had come after nine days, 10 hours, and 30 minutes in the lifeboat, through rough seas, thirst, privation, and frustrating hoped-for recoveries after being sighted a day earlier by an American long range patrol aircraft that dropped a little food and cigarettes and signaled them to "Hang on a while longer. A Coast Guard cutter is coming to pick you up." At 0200 hours the morning of the 27th they fired their last pistol flare to catch the attention of another patrol plane. The desperate survivors then held the aircraft near them using coston lights, varied color lights used in life saving work at sea.[11]

More pertinent to Convoy 4032's future was the absence of Japanese submarine attacks off the mainland's West Coast the day the formation sailed out of Honolulu. The 26th, the attacks ceased as suddenly as they began, the result of low fuel states on board the nine submarines that had arrived in their assigned operating areas the night of the 17th. Both the Western Defense Command and the West Coast Naval Districts were initially uncertain of the implications of the sudden quiet.

They were unaware the submarines were withdrawing toward Kwajalein in the Marshall Islands, for refueling before proceeding on additional patrols or returning to the home islands. Nevertheless, as the convoy continued toward its San Francisco destination, the destination still not revealed to passengers, West Coast radio news broadcasts and newspapers took note of the sudden silence—while the threat of submarines had not entirely disappeared. Unknown to the task force, the withdrawing submarines were moving generally in the opposite direction the convoy was proceeding, with the possibility that one or two might encounter the task force. Captain Rood, on board *St. Louis*, was also unaware of the decreasing attacks, but was taking no chances. Somewhere off the West Coast a Japanese oiler, with a submarine tender, might be waiting to refuel and transfer provisions to submarines capable of remaining on station.[12]

The night of the 26th, and every night during the *Tennessee*'s return to the mainland, Bob Border wondered where Joey might be. Task Force 16, which was pushing into increasingly heavy weather, unknown to Bob, was well to the north, northeast of Convoy 4032. Saturday, Sunday and Monday, the 20th through the 22nd, Admiral Anderson, the Senior Officer Present Afloat, on board the *Maryland*, had overseen varied task force speeds and courses with frequent zigzagging when weather prevented launching scout planes. On the 22nd, the *Pennsylvania* had sighted a submarine at 0725 hours, northeast of Oahu, the formation promptly took evasive action, and there were no further encounters that day. On Tuesday, Wednesday and Thursday—Christmas Day—during daylight hours, all three battleships catapulted scout planes on a coordinated schedule to scour the ocean ahead of them for enemy submarines and surface vessels—while *Pennsylvania*'s radar was in operation. At 1605 on Christmas Day, the destroyer *Flusser* established a suspected enemy submarine contact via hydraphone. Subsequent investigation revealed the contact apparently false.

On the morning of the 27th, with Task Force 16 moving through heavier weather, time was drawing near when the three battleships would, with additional destroyer escorts, split into two formations, with *Pennsylvania*'s planned departure for San Francisco. The dividing of the force began at 1215 hours when three PBY long range patrol planes rendezvoused overhead, and at 1227 the destroyer *Sands* (DD-243) reported for duty from San Francisco.

At 1345 hours the watch on the *Tennessee* sighted three more destroyers which subsequently joined the formation. The destroyers *Brooks* (DD-232), *Williamson* (DD-244), *Gilmer* (DD-233), and *Case* remained with *Maryland* and *Tennessee*, bound for Puget Sound, when at 1419 hours on the 27th, the

Pennsylvania with the destroyers *Tucker* and *Sands* left the formation, turning southeast toward San Francisco.

While Task Force 16 was rendezvousing with the additional destroyers inbound to screen the dividing battle force, at 1326 hours *Pennsylvania's* watch officers sighted an unidentified ship at a range of approximately 28,000 yards, bearing 150 degree true (south, southeast). *Pennsylvania* signaled the ship's presence to the combat force. *Pennsylvania*, now commanding Combat Division Two, was ordered by Admiral Anderson on the *Maryland*, to take charge of the unidentified ship.

Pennsylvania's commander, Captain Charles M. Cooke, Jr., ordered her forward turrets manned, as the unidentified ship entered a rain squall. At 1412 the ship was again sighted, now at 26,000 yards, on a northwesterly course of approximately 315 degrees. At 1424, Captain Cooke ordered the *Tucker* to investigate the ship, which appeared to be a tanker, and simultaneously ordered the battleship's forward turrets to train on the potential target, now bearing 135 degrees true, target angle 000 degrees, range 14,000 yards. While holding the forward turrets trained on the still unidentified ship, Cooke signaled the destroyers his intent to zigzag, and at 1434 commenced zigzagging for 15 minutes.

At 1510 hours *Tucker*, which had left the formation for a closer look at the stranger in their midst, reported it's findings: "Ship was '*Menjsnskii*,' bound for Russia from San Francisco. Nothing suspicious noted."

Combat Division Two changed course to 190 degrees true, heading for San Francisco, speed 14 knots, and at 1542, on a base course of 185 degrees, running roughly parallel with the West Coast, *Pennsylvania* commenced zigzagging on into the early morning hours of the next day.[13]

Aboard *St. Louis* early the morning of the 27th, Lieutenant Charles M. MacDonald, officer of the deck from midnight to 0400, logged the task force and convoy formation courses and speeds. The cruiser remained in the lead, 1,000 yards ahead of *Lurline*, with *Matsonia* and *Monterey* in column astern of *Lurline*. Course 062 degrees, speed 19 knots. The destroyers *Preston* and *Smith* were on anti-submarine screen on *St. Louis's* port and starboard bows respectively. The day began with general quarters called at 0600, followed at 0630 with catapulting the first of two scout planes to search ahead of the convoy, and at 0644 the formation began zigzagging for more than three hours, using Plan No. 21.

Preston and *Smith* continued anti-submarine screening while the *St. Louis* briefly left the formation, maneuvering and changing speed to 15 knots to recover the last of the two aircraft at 1005. The cruiser accelerated to 20 knots to return on station in the lead position, while signaling the formation to again prepare to zigzag using Plan No. 21. Back on station at 1018, *St. Louis* signaled the "Execute" and the six ships immediately commenced zigzagging again. While zigzagging at 1027, *St. Louis* changed convoy speed to 19 knots.

Twice in the succeeding three and a half hours the formation passed through brief rain squalls, the first at 1217 for three minutes, and again at 1350 hours for ten minutes, during which visibility decreased to 1500 yards. Between the two rain squalls, at 1335 hours, approximately 450 miles northeast of Oahu, all three of the Navy combatants sighted, and *St. Louis* challenged, a Navy PBY long range patrol bomber which was ten miles just east of due north of the formation. The PBY, undoubtedly ordered to patrol the sea lane leading to the mainland, and possibly provide more cover for the convoy, correctly answered the cruiser's challenge. As soon as the formation emerged from the second rain squall, at 1400 *St. Louis* again maneuvered to launch another pair of scout planes. After launching the scouts, the gun crew on No. 3 mount, at 1445 hours, responded to orders to test fire 20 rounds from its 1.1-inch anti-aircraft, four-barrel battery.

Meanwhile, on board the *Smith* at 1415 hours, the destroyer's crew received an order from its skipper, Commander Francis X. McInerney, to conduct an "abandon ship" drill.

St. Louis recovered the last scout plane at 1655 hours, maneuvered back on station, and again, as darkness set in along with the period of highest threat, the crew came to general quarters and the formation zigzagged for 15 minutes, until 1741 hours, when the convoy and screens began their night time dash. While the escorts continued their hard-driving daytime submarine defense, life on board the ships in the convoy was equally fast-paced.[14]

On *Lurline* the morning of the 27th, Joey Border arose at 7:30, ate breakfast, walked about the ship and volunteered to help in the sterilizer room, where babies' bottles were washed. She then tended seasick people, and at 10:42, while the entire convoy formation was zigzagging, mustered at her lifeboat station in the "abandon ship drill." Afterward she paused a bit to play some bridge. All day the 27ᵗʰ, she and Barbara Morrison were becoming acquainted with more "gals," including more *Tennessee* wives— eleven others to be exact, some Joey already knew: Anne Shertz, Peg Batchelder, who was pregnant and having a prolonged struggle with seasickness, Nida Renfro, and Nancy Meyer.

The Noble Purser

Among the ship's officers she saw some familiar faces. She particularly recognized one officer. She had danced with him in September, the last night of the voyage to Oahu when she sat at Commodore Berndtson's table for the traditional "Captain's Party." Mr. J.C. "Jack" Fischbeck, the ship's purser.

A pleasant man with a good sense of humor, he was the officer responsible for accounting and bookkeeping on *Lurline*, and much more. He was easy to talk to, thoroughly enjoyed and was proud of his work, was duty-conscious, experienced in making people comfortable and able to enjoy their often "once-in-a-lifetime" voyages—and truly liked people. Whatever occurred on the ship, whatever was planned as an expenditure of time, energy and dollars—particularly activities such as entertainment, which contributed to the welfare and happiness of the passengers and crew, he was the officer to get help to the wounded, the few returning tourists, and help the "thousands of women and children" help themselves—this large, most unusual group of passengers.

Mr. Fischbeck and his pursers had had their hands full, absolutely no doubt, and more than their share of changes in the past nineteen days. First, they had left Oahu on 5 December with their relatively normal load of passengers intent on helping passengers enjoy a vacation at sea on a grand luxury cruise liner sailing to San Francisco—homeward bound. Then came the emergency signal from the *Cynthia Olson*, attacked by a submarine, the Japanese attack on Pearl Harbor, and the abrupt change from peace to war en route, followed in San Francisco with the immediate handover of the *Lurline* and the entire inventory of Matson ships to the United States Maritime Commission, chartered to the U.S. Navy and the conversions of the last two of the three great white ships to troop ships—an abrupt, heavy dose of austerity. The days of commercial adventures and international ports of call were over for the foreseeable future. The Matson Line was to continue managing and operating their ships, but their voyages would be determined by the nation's wartime needs, and during the war they would seldom sail without a naval escort. All their movements on the seas were to be highly classified. And there would be no frills.

Six days later came their first wartime voyage from San Francisco to Oahu. Gaiety and luxury were left behind when they loaded their new passengers and sailed outbound beneath the Golden Gate. The soldiers were adaptable, easily entertained themselves, and were easy to entertain. Enforced sobriety, no bars or lounges where alcohol would be served, and the absence of professional entertainment didn't seem to bother them, while galley and waiter staffs were confronted with more than twice the number of meals to serve—and all the traditional gripes about food normally heard from soldiers far from home.

On the way to Oahu the ship's officers and crew heard on radios and read words in messages about submarines on the attack. As men in the military, the soldiers and their officers had been trained for emergencies, paid attention to the lifeboat drills, and could respond if called upon in an emergency. Nevertheless, the abrupt change from peace to war had had its effects. The *Lurline* had arrived in Oahu on the 21st, and Commodore Berndtson, through Crown and Cooke, had informed the Navy their crew was short 100 people, and morale was low. The Navy sent sailors and junior officers to augment. Now this.

Another dramatic change—with submarine warnings increasing—a temporary hospital occupied what was once a beautifully appointed ballroom, with wounded on cots lining the ballroom floor, so close together there was barely room to pass between them. Some were grievously wounded, especially the burn victims, men with multiple shrapnel and fracture wounds and compound fractures immobilized in casts. One doctor and two nurses, plus the ship's doctor and medical staff. If *Lurline* is torpedoed, how will we get the totally helpless wounded up to the boat deck and into the lifeboats? That will take some thought, planning, preparation, assignment of responsibilities and drills.

But the great majority of passengers were worried, if not frightened, women and children abruptly ordered to leave their husbands, fathers, sons and brothers behind. Many had received two hours notice or less to evacuate, and came with little in hand to face an uncertain future at unknown destinations. Little time to plan, prepare and pack. Worse, it had all happened at Christmastime. Not a good time to say goodbye. Children with absent fathers, many with no time or wherewithal to celebrate Christmas, one small Christmas tree on board ship, no parties or gifts, Santa Claus nowhere in sight. The attack had seemed to devastate Christmas along with everything else, but fortunately, not the spirit of Christmas. The spirit was still alive in the midst of a tumultuous time.

Then there were the worried tourists, trapped in their vacation paradise. They had wondered for days if or how they would ever get home. Equally worried were old time islanders not wanting to leave Hawaii—ever—now faced with the prospect of sailing through waters patrolled by Japanese submarines to an unknown interim destination, and then travel to some final destination they had never seen.

Mr. Fichbeck and Commodore Berndtson needed help. Joey, the *Tennessee* wives—indeed, all the wounded, wives, mothers and children—needed help and some smiles. And that meant get organized, cooperate, and work together to deliver help, encouragement and cheer where needed.

The *Lurline*, like the *Tennessee* and all the Navy combatants, had a speaker system. If Commodore Berndtson granted permission for Joey to use the speaker system, which was accessible on the *Lurline*'s bridge, it offered a way to communicate and organize. A woman's voice on the speaker system, heard by a shipload mostly of women and children, might lift spirits. While there was no longer an orchestra or dance band, dance troupe, a bar selling drinks, gambling tables or slot machines on board, there was a piano, at least one actor and an actress. Joey contacted seven *Tennessee* wives, explained the circumstance, asked for volunteers to take charge of committees and started regularly using the speaker system to ask passengers to participate in the committees' activities.

The wounded, widows, and children should receive priority attention. Joey went to Mr. Fischbeck. He was genuinely interested in bringing order out of an unhappy, chaotic situation, and because of his years of experience in pleasing people, offered advice to her. "How can we best help the widows?" she asked. "Keep them busy," he replied. "Put them to work on the census committee. By feeling needed and accomplishing something, they will keep their minds off themselves and their sadness. We need to know precisely how many passengers are on board, and we don't have a count." From that time on, the speaker system regularly transmitted the voice of Joey Border calling for volunteers to get things done—always with Commodore Berndtson's permission.

"Mighty Mouse" and Committees

The *Tennessee* wives enlisted all the widows they could and obtained a passenger count on the 27th. There were 1807, plus 57 wounded, the doctor and two nurses, more than twice the *Lurline*'s designed, peacetime passenger load. They organized a letter writing committee to work with the wounded, offering to those who couldn't write—not pushing them—to write letters. The ladies would ask the men if they wanted letters written to anyone, what they wanted said in the letters, write, then read them to the men, make corrections or rewrite them if need be, and drop them in the ship's mail for offload at the destination. They read to the wounded, magazines or books, if the men wanted—or simply talked with them. The wounded confined in the makeshift hospital mostly wanted to know about the war. "What's happening? What have you heard or read about the war?" In spite of their wounds, they were defiant and frustrated at their circumstance, wanting to get back at the Japs and into the fight.

There were several seriously wounded men who were quiet and withdrawn, but the great majority were an inspiration to passengers because they maintained positive, light-hearted demeanors in spite of their pain, prolonged recovery prognoses, and anxiousness to again battle the enemy. They didn't complain and were unerringly courteous and thankful for everything done for them. But one wounded sailor was particularly sad. He frequently cried.

Joey held his hand and soon cried with him, as did many others who sought to comfort him. The first time she sat down beside him to talk, and asked him about home, he responded, "You know what I'm going home to?"

"What?" Joey asked. "I'm engaged," he replied. "How am I going to tell her I got my balls shot off?" he blurted out tearfully. They both wanted children, but there would be none. Not ever.

He would have to tell her he could never father children. He didn't know how he was going to tell her, and under the circumstances felt he must break their engagement. There seemed no way to console him.

One of the saddest, yet most inspirational cases among the wounded was an 8-year-old boy in a full body cast. He was wounded in the town of Wahiawa during a strafing attack. The boy never complained, was sweet and gentlemanly.

On the 27th, the children's entertainment committee planned a Christmas party for all the children on board, for Sunday, the 28th, and Joey announced it in advance. The hectic preparations for the rushed 25 December boarding of *Lurline*, the processing of baggage and wait on the docks that morning before the boarding began at 1:00 p.m., and all that had occurred in the days leading to the evacuation, virtually eliminated the normal family Christmas celebration for everyone. The Christmas party committee collected from willing passengers all they could find which might reasonably be given as gifts, and passengers bought more gifts from the ship's store.

There would be a community Christmas carol sing, and Joey, with the singing voice Bob Border loved to hear, volunteered to lead. In fact, during the last days of the voyage, there would be several ad hoc sing-a-longs, in which Joey and the *Tennessee* wives would round up passengers and the wounded and encourage them to join in. The "Star Spangled Banner" and "California, Here I Come," sung as "California, Here We Come," was sung many times throughout the remainder of the voyage.

The *Tennessee* Twelve and Joey—who was gaining the nickname "Mighty Mouse" because of her diminutive stature and ability to obtain results—formed a warm clothes committee and a diaper washing committee, and she announced them on the ship loud speaker. The sterilizer committee was needed to daily assist in washing the large number of diapers and children's clothes. Numerous wives, including some widows who had never been to the mainland and were sailing into colder winter weather, were going to travel into much colder climates when they left the port to travel into the American heartland. Joey and her committee asked passengers who could spare warm clothes to donate them for use by women and children ill-prepared for the cold winter.

Joey's day was full and busy. She was tired when she went to bed at 10:00 p.m., but took the time to remark in her diary,

"Really interesting experience—1807 people aboard—know the pursers quite well—met swell group of gals." As the day drew to a close and the clock moved toward midnight, Convoy 4032 and its escorts, on a course of 058 degrees at 19 knots entered colder weather, with higher winds and a sea state which kept *St. Louis*'s scout planes on their catapults all day the 28th.[15]

Anti-submarine screening was hobbled somewhat in the absence of planes that could search hundreds of square miles along the formation's projected course, but two fast destroyers and a powerful cruiser; the entire formation unpredictably, periodically zigzagging, with underwater listening devices, armed with depth charges, heavy guns, torpedoes and many pairs of binoculars and eyes scanning the rough ocean's surface, presented any submarine commander a formidable, dangerous screen to penetrate. To make matters worse for the enemy, long range patrol bombers were beginning to join picket ships in anti-submarine patrol along and across routes leading into West Coast harbors, the bombers weaving overhead and around convoys and adding to the surface escorts' already substantial power. In spite of all that had happened over the last three weeks, and today's deepening cold, the rough, wind-swept swells, and the nagging fear of submarine attacks, a modest but important Christmas came to the children on board the *Lurline* that morning.

A Late Christmas at Sea

The morning of the 28th, *St. Louis* rang general quarters and simultaneously called flight quarters at 0600, but in the face of the continuing unsatisfactory sea state, secured from flight quarters at 0645. At 0656, after *St. Louis* signaled the formation, the six ships commenced zigzagging according to Plan No. 21, continued zigzagging throughout the entire day, and ceased at 1750 hours, as darkness was closing in. Neither the cold nor the constant zigzagging dampened the spirits of *Lurline*'s passengers.

Joey was up at 7:00, ate breakfast, and then, joining with the children's Christmas party committee, completed the dining room set-up. A small Christmas tree with presents underneath and around its base, a volunteer St. Nick and Christmas carols brought a modicum of joy to many mothers and children on

Lurline that day. The gathering warmed with the singing of traditional Christmas carols such as "Oh Holy Night," "Good King Wenceslas," "It Came Upon a Midnight Clear," "Oh Come All Ye Faithful," and "Silent Night." The ambulatory wounded who came joined in, and afterward, Joey and others went to *Lurline*'s temporary hospital and sang carols for the wounded who couldn't come to the "mess hall" for the children's party.

Joey, mindful of being a mother someday, was particularly taken by the children, and after the party made her way to the sterilizer room to help wash baby diapers and clothes. Later in the day she played bridge, did some typing for Mr. Fischbeck and the pursers, and led more community singing. To celebrate the day, the *Tennessee* wives gathered afterward, and one of the wives, who had slipped a bottle of Scotch on board, passed the bottle around. To Joey, it seemed one thimble full knocked her for a loop. She fell into bed at 11:00, telling her diary, "so tired—. "[16]

Far to the south of Hawaii on the 28th, Christmas finally came to a much smaller boat, ending a far different drama at sea. Captain George Sidan, the master of the torpedoed Matson freighter *Manini*, and the exhausted fourteen other survivors in his No. 2 lifeboat, were overwhelmed with joy to see the destroyer *Patterson* (DD-392) come steaming over the horizon directly toward them. For 64 hours following the *Manini*'s 17 December sinking, they had been constantly at the oars, an hour rowing, two hours resting, battling heavy seas to keep the bow into the wind. On 20 December they were finally able to raise the mast and set sail. Two days later an American bomber passed 800 feet overhead. Certain they had been seen and were about to be rescued, they celebrated with a feast of three cans of tomatoes. But no rescuers appeared.

On Christmas Eve, after vainly attempting to attract the attention of several other patrol planes seen in the distance, the survivors decided to use their last pistol flare. Convinced again their lifeboat had been spotted, they decided to "celebrate our good luck and Christmas Eve," according to the log. Each man received one cup of water. "We are hopeful of being rescued tomorrow," the log stated. It was not to be. Christmas Day brought only more crushed hopes and the disheartening fear that their "SOS" had not been understood. No plane appeared.

On 26 December, Messman Jules H. Simmons died of thirst, hunger and exposure, and was buried at sea. The 27th, the survivors joined in prayer while Captain Sidon read the traditional ceremony and conducted a service. Their prayers must have been heartfelt. An hour later, three Navy planes sighted them and circled overhead, exchanging signals with the boat. A half hour later, a large plane joined the watch over the boat, signaled, "Help is coming," and the next day, over the horizon came the *Patterson*, which was returning to Pearl Harbor from patrol duty.[17]

On the 28th, Christmas came late for another lifeboat of thirteen survivors who arrived in Honolulu, these from the freighter *Prusa*, torpedoed 120 miles south of Hawaii on 18 December. When the *Prusa* was torpedoed, 9 of the 34 crew members were killed by the explosion, including the sole female crew member, Fireman/Water tender Dolores Martinez. The first survivors were picked up on the 27th, and brought to Honolulu, and the second lifeboat sailed 2,700 miles in 31 days until picked up by a Fiji government ship. One of its crew died of exposure.[18]

Another Surprise Attack

Off the mainland's West Coast at 0300 hours the morning of the 28th, the battleship *Pennsylvania* with two destroyers, *Tucker* and *Sands* on submarine screening duty, ceased zigzagging and continued steady on a course bound for San Francisco. *Pennsylvania*'s radar was on and operating. One hour later the formation turned port to 114 degrees. All was quiet. No submarine contacts since the 22nd.

After calling general quarters at 0540, setting condition Zed, all engines full at 15.8 knots, the formation commenced zigzagging at 0608, base course still 114 degrees. At 0715 orders came over the battleship's voice activated speaker system, "Secure from general quarters and condition Zed. Set condition Yoke, set battery defense condition III watches, and set condition III in aircraft." Weather didn't permit launch of her scout planes. Still holding course 114 degrees, in a somewhat more relaxed state of readiness, Combat Division Two's lone battleship and two screening destroyers plowed steadily toward the West Coast.

At 0903, while far to the south, southwest, the passengers on board *Lurline* were enjoying their belated Christmas party on a cold day, *Pennsylvania* received a genuine surprise. With no warning, came a report, "Three torpedo wakes sighted passing port to starboard bearing zero degrees relative!" When sighted, the wakes were crossing dead ahead, distance not specified.

On the battleship's bridge the response was immediate. Flank speed. Turn starboard 50 degrees to 164, a rapid turn away from the attacker and acceleration to top speed. Captain Cooke was presenting the smallest targets possible, *Pennsylvania*'s and her screening destroyers' sterns, while turning back and forth across the base course. The attacker had apparently been lying off the formation's port beam when the torpedoes were fired, and at the enemy's best submerged speed the surface formation was proceeding directly away, opening up distance at a rate of approximately ten knots, almost 1,000 feet per minute, while still zigzagging.

The formation continued zigzagging while opening up the distance to more than three miles from the attacker over a period of 17 minutes. At 0920 *Pennsylvania* and the two destroyers reduced speed to standard while holding the base course of 164, still zigzagging, until 0950 hours, when the formation turned back port to base course 114 degrees. Zigzagging continued. If the submarine's commander chose to give chase at top submerged speed for the entire 47 minutes the formation held a southerly course, his undersea-boat would have been left hopelessly far behind, while rapidly draining battery power and reducing the time it could remain submerged.

The submarine threat wasn't gone. Not yet. *Pennsylvania* had apparently encountered one of the submarines which had been lying off the U.S. northwest coast, perhaps as it was withdrawing. Nothing would please a Japanese submarine commander more than dealing a fatal blow to an American battleship near its homeland—especially one that had survived the Japanese Naval Air Force attack at Pearl Harbor. But fortunately the brace of three torpedoes missed their intended target, and undoubtedly the submarine immediately left the area when its commander became aware his shots had missed and had been observed. Vigilance and readiness to defend against submarines would remain high on board *Pennsylvania* and her screens the remainder of the way to San Francisco.[19]

To the north of *Pennsylvania*'s formation the morning of the 28th, the remainder of Task Force 16, *Maryland*, with *Tennessee* still in column, and five screening destroyers, *Flusser*, *Case*,

Williamson, Gilmer and *Brooks*, began varying their formation's courses at 0611 hours. The first turn was port from 042 degrees to 007—almost due north—then at specified intervals came turns to 032, further right to 064, back to 030, 031, 032, and finally, at 0707 hours the formation commenced zigzagging according to Plan No. 6. Aboard *Maryland*, came the sound of "Church call" at 0955, followed at 1000 with "Divine Services." The day's routine of anti-submarine precautions remained strapped by the weather's denying the safe use of scout planes, and three events that interrupted an otherwise quiet day.

At 1310 hours the *Brooks* signaled a breakdown, but rejoined the formation at 1320, and *Tennessee* sheared out of the formation to port at 1326 hours, also signaling a breakdown. Her crew had temporarily shifted steering to its alternate, as a test, but on return of steering to the bridge, a temporary failure occurred. The problem was resolved rapidly, and *Tennessee* returned to station at 1410.

At 1422 the *Flusser*, listening with a hydraphone, veered out of the formation to investigate a submarine contact, while the *Maryland* accelerated to flank speed and turned to course 042 degrees. *Flusser* reported no submarine contact, but dropped a depth charge over the suspected spot at 1430 hours, as the task force commenced zigzagging on a base course of 005 degrees, using Plan No. 6. At 1700 the formation changed course to 087 degrees, almost due east, then three hours later, while still zigzagging, changed the base course again, to 046 degrees.

At midnight, 28-29 December, Bob Border was only fourteen hours from Puget Sound Navy Yard where he and Joey had met. Tomorrow, perhaps he would be able to leave *Tennessee* and surprise Captain Springer and Florence, Joey's father and mother, and call his mother, father and brother Karl, in Mobile and Pensacola. Nevertheless, aboard *Maryland*, *Tennessee*, and their five screening destroyers, more caution was in order. They were not yet home free.[20]

On Monday the 29th, Task Group 15.6, *St. Louis*, *Preston* and *Smith*, and Convoy 4032, *Lurline*, *Matsonia* and *Monterey*, were beyond the halfway point to the West Coast, holding the same formation held throughout the crossing thus far. The final destination, still unknown to the passengers and crews on the Matson liners, was ever a topic of discussion and speculation. Weather that morning was satisfactory for catapulting scout planes to search ahead of the convoy. At 0652 the first of two launches occurred, and at 0703 the task force commenced zigzagging. The weather didn't hold, however, turned blustery and rough, and recovery operations by *St. Louis* began a little more than an hour later, with no further flight operations the entire day.

Joey Border, wrung out by the previous day's activities, slept until noon, while the purser, Mr. Fischbeck, continued grappling with a load of passengers like none he had ever encountered. He was learning that a pitching and rolling ship full of women and children in crowded conditions, and the women unable to bathe in fresh water, didn't earn a cheerful outlook or smiles at him, but did earn a lot of grumbling and complaints.

As for Joey, a Navy wife, she understood the circumstance, realized it was all for a short time, and the best that could be done had to be done with what was on hand—although she wished it otherwise. She spent her day helping with washing diapers and baby clothes in the sterilizer room, working in the pursers' office, and began spending more time with the warm clothes committee. While the pursers, all *Lurline*'s crew, Joey and the "*Tennessee* Twelve," doctors and nurses, and many other passengers volunteering to help, were daily working to make life as pleasant as possible on board a ship sailing in rough waters, it wasn't easy. The dangerous, wartime circumstances, crowded conditions coupled with tension, frustration, and an undercurrent of fear inevitably triggered some angry outbursts.

Climbing up a "ladder"—an outside stairway—to an upper deck, Joey encountered a seasick Navy wife struggling down the ladder with two children, one a baby she was holding. She caught Joey's eye and muttered and cursed as she went past. "I hate the fucking Navy. Why did my husband ever get into this?"

At least one baby was born on *Lurline* during the return to the mainland, and Joey unintentionally found herself enmeshed in the blessed event, which didn't seem so blessed at the time. She was walking past a stateroom when she heard a woman's loud voice expressing obvious, tortured pain. Joey knocked on the door, and on hearing an anguished reply, entered to discover the woman in the midst of giving birth—alone. The baby's head was already out. Not a mid-wife, and totally inexperienced in this kind of emergency, Joey's immediate response was "I'll go for help," and she started to leave. The woman almost screamed at her. "No! Don't leave me alone!" Joey had no choice. She had to get a doctor or at least a nurse from the "hospital" to help, which she did. Then she stayed and assisted the nurse in birthing the child, an apparently healthy little girl.

When the woman gave her last desperate push and groan of pain, and the nurse was about to give the mother her first glimpse of the newborn infant, the mother's sharp response stunned Joey. Nodding toward the nurse, the labor-worn mother found the energy to snap, "You keep it! I don't want the damn thing!" In due time, the woman calmed herself, the anger subsided, and she kept her baby. Such was the rough beginning for a child born on a bunk, in a stateroom, on a ship carrying her to safety in the early days of the war against Japan.

A Song From the Nifty-Nine Club

The community sings had given Joey and the *Tennessee* wives an idea. A humorous theme song for this trip was needed. Something that would capture the moment, and tell about the Navy wives' travails, and the journey home. There wasn't time to write the music, but the lyrics? They could do that. But to what music? A college fight song. That was it. How about the Georgia Tech (Georgia Technical Institute) fight song? We're in a fighting mood. "I'm a Ramblin' Wreck from Georgia Tech and a hell of an engineer . . . " That's known all over the country, and other colleges and more than a few high schools have adopted the music and composed lyrics to sing their alma maters' and athletic teams' praises. The original music grew out of an old folk ballad, "The Sons of the Gamboliers," and by the early 1900s, "The Ramblin' Wreck" was an established tradition at Georgia Tech. The music had just the right meter, the right attitude to tell the Navy wives' story. They dispensed with the original words, which were:

> I'm a Ramblin' Wreck from Georgia Tech and a hell
>   of an engineer,
> A helluva, helluva, helluva, helluva, hell of an engineer,
> Like all the jolly good fellows, I drink my whiskey
>   clear,
> I'm a Ramblin' Wreck from Georgia Tech and a hell
>   of an engineer.

Oh, if I had a daughter, sir, I'd dress her in White and
   Gold,
And put her on the campus, to cheer the brave and
   bold.
But if I had a son, sir, I'll tell you what he'd do.
He would yell, "To Hell with Georgia," like his
   daddy used to do.
Oh, I wish I had a barrel of rum and sugar three
   thousand pounds,
A college bell to put it in and a clapper to stir it around.
I'd drink to all good fellows who come from far and
   near.
I'm a ramblin', gamblin', hell of an engineer.

In their place they used these words. Joey typed them up, and
at the first opportunity, with the nine *Tennessee* wives who had
been singing Christmas carols and helping with community sing-
a-longs, sang them for the benefit of Mr. Fischbeck, his pursers,
and passengers on *Lurline*:

HAWAIIAN WAR CHANT, OR
NAVY WIVES' LAMENT

I'm a refugee from Waikiki
And haven't had a bath.
We roll and pitch and itch and bitch;
We're on a stormy path.
The children drive us crazy,
The mothers drive us mad.
I'm a refugee from Waikiki,
And crying for a bath.

On Army cots we sleep at night,
With six it's quite a crowd.
We smoke and drink and play and stink,
The noise is awful loud.
I haven't slept a wink, sir;
I'm really in a stew,
And I'm sagging in the middle,
Like a bay horse used to do.

All the seasick girls have manned the rails,
Our glamour's at a low.
Salt water is in all the taps,
We'd love some H2O
And when this trip is over
We'll all be awful glad.
I'm a refugee from Waikiki
And haven't had a bath.

Nifty-Nine Club fecit.

Mr. Fischbeck and his pursers reacted predictably when they heard THE HAWAIIAN WAR CHANT, OR NAVY WIVES' LAMENT. There had to be an answer, with some creativity of its own. But it would take awhile. There were more than enough women, children and related tasks to keep them busy, but they got started on a retort.

Joey's close work with the pursers, among them a young man named Bob Winn, was having its effects—and it was all positive, at least she was convinced of that. But a lovely, petite, honey blonde, personable, energetic, hard driving, hard working young woman apparently confused Bob Winn, who saw her as more than a helpful passenger—in fact someone who might be romantically interested in him—wedding ring or no wedding ring. She wasn't, and when she recognized the signs of more than professional interest he learned quickly it was best to change his behavior and expressed attitude toward her. His shipboard romance never got beyond his imagination.[21]

While Convoy 4032 was closing on the West Coast, to the north, northeast, the now-divided Task Force 16 was in its last day at sea, the three damaged battleships nearing safety, repair and modernization—resurrection as the enemy would learn in the years ahead.

After the early morning surprise of three torpedo wakes on Sunday, the 28th, *Pennsylvania*'s Captain Cooke was taking great care on a moonlit night. Throughout the hours after midnight, 28-29 December, until sunrise on the 29th, he kept the formation zigzagging on the base course of 093 degrees, toward San Francisco. No other destroyers were sent to meet the battleship and her submarine screen, the *Tucker* and *Sands*.

Weather was satisfactory for flying operations west of San Francisco that morning. At 0615, while still on course 093 degrees at 17 knots, general quarters sounded and the command for flight quarters came over the speaker system. While preparations were underway to launch the scout planes, at 0627, after signaling the two destroyers, the *Pennsylvania* commenced zigzagging. Beginning at 0710, the crew catapulted her three OS2U-2 Kingfisher scouts into the air, to add strength to the submarine screen. While the launches were in progress, at 0718, the *Pennsylvania*'s Officer of the Deck, Ensign Charles J. Beers, logged sighting the Farallon Island light, and the formation passed the light, abeam to port at 0851. Four minutes later, the watch sighted the San Francisco light ship and Golden Gate Bridge, bearing 20 degrees north of due east, at 25 miles. At 0937, on orders from the bridge, the crew shut down the ship's radar.

Passing beneath the Golden Gate Bridge at 1042, an event which must have brought a round of wild cheering to her crew, *Pennsylvania* continued on various courses and speeds to Berth One of the San Francisco Naval Anchorage, and anchored at 1142 hours, her journey to resurrection completed.

Battlesnhip *Pennsylvania* (BB-38) undergoing repair and modernization, Mare Island Navy Yard, 2 March 1942. NAPR

Just past noon, the crew hoisted the three scout planes aboard, after they landed nearby in San Francisco Bay, and men began leaving the ship for new assignments. At 1605 hours, the Officer of the Deck, Ensign Terry T. McGillicuddy, logged an event, the details of which are not recorded in history. Captain Cooke asked that the crew be assembled on the quarterdeck, that he might address them, probably for most, the last time.

His words can only be imagined. He may have written them down, but there is no official record. What he did say probably carried a great deal of emotion, a powerful meaning, and perhaps a promise. "On the *Pennsylvania*, we have, together, been through difficult times, the most difficult of which began the early morning hours of 7 December. We have suffered the loss of great ships and thousands of good men, including some of our shipmates. But our shipmates, and those from other ships who came on board to serve with us that morning, will be remembered, and their loss will not have been in vain. Because of those losses, this ship and its crew will never be the same. But we will be back in the fight, and in memory of those who were lost, and for all this nation stands for, we will bring to them, and to our countrymen, the ultimate victory. Good luck, and God speed."[22]

Tennessee Comes Home

Far to the north on the 29th, another drama played out as the *Maryland*, *Tennessee*, and the five destroyers screening them approached the Strait of Juan de Fuca, the strait through which they must pass to arrive at their destination, Puget Sound Navy Yard. Contrary to the relative quiet that greeted the *Pennsylvania*, *Tucker* and *Sands* as they neared the Golden Gate Bridge that morning, Admiral Anderson and the seven remaining ships of Task Force 16 had another surprising round of excitement, and it began shortly after midnight, assisted by light from the moon.

At midnight the remainder of Task Force 16 was steaming at 15 knots, course 046 degrees, ships darkened, with *Maryland*'s crew manning the Number 2 turret and one fourth of her anti-aircraft and secondary batteries. At 0047 hours, with *Maryland* still leading *Tennessee* in column on a northeast course of 046 degrees, the *Case* ahead of *Maryland*, and the four other destroyers arrayed, one on each flank of the battleships, *Maryland*'s watch officers sighted an unidentified flashing light almost due east from their position. Just four minutes earlier, at 0043, the watch on the destroyer *Flusser* sighted a submarine on the surface, to port of the large formation. A flurry of activity immediately occurred on the destroyer's bridge. *Flusser*'s Officer of the Deck, Ensign Donald C. Smith, noted the sighting as the crew heard the "clang, clang, clang" of general quarters and scrambled toward battle stations.

Simultaneously, while ordering the sighting to be signaled to the task force commander on *Maryland*, orders for "flank speed" went to the engine room, to the helmsman to turn to intercept and cross directly over the now-diving submarine's projected position, and the crew was told to get depth charges ready. The probability of sinking the submarine was low, but *Flusser*'s skipper, Lieutenant Commander Beecher, like all destroyer commanders, was trained to take the initiative and pursue an aggressive attack that would at least cause the submarine to turn away from the formation.

At 0050 *Flusser* released a depth charge over the suspected position of the potential attacker, at the same time *Maryland* signaled and logged "Flank speed" and "change course right to 082 degrees true." Admiral Anderson was turning the task force away from the submarine's last known position, again presenting the smallest possible targets to a potential torpedo attack. Five minutes after dropping the one precautionary depth charge, *Flusser* turned to rejoin the formation, and another five minutes later the formation came further right to 097 degrees. By 0113 hours the formation had accelerated away from any submerged Japanese submarines a total distance of nearly four miles, and was opening an ever-increasing distance between them. But prudence suggested the enemy might be operating more than just singly. There could be additional submarines along the course into Puget Sound Navy Yard. Indeed, after changing course left to 077 degrees, more difficulties and greater caution lay ahead, though at 0135 hours the watch on *Maryland* sighted Cape Beale Light.

At 0145 the destroyer *Case*, equipped with the emerging British-invented, anti-submarine detection device, nicknamed ASDIC for its inventors, the Anti-Submarine Detection Investigation Committee, early SONAR (SOund Navigation And Ranging) to the Americans, began "echo-ranging," searching ahead of the formation for the presence of submarines. The device, mounted on the hull, on or near the keel of the destroyer, sent out electronic pulses in a rather narrow, fixed cone of approximately 16 degrees. The electronic pulses bounced off a potential intruder's steel hull within the cone of search, and if a "target" was detected the time lag for the signal to return as an "echo" in the receiver and headset of the operator, provided approximate range and bearing to the target.

Additional course changes, with speed holding 17 knots, kept the formation heading generally east into the Strait of Juan de Fuca, when at 0341 hours the watch sighted Cape Flattery Light 10 degrees off the starboard bow, approximately 21 miles. The task force was coming toward the approximate 14-mile-wide strait from the northwest, and at 0400, at a speed of 17 knots, commenced maneuvering on various courses preparing to enter the strait. Admiral Anderson was bringing the task force into the strait with a plan used in anti-submarine operations in the Atlantic, should the presence of submarines inside the strait be detected. On entry in the Strait of Juan de Fuca, Puget Sound Navy Yard was approximately 180 miles distant.

The signal from *Case* to *Maryland* arrived at 0455. "Enemy submarines present." While the technology was new; and perhaps the operator on board *Case* was new, inexperienced, or was receiving an erroneous reading, the task force commander, as prearranged, signaled for the destroyers to begin dropping precautionary depth charges according to Plan No. 3. The charges began exploding at 0504 and continued until 0515 hours. The precautionary counterattack was intended to either sink any undersea intruders, or cause them to give the formation wide berth. In the meantime, task force speed would take the seven ships out of range.

Additional course changes followed the depth charges as the task force proceeded through Puget Sound. At 0737 the *Tennessee* catapulted an OS2U-2 Kingfisher on inner air patrol, and at 0813 *Maryland* catapulted their first Kingfisher that morning, for intermediate air patrol. At 1000 hours *Maryland* catapulted a second scout plane, and five minutes later the destroyers began one last time, dropping precautionary depth charges according to plan, with *Case* dropping her one charge, set to explode at a depth of 200 feet. After each aircraft launch and release of precautionary depth charges, the formation varied courses and speeds. At 1145, *Case* fell into the Number 2 position in the column with the destroyer *Gilmer* taking the lead position as column guide, 1,000 yards ahead. The two battleships and three other destroyers commenced following the motions of *Gilmer* as she swept the channel.

Aboard *Tennessee*, Bob Border and the crew heard the explosions, and knew depth charges were being dropped. For Bob, it was the last, anti-submarine warfare—or training—he would ever witness or participate in, aboard *Tennessee*, the ship on which he had served since graduating from the Naval Academy with his brother, Karl, on 1 June 1939.

At noon *Tennessee* was maneuvering at various courses and speeds to conform to the channel leading to Puget Sound Navy Yard, and at 1254, harbor pilot, Captain C. Christenson came aboard and took the conn to bring the ship into the Yard. At 1357 hours, *Tennessee* anchored in the Puget Sound Navy Yard, to "swing the ship," in order to go alongside a berth, while *Maryland* proceeded toward the anchorage in Port Orchard Inlet. Three minutes later the tugs *Mahopeg* and *Taknuck* came alongside *Tennessee*, followed at 1418 by unamed tug *132*, to bring the battleship into the dock. At 1456 hours, the Officer of the Deck, Lieutenant Arthur L. Benedict, Jr., logged the *Tennessee*, "Moored port side to dock 6C, Puget Sound Navy Yard, Bremerton, Washington." With 7 December now more than three weeks past, war for her and her crew, was suspended.[23]

After Bob Border's ship anchored in the Yard where he and his family had twice lived in years past, and where he had met Joey little more than a year ago, the wait began for orders for Pensacola Naval Air Station and Naval aviator training. When the day for his departure does arrive, he will gather his personal belongings, pack his sea bag, render his last hand salutes to the Officer of the Deck and the colors flying on *Tennessee*'s stern, say goodbye to a ship that has been his home away from home for almost two and a half years, and walk down her gangway for the last time.

But today, Monday, 29 December 1941, the quarters of Marine Corps Captain George Springer and his wife Florence, Joey's dad and mother, and perhaps Joey, are a short distance from the Yard's Berth 6C. An eternity had passed since the morning of Sunday, 7 December, when he had dashed out of their apartment leaving Joey behind to reach his burning ship and an unprecedented disaster in Pearl Harbor, a lifetime since last he was in her arms in their Honolulu apartment ten days later, nine days since he last talked with her on the phone. He didn't know at this moment where she was, or what she was going through.

The newspapers and radio stations had been peppered with news of submarine attacks along the West Coast and in Hawaiian waters, and Task Force 16 had had its share of encounters leaving Oahu and entering Puget Sound. Joey was at Barbara Morrison's when last they spoke on the phone, she had told him she was going home, and that afternoon the task force had sailed out of Pearl Harbor, destination unknown. Neither he nor Joey had the slightest idea precisely when, or on what ship she would "come home"—nor did either know where on the West Coast she would arrive. The war had separated them in a way neither expected, and both were wondering where the other was, where and when they would be reunited.

Early the morning of the 30th, off the West Coast hundreds of miles to the south of Puget Sound, Task Group 15.6 and Convoy 4032 held a steady course of 067 degrees, making 20 knots. The night had been uneventful, and the daylight was bringing weather satisfactory for flight operations. After *St. Louis* sounded general quarters at 0620, followed by flight quarters, the cruiser catapulted the first of two scout planes at 0659, and at 0710, after signaling the five other ships in the formation, commenced zigzagging according to Plan No. 21.

Following the crew's mid-morning recovery of the two aircraft, and the ship's resuming its station ahead of *Lurline*, Captain Rood initiated *St. Louis*'s afternoon flight operations at 1230, which began with the catapulting of two more aircraft to search ahead for enemy submarines.

After arising at 7:00 a.m. and eating breakfast, Joey spent the entire day helping the warm clothes committee and doing work for the pursers. The further north the convoy sailed, the more pronounced became the need for warm clothes for people who had never confronted cold weather of any consequence. From among women and children, which constituted the great majority of passengers on *Lurline*, *Matsonia* and *Monterey* came the greatest need.

Numerous women and children had been in Hawaii for years, with year round temperatures considerably warmer than on the mainland. Many passengers were headed for the northern tier and heartland of the United States, where winter temperatures were far more severe than they were on the Pacific Ocean stretching southwest to the islands. To compound their shortage of warm clothes, the abrupt evacuation gave them little time to grab absolute necessities, and certainly gave them insufficient time to make thoughtful preparations, including local purchases from already scarce supplies of warm clothes on Oahu, or orders from the mainland—which required weeks of lead time, and now was made impossible by the wartime circumstance. The low pay and the necessary thrift-driven purchasing habits of enlisted families added to the already aggravated shortage. And adding to it all, when departure time arrived, many of the husbands and fathers who would have otherwise been available to help plan for and assist in meeting their clothing and packing needs, were either deployed elsewhere on the island for indeterminate periods or on extended duty hours.

Work on the committee was particularly detailed and time consuming. Warm clothes for children were not readily available except for a few who might have an extra sweater or jacket. Passengers who might contribute to existing needs had to be asked to help, clothes they could give had to be identified, and then they had to be delivered to collection points specified in Joey's announcements. Although Joey had borrowed the ship's speaker system to explain the committee's purpose, to elicit volunteers, and establish collection points, it was necessary to repeat the announcement to ensure it reached all on board. Nothing on this voyage was easy, but passengers graciously responded.[24]

In Pearl Harbor, approximately 1,600 miles southwest of Convoy 4032's position, at 1016 hours Hawaiian time, the cruiser *Phoenix* got underway in conformance with Commander, Task Force 15.0, operation order #2241. At 1220 hours, *Phoenix* was on station, leading another convoy bound for San Francisco, carrying more evacuees home to the mainland. Escorting as plane guards and submarine screens were the destroyers *Perkins* (DD-377) and *Aylwin* (DD-355), and the minelayers *Montgomery* (DM-17) and *Gamble* (DM-15). In the convoy were the passenger carriers USAT *Tasker H. Bliss*, SS *President Garfield*, and the cargo ship *Procyon* (AK-19)—which, under emergency orders, had carried a cargo of plasma and medical supplies from San Francisco, arriving 19 December. Once again aircraft were overhead as an anti-submarine escort until late afternoon of the 30th. At 1930 hours *Montgomery* and *Gamble* peeled out of the formation and returned toward Hawaiian waters while the third evacuation convoy of the month proceeded toward San Francisco, and would arrive 6 January 1942.

The Pursers' Reply

While Joey and the "Nifty-Nine" were busy with the warm clothes committee on another blustery day, the purser, Mr. Fischbeck, and his assistants, had the entire passenger list to consider—for quite different reasons. By the time *St. Louis* catapulted the task group's scouts into the air in early afternoon, Convoy 4032's destination was less than 24 hours ahead. He and the *Lurline* crew had plenty to do to get ready to dock and disembark the passengers, and time was running out for a retort to the HAWAIIAN WAR CHANT, OR NAVY WIVES' LAMENT. Nevertheless, he was not to be outdone and found time to write some lyrics of his own, though he had the same problem as the "Nifty-Nine," with respect to time and musical creativity. Time was short, and he chose to set his original lyrics to the same musical notes of the Georgia Tech fight song.

PURSER'S DIRGE OR PILIKIA MELE

We're off from Honolulu
With Navy wives aboard,
They came aboard in thousands,
A howling screaming horde.

They had more baggage than
The Shah of Persia's train.
The babies, brats and grownups
Give us all a pain.

The ship's full of women,
They lead us an awful pace.
They've trampled us down and kicked us
All over the bloody place.

They beef about the staterooms,
Salt water and the food.
They kick about the baggage
And everyone else's brood.

They don't want to wear
Life jackets all day long,
They've even had the crust to go
And write an insulting song.[25]

Mr. Fischbeck ensured his ditty was delivered to the "Nifty-Nine," on paper and in voice. The word PILIKIA has several closely related meanings such as troubles, problems or bother, and in this instance, the most accurate translation of PILIKIA MELE is MISERY SONG.

The formation continued to zigzag nearly all day, except when launching and recovering aircraft. *St. Louis* recovered the second of its two afternoon flights at 1608 and commenced maneuvering on various courses at 23 knots. Thirty minutes later, with nighttime approaching, came the order "Darken ship," and all vessels in the convoy began shifting to the same status. There had been no submarine warnings all day. At 1703 *St. Louis* ceased zigzagging, holding to the base course of 076 degrees. Joey noted in her diary that night, "-almost there!-"

But where was "there?" That was the question still unanswered for passengers on board the ships of Convoy 4032. The captains and navigators on the three former liners had done a magnificent job of holding tight to information regarding the planned destination. They didn't want to get passengers' hopes up, then have them dashed by an abrupt change in plans. Though the pursers were probably praying there would be no change in destination—an extra day or more at sea with 1,500 women and children would be mind-numbing—there was still no guarantee the enemy or unanticipated wartime circumstances might force a last minute change.[26]

While the absence of enemy submarine attacks off the West Coast suggested Japanese commanders were pulling back their undersea forces beginning 26 December, three deck gun attacks on port cities in the Hawaiian Islands occurred over a two-and-a-half hour period the night of 30-31 December. It was a bright moonlit night in the islands when Hilo on the big island of Hawaii, Kahului on Maui, and Nawiliwili on Kauai, experienced the shelling.

The crew of Japanese submarine *I-2*, responding to orders received on 27 December, first conducted periscope reconnaissance, then surfaced their boat and fired 10 high explosive rounds from her 5.5-inch deck gun at a small merchant vessel moored at Kahului's Pier 2. Several shells fell short, and the others went over the town in the direction of Puuene. Army guns on Maui unsuccessfully returned fire.

At Nawiliwili, *I-3*, responding to similar 27 December orders, fired 20 rounds from her 5.5-inch gun at the breakwater for the Wailua River estuary, but most rounds fell short and damage was limited to a cane field blaze, small shrapnel holes in a gasoline tank and a home, amounting to a total of $500.

In Hilo residents were roused from their sleep when *I-1*, captained by Commander Eitaro Ankyu, surfaced three miles offshore and opened fire on what the crew believed to be a small transport moored in the bay. Actually, the ship was a former World War I "four stacker" destroyer converted to seaplane tender *Hulbert* (AVD-6)—one of the first Pearl Harbor veterans along north side of "The Bowling Alley" to open fire against attacking torpedo bombers on 7 December. With ten rounds of 5.5-inch high explosive shells, the *I-1* crew claimed "moderate damage" to *Hulbert*, a hit to the pier next to *Hulbert*, and one round starting a fire in the vicinity of the Hilo Airport. *Hulbert* unsuccessfully returned fire as did a local Coast Artillery unit.

According to local reports, the submarine sent two rounds ripping through the roofs of piers and among *bala* trees beyond the airport in an evident effort to hit nearby oil storage tanks. The camouflaging of these tanks and other port installations, which had been postponed pending further consideration of coast and authority from home offices, was begun at daylight.[27]

Flight to Joy

Off the coast of central California the morning of the 31st, New Year's Eve, was cold. At one minute past midnight *St. Louis* was still holding course 076 degrees true, making 20 knots, 1,000 yards ahead of *Lurline*, the column guide for *Matsonia* and *Monterey*. Destroyers *Preston* and *Smith* were still on their same stations, *Preston* on *St. Louis*'s port bow, and *Smith* on the starboard bow. Thirty minutes past midnight, *St. Louis*'s Officer of the Deck, Lieutenant (jg) MacDonald, noted in the ship's log, ". . . set clocks ahead one half hour, changed zone description to plus eight." Convoy 4032 had entered the mainland's Pacific time zone.

At 0537 hours, with the *St. Louis* holding on course 076,

the watch on her bridge sighted the loom of Farralon Light approximately 45 miles distant, on the port bow. The Western Defense Command and the 12ᵗʰ Naval District, both of which encompassed the city of San Francisco and San Francisco Bay, had been made aware a convoy from Hawaii was inbound, because eight minutes later the watch sighted a patrol bomber, with running lights on, coming almost head-on toward Task Group 15.6. It was a screening patrol bomber that joined overhead to escort the ships into San Francisco Bay.

General quarters rang at 0620, and at 0645 the formation came left to 049 degrees and began zigzagging, while *St. Louis* prepared to catapult its two scouts to give additional screening coverage. While there had been no submarine warnings during the last days of the crossing, this was not the time to relax. At night, a determined, aggressive submarine captain could have slipped his boat in close to the Bay entrance and waited quietly in the right position to strike.

At 0652 *St. Louis* catapulted the first scout, manned with pilot, Lieutenant (jg) Richard G. Jack, and his observer, Radioman Third Class Robert H. Whalen, followed almost immediately by the second scout, with pilot, Ensign Raymond E. Moore, and his observer, Radioman Third Class Hal C. Norman. At 0710, Officer of the Deck, Ensign George H. Stone, Jr., noted in the *St. Louis* log, ". . . sighted second patrol bomber bearing 045 True . . . " The aircraft was inbound almost dead ahead, to add one more to the three already in the overhead submarine screen.

With a port turn to due north, then back right to 048 degrees—northeasterly—the formation drew closer and passed Farralon light five miles on the port beam. As the six ships approached the entrance to San Francisco Bay, the two destroyers began falling slowly back, protecting the column of Matson liners, then, as the column entered the channel, falling into line with the destroyer *Preston* last.

The evacuees were packing up their belongings they could carry off the ship, leaving them in their staterooms and coming out on decks, a few at a time. They knew they were getting close to "somewhere in California." Talk in small groups at the drinking fountains and in staterooms throughout the days at sea had been of politics, the war and "where will we land in the States?" There had been hundreds of rumors and nothing to verify them. Not one passenger knew where in America they

SUNDAY IN HELL 853

would land, and the officers who did know did an excellent job of keeping it to themselves.

Approximately 8:00 a.m., cheers could be heard erupting as passengers on *Lurline* first glimpsed the Golden Gate Bridge looming ahead of them. Some had tears in their eyes as they cheered in unison. The parade of cheers continued and rolled across the water as the *Matsonia* and *Monterey* slipped beneath the bridge. Home. The Golden Gate. Home safely. Many had wondered if they would ever get home. An unforgettable, emotional event. Now they knew exactly where they were. So did Joey Border, and she knew where she was going—home to the Puget Sound Navy Yard. There was a chance the *Tennessee*, Bob and the husbands of the other *Tennessee* wives might be there.[28]

At 8:27 a.m. *Lurline*'s Officer of the Deck logged her arrival, *Matsonia*'s, 8:32, and *Monterey*'s 8:33. It would take two and one half hours for *Lurline* to dock at Pier 30 N, and in the

Port of San Francisco circa 1938. In this photograph, one of Matson Navigation's passenger liners is moored at Pier 32S, the third slip to the left of the Oakland Bay Bridge. On 31 December 1941, *Lurline* moored at Pier 30N, on the north side of the U formed by Piers 30 and 32. SFHC

meantime *St. Louis*, *Preston* and *Smith* continued underneath the San Francisco Bay Bridge to the Navy anchorage, their mission as Task Group 15.6 complete. Unsung heroes—all.

The cruiser and two destroyers and their crews had now completed two such missions, silently, without fanfare or accolades, almost unnoticed, theoretically routine missions, escorting ships carrying a total of 13,065 passengers under wartime conditions. They had brought the greater part of two Army regiments, with arms, ammunition, equipment, and airplane parts to Oahu to reinforce the island's defenses two weeks after the attack and returned with 3,504 evacuees, including nearly three thousand women and children, from Oahu to San Francisco. The crews on the three escorts, along with passengers and crews on the three Matson liners, had watched endlessly for enemy submarines, zigzagged, weaved, varied speeds and courses day in and day out, dashed full out at night. While leading the task group and convoy, *St. Louis* catapulted and sent scouts ahead in marginal, potentially hazardous weather conditions, and all the escorts and convoy crews had been especially watchful at dawn and dusk when the submarine threat was highest.

Enormous undertakings of great responsibility, under potentially dangerous conditions, and for obvious reasons done in utmost secrecy. Deeds not recorded or given detailed official notice or recognition, except ever-so-briefly in the ships' logs and histories, the letters, diaries and memories of crew members, and perhaps a few passengers.[29]

While coming into San Francisco Bay and during the period harbor pilots and tugs were easing the liners toward their docks, Joey went to thank and say goodbye to the purser, Mr. Fischbeck. In her mind he had done extraordinary work—even noble work—in behalf of all the passengers, particularly in behalf of the wives and children. After she spoke, he thanked her profusely and said, "You've been such a help. What can I do for you?"

She didn't hesitate with a request that surely came as no surprise. "I want a bath."

"Alright. I'll send someone to my stateroom with a bucket of warm water. You can go in and bathe, but don't tell anyone. If word gets out, we'll all be in trouble."

Joey—"What about some of the *Tennessee* wives? Can you send some extra water for them?"

"I'll have a few more buckets brought—but that's it. Word will get out if you bring in too many."

"And I and twelve others need to be the first passengers off the ship. I'm going home today and will take the twelve *Tennessee* wives with me, if possible. I have much to do and can't afford to wait, or we won't make it to Seattle today."

Mr. Fischbeck replied, "I'll let you use the crew gangway, the one I use."

There was a brief pause. Joey had done much to help him, the *Lurline* passengers and crew. After their first meeting during the September voyage to Honolulu, their cooperative work during this far different, five-day return trip had yielded a strong mutual admiration and respect. Just for a moment, a hug for Mr. Fischbeck seemed the right way to part, but both stopped short. Holding to his proper professional distance as an officer on the *Lurline*, he ended their brief acquaintance with, "I don't know if I should get close to you. You might put me on a committee."

Joey and five other *Tennessee* wives, including Barbara Morrison, took their glorious, but sparse freshwater baths in the purser's stateroom. Then, as soon as the ship docked, and the cross-passageway doors were opened to the crew gangway, all thirteen *Tennessee* wives left the ship. She was surprised by the first person to greet her—a Navy chaplain.

After he introduced himself, he asked, "Where are you going?"

At first puzzled, she glanced toward the passenger gangway to see an unusually large number of chaplains waiting on the dock. Then she remembered the wounded on board, and the thousands of wives and children who had been abruptly ordered to leave their husbands and fathers behind. Joey had been anxious to leave Oahu once she understood what she and Bob faced had she stayed. She had been fortunate, decided early she wanted to go home, prepared herself, and tried three days in succession to board the ship. But many of those leaving the *Lurline* today weren't nearly so fortunate, having been ordered to pack and leave on short notice. They might well need a chaplain's counsel and assistance, as well as the assistance of others.

"I'm going home, to Puget Sound Navy Yard."

"That's your home?"

"Yes, my dad is a Marine officer stationed there."

"You *do* know where you're going, don't you?" he smiled.[30]

In spite of the tight secrecy involving ship movements, as

had occurred when the first convoy arrived on Christmas Day, the Navy, Army, Red Cross, and the city of San Francisco were well-prepared for their arrival. The tired, travel-worn passengers received a warm welcome on a cold day.

Once again, a security cordon was set up by the Army, Navy and San Francisco police, keeping the general public several blocks from the waterfront, but this time the press was permitted closer to the wounded and other passengers coming off the great, gray ships. Four receiving stations had been set up quickly as soon as soon as the ships were sighted coming in the Golden Gate. The Civic Auditorium, the Y.W.C.A., the Jewish Community Center and the Women's City Club were ready with beds, food, doctors, nurses, cradles and social service workers.

First to pick up passengers were the ambulances. Down the passenger gangways came the walking wounded, then those carried on stretchers. Arms, legs and heads with bandages on them. Those who could walk limped, leaned on companions, hopped, and hobbled on crutches along the piers, some with cigarettes dangling from smiling lips. Most, including the stretcher cases, grinning, thrilled to be home, but anxious to heal and return to the fight. "Hi ya, ma! Hello, sis! Here I am, baby!" "Fix me up quick, brother, and let us get back. There's work to be done out there."

Some were still and quiet. Others freely told reporters of their and their buddies' difficult and painful experiences the terrible morning of 7 December, without naming their ships or units, each voicing his frustration, anger and determination to get back into the fight. Some were quick to take up San Francisco newspapers, eager to know what was happening in the war world they left behind.

Scores of doctors and nurses worked swiftly but calmly, making them comfortable for the trips to the hospitals in olive drab Army and white Navy ambulances. Some civilians could be seen shedding tears, not of sadness, but of anger at the sight of young men terribly wounded in the attack.

While the wounded were going down the gangways, Navy and Army wives and children crowded the corners and passageways of the ships. Stacks of life preservers were piled high in the corridors, and many of the women and small children were sitting on them, waiting their chance to get off or wondering where to go. Down on the piers, the Navy League Emergency Service girls and trim Red Cross volunteers in light blue uniforms were ready to help. But there on the ships some of the civilian passengers appeared lonely and bewildered. Still, there was no falling of spirit. They had survived, and they would keep on surviving. Finally, down the gangway behind the wounded came the hundreds of women and children and a few men—the vast majority wives and children.

Several hundred private automobiles, buses and taxicabs were waiting at the piers. The National League for Women's Service alone supplied 101 private cars and drivers. The Red Cross sent many more to the piers. As swiftly as possible the civilians were taken away to the four receiving stations. They came from every state in the Union and The Territory of Hawaii. Many of them still had long transcontinental journeys ahead of them.

The children tugged at observers' and hard-bitten reporters' heartstrings. Some gazed grimly at the San Francisco skyline, and when asked questions, they looked up cautiously and answered with care. The reporters knew they, too, were looking back at that day and all that followed. A few talked proudly of their dads' accomplishments, or what they and their mothers had to do and where they hid when the attack occurred. There was little doubt that some of their memories would last a lifetime.

Passengers who needed time and a place to stay while making arrangements for further travel, were taken to the receiving stations. There, food and warm clothing were available for those whose needs weren't met by *Lurline's* warm clothes committee.

As for Joey, her first order of business after leaving the ship with her small carrying case, was to call home and surprise her parents. It was New Year's Eve, and she was certain her dad would be home. "I'm coming home!" Then came even more exciting news. Bob is home! Though her dad and mother couldn't mention the *Tennessee's* presence in Puget Sound, Joey knew by implication his ship was in the harbor. He must have phoned them from the ship. Everything was falling into place. Everything! All she loved was where it should be, in spite of the attack on Pearl Harbor and all the other bases on Oahu, in spite of martial law, the constant worrying about additional attacks, a possible invasion, blackouts, the hectic days and nights after the attack, rationing, the sad funerals, the rough voyage and the threat of Japanese submarines. All she hoped for, all her efforts, and all her determination had paid off. She and Bob were keeping their promises to one another. "Stay as close to one another as humanly possible, under any circumstance." They had been blessed. They both made it home. But she wasn't home yet.

"Unfortunately, dad, I've no money to make it home, or anywhere else—and there are twelve *Tennessee* wives with me whose parents don't live in Seattle or the Yard. If I can get airline tickets and the prices for all thirteen of us, can you wire us the money to fly home? I'll make sure you are reimbursed. I know they will make good on repaying. They'll be thrilled to see their husbands again after all we and the men on the *Tennessee* have been through. Can you and mother make room for them to stay until they can make other arrangements?"

He was a tough Marine officer, knew how to say no. But he couldn't say "no." Not this time, most assuredly not this time. He would do whatever was necessary to get them to Seattle. The Springers could set up twelve beds in the attic. She was elated when he agreed. Joey gave him the names of the *Tennessee* twelve, asked him to notify Bob and the other husbands, told him she would call or wire the total charges, and he could wire the money to the United Airlines ticket office.

She next hailed a taxi waiting at the Embarcadero. The driver was in the line of taxi's waiting to pick up passengers leaving the ships, and knew they were evacuees from Hawaii. "Where to Miss?" he asked.

"Take me to a travel office or airline ticket office," she replied. "I need to purchase tickets to Seattle." Joey was in luck. The A.T. Cab Company serviced the United ticket office at 400 Post Street, on Union Square, and United was the only line flying the San Francisco to Seattle route. On the way to the ticket office, the cab driver, filled with curiosity, began peppering her with questions.

"You just got back from Hawaii, Miss?"

"Yes," she replied.

"Were you there when the attack occurred?"

"Yes."

"Your husband in the military?"

"Yes, he's a Navy officer."

"Was he on a ship?"

"Yes, but I can't talk about it."

"Oh, sure. I understand. Sorry. Didn't mean to pry. It's just that people here get all their news from the paper and radio, and I've never had a chance to talk with anyone who was actually there."

"Did you live at the Naval Base or in Honolulu?"

"In Honolulu."

"Did the Japs bomb Honolulu like the papers said?" "Yes, a bomb fell a couple of blocks from our apartment."

"Yeah, the papers said they bombed Honolulu and strafed cars and people on the streets and roads."

"How was your trip back to the states?"

"Not easy. We didn't know for sure where we would land in the states. Winter weather was cold, windy, and the sea rough at times. Lot of women, children, and seasickness—and it was crowded. But we made the most of it."

"Submarines? I guess you heard that the Japs have been sinking ships just off the coast."

"Yes, there were submarine alerts on our way back, but that's all I can say. We've been told not to discuss military operations of any kind. I realize you want to know what happened, and I would like to be able to tell you. Before I went to Hawaii in September

United Airlines ticket office at 400 Post Street and the intersection of Powell Street, at the northwest corner of Union Square, where Joey Border purchased tickets to Seattle, Washington, for her and "the *Tennessee* Twelve," 31 December 1941. Note the bus parked in front of the ticket office, the same means of transportation they took to the San Francisco Airport at 5:00 pm for a 6:50 pm departure on Flight 11. SFAMC

to join my husband, I was a newspaper reporter in Bremerton, Washington. So believe me, I want to tell you everything I saw and heard, but I can't. We're simply thrilled to be home. "

"Yeah—yeah, sorry, understand. Won't ask any more questions. But I want you to know I'm so happy you and everyone else on those ships came home safe today. People have been wondering, hopin' ever since the first two ships arrived Christmas Day. Thank God you're safe. You are a survivor. You all are survivors. We're just happy to be able to help."

The cab arrived at the ticket office and she asked him to come in with her while she checked on reservations. She introduced herself to the ticket agent and told him she just arrived from Hawaii with hundreds of other evacuees, and she wanted to get home to the Puget Sound Navy Yard, near Seattle, as soon as possible. "Are there any flights available to Seattle today?"

"Yes, Mrs. Border, we have one left late today. United Flight 11 departing at 6:50 p.m."

"There are thirteen of us traveling together. Can you take all of us?"

"Just a moment. Let me check." After a call to the United desk at the San Francisco Airport, he replied, "You're in luck. It's a 21-passenger, Douglas Mainliner Club DC-3, and things have slowed down a bit since the war started, except for business and government travel. And besides, this is New Year's Eve, the middle of the week, and not many people are traveling today. Seats are available. Flight 11 is scheduled to arrive in Seattle at 11:57 p.m. after three brief stops en route. If the weather will allow the flight to go on schedule, you'll make it to Seattle just in time for the New Year."

Joey was elated. "How much are the tickets? And give me the total for thirteen."

"Per ticket, $33.80." Then, turning to his adding machine, "Let me see, $33.80, times 13, is . . . $439.40, plus tax."

"How long does it take to get from here to the airport?"

"It takes an hour by taxi, but we have bus service that can take all of you, with a departure from here at 5:00 o'clock. There's no charge for the bus."

"My dad is going to wire money for the tickets. Can you hold the reservations for us?"

"Under the circumstances, we'll be glad to."

Before she wired her dad, Joey had to quickly calculate other

Exterior of the San Francisco Airport, circa December 1941. SFAMC

Interior of the San Francisco Airport, circa December 1941. SFHC

United Airlines Flight 11, the 21-passenger, Douglas Mainliner Club DC-3 named "City of Seattle," which flew Joey Border and the Tennessee Twelve to Seattle, the night of 31 December 1941. They arrived in Seattle at midnight. SFAMC

expenses, such as cab fees to the airport. Then it was to the Western Union to dash out a telegram to her dad. She now had to shop for one other important item. A negligee. This occasion called for a negligee. She had enough money to pay for the negligee.

She and the driver hurried back to the cab, and she told him to take her to the best lingerie shop he could find. She wanted to buy a negligee—and she wanted him to come into the shop with her, to help select the right one. He knew right where to go, pulled into a parking place, and they went inside.

While she quickly perused the negligees on display, the cab driver was at the front of the shop talking with the manager, explaining who Joey was and where she had come from. She found the one she liked, showed it to the driver for his approval—which he gave with a knowing smile and a nod. When she turned, handed it to the manager to be put in a sack for her carrying case, she asked the price. The store manager, without a pause, quietly said. "No charge, Mrs. Border. Welcome home, and have a good flight to Seattle."

Joey was at first speechless. Then, "Thank you. How very kind." While her dad worked on the money for the reservations, she had to return to round up the *Tennessee* wives, explain what she had done, and ensure they all made it to the airport for the 6:50 flight.

Baggage! Her trunk with the rest of her most prized possessions. The twelve *Tennessee* wives and their baggage. She had the driver take her back to the pier to pick up the wives. They could bring their carrying cases, and any other baggage, like her trunk, they would have to have Matson ship it to Seattle. En route back to Pier 30N, she asked him what all the time on the cab would cost.

His answer once again was an unforgettable surprise. "Nothing, Mrs. Border. No charge. I'm glad to do it. I'll bring the other ladies from the pier to the ticket office, for transportation to the airport."

He made good on his promise. He made enough trips back and forth to deliver all 13 to the ticket office for their rides to the airport. Pregnant, frequently-seasick Barbara Batchelder threw up in the car on the way to the ticket office, but they got their baggage shipped, made it to the airport on time, Barbara got freshened up, and they left for a grand night flight to Seattle.

In the quarters of Captain and Mrs. George I. Springer in Puget Sound Navy Yard there was a flurry of activity as Captain Springer located the twelve cots and bedding to set up in the attic for the arriving guests who were coming home from Hawaii and war in the Pacific.

United Airlines Flight 11 made brief stops in Oakland for sixteen minutes, Medford, Oregon for five minutes, and Portland for ten minutes. At each stop the pilot taxied the DC-3 Club Mainliner, named "The City of Seattle," to the terminal, shut down one engine to offload and onload passengers and baggage, and then took off again. The weather was kind for the flight home, and they arrived in Seattle at midnight.

It was the end of a long, perilous, unforgettable journey, a joyous flight home, and joy was there to greet her. Bob had rounded up husbands and transportation for the other twelve wives and driven Joey's mother to meet her. They arrived at the Springer's quarters, and the next morning, she wrote the last diary entry in her entire life. The last words were. ". . . Beautiful flight—landed at midnight—Bob & mom met me in Seattle—So happy & so thrilled—home & in bed at 2:30— . . . ———And so on for life———"[31]

CHAPTER 14

Love and Sacrifice

Desperate affairs require desperate measures.

Admiral Viscount Nelson

The Japanese attack on Pearl Harbor provoked a profoundly righteous anger among the American people. A wave of patriotic indignation over Japanese duplicity and brutality swept the country. Isolationism virtually evaporated as a public issue, and all political parties closed ranks in support of the war effort.

While the country rapidly united in confronting enemies across both the Pacific and Atlantic Oceans, the pain of the shattering surprise, bitter losses, and unrelenting controversies growing out of the attack eventually mandated an intense, deep look into the events leading to the disaster. On 9 December 1941, Secretary of the Navy Frank Knox, in his visit to Oahu, began the first of eight official investigations leading to the post-war Joint Congressional Committee investigation, which lasted from 15 November 1945 until 23 May 1946.

The committee's exhaustive examination of facts led to twelve major conclusions and twenty-five recommendations, the recommendations couched in terms of "principles" addressing supervisory, administrative and organizational deficiencies found in the Military and Naval establishments. President Harry S. Truman released the Congressional report to the public on 20 July 1946.

Not too surprisingly, the questions the committee posed and the conclusions and recommendations reached did not—and probably never will—satisfy the suspicious, the cynics, or those naturally disposed to conspiracy theories regarding cyclically-restated beliefs President Roosevelt and perhaps a small group of conspirators knew how, from where, and when the attack on Pearl

Harbor was coming, deliberately withheld the information—and restrained the Army and Navy's daily operations that might have otherwise discovered the oncoming enemy fleet. Nevertheless, the committee found no evidence of a conspiracy, and over the years, after repeated examinations of existing and purported "new" evidence, such allegations have been firmly refuted with facts and logic.

On 11 December 1941, the United States declared war on Germany and Italy, the same day the two Japanese allies announced earlier they were at war with the United States. Indeed, in retrospect, despite the immediate tactical success the Japanese achieved at Pearl Harbor and in the six months afterward, the attack proved to be a monumental blunder. Allied with Nazi Germany and Fascist Italy after signing the Tripartite Agreement of 27 September 1940, Japan, firmly seated in the brutal triumvirate of new totalitarians, had fully unleashed the dogs of war in the Pacific. To this day, World War II remains the ultimate measure of worldwide catastrophe and the most destructive war in human history, having taken an estimated 60 million lives.

On 31 December 1941, later the same morning Joey Border and twelve other *Tennessee* wives arrived in San Francisco hoping to be reunited with their husbands at the Puget Sound Navy Yard, Admiral Chester W. Nimitz formally took command of the United States Pacific Fleet. Early the following month, President Roosevelt dramatized the magnitude of the effort the war demanded by proclaiming a new set of production goals—60,000 airplanes in 1942 and 125,000 in 1943; 45,000 tanks in 1942 and 75,000 in 1943; 20,000 antiaircraft guns in 1942 and 35,000 in 1943; half a million machine guns in 1942 and as many more in 1943; and 8 million deadweight tons of merchant shipping in 1942 and 10 million in 1943.

Vanished were the two illusions that America could serve only as an arsenal of democracy, contributing weapons without the men to wield them, or, conversely, that the nation could rely solely on its own fighting forces, leaving other anti-Axis nations to shift for themselves. "We must not only provide munitions for our own fighting forces," Roosevelt advised Secretary of War Henry L. Stimson, "but vast quantities to be used against the enemy in every appropriate theater of war." A new Victory Program boosted the Army's ultimate mobilization goal to 10 million men, and the War Department planned to have 71 divisions and 115 combat air groups organized by the end of 1942, with a total of 3.6 million men under arms. As Army planners had predicted back in the spring of 1941, the United States now seemed destined to become "the final reserve of the democracies both in manpower and munitions."

Late in December 1941 President Roosevelt and Prime Minister Churchill met with their advisers in Washington (the ARCADIA Conference) to establish the basis of coalition strategy and combine immediate measures to meet the military crisis. They faced an agonizing dilemma. Prompt steps had to be taken to stem the spreading tide of Japanese conquest. On the other hand, it seemed likely that the coming year might see the collapse of Soviet resistance and of the British position in the Middle East. In this difficult situation the Allied leaders made a far-reaching decision that shaped the whole course of the war. Reaffirming the principle laid down in Anglo-American staff conversations in Washington ten months earlier, they agreed that the first and main effort must go into defeating Germany, the more formidable enemy. Japan's turn would come later. Defeating Germany would involve a prolonged process of "closing and tightening the ring" about Fortress Europe. Operations in 1942 would have to be defensive and preparatory, though limited offensives might be undertaken if the opportunity offered. Not until 1943 at the earliest could the Allies contemplate a return to the European continent "across the Mediterranean, from Turkey into the Balkans, or by landings in Western Europe."

Another important action taken at the ARCADIA Conference was to establish the Combined Chiefs of Staff (CCS). This was a committee consisting of the professional military chiefs of both countries, responsible to the President and Prime Minister for planning and directing the grand strategy of the coalition. Its American members were the Army Chief of Staff, General Marshall; the Chief of Naval Operations, Admiral Harold R. Stark (replaced early in 1942 by Admiral Ernest J. King); and the Chief (later Commanding General) of the Army Air Forces, Lieutenant General Henry H. Arnold. In July 1942 a fourth member was added, the President's personal Chief of Staff, Admiral William D. Leahy.

Since the CCS normally sat in Washington, the British Chiefs of Staff, making up its British component, attended in person only at important conferences with the heads of state. In the intervals they were represented in Washington by the four senior members of the permanent British Joint Staff Mission, headed until late in 1944 by Field Marshal Sir John Dill, the former Chief of the British Imperial General Staff. Under the CCS a system of primarily military subordinate committees grew up, specifically designated to handle such matters as strategic and logistical planning, transportation, and communications. In summary, in the Pacific theater of operations, the United States and its Allies were to remain essentially on the defensive—but that didn't last long.[1]

Mobilizing American Military and Industrial Might

In response to the attack on Pearl Harbor and declarations of war against Japan, Germany and Italy, the United States mobilized armed forces and a war production base like none ever seen in the history of the world. With the 1940 census reporting a population of slightly more than 131 million, America built the mightiest seagoing fighting force in the history of the world, consisting of 40 aircraft carriers, 24 battleships, 24,000 aircraft, manned by 3.3 million men, plus a Marine Corps of 480,000 men.[2]

Complementing the two-ocean power of the United States Navy, Marine Corps and Coast Guard, the nation's shipbuilding industry produced an incomparable sealift capability. When the war began, the United States had only about 1,340 cargo ships and tankers. Despite the loss of 733 merchant ships of more than 1,000 gross tons prior to the September 1945 victory over Japan, the number of ships controlled by the War Shipping Administration grew to 4,221 with a deadweight tonnage of 44,940,000. Liberty ships and Victory ships comprised the great majority of additions to the merchant fleet, with approximately 2,400 being Victory ships (with another 300 built in Canada), an improved and faster cargo carrier constructed beginning in 1942.[3]

This vast fleet of merchant ships carried the materials and men needed for victory to all parts of the world. Between 7 December 1941 and the surrender of Japan 268,252,000 long tons of cargo left United States ports. About three fourths of this cargo was carried in ships controlled by the War Shipping

Administration. Imports during the war ran to 70,652,000 tons of dry cargo and 35,118,000 tons brought back in tankers. A large part of this cargo was carried on ships defended by Navy Armed Guards. From the outbreak of war to 30 November 1945, over seven million Army personnel and more than one hundred and forty-one thousand civilians were transported overseas. The great majority was carried in Army and Navy transports and in merchant ships.

The Navy armed 6,236 of these ships to the end of World War II. Of this number 4,870 were United States flag ships; 244 were United States owned but under foreign flag; the rest were foreign owned and foreign flag ships. Armed Guards were placed aboard nearly all of the 5,114 United States owned and United States flag ships.[4]

The Japanese attack on Pearl Harbor and the Philippines resulted in a significant, but temporary, loss of strength for the U.S. Navy and initially placed the Navy in a defensive posture in the Pacific. The only weapon system immediately available to take the war to the enemy was the U.S. Submarine Force. President Roosevelt's pre-war decision to conduct "unrestricted submarine warfare" in the event of hostilities with Japan, hastened the wartime success. Throughout the war, the growing U.S. submarine force was employed in attacks on Japanese merchant shipping as well as on Japanese fleet units when the opportunity presented itself. In both these tasks, the American submarine force was aided by *magic*-intelligence derived from broken Japanese codes. The Japanese Navy, with Mahanian intellectual roots, prepared tardily and insufficiently for an undersea onslaught not directly related to the "decisive battle" like those the Empire had waged in wars past. The American Navy won a spectacular victory.

The Japanese Merchant Marine lost 8.1 million tons of vessels during the war, with submarines accounting for 4.9 million tons (60%) of the losses. Additionally, U.S. submarines sank 700,000 tons of naval ships (about 30% of the total lost) including 8 aircraft carriers, 1 battleship and 11 cruisers. Of the total 288 U.S. submarines deployed throughout the war (including those stationed in the Atlantic), 52 submarines were lost with 48 destroyed in the war zones of the Pacific. American submariners, who comprised only 1.6% of the Navy, suffered the highest loss rate in the U.S. Armed Forces, with 22% killed.[5]

When war came with the attack on Pearl Harbor, Army

leaders envisaged the eventual mobilization of 215 divisions, 61 of them armored, and 239 combat air groups, requiring a grand total, with supporting forces, of 8.8 million men. Five million of these would be hurled against the European Axis. War planners emphasized that victory over the Axis Powers would require a maximum military effort and full mobilization of America's immense industrial resources.[6]

On 7 December 1941 the Army consisted of 1,685,403 men (including 275,889 in the Army Air Force) in 29 infantry, five armor, and two cavalry divisions. While this 435 percent increase since September 1939 was a magnificent achievement, brought about in large measure by bringing the National Guard and Reserves on active duty, shortages of equipment and trained personnel were still serious. Over the following three and a half years the Army expanded a further 492 percent, to 8,291,336 men in 89 divisions: sixty-six infantry, five airborne, sixteen armored, one cavalry, and one mountain infantry.

On 16 December 1944, forty-three divisions were deployed in the European Theater of Operations (ETO), including two airborne, ten armored and thirty-one infantry. Sixteen more divisions were preparing to join them. One armored division was on its way to the front. One airborne, one armored, and two infantry divisions were in England awaiting shipment to France. One airborne, three armored, and seven infantry divisions were in the final stages of training in the United States or were en route to Europe, but would not be deployed as complete units on the continent prior to the end of 1944.

At the end of the war in Europe there were a total of sixty-one divisions in the ETO: fifteen armored, forty-two infantry, and four airborne (one airborne division, the 13th, did not enter combat). Also, there were seven divisions in the Mediterranean Theater of Operations (MTO): one armored, five infantry (including one composed of African-American troops, the 93rd [designated Colored in the segregated Army of that era]), and the 10th Mountain. There were twenty-one divisions in the Pacific Theater of Operations (PTO); one cavalry (dismounted), nineteen infantry (including one that did not enter combat, the 98th, and one that was Colored, again, units of the 93rd), and one airborne.

The nation's factories produced a total of 100,408 light, medium and heavy tanks; tank destroyers, self-propelled artillery (officially called gun motor carriages or howitzer motor carriages) and other armored vehicles, to equip the Army and Marine Corps divisions, and provide lend lease supplies to our Allies.[7] In addition, literally hundreds of thousands of trucks and jeeps came off America's assembly lines to help move American and Allied armies forward against the enemy.

The Army Air Force expanded to a maximum of 16 Air Forces, 8 Air Divisions, and 91 Wings totaling a maximum, in July 1944, of 2,403,056 men and women serving at 1,479 airfields or bases and other locations during World War II. At peak strength that year, the Army Air Force was 31 percent of the total Army. To equip the Air Force, Navy, and Marine Corps with aircraft and send lend lease aircraft to Allies, American manufacturers delivered 295,959 aircraft: 158,880 to the Army Air Force; 73,711 to the Navy and Marines; and another 3,714 to other U.S. units, such as ground forces. The United Kingdom received 38,811; the Soviet Union 14,717; China 1,225, with an additional 4,901 to other nations. Among the totals, the Army Air Force received 99,487 combat aircraft; the Navy and Marines, 56,695; 8 went to other services; the United Kingdom 27,152; the Soviet Union 13,929; and other nations 3,172.[8]

The build-up in America's armed forces included women and black Americans in unprecedented numbers. There were 140,000 women in the Army—including 38,000 in the Army Air Force; 100,000 in the Navy; 23,000 in the Marine Corps; 13,000 in the Coast Guard; 74,000 in the Army and Navy Nurse Corps; and over 1,000 Women's Airforce Service Pilots (WASPs). More than 25,000 women applied for WASP training, 1,830 were accepted and paid their own way to training in Texas. The program graduated 1,078 pilots who flew 60 million miles during operations—including overseas—ferrying aircraft of all makes and models. Accidents took the lives of 38, some in training. The WASP organization was disbanded 20 December 1944. They were considered civil service workers and weren't recognized for their military service until 1977, the year the Air Force graduated its first post-WASP women pilots. Congress granted veteran status to those who served as WASP, and in 1979 issued official honorable discharges.[9]

Though blind biases and crippling prejudices against black Americans continued throughout the war to foment a tragic state of race relations in the United States—a blight on the nation's enshrined ideals and evolving American culture—America's black

SUNDAY IN HELL 871

men and women answered the call to arms in unprecedented numbers. In the Army and Army Air Force, though black leaders repeatedly protested the services' practices of segregation and restraint in placing black Americans in combat units, between December 1941 and June 1945, the number of black Americans serving increased from 99,206 to 694,818.[10] Similar practices affected the placement of black Americans almost entirely in service organizations in the Navy and Marine Corps, nevertheless, approximately 165,500 blacks served in the Navy, 19,168 served in the Marine Corps, and another approximately 5,000 in the Coast Guard.[11]

In spite of numerous burdens and obstacles imposed by the state of race relations in America, and continued segregation in the armed forces, black sailors, soldiers, Army Air Force, and Coast Guardsmen—both individuals and combat units— repeatedly distinguished themselves in the war. The first was Mess Attendant First Class Doris "Dorie" Miller, aboard the battleship *West Virginia*, at Pearl Harbor. His performance of duty that day was recognized with the Navy Cross, the nation's second highest decoration for valor, awarded him personally by Admiral Nimitz aboard the carrier *Enterprise* on 27 April 1942.[12]

Without question perhaps the most famous all black units of World War II were the Army Air Force's Tuskegee Airmen, the men and four squadrons of the 332nd Fighter Group, which served with distinction in North Africa, Sicily, and Italy. Eventually commanded by Colonel Benjamin O. Davis, Jr, at that time one of West Point's few African American graduates and the son of the first black general in the Army, the men of the 332nd flew P-40s, P-47s, and finally P-51s—the airplane for which they were best known—in compiling one of the most distinguished combat records of the entire war in the ETO.[13]

In the United States as in those countries heavily engaged in World War II, enormous resources were diverted from domestic uses to military uses. Some analysts calculate the United States spent as much as 30 percent of its Gross Domestic Product on the war effort. The domestic workforce fell as men and women went into uniform, and even though women filled some of the openings left by those who went into the military or into war production jobs, domestic production fell as well—while military production skyrocketed.

As women were traditionally the managers of the home, the

rationing and shortage of domestic resources fell more heavily on women to accommodate. Women's shopping and food preparation habits were affected by having to deal with ration stamps or other rationing methods, as well as the increased likelihood that she was working outside the home in addition to her homemaking responsibilities. Many worked in volunteer organizations connected with the war effort.

In the United States, women were urged to practice frugality, to carry groceries instead of using the car to preserve tire rubber for the war effort, to grow more of their family's food, in "Victory Gardens" for example, to sew and repair clothing rather than buy new clothes, to raise money for and contribute to war bonds, and generally to contribute to the morale of the war effort through sacrifice.[14]

Other than the peak strength of more than 12 million men and women in uniform, reached in 1944, and the huge diversion of domestic resources to sustain the military effort, on the home front, one of the most evident means of wartime sacrifice was rationing.

At the outset of World War II, numerous difficulties confronted the American people. The government found it necessary to ration food, gas, and even clothing during that time. Americans were asked to conserve on everything. With not a single person unaffected by the war, rationing meant sacrifices for all. In the spring of 1942, the Food Rationing Program was set into motion. Rationing would deeply affect the American way of life for most. The federal government needed to control supply and demand. Rationing was introduced to avoid public anger with shortages and not to allow only the wealthy to purchase commodities.

While industry and commerce were affected, individuals felt the effects more intensely. People were often required to give up many material goods, but there also was an increase in employment. Individual efforts evolved into clubs and organizations coming to terms with the immediate circumstances. Joining together to support and maintain supply levels for the troops abroad meant making daily adjustments. Their efforts also included scrap drives, taking factory jobs, goods donations and other similar projects to assist those on the front. Government-sponsored ads, radio shows, posters and pamphlet campaigns urged the American people to comply. With a sense of urgency, the campaigns appealed to America to contribute by whatever means they had, without complaint. These appeals were highly effective tools in reaching the masses.

Rationing regulated the amount of commodities that consumers could obtain. Sugar rationing took effect in May 1943 with the distribution of "Sugar Buying Cards." Registration usually took place in local schools. Each family was asked to send only one member for registration and be prepared to describe all other family members. Coupons were distributed based on family size, and the coupon book allowed the holder to buy a specified amount. Possession of a coupon book did not guarantee that sugar would be available. Americans learned to utilize what they had during rationing time.

While some food items were scarce, others did not require rationing, and Americans adjusted accordingly. "Red Stamp" rationing covered all meats, butter, fat, and oils, and with some exceptions, cheese. Each person was allowed a certain amount of points weekly with expiration dates to consider. "Blue Stamp" rationing covered canned, bottled, and frozen fruits and vegetables, plus juices and dry beans, and such processed foods as soups, baby food and catsup. Ration stamps became a kind of currency with each family being issued a "War Ration Book." Each stamp authorized a purchase of rationed goods in the quantity and time designated, and the book guaranteed each family its fair share of goods made scarce, thanks to the war.

Rationing also was determined by a point system. Some grew weary of trying to figure out what coupon went with which item, or how many points they needed to purchase them, while some coupons did not require points at all. In addition to food, rationing encompassed clothing, shoes, coffee, gasoline, tires, and fuel oil. With each coupon book came specifications and deadlines. Rationing locations were posted in public view. Rationing of gas and tires highly depended on the distance to one's job. If one was fortunate enough to own an automobile and drive at the then specified speed of 35 mph, one might have a small amount of gas remaining at the end of the month to visit nearby relatives. Added to the mix were the suspension of domestic automobile manufacturing and the near overwhelming commitment of the nation's transportation systems to the movement of the military, its equipment, and millions of tons of supplies to bases, ports and overseas Allies.

Rationing resulted in one serious side effect, the black market, where people could buy rationed items on the sly, but at higher prices. The practice provoked mixed emotions from those who banded together to conserve as instructed, as opposed to those who fed the black market's subversion and profiteering. For the most part, black marketers dealt in clothing and liquor in Britain, and meat, sugar and gasoline in the United States.

While life during the war meant daily sacrifice, few complained because they knew it was the men and women in uniform who were making the greater sacrifice. A poster released by the Office of War Information stated simply, "Do with less so they'll have enough." And yet another pleaded, "Be patriotic, sign your country's pledge to save the food." On the whole, the American people united in their efforts.

Recycling was born with the government's encouragement. Saving aluminum cans meant more ammunition for the soldiers. Economizing initiatives seemed endless as Americans were urged to conserve and recycle metal, paper and rubber. To provide war funds, war bonds and stamps were sold, and the American people also united through volunteerism. Communities joined together to hold scrap iron drives, schoolchildren pasted saving stamps in bond books, and even elementary schools "bought" tanks or other equipment through purchases of savings stamps and bonds.

Others planted "Victory Gardens" to conserve food. For a small investment in soil, seed and time, families could enjoy fresh vegetables for months. By 1945, an estimated 20 million victory gardens produced approximately 40 percent of America's vegetables.

Training sessions were held to teach women to shop wisely, conserve food and plan nutritious meals, as well as teach them how to can food items. The homemaker planned family meals within the set limits. The government's persuading of people to give up large amounts of red meats and fats resulted in people eating more healthily.

The government also printed a monthly meal-planning guide with recipes and a daily menu. *Good Housekeeping* magazine printed a special section for rationed foods in its 1943 cookbook. Numerous national publications also featured articles explaining what rationing meant to America.

Then there were the food manufacturers who took advantage of the wartime shortages to flaunt their patriotism to their profit. Kraft Macaroni and Cheese Dinner in its familiar blue box, gained great popularity as a substitute for meat and dairy products. Two boxes required only one rationing coupon, which resulted in 80 million boxes sold in 1943. Food substitutions became evident with real butter being replaced with Oleo margarine. Cottage cheese took on a new significance as a substitute for meat, with sales exploding from 110 million pounds in 1930 to 500 million pounds in 1944.

After three years of rationing, World War II came to a welcome end. Rationing, however, did not end until 1946. Life resumed as normal, and the consumption of meat, butter and sugar inevitably rose. While Americans still live with some of the results of World War II, rationing has not returned.[15]

The Accounting

While Japanese tactical and strategic successes mounted in the nearly six months following the attack on Pearl Harbor, the relentless mobilization and build-up of the American industrial base and armed forces continued. Throughout the first five months of 1942, the Japanese drove deeper into the South Pacific and Southeast Asian regions, inflicting a string of defeats on America and its Allies.

Japan's operation plan for phase one of their war plan was based upon a finely calculated distribution of forces. Their Army was comprised of 51 divisions and 59 brigades in December 1941, but only ten divisions and four brigades each were allocated to their four offensive armies, the remaining 11 divisions and 43 brigades held in Japan and China in the event that alternative courses of action had to be adopted. The primary objective of the offensive was the rich Southern Resources Area, whose seizure, the Japanese believed, would not be possible without also capturing the Philippines and neutralizing the United States Pacific Fleet.

Operations began with the attack on Pearl Harbor. Similar strikes followed almost simultaneously in the Philippines, Malaya, Hong Kong, Guam and Wake Islands. Then landings were made in the Philippines and Malaya to initiate a two-pronged drive on Java. Concurrently, the Japanese planned to occupy Guam, Wake, and Hong Kong, and invade Borneo. The almost simultaneous execution of operations against widely separated objectives attests to the thoroughness of Japanese planning.

From the Chinese mainland, the Japanese invaded the British Crown Colony of Hong Kong at 0800 hours, 8 December, and the garrison surrendered on Christmas Day. The Japanese suffered 2,754 casualties. The British lost 11,848.

The attack on Malaya also came with startling swiftness early on 8 December, when at 0430 in the morning the Japanese bombed airfields in Singapore and northern Malaya. On 10 December enemy aircraft sank the British battleship *Prince of Wales*, and the battle cruiser *Repulse* off Kuantan, Malaya, another demonstration of the demise of surface fleets which have no effective air cover. The Malayan campaign lasted until 15 February 1942, when British Lieutenant General Arthur Percival surrendered Singapore to Lieutenant General Tomoyuki Yamashita the commander of the Japanese 25th Army. The fall of Singapore came when Percival had only two days supply of ammunition remaining, and followed a string of battlefield defeats and some brutal atrocities by Japanese troops, including the killing of over 300 doctors, nurses and patients—most by bayonets—at the Alexandra Hospital in Singapore, and other atrocities committed against British troops. When Yamashita learned of the incident at the hospital he had the Japanese soldiers responsible executed at the hospital.

The British sustained 138,708 killed, wounded and captured, and Yamashita's Army suffered 9,824 total casualties. Their crushing defeat of the Allies in Malaya opened the Indian Ocean to the Japanese and imperiled Sumatra, Java, and Borneo.[16]

Then, in another string of successes January through March 1942, the Japanese took Sumatra, Java, Borneo, the Celebes, Bali and Timor, pressing ever closer to New Guinea and Australia. The Netherland East Indies, rich in oil, rubber, and other strategic materials, were to be the treasure house of Japan's Greater East Asia Co-Prosperity Sphere. During the Japanese advance into the Dutch East Indies, on 27 February their Navy inflicted a defeat on a combined American, British, Dutch, and Australian fleet in the Battle of the Java Sea. The defeat cost eight Allied warships sunk with the loss of approximately 2,000 officers and sailors.[17]

While the Japanese pressed their assault toward the south and southeast in the treasure house of the Dutch East Indies, behind their advance they continued their offensive against the Philippines, while other task forces fanned out to seize the strategic island chains that were to form the defensive perimeter about their rich conquests. As part of this operation, the Japanese Fourth Fleet steamed south in late January and on the 23rd seized Rabaul on the island of New Britain in the Bismarck Archipelago. Most of the available Australian forces had been sent to Singapore and the East Indies. Their few remaining soldiers and planes did what they could to defend a wide area of territory under the jurisdiction of Australia, but were overwhelmed. Rabaul had one of the finest natural harbors in the Pacific and ample terrain suitable for airfields. From Rabaul, they continued their methodical, leapfrog advance, constructing airfields as they moved southward, island by island.[18]

As the Japanese tightened their grip on their island targets, on 19 February they unleashed another devastating surprise air raid, this time on Darwin Australia. It was to be the first of 63 raids on Darwin, through 1943, and the Japanese veterans of Pearl Harbor had major roles in the raid.

Most of the attacking planes came from the four aircraft carriers of the Imperial Japanese Navy's Carrier Division 1 (*Kaga* and *Akagi*) and Carrier Division 2 (*Hiryu* and *Soryu*) commanded by Admiral Chuichi Nagumo, who led the Japanese carrier strike force at Pearl Harbor. Land-based heavy bombers were also involved. The Japanese launched two waves of planes, comprising 242 bombers and fighters. Darwin was relatively well covered by antiaircraft guns. However, the only operational Royal Australian Air Force (RAAF) fighter squadrons were in Europe, North Africa, or the Middle East; the only modern fighters based in Darwin were 11 P-40s from the US Army Air Force's 33rd Pursuit Squadron, in addition to lightly armed and obsolete training and patrol aircraft belonging to the RAAF. An experimental radar station was not yet operational.

The first wave of 188 Japanese planes, led by naval Commander Mitsuo Fuchida, their mission leader at Pearl Harbor, took off at 8:45 a.m. At about 9:15 a.m., it was spotted by an Australian Coast Watcher on Melville Island (Northern Territory), then by Father John McGrath, a Catholic Priest conducting missionary work on Bathurst Island (Northern Territory). The latter would send the message, "An unusually large air formation bearing down on us from the northwest." Darwin received both warnings at least twice by radio, no later than 9:37 a.m., however, ten US P-40E

Kittyhawk fighters and an LB-30 Liberator had just departed Darwin, and the Australian duty officer assumed this was the same formation. The warnings were not acted upon. Thus, as had occurred at Pearl Harbor just months earlier on 7 December, Darwin's final chance to make last-minute preparations for the impending raid slipped away. The attackers arrived at their target just before 10:00 a.m.

Fuchida later wrote of the raid:

> The job to be done seemed hardly worthy of the Nagumo Force. The harbor, it is true, was crowded with all kinds of ships, but a single pier and a few waterfront buildings appeared to be the only port installations. The airfield on the outskirts of the town, though fairly large, had no more than two or three small hangars, and in all there were only twenty-odd planes of various types scattered about the field. No planes were in the air. A few attempted to take off as we came over but were quickly shot down, and the rest were destroyed where they stood. Anti-aircraft fire was intense but largely ineffectual, and we quickly accomplished our objectives.

In fact, the Japanese encountered five of the USAAF P-40s, which had recently returned from an aborted mission over Timor and were still carrying drop tanks. With both numbers and surprise on their side, Japanese fighters shot down all of the US planes, except one piloted by Lieutenant Robert Ostreicher. A total of 81 Nakajima B5N "Kate" torpedo bombers then attacked shipping—at least 45 vessels—in the harbor, while 71 Aichi D3A "Val" dive-bombers, escorted by 36 Mitsubishi A6M Zero fighter planes attacked RAAF bases, civil airfields, and a hospital. Ostreicher shot down two Vals and managed to survive the attack, but no Allied planes successfully took off, and all were destroyed or rendered unable to fly after the first attack. By about 10:40 a.m. the first wave of Japanese planes had left the area.

Just before midday, there was a high altitude attack by land-based bombers, concentrated on the Darwin RAAF Airfield: 27 Mitsubishi G3M "Nell" bombers, the same type to launch the first raid on Wake Island, flew from Ambon and 27 Mitsubishi

G4M "Betty" bombers from Kendari, Sulawesi. This second raid lasted for 20-25 minutes.

In spite of Fuchida's assessment of the anti-aircraft fire as "largely ineffectual," the lack of armor and self-sealing fuel tanks in many Japanese planes, as well as the prolonged low-level strafing runs carried out, made pilots and planes exceptionally vulnerable to ground fire. Most Australian sources say that four Japanese planes were destroyed in Australian airspace; it has been suggested that several more failed to return to their carriers or bases.

Casualties, damage, and consequences following the attack included sunken ships, a burnt-out wharf in Darwin Harbor, and 243 civilians and military personnel killed, most of them on the sunken ships. Over 400 people were wounded and 200 of these were seriously injured. The total number of these people who died from their wounds was not recorded.

The air raids caused chaos in Darwin. Most of the essential services were destroyed. Fear of an imminent invasion spread, and there was a wave of refugees as half of the town's civilian population fled. There were reports of looting and in some cases— it was alleged—the culprits were Provost Marshals. Many civilian refugees never returned or did not return for many years, and in the post-war years some claimed that land they owned in Darwin had been expropriated by government bodies in their absence.

According to official figures, 278 servicemen were considered to have deserted as a result of the raids, although it has been argued that the "desertions" mostly resulted from ambiguous orders given to RAAF ground staff during the attack.

Eight ships were sunk in Darwin Harbour: the United States Navy destroyer *Peary*, the USAT *Meigs*, which had arrived in Brisbane with the *Pensacola* Convoy on 22 December, the Australian patrol boat HMAS *Mavie* and the merchant ships *British Motorist*, *Kelat*, *Mauna Loa*, *Neptuna* and *Zealandia*. Among the ships damaged but not destroyed was a hospital ship, AHS *Manunda*.

The USAAF lost 10 P-40s, one B-24 bomber, and three C-45 transport planes. The US Navy lost three PBY Catalina flying boats. The RAAF lost six Lockheed Hudsons.

The success of the Darwin raid led to calls within the Japanese Navy for an invasion of Australia. Admiral Osami Nagano, the Chief of the Navy General Staff, was in favor. But the Imperial

Japanese Army lacked the troops for such an undertaking and Admiral Isoroku Yamamoto's plan for an attack on Midway Island was preferred.

The Allied navies largely abandoned the naval base at Darwin after the attack, dispersing most of their forces to Brisbane, Freemantle and smaller ports. Conversely, Allied air commanders launched a major build-up in the Darwin area, building more airfields and deploying many squadrons.[19]

Internment of Japanese and Japanese-Americans in the Continental United States

One day before the Japanese raid on Darwin, Australia, President Roosevelt issued United States Executive Order 9066, using his authority as Commander-in-Chief to exercise war powers to send ethnic groups to internment camps.

This order authorized U.S. Armed Forces commanders to declare areas of the United States as military areas "from which any or all persons may be excluded." It was eventually applied to one-third of the land area of the U.S. (mostly in the West) and was used against those with "Foreign Enemy Ancestry."

The order led to the Japanese American internment in which some 110,000 ethnic Japanese people were held in internment camps for the duration of the war. Of the Japanese interned, 62 percent were *Nisei* (American-born, second-generation Japanese American) or *Sansei* (third-generation Japanese American) and the rest were *Issei* (Japanese immigrants and resident aliens, first-generation Japanese American).

Secretary of War Henry L. Stimson was to assist those residents of such an area who were excluded, with transport, food, shelter, and other accommodations. Americans of Japanese ancestry were by far the most widely affected, as all persons with Japanese ancestry were removed from the West Coast and southern Arizona, including orphan infants. Americans of Italian and German ancestry were targeted by these restrictions, including internment.

Contrary to conventional wisdom, there was opposition to

President Roosevelt's impending signature on the order. Notably, one of the few voices in Washington opposed to internment was FBI Director J. Edgar Hoover. By the time of World War II, after nearly a decade of Democratic control of Washington under President Roosevelt, Hoover was one of the few Republicans left with any power. His opposition to internment is ironic, considering how some labeled his career as one in opposition to civil liberties. Eleanor Roosevelt was also opposed to Executive Order 9066. She spoke privately many times with her husband, but was unsuccessful in convincing him not to sign it.[20]

Simultaneously with planning for a mass evacuation of Japanese residents from the West Coast of the United States, Army authorities in Hawaii and Washington proposed a similar mass evacuation from Hawaii as a measure of defense. Martial law had given the Army almost plenary authority over both citizens and aliens. As a result, there were no legal barriers to prevent the Army from handling the large Japanese population as it wished, but there were other factors. Among them were the Hawaiian climate of racial tolerance, the fact that most of the pressure for mass evacuation came from outside the Army, and the unquestionable importance of the Japanese in the civilian labor force—as farmers, fishermen, everyday workers and shop owners. All these factors operated as powerful checks on proposals to move a large part of the Japanese population from Oahu to another island or the mainland.

Two other factors operative in the eventual resolution of this vexing problem, were the needs for additional manpower to perform the expanded missions of units already defending the islands, and the decision to evacuate more than 20,000 American civilians from the island—already under way with the three convoys which left Oahu by the end of December—and which the Army and Navy considered higher priority.

After a prolonged discussion within the government and military, in which, on the one hand, President Roosevelt and Secretary of the Navy Frank Knox favored moving the Japanese population on Oahu to an outlying island, and General Emmons and Admiral Bloch on Oahu favored evacuation of a limited number of the "more dangerous" elements of the Japanese population to the mainland, the government finally concluded it couldn't incarcerate the entire population of some 155,000 to158,000 Japanese-Americans. (General Emmons estimated the population was 118,000.) In the end, approximately 2,000 Japanese-Americans—influential Buddist priests, political figures, and business leaders—were treated as enemy aliens—and sent to the mainland to be interned. There was to be one other indignity suffered by Japanese Americans, one which they would overcome by their voluntary service in World War II.[21]

After the bombing of Pearl Harbor, with the loyalty of the Japanese Americans in sharp question, they were classified 4C (Enemy Alien), making them ineligible for the draft. In Hawaii, where in 1941 an increasing number of Japanese Americans had joined the Hawaiian Territorial Guard during the pre-war build-up, and the 298th and 299th Regiments of the National Guard of Hawaii were—immediately after the attack—engaged in providing for the defense of Oahu, General Emmons disbanded the regiments, without explanation, in the period after the Army's 34th and 161st Regiments and other reinforcements began arriving.

Swallowing their outrage, the discharged veterans of the Hawaiian Territorial Guard offered their services in whatever capacity that the Army might choose to use them. These tasks usually consisted of cleaning up the grounds, building new installations, and other menial jobs that the volunteers performed with diligence, dedication, and no complaints. On 25 February 1942, the all-*nisei* Varsity Victory Volunteers (Triple V) formed in Hawaii as part of the 34th Combat Engineers. As a result, General Emmons reversed his decision and recommended to the War Department that the Japanese Americans should be formed into a special unit and be sent to the mainland for training.

On 26 May 1942, days before the decisive naval battle at Midway, General George C. Marshall issued orders establishing the Hawaiian Provisional Battalion. On 5 June, one day after news of the resounding Japanese defeat at Midway, the Provisional Battalion, consisting of 1,300 men and 29 officers under the command of Lieutenant Colonel Farrant Turner sailed for the mainland and training. On 12 June 1942, the 100th Infantry Battalion was activated and assigned to the Second Army at Camp McCoy, Wisconsin. Because of their excellent training record and a steady stream of petitions and interventions by prominent Americans, both civilian and military, the War Department was forced to reopen military service to Americans of Japanese ancestry.

The Army began activating the 442nd Regimental Combat

Team on 1 February 1943. President Roosevelt announced the forming of the 442nd RCT with the famous words, "Americanism is not, and never was, a matter of race or ancestry." The call to arms was sounded, and those that answered astounded the Army. The original plan called for a quota of 3,000 volunteers from the mainland and 1,500 from Hawaii. Nearly 10,000 Hawaiian *nisei* volunteered, and over 2,600 were accepted. From the Japanese in the internment camps on the mainland, only 1,256 *nisei* volunteered. There were some 23,606 *nisei* of draft age in the camps. From the camp volunteers, around 800 were inducted into the Army.

By June 1943, the 442nd RCT arrived at Camp Shelby, Mississippi, where the 100th Battalion was just finishing up advanced training. There were reunions of cousins and old friends in addition to some sibling rivalry. The island boys were known as "buddaheads" (a pidgin English and Japanese term, butahead, meaning pig headed), and *nisei* mainlanders were called "kotonks" or "stone head." Kotonk is sometimes described as the sound of an empty head hitting the ground.

Many fights broke out between the two units during their time together at Camp Shelby, but slowly a mutual respect developed, and soon the 100th Battalion was called and went overseas while the 442nd started their training.

In July 1943, the 100th Infantry Battalion received its colors emblazoned with the motto, "Remember Pearl Harbor." It was time for the men of the 100th Battalion to set off and prove themselves. On 11 August 1943, they left Camp Shelby for North Africa. It would be nine long months of heavy fighting before the 442nd would team up with the 100th in Italy. There, in Italy, at the battle for Monte Cassino, one of the longest, bloodiest battles in Italy, was the beginning of two of the most distinguished combat records found in the United States Army of World War II. The "original" 100th Battalion became known as "The Purple Heart Battalion" and "the little iron men," and units of the 442nd RCT fought in Italy, France and Germany, and were involved in the liberation of the Dachau prison camp outside Munich.

In July 1945, there were 20,289 *nisei* men in the Army, and in all, over 33,000, including women, served in World War II. Nearly 800 Japanese Americans made the ultimate sacrifice.[22]

The Turning

While Japanese Americans were being interned in the continental United States in early 1942, Hawaii and Australia were being reinforced, and the American mobilization was moving at a sharply accelerated pace, the Japanese Army and Navy continued making astounding gains in the Pacific. Nevertheless, their Navy's anticipated six months of holding their flanks free of the Pacific Fleet's interference with their Empire war plan would soon run afoul of an American military trained and geared to take the offensive. The first hint of trouble ahead came in the Philippine Archipelago, comprising 7,000 islands lying only 500 miles from the China coast, and dominating the eastern approaches to the South China Sea.

Though the Japanese virtually destroyed the small American Asiatic Fleet (only three destroyers escaped to Australia) and inflicted shocking defeats on the Allies in the South Pacific and South China Sea, General Douglas MacArthur's United States Army Forces Far East (USAFFE), composed of American and Philippine Army units fought determinedly on the main island of Luzon against a better trained, experienced 43,110-man Japanese Fourteenth Army, commanded by Lieutenant General Masaharu Homma.

General MacArthur had been designated military advisor to the Philippine Commonwealth in 1935, and in the years that followed assisted the Filipinos in building their Army toward maturity and promised national independence in 1946. Ably assisted by a small group of military men, including Major Dwight D. Eisenhower, he prepared plans for a Philippine defense establishment. As tension increased between the Japanese and American governments following the outbreak of the war in Europe, he was recalled to active duty 26 July 1941. In spite of the "Germany First" strategy conceived in January 1941 and written into the Army's over-all Rainbow-5 war plan, he immediately injected optimism—primarily based on claims for the offensive capabilities of the new B-17 bomber and the spirit of the offensive built into the plan for the defense of the Philippines. Defeat was no longer conceded, the enemy would be met on the beaches, and the entire archipelago would be defended. Reinforcements began moving to Luzon, and it was expected that by April 1942, USAFFE would be strong enough to hold the islands. But the Japanese had other ideas.

On 27 November 1941, the day the war warning message came from General Marshall, USAFFE went on full alert. In spite of the approximate 130,000-strong USAFFE, which included 13,507 U.S. ground troops, the Japanese Fourteenth Army expected to complete the capture of Luzon in fifty days—after successfully completing the preliminary landing of its first unit of 2,000 men at Aparri on northern Luzon on 10 December. The landing was the same day Japanese bombers from Formosa devastated USAFFE by striking airfields and destroying half its new, B-17 heavy bombers and modern fighters on the ground, most at Clark Field.

The Philippine and American units on Luzon mounted a spirited defense, but were gradually pushed toward southern Luzon, until 7 January, when the remaining USAFFE units withdrew and were compressed behind a line across the upper Bataan Peninsula, which was across Manila Bay, to the west of the capital. By then it was clear USAFFE would have to fight with what they had. There would be no reinforcements or effective re-supply—which had even been attempted by submarines when only three ships had managed to slip through the Japanese Army and Navy's tightening noose. The defenders, cut off from re-supply, were growing weaker by the day with malnutrition and casualties. Also, as medical supplies dwindled, diseases such as malaria, dengue, dysentery, and beriberi made inroads, sanitation dropped, convalescent periods lengthened, and significantly, nerve fatigue—in the absence of rest areas—became more serious.

General MacArthur declared his intent to remain to the last, but on 23 February President Roosevelt ordered him to Australia to assume command of Allied forces in the Southwest Pacific. On the night of 12 March, accompanied by his family and some of his staff, he left the island fortress of Corregidor via PT boats for the island of Mindanao, and transferred to B-17s for the last leg of the journey. Just before departing, MacArthur reorganized his forces into four commands, the Mindanao, Visayas, Harbor Defenses, and Luzon Force, all to be responsible to him in Australia through an advance headquarters on Corregidor.

On 9 April, the Luzon force of 76,000 surrendered, and began the infamous "Death March" to Camp O'Donnell. Homma, angered that the surrender had not included all the troops in the Philippines, turned to Corregidor. The Japanese had kept the island fortress under sporadic air and artillery attack since early February, but the defenders now received the concentrated fire of all the Japanese heavy artillery and aircraft. By early May, Corregidor's defenders were dazed from the continuous bombardment, and their water supply was critically short. On the night of 5 May, the Japanese managed to land one battalion near the west end of the island and soon reinforced it with another. Their plan to land a larger force near the east end of the island the next night, though undertaken, proved unnecessary, for by noon on 6 May, Major General Jonathon M. Wainwright had initiated negotiations to surrender the 11,000 troops in the island forts.

For General Homma, his command and victory in the Philippines proved hollow and eventually brought his undoing. His planned fifty-day campaign lasted 157 days. He was soon relieved of command and ordered to Tokyo, retired, and lived in semi-seclusion until the end of the war. The man the Japanese called "The Poet General," who reportedly wrote poetry and painted while his men fought, spoke English, had gone to military academies and Oxford University in England, served beside the British for eight years that overlapped World War I and service in France, was brought back to the Philippines to stand trial for war crimes. The charges were based upon the "Bataan Death March" and other atrocities against prisoners and the Filipino population, committed by troops under his command. He was executed by firing squad outside Manila on 3 April 1946.[23]

While USAFFE forces in the Philippines were defending doggedly, without logistical support to sustain them, and upsetting the Japanese timetable of conquest, on 18 April, nine days after the Luzon Force surrendered on Bataan, the Pacific Fleet's carriers, *Hornet* (CV-8) in Task Force 18, supported by *Enterprise* in Task Force 16, launched Lieutenant Colonel Jimmy Doolittle's specially modified, sixteen B-25 bombers on a daring raid on Tokyo. In January President Roosevelt began pressing—demanding—the military strike Tokyo, in retaliation for the Japanese attack on Pearl Harbor.

Though the raid did comparatively little military damage, it was an enormous lift for America's sagging morale, and damaged Japanese civilians' morale. Though the Japanese government and its militarists publicly brushed off the "Do-nothing Raid," they had received a small foretaste of the catastrophe that would befall the homeland in the years ahead. There were also important military effects, including the recall of some fighter units from the Pacific to defend the homeland, and a substantial diversion of other antiaircraft defense capabilities to augment air defenses.

In addition to the two carriers in the combined Task Force 16, under the command of Vice Admiral William F. Halsey, were fourteen other ships, several of which had been at Pearl Harbor. The escorting ships were the heavy cruisers *Salt Lake City* (CA-25), *Northampton* (CA-26) and *Vincennes* (CA-44), along with the light cruiser *Nashville* (CL-43). The eight destroyers were the *Balch* (DD-363), flagship of Captain Richard L. Conolly's Destroyer Squadron Six, *Benham* (DD-397), *Ellet* (DD-398), *Fanning* (DD-385), *Grayson* (DD-435), *Gwin* (DD-433), *Meredith* (DD-434) and *Monssen* (DD-436).* Two oilers integral to TF-16, which needed refueling en route, were the *Cimarron* (AO-22) and *Sabine* (AO-25).

Modifications to the aircraft included removal of the lower gun turret, installation of de-icers and anti-icers, steel blast plates mounted on the fuselage around the upper turret, removal of the liaison radio set, installation of additional fuel tanks and support mounts to increase fuel capacity from 646 to 1,141 U.S. gallons, mock wooden gun barrels installed in the tail cone, and replacement of the Norden bomb sight with a makeshift aiming sight.

Throughout their training, the bomber crews, all volunteers, were never told of their destination, only that it was "an extremely hazardous mission." Not until the task force was at sea did they learn their destination—Tokyo. Because Japanese picket ships discovered the presence of the task force and warned of the sighting before the carriers arrived at their planned aircraft launch point,

---

**Monssen was the newly commissioned destroyer Joey Border had had dinner aboard in Puget Sound Navy Yard fifteen months earlier. The skipper's wife, Sally Smoot, also a close friend of Joey's mother, had acted as bridesmaid and stood in for Joey's father to give Joey away at the Border's 15 July 1941 wedding in Long Beach. Lieutenant Commander Roland N. Smoot was still in command when the *Monssen*, after five months of neutrality patrol duty in the northeast Atlantic, rejoined the Pacific Fleet following the attack on Pearl Harbor.

the decision was made to launch as soon as possible, ten hours earlier and 170 miles further from the target. The earlier launch adversely affected Lieutenant Colonel Doolittle's air tactics plan. To the bomber crews, with each airplane carrying four specially modified 500-pound bombs, including one incendiary, the decision meant a daylight attack, in single file, instead of a night raid, and Lieutenant Colonel Doolittle couldn't proceed to their target two hours ahead of the remaining fifteen and drop incendiary bombs to light the way for a concentrated night attack on the target.

The early launch also ensured none could possibly reach their intended destination airfield in China. Admiral Halsey's 24 April action report to Admiral Nimitz, completed while the task force was still at sea and quoted in part below, tells of the decision.

> After fueling of the heavy ships on 17 April, these ships (carriers and cruisers) proceeded west without destroyers and oilers in order to permit high speed operations. Fuel conservation for destroyers was another consideration. High winds and heavy sea conditions prevailed. The destroyers rejoined the morning following the attack (19th) and the oilers (with destroyer escort) two days later (21st).
>
> The necessity for launching the Army planes at 0820 on the 18th about 650 miles east of Tokyo was regrettable. The plan was to close to the 500 mile circle and there launch one plane to attack at dusk and this provide a target for the remaining planes which would strike about two hours later. This plan was evolved by Lieutenant Colonel Doolittle, in command of the Army flight, and was designed to inflict the greatest damage with the least risk. The remote location of the desired terminus for the flight was also a factor influencing the selection of this plan of attack. However, contacts with enemy surface vessels early in the morning compromised the secrecy of the operation, and after the third contact, at 0744, the decision was made to launch. Japanese radio traffic was intercepted indicating that the presence of the raiding force was reported. The prime consideration then was the launching of the Army planes before the arrival of Japanese bombers.

The successful launching of the 16 Army bombers from the HORNET in unfavorable wind and sea conditions reflected great credit on the Army pilots and on the Commanding Officer of the HORNET . . .

Captain Marc Mitscher, *Hornet*'s skipper, made the decision to launch. The aircraft were respotted on the *Hornet*'s deck to allow for engine starting and run-ups, leaving Doolittle in his lead aircraft 467 feet for takeoff distance. Despite the fact none of the B-25 pilots had ever taken off from a carrier before, all 16 aircraft launched safely between 0820 and 0919. To avoid radar detection they flew just above wave top level and began arriving over Japan about noon (Tokyo time), six hours after launch, and bombed military and industrial targets in Tokyo, two in Yokohama, and one each in Yokosuka, Nagoya, Kobe and Osaka, the latter targets all to the southwest of Tokyo. Although some B-25s encountered light antiaircraft fire and a few enemy fighters over Japan, no bomber was shot down or severely damaged. Fifteen of the 16 then proceeded southwest along the southern coast of Japan and across the East China Sea towards unoccupied areas in eastern China, where recovery bases supposedly awaited them. They faced unforeseen challenges during their flight to China: night was approaching, the aircraft were running low on fuel, and the weather was rapidly deteriorating.

Fifteen aircraft reached the China coast after thirteen hours of flight and crash-landed or the crews bailed out. One B-25, extremely low on fuel, headed instead for the closer land mass of the Soviet Union and landed 40 miles beyond Vladivostok, where their B-25 was confiscated and the crew interned until they managed to escape through Iran in 1943. The raid was the longest combat mission ever flown by the Mitchell B-25 bomber, averaging approximately 2,250 miles.

There were 10,000 Navy men in the task force. Eighty Army Air Force men took part in the raid, five men in each of the sixteen B-25s. One man, Corporal Leland Faktor, was killed on bail-out after the mission. Two men from Crew #6 drowned as a result of a crash landing in the water off the China coast: Sergeant Donald E. Fitzmaurice and Staff Sergeant William J. Dieter. The Japanese captured eight men, and all were held for a time in the Japanese police headquarters in Shanghai: Lieutenants Dean E. Hallmark, Robert J. Meder, Chase J. Nielsen, William G. Farrow, Robert L.

Hite, and George Barr, and Corporals Harold A. Spatz and Jacob DeShazer. On 28 August 1942, after a mock trial the Japanese executed three by firing squad: pilots Hallmark and Farrow, and gunner Spatz. Lieutenant Meder died of beriberi and malnutrition while in prison.

Four survived 40 months of prison, most of which was in solitary confinement. Most raiders flew additional combat missions after the Tokyo raid. Four raiders became POWs of the Germans later in the war. Thirteen died later during World War II, most in action against the enemy.

Immediately following the raid, Doolittle told his crew that he believed the loss of all 16 aircraft, coupled with the relatively minor damage the aircraft had inflicted on their targets, rendered the raid a failure, and he expected a court martial after he returned to the United States. Instead, the raid bolstered American morale to the extent that President Roosevelt awarded him the Medal of Honor, he was promoted two grades to Brigadier General, skipping the rank of colonel. He went on to command the 12th Air Force in North Africa, the 15th Air Force in the Mediterranean, and the 8th Air Force in England in the next three years. Additionally, Corporal Dave Thatcher, an engineer-gunner and Lieutenant Thomas White, flight surgeon-gunner, each received the Silver Star for their brave efforts in helping several wounded crew members evade Japanese troops in China. All the remaining raiders, including Thatcher and White, were awarded the Distinguished Flying Cross and those who were killed, wounded or injured as a result of the raid also received the Purple Heart. Additionally, every Doolittle Raider received a decoration from the Chinese government.[24]

On Wednesday, 4 March 1942, while the battle for Bataan was still in progress, and planning for the Doolittle Raid was under way, President Roosevelt signed the letter posthumously awarding the Medal of Honor to Ensign Herbert C. Jones, whom Joey Border had met when he came to the Springers' quarters in January 1941. Ensign Jones, who had been a crew member on the *California* at Pearl Harbor, was among fourteen men who received Medals of Honor, eleven posthumously, as a result of their actions on 7 December. Another 48 men were awarded the Navy Cross, three posthumously, and one officer, Lieutenant Clarence E. Dickinson from the *Enterprise*'s VS-6, received two Navy Crosses, the second awarded in the form of a Gold Star for sinking a Japanese submarine on 10 December 1941. The Navy also awarded 63 Silver Star Medals, while separately the Army and Army Air Force awarded a total of five Distinguished Service Crosses and 66 Silver Stars.

The Navy later named a ship after each man who posthumously received the Medal of Honor for their acts of courage and valor at Pearl Harbor. The Destroyer Escort *Herbert C. Jones* (DE-137), sponsored by his widow, Mrs. Herbert C. Jones of Menlo Park, California, slid down the ways at the Consolidated Steel Corporation shipbuilding division yard at 12 noon on Tuesday, 19 January 1943. In addition to Mrs. Jones' presence, the late twenty-three year old ensign's father, retired Navy Captain Herbert A. Jones, who once also served on the battleship *California*, observed the launching and spoke with pride of his son.

> The Navy blue ran deep in his veins. Navy customs. Navy spirit, Navy traditions—those were his life. The only duty well done as far as he was concerned was one done beyond the call of duty. The USS *Herbert C. Jones* has built into her for her officers and men the soul and spirit of Ensign Herbert C. Jones.

Following the Doolittle raid and the 6 May surrender of the garrison on Corregidor, two major Naval battles, Coral Sea and Midway, turned the tide of the Pacific war and finally relieved the heavy pressure felt in Hawaii since the attack on Pearl Harbor—though more than thirty-seven months of heavy fighting were to follow the disastrous defeat suffered by the Imperial Japanese Navy at Midway.

In May 1942, while Bob and Joey Border were in Pensacola, Florida for Bob's naval aviator training, Imperial Japan was nearing the apex of its power, with occupying forces providing a sphere of influence stretching from Burma to Java, the Bismarck Archipelago, north of New Guinea, and were threatening New Guinea, the Solomon Islands, Australia, and the lengthy supply line stretching from the United States' West Coast through Hawaii, Samoa, the Fiji Islands, and New Caledonia to Australia and New Zealand. Far to the north they were pressing across the Aleutian Island chain toward Alaska.

Still reeling from a long series of humiliating defeats, the Allies were just beginning to develop the skills and gather the resources needed to survive, protect the supply line and sea lanes to Australia and New Zealand, and eventually roll back the enemy's territorial gains. Allied strategy at this time was focused on a defensive buildup of the United States Army and Marine Corps strength on New Caledonia—well to the south, southeast of the Solomon Islands—and Australian Army and Royal Australian Air Force units in the south and east of the Australian Territory of New Guinea, just north of Australia.

On 12 March the Japanese Prime Minister, General Hideki Tojo had said, "Australia and New Zealand are now threatened by the might of the imperial forces, and both them know that any resistance is futile. If the Australian government does not modify her present attitude, their continent will suffer the same fate as the Dutch East Indies."

In April, after the Doolittle raid, when the Japanese realized the homeland was vulnerable to air attack, and were still convinced of their invincibility, the Japanese forces chose to expand their perimeter instead of rapidly consolidating its defenses. A major expedition would be launched against Midway to draw the American Fleet into battle and destroy it. As a diversion, a smaller Japanese force would seize Attu and Kiska in the western Aleutians, making its strike one day ahead of the main force. Later, once the Japanese had established bases at Port Moresby on the south coast of New Guinea and the island of Tulagi in the Solomon Islands, further operations could be launched to isolate Australia and New Zealand by capturing New Caledonia, Fiji, and Samoa.

Japanese forces left their new stronghold of Rabaul, on the island of New Britain, just north of New Guinea, to launch a two-pronged campaign: an amphibious assault against Port Moresby (Operation "MO"), on New Guinea, and another against Tulagi, the latter with the intent to establish seaplane bases at Tulagi and in the Louisiade Archipelago off the eastern tip of New Guinea. To accomplish their Port Moresby objective, guard their invasion force, and engage any Allied naval warships that approached to contest the invasion force, the Japanese assembled a large force split into several elements, consisting of two heavy aircraft carriers, the *Shokaku* and *Zuikaku*, both of which were veterans of Pearl Harbor; a smaller carrier, *Shoho*, a seaplane tender, nine cruisers and thirteen destroyers. The smaller carrier and its force were to support and cover the troop transports. Intercepted radio messages and the previously broken Japanese code warned the Allies of the move of Japanese land-based bombers south, and that an offensive operation was impending.

In the Allied forces as they converged in the Coral Sea were three main groups. Task Force 17 centered around the carrier *Yorktown*, led by Rear Admiral Frank Jack Fletcher, who would later take command of the three task forces and reorganize them into five task groups. In Task Force 11, led by Rear Admiral Aubrey Fitch, was the carrier *Lexington* which on 4 May had launched a damaging, surprise series of four air strikes on the enemy's Tulagi forces. Task Force 11 had 69 planes, two heavy cruisers, and six destroyers while TF-17 had 67 planes, three heavy cruisers, six destroyers, and two fleet oilers. The third was Task Force 44, a group of Allied warships, including the two Australian ships, heavy cruiser HMAS *Australia* and the light cruiser HMAS *Hobart*, commanded by Australian Rear Admiral John Crace. In TF-44 with *Australia* and *Hobart*, were the American cruiser *Chicago*, and destroyers *Perkins*, *Farragut*, and *Walke*.

When Admiral Fletcher took command of the combined Task Force 17, the re-designated and reorganized order of battle was: Task Group 17.2 (Attack Group), commanded by Rear Admiral Thomas Kinkaid, composed of the cruisers *Minneapolis*, *New Orleans*, *Astoria*, *Chester*, and *Portland*; and the destroyers *Phelps*, *Dewey*, *Farragut*, *Aylwin*, and *Monaghan*. The cruiser *New Orleans*, with its growing legend of "... pass the ammunition," was at Pearl Harbor, as were all five destroyers, including *Monaghan*, which had rammed, depth charged and sunk the midget submarine inside the harbor that morning.

Task Group 17.3 (Support Group), commanded by Australian Rear Admiral Crace, was all the combatants in TF-44, less the destroyer *Farragut*, now in the Attack Group.

Task Group 17.5 (Carrier Group), commanded by Admiral Fitch, included the *Lexington* and *Yorktown*, and destroyers *Anderson*, *Hammann*, *Russell* and *Morris*—the destroyer Bob Border had been ordered to ride back to Pearl Harbor to return to the *Tennessee* after he proposed to Joey in February 1941.

In Task Group 17.6 (Fueling Group), commanded by Captain John S. Phillips on his oiler and Pearl Harbor veteran, *Neosho*, was a second oiler, the *Tippecanoe*, with destroyers *Sims* and *Worden*—another Pearl Harbor veteran. Task Group 17.9

(Search Group) was one ship, the seaplane tender *Tangier* with 12 PBY-5 Catalina flying boats. *Tangier*, too, was a Pearl Harbor veteran, having been moored aft of the capsized *Utah* with its still-entombed 47 crewmembers. *Tangier* now had a new skipper, Commander George H. DeBaun.

In Task Force "MO" confronting the Allied force, was the Carrier Striking Force, commanded by Vice Admiral Takeo Takagi, with the carriers *Shokau* and *Zuikaku*; the cruisers *Myoko* and *Haguro*; two Division 7 destroyers, *Ushio* and *Akebono*; four Division 27 destroyers, *Ariake*, *Yugure*, *Shiratsuyu*, and *Shigure*; and the oiler *Toho Maru*.

The Port Moresby Invasion Group, commanded by Rear Admiral Sadamichi Kajioka, included the cruiser *Yubari*; destroyers *Oite*, *Asanagi*, *Uziuki*, *Mutsuki*, *Mochizuki*, and *Yayoi*, plus the transport unit commanded by Rear Admiral Koso Abe. The invasion Support Group, commanded by Rear Admiral Kuninori Marumo, was composed of the cruisers *Tenryu* and *Tatusta*; the *Kamikawa Maru*; and three gunboats, the *Keijo Maru*, *Seikai Maru*, and *Nikkai Maru*. The Covering Group, commanded by Rear Admiral Goto, was composed of the carrier *Shoho*; the cruisers *Aoba*, *Kako*, *Kinugasa*, and *Furutaka*, and the destroyer *Sazanami*. The submarine force was commanded by Captain Noburu Ishizaki.

The Tulagi Invasion Group, which had come and gone—except for some supporting ships—when *Lexington* launched her four strikes on 4 May, was commanded by Rear Admiral Kiyohide Shima, and was composed of the minelayers *Ikinoshima* and *Koei Maru*; the transport *Azumasan Maru*, and destroyers *Kikuzuki* and *Yuzuki*.

On 6 May, after the Port Moresby invasion and carrier support forces had been sighted heading toward New Guinea by American B-17 bombers which fruitlessly attempted to bomb them, the battle was joined. Admiral Fletcher, mindful his role was to protect Port Moresby, and concerned about separating his carrier forces in the face of possibly three Japanese carriers, made the difficult decision to split his surface forces instead, sending Admiral Crace's TG-17.3 to block the invasion force. Both he and Crace were aware of the lessons learned from the sinking of the *Prince of Wales* and the *Repulse* when they were without air cover to defend against land-based bombers. Their fears were nearly realized when the cruisers were spotted and came under intense air attack from a squadron of torpedo bombers the afternoon of 7 May. The ships escaped with a few casualties and little damage. Only a few minutes after the Japanese raid, Crace's force was inadvertently attacked by friendly B-17s, and the *Perkins* and *Farragut* once again had to endure near misses.

The complex, maneuvering battle, which occurred southwest of the Island of Guadalcanal in the Coral Sea, 7-8 May 1942, became the first of six major battles in the war in which the two contending fleets never fired a gun directly at one another, but fought at a distance beyond gun range, with exchanges of air strikes. The weapons were torpedoes, bombs and machine gun bullets dropped and fired at ships by aircraft.

When the battle ended, the Japanese had lost 77 aircraft, 1,074 men, the smaller carrier *Shoho*, several auxiliaries, and a destroyer; suffered damage to the *Shokaku* so that she couldn't launch or recover aircraft and took six months to repair. The *Shoho* was small by carrier standards, but the laconic phrase "scratch one flattop" radioed back to *Lexington*, announced the first major Allied naval success of the Pacific War. *Zuikaku* suffered slight damage and had only 40 aircraft left. She, too, had to return to Japan for repairs and replenishment.

The Americans lost the *Lexington*, hit by both bombs and torpedoes, the oiler *Neosho*, which had managed to escape destruction at Pearl Harbor, and one of *Neosho's* escorts, the destroyer *Sims*. Although the larger of the two carriers, the slower *Lexington*, survived the immediate damage and was thought to be repairable, leaking aviation fuel exploded over an hour later. She had to be abandoned and scuttled to prevent her capture.

The Americans lost 66 aircraft and 543 men killed or wounded. The *Yorktown*, struck by one bomb which started a fire on the hangar deck and believed to be sufficiently damaged to require a 90-day refitting, returned to Pearl Harbor and was turned around, ready to fight, in an astounding three days.

Though the Japanese achieved a narrow tactical victory, with the loss of one small carrier, a large carrier severely damaged with the other lightly damaged, and a destroyer sunk, compared with the Americans' loss of a large carrier and significant damage to another, plus the loss of a destroyer and the oiler *Neosho*, in strategic terms the Japanese suffered a defeat that substantially affected the course of the war and the morale of both sides.

When the *Shoho* was sunk, the Port Moresby invasion force

lost its air cover and turned back. This was the first time a Japanese invasion force had been turned back without achieving its objective. Port Moresby was vital to Allied strategy and could not have been defended by the ground forces stationed there. Without a hold on New Guinea, the subsequent Allied advance in the Pacific, difficult though it was, would have been much harder still. As a result the Japanese were forced to attack Port Moresby overland. The delay was long enough to permit the arrival of the veteran Second Australian Imperial [Army] Force to fight the Kokoda Track campaign, defending against the Japanese overland offensive toward Port Moresby.

In 1942 many people in Australia believed their country had been saved from invasion by the Battle of the Coral Sea. A speech at the time by Prime Minister John Curtin made that clear:

> Events that are taking place today are of crucial importance to the whole conduct of the war in this theatre . . . I should add that at this moment nobody can tell what the result of the engagement may be. If it should go advantageously, we shall have cause for great gratitude and our position will then be somewhat clearer. But if we should not have the advantages from this battle for which we hope, all that confronts us is a sterner ordeal and a greater responsibility. This battle will not decide the war; it will determine immediate tactics which will be pursued by the Allied forces and by the common enemy.

In Australia, those who knew what was happening were ready for the worst, though historians have never found conclusive evidence the Japanese planned to invade their country. Nevertheless, until more recently, each year since 1946 Coral Sea Week has been celebrated in Australia with marches by service personnel from both Australia and the USA, and official functions for American dignitaries. These celebrations express gratitude to the United States for its part in the battle and the support given Australia in World War II.

More recently the commemorative emphasis has moved from the "Battle that saved Australia" to the broader concept of the "Battle for Australia," held on the first Wednesday in September. This now marks not only the Battle of the Coral Sea, but the contribution and significance of all those who helped defend Australia at its most vulnerable time.

For the United States Navy, the Battle of the Coral Sea had other positive consequences. The Japanese had at least two and possibly three less carriers available for the battle of Midway, waged 3-6 June. Midway was to be the decisive battle Admiral Yamamoto had planned in the months since Pearl Harbor. It was a decisive battle, but not the way he intended.[25]

The Decisive Battle of Midway

The great, complex, swirling, naval Battle of Midway will not be treated in any depth or adequate summary in this work. Suffice it to repeat what Gordon Prange and his co-authors Dr. Donald M. Goldstein and Katherine V. Dillon found years later in their diligent research for another of his classic works, *Miracle at Midway*. The Battle of Midway was the turning point in the Pacific war.

In the introduction to their book, they acknowledged their "... volume complements, rather than supplants, other fine works in this area." Particularly, they cited *Midway: The Battle That Doomed Japan*, by Mitsuo Fuchida and Masatake Okumiya, edited by Clarke H. Kawakami and Roger Pineau, as a prime source from the Japanese side, and expressed their indebtedness to them. A special salute was also given Samuel Eliot Morison's naval history, *Coral Sea, Midway and Submarine Actions*, and to Walter Lord's "... wonderfully human *Incredible Victory*."

In the preface of *Miracle at Midway* are these words:

> Less than six months after their victory at Pearl Harbor, the Japanese sent forth an enormous, combat-seasoned fleet of eighty-eight surface warships [including the Guard Force which sortied with the Japanese Main Body] with the dual mission of capturing Midway and luring the remains of the weakened U.S. Pacific Fleet to their destruction. This was to be the opening salvo of their second phase operations which contemplated the isolation

of Australia at one extreme and possible capture of Hawaii at the other.

But events did not conform to the Japanese pattern. Forewarned through superior cryptanalysis and radio intelligence, American naval forces much inferior numerically to the Japanese (twenty-eight surface warships), but superbly led and manned, sped past Midway and were waiting on the enemy's flank.

The result was by no means a foregone conclusion. The Japanese spearhead held the veteran carriers *Akagi*, *Kaga*, *Hiryu*, and *Soryu*, under the command of Vice Admiral Chuichi Nagumo. This was the admiral and four of the six carriers which had attacked Pearl Harbor on December 7, and since then the Nagumo task force had scored one victory after another in the south Pacific and Indian Oceans.

The immutable before and after facts of Midway make clear who won and who lost.

	United States	Japan
Casualties	307	2,500
Carriers	1	4
Heavy Cuisers	0	1
Destroyer	1	0
Aircraft	147	332

The destroyer *Hammann* (DD-412) was sunk north of Midway by the Japanese submarine *I-68* (later designated *I-168*). The submarine had participated in the Pearl Harbor operation and on 12 December had withdrawn to Kwajalein after being damaged during attacks totaling 21 depth charges southwest of Oahu while attempting to penetrate the carrier *Saratoga*'s destroyer screen. *Hammann* sank approximately four minutes after being struck by one of *I-168*'s four torpedoes, and the destroyer's survivors suffered additional losses when an underwater explosion followed moments after the *Hammann* went down. Of a total of

13 officers and 228 men, 80 of her crew were lost, many killed by the underwater explosion.

Ironically, *I-168* had been ordered to sink the drifting, already-abandoned, badly-damaged, carrier *Yorktown* (CV-5), which Captain Elliot Buckmaster and a skeleton crew were attempting to salvage. When *I-168* found her quarry, *Hammann* was close alongside aiding in the attempted salvage. One of the four torpedoes missed both ships, but the other two eventually proved fatal to the *Yorktown* as well. Struck by *I-168's* torpedoes the afternoon of 6 June, the carrier amazingly stayed afloat until 0458 the morning of 7 June 1942, when she finally succumbed to the numerous hits she had taken in the Battle of Midway.

Slipping in close to attack a ship with a submarine is generally the easy part. Escaping is another matter entirely. This time *I-168* desperately maneuvered until after dark with more than 60 depth charges dropped in attempts to sink her. Pursued by the destroyers *Monaghan*, *Gwin* and *Hughes*, miraculously, *I-168* did manage to escape again, but not without serious damage—again.[26]

Aircraft from the carrier *Enterprise*, including crewmembers from Scouting Squadron Six (VS-6), the bloodied veterans of Pearl Harbor, were heavily involved in the Battle of Midway. The squadron had suffered the loss of six SBDs on 7 December, five to the Japanese, one to American guns, two pilots and four radiomen/gunners, with two more wounded. Bombing Six (VB-6) had lost one SBD the same morning, and that night Fighting Six (VF-6) tragically lost five F4F Wildcats to American guns. On 1 February, in a raid in the Marshall Islands, VS-6 lost four more SBDs and all eight crew members, including its squadron commander, Lieutenant Commander Hopping, and VF-6 lost an F4F and its pilot on takeoff. On 24 February VS-6 lost another SBD radioman/gunner, who had survived Pearl Harbor, when the aircraft went over the side of the carrier in a night accident. Later in the day, in a raid on Japanese held Wake Island, VS-6 lost yet another SBD and its crew.

The *Enterprise* and its task force turned south from Wake Island and on 4 March launched a raid on Marcus Island. This time, SBD 6-S-7, with pilot Dale Hilton and radioman/gunner Jack Leaming, both Pearl Harbor veterans, were shot down by enemy guns, ditched the Douglas Dauntless in the ocean, were captured, taken to Japan and interned for the duration of the war. In the Battle of Midway only 19 of 54 aircrews from the

Enterprise who flew against the enemy survived, and of these, three were wounded.[27]

In addition, as a result of the Battle of Midway there were other tangible damages to both sides, but the intangibles were perhaps far more important.

For the second time, a Japanese invasion force was turned back from its objective. Further, a valuable U.S. Naval War College study quoted in *Miracle at Midway* succinctly stated the battle's more profound effects:

> It had a stimulating effect on the morale of the American fighting forces; . . . it stopped the Japanese expansion to the east; it put an end to Japanese offensive action which had been all conquering for the first six months of the war; it restored the balance of naval power in the Pacific which thereafter steadily shifted to favor the American side; . . . it removed the threat to Hawaii and the west coast of the United States; . . . [and] . . . the Japanese were forced to a defensive role.

Gordon Prange and his co-authors went on to say, "This is the ultimate meaning. At Midway the United States laid aside the shield and picked up the sword, and through all the engagements to follow, never again yielded the strategic offensive."

In the meantime, in Hawaii, controversy surrounding the imposition of martial law was growing. The military judiciary which replaced the civil courts consisted of two types of bodies: a military commission, which tried cases involving punishment of more than $5,000 fine and five years' imprisonment; and several provost courts—three were in Honolulu—each with a single judge, which heard lesser offenses.

Controversy had begun almost immediately after the declaration of martial law when a joint military-civilian commission was appointed to deliberate the more serious class of offenses. In the commission's first meeting, the civilian members questioned the legality of martial law and the authority of the military governor to appoint the commission. They were apprehensive of their personal liabilities should they participate in the commission's proceedings. The atmosphere of the meeting became quite tense. A few days later, the military governor issued a new general order appointing a new commission consisting entirely of Army officers. In the coming months lawyers and others began increasingly criticizing the provost courts' functions.

The summer of 1942, Governor Poindexter's term of appointment ended, and Ingram M. Stainback succeeded him. The new governor immediately appointed Garner Anthony, Hawaii's most vocal critic of martial law, as his attorney general. The shattering defeat of the Japanese at Midway had considerably reduced enemy military pressure on Hawaii, which accelerated the questioning of continued martial law. Successful steps were begun through various avenues almost immediately to back the military away from its tight control of Hawaii's civilian authority, but not until 24 October 1944 was martial law finally ended.[28]

The Death of Imperial Japan's 7 December Carrier Striking Force

Not one Japanese ship or submarine involved in the attack on Pearl Harbor survived World War II. Following the loss of the first midget submarine to the guns and depth charges of the destroyer *Ward* outside the harbor early the morning of 7 December, the first major submarine sunk was *I-70* on 10 December, the victim of Lieutenant Clarence Dickinson's dive bomb attack launched from the carrier *Enterprise*. The first Japanese surface vessel lost was the carrier *Soryu*, at 1910 hours on 4 June 1942, in the Battle of Midway, followed fifteen minutes later by the sinking of the carrier *Kaga*.[29]

Akagi and *Hiryu* were also sunk at Midway. They were the last of four veteran Pearl Harbor carriers sunk at Midway. The final two Pearl Harbor carriers, *Shokaku* and *Zuikaku*, which were at the Coral Sea but missed Midway remained in operation until the United States was deep into its strategic offensive in 1944. The *Shokaku* was sunk 19 June 1944, during the Battle of the Philippine Sea, by the submarine *Cavalla*, operating from Pearl Harbor. The *Zuikaku* was sunk off Cape Engano by American carrier aircraft on 25 October 1944.

Ironically, on 15 June 1944, after Vice Admiral Jisaburo Ozawa's failed naval Battle of the Philippine Sea, in which the Japanese lost 500 aircraft, Vice Admiral Chuichi Nagumo, who commanded the Carrier Striking Force at Pearl Harbor, and his Army peer, General Yoshitsugu Saito, attempted to defend the island of Saipan against the American assault. On 6 July, in the final stages of the Battle of Saipan, Nagumo committed suicide, not in the traditional method of seppuku, but rather a pistol to the temple. His remains were later found by American Marines in the cave where he spent his last days as commander of the Saipan defenders. The Japanese posthumously promoted him to admiral.

The last survivor of Admiral Nagumo's 7 December Carrier Striking Force was the heavy cruiser *Tone*. She was caught and sunk at her moorings at Kure, in the Inland Sea, in the great raid of 24 July 1945 when American and British carrier groups put 1,747 of their aircraft over the Inland Sea, its bays, its harbors, and its islands.

On 18 April 1943, by coincidence Easter Sunday and the first anniversary of the Doolittle Raid on Tokyo, Admiral Isoroku Yamamoto, commander of the Combined Fleet and architect of the Japanese attack on Pearl Harbor, was killed on Bougainville Island, in the Solomons, when his Mitsubishi G4M "Betty" transport bomber was shot down by Army Air Force P-38G aircraft flying out of Henderson Field on Guadalcanal. On 14 April, the U.S. Naval intelligence effort code-named "Magic" intercepted and decrypted orders alerting affected Japanese units in the *I-Go* operation—the disastrous Japanese withdrawal from Guadalcanal—to a morale building tour of the units by Yamamoto.

Information was passed to President Roosevelt who requested Secretary of the Navy Frank Knox, "Get Yamamoto." Admiral Nimitz consulted with Admiral Halsey, and, because Navy fighters hadn't the range to carry out the mission, it fell to the Army Air Force's 339th Fighter Squadron, 347th Fighter Group, Thirteenth Air Force. In a near perfectly planned and flown mission assigned the 18 aircraft in the 339th, Yamamoto's aircraft was intercepted and shot down after a two hour and nine minute flight to the planned intercept point. (Ten of the pilots came from the other 347th squadrons.)

A "Killer Flight" of four P-38s led the low level mission fifty feet above the wave tops to a point short of the intercept where the remaining fourteen, which included two spares, climbed to 18,000 feet and provided top cover against expected reactions by

Vice Admiral Chuichi Nagumo, who commanded the Carrier Striking Force at Pearl Harbor, and his Army peer General Yoshitsugu Saito attempted to defend the island of Saipan against the American assault. On 6 July, in the final stages of the Battle of Saipan, Nagumo committed suicide. NHHC

Admiral Isoroku Yamamoto, Imperial Japanese Navy, was killed on Bouganville Island in the Solomons 18 April 1943, by coincidence Easter Sunday and the first anniversary of the Doolittle Raid on Tokyo, when his Mitsubishi G4M "Betty" transport bomber was shot down by Army Air Force P-38G aircraft flying out of Henderson Field on Guadalcanal. Portrait photograph, taken during the early 1940s, when he was Commander in Chief, Combined Fleet. NHHC

Japanese Zeroes flying top cover for the two Bettys. The mission proved to be the longest intercept mission of the war. Both Betty's were shot down, the second carrying members of Yamamoto's staff.[30] But the war's road to that point for the Allies had been long and hard.

Ghosts of Pearl Harbor: Tragedy, Irony and Inspiration

Two of America's Pearl Harbor battle line could never be resurrected, *Arizona* and *Oklahoma*. *Arizona* and her 1,177 men lost with her, in death became at once the living symbols of ". . . a date of which will live in infamy . . . " and individual courage, valor and sacrifice in behalf of a free people. Following the "Battle of the Bands" on the night of 6 December 1941, and the next day's attack, the *Arizona* band was later posthumously recognized as the best of all in the musical contest.

On 12 December 1950 a plaque was placed on the *Arizona*, in memory of all who died on the ship. The *Arizona* Memorial grew out of a wartime desire to establish some sort of memorial at Pearl Harbor to honor those who died in the attack. President Dwight D. Eisenhower, who helped achieve Allied victory in World War II, approved the creation of the Memorial in 1958, construction was complete in 1961, and it was dedicated in 1962.

The architect, Alfred Preis, describes the design of the Memorial, which attracts over a million and a half visitors a year:

> Wherein the structure sags in the center but stands strong and vigorous at the ends, expresses initial defeat and ultimate victory . . . the overall effect is one of serenity. Overtones of sadness have been omitted to permit the individual to contemplate his own personal responses . . . his innermost feelings.[31]

The first chaplain to die in World War II, was Chaplain Thomas L. Kirkpatrick, on the *Arizona*, followed in death a few minutes later by Father Aloysisus Schmitt, on the *Oklahoma*. Chaplain Kirkpatrick is still on the *Arizona*.

Beginning 15 July 1942, the *Oklahoma* was the subject of

a massive salvage undertaking, involving turning her upright, patching her damages and re-floating her. Twenty officers and 395 enlisted men were either killed or missing.

Preparations for righting the overturned hull took 7 ¾ months. The actual righting took 3 ¼ months, between 8 March 1943 and 16 June, with Oklahoma towed into dry dock on 28 December. She was stripped of guns and superstructure, and repaired sufficiently to make her relatively watertight. Determined to be too old and badly damaged to be worth returning to service, *Oklahoma* was formally decommission in 1 September 1944. She was sold for scrapping on 5 December 1946, to Moore Drydock Company of Oakland, California. *Oklahoma* sank in heavy weather on 17 May 1947, 540 miles out of Pearl Harbor while being towed to San Francisco.[32]

The capsized older battleship-turned-target ship, *Utah*, remains where she sank that terrible morning. Of *Utah*'s complement, 30 officers and 431 enlisted men survived the ship's loss. Six officers and 52 men died. Four of the latter were recovered and interred ashore, as are seven Unknowns from *Utah*. One of those known interred ashore and was a survivor of the sinking in the harbor, was Seaman Pallas F. Brown, who was tragically killed on board the repair ship *Argonne* by a stray bullet the night of 7 December when gunners on the ships and in nearby ground antiaircraft positions opened fire on the F4F's attempting to land at Ford Island. In 1972, a memorial in honor of *Utah*'s crew was dedicated on the northwest shore of Ford Island, adjacent to the ship's wreck.[33]

When the *West Virginia* was pumped out and re-floated on 17 May 1942, then went into Dry Dock Number One on 9 June, it was discovered she had taken seven torpedo hits, not five. During ensuing repairs, workers located the remains of 70 West Virginia sailors who had been trapped below deck. In one compartment, a calendar was found, the last scratch-off date being 23 December 1941.

West Virginia and all battleships in Pearl Harbor on 7 December that eventually returned to the fight, accumulated distinguished war records, survived the war, and their surviving crew members would proudly remember the great ships' service the rest of their lives. The battleships' returns to war generally coincided with the United States' mounting of its strategic offensive aimed at the unconditional surrender of Japan. The enemy felt the presence and sting of one or more in the invasions to recapture the Philippines, Attu and Kiska in Alaska's Aleutian Island chain, the Battles of Leyte Gulf, Lingayen Gulf, and the Surigao Strait; the campaigns in the Gilbert and Marshall Islands, the Palaus, Tarawa, Kwajalein, Eniwetok, Guam, Saipan, Tinian, Iwo Jima, Okinawa—and some carried occupation forces to Japan and brought other men home from the mid-Pacific after the war.

The *Nevada* participated in gunfire support for the invasion of Normandy and landing operations in Southern France before returning to the Pacific for more campaigns against the Japanese toward the end of the war.

Early the morning of 19 October 1944, the once-badly-damaged *West Virginia* returned to war and provided gunfire support for the invasion of the Philippines. In the period 23-26 October, while operating in support of the Philippines campaign, she participated in the last major naval battle of World War II, the Battle of Leyte Gulf—another disastrous defeat for the Japanese. One of several Leyte Gulf engagements was the 25 October Battle for Surigao Strait, in which the *West Virginia* and five other battleships—four of them also ghosts of Pearl Harbor: *Tennessee, Maryland, California* and *Pennsylvania,* reappeared to help administer the defeat. At the Surigao Strait, with the sixth battleship, *Mississippi* (BB-41), the five ghosts of Pearl Harbor were taking part in the final line battle to date in naval history, and the last battle in World War II in which battleships engaged battleships. The "crossing of the Japanese T," firing broadsides at a column of Japanese combatants that included two battleships proceeding through the Strait toward Pearl Harbor's ghosts and American forces landed further north, resulted in a resounding Allied victory and the mastery of a tactical situation of which every surface admiral dreams.[34]

The Philippines in October 1944 also saw the beginning of the "suiciders' war," the Kamikaze's—Japanese translation, "The Divine Wind," aircraft flown on suicide missions and deliberately crashed into their targets. On 21 October a Kamikaze hit the Australian heavy cruiser HMAS *Australia,* and the organized suicide attacks by the "Special Attack Force" began on 25 October. The Kamikaze attacks began slowly, and at first increased slowly, as the Allies advanced toward the Japanese homeland. Several of Pearl Harbor's ghosts were hit by Kamikazes. Years later historians glorified the heroics of "The Divine Wind," which was neither divine nor a wind, took thousands of lives on both sides, and in the end was disastrous for the Japanese.[35]

In the Allies' five-month Okinawa campaign beginning in April 1945, the Japanese launched operation *Ten-Go* on 6 April, ten mass suicide attacks by aircraft, which included hundreds of fighters, bombers and torpedo planes escorting the Kamikazes; a total of 48 MXY-7 Ohka ("cherry blossom") suicide rocket-powered, flying bombs designated by the Allies as Baka ("idiot" in Japanese), intended to be air launched against Allied ships by G4M2e "Betty" Bombers; and finally a one-way suicide attack by a naval force that included the largest surviving Japanese battleship, *Yamato*—which was sunk within two hours after she was first sighted. Fewer than 300 of her crew survived and nearly 2,500 were lost. One hundred ninety ships in the Okinawa invasion force suffered casualties. Thirty-four were sunk. Casualties suffered at sea were 5,400 hundred killed and 6,700 wounded.[36] The enemy's increasing suicide attacks in the air, on the sea, and in ground campaigns on the islands, strongly influenced the decision to use atomic weapons to attempt to end the war before having to sacrifice hundreds of thousands of lives, perhaps millions on both sides, in an invasion of the Japanese homeland. A massive shift in Allied forces, by sealift from the ETO into the Pacific theater after Germany surrendered, was already in progress when the atomic bombs were dropped at Hiroshima and Nagasaki.

Among the cruisers in Pearl Harbor the morning of 7 December, or escorted convoys to or from Pearl Harbor in the month of December 1941, the *St. Louis*, *Raleigh*, *Detroit*, *New Orleans*, *Phoenix*, *San Francisco*, and *Honolulu* all survived the war with distinguished records of service.

The cruiser *San Francisco* was the intended victim of Japanese submarine *I-26* the morning of 13 November 1942, but survived while still struggling to recover from heavy damage she received early that morning in the fierce first engagement of the "Battle of Guadalcanal." *San Francisco* had taken 45 hits during the engagement with Japanese forces that included two battleships, one cruiser and 25 destroyers—and her crew fought 22 fires on board in the hours during and following the battle. Two of those 45 rounds struck the Flag and Navigation Bridges, killing or wounding all the officers present, including the task group commander, Rear Admiral Daniel J. Callaghan, who, as a captain, had commanded the *San Francisco* at Pearl Harbor. Admiral Callaghan was on the Flag Bridge, and in a particularly tragic irony, Captain Cassin Young, the *San Francisco*'s skipper, received fatal wounds. He had received the Medal of Honor for his actions at Pearl Harbor. As Commander Cassin Young on 7 December 1941, he was the feisty, hard-fighting captain of the repair ship *Vestal*, which was alongside the *Arizona*.

The courageous fight Admiral Callaghan's task group and *San Francisco* gave, and the battering she and her crew took the early morning hours of 13 November resulted in four Medals of Honor, three for crew members who fought heroically to save and keep fighting their heavily damaged ship. Lieutenant Commander Bruce McCandless, the Communications Officer, and Lieutenant Commander Herbert E. Schonland, the Damage Control Officer, were two of the crewmembers. Boatswain's Mate First Class Reinhardt J. Kepler, from Washington State, was the third, and with Admiral Callaghan, received the award posthumously.

In another terrible bit of irony, the *I-26*, which sank the SS *Cynthia Olson* 1,000 miles northeast of Oahu as Pearl Harbor was being attacked, and was to become one of the Imperial Japanese Navy's most notorious submarines, had struck again with devastating effects. The morning of the 13th, while engaged in one of several patrols following the sinking of the *Cynthia Olson*, *I-26* raised her periscope to see *San Francisco* crossing her path in torpedo range. Commander Minoru Yokota "snap-shot" three torpedoes that missed his intended target, the heavily-damaged *San Francisco*. The American task force of three cruisers and three destroyers was zigzagging, headed for repairs at the Island of Espiritu Santo in the New Hebrides. The second cruiser was the *Helena*, like *San Francisco* also a Pearl Harbor veteran, was also heavily damaged as a result of the battle during the hours after midnight.

Also in the formation was the light cruiser *Juneau* (CL-52), on *San Francisco*'s starboard quarter. The *Juneau* had been heavily damaged by a torpedo which exploded in her port side during the battle. The explosion was believed to have broken her keel and killed 17 crewmembers. She was 12 feet down by the bow, listing slightly to port and struggling to maintain 18 knots. Nevertheless, casualties on board *San Francisco* had been so heavy—77 dead and 105 wounded—that *Juneau*'s senior medical officer, Lieutenant Commander James G. Neff, who had himself been injured in the previous night's torpedo attack and was undoubtedly acting on *San Francisco*'s request, asked his junior medical officer, Lieutenant Roger W. O'Neill, if he wanted to go aboard *San Francisco* to assist her medics. A short time later the destroyer *O'Bannion* sent a boat to take O'Neill and three of *Juneau*'s medical corpsmen to *San Francisco*.

One of the torpedoes fired by *I-26* continued past the *San Francisco*, and at 1101 struck the *Juneau* amidships, between frames 42 and 45, close to the same area she had been struck by the torpedo early in the morning. At that moment, Lieutenant O'Neill was in the Admiral's cabin on *San Francisco*, donning his surgeon's mask prior to assisting Lieutenant Commander Lowe in operating on the fatally wounded, but still-living Captain Young. About one minute later, *Juneau*'s main magazine violently exploded, which broke her in half, killed most of her crew, and she sank in about 20 seconds. Among her crew were the five Sullivan brothers from Waterloo, Iowa, two of whom survived the explosion and sinking and were in the water among a total of approximately 115 men.

San Francisco immediately swung to starboard, and within 30 seconds Lieutenant O'Neill saw the spot where *Juneau* had been. The spot was 2,000 to 3,000 yards distant and he could see nothing but "tremendous clouds of grey and black smoke." Uncertain as to enemy ships and submarines in the area, the task group commander, aboard a damaged *Helena*, made a decision not to stop and pick up survivors, but continue toward Espiritu Santo. A message from *Helena* to a nearby B-17 search plane gave the location of *Juneau*'s loss. Unfortunately, *Helena*'s message didn't reach Noumea, and owing to continued uncertainty about the number of Japanese ships in the area, rescue efforts didn't begin for several days. Tragically, exposure, exhaustion and shark attacks whittled down the survivors, and only ten men were rescued from the water eight days later. None of the Sullivan brothers survived.[36]

The cruiser *New Orleans* survived the war, but not without a near disastrous close call. With four other cruisers and six destroyers in Task Force 67, commanded by Rear Admiral Carlton H. Wright, she fought in the Battle of Tassafaronga on the night of 30 November 1942, engaging a Japanese destroyer-transport force, which included eight destroyers, six acting as transports. It was a night when "Praise the Lord and Pass the

The cruiser *New Orleans* (CA-32) Camouflaged at Tulagi, Solomon Islands, some days after she was torpedoed during the Battle of Tassafaronga on 30 November 1942. Note that her stern is riding high, and that her forward end is low in the water. The torpedo and subsequent explosion had severed her bow between # 1 and # 2 eight-inch gun turrets. NA

Ammunition" would have a special significance to Chaplain Howell Forgy and the entire surviving ship's company. Unknown to them, the battle occurred about the time songwriter Frank Loessor was completing and copywriting the song that brought the Chaplain's Pearl Harbor legend to life, and in early 1943 would begin sweeping the nation as one of America's great wartime anthems.

When the TF 67 flagship *Minneapolis* (CA-36) was struck by two torpedoes, *New Orleans*, next astern, was forced to sheer away to avoid collision, and ran into the track of a torpedo which exploded, triggering a secondary explosion of a bomb and ammunition magazine. The combined explosions ripped off her bow. Bumping down the ship's port side, the severed bow punched several holes in *New Orleans'* hull. A fifth of her length gone, slowed to 2 knots, and blazing forward, the ship's crew fought for survival. Individual acts of heroism and self-sacrifice along with skillful seamanship kept her afloat, and under her own power she entered Tulagi Harbor near daybreak 1 December. On board were numerous wounded and more than 70 dead, with more lost when the number one turret and bow were ripped from the hull and sank. Among the dead on board was the ship's senior medical officer, Lieutenant Commander Edward Evans, who had been Chaplain Howell M. Forgy's close friend.

Camouflaging their ship from air attack, the crew jury-rigged a bow of coconut logs, and 11 days later, *New Orleans* sailed to replace a damaged propeller and make other repairs in Sydney, Australia, arriving 24 December. On 7 March 1943, she was underway for Puget Sound Navy Yard, where a new bow was fitted and all battle damage repaired. That fall, on 5-6 October she returned to the fight as part of a cruiser-destroyer force that bombarded Japanese-held Wake Island and repulsed a Japanese torpedo-plane attack during the sortie.

In yet another cruel twist of fate, similar to that of Captain Cassin Young on *San Francisco*, Officer's Cook Third Class Doris Miller, the African-American sailor who had been awarded the Navy Cross by Admiral Nimitz for "Dorie's" actions in repeatedly carrying wounded sailors to safety on the burning, sinking battleship *West Virginia*—lost his life to another Japanese veteran of Pearl Harbor, submarine *I-75*.

Reporting to Puget Sound Navy Yard on 1 June 1943, he was assigned to the new carrier, *Liscome Bay* (CVE-56), which was commissioned 7 August. That fall the escort carrier participated in her first and last battle, the Battle of Tarawa, which began on 20 November. On 24 November, at 0505 hours, while the three escort carriers and the battleship *New Mexico* (BB-40) were steaming at 15 knots, *Liscome Bay* sounded routine general quarters preparatory to launching aircraft at dawn.

Then, at 0510, with no warning of submarines present, a lookout shouted, ". . . here comes a torpedo!" One of four torpedoes fired by *I-75* hit the carrier on the starboard side, aft of the engine room with a shattering roar. The aircraft bomb magazine detonated a few moments later, disintegrating the ship's stern, and the entire interior burst into flames. The *New Mexico*, a mile away was showered with metal fragments and body parts. At 0533, *Liscome Bay* listed to starboard and sank, carrying Rear Admiral Henry M. Mullinix, Captain Irving D. Wiltsie, 53 other officers, and 591 enlisted men down with her. There were 242 survivors rescued. The rest of the crew was listed as missing and presumed dead. On 7 December 1943, Mr. and Mrs. Connery Miller were notified their son was "Missing in Action."[37]

The *Helena*, which was moored inside the minelayer *Oglala* at Dock 1010 the morning of 7 December 1941, and was struck by a torpedo that passed beneath *Oglala*, also accumulated a distinguished record of service, but didn't survive the war. On leaving Solomon Island waters after the Battle of Iron Bottom Sound, she underwent overhaul in Sydney, Australia, and was back to Espiritu Santo in March 1943 to participate in the bombardments of New Georgia Island, soon to be invaded. In the force escorting the transports carrying the initial landing parties, *Helena* moved into Kula Gulf just before midnight 4 July, and shortly after midnight on the 5th, her big guns opened up in her last shore bombardment.

The troops were landed successfully by dawn, but on the afternoon of 5 July, intelligence indicated The Tokyo Express was ready to roar down once more, and the escort group, composed of three cruisers and four destroyers turned north to meet it— three groups of destroyers totaling ten enemy ships. The battle began at 0157, and unfortunately the flashes of her rapidly firing guns lit her well. Hit by three torpedoes which broke her back, the cruiser jackknifed, broke into three parts and sank—except for the bow section which stayed afloat until the next day, with approximately 200 men clinging to it like a life raft. An inspiring series of events that day resulted in saving all but 168 of her nearly 900-man crew.[38]

The relatively new destroyer, *Monssen*, didn't survive the war. Not a Pearl Harbor veteran, her skipper was Lieutenant Commander Roland N. Smoot when the 1,630-ton ship was commissioned at Puget Sound Navy Yard 14 March 1941, a ceremony attended by his wife Sally and Joey Border, whom Sally gave away at the Border's wedding. After returning from five months of duty in the Atlantic, overhaul in the Boston Navy Yard, and sailing with Admiral Halsey's Task Force 16 on the Doolittle Raid, she was in Task Force 17 at the Battle of Midway and supported various operations in the Solomon Islands, beginning with the first of the Navy's giant amphibious landings 7-8 August. Lieutenant Commander Smoot had given up his command before *Monssen* fought her last battle. She, too, was at Iron Bottom Sound early the morning of 13 November 1942, as part Admiral Callaghan's Task Group 67.4—the same group the cruisers *San Francisco*, *Helena* and *Juneau* were in that morning.

The task group had escorted transports with reinforcements for Marines already ashore on the 12th, and after the transports were 90% un-laden of their cargo, were subjected to torpedo plane attacks, one of which cost use of *Monssen's* fire control radar. Shortly after 0140 on the 13th, the task group sighted the enemy fleet, which they had learned was inbound. The enemy was headed toward Henderson Field to bombard it and sneak in 11 of their transports, then en route to relieve their beleaguered comrades fighting on Guadalcanal. Ten minutes later the battle began.

At about 0220 hours *Monssen*, forced to rely on radio information and optics, was spot-lighted in a battle fought often at point blank range, hit by some 37 shells from Japanese destroyers, and reduced to a burning hulk. Twenty minutes later, completely immobilized in all departments, the ship was ordered abandoned. After daybreak, *Monssen* was still a floating incinerator when three crew members climbed aboard and rescued eight men still on the ship—five of whom lived after they were taken ashore. At about 0800 that morning the survivors were picked up and taken to Guadalcanal. The ship continued to blaze until early afternoon, when the waters of Iron Bottom Sound closed over her. The fierce battle took the lives of approximately 60 percent of her crew, a loss of 130 men.[39]

The destroyer *Reid*, which participated with the cruiser *Detroit* and destroyer *Cummings* in Task Force 15.2 in the first 46 hours of escorting the SS *President Coolidge* and USAT *General Hugh L. Scott* from Honolulu to San Francisco, 19-25 December, sank in approximately two minutes after being hit by two Kamikazes in Ormac Bay, Leyte, the Philippines, on 11 December 1944. One of the landing craft (LSM 42) accompanying the force of seven destroyers picked up over 100 of her crew members, many seriously wounded.[40]

The destroyer *Preston*, which participated with the cruiser *St. Louis* and the destroyer *Smith* in escorting the three Matson liners from San Francisco to Honolulu and back (Convoys 2005 and 4032) in December, was sunk by gunfire from the Japanese cruiser *Nagara*, off Guadalcanal the night of 14-15 November 1942, with the loss of 116 of her crew.[41]

Both the destroyers *Cushing* and *Perkins*, which participated with the cruiser *Phoenix* in escorting the six-ship Convoy 2004 from San Francisco to Honolulu and Pearl Harbor 17-24 December, were lost. Gunfire from Japanese warships sunk *Cushing* off Guadalcanal 13 November 1942, with the loss of 69 of her crew. The *Perkins* sank on 29 November 1943, with the loss of nine members of her crew, after colliding with the Australian troopship HMAS *Duntroon* off Cape Vogel, New Guinea.[42]

The destroyer *Monaghan*, which rammed, depth charged and sank the Japanese midget submarine in Pearl Harbor's Midde Loch on 7 December, fought in the Battles of Coral Sea and Midway and earned a total of 12 battle stars as part of her distinguished record. One action she was involved in was chasing and driving a Japanese submarine up on rocks near the Island of Kiska in the Aleutians, where the sub's crew abandoned her. The submarine was later identified as the *I-7*, which was another Pearl Harbor veteran. But *Monaghan*, en route to join escort for three oilers bound for a rendezvous with Admiral Halsey's Task Force 38, came to a tragic end 17 December 1944. That day a giant typhoon claimed 790 lives in the 3rd Fleet, and sank two other destroyers, *Spence* (DD-512) and *Hull* (DD-350), the *Hull* another Pearl Harbor veteran. For three days the only six survivors of *Monaghan*'s crew, plus 18 from *Hull*, awaited rescue until the two groups of survivors were picked up by the destroyer *Brown* (DD-546). *Mongahan*'s survivors described how the ship had repeatedly righted herself from starboard rolls, before finally rolling over.[43]

The destroyer *Tucker*, another Pearl Harbor veteran that

escorted the three battleships in Task Force 16 toward Puget Sound Navy Yard 20-27 December 1941 before leaving the formation for San Francisco with the battleship *Pennsylvania*, didn't survive the war.

After escorting convoys between San Francisco and Hawaii the next five months, *Tucker* was ordered to the South Pacific and spent the next four months on escort duty to Fiji, Australia, and New Zealand. On orders to escort the freighter SS *Nira Luckenbach* from Suva in the Fiji Islands to Espiritu Santo, the two ships departed Suva on 1 August 1942. As a result of a tragic communication error, in which the ship never received a "Q message," routinely sent to warn of a defensive minefield, *Tucker*

The destroyer *Ward* (APD-16), converted to a fast transport, burning in Ormoc Bay, Leyte, Philippine Islands, after she was hit by a Kamikaze on 7 December 1944. The destroyer *O'Brien* (DD-725) is fighting fires from alongside, as landing craft circle to rescue survivors, and later sunk the *Ward* with gunfire. Photographed from the *Crosby* (APD-17). Ironically, the commanding officer of the *O'Brien* that day was William W. Outerbridge, who commanded the *Ward* three years to the day earlier, when her crew sunk the Japanese midget submarine outside the entrance to Pearl Harbor. NA struck a mine at 2145 hours on 3 August as she was about to swing north to enter the Segond Channel, Espiritu Santo.

The explosion tore into her amidships, broke her keel, instantly killed three men, promptly slowed her to a stop, and her hull began folding like a jackknife. She was abandoned, then drifted most of the next day without sinking, was later taken under tow and grounded in hopes of salvage, but eventually sank in ten fathoms of water about 2100 hours on 4 August. Three other men were later determined missing, never found, and were assumed to have been lost when the ship sank. She sank having been struck by a mine from one of three minelayers that were also Pearl Harbor veterans: *Breese, Tracey,* and *Gamble*. The three minelayers were anchored at Espiritu Santo when *Tucker* struck the mine, and the mines had been laid across the south entrance to Segond Channel the day *Tucker*'s skipper, Lieutenant Commander W.R. Terrell, unknowingly brought his ship and crew into dangerous waters.[44]

The USS *Ward*, the World War I-era destroyer which fired the first shot of the Pacific war at a Japanese midget submarine outside the entrance to Pearl Harbor, and in the same attack depth charged the intruder an hour before the 7 December air raid, didn't survive the war. Sent to the West Coast for conversion to a high speed transport in 1942, she was re-designated APD-16. During the conversion her Number 3 gun, which had fired the first shot, was removed. In February 1943 *Ward* steamed to the Pacific to operate with U.S. forces in the Solomon Islands area, where she helped fight off a heavy Japanese air attack on Tulagi, 7 April 1943. After participating in several Southwest Pacific amphibious landings, she was sent to assist in recapturing the Philippines, and in early December 1944 transported Army troops during landings at Ormoc Bay.

On 7 December 1944, three years to the day after Number 3 gun fired the opening shot of America's involvement in the War, she was patrolling off the invasion area when she came under attack by three Japanese twin engine bombers, which broke away from the remnants of a larger formation of nine under attack by Army Air Force P-40s and P-38s and entered a 45-degree dive from approximately 5,000 feet altitude. As soon as the bombers broke away and turned for the destroyer, her gunners opened fire with 3-inch and 20-millimeter batteries, and the ship began a full left rudder turn to port. The lead plane was smoking, either hit by one of the American fighters, or firing its machine guns at *Ward*, while aiming for a Kamikaze attack. Moments before impact, the airplane leveled from its dive, crashing into her hull amidships about six inches above the water line on the port side, and within minutes bringing her to a stop. Debris, including one or both aircraft engines passed completely through the hull and tore large holes in the hull on the starboard side. Amidships the aircraft gasoline had started a huge, rapidly expanding fire. She took on a ten degree list to starboard, began losing steam because of repeated blow-back through the boilers, making it necessary to stop the engines, shut off valves to avoid an explosion—a complete loss of power. The resulting fires could not be effectively fought or controlled, and *Ward*'s crew was ordered to abandon ship. Still burning fiercely and obviously not salvageable, she was sunk by gunfire from the destroyer *O'Brien* (DD-725), whose commanding officer, William W. Outerbridge, had been in command of *Ward* during her action off Pearl Harbor three years before. There was no loss of life on the *Ward*, despite the successful Kamikaze attack.

In 1956, the 4-inch Number 3 gun was installed as a memorial at the Minnesota State Capitol in St. Paul, as the men who fired the gun that fateful morning of 7 December were members of the Minnesota Naval Reserve. The ship's bell is now displayed in the St. Paul, Minnesota City Hall, on the 3rd floor between the council and mayoral offices.

There nearly always are uncertainties and doubts surrounding a claimed sinking of an enemy submarine, and for years a minority of academics doubted whether the *Ward* had really sunk a Japanese midget sub, since undersea searches off Pearl Harbor had previously failed to locate the midget submarine. On 28 August 2002, a team of scientists from the University of Hawaii discovered the submarine 1200 feet underneath the sea in American waters about 3-4 miles outside the harbor. The starboard side of the conning tower exhibited two shell holes— evidence of damage from a 4-inch shell from the *Ward*'s guns. While *Ward*'s depth charges were sufficient to fully lift the 46-ton, 78-foot midget out of the water, they did no apparent structural damage to the submarine, which sank due to water flooding into the vessel from two shell holes.[45]

There was more than a bit of irony associated with the first four convoys related to the December 1941 reinforcement of Hawaii

The *President Coolidge*, sinking on 26 October 1942 after hitting two mines while traversing the Scorff Passage into Segond Channel, Espiritu Santo Island, New Hebrides. Troops of the 172nd Regimental Combat Team, the 43rd Division, climb down ropes and cargo nets to escape as the ship lists to port at a rate of about one degree per minute. Some are fortunate to be taken to shore by lifeboat or raft, others must swim. Two men lost their lives in the tragic accident, which could have been far worse were it not for the actions of Captain Henry Nelson, his crew and the disciplined response by the officers and men of the 172nd RCT. NA

and evacuations of wounded, tourists, non-essential government employees and their dependents, dependents of contractor personnel and military dependents from Oahu. Neither *President Coolidge* nor the *General Hugh L. Scott*, which comprised the first convoy to San Francisco, survived the war. The USAT *Tasker H. Bliss*, in Convoy 2004 with five other ships, the SS *President Garfield*, the USS *Aldebaran, Harris, Platte*, and *Sabine*, met her end at the hands of a German U-Boat in waters off North Africa during Operation Torch—as did the *Hugh L. Scott*.

The *Tasker H. Bliss* was transferred to the Navy on 19 August 1942, converted for use as a Navy transport by the Maryland Drydock Co., Baltimore, Maryland, commissioned on 15 September, and arrived in Norfolk, Virginia on 22 September to join Task Force 34. Similarly, the *Hugh L. Scott* was taken over by the Navy 14 August 1942 and converted to an attack transport in Hoboken, New Jersey, sailed to join the same task force. After loading troops and equipment for Operation Torch, the invasion of North Africa, the task force sailed on 24 and 25 October for the coast of Morocco. Assigned to Task Group 34.9, Center Attack Group, *Bliss* and *Scott* arrived off Fedhala, Morocco on 8 November.

The evening of 12 November, they were riding at anchor in Fedhala Roads when the German submarine *U-130* slipped in among the ships and fired five torpedoes at three transports. All torpedoes hit their targets, and they burst into flames. *Bliss, Scott,* and the *Edward Rutledge* (AP-52) were *U-130*'s victims. The crews abandoned all three and the *Rutledge* and *Scott* sank shortly. The *Bliss* burned until 0230 the next morning, and then sank. Casualties were eight officers and 51 men.[46]

On 26 October 1942, while the major naval battle of Santa Cruz was in progress three hundred miles north, another drama was taking place at Espiritu Santo. The former great American President's Line cruise ship, *President Coolidge*, converted to a troop ship following the attack on Pearl Harbor, and with the *Hugh L. Scott*, the first to carry evacuees from Honolulu to San Francisco after the attack, was carrying 5,050 Army troops, 50 Navy Armed Guard and Signal personnel, plus 340 ship's crew when she struck two mines in a defensive minefield and sank in ninety minutes. Bound for Espiritu Santo in the New Hebrides Islands, from Noumea, New Caledonia, Captain Henry Nelson's ship attempted to enter Segond Channel from the east, through

Scorff Passage, rather than from the south between Acore Island and Tutuba Island. The tragic accident came thirteen weeks after the destroyer *Tucker* fell victim to another minefield at the south entrance to Segond Channel while turning north from Bruat Channel. The two mines which *Coolidge* struck were part of a barrier of mines intended to block enemy penetration of the anchorage and huge staging base through Scorff Passage.

Though the *Coolidge* was a great loss to the Allied cause, and the sinking was intensely controversial and later the subject of three courts of inquiry, Captain Nelson averted a major disaster by acting quickly after the two mines exploded, the first on the port side beneath the engine room at 0935 hours. The ship maintained forward momentum and 30 seconds later the second mine blasted the starboard bottom plates amidships, also near the engine room. After rapidly obtaining sketchy damage reports, he correctly concluded he was going to lose the ship, ordered all watertight doors closed, followed by "hard right rudder" to take advantage of the headway to turn the ship directly into shore, and beach her in shallow water. At 0938 the ship struck the coral ledge fifty meters from the shore, and Captain Nelson immediately called "Abandon Ship."

Miraculously, in the next 90 minutes all but two men escaped the sinking *Coolidge*, which heeled to port, capsized as she was going down, and slid stern-first down a steep bank toward deeper water. The first was Fireman Robert Reid, who was working in the engine room and was killed by the initial mine blast. The second was Captain Elwood J. Euart, of the 103rd Field Artillery, attached to the 172nd Infantry Regiment aboard, who was the Troop Mess Officer on duty in the enlisted men's mess hall, and personally checked the clearing of the area when the alarm sounded. On arriving at his abandon-ship station he learned of men trapped in the hold and went there. By lashing himself to the low end of a rope he was able to hold tight enough for men to climb up it to safety, even though the ship was listing badly. Finally, as he attempted to climb up, almost vertically by that moment, with the help of a few men at the other end of the line, the ship sank very quickly. "For his unselfish, heroic action and with utter disregard for his own safety, Captain Euart conducted himself far above and beyond the call of duty, saved countless lives and gave his life that others might live." So stated the citation accompanying the posthumous award of the Distinguished Service Cross.[47]

The Matson Line's *Lurline*, *Matsonia* and *Monterey*, which carried the first full load of evacuees home from Hawaii in December 1941, all survived the war with distinguished records of service—along with Matson's fourth great passenger liner of that era, SS *Mariposa*, the sister-ship of *Lurline* and *Monterey* not mentioned in this work.

The following tells of the liners' magnificent wartime contributions to the nation and its armed forces:

Vessel	Number of Voyages	Miles Steamed	Total Passengers Carried	Total Meals Served
Lurline	31	388,847	199,860	9,322,706
Average/ Voyage		12,544	6,447	300,732
Matsonia	33	328,301	163,732	6,526,524
Average/ Voyage		9,949	4,962	197,773
Monterey	26	328,490	170,240	8,663,471
Average/ Voyage		12,634	6,547	333,210
Mariposa	29	414,589	202,689	10,571,670
Average/ Voyage		14,296	6,989	364,540
Grand Total	119	1,460,227	736,521	35,084,371
Average/ Voyage		12,271	6,189	294,827[48]

Japanese submarine attacks off the West Coast diminished somewhat after 25 December 1941; however, they remained a threat to be reckoned with into the fall of 1942, requiring the continued escort of convoys and aggressive anti-submarine warfare. On 25 February 1942, Japanese submarine *I-17* shelled the Ellwood oil production facilities at Goleta, California, near

Santa Barbara. It was the first enemy shelling of a U.S. mainland military installation since the War of 1812. The notorious *I-26* shelled and sank the 3,268-ton American freighter, *Coast Trader*, 35 miles southwest of Cape Flattery near the Straits of Juan de Fuca, on Sunday, 7 June 1942. After sunset on 20 June, *I-26* surfaced and shelled the Estevan Lighthouse and radio station on Vancouver Island, British Columbia, Canada. It was the first attack on Canadian soil since 1812.[49]

On 21 June, *I-25* fired 17 rounds at coastal defenses at Ft. Stevens at the mouth of the Columbia River, on the Oregon side. On 9 September *I-25* again appeared in coastal waters and catapulted a Watanabe Tekkosho E14Y-1 "Glen," piloted by Warrant Officer Nobuo Fujita and carrying two incendiary bombs intended to cause a large forest fire and force repositioning of the Pacific Fleet to the West Coast. Warrant Officer Fujita dropped them near Mount Emmily, but rain had saturated the woods, making the attempt unsuccessful. It was the first time in history the mainland had been bombed by an enemy aircraft. The next day an Army Air Force Lockheed

A-29 Hudson on patrol from the 42nd Bomb Group spotted the surfaced *I-25* when some of her crew were on deck. Commander Neiji Tagami ordered a crash dive and the submarine was at 230 feet depth when the A-29 dropped three depth charges. One exploded at 80 feet, the others at 100 feet, damaging an antenna lead and causing a leak in the radio room. While Tagami tried to escape seaward, the plane dropped seven more depth charges, but inflicted no damage.

On Tuesday night, 29 September, *I-25* surfaced again 50 miles west of Cape Blanco, and at 2107 hours catapulted Fujita's aircraft in another attempt to start a forest fire, this time starting one fire that went out before the Forest Service arrived to suppress it. On Sunday, 4 October *I-25* sank the American freighter *Camden* off the south coast of Oregon, with one crewman killed. The following Tuesday *I-25* sank the tanker *Larry Doheny* off Cape Sebastian, with the loss of two crewmen and four U.S. Navy armed guards.[50]

There were additional reports of submarines present in Hawaiian waters during January 1942, but attacks tapered off after the *I-71*, captained by Commander Rokuro Kawasaki, attacked a small three-ship convoy and sank the Army Transport *Royal T. Frank* in the channel between Maui and Hawaii on 28 January with the loss of 24 island men. A survivor reported, "The ship did not seem to blow up or sink, she just disintegrated and disappeared in 30 or 40 seconds." The motorship *Kalae* rescued 36 men from the oily waters and rushed them to Hana, Maui, where the 13 seriously injured were treated at the Hana Hospital. Seventeen of the missing were Island-born soldiers en route to the Big Island to serve as garrison troops. The others were crew members.[51]

On Friday, 20 February 1942, Sara Hill Heaton and Sara Dudley Heaton, wife and daughter of Major Leonard D. Heaton, the Army surgeon at the North Sector General Hospital in Schofield Barracks on 7 December, left Oahu for the mainland on the *Lurline*. An anguished Dr. Heaton wrote in his diary the night after his wife and daughter departed Honolulu into waters still haunted by Japanese submarine attacks, from an island still deeply worried about another air raid—or worse.

> What can I write—all I love near aboard the Lurline at 10:45 AM today. Oh God please please help me to bear up under this cross. And God please be with them every step of the way. Sara Hill held up well and I would have too but Sara Dudley started crying and then I was literally torn to shreds—this is almost like going thru the Valley of the Shadow of death—but I pray God that it is his will that in some distant day we shall draw together again. I can't write more—tears just can't be held back.

Three days after they left on the *Lurline*, Japanese submarine *I-17* shelled the oil production facility at Goleta, California, north of Santa Barbara. En route, Mrs. Heaton wrote in her diary, describing the convoy and conditions similar to those experienced by Joey Border and other passengers in the December 1941 convoys. ". . . 9 beds in a stateroom . . . put on and told to keep on life belts . . . 1700 women—800 children and quite a number of men . . . sea sickness . . . twins and other babies born en route . . . heard some women lost babies . . . zigzagging."

The relatively large convoy she described in part in a simple diagram in her diary included a destroyer in the lead, the *President Garfield* on the port bow of *Lurline*; on her starboard bow was the British-owned Curnard Line's giant, 901 foot-long, 45,647-gross ton SS *Aquitania*, which took her maiden voyage from Liverpool, England in May 1914, and was built to carry 3,230 passengers as a grand cruise liner.

A cruiser was in the formation, beyond *Aquitania*, and the *President Grant* was on the starboard abeam of *Lurline*. An unnamed transport and another cruiser were off *Lurline*'s starboard quarter, and the 13,788-gross ton transport USS *Wharton* (AP-7), was off *Lurline*'s port quarter. Astern of *Lurline* came the aircraft transport *Kitty Hawk* (AKV-1), which in early February had carried a load of airplanes to Pearl Harbor to replace those lost in the 7 December attack—and another destroyer off the starboard quarter of *Kitty Hawk*. She described Navy and Army airplanes overhead, escorting the convoy from Honolulu "for some distance, then disappeared." When they were en route the *Grant* broke down, which slowed progress considerably. Then, because of the submarine threat off the West Coast, the convoy veered considerably off the great circle route, all of which stretched five days into nine. Sara Heaton was heartened and the passengers were cheered considerably to see a Catalina PBY aircraft meet and begin escorting the convoy into its destination.[52]

Sara Hill Heaton's husband completed a distinguished 40-year career as a surgeon in the Army, devoting his life to healing and saving the lives of soldiers and their families. The first surgeon in the Army to become a lieutenant general, he was named the Army's Surgeon General from 1959 to 1969, which spanned in part the Vietnam War. During that period he became President Dwight D. Eisenhower's personal physician and provided devoted treatment to retired General of the Army Douglas MacArthur in the days before he died in 1964.[53]

No Greater Love . . . .

By 1 March 1942, approximately 10,000 people were evacuated from Oahu, and some 20,000 more followed safely before the end of the year. The evacuees were convoyed on ships that had taken thousands of American servicemen, their equipment and supplies to Oahu and other huge staging bases building up to prosecute the war in the Pacific.[54] The additional 10,000 above original estimates can be accounted for in part by approximately 2,000 Japanese Americans brought to the United States for internment,

1,500 more who volunteered to serve in the armed forces, most in the 100ᵗʰ Battalion and 442ⁿᵈ Regiment.

In World War II, from 7 December 1941 until Japan surrendered 2 September 1945, the United States fought a war lasting 1,364 days, or 44 months and 24 days. American casualties were 435,399 dead, including non-combat deaths and 78,976 missing later declared dead, with 670,846 wounded for a total of 1,106,245. Seen from a different perspective, the nation suffered an average of 319 dead, and total of 811 killed and wounded a day, every day at war.

On 5 January 1941, Karl Frederick Border celebrated his 26ᵗʰ birthday—flying solo out of Pensacola Naval Air Station, Florida. His mother, Missy, and his dad gave him a magazine subscription for a gift, and he received a decorated birthday cake from Mary Mather, a young woman who was a long time friend.

Nineteen days later, in Puget Sound Navy Yard, Bob Border said goodbye to his shipmates and was detached from the *Tennessee*. A few days afterward he and Joey said their goodbyes to Captain and Mrs. Springer, Joey's parents, and left Seattle by train for Mobile, Alabama, arriving at 1520 hours on 5 February. They were overjoyed to be home. Bob was happily on his way to Naval Aviators' Training in Pensacola, looking toward a future as a Navy fighter pilot, a dream finally come true. Karl was in Pensacola while they were still en route that morning, and he later remarked in his diary, ". . . Luckily was able to meet them and we had a big dinner afterward. Sure is good to see Minimus and his 4.0 wife."

Joey met Bob's mother and father in person for the first time and was able to stay with them almost a week, which spanned Missy's birthday. Karl noted they "bought her many fine presents," and he took her some flowers and a compact. On 11 February Joey and Bob went to Warrington, Florida, near Pensacola, to see the new house Karl had picked out for them at 304 2ⁿᵈ Street. He was delighted to know "[they] like it, thank goodness."

On 1 April Bob Border flew his first training mission out of Pensacola, and on 4 April, an excited Karl Border, his class having completed its training, remarked in his diary, "Received our wings today! It seems impossible that we are Naval Aviators now but it's a swell feeling . . . " Four days later he told his diary, "Bob evidently is getting this flying very well—the little scoundrel is doing as I expected and I expect him to be an ace." By 8 April, Bob had flown six training missions in the N3N-3, a yellow bi-wing airplane nicknamed by the men who flew it, "The Yellow Peril," and was enjoying flying immensely. Two days later he soloed, and in his mind flying progressed from enjoyable to exhilarating.

On the 17th Karl wrote, "Had one of the best evenings I've ever had tonight. Missy, Dad, and I went to a cocktail party together at Lt. Cmdr Goldenberg's and afterward to a Mobile Junior League Dance. Missy enjoyed it, I think, and I had a deuce of a good time dancing with her and watching her have a good time." Two days later—"Said Aloha to Missy, Dad, Bob, Joey, and Bunky [the family air dale dog], and then Margaret, and headed west on a trip I hope will stop by Tokyo. Saw two ships launched at the yard this morning and a photographer took Dad and Bob and my picture."

He drove through southern Louisiana, Texas, New Mexico, and Arizona, arriving in San Diego on 22 April for assignment to the Advanced Carrier Training Group. The Springers were now living in San Diego, as Captain Springer would soon be preparing for further assignment somewhere in the Pacific. When Karl arrived about 9:00 p.m. they greeted him warmly, invited him to stay with them while he looked for an apartment and began advanced carrier qualification training, first in the SNJ-3, then in the Douglas Dauntless dive-bomber, the SBD. They had a room ready to provide him, and the warmth of their reception eased his delighted acceptance of their offer.

On 12 May, the Springers brought him "... lots of nice things," the beginning of a red letter day. That was the day he met Mary Chubbock, "... a pretty little nurse [at the Navy hospital] who [had] been in England," during the early days of the war. On the 16th, without elaborating, he noted in his diary, "In the last seven days 5 pilots have been killed in A.C.T.G."—a measure of the hazards inherent in advanced carrier training, and on the 19th he remarked with obvious pleasure, "Captain Springer made major today, and I'm damn glad!"

Mary Chubbock had attended school in England, and Karl was enthralled with her personality and beauty. During later encounters, including movies, parties, dancing, dinners at restaurants and at the Springer's home, a whirlwind romance ensued. On Friday, 30 May he proposed to her, and she accepted. Wedding plans proceeded apace, with enthusiastic help from the Springers; a Saturday, 7 June drive to Los Angeles to meet

Mary's mother and father, Bob and Jeanette "Jay" Chubbock; on Sunday eight days later, a day with Mary at the Springers with a phone call and ". . . wonderful talk with Missy, Dad and Bob." Then came Friday, 20 June, and the words, "Mary and I were married at eight o'clock tonight by Canon Barnes, making this the happiest day of my life . . . "

Karl and Mary Border left that night for their honeymoon in Idyllwild, California, and he wrote in his diary the next day, "Idyllwild is a marvelous place—mountains, giant pines, trails, streams—and above all, Mary. Last night was a night of happy and perfect love." On Monday, he was back on duty, and remarked, "Back to work at North Island and our honeymoon is over—the happiest two days and nights of my life. With Mary as a wife I expect to fly and fight better."

Six joyous weeks followed their wedding. They moved into their first home on 10 July, described by Karl as a "nifty" apartment at 910 4th Street in San Diego, amid more movies, parties, picnics, swimming, a rodeo; dinners at clubs, restaurants, and with Springers; Charlotte Springer's silver wedding anniversary, visits with Mary's family, his discovery that Mary was a "4.0 cook," his promotion to "full lieutenant," more flying—which he loved—and all the while Karl's departure for the Pacific war drew nearer.

On 24 July, still at North Island, Karl and three other pilots from the A.C.T.G. reported to their new squadron, Bombing Squadron Ten, VB-10, a squadron in Air Group 10—and he met the squadron's Skipper, Lieutenant Commander Frank T. Corbin, and the Executive Officer, Lieutenant Commander James A. Thomas. To Karl, "They both seem fine and it looks like a good outfit." On Thursday, 30 July, VB-10 bombed a target boat, and Karl was elated by his results, ". . . I think eight of my ten bombs would have sunk a carrier." The next day Air Group 10 exercised as a unit three long hours—scouts, bombers, torpedo planes, and fighters. Karl flew again on Saturday, on the wing of the squadron exec, and on Sunday, 2 August, the Group packed all day, ordered to be ready to leave for Hawaii immediately.

On Tuesday evening, Karl and Mary attended a party given by Tom and Shel Gary for all the new "full lieutenants" and their wives in the Naval Academy class of '39—the Malones, Harris's, Millers, Gardners, Nortons, Abbots, Wallaces, MacConnagheys, Kilpatricks, Eckhardts—"before we're off to war!" as he remarked in his diary. The next day, he wrote, "[In] Coronado. Kissed my Mary 'Aloha,' and started for Hawaii and wherever else the war may take us. What a lovely and perfect wife the little gal has been! Took the train with all of A.G. X [10]." The train went to San Francisco, and as soon as it arrived, he went to Vallejo and "Saw Grandma and Aunt Carrie, Elizabeth. Bill and Gail had a nice dinner and he stayed all night."

The next day, 8 August, he was aboard ship en route to Hawaii when the squadron executive officer told him he would have the additional duty of squadron "Engineering Officer," the officer responsible for aircraft maintenance. Delighted with his expanded responsibilities, he wrote that night, ". . . It will be a lot of work but also the best training and I intend to work like hell . . . "

The roll of a ship under his feet felt good, and on the way he thought of the *Tennessee*, his leaving her a year earlier—and this had been the best year of his life. The week en route was busy, with briefings and lectures on anti-aircraft artillery, radar, duties of the squadron's executive officer and commander. Additionally, he practiced sending Morse Code and was becoming proficient. But most of all, he missed Mary. Thought of her. Wrote about her. Wondered what she was doing. He was deeply in love with his wife, wished she were with him. Simply couldn't think of much else when he had a few free moments.

They arrived in Pearl Harbor on 15 August, and there was the *Tennessee*. Karl enjoyed a fresh look at her, repaired and fit to fight. But there was no time to lose. The next day the entire squadron was sent to Kaneohe, and they began settling in—until the 18th, when they were told to move again, to Ewa, where training began in earnest. On the 19th VB-10 trekked by highway, over the Pali, and resettled at Ewa. Karl noted ". . . Hawaii is very changed & warlike . . . Ewa is about as crude as they make them but will have fun and get started flying at last. Took our desk from Kaneohe. Wrote Missy, Mary, and Mary's mother by V-[mail]."

In the following week the squadron worked hard to settle in at Ewa, arranged for base support by the Marines, learned their field operating procedures and how Ewa fit in with other airfield operations on the island, organized aircraft operations and maintenance, got oriented on island defenses, gunnery and bombing ranges before beginning flying training on 26 August— the day Karl, now a pilot on a combat aircraft, for the first time got back into the air over Hawaii.

The next day he learned of the first American offensive land campaign of the war, the invasion of Guadalcanal, the beginning of what was to be a long, bloody battle on many islands in the Solomons. Major George Springer was in fact there, in the role of a comptroller and paymaster, and survived the war, although Karl didn't know for certain Joey's dad was on Guadalcanal when he wrote the night of the 27th, "Major Springer must be with them, and I hope to hell is all o.k. The Marines are really a damn good outfit and I'm proud of them . . . " The next evening, after working in squadron engineering, he noted ". . . some trouble with dirt in the [aircraft] gas coming from heaven knows where."

Karl had begun receiving letters from Mary within a day or two after the squadron arrived in Pearl Harbor, and the flow of letters continued, with Karl noting he had received more letters from Mary than any other officer in the squadron received from their wives or sweethearts, saying, "[I] get a tremendous thrill out of each one. She is taking care of things in fine shape at home but must be a bit at loose ends so she's thinking of getting a job. It worries me a little bit but she has lots of sense and will do the best thing I'm sure. Give most anything to have the little sweetheart with me."

Then came September and a whirlwind of flying training, except on the 7th he managed to get a station wagon and drive to Pearl Harbor and Honolulu, where he bought a jade necklace for Mary's birthday and mailed it the next day. Dive bombing, glide bombing, gunnery, formation flying and tactics, dive bombing from 16,000 feet—for the first time using oxygen. Target ship attacks from 16,000 two days later. Gunnery missions to give radiomen/gunners in SBD rear seat practice at shooting airborne target sleeves towed by other aircraft. Following a 14 September gunnery mission, he observed, "Margarido, my gunner, did very well on the sleeve and I hope he'll be able to do as well on the Jap Zeroes . . . "

The next day Karl was delighted to learn ". . . Bob got his wings, his lifelong ambition, and I'm very proud and glad. Hope we will be flying together in the not too distant future." Plans were under way between Mary Chubbock Border in San Diego and Mary Joleen Border in Warrington, Florida. Bob already had orders for Navy North Island. His father had tried to "help him" get his long-dreamed-of fighter assignment, but the Bureau of Personnel needed dive bomber pilots, and he was going to fly

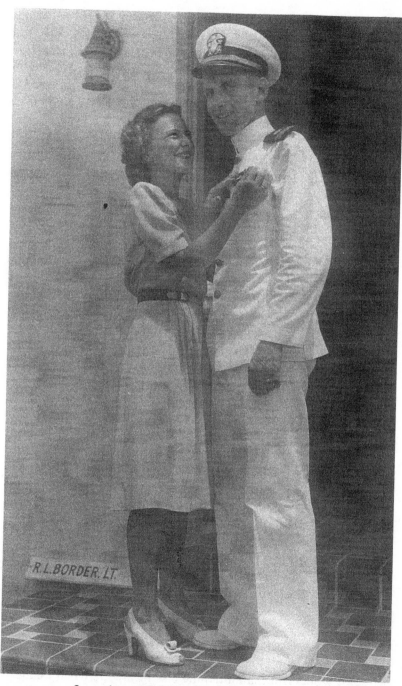

Joey pins on Bob Border's Navy wings of gold, Pensacola, Florida, September 1942. Borders' Collection.

the SBD. The two Mary's agreed Mary Chubbock Border would hold her apartment at 910 4th Street in San Diego for Mary Joleen Border and Bob, and Karl's Mary would go visit and personally introduce herself to Captain and Missy Border in Mobile, for an overdue visit and "get acquainted" period. A perfect arrangement, and a way for Bob and Joey to avoid house hunting when time together was already scarce.

Since the day Karl came into VB-10 at San Diego's Naval Air Station North Island, his squadron commander and executive officer had been observing and evaluating the performance of every officer, pilot, radioman/gunner, petty officer and sailor in the squadron, to organize and develop the most cohesive, effective combat squadron they could. On September 18, he received a pleasant surprise. "I have been given the second division, quite some responsibility. Am going to have to whip the boys into shape for a quick, accurate dive bombing attack and a tight defense against Zeroes." He would be leading three two-plane sections in combat. "It's a hell of a responsibility and a great privilege. We had a night of flying tonight." This was the prelude to night practice carrier landings.

In the days ahead he began welding his division into a team. On the 22nd, he tested his "permanent plane, B-7 [Bureau Number 40 6654], and found it pretty good. Took the lads around the island, through the clouds, close to the surf; tail chased & dive bombed." The next day he flew a scouting hop with his new wingman, Bob "Hoot" Gibson. "Bob is a veteran with two subs to his credit and is an excellent flier and a good fellow." The 24th Karl put the second division "through a good workout—clouds, surface flying—the boys are learning to fly tight." And then he added, "The moon is full and miss Mary more than ever. How I wish we were together."

> 26 September 1942. Barbers Point, TH—My darling Mary sent me two letters, and I've been happy all day. Her brother Bob is going to prep school in Long Beach and I hope will get an appointment to the Academy. Each day I miss Mary more and more and I long to be back with her. It will be more wonderful than anything else in my life when I can get back to her.

He continued to work hard to weld his second division into a strong unit within VB-10. On Sunday, the 27th, he drew a truck from the motor pool and took 12 "boys" to Pearl Harbor. Knowing it wouldn't be long until the squadron was aboard an aircraft carrier, they looked at the "Big E"—the *Enterprise*—the battleship *South Dakota*, and the carrier *Saratoga*—and then it was off to Oahu Country Club for 18 holes of golf. The artist came out in him again when he observed, "Nussover valley was shrouded in clouds and mist, a beautiful contrast to the blue sky over Honolulu and the Aloha Tower. Wrote Mary and Missy and Dad, wished I were with my wife."

On Monday, it was back on the flying training schedule, a heavy schedule, with three flights each Monday and Tuesday. After a hard day on Monday, he wrote, ". . . Received a long letter from Mary, whom I miss more each day. She is the best and loveliest of wives and I expect to spend all my life making her happy." On Tuesday, the division dive bombed, fought fighters, and practiced carrier landings. He judged his division to be ". . . very effective against attacking fighters, but it requires one hell of a lot of flying. My division—Border, Gibson, Goddard, Czarvecki, Leonard, and Winograd improves every day and soon we should be a crack outfit . . . "

Then on Wednesday, 30 September, VB-10 had its first fatality, a sobering event Karl wrote of that evening. Karl had led his second division in a dive bombing attack on a target boat, following Lieutenant Commander Thomas' division. He pushed over, extended his plane's dive flaps—speed brakes to keep the aircraft from accelerating beyond its aerodynamically limiting speed—and dove on the target. One aircraft flown by Lieutenant Czarnecki, from the other division, somehow got out of position and pulled up into Goddard's propeller, which cut Czarnecki's fuselage apart just aft of the rear cockpit. Czarnecki bailed out but was hit by a piece of the wing, and his throat was cut. His radioman/gunner, Bode, went in with the plane. Karl's reaction was typical of men who daily would face danger, even in flight training. ". . . -tough luck for two good fellows."

The 1st of October was another red letter day. Karl and the men of VB-10 received the words they had been preparing and training for, "The Squadron is preparing to put to sea on the *Enterprise* loaded for Japs. We are all working like hell and I expect we will be in fair shape by the time we go aboard . . . "

Then, for the next three days, it was more flying, a talk from a representative of the Sperry Gyro about the SBD's automatic pilot, and yet another on the landing procedure by the *Enterprise* landing signal officer.

On 4 October, another letter from Mary, and on the 6th he wrote, "Had another wonderful letter from Mary—how I love that gal and wish I were with her. We had squadron tactics for 2 ½ hours this morning and another 2 hours tonight. Tonight was a hell of a mess."

Not until 7 October did time and events permit him to record the day's events. Again, the sensitive artist flowed through his pen onto the diary's page. "VB-10 took a cross country hop to Hilo, Hawaii. We left Kaneohe, passed Molokai, Lanai, Maui, Kahoolawe, and finally picked up the big island. The cliffs and waterfalls of Molokai and Hawaii are beautiful."[55]

It was Monday afternoon, 19 October 1942, at 910 4th Street in San Diego, when a knock came at Joey's and Bob's apartment door. Bob was on duty, flying that day in the Advanced Carrier Training Group. When Joey opened the door, a Western Union deliveryman asked, "Mrs. Mary Border?"

"Yes," Joey replied.

"I have a telegram for you, Ma'am. Please sign here."

Joey signed, handed him the pen with a "thank you," and closed the door. She was curious about who might have sent her a telegram. Her mother was nearby while her dad was in the Pacific, and Bob's parents were in Mobile where she had left them in good health less than a month ago. Yet, on more than one occasion telegrams had been used to communicate among the families. Still somewhat puzzled she opened the envelope, and in astonished disbelief read the words, "We regret to inform you that Lieutenant Karl Frederick Border . . . "

Almost immediately she was overcome with sorrow and tears began to flow. Then abruptly, realizing the intended recipient of the telegram, she regained her composure. She had just accepted the telegram intended for Karl's Mary. The Navy wasn't aware Mary C. Border, the person Karl had rightly named to contact in case of an emergency, had moved from the address he listed. "Good God in heaven. What can I do? What must I do?" Mary Border was in Mobile, Alabama, visiting Captain and Missy Border, Mary's new mother and father-in-law, whom she hadn't met before she and Karl were married on 20 June. Joey knew what she must do, without hesitation.

The agonizing phone call to Mobile was first, in which she had to attempt hiding the sadness in her voice and ask to speak to Bob's father first—then tell him and let him tell Missy and Karl's Mary. Next came the call to Bob's training squadron. She asked that he come to their apartment as soon as possible. "There is an emergency." The message conveyed to Bob was troubling.

When he arrived, he could tell by the expression on her face something was terribly wrong. She asked him to sit down on the couch, she had something to tell him. Controlling her emotions as best she could, she gently described the arrival of the telegram she had in her hand, and how she mistakenly accepted what was obviously intended for Mary, Karl's wife. "Karl has been killed," she said. "Here's the telegram. I called your father just before I called the squadron to ask that you come home."[56]

Typically, like all those before Karl, the death notification from the Department of the Navy gave no details or explanation of the cause, thus Karl's father, a highly respected senior officer in the Navy, immediately began inquiring of the facts and circumstances, and the outlines of his last flight began to emerge. In the end, the accident presented a set of facts entirely consistent with the strong, caring, duty-bound, conscientious man, Karl Frederick Border.

Sunday, 11 October, Karl, with Aviation Radioman/gunner First Class Arthur S. Margarido in the aft cockpit, took off for a dive bomb training mission to drop live ordnance from SBD-3 Bureau No. 40 6654. The aircraft was carrying a 500-pound bomb, hung underneath the fuselage, on the plane's centerline, almost directly below the front cockpit. The flight was from Naval Air Station Barber's Point, a new field built after the attack on Pearl Harbor and before Karl returned to Hawaii.

Once airborne, just past the end of the runway, he immediately retracted the landing gear, and continued in a straight, very slow climb for about ten seconds, after which he made an S-turn starting to the right into Ewa Field, which was about 1 ½ miles distant along the axis of the Barber's Point runway. The landing at 0910 hours was apparently forced, judging by the nature of the approach and the fact his landing gear was not extended. The landing was good and the plane skidded along the runway 500 feet, resting on the bomb all the way. According to the accident report, Karl and Arthur were just preparing to step out of their cockpits when the bomb exploded, disintegrating the center section and breaking the plane in two at Karl's cockpit. The bodies of both were thrown about twenty feet by the explosion. The airplane was demolished with only slight damage to the engine, and the cause of the accident was undetermined.[57]

Bob and Joey were later told that Karl was exiting the front cockpit when he saw Arthur Margarido having trouble getting out of the aft cockpit. He went to help, and they were both killed by the explosion. As well attested to by men who flew in the aft cockpit of the SBDs, the rear seat was always more difficult to escape in an emergency, due to the presence of the .30-caliber machine guns and ammunition, parachute, survival gear, and other complicating factors associated with the swivel seat, which could rotate 360 degrees in a confined space.

Carrier Air Group Ten, on *Enterprise*, which Karl would have boarded with VB-10 and his second division, entered the fierce battle for Guadalcanal 13-14 November 1942. Though VB-10 lost four airplanes and their crews, one plane and its crew from VS-10, and two pilots in VF-10 received wounds, none of the eight men from VB-10 were from the second division. His former wingman, Lieutenant (jg) "Hoot" Gibson and the crews of second division acquitted themselves admirably, with "Hoot" given credit for badly damaging a Japanese cruiser in a dive bomb attack.[58]

Karl Border didn't fight in the war he trained for and longed to enter—and didn't complete the trip to Tokyo of which he wrote. He didn't return to Mary, whom he loved so deeply and with whom he had shared so few days in his young life. Neither did he return to his family who were so proud of him, nor did he and Bob serve together again in the Navy as Karl hoped. Bob Border, however, did enter the war in the South Pacific—not as the fighter pilot he sought to be, rather as a dive bomber pilot in the Douglas Dauntless SBD, the same type of airplane Karl was flying when he made the emergency landing at Ewa and died attempting to assist Arthur Margarido to safety.

In August 1942, as Karl was preparing to return to the Hawaiian Islands, the United States had first taken the offensive in the Pacific in a joint land, sea and air campaign to stop Japan's aggressive moves toward the New Hebrides Islands, New Caledonia, the Samoan and Fiji Islands. The enemy intended to cut the supply lines to New Zealand and Australia and possibly isolate both Allied nations. After the 1st Marine Division landed on Guadalcanal in the Solomon Islands on 7 August, there followed a series of bloody naval, land, and air battles to retake Guadalcanal from the Japanese, seize the airfield they were building on the island, blunt their advance into the South Pacific, and expand Allied holdings in the Solomons. Joey Border's father had left San Diego, assigned to support the marines during their campaign.

Following Bob Border's assignment to the Advanced Carrier Training Group at Navy North Island, where Bob began flying the SBD on 20 November 1942, he completed carrier qualification training in the SBD on 16 February 1943. In early March, with others in his class, he deployed to Tongue Point Naval Air Station, Astoria, Oregon. The Navy was forming a new squadron, VC-60, Composite Squadron 60, equipped with SBDs and the FM-1, an F4F Wildcat fighter built by General Motors. Joey went with him, and they lived in a small, single, motel-like housing unit on the coast. Equipped with an old pot-bellied, wood-burning stove, the new quarters didn't include exactly the kind of cooking equipment Joey loved.

But Bob was excited about his new squadron's airplanes. It included fighter aircraft. He believed he might finally achieve his goal. On 24 March he flew an FM-1 for the first time. A fighter! What he had always yearned to fly. The next day it was another training mission in the FM-1. Then, in the weeks leading to 31 May, he flew 30 more training sorties in the FM-1, intermixed with flights in the SNJ-4 and the SBD-4, newer models of the SNJ trainer he flew at Pensacola, and the SBD, which he began flying at Navy North Island.

On 1 June 1943, circumstances changed again, and Bob had to leave his dream of flying fighters behind. Another squadron was being formed in San Diego. Bob's squadron commander in VC-60, Lieutenant Commander John H. "Red" Pennoyer remained his squadron commander, but was given command of the new Composite Squadron 40 (VC-40) equipped with newer SBD-5s and TBMs, the new, larger Avenger torpedo bombers. Bob and all the SBD crews were abruptly ordered back to San Diego, to join with the TBMs and begin training in their new squadron organization. They rapidly packed up and flew their SBD-5s from Tongue Point to North Island Naval Air Station, and were told to be prepared to leave at a moment's notice.

He began training in earnest again in the SBD, and on 9 June flew his first mission with Ordnanceman First Class R.W. Walcott, the man who in the weeks and months ahead became the primary crew member to fly missions with him in the Douglas Dauntless dive bomber.

Joey arranged to leave their rental bungalow near Tongue Point, packed their car and followed him to San Diego. She drove alone, late into the two evenings, using headlights—blackout lights—the small slits through which light filtered from blue painted headlamps. The trip was far less pleasant than the drive north to Tongue Point.

She decided to stay with her mother in the rented home her parents had moved into in San Diego. The "hurry-up" notice resulted in a lengthy wait before the entire squadron, in early August, went aboard a "jeep carrier," which would take them from San Diego to Espiritu Santo in the New Hebrides.

This time Joey and Bob parted with a passionate kiss and an embrace filled with the certain knowledge he was leaving to fight a war that had already cost so many thousands of lives and savaged the lives of the families who lost their loved ones. Karl, who lost his life in an accident and would never make his trip to Tokyo, had been gone ten months. A wrenching blow to the Borders, Chubbocks, and only slightly less to the Springers, time had lessened the pain's intensity—but the memory was still present. Nevertheless, both Bob and Joey, deeply in love, ever optimistic and positive in their determination to be together whenever possible—for a lifetime—pushed aside every notion of fear, and held tightly to the ones that would hold them together. Joey, "Write every day humanly possible. I will do the same. Take care of yourself. I will be waiting." Bob, "I will, and I will come home safely. Plan on it." Then he was gone.

After VC-40's long voyage to Espiritu Santo, the squadron resumed training for combat operations on 28 August, and in the period 28 August through 13 September Bob flew 15 sorties from "Buttons," a large airfield on the huge and growing staging base at Espiritu Santo. The squadron was concentrating on gunnery, bombing, navigation and search. Among Bob's missions with R.W. Walcott in the rear cockpit was the delivery of live ordnance—in one instance, a 1,000-lb. bomb. They were now ready to join the fight, but they weren't going to be flying combat from an aircraft carrier. They would be flying from a South Pacific island airfield.

On 13 September VC-40, composed of SBD-5 Douglas Dauntless dive bombers and TBM Avenger torpedo bombers, led by a navigation guide R-4D aircraft, the Navy version of the Army Air Forces' C-47 "Gooney Bird," flew four and a half hours to Henderson Field on Guadalcanal Island in the Solomons. The squadron was now under the operational command of COMAIRSOLS (Command, Aircraft, Solomons), a Navy command of land-based attack aircraft reporting to Admiral Nimitz at Pearl Harbor. The Pacific Command was steadily building its forces, driving the Japanese further to the northwest up the Solomons' chain, toward their homeland.

The next day he flew with VC-40 on their first combat mission, a raid on Ballale Airfield, on a small island off the southeast tip of the heavily defended island of Bougainville. The mission lasted over five hours, and due to the approximate 290 nautical mile outbound flight to the target area, weather encountered on the return flight, and fuel limitations, landed at Munda Airfield on New Georgia Island. The next day, in an hour and a half flight, the squadron returned to Henderson Field, over-flying friendly-controlled Segi Airfield on southern New Georgia en route to "Cactus," the call sign given Guadalcanal's Henderson Field by the Americans.

On the 16th, he flew with VC-40 on another lengthy, nearly four and a half hour bombing mission against Ballale, recovering this time at Segi Airfield to refuel before returning to "Cactus." He was excited about the prospect of frequent strike missions against the Japanese, but once again frustrating circumstances and his Naval Academy background intervened.

A message from the Pacific Command arrived directing that two Naval Academy graduates be assigned to the COMAIRSOLS' joint and combined staff. The staff, initially formed at "Cactus" was to manage day-to-day flying operations in behalf of the Navy command's boss. Army and Army Air Force representatives were part of the command, primarily as liaison officers, as well as Australians and New Zealanders, with the intent of integrating air operations of all Pacific Command services and the three allies in the campaign to secure the Solomon Islands, including the northernmost island of Bougainville. A primary objective of the campaign was to eventually isolate and bypass the large, heavily-defended Japanese base at Rabaul, on the island of New Britain.

Bob was clearly disappointed at being taken out of flying duties and placed on a staff. On 18 September it was back to "Buttons" to prepare for setting up the staff operation. With R.W. Walcott in the rear cockpit, he returned to Espiritu Santo on an SBD ferry flight lasting over four hours.

On 24 October he managed to fly one strike mission against Kahili Airfield on the southern tip of Bougainville, after flying an SBD-4 into "Cactus" on 5 October by way of the Russell Islands and Tulagi, then hitching a ride on an R4D to Munda Airfield. From that day forward into January, it was all staff duty and flying time was scarce to non-existent, with only one flight each in November and December—and no more strike missions until January 1944 when he flew two more. One was a raid on Japanese ships in Rabaul Harbor, a seven and one half hour mission, the other against Lakunai Airfield near the enemy base at Rabaul, a tough seven-hour mission.

The missions were much longer, but at least his flying hours and sorties were increasing in January, with nearly 38 hours and six sorties in the SBD. Two of the other four were missions labeled as "false starts" due to weather or some other complicating factor, in which the raiders returned home after extended periods airborne.

After a one-week R&R (Rest and Recuperation) in Sydney, Australia, he returned to Espiritu Santo on 7 February and began training to rejoin VC-40, which had moved forward to Piva Uncle strip at Torokina, Bougainville, near the Navy's recently-seized anchorage at Empress August Bay on the west side, center of the island. After flying six training sorties out of Espiritu Santo, R.W. Walcott rejoined him and on 24 February they ferried an SBD to Segi, on southern New Georgia.

By the time he and Walcott were ready again to begin flying strike missions in early March, the men of VC-40 had given themselves the nickname "Red's Raiders" for their highly respected skipper, Lieutenant Commander "Red" Pennoyer, who had brought them together at Tongue Point Naval Air Station, Oregon, taken them to war, and aggressively led and leapfrogged his raiders up the Solomon Island chain to Torokina—with Japanese ground forces still occupying positions on the island.

The still unresolved ground battle on Bouganville made life more than uncomfortable on several occasions, with night time Japanese infantry attacks on the field's defense perimeter and artillery rounds frequently fired into the airfield. At one point, some of the men in aircraft engineering (maintenance) decided to join the marines' infantry battle and returned early the next morning with a number of battle souvenirs, including Japanese officers' swords. They suffered no casualties, and word spread of their easy success in obtaining infantry experience, along with noteworthy war souvenirs.

Momentum for a return to the ground fight gathered as the scuttlebutt continued, but in the next engagement they were not so fortunate. Several were wounded and more than one was killed in action. The base commander ended VC-40's participation in the ground war.

Composite Squadron 40 flew 1,084 sorties against heavily defended targets on northernmost Bougainville Island in the Solomons and New Britain Island in the Bismarck Archipelago, including the huge Japanese base at Rabaul, New Britain, from September 1943 through April 1944. Their attacks resulted in the destruction of enemy aircraft, ships, and antiaircraft positions. During an intense period of offensive operations from 6 March 1944 through 8 April, Bob Border flew additional combat missions against airfields, gun positions, ships and shore installations in these areas, bringing his total to 25, with missions averaging four hours in duration.

Because of accuracy in weapons delivery, dive bombers were typically the preferred means of attack on flak suppression missions against antiaircraft guns, a particularly dangerous mission that almost invariably resulted in a deadly, heavily one-sided duel between the guns and the airplanes pressing their attacks. The enemy, which could man numerous guns within range of approaching aircraft, knew they are seeing airborne targets that were carrying powerfully destructive payloads, and the aircraft must be destroyed before bomb delivery, if humanly possible.

The intensity of a concentrated, well-coordinated antiaircraft defense was both disconcerting and dangerous, complicated by steep, sometimes near-vertical dives from high altitudes, or lower angle attacks, all of which were normally made singly, in a string, and lengthened the number of seconds the bomber was on a relatively stable flight path before bomb release. The longer the dive, the more time gunners had to better their aim, concentrate, and lead the aircraft with their fire.

Japanese gun emplacements were in deeply dug, sandbag and concrete-reinforced revetments, and required almost direct hits to destroy them. Shallower dive angles created even more AA exposure for the attacking crews. Despite intense antiaircraft fire on 14 September, Bob had scored a direct hit, completely destroying an antiaircraft gun defending the enemy airfield on Ballale Island. Before he completed his twenty-fifth combat mission, he would participate in six such attacks on enemy gun emplacements.

On 14 January 1944, he attacked an enemy destroyer, which by 1944, like nearly all naval combatants, both enemy and friendly, literally bristled with antiaircraft guns. What's more the destroyer was in Simpson Harbor, on Rabaul, the major Japanese Base also peppered with antiaircraft guns. In spite of the fierce response by defenders, he scored a damaging near miss on the destroyer.

On 23 January, he led the attack that destroyed an automatic gun position and nine parked aircraft at Lakunai airfield, Rabaul, New Britain. On numerous other occasions, he destroyed antiaircraft guns and scored effective hits on airfield installations that materially contributed to neutralizing those airfields. For meritorious achievement in aerial flight, in his 25 missions, all dangerous by any measure, he received an Air Medal with three Gold Stars, one Air Medal for each five missions. For heroism and extraordinary achievement in aerial flight as a dive bomber pilot he was awarded the Distinguished Flying Cross for pressing aggressive, damaging attacks against enemy gun positions on New Britain and Bougainville in the period 19 to 29 March 1944.[59]

None of his missions were without peril, and several painted vivid images in his memory by the time he left Composite Squadron 40. One was a large, 6 April strike by 54 SBDs and 36 TBMs from VC-40, VB-98 and other Navy and Marine squadrons, escorted by more than 90 fighters—including Army Air Force P-38s weaving high overhead, Navy F6Fs, and New Zealanders flying P-40s below them—against a Japanese base at Talili Bay, west of Rabaul, recorded by H. Paul Brehm's camera.

But his most memorable mission, his last scheduled with VC-40, came two days later, another strike on enemy antiaircraft gun positions on a ridge line at Rabaul, a base always heavily defended. The event was to be indelibly etched as a warm, glowing, lifelong memory for both Bob and Joey. It is a story told quietly, softly, in measured tones, with unmistakable clarity and gentle reverence.

He was in a section of SBDs positioning their aircraft at 12,000 feet altitude to attack the antiaircraft battery. Carrying a 1,000-pound high explosive bomb on the centerline of his

With a 1,000 lb. bomb on the centerline and a 100 lb. bomb on each wing, an SBD-5 Dauntless dive bomber of Composite Squadron (VC) 40 taxis to the end of the runway on Torokina for take off on a strike against Talili Bay west of Rabaul on 6 April 1944. This aircraft was part of a ninety-plane strike group consisting of both Navy and Marine planes. NNAM

airplane's fuselage, he had plenty to keep him busy, flying formation and preparing to launch their attack. American fighters were battling Japanese fighters that were trying to break through to attack the bombers. The aircraft were spread safely apart, staggered in echelon downward to the right from the lead aircraft. The lead had the bombers offset from the target to provide space for the planned dive angle. Offset from the target, Bob could dip his port wing toward the target slightly, look over the side and keep his target in his field of view.

Bomb-arming procedures were complete, with reminders from R.W. Walcott in the aft cockpit. There was one other reminder— dive brakes. But they wouldn't be opened until Bob, in his turn, began peeling off the echeloned formation, rolling nearly inverted into a diving turn to align the aircraft with the planned direction of approach to the target. Before rolling out, wings level, nose and bomb-sight initially well below the target, speed would begin increasing, causing aircraft trim to change and the nose to rise toward the proper dive angle of attack and bomb release.

As he was rolling into his dive, he caught sight of a Japanese Zero apparently positioning for an attack on his SBD. He moved the lever to open his big, room-door-like dive brakes, which had large, circular holes in them to keep aircraft speed reasonably steady yet avoid airframe vibration and exceeding designed limiting speed in the 45 to 50 degree dive. The normal procedure was to ease the throttle back slightly as the airplane began accelerating. He glanced at the trailing edge of his wings to ensure the large dive brakes were opening, top and bottom. They were beginning to open as he had seen them do many times previously.

His best alternative to escape the much faster, more maneuverable enemy fighter was to continue the dive bomb pass, pulling Bob's pursuer toward the Japanese antiaircraft guns—if he chose to follow. Bob rapidly crosschecked the sight picture and instrument readings, and concentrated on arriving at exactly the right point in space, at the right dive angle and speed for bomb release. He began to sense something wasn't right well before he released the bomb. Something, in fact, was wrong.

He was having to apply too much nose-down trim to keep the nose from coming up sooner than normal. The airspeed and attendant noise heard in the cockpit told him the airplane was accelerating far too rapidly. He began applying back pressure on the stick, which confirmed immediately the stick and nose of the airplane were becoming increasingly heavier because of nose down trim now forced by aircraft acceleration and attendant nose down pitch caused by the change in airflow over the plane's horizontal stabilizer—commonly called the tail-plane or elevator.

His speed was increasing far too rapidly and was going to increase right through acceptable terminal dive and bomb release speed. Acceleration beyond red-line speed could cause complete loss of control. An instant check of the dive flaps told him they were either not open at all, or barely open. He was in serious trouble. Concentration on dive recovery became the immediate priority

As the SBD plummeted toward the release altitude, instinct told him he couldn't wait. He pulled the bomb release handle early, felt the bomb leave the airplane, pulled the throttle to the idle position, and began firmly pulling back on the stick with his right hand and arm for what should have been an approximate normal feeling pullout. The control stick didn't want to move, and in a flash he ignored the trim wheel and began applying back-pressure with both hands, his feet braced hard against the rudder pedals.

In dive-bombing, pressing the attack through normal bomb release altitude—which routinely gives only split-second margins for error—is to court flying through the bomb's violent explosion or a collision with the ground, and death for him and his gunner-radioman. And it is the radioman-gunner who, throughout the dive attack faces aft with his machine guns, protecting the airplane's stern quarter, the pilot's blind side, while trusting his life to his pilot's abilities and experience. With all his might, Bob Border pulled back on the stick, and finally the airplane began responding.

Pullout from the dive was a desperately close-run thing. But there was more. He had to continue the pull up while pushing the throttle to full power to keep his airspeed up and clear the ridge he was headed toward, then begin to weave, twist, turn and climb to escape the antiaircraft hotbed they were in. With feet to spare, the SBD cleared the ground, and the bomb's explosion was safely behind their airplane. They barely cleared the hilltop. The entire time enemy guns were firing at them—and missed.

The experience left both men badly shaken and more than thankful to be alive. When Bob landed at Torokina, he and R.W. Walcott were astounded to see their airplane's sturdy, three to four foot radio antenna, mounted vertically on the top centerline of the fuselage, had been collapsed, bent so sharply to one side by the force of gravity during the pull-out it was laying against the fuselage.

Typically, Bob didn't write Joey or his mother and father telling them of his close call. He flew three more flights in VC-40, two with R.W. Walcott. He had orders for his next assignment. None of the three were strike missions, and the last, to "Cactus," was with R.W. Walcott, the man with whom Bob had flown the great majority of his combat missions.

At "Cactus" they wished one another well, and Bob left on an Army Air Force DC-3 for Espiritu Santo. He didn't know what caused his and his radioman-gunner's brush with disaster, or how they managed to escape, but it was all in a day's work in a war far from home. Maybe someday he would tell Joey and his family, but he didn't want to frighten them or cause undue concern. They had enough to worry about. The war wasn't over, and he didn't know what its future might hold.

Not too surprisingly, Joey didn't write Bob about a visit to her that occurred that same evening as his nearly disastrous 8 April mission against enemy guns on an island in the Pacific. She would tell him later, when the time was right.

She had stayed in San Diego at her mother's home at 2421 West 5th Avenue while Bob and her father were overseas, and was lying on her side, in bed, with a small lamp behind her on an end table next to the head of the bed. The lamp was on, and she had been lying there, quietly, thinking about Bob and wondering what he was doing, when she decided it was time to turn off the lamp. As she rolled over to reach for the switch, she suddenly felt someone else was in the room. She stopped, slowly sat up, and glanced toward the foot of the bed—to see Karl standing there, silent, gazing at her. He was dressed in his Navy tans, complete with the tan shirt, black tie, pressed tan blouse and trousers, with the black shoulder boards bearing the gold lieutenant's stripes. On his blouse were his gold Navy aviator's wings. For a moment he simply stood there, still gazing at her, both his hands inserted in his blouse pockets at his hips, a somewhat unusual habit she had frequently seen in him and his father when they were more formally dressed.

Finally, she spoke, asking, "Karl Frederick? . . . " A brief pause, then a response. His voice was clear and unmistakable.

"Yeah. I came to tell you I was with 'Minimus' today. My hands were on the stick, too." He paused again, still gazing into her eyes, and added, "I'm there if he needs me." Another momentary pause, and he turned and walked out of the room. As he walked toward the door, Joey said softly, "Thank you," and he was gone.

Joey lay there, gazing toward the door. She had felt no fear. Rather, she felt good, warm, comfortable—and comforted. Her comfort would turn to joy only if Bob came home safely from the most destructive war in human history. And he did.[60]

SOURCE NOTES

Chapter 1 The New Totalitarians

1. Deck Log of the USS *Tennessee*, 19-29 December 1941. (Hereinafter referred to as *Tennessee* Log.); Deck Log of the USS *St. Louis*, 26-31 December 1941. (Hereinafter referred to as *St. Louis* Log); *Maryland, Pennsylvania, Tucker, Flusser, Case,* and *Conyngham* Logs, 20-29 December 1941.; *Preston* and *Smith* Logs, 26-31 December 1941.; *Lurline, Matsonia* and *Monterey* Logs, 16-31 December 1941.; Mary Joleen Border diary entries, 20-31 December 1941. (Hereinafter referred to as Joey's diary); Karl Frederick Border's diary entries. (Hereinafter referred to as Karl's diary) Author's interviews, Mary Joleen Border and Robert Lee Border. (Hereinafter referred to as Joey or Bob Border interviews.)
2. Sulzberger, *The American Heritage Picture History of World War II*, 19. (Hereinafter referred to as *Picture History of World War II*.)
3. Ibid.
4. Ibid., 42.
5. Ibid., 19.
6. "Three Lurlines," "Hail to the Lurline!:" Elwin M. Eldridge Collection.
7. *Dictionary of American Naval Fighting Ships*, Online.
8. Sulzberger, Ibid.,18 and 25.
9. Ibid., 25.
10. Carruth, *What Happened When*, 738.
11. Ibid.
12. Ibid., 738-9.
13. Ibid., 741-2.
14. Ibid., 739-40.
15. Author's interviews, Bob and Joey Border.
16. Carruth, Ibid., 739.
17. Allen, *Hawaii's War Years*, 65-71.
18. Siddiqi, "Air Transportation: Pan American's Flying Boats." Online.
19. Sulzberger, Ibid., 20.
20. Carruth, Ibid., 742-43, 745-6.
21. Sulzberger, Ibid.
22. Ibid., 20-1.
23. Siddiqi, Ibid.
24. Carruth, Ibid., 742-4.
25. Ibid., 747-8.
26. Willmott, *Pearl Harbor*, 14; Carruth, Ibid., 748; Part Two: "The Wreck of the *SS President Hoover*," The Takao Club" online; "The Sinking of Panay, 12 December 1937," online.

27. Author's interview, Bob Border.
28. Sulzberger, Ibid., 19-20, 50.
29. Carruth, Ibid., 752-7.
30. Siddiqi, Ibid.
31. Carruth, Ibid., 753-7.
32. Allen, Ibid., 68.
33. Willmott, Ibid., 25.
34. Carruth, Ibid., 758-61.
35. Karl's diary, 1 and 24 June 1939; Author's interview, Bob Border.
36. *Dictionary of American Naval Fighting Ships*, Vol II, 88-89.
37. Carruth, Ibid., 758-61.
38. The Department of Military Art and Engineering. *The West Point Atlas of American Wars, Volume II, 1900-1953*, Maps 8-10.
39. Ibid., Map 11.
40. Ibid., Maps 12-17.
41. Ibid., Map 18.
42. Willmott, *Pearl Harbor*, 25.
43. "Almanac," Las Vegas Review-Journal, 5 February 2005.
44. Carruth, Ibid., 763-7.
45. Campbell, Richard M.; Painter, John D.; Straziscar, Sean W. *NCAA Football, The Official 1996 College Football Records Book*, 251-2.
46. Prange, *At Dawn We Slept*, 37; *Dictionary of American Naval Fighting Ships*, Vol. II, 89.
47. Allen, Ibid., 64-8.
48. Sidiqi, Ibid.
49. Prange, Ibid., 89-93.
50. *Dictionary of American Naval Fighting Ships*, battleships' histories.
51. Karl's diary.
52. "Tacoma Narrows Bridge (1940)," *Wikipedia*, online.

Chapter 2 A Diary of Happy Times

1. Karl Border's diary, 1 and 24 June 1939.
2. Karl and Joey Borders' diaries; Author's interviews, Bob and Joey Border.
3. Author's interviews, Joey Border.
4. Prange, Ibid., 4.
5. Karl and Joey Borders' diaries; *Tennessee* Log; Ships' histories, *Dictionary of American Naval Fighting Ships*.
6. Author's interviews, Joey Border.
7. Joey's diary.
8. Ibid.
9. Author's interviews, Bob Border.
10. Ibid., Joey Border.
11. Author's interviews, Joey Border; Battleships' Logs.
12. Joey Border's diary; Author's interviews, Bob and Joey Border.
13. Author's interviews, Bob Border.
14. Ibid., Bob and Joey Border.
15. Ibid.

16. Ibid., Bob Border.
17. Ibid., Bob and Joey Border.
18. Joey Border's diary, 1 Jan 1941; Author's interviews, Joey Border.
19. Karl Border's diary, 25 December 1940-1 January 1941; Author's interviews Bob and Joey Border.
20. Joey Border's diary, 1-6 January 1941.
21. Ibid., 7-11 January 1941; Author's interviews, Joey Border.
22. Ibid., 12-18 January 1941; Author's interviews, Joey and Bob Border.
23. Author's interviews, Bob Border; *Tennessee* log, 20 Jan 1941.
24. Joey Border's diary, 19-21 January 1941; Author's interviews, Bob and Joey Border.
25. Ibid.
26. Ibid.
27. Author's interviews, Joey Border.
28. Ibid.
29. Joey Border's diary, 22-26 January 1941; Author's interviews, Bob and Joey Border.
30. Ibid., 27 January 1941; Ibid.
31. Ibid., 27 January-1 February 1941; Ibid.
32. Official Chronology of the U.S. Navy in World War II, 1941, online.
33. Joey Border's diary, 1 February 1941.
34. Ibid., Official Chronology of the U.S. Navy in World War II, 1941, online.
35. Joey Border's diary, 2-3 February 1941; Author's interviews, Bob and Joey Border.
36. Ibid., 4-5 February 1941; Ibid.
37. Author's interviews, Bob and Joey Border.
38. Joey Border's diary, 8-14 February 1941; Author's interviews, Bob and Joey Border.
39. Endorsements to Ensign Robert L. Border's official orders, 22 February 1941; Arakaki and Kuborn, *7 December 1941, The Air Force Story*, 41-4.
40. *Morris* Log, 137,143 and 147.
41. Author's interviews, Bob Border and Harry Keneman.
42. *Morris* Log, 163; Karl Border's diary, 1 March 1941.
43. U.S. Navy Chronology of World War II, 1941, online.
44. Ibid., Official Chronology of the U.S. Navy in World War II, 1941, online; Karl Border's diary, 11 March 1941.
45. Karl Border's diary, 17 March 1941.
46. Ibid., 26 March 1941.
47. Ibid., Official Chronology of the U.S. Navy in World War II, 1941, online.
48. Karl Border's diary, 5 April 1941.
49. Swanborough, Gordon; Bowers, Peter M. *United States Navy Aircraft Since 1911*, 159 and 447.
50. *Wikipedia* online, SCR-270 radar, 1-3.
51. *Wikipedia*, Ibid.; Swanborough, Bowers, Ibid.,159 and 447; Keneman, "The Famous Cruiser Aviators and Their SOC's."
52. Ibid., Official Chronology of the U.S. Navy in World War II, 1941, online; Bennighof, *Avalanche Press*, May 2006, online.
53. Allen, *Hawaii's War Years*, 73.

54. Ibid, 72.
55. Karl Border's diary, 13 April 1941; Author's interviews, Bob Border.
56. Ibid., Official Chronology of the U.S. Navy in World War II, 17 April 1941, online.
57. Franklin D. Roosevelt Presidential Library and Museum, online.
58. Karl Border's diary, 28 May-28 June 1941.
59. *Dictionary of American Naval Fighting Ships*, online; Author's interviews, Bob and Joey Border, and Harry Keneman.
60. *Dictionary of American Naval Fighting Ships*, online.
61. Joey Border's diary, 14 March-7 April 1941; Author's interviews, Joey Border.
62. Ibid., 10 May-24 June 1941; Author's interviews, Joey Border; Letter, Sally Smoot to Florence Springer, 18 July 1941.
63. Ibid., 25-26 June 1941; Ibid; *Dictionary of American Naval Fighting Ship*, History of USS *Monssen*.
64. *Tennessee* Log, 3-4 and 6-10 July 1941; Karl Border's diary, 3-14 July 1941.
65. Joey Border's diary, 10-11 July 1941; Author's interviews, Bob and Joey Border.
66. Ibid., 12-15 July 1941; Ibid.; Letter, Sally Smoot to Florence Springer, 18 July 1941.
67. Ibid., 15-25 July 1941; Karl Border's diary, 15 July-3 August 1941; Author's interviews, Joey Border.

Chapter 3 Voyages

1. Joey's diary, 13 Aug 1941.
2. Karl's diary, 13 Aug 1941.
3. Ibid, 14 Aug.
4. Author's interviews, Bob Border.
5. Joey's diary, 14 Aug.
6. Ibid, 15 Aug; Karl's diary, 15 Aug.
7. Joey's diary, 16 Aug.
8. *Tennessee* Log. 16 Aug.
9. Joey's diary, 16 Aug.
10. *Tennessee* Log, 17 Aug
11. Joey's diary, 17 Aug; Author's interviews, Joey Border.
12. Ibid. 18 Aug; Ibid.
13. Ibid, 19 Aug; Ibid.
14. Karl's diary, 19 Aug.
15. Karl's and Joey's diaries, 20 Aug; Author's interviews, Joey Border.
16. Joey's diary, 21 Aug.
17. Joey's diary, 22 Aug 22; *Tennessee* Log, 22 Aug.
18. Ibid, 23 Aug; Author's interviews, Joey Border; *Tennessee* Log, 23 Aug.
19. Joey Border's diary, Aug 24-31.
20. Ibid, 1-12 Sept; Author's interviews, Joey Border; *Wikipedia*, "HMS Warspite," online.
21. Sulzberger, *The American Heritage Picture History of World War II*, 134.
22. Joey's diary, 13-17 Sept.
23. Official Chronology of the U.S. Navy in World War II, online.

24. Joey's diary, 16-19 Sept.
25. *Tennessee* Log, 18-19 Sept.
26. Joey's diary, 20-24 Sept.
27. *Tennessee* Log, 20-27 Sept; Karl's diary, 7 Oct; Author's interviews, Bob and Joey Border.
28. Official Chronology of the U.S. Navy in World War II, online.
29. Prange, *At Dawn We Slept*, 96.
30. McNaughton, *United States Army, Pacific*, "The Hawaiian Department, 7 December 1941," online.
31. Karl's diary, 7 Oct.
32. Tennessee Log, 8-18 Oct; Joey's diary, 18 Oct.
33. Joey's diary, Sept 25-31 Oct; Author's interviews, Bob and Joey Border; *Tennessee* Log, Sept 24-Nov 3.
34. Knox, Frank. Directive to Chief of Naval Operations. "Evacuation Plan for Dependents of Navy Personnel from the Outlying Bases," October 31, 1941.
35. Joey's diary, 1 Nov.
36. *Tennessee* Log, 1-3 Nov.
37. Willmott, *Pearl Harbor*, 78-79, 82-83, 196. Prange, *At Dawn We Slept*, 336-339; Masataka Chihaya, "The Japanese Fleet Task Organization: 7th December 1941," circa 1950, Prange Collection, University of Maryland.
38. *Tennessee* Log, 18 Nov.; Joey's diary, 18-19 Nov.
39. Ibid., 19 Nov; Willmott, 82-83; Masataka Chihaya, "The Japanese Fleet Task Organization: 7th December 1941," circa 1950, Prange Collection, University of Maryland.
40. Marine Exchange Ledger, San Francisco Harbor, 21-22 Nov 1941; Feuer, "Pawn of Fate: The Pensacola Convoy," online.
41. *Tennessee* Log, 22 and 28 Nov.
42. Willmott, *Pearl Harbor*, 78-79; Masataka Chihaya, "The Japanese Fleet Task Organization: 7th December 1941," circa 1950, Prange Collection, University of Maryland.
43. Prange, Ibid, 396.
44. *Oregon Statesman*, "Cat Gridders Off for Hawaii This Morning," 26 November 1941; San Jose State College, *1942 La Torre*, 184; *San Jose Mercury*, "Spartan Team Surprise Return From Hawaii," 26 December 1941.
45. Prange, Ibid., 400-2.
46. Leaming, *From 6-S-7*, 7.
47. Feuer, "Pawn of Fate: The Pensacola Convoy," online.
48. Joey's Diary, 28 Nov.

Chapter 4 Prelude

1. Young, *December 1941, America's First 25 Days at War*, vi.
2. Ibid., vi-vii.
3. Joey's diary, 2 Dec.
4. Ibid. vii.
5. Joey's diary, 3 Dec.

6. Young, Ibid.
7. Ibid., vi-vii.
8. Ibid.
9. Ibid., viii.
10. Joey's diary, 4 Dec.; *Tennessee* Log, 30 November end of month officers' roster; Cutler and Cutler, *Dictionary of Naval Terms*, 200.
11. Statement by Captain L. F. Safford, US Navy, Regarding Winds Message, Before the Joint Committee on the Investigation of the Pearl Harbor Attack, 79th Cong., 1st sess., pursuant to Congressional Resolution 27.
12. Prange, *At Dawn We Slept*, 445.
13. Leaming, *From 6-S-7*, 7-9; *Enterprise* Log, 4 Dec.
14. *Saratoga* Log, 30 Nov-5 Dec.
15. *Lexington* Log, 5 Dec; Naval History and Hertitage Command, Frequently Asked Questions, "Where Were the Carriers, 7 December 1941," online.
16. Willmott, *Pearl Harbor*, 78-9.
17. *Lexington* Log, 5 Dec; Ships' histories, *Dictionary of American Naval Fighting Ships*, online; Prange, 456 and 460.
18. Willmott, Ibid., 91-5; *Pensacola* Log, 5 Dec.
19. *Ampersand*, 5.
20. *Tennessee* Log, 6 Dec; Joey's diary, 5 Dec.
21. Letter from Joey to Springers (her parents), 6 Dec.
22. *Lexington* Log, 6 Dec.
23. *Enterprise* Log, 6 Dec.
24. Hop, *Honolulu Star-Bulletin*, 3 Dec 1941.
25. Ibid., "Willamette's Short High Passes May Whip Hawaii"; Misukado, "Ramblin Around," *Honolulu Advertiser*, 4 Dec; McQueen, "Hoomalimali," *Honolulu Advertiser*, 6 Dec.
26. *Louisville* Log, 6 Dec. ; Ship's history, *Dictionary of American Naval Fighting Ships*, online.
27. Navy Music Program, "Pacific Fleet Band," online; Navy School of Music, *Wikipedia*, online; Lord, *Day of Infamy*, 7; Author's interview, Ira Schab.
28. Prange, Ibid., 481.
29. Young, Ibid., viii.
30. Joey's diary, 6 Dec.
31. Goldstein and Dillon, *Pacific War Papers*, 234-5.
32. Ibid.
33. Willmott, Ibid., 94-5, 196.
34. Delgado, *Japanese Midget Submarine HA-19 National Historic Landmark Study*, online.
35. Grannis, USS *Antares* Action Report to CINCPAC, 10 Dec, online; *Dictionary of American Naval Fighting Ships*, USS *Antares* history, online.
36. Willmott, Ibid. 95; *Dictionary of American Naval Fighting Ships*, USS *Ward* history, online.
37. *Dictionary of American Naval Fighting Ships*, Ibid.
38. Prange, Ibid., 484.
39. Prange, Ibid., 496; Outerbridge, USS *Ward* Action Report to CINCPAC, 13 Dec, online; *Dictionary of American Naval Fighting Ships*, USS *Ward* history, online; Grannis, Ibid.; "Patrol Squadron 14, NAS Kanehoe Bay War

Diary," online; Tanner, "Narrative of Engagement with enemy submarine on December 7, 1941," online; *Condor-Ward* Dispatches, Radio Transcript USS *Ward* (DD-139), Naval Radio Station Bishop Point, 7 December 1941, online.

40. Prange, Ibid., 496-7.
41. Willmott, Ibid., 95-101; Prange, Ibid., 490-91.
42. Willmott, Ibid., 100, 186.
43. Enterprise Log, 7 Dec; Leaming, *From 6-S-7*, 10-12.
44. Arakaki and Kuborn, *7 December 1941, The Air Force Story*, 69-72.
45. Prange, Ibid., 500-1; Willmott, Ibid., 97-8; Butowsky, "Early Warnings: The Mystery of Radar in Hawaii," online.
46. Prange, Ibid., 477, 480-1.
47. Hickam Air Force Base Public Affairs, "Account of the 38th Reconnaissance Squadron," December 1997, online; Prange, Ibid., 476; Arakaki and Kuborn, Ibid., 157-59.

Chapter 5 "AIR RAID, PEARL HARBOR. THIS IS NOT DRILL"

1. Arakaki and Kuborn, Ibid., 61; Prange, Ibid., 382 and 503; Willmott, Ibid., 100-1, 186; Young, H.L. "Report of Action with Japanese Air Force at Oahu, T.H., 7 December 1941,"online.
2. Willmott, Ibid., 102-3, 123; Arakaki and Kuborn, Ibid., 62; Goldstein and Dillon, Ibid., 264.
3. *Amperand*, 6; Hackett and Kingsepp, "*Sensuikan*," Tabular Records of Movement (TROMs) of Imperial Japanese Navy submarines, online; Prange, Ibid., 51; Kells, letter to Mrs. Berthel Carlsen, 26 December 1941.
4. Prange, Ibid., 518-19; Bellinger, Task Force NINE Operations on 7 December 1941, online; Hanson, written recollections of the Japanese attack on Kaneohe Naval Air Station, December 1979; Author's interview, James K. Poppleton.
5. McGinnis, "Report of Japanese Air Attack on Kaneohe Bay, T.H.—7 December 1941,"online.
6. Prange, Ibid., 518-19.
7. Navy Patrol Bombing Squadrons 102/14 Association, Citation Accompanying the Medal of Honor Awarded to John W. Finn, on line; John William Finn, Association of Aviation Ordnancemen, online; Author's interview, James K. Poppleton.
8. Arakaki and Kuborn, Ibid., 128.
9. Ibid., 58, 66 and 128.
10. Ibid., 128.
11. Ibid., 3-5, 48.
12. Ibid.
13. Kamaka, undated written recollections.
14. "San Jose Home From Hawaii," *San Francisco Examiner*, 26 Dec.
15. Merrick, "Spartan Team in Surprise Return from Hawaii," *San Jose Mercury Herald*, 26 Dec.
16. Gemmell, *The Oregon Statesman*, 26 and 27 Dec.
17. Gemmell, "Salem Welcomes Home Willamette Party," Ibid.; *Willamette Collegian*, "Hawaiian Trip Filled With Action," 10 Jan 1942.

18. Arakaki and Kuborn, Ibid., 112-3.
19. Ibid., 111.
20. Ibid., 113.
21. Ibid., 115-8.
22. Ibid., 122-23.
23. Ibid., 117-8.
24. Prange, Ibid., 524, 534-5; "The Attack on Pearl Harbor," *Aviation History* online.
25. Arakaki and Kuborn, Ibid., 5, 65-6.
26. Dr. Heaton's diary, 7 Dec.
27. Willmott, Ibid., 92-3; Arakaki and Kuborn, Ibid., 5, 66.
28. Arakaki and Kuborn, Ibid., 66-7.
29. Written recollections of Joseph Honish; Author's interview, Joseph Honish.
30. Author's interview, Margaret Littmann Baccelli; Speight, "USS *Oglala* (CM-4) Action Report", 11 Dec, online.
31. Arakaki and Kuborn, Ibid., 72-76, 131, 157-160, and 190; Prange, Ibid., 522; "Account of 38th Reconnaissance Squadron, online.
32. Author's interview, Edward E. Hall; Edward Hall's written recollections, undated.
33. Arakaki and Kuborn, Ibid., 97-102.
34. Cressman and Wenger, "Infamous Day: Marines at Pearl Harbor, 7 December 1941," 15-16, online.
35. Hinz, written recollections, 16 Jan 2007; Author's interview, Earl Hinz.
36. Prange, Ibid., 524-25; Cohen, *East Wind Rain*, 122; Hinz, Ibid.; Willmott, Ibid., 190.
37. Willmott, Ibid.
38. Hinz, written recollections; Author's interview, Earl Hinz.
39. Cohen, Ibid.; Willmott, Ibid., 125 and 190.
40. Prange, Ibid., 524-5.
41. Copy of Order provided by Earl Hinz; Author's interview, Earl Hinz.

Chapter 6 Inferno, Carnage, and Valor: Attack on the Pacific Fleet

1. Prange, Ibid., 505.
2. Ibid., 517-8; Cressman and Wenger, *Infamous Day: Marines at Pearl Harbor 7 December 1941*, online.
3. Ibid., 505-6.
4. *Oklahoma* Action Report and Statement by Ensign H.F. Rommel, 18 Dec.
5. Prange, Ibid., 509.
6. *Oklahoma* Action Report with accompanying statements by crew members, Ibid.; Wallin, Naval History and Heritage Command, "Reports of Survivors of Pearl Harbor Attack," 297-327, online; Prange, Ibid., 513; *California* Log, 0815, 7 Dec.
7. Prange, Ibid.; "Profiles in Courage, True Stories of Great American Heroes," online; Chambers, "What the Pearl Harbor Chaplains Were Doing at Pearl Harbor on December 7th 1941," online; Author's interview, Raymond J. Turpin; *Maryland* deck log, 7 Dec 1941, and 1 Jan1942; Godwin, *Maryland* Action Report, 15 Dec 1941, online.

8. Ibid., 506, 508.
9. *West Virginia* Action Report, 11 Dec.
10. Ibid.
11. Ibid.
12. Ibid.
13. Ibid.
14. Ibid.
15. Ibid.
16. Ibid., Prange, Ibid., 514-5.
17. *West Virginia* Action Report, Ibid.
18. Ibid.
19. *Tennessee* Log, 7 Dec.
20. *Arizona* Action Report, 13 Dec, online; *Vestal* Action Report, 11 Dec, online.
21. Arizona Action Report, Ibid.
22. Ibid.; Samuel G. Fuqua, *Wikipedia*, online.
23. *Arizona* Action Report, Ibid.
24. Ibid.
25. Ibid.
26. Ibid.
27. Willmott, Ibid., 116.
28. *Arizona* Action Report, Ibid.
29. Ibid.
30. Ibid.
31. Ibid.
32. Ibid.; "Profiles in Courage, True Stories of Great American Heroes," online.
33. *Vestal* Action Report, 11 Dec.
34. Young, *Above and Beyond*, 196-8.
35. *Vestal* Action Report, Ibid.
36. Willmott, Ibid., 101; Olsson, "Today in History," online.
37. *Utah* Action Report, 15 December 1941, online; History of USS *Utah*, online.
38. "Profiles in Courage, True Stories of Great American Heroes," online; Chief Watertender Peter Tomich, *Wikipedia*, online.
39. Prange, Ibid., 506; *Raleigh* Action Report, 13 Dec, online.
40. *Raleigh* Action Report, Ibid.
41. Ibid.
42. *Oglala* Action Report, Ibid.; Furlong, Minecraft Battle Force Reports, 7 Dec, online; *Helena* Action Report, online.
43. *Oglala*, Ibid., *Helena*, Ibid., History of USS *Oglala*; History of USS *Helena*.

Chapter 7 "Praise the Lord and Pass the Ammunition . . . "

1. Willmott, Ibid., 162-3; Prange, Ibid., 161-2.
2. Prange, Ibid.
3. Ibid., 510.
4. Ibid., 508.
5. Ibid.

6. *Pennsylvania* Action Report, 16 Dec; USS *Arizona* Memorial, "The First Casualties," 22 Dec 2004, 17, online; *Oglala* Damage Report, 31 Dec.
7. All ships named Action Reports, online.
8. Forgy, . . . *And Pass the Ammunition*, 1-4.
9. Action Reports from all except *California* and *Cummings*, online.
10. *San Francisco* Action Report, online.
11. *New Orleans* Action Report, online; Forgy, Ibid., viii.
12. Forgy, Ibid., 5-11; Song Sheet: Remember Pearl Harbor, online.
13. *St. Louis* Action Reports, 10 and 25 Dec, online.
14. *Tautog* Action Report, 12 Dec, online.
15. *Thornton* Action Report, 17 Dec, online.
16. *Hulbert* Action Report, 8 Dec, online.
17. Motor Torpedo Squadron One, "Offensive Measures Taken During Air Raid," 12 Dec, online.
18. Prange, Ibid., 515; Willmott, Ibid., 187.
19. Nimitz, CinCPac Report, 15 Feb, online.
20. Young, H.L., *Enterprise* Air Group Commander's Report, 15 Dec, online.
21. Leaming, *From 6-S-7*, 21-28; Swanborough and Bowers, *United States Navy Aircraft Since 1911*, 183-5; Dickinson, *The Flying Guns*, 1-20; Commander, Scouting Squadron Six Action Report, online.
22. *California* Action Report, 13 and 22 December, online.
23. "Profiles in Courage, True Stories of Great American Heroes," Jackson C. Pharris, online.
24. Ibid., Robert R. Scott.
25. *California* Log, 7 Dec; *Oklahoma* Action Report, 18 Dec, online.
26. "Profiles in Courage, True Stories of Great American Heroes," Herbert C. Jones, online; *California* Action Report, 13 Dec; Cressman and Wenger, J. Michael. *Infamous Day: Marines at Pearl Harbor 7 December 1941*, online.
27. "Profiles in Courage, True Stories of Great American Heroes," James T. Reeves, online.
28. *California* Action Report, online; Nimitz, CinCPac Report, 15 Feb, online.
29. *California* Action Report, online.
30. Battleship Action Reports, online; USS *Arizona* Memorial, "The First Casualties," 22 Dec 2004, online.
31. *Maryland* Log, 7 Dec; *Maryland* History, online; *Maryland, Tennessee, Helena* and *Oglala* Action Reports, online.
32. *Maryland* Action Report, 15 Dec, online.
33. *Maryland* Log, 7 Dec.
34. Reports of Survivors of Pearl Harbor Attack, online; Wallin, *Pearl Harbor: Why, How, Fleet Salvage and Final Appraisal*, Ibid.
35. Ibid.
36. *Maryland* and *Tennessee* Action Reports, online; *Maryland* and *Tennessee* Logs, 7 Dec.
37. *Maryland* Action Report, 15 Dec,3, online.
38. Ibid.
39. Ibid.
40. Ibid.
41. *Tennessee* Log, 7 Dec; *Tennessee* Action Report, 11 Dec, online.

42. *Helm* Action Report, 11 Dec, online.

43. Commander, Destroyer Flotilla 1 Action Report, 19 Dec, online.

44. *Monaghan* Action Report, 21 Dec, online.

45. All ships' Action Reports, online.

46. Ibid.

47. *Tangier* Action Report, 2 Jan 1942, online; Bates, "Pearl Harbor: Remembered," online.

48. *Tangier* Action Report, Ibid., online.

49. *Zane* Action Report, 10 Dec, online; Submerged Cultural Resources Study, Chapter II, online.

50. *Perry* Action Report, 22 Dec, online.

51. *Medusa* Action Report, 16 Dec, online.

52. *Curtiss* Action Report, 16 Dec, online; *Monaghan* Action Report, 21 Dec, online; *Tangier* Action Report, 2 Jan 1942, online.

53. *Monaghan* Action Report, Ibid., online; Prange, Ibid., 531.

54. *Monaghan*, Ibid.; Prange, Ibid.; *Curtiss*, Ibid.; *Medusa*, Ibid.; *Tangier*, Ibid., online.

55. *Nevada* Log, 7 Dec; *Nevada* Action Report, 15 Dec, online.

56. *Nevada* Action Report, Ibid.; Prange, Ibid., 515.

57. *Nevada* Log, Ibid.

58. "Profiles in Courage, True Stories of Great American Heroes," online.

59. Prange, Ibid., 535-6.

60. Ibid., 536.

Chapter 8 The Second Wave

1. Willmott, Ibid., 127; Prange, Ibid., 530.

2. Ibid., 190-1.

3. Ibid., 110-1.

4. Prange, Ibid., 532.

5. Joey Border's diary, 7 Dec; Author's interviews, Bob and Joey Border.

6. *Shaw* Action Report, 29 Jan 1942, online; Shaw History, *Dictionary of American Naval Fighting Ships*, online; USS *Arizona* Memorial, "The First Casualties," 22 Dec 2004, 26, online.

7. *Downes* Action Report, 17 Dec, online.

8. *Cassin* Action Report, 13 Dec, online.

9. *Pennsylvania* Action Report, 16 Dec, online; Action Reports from five ships named, online; Author's interview, Andrew Hoover; Written recollections, Andrew Hoover; USS *Arizona* Memorial, "The First Casualties," 22 Dec 2004, online.

10. Author's interview, Andrew Hoover; Written recollections, Andrew Hoover.

11. *Pennsylvania, California, Nevada, Avocet,* and *Cachalot* Action Reports, online.

12. *Nevada* Log, 0850, 7 Dec; *Nevada* Action Report, 15 Dec; *Neosho* Action Report, 11 Dec, online.

13. *Nevada* Log, 7 Dec; *Nevada* Action Report, Ibid.; "Profiles in Courage, True Stories of Great American Heroes," online.

14. *California* Log, 7 Dec; *California* Action Report, 13 Dec, online.

15. *California* Action Report, Ibid.

16. USS *Arizona* Memorial, "The First Casualties," 22 Dec 2004, 13, 15-6, online.

17. *Tangier* Action Report, Ibid., online.

18. *Raleigh* Action Report, Ibid., online.

19. *Detroit* Action Report, Ibid., online.

20. *Curtiss* Action Report, 16 Dec, online; *Tangier* Action Report, Ibid., online.

21. *Medusa* Action Report, 16 Dec, online.

22. *Curtiss*, *Medusa*, and *Montgomery* Action Reports, Ibid., online.

23. *Tangier* Action Report, Ibid., online.

24. Willmott, Ibid., 90-1.

25. Destroyer Flotilla 1 Action Report, 19 Dec, online.

26. *Dobbin* Action Report, 11 Dec, online.

27. All ships' Action Reports, online.

28. Prange, Ibid., 532.

29. Ibid.

30. Arakaki and Kuborn, Ibid., 128-9.

31. Ibid., 129-30.

32. Ibid., 131.

33. Ibid., 194-5; Prange, Ibid., 532.

34. Prange, Ibid.; Patrol Wing One Action Report, 1 Jan 1942, 1, online.

35. Author's interview, Clifton E. Dohrmann; Patrol Squadron 11 Action Report, 1 Jan 1942, online.

36. Prange, Ibid., 532-3; Author's interview, James K. Poppleton.

37. Patrol Wing One Action Report, 1 Jan 1942, online; Meyer, Report of engagement with hostile aircraft, 25 December 1941.

38. USS *Arizona* Memorial, "The First Casualties," 22 Dec 2004, 4, 30-1, online.

39. Arakaki and Kuborn, Ibid., 76.

40. Ibid.; Willmott, Ibid., 190.

41. Arakaki and Kuborn, Ibid.; Prange, Ibid., 534.

42. Prange, Ibid., 524-5; Cohen, *East Wind Rain*, 122; Author's interview, Earl Hinz; Earl Hinz written recollections, 16 Jan 2007.

43. Arakaki and Kuborn, Ibid., 76-80; Prange, Ibid., 534-5.

44. Willmott, Ibid., 191.

45. Arakaki and Kuborn, Ibid., 98.

46. Willmott, Ibid.

47. Arakaki and Kuborn, Ibid., 97-8.

48. Ibid., 97-102, 107-8.

49. *Helms* Action Report, 11 Dec, online.

50. All ships' Action Reports, online.

51. *St. Louis* Action Report, 10 and 25 Dec, online.

52. Prange, Ibid., 538.

53. *St. Louis* and *Honolulu* Action Reports, 10 Dec, online; *Honolulu* Damage Report, 15 Feb 1942, online; Prange, Ibid., 538.

54. *St. Louis* Action Report, 10 Dec, online; Prange, Ibid.

55. *St. Louis*, Ibid.

56. Prange, Ibid.

57. *St. Louis*, Ibid.

Chapter 9 The Aftermath: 7 December

1. *Enterprise* Log, 7 Dec.
2. Willmott, Ibid., 133.
3. *Enterprise* and *St. Louis* Logs, 7 Dec.
4. Cohen, *East Wind Rain*, 44.
5. Prange, Ibid., 539.
6. Prange, Ibid.; Arakaki and Kuborn, Ibid., 157-8.
7. Prange, Ibid., 541.
8. Willmott, Ibid., 133 and 187.
9. Prange, Ibid.
10. Ibid.; Willmott, Ibid., 132.
11. Prange, Ibid.
12. Ibid., 542.
13. Ibid.
14. Ibid., 542-3; *Enterprise* Log, 7 Dec.
15. Prange, Ibid., 543-50.
16. *Lexington* Log, 7 Dec.
17. Willmott, Ibid., 133.
18. Ibid.
19. Ibid.
20. Prange, Ibid., 563.
21. Ibid.; Willmott, Ibid; Meyer, "Report of engagement with hostile aircraft," 25 December 1941; Bellinger, "Task Force NINE (Patrol Wing Two) Operations on 7 December 1941," online; Author's interview, James K. Poppleton.
22. Prange, Ibid., 564.
23. Arakaki and Kuborn, Ibid., 108-9; Prange, Ibid., 520-1, 565; Cressman and Wenger, "This Is No Drill," *Naval Aviation News*, November-December 1991, online.
24. Prange, Ibid.
25. Arakaki and Kuborn, Ibid., 137.
26. Prange, Ibid.
27. Arakaki and Kuborn, Ibid.
28. Prange, Ibid.
29. Prange, Ibid., 565-6; Author's interview, Earl Hinz; Earl Hinz written recollections of 7 December, undated; "Douglas B-23 Dragon," online.
30. Arakaki and Kuborn, Ibid., 137-8; Chapter VIII: The Hawaiian Defenses After Pearl Harbor, online, 197, 205.
31. *Enterprise* Air Group Commander's Report, 15 December 1941, online.
32. Leaming, Ibid., 28-31.
33. *Enterprise Log*, 7 Dec; Leaming, Ibid., 31.
34. Emory, author's interview; Dunlop, "Annual Report for the Calendar Year 1941." Hawaiian Department, Office of the Department Surgeon, 11 May 1942.
35. Dr. Leonard Heaton's diary, 7 Dec; Wilson, Letter of Commendation for Major Leonard J. Heaton, 7 Jan 1942.
36. Wilson, Ibid.
37. Arakaki and Kuborn, Ibid., 98-100; Dunlop, "Annual Report for the Calendar Year 1941," Ibid.

38. *Solace* Action Report, 12 Dec, online; *Arizona*, and *West Virginia* Action Reports, Ibid., online; "Pearl Harbor Navy Medical Activities," *The United States Navy Medical Department at War, 1941-1945.* Vol. 1, parts 1-2, 1946, online.

39. "Pearl Harbor Navy Medical Activities," Ibid., online; Chambers, "Pearl Harbor Commentary, What Were the Chaplains Doing on the Day That Will Live in Infamy?" online.

40. "Pearl Harbor Navy Medical Activities," Ibid., online.

41. *Tern* Action Report, 15 Dec, online.

42. *Rigel* Action Report, 9 Dec, online.

43. *Tennessee* Log, 7 Dec, online; *Tennessee* Action Report, 11 Dec, online.

44. *Tennessee* Log, Ibid.

45. Ibid., Author's interview, J.R. Johnson.

46. *Tennessee* Log, Ibid.

47. Ibid.; Author's interview, J.R. Johnson.

48. *Tennessee* Log, Ibid.

49. Commander Battleships, Battle Force Action Report, 19 Dec, online.

50. *Tennessee* Log, Ibid.; *Tennessee* Action Report, Ibid.

51. *Maryland* Action Report, 15 Dec, online.

52. Raymer, *Descent Into Darkness*, 11-13.

53. Krupnick, *Pan American's Pacific Pioneers*, 402 and 420; Glines, C.V. "Clippers Circle the Globe," *Aviation History*, 34 and 36; Silverman, "Hell Broke Loose, Anzac Clipper's Officer Tells How Plane Dodged Japanese," *The San Francisco Chronicle*, 10 Dec, 17; "Clipper Back, Dodges Bombs At Honolulu," *The San Francisco Examiner*, 10 Dec, 2.

54. Glines, "Clippers Circle the Globe," Ibid.

55. Ibid., 34-35; Silverman, Ibid.; "Clipper Back, Dodges Bombs At Honolulu," Ibid.

56. Ibid.; Krupnick, Ibid., 420; Glines, Ibid.; "Clipper Passengers Here," Hilo Herald-Tribune, 8 Dec, A1.

57. "War Witness! How the Clipper Escaped From Wake," *The San Francisco Chronicle*, 11 Dec,1; "Huge Clipper, Strafed by Japs, Safe in S.F.," *The San Francisco Examiner*, 11 Dec, B; Krupnick, Ibid., 431-2; Rickard, J. (20 January 2007), *Battle of Wake Island, 8-23 December 1941*, online; Cressman, *A Magnificent Fight: Marines in the Battle for Wake Island*, online.

58. Krupnick, Ibid.

59. Ibid.; Glines, Ibid., 34 and 36; *The San Francisco Chronicle*, Ibid.; *The San Francisco Examiner*, Ibid; Cohen, *Wings to the Orient*, 190-2.

60. Glines, Ibid., 34-6; Cohen, Ibid., 190-2.

61. *Amperand*, 6-8; *Ships in Gray, The Story of Matson in World War II*, 11.

62. *Ships in Gray*, Ibid.

63. *Enterprise* Log, 29 Nov; *Louisville* Log, 29 Nov.

64. Lenn, "Ships With Hawaii Injured Reach S.F., *The San Francico Examiner*, 26 Dec, 1 and B.

65. *Louisville* Log, 25 Nov-16 Dec; "10,000 Miles of Waiting for Jap Subs," *The San Francisco Chronicle*, 27 Dec, 1 and 5.

66. *Louisville* Log, 16 Dec.

Chapter 10 ". . . A Date Which Will Live in Infamy . . . "

1. Allen, *Hawaii's War Years*, 1941-45, 9-10.
2. Darcy and Emory, "Finding America's Missing," undated, online.
3. *Argonne* Action Report, 28 Jan 1942, online.
4. *Honolulu Star-Bulletin*, 1st Extra, 7 December 1941.
5. Prange, Ibid., 555-6.
6. Allen, Ibid., 7-8.
7. USS *Arizona* Memorial, "The First Casualties," 22 Dec 2004, 3-4, online.
8. Allen, Ibid., 29.
9. Ibid., 30-1.
10. Ibid.
11. Ibid., 31.
12. Ibid.
13. *Hawaii Medical Journal*, six series articles, each titled "Reminiscences of December 7th,"from Volume 7, issue numbers 1 through 6, page numbers 49, 143, 246, 329, 412, and 497.
14. Allen, Ibid., 10.
15. Presidential Papers, Franklin D. Roosevelt Library, OF 400, Hawaii, 1943 folder.
16. Ibid.
17. Ibid.
18. Prange, Ibid., 562.
19. Allen, Ibid., 37.
20. Ibid., 36-9.
21. Brachman, "San Jose Home From Hawaii," *San Francisco Examiner*, 26 Dec, 16-8.
22. Allen, Ibid., 36-9.
23. Journal, 25th Infantry Division, 7 Dec, 2.
24. Allen, Ibid., 32.
25. Arakaki and Kuborn, Ibid., 134.
26. Author's interview, Sherry (Sardis) Richey.
27. Author's interview, Margaret (Littmann) Baccelli
28. Dr. Leonard Heaton's diary, 7-8 Dec.
29. Conn, Engelman and Fairchild. *US Army in World War II, The Western Hemisphere, Guarding the United States and Its Outposts*, Chapter VI, "The Reinforcement of Oahu": Conn, Engelman, & Fairchild, 168, online.
30. Journal, 25th Infantry Division, 7 Dec.
31. "The 25th Infantry Division on December 7th 1941, 25th Infantry Division Association, online; Shettle, *United States Marine Corps Air Stations in World War II*, 89.
32. Arakaki and Kuborn, Ibid., 139.
33. Crown, Eller, Matson, Rico, and Shepard.161st Regiment History, New Caledonia, 10 Sept 1944. (Hereinafter referred to as 161st Regiment History.)
34. War Diary, 34th Infantry Regiment, 7 December 1941-1 January 1942.
35. Joey Border's diary, 7 Dec.
36. Martial Law Declaration, *Honolulu Star-Bulletin*, 1st Extra, 7 December 1941.
37. Allen, Ibid., 38.

:2?

38. Kamaka, Frederick K. Written recollections of the attack on Pearl Harbor, undated, with 18 April 2005 and 20 April 2007 letters of explanation.
39. Blackwell, Herbert H. Letter to his family. 9-14, 25 Dec.
40. Arakaki and Kuborn, Ibid., 139-40.
41. Ibid., 140-1.
42. Ibid., 141; Prange, Ibid., 523.
43. Arakaki and Kuborn, Ibid., 141-2.
44. *Enterprise* Log, 7 Dec.
45. *Tennessee* and *Maryland* Logs, 7 Dec; Cohen, *Attack on Pearl Harbor*, 45.
46. 251st Coast Artillery War Diary, 7 Dec.
47. 25th Infantry Division Journal, 7 Dec.
48. *Argonne* action report, 28 Jan 1942.
49. Cohen, *East Wind Rain*, 30.
50. Dr. Heaton's Diary, 7 Dec.
51. Arakaki and Kuborn, Ibid., 140.
52. US Navy and US Marine Corps Aircraft Serial Numbers and Bureau Numbers—1911 to Present. Second Bureau Number Series (1935-1940), 0001 to 5029, online; Arakaki and Kuborn, Ibid., 140; Leaming, Ibid., 31; *Vireo* Action Report, 10 Dec.
53. Leaming, Ibid., 31.
54. *Maryland* Log, 8 Dec.
55. 161st Infantry Regiment History, 10 Sept 1944, 13.
56. Young, *December 1941*, 9.
57. Franklin D. Roosevelt Library, President Roosevelt's address to Congress, 7 Dec, online.
58. Arakaki and Kuborn, Ibid., 142-4.
59. *Maryland* Log, 8 Dec.
60. Raymer, *Descent Into Darkness*, 16-25.
61. Joey Border letter to Captain and Mrs. Springer, 7-8 December 1941.
62. Joey Border's diary, 11 Dec; Author's interview, Joey Border.
63. "Pearl Harbor Navy Medical Activities," *The United States Navy Medical Department at War, 1941-1945*, Ibid., online; USS *Arizona* Memorial, "The First Casualties," 22 Dec 2004, online.
64. *Enterprise* and *Maryland* Logs, 8 Dec; Hackett and Kingsepp. *Sensuikan!* Japanese Submarines: Tabular Record of Movements (TROMs), *I-70* and *I-8*, online.
65. Leaming, Ibid., 33.
66. *Enterprise* Log, 8-9 Dec.

Chapter 11 Reverberations

1. *Ships in Gray, the Story of Matson in World War II*, Matson Navigation Company, 1946, 11.
2. Ibid., 12; 161st Infantry Regiment History; War Diary, 34th Infantry Regiment, 1.
3. War Diary, 34th Regiment, Ibid.; "World War II in the San Francisco Bay Area," National Park Service, online.
4. Young, *December 1941, America's First 25 Days at War*, 1-5.
5. Ibid., 13.

6. Ibid., 14.
7. Ibid.
8. Ibid., 16.
9. Ibid.
10. Ibid., 17.
11. Ibid., 16-23.
12. Willmott, *Pearl Harbor*, 196.
13. Goldstein and Dillon, *The Pacific War Papers*, 239; *Enterprise* Log, 8-9 Dec; Hackett and Kingsepp, *Sensuikan! I-70 TROM*, online.
14. *Enterprise, Lexington, Saratoga* Logs, 7-15 Dec; Stafford, *The Big E*, 37-8.
15. Goldstein and Dillon, Ibid.; *Enterprise, Lexington* and *Saratoga* Logs, 9 Dec; Hackett and Kingsepp, *Sensuikan! I-69, I-6, I-10, I-26*, and 1st Submarine Group *TROMs*, online.
16. Goldstein and Dillon, Ibid., 238-40; Hackett and Kingsepp, Ibid., online.
17. Anderson, "Contact with Enemy Submarine, 10 December 1941," 15 Dec, online.
18. Walters, "Contacts for War Diary," 13 Dec, online.
19. Hackett and Kingsepp, Ibid., *I-25 TROM*, online.
20. Willmott, Ibid.
21. Hackett and Kingsepp, Ibid., *I-70 TROM*, online.
22. Dickinson, *The Flying Guns*, 54-61.
23. *Enterprise* Log, 10 Dec.
24. Hackett and Kingsepp, Ibid., *TROMs*, online; Goldstein and Dillon, Ibid., 240.
25. *Saratoga* Log, 8-10 Dec.
26. Ibid., 12 Dec.
27. Ibid., 15-16 Dec.
28. *Lexington* Log, 7-13 Dec.
29. Ibid., 13 Dec; Hackett and Kingsepp, Ibid., *I-68 TROM*, online.
30. Ibid., Ibid.
31. *Lexington* and *Saratoga* Logs, 14-17 Dec.
32. Thiele, *Kennedy's Hawaiian Air.* 82-6; Forman, *Wings of Paradise, Hawaii's Incomparable Airlines*, 78-80; *St. Louis* and *Phoenix* Logs, 11 Dec.
33. *St. Louis* and *Phoenix* Logs, Ibid.
34. *Ampersand*, 18-19.
35. Willmott, Ibid., 195; Hackett and Kingsepp, Ibid., *I-9 TROM*, online; *Ampersand*, Ibid.
36. *Ampersand*, Ibid.
37. *St. Louis* and *Phoenix* Logs, 12 Dec.
38. *St. Louis* and *Phoenix* Logs, Ibid; *Pensacola* Log, 12-14 Dec.; *Pennsylvania, Maryland,* and *Tennessee* Logs, 7-12 Dec.
39. Allen, Ibid., 32; Joey Border's diary, 7-13 Dec; Author's interviews with Joey Border.
40. Allen, Ibid., 40.
41. Karl Border's diary, 14 Dec; Joey Border's diary, 7-15 Dec; Author's interviews with Joey and Bob Border.
42. Sevier letter to Captain Frucht, 12 Dec; Bloch letter to Randolph Sevier, 14 Dec.
43. Frucht memo to Admiral Bloch, Commandant, 14th Naval District, 15 Dec.
44. Hackett and Kingsepp, Ibid., *I-4 TROM*, online; Allen, Ibid., 58.

45. Memorandum from Rear Admiral Bloch to The Commander-in-Chief (Pacific Fleet), 15 Dec.
46. Earle, J.B. 14th Naval District Memorandum, 16 Dec.
47. Captain Frucht's Press Release, 17 Dec.
48. *US Army in World War II*: "Fall of the Philippines," Chapter 9, 146-8, online; *American Military History*, Chapter 20, "World War II: The Defensive Phase," 432-4, online.
49. Prange, Ibid., 584-90.

Chapter 12 Surprise Departure, and ". . . Am Going Home"

1. *St. Louis* and *Phoenix* Logs, 16 Dec.
2. *St. Louis* Log, Ibid.
3. *Louisville* Log, 16 Dec.
4. *St. Louis* Log, Ibid.; *Ships in Gray*, 14, 17 and 31; 34th Regiment War Diary; 161st Regiment History, 15.
5. *Phoenix* Log, 16-17 Dec; *Aldebaran* Log, 10-17 Dec; *Aldebaran, Tasker H. Bliss* Ships' Histories, Navsource online.
6. 161st Regiment History, 15.
7. *St. Louis, Phoenix* Logs, 17 Dec; *Matsonia* Log, 17-19 Dec.
8. Hackett and Kingsepp, *I-15 TROM*, online.
9. *St. Louis, Phoenix* Logs, 18 Dec; *Harris Log*, 7-18 Dec: *Sabine, Aldebaran, Platte* Logs, 10-18 Dec; Ships' histories, *Dictionary of American Naval Fighting Ships*.
10. Hackett and Kingsepp, *TROMs* for submarines identified, online.
11. Young, *December 1941*, 77-8.
12. Joey Border's diary, 15-8 Dec.
13. Raymer, *Descent Into Darkness*, 27-8; *Tennessee, Maryland* and *Pennsylvania* Logs, 8-16 Dec; *Tennessee* Action and Damage Reports, 11 Dec.
14. Erickson, "Oral Histories of the Pearl Harbor Attack: Lieutenant Ruth Erickson, NC, USN," 7 Dec, online.
15. Joey Border's diary, 16-9; *Tennessee* Log, 16-9.
16. Erickson, Ibid.; Logan, "Convoy Nurse."
17. Terrell, "War Comes to the Coast . . . Ambulances Pick Up the Injured as Crowds Mill Around Seeking Relatives," *The San Francisco Chronicle*, 26 Dec, 5.
18. Letter from A.J. Pessel to Captain M.M. Frucht, U.S. Naval Representative of Evacuation; Honolulu, Hawaii December 30, 1941.
19. Erickson, "Oral Histories of the Pearl Harbor Attack: Lieutenant Ruth Erickson, NC, USN," 7 Dec, online; Logan, "Convoy Nurse," undated recollections of a Red Cross Nurse.
20. Brachman, "San Jose Home From Hawaii," San Francisco Examiner," 26 Dec; Gemmell, "Salem Welcomes Home Willamette Party," *The Oregon Statesman*, 27 Dec.
21. Brachman, Ibid.; Gemmell, Ibid.; Merrick, "Spartan Team in Surprise Return from Hawaii," *San Jose Mercury Herald*, 26 December 1941.
22. *Detroit, Reid, Cummings* Logs, 19 Dec; USS *Procyon* Log 12-19 Dec.; *Wikipedia*, USS *Procyon* (AKA-2), online.
23. Ibid.
24. *St. Louis, Smith, Preston* Logs, 19 Dec.

25. *Tennessee* Log, 20 Dec; *Maryland* Log, 8 Dec.
26. Young, Ibid. 86-8.
27. Ibid., 86, 88-90.
28. *Tucker, Flusser, Case* and *Conyngham* Logs, 20 Dec.
29. *Tennessee, Maryland* and *Pennsylvania* Logs, 10-20 Dec.
30. Author's interviews, Joey Border.
31. *Tennessee, Maryland* and *Pennsylvania* Logs, 20 Dec.
32. Ibid., *Tucker, Flusser, Case* and *Conyngham* Logs.
33. Ibid.
34. *Ampersand*, 18; Young, *December 1941*, 93.
35. *Detroit, Reid* and *Cummings* Logs, 21 Dec.
36. Logan, "Convoy Nurse."
37. Terrell, "War Comes to the Coast . . . Ambulances Pick Up the Injured as Crowds Mill Around Seeking Relatives," *The San Francisco Chronicle*, 26 Dec.
38. *St. Louis* Log, 21 Dec; *Lurline, Matsonia* and *Monterey* Commanders' Logs, 1941.
39. 161ˢᵗ Regiment History, 16.
40. 34ᵗʰ Regiment War Diary, 21-23 Dec.
41. 161ˢᵗ Regiment History, Ibid.
42. Springer, Letter to Joey Border, 17 Dec.
43. *Detroit* Log, 22 Dec; *Pensacola* Log, 22 Dec.
44. Young, Ibid., 105-7.
45. *Detroit* Log, 23 Dec.
46. Young, Ibid., 107.
47. Joey Border's diary, 23 Dec.
48. Frucht Memo to Commandant, 14ᵗʰ Naval District, 15 Dec; Hoddick Memorandum to Commander Rice, 22 Dec.
49. Pessel, 23 and 30 Dec letters to Captain Frucht; Frucht, 24 Dec letter to Castle and Cooke.
50. Pessel, 23 Dec letter to Frucht.
51. Grossman, *A Magnificent Fight: Marines in the Battle for Wake Island*, online.
52. Bloch, Letter from Admiral Bloch to steamship owners, operators and agencies, 23 Dec.
53. Lenn, "Ships With Hawaii Injured Reach S.F.", *San Francisco Examiner*, 26 Dec; Logan, "Convoy Nurse," 4.
54. *Maryland, Tennessee, Pennsylvania* Logs, 23 Dec.
55. Young, Ibid., 109.
56. *Phoenix, Cushing, Perkins, Harris, Aldebaran, Platte*, and *Sabine* Logs, 23 and 24 Dec.
57. Young, Ibid., 111-117.
58. Frucht letter to Castle and Cooke, 24 Dec; Joey Border's diary, 24 Dec.
59. Hackett and Kingsepp, *I-15* and *I-17 TROMs*, online.
60. Lenn, "Ships With Hawaii Injured Reach S.F.", *The San Francisco Examiner*, 26 Dec; Silverton, "Isle Evacuees Mix Sorrow With Elation," *The San Francisco Chronicle*, 26 Dec, 1, 3.
61. Erickson, "Oral Histories of the Pearl Harbor Attack: Lieutenant Ruth Erickson, NC, USN," 7 Dec, online.
62. *Detroit* Log, 24 Dec.

63. "Hawaii Wounded in S.F., Evacuee Ships Escorted By U.S. Planes," *The San Francisco Call Bulletin*, 26 Dec, B.

64. Logan, "Convoy Nurse," 4.

65. *Detroit* Log, 24-5 Dec.

66. Lenn, "Ships With Hawaii Injured Reach S.F.", *The San Francisco Examiner*, 26 Dec, 1; Terrell, "War Comes to the Coast . . . Ambulances Pick Up the Injured as Crowds Mill Around Seeking Relatives," *The San Francisco Chronicle*, 26 Dec, 1, 3, 5; Silverton, "Isle Evacuees Mix Sorrow With Elation," *The San Francisco Chronicle*, 26 Dec, 1, 3.

67. Logan, "Convoy Nurse," 4-5.

68. Terrell, Silverton, *The San Francisco Chronicle*, Ibid., 26 Dec; *The San Francisco Examiner*, Ibid., 26 Dec; Lenn, *The San Francisco Examiner*, Ibid., 26 Dec.

69. Brachman, "San Jose Home From Hawaii," *San Francisco Examiner*, 26 Dec, 16; Gemmell, Ron. "Salem Welcomes Home Willamette Party," *The Oregon Statesman*, 27 Dec, 1.

70. Logan, "Convoy Nurse," 4-5; Ericson, Oral History, online; Lenn, Ibid., *The San Francisco Examiner*, 1.

71. Hicks, Letter from Commander, Harbor Defense of Los Angeles to The Adjutant General, Washington, DC; 21 April 1944; Young, Ibid., 120.

72. Young, Ibid., 121.

Chapter 13 Three Matson Ladies Plus Escorts: Convoy 4032

1. Peisner, Interview of Captain (USN Ret) Frank L. DeLorenzo, 2002, online.

2. Joey Border's diary, 25 Dec.

3. Bloch, Letter to Commander-in-Chief, Pacific Fleet, 26 Dec.

4. Author's interviews, Joey Border.

5. Terrell, "More Injured and Civilians Arrive—-Mad!," *San Francisco Chronicle*, 1 Jan 1942, 1 and 13.

6. "Wounded Stir Victory Vow," *San Francisco Call-Bulletin*, 1 Jan 1942, 6-7.

7. Pearce, "More Hawaii Wounded Arrive," *San Francisco Examiner*, 1 Jan 1942, 1, 8.

8. *St. Louis*, *Preston* and *Smith* Logs, 25-26 Dec; *Lurline*, *Matsonia* and *Monterey* Commanders' Logs, Dec 1941.

9. *Matsonia* Commander's Log, Ibid.

10. *St. Louis* Log, 27 Dec.

11. *Ampersand*, 14-17.

12. Hackett and Kingsepp, *Sensuikan! TROMs*, online.

13. *Tennessee*, *Maryland* and *Pennsylvania* Logs, 20-27 Dec.

14. *St. Louis*, *Preston* and *Smith* Logs, 27 Dec.

15. Joey Border's diary, 28 Dec; Author's interviews, Joey Border.

16. Ibid.

17. *Ampersand*, 12-14; *Patterson* History, *Dictionary of American Fighting Ships*, online.

18. Allen, Ibid., 58; American Merchant Marine at War, "American Women Mariners in World War II," online.

19. *Pennsylvania* and *Tucker* Logs, 28 Dec.

20. *Maryland*, *Tennessee*, *Case* and *Flusser* Logs, 20-9 Dec.

21. *St. Louis, Smith, Preston* Logs, 29 Dec; Joey Border's diary, 29 Dec; Author's interviews, Joey Border; "Navy Wives Lament" courtesy of Joey Border;
22. *Pennsylvania* and *Tucker* Logs, 29 Dec.
23. *Maryland, Tennessee, Case* and *Flusser* Logs, 29 Dec.
24. *St. Louis* Log, 30 Dec; Joey Border's diary, 30 Dec; Author's interviews, Joey Border.
25. Phoenix Log, 30 Dec.; "Purser's Dirge," courtesy of Joey Border.
26. *St. Louis* Log, 30 Dec; Joey Border's diary, 30 Dec.
27. Allen, Ibid., 59; Hackett and Kingsepp, *Sensuikan! TROMs*, online.
28. St. Louis Log, 31 Dec; Joey Border's diary, 31 Dec; Williams, "Story of the Crossing: 'Blackouts . . . Lifebelts . . . and Always Rumors . . . but Morale Was High to the End," *San Francisco Chronicle*, 1 Jan 1942, 6.
29. *Ships in Gray*, Ibid., 14, 17, 31.
30. Author's interviews, Joey Border.
31. Author's interviews, Joey Border; San Francisco Airport name, United Airlines Schedule to Seattle, type of aircraft, and ground transportation information via a series of E-mails ending 18 July 2007, courtesy of Ms. Alissa Chadburn, San Francisco Airport Commission Aviation Library.

Chapter 14 Love and Sacrifice

1. *Investigation of the Pearl Harbor Attack*, Part V. "Conclusions and Recommendations," online; *American Military History*, Army Historical Series. Chapter 20, "World War II: The Defensive Phase," 426-28. Online.
2. Blair, *The Forgotten War*, 8.
3. *Sealift in World War II*, online; "Liberty Ship" and Victory Ship," *Wikipedia*, online.
4. *Sealift in World War II*, online.
5. *Results of the American Pacific Submarine Campaign of World War II*, online.
6. *American Military History*, Chapter 20, 427, online.
7. *American Armored Fighting Vehicle Production During World War II*, *Wikipedia*, online.
8. *United States Aircraft Production During World War II*, online; The United States Army Air Forces in World War II, *Army Air Forces Statistical Digest, World War II*, Table 3, *Wikipedia*, online.
9. Lewis, Jone Johnson, *Women and World War II—Women and the Military*, online; Ibid., "WASP—Women Pilots of World War II," online; *Employment of Negro Troops*, Chapter XIV: "Manpower and Readjustments," online.
10. Krawczynski, *Historic Context of the African American Experience*: Section 7, online.
11. Krawczynski, Ibid.
12. *Doris "Dorie" Miller, African American Sailor*, Naval History and Heritage Command, online.
13. *Tuskegee Airmen, Wikipedia*, online.
14. Lewis, Jone Johnson, *World War II Homefront –Women at Home*, online.
15. *World War II Rationing*, online.
16. Stamps, *The West Point Atlas of American Wars*, Volume II, Maps 116-18; Chen, World War II Database, *Invasion of Malaya and Singapore*, online.

17. Stamps, *The West Point Atlas of American Wars*, Volume II, Map 128; Chen, World War II Database, *Java Campaign*, online.
18. Stamps, Ibid.
19. *Bombing of Darwin (February 1942)*, *Wikipedia*, online.
20. "Executive Order 9066," *Wikipedia*, online.
21. Chapter VIII, "The Hawaiian Defenses After Pearl Harbor," 206-211, online; National Japanese American Memorial Foundation, *World War II Service*, online.
22. National Japanese American Memorial Foundation, *World War II Service*, online; Toth, "Timeline of AJA's Joining the World War II Fight," online.
23. Stamps, Ibid., Maps 119-125; "Masaharu Homma," *Wikipedia*, online.
24. "Doolittle Raid on Japan—Army B- 25s," Naval History and Heritage Command; "Doolittle Raid on Japan—People." Naval History and Heritage Command; "Doolittle Raid on Japan—Ships," Naval History and Heritage Command, online; "Doolittle Raid." *Wikipedia*, online; Halsey, "Doolittle Raid—18 April 1942," online.
25. McIntyre, MEMORANDUM TO THE SECRETARY OF THE NAVY, 4 March 1942; "Award 62 Medals to Heroes of Navy," *The New York Times*, 15 March 1942, 29; *The Orange Leader*, 19 January 1943, 1; "Battle of the Coral Sea, 7-8 May 1942," online; "Battle of the Coral Sea," *Wikipedia*, online; Lewis, *The Battle for Australia*—"The Battle of the Coral Sea," online.
26. Hartigan, *Hammann* Action Report, online; Destroyer Photo Index DD-412 USS *Hammann*, online; Prange, *Miracle at Midway*, 348-352.
27. Leaming, *From 6-S-7*, 34-48; Dickinson, *The Flying Guns*, viii.
28. Prange, Ibid., 396-7; Allen, *Hawaii's War Years*, 174-5.
29. Ibid., 308, 312.
30. Willmott, *Pearl Harbor*, 175; *Wikipedia*, "Death of Isoroku Yamamoto," online; *Wikipedia*, "Chuichi Nagumo," online.
31. USS *Arizona* National Memorial—History and Culture (U.S. Park Service), online.
32. Chambers, "Pearl Harbor Commentary, What Were the Chaplains Doing on the Day That Will Live in Infamy?" online; "USS Oklahoma (BB-37), 1916-1946," Naval History and Heritage Command, online; "USS *Oklahoma* (BB-37)," *Wikipedia*, online.
33. "USS *Utah* (BB-31)," *Wikipedia*, online.
34. "Battle Experience for Leyte Gulf," online; "*West Virginia*," *Dictionary of American Naval Fighting Ships*, online; "USS *Nevada* (BB-36), 1916-1948," Naval History and Heritage Command, online; "USS *Maryland* (BB-46), 1921-1959," Naval History and Heritage Command, online; "USS *Pennsylvania* (BB-38), 1916-1948," Naval History and Heritage Command, online; "USS *Tennessee* (BB-43), 1920-1959," Naval History and Heritage Command, online.
35. Ibid. "Okinawa Kamikazes," online; "Ohka," *Wikipedia*, online.
36. Young, *Above and Beyond*, 206; "Sansuikan!" *I-26*: Tabular Record of Movement, online; O'Neill, "The Sullivan Brothers: Report on the Loss of the USS Juneau," online; "USS *San Francisco* (CA-38)," *Wikipedia*, online; "USS *Juneau* (CL-52)," *Wikipedia*, online.
37. "USS *New Orleans* (CL-32)," Dictionary of American Naval Fighting Ships,

online; Forgy, . . . *And Pass the Ammunition*, 193-206; "Sansuikan!" *I-75*: Tabular Record of Movement, online; "Doris Miller," *Wikipedia*, online; *Doris "Dorie" Miller, African American Sailor*, Naval History and Heritage Command, online; "*Liscome Bay* (CVE-56)," Dictionary of American Naval Fighting Ships, online.

38. "USS *Helena* (CL-50)," *Wikipedia*, online.

39. "USS *Monssen* (DD-436)," *Wikipedia*, online; "USS *Monssen* (DD-436), 1941-1942," Naval History and Heritage Command, online.

40. "USS *Reid* (DD-369)," NavSource, online.

41. "USS *Preston* (DD-379)," NavSource, online.

42. "USS *Perkins* (DD-377)," NavSource, online; USS *Cushing* (DD-376)," NavSource, online.

43. "USS *Monaghan* (DD-354)," *Wikipedia*, online; "USS *Monaghan* (DD-354)," Dictionary of American Naval Fighting Ships, online.

44. "USS *Tucker* (DD-374)," *Wikipedia*, online; Stone, *The Lady and the President*, 74-7.

45. Wiltshire, John C. "The Search for the Japanese Midget Submarine Sunk Off Pearl Harbor, Dec. 7, 1941, " online; "USS *Ward* (DD-139)," *Wikipedia*, online; Farwell, USS *Ward* (APD-16) Action Report, 16 January 1945, online.

46. "USS *Hugh L. Scott* (AP-43)," *Wikipedia*, online; "USS *Tasker H. Bliss* (AP-42)," *Wikipedia*, online.

47. Stone, *The Lady and the President*, 97, 103-4; "*SS President Coolidge*," *Wikipedia*, online.

48. *Ships in Gray, The Story of Matson in World War II*, 37.

49. "*Sensuikan!*" *I-17*, online; "*Sensuikan!*" *I-26*, online.

50. "*Sensuikan!*" *I-25*, online.

51. Allen, *Hawaii's War Years*, 58-9; "*Sensuikan!*" *I-71*, online.

52. Sara Hill Heaton's diary, 20 Feb-1 Mar 1942; Dr. Heaton's diary, 20 Feb 1942.

53. Pearson, "Army Surgeon General to Four Presidents," 12 September 1983.

54. Chapter VIII: "The Hawaiian Defenses After Pearl Harbor," online, 202.

55. Karl Border's diary, 5 January-7 October 1942.

56. Author's interviews, Joey and Bob Border.

57. Aircraft Accident Report, SBD-3 #06654, October 1942.

58. Hardison, USS *Enterprise*, CV-6 Action Report, 19 November 1942, online.

59. Author's interviews with Bob Border; Bob Border's Aviators Flight Log Book, 1 April 1942-14 April 1944; Bunch, J.M. Citations to Accompany Award of Air Medal and Three Gold Stars, 29 October 1947; Newton, J.H., Vice Admiral, U.S. Navy; Citation to Accompany the Award of the Distinguished Flying Cross to Lieutenant Robert L. Border, undated (circa June 1944); National Museum of Naval Aviation, VC-40, online.

60. Bob Border's Aviators Flight Log Book, Ibid.; Author's interviews, Joey and Bob Border.

BIBLIOGRAPHY

Interviews with the Author

Baccelli, Margaret (Littmann)
Border, Mary Joleen
Border, Robert Lee
Dohrmann, Clifton E.
Emory, Raymond
Hall, Edward E.
Honish, Joseph
Hoover, Andrew
Hinz, Earl
Johnson, J. R.
Kamaka, Frederick K.
Keneman, Harry L.
Latta, Robert L.
Poppleton, James K.
Richey, Sherry (Sardis)
Schab, Ira
Turpin, Raymond J.

Books

Allen, Gwenfread. *Hawaii's War Years, 1941-45*. Honolulu, HI: University of Hawaii Press, 1950.

Arakaki, Leatrice R. and Kuborn, John R. *7 December 1941, The Air Force Story*. Pacific Air Forces Office of History, Hickam Air Force Base, HI, 1991.

Blair, Clay. *The Forgotten War*. New York, NY: Doubleday, 1987.

Campbell, Richard M.; Painter, John D.; Straziscar, Sean W. *NCAA Football, The Official 1996 College Football Records Book*. United States of America: The National Collegiate Athletic Association, July 1996.

Carruth, Gorton. *What Happened When, A Chronology of Life and Events in America*. New York, NY: The Penguin Group, 1991.

Cohen, Stan. *Attack on Pearl Harbor, A Pictorial History*. Missoula, MT: Pictorial Histories Publishing Company, 2006.

Cohen, Stan. *East Wind Rain*. Missoula, MT: Pictorial Histories Publishing Company, 1981.

SUNDAY IN HELL 973

Cohen, Stan. *Wings to the Orient, A Pictorial History, Pan American Clipper Planes 1935 to 1945*. Missoula, MT: Pictorial Histories Publishing Company, 2005.

Cutler, Deborah W. and Cutler, Thomas J. *Dictionary of Naval Terms*. Annapolis, MD: Naval Institute Press, 2005.

Dickinson, Clarence E. *The Flying Guns*. Excerpts reprinted with the permission of Scribner, a Division of Simon & Schuster, Inc., from *The Flying Guns* by Clarence Dickinson & Sparkes Boyden.

Conn, Stetson; Engelman, Rose C.; Fairchild, Byron. *United States Army in World War II, The Western Hemisphere*, Volume II. Washington, DC: Office of the Chief of Military History, 1962.

Forgy, Howell M. . . . *And Pass the Ammunition*. New York, NY and London, U.K.: D. Appleton-Century Company, 1944.

Forman, Peter N. *Wings of Paradise, Hawaii's Incomparable Airlines*. Kailua, HI: Barnstormer Books, 2005.

Goldstein, Donald M. and Dillon, Katherine V. *The Pacific War Papers, Japanese Documents of World War II*. Washington, DC: Potomac Books, Inc., 2004.

Krejcarek, Captain Kevin K. *Hickam, The First 50 Years*. Hickam Air Force Base, HI: Public Affairs Division, 1985.

Krupnick, Jon E. *Pan American's Pacific Pioneers, The Rest of the Story*. Missoula, MT: Pictorial Histories Publishing Co., Inc., 2000.

La Torre. San Jose State College Annual, 1942. San Jose, CA.

Leaming, Jack. *From 6-S-7*. Las Vegas, NV, 1998.

Lord, Walter. *Day of Infamy*, New York, NY: Bantam Books, Inc., 1957.

Morison, Samuel Eliot. Volume III, *History of United States Naval Operations in World War II, The Rising Sun in the Pacific 1931-April 1942*. Boston, MA: Little, Brown and Company, 1959.

Perry, Mark. *Partners in Command, George Marshall and Dwight Eisenhower in War and Peace*. New York, NY: The Penguin Press, 2007

Prange, Gordon W.; Goldstein, Donald M.; Dillon, Katherine V. *At Dawn We Slept, The Untold Story of Pearl Harbor*. New York: McGraw-Hill Book Company, 1981.

Prange, Gordon W.; Goldstein, Donald M.; Dillon, Katherine V. *Miracle at Midway*, New York, NY: Penguin Books, 1983.

Raymer, Commander Edward C. *Descent Into Darkness, Pearl Harbor, 1941*. Novato, CA: Presidio Press, 1996.

Shettle, M.L., Jr. *United States Marine Corps Air Stations in World War II*. Bowersville, GA: Schaertel Publishing Co., 2001.

Stafford, Edward P. *The Big E*. Annapolis, MD: Naval Institute Press, 1962.

Stamps, Colonel Vincent J. (Chief Editor) *The West Point Atlas of American Wars*, Volume II, 1900-1953. New York, NY: Frederick A. Praeger, Inc., 1959.

Stern, Rob; *SBD Dauntless in Action*. Carrollton, TX: Squadron/Signal Publications, 1984.

Stone, Peter. *The Lady and the President, The Life and Loss of the S.S. President Coolidge*. Victoria, Australia: Oceans Enterprises, 1997.

Sulzberger, C.L. *The American Heritage Picture History of World War II*. New York: The American Heritage Publishing Co., Inc., 1966.

Swanborough, Gordon; Bowers, Peter M. *United States Navy Aircraft Since 1911*. Annapolis, MD: Naval Institute Press, 1990.

Thiele, Ray. *Kennedy's Hawaiian Air*. Kaila, HI: Olomana Publishers, 1994.

Willmott, H.P. *Pearl Harbor*. London, England: Cassell & Co., 2001.

Young, Donald. *December 1941, America's First 25 Days at War*. Missoula, MT: Pictorial Histories Publishing Company, Inc., 1992.

Young, Richard et al. *Above and Beyond*. Boston, MA: Boston Publishing Company, 1985.

Booklets

Ships in Gray, the Story of Matson in World War II. San Francisco, CA: Matson Navigation Company, 1946.

Magazines

Ampersand. Honolulu, HI: Alexander & Baldwin, Inc. Winter 1991.

Aviation History. Harrisburg, PA: Cowles Magazines, March 2007.

Hawaii Medical Journal. Honolulu, HI: Six series articles, each titled "Reminiscences of December 7th," from Volume 7, issue numbers 1 through 6, September 1947-August 1948.

Articles

"Award 62 Medals to Heroes of Navy," *The New York Times*, 15 March 1942.

Brachman, Bob. "San Jose Home From Hawaii," *San Francisco Examiner*, 26 December 1941.

"Cat Gridders Off for Hawaii This Morning." *The Oregon Statesman*, 26 November 1941.

"Clipper Back; Dodges Bombs At Honolulu," *The San Francisco Examiner*, 10 December 1941.

"Clipper Passengers Here," *Hilo Herald-Tribune*. Hilo, Hawaii, T.H., 8 December 1941.

"D.E. Vessel 'Jones' Is Launched Here," *The Orange Leader*, Orange, TX, 19 January 1943.

Gemmell, Ron. "Group Returns on US Convoy, Coach Advises," *The Oregon Statesman*, 26 December 1941.

Gemmell, Ron. "Salem Welcomes Home Willamette Party," *The Oregon Statesman*, 27 December 1941.

Glines, C.V. "Clippers Circle the Globe." *Aviation History*, March 2007.

"Hawaii Wounded in S.F., Evacuee Ships Escorted By U.S. Planes," *The San Francisco Call Bulletin*, 26 December 1941.

Hop, Loui Leong. "Teams' Arrival Marks the 22nd Annual invasion by Mainland Elevens," *Honolulu Star-Bulletin*, 3 Dec 1941.

Hop, Loui Leong. "Willamette's Short High Passes May Whip Hawaii," *Honolulu Star-Bulletin*, 3 December 1941.

"Huge Clipper, Strafed by Japs, Safe in S.F.," *The San Francisco Examiner*, 11 December 1941.

Lenn, Earnest. "Ships With Hawaii Injured Reach S.F., *The San Francisco Examiner*, 26 December 1941.

McQueen, Red. "Hoomalimali (Kid 'em along)," *The Honolulu Advertiser*, 6 December 1941.

Merrick, Fred. "Spartan Team in Surprise Return from Hawaii," *San Jose Mercury Herald*, 26 December 1941.

Mitsukado, Andrew. "Rambling Around," *The Honolulu Advertiser*, 4 December 1941.

Pearce, Dick. "More Hawaii Wounded Arrive," *San Francisco Examiner*, 1 January 1942.

Pearson, Richard. "Army Surgeon General to Four Presidents," *Washington Post*, 12 September 1983.

Silverton, Milton. "Hell Broke Loose, Anzac Clipper's Officer Tells How Plane Dodged Japanese Bombs," *The San Francisco Chronicle*, 10 December 1941.

Silverton, Milton. "Isle Evacuees Mix Sorrow With Elation," *The San Francisco Chronicle*, 26 December 1941.

Terrell, John U. "More Injured and Civilians Arrive—-Mad!," *The San Francisco Chronicle*, 1 January 1942.

Terrell, John U. "War Comes to the Coast . . . Ambulances Pick Up the Injured as Crowds Mill Around Seeking Relatives," *The San Francisco Chronicle*, 26 December 1941.

"Vessel Named After Ensign Killed At Pearl Harbor To Be Launched Here," *Orange Leader*, Orange, TX, 17 January 1943.

"War Witness! How the Clipper Escaped From Wake," *The San Francisco Chronicle*, 11 December 1941.

Williams, Will. "Story of the Crossing: 'Blackouts . . . Lifebelts . . . and Always Rumors . . . but Morale Was High to the End'," *The San Francisco Chronicle*, 1 January 1942.

"Wounded Stir Victory Vow," *The San Francisco Call-Bulletin*, 1 January 1942.

"10,000 Miles of 'Waiting' for Jap Subs," *The San Francisco Chronicle*, 27 December 1941.

Newspapers

Hilo Tribune-Herald, Hilo, HI, 8 December 1941.
Honolulu Star-Bulletin, Honolulu, HI, 3 December 1941.
Honolulu Star-Bulletin, 1st Extra, Honolulu, HI, 7 December 1941.
Honolulu Star-Bulletin, 3rd Extra, Honolulu, HI, 7 December 1941.
Las Vegas Review-Journal, Las Vegas, NV, 5 February 2005.
San Francisco Call Bulletin, San Francisco, CA, 26 December 1941.
San Francisco Call Bulletin, San Francisco, CA, 1 January 1942.
San Francisco Chronicle, San Francisco, CA, 10 December 1941.
San Francisco Chronicle, San Francisco, CA, 11 December 1941.
San Francisco Chronicle, San Francisco, CA, 26 December 1941.
San Francisco Chronicle, San Francisco, CA, 27 December 1941.
San Francisco Chronicle, San Francisco, CA, 1 January 1942.
San Francisco Examiner, San Francisco, CA, 10 December 1941.
San Francisco Examiner, San Francisco, CA, 11 December 1941.
San Francisco Examiner, San Francisco, CA, 26 December 1941.
San Jose Mercury, San Jose, CA, 8 December 1941.
San Jose Mercury, San Jose, CA, 26 December 1941.
The Honolulu Advertiser, Honolulu, HI, 10 December 1941.
The Honolulu Advertiser, Honolulu, HI, 4 December 1941.
The Honolulu Advertiser, Honolulu, HI, 6 December 1941.
The New York Times, New York, NY, 15 March 1942.
The Orange Leader, Orange, TX, 17 January 1943.
The Orange Leader, Orange, TX, 19 January 1943.
The Oregon Statesman, Salem, OR, 26 November 1941.
The Oregon Statesman, Salem, OR, 27 November 1941.
Washington Post, Washington, DC, 12 September 1983.
Willamette Collegian, Salem, OR, 12 December 1941.
Willamette Collegian, Salem, OR, 10 January 1942.

Videos

"Pearl Harbor . . . the real story," Terra Entertainment; Los Angeles, CA, 2001.

Unpublished Sources

Border, Mary Joleen "Joey" (Springer). Personal diary, 1 January 1941-1 January 1942.

Border, Karl Frederick. Personal diary, 28 July 1935-31 December 1939.

Border, Karl Frederick. Personal diary, 1 January 1940-7 October 1942.

Border, Robert Lee. Aviators Flight Log Book, 1 April 1942-19 January 1948.

Bloch, C.C. "War Diary for period 7 December to 1 January." Fourteenth Naval District and Navy Yard, Pearl Harbor, Hawaii, U.S.A., 5 February 1942.

Bunch, J.M. Citations to Accompany Award of Air Medal and Three Gold Stars, Navy Department Bureau of Navy Personnel, 29 October 1947.

Crown, Keith G., Matson, Elson L., Eller, Jerome N., Rico, Bernard G., Shepard, Paul R. 161st Regiment History. New Caledonia, 10 September 1944. National Archives.

Chihaya, Masataka, "The Japanese Fleet Task Organization: 7th December 1941," prepared for Dr. Gordon W. Prange, circa 1950, Prange Collection, University of Maryland.

Deck Logs:
Aircraft Carriers: *Enterprise, Lexington, Saratoga*
Battleships: *Arizona, California, Maryland, Nevada, Oklahoma, Pennsylvania, Tennessee, West Virginia*
Cruise Liners: *Lurline, Matsonia, Monterey*
Cruisers: *Chester, Detroit, Louisville, New Orleans, Northampton, Pensacola, Phoenix, Raleigh, St. Louis*
Destroyers: *Blue, Case, Conygham, Cushing, Flusser, Humphreys, Lawrence, Morris, Perkins, Preston, Reid, Smith, Southard, Tucker*
Minelayers: *Breese*
Minesweepers: *Chandler*
Oilers: *Platte, Sabine*
Stores Ship: *Aldebaran*
Transports: *Harris, Procyon*

Dulop, Robert H. "Annual Report for the Calendar Year 1941." Ft. Shafter, T.H.: Headquarters Hawaiian Department, Office of the Department Surgeon, 11 May 1942. National Archives.

Endorsements to Basic Orders for Ensign Robert L. Border. Naval Air Station San Pedro, California, 6 and 22 February 1941.

Frucht, Max M. Press Release for 17 December 1941. National Archives.

Hall, Eward E. Written recollections of the attack on Hickam Field, undated.

Hanson, Murray. Written recollections of the attack on Kaneohe Naval Air Station, December 1979.

Heaton, Leonard J. Personal diary, December 1941, courtesy of Sara Dudley Heaton Mayson.

Hinz, Earl. Copy of Offical Order, issued by Commander, MAG 21, 7 December 1941.

Hinz, Earl. Written recollections of attack on Marine Corps Air Station Ewa on 7 Dec, dated 16 January 2007.

Hinz, Earl. "Good to the Last Drop," a written recollection of an event of 7 December 1941 at Marine Corps Air Station Ewa, undated.

Honish, Joseph. Written recollections of the attack on Pearl Harbor, undated.

Journal, 25th Infantry Division, 7 December 1941. National Archives.

Kamaka, Frederick K. Written recollections of the attack on Pearl Harbor, undated, with 18 April 2005 and 20 April 2007 letters of explanation.

Keneman, Harry L. "The Famous Cruiser Aviators and Their SOC's." Undated.

Knox, Frank, Directive to Chief of Naval Operations. "Evacuation Plan for Dependents of Naval Personnel from the Outlying Bases," October 31, 1941.

Logan, Margaret C. "Convoy Nurse," undated, written recollections of a Red Cross Nurse: Honolulu, T.H., University of Hawaii Special Collections.

Meyer, Ensign O.F. Jr., Report of engagement with hostile aircraft, 25 December 1941.

Newton, J.H., Vice Admiral, U.S. Navy; Citation to Accompany the Award of the Distinguished Flying Cross to Lieutenant Robert L. Border, United States Navy, South Pacific Area and Force, undated. (circa 1944)

Poppleton, James K., "Pearl Harbor December 7, 1941." Written recollections, undated.

Tanner, William P. Jr., Ensign, U.S. Navy; Official Report to Commander Patrol Squadron Fourteen, "Narrative of Engagement with enemy submarine on 7 December 1941," 7 December 1941

United States Navy Aircraft Accident Report, SBD-3 #06654, October 1942.

War Diary, 34th Infantry Regiment, 7 December 1941-1 January 1942. National Archives.

War Diary, 251st Coast Artillery, 7 December 1941. National Archives.

Letters and Memos

Bloch, C.C. Memorandum for Commander-in-Chief (Pacific Fleet), 15 December 1941.

Bloch, C.C. Letter from Commandant of 14th Naval District to Mr. Randolph Sevier, Castle and Cooke, Ltd., 14 December 1941.

Bloch, C.C. Commandant of 14th Naval District letter to Commander-in-Chief, Pacific Fleet, "Evacuation of dependents," 26 December 1941.

Border, Joey. Letter to her parents, Captain and Mrs. Springer, 6 December 1941. (Courtesy of Joey Border)

Border, Joey. Letter to her parents, Captain and Mrs. Springer, 7-8 December 1941. (Courtesy of Joey Border.)

Earle, J.B. Memorandum to 14th Naval District, 16 December 1941. National Archives.

Frucht, Max M. Letter to Castle and Cooke, Ltd., 24 December 1941. National Archives.

Frucht, Max M. Memo to the Commandant, 14th Naval District: Honolulu, T.H., 15 December 1941. National Archives.

Frucht, Max M. Memo to Commandant, 14th Naval District, from Evacuation

Manager, United States Maritime Commission, Honolulu, T.H., 15 December 1941. National Archives.

Frucht, Max M. Memo to Commandant, 14th Naval District, From Evacuation Manager, 23 December 1941. National Archives.

Hicks, W.W. Letter from Commander, Harbor Defense of Los Angeles to The Adjutant General, Washington, DC; 21 April 1944. National Archives.

Hoddick, F.G. Memorandum to Commander Rice, 14th Naval District, 22 December 1941. National Archives.

Kells, C.H. Letter for the Quartermaster General to Mrs. Berthel Carlsen (wife of Berthel Carlsen, the Master, SS Cynthia Olson), 26 December 1941.

Pessel, A.J. Letter to Captain Frucht from Castle and Cooke, Ltd., 23 December 1941. National Archives.

Pessel, A.J. Letter from Castle & Cooke, Limited, General Agents, Matson Navigation Company, to Captain M.M. Frucht, U.S. Naval Representative of Evacuation; Honolulu, Hawaii December 30, 1941. National Archives.

Sevier, Randolph. Letter from Castle and Cooke to Captain Max M. Frucht, 12 December 1941. National Archives.

Smoot, Sally. Letter to Florence Springer, 18 July 1941. (Courtesy of Joey Border)

Springer, George I., Letter to Joey Border, 17 December 1941. (Courtesy of Joey Border)

Walton, A.S. Letter A16-3/Evacuation, Subject: The Steamship Lurline—Addition of Crew Members, to The 14th Naval District Personnel Officer, 23 December 1941. National Archives.

Wilson, Earle M. Letter of Commendation for Major Leonard J. Heaton to The Adjutant General in Washington, D.C. from the Commander, Schofield Barracks, 7 January 1942. (Courtesy of Sara Dudley [Heaton] Mayson)

Library and Museum Collections

Blackwell Letter, 9-14, 25 December 1941. Military History Institute Collection, U.S. Army War College, Carlisle Barracks, Pennsylvania.

Elwin M. Eldredge Collection. The Library at The Mariners' Museum, Newport News, Virginia.

Franklin D. Roosevelt Library, MEMORANDUM FOR THE SECRETARY OF THE NAVY from M.H. McIntyre (Secretary to the President), 4 March 1942.

Franklin D. Roosevelt Library. Presidential Papers, OF 400, Hawaii, folder 1943.

Lurline Commander Log 1941, Matson Navigation Company Collection, San Francisco Maritime National Historical Park.

Marine Exchange Ledger, San Francisco Maritime National Historical Park, San Francisco Harbor, California.

Matsonia Commander Log 1941, Matson Navigation Company Collection, San Francisco Maritime National Historical Park.

Monterey Commander Log 1941, Matson Navigation Company Collection, San Francisco Maritime National Historical Park, San Francisco Harbor.

Online Primary Sources

Action Reports:

Agnew, D.M. USS *Trever*, 12 December 1941. http://www.history.navy.mil/docs/wwii/pearl/ph92.htm

Anderson, E.L. "Contact with Enemy Submarine, 10 December 1941"; 15 December 1941. http://www.cv6.org/ship/logs/ph/ela19411210.htm

Anderson, William S. Commander Battleships, Battle Force. Action Report, 19 December 1941. http://www.history.navy.mil/docs/wwii/pearl/ph3.htm

Atkins, J.G. USS *New Orleans*, 13 December 1941. http://www.history.navy.mil/docs/wwii/pearl/ph60.htm

Beck, E.L. USS *Phelps*, 30 December 1941. http://www.history.navy.mil/docs/wwii/pearl/ph68.htm

Bellinger, P.L.N. "Task Force NINE (Patrol Wing Two) Operations on 7 December 1941." http://www.history.navy.mil/docs/wwii/pearl/ph11.htm

Bode, H.E. USS *Oklahoma*, 18 December 1941. http://www.history.navy.mil/docs/wwii/pearl/ph62.htm

Bunkley, J.W. USS *California*, 13 December 1941, Revised 22 December. http://www.history.navy.mil/docs/wwii/pearl/ph29.htm

Burford, W.P. USS *Monaghan*, 20 December 1941. http://www.history.navy.mil/docs/wwii/pearl/ph54.htm

Callaghan, D.J. USS *San Francisco*, 10 December 1941. http://www.history.navy.mil/docs/wwii/pearl/ph80.htm

Carroll, C.E. USS *Helm*, 11 December 1941. http://www.history.navy.mil/docs/wwii/pearl/ph45.htm

Christensen, W.N. USS *Cachalot*, 10 December 1941. http://www.history.navy.mil/docs/wwii/pearl/ph28.htm

Connor, F.W. USS *Argonne*, 28 January 1942. http://www.history.navy.mil/docs/wwii/pearl/ph110.htm

Cooke, C.M. USS *Pennsylvania*, 16 December 1941. http://www.history.navy.mil/docs/wwii/pearl/ph66.htm

Crandeli, D.A. USS *Gamble*, 13 December 1941. http://www.history.navy.mil/docs/wwii/pearl/ph43.htm

Detzer, A.J. USS *Dewey*, 13 December 1941. http://www.history.navy.mil/docs/wwii/pearl/ph38.htm

Dodd, Harold. USS *Honolulu*, undated (prior to 15 February 1942). http://www.history.navy.mil/docs/wwii/pearl/ph47.htm

Dudley, R. USS *Rigel*, 9 December 1941. http://www.history.navy.mil/docs/wwii/pearl/ph78.htm

Earle, Ralph Jr. USS *Ralph Talbot*, 12 December 1941. http://www.history.navy.mil/docs/wwii/pearl/ph74.htm

English, R.H. USS *Helena*, 14 December 1941. http://www.history.navy.mil/docs/wwii/pearl/ph44.htm

Farwell, R.E. Ormac Bay, Leyte: USS *Ward* (APD-16) Action Report, 16 January 1945. http://www.ibiblio.net/hyperwar////USN/ships/logs/APD/apd1

Fischer, H.E. USS *Phoenix*, 11 December 1941. http://www.history.navy.mil/docs/wwii/pearl/ph69.htm

Furlong, William R. Commander Minecraft, Battle Force, Reports for Pearl Harbor Attack, 7 December 1941. http://www.history.navy.mil/docs/wwii/pearl/ph5.htm

Geishlean, E.H. USS *Arizona*, 13 December 1941. http://www.history.navy.mil/docs/wwii/pearl/ph21.htm

Godwin, D.C. USS *Maryland*, 15 December 1941. http://www.history.navy.mil/docs/wwii/pearl/ph51.htm

Grannis, L.C. USS *Antares*, 10 December 1941. online.http://www.history.navy.mil/docs/wwii/pearl/ph20.htm

Guthrie, R.A. USS *Montgomery*, 12 December 1941. http://www.history.navy.mil/docs/wwii/pearl/ph55.htm

Halsey, William F. "Doolittle Raid—18 April 1942." http://www.cv6.org/ship/logs/action19420418-19.htm

Hardison, O.B. USS *Enterprise*, CV-6, 19 November 1942. http://www.cv6.org/ship/logs/action19421113.htm

Hartigan, C.C. Jr. USS *Hammann*, DD-412. http://www.ibiblio.net/hyperwar////USN/ships/logs/DD/dd412-Midway.html

Hillenkoetter, R.H. USS *West Virginia*, 11 December 1941. http://www.history.navy.mil/docs/wwii/pearl/ph98.htm

Hopping, H.L. Scouting Squadron Six, USS *Enterprise*, December 1941. http://www.history.navy.mil/docs/wwii/pearl/ph16.htm

Hunter, G.P. USS *Farragut*, 13 December 1941. http://www.history.navy.mil/docs/wwii/pearl/ph42.htm

Ilsemann, F.J. USS *Vireo*, 10 December 1941. http://www.history.navy.mil/docs/wwii/pearl/ph96.htm

Johnson, W.G. Jr. USS *Avocet*, 12 December 1941. http://www.history.navy.mil/docs/wwii/pearl/ph22.htm

Jones, F.R. Patrol Squadron 1, 1 January 1942. http://www.history.navy.mil/docs/wwii/pearl/ph39.htm

Jones, W. Glenn. USS *Shaw*, 29 January 1942. http://www.history.navy.mil/docs/wwii/pearl/ph117.htm

Kendall, H.S. USS *Curtiss*, 16 December 1941. http://www.history.navy.mil/docs/wwii/pearl/ph35.htm

Kline, W.F. USS *Thornton*, 17 December 1941. http://www.history.navy.mil/docs/wwii/pearl/ph90.htm

Lane, J.M. USS *Hulbert*, 8 December 1941. http://www.history.navy.mil/docs/wwii/pearl/ph48.htm

LeHardy, L.M. USS *Zane*, 10 December 1941. http://www.history.navy.mil/docs/wwii/pearl/ph101.htm

McGinnis, K. "Report of Japanese Air Attack on Kaneohe Bay, T.H.—7 December 1941," 1 January 1942. http://www.history.navy.mil/docs/wwii/pearl/ph12.htm

McIsaac, J.M. USS *MacDonough*, 14 December 1941. http://www.history.navy.mil/docs/wwii/pearl/ph112.htm

Miller, L.H. USS *Perry*, 22 December 1941. http://www.history.navy.mil/docs/wwii/pearl/ph67.htm

Nimitz, C.W. Commander-in-Chief Pacific (CinCPac) Report, 15 February 1942. http://www.history.navy.mil/docs/wwii/pearl/CinCPac.htm

O'Neill, Roger. "The Sullivan Brothers: Report on the Loss of the USS *Juneau*," 17 November 1942, Naval History and Heritage Command. http://www.history.navy.mil/faqs/faq72-2a.htm

Outerbridge, W.W. USS *Ward*, 13 December 1941. ibiblio.org/hyperwar/USN/ships/logs/DD/dd139-Pearl.html

Paddock, H.E. USS *Dobbin*, 11 December 1941. http://www.history.navy.mil/docs/wwii/pearl/ph39.htm

Pendleton, W.B. USS *Tern*, 15 December 1941. http://www.history.navy.mil/docs/wwii/pearl/ph118.htm

Perlman, Benjamin. USS *Solace*, 12 December 1941. http://www.history.navy.mil/docs/wwii/pearl/ph83.htm

Phillips, John S. USS *Neosho*, 11 December 1941. http://www.history.navy.mil/docs/wwii/pearl/ph58.htm

Pogue, W.C. USS *Worden*, 9 December 1941. http://www.history.navy.mil/docs/wwii/pearl/ph100.htm

Pullen, H.F. USS *Reid*, 12 December 1941. http://www.history.navy.mil/docs/wwii/pearl/ph77.htm

Rainer, G.B. USS *Dolphin*, 12 December 1941. http://www.history.navy.mil/docs/wwii/pearl/ph40.htm

Reordan, C.E., *Tennessee*, 11 December 1941. http://www.history.navy.mil/docs/wwii/pearl/ph89.htm

Rodgers, R.H. USS *Aylwin*, 12 December 1941. http://www.history.navy.mil/docs/wwii/pearl/ph23.htm

Rorschach, A.L. USS *Dale*, 28 December 1941. http://www.history.navy.mil/docs/wwii/pearl/ph36.htm

Scanland, F.W. USS *Nevada*, 15 December 1941. http://www.history.navy.mil/docs/wwii/pearl/ph59.htm

Schrader, A.E. USS *Medusa*, 16 December 1941. http://www.history.navy.mil/docs/wwii/pearl/ph52.htm

Shea, D.F.J. USS *Cassin*, 13 December 1941. http://www.history.navy.mil/docs/wwii/pearl/ph30.htm

Simons, R.E. USS *Raleigh*, 13 December 1941. http://www.ibiblio.org/hyperwar/USN/ships/logs/CL/cl7-Pearl.html

Sims, G.L. USS *Ramsay*, 13 December 1941. http://www.history.navy.mil/docs/wwii/pearl/ph76.htm

Smith, Robert H. USS *Henley*, 15 December 1941. http://www.history.navy.mil/docs/wwii/pearl/ph46.htm

Specht, W.C. Motor Torpedo Squadron One, "Narrative of Offensive measures taken during air raid," 12 December 1941. http://www.history.navy.mil/docs/wwii/pearl/ph10.htm

Speight, E.P. USS *Oglala*, 11 December 1941. http://www.history.navy.mil/docs/wwii/pearl/ph61.htm

Sprague, C.A.F. USS *Tangier*, 2 January 1942. http://www.history.navy.mil/docs/wwii/pearl/ph87.htm

Steele, J.M., Isquith, S.S. USS *Utah*, 15 December 1941. http://www.history.navy.mil/docs/wwii/pearl/ph94.htm

Stout, H.F. USS *Breese*, 9 December 1941. http://www.history.navy.mil/docs/wwii/pearl/ph27.htm

Stout, R.F. USS *Hull*, 9 December 1941. http://www.history.navy.mil/docs/wwii/pearl/ph49.htm

Terrlell, W.R. USS *Tucker*, 15 December 1941. http://www.history.navy.mil/docs/wwii/pearl/ph93.htm

Thayer, W.R. USS *Downes*, 17 December 1941. http://www.history.navy.mil/docs/wwii/pearl/ph41.htm

Theobald, R.A., Commander, Destroyer Flotilla 1; 19 December 1941. http://www.history.navy.mil/docs/wwii/pearl/ph4.htm

Walker, Frank R. USS *Patterson*, 12 December 1941. http://www.history.navy.mil/docs/wwii/pearl/ph64.htm

Walters, C.R. "Contacts for War Diary," 13 December 1941. http://www.cv6.org/ship/logs/ph/crw19411210.htm

Wilfong, J.L. USS *Wasmuth*, 12 December 1941. http://www.history.navy.mil/docs/wwii/pearl/ph120.htm

Wilkins, C.W. USS *Narwhal*, 12 December 1941. http://www.history.navy.mil/docs/wwii/pearl/ph57.htm

Williams, H.N. USS *Blue*, 12 December 1941. http://www.history.navy.mil/docs/wwii/pearl/ph25.htm

Willingham, J.H. USS *Tautog*, 12 December 1941. http://www.history.navy.mil/docs/wwii/pearl/ph88.htm

Wiltse, L.J. USS *Detroit*, 10 December 1941. http://www.history.navy.mil/docs/wwii/pearl/ph37.htm

Young, C. USS *Vestal*, 11 December 1941. http://www.history.navy.mil/docs/wwii/pearl/ph95.htm

Young, H.L. *Enterprise* Air Group Commander's Report, 15 December 1941. http://www.history.navy.mil/docs/wwii/pearl/ph17.htm

Other online sources

American Armored Fighting Vehicle Production During World War II, *Wikipedia*. http://en.wikipedia.org/wiki/American_armored_fighting_vehicle_production_during_World_War_II

American Military History, Army Historical Series. Chapter 20, "World War II: The Defensive Phase." http://www.army.mil/cmh-pg/books/amh/AMH-20.htm

American Merchant Marine at War. "American Women Mariners in World War II." http://www.usmm.org/women.html

Bates, Lawrence N. "Pearl Harbor: Remembered," USS *Tangier*. http://my.execpc.com/~dschaaf/bates.html

"Battle Experience for Leyte Gulf," online. http://www.ibiblio.org/hyperwar/USN/rep/Leyte/BatExp/index.html

"Battle of the Coral Sea, 7-8 May 1942 . . . " Naval History and Heritage Command. http://www.history.navy.mil/photos/events/wwii-pac/coralsea/coralsea.html

"Battle of the Coral Sea," *Wikipeida*. http://en.wikipedia.org/wiki/Battle_of_the_Coral_Sea

Bennighof, Mike, *Avalanche Press*, "Americans and the 'Bismarck,'" May 2006. http://www.avalanchepress.com/Americans-Bismarck.php

"Bombing of Darwin (February 1942)," *Wikipedia*. http://en.wikipedia.org/wiki/Bombing_of_Darwin,_February_19,_1942

Butowsky, Harry A. "Early Warnings: The Mystery of Radar in Hawaii." http://crm.cr.nps.gov/archive/15-8/15-8-2.pdf

Chambers, Chaplain Samuel D. (USN, Retired"What the Pearl Harbor

Chaplains Were Doing at Pearl Harbor on December 7th 1941." http://www.airbornepress.com/pearlharbor.html

Chapter VIII: "The Hawaiian Defenses After Pearl Harbor." http://www.army.mil/CMH-pg/books/wwii/Guard-US/ch8.html

Chen, C. Peter. World War II Database, *Invasion of Malaya and Singapore*. http://ww2db.com/battle_spec.php?battle_id=47

Chen, C. Peter. World War II Database, *Java Campaign*. http://ww2db.com/battle_spec.php?battle_id=23

"Chuichi Nagumo," *Wikipedia*. http://en.wikipedia.org/wiki/Chuichi_Nagumo

Condor-Ward Dispatches, 7 December 1941. http://www.geocities.com/subskipper/dispatch2.htm

Conn, Engelman and Fairchild. *US Army in World War II, The Western Hemisphere, Guarding the United States and Its Outposts*, Chapter VI, "The Reinforcement of Oahu": Conn, Engelman, & Fairchild. http://www.ibiblio.org/hyperwar/USA/USA-WH-Guard/USA-WH-Guard-6.html

Cressman, Robert J. *Marines in the Battle for Wake Island*. http://www.ibiblio.org/hyperwar/USMC/USMC-C-Wake.html

Cressman, Robert J., Wenger, J. Michael, "'This Is No Drill.' U.S. Naval Aviation and Pearl Harbor, December 7, 1941." *Naval Aviation News*, November-December 1991. http://www.history.navy.mil/download/ww2-14.pdf

Cressman, Robert J., Wenger, J. Michael. *Infamous Day: Marines at Pearl Harbor 7 December 1941*. http://www.ibiblio.org/hyperwar/USMC/USMC-C-Pearl.html

Darcy, Ted and Emory, Ray. "Finding America's Missing," undated. http://www.soft-vision.com/ao_vets/pdf/FindingAmericasMissing.pdf

"Death of Isoroku Yamamoto," *Wikipedia*. http://en.wikipedia.org/wiki/Death_of_Isoroku_Yamamoto

Delgado, James P. Japanese Midget Submarine HA-19 National Historic Landmark Study, "Japanese Midget Submarines and the Pearl Harbor Attack." http://www.nps.gov/history/maritime/nhl/ha19nhl.htm

Destroyer Photo Index—DD-412 USS *Hammann*, NavSource. http://www.navsource.org/archives/05/412.htm

Dictionary of American Naval Fighting Ships Online. http://www.hazegray.org/danfs/

"Doolittle Raid." *Wikipedia*. http://en.wikipedia.org/wiki/Doolittle_Raid

"Doolittle Raid on Japan—Army B-25s." Naval History and Heritage Command. http://www.history.navy.mil/photos/events/wwii-pac/misc-42/doolt-a.htm

"Doolittle Raid on Japan—People." Naval History and Heritage Command. http://www.history.navy.mil/photos/events/wwii-pac/misc-42/doolt-p.htm

"Doolittle Raid on Japan—Ships." Naval History and Heritage Command. http://www.history.navy.mil/photos/events/wwii-pac/misc-42/doolt-s.htm

Doolittle's Raid on Tokyo. http://www.angelfire.com/ia/totalwar/DoolittleRaid.html

"Doris Miller," *Wikipedia.* http://en.wikipedia.org/wiki/Doris_Miller

Doris "Dorie" Miller, African American Sailor, Naval History and Heritage Command. http://www.history.navy.mil/faqs/faq57-4.htm

"Douglas B-23 Dragon."

http://www.aero-web.org/specs/douglas/b-23.htm

Employment of Negro Troops, Chapter IV: "Expanding Negro Strength." http://www.army.mil/cmh-pg/books/wwii/11-4/chapter4.htm

Employment of Negro Troops, Chapter XIV: "Manpower and Readjustments." http://www.army.mil/cmh-pg/books/wwii/11-4/chapter14.htm

Erickson, Ruth. "Oral Histories of the Pearl Harbor Attack: Lieutenant Ruth Erickson, NC, USN," 7 Dec. http://www.history.navy.mil/faqs/faq66-3b.htm

"Executive Order 9066," *Wikipedia.* http://en.wikipedia.org/wiki/Executive_Order_9066

Finn, John William. Association of Aviation Ordnancemen. http://www.aaoweb.org/AAO/finn.html

Franklin D. Roosevelt Presidential Library and Museum. http://www.fdrlibrary.marist.edu/research.html

Franklin D. Roosevelt Library. Roosevelt, Franklin D. Text of address to Congress, 7 December 1941. http://www.fdrlibrary.marist.edu/images/decwarp1.jpg

Feuer, A.B., *Sea Classics* Magazine and Challenge Publications "Pawn of Fate: The Pensacola Convoy," July 2004. http://findarticles.com/p/articles/mi_qa4442/is_200407/ai_n16065359

Grossman, Robert J. *A Magnificent Fight: Marines in the Battle for Wake Island.* http://www.ibiblio.org/hyperwar/USMC/USMC-C-Wake.html

Hackett, Bob; Kingsepp, Sander. "Sensuikan!" Japanese Submarines: Tabular Record of Movements (TROMs). http://www.combinedfleet.com/sensuikan.htm

Hackett, Bob; Kingsepp, Sander. "Sensuikan!" *I-17*: Tabular Record of Movements. http://www.combinedfleet.com/I-17.htm

Hackett, Bob; Kingsepp, Sander. "Sensuikan! *I-25*: Tabular Record of Movements. http://www.combinedfleet.com/I-25.htm

Hackett, Bob; Kingsepp, Sander. "Sensuikan!" *I-26*: Tabular Record of Movements. http://www.combinedfleet.com/I-26.htm

Hackett, Bob; Kingsepp, Sander. "Sensuikan!" *I-75*: Tabular Record of Movements. http://www.combinedfleet.com/I-175.htm

Hearings Before the Joint Committee on the Investigation of the Pearl Harbor Attack Congress of the United States Seventy-Ninth Congress, *Investigation of the Pearl Harbor Attack*, Part V. "Conclusions and Recommendations." http://www.ibiblio.org/pha/pha/congress/part_5.html—253

Hickam Air Force Base Public Affairs, "Account of 38th Reconnaissance Squadron," December 1997. http://www.hawaiischoolreports.com/history/wwiimilitary.htm

National Japanese American Memorial Foundation, *World War II Service*. http://njamf.com/index.php/world-war-ii-service

History of USS *Helena*, Naval History and Heritage Command. http://www.history.navy.mil/photos/sh-usn/usnsh-h/cl50.htm

History of USS *Oglala*, NavSource online. Mine Warfare Vessel Photo Archive. http://www.navsource.org/archives/11/0604.htm

History of USS *Utah*, NavSource online: Battleship Photo Archive. http://www.navsource.org/archives/01/31c.htm

Joyce, R.O. The Doolittle Tokyo Raiders, Richard O. Joyce Memorial Site, "Facts About the Doolittle Tokyo Raid." http://www.doolittleraider.com/

Krawczynski, Keith. *Historic Context of the African American Experience*: Section 7, "African American Navy, Marine Corps, Women's Reserves, and Coast Guard Service During World War II." https://www.denix.osd.mil/denix/Public/ES Programs/Conservation/Legacy/AAME/aame3a.html

Lewis, Jone Johnson. "WASP—Women Pilots of World War II," About.com. http://womenshistory.about.com/od/waspwwiiaviation/a/wasp.htm

Lewis, Jone Johnson. *Women and World War II—Women and the Military*. About.com. http://womenshistory.about.com/od/warwwii/a/military.htm

Lewis, Jone Johnson, *World War II Homefront –Women at Home*, About.com. http://womenshistory.about.com/od/warwwii/a/women_at_home.htm

Lewis, Robert. *The Battle for Australia*—"The Battle of the Coral Sea." http://www.anzacday.org.au/history/ww2/bfa/coralsea.html

Lewis, Robert. *The Battle for Australia—Battle of the Coral Sea*, "The Battle of the Coral Sea." http://www.anzacday.org.au/history/ww2/bfa/coralsea.html#battlemap

"Liberty Ship," *Wikipedia*. http://en.wikipedia.org/wiki/Liberty_ship

"*Liscome Bay* (CVE-56)," *Dictionary of American Naval Fighting Ships*. http://www.org/danfs/carriers/cve56.txt

Mamiya Medical Heritage Center, Archives Museum, and Special Collections at Hawaii Medical Library. "Medicine in Hawaii: The World War II Experience." *Hawaii Medical Journal* from 1947 to 1948. "Remembrances of December Seventh." http://www.hml.org/mmhc/ww2/ww2index.html

"Masaharu Homma," *Wikipedia*. http://en.wikipedia.org/wiki/Masaharu_HommaHMS *Warspite*, 2-7; *Wikipedia*. http://en.wikipedia.org/wiki/HMS_Warspite_(03)

McNaughton, James C. *United States Army, Pacific*, "The Hawaiian Department, 7 December 1941," 20 November 2001. http://www.usarpac.army.mil/history/dec7_hawndept.asp

Mongell, John. *John Mongell's Flying Tigers Tribute—A Photo History of the 11th Bomb Squadron*. http://www.angelfire.com/ma/MONGELL/photohist1.html

Morton, Louis; *U.S. Army in World War II, The War in the Pacific*, "The Fall of the Philippines;" Chapter IX: "Strategy and Logistics," 145-48.

http://www.ibiblio.org/hyperwar/USA/USA-P-PI/USA-P-PI-9.html

National Museum of Naval Aviation, Pensacola, FL. http://www.navalaviationmuseum.org/getdoc/91d59f24-7e8c-4bb5-9e0a-58dc714b7ee7/Featured-Collections.aspx

Naval History and Heritage Command. "Statement Regarding Winds Message." http://www.history.navy.mil/library/online/winds.htm

Naval History and Heritage Command. "Frequently Asked Questions," "The Pearl Harbor Attack, 7 December 1941: Where were the Carriers, 7 December 1941?" http://www.history.navy.mil/faqs/faq66-9.htm

Navy Music Program, "Pacific Fleet Band." http://www.cpf.navy.mil/cpfband/other/history.shtml

Navy Patrol Bombing Squadrons 102/14 Association, Citation Accompanying the Medal of Honor Awarded to John W. Finn. http://members.tripod.com/~vpb_102/unitmembercitations/finn.html

Navy School of Music, *Wikipedia*. http://en.wikipedia.org/wiki/Navy_Music_Program#Navy_School_of_Music

Official Chronology of the U.S. Navy in World War II, Chapter III, 1941. http://www.ibiblio.net/hyperwar/USN/USN-Chron/USN-Chron-1941.html

"Ohka," *Wikipedia*. http://en.wikipedia.org/wiki/Ohka

"Okinawa Kamikazes." http://www.history.navy.mil/download/ww2-31.pdf

Olsson, Ken P. "Today in History," 7 December 1941. http://www.islandnet.com/~kpolsson/today/1207.htm

"Pearl Harbor Navy Medical Activities," *The United States Navy Medical Department at War, 1941-1945*. Vol. 1, parts 1-2, Manuscript #68-A; Bureau of Medicine and Surgery: Washington, DC, 1946. http://www.history.navy.mil/faqs/faq66-5.htm

Peisner, Allen. "Interview of Captain (USN Ret) Frank L. DeLorenzo, 2002." http://www.johngreavesart.com/delo.htm

"Profiles in Courage, True Stories of Great American Heroes." http://www.homeofheroes.com/pearlharbor/pearl_8moh.html

Reports by Survivors of Pearl Harbor Attack. http://www.history.navy.mil/docs/wwii/pearl/survivors3.htm

Results of the American Pacific Submarine Campaign of World War II. http://www.navy.mil/navydata/cno/n87/history/pac-campaign.html

Rickard, J. (20 January 2007), *Battle of Wake Island, 8-23 December 1941*. http://www.historyofwar.org/articles/battles_wake_island.html

Sealift in World War II. Global Security.org.http://www.globalsecurity.org/military/systems/ship/sealift-ww2.htm

Siddiqi, Asif. "Air Transportation: Pan American's Flying Boats." http://www.centennialofflight.gov/essay/Commercial_Aviation/china_clipper/Tran5.htm

"Song Sheet: Remember Pearl Harbor." http://my.execpc.com/~dschaaf/praise.html

"*SS President Coolidge*," *Wikipedia*. http://en.wikipedia.org/wiki/SS_President_Coolidge

"Statement Regarding Winds Message" by Captain L.F. Safford, U.S. Navy. Department of Navy Library. http://www.history.navy.mil/library/online/winds.htm

Submerged Cultural Resources Study: "USS *Arizona* and Pearl Harbor National Historic Landmark," Chapter 2. http://www.nps.gov/archive/usar/scrs/scrs2.htm

"Tacoma Narrows Bridge (1940)," *Wikipedia*. http://en.wikipedia.org/wiki/Tacoma_Narrows_Bridge_(1940)

Tanner, William P. Narrative of Engagement with Enemy Submarine on 7 December 1941. http://www.crockermediaexpressions.com/PBY/pdfs/chapter01-insert.pdf

The Attack on Pearl Harbor, "George Welch, Ken Taylor, Fritz Hebel," Aviation History online, 2002. http://www.aviation-history.com/airmen/pearl.htm

"The Sinking of Panay, 12 December 1937," online. Excerpted from Morison, Samuel Eliot. *History of United States Naval Operations in World War II*, Volume 3: *The Rising Sun in the Pacific*, 16-18. http://www.ibiblio.org/hyperwar/USN/ships/dafs/PR/pr5-sinking.html

The Takao Club, Part Two: "The Wreck of the SS President Hoover." http://www.takaoclub.com/hoover/wreck.htm

The United States Army Air Forces in World War II. http://www.armyairforces.com/

The United States Army Air Forces in World War II, "Army Air Forces Statistical Digest, World War II," Table 4. http://www.usaaf.net/digest/t3.htm

"The 25th Infantry Division on December 7th 1941." 25th Infantry Division Association. http://www.25thida.com/pearlharbor.html

"The USS *Juneau* (CL-52)," *Wikipedia*. http://en.wikipedia.org/wiki/USS_Juneau_(CL-52)

Toth, Catherine E. "Timeline of AJA's Joining the World War II Fight," *Honolulu Advertiser*.com. http://the.honoluluadvertiser.com/article/2007/Jun/17/ln/ln01a.html

"Traditions: Georgia Tech Yellow Jackets," "Ramblin' Wreck Song." http://ramblinwreck.cstv.com/trads/geot-trads.html

"Tuskegee Airmen." *Wikipedia*. http://en.wikipedia.org/wiki/Tuskegee_Airmen

United States Aircraft Production During World War II, Wikipedia (Army Air Forces Statistical Digest, World War II, Aircraft and Equipment, Table 79.). http://en.wikipedia.org/wiki/United_States_aircraft_production_during_World_War_II

USAT Tasker H. Bliss, History. http://ww2troopships.com/ships/t/taskerhbliss_USN/default.htm

US Army in World War II: "Fall of the Philippines," Chapter 9. http://www.ibiblio.org/hyperwar/USA/USA-P-PI/USA-P-PI-9.html

US Army in World War II, Military History. http://www.militaryhistoryonline.com/wwii/usarmy/introduction.aspx

U.S. Navy Patrol Bombing Squadron 14—07 December 1941, "Patrol Squadron 14 NAS Kanehoe Bay War Diary." http://members.tripod.com/~vpb_102/information/07_december_1941.html

"US Navy and US Marine Corps Aircraft Serial Numbers and Bureau Numbers—1911 to Present." Second Bureau Number Series (1935-1940), 0001 to 5029. http://home.att.net/~jbaugher/navyserials.html

USS *Aldebaran* (AF-10) History, 1941 Log. http://home.epix.net/~nooyawka/1941.htm

USS *Arizona* Memorial, "The First Casualties," 22 Dec 2004. http://www.nps.gov/archive/usar/phcas.html

USS *Arizona* National Memorial—History and Culture (U.S. Park Service). http://www.nps.gov/usar/historyculture/index.htm

"USS *California* (BB-44), 1921-1959," Naval History and Heritage Command. http://www.history.navy.mil/photos/sh-usn/usnsh-c/bb44.htm

"USS *Cushing* (DD-376)," Destroyer Photo Index DD-376 USS Cushing, NavSource. http://www.navsource.org/archives/05/376.htm

"USS *Helena* (CL-50)," *Wikipedia*. http://en.wikipedia.org/wiki/USS_Helena_(CL-50)

"USS *Hugh L. Scott* (AP-43)," *Wikipedia*. http://en.wikipedia.org/wiki/USS_Hugh_L._Scott_(AP-43)

"USS *Maryland* (BB-46), 1921-1959," Naval History and Heritage Command. http://www.history.navy.mil/photos/sh-usn/usnsh-m/bb46.htm

"USS *Monaghan* (DD-354)," Dictionary of American Naval Fighting Ships. http://www.hazegray.org/danfs/destroy/dd354txt.htm

"USS *Monaghan* (DD-354)," *Wikipedia*. http://en.wikipedia.org/wiki/USS_Monaghan_(DD-354)

"USS *Monssen* (DD-436)," *Wikipedia*. http://en.wikipedia.org/wiki/USS_Monssen_(DD-436)

"USS *Monssen* (DD-436), 1941-1942," Naval History and Heritage Command. http://www.history.navy.mil/photos/sh-usn/usnsh-m/dd436.htm

"USS *Nevada* (BB-36), 1916-1948," Naval History and Heritage Command. http://www.history.navy.mil/photos/sh-usn/usnsh-n/bb36.htm

"USS *New Orleans* (CL-32)," Dictionary of American Naval Fighting Ships. http://www.hazegray.org/danfs/cruisers/cl32.txt

"USS *Oklahoma* (BB-37), 1916-1946," Naval History and Heritage Command. http://www.history.navy.mil/photos/sh-usn/usnsh-o/bb37.htm

"USS *Oklahoma* (BB-37)," *Wikipedia.* http://en.wikipedia.org/wiki/USS_Oklahoma_(BB-37)

"USS *Pennsylvania* (BB-38), 1916-1948," Naval History and Heritage Command. http://www.history.navy.mil/photos/sh-usn/usnsh-p/bb38.htm

"USS *Perkins* (DD-377)," Destroyer Photo Index DD-377 USS *Perkins*, NavSource. http://www.navsource.org/archives/05/377.htm

"USS *Preston* (DD-379)," Destroyer Photo Index DD-379 USS *Preston*, NavSource. http://www.navsource.org/archives/05/379.htm

USS *Procyon* (AKA-2), *Wikipedia.* http://en.wikipedia.org/wiki/USS_Procyon_(AKA-2)

"USS *Reid* (DD-369)," Destroyer Photo Index DD-369 USS *Reid*, NavSource. http://www.navsource.org/archives/05/369.htm

"USS *San Francisco* (CA-38)," *Wikipedia.* http://en.wikipedia.org/wiki/USS_San_Francisco_(CA-38)

"USS *Tasker H. Bliss*, (AP-42)," *Wikipedia.* http://en.wikipedia.org/wiki/USS_Tasker_H._Bliss_(AP-42)

"USS *Tennessee* (BB-43), 1920-1959," Naval History and Heritage Command. http://www.history.navy.mil/photos/sh-usn/usnsh-t/bb43.htm

"USS *Tucker* (DD-374)," *Wikipedia.*http://en.wikipedia.org/wiki/USS_Tucker_(DD-374)

"USS *Utah* (BB-31)," *Wikipedia.* http://en.wikipedia.org/wiki/USS_Utah_(BB-31)

"USS *Ward* (DD-139)," *Wikipedia.* http://en.wikipedia.org/wiki/USS_Ward_(DD-139)

USS *West Virginia*, *Dictionary of American Naval Fighting Ships*. http://www.history.navy.mil/danfs/w6/west_virginia-ii.htm

"Victory Ship," *Wikipedia.* http://en.wikipedia.org/wiki/Victory_ship

Wallin, Homer N. *Pearl Harbor: Why, How, Fleet Salvage and Final Appraisal.* Washington, DC: US Government Printing Office, 1968. http://www.history.navy.mil/docs/wwii/pearl/survivors2.html

Wiltshire, John C. "Japanese Midget Submarine, The Search for the Japanese Midget Submarine Sunk Off Pearl Harbor, Dec. 7, 1941," University of Hawaii Undersea Research Laboratory, 20 December 2003. http://www.soest.hawaii.edu/HURL/midget.html

World War II in the San Francisco Bay Area, National Park Service. http://www.
 nps.gov/nr/travel/wwiibayarea/ben.HTM

World War II Rationing, United States History. http://www.u-s-history.com/
 pages/h1674.html

Photograph Credits Guide

Hawaii State Archives: HA

Imperial Japanese Navy: IJN

Matson Navigation Company: MNC

National Archives: NA

National Archives Pacific Alaska Region: NAPAR

National Archives Pacific Region: NAPR

National Naval Aviation Museum Collection: NNAM

National Park Service, *Arizona* Memorial: NPSAM

National Park Service, San Francisco Maritime Museum and National Historical
 Park Library: NPSSFHMML

Naval History and Heritage Command: NHHC

San Francisco Airport Museum Collection, gift of United Airlines: SFAMC

San Francisco History Center, San Francisco Public Library: SFHC

University of Detroit Mercy Library, Photographic digital image from the Fr.
 Edward J. Dowling, S.J. Marine Historical Collection: UDML

University of Hawaii, Hamilton Library Archives and Special Collections:
 UHHL

Pan American World Airways, Inc. Records, Special Collections, University of
 Miami Libraries, Coral Gables, Florida: PAAR/UMLSCF

US Air Force: USAF

US Air Force Museum: USAFM

US Army: USA

U.S. Army Military History Institute, World War II Signal Corps Photograph
 Collection: USAMHI

USMC Archives and Special Collections, Jordan Collection: USMCASC

US Marine Corps History Center: USMCHC

US Navy: USN

Robert Lee and Mary Joleen Border: Borders' Collection

ACKNOWLEDGMENTS

Surprise and wonder never cease when researching and writing history. The decision to write a history sometimes comes slowly. In this instance, courageous people who lived the events drew me toward researching another world and another era. When I first met Robert Lee "Bob" Border and his lovely wife of sixty-two years, Mary Joleen "Joey" Border, it was Saturday morning, 6 December 2003, an auspicious date. The day we met was the 62nd anniversary of the last day of peace for The Territory of Hawaii and the United States of America, before the nation and its territories were thrust headlong into World War II.

There was a gathering of West Point and Annapolis graduates to watch the traditional Army-Navy football game on a large-screen television. Paul Adams, the host for the morning's activities, was aware of my first two military history books, and urged me to ". . . go meet Bob Border. He's a 1939 graduate of the Naval Academy, and was assigned to the USS *Tennessee* at Pearl Harbor." Curiosity seized the moment. In the intervening years since the Japanese attack I had never talked in any detail with anyone who was at Pearl Harbor or anywhere on the island of Oahu on December 7, 1941.

After walking to the table, introducing myself and explaining I was a writer, I asked Bob, a retired Navy commander, if he would permit me to take a photograph. As I was to learn, he was truly an officer and a gentleman. While taking the snapshot, I heard a small woman's voice from across the table. "Why don't you tell *her* story?"

She was Joey's friend, and began to describe some of Joey's experiences during that December so long ago. An introduction and conversation with Joey revealed she had written recollections of her journey home from Hawaii in late December of 1941. "Would you be willing to send a copy to me?" I asked. "Perhaps someone will publish your story." She said she would, and I handed her a business card.

Four days later, the copy arrived, a brief, unforgettable story. I had to know more, and called, asking for an interview. The first of many sessions was 22 January 2004. At the time, a book wasn't yet on the horizon—but the belief this would be an article soon receded into the background. By the end of April 2004, facts derived from interviews and early research whetted my curiosity even more, and convinced me there was considerably more than an article to be written. Thus began my third passage into researching and writing a major history.

This would not be about a fierce, five-day, Korean War infantry battle for a single hill along a 155-mile front that was a throw-back to the bloody trench and bunker warfare of World War I. This time, the work reflects the coming of age of air power combined with naval power and land-based air power, and would be about a single, savage, earth-shaking, surprise air attack—a raid scarcely two hours in duration—launched from six aircraft carriers into a complex of interrelated air, sea and land battlefields, as the foreword states, in a far different era.

In 1930, Albert Einstein also wrote these words in *What I Believe*. "The most beautiful thing we can experience is the mysterious. It is the source of all true art and science." In addition to *At Dawn We Slept*, seven other works were of great value in viewing Pearl Harbor through a different, complementary lens.

British author, Mr. H.P. Willmott, with Tohmatsu Haruo and W. Spencer Johnson, in his work, *Pearl Harbor*, provided another thoughtful, fact-filled examination of Japan's and America's road to war, followed by a detailed, factual insight into the attack, and assessments of its effects. The book is filled with outstanding, beautifully-rendered, color photographs, maps, diagrams and tables which enhance a comprehensive look at the attack and its immediate aftermath.

In 1950, the University of Hawaii Press published *Hawaii's War Years, 1941-1945*, by Gwenfread Allen. A most excellent, invaluable one-of-a-kind reference and source, the book laid before readers a wonderfully crafted history and analysis documenting The Territory of Hawaii's American role in the great Pacific, the islands' preparations for war, and subsequently their total immersion in efforts to defeat the Japanese Empire and its Axis allies.

For the fiftieth anniversary of the attack, the Pacific Air Force's Office of History, sponsored a landmark work, titled *7 December 1941, The Air Force Story*. Written by Leatrice R. Arakaki and John R. Kuborn and filled with outstanding photographs, diagrams, maps, and fascinating human interest, the book presents yet another important perspective on the events of that day, including a detailed accounting of Army Air Force casualties and aircraft losses.

In 1992, Pictorial Histories Publishing Company released Donald Young's *December 1941, America's First 25 Days at War*. The work proved invaluable in surveying the immediate impacts of 7 December on the nation, and more particularly on the West Coast and its Pacific waters. The book brought readers the history of publicly obvious American defense responses, and equally obvious Japanese submarine attacks in the Pacific waters off the coast—along with the beginning of the round-up and internment of Japanese-Americans in the first days of World War II.

Three other wonderful books, primary sources from men who were at Pearl Harbor, were inspiring, for they captured and exuded so well, the spirits of men who were there and later heavily engaged in the Pacific war. The first, *From 6-S-7*, by Jack Leaming, a radioman-gunner in the rear cockpit of a Douglas Dauntless SBD scout bomber in Scouting Squadron Six (VS-6) on the carrier USS *Enterprise* (CV-6). A marvelous, courageous, giving American, Jack Leaming and his pilot, then Lieutenant (USN) Dale Hilton, had been shot down early in World War II and spent the balance of the war in Japanese prisoner of war camps. Jack gave me unqualified permission to quote and paraphrase from his work, which told of the wrenching experiences of his squadron that fateful day, including their unsuspecting early-morning flight into the maelstrom of the Japanese air raid, and their role in the search for the Japanese carrier strike force after the attack.

The second, the 1942 book *The Flying Guns*, by then Lieutenant (USN) Clarence E. Dickinson, a Douglas Dauntless pilot on the *Enterprise*, was filled with firsthand accounts of events important to a complete history of the attack on Pearl Harbor. Coupled with Jack Leaming's work and action reports written by other pilots within days after the attack, *The Flying Guns* filled out important details in the story of Scouting Squadron Six (VS-6).

The third work, a 1944 book by Navy Chaplain Howell M. Forgy, chaplain on board the heavy cruiser USS *New Orleans* (CA-32) at Pearl Harbor and later, with his shipmates, he described the ship's participation in bloody naval battles. His work was inspiring beyond words. This good man's love and deep respect for the men who went down to the sea in ships, sparkled like a bright light in his every word.

Without the assistance of so many others willing to give of their time and energies during the period 2004-2011, this work would have been impossible. Numerous archivists, librarians, photograph custodians, historians and others in the National and Hawaiian Archives; the Naval History and Heritage Command; United States Marine Corps History Division; National Park Service historical sites, National Museum of Naval Aviation, maritime and airport museums; the Army's Military History Institute; the Franklin D. Roosevelt Presidential Library, public and university libraries, who retrieved, copied, and mailed or E-mailed the documents and photographs indispensable to fact-finding and a complete work.

I would be remiss if I didn't name the following and acknowledge their kind, responsive assistance and warmly courteous contributions: David A. Giordano, Gibson B. Smith, Terrence Johnson, Jason D. Staton, John Vernon, Nathaniel S. Patch, Barry Zerby, and Regina Davis at the National Archives in College Park, MD; Robert Glass at the National Archives Pacific Region in San Bruno, CA; Hill Goodspeed at the National Museum of Naval Aviation in Pensacola, FL; Susan Karren and Kathleen Crossman at the National Archives Pacific-Alaska Region in Seattle, WA, and Deborah Franz-Anderson, Puget Sound Navy Yard Public Information Office; Matthew C. Hanson at the Franklin D. Roosevelt Presidential Library in Hyde Park, NY; Jason Achiu at the Hawaii State Archives and James Cartwright, Archivist, and DeeDee Acosta, Special Collections, at the University of Hawaii at Manoa Hamilton Library, HI; Sara Diamond and Bill Kooiman, National Maritime Museum Library in San Francisco, CA; Josh Graml and Claudia Jew, The Library at The Mariners' Museum, Newport News, VA; Marti Goddard and Christina Moretta at the San Francisco Public Library, San Francisco, CA; Mr. Daniel Martinez, National Park Service Chief Historian, World War II Valor in the Pacific National Monument, at Pearl Harbor, HI, for assisting with numerous photographs and important suggestions for additional manuscript reviews; Donald Gill, U.S. Merchant Marine Academy Library, Kings Point, NY; Edwin Finney, Jr., Naval History and Heritage Command, Laura Waayers and Cory Black, Naval Historical Foundation, Washington, DC; Tim Wooldridge, Archivist, History Reference and Preservation Library, United States Naval Institute, Annapolis, MD; Bill

McQuade at the U.S. Naval Academy Library, Annapolis, MD; Ford Schmidt, Mark O. Hatfield Library, Willamette University, Salem, OR; Linda Sueyoshi, Hawaii State Library, Honolulu, HI; Helen Wong Smith, Librarian, Hawaiian Collection and Mookini Library, Hilo, HI; Julie Tashima Takata and Alissa Chadburn at the San Francisco Airport Commission Aviation Library, San Francisco, CA; Michael Nerney, Port of San Francisco, CA; Bob Johnson at the Dr. Martin Luther King, Jr. Library, a San Jose and San Jose State University Collaboration, San Jose, CA; Greg Cina and Sue Dillon, at the U.S. Marine Corps Archives and Special Collections; Ryan D. Meyer, David Keough, and Dr. Arthur W. Bergeron, Jr., Military History Institute, U.S. Army War College, Carlisle, PA; Karen Phares at the Orange, TX Public Library; Cindy A. Gillam, University of Detroit Mercy Library Special Collections and Margaret E. Auer, Dean of Libraries, McNichols Campus Library, University of Detroit; Caroline Harzewski and Laura Capell, Richter Library, University of Miami (FL) Libraries; Henry Pazos of OfficeMax for his invaluable assistance in updating and improving maps and diagrams to better depict the key events in the work; and good friend and West Point classmate Roy T. Thorsen, Thousand Oaks, CA, for his kind assistance in restoring photographs important to portraying this history to readers.

To Jeff Hull, public affairs officer in the Matson Navigation Company, a special thanks for all he gave—a clear expression of his great admiration for Matson's long colorful history: the numerous photos of the magnificent ships of that era, the copies of *Ampersand* (Winter 1991); and *Ships in Gray, the Story of Matson in World War II* (1946).

To my good friend of many years, Dan Nelis, thank you for turning me toward the grand, romantic history of the *Pan American Clippers*. To another good friend, Australian author and free lance writer Kate Doolan, a special thank you for sending a copy of *The Lady and the President, The Life and Loss of the SS President Coolidge*, a tragic yet inspiring sea story containing important contributions to this history.

My deep and sincere appreciation for the kind and invaluable assistance of Mr. Sidney Hayes of Tampa, Florida, who so readily volunteered to give of his time, energy and editorial skills in critically reading the entire narrative and providing numerous suggestions to improve the work's quality and readability. To J.

Michael Wenger, the widely acclaimed Pearl Harbor and military historian and expert on the Japanese attack, for his seminal, factual works on the Hyperwar website, with another renowned military historian, Robert Cressman, and his willingness to assist with a short notice technical review of selected manuscript excerpts, to develop guidance for further review of the entire manuscript. To a good friend and former Navy officer, John Gould, who read the manuscript and gave his comments leavened always with kind encouragement and good humor.

And to my wife, the love of my life, Veronica, who made it all possible, my everlasting gratitude and adoration. Without her patient understanding and support, listening to and reading the stories; her steadfast willingness to assist, and doing work I should ordinarily have done, this book would never have been completed.

The growth and maturity of computer technology, the worldwide web, and centers of history that have taken full advantage of both, must be acknowledged because of their role in this work. Were it not for upgraded computer capabilities, research would have taken more than twice as long and documents and photographs would have filled many more drawers and storage boxes. The trend toward putting more and more history on line is accelerating, permitting researchers and nearly all citizens easy access to our past, access invaluable to the accumulation of knowledge, and to our future national security.

There were well over 200 documented online sources used to help bring this history to life, and there were probably twice that many examined that were not used. In many instances there were multiple online sources used in reconstructing one event or a series of events. As an example, online Pearl Harbor action reports from the Naval History and Heritage Command were invaluable. Nearly all written within four to fifteen days by captains, acting captains and other officers aboard ships in the harbor the morning of 7 December, complete with additional statements by other crew members, these marvelous action accounts, along with online damage reports, were used in concert with other online documents such as ships' histories and citations accompanying awards—plus hard copies of ships' deck logs from the National Archives—to reconstruct the stories of the ships struck in the attack.

Another online work, *Sensuikan!* by Bob Hackett and Sander

Kingsepp, proved invaluable. Their website provided operational histories of Japanese submarines in World War II, with over 200 initial submarine Tabular Record of Movements (TROMS) that were stories and battle histories. The TROMS, regularly updated, are helping fill in numerous historical blanks and connect World War II events and people from the two former enemies.

As was the case in each of the two prior histories I've been privileged to write, this story was given life by those who lived it, or were close to those who "had gone before." Age and its infirmities are all too rapidly diminishing their numbers; nevertheless, their legacy grows stronger and shines more brightly with each passing day. Of those listed as "Interviews with the Author," fifteen were on Oahu that day: Margaret (Littmann) Baccelli, Clifton E. Dohrmann, Raymond Emory, Edward E. Hall, Joseph Honish, Andrew Hoover, Earl Hinz, J.R. Johnson, Frederick K. Kamaka, James K. Poppleton, Sherry (Sardis) Richey, Ira Schab, Raymond Turpin and two more to whom this work is dedicated. All were kind, thoughtful, and generous in sharing their time and recollections in telephone or personal interviews, letters, written recollections recorded long ago, E-mails and photographs. Every single one provided recollections and information that brought substance, enthusiasm, and excitement to the work, and breathed life into the story.

Particularly, I want to acknowledge a grand lady and her husband, Mary Joleen "Joey" Border and Robert Lee "Bob" Border, who opened their lives and took me on a journey to Pearl Harbor and back on the Matson Line's SS Lurline and the great battleship, USS Tennessee. When we met, Joey had just turned 83, and Bob was 85. I lost count of the hours spent with them, always with more questions than time or memory could answer. She gave complete, unfettered access to the one small diary she had religiously kept one year in her entire life—1941, which permitted me to pose more questions, probe deeper and help them recall lost details of days long ago.

Her first diary entry at the end of the first day of that tumultuous year was little more than a month after her twentieth birthday, and less than two weeks after she was first introduced to Bob in the junior officers' wardroom on board the Tennessee. The diary was a wonderful treasure trove, a window into another time, when life was far simpler and more innocent. It was also a window into the inner life, heart and soul of a beautiful young woman at perhaps the most joyful time of their lives, for it told of his pursuit of her, her response to him every step of the way, their falling in love, marriage, and their trials that first year. The diary, with its revelations, and their responses to the numerous questions asked, painted a marvelous, unforgettable picture that will be with us always.

Joey and Bob made the mosaic more vivid with copies of personal letters, telegrams, military records, newspaper clippings, individual and family photograph albums and treasured keepsakes, high school and Naval Academy class yearbooks, access to another treasure, the two diaries of Karl Border, Bob's older brother, and to Bob's Aviation Log Book. Finally, after three years and nine months and many hours of questions, answers and discussion, the manuscript was nearly complete. They had read bits and pieces, and shortly I would be ready for them to read the entire history, which contained their story. It was not to be, not for Joey.

On Tuesday, 14 August 2007, I learned from Bob that Joey had entered the hospital two days earlier. After a necessary surgical procedure, she began to decline. Always strong, private, proud, and wanting no expressions of sympathy, she told Bob and the hospital staffs emphatically she wanted no visitors. Bob, now 89 years of age, drove to the hospital and visited her all day, every day. On 18 September, I wrote them a letter, asking Bob to take it to the hospital and read it to her. The letter told her the manuscript was complete, we were anxious for her to return home and read it. She took her magnifying glass, read the letter herself, handed it back to Bob and told him to put it on her desk. She would answer it when she got home.

On Sunday, 7 October, Bob brought her home for a brief stay before returning her on Wednesday to the rehabilitation hospital to which she had been transferred. Ironically, that night I took the evening at home to watch television and saw the Navy football team defeat the University of Pittsburg in triple overtime—as did a somewhat weary Bob Border after he returned to their apartment in the retirement home. Joey left us that night, quietly, in her sleep. Her journey was over, and I suspect she was cheering Navy all the way—while God was taking her home.

And so, Mary Joleen "Joey" (Springer) Border, this acknowledgment is for you. You have taken all of us on a voyage toward love and the mysterious, ". . . the source of all true art and science." This book is for you and Bob.

ABOUT THE AUTHOR

Bill McWilliams was born in Brownsville, Texas, was raised in small towns in Texas, New Mexico, and Colorado, and received an appointment to the United States Military Academy at West Point, New York, from the third congressional district of Colorado. He graduated with a bachelor of science degree and earned a master of science in business administration from the George Washington University while attending the Air Command and Staff College at Maxwell Air Force Base, Alabama. He later attended the US Army War College in Carlisle Barracks, Pennsylvania, where he completed ten months of senior management training.

His air force service included work as a flight and classroom instructor in undergraduate pilot and fighter training; a seven-month combat tour in the Republic of Vietnam, where he flew one hundred twenty-eight fighter-bomber close-support and interdiction missions; and posts at the United States Air Force Academy as commanding and flight instructor for cadets receiving familiarization training in light aircraft. Later he served in the Republic of Korea for two years, and at the Air Force Tactical Fighter Weapons Center in Las Vegas, Nevada. After leaving the Air Force he served more than eight years in systems engineering and management positions in the aerospace industry.

McWilliams's writing includes two Korean War histories—*A Return to Glory: The Untold Story of Honor, Dishonor, and Triumph at the United States Military Academy, 1950–53* and *On Hallowed Ground: The Last Battle for Pork Chop Hill*—plus numerous articles, including series in newspapers and magazines. The ESPN made-for-television movie *Code Breakers*, which premiered in December 2005, was based on McWilliams's first book.

OPEN ROAD
INTEGRATED MEDIA

Open Road Integrated Media is a digital publisher and multimedia content company. Open Road creates connections between authors and their audiences by marketing its ebooks through a new proprietary online platform, which uses premium video content and social media.

Videos, Archival Documents, and New Releases

Sign up for the Open Road Media newsletter and get news delivered straight to your inbox.

Sign up now at
www.openroadmedia.com/newsletters

FIND OUT MORE AT
WWW.OPENROADMEDIA.COM

FOLLOW US:
@openroadmedia and
Facebook.com/OpenRoadMedia